John C. Calhoun

J. C. Calhoun

CALHOUN AS SECRETARY OF WAR

From the portrait by John Wesley Jarvis in the Department
of the Army, Washington, D. C.

John C. Calhoun

AMERICAN PORTRAIT

By Margaret L. Coit
With a new introduction by Clyde N. Wilson

University of South Carolina Press
Published in Cooperation with
The Institute for Southern Studies
and the South Caroliniana Society
of the University of South Carolina

Southern Classics Series
John G. Sproat, General Editor

King Cotton and His Retainers:
Financing and Marketing the Cotton
Crop of the South, 1800–1925
By Harold D. Woodman

The South as a Conscious
Minority, 1789–1861:
A Study in Political Thought
By Jesse T. Carpenter

Red Hills and Cotton:
An Upcountry Memory
By Ben Robertson

John C. Calhoun:
American Portrait
By Margaret L. Coit

The Southern Country Editor
By Thomas D. Clark

Copyright © 1950, Margaret L. Coit
Copyright © University of South Carolina 1991

Published in Columbia, South Carolina by the
University of South Carolina Press in cooperation
with the Institute for Southern Studies and the
South Caroliniana Society

Manufactured in the United States of America

First published by Houghton Mifflin Company
Boston, Massachusetts, 1950

Library of Congress Cataloging-in-Publication Data

Coit, Margaret L.
    John C. Calhoun : American portrait / Margaret L. Coit : with a
new introduction by Clyde N. Wilson.
        p.   cm. — (Southern classics series)
    Reprint. Originally published: New York : Houghton Mifflin, 1950.
    Includes bibliographical references and index.
    ISBN 0–87249–774–7. — ISBN 0–87249–775-5 (pbk.)
    1. Calhoun, John C. (John Caldwell), 1782–1850.   2. Legislators—
-United States—Biography.   3. United States.   Congress. Senate—
-Biography.   4. United States—Politics and government—1815–1861.
5. South Carolina—Politics and government—1775–1865.   I. Title.
II. Series.
[E340.C15C63   1991]
973.5'092—dc20
[B]   91-9605

General Editor's Preface

The Southern Classics Series returns to general circulation books of importance dealing with the history and culture of the American South. Under the sponsorship of the Institute for Southern Studies and the South Caroliniana Society of the University of South Carolina, the series is advised by a board of distinguished scholars, whose members suggest titles and editors of individual volumes to the general editor and help to establish priorities in publication.

Chronological age alone does not determine a title's designation as a Southern Classic. The criteria include, as well, significance in contributing to a broad understanding of the region, timeliness in relation to events and moments of peculiar interest to the American South, usefulness in the classroom, and suitability for inclusion in personal and institutional collections on the region.

*   *   *

A combination of John C. Calhoun, Margaret L. Coit, and Clyde N. Wilson is an especially fortuitous one for the Southern Classics Series. Surely, no one epitomizes the term "southern classic" better than Calhoun. Of all the studies of this giant of southern—and American—politics, none has had wider appeal and more acceptance (among scholars as well as general readers) than Coit's Pulitzer Prize-winning biography of 1950. And no scholar of our time knows more about the subject than Wilson, the discerning editor of *The Papers of John C. Calhoun.* In his spirited introduction to this edition of *John C. Calhoun: American Portrait,* Wilson reaffirms both the continuing appeal of Coit's biography and the centrality of its subject to an understanding of antebellum America.

JOHN G. SPROAT
General Editor, Southern Classics Series

Introduction to the Southern Classics Edition

During the great middle period of American history between Jefferson's presidency and the Civil War, the legacy of the Founding Fathers clashed and mingled with the historical force of modernization and a geometric explosion of population, territory, economy, and culture. Out of this formative period—complex, varied, and problematic—emerged a synthesis that is the America we now know. The period coincides with the career of John C. Calhoun as a national statesman.

From 1811 to 1850—as representative from South Carolina, secretary of war, vice president, twice presidential contender, secretary of state, and senator for fifteen years—Calhoun was a central figure in the American experience. He was never predominant in influence, even in the South in his own lifetime, but there was never a time when he was not a major player who had to be taken into account.

He had many admirers and disciples, northern as well as southern, but he never enjoyed a large political base, an effective party organization, significant power over patronage, or national mass popularity. For most of his career he was either outside the two-party system or at odds with the leadership of the party with which he was identified. Despite the absence of all these hallmarks of political power, from the beginning to the end of his forty-year career Calhoun arrested public attention and influenced public opinion. Calhoun had a major if not always decisive influence on every issue of the period—in regard not only to state-federal conflict and slavery, with which he is most commonly associated by later generations, but also to free trade and tariff, banking and currency, taxation and expenditure, war and peace, foreign relations, Indian policy, the public lands, internal improvements, the two-party system, and the struggle between congressional and presidential power.

With Henry Clay and Daniel Webster, Calhoun made up "The Great Triumvirate," which, as Merrill D. Peterson has reminded us in a recent work of that name, for forty years "triangulated the destiny of the nation." Together with General Andrew Jackson (whom the triangle was largely designed to contain), the Great Triumvirate *were* American political life between that time when Jefferson crossed the Potomac going South for the last time, leaving behind a modest federal establishment for a Union of the States, and that time when Lincoln, with the help of Generals Grant and Sherman, forged the modern American state out of blood and fire.

Calhoun was, then, as every one at the time and later recognized, a major protagonist in the drama of expansion and conflict that is at the heart and center of American history in the nineteenth century. Whatever road one travels, Vernon L. Parrington observed well over half a century ago in *Main Currents in American Thought,* one finds Calhoun standing at the crossroads. And while Calhoun is very far from being the most admired of American statesmen, and in some calculations is one of the great villains of American history, it is curiously true that never at any time, during his life or since, has he lacked weighty admirers, who often appear from quite unexpected quarters.

But Calhoun has an additional importance not shared with the other great public men of his time or later and in which he resembles the generation of the Founding Fathers. Though a public man speaking on pressing public issues, Calhoun always cast his political positions and arguments in principled and philosophical terms and always disdained the superficial and opportunistic view for the long-range one. As Margaret Coit observes in her summation of Calhoun's career (p. 516): "He had been a statesman, not a politician."

Calhoun was, then, a political thinker as well as a political actor, and this has given him a certain enduring and even prophetic quality. Calhoun qua political thinker has received continuing, international, and interdisciplinary interest from diverse generations, countries, and viewpoints. Except for Jefferson and Lincoln, it is hard to think of any American statesman who has had admirers from more points of the compass and the political spectrum, and for reasons that transcend the issues of his own time, than has Calhoun.

Margaret Coit knows this, and it is significant that her account of Calhoun's life and ideas has been admired by both Arthur M. Schlesinger, Jr., the paragon of American liberal historians, and Russell Kirk, the dean of modern American conservative thinkers. In their company is President John F. Kennedy, who included *John C. Calhoun: American Portrait* on the list of his ten favorite political biographies.

Calhoun's importance has always been evident but has not always been readily acknowledged in some quarters. That we can now assert with confidence and without fear of successful contradiction Calhoun's enduring importance as a political thinker is in part due to the achievement represented by *John C. Calhoun: American Portrait*. This honor Coit shares with Charles M. Wiltse, whose three-volume *John C. Calhoun*, a different though equally admirable biography, appeared at approximately the same time.

The timing of the revival of interest in and appreciation for Calhoun at the midpoint of the twentieth century was significant. In the years after World War II many Americans were in a mood to be receptive to old wisdom that might shed some light on pressing and troubling problems of democracy—problems of consensus, pluralism, economic concentration, and minority rights.

"Miss Coit's book provides far and away the most detailed, vivid, and convincing personal characterization of Calhoun we have," wrote Schlesinger in 1950 on the first appearance of *John C. Calhoun: American Portrait*.[1] The passage of four decades and a Niagara of additional published material on the great Southern statesman leaves no reason to reverse Schlesinger's judgment, a judgment confirmed by the award of the 1951 Pulitzer Prize for Biography.

Another early reviewer, Gerald W. Johnson, agreed: "The book has many merits—learning, logical form, obvious sincerity, lucidity. . . . The net result is that she has taken what is commonly regarded as one of the dryest stories in American history and turned it into a colorful, somberly gorgeous portrait that enthralls the attention and stirs the emotions as few modern biographies do."[2] High praise for the first book of a young newspaperwoman, barely out of her twenties and with no advanced degrees in history, but entirely justified.

That the book contains the best extant characterization of Calhoun does not exhaust its merits. It presents a vivid history of Calhoun's times. To quote another early reviewer: "Miss Coit has the art of creating historical characters of almost Shakespearean stature: not only Calhoun of the tortured doubts, intense affections, discouragements, but also the men who ruled with him, Jackson, Webster, Clay."[3] The book also contains an original and arresting interpretation of Calhoun's ideas and their continuing relevance for later times.

Further, it is a wonderful example of historical work of an increasingly rare type—a work that speaks equally to the general and the scholarly reader. Claude G. Bowers, probably the most successful American popular historian of the first half of the twentieth century,

1. *Nation* (April 1, 1950), 170:302.
2. *New York Herald Tribune Book Review,* March 5, 1950, p. 1.
3. Clorinda Clarke in *Catholic World* (July 1950), 171:316.

hailed the biography on its publication as "a brilliant achievement, scholarly and at the same time a work of art steeped in charm."[4] The reading and re-reading of *John C. Calhoun: American Portrait* can actually be enjoyed by a large and varied audience, which is sadly untrue of the productions of most academic historians, in 1950 or 1990.

Coit's deep and sympathetic recovery of the most Southern of all statesmen is all the more surprising when we remember that she is a New England native, though raised and educated in North Carolina. The combination of contrasting influences proved a happy one. While pursuing a career in big-city journalism after graduation from the Woman's College of the University of North Carolina (now the University of North Carolina at Greensboro) on the eve of World War II, Coit undertook the audacious assignment of a thorough biography of one of the most difficult and contentious figures in American history.

Even more audaciously, the biography was not to be a quick publisher's knockdown. It was to be based on extensive scholarly research, incorporate both narrative and interpretation, appeal to both general readers and scholars, and have contemporary relevance as well as historical interest.

The result was a classic of the biographer's craft which remains the best one-volume treatment of its subject. *John C. Calhoun: American Portrait* has been a remarkable success that has gone through many printings in hardback and paperback.

Coit has since published a number of other books on the "Jacksonian" era of American history, as well as a prize-winning biography of another difficult subject, Bernard Baruch, in 1958. Leaving journalism, she was for some years professor at Fairleigh Dickinson University in New Jersey. She now lives with her husband, Albert Elwell, farmer and poet, at Strawberry Hill in West Newbury, Massachusetts, where she is active in local affairs and has been moderator of the town meeting. All of Coit's books are marked by independence of thought, original historical insight, and good writing.

Even though conditions were in some respects favorable, the task of redeeming Calhoun's personality from distortion and his political thought from neglect and condescension in the middle of the twentieth century was formidable. As Coit wrote (p. 382): "With the possible exception of George Washington, no American statesman has been more thoroughly dehumanized than John C. Calhoun."

The Calhoun fixed almost indelibly in American folklore and even in widespread "scholarly" understanding was still the dour and

4. *New York Times Book Review,* March 5, 1950, p. 1.

fanatical "cast-iron man" of the English writer Harriet Martineau, who knew him only slightly. This Calhoun stared out of the textbooks (as indeed he often still does) from the Matthew Brady daguerreotype taken near the end of his life when he was wasted by disease, to frighten generations of northern schoolchildren: the evil genius who personified the perfidy of the South, and so obviously looked the part.

It was always a superficial image, designed to bolster the confidence of the winning side in the Civil War. But it was Margaret Coit who more than any other writer gave it the coup de grace and restored to the national consciousness the real Calhoun—the handsome, brilliant, patriotic, charming figure who was known to most of his contemporaries for most of his life.

For there was a Calhoun, as Coit shows us, whose influence depended upon personal charm and impregnable integrity, next only to intellect, and who at any time could win the undying admiration of army officers or intellectuals or hard-fisted labor leaders, or even, sometimes, unwilling young abolitionists.

There was a Calhoun who was most happy when engaged in the pursuits of a farmer; who was the too-indulgent father of many children; who had such a characteristically American enthusiasm for technology and material progress that in his fifties he spent nine days on horseback clambering over the most rugged part of the Appalachians to satisfy himself as to the best route for a railroad; who could charmingly whisper verses in the ear of President Tyler's young bride. Most of all, there was the tragic patriot who struggled heroically, not to destroy the Union but to find a way to save it from the chaos of clashing imperatives.

Coit restored to our national pantheon this lost figure, surely a constructive and consoling achievement. Her book was probably the decisive factor in the United States Senate's designating Calhoun as one of its five greats in 1959, on the finding of a committee chaired by John F. Kennedy.

If one wished to criticize *John C. Calhoun: American Portrait,* one might suggest that this redemption was achieved at the price of a certain amount of romanticism and imaginative amplification of bare fact. This was a line taken by a few reviewers at the time of the book's first publication, though the critical reception, in both academic and popular journals, was overwhelmingly positive.[5]

Where adequate documentary evidence is and forever will be lacking—for instance, in regard to Calhoun's childhood, his relationship with his wife, and his encounters with Thomas Jefferson—

5. *Book Review Digest 1950,* pp. 188–189.

Coit has supplied us with a plausible version of what can never be known for sure. We are always aware that this is what she is doing. The pedantic critics took too narrow a view of what history is and how it should be written. It is not a question of accurate or inaccurate, it is a question of the proper strategy for presentation of an inescapably imperfect documentary record.

We do not know, for instance, from direct evidence, what suit Calhoun wore on a particular occasion of a great and dramatic speech in the Senate. But we do know, from direct evidence, what sort of suit he is likely to have worn, and are entitled to say so without too much quibbling. Contrary to what many pedants seem to think, literal-mindedness is not at all the same thing as truth. What is important is the historian's integrity and responsibility in determining probabilities where there are no certainties.

History must adhere to the documentary record. This is what distinguishes it from other forms of examination of the human experience. But no great history, certainly no successful narrative history, has ever been written without the use of the imagination. Facts do not tell their own story. They have meaning only in a relationship to a total picture which is, in part, a product of the historian's imaginative arrangement. To put it another way, the line between fact and imagination is real and significant but not absolute, any more than is, as we know from modern physics, the line between time and motion.

It is the loss of this basic truth of historical knowledge, a truth that has always informed the greatest historians, that renders so much contemporary historical output, unlike *John C. Calhoun: American Portrait*, unreadable to the non-specialist and bereft of cultural significance, human impact, and enduring meaning.

I have defended this book from a charge of romanticism because the charge has been made from time to time, but the defense is not really necessary. We would have to look far and wide to find a more controlled and responsible and creative exercise of the historical imagination. As another early reviewer commented, Coit makes "it possible for any reasonable reader to reach a reasonable conclusion."[6]

Having spent two decades in intimate daily communion with the hard documentary record of Calhoun, I find only few and minor errors (such as can be found in any ambitious work) and few and minor places to take issue with in Coit's account of Calhoun's life and personality. Any significant points of disagreement I have with the book have to do with the larger historical context, the inevitable

6. A. B. Miller in *Annals of the American Academy* (November 1950), 272:219.

disagreements a thoughtful historian will have with any work on a period with which he or she is familiar.

And even where I am not in accord I am compelled to recognize *John C. Calhoun: American Portrait* as a significant, original, and persuasive interpretation of the period of American history that is the least amenable to simple synthesis and that is littered with the debris of historiographical dispute.

Many historians of recent day prefer the quantitative and literal and eschew the kind of deep cultural background that suffuses this biography. For them Coit is out of step. For instance, she describes Southern society as a fusion of the low country aristocrat and the Celtic backcountryman, an image that she uses to account for both Calhoun and Andrew Jackson. Before we dismiss this as poetic license, we should note that she has merely anticipated by four decades an extremely sophisticated recent cultural history of American origins, which elaborately, with a vast array of evidence, makes the same point. (I refer to David Hackett Fischer's *Albion's Seed: Four British Folkways in America.*)

One suspects that what some critics mean by romanticism is simply that Coit finds Calhoun a sympathetic figure and is willing to give him the benefit of a reasonable doubt. They find this ideologically unacceptable, because the great evil genius of the South must not be treated sympathetically. But an equally romanticized negative treatment would be quite acceptable; and this is, indeed, what has often happened in Calhoun biography and in the treatment of Calhoun in works on the "Jacksonian" era, both before and after the publication of *John C. Calhoun: American Portrait.*

Calhoun's most recent biographer, for example, makes the completely subjective judgment that Calhoun was "out of touch with reality" at the time of the Nullification crisis.[7] This estimate reflects the propaganda of some of his opponents at the time. But Calhoun was not out of touch with reality; he simply viewed reality in a different framework than did ordinary pragmatic politicians. In the Nullification crisis, though he did not completely carry the day, Calhoun fought all the powers arrayed against him—all three branches of the federal government, both major political parties, overwhelming public opinion, and the formidable temper and popularity of

---

7. John Niven, *John C. Calhoun and the Price of Union: A Biography* (Baton Rouge: Louisiana State University Press, 1988). A comprehensive evaluation of the writing on Calhoun can be found in Clyde N. Wilson, *John C. Calhoun: A Bibliography* (Westport, Conn. & London: Meckler, 1990).

Andrew Jackson—down to a compromise of the issue that most concerned him. No small accomplishment for a political leader "out of
touch with reality."

Coit's biography is subjective in that she is sympathetically engaged with her subject. But her historianship compares favorably with
many works on the "Jacksonian" period which are accepted by academic historians without cavil, apparently because their subjectivism is
in the service not of Calhoun but of a romanticized "Jacksonian
democracy." The book provides a ready and persuasive antidote for
such accounts.

The work should surely redeem Calhoun, for all time, from the
sillier charges of ambition and opportunism that have marked much
of the literature about him. One conventional school of interpretation
portrays Calhoun's career as explained by an overwhelming lust for
the presidency—to the degree that Gerald M. Capers entitled his 1960
biography *John C. Calhoun: Opportunist.*

Coit provides a more complex and plausible account. Opportunism is a strange description for a public man, widely admired, who
resigned the vice presidency, to which he had been twice elected by
large majorities, to accompany his own small state in a dangerous
pursuit of principle. It should be clear that something other than
conventional ambition governed the actions of such a man. Coit
comes the closest of any of Calhoun's many biographers to giving us
an understanding of what that was. In so doing, she helps to redeem a
whole era of American history from distortion.

A little less difficult but perhaps more important than Coit's
recovery of Calhoun the man was her recovery of Calhoun the political thinker. The outcome of the Civil War had fixed an image of
Calhoun as a fanatic whose intellect was bent to the one, indefensible
goal of preserving slavery. The first serious biography after the Civil
War, that of the German-American Hermann E. von Holst (*John C.
Calhoun*, 1881), pursued this theme relentlessly, even though there
was in his book itself evidence against so oversimplified a view of
American history.

Yet, as preposterous as it now seems, such a view, though not
unchallenged, long held sway. Holst dealt with the polemics of the
sectional struggle of the late antebellum period. He knew nothing of
the ancient and important role that state rights had played in the
American mind, nor of the early history of slavery. With much superior historical scope, Coit reminds us that the young Calhoun was
educated in a Connecticut where slavery was still known and state
rights still preached by many.

In the recovery of the complexities and timeless elements of

Calhoun's ideas, *John C. Calhoun: American Portrait* had substantial allies. As early as 1927, in a work called *The American Heresy*, the English writer Christopher Hollis had linked Calhoun with Jefferson, Lincoln, and Wilson as the great definers of the American regime. There was also Charles M. Wiltse's careful and detailed study of the life in political context (*John C. Calhoun*, 3 vols., 1944–1951). Wiltse's portrayal of the modern relevance of Calhoun's thought was his own, but in most respects was compatible with Coit's

August O. Spain's *The Political Theory of John C. Calhoun*, a dispassionate exposition, appeared the year after *John C. Calhoun: American Portrait*. At about the same time Coit began her work, Robert L. Meriwether started collecting and planning at the University of South Carolina for a comprehensive edition of *The Papers of John C. Calhoun*, a series of which nineteen volumes had appeared as of 1990.

At about the same time, there was a host of writers, popular and scholarly, on both sides of the Atlantic, who began in articles to point to Calhoun as a prophet of enduring significance and with concrete application to the plight of men and nations in an era of class conflict, economic concentration, totalitarianism, and global strife. The stature that Calhoun had achieved was indicated by the title of a celebrated 1948 article in political science: "A Key to American Politics: Calhoun's Pluralism,"[8] and by Felix Morley's 1951 book, *Freedom and Federalism*, which strenuously argued Calhoun's relevance to the situation of America in the twentieth century.

By midcentury, serious thinkers, whether they admired Calhoun or not, no longer viewed him as only the defender of a peculiar outmoded and beleaguered sectional interest. Not every one would have taken the claim for Calhoun as far as did Coit, but they would have understood the point: "Calhoun stands in the first rank of men America has produced. For as thinker and prophet, he was more important for later times than for his own" (p. 531).

Most earlier biographers had restricted their treatment of Calhoun's political thought largely to questions of constitutional interpretation in regard to slavery and state rights. Coit was quite right, and in good company, in avoiding this trap and portraying Calhoun as a statesman of broad views and interests. Calhoun made more speeches on banking and currency, and on protection and free trade, than he did on slavery, and for most of his career economic issues loomed larger than sectional conflict.

A number of economic historians have, in fact, found Calhoun's

---

8. Peter F. Drucker in *Review of Politics* (October 1948), 10:412–426.

grasp of fiscal and monetary policy superior to that of other public figures of his day. Neither Coit nor any other writer has yet completely exhausted all that might be said about Calhoun's political economy. This remains a fruitful line of research for the alert. But Coit struggles mightily to bring the complex knot of issues involving banking, currency, the tariff, and other aspects of economic conflict and development, under our understanding. This is in stark contrast with many other biographers, who do not seem to be aware that Calhoun had a fully developed political economy, distinct from that of both the Democrats and the Whigs, and who tend to treat such issues merely as political tactics.

Historical understanding, unfortunately, is not always cumulative. We do not necessarily always progress to more sophisticated and inclusive interpretations, and we sometimes discover that old works are not, after all, superseded. We need to go back now and then and recover insights that have been lost. That we can do splendidly in this work.

One, though not the only, virtue of Coit's treatment of Calhoun as a political thinker, a treatment skillfully developed against the narrative of his life, is precisely the fact that the book is very much a product of its time, the immediate post-World War II era. As such, it instructs us usefully not only about Calhoun but also about certain lost alternatives that flourished in the intellectual climate of a few decades ago.

Coit's Calhoun, slavery aside, is an adherent neither of the welfare state nor of big business. He is, rather, the advocate of another way, of what used to be known as Jeffersonian Democracy. Coit's Calhoun is a conservative Democrat who, if we may be permitted an anachronistic reference, would not have been satisfied with either a Reagan or a Mondale, and who would not have agreed that between them they subsumed all the policy alternatives available to America.

So far as participation in the national dialogue goes, the breed of Jeffersonian Democrat appears almost extinct. However, a specimen can still be sighted now and then in the hinterland, and there may be a great many more of them out there than is currently believed. At any rate, for historical perspective we badly need to be reminded that they loom very large indeed in the American record; were once, in fact, the predominant national type. Coming at the time and from the direction that it did, this book provides us with insight into certain forgotten potentialities of its own time as well as Calhoun's and reminds us of a tradition that links both and that is perhaps even yet not quite dead.

Here it may be useful to remember Calhoun's own long-range

view of political victories, as summarized by Coit: "the potential success of a cause had nothing whatever to do with its abstract merits."

John C. Calhoun is an important and problematic figure at the heart of American history and a prophet of whose ideas we can usefully take account in our present concerns. This book is the best place to begin a study of the subject. That is true despite many turns of the wheel of history since it was written, and will likely remain true whatever turns of the wheel of history are to come.

CLYDE N. WILSON

TO MY MOTHER AND FATHER

Acknowledgments

First, I want to express my gratitude to my editors at Houghton Mifflin Company, Paul Brooks, Dorothy de Santillana, Craig Wylie, and Esther Forbes, who with infinite patience and understanding have worked with me on this book through the years. Special thanks are also due Arthur M. Schlesinger, Junior, of Harvard, who read *American Portrait* while it was still in manuscript, and to whom I am indebted for enlightenment on obscure aspects of the slavery question, and on the modern significance of Calhoun's philosophy. I have accepted without material alteration his interpretation of Calhoun's state of mind in the 'Years of Decision' (1837–38), as depicted in *The Age of Jackson*. Bernard DeVoto of Cambridge also read this book in its original eleven hundred pages of manuscript, and is responsible for pruning of much surplus material, and for directing my attention to the significance of the soil depletion in the Southern states and the interrelationship of the consequent Western expansionist and abolitionist movements.

I wish to thank Little, Brown and Company for permission to quote from Claude M. Fuess' *Daniel Webster*, two volumes, Boston, 1930; Charles Scribners' Sons for quotations from Margaret Bayard Smith's *The First Forty Years of Washington Society*, Gaillard Hunt, editor, New York, 1906; E. C. McClurg and Company, publishers of Eva E. Dye's *McLoughlin and Old Oregon*, Chicago, 1900; John Perry Pritchett, for material quoted from his *Calhoun and His Defense of the South*, Poughkeepsie, 1935; the Chapel Hill Press for quotations from the *Reminiscences of William C. Preston*, Minnie Clare Yarborough, editor, copyright, 1933, by the University of North Carolina Press, and especially G. P. Putnam's Sons, for quotations from *The American Heresy* by Christopher Hollis, copyright, 1930, by Christopher Hollis.

The search for the essence of Calhoun must, of course, begin in his own South Carolina. At Clemson Agricultural College his great mass of personal papers and other contemporary material were made available to me; and I wish to express my thanks to the librarian, Miss Cornelia Graham, to Professor and Mrs. A. G. Holmes and Professor Mark Bradley for their assistance. I am deeply grateful to Mrs. Francis Calhoun, who nearly fifty years ago wrote down her personal interviews with the last of the Calhoun slaves at Fort Hill, which are here used for the first time.

Help has also come from other members of the Calhoun family, including anecdotes and reminiscences from the last grandson, the late Patrick Calhoun of Pasadena, California; from Miss Lilian Gold, Flint, Michigan; Mr. John C. Calhoun, Columbia, South Carolina; and Mr. Louis Symonds, Mr. and Mrs. John C. Calhoun Symonds, and Miss Eugenia Frost, all of Charleston.

Mr. Alexander S. Salley, Junior, head of the South Carolina Historical Commission, gave me invaluable help in unraveling the early legislative proceedings of South Carolina, still in manuscript. Others assisting me in Columbia were Professor Robert L. Meriwether of the University of South Carolina Faculty, Miss Elizabeth Porcher of the University Library, Colonel Fitz Hugh McMaster, Mr. J. Gordon McCabe, and Mr. James T. Gittman. I also wish to thank Miss Virginia Rugheimer of the Library of the College of the City of Charleston, Miss Ellen FitzSimons, librarian of the Charleston Library Society, and Miss Kitty Ravenel and Dr. W. W. Ball, also of Charleston.

In Washington, D.C., I am under obligation to Mr. St. George L. Sioussat of the Manuscript Division of the Library of Congress; also to Mr. Thomas P. Martin and Miss Elizabeth McPherson; and to Miss Bess Glenn of the National Archives.

I am deeply grateful to Professor Hollen Farr, curator of the Yale Memorabilia Room, who reconstructed for me the 'Yale College' of 1804. Also assisting me at Yale University were Miss Anne Pratt, Professor Gerard Jensen, Mrs. Sara Jane Powers, Mr. James T. Babb, Mr. C. B. Tinker, Professor R. D. French, and Doctor John Charles Schroeder, headmaster of Calhoun College.

The staffs of the Public Libraries of Boston, Newburyport, Haverhill, and West Newbury, Massachusetts; the Boston Athenaeum, the Library of the University of North Carolina at Chapel Hill and of the Woman's College at Greensboro, North Carolina, have all been generous with their assistance.

The following individuals, by advice or information, have also aided in the preparation of this book: Dr. Clarence Saunders Brigham and Mr. Clifford Shipton of the American Antiquarian Society, Worcester; Mr. Louis H. Dielman, former librarian of the Peabody Institute, Baltimore; Mr. Gerald Johnson, Baltimore; Mr. Robert Richards, Memphis; the Honorable Thomas Salley, Orangeburg, South Carolina; Professor Fletcher Green and Professor Paul Green, Chapel Hill, North Carolina; Mr. Theodore Morrison, Cambridge, Massachusetts; Mr. John N. Burk, Boston; Mrs. Ralph Boas, Norton, Massachusetts; Miss Evelyn Crosby, Centerville, Massachusetts; Mr. John B. Osgood, Lawrence, Massachusetts; Mr.

ACKNOWLEDGMENTS   xxiii

Robert W. Lull, Newburyport, Massachusetts; Miss Mildred Gould and the late J. E. Latham, Greensboro, North Carolina; Mr. Cornelius D. Thomas, Junior, New Orleans; Mrs. Howard F. Dunn and Mrs. Mildred I. Hallihan, Litchfield, Connecticut; Mr. Eugene F. Dow and Mr.- Fletcher Pratt, New York City; Mr. and Mrs. Carl Kuhlmann, Riegelsville, Pennsylvania, and Mr. E. Austin Benner, Haverhill.

Finally, I wish to mention two of my professors at the Woman's College of the University of North Carolina, the late Benjamin B. Kendrick and the late Alex Mathews Arnett, whose advice, encouragement, and understanding enabled me to write this book.

Contents

Illustrations

John C. Calhoun

I

The Heritage

THE YEAR was 1782; the place, Abbeville on the South Carolina frontier. John Caldwell Calhoun was born on the eighteenth day of March in the first frame house in the Long Cane country. That year the last guns of the Revolution sounded along the mountain borders. That year a son was born to another pioneer and soldier in a cabin on the New Hampshire frontier, a region rough and primitive as Abbeville. His name was Daniel Webster.

At first, John's world was small. Tossing on a quilt, his back braced to the hard planks beneath, he could lie and kick for hours. Full skirts brushed across the floor; faces, black and white, bent over him and vanished; his young nose quivered to the scents of cornbread and frying pork; his ears heard the thumping of the churn and the whirr of the spinning wheel. Near, but not too near, orange flames licked at the black hollow of the fireplace, and on cool days he might roll closer, sinking his small fists into the heaps of fresh-picked cotton that lay drying on the hearth. But this pleasure was brief—a swift slap across the knuckles, or the hasty substitution of a gourd filled with dried peas, suspended investigations. Cotton was not for baby boys, but in a very few years he and his younger brother, Patrick, would be seated before that same fireplace, fingers busily searching the warm cotton for the seed, of which they would be required to find an ounce before bedtime.[1]

Slowly the horizon widened. The baby could creep about the kitchen, sinking his knees into the softness of a bearskin, or scraping them raw against the splintery pine flooring. And if in his explorations he rammed his head against a table with the usual wailing results, it is safe to assume that he got his share of kissing and consolation.

For the time and the place his was a normal but solitary boyhood. Cheerful, it could not have been. It was hard growing up to be a Puritan in South Carolina.[2] Sin was a dark and evil thing in even the youngest heart—so ran the tenets of that stern Calvinistic faith which burned across the Southern highlands in all the primitive fury with which it had seared New England a century earlier or still smouldered on the moors of Scotland. For young children the code was severe. Strict obedience. No contradiction of parental authority. Honor thy father and mother. Keep holy the Sabbath day. A solitary lie or theft was 'a stain for life.'[3] Always they must hold themselves in check, try to make something of themselves. Self-discipline and self-control were emphasized, but these were not enough. When the flesh weakened, when even threats of hell-fire failed, the 'pear tree sprouts,' found in the corner of virtually every up-country kitchen, spoke a language not even the youngest child could fail to understand.

Calhoun understood it. 'Life is a struggle against evil,'[4] he once declared, and would believe until his dying day. There is no evidence that by the standards of his times he was harshly treated. There is abundant evidence of his love for his family, of his contentment, if not happiness, in his mode of life. Happiness was something that his code neither expected nor sought, but he had a keen capacity for spiritual as well as for bodily suffering, and his overindulgence of his own children would indicate a reaction from the harsh teachings of his youth. For good or for evil, this Calvinism stamped his character. And the wonder is not that he was as narrow as he was, but as broad; that he could see not only sin in man, but good; that he could condemn, but also pity.

2

He was his father's boy. Around the Calhoun fireside the old wounds of war were opened once more; and almost with their mother's milk, the children drank in the tales of murders and marauding partisan bands, stories that festered in the mind because they were too horrible for the history books.[5] Living it all was five-year-old John, his mind aflame, his small body tight clasped between his father's hard knees, the firelight hot on his face, and voices 'roughened with feeling' thundering in his ears. Out of John's earliest memories faces would loom, gaunt, bearded; eyes burning in the darkness. These were the 'rough but high-strung men who had challenged oppression,' in Scotland, in Ireland, and in their new haven across the seas; and they had stories to tell—of worship in the crude log meeting-houses where they had ridden on horseback in the days before the Revolution, muskets slung across their saddles. Outside, a guard was posted; inside, the Bible lay open before the preacher, but a powder-horn had swung from his shoulder and a gun was clenched in his hand.[6] Thus had the forbears of the Long Cane settlers huddled together on the moors, their horses picketed in the rear, their pikes, swords, and muskets heaped between the congregation and the pulpit where the preacher stood, the Book in one hand and a short sword in the other. It had been 'watch and ward' in the Old World; it was 'watch and ward' in the New, danger like a bridge spanning the years.

Young John heard stories of that winter of 1780 when the whole

Carolina hill-country was surrendered to the British forces—Patriot
against Tory, Carolinian against Carolinian, women and children 'slain
in cold blood'[7] by their own neighbors. Death had walked the hills . . .
a hushed knock against a doorway . . . broken voices in the night and
the hard breathing of hunted men . . . a 'Brown Bess' . . . a few shreds
of a buckskin jacket or a broken powder-horn to show that once a man had
lived and died . . . the entire District of Ninety-Six * under siege.[8]
Stories of Cowpens and Camden and King's Mountain; of Francis Marion,
'the Swamp Fox,' and the gay-faced Quaker boy, Nathanael Greene; of
John's own family, his old Scottish grandmother, slaughtered by Indians
in the grim winter of 1760; of the uncle who fell at Cowpens with thirty
saber wounds, and of the uncle who rotted in a hell-ship off St. Augustine;
of that Major John Caldwell, for whom he had been named, cut down by
the 'Bloody Scout' in his own back yard.[9]

It was not history yet. It was too near and too real. Nearby at Hopewell stood Treaty Oak, where only three years after John was born, the
tribes had gathered for a ten-day parley; there to surrender, to a Calhoun
cousin, General Francis Pickens, lands west of the Blue Ridge, encompassing a third of Georgia, Tennessee, and Alabama. And there, too, had
been surrendered and returned John's cousin, Anna, seized in the Long
Cane Massacre, twenty-five years before.

It must have been hard for John to see in his aging father, the surveyor
and county judge, one of the wiliest and most ruthless Indian fighters
in the entire Southern back-country, a scout who only a few years before,
had headed a group of mountain rangers, patrolling the South Carolina-
Georgia border in a ceaseless watch for enemy Indians.

For Patrick Calhoun was a fighter. The whole life of this Scotch-Irishman from Donegal was a battle, political or military. He was a prayer
and a killer, and he could kill and pray with equal fervor, even with
dedication. Grim, rough-hewn, there was little that was lovable about him.
He was tough in mind and tough in body, devoid either of humor or of
imagination. He was stubborn and wrong-headed, the kind of man who
could unfailingly mistake a prejudice for a conviction;[10] but hardened
for conflict as he was, he was the ideal leader of a frontier community.

Pat Calhoun had grown up in the wilderness. He was only five in 1733
when his family stepped off a dank waterlogged sailing vessel at the port
of Philadelphia.[11] Along the borders of the frontier the Calhouns had
moved, to the drumbeat of Indian warfare; from old Fort Duquesne to
the valley of the Shenandoah, on down through the lush farmlands of
Wythe County, Virginia, to the Waxhaws 'where the Carolinas meet,' and
the hunters told of the land beyond the Catawba where the buffalo ran
and the rich black soil had never known the touch of a plow.[12]

* Legal name for the Long Cane section.

In 1756 the Calhouns had moved once more, beyond the pine barrens and the sand hills to the District of Ninety-Six, the Long Cane country, where the vast brakes grew five to thirty feet in height, and the hills were tangled in peavine, high as a horse's back. There, on the right bank of a stream, Pat Calhoun framed the house to which he brought his third wife, Martha Caldwell, in 1770, and where his five children were born. And there in the wilderness he organized a church, the Long Cane congregation; and for a generation, with his few neighbors, held off attack from the Indian frontier.

He had survived the Long Cane Massacre of February, 1760, and returning to bury the twenty victims had looked down on the body of his brother, James, and his old mother, 'most inhumanly butchered.' [13] Aided by only thirteen neighbors, he had held forty Cherokees at bay for uncounted hours, retreating only when seven of his comrades had been slain and twenty-three Indians lay dead on the ground.[14]

There on the wall hung his old hat, with four bullet holes through the crown—memento of the long hours when he, behind a log and a chief behind a tree, had waited to kill each other. Weary of shooting at the hat, as Calhoun again and again lifted it up on a ramrod, the Indian at last peered out. Instantly Calhoun shot him through the shoulder.[15]

This was John's heritage: stories of Tory atrocities, of Redskin barbarities. Small wonder that a boy, brought up on these tales of heroism and suffering, had fibers of bitter sternness running through his gentle nature.

And always at the fireside was talk of politics. For it had been Pat Calhoun who had led the battle for political representation for the Carolina up-country. Nearly half the population of the state was scattered through the hills, but so far as Charleston was concerned, the up-countryman might have lived in another world. Horse-thieves, cattle rustlers, gunmen, all the riffraff of civilization swept the region with terror—in orgies of pillaging, arson and rape—against which the outraged settlers had no legal redress at all.

So before the assembled dignitaries of the Provincial Assembly, an uninvited guest named Patrick Calhoun appeared to plead for courts, churches, roads, schools, and, above all, for political representation. His demands went unheeded. And in 1769, his coonskin cap on his head, his rifle over his shoulder, Calhoun led his neighbors two hundred miles on foot down to the voting booths, within twenty-three miles of Charleston. There, at the point of the gun, they seized and cast their ballots and voted their leader into the State Legislature.[16] The battle for up-country representation was over.

With Patrick Calhoun, as later with his son, the potential success of a cause had nothing whatever to do with its abstract merits. Among the gentlemen from St. John and Prince George Parishes, the up-country legislator distinguished himself by his vote against adoption of the Federal

Constitution, on the ground that it permitted other people to tax South Carolinians, which, he asserted, was taxation without representation. While young Daniel Webster was puzzling out the words of the Constitution of the United States, written on a general-store pocket handkerchief, the five-year-old Calhoun heard his opinionated father denouncing the Constitution to an eager audience of back-country trappers and amateur politicians.[17]

History has condemned the elder Calhoun for bringing his child up on an intellectual diet of politics. But Patrick, the leading citizen in a community where gambling, drinking, hunting, and political conversation were the only recreation from the drudgeries of farm work, had little time to nourish his own hair-splitting mind. He had learned to read and to write with some difficulty; he had somehow taught himself the business of surveying. What books there were in the Abbeville district he had read, and sometimes on his return home from the Legislature, he brought with him one of the English classics for which he had developed a fondness. Whether young John, the third of his four sons, had access to these volumes is unknown. It is probable that he did. For it is known that by the time he was thirteen, he had memorized certain significant passages in *The Rights of Man,* which book was probably a background for his father's sentiments.

Yet Patrick was content to have his four sons grow up as he had, almost unlettered. Hollis has written of John Calhoun that his mind had been stamped into its pattern for life before it was touched with education. John learned to reason before he could read, and lived in his intellect because he had no library.[18] Always he hated the bad logic of half education; had the narrow but deep clarity of a mind trained in solitary thought, undiverted by conflicting theories and prejudices, which he could have acquired from too early and too generalized an education.

From his father, indeed, John Calhoun did inherit a set of prejudices. He inherited a prejudice against lawyers, but he reluctantly became one. He inherited a prejudice against aristocrats, but he—not at all reluctantly—married one. The father feared and distrusted the eastern portion of his state; the son would fear and distrust the northern portion of his nation. But John's primary legacy from his father was a sturdy-fibered, independent mind, unwilling to accept anyone's opinion but his own, arrived at by tortuous self-analysis and mental agitation. Patrick Calhoun left his son the blood and backbone of a fighter, who would spend his whole life supporting lost causes, unpopular causes, fighting until within two weeks of the grave. The sturdy old pioneer left his boy a rugged, typically American, heritage.

One other legacy Patrick Calhoun bequeathed to his more famous son. John once told his friend, Duff Green, that at the age of nine he remembered his father saying that the best government was that which allowed the individual the most liberty, 'compatible with order and tranquillity,'[19] and that the objective of all government should be to 'throw off needless restraints.' This was pure Jeffersonian doctrine. Young John Calhoun rejected his father's distrust of the Constitution with characteristic independence, but he accepted Jefferson's American principle. He carried it before him like a flag throughout his life; it was buried with him in his grave. It was a pioneer's dream of America.

3

The year 1795 marked a turning point in the life of young John Calhoun. It was the year, too, when he knew personal loss, the desolation that comes when those closest are torn away. It was the year when he studied his first books, learning then what a great and undreamed-of world lay inside them. So far, he had had only a few months of schooling. When he was seven or eight, he had trudged several miles a day through the almost unsettled frontier country to a log-cabin school at Brewers, the same kind of school that Abraham Lincoln would attend thirty years later.[20] He could read and write his name, do a bit of figuring, but he had learned all that the school had to teach him; and his education might have ended there, had it not been for Moses Waddel.

Moses Waddel was John's brother-in-law. A young 'preaching Irishman,' but a generation removed from County Down, he had wandered into the up-country two years before, sickened by the worldliness of his parishioners in Charleston, 'the rich, the rice, and the slaves.' His first night in the Long Cane country he had spent with the Calhouns and before their fireplace had been struck by the vivid, strongly marked features and tousled hair of a shy twelve-year-old, John, who had opened a door, peered in, and fled; and stirred by the lovely face of the boy's older sister, Catherine. That night Waddel had had a dream. He had dreamed that he had married Catherine Calhoun, and that she died within a year. Yet the next morning, shaken and wondering, he had known that at least the first part of his dream must come true.[21]

Waddel took his bride to Columbia County, Georgia, where he opened a law school and academy. He was only too glad to enroll his younger brother-in-law. It has been said that John was delighted with his studies, but he had scarcely begun when his sister sickened and died. Moses Waddel's dream had ended.

Waddel was in despair. For a time he had no heart to continue his school, and dismissing the pupils, he impulsively set off on an itinerant preaching tour through the Georgia wilderness.

He left behind his grief-stricken young brother-in law. There were no neighbors; the great forest-bound plantation was deserted for days at a time. For over six weeks John scarcely saw the face of a white man or woman.[22] Finding loneliness at an early age, John never quite escaped it again.

He did not surrender to his grief. Boys of thirteen, brought up as he had been, with few necessities and no comforts, were often mature enough to be left to their own devices. John, then as later, was vividly conscious of his surroundings, and especially sensitive to the beauties of the Southern countryside.

The northern Georgia county of Columbia was beautiful. Here black pines stand in blurred masses against the hard blue sky, one now and then pointing above the others like a long finger. Here great shoulders of granite push their way through blood-red slashes of clay, the red clay of southern Virginia, North and South Carolina, clay prophetic then, reminiscent now, of that scattered American blood laid waste by American arms on American soil. But in 1795 there were more pine and sturdy, close-growing cedar instead of white blankets of cotton strewn over the red earth; there were the gloom and the loneliness of a half-settled frontier.

John had no time to be lonely. For there were books in the Waddel home, and in books the boy could find escape from more sad reality. He took to the library. Almost forgetting to eat or sleep, he consumed Rollin's *Ancient History*, Robertson's *America* and *Charles the Fifth*, the large edition of Cook's *Voyages*, Browne's *Essays*, and a volume and a half of John Locke on *The Human Understanding*.[23]

The choice of books was limited, theology, of course, predominating; but without hesitation John had unearthed the works of history and philosophy. His luck was good: Parton has called *Charles the Fifth* the best book ever written for a boy.[24] John gained a knowledge of the past from the histories and travel books; and of the world of abstractions from the essays of Locke, which laid solid foundations for all his subsequent thought.

Even at this early age he revealed a characteristic mental intemperance; he read with such indifference to rest and eyestrain that his health gave way. Lacking any supervision that he would respect, he rapidly lost color and weight. His appearance so alarmed Moses Waddel on his return that he notified Mrs. Calhoun, who immediately sent for her son.[25]

John would have been glad to see his mother again. The books with which he had grappled so fiercely may have dulled the edges of his pain, but it was not only his sister that he mourned now. For months, old Patrick had been troubled with 'a lingering fever' and 'a bleeding at the nose . . . which exhausted him gradually.' He died on the fifteenth of February, 1796, probably of tuberculosis.[26] It took three weeks for the news to reach Charleston.

John's father died a relatively prosperous man. Only one man in the neighborhood had accumulated more than the thirty-one Negroes which the census of 1790 credited to Pat Calhoun. He left not one but five farms to his widow and four sons; riches indeed for the hill-country, in which the old wills show that items such as 'one pair of silver knee buckles,' 'a horse named Tumbler,' '1 pair of spoon molds,' and 'two pewter plates,' or 'a compact little farm with a Negro servant named Modesty,' represented the heights of luxury attainable. Needless to say the self-educated and superbly self-confident Pat would not have instructed his survivors, as did one up-countryman, to see that his son 'received a good English education.' More likely his final wish would have been akin to that of the Anderson County farmer who willed his son 'a bay cold [sic], saddle and bridle, and a Rifle gun, and if he stay with his Mother and assist in supporting the younger Children,' [27] an extra share of the profits from the plantation and the grist mill.

Only his mother and his younger brother, Patrick, were there to greet John when he returned home. The big house was empty now, with the echo of old Pat's restless footsteps stilled, and the two tall brothers gone their own way into the world. The old veterans and hunters, the storytellers who used to cluster around the great fire came no more. Outside, beyond the walls of the house, it was lonelier still. It had always been lonely up in the hills, and now, a decade and a half after Cornwallis's defeat, it was like a forgotten corner of the world. The men who had broken the wilderness were themselves old and broken now, and the sons who might have carried on the work of their fathers slept at Camden, Cowpens, or under the blood-red clay of King's Mountain. In scattered cabins and small hillside farmhouses, old women and widowed or unwed girls lived solitary lives, walled in 'by the bounds of self,' [28] speaking the crabbed speech of Elizabethan England or the Scottish Highlands, haunted by fears of ghosts and witches.

Down in the village, of course, a certain community life prevailed: quilting parties and husking bees, log-rolling and wrestling. 'The youth who could pull down his man at the end of the handstick, throw him in a wrestle, or outstrip him in a footrace' could be sure of a cheer from the older men and 'a slap on the shoulder by the old ladies.' [29] There was plenty of hunting, too, for the Long Cane country abounded with game, and on moonlit nights young John may have stirred in the depths of his feather bed to hear the mournful echo of a hound-pack on the far-off trail of a coon.

4

In the world outside, George Washington was ending his second Presidential term. In France, mobs that had fought to dip their fingers in the blood of Louis XVI were 'cannonaded out of existence' by a young officer named

Bonaparte. The 'Terror' that had ended in France was rising in Europe; in Egypt, at the naval battle in Aboukir Bay at the mouth of the Nile, the genius of a frail, hollow-eyed Vice-Admiral of the King's Navy, not yet forty, had destroyed the French fleet, and in England the name of Horatio Nelson was already a legend. An era and a century were ending.

Meanwhile, young John Caldwell was living the arduous and withdrawn life of the Southern frontier. Probably none of our American statesmen, not even Abraham Lincoln, spent his formative years in such utter solitude. While Calhoun was growing up in the empty Long Cane country, young Daniel Webster was struggling with Latin and table manners at Phillips Exeter Academy in New Hampshire, and Henry Clay was learning the ways of men and the wiles of women at the race-tracks and dancing assemblies of Lexington, Kentucky. But what the South Carolina boy learned, he had to learn for himself, slowly, painfully, with infinite groping and self-questioning. He lived entirely within himself, was thrown back always on his own resources and his own decisions. By temperament the student, his character was far more that 'of the lonely, thoughtful, meditative boy . . . than the careless, happy, healthy comrade of other boys.' [30] A solitary walk through the woods in the fall, carrying a rifle; a hot afternoon at the side of the creek, his long hands tensed on the rod, and the Negro, Sawney, asleep at his side—moments like these were all he asked of happiness. Physically he was 'active and energetic'; he 'shot and angled with skill'; [31] but these were solitary sports; and he was too young to join the farmers of the neighborhood in political discussions at the polling booths or around the tavern firesides. There was no time for visits to the town or rides to the cabins of the neighbors. There was too much work to be done. For this was the farming South, not the plantation South; there were no house-parties or barbecues; the horses were for plowing, not for visiting; and wagons, not carriages, stood in the stables.

For John Calhoun childhood was already over. He had a man's burdens now, and he bore them manfully. The institution of the overseer had not yet been invented; and upon his and his mother's shoulders fell the responsibility of the five farms and all the Negroes. Nor was mere management all. There was plenty of hard physical work to be done, and of this the frail boy of fourteen did his full share. Not yet had Southerners discovered that black bodies alone were able to endure the fierce heat of the cotton field. Years later, John's playmate, Sawney, basking in reflected glory, would gleefully recall: 'We worked in the field, and many's the time in the brilin' sun me and Marse John has plowed together.' [32]

The days were not long enough for all that had to be done. All his life, sleep was over for Calhoun at the first glow of dawn, a habit which can be traced back to his farming boyhood. Out of bed in an instant, he would pull on shirt, breeches, and moccasins, then hurry out to the barn where the sheep and cattle were waiting. Feeding and milking over, he could

walk into the field, gather apples or melons with the damp chill of the
night still on them, smell the clean tang of the pennyroyal, and feel the
wet weeds along the footpaths lashing his ankles.[33] Breakfast would be a
hearty meal: ham and red gravy, fried eggs, grits, and milk cool from the
spring, all eaten hastily while plans for the day worked through his nimble
brain. There might be oats or corn to be tended, wheat to be harvested,
with the whole neighborhood pitching in; peach brandy to be distilled for
their entertainment, fruit to be picked, or stock to be bred. This was a
subsistence farm, operated for its owner's livelihood, not for a landlord's
profit. Provision crops secured the first attention; market crops were
secondary.

Breakfast over, Calhoun was off to the cotton rows, the soft earth hot
under his feet, the sun blazing upon his head, and the linsey-woolsey shirt
heavy and wet upon his bowed shoulders. Up and down, up and down the
rows he moved, setting his course diagonally from one curving terrace to
another, so that the rough brown stalks from last year's crop would not
scratch the legs of the horses. Sawney would be close behind, dropping
the seed into the hills or the open crests of the ridges.[34] Weeks later, the
young plants would appear, thin and frail, with their two or three minute
leaves, and then were the aching hours of thinning them out to clusters
twelve inches apart. And once these had grown beyond the danger of
cutworm, the young sprouts would be chopped down to fertilize the one
sturdy plant selected for survival.

Next came the hoeing and the cultivating—the 'light plowing,' John
would have called it—while on the young plants the small buds hardened
and swelled. And then, at last, the morning when the flowers were the
color of fresh cream on the cotton stalks and by noon were white as the
clouds floating overhead. Through the slow hours of afternoon the tint
would change to the most delicate and softest rose, deepening onward hour
by hour, almost so you could watch it, if you had time to watch; glowing
from pink into red as the afternoon was lost in twilight, and from red to
flame in the quick hot blaze of the Southern sunset. It was over then; the
blossoms tarnished under the moonlight; by morning the fallen petals
would lie in a circle around each plant. The beauty was gone, but for
John this would have been the best time of all; for where the blossoms
had been were round balls, turning slowly to a harsh brown, until on some
hot sleepy day the fibers would yawn apart and the white 'locks' of the
cotton burst forth, ready for the picking.

All these things Calhoun knew would happen as surely as dark came at
night and cold in the autumn, not through the turn of the hours and seasons
alone, but from the aching effort of his body and the workings of his brain.
He knew little, but what he did know, he understood; and what he felt,
he felt deeply. Solitude and retirement 'had intensified all his impressions.'
Now and then the restlessness of his forbears who had broken the wilder-

ness trails would come upon him, and flung down upon the top of a wind-swept hill he would know a soaring freedom. He knew the pure unearthly feeling of the early morning; the depths of blue shadows streaked along the logs of the barn and the corn crib; the deceptiveness of the noontime shade and a water bucket that were never so cool as they looked from the cotton row. There were moments when he could give himself up to dreaming, to plumbing the depths of his own nature, contemplating rather than working, like all who live alone and within.[35] He could rest his horse and his back for a moment and scoop up one of those tiny cross-shaped stones the angels had dropped when they brought the story of the Crucifixion to America; or, like the psalmist, lift his eyes to the hills. He was content. Knowing no life other than the one into which he had been born, taught that duty, not happiness, was the chief end of man, he was only surprised at how much happiness he actually found. Perhaps for the only time in his life he was at peace with himself, in utter harmony with the world around him. He loved the land, not with any mystic idolatry, but with the physical love of a man who has worked the soil with his own hands and found it good. For Calhoun, the love of the land was fundamental. It was a part of his emotional and physical being. Everything that he said or did in later life can be traced back to this love and understanding of the earth from which he sprang. To him, agriculture was not a means to an end, but a life, complete and satisfying in itself. All his years, even at the summit of his fame, he would find his greatest happiness in the few months when he could be the planter that he had always wanted to be.

He was a born farmer. Several years after this period he is said to have taken charge of his brother's property, 'made the largest crop ever made, and saved him from bankruptcy.'[36]

Much of his proficiency, however, he owed to his mother. Little, pitifully little, is known of this 'tall, stately' mother of John Calhoun. She is said to have been a woman of some 'culture,' and hers was now the task of tempering the rugged heritage Patrick Calhoun had left his son. Her gentle influence and association with the few Huguenots of Abbeville, whose race was to become a synonym for 'Southern aristocracy,' gave Calhoun the grace of manner, the aura of Old-World courtliness, intermingled with frontier reserve, that was to characterize him in Washington society.[37] Society, too, in Calhoun's youth was wont to trace his dark Irish beauty to his mother, although it was tempered with no small degree of the physical and mental austerity, inherited from old Patrick.

The boy inherited more than grace and good looks from his mother. She left him ardency and enthusiasm, emotional intensity,[38] balanced by a shrewd business head, unusual in a woman, but essential to a man with a plantation to direct, to say nothing of the affairs of government. 'She was a great manager,' wrote a contemporary, and in teaching her son the management of a plantation she was giving him more than even he knew.

No better training for a future leader of men could have been devised. 'A well-governed plantation was a well-ordered little independent state.'[39] There was a whole economy to be controlled, a whole community to be governed. From this school, before the rise of the overseer had absorbed personal responsibility, rose a whole generation of Southern spokesmen to whom command, duty, and personal responsibility were as automatic as breathing.

There was much else that Martha Caldwell taught her son. From her he learned to reverence the Bible as sacred, and, although never religious in the orthodox sense, he was always devout. She taught him to revere God, to honor his parents, and to do justice. And these were lessons that remained with him, just as his father's theories of government became a part of his being.

Furthermore, she was a good listener. During the long hours behind the plow, John had time to mull over the ideas that he had gleaned from the books in Moses Waddel's library and to make them a part of his own fine-spun thinking. He had absorbed with delight, and he remembered 'an accumulation of facts to be slowly digested into mental substance during the coming years.'[40] More and more he was thinking for himself, and what he said was flavored with his own originality. Already, he is said to have become something of a conversationalist—with his mother as his audience.

Once, in all these years, he obtained a single copy of a newspaper. There was no postoffice in Abbeville then; few newspapers ever made their way to the up-country. To Calhoun his one issue of the South Carolina *Gazette* was as precious as a book, and he treasured it all his life. It was his first political textbook, and his faded pencil marks still remain, underlining an account of the proceedings of Congress for April 11 and 13, 1798, including a debate on relations with France, a public meeting at Charleston, and an address by President John Adams.[41]

In the evening, after watering and feeding the stock, locking the barn for the night, and hanging the keys beside the fireplace, the lanky, bushy-haired boy of sixteen lit a home-made tallow candle and studied his newspaper. There is no evidence that he had developed any political ambition. He was not dissatisfied with his lonely, hard-working life, but had merely a healthy interest in those scant items from the world outside. He had pitifully little reading material; and almost as difficult as getting the books to read would have been finding the time to read them. But Calhoun's ingenuity was successful. A contemporary account tells of a farmer who rode by the Calhoun lands, and there saw John, hard at work in a field, whistling cheerfully, with a book 'tied to the plow.'[42]

Neighbors in the tavern now had something to talk about for the rest of the summer. Books and education—these were not matters to be taken lightly. Probably most boys in the neighborhood were far more concerned over the next coon hunt than over their lack of schooling, but with their fathers it was not so. Scant as education was in the hills, to those unlettered but ambitious men it remained the highest of human ideals. If not for them . . . perhaps for their children.

Obviously, Pat Calhoun's son was a 'young man of worth and promise.' He was too bright and quick a youth to be a farmer for the rest of his life. He 'ought to be educated.' [43]

The neighborhood clamor at first left Mrs. Calhoun unmoved. She needed her son on the farm. But 'so frequently and urgently' was 'the feeling of the people . . . pressed upon her' that at last in the summer of 1800 she sent for her two older sons.

It was these two brothers, shop clerks in Augusta and Charleston, who, as instruments of Providence or of history,. diverted their stubborn, somber-eyed younger brother from his peaceful existence to the rocky road of politics. Had not James and William returned to the family farms while John was still young enough for formal education, he might have only been remembered as a neighborhood individualist.

Already he had become set in his habits of living. This was no child that James and William had to deal with, but a man who had found his place in the world and was content. This was the self-assured master of the plantation, his lips, above a square cleft chin, set with a firmness startling in one so young. Tentatively, the two brothers approached the question. Moses Waddel had reopened his school. John should go back there for a few months, to fit him to practice law.

John shook his head. He could not think of leaving his mother, he said, and he did not want to be a lawyer. He had determined to be a planter; a planter he would remain. To convince him of the necessity of his own education was even more difficult than winning over his mother had been. But his brothers persisted. They put a far higher estimate upon his abilities than he did himself.

At last John gave way. Yes, if his mother gave her free consent, he would return to school. But he would not be contented with a few months. He faced the family council with an ultimatum.

'To . . . a partial education I answer decidedly, no; but if you are willing and able to give me a complete education, I give my consent.'

'What is your idea of a complete education?'

'The best school, college, and legal education to be had in the United States,' John replied.

'In that case we would be obliged to send you to a New England college and maintain you there for several years.'

'True, but I will accept nothing less.'

'How long will you require for the accomplishment of such an education?'

'About seven years.' [44]

John himself chose Yale College.

II

For God and Timothy Dwight

JOHN C. CALHOUN was graduated at the age of twenty-two from Yale College with the class of 1804. Although he had entered the college at the start of his junior year, transferring from Dr. Waddel's Academy, he received high honors. This is all the more remarkable when it is remembered that twenty-four months of intensive study had comprised his entire scholastic preparation. Despite this short period in which to learn the work of fourteen years, Calhoun by the excellence of his teaching and the brilliance of his mind did escape that specter of half education which he feared. He was graduated from Yale a man better educated than many of his classmates. He had learned to study, but, more important, he had learned to think.[1]

Although, as he said upon his entry into college, he was 'fresh from the backwoods,' he had attained a far more solid scholastic foundation than he himself realized. For in the rural South of his day there was no better education available than in those 'log colleges,' like Dr. Waddel's, where all over the up-country, young Scotch-Irishmen, safely removed from the distractions of both city and plantation life, were memorizing thousands upon thousands of lines of Virgil, Horace, and Cicero. Even on Sundays there was no rest from mental and spiritual discipline, as the stern-browed Calvinistic schoolmasters poured their grim and unbending doctrine into the always intense and sometimes fanatical minds of their young listeners.[2]

And the results were good. Orthodox as was the curriculum, it was designed, not so much to impart knowledge as to develop the power for independent work and the qualities of judgment and imagination. Greek and Roman classics were stressed because of their wealth of general principles which could be applied to contemporary ethics and politics, the two matters which were of primary concern to a gentleman. And the object of these schools was to develop gentlemen, or, at least, 'good men, with command over themselves,' men of the world, with 'spiritual roots in their own communities.'[3]

There was a rigorous selection of talent in schools like the Waddel Academy. Intellectually, it was not democratic. It denied that all men were equal, in the sense that the unlettered poor white, in his innate judgment and ability, was as capable of ruling as a Jefferson, merely because he had the political right to rule. The school consciously sought for and aided those whom 'Nature had endowed with genius'; and with Waddel, at least, students like Calhoun could advance as fast as their capacities would carry them. No brilliant pupil had to slow his pace to the drudge. Such schools were answers to Jefferson's dream that the poor but intelligent child could have an equal opportunity with the rich and lazy one. Calhoun himself judged Dr. Waddel's Academy by the quality of leadership it provided, noting such examples as George McDuffie, James Louis Petigru, Hugh Legare, and William H. Crawford. Whatever its limitations, 'enough teaching talent was available to give us a Calhoun,' and to satisfy the cravings of his hungry mind.

Socially, the school was democratic in the extreme. Bucks in broadcloth might arrive to scoff at the cruder country youths in their twilled homespun, yet, only a few years later, these sons of small farmers, through the vigor of their intellects and the strength of their ambitions, had themselves entered the planter class.

Even more democratic than the student personnel was the whole mode of life. 'The Waddel school stressed high thinking, hard work, and plain living.' If minds were nourished, bodies were another matter. Three times a day fifteen minutes were snatched from study hours for that pitifully inadequate diet of cornbread and bacon, upon which Northern troops perished in the Southern prison camps of the eighteen-sixties. In primitive log cabins, lit by pine torches or flickering tapers, the boys lived in groups, studying from sunrise until nine o'clock at night. A horn roused them at 'first dawn streak,' and after breakfast they gathered in the schoolroom for prayer. They studied in the woods, each in his own chair, with his name carved on the back; and on cold days obtained heat and exercise from chopping trees and building 'log-heap fires.' [4] Though not under the teacher's eye, they studied their grammar and syntax, their Virgil and Homer, with intensity. A hundred and fifty memorized lines a day would be the quota for the slower pupils; over a thousand, for the brilliant ones. There were no organized athletics to distract their interest and their energies; their competitive spirit was largely satisfied in the classrooms.

Pent-up energy found release in fighting, and overdisciplined youths would insert long burning sticks into the cabins, applying them to the seat of the pantaloons of some unlucky victim. On Saturdays a certain degree of freedom was allowed, the older boys spending the night 'possum and coon hunting or shooting squirrels and turkeys. There were races and games of 'bull-pen'; and it is known that Calhoun 'played town ball . . . and gathered nuts' with the others and joined in the long discussions of the books that had been read. But the Friday debating club, which to some of the boys was the high spot of the week,[5] he could not have enjoyed. He was struggling with a speech impediment, or hesitancy, which, 'added to his unusual diffidence, rendered his prospects of eminence as a speaker quite unflattering.'[6] Probably this difficulty lowered his self-esteem, for until he entered Yale he had no realization of his superior abilities.[7]

It would have been hard, too, for Calhoun at this period not to have given way to discouragement. The greatest sorrow of his life, thus far, had broken over him. On the fourteenth of May, 1801, he went home for a visit and found that his mother had been ill. She seemed to be 'in no danger,' and in the evening he returned to school. The next day the news came that his mother was dead. It was well into September before he was sufficiently recovered from 'a severe spell of the fever,' with which he battled throughout the summer, to write the tragic news to a friend. 'How can I express my feelings when it was announced to me?' he wrote.[8] But he owed himself a reckoning, himself and the memory of the mother who had believed in him. He resumed his studies. There was nothing left to do but to go on. . . .

Schools of the kind he was leaving were revolutionizing Southern thought, in theology and politics as well as education. It is not at all remarkable that Calhoun and the leaders of his generation led an only too willing South toward the ideal of a Greek Republic.[9] Nor is it remarkable that Calhoun himself, for all his underlying gentleness, could never, despite momentary lapses, entirely escape the Puritan heritage of his youth. He emerged from Waddel's classroom, disciplined, controlled, his intellect broadened, but with all the sterner side of his nature intensified. Under the easy manner of the Southern 'gentleman,' the 'lean, eager' young man who entered Yale in the fall of 1802 was as rigid and fatalistic as the New England Puritans with whom he was thrown.

2

The Yale College that Calhoun knew has vanished so completely in the rebuilding energies of a hundred years that it is now useless to look for it. Of that mellowed 'Brick Row' under the elms, which to Calhoun would symbolize Yale, Connecticut Hall alone remains. And even it, quaintly hip-roofed, as it was built in 1750—engulfed on three sides by the grim brownstone of the eighteen-eighties—is very different from the square four-storied structure of Calhoun's day. On the Green three steeples reach into clouds that still hang so low over the New Haven rooftops, but the stately brick churches are not the old meeting-houses where Calhoun sat, his head bowed in prayer; and successively a Greek temple and a frame 'Gothic' church have replaced the little brick State House where 'Old Pope Dwight,' as the irreverent secretly called him, toasted the Phi Beta Kappa students with 'rational conviviality.'

Only the street names are the same: College, fronting the Green, the cement smooth where the elms once stood; Chapel, to the right, a plaque marking the site of 'Sally' Sherman's house; and parallel to College, Old High, now sucked into the campus itself. Today, only the contours of the city, the huddle of shanties, houses, towers, and churches, backed up against East and West Rocks, suggest the dim outlines of Calhoun's New Haven—a country village of sandy streets and cows grazing on the Green.[10] But to a boy only a generation removed from the frontier, the little town, with its rows of pre-Revolutionary houses, trim behind picket fences, must have seemed a metropolis indeed.

That he roomed in the dormitory, we know. The old Treasurer's account books at Yale show payment of his 'study rent,' [11] and in this he was fortunate, whether he had to share quarters with one roommate or two. For Yale was growing fast, too fast to house her flock, which had spilled out into dwelling houses all over New Haven, charging the sedate little town with their infectious vitality. Whether it was in Old Connecticut, or the 'new' Union Hall, where Calhoun first lowered his trunk onto the broad floor-boards of his room, has long been forgotten. But Connecticut set the pattern for both, with its long hallways running from front to rear, its ninety-six rooms, ample closets, and broad open fireplaces.

From small-paned windows, Calhoun could look out on the sights of New Haven; and if he was on the first floor, in summer at least he would have become thoroughly acquainted with the sounds and smells of the town as well. For the windows were but a foot from the ground—temptingly near, as the monthly bills for unconfessed glass breakages show—and in all but the coldest seasons students often removed the casements from their frames. So the breath of New Haven permeated the rooms of Yale: the scent of the sea when the wind was fresh—strange and disturbing to a hill-born Southerner—and in the spring the heady odors of fruit-blossoms and cow-stables could only make the homesickness of the farm-bred boys all the more keen.

Less idyllic were the sounds of New Haven, for but a step away from the College were grouped the jail, the poorhouse, the house of correction, and the insane asylum; and thoughts of God and Life Eternal and songs of praise in the College chapel were broken by 'moans, cries,' and the shrill screams and wild laughter of the insane.[12] Not even in their own world were the boys free from the vision of the world to which they, without God's help, might descend.

Calhoun's first day would have been a busy one. As an upperclassman, he was spared the grueling oral examination by the tutors; but like the more lowly freshmen, he had to present 'satisfactory evidence of a blameless life.' [13] Sometime during the day he would have been subjected to an interview with 'Old Pope Dwight,' but this would have been more terrifying in prospect than in reality. Domineering as Dwight was, outside of the pulpit his smile was 'irresistable,' and his manner 'gentle,' [14] although his initial scrutiny of a new student—black eyes piercing through shell-rimmed lenses—was disconcertingly thorough.

Calhoun was not even yet a part of Yale College until, having pocketed his receipt for $30.60 of 'Tuition-money' [15] he could affix his signature to the 1800 edition of *The Laws of Yale College*.[16] Later, he would learn that this formidable list of 'Thou Shalt Not's' was little read and less enforced, but now, in the serious moment of college entrance, he, who had virtually grown up with a gun in his hand, would have been quick to note that no firearms or gunpowder could be kept in the rooms, and 'If any Scholar shall go a-fishing or sailing . . . he may be fined not exceeding thirty cents.' For restrictions against attending 'any comedy or tragedy,' playing billiards, 'or any other unlawful game . . . for a wager,' Calhoun would have cared little; college for him was 'no season of recreation.' But he may have paused for a second reading of the more serious 'Crimes and Misdemeanors,' such as calling 'for strong drink in any tavern,' and the grim warning that 'Any Scholar' so bold as to 'deny the Holy Scriptures . . . to be of divine authority . . . shall be dismissed.' [17]

3

Tired though he was when he lay in bed, the breathing of his roommate sounding in his ears, and the dying firelight throwing dancing patterns across the ceiling, sleep would have eluded Calhoun. Forebodings nagged at his overactive brain. What chance had he, with his limping Latin and scant Greek, his 'limited' educational opportunities, against these primed and charging young graduates of Exeter and Andover, these boys who knew libraries as he knew a cotton field? So it must have been with an extra-sized chip on his shoulder that he entered Josiah Meigs's mathematics class the next morning.

Gripping his slate, Calhoun sat down and mechanically scrawled several 'arithmatical questions' which the professor was dictating. He bent over his work. Surprise swept over him. Why, this was 'no difficulty' at all! Instantly he solved the first problem, and looking up was surprised 'to find the others busy with their slates.' Meigs caught his eye. 'Have you got the answer?'

Calhoun passed him his slate. 'The answer proved to be correct.' Once again he bent over his desk, looked up, and found his classmates still at work. Again he passed up his slate, and again it was returned. It happened again and again. 'The same thing happened every time.'

Calhoun was gripped with excitement. For the first time, the thought crossed his mind that his abilities were above those of other men. He was worth the money that his brothers were spending on him. He could justify his family's faith in him, and he felt 'gratified.' [18]

Thus assured, Calhoun swung into the tempo of his new work. As an upperclassman, he had greater freedom than the overtasked freshmen and sophomores, who from six in the morning until ten at night were allowed but two hours for recreation. Nevertheless, he too would have been kept 'hard at worke.'[19] Languages, English, grammar, trigonometry, navigation, surveying, 'and other mathematics,' natural philosophy and astronomy were the subjects prescribed for his junior year, and as a senior, 'Rhetoric, Ethics, Logic, Metaphysics, history of Civil Society and Theology,[20] would demand his attention. Scientific studies, although virtually 'the promised land,'[21] to Calhoun were so new in the curriculum that they were not even listed in the 1800 program.

No record of Calhoun's grades has been preserved. All evidence—his place in the college graduating exercises, the testimony of his teacher, Benjamin Silliman, plus his addiction to study—indicates that he was a brilliant student. His best subjects, according to an early biographer, were 'metaphysics, mathematics, and the precise sciences.'[22] History and moral philosophy are not mentioned. But in the political hydrophobia then raging at Yale, it would have been impossible for Dr. Dwight to have judged the work of a Jeffersonian with any notable impartiality.

4

Calhoun had more responsibilities than his studies. As a senior he had 'to inspect the manners of the lower classes . . . to instruct them . . . in graceful and decent behavior';[23] and unwritten custom permitted him to 'trim' the freshmen, keeping them bowing to their own shadows, although it is doubtful if he wasted much time on such amusements. Fresh from the South, however, he would have been only human if he had not stolen a few moments' extra warmth in bed on zero mornings and let a Yankee-born freshman light his fire and plow through the unbroken snow to the well to fill his pitcher with ice water; for the laws of Yale required that freshmen run errands for their superiors, if not 'needless, unreasonable, or vexatious.'[24]

It is unfortunate that we know so little of Calhoun's inner life at Yale. From the diaries of teachers and students, from their private letters and published reminiscences, we can indeed piece together the externals of his day-to-day living. We can see him jerked from sleep into the black dawns, the chapel bell 'howling and tumbling' like a 'noisy demon'[25] in his ears; and hear the crunch of his footsteps on the snow. We can see him in the chapel, evenings and mornings, knees bent, as Dr. Dwight or one of the tutors read 'suitable' Scripture, or exhorted on religious and moral subjects.[26] We can see him in the half-hour before breakfast, as some boys studied and some played backgammon or football on the

Green,[27] waking himself up with a quick walk under the elms. The meals were ample: coffee, chocolate, and hashed meat were served every morning; and for dinner, roast beef and steaks were served twice a week, oysters occasionally, and turkeys and geese at least once a fortnight. Calhoun, who had somehow survived the Waddel 'hog and hominy' had not been so well nourished in years. For Dwight was mindful of the health of his students; 'exercise and activity' were his indiscriminate remedies for all boys who felt themselves 'weak and tired.'[28] The Spartan life was too much for the frailer boys, however, and it was observed that 'many, while here, lay the foundation of diseases which terminate fatally.'[29] Calhoun, hardened from his years in the field, bore up well; enjoying what was rare with him, 'almost uninterrupted health'[30] throughout the two years.

We can see him mulling over the crabbed old books: *Distempers of Sea-Going People*, Norris's *Ideal World*, Pearce on *The Nature of Sin, Contemplations on Death and Immortality*. Only by courtesy could the stark little room on the second floor of the chapel, with its low table and high-backed armchair, its single door open only to the faculty and upper-classmen with money to rent desired books, be called a library, although in his few years of administration, Dr. Dwight had succeeded in raising the number of volumes from two thousand to five thousand. There was enough, however, for Calhoun's hungry intellect; and if there was more of Edwards and Mather than of plays and poetry, there were Locke and Calvin, Sophocles and Euripides, Shakespeare and Milton, Euclid, Adams on the Constitution, and mathematical works, ranging from plain arithmetic to Marolois on *Fortifications*.[31]

And we can see him in his rare moments of relaxation, when the repressed students would cluster in one of the rooms secretly to 'help despatch . . . a few glasses of wine,' and to argue fiercely on women, 'politics . . . the corruption of . . . our great men,' on whether minorities were ever justified in rebelling against majorities, and if want of religious principles should 'exclude a man from public life.'[32]

It was a stirring time to be alive. Calhoun, bred to the tradition of hatred for the British, could look with complacency on newspaper forecasts of a coming French invasion which would 'put an end to the existance . . . of Great Britain,' yet could heed President Jefferson's words of warning: 'We have seen with sincere concern the flames of war lighted up again in Europe . . .' What did it mean—a humbled Britain, 'Boney' astride France, astride Europe, astride the world? And in America, world events echoed in the Louisiana Purchase Treaty? Did New England, quaking lest her 'balance of power' be overthrown, deny that the United States had authority to annex more territory? John Randolph, Jefferson's brilliant House floor leader, had an answer. 'The Constitution,' he declared, 'did not describe any particular boundary beyond which the United States could not extend.'[33]

5

Yale was seething with life. It was a young man's school: Dwight himself was only fifty, at the height of his powers; Benjamin Silliman, elected Professor of Chemistry the previous year, was twenty-two, and Jeremiah Day, Professor of Mathematics and Natural Philosophy, not yet thirty. The bulk of the teaching fell on the shoulders of the tutors, only youngsters themselves, and fired with the kind of zeal that led one to comment upon another: 'In six months you will make the young men . . . feel that a knowledge of Hebrew is as essential to success in the ministry as air is necessary to animal life.' [34]

There were eight tutors when Calhoun arrived, including the politically and legally minded George Hoadley, later to serve as Mayor both of New Haven and of Cleveland, Ohio; and Ebenezer March, whose death early in 1803 furnished inspirational material for the entire city clergy. Progress jostled reaction at Yale. In 1801 had come the Law School, with its own professor, Elizur Goodrich, and although Silliman could still carry the entire contents of the mineralogical cabinet around in one candlebox, the collection—and collegiate curiosity about it—was growing every day.

Dwight was Yale and Yale was Dwight in the year 1802. Only five years had passed since the burly ex-soldier of the Revolution had started to draw the straggling college into a focus in which the outlines of the future university were already visible; [35] but the name of Timothy Dwight was already as strong a factor in bringing Carolina 'gentlemen' to the college as were the packet-boats, which ran their rum cargoes so assiduously between New Haven and Charleston. Timothy Dwight, hymn-writer, religious and political fanatic, arrogant and incurable Federalist, was a man born to perform miracles and to move mountains—and he had need of these talents at Yale.

Yale had been a gay place back in 1797, far more satisfying to the young gentlemen who passed their study hours smoking, drinking, and enjoying 'sprightly conversation,' [36] than to their Puritan parents. Dr. Dwight had found himself confronted with a rebellious and even roistering student body, who at best contented themselves with howling down a guest speaker at chapel, to a thunder of stamping feet; and at worst, danced, gambled, stored liquor in their rooms, and according to accusation engaged in 'the violation of the most sacred of all ties between men and women.' [37] The Age of Reason had arrived, or so the students thought. Rules were on the books and so were the Blue Laws, but human nature had long since prevailed.

By 1802, the year Calhoun arrived at Yale, a seeming miracle had been worked. Where only two years before but a single student had partaken of the Lord's Supper, now half the student body were converted within twelve months' time, and of the class of 1802 'the greater part settled down in quiet country parishes, where their lives glided away in . . . peace.'[38] Now the students of Yale spent their time in such 'stormy dark debate' as they hoped 'might be rare for the sake of human nature,' arguing such questions as 'Is a Divine Revelation Necessary?' or 'Did all mankind descend from Adam?'[39] God and Timothy Dwight had done their work.

But youth is youth, and 'human nature is the same everywhere,' as Captain Marryat grimly observed; and although the godly Captain's opinion may be exaggerated, that the college students were still 'in the secret practice of more vice than is to be found in any other establishment of the kind in the Union,'[40] it is certain that even God and Timothy Dwight faced difficulties in attempting to reverse the trends of the times—the French Revolution and the 'licentious democracy of Thomas Jefferson.'

Dwight stinted no efforts. Culprits were invited to his rooms, and for a man who had been convinced of his own utter depravity at the age of six, it was no great task to break down the most hardened of eighteen- to twenty-year-old sinners, and to send them away in tears.[41] In chapel, the fiery zealot denounced the 'grossness and immorality of the theater,' defining Shakespeare as 'the language of vice,' and warning that he who visited 'the strange woman' would never look upon the face of God. 'There hath no temptation befallen you,' Dr. Dwight told his stricken-faced sinners, 'except what is common to all men.'[42]

Nor did Dwight depend upon emotionalism alone to win his converts. Already a legend at Yale in Calhoun's time was the story of the new young president, confronting a class of scoffing non-believers with the question: 'Is the Bible the Word of God?' Written and verbal refutations were invited, but once the last 'proof' of 'the hypothesis of God' was handed in, Dwight proceeded to take the case for his maker, tearing apart the reworked French agnosticism of his young skeptics as easily as the papers they were written on. From then on, the issue was decided: God was no longer a subject for debate at Yale. 'Christianity was supported by authority, and not by argument.'[43]

Thus was formed the goal of education at Yale: to give men the tools to build a changing world upon a foundation that would never change. Not facts, whose importance dimmed from one generation to the next, but the use of facts; not how to make a living, but the purpose in living, were the essentials. Consciously, Yale was training men for leadership, both in theology and statecraft; and more important than their knowledge would be the standards upon which their knowledge was built.

6

Calhoun's class, with its sixty-six members, was one of the largest in Yale history. Traditionally, almost half had their thoughts turned toward a spiritual career, but individualists did crop out, and the personnel ran all the way from Ezra Ely who had 'made a profession of religion before he was fourteen,' to the wild young Georgian, Amos Whitehead, who died 'from the results of dissipation' in 1808.[44]

If the warmth and self-revelation of letters written in later life is evidence, Calhoun's most intimate friend among his classmates was a young Scotch-Irish South Carolinian named James MacBride. Nor was his choice surprising, for it was MacBride of whom a brilliant South Carolina scholar later said he was one of the two men in Charleston, 'whose intercourse ever tended to keep alive the languishing flame of intellectual desire in my breast.'[45] Now doggedly working his way through the medical course, MacBride's interests were feverishly intensive; Calhoun once complained to him: 'I was always fond of your pursuit, the study of nature; you indifferent to mine.' Yet each had the kind of clear, keen-edged mind the other could appreciate, and their friendship lasted to the close of MacBride's short life. Calhoun could talk to MacBride. He could let his barriers down, boast, scoff, condemn, and reveal 'in strick confidence,' his secrets, his hopes, and his 'dispondency.' 'If I could see you,' he once wrote, 'I could fill a volume, almost.'[46]

With only two of his other classmates, John Felder and Micah Sterling, both later members of Congress, does Calhoun appear to have continued any close friendship after college. Both were brilliant; Sterling excelled as speaker and writer, and Calhoun had high regard for his opinions. Years later we find him writing: 'I receive with unmixed pleasure the approbation of my old friend.' When Sterling achieved election to Congress, Calhoun immediately sent him his instructions. 'I hope that you will quarter near to me, and that you will make my house as familiar as your own home. . . . I hope my namesake is growing finely.'[47]

John Felder of Orangeburg, South Carolina, Calhoun's only rival in the mathematics class, was a lovable eccentric, of whom it was said: 'No one could look so earnestly as he.' He read intensively, but hid his knowledge; temperamentally and politically he differed from Calhoun; yet their friendship lasted a lifetime.

7

Calhoun 'mixed not much with his class.' Never able to give himself easily to intimacies, at Yale he 'indulged his propensity to solitude.' He

walked alone under the elms, runs a highly colored account, 'his head among
. . . the stars.' [48]

So Yale would remember him. All knew of him; yet few really knew
him. Men remembered his tall figure, six feet two inches in his stocking
feet; and his mass of springy dark hair, which seemed to rear almost
erect 'when the fire was in him,' carrying his stature 'to an almost incredible height.' But the living, human man, who 'ate and drank like
other mortals,' [49] who argued forbidden politics and prepared the refreshments at the Phi Beta Kappa meetings, is lost in the mist of tradition.
Almost within his own lifetime, Calhoun became a legend at Yale. He was
a towering but remote figure in far-off Washington, a giant in the land,
and a myth to the college that he had attended only a generation before.

The impression gathered seems fantastic, but there is really nothing
fantastic about it. He was 'a man among boys.' Actually a number of his
classmates were his own age, or older, but in mental maturity they were
years behind him. He had grown up too soon. Facing the difficult social
adjustment that confronts any mature student of a background different
from that of his classmates, it is not surprising that he kept to himself.

Yet he was capable of both feeling and showing affection. Under-
standably, his closest friends included the young professors and tutors,
some of whom were only two or three years his seniors. Among these
were Benjamin Silliman, not 'the great Silliman' then, but 'a fair and
portly young man,' with thick hair clubbed into a queue and a perpetual
blush when confronted with new problems; [50] and James Kingsley, tutor
of Latin and Greek, dark, classic-featured, so timid . . . that he could
scarcely . . . look a scholar in the face . . . yet such a scholar himself
as to inspire with fear all who came to recite.' The keen intelligence of
these young men was a stimulus to Calhoun, and to both he showed
'feelings of warm attachment.' For them, Silliman was the spokesman.
'We, in turn, esteemed and loved him.' [51]

Already Calhoun was showing the power over the minds and imaginations of men younger than himself, so striking in his mature years. It is a
contemporary account that speaks of Calhoun's influence over classmates,
who, admiring his integrity and intellect, 'cultivated his friendship.' [52]

A genuine tribute to his personal appeal was accorded in his election
to the Alpha Chapter of Phi Beta Kappa. For although the Phi Beta
Kappa of 1803 demanded high standards of scholarship, it was first a
social fraternity. It had its ritual and secret grip, and the most brilliant
student in the college, lacking the required standards of morality and
general popularity, might fail of the unanimous vote necessary for membership.

Calhoun was not only a member, but one of the leading members. Immediately after his initiation on July 11, 1803, 'Mr. Calhoun was . . .
then appointed treasurer'; and to a committee to 'devise . . . a plan for

raising a permanent fund for the benefit of indigent Brethren residing at the University.'[53] In addition, he had to prepare his part in the debate for the next meeting, a task which, in view of his intense self-consciousness and his past difficulties at Dr. Waddel's school, must have caused him no little strain. Nevertheless, on July 25, his name first appears on record as a public speaker, as with three of his fellow members he discussed the question: 'Is government founded on the Social Compact?'[54] In December he took the floor again, this time on the question, 'Is Language of Divine Origin?'[55] The Alpha Chapter decided that it was.

Calhoun enjoyed the Phi Beta Kappa Society. Several of his best friends belonged, including MacBride and Felder, as well as the Charleston contingent of students: Jacob I'on, Amos Northrup, and the Gadsdens. Even socially Calhoun played an active part. He took upon himself the most difficult of all tasks, that of trying to find a speaker for an oration on June 18, 1804; an inconvenient honor that he himself would years later politely decline.[56] He assisted with the anniversary celebration on December 10, 1803, and on the twentieth, after his reelection as treasurer, marched with his 'brothers' in the traditional procession to the brick meeting-house on the Green, where an 'elegant oration' was heard; and from there to the State House, where, with Dwight himself as toastmaster, an 'excellent entertainment'[57] was enjoyed.

8

Socially omnipotent at Yale in Calhoun's day were the 'Literary' societies, 'Linonia' and 'Brothers in Unity.' In both members were drawn by lot, and in Calhoun's time every student at Yale belonged to one society or the other; that is, every student but John C. Calhoun.

Just what happened was a mystery for twenty-five years, as Calhoun's fame mounted, and both societies fought for the honor of his name. Faint, but clear, Calhoun's signature does appear on the rolls of the Linonian Society; but the Brothers in Unity, declaring that they 'had from himself assurances of his undiminished attachment to us,' fortified claims by squeezing in a palpable forgery of the great man's signature between a couple of neatly spaced names—and in the record book for the wrong year![58]

By 1840 the clamor compelled Calhoun to make a statement that 'he was not a member of either of the Literary Societies . . . he was appointed to the Linonian Society. Most of his friends (who were from the South) being members of Brothers in Unity, he preferred to belong to that society: but the rules preventing this, he attached himself to neither.'[59]

One might expect these words to have ended the controversy, but in

1858 a member of the Linonian Society produced a sheet of yellowed paper, written in a cramped nervous hand, almost unmistakably that of Calhoun. Addressed to his mother, in September, 1802, it stated that he had just been admitted to the junior class and had joined the Linonian Society. The question of whether Calhoun would have written a letter to a mother, already dead two years, did not seem to dampen the Lino- nian ardor. Regretfully, the Brothers in Unity conceded their claims. Not until years later was it discovered that in 1802 Yale did not open until October! [60]

So far as Calhoun's future was concerned, it might have been better had he belonged to one of the societies. For in their meetings questions were being considered that would have deep meanings in the life of the na- tion and in the life of John C. Calhoun. Such liberality of thought as could be tolerated at Timothy Dwight's Yale was rampant in the Linonian Society, which Calhoun had so casually spurned. Their answer was yes to the question, 'Can the aggrandizement of a neighboring power, by which a nation fears it may one day be oppressed, authorize a war against him?' It is easy to imagine Calhoun's interest in such questions as: 'Would it be desirable for the New England States to be separated from the others?' 'Ought the president to be endowed with power to remove of- ficers of government, except for misdemeanor?' [61] Meanwhile, over at the more conservative Brothers in Unity the problem, 'Is it politick for the United States to encourage manufactures?' was under consideration.[62] But the Phi Beta Kappa members, debating always under the eyes and ears of faculty members, decided that a division of the Union would not be 'politick,' agreed that infidels should be excluded from public affairs, that property should be a necessary qualification for voting, and that debtors should be imprisoned 'at the mercy of the creditor.' [63]

9

Calhoun did not depend exclusively on Yale Literary Societies for his social outlets. He had good times that fellow students in the predominantly mas- culine world of Yale must have envied. For there was Sarah Sherman!

It was but a step across Chapel Street from Brick Row to the two-story Colonial house where the three Sherman sisters lived. Two were already spoken for, but all three—Martha, Mehitabel, and Sarah—liked 'brilliant, devout, and public-spirited young men;' [64] and John Calhoun filled these qualifications admirably. Furthermore, he was a 'Carolina gentleman,' and although this species was often suspect on the score of lax morals and caressing, soft-edged speech, no others were such 'gentlemen of style,' and in Connecticut, at least, no attention was too much for visitors from South Carolina.

Calhoun rapidly became very intimate in the home of Roger Sherman's daughters. In later years he would always inquire 'with great interest after the young ladies of the family.' But it was no secret that it was the twenty-year-old Sarah for whom he 'had a special liking.' [65] Whether or not she was one of those legendary women of New Haven, so famous for their beauty, contemporary records fail to say; nor is there any indication that Calhoun's feeling for her was more than a natural enjoyment of apples and tea with a girl in the candlelight, or walks under the fruit trees when spring was in flower. Purpose was driving Calhoun; he had no time for romance.

But Sarah may have felt differently. Evidence hints that her dark-eyed Carolina visitor may have made an impression upon her heart not easy to erase. At any rate, she was well past thirty when she married the scholarly, politically ambitious man who would become Congressman Samuel Hoar, and by then she was quite an old maid.

10

It was not until his senior year that Calhoun came directly under Timothy Dwight's eye. For although 'father-confessor to all of his student body,' the seniors were Dwight's special charge. Nor was.it only sermons and textbooks that he expounded; manners as well as morals held sway in his discussions. Seated in the drafty classroom on a winter morning, his back to the students and feet within an inch of the blaze, Dwight's organ-like voice boomed forth, effortlessly holding the attention of thirty or forty at a time. Truth, honor, and manliness were words that slipped freely from his lips; and 'To be always a gentleman,' [66] was his credo. He advised the individual always to discuss the subject in which his companion was most interested, a teaching which Calhoun's admirers would later testify that he followed to the letter. And we can even trace the origin of Calhoun's strenuous physical régime to Dwight's lectures on keeping a robust body.

These were incidentals. Dwight's doctrine, as such, Calhoun rejected without equivocation. Outwardly, in insignificant matters, he conformed readily enough, but in the things that mattered he was a rebel. He would neither absorb Yale nor let himself be absorbed. He would not join the Moral Society. He would not join the Church of Christ. He would not even profess Christianity! Worst of all, not only in the classroom would he refuse to accept any doctrines whatsoever 'unless he could imagine them in practical operation and foresee their results,' but outside, wherever he was and whenever he got a chance, he 'avowed his Republican principles in an atmosphere where the very name of Republican was odious.' [67] His heresies were not held against him; were, no doubt, secretly envied.

But his friends were compelled to accept him on his own terms; and might concede, like the troubled Silliman, that John was 'a first-rate young man . . . for pure and gentlemanly conduct . . . but that his mind was of a peculiar structure, and his views also were often peculiar.' [68]

Not even Dr. Dwight could instill the fear of hell-fire and damnation in the young Southerner, who had already a thoroughly developed faculty for absorbing only such material as coincided with his own preconceived opinions. Dwight's failure to achieve conversion might have been expected to anger the dogmatic Puritan; for to him indifference was worse than 'direct opposition.' But no one who looked twice into Calhoun's intense face and deep eyes would have accused him of indifference—to religion or anything else. He was merely going through a period of rebelliousness and skepticism normal to his years and to an intellect 'so independent of authority.' Yet all unconsciously, the Puritanism then rampant at Yale left its mark. It fitted Calhoun's own temperament, his own Calvinistic heritage. He could never escape it entirely. It would be years before he could free himself from the conviction that dancing, that the theater, that actual happiness in work or in play, were all to be classified as sin.

At this period, however, politics were uppermost in his mind. Dwight had a grasp of fundamentals, and questions thrashed out in his classroom would later be fought out on the battlefields. 'The people of the Southern States,' Dwight would remark, 'suppose their interests to be different from ours. . . . The Southern States clash with the Northern and Western, and the question is whether a division should be made in the country, that each portion may pursue its own course.' [69]

Secession was Timothy Dwight's answer. And there were other questions: Foreign immigration? Union or disunion? Ought the poor to be supported by law? In discussions such as these, even Dwight, bitter Federalist that he was, could stimulate Calhoun's love of politics and government.

This is not to say that John learned much from Dr. Dwight, unless testing the strength of one's own opinions against a strong antagonist can be called learning. Dwight's disunionist theories Calhoun may have heeded somewhat, because of the distrust of the Union already sown in his mind by his own father. His reason for suspicion, however, was very different from Dr. Dwight's; the opinionated Federalist hated the Union because it gave too much power to the people; Calhoun distrusted the Union because he thought it was not fulfilling its original purpose, to give liberty to the people.

John Calhoun knew the answer the day when Dwight confronted his Moral Philosophy class with the question, 'What is the legitimate source of power?' John knew what Dr. Dwight expected him to say. Stretching himself erect, the indignant fires of old Pat Calhoun ablaze in his eyes, he answered defiantly, 'The people.'

The Moral Philosophy class was probably no more startled by this response than Dr. Dwight himself. But it interested the teacher to have his fundamental tenets challenged by a young frontiersman with the accents of the Deep South on his lips and the democratic heresies of the Jeffersonians in his mind. Sharply, Dwight threw forward an assertion; Calhoun denied it, not only with emotional heat, but with cold logic. Dwight became more interested, led the Carolinian on, and heard an exposition of Patrick Calhoun's theories on government, interspersed with a smattering of Locke and Paine.

The forgotten class in Moral Philosophy listened with a growing consciousness of the abilities of their classmate and perhaps a reluctant admiration for his foolhardy courage which dared praise Dwight's bitterest political enemy, Thomas Jefferson.

At dinner time the class adjourned, leaving Dr. Timothy Dwight in a state of mingled emotions. Unconvinced himself, he realized that the stubborn Carolinian was equally unconvinced, and that his dogmatic assertions were braced with keen logic. Suddenly Dwight discovered that he admired young John Calhoun for standing so staunchly by his Republican principles. In fact, he went so far as to say to a friend that Calhoun had ability enough 'to be President of the United States,' and that he would not be 'surprised to see him one day occupy that office.' [70]

Eventually this prediction found its way back to Calhoun. There is no way of telling what this revelation may have wrought in the depths of his introspective mind. He took it with perfect seriousness; 'he took everything seriously.' He was never able to forget it, never able to understand why having the ability for the office did not automatically mean that he should attain it. Certainly now he realized, more acutely than even on that first day in the mathematics class, that his natural abilities might, with education, carve a far deeper niche in life than the mere practice of law would ever do. Perhaps then he realized how far even a poor farm boy might aspire under a democratic government. His commencement address indicated that he did: it was entitled 'The Qualifications Necessary to Make a Statesman.' [71] John Calhoun with the shrewd bright eyes and stubborn set to his mouth had begun to dream, to plan, and to wonder.

Momentarily, it must be admitted, he became something of a prig. He threw himself into his work with a startling intensity; awakened ambition was driving him like a goad. Already he was beginning to develop those powers of intense concentration which were to mark him through life. Now, whenever he went for a walk or a ride alone, he made it a point to fasten his mind upon some one subject and, whatever the distraction, not permit his attention to break from its self-imposed walls.

This program was not lost upon his fellow students. Calhoun snapped back at their ridicule, declaring that he was compelled to study so hard 'in order that he might acquit himself creditably when he should become a

member of Congress!' 'I would leave College this very day,' he declared,
'if I doubted my ability to reach Congress within three years.' [72]

A hint of how the Carolinian impressed his classmates during this period
is revealed in the campaign song, popular in the eighteen-forties:

> 'John C. Calhoun, my Jo, John,
> When first we were acquaint
> You were my chum at Yale, John—
> And something of a saint.
> And Dr. Dwight, God bless him, John,
> Predicted as you know
> You'd be the Nation's President,
> John C. Calhoun, my Jo.' [73]

11

Three months more. Calhoun's time was more crowded than ever now, and
yet he must have stolen moments in that summer of 1804 to scan the finely
printed columns of the New Haven Herald or Register. These were strange,
tense days, with old empires dying and new ones not yet born; with
Boney fitting out his flat-bottomed landing craft for the invasion of England, and England fighting back with words instead of guns. 'The zeal
which has been displayed by the people of England,' [73] declared Fox in
the House of Commons, 'will ever be inseparable from the breast of Englishmen, that of a determined resolution to resist the menaces of a foreign
enemy.' [74]

At Calais gunboats tugged restlessly at their moorings. Those same
revolutionists who had once shouted of liberty, fraternity, and equality
ducked knees before a self-styled Emperor, who spoke not of liberty but
of glory; not of fraternity but of conquest. It was indeed a confusing
world, and that Calhoun could have been indifferent to the events overseas
is impossible to imagine.

Meanwhile, with his college days all but over, Calhoun still had tremendous gaps remaining in his education. He had a simple, logical command of the English language, but no literary polish whatsoever. Strangely
enough, his speeches read better today than those of his great rivals,
Webster and Clay, simply because of his bare, austere language.

Calhoun had no time for 'little things.' He did not strive for grace or
style in either his speech or writing, but concentrated on developing the
reasoning powers of his mind. So successful was he in this attempt that his
lean language became a reflection of the Grecian clarity of his thought.
He believed in language for what it could do rather than for what it was;
and this belief later became the core of his political philosophy.

He learned his Greek and Latin, but the most that could be said for his spelling was that it was a dubious improvement upon the English language, and his tense, spindling handwriting was conspicuously illegible. Later, he would write discourses on government that became a part of the political philosophy of America, but his idea of punctuation was to insert a comma at the end of every phrase. Yet by sheer force of willpower and natural abilities he had won his struggle, and at the close of his senior year he stood where he had wanted to stand, in the top rank of his graduating class.

Calhoun had been happy at Yale. He never regretted his choice. Scattered through the manuscript collections at the University today are numerous gracious notes from Calhoun, all revealing his 'affectionate regard' [75] for his *alma mater*. 'I have every reason to feel the strongest gratitude to Yale College, and shall always rejoice in her prosperity,' [76] he wrote Silliman in 1818. A check for a hundred dollars that he mailed in 1824, he regretted fell 'much short' of his inclination, as he had suffered severe losses in a fire. However, 'as one of her sons,' should Yale fail to raise the funds needed, he would 'very cheerfully [77] increase his contribution, 'I consider it as one of the fortunate incidents of my life,' he wrote in 1826, 'that early inclination led me to Yale.' [78]

III

Years of Growth

JOHN CALHOUN never delivered the oration on 'The Qualifications Necessary to Make a Statesman,' which he had prepared so carefully. The months of concentrated study had taxed his strength, and in August, 1804, he came down with 'a serious illness which . . . well nigh put an end' to his life. By the end of the month he thought himself improved, but at commencement on September 12, he was 'so low' that he could take no part in 'either the pleasures or the exercises of the day.' Throughout his life, even if Calhoun felt the desire for physical excesses, he never had the health to indulge in them. The fierce energies of his mind sapped his strength, leaving him only enough for the performance of what he considered his duties.

Just what Calhoun had planned to do that fall is uncertain. Had he not then met the widow of his late cousin, John Ewing Colhoun, he might never have gained the friendship of an extraordinary woman, whose influence made him acceptable to Charleston society—and to Charleston voters. She had done as much for her husband, himself a frontiersman, who had won a seat in the United States Senate before his death in 1802. His strong-minded Huguenot widow did not even call herself Calhoun, but Colhoun, which was closer to the old Scottish Colquhoun. Every summer, with her three children, John, James, and Floride, she made the long trip from Charleston to Newport, Rhode Island, in a luxurious family coach, drawn by four gray horses, and topped by a British coachman in full livery.

Relatives eight hundred miles from home were rare in those days, and Mrs. Colhoun, hearing of the South Carolina cousin ill at Yale, impulsively wrote, urging him to complete his recovery at Newport.

Late in September, John arrived at his cousin's, where he slowly regained his strength. In the early eighteen-hundreds Newport was an out-of-the-way sort of place, lingering wistfully in the twilight of pre-Revolutionary glories, when it had been a great port and one of the most fashionable of summer resorts. The old mansion houses still stood; and the beaches were as hard and wind-swept and the churning waves as white as in the past, but Newport was stranded in a gulf between two eras of time.

Nevertheless, wealthy and fashionable Southerners still congregated there, and Calhoun looked upon his surroundings with wary disapproval. To a friend, he wrote: 'Newport is quite a pleasant place, but it has rather an old appearance which gives it a somewhat melancholy aspect. I have found,' declared the dogmatic youngster out of the vast experience of two years in New Haven and two weeks in Rhode Island, 'no part of New England more agreeable than the island of Rhode Island. . . . But as to its manners, customs, moral and religious character, it seems much inferior . . . to every other part of New England.'[1] The verdict had been delivered.

The wealth and living standards of his Huguenot cousins did not arouse Calhoun's envy. He made no pretenses of being anything but what he was. Large-boned and shaggy-haired, he looked a 'typical Ulsterman'; yet there was dignity and some grace in his demeanor.[2] His mouth was too large for classical standards, but the thin lips were startlingly sensitive and the deep-set eyes had a searching intensity. Young as he was, he had presence which could focus the attention of an entire room.

Here in Newport, for the first time he mingled with an aristocratic, cultivated society and betrayed no sense of inferiority. His letters show that he thoroughly enjoyed himself. He made friends. The training that his mother had given him, the shy yet charming grace of his manners, eased his way and captivated Mrs. Colhoun.

Into her family circle Calhoun fitted as easily as if he had always belonged there. Almost automatically he assumed the position of the older brother, the man of the household. He shouldered some of the responsibilities of the children's rearing, agreed with their mother that Newport was 'not a very fit place for boys of the age of James and John,' and offered intelligent suggestions on their schooling. He listened to them read the Bible. To him it was 'not . . . a duty, but a delight to pay them particular attention,' for he loved children, and with them even a lingering boyishness in his nature came into play. He could not resist teasing his young cousins occasionally, and the seven-year-old was infuriated when John promised him that the next time he wrote a certain 'Miss ———,' he would not forget 'to request a kiss for James.' Apparently this cousinly attention was received in the spirit in which it was offered, for it was four months later that John was writing Mrs. Colhoun: 'I dare say James has forgot his jealousy and will be glad to see me.'[3]

Upon the entire Colhoun family John lavished all the pent-up fondness of a warm and family-loving nature. He was, in fact, starved for affection. Scotch clannishness was embedded in his nature; 'all the weavings and interweavings of kin'[4] held him closely. And Mrs. Colhoun responded to his need. She could understand a man like Calhoun because she had married one. She had felt the power in him, and she sensed the latent strength in this young cousin of his. She had the gift, common among Southern women of her generation, of being able to talk well on subjects that interested men, and John found that he could talk to her as he could to no one else. Perhaps he never had a closer friend than Mrs. Floride Bonneau Colhoun, and from association with her he became an early and ardent believer in the equality of the sexes.

She gave him more than affection and understanding. She brought a softening influence into his life; kept an anxious eye on his health, his interests, and his moods. Her interest was genuine, for he had won her heart almost as if he had been one of her own children. Whether she already had designs upon him as a son-in-law it is impossible to say; if she had, she was sensible enough to wait and let the young people discover their love through constant association.[5]

Family legend contends that at first Calhoun's unfulfilled romantic longings came near centering upon Mrs. Colhoun herself, which a hint here and there in his letters would substantiate.[6] For her part she firmly established herself on a maternal plane, which her ardent protégé soon realized. 'From my first acquaintance with you at Newport,' he wrote in later years, 'I have loved you as a mother. Sure am I, that, I would not from a mother experience more kindness and tender affection. . . . Never shall I be able to make you suitable return.'[7]

2

At the season's end Calhoun returned home. Though he had had no formal legal training, he seems to have spent the winter practicing law in Chancellor Bowie's office in Abbeville. A record 'of the judgment of the Court,' now at Yale, shows that on the fourth Monday in March, 1805, John Calhoun appeared at the Edgefield County Courthouse as attorney for one John Brooks versus Wiley Kemp in a debt claim amounting to $253.76. Attorney Calhoun received a fee of $24.40.[8]

In April there was a stir in the little village. A coach and four rattled through the dusty main street; Mrs. Colhoun had arrived to take John to Newport once more, before he entered the Litchfield, Connecticut, Law School in the fall.

At Charlottesville, Virginia, Calhoun left the coach. His walk was long. By a crude bridge he crossed 'a wild and romantic little river,' foaming from the floods of spring. Ahead, the slope mounted steeply, but breathless a few minutes later he gained the summit. On all sides stretched a sixty-mile tangle of woodland, fresh in new green, scattered strippings of plowed fields, and to the west the blue lift and rise of the mountains. Before him was an expanse of lawn bordered with shade trees and a brick house with a dome and a small Roman portico with gracious wings and French doors—the most beautiful house that Calhoun had ever seen.

Family legend tells us that he had persuaded Mrs. Colhoun to divert her route that he might visit Thomas Jefferson at Monticello.* And there is no greater proof of the simplicity of American democracy in those early days than an unknown young frontier American walking up to the door of Monticello, seeking and winning an audience with the President. Jefferson's bedtime was nine o'clock, but that night he sat up until past twelve, talking to his strange visitor. He insisted then on keeping John with him overnight and on giving him breakfast in the morning.

They were much alike, Thomas Jefferson and John Calhoun, both democrats and both slaveholders, both believers in state rather than national control of the slavery problem. They were alike in their intellectuality, their simplicity of manner, and in their very nerves. One was young and the other was old, but each had a grip on fundamentals. Each was by instinct close to the soil, each convinced that only as America recognized her dependence upon the soil could her way of life be healthy. Future history of an industrialized scientific America might prove both bad prophets, but not necessarily false leaders.

What words, what insights into the meaning and destiny of America passed between those two men during the late April night is regrettably lost to history. Their understanding seems to have been complete. The family tradition is that President Jefferson, the next morning, saw Mrs. Colhoun in Charlottesville and spoke about the young man 'in a manner quite gratifying to her.' Even more reliable is the testimony of Philadelphia's Richard Rush, who knew well both Calhoun and Jefferson. 'Jefferson loved him,' [9] Rush declared. As for Calhoun himself, all his life he would bear himself as the spiritual heir to Thomas Jefferson.

Southerners saw romanticism in this interview. The story of a single midnight conversation at Monticello, with Jefferson and Calhoun both fearing to destroy the illusion by a second meeting, seemed to them akin to the old Greek mystic torch race, where the wearied runner passed the lighted torch up to a fresh hand which carried it on to the goal. There is

---

* It has been maintained that this meeting never took place. Had it happened, asserts Charles M. Wiltse, Calhoun would not have failed to have mentioned it, or to have made political capital of it. That the story of the meeting rests solely upon the testimony of Mrs. Colhoun's son, James, aged seven, seems also to have laid its authenticity open to doubt.

As far as dates are concerned, the meeting was perfectly possible. Jefferson was at Monticello until mid-April, 1805; and Mrs. Colhoun's party could well have started north early in the month, as their way was long, and already fevers would have been breeding in Charleston. Wiltse's contention, that if the trip was made as early as April 'the party should have reached Newport long before July,' is irrelevant, for no attempt is made to show that Newport was not reached before July. During July Calhoun left Newport for Litchfield, but there is no indication as to how long he had already been at the resort. As for young James's testimony, even a seven-year-old can conceivably remember, years later, a kinsman calling upon the President of the United States.

truth in the romanticism of the legend, for a friendship did exist between Jefferson and Calhoun, and Calhoun never used the fact as political capital. It is not recorded in the history books, yet it seems to have been generally known to Calhoun's friends. 'Should you see Mr. Jefferson,' we find Calhoun writing Monroe in June, 1820, 'I would thank you to make my respects to him.' And in John Quincy Adams's monumental *Diary,* an entry for September 27, 1822, quotes Calhoun as remarking that 'Mr. Jefferson told him two years ago that we ought to seize Cuba.' [10]

Nor would Calhoun's nationalism have necessarily alienated Jefferson's support. Jefferson, too, would favor the tariff of 1816. Jefferson, too, would realize that the bonds of the agrarian democracy he had created must stretch to encompass the men of the mines and the machine shops whom he had once seen as the enemies to human liberty.

It is even possible that the tortuous development of Calhoun's thought through the eighteen-twenties may have been the product of conversations with a saddened and fear-haunted Jefferson. For it was only two years after the Sage of Monticello had died that Calhoun, in defense of violated minority rights, wrote his South Carolina *Exposition and Protest,* asserting in virtually the same words that same 'right' of nullification which Jefferson had espoused thirty years before.

3

In July, 1805, Calhoun left Newport for Litchfield. At Hartford, as he swung himself into the red-and-yellow stage, one of his companions caught his eye. He was a tall man of sixty or sixty-five and much stooped, dressed in elegant small-clothes, his hands clasped over a gold-headed cane. His face was arresting, 'soft dark eyes' glowing from beneath arched brows, high cheekbones, a mouth straight and chiseled, the whole contour almost an unearthly blending of the austere Puritan and the pagan Greek—the look that Jonathan Edwards must have had.

Calhoun heard the stranger's name, Judge Reeves. Curiosity stirred in him. Could this be the great head of the Law School to which he was now bound? Hesitantly, the young man ventured a question, received an answer, and passed over his letter of admission to the school. The day passed quickly. Calhoun found himself 'peculiarly fortunate' in the companionship of the 'open and agreeable' old jurist, whose streams of talk flowed freely over the jolting and creaking of the stage.[11]

As they entered the little village, its four main streets stretching out like a cross from the central Green, Reeves would have been busy pointing out landmarks. To the west the dark peak of Mount Tom brooding over the town, and nearer-by the smooth slope of Prospect Hill, where the law students loved to hunt. Nearby shimmered the bright waters of Bantam Lake. The rows of sturdy 'salt-box' houses were gay with color, 'earthy

Indian red,' gray-green, or bright yellow. From open windows came sounds pleasingly reminiscent of the Carolina plantations: the buzz of the spinning wheel, the clang of the loom, and the thumping of a churn. Children in 'brown tow crash' played at the roadside, waving a greeting as the stage thundered past; and well-mounted young bloods from the law school dashed by, dust rising in whirlwinds about the flying hooves of their horses.[12]

The new student did not arrive unwelcomed. As the stage lumbered its way down a grassy street, John Felder hurried forward to give his former Yale classmate a warm Carolina greeting. He had been 'anxiously' awaiting him for some time. He had already been at the school for five weeks and was 'pleased with the place.' [13] And as Calhoun straightened his stiff legs and assembled his luggage, Felder, too, was eagerly pointing out landmarks. Over on the Green was the 'whipping post,' where according to Connecticut Blue Law offenders 'pernicious to the publique weal' could be stripped and 'whipped upon the naked body.' [14] That huge four-story building on East Street with the double-galleried porch—that was Catlin's Tavern. The law students held their dances there in the assembly room with its high-arched ceiling and maroon-covered divans, and with luck you might even receive an invitation to one of Miss Sally Pierce's school dances, written on a blank playing card, the hours carefully specified, six to nine.

Felder had rented a room for Calhoun and himself in a house on the corner of West and Spencer Streets. Later, they moved to the home of Reuben Webster on Prospect Street, where the admiring young son of the family, Hosea, tagged happily after the long-legged Calhoun, and on a warm day in spring had the joy of holding tight to the slender trunk of a tree as Calhoun shoveled the dirt in around the roots, thus planting the elm which tradition demanded of every Litchfield law student.

Probably both houses would have been much the same with bare floors and whitewashed walls, cucumber vines curling around the outside of the tiny-paned windows and curtains of gay calico hanging within; the cellar crammed with salted meat and the attic beams mellow with the pungent odors of garden herbs and dried apples and peaches swinging from the rafters.[15]

Calhoun's room rent would total about $45 a year, plus $2.75 a week for husky meals of salt beef and pork, rye bread, potatoes, and cabbage. Tuition would be $100 for the first year, and $60 extra if he remained for a second.[16]

Calhoun seized his first spare moment to write to Mrs. Colhoun. He was 'lonesome,' he admitted, but hoped that a 'few days' application to studies which to me are highly interesting' would cure this particular ailment. He faced the future with zest. 'I return, I assure you,' he wrote, 'with much pleasure to the cultivation of Blackstone's acquaintance.' [17]

It was in this mood of enthusiasm that Blackstone's newest devotee walked over to the square house with hipped roof and rambling pillared porch where Judge Reeves lived. Considering the size of its reputation, the law school was incredibly small, housed in a white one-story building with four windows and a single fan-lit door. Inside waited a being as classic as his shelter. Judge Gould, 'the last of the Romans,' was a young man still, scarcely half the age of his distinguished partner, but a figure to inspire respect. However, no two men could have been more unlike. Both were Federalists—and of the most extreme sort—disunionists, if you will. Both were undeniably gentlemen. Here the resemblances ceased. Gould's manner was 'genial and refined,' his expression pleasant enough, but black brows gloomed over a large nose, and the froth of ruffles at his throat only emphasized the sharp-pointed chin. 'All intellect,' men called him, yet he showed no trace of pedantry. His exposition was as logical as a problem in mathematics, brief and clear even to newcomers. He read his lectures slowly, and at the end discussed the more critical parts. Where Gould's every sentence was 'transparent and penetrating as light,' Reeves's lectures were 'a huddle of ideas,' of scrappy notes and ragged sentences, torn off in the middle and left dangling in the air. His voice was only a whisper, but a whisper of such vibrance that a hundred students could hear it. None could deny Gould's talents or his genius for leadership; he was generally conceded to be more 'learned and lucid' than Reeves; but it was the older man whom Nature had touched with genius, and whom all students loved. Generations of schoolboys cherished his quip that he had never seen a little girl but what he wanted to kiss her; but, as for little boys, he wanted only to thrash them, for if they were not bad now, they would be some day. Legal experts were quick to point out that Reeves's *Treatise on Domestic Pleading* leaned entirely too far in the direction of Women's Rights, but this criticism would have impressed Tapping Reeves as a compliment. He glorified, idealized 'the fairer sex.' Certainly they had wills of their own, 'most happily for us.' Students left his classroom with occasional misgivings on the subject of torts, but fired with eagerness to 'be the defenders of the right and the avengers of the wrong.'[18]

To Litchfield, Tapping Reeves was the typical absent-minded professor. Lost in thought, his long gray hair floating to his shoulders, he was a familiar sight on the elm-shaded streets, ambling along, carefully holding the bridle rein of a horse that had eluded him and was happily grazing in someone's garden, blocks away.[19]

Reeves did have much upon his mind. In April of 1806, during Calhoun's residence, a Federal Grand Jury did not hesitate to indict Reeves for a 'libelous' attack on President Thomas Jefferson. And there was his brother-in-law and one-time student, Aaron Burr, to consider—a fallen angel indeed! It was only five years before that Burr had tied with

Jefferson on the electoral vote for President of the United States, and shortly afterward had rapped his first gavel as Vice-President of the nation. Two years later, dark, dapper, and debonair, with all of his grandfather Jonathan Edwards's genius and none of his morals, he had killed Alexander Hamilton, and from then on Burr, 'the beautiful and damned,' was a man to be spoken of in whispers. Litchfield saw him no more, but rumors filtered into the little town of empires far to the Southwest, of uprising and revolution, of a trial for treason, and a defending lawyer from Kentucky, named Henry Clay.

4

Litchfield was a sleepy town. The calendar might declare the year was 1805, but the little Connecticut village still lingered in the twilight of the eighteenth century. Litchfield was sure that the end of the Republic was at hand. Symbolic was the dress of Judge Reeves and all male citizens with any claim to respectability: the buckled breeches and ruffled stocks, the cocked hats with powdered queues hanging behind. Even the law students —although dandified young Southerners disported themselves in 'pink ging- ham frock coats'—were expected to conform. Bold was the youth who defied custom, for 'tight trousers . . . pantaloons,' disheveled hair and laced shoes, had an unholy significance; they were the trade-mark of Sabbath-breakers, tipplers, and 'ruff-scuff'; in short, of the followers of the 'atheist and libertine,' Thomas Jefferson.[20]

But Calhoun dared assert himself. The young man who had flouted 'Pope' Dwight, who had followed his dreams and yearnings up the slope of Monticello, who had clasped the warm freckled hand of the most hated and beloved man in America, who had shared his food and slept under his roof, was in no mood to hold his tongue, remove his pantaloons, or conform to Litchfield opinion. With his shaggy hair falling in loose masses over his forehead and temples, he was 'free in his conversation,' and soon all Litchfield knew exactly where he stood. And he paid for his political opinions. 'This place is so much agitated by party feelings,' he wrote in December, 1805, 'that both Mr. Felder and myself find it prudent to form few connections in town. This, though somewhat disagreeable, is not un- favorable to our studies. . . . I take,' he confessed, somewhat wistfully, 'little amusement and live a very studious life.[21]

But Sunday was the day of reckoning. Amidst a congregation of 'lean and sturdy' farmers, of women in silver or steel-rimmed spectacles, sur- reptitiously nibbling orange peel to keep awake, of schoolgirls pricking each other with pins, eyes would have been quick to ferret out the slim form of John Calhoun. Public interest in his appearance at church must have been especially keen, for a young man of such avowed political heresies would have been all the more suspect on the score of morals and religion. Attendance under these circumstances must have been a virtual spiritual exposure in the stocks.

Calhoun could not endure it. He was not irreligious. He was as much at peace with his soul as any intensely thinking and questioning young man of twenty-three can be. He could receive with 'gratitude' Mrs. Colhoun's 'anxious solicitude' for his welfare on 'the all important subject of religion'; and assure her that whatever she might say would be 'kindly received.' But religion, then as later with him, was a distinctly personal thing. He would not be bullied into churchgoing nor made the cynosure of the staring eyes of the town. And yet he suffered under his ostracism. He was far from home, and his friends' letters became fewer and fewer. 'I know not when, I have been so unfortunate in hearing from my friends, as I have been since my arrival here,' he wrote Mrs. Colhoun. He had not received 'a scrap of a pen' from South Carolina, although he had written to nearly everyone he knew. He haunted the postoffice at every mail, but 'uniformly had the mortification of disappointment.' [22]

Then he found escape. In the neighboring town of Cornwall lived another John Calhoun, a country doctor of 'the best man God ever made' variety. Just how closely they were related is impossible to determine; the roots of both struck back to the same soil in Scotland, but the lonely South Carolinian was quick to seek out his namesake and to seize on even the most fragile ties of relationship. Soon the young law student had a standing invitation to spend every weekend at the doctor's home. Blue Laws might pronounce that 'No one shall run of a Sabbath-day, or walk in his garden, or elsewhere, except reverently to and from church'; [23] but Calhoun cared little.

As Cornwall was a good fifteen miles from Litchfield and Calhoun walked the entire distance, the doctor's company must have presented unusual attractions. Soon the two men became really fond of each other; and the story of their friendship has been handed down in the annals of the Connecticut Calhouns.[24] Perhaps it was then that Calhoun gained his understanding of New England's basic patriotism running like bedrock under the foam of party feeling—knowledge which was to be reassuring during the dark days of the War of 1812.

His ostracism did nothing to cure Calhoun of his taste for politics. He took a lively interest in town government, and later confessed that he gained his knowledge of caucus politics from the manipulations at town meetings. As a keen-eyed observer he could have seen 'the paupers of the Town . . . sold at auction to those who keep them cheapest, taking into account the work they were capable of doing!' For the 'pauper was a slave . . . sold yearly as long as he lived'; [25] and critics who have wondered how Calhoun could have lived four years in New England with no qualms as to the righteousness of the South's 'peculiar institution' may have forgotten that black slavery was still legal in Connecticut, although owners were finding it more profitable to sell the Negroes South and to auction off the whites at town meeting.

5

Calhoun's zest for his new profession quickly waned. Not all Reeves's digressions and Gould's lucidity could keep the journey through the 'exterior fields of law' from being 'dry and solitary.' Often, when submerged in a welter of bills, notes, and pleading, Calhoun looked with wistful envy on his friend Alexander Noble, who 'intirely relinquished the business of a merchant for that of a farmer . . . Tho' less profitable it certainly is more peacable and favourable to happiness.' Would his time ever be his own again? Perhaps, when he had gained 'a pretty thorough knowledge' of his profession; but perhaps this, too, was only a 'pleasant dream,' as each succeeding year would pile on its 'own particular cares and business.' [26]

To study the law lectures, not as they usually were studied, but as he was convinced 'they ought to be,' absorbed his time. Although longing to be with Mrs. Colhoun and 'the children' in Newport, he held out firmly against this temptation. Grimly he forced himself to admit that the lack of 'social pleasure' was exactly what he needed to stimulate his 'studious habits. . . . I have always found,' he explained to Mrs. Colhoun, 'that just . . . as the number of friends . . . increases around me, and a consequent opportunity of interesting conversation, my attention to my studies has relaxed.'

Hard work was the result of equally hard self-discipline. There were exasperated moments when he would toss it all 'aside for the more delicious theme of the muses, . . . interesting pages of history,' or the newspapers. Always, too, he would 'throw away with joy' his studies to hear from his Carolina correspondents. 'You do me injustice in supposing your letters intrude on my studious disposition,' he wrote Andrew Pickens. 'Many things I study for the love of study, but not so with law. I can never consider it, but as a task. . . . But, I confess from my aversion . . . I draw a motive to industry. It must be done, and the sooner the better, is often my logick.' [27]

Despite his distaste for law, Calhoun was distinguishing himself in it. Nor did he neglect that most essential part of the Southern lawyer's or statesman's equipment—oratory. The promise that he had shown at Yale was being fulfilled. He was cultivating his newfound talent for public speaking with such thoroughness that despite his early speech impediment, he now 'excelled all his companions.' His powers of logic, too, were commanding attention. At a moment's notice he would gather up the threads of half a dozen desultory arguments, weave them together, and answer them all in 'a logical, lucidly arranged speech, indicating no formal preparation.'[28] He owed much to Gould's clear logical exposition. But Calhoun was learning more than law at Litchfield. The startling fact is that every principle of secession or states' rights which Calhoun ever voiced can be traced right back to the thinking of intellectual New England in the early eighteen-hundreds. Not the South, not slavery, but Yale College and Litchfield Law School made Calhoun a nullifier. In the little classroom, Reeves at white heat and Gould with cold logic argued the 'right' of secession as the only refuge for minorities. Logically, their argument was unimpeachable. Messrs. Dwight, Reeves, and Gould could not convince the young patriot from South Carolina as to the desirability of secession, but they left no doubts in his mind as to its legality.

Calhoun was not wholly unhappy in Litchfield. Not all the bitterness and bickering of small-town politics could break the spell of that late and fragile spring of 1806 for which he waited longingly, week after week, until June came at last with its showers of dropping blossoms and overhead the fresh and swaying green. It was then that Litchfield seemed to him 'among the most pleasant towns I have ever been in';[29] and the magic of that late spring lingered. Fall brought new pleasures, rambles through the underbrush on Prospect Hill, and even an occasional pigeon hunt. Life was good.

He returned from two weeks' summer vacation in Newport, reluctant, yet feeling 'a secret satisfaction on returning to a place, in which I have spent so many agreeable moments.' Home-loving even in a rented room, he enjoyed arranging his few belongings as attractively as possible. 'I always endeavor to make the place I reside in agreeable; from a conviction, that it is necessary to every other enjoyment,'[30] he told Mrs. Colhoun.

He had more time for recreation this year. Litchfield was Puritan New England, to be sure, but it was old New England still; and in the great kitchen fireplaces a blue dye-pot, covered with a plank, waited invitingly for courting couples; and the bundling bed and the bundling board were still more than memories. If Calhoun chose to linger late into an autumn evening, strolling with his girl through a shadowy field at the foot of Chestnut Hill, or sitting on a stone wall watching the moon lift itself over the branches of an apple tree, no rebuke would be offered on their return. For all their Blue Laws, Connecticut folk were as lenient toward youth as they were strict in religion; chaperonage was the product of a later age, and young boarders were expected only to obey the rules of the household in which they lived.[31]

Sleigh-riding delighted him. 'I was out last evening . . . and found it very agreeable,'[32] he wrote Mrs. Colhoun. Often twenty sleighs, ringing with bells and laughter, would jounce across the hard-packed country roads, and it is most unlikely that one of Miss Sally Pierce's girls would not have shared the warmth of a bearskin with Calhoun. Connecticut youth would defy the coldest night of the year and a blizzard so thick that the ears of the horses were blotted out, to drive seven or eight miles to some country tavern, tumbling down for handfuls of snow to rub against a frozen ear or cheek; one or two of the boys shaking icicles from their very ears; then into the tavern for supper, dancing, and hot rum and cider, emerging hours later to pile into the frosty sleigh and speed back against the glittering roadway as if to win a race against the dawn.

That Calhoun enjoyed the rigors of the New England climate would be asking too much of outraged Southern nature. This winter was an aching cold, a cold with the feel of the first spring plunge in a Carolina river, but it set his blood atingle. He had put on some much-needed weight; and although believing that he was always 'in the best of health when studying closely,' he paid careful attention to exercise and temperance. When, for the last time, he left the wind-swept hills of Litchfield and boarded the stage for Philadelphia on his way home, he had not felt so well in years. Years later he would write a friend that no time of his life had been spent so advantageously as at Litchfield. 'I love to dwell on it.' [33]

6

There could have been no greater contrast to the austerity of Litchfield than Charleston, South Carolina, in 1806. Charleston was not the fragile shell of its post-bellum days, a city of dreams and mellowed, wistful memories, but a trading port, vividly alive, looking to foreign visitors, a blending of Southern Europe and the Orient. Calhoun's senses were lashed with stimuli, overpowered by the headiness of gardenias, magnolias, and camellias, the scents of orange blossoms, sweet olives and figs, all contrasted to the reek of low tide when the Ashley and the Cooper receded from the mud-flats and buzzards perched themselves on long posts, rising inch by inch from the water.[34]

Even the cramped streets could not shut out the tropic sunlight as it sparkled against the great hedges of Cherokee roses with their shimmering leaves and glanced off the white stuccoed houses. If Calhoun had climbed the spire of Saint Michael's, as so many travelers did, he would have seen the city spread out before him like a fan, and looked down through swimming haze on hip roofs, where red tile had faded into pink and lavender, on buildings early aged by mold and damp; on yucca and palmetto and bright-leaved magnolias.[35]

Descending to the street, he would have jostled full-figured mulatto girls, sweating West Indians; perhaps an old man in the knee-breeches and diamond-buckled shoes of an earlier era, his powdered hair tied back in a queue, his Negro body-servant in coat of broadcloth and satin pantaloons. He would have passed pale girls, their hair a tumble of curls upon their shoulders, eyes gazing 'soulfully' out from willow bonnets or picture hats of straw tied with ribbons; young Jeffersonians like himself with cropped hair and 'slovenly' pantaloons; [36] a slave woman carrying a gaudy basket of fruit upon her turbaned head; another gracefully balancing a jug of water.

Following the crowds, Calhoun would have sought the docks, for there activity was greatest. Sails moved along the tawny river water; green heaps of bananas and pyramids of coconuts, sacks of coffee, sugar, and flour were piled upon the wharves; burly stevedores, sweat dripping from their black foreheads and great muscles rippling across their bare backs, moved past, shoulders sagging under sacks of rice or bales of cotton, eyes rolling toward a Negro woman who stood nearby, her child balanced upon her hip. The very air was alive with sound; the chanting wail of the dock laborer, the distant shout of the slave auctioneer and the crack of his gavel; and over all, the chiming, silvery sweetness of the bells of Saint Michael's.[37]

To this riot of scent and sight, color and sound, Calhoun could not have been indifferent. Were more of his Charleston letters preserved, it is possible that we should find that he described the panorama in the words which he applied to the scenery of the hill-country, as 'romantick in a high degree.' [38] But he did not approve of it. He did not approve of it at all. His reactions were perfectly normal, perfectly characteristic of any young Puritan taught to think that Charleston was a sort of Paris, dedicated to the pleasures of this world. A glance at the South Carolina *Gazette* would only have confirmed his suspicions. Lottery agents promised him $30,000 for 800 cents; Robinson's Summer Coffee House lured with enticements of 'cool creams and jellies'; the Dock Street Theater beckoned with *The Prisoner at Large,* and *Love Laughs at Locksmiths;* the bookstore flaunted *The Wild Irish Boy,* and *The Pleasures of Love, being Amatory poems.*[39]

History has it that another young Scotch-Irishman dallied gaily in the pleasures of Charleston, with special attention to horse-racing, cockfighting, drinking, and gambling, with disastrous results, both to his self-esteem and his pocketbook.[40] But Calhoun did not follow Andrew Jackson's example. He was sophisticated enough to realize the cynical amusement of the cultivated Charlestonians at raw 'up-country gentlemen,' and, furthermore, a consciousness of sin weighed him down. Still convinced that He whom he called 'the author of good' was giving His personal attention to everything that he did, Calhoun was distressed at the indifference to religion which he found in Charleston. Indeed, in the South Carolina metropolis, which had not yet outgrown its youthful coarseness, Sunday was a sort of gala day, devoted to visiting and horse-racing. To young John Calhoun the situation was appalling, and he wrote sadly of that city 'so corrupt . . . so inattentive to every call of religion.' [41]

'Since my arrival here, I have been very much of a recluse,' he wrote in December, 1806. 'I board with the French protestant minister Mr. Detargeuy. . . . It is a quiet house and answers my purpose well.' [42] Absorbed in his studies in Chancellor De Saussure's law office, he had withdrawn into himself, condemning Charleston on surface appearances. Indeed, after this period Calhoun never lived again in Charleston, and took no part in its life at all.

IV

The Birth of a Patriot

THOUGH Calhoun did not know it, his public life was born on a spring day in 1807, when a British man-of-war, the *Leopard*, lurking off the Virginia capes, opened fire upon the American frigate, the *Chesapeake*. With disciplined coolness English seamen boarded and carried off three Yankee sailors for impressment into His Majesty's service and the war against Napoleon.* Twenty-one Americans were left dead or wounded. Across the United States anger spread like a prairie fire, and with wounds from the Revolution scarcely healed, the country clamored for war and punishment of the aggressor. Despite President Jefferson's efforts at appeasement, bitter farmers and townspeople all over the states gathered into informal assemblies and passed resolutions of censure and indignation.

Nowhere was the public temper at higher pitch than in Abbeville, South Carolina. In front of the old red-painted log cabin where Calhoun had opened his law office, the new attorney could often be seen standing bareheaded in the midst of a large and milling group of townspeople, talking fervently. His indignation must have been in accord with the general sentiment, for he was the man selected to draw up appropriate resolutions for a public meeting on June 22. An overt act of foreign aggression had served to open his career.[1]

No doubt he spent hours in preparation, for he could not have been unaware of the honor bestowed upon him. Resolutions were the free speech of a people at one with their government, aware of the importance of the individual in the general scheme. Though Washington was three weeks' hard travel from Abbeville, actually the little country village in the foothills and the overgrown village on the Potomac were closer to each other than automobiles and railroads would make them a century later. The government in Washington was no abstract mechanism, where responsibility to the people was lost in a tangled mesh of weavings and interweavings. It was a vital living organism, dreamed and shaped by men still alive, who had given their personal consent to its formation and who

---

* These three Americans had previously been impressed by the British and had escaped. A fourth sailor, one Jenkin Rafford, was a true deserter from the British Navy and was also removed from the *Chesapeake*.

could, at will, withdraw it.[2] It was a government of men who still believed that in voicing their honest opinions in resolutions of praise and censure, they could sway public policy.

As Calhoun would for the first time appear 'before his assembled countrymen,' he dressed carefully for the occasion, in a dark coat, light 'weskit,' and the newly fashionable trousers of the same color. Holding himself proudly erect, he looked even taller than his six feet two inches, for he was thin to the point of gauntness. Already, the hollows were deep under his cheekbones. But if his bone contours were Scottish, his coloring was Irish, and black Irish at that. His hair, short-clipped and parted on the side, was dark and thick, appearing from a distance almost black, and the dark, clear eyes flashed with an 'intense light' from under bushy black brows.[3]

Calhoun's actual remarks have been lost, but there is plenty of evidence that they were highly satisfactory. The words 'freedom,' 'glory,' and 'public honour' had a fresh-minted ring in those days, and a speaker far less eloquent than Calhoun would have had no difficulty in arousing indignation. Though no demagogue, he had only to recall the stories from his own childhood—the prison camp at Camden where men from all over Carolina had died of untended wounds, smallpox, and starvation, and of the hell-ship at St. Augustine—to have his audience kindle into flame. As yet, he was no great orator; he had various minor defects to correct in his delivery; but his 'fiery zeal,' 'nervous impetuosity,' and keen indignation saw him through very well.

Although the passage of Abbeville's indignation resolutions had no perceptible effect upon the British Navy, they made a great difference in the future career of their author. For he was a lawyer, and the people of Abbeville had long cherished an ardent dislike of lawyers.[4] Old Patrick Calhoun had voiced the community opinion several years before when he announced that he 'would sooner gie a poound for a lawyer's skelp, than an Indian's.'[5] Now Abbeville's sentiment changed, changed so completely that by general acclaim in the fall of 1807 John Calhoun was elected, without opposition, to the legislative seat so long held by his father. For years, no lawyer in the district had dared offer himself as a candidate.

2

Calhoun had more than a year to wait before he took his seat in the Legislature. Meanwhile, he was besieged by clients. His teacher, Chancellor Bowie, commented that 'Perhaps no lawyer in the State ever acquired so high a reputation from his first appearance at the bar as he did.'[6] Popular throughout the district, he had also a large practice in Newberry, the home of his mother's relatives. And yet he was miserably unhappy. He was going through a struggle common to most young lawyers, as to whether his duty was to do the best he could for his client or for the claims of society. He took the problem seriously, and would have seen no humor at all in Henry Clay's courtroom declaration to a client charged with stealing a beehive: 'We lost our case, but by God, we still have our bee-gum.'[7] Criminal practice, of which there was always a sufficiency, was congenial to Calhoun only when he could break loose from 'the shackles of an arbitrary technical system,' and expound in 'the wider field of natural justice.'

Justice, however, was not natural to the Southern back-country. Chastisements were severe: the horse-thief, although not ordinarily lynched, might well have preferred to be; instead, he was seated four hours in the pillories, given 'three good whippings' of thirty-nine lashes each, and finally branded upon the shoulder. Imprisonment for debt was common, and a prisoner's freedom depended not nearly so much upon his guilt or innocence as upon the eloquence of his attorney. A lawyer could spend hours and days rooting through the statutes of the state, only to be defeated by an opponent more adept at boldly asserting and maintaining his arguments. A fluent tongue counted for far more than a well-stocked brain. It would have taken Calhoun, brilliant, but unpredictable, long to live down the day when he put in a plea of manslaughter for a client accused of murder. Only the hastily assembled emotional forces of Calhoun's senior colleague could convince the jury that the accused was 'Not guilty.' Potentially, John Calhoun might be 'the greatest logician in America,' but his powers of cold, clear analysis were far more suited to the corporation practice of a later day, or even to the Supreme Court, than to the Carolina back-country. Fresh from the best law school in the nation, Calhoun had no desire to lower his arguments to the mentalities of men less intelligent than he, nor to play on the emotions of an ignorant, frontier jury. 'I feel myself,' he wrote Mrs. Colhoun, 'a slave chained down to a particular place and course of life.'[8]

Yet to most of those hard-living, hard-fighting young lawyers of the back-country, life was a rollicking, roistering affair. They were like a band of strolling players on their geldings or in their two-wheeled sulkies, the judge in 'finest broadcloth' at the procession's head, as they rode the circuit all the way from the blue-misted foothills to the black swamp waters near Craytonville. They fought their way through the lurching farm wagons and saddle horses around the public squares, rubbed shoulders with the 'drinking, fighting, and jollifying' mob of court day, who wrestled, shot, gambled, 'snuffed the candle,' raced their horses and fought their cocks, challenged the roarer 'to make good his roarings,' and 'drank each other under the table.' Inside the courtroom, before a judge sprawled on the bench 'half asleep, with his hat on' and bare toes sticking from 'a pair of old worsted stockings,' the lawyers of the circuit matched wits, shouting that right was wrong, or black, white.

Nights were scarcely less strenuous. Too keyed up for sleep, the young attorneys frequented taverns and 'houses of pleasure,' only to be bedded down at last often in rows in the tavern ballroom, 'not less than two, nor usually more than three to a bed,' with 'bugs hunted out,' against the arrival of its occupants. Then came the story-telling, the battles of the courtroom refought and rewon, the 'feverish gambling' at loo, brag, whist, and twenty-deck poker, when Blackstone's winner of the morning might lose to Hoyle at night.[9]

Knowing the fastidious Calhoun, it is easy to understand how little appeal this rough-and-tumble life held for him. He lacked the animal spirits, the vitality, perhaps, that made the circuit a gala holiday to Henry Clay and endurable even to Abraham Lincoln. Mentally he was a splendid lawyer; but temperamentally he was too constrained for his profession. But he won recognition upon his own terms. If he was adequate during the two months on the circuit, he shone during the long warm evenings on the porch of his Abbeville home, when surrounded by fellow lawyers and students who were already striving for places in his office, he would talk on and on in words fresh with the flavor of his own keen thinking. As the cool air from the foothills worked its way through the shadows, talk would be enlivened with foot-races, with the more agile Calhoun beating the more vigorous Bob Yancey.[10]

But all this was small outlet for a man of Calhoun's drive and magnetism. His ideas extended beyond the mediocrities of practice in a small Southern town; and he suffered from the frustration of wasted abilities that could only find employment in unraveling causes and seeking effects. His one hope was that the law might prove a stepping stone upward, a hope consummated in his election to the Legislature. Meanwhile, restless, bored, and unhappy in his work, he sought—and found—diversion.

3

The diversion, as is usual in such instances, was a woman. Legends lingering in the Carolina up-country have named her Nancy Hanks; and by strange historical coincidence she may even have been related to the Kentucky girl who became the mother of Abraham Lincoln.[11] Nancy's mother was Ann Hanks, who in the early years of the nineteenth century kept an old cross-roads tavern between Abbeville and Pendleton at Craytonville, where veilings of gray moss hid secrets in the woods, and swamp forests glowed green and pink at the first dawning of spring.

It is easy enough to imagine this old ordinary, crude, vigorous, brawling, like hundreds tossed along the fringe of the frontier, all the way from Georgia to New England—its puncheon floor and smoke-stained rafters, the yawning fireplace, seven or eight feet in length, a huge poker hanging at the side, and next it the flip iron, which sizzled invitingly when dipped, hot from the flames, into a jug of toddy. Soft feather beds, country bacon and buckwheat cakes, a bar stocked with rum, cider, brandy, and raw whiskey for the frontiersman, who North and South alike demanded 'hard liquour' as well as 'hard doctrine,'[12]—these were the allurements. Planters, wagoners, trappers, horse-drovers, and farmers met, mingled, bedded themselves down together on loose blankets before the fire when the rooms were full, and talked into the night. Outside was the sound of horses munching and of wind whipping through the pine trees; inside rose the voices of free Americans who could say what they saw fit, and what they lacked in learning made up in conviction and originality.[13]

Here in this old tavern, fragrant with scents of tobacco and home-cured ham and wood-smoke, Calhoun met the girl. Little is known about her. She is said to have been about nineteen years old, the youngest of her mother's eleven children.[14] She is said to have worked behind the bar and passed the cornbread and 'long sweetnin'' to the young lawyers of the county circuit who stopped there from time to time for their evening meal.

Calhoun, it is said, stopped more often. Time and again that year he was racked with headaches which so prostrated him he was unable to go home. Instead, he would spend the night at the tavern, and it became a standing joke among the lawyers that his headaches always developed when he came within riding distance of the young barmaid. Possibly a physician would have attributed his ailment to his unhappiness in his work and to the years of repression and self-discipline he had undergone. At any rate, a young man, whose self-righteousness had brought him to a point where he believed that a Charleston yellow-fever epidemic was God's curse for the inhabitants' 'sins and debaucheries,'[15] stood in serious need of deflation.

The reaction came quickly. In later years, Calhoun's friends marveled at his youthful self-restraint in withstanding the more popular temptations of those tempestuous times. He could drink without getting drunk, could frequent the taverns and yet remain free from brawls and gambling debts. Life for him had been a serious matter. Burdened from boyhood with work and responsibility, he had never really learned to play. He had neither the time nor the surplus energy for casual romance, and was to become more and more ascetic, controlled, struggling to hold his emotions 'in strict subjection to his reason.' But now he was only twenty-five, and his deep feeling for beauty eagerly responded to feminine loveliness. And Nancy was lovely. One account calls her 'a handsome Irish beauty'; another, a country girl, 'said to be possessed of unusual beauty.'[16] She was probably one of those hard-working, excitable women of the hill-country who bloom into a haunting beauty before years of toil and childbearing wear them down to gaunt contours of sinew and bone.

Evidence indicates that Nancy had fallen in love with Calhoun. No doubt she, too, found him physically attractive. It was his eyes and his smile that would have won her heart; 'eyes glowing like stars at the depths of caverns,' a smile which, flashing across his unusually mobile lips, lent 'something seductively winning' to his grave features that made him 'comely in the eyes of women and won for him even the friendship of men.' [17]

It is said that he considered the possibility of marriage. But actually he was probably not even in love with the girl; for his letters to Floride and her mother, written a few years later, are all full of the wonder and freshness of a man deeply in love for the first time in his life and bewildered by the power of his emotions.

Here a curtain falls over the story. From the midsummer of 1807 to the spring of 1809 there is a significant gap in Calhoun's correspondence. If a single letter has been preserved, it has not been made public. Whatever emotions swayed him, whatever he thought, felt, and did during those months, can only be conjectured. We only know that in the spring of 1808 he mounted his horse and rode all the way from Abbeville to Bonneau's Ferry near Charleston, where he spent several days visiting the Colhouns. There he saw young Floride, now sixteen, 'a very gay vivacious miss,' [18] and realized that it was she, and not the girl in Craytonville, with whom he was really in love. He went home in emotional turmoil, for he could no longer consider the thought of marrying his barmaid. She had never been the choice of his intellect; now she was no longer the choice of his heart.

In a heart-searchingly frank letter to Floride, several years later, Calhoun admitted how 'violent' the attraction of 'mere personal charms' [19] could be. 'His blood ran warm, always.' Unquestionably he felt that he had wronged the girl in Craytonville in some way, and was said, in later years, to have 'looked back on his youth with regret for one mistake.' [20] A less principled man could probably have thrust her aside and forgotten her in two weeks, but not Calhoun, for he was 'keenly sensitive,' [21] and shrank always from injuring the feelings of others. Nevertheless, he was equipped with a goodly share of Scottish realism, which warned him of family obligations and family pride; of ambition, whose fulfillment could only be furthered by a wife who could promote his social as well as his political interests. Yet 'worldly considerations' were not the only factor in his decision. He knew that if he were so foolish as to marry a girl he did not love, he surely could not make her happy.

He was for a time, however, so bitterly unhappy that Dr. Waddel is said to have feared that anguish and despair might permanently affect his reason. In letters to Calhoun's brothers, Waddel is said to have urged that John be encouraged to 'active outdoor exercise,' [22] such as hunting and fishing, with the hope that in bodily exertion he could find relief from his mental tensions.

Time and the bracing air of autumn gradually swept away his brood-

ings, and with the approach of the legislative session, new interests began
to fill his mind. Yet all his life Calhoun would fight off a tendency 'to
melancholy.' [23] Lacking a balance wheel of robust humor, he was obliged
to force himself into the semblance of optimism. So successful were his
efforts that at least two friends declared him the most 'undespairing' man
they ever knew.[24]

Nor did Nancy Hanks die of 'a broken heart.' She was said to have
'disappeared,' but upon the partitioning of her father's estate, she turned
up again in Alabama, the wife of a man named South.[25] She lived to see
her youthful lover become Vice-President of the United States and excluded from the highest office of all, because his wife's social pretensions
would not permit her to 'receive' a former barmaid. Did Nancy Hanks
South, barmaid at Craytonville, laugh? Did she wonder?

From what had proved to be 'a very serious period in Calhoun's young
life,' he emerged, humbled, more tolerant, no longer inclined to prate of his
and God's judgments on the sins of his fellow Carolinians. He could understand now the temptations to which human nature was subject; and never
again would he condemn or judge other men on any but their political
actions, or set himself up as the guardian of anyone's morals but his own.
The young man who came down to Columbia in November, 1808, to take
his seat in the Legislature had a new maturity, new depths of understanding.

4

The capital of South Carolina was an attractive city in which to be. Its
criss-crossed streets of tawny yellow or rusty red were lined with high brick
walls, dripping with ivy, and large oak trees shaded the sidewalks. Beyond
the capitol several bare whitewashed buildings, snug behind a wall and
facing each other across a small green, formed the nucleus of the seven-
year-old State University. Columbia had its society, too, 'refined and cultivated,' [26] according to a French visitor; even in November it had tropic
warmth and luxuriance, with palmettos, magnolias, and shady, white-
sanded yards around the large dwelling houses.

Shortly after his arrival, Calhoun was appointed an 'Aide de Camp' to
Governor John Drayton, with the rank of Lieutenant Colonel.[27] No doubt
he received his share of admiring glances from the Columbia belles when
he strode forth, in full uniform, his sword upon his hip, but with his past
experience and future hopes he was in no mood for romantic entanglements.

The Speaker of the House was Joseph Alston of Charleston, 'short,
stocky, rakishly dressed, and smelling of the stable.' A low-country rice
planter and son-in-law of the sinister Aaron Burr, Alston himself was not
lacking in abilities as a tricky and resourceful party leader. But it was
Daniel Elliott Huger, who would have attracted Calhoun's or any new-

comer's attention. A striking-looking man, his swarthy complexion, bristling eyebrows, and 'sardonic grin' had won for him the title of Milton's Satan, 'and all Hell grew darker at his frown.' Actually he was Charleston's typical 'gentleman of the old school,' and his labored oratory of 'short sentences and long pauses' belied his dramatic appearance. He was, however, the unquestioned party leader of the House, and it was to him that Alston brought the problem of young John C. Calhoun.[28]

For Calhoun was a problem. He would not have been old Patrick's son had he proved otherwise. He had all his father's stubborn independence and utter confidence in his own judgment, characteristics which Alston observed with concern. 'I'm afraid,' he told Huger, 'that I shall find this long, gawky fellow from Abbeville hard to manage.' [29]

Mr. Alston's estimate of human nature—or at least Calhoun nature—was perfect. Calhoun was not easy to manage, and his 'cutting tongue' got him into trouble immediately. In characteristic fashion he had leveled his guns against as powerful an opposition leader as he could possibly have chosen; and although the opponent himself did not show any concern, an enraged follower decided to confront the 'fellow from Abbeville' and teach him wisdom with a pair of hard fists—or a good horsewhip!

Calhoun was walking up and down the porch of his hotel when he was warned of approaching attack. Several moments later, the self-appointed instrument of vengeance rushed up the steps and planted himself in his victim's path. Calhoun, smiling pleasantly, approached him, said good-morning, side-stepped, and calmly continued his exercise. The other man stared after him, suddenly 'burst into tears,' [30] apologized, and politically, at least, came over to Calhoun's side.

Actually the 'father of fire-eating had no great appetite for flame.' [31] His legislative history was so quiet that had he not later become South Carolina's 'great king,' little of it would have found any place in history. True, his bill 'to enable parties to give in evidence copies of wills in actions where the Titles to land may come into question,' appeared to be the only measure of the session of which as many as five hundred copies were printed and distributed to the members. But his bill 'to provide for the more . . . expeditious administration of justice in the Courts' [32] had a vagueness which added little to Calhoun's reputation. Huger, noting his struggles to draw up readable resolutions, at which he later became so adept, little dreamed that he would one day describe the young man from Abbeville as 'the greatest metaphysician in the world.' [33] Still less did he imagine himself delicately withdrawing from the Senate of the United States that South Carolina might be served by the superior abilities of John Calhoun.

Recorded on the House roll as John C. Colhoun (sic) [34] the newcomer attended sessions with reasonable regularity, but occasionally he paid a twenty-five-cent fine for failure to be in his seat at convening time. Legislative rules were few, but designed to reimburse the Treasury for money wasted upon lazy legislators. A member absent without leave was sent for at his own expense and kept in custody. Breaking a quorum cost fifty cents, and the cashier promptly deducted a similar sum from the pay of any member so impudent as to leave the chamber before the Speaker. [35] On Tuesdays each member was publicly informed of his accumulated fines; and lucky indeed was the man sufficiently wary to break even on his meager salary.

Delvers into the by-paths of American history can find the notations of Calhoun's 'Ayes' and 'Nays' in the yellowed, hand-written records of the Legislature of South Carolina. He served upon a special committee 'concerning illegal and improper conduct to an infant.' [36] He cast a minority 'Nay' against the establishment of courts of appeal in the state, and persistently and consistently voted 'Nay' on political attempts to throw the legislative body into abortive adjournment. Certainly in none of these routine actions is there forewarning of the statesman. But monotony was not made for Patrick Calhoun's son, nor he for monotony. His opportunity came; he seized it unhesitatingly, revealing all the keen insight and prophetic power that brought him to fame.

5

The scene was a Republican caucus meeting; the task, to nominate candidates for the Presidency and the Vice-Presidency of the United States. James Madison was nominated without opposition, but on the renomination of Vice-President George Clinton a hitch occurred. Calhoun had arisen. He spoke rapidly. American rights as a neutral were being trampled underfoot. War with England was inevitable. Hence, the party must be unified. Clinton was old and conservative; should he be renominated, he would become the nucleus of party discontent, making a formidable division when the country was at last forced into war. Calhoun's choice was John Langdon of New Hampshire, and so strong were his urgings that the nomination was actually offered to the New England statesman.* With this show of power, Calhoun stepped instantly into a leading position in the Legislature.[37]

What happened during those two legislative sessions in which Calhoun served is far more important than his presence there. For those were the years when the conflict between the planters of the coast and the farmers of the hills reached the breaking point. The 'backward and neglected' regions of the state, so far as their actual population went, now outnumbered the old coastal parishes. They were not unaware of this fact.

* Langdon was 'nominated' by several states, but Clinton was re-elected.

They were loudly demanding legislative representation in proportion to their numbers. And they were powerless.

Until the Revolution, as we have seen, the up-country had had no voice at all in the state government. Until 1790 its weight had been scarcely felt; and even now it was distinctly in the minority. Such power as it had had been won by pioneers like Patrick Calhoun, almost by threat of force alone. The legislative gentlemen well remembered these occurrences. And looking on the square chin and stern lips of old Pat's twenty-six-year-old son, they may even have feared a recurrence of them.

They might have spared themselves their anxiety. The rule that no man could sit in the governing body unless he owned at least one hundred acres of land and fifty slaves gave ample protection against dominance by the wild men of the hills. There was no place for 'mudsills' in the Legislature of South Carolina. And yet the governing gentlemen knew that land and slaves alone did not insure either education or a capacity for judgment. For all their narrowness and distrust of 'the people,' the legislators were not fundamentally unjust men. They could not and would not turn their whole state over to the questionable mercies of the frontier, but they were willing to compromise the question.

To their surprise, the back-country proved equally willing to modify its demands. An agreement was reached, the coast retaining control of the Senate, the hills winning the power in the House. New electoral districts were determined with equal regard to population and taxation, so that money and political power would not necessarily be synonymous.[38] Years later, Calhoun was to acclaim this compromise as an example of the 'concurrent' rather than the numerical majority of the South Carolina government 'not of one portion of its people over another portion.' Two great 'interests' had been given protection against each other, and, according to Calhoun, this very action was responsible for the mutual attachment'[39] which grew up between the two previously warring sections, welding the state into an unbreakable unit.

Calhoun's future career would prove how deeply this lesson in government had impressed him. A patriot was born when the *Leopard* attacked the *Chesapeake,* but a political philosopher had been conceived during those tedious hours when legislators debated checks and balances, argued and gave birth to a doctrine which was to revolutionize American thought. It was a device for securing justice for all minority economic groups within a population. Perfected, it was to be Calhoun's great contribution to the science of government.[40]

Yet it was twenty years before he himself knew it.

V

Of Courts and Courting

IT WAS APRIL in South Carolina.

April, and the pungent, burnt-honey scent of pear blossoms in the air, garnet stains on the sidewalks, where the maple buds were falling, tree branches blurred in masses of tiny new leaves, yellow as sunlight. It was April of 1809, and Court was in session at Newberry. In an anteroom, below the court chamber, a man in dark, long-tailed coat, high white stock and ruffled shirt, at his side the familiar green bag of the circuit-riding lawyer, dipped a pen and bent over a sheet of paper. He was writing Mrs. Floride Bonneau Colhoun, his thoughts leaping ahead of the eager quill, his black hair tumbled over his forehead.

Within a few moments the courthouse bell would ring, and Attorney Calhoun would hurry up a steep flight of stairs in the rear of the hall, entering through a door beside the judge's platform. The chamber would be small, noisy, crowded with the usual courthouse array of South Carolina 'sand-lappers,' heavy with the usual courthouse smells of dust and splintering pine floors deep under trodden sawdust, or oil lamps and corn whiskey and musty calf-bound law books; of clean, pressed broadcloth, and of sweated linsey-woolsey and homespun.[1]

To Calhoun the scene was entirely familiar and completely distasteful. Yet he could not leave. He could not visit Bonneau's Ferry that spring without 'a considerable neglect' of his 'professional duties. . . . It is perhaps one of the most disagreeable circumstances in our profession,' he wrote, 'that we cannot neglect its pursuit, without being Guilty of . . . a breach of confidence, reposed in us by our clients.' He had been 'very successful' in obtaining practice, he wrote, but 'I still feel a strong aversion to the law; and am determined to forsake it as soon as I can make a decent independence; for I am not ambitious of great wealth.'[2]

He finished his letter. He sprinkled it with sand, folded it, sealed it, and addressed it. His resolutions had been noble. Duty before pleasure. And within a month, in defiance of clients, resolutions, and the 'country fever,' * he was in Charleston.[3]

* 'Country fever' was a malarial condition to which people unaccustomed to the Charleston climate were especially susceptible on visits to the city.

For John Calhoun was in love. Now there were no doubts, no fears, no self-questionings. He was in love; he had never been in love before; and he would never be in love again.

2

To him, his discovery may have seemed original. Actually Mrs. Colhoun had been gently but firmly propelling him toward his objective for some time. Now she could bring her campaign into the open. Even before her daughter's maturity, Mrs. Colhoun, in the most approved fashion of French *mamans,* had been searching for a 'suitable' son-in-law. But unlike the usual ambitious mother, she had no need to find those all-important symbols of eligibility—wealth and aristocracy—in her daughter's husband-to-be. The Bonneaus of Charleston had a surplus of these qualities. With rare wisdom Mrs. Colhoun sensed the decadence of the hard-living, inbred young blades of the low-country. Floride's husband must be a man of virility, of mental brilliance, possessing those more subtle and forceful qualities that indicate not only success but future greatness. John Calhoun with his drive and ambition,was an embodiment of Mrs. Colhoun's goal.[4]

Furthermore, he was a gentleman. Although by die-hard Charlestonians he was excluded from the halls of aristocracy by his failure to choose a birthplace somewhere between the Battery and Broad Street, to the world outside he was a gentleman. He was a man of education and breeding, a planter and a slaveholder; and to the North and West, at least, he came to epitomize the Southern aristocrat. But not to Charleston—not for a long time.

Calhoun was no unwilling victim of his kin. 'If I should finally be disappointed,' he wrote Mrs. Colhoun, 'which heaven forbid, it will be by far the most unlucky accident in my life. . . . Nothing can shake my regard.'[5] As Floride's father was dead, convention demanded that a prospective suitor first 'address' himself to her mother. For Calhoun there could have been no task less difficult. All his life it was only with women with whom he had been intimate for a number of years that he was able to break down the self-imposed, protective barriers of the introvert—which had left him romantically unattached at twenty-seven—and reveal the deep affections of his nature. The women in his family were always his confidantes; and the stages were easy from his mother, to his mother-in-law, to his wife, and finally to his daughters. Since that first summer in Newport, it had been Mrs. Colhoun whom he had told 'of the things he hoped to do, and she encouraged him in all his dreams.'[6]

To the casual observer at this period, Calhoun appeared 'proud and reserved'; in actuality he was painfully shy. It was 'all politics' with this shaggy, rough-hewn young man; serious and intense, he had had no time to cultivate the graces of small-talk, nor to perfect his dance steps. Intellectually he was mature beyond his years, but emotionally just reaching his full development.

Such few of his letters as have survived show that his reserve was never wholly broken down, at least on paper. Even for their day they are stiff and stilted, and yet they tell us something of the young man. His courtship may have 'brought out the romantic side of his nature,' but his dreams of love and marriage seem strangely abstract: those of a man idealistic and comparatively inexperienced. Eventually he is said to have become quite a 'masterful' lover, but in those first months he found it 'easier to pour out his feelings to the older woman, who had been the friend of his heart for many years.' [7]

So we find him writing to Mrs. Floride Bonneau Colhoun in the early days of his courtship that 'to you I make the full and entire disclosure of the most inward recesses of my thoughts while to all the world, even to my own brothers, I am quite silent.' He was pleasantly surprised at the novel sensations he was undergoing, but his excitement was apparently self-generated, for he had not revealed his feelings to Floride. 'I formerly thought that it would be impossible for me to be strongly agitated in an affair of this kind, but that opinion now seems . . . wholly unfounded, since . . . in the very commencement, it can produce such effects. . . . I have a strong inclination to lay open my intentions to the object of my affection by letter; if this meets with your approval . . . nothing will prevent my doing so.' *[8]

At the Christmas season of 1809, he appears to have spent several days visiting the Colhouns at Bonneau's Ferry. Here he must have put in an intensive courtship, for in his very next letter he writes, 'Tell my *most esteemed Floride* that nothing could prevent me from the pleasure of writing, but that there is so much suspicion on the subject, that I am fearful of the fate of a double letter . . . in my handwriting.' It was evident that he was referring to Floride's young brothers, who were beginning to suspect that his relationship was something more than cousinly. 'Tell Floride that neither time or distance can in the least abate my affection, but that absence only proves how much my happiness depends on her good opinions.' [9]

Floride's opinions were not yet settled. She would wait a little and enjoy the courtship. She was only seventeen, gay and high-spirited, and although possessed of many 'solid qualities,' [10] she was not nearly so much like

---

* Several times in Calhoun's correspondence with Mrs. Colhoun he refers to letters written or enclosed to Floride. (See J. F. Jameson's collection of Calhoun's correspondence, pp. 111–112, 115–116, and 121.) Several writers, most notably G. W. Symonds in his article, 'When Calhoun Went A-Wooing' (*Ladies' Home Journal*, May, 1901), have fallen into the error of believing that because only one of Calhoun's love-letters has been reproduced, it was the only one that he ever wrote.

Calhoun, as a complement to him. He could write of his recent visit, 'Should it contribute in any degree to an event I have so much at heart, how happy a man I shall be.' [11] But Floride was in no haste to make up her mind. With her slim figure and feet made for dancing, she betrayed no undue eagerness to settle down into matronhood and child-bearing. Furthermore, Calhoun was too familiar to her to hold the romantic appeal of novelty. If he were to win Floride, he must court her at length.

This, he was fully prepared to do.

3

Already, one year of belledom lay behind this graceful, dark-haired girl, who was described as 'beautiful in . . . feature,' with all the vivacity of her French blood, blended with the practical common-sense of the Huguenots. Like other low-country women, she would have been pale and shadow-eyed from hot sleepless nights, tossing on a silk-hung bed draped with pavilion gauze, windows tight-closed against mosquitoes and damp; and from constant attention to face and arms with alum, rosewater, and Pear's soap; [12] but actually she was not nearly so fragile as she appeared. Apparently her mother was not in the least deceived, and had no compunctions in guiding her daughter toward the rigorous existence of an up-country planter's wife.

Floride Colhoun knew how to dance and how to flirt, as her suitor might ably have testified. She could cook and sew. She could make soap and candles, doctor the sick and soothe the dying. For she was a Southern woman, a plantation woman of 1809, and whatever her future, whether as the bride of one of those drawling, fast-shooting gallants of the low-country, or of the frontier lawyer, John Calhoun, her tasks were preordained. Judge of the sinners, teacher of the ignorant, manager of the house and even of the plantation, sweetheart, wife, and mother—this was her career.[13] This was marriage in South Carolina, 'the whole duty of womankind.'

Marriage was a serious responsibility, Floride's mother would tell her, and marriage to a man like Calhoun would be especially so. As planter and politician, his would be a strenuous life, and his domestic arrangements must be quiet and orderly. Her charm and beauty may have won his heart before marriage; it would be her good temper and good sense that counted later. She must always be ready, serene and unruffled, to entertain unexpected guests, regardless of their number. If he spent the entire evening talking of crops and politics, she must keep awake, keep smiling, keep ready to flirt her fan and pass the gentlemen their juleps or Madeira. She might dream of 'an independent sway over her household,' and of unbroken companionship with her husband, but this was only part of the story. She might consult him about such household matters as really interested him, but never must she annoy him with trifles. If he chose to spend an evening crouched in his easy-chair, lost in thought or in a book, she must wait in silence until he was ready to communicate his ideas.

No matter how tired she might become, no matter even if ill, 'a good wife must smile and clear her voice to tones of cheerfulness' on the arrival of her husband; for men, beset by trials or illness, would expect to 'find her ear and heart a ready reception.' And if he sinned, if he came home roaring, to be put to bed in his boots, or to spend the night in the quarters, not bothering to come home at all, a good wife must forget and forgive, for the spirit of marriage could be broken in South Carolina, but never, never the letter. And the smaller sins, the sins of misunderstanding that a man like Calhoun would inevitably commit—she must forgive these, too. He was not unreasonable; he would wound through ignorance and be surprised at having hurt her. He was easily depressed, given to moods and abstractions; he would be difficult to understand. Floride must remember to 'forbear from self-defense,' whoever was right or wrong, 'to hold back her harsh answers and confess her faults,' for these were 'the golden threads with which domestic happiness is woven.' [14]

Floride needed her mother's training. She came from the low, flat, sandy country near Charleston, from the family mansion on the Cooper where cypress canoes loaded with rice floated languidly down the brown waters toward the city, which had been the focus of her life. Hers was the world of town houses, of a pew at Saint Michael's, where the gallery was reserved for outsiders and Negroes; and of the legendary Saint Cecilia balls. Floride could wander in those fabulous gardens, which those like Calhoun had glimpsed only in snatches through wrought-iron gateways, their 'graceful tangle of rosettes and spirals, topped by a quaint old lantern,' or patterned in urns and interlocking circles, whirling around a great wheel. She could drowse in the shade of orange and Pride-of-India trees, breathe in the scents of arborvitae, sun-warmed figs, and oleanders, and as late as December, pick the old-fashioned damask roses.[15] She would dine at three on boned turkey, game, terrapin, and doves of blanc-mange in a nest of shredded, candied orange peel, and sup lightly at eight on a Huguenot meal of bread and butter and fresh figs.[16]

And Floride knew the other Charleston, that restless, vibrant Charleston of the travelers' stories, of concerts and dancing assemblies, of musical or dramatic evenings at the Dock Street Theater with its orchestra of French refugees from Santo Domingo, the Jockey Club and Race Week, when the streets were thronged with planters from the coastal parishes; afternoon tea at the sidewalk cafés. And she knew, too, the quieter, more intellectual side of a city that boasted a library of four thousand, five hundred volumes, and a society so close to that of the best in Europe that of all American cities foreign visitors found Charleston 'the most agreeable.' [17]

To Calhoun, Floride must have seemed from another world. But he had no fear of their differences; the lovely Huguenot girl had brought a lilt into his life that he had never felt before. 'I am not much given to enthusiasm,' he wrote Mrs. Colhoun, 'nor to anticipate future happiness. But I cannot now restrain my hopes of joy. . . . Let me add . . . that to be so nearly related to yourself, is a . . . source of happiness. . . . Sure am I, that I could not from a mother experience more kindness and tender affection.' [18]

Though aroused by the surge of an emotion wholly new to him, Calhoun was not too far gone to keep his cool logic from analyzing the girl he loved. 'After a careful examination,' he frankly wrote her mother, 'I found none but those qualities in her character which are suited to me. . . .[19] Could I suppose that she was . . . fickle . . . I should be wretched. But there I am happy; my trust in her constancy is extreme. The more I . . . compare her with others . . . the stronger does my reason approbate the choice of my affection. . . . Heaven has been kind to me in many instances; but I will ever consider this as the greatest of its favors. I know how much happiness, or how much misery is the consequence of marriage. As far as the former can be secured by prudence, by similarity of character, and sincerity of love, I may flatter myself with no ordinary share of bliss.' [20]

He was happy. He was unhappy. He was 'madly in love,' [21] with no outlet to his feelings but the scratching of words across a sheet of paper, and half-waking, half-sleeping dreams as he tossed about on the long, hot summer nights. Never had the wrangles and tangles of the courtroom, nor the slow-paced hours in the law office so palled upon him. He was twenty-eight, an ardent and self-confessedly 'impatient' [22] man; he had waited years for the consummation of his hopes, but these last few months seemed almost more than flesh and blood could endure. 'If possible, I will be in New Port next fall,' he wrote Mrs. Colhoun. 'I wish much that Floride would consent to that time. I will write to her about it by my next. . . . If you know her sentiment I would be glad you would let me know in your next, for it will be a great inducement for me to go on, if she agrees to that time; and . . . will furnish a good excuse for my leaving my professional business at the fall court.' [23]

But Floride was coy. She manifested no desire to wed her lover in the fall at Newport, nor did she show any interest in rescuing him from the tortures of the law court. So he remained in Abbeville, working out his ardor in letter after letter to his beloved and to his future mother-in-law. 'I formerly was considered the most indolent in letter-writing,' was his confession. 'But now it is my delight. I could write you by every mail. . . .' [24] But his persistency reaped results; by midsummer Floride gave him her promise that in the winter she would become his bride. Calhoun was ecstatic. 'I am not only happy in the love and esteem of your daughter,

but in the concurring assent of all our mutual friends,' Calhoun wrote his
ally. 'How shall I be sufficiently grateful?' [25]

With this new impetus to his hopes, not even the intense summer heat
could sap his energies. He spent weeks looking out 'for a place' to establish himself 'permanently for life.' He decided, at last, on a farm near his
brother Patrick's, but reluctantly postponed building until he could consult the taste of his future bride.[26] He even succumbed to an attack of
poetry, but his recovery was swift and complete. Every one of his labored
verses began with the word, 'Whereas.' [27]

Introspective though he was, Calhoun's letters show that his self-analysis
was giving way to sympathy and solicitude for the girl who had consented
to place her life's happiness in his care. Late in the summer he received
shocking news. Floride had been seriously bruised in an accident. The
letter from Newport filled him with 'joy and sympathy at the same time.
Joy for her preservation and sympathy for the pain she endured. . . .
Had her life not been spared . . . I know not where I should have look
for relief. . . . I never was so anxious to see Floride and yourself.' [28]

Thus in hopes and reading and letter-writing the long days passed. On
the hillsides the corn stalks were thickening; the warm juice was running
through the ears. The cotton fields flamed in seas of red fire. These were
growing days, days when Calhoun could lift his shaggy head from the dust
of the old law books to scan his own inner horizons, to take time out to
grow, to dream, to plan.

4

No mere state legislator would become Floride's husband. Calhoun was
running for Congress. Lovesick he might seem to himself, or to the recipient of his letters. Yet night after night through this summer of 1810 he
was out on the stump at all the little cross-roads villages of the district—
Abbeville, Greenwood, Ninety-Six, and Hodges—fighting out the battle
of the past versus the future, of submission to British depredations versus
resistance. It had been a three-way race at first, between Calhoun, his
cousin James, and the elderly General Elmore,* a 'hero of the late war,'
whose grueling memories had long since tempered his taste for flame.

Calhoun was the outsider, the avowed advocate of the swamp-dwellers,
hunters, and back-country farmers, all the rough-and-tumble hierarchy
of the new frontier democracy. He was caught in the surge of the new
times; and from the first, the trend was clear. James Calhoun saw wisdom
early, and withdrew in favor of his young relative. Calhoun was guilty
of no crime worse than complacency when he informed Floride in Sep-

* John A. Elmore, father of Franklin P. Elmore.

tember, a week before election day: 'It is thought that I will succeed by a large majority,' [29] for when the smoke and fire had cleared away, it was discovered that he had won, not only by a majority, but by a landslide! [30]

5

It was almost September when Calhoun sat down and wrote to Floride the only one of all his love-letters which has been reproduced for public view.* It was a strange letter, not lacking in warmth, nor even in a certain formal beauty of its own. It was the letter of a Puritan idealist, not a Southern courtier. But there was no doubting its tenderness nor its sincerity.

> *I rejoice, my dearest Floride, that the period is fast approaching when it will be no longer necessary to address you through the cold medium of a letter. At furthest it cannot be much longer than a month before I shall behold the dearest object of my hopes and desires. I am anxious to see you and my impatience daily increases. May heaven grant you a safe return. What pleasure I have experienced in your company, what delight in the exchange of sentiment, what transport in the testimonies of mutual love. In a short time this with the permission of heaven will be renewed, and I shall be happy. To be united in mutual virtuous love is the first and best bliss that God has permitted to our natures. My dearest one, may our love strengthen with each returning day, may it ripen and mellow with our years, and may it end in immortal joys . . . time and absence make no impression on my love for you; it glows with no less ardour than at the moment of parting, which must be a happy omen of its permanent nature. When mere personal charms attract, the impression may be violent but cannot be lasting, and it requires the perpetual presence of the object to keep it alive; but when the beauty of mind, the soft and sweet disposition, the amiable and lovable character embellished with innocence and cheerfulness are united to . . . personal beauty, it bids defiance to time. Such, my dear Floride, are the arms by which you have conquered, and it is by these the*

---

* The most intimate of Calhoun's family secrets belong to him alone. Only three of his other letters to Floride have been made public. Only three of her letters to him are in his collected papers, and these of little importance. It may be true, as Gerald Johnson believes, that Calhoun destroyed all his more personal papers before his death, solely to keep them from the prying eyes of biographers. Some of them, however, may have been in the correspondence entrusted to R. M. T. Hunter of Virginia, of which much was lost during the Civil War. The absence of these letters leaves a gap in the story of Calhoun's life, which only legend, family tradition, and a few hints in his more impersonal correspondence have been able to fill.

durability of your sovereignty is established over your subject whom
you hold in willing servitude. . . . Adieu my love; my heart's de-
light.[31]

I am your true lover.[32]

By November the 'sweet pain' of waiting was over. Calhoun arrived at
Bonneau's Ferry, and for six weeks, perhaps the happiest he was ever to
know, he surrendered himself to the joy of courting. Informally chap-
eroned by her thirteen-year-old brother, James, Floride's cambric-fringed
shawl or 'camel-heir' cape tossed over a large basket of ham and fowl,[33]
the lovers were off for the country, a whole day stretching ahead of them.

Winter was near, but there were still 'mild and balmy' days, and along
the river banks the last few bronzed rice grains were waving in the wind.
Foliage was scant now, but red-birds, 'bright as if painted in new colors,'
flashed through the gray veils of moss, and the salt-marshes glowed saf-
fron and gold in the sun.[34] In the long sweetness of these hours all thoughts
of politics, all frets and tugs of ambition were pushed from Calhoun's
mind. He was the lover now, eager and gay; he wooed Floride with his
'sweet smile,' and the voice that could sound clear over the bustle of an
Abbeville Court Day was softly modulated and gentle when whispering
words like 'my dearest one,' or 'my heart's delight.'[35]

Their lovemaking, their 'testimonies of mutual love' were stolen and in
secret, for their engagement was still concealed. But Calhoun was quick
to seize both the opportunity and the girl, once young James's back was
turned, and the day the boy discovered John in the carriage 'slyly' kissing his sister, his indignation was unbounded, and he could not get home
fast enough to tell his mother. To his bewilderment she expressed neither
surprise nor anger. The secret was a secret no longer.[36]

That day, the day which Calhoun had said would be 'the happiest
. . . of my life,'[37] dawned on January 8, 1811. Here, in this tropical
coast-country, there was already a promise of spring in the air, and over
the mirrors the first pale sprigs of 'January Jasmine' touched sprays of
holly and branches of wild olive and magnolia. The 'great house' was
alive with expectation. 'It was a grand affair, that wedding,' young James
Colhoun noted; 'an old-time wedding; everybody was there.'[38]

'Everybody,' meaning, of course, the clans of Colhoun and Bonneau,
all the assorted 'kin' and 'kissing kin' from Charleston and the low-
country parishes: women in clinging dresses of 'soft crepe and white
Peelong,' stepping down from round, velvet-lined coaches; men in ruffled
shirts and waistcoats of white satin, swinging off their horses.[39] Brooding 'Brother Patrick' from the home farm in Abbeville would have been
there, and the older brothers, William, the Augusta clerk, and James, the
Charleston shopkeeper, awkward and self-conscious, perhaps, marked as

they were with the stigma of 'trade,' but aglow with pride. Yes, they had done well by this young brother of theirs.

From the wedding guests, however, more appraising glances were cast upon Floride's bridegroom. So this was he, this gaunt young man, the up-country cousin, who from two brief terms in the Legislature had stepped to the halls of Congress in a single stride. Now the last of the protective barriers of the aristocracy was to be broken by intermarriage. Pat Calhoun had been a tough nut, 'too tough for the lowlanders to crack.' Now they were faced with the challenge of swallowing his son—or of being swallowed by him.

Meanwhile, sequestered in her own bedchamber, Floride had no time for fears. Her bridesmaids were dressing her, flying about like eager birds, one draping the floating veil over her shoulders, another pinning orange blossoms against her dark hair. Finally, when the last lock was braided, the last glittering jewel slipped on her fingers and a single rose placed in her hand, the bridegroom was called; and for one long moment, shut away from the scrutiny of the guests, he could have his fill of looking and of adoring, taking with him a picture to be treasured and carried in his memory always.[40]

Then came the wedding, the ring and the words, the congratulations, the handshakes, and the cry of the girl who found the ring in the cake, for she would be the first to wed. And afterward, the marriage feast, the 'old wine,' the 'intemperate revel' of the younger men, and the valiant and alcoholic attempts at wit and wisdom from the old. Twilight was stealing through the windows before the party arose; and from outside came the shuffling sound of footsteps as the Negroes marched 'round and 'round the house, peering shyly through the open door in passing, and singing such old-time airs as 'Joy to the Bride,' and 'Come Haste to the Wedding.'[41]

6

They took no wedding trip. Instead, they lingered in the big house on the Cooper until young spring swelled the first buds against the stiff leaves of the winter, when they started for the 'upper country' and their new home, Bath, on a ridge high above the Savannah. It was only a small plantation, but 'fit for the residence of a Genteel family,' and probably akin to those described in the Courier with 'three decent rooms,' and 'two good brick chimnies.'[42] There would be saddle-horses and slaves, but Floride would have to submit to a far simpler style of living than that to which she had been accustomed.

History has credited Floride with having brought 'a small fortune' as her wedding dowry, enabling her husband to devote his energies to politics.

On 'the settlement of Floride's property,' Calhoun had taken the advice of his old friend, 'Judge Desassure,' and written Mrs. Colhoun that his own sentiment was that in marriage all property should be in the husband's name. Yet there is much circumstantial evidence to indicate that Calhoun's lifelong determination was to support his wife by his own efforts, and that 'the fortune [was] her's' alone.[43] Either he refused to use her money for common household expenses or Floride's share of her mother's estate was much smaller than is generally supposed, for in all the years of their marriage, freedom from financial care was something the Calhouns never knew.

In that first year, however, the couple were in Charleston in the 'proper season.' Together, they could visit Coit and Fraser's [44] for final purchases for their household; and they were in time for the post-Lenten gaieties, with Floride, true to her heritage, joining a lively theater party, and Calhoun, true to his prejudices, remaining at home. They were honeymooners still, struggling to surmount their differences of temperament, taste, and tradition; and in this first difference, Calhoun emerged the victor. Floride returned 'not at all pleased,' and feeling 'less sickness than what I believe is usual in her condition.' [45] They had been married five months; to him, she was his 'dearest Floride'; [46] but to her, he was her 'dear husband,' or 'Mr. Calhoun.'

VI

The Second American Revolution

IN THE YEAR 1811, Washington was stagnant. The adjective is descriptive of the political and the physical atmosphere. The war drums beating in the Southern and Western hinterlands were but faint echoes in the capital. Four years had passed, but the blood-stained decks of the *Chesapeake* were not forgotten. Embargo, non-importation, non-intercourse, impressment, were being endured with less and less resignation by the people of America as a whole. They suffered in their homes, their business, and the entire normal course of their lives; but Washington, the straggling little 'city of magnificent distances' rested comfortably on its marshes and mudflats, almost unaware of the effect that its ill-received political measures were having upon the country.

Now and then an especially virulent foreign insult caused a slight ripple across the consciousness of the capital. Old-line Federalists wondered vaguely if mild little 'Jemmy' Madison might actually be forced into war some day, while equally listless Republicans merely conjectured as to how long the President, with his policy of inactivity, would be able to postpone the conflict.

It had taken an off-year Congressional election to change Washington to the true capital of an aroused, virile, and increasingly Unionistic nation.

Through the weeks of October and early November they flooded into the capital, frontier lawyers and planters, riding in on horseback, walking unsteadily off packet-boats, or stiffly descending from crude stagecoaches. Fully half the members of the House of Representatives for the session of 1811–12 were newcomers to Washington.

Although these men were young, there was the hardness of frontier life on their faces. Their childhood had been spent in the shadow of the Revolution, and there was grimness in their resolve not to let England reimpose her authority on the fledgling Republic. If there was passion in the flash of their eyes and in the curve of their lips, it was controlled by the responsibility that dominated them, their belief that they held a mandate from the people-at-large to thrust aside the decadent and faltering conservative régime, and to return young America to the virility of its heritage.

Although there might be a hint of the aristocrat in the proud lift of their heads, in their poise and self-discipline, they scorned the knee-breeches and buckled shoes, the mincing steps and courtly manners of the early days of the Republic. These were plain men, simple in their dress, simple and direct in their objectives. They strode out like Indians, with the free-and-easy grace of men used to long rides over fields and through woods, used to flinging themselves upon swift horses and riding twenty or thirty miles a day.

Their voices, their cadences of speech were new also. Mingled with the near-British accents of the 'Virginia Dynasty' and the flat speech of the coastal aristocrats were new voices and new pronunciations. Washingtonians now heard the twang of the mountaineer, the musical drawl of the Southwesterner, the soft slur of the central Georgian. New faces and new voices, a new power in American government, all these Washington saw and sensed and feared.

First business for the newcomers was the election of a Speaker of the House. Because of its accompanying power of committee appointments, this post was considered second only to the Presidency. On the choice of a Speaker might depend the fundamental issue of war or peace for the nation. That the newcomers meant war, Washington well understood. United in their backgrounds, they needed only the additional unity of political leadership to shake the incumbent Administration from its foundations.

United they would select the new Speaker. He would be for war—or those who had chosen him would displace him. Who would he be—Macon of North Carolina, Nelson of Virginia, Bassett of Virginia? Doubts were somewhat dispelled when on the night of November 3, 1811, the newcomers began to gather at Mrs. Bushby's boarding house. There a former Senator, now a newly elected Representative, had taken rooms, a tall, imperious young Kentuckian named Henry Clay.

The thirty-five-year-old Clay was not unknown to Washington. He had burst upon the capital six years before, a one-man vanguard of the Western invasion. Although a year under the constitutional age limit, with characteristic impudence he had forced his way into the United States Senate, where he had spent his time challenging the votes, opinions, and leadership of his elders, most of them antiquated relics of Revolutionary days.

Impudence, indeed, was his outstanding quality on and off the Senate floor. It was visible in the very tilt of his shoulders, the flair of his shapely legs, as he swaggered along the muddy streets of the capital, his feet pointing straight ahead in his characteristic Indian stride.

Politically, his luck had not been very good. He had called for the abolition of the slave-trade, for the annexation of Florida, for protection of domestic manufactures, for rearmament and national defense, and, above all, for war and national honor. The Senate had declined debate with him, and had rejected the majority of his proposals. Unwilling to follow, he had been unable to lead, and was suffering from political frustration.

Now the wind had turned. Scenting the inevitable approach of war, aware of the tremendous shift of public opinion, Henry Clay was weary of seeing his nation 'eternally the tail to Britain's kite.' His day had come and his lips were ready to sound the trumpet call of young America.

So it was that the young 'War Hawks' of the 'Second American Revolution' were wading through the mud and drizzle of early November to the dreary boarding house where Henry Clay was awaiting them. Aware of their cause, they were discovering their leader. Henry Clay had found his army.

The blond Kentuckian, a bottle of Bourbon close to his elbow, a confident smile on his petulant mouth, sat sprawled in a chair, eyeing the young Representatives who were filing beneath his banner. The names of many were already familiar to him: William Wyatt Bibb of Georgia, Peter Buell Porter of western New York, Langdon Cheves of South Carolina, Felix Grundy of Tennessee, George Poindexter of Natchez, Mississippe, William Lowndes of South Carolina, Samuel McKee of Kentucky, John Caldwell Calhoun of South Carolina.

Here were young fire-eaters, whose care for their country's glory and honor was as keen as Clay's own. They were waiting for leadership, and he was the leader. He spoke to them out of a common heritage. 'Rocked in the cradle of the Revolution,' he could remember as a child of four seeing the British armies swooping down upon southern Virginia. Nor did he forget the British soldier who in a hunt for concealed family treasures had thrust his sword into the grave of his father, buried four hours before. And Clay did not even need to tell the group that Lord Dorchester, the Governor-General of Canada, was already negotiating with England for the purchase of American scalps.[2]

Clay's emotion was contagious. He saw the brooding horror in the eyes of Felix Grundy, who had seen Indians kill and scalp members of his own family. Henry Clay, the most imperious and lovable leader the American Congress was ever to know, was captivating the group before him with the same weapons with which he later won the hearts of the American people.

At the conclusion of the caucus, one group stayed behind. They were Clay's messmates, young men whose known talents and eagerness for war had given them advance reputations in Washington. From them Clay would choose his leaders; with them he would draft the new program of the American government. Upon their arrival in Washington, Bibb, Calhoun, Cheves, Grundy, and Lowndes formed the 'War Mess,'[3] with Clay at the head.

Already Calhoun was chosen as second-in-command.* It was a strange alliance, for no two men could have been more unlike. Both were highstrung, but the Kentuckian was expansive, revealing, eager for self-expression.[4] The shy and introverted South Carolinian was, on the other hand, constantly holding himself in check, yet, despite this repression, his whole being radiated dynamic intensity. Clay quickly recognized Calhoun's latent strength, saw him as a valuable lieutenant and potential leader of men, but it is doubtful if he recognized the genius of the unassuming Southerner, or viewed him as a rival to his own ambitions. If so, he would scarcely have entrusted him with so much authority. Calhoun's greater qualities were not obvious ones, and it was impossible for Clay fully to understand a man so unlike himself.

Calhoun, being of a more thoughtful disposition, had a better though incomplete understanding of Clay. He vividly realized Clay's talents, and saw him as a man to support and follow. Ambitious himself, Calhoun understood that association with Henry Clay would place him high in the group that was seizing control.

Calhoun was no starry-eyed dreamer at this, the start of his national career. His ideals were high and his hopes also; he would frankly admit that 'I love just renown.' But he had learned his politics in a tough school. Easy as his election to Congress had been, it had left its own trail of bitterness and disillusion. In a rhetorical outburst to MacBride in September, 1811, he had thanked his friend for putting him on his guard against enemies masquerading under the guise of friendship. 'I love my country . . . too much . . . to be subordinate to their selfish views . . .' Calhoun wrote. 'This is my sin; this is my want of firmness. This is my dubious conduct.' He had failed to place them in 'lucretive' political posts. 'Want of firmness! I would have supposed it the last fault imputable to me. . . . I have ever stood obstinate against all local, party, or factious interest.' He had often advocated unpopular questions, 'and was determined that neither private censure, nor that of the whole community will ever drive me from the path of duty.'[5]

Calhoun faced the future forearmed.

2

It was November 6, 1811, when Calhoun first looked upon the makeshift city of Washington, with its aimless avenues and meandering foot-

---

* Actually Calhoun did not arrive in Washington until November 6, 1811, two days after the opening of the session, but his reputation had preceded him, and his place of leadership was assured.

paths, its tangled marshlands and croaking frogs. Even to men from the half-charted frontier, Washington bore small resemblance to their preconceived dreams of a city; and to men like William Lowndes, who knew Piccadilly better than Pennsylvania Avenue, or even to Calhoun, the half-realized capital must have seemed appalling indeed. Discerning men might detect in unfinished buildings and grass-grown streets that same decay that was rotting away the national spirit. Still true was the observation six years before of the actor, William Dunlap: 'No houses are building; those already built are not finished and many are falling rapidly to decay'; and Calhoun with his classical turn of mind might have seen the capital as Dunlap did, like 'some antique ruin,' reminding one of 'Rome or Persepolis.' [6]

Now, standing under the double row of poplar trees that lined Pennsylvania Avenue, Calhoun saw it all: to the west, the 'President's House,' on either side the 'two handsome Brick buildings in which the public offices are kept.' To the east loomed Capitol Hill, the white blocky wings of the unfinished legislative building connected only by a wooden runway.[7]

Once inside the Capitol itself, however, the story was different. Observers might find the Senate Chamber 'much more elegant than that of the House,' but to the 'brawling boys' from the backwoods, what the House lacked in beauty it made up in grandeur.[8] The pillars were only of sandstone, but of the purest Corinthian design, beautifully fluted, and encircled with draperies of crimson. Stone steps spiraled up to the visitors' galleries, now packed with spectators, all eyes centered on the rostrum and the great canopy, resplendent with scarlet and green velvet and golden fringe. Above perched a huge stone eagle, wings defiantly spread; below stood the ornate chair of the Speaker—Henry Clay.

From thick skylights shafts of sunlight fell against heads, bald, powdered, curled, bewigged; on coats of blue, green, or plum. The room was a whirlpool of rapping knuckles and clashing voices, of stagnant air and stumbling page boys; the floor a litter of discarded newspapers, letters, quills, and novels; the 'turkey carpets' stained with pools of tobacco juice. Under one desk a pair of hounds lay coiled; from the top a pair of pipestem legs slanted upwards.

Other than the war leaders, Calhoun would have seen few familiar faces. Only a sprinkling of the veterans were left: North Carolina's graying 'Father Macon,' with his round pleasant face and his white-topped boots, and the cluster of irreconcilables, the Federalists of New England: Boston's bitter Josiah Quincy, openly avowed disunionist; dour Abijah Bigelow, and the fat and Calvinistic Reverend Samuel Taggart. But that weird figure with the hounds, long black hair stringing down over a velvet collar—was he a page boy dressed up in his elders' clothes or a sick old man? The frail form was slim as a boy's, but Calhoun could see that the face was white and seamed with lines of pain, and that the Indian-black eyes glowed with a feverish brilliance. Calhoun knew him now: 'Mad Jack' Randolph of Virginia, thirty-eight years old, a nephew of Thomas Jefferson's and once his brilliant young floor leader in the House; now in chronic opposition, invalid, erratic, embittered.

First on the agenda two days earlier had been the election of a Speaker. The balloting was brief: three votes for former Speaker Macon, thirty-five for the young Georgian physician, William Wyatt Bibb, and seventy-five for Henry Clay. That 'clever man,' the 'Western Star,' in the sneering words of John Randolph, 'strided from the door . . . as soon as he entered it, to the Speaker's chair.' [9]

Clay had arisen, faced his subjects, relaxed, poised, the sunlight bright on his face, the gavel in his hand. He spoke a few words, promising the transaction of all business 'in the most agreeable manner.' [10] He lowered his gavel. The Second American Revolution had begun!

3

Primary business for the new Speaker had been the appointment of standing committees. A Federalist seized the floor. Should not the appointments be postponed until the next day, 'in order to give the Speaker further time to become acquainted with the members.' [11]

Mr. Clay had no need of such consideration. He was thoroughly acquainted with the members whom he proposed to appoint, and the mere announcement of his selections was enough to convince the opposition that their day was gone indeed. Seniority had been tossed to the breezes. Clay packed the committees with youngsters who lived and breathed the spirit of war. Of the important Committee on Foreign Relations he named Peter Buell Porter of New York chairman,[12] but on his withdrawal from Congress shortly afterward, the members selected John Calhoun as their acting head.*

The South Carolinian shouldered his responsibilities with gravity. 'Your friend is now an actor on the political stage,' he wrote the sympathetic James MacBride, later in the session. 'This is a period of the greatest moment to our country. No period since the formation of our Constitution has been equally . . . important.' [13]

President Madison's Message of November 5, although urging that the Republic assume 'an armour and an attitude demanded by the crisis,' [14] was nevertheless noncommittal. Impressment was not mentioned, although

* Proof of Calhoun's leadership was to be given in the next session when, in the newly formed Committee on Foreign Relations, John Smilie of Pennsylvania was named head. At the first meeting Smilie suddenly moved that Calhoun be made chairman in his place. Vehemently, Calhoun protested, asserting that someone older, someone from another state would be far more suitable, and that he would serve under Smilie with 'perfect willingness.' But Smilie insisted, and Calhoun was unanimously elected. (Calhoun, *Life*, pp. 12–13.)

a line referred to 'war on our lawful commerce.' England was condemned for her 'hostile inflexibility'; but bitter rebuke of France made certain that Napoleonic 'assistance' would neither be offered nor desired in any American struggle against British power.

As anti-French as it was anti-British, the Message was more illustrative of Madison's grasp of international realities than of his understanding of the American people. Vacillating the President undoubtedly was, but he at least realized that American wrongs were as nothing beside the threat which Napoleonic dictatorship posed, not only to Europe but to the world at large. Repeatedly, Jonathan Russell in Paris was warning the President that Napoleon's greatest hope 'was to entangle us in a war with England,' so that he might be free to complete his enslavement of the European Continent. Britain, weary, alone, drained of her man-power by years of blood-letting, could not quibble about the 'citizenship papers' of so-called 'Yankee' seamen, speaking the English of Bow's Bells or Yorkshire.

On November 29, 1811, the Foreign Relations Committee Report, largely although not entirely the work of Calhoun, sounded the first official note of war. It called for fifty thousand volunteers, for the arming of all merchant ships and the outfitting of warships. 'The period has now arrived,' the Report proclaimed, 'when . . . it is the sacred duty of Congress to call forth the patriotism and the resources of the country.' [15]

Public opinion agreed with Calhoun. By December, foreign visitors might well have assumed that the conflict had already begun. A frontier skirmish at Tippecanoe on November 7, in which sixty-eight white settlers under the leadership of General William Henry Harrison had fallen to Indian attack, was the sole incident needed to set the Western press off into a cry of 'WAR! WAR! WAR!' and 'BRITISH SAVAGE WAR. THE BLOW IS STRUCK.' [16] Nor was the alliance of Redcoats and Redskins mere journalistic headline writing. News of Tippecanoe revealed the seizure of at least '90 fusees and rifles from the enemy, most of them new and of English manufacture.' [17] Here alone was proof of the ugly truth, known at first-hand by many of the young War Hawks themselves. Square-jawed, grim-faced Felix Grundy sounded off the Congressional attitude. 'Why, sir,' he addressed Speaker Clay, 'the fighting has already begun! The Indians are up along the whole frontier with British weapons.' Impressment was the issue on paper, the issue of the coastal colonies all the way from Charleston to Portsmouth, but no backwoodsman could forgive the crime of English rifles in red-skinned hands.[18]

4

A one-man opposition to the whole war program was John Randolph. Randolph was no frontiersman. He knew nothing about Indian blood, save

for the diluted portion flowing through his own veins.* Vehemently, he
turned upon the 'Liberty Boys.' 'You may make war, if you please,' he
chortled. 'I will make peace.'[19]

Life was far from pleasant for Mr. Randolph. Disciplined by Speaker
Clay, daily challenged and contradicted by an impudent young 'puppy'
from South Carolina, the discursive Virginian saw his rule sweeping away
on the flood of the new congressional invasion. That red-haired, young
'Dick' Johnson was the author of a *Rationale of Tactic for Mounted Rifle-
men*, which even Bonaparte had pronounced 'not bad,' would have interested Randolph little; but that Johnson's octoroon mistress was 'the
most beautiful girl in the West' would have made him writhe with im-
potent fury. That Henry Clay was the youngest man ever elected to the
United States Senate was nothing beside the bitter realization that only
a few scant years ago this bumptious cockerel had been passing Italian
stays and imported brandies over the counter of a Richmond department
store. And Calhoun, with his talk of the Founding Fathers and demands
for the building of thirty-two new ships, his 'haughty assumptions of
equality with the older members,' who was he but the son of an unlettered immigrant Irishman, a backwoodsman, 'who never saw a ship?' Between 'the tyro in the chair and the tyro on the floor,' Randolph's misery
was complete.[20]

Calhoun had incurred his particular hatred, for of all the men in the
House of Representatives, the South Carolinian had alone dared challenge
the assertions of John Randolph of Roanoke. By his colleagues Calhoun's
courage was regarded as little short of foolhardy. Randolph's predilection
for duels was already a national scandal. Yet with a finesse that would
have done credit to men twice his years, pitting cold logic against the
Virginian's bursts of fury, Calhoun maintained the bounds of courtesy
as well as the strength of his position. So far his exchanges were merely
in the hasty encounters of running debate, but no disinterested observer
failed to sense his hidden reserves of strength. 'His high character as a
scholar . . . the Herculean vigor of his understanding of American liberty
cannot fail to find a most powerful support,'[21] wrote an admiring correspondent for the Hartford *Mercury*.

He won no support from Randolph. Although his own ravings had
played no small part in preventing rearmament, the Virginian now hurled
curses upon the heads of those who would throw their country into war,
unprepared. Thwarted, he even seized upon a comet as one of the 'signs
of the times' that 'bespoke the inadvisability of war.'[22]

This procrastination was too much for Calhoun. 'Are we to renounce
our reason? Must we turn from the path of justice . . . because a comet
has made its appearance . . .?'[23] But if Calhoun was exasperated, so
was President Madison, bending pale and haggard over his desk until

* Randolph was descended from Pocahontas and John Rolfe.

dawn faded his candles. 'The Damned Rascal,' was the Presidential comment. 'I wonder how he would conduct the Government. It is easy . . . to make speeches.' [24]

Day by day Calhoun watched Randolph choking the columns of the public press with his brilliant, mischievous diatribes. Threats of the invasion of Canada he countered with threats of Southern secession from the Union; this 'tid-bit Canada,' he declared, would destroy the balance of power between the sections. He discussed female card-players and Yankee peddlers. He asserted that the Louisiana Purchase would cause both the Union and the Constitution to 'crumble into ruin'; and that 'Tom Paine and the Devil would not make universal suffrage work.' [25]

Calhoun listened in baffled fury. Temperamentally, the Southerner, in spite of his almost incredible self-control, was a far from patient man. These months of 'suspense, ennui, and anxiety' were a severe strain upon him. 'The greatest impediment' to his program, he had originally believed, was the President, who lacked the 'commanding talents,' * [26] to unify the country and fire Congress with the courage to proceed. But Randolph was different. Randolph was deliberately malicious, deliberately thrusting himself against what Calhoun was convinced was the united will of the American people. Upon the public, who read his harangues as the voice of Congress itself, Randolph's effect was becoming dangerous. Never did Calhoun realize this more clearly than in the Virginian's violent attempt of December 10, 1811,[27] to disrupt American war morale before it had been fairly born.

It was Calhoun's Foreign Relations Committee Report that drew Randolph's fire. Sarcastically he demanded if the Report actually meant war —war not only against the interest of the country but of humanity itself. The merchants of Salem would not sacrifice their scant remnants of foreign trade to a war that would destroy the very rights which it proposed to protect. Nor would the planters of Virginia be taxed for a useless conflict which would only aggravate their present distresses.

And what, demanded Randolph, of the South's most dreaded nightmare —slave insurrections? What of the Yankee peddlers seeping through the Southern states, poisoning the minds of the blacks with their talk of the Revolution in France, of liberty and equality? What of the women and children, alone on the plantations, open to the murderous wrath of a slave uprising? How could men talk of taking Canada when 'some of us are shuddering for own safety at home? . . . The night-bell never tolls for fire in Richmond that the mother does not hug the infant more closely to her bosom.'

On he ranted, of Shakespeare and Chatham, of American greatness drawn from British strength; and then, with characteristic lack of transi-

* Calhoun's comment was actually uttered in April, 1812, but summarized his opinion of Madison, generally. (See MacBride MSS, Library of Congress.)

tion, railing against the 'mother country,' reminiscing of his own childhood, when his mother and her newborn son fled the armies of the traitor
Arnold and the British Phillips. Sneering, the Virginian turned on Calhoun. 'I,' he proclaimed, 'must be content to be called a tory by a patriot
of the last importation.' [28]

What of the cost of war? Randolph queried. Had not the Republicans
pledged not to burden the country with standing armies and to pay off
the national debt? Shaking his finger, long and white as the bone of a
skeleton, in the faces of the War Hawks, Randolph screeched his warning:
'You sign your political death-warrant.' The prediction was somewhat
alleviated by his remark off the House floor that Clay and Calhoun 'have
entered this House with their eyes on the Presidency, and mark my words,
sir, we shall have war before the end of the session.' [29]

Calhoun pondered the outburst for forty-eight hours, then chose his
own ground for a reply. This was wise strategy; he knew that in a battle
of emotions he would have no chance. Even tempestuous Henry Clay was
no match for the erratic Virginian. And wittingly Calhoun determined
to strike at Randolph's weakest point, using strong logic to devastate his
opponent.

For this, his first major address, the tall South Carolinian had diffidence in his bearing, restraint in his measured phrases. But in his austere
language and flawless logic, he was already the Calhoun the world came
to know.

He acknowledged that the Committee Report did mean war, nothing but
war, and he believed that it was so understood by every member except
the gentleman from Virginia. 'War,' he admitted, 'ought never to be
resorted to but when it is clearly . . . necessary; so . . . much as not
to require logic to convince our understandings, nor . . . eloquence to inflame our passions.' But to prove the necessity of war now, in the face
of the impressed seamen, the shattered commerce, and the intimidation
and destruction of American rights by British arms, would be as foolish
as if he were to state the obvious fact that the House was now in session,
and then go on to prove it.

'It is not for the human tongue to instil the sense of independence and
honor. This is the work of nature; a generous nature that disdains tame
submission to wrongs. . . . This part of the subject is so imposing as to
enforce silence upon even the gentleman from Virginia,' shouted Calhoun,
with the same defiance with which he had bearded Timothy Dwight in the
classroom at Yale, six years before.

More calmly, Calhoun announced that he would answer Randolph's
arguments, but only those, he hastened to add, that were worth answering.
The opposition had declared the country unprepared. Then it must be
prepared, and swiftly. Abruptly he turned upon Randolph, 'who . . .
for many years past' had 'seen the defenceless state of his country . . .

under his own eyes, without a single endeavor to remedy so serious an evil.'

Indignantly he challenged Randolph's assertion that the people would refuse to pay war taxes, because their violated rights were not worth defending. 'The people . . . are against hesitation and wavering. They are not prejudiced against taxes laid for a great and necessary purpose.' To produce 'the real spirit of union,' the government must 'protect every citizen in the lawful pursuit of his business. . . . Protection and patriotism are reciprocal.' He would scorn 'to estimate in dollars and cents the value of national independence. I cannot measure in shillings and pence the misery, the stripes, and the slavery of our impressed seamen; nor even the value of our shipping, commercial, and agricultural losses, under the Orders in Council and the British . . . blockade.'

Calhoun's self-consciousness had left him. He drew his thin frame erect; his eyes darkened; his voice rang clear across the Chamber. Slave uprisings would be ridiculous, with a whole nation on armed guard. Personally, he doubted that Southern slaves had ever heard of the French Revolution. Charges that the Southwest was for war because of the declining prices of hemp and cotton were 'base and unworthy.' Nevertheless, the South had no desire to be relegated to the colonial state, even for the benefit of England. And she was for a war of defense, not aggression, a defense of violated rights.

If the gentleman from Virginia really wanted to 'promote the cause of humanity,' Calhoun suggested, 'let his eloquence be addressed to Lord Wellesley or Mr. Percival, and not the American Congress. Tell them if they persist in such daring . . . injury that, however inclined to peace,' our nation 'will be bound in honor . . . to resist . . . that . . . war will ensue, and that they will be answerable for all its . . . misery.' [30]

The House broke ranks. The War Hawks swarmed around their champion, battling to shake his hand. From the gallery, Thomas Ritchie, brilliant young editor of the Richmond *Enquirer,* wrote down that the South Carolina speaker would become 'one of the master-spirits, who stamp their names upon the age in which they live.' [31] It was Calhoun's audacity which won admiration, the courage of a young and inexperienced member who had dared touch the untouchable, to measure his intellect against Randolph's emotion and emerge victorious. But his triumph was not complete.

For the moment, he had silenced his opponent; but Calhoun had failed to answer Randolph's most telling argument: that the merchants of New England would not support a war which destroyed their commerce. He had no answer. Yet he had reason for misjudging New England's taste for conflict. Was not the Newburyport, Massachusetts, *Herald,* in that very fall of 1811 trumpeting: 'If it be necessary in defense of our injured country to take up arms, let us know the worst of it? The popular

pulse . . . beats high. Should the National Legislature . . . dilly-dally
. . . should they fail to come to some decisive conclusion . . . we fear
that an insulted and exasperated nation will endure it no longer.'[32] Was
not even the former President, John Adams, contending that for all its
surface bickering, the nation was never 'better united'? Calhoun's own
idealistic contempt for 'low and calculating avarice' had betrayed him.
Not all of Randolph's warnings had convinced him that violated rights
were nothing to New England beside the practical fact that war would
destroy the last of the scanty commerce left her by blockades and embargo. In Calhoun's opinion, the 'common danger' would unite all. 'Tie
down a hero and he feels the puncture of a pin, but throw him into battle,
and he is scarcely sensible of vital gashes.'[33]

5

Blissfully unimpressed by the rising storm was Augustus J. Foster, His
Britannic Majesty's representative in Washington. 'No person appears
to receive less impression from our measures than the British Minister,'
wrote J. A. Bayard in February, 1812. 'He gives dinners to Gentlemen
of all Parties in the most friendly style possible.' Dinner was 'displayed
on tables spread in four different rooms,' and apparently Foster, who was
not lacking in his own brand of humor, derived a superior British enjoyment from the spectacle of the recent backwoods graduates from buckskin into broadcloth gorging themselves on his canvasback ducks and
directing tentative sniffs at his ices. Even Foster must have had difficulty in maintaining his 'British tranquillity,' when guests at one of
his dinner parties mistook the caviar for 'excessively nasty' black raspberry jam, and 'spit it out' at the first mouthful.[34]

At first, Calhoun attended few of these functions. He had been
burdened with a 'load of anxiety' on leaving Floride and his newborn
'little son at so critical a period,' and on receiving letters from home was
almost frightened to open them 'for fear that all was not well. . . . I am
as comfortably fixed here as I could be,' he wrote his mother-in-law, 'and
have nothing to render me uneasy but my solicitude for those I have left
behind. . . . This place is quite gay . . . but I do not participate in it
much myself.'[35]

As the session wore on, however, Calhoun's taste for solitude wore off.
He was only twenty-nine, eager and energetic, not constituted to stay
alone in his room writing letters night after night. Reckless of the 'requirements of good breeding,' as Jack Randolph might be in the House,
who was more fascinating as a dinner companion? He had friends who
had known Nelson from childhood and 'seen Fox naked'; he could leap
from denunciation of Napoleon as 'the arch-fiend . . . of mankind' to a
story of the jolly parson who cheated at cards.[36] There was escape for

Calhoun and the 'War Boys,' too, in small parties at the 'President's House,' where talk of the spring snowfall in North Carolina, the earthquake in Caracas, or the new French coffee made from sugar beets, flowed easily over glasses of ginger-wine; and at dinner at Mrs. Bushby's, with the whole mess entertaining Mr. Foster, now bandying 'ill-timed' jests on the imminence of their guest's departure, now vying with one another to purchase his imported wines. 'I,' declared the British Minister, in secret exasperation, 'am tired of Washington and the Congress.' [37]

Calhoun exchanged greetings with Foster at the 'Queen's Birthday Ball,' to which the War Mess was invited for a surface appearance of impartiality, and again at the banquet celebrating Louisiana's admission to the Union, with champagne corks popping from a corner, and Robert Wright singing a 'b—y song,' and giving a 'b—y toast.' Although Calhoun sought relief from the constant 'state of suspense,' he could not relax, even at play. In the 'cool decided tone of a man resolved,' he bitterly told Foster that 'the Merchants would put up with any wrong and thought only of gain, but a Government should give protection.' [38]

6

With every month, however, the war machine rolled slowly on. On January 31, 1812, an Army 'Volunteer' Bill was rammed through in the House, but when Secretary of the Treasury Gallatin appeared in person to recommend that the sum of five million dollars be raised by 'internal taxes,' war fever cooled instantly. 'Nothing has depressed the war spirit more than the frightful exhibit made by Gallatin of war taxes,' wrote one observer. 'Many who voted for the Army Bill will not vote for the taxes.' [39]

Henry Clay, however, spoke the truth. 'If pecuniary considerations alone are to govern,' he had told the House on December 31, speaking for the Army Bill, 'there is sufficient motive for war . . . the real cause of British aggression is . . . to destroy a rival. . . . She sickens at your prosperity.' That England was locked in a death-grip with 'the archenemy of mankind' was none of our concern. American rights had been invaded; French aggressions were beside the issue. 'Must we drink British poison that we may avoid an imaginary French dose?' [40] demanded the outraged Kentuckian.

Eloquence such as this silenced the floor, hushed the galleries. Men leaned forward eagerly, heard again the echoes of '76 and the young 'fathers' of the infancy of the Republic. True, there were those who sensed uncertainty behind the bluster, who knew the young War Hawks' fear of being scorned by that very England they pretended to despise; and that underneath the coming war burned the old, old war between age and youth. But there were others who thrilled to Harry Clay's soaring eloquence and saw in the thoughtful but 'spirited' Calhoun 'one of the sages of the old Congress, with all the graces of youth.'[41]

7

The tide was turning, but in Calhoun's opinion it was turning slowly. These had been tense weeks during this spring of 1812, with early heat swathing Washington in a damp, clinging blanket, with Calhoun chafing at the divisions in Madison's Cabinet, and 'constantly urging on the reluctant executive.'[42]

Madison's reluctance was indeed extreme. As late as March he was still daring to hope that if war came, it would be with France and not with England. A ninety-day embargo on British commerce, passed by Congress and signed by the President on April 4, was acknowledged by Madison himself, in a letter to Jefferson the day before, as 'a step'[43] to war. Yet privately Madison was still promising Foster that the door of reconciliation would be held open!

Not until April 18 could Calhoun write to James MacBride that war was 'now seriously determined upon.'[44] One month later, Madison was renominated for President of the United States, and between the two dates runs a series of events which adds no luster to James Madison's fame.

The war group controlled the Republican Party. For Madison the choice was plain—war or defeat—and his biographer is frank in stating that his nomination was 'the price' of a change of policy.[45] To insure his second term in the 'President's Palace,' the Father of the Constitution surrendered his country to war.

By May, eighty-two of the War Hawks met to plan the 'new States to be cut out of Canada,' and to proclaim the Virginia families like the Randolphs ruined by too much 'good living.' From the House gallery Augustus Foster watched proceedings with mounting despair. 'Young men . . . violent measures' was his own youthful verdict. 'Mr. Calhoun and his Friends . . . seemed to have great confidence and were very cool and decided upon the question of going to war.'[46]

Actually the War Boys were less cool than they looked. And on a soggy day in May, when John Randolph climaxed two months of irrelevant and abusive tirades with a long discourse on the evils of Napoleon, Calhoun's patience broke. 'Hotly,' he silenced the buzzing of the Virginia gadfly with a sharp call to order. Why 'was the honorable member speaking? There was no question before the House.' Caught, Randolph stammered that he was making remarks prefatory to a resolution. He thanked the gentleman for the interruption. It had given him a chance for rest.

'As the gentleman is so grateful for his rest, I will give him some more,' snapped Calhoun. 'Do not the rules of the House require that a resolution shall be laid before the Speaker in writing before remarks are made on it?'

Randolph hesitated, and up popped Speaker Clay. Invoking a long-forgotten rule, he ordered the marathon orator to submit his resolution in writing. A moment later, the House made short shift of it and him, voting down by a count of 72 to 37 his contention that 'it was inexpedient to resort to war.'[47] For the madcap Virginian his reign of fourteen years was over.

8

On June 1, 1812, Calhoun received a letter from Secretary Monroe, which 'he gave to Grundy who looked grave.'[48] That same day the President's Message arrived. It was conclusive this time. Now at last England was charged with 'violating the American flag on the great highway of nations . . . seizing and carrying off persons sailing under it.'[49] Violated coasts, plundered commerce, Indians and Canadians plotting against American sovereignty—the charges were old, but sufficed.

Calhoun's War Report was submitted from the Foreign Relations Committee, June 3. The House approved immediately, 79 to 49, but for two more weeks the question hung fire in the Senate. All were 'dumb on the subject of politics.'[50] At an evening party on the seventeenth, Calhoun had 'a long tiresome conversation' with Foster on Spain and Portugal, anything and everything to avoid the one subject of which everyone was thinking and which everyone wanted to discuss.[51]

It was all over. The Senate had balloted that very day—by an ominous vote of 19 to 13, but the verdict was clear-cut. The next morning the bill was referred back to the House for concurrence in amendments, and signed by Madison a few hours later.[52] That evening Foster made his last call at the Presidential Mansion, saw Madison 'ghastly pale,' flanked on either side by the 'flushed and smiling' Clay and Calhoun. They were 'all shaking hands.'[53] The first battle had been won.

VII

Young Hercules

YOUNG BILLY PHILLIPS swung to the saddle, gouged his heels into his horse, and was off 'in a cloud of dust, his horse's tail and his own long hair streaming . . . in the wind.' Mile after mile, hour after hour, day after day, he galloped on, stopping only to leap from a steaming horse to a fresh one, to seize a few mouthfuls of food, a few hours of sleep, and then on again. He tore through town after town, fifteen hundred miles in twenty days, swinging his wallet over his head as he neared the taverns and shouting across the wind: 'Here's the stuff! Wake up! War! War with England! War!' And then he was gone, President Madison's little express courier, who roused the Southwestern frontier just as Revere had roused New England a generation before, gone in a ringing of hooves and a swirl of dust, back into the oblivion from which he had come.[1]

War! This was the news the Southwest had been waiting for. Not healed, but festering still were the terrible wounds of thirty-odd years before; the memories of burnings and massacres, to be rekindled again for this war in the late summer of 1813, when at Fort Mims on the Indian frontier a 'heap of ruins ghastly with human bodies' would send a shudder across the nation.[2] This horror, the Southwest believed, was as much the work of the British as of the Redskins. And for a chance of sweeping British and Indians alike back from the American borders, back even from Canada itself, no war was too terrible to endure.

At Nashville, Tennessee, a stocky horseman turned toward a nearby plantation. At 'The Hermitage' the scene was peaceful. Outside, the rain was falling and inside, before the fire sat Andrew Jackson, lean, red-haired, forty-four years old, between his sharp knees a baby boy and a lamb. And as Thomas Hart Benton of the Tennessee militia stripped off his coat, his embarrassed host explained that 'the child had cried because the lamb was out in the cold, and begged him to bring it in.'[3]

Peace was ended for that evening. Planter Jackson received Benton's news with the same fierce enthusiasm that his fellow Westerners had shown. No one knew war better than Andrew Jackson. He was only fifteen when the Revolution ended, but it had cost him bitterly. It had taken his mother and his two brothers. It had wrecked his health, stripped him of boyhood and all its illusions. He had been beaten and wounded, imprisoned and diseased. He had become a hardened veteran before his sixteenth birthday, with hatred seared into his memory. And for a chance at revenge, he would face it all again. Nothing could happen to him worse than what he had already undergone.

Vehemently, he inked his pen:

> *Citizens! . . . the martial hosts . . . are summoned to the tented fields. . . .*
>
> *Are we the titled slaves of George the third? the military conscripts of Napoleon? or the frozen peasants of the Russian Csar? No—we are the free born sons of. . . the only republick now existing in the world. . . .*
>
> *We are going to fight for re-establishment of our national character . . . for the protection of our maritime citizens, and the rights of free trade!*[4]

2

Since the November morning when Henry Clay of Kentucky had swaggered up to the Speaker's stand and with the first stroke of his gavel sounded the drums of war, eight months had passed. America was at war. America, with a navy of fifteen seagoing ships, with an army of less than ten thousand men, staffed by motheaten relics of the Revolution, had dared challenge 'Mother England,' the greatest power on earth. It was a wild gesture, foolhardy, unbelievable. But it was typically and boldly American.

Congress reconvened in September, 1812. Only then was the news of the first American victories beginning to trickle into the capital. The tiny fleet had indeed done well. Commodore Rodgers had been wounded off Jamaica in the first battle of the war, but in a month's time his small squadron had taken seven prizes and recaptured an American vessel. On September 7, Captain David Porter's *Essex* returned to New York, with a total of ten prizes. Scantily armed, but with a hard-bitten crew brandishing cutlasses, the *Essex* had captured a transport of two hundred men, and later disarmed the British ship *Alert*. Most spectacular of all had been the triumphs of the *Constitution*, which in July in a wild three-day chase had outdistanced an overwhelming British force of fifteen ships. One month later, the vessel staggered into Boston Harbor, a battered wreck, loaded down with two hundred and fifty British prisoners of war. She had clashed with the great *Guerrière* on August 19, and after enduring twenty minutes of murderous fire, the British ship had struck her colors.

In the sitting room of their new lodgings at Mrs. Verplanck's boarding house, Clay, Calhoun, Lowndes, and Cheves heard the news, sprang to their feet, joined hands, and danced a jig of rejoicing across the floor.[5] Calhoun, as 'the uniform advocate of a Navy,' could take his full share of the glory.

But there was another—and a more sobering—side to the picture. Up in Michigan the aging General William Hull had begun the war by surrendering Detroit without a shot. Elderly Major-General Henry Dearborn had marched into Canada and marched out again, his men having fired on each other instead of on the enemy. Calhoun was in near despair, his mind 'in such a state of perplexity' that it discouraged him from writing even to James MacBride until well into December. 'Our officers are most incompetent men,' he bitterly confided to his friend. 'I do believe the Executive will have to make a disgraceful peace.' He felt himself obliged, however, 'to give the Administration support on the war; when I have not the least confidence in them.'[6] The tragedies of the military had indeed been crushing to the personal and national pride of a man who had predicted that within four weeks from the declaration of war the whole of upper and part of lower Canada would be in American hands.[7]

3

More battles were waiting on the floor of Congress. A newcomer took his seat in the House that spring, a swarthy man with high cheekbones, coarse black hair, and eyes black and burning 'as anthracite.' His manner was 'haughty, cold, and over-bearing'; in appearance he was as striking as Calhoun himself, but there was a theatrical quality about him which some observers found displeasing. At first glance he seemed unusually tall; actually he was not more than five feet nine or ten, but his slender frame, contrasted with massive shoulders and a large rugged head, gave him an overwhelming presence.

This was Daniel Webster—thirty-one years old, a small-town lawyer from Portsmouth, New Hampshire, but with a reputation behind him. Elected on an avowed 'peace-ticket,' his declarations of the summer that the Constitution itself had been adopted 'for the protection of commerce,' and that the war was 'premature and inexpedient,' had won him his seat and his fame. Unlike the War Boys, there was nothing of passion or impetuosity about him. 'Caution, deliberation, and diffidence' were the watchwords of this young man, but underneath a surface languor was a bedrock of purpose.[8]

Impishly Speaker Clay appointed the newcomer to John Randolph's old seat on the Foreign Relations Committee. And if Calhoun had dared hope that life would be easier for him with the Virginia gadfly buzzing in his native hills, he was rapidly disillusioned.

Across the committee table, the two men eyed each other. What Cal-

houn thought of Daniel Webster at this period we do not know. But
Webster had foreknowledge of Calhoun. Warm in his pocket lay a letter
from his friend, William March: 'Calhoun I don't know personally, but
have a high respect for his talent. He is young, and if honest may yet be
open to conviction.' ⁹

Honest? Good Lord, yes! but 'open to conviction'—that intense young
zealot! You might as well try to convince a hurricane! But the New
Englander spared no efforts to convince the more placable. On June 10,
1813, he launched a searing attack on the entire war program. Unflinchingly he accused the Administration of having deliberately withheld,
until the declaration of war, the publication of the new French Decrees
which would have automatically produced repeal of the British Orders
in Council, a major cause of the war.

These were serious charges. Back in 1805, after Trafalgar had left
Britain the mistress of the seas, with Napoleon still master of the Continent, the two empires had tried to starve each other out by destruction
of commerce. Britain's Orders in Council forbade neutrals to trade with
ports on the Continent, and Napoleon's Berlin and Milan Decrees authorized seizure of all ships which traded with the British Empire. Britain
followed up with a subsequent Order, commanding every neutral vessel
to pay 'protection' duties at British ports or risk seizure; and Jefferson's
retaliatory Embargo cutting off all American trade, both from Britain
and the Continent, had almost completed the ruin of America's $157,-
000,000 shipping industry.

For American ears alone, Napoleon's Foreign Minister had announced
repeal of the French Decrees as early as August, 1810. This was, of
course, a trick to restore American trade with France, and Britain recognized it as such. Hence, His Majesty's government was deaf to Madison's
warning that unless the Orders in Council were repealed by February,
1811, no trade would be permitted between America and the British Empire.

As late as May 19, 1812, England had repeated her determination to
maintain her Orders until convinced that France had actually repealed
her Decrees in good faith. Then was staged a tragedy of errors on both
sides of the Atlantic. Had modern communications existed, the bloodshed
and sufferings of the War of 1812 might all have been averted. For under
American diplomatic pressure, England had agreed to repeal, two days
before the declaration of war!

Whether or not, as Webster believed, Napoleon's reiteration that he
would revoke the Decrees was influential in producing the British action
is impossible to determine. But in this, his maiden speech, not even the
bitterest of the New Englander's opponents failed to feel his power. Members left their seats that they might more easily see the glowing face of
the speaker, and 'sat down or stood on the floor fronting him.' 'No mem-

ber,' declared the reporter for the Boston *Messenger,* 'ever riveted the attention of the House so completely in his first speech.' [10] All the frayed, dusty old phrases of congratulation that had marked Calhoun's initial effort were revived for Webster.

Calhoun, of course, leaped to the defense of the beleaguered Administration. There was justice in Webster's challenge to prove the conflict 'strictly American . . . the cause of a people and not of a party.' This was, to a degree, a sectional war, favored by the majority but by no means the whole of the American people. This sectional opposition was a sharp blow to Calhoun's happy belief that 'the common danger unites all.' Perhaps already the perceptive South Carolinian was aware of the cleavage in vital interests that would one day divide the nation.

Nevertheless, the bulk of Webster's charges boomeranged. Unimpeachable authority revealed that the American government's first intimation of the revocation of the French Decrees had not reached the country until July 13, 1812, a good three weeks after war had been declared. Vindication was complete, but Webster was not there to acknowledge it. Hot weather had driven him home for the remainder of the session.

He returned in December, 1813, late as usual, but in time to vote for a resolution requesting the President to give information explaining the failure 'of the arms of the United States on the Northern frontier.' Wholesale failure through a second summer had equipped the bitter New Englander with plenty of ammunition for his charges; and there must have been times when it was difficult for the hard-pressed congressional leaders to decide whether they were carrying on a war against England or New England and Daniel Webster. 'We in New England are no patriots—we will do what is required—no more,' [11] said the New Hampshire man.

Calhoun, meanwhile, in 'ringing' speeches, which along with Henry Clay's were read at the head of the armies to inspire the troops, strove to nationalize and focus the war sentiment. For the anti-war faction he had stern rebuke. 'It is the duty of every section to bear whatever the general interest may demand,' Calhoun reminded the rebellious elements. 'Carolina makes no complaint . . . she turns her indignation, not against her own government, but against the common enemy.' Carolina did not compare her sufferings 'with those of the other States. She would be proud to stand pre-eminent in suffering if . . . the general good could be obtained. It seems the injury and insult go for nothing with the opposition,' said Calhoun bitterly. 'War has been declared by a law of the land . . . the worst of laws ought to be respected while they remain laws. . . . What would have been thought of such conduct in the war of the Revolution?'

Despite his condemnations, however, he refused to give way to despair. He had lived in New England long enough, he felt, to be convinced of its citizens' 'basic loyalty.' The 'interest of the people and that of the leaders . . . are often at war.' [12]

4

What with committee meetings and debate and preparation of oratory, during the daytime Calhoun's energies were well absorbed. But at night life was dull. For the six-dollar-a-day Congressmen there were only the fifteen-dollar-a-week boarding houses, crude, comfortless, and scantily furnished, of which fifteen or sixteen huddled around the Capitol. In one of these, amidst a maximum of noise and a minimum of privacy, Calhoun and the rest of the War Mess took 'genteel board and lodging,' with 'two gentlemen to each room.' They shivered when the expected supplies of coal failed to arrive; gulped down coarse meals of tough steak and stewed peaches; tossed on lonely and lumpy beds, picked bugs out of the closets and red ants from the washstand; and for entertainment were offered the pleasure of hearing one of their company read aloud from Shakespeare or a similar 'improving' work; or on Sunday night a psalm-singing session if the house was lucky enough to boast the dual attractions of a piano and a girl.[13]

Morning after morning they struggled up Capitol Hill through yellow mud or swirling dust, buffeted by wind that 'almost takes your breath away.' Though war had silenced the social festivities, there were occasional presentations of dramas such as *Youth's Errors* or *The Marriage Promise;* there was aplenty of snipe and 'even partridge shooting . . . on each side of the Main avenue and even close under the walls of the Capitol'; and those to whom solitude was essential could ride horseback for hours in the outskirts, completely undisturbed.[14]

For the War Mess as a whole, however, these outlets were not enough. 'Wild and irreverent,' off as well as on the Congressional floor, they curled their hair, swaggered forth in 'wonderful waistcoats,' washed down their indifferent food with inordinate quantities of the brandy and whiskey which were included in their board bills, gambled at brag, 'that game of bluster and look and talk big,' danced 'indecent dances' and 'chased women,'[15] although the almost 'unvarying masculinity of the society,' of which Daniel Webster complained so bitterly, made conquests few while whetting ardor all the more.

Doubtless some relief was offered in March by a famous—or infamous —art exhibit. Vehement little Amos Kendall, purported to be 'stirred by the power of the painting,'[16] but other observers were more forthright. Unfortunately, history leaves no record as to what Calhoun thought of the picture, but he probably shared the viewpoint of his friend, William Lowndes, with whom he may even have attended the exhibit. To his wife the Charleston statesman observed sadly that 'all the ladies go,' and revealed the cause of the excitement as 'an exquisitely beautiful woman, who had no other dress than a braid of pearls for her hair.' He would give no

further description 'of this fascinating picture, for though it may do you
no harm to read, it may do me some to write or think of it.' A 'draping
of . . . lace,' [17] thought the modest South Carolinian, would 'heighten the
effect.' Just what effect was to be heightened, he failed to say.

5

As far as male companionship was concerned, the young men of the Congress offered a wide and satisfying variety. Calhoun could spend an evening
with young Carolina-born Israel Pickens, scientist and mathematician,
whose mind was as cold and clear as his passions were hot; or with absent-
minded Langdon Cheves, never so happy as when hunched over a table
drawing mansions by candlelight. Between Clay and Calhoun strong feeling always existed, whether of affection or hatred, and at this period each
felt keen personal admiration for the other, although they were already
too aware of the surge of each other's ambition to achieve real intimacy.
But of Calhoun's friendship for one man, we have clear proof.

'Mr. Calhoun of South Carolina has joined us,' William Lowndes had
written early in the session of 1811–12, '. . . a man well-informed, easy in
his manners . . . amiable in his disposition. I like him already better than
any man of our mess.' [18]

Thus, for Calhoun and Lowndes began one of those rare friendships that
are ended only by death. Almost instantaneously, these two, neither of
whom gave his intimacy easily, became inseparable; and their tall figures
walking side by side became a familiar sight on the streets of the capital,
Lowndes' lank, loose-limbed six-foot-six frame dwarfing even his companion. Had this stooped, cadaverous man with his craggy features lived
a generation or so later, he would have been said to look like Abraham
Lincoln; had he lived a few years longer, Lincoln might have been said to
look like him.

But there was nothing of Lincoln in his background. All the 'advantages'
that Fate had denied Calhoun were his friend's in abundance: European
travel and education, all the books that he could read, and all the horses
that he could ride. In his Commonplace Book, filled with architectural
drawings and plans for farm machinery of his own invention, were notes
of long conversations with Madison on the formation of the Constitution—
whether or not the President should have the authority 'to choose peace
or war,' and if Congress 'should have a negative upon the State Laws'—
subjects which would have greatly interested Calhoun had he had access
to them.[19]

Even superior Europe had granted William Lowndes admiration; on a
London street one man remarked to another: 'I have just been talking
with a young American . . . who is the tallest, wisest, and best-bred

young man I have ever met.' 'It must have been Mr. Lowndes of South
Carolina,' was the speedy response.[20]

Everyone admired William Lowndes. Congressional old-timers, who
dismissed the rest of the Liberty Boys as half-grown hotheads, 'their pin-
feathers still on,' would leave their seats to cluster around this pale, hollow-
chested young man whose whisper of a voice spoke words of such mellowed
wisdom that he was compared even to Washington himself. As he never
spoke unless he had something to say, and never had anything to say unless
it was constructive, he had become something of an oracle. And yet 'there
was nothing pompous in him, no blustering, no rant.' [21] Only once, on the
news of the great victory on Lake Erie, his reserve dropped from him, and
for an hour he spoke with a fire that electrified the House.[22] And yet it
was his gentleness even more than his great intellect that won. To hurt
another, even to protect himself, was beyond his powers. To discuss before
him the petty bickerings of party politics seemed to his friends like sacri-
lege.[23]

He was utterly void of ambition. Tubercular from childhood, he was
little more than an invalid, and under the strain of Washington life his
strength ebbed from month to month. He knew that he had not long to
live and his mind was not on the rewards of living. Upon Calhoun's eager
strivings he could look with wistfulness, but also with sympathy. Between
the two men understanding was complete. Twenty years later, Calhoun,
shaken with 'an emotion rare in that great man,' would tell Lowndes'
widow that there had never 'been a cloud' [24] between his friend and himself.

For Calhoun, however, home seemed far away during the wearing winter
months, and letters were few and unsatisfying. There was so much he
wanted to say. 'It is impossible for me in . . . an ordinary letter to communicate half the observations . . . which I have made since the commencement of my publick life' he wrote MacBride. 'My friend,' he hinted,
'will not let many days elapse before he will gratify me with his presence.' [25]

But he could not summon Floride. 'If Floride bears my absence as badly
as I do hers, she must occasionally be very impatient,' he confessed to his
mother-in-law. By day he could absorb himself in his work; but at night
he could not escape homesickness even in sleep. 'I Dreamed all night the
last night of being home with you; and nursing our dear son,' he wrote
Floride, 'and regreted when I awoke to find it a dream. I was in hopes
that the morning's mail would bring me a letter from you; but was disappointed. It is near a month since I had one.' * [26]

Through the dour weeks of January, 1814, Calhoun waited every mail-
day with a rising sense of anxiety. It was not until February 6 that he tore
open the letter from South Carolina signed by 'Dr. Casey.' 'Relief and

* Written in March, 1812, but typical of his state of mind when away from home.

joy' swept over him. His first daughter had arrived, and Floride had had 'comparatively easy times.' [27] He took time out from the questions of conscription and banking to consider a name for the 'addition to our family.' To his wife he wrote that his 'inclination would be to call her by the name which you and your mother bear.'

Despite his excitement, Calhoun did not neglect the small bystander in the family drama. The year before, he had written his 'dearest Floride' detailed advice on the necessity of weaning their son; now Calhoun remarked that 'Andrew appears . . . forgot. None of the letters . . . mention a word of him. . . . Kiss him for me.' [28]

6

It was with genuine conviction that Calhoun on April 6, 1814, delivered a successful speech urging repeal of Madison's abortive embargo. Commercial restrictions were particularly distasteful to Calhoun in a supposed war for 'free trade,' and he had supported the three-months' Non-Intercourse Act of April 4, 1812, only as an emergency measure. Already fearful of the undue stimulus embargoes gave industry and manufacturing, he vehemently fought down an attempt at renewal in December of 1812, on the ground that he was against anything that the government was powerless to enforce.

As Administration floor leader, however, Calhoun was forced to give a reluctant vote to the Embargo of December 17, 1813, passed to prevent 'leaks' to Canada and England. Now, four months later, in the face of taunts from Daniel Webster, Calhoun saved 'face' for the Administration by adroitly concocted explanations as to why the measure had been a mistake, after all. His words now re-echoed his more eloquent argument of two years before. We think that 'prohibition in law is prohibition in fact,' Calhoun had then contended. This 'mistake' he daily saw reflected in shops 'lined with English manufactures. . . . In all free governments, the laws cannot be much above the tone of public opinion.' Why not let British goods in—as they were coming in anyway? Why not let the government reap the profits, win additional millions for 'our gallant little Navy?' Such action, maintained the surprisingly realistic Carolinian, 'will yield . . . more revenue than the whole of the internal taxes, and this on goods which will be introduced in spite of . . . laws.' He had condemned proposals to lay penalty taxes upon those who had illegally profited in British goods. Was the object profit, or the execution of the law? 'If our merchants are innocent, they are welcome to their good fortune; if guilty, I scorn to participate in their profits.'

'To say to the most trading people on earth, you shall not trade . . . does not suit the genius of our people. . . . Our government is founded on freedom and hates coercion.'

'Men do not look beyond immediate causes,' Calhoun had warned. If the Embargo ruined commerce, they would blame the government that imposed it, not 'those acts of violence and injustice' which it was 'intended to counteract.' Thus would government be 'rendered odious.' * [29]

For Calhoun, back at home that summer of 1814, the war seemed very far away. Not even his pending candidacy for re-election caused him concern. He had won easily two years earlier against a Federalist tide, on the heels of the military defeats. Such had been his popularity in his home district that no opponent had dared stand against him. And now, despite two more years of external defeats and internal divisions for the nation, Calhoun's personal standing was still unchallenged. He won again, by a high vote and without opposition.

7

Fear weighed heavily on the national capital during those hot, thunder-blurred days of summer, as the press screamed boasts that 'the insolent foot of the invader would never touch American soil.' It was July 20, 1814, and the Tenth Military District—Maryland, Washington, and all Virginia north of the Rappahannock—awaited the attack of the British armies—with a defensive force of six hundred men! Not until nearly August did the Maryland Governor call out three thousand members of the state militia. It was not until August 19 that seven hundred Virginia militiamen came forth for the 'glorious cause'—minus flints and muskets. That same day British barges were up the Patuxent River, pouring an army of 'Wellington's Invincibles' out upon the village of Benedict—forty miles from the capital! [30]

In Washington, the twenty-fourth of August, 1814, dawned hot and still. Clouds darkened the sky, but the faint rumbling in the east was not thunder. Cannon were booming at the little Maryland hamlet of Bladensburg. There British troops sent a motley and hastily assembled army of clerks, mechanics, and 'regulars' under the doddering General Winder, fleeing 'pell-mell' in such speed that more than one Britisher suffered a sunstroke trying to keep up with them!

In Washington, the women waited, but they could not see what Dolly Madison saw. Dolly had a spyglass in her hand. Since sunrise she had been turning it 'in every direction,' hoping to see her husband, 'but without success.' All she could see were 'groups of military wandering in all directions, as if . . . there was a lack of . . . spirit to fight for their own firesides.'

Twelve o'clock. Two. Three. Two messengers, gray with dust and weariness, stumbled up the steps of the 'President's Palace' to bid Dolly

* The quotations are from Calhoun's speech on 'Merchants' Bonds,' of December 4, 1812.

'fly.' She seized paper and pen and poured out her fears: 'Mr. Madison comes not. May God protect us . . . here I mean to watch for him.'[31]

From her own window a Washington society woman, Mrs. Margaret Bayard Smith, was watching 'our troops . . . pale with fright, retreating by, hour after hour.' And over pounding footsteps and echoing cannon sounded the voice of a Negro cook: 'I done heard Mr. Madison done sold the country to the British!'[32]

Dolly Madison at last was reading a penciled note from her husband. She must be ready to leave the city 'at a moment's notice.' The enemy 'seemed stronger than reported, and . . . might . . . reach the city with intention to destroy it.' A wagon was pulled up to the front door and Dolly and her servants rushed to and fro, their arms piled with silver, china, and jewelry. A few moments later the President's wife stood taut before Gilbert Stuart's portrait of Washington, waiting to catch 'the precious canvas' as sweating workmen frantically hacked the frame apart.[33]

Four o'clock. At the windows of her Sixth Street home a weary young New England matron, too far gone in pregnancy to risk the jostling ride to the woods beyond the city, watched the dust settle back into the empty streets and heard the echoing footsteps and creaking wagon wheels die away. Through the sodden hours of morning she had felt the tightening band of panic close in on the city; watched neighbors 'pressing into service everything in the shape of an animal or a vehicle,' and following their army into headlong flight. Now she noted: 'Nearly the whole of the more aristocratic population had decamped.'

There were those, however, who remained behind. The New England girl heard their voices: 'The President! The President!'

She peered from the window, caught a glimpse of Madison's thin, sunburned face and bare head. The dust whirled into her face as the coach dashed past.[34]

Hour by hour the waiting dragged on. The red ball of the sun dropped lower, but not a leaf stirred. Then, like the voice of an approaching storm, came the lift of the dust . . . the footsteps . . . hoofbeats. . . . The British had entered the city.

Ragged, stumbling, almost as weary as the men they had beaten, the Redcoats streamed through the deserted streets, crashed in locked doors, emerged with food and fresh clothes. Silently the citizens watched the proud Admiral Cockburn ride by on a white horse followed by its foal, which was vainly attempting to nurse. A child sat sobbing in a doorway; General Ross shouted to her as he passed. 'Don't cry, little girl; I will take better care of you than Jemmy did.'

At the Capitol, the triumphal march ended. A single volley shattered the windows; the Redcoats swarmed up the steps. General Ross himself escorted the conquering admiral to Henry Clay's rostrum, and laughter and cheers broke out as Cockburn called the body to order and put the question: 'Shall this harbor of Yankee democracy be burned? All for it say aye!' The question was 'carried unanimously' amidst a clamor of shouts: 'Fire the building! Fire the building!'

'The Cossacks,' boasted the British leaders, 'spared Paris, but we did not spare the Capitol of America.' Officers and men dashed for the Library, where they tore paintings from the walls, pulled handfuls of books and papers from the shelves, tossed them on the velvet canopies and 'Turkey carpets' of the House, and applied the torch. Outside, fifty men armed with poles topped with fireballs, thrust their weapons through the Capitol windows. Flames soared up and a red stain spread against the sky.[35]

It was a still moonlit night. On her portico the young New England housewife stood helpless beside her husband, her fists clenched. 'We . . . stood and gazed, as if it had been a play upon a stage. . . . Not a breath stirred the flames which rose up straight, mighty pillars of fire. . . . Gradually they widened and brightened until the Capitol, the buildings of the several departments and the bridge over the Potomac were wrapt in one sheet of fire.' Meanwhile, over at the White House Ross, Cockburn, and their troops were gorging themselves on the meat, wine, and melted ices which Dolly Madison had left on the dinner table a few hours before.[36]

In stagnant heat the next morning the work of demolition continued. Overhead, the sky darkened. Thunder muttered intermittently. Gusts of wind whipped through the poplar trees. Rain began to fall, slowly at first, and then faster and more heavily. Minute by minute the sky grew darker. By noon the blackness of midnight shrouded the surrounding hills. A panicky British officer peering through the dusk fancied he could see a great army of American troops gathered on the heights of Georgetown, poised to swoop down upon the city. His story spread; and as a roaring hurricane swept across the smoking ruins, uprooting trees, ripping off roofs, and tossing about the great cannon on Capitol Hill, the call for retreat sounded.

Then an explosion shook the ravaged city. A soldier had dropped a torch into a well where the Americans had stored their surplus gunpowder. Tiny groups of burned and bleeding Redcoats staggered back into the city to report the death of a hundred of their number.[37]

The invasion of Washington was over. Like ants from a crushed hill the invaders fled the death and destruction. Slowly the dazed citizenry began to creep through the streets. Now and then came a sweetish whiff of death from open ditches and underbrush, where under the hot sun unburied bodies still lay. The government buildings were destroyed, but most of the dwelling houses still stood. Life could go on. But it was not expected that Washington would 'ever again be the seat of government.' [38]

8

On September 19, 1814, a Special Session of the Thirteenth Congress
assembled amid the ruins. Bitter Federalists introduced and lost a long-
cherished dream of moving the capital to another city; and Washingtonians set to work building a temporary Capitol, later to be known as
Hill's boarding house, and later still, as the Old Capital Prison. For immediate use Congress was assigned a tumbledown shanty on Seventh
Street, which had seen service as Post Office, Patent Office, theater, lodging
house, and tavern. House members packed themselves into a tiny room,
heated by a single wood-burning fireplace, and with so few desks that
Calhoun and other late comers had to take their chances on a spot on the
window seat or in the very fireplace itself.

The South Carolinian was not present for the opening. Months of work
and strain had lowered his resistance, and he had caught a 'very severe
fever,' which lingered for several weeks. Not until October 19 could the
National Intelligencer report that 'Mr. Calhoun . . . appeared and took
his seat.'

He found his fellow legislators engrossed, not in plans for reconstruction,
but in feverish debate as to whether or not the library of Thomas Jefferson was fit for the government to accept as a gift to the nation. The trouble
was with the books themselves—works of Newton and Locke—strong meat
for legislators whose literary tastes, if any, were satisfied by *Tales of
Horror* and *King Arthur's Knights*. The great objection, however, according to press reports, was to 'the works of Voltaire.' It is easy to imagine
Calhoun's disgust at this nonsense, and doubtless he cordially shared the
view of the Petersburg *Courier*, which asked: 'What can be a greater stigma
upon the members of our National Legislature than to assert that books
of a philosophical nature are improper for their perusal?' [39]

Calhoun lost no time in distracting the legislative attention. His worry
was the currency—or rather the lack of it. The creaking framework of a
government had risen out of the ashes of defeat, but of that *sine qua non*,
money, there was none at all. A national bank offered hope for resurrection
of the dying currency and replenishment of the depleted Treasury; but
Secretary of the Treasury Dallas's plan for 'a vast government engine'
with a capital of fifty million dollars, of which only five million would be
in coin, with the government free to borrow thirty million, seemed to Calhoun an 'odious' scheme.

For the first time Calhoun, the Administration spearhead, 'the young
Hercules who had borne the war upon his shoulders,' showed that 'proud
independence of party spirit,' later so characteristic of him. His one concession was a refusal to have his speech of opposition published, reluctant

as he was to defy both the Administration and his own close friends. Yet, despite his personal scruples, the 'slender, erect, and ardent' orator held none of his fire. A listener cites this lost speech as 'one of the most luminous and irresistable arguments ever delivered in Congress.' [40]

The House thought so, and promptly rejected the Dallas plan. On November 16, 1814, Calhoun presented his substitute. Where in Dallas's bank the capital would have been in government stock, Calhoun's measure provided for a $45,000,000 capitalization of Treasury notes. In Dallas's measure the President could suspend specie payments as necessary, and a loan of three-fifths of the capital was to be made to the government; but in Calhoun's bank the government could not suspend, nor, in the South Carolinian's opinion, would there be any necessity for a loan. Calhoun was not over specific on the details of the scheme; but as the Treasury notes, already in circulation, had nose-dived to seventy cents on the dollar, the new issue, $45,000,000 in face value, would actually have been worth only $31,500,000. Consequently, Calhoun's bill provided that the new notes were to be convertible into bank stock. As the stock was a good buy, the new notes would immediately soar to par, carrying with them, so Calhoun seems to have thought, all notes previously issued by the Treasury Department. Thus, the government would have gained thirty cents on every dollar of the outstanding notes and have 'made' enough money not to require a loan.

The scheme was certainly more ingenious than sound, but there was an intriguing plausibility about it which appealed to Congress. Calhoun's bill was passed on November 27; its author experienced a brief twenty-four-hour triumph before the terrified Dallas rallied an emergency coalition to defeat it by a handful of votes.

On December 9, Dallas introduced a new bill, incorporating several features of Calhoun's plan, but still providing for a paper as opposed to a specie bank. Under the plea of war necessity, he managed to ram the measure through the Senate, but its defeat in the House on January 2, 1815, was guaranteed by Daniel Webster, who galloped forty miles from a Christmas vacation in Baltimore to his party's rescue. The vote was close, 81 yeas to 80 nays. Then Speaker Langdon Cheves, later to be President of the United States Bank, arose, seconded Webster's objections, and killed the bill with a tie.

To Calhoun, tired and overwrought, the humiliation was especially keen. He had voted against the bill in its original form, but few realized more keenly than he that something had to be done, and he still believed that Dallas's plan, objectionable as it was, might be revised into something sound and satisfactory. Calhoun had stood for reconsideration three days earlier, and had been howled down. Now the hopelessness of the months of waiting and wrangling flooded over him. Impulsively he arose and, holding out both hands in appeal, strode across the House floor to Webster, whom he begged for assistance in writing a bill that would gain the support of all parties. The surprised New Englander readily promised his help, at which point Calhoun 'burst into tears.' [41]

The next day the House voted to reconsider. The new bill was ready by January 6, 1815. The bank's capitalization was to be part in specie, part in new stock, and part in Treasury notes, with Calhoun's proposals incorporated in the clauses forbidding the suspension of specie payments and in placing no obligation upon the Bank to lend to the government. It passed the Senate. It passed the House. But it died stillborn at the hands of a Presidential veto; and was replaced promptly by another 'paper Bank' bill from the office of the exasperated Dallas. Again, the weary wrangle was on.

9

The ranks of the War Boys were noticeably thinned. Several were fighting in the front lines; Clay was in Belgium, caught in a tangle of peace negotiations which had dragged on so long now that few hoped for anything better than an honorable surrender. The empty Speaker's chair had been offered Calhoun, but he had hastily declined it. National unity was imperative, and none knew better than he that, although in actual votes he could command the office, no man had more bitter enemies. To the resentful and reluctant New Englanders, to the rebel aristocracy of the breed of Randolph, Calhoun was the hated personification of the flagging cause of the war.

But to him, the cause was not lost. 'I am not without my fears and my hopes,' he had earlier admitted to the assembled Congress, but now he dared voice no fears. Weary, tormented with his own forebodings of disaster now that the fall of Napoleon had freed England to thrust her entire strength against America, Calhoun pitted his own faith and the intensity of his convictions against the flooding counsels of despair. Speaking time and again during those dark months of 1814 and '15, until candles flickered against the faded walls and sheer physical exhaustion compelled him to drop into his seat, he fought back with the only weapons left to the once cocksure war leaders, courage and words. 'From the flood the tide dates its ebb,' he promised. Even if America bowed to British arms, the fight would be taken up again when the population had jumped from eight millions to twenty. 'The great cause will not be yielded. No; never! never! We cannot renounce our rights to the ocean which Providence has spread before our doors. . . . We have already had success. . . . The future is audibly proclaimed by the splendid victories over the *Guerrière, Java,* and *Macedonia.* . . . The charm of British naval invincibility is broken.' Bold words these, for the die-hards, such as Webster, were railing far more against the government that had invited the destruction than the destruction itself.[42]

A conscription bill, strongly supported by Calhoun, the New Englander termed a 'horrible lottery . . . to throw the dice for blood.' Conscription was unconstitutional. It must be prevented. 'It will be the solemn duty,' he informed the Congress, 'of the State Governments . . . to interpose between their citizens and arbitrary power. These are among the objects for which the State Governments exist.' Thus, twenty years later, in time of peace, Calhoun would define the purposes of nullification; and thus, in time of war, spoke Daniel Webster, 'the defender of the Union.' True, he came to the Union's defense, and in the very way that Calhoun would later defend it; asserting that 'Those who cry out . . . that the Union is in danger are themselves the authors of that danger. They put its existance to hazard by measures of violence, which it is not capable of enduring.' True Unionists, Webster declared, were those who 'preserve the spirit in which the Union was framed.'[43]

Meanwhile, as Webster was threatening state nullification of federal law and gleefully writing in his diary 'The Government cannot execute a Conscription Law. . . . It cannot enlist soldiers . . . It cannot borrow money . . . What can it do?'[44]—remnants of the Massachusetts 'Essex Junto' which since Jefferson's time had 'meditated the creation of a Northern Confederacy,' were gathering in the State House at Hartford, Connecticut. And, as under the dome of the old Council Chamber, men born and bred in the shadow of Bunker Hill coolly calculated the value of the Union, in terms of finance and commerce, Madison broke down. To be driven from his home, to be scorned as a coward, to see the nation which he had sworn to protect and defend, invaded and shattered, all that he could stand. But this was too much. 'No foreign foe has broken my heart,' wrote the President. 'To see the capital wrecked by the British does not hurt so deeply as to know sedition in New England.'[45]

Calhoun, younger and of sterner fiber, was undaunted. Of New England's right to secede he had no doubts, but of her basic loyalty he was equally sure. Yet he warned his fellow legislators of the dangers inherent in 'a false mode of thinking.' A minority had no 'right to involve the country in ruin. . . . How far the minority in a state of war, may justly oppose the measures of Government, is a question of the greatest delicacy. . . . An upright citizen will do no act, whatever his opinion of the war, to put his country in the power of the enemy. . . . Like the system of our State and General governments,—within they are many,—to the world but one,—so . . . with parties . . . in relation to other nations there ought only to be the American people. . . . This sympathy of the whole with . . . every part . . . constitutes our real union. When it ceases . . . we shall cease to be one nation.'[46]

Such was his ideal, but he wasted little time in lamentation. There was work to be done; men and money to be raised, the warfare at home to be put down and the war against the enemy to be pursued. Time was 'precious.' Though feeling 'pressed on all sides by the most interesting topics,' he held himself under strict control, fearful that he, 'who admonished against the consumption of the time of the House in long debate, should set an example of it.' [47]

If he spoke briefly, however, he spoke frequently. In answer to the cry for a defensive rather than an offensive war, he countered that any nation fighting in defense of violated rights was fighting a defensive war. 'The ambition of one nation,' Calhoun warned, 'can destroy the peace of the world.' With Bonaparte defeated, England could no longer claim to be fighting 'in defense of the liberties of mankind.' As for us, we were fighting for the trade rights of a free world. From 1756 on, had it not been England's unshakable policy to enlarge her trade at the expense of her neighbors? Had she not violated rights guaranteed to her fellow nations under international law? 'It is her pride and her boast,' declared Calhoun. 'A policy so injurious to the common interest of mankind must . . . unite the world against her.' [48]

10

United the world may have been against the pretensions of His Majesty's Empire, but not so the Congress of the United States. Debate raged on, despite Calhoun's appeals to the opposition at least to 'coldly look on' and not to impede the progress of the war by 'idle and frivolous' chatter. 'Now is the time, not for debate but action.' Fifty thousand men must be recruited. The enemy must be crushed on land and on sea. Canada must be invaded. Did the member from New Hampshire * object? The member from New Hampshire preferred surrender? Did the member from New Hampshire realize what surrender would mean to New England—the loss of Maine—the loss of the codfisheries? † [49]

Thus, with the Hartford Convention adjourning in hazy talk of constitutional amendments to protect the rights of the Northern States against the 'hostile . . . Southern interest,' and Henry Clay deep in games of bluster and brag at Ghent, Calhoun pitted words against defeat—and waited. Discouragement he would not admit, even in private letters. 'No menace, no threat of disunion shall shake me,' he told MacBride. 'I know the difficulties. . . . To me they are nothing. I by no means despair.'

* Daniel Webster.
† All quotations from Calhoun in the latter half of this chapter are from his great speech on the Loan Bill of February 25, 1814, in which he more eloquently covered all issues of the last year of the war than in any of his subsequent, briefer addresses.

America was too great to 'permit its freedom to be destroyed by either domestick or foreign foes. . . .'[50]

On a night in late January, 1815, it happened. A rumor rippled across the surface of Washington, stirring the seething depths, roaring into a storm of hysteria and hero-worship. News had arrived, so fantastic and incredible that the entire country reeled out of its lethargy and despair.

There had been a battle over the heaped cotton bales outside New Orleans. There had been a victory, an undreamed, unbelievable victory. Nearly two thousand Redcoats lay dead in the dank swamplands of Louisiana, while the opposing Americans had lost but sixty-three. A ragtag army of Kentucky hunters, Tennessee frontiersmen, and Georgia wildcats, under the command of lean red-haired Andrew Jackson, had smashed the last British invasion of American soil. 'The affair at New Orleans,' exulted Calhoun, 'must indeed be a strong sedative to any scheme of conquest the British Government may have formed. . . . It sees how little is to be gained by war.'[51]

The Battle of New Orleans! Candles and torchlights flaring against the skies of Boston, New York, and Washington, dark streets surging with shouting mobs, bunting flung across the rotting ships in the harbors of New Bedford and Portsmouth.[52] The war was won, and the fact that the decisive battle had been fought and the enemy repulsed, fifteen days after a treaty of peace had been signed at Ghent, mattered not at all.

In the governmental councils, opposition to the war collapsed like a punctured soap bubble. Those who had declined to bear the burdens were only too glad to partake of the victory.

Though unaware of the Christmas Eve Treaty at Ghent, it took no great foresight on the part of Calhoun to predict, as he encountered the latest Dallas scheme for a 'paper bank,' that should news of peace arrive that day, the measure would not receive a single vote. The news arrived that very hour. For the second time in a month, all America turned out for an orgy of celebration. In Washington, bonfires threw weird shadows across the ruined buildings; at the Octagon House, Calhoun, caught in a 'stifling' mass of humanity, saw the President, smiling and confident once more, and beside him Queen Dolly, her cheeks aglow under her paint. Politics melted away in congratulations. The Marine Band blared; wine flowed freely in the Presidential reception rooms and the servants' hall. The war was over!

11

A useless war, history would call it. History would deal harshly with those 'brawling boys' from the frontier, who, drunk on dreams of Canada and Florida and 'a new United States, whipped and bullied their country into a world holocaust for which it was as unprepared as it was unwilling.'

Yet from all the blaze of surplus powder and shot, one fact rises clear.
We emerged from the war thinking we were a great nation. And armed
with this delusion we were able to exist most comfortably until the
thought became fact.

If America and England are united in a common destiny and a common responsibility to the world of the future, it was the War Hawks of
1812 that made the fulfillment of this destiny possible. In 1783, America
had won her independence, but not her equality. And only as an equal
could she play the role that she was fated to play. The war had been
a psychological necessity. We see this in the War Boys' own words, in
their braggart boasts and bluster. We can see the wrinkled brow of the
young British Minister, Foster, when Henry Clay talked glibly of war
as a 'duel' which a proud young nation might fight 'to prevent . . . being bullied and elbowed.' We find it in the observation of the shrewd
Thomas Lowe Nichols, who could not 'remember the time when the idea
of a war with England was not popular'; and in the assertion of a Congressman that 'The only way to please John Bull is to give him a good
beating, and . . . the more you beat him, the greater is his respect.' We
find it in Calhoun's cry for a 'Second American Revolution,' and in Clay's
embarrassing appeals to the British Minister as to what his country would
think of us if we didn't fight; and his fervent boasts that we could 'wait
a little longer with France' after silencing 'the insolence of British cannon.' In the opinion of the War Hawks war alone would compel Britain
and the world to recognize the United States as a sovereign and equal
member of the family of nations. Only by the sword could we win a
friendship based upon mutual respect. The war, said Henry Clay, would
leave the two nations 'better friends than they had ever been before.' [53]

VIII

Toward a Broadening Union

NOW THAT THE WAR WAS OVER, no one was more surprised than the War Hawks to discover how popular it had been. As Albert Gallatin said: 'The war . . . renewed the national feeling which the Revolution had given. . . . The people . . . are more Americans; they feel and act as a nation.' [1]

His words were true. The unity, so sought for in the hardships of war had become a reality in the joy of peace. The naval victories of Hull and Decatur were American victories; the Battle of New Orleans was a Western victory; and of the entire country, the West was most nationalistic in spirit. The abortive Hartford Convention had united the people as only a major battle could have done. It had become a sneering byword across the country, and the label of Federalist was enough to damn the political prospects of any man. 'Clay, Calhoun, Grundy, and Company' found themselves undisputed leaders, not of their party alone, but of the country at large.

Internationally, too, the victory had repercussions. By the great powers of the world—France, as well as England—the United States had been 'kicked and cuffed about' like 'an illegitimate child in the family of nations.' Now, as Calhoun exulted, America 'ceased to have merely a putative rank among the great countries of the world.' She had shaken off her 'thralldom of thought.' [2]

2

For Calhoun, in the spring of 1815, the 'extreme delight' he had felt at the defeat of John Bull was of short duration. It was good to be home again, to look into the eyes of his young wife from whom he had been separated so long, to walk through the quiet of his own fields and to feel the cool, wet noses of his hounds pressing into his hands. Little Andrew was there, three years old now, and running to meet his father; and baby Floride, toddling across the floor in her first few steps. She was fourteen months old, just beginning to walk and talk, and her father never tired of watching her as she chattered and laughed and ran all over the house.

Then on a balmy April night he and Floride were aroused by the sound of vomiting. The baby was sick! Floride could reach out her hand and feel the hot little body in its three-sided crib, fitted against their own bed. They arose, lighted candles. It was nothing, they were sure. Young children were often taken so.

An hour passed. The child was no better. Her flesh was burning hot. Slowly, light crept around the curtains. Calhoun could see 'the wildness' in the baby's eyes. Terrified, he sent a servant for the doctor. They waited. At last the slave returned—alone. Dr. Casey had gone to Augusta.

'Everything was done . . . but in vain,' Calhoun wrote afterward. Morning light poured into the room, on the tumbled crib where the little body lay, limp and still; on Calhoun's haggard face and Floride's swollen eyes. Calhoun stooped over the body of his firstborn daughter . . . a part of himself wrenched away . . . his own flesh and bone and blood.

Floride broke down. Fighting back his own pain, Calhoun turned to his grief-stricken wife. Perhaps, he suggested, it was God's plan. 'Providence may have intended it in kindness to her.' Who could know whether she would have been happy had she lived? . . . 'We know that she is far more happy than she could be here with us.' But Floride broke into fresh paroxysms of grief. It was in vain that Calhoun told her that almost all parents had suffered the same calamity; every word of consolation that he clumsily attempted only grieved the broken-hearted mother the more. 'She thinks only of her dear child . . . every thing that made her interesting, thus furnishing additional food for her grief.'[3]

The house quiet at last, Calhoun wrote his mother-in-law of 'the heaviest calamity that has ever occured to us . . . our dear child . . . but a few hours before . . . our comfort and delight. So healthy, so cheerful, so stought. . . . She could hardly walk when I returned. . . . She is gone alas! from us forever; and has left nothing behind but our grief and tears.'[4]

3

It was harder than ever for Calhoun to leave Floride that fall. That there would be another child in the spring to take the place of little Floride added to his cares, for he had lost all faith in the availability of country doctors, and was determined that his wife should go to Charleston for her labor. Little Andrew was ill with a lingering fever; and it was of home, not Washington, that Calhoun thought as he stood beside the aging John Taylor of Caroline on the deck of the steam packet to Washington. Only the trust that Floride would write him by every mail eased his mind.[5]

Conversation with Taylor was little calculated to lift Calhoun from his depression. The future looked dark to the old Jeffersonian agrarian. He was dubious of this 'shifting restless' acquisitive nation, sprung full-grown from the battlefield, with progress the first law of its being and realism laid away with powdered wigs and small-clothes.

The war had brought into focus the differing interests of the three sections of the country. Landless masses were piling pell-mell into the cities of the East; farms were dotting the democratic West; beyond, lay an unbroken immensity, too broad for dreams, too great for individual enterprise. In the South was the trend from the farm to the plantation, from self-sufficiency to cotton. Already North and South meant a criss-cross of opposing economic interests, and where would it end? [6] Agriculture, said Taylor, was 'the only productive class of labor'; monopoly and incorporation were spreading over Europe; and 'America would be forced to a choice between agrarianism and capitalism, for the two were utterly incompatible.' [7]

True democracy, Taylor could have told Calhoun, was only possible among equals. Economic inequalities had wrecked every democratic program of the past. What hope could there be for a middle-class society, frankly based on the exploitation of the laboring by the moneyed classes?

Calhoun understood. He had been aware of sectional conflicts from the beginning. Perhaps the most remarkable prophecy of his life was uttered, not in the eighteen-thirties or forties, but on a fall night in 1812 in Mrs. Bushby's sitting room. There, young Charles Stewart, later captain of the U.S.S. *Constitution*, had told Calhoun that he was 'puzzled' at the alliance of the Southern planters with the 'Northern Democracy. . . . You are decidedly the aristocratic portion of this Union. . . . You neither work with your hands, heads, nor any machinery . . . have your living by the sweat of slavery, and yet . . . assume the professions of democracy.'

Calhoun had admitted it. 'That we are essentially aristocratic, I cannot deny; but . . . we yield much to democracy.' Stewart was losing sight 'of the political and sectional policy of the people.' The South was 'from necessity' wedded to the Northern Democracy, for it is through 'our affiliation with that party in the Middle and Western States that we hold power.' Yet, prophesied Calhoun, when the South ceased 'to control this nation' it would 'resort to the dissolution of the Union.' The constitutional compromises were 'sufficient for our fathers, but, under the altered conditions of our country from that period, leave to the South no resource but dissolution.' [8]

Thus, in 1812, could the young man, who had grown up in the school which looked upon the Union only as an experiment, contemplate its inevitable disruption. He was unshaken at this early period by the love of country which grew upon him year by year, so that he exhausted a lifetime of strength in futile attempts to stave off the doom which from the first his pitiless logic showed him was inevitable. Now, his patriotism, fused in the fire of war, failed to recognize defeat. Already he knew that in statecraft his task would be to fit the political framework, designed for a compact, pastoral republic, to a sprawling, fast-growing, industrial democracy.

He knew the dangers that diversity would bring. To him, the Union seemed a fragile thing, too delicately wrought to stand 'on the cold calculation of interest, alone . . . too weak to stand political convulsions. . . . I feel no disposition to deny,' he had said, as early as 1814, that if the majority ceased 'to consult the general interest . . . it would be more dangerous than a factious minority.'[9] Party 'rage,' he saw as the great 'weakness of all free governments,' and precedent as scarcely less dangerous. 'It is not unusual,' he had said two years earlier, 'for executive power, unknown to those who exercise it, to make encroachments. . . . What has been the end of all free governments, but open force, or the gradual undermining of the legislative by the executive power? The peculiar construction of ours by no means exempts us from this evil. . . . Were it not for the habits of the people we would naturally tend that way.' What he desired was 'the whole' of the government in 'full possession of its primitive powers, but all of the parts confined to their respective spheres.'[10] So he spoke in 1812; and again in 1833 and 1848.

Fragmentary as these observations are, their remarkable prophecies alone make them worthy of serious study. More important, they offer conclusive proof of an assertion that 'if the young Calhoun had been asked to define the relations of the State to the General Government, he would have used language not very different from that with which he was afterwards to defy Webster or Jackson.'[11] Clearly, what he was already defining as 'the conflict between the States and General Government' was not yet uppermost in his mind. Nevertheless, he had said enough to show that basically the Calhoun of 1815 and the Calhoun of 1833 were one man.

For eighty years historians have divided Calhoun's public career into two sharply defined sections: one, nationalist, the other, sectionalist. This is an oversimplification. Basically Calhoun was at once a nationalist and a sectionalist from the beginning to the end of his career. In 1815 he represented a majority; by 1833 those who thought as he did were in the minority, which explains where the difference lay. In 1815 he was as representative of the frontier farmers as he later became of the planting South; but in 1815 the frontier stretched all the way from rock-tipped Maine to the Alabama border. Like other nationalists, Daniel Webster included, Calhoun was always to demand first protection for his immediate constituency.[12]

Now, despite John Taylor's warnings, Calhoun saw no interest inimical to that Southern life he loved. The difference between the Calhoun of 1815 and the Calhoun of 1833 is a matter of knowledge, not of philosophy. Bitter experience divides the confident young patriot who had yet to learn the dangers of nationalism and the worn-out statesman in whom hope was almost dead. For it is 'not inconsistent that a man should allow much freedom to a partner whom he still trusts, which he would be reluctant to allow to one of whom he has come to be suspicious.' [13]

To Calhoun, the future was a 'could be,' not a 'would be.' He failed to heed his own warnings. He trusted his heart, not his head. He had faith and hope; he had confidence in the 'virtue and intelligence of the American people' Later, he would change his mind. A nationalistic America, which practiced as well as preached 'the general welfare' could conceivably have endured on the principle of majority rule; but a nation which had divided into states, regions, and groups must find other means for that 'justice' which Calhoun in 1813 defined as the 'prime objective of government' to survive. It would be Calhoun's task to seek ways of both restraining and satisfying the 'cold' calculations which he had predicted might destroy the Union, so that, in disproof of his own predictions, the Union would endure.

4

Never had Washington been more brilliant than in that triumphant postwar fall of 1815. Never had there been such feverish pursuit of pleasure nor such beautiful women to join the pursuit. In tiny hamlets and farms, all the way from southern Maine to northern Georgia, fathers and mothers mourned sons buried at Lundy's Lane or Tippecanoe, or drowned off Jamaica; young widows mourned the happiness they had lost, and unwed and unsought girls the happiness they could now never know. But for those with politically hopeful or successful parents, a future still beckoned. There were men enough in Washington, and, it was said, never enough girls to go around. So while outside a nation mourned, inside Washington girls in lace ruffs and 'macaroni' gowns of velvet and satin, their eager lips 'pink with cherry paste,' their slim arms leaving white streaks along the dark coats of their partners, laughed and flirted with great men in rooms so crowded that onlookers 'could only see the heads,' and stood upon the benches, 'the heat was so great.' [15]

Dolly Madison, Queen Dolly, who could rouge her cheeks and serve cabbage and fried eggs at a State dinner and still be a great lady, was queening it at the Octagon House. The 'President's Palace' was still a mass of smoke-stained rubble, but the stately mansion on the corner of New York Avenue and Eighteenth Street made up in beauty what it lacked in size. Visitors could step from the circular marble hall on the ground floor into one of the drawing rooms where Dolly and her 'withered little applejohn, Jemmy,' were waiting before the mantel. Feminine visitors would note the window curtains of blue 'embossed cambric' with red silk fringe, the two little couches covered with blue 'patch' and the 'pretty French chairs . . . covered with striped rich blue silk,' as Mrs. Mary Crowninshield noted. They chattered of Commodore Porter's young wife, who was conceded to be 'a very pretty little woman'; and of Mrs. Henry Clay, who dashed the hopes of innumerable 'mantrap' girls by her appearance in the capital early in 1815. Her white merino dresses were 'very tasty'; there was praise, too, for her children, all in white or black silk aprons; but all agreed that although Mrs. William H. Crawford's husband may have been Minister to the Court of France, she had 'never before been from the country . . . and seldom looks neat.'[16]

And through the drawing rooms walked Dolly Madison, 'a tall, portly, elegant lady with a turban on her forehead and a book in her hand,'[17] charming Henry Clay as she took a pinch from his gold snuffbox, pushed it up her nose with a red handkerchief 'for the rough work, Mr. Clay,' and dusted off with a tiny lace 'polisher'; soothing the jangled nerves of an admiring young countryman by ignoring the fact that, in his excitement at seeing the President's wife, he had hastily slipped a full cup of hot tea into his breeches' pocket;[18] intriguing John Calhoun as she matched the nimbleness of his eager mind with her witty knowledge of men and books and affairs.

Calhoun liked Dolly Madison. And of all the War Mess, Clay and Calhoun were her favorites. Now with the war over, Calhoun went to the Presidential receptions, although he probably would have heartily seconded the New Englander, Amos Kendall, who declared he would rather give the girl he loved 'one kiss than attend a thousand such parties.'[19]

Even Madison could relax now from the 'cold and stiff' manner of his war years. 'The bottle circulated freely' at his dinner table, and warmed by wine the President would tell 'with great archness' anecdotes of 'a somewhat loose description.' Red-haired, fastidious young William Campbell Preston, who was proud of being 'much with the War Hawks,' was disgusted by the 'habitual smut' of these stories. He noticed admiringly, however, that his hero, Calhoun, although a favorite at parties, was the only one of all of them whose own 'conversation was uncontaminated by such impurity.' *[20]

It was a man's world. For the men's pleasure were the drinks poured and the hostesses selected, 'young enough to look entrancing in candlelight and old enough to juggle discreetly with small gossip and large public affairs.' The men were lionized; the men were the heroes. You saw them all at the Madisons', the last of the great dynasty of Virginia: tall, shambling John Marshall, with his rough hair and hearty laugh and the tumbled clothes that looked as if he had picked them out in some forgotten second-hand shop; little James Monroe, exquisite in small-clothes and flashing knee-buckles; 'our western hero,' gaunt, horse-faced William Henry Harrison; and the skeleton-like figure of John Randolph, silver

---

* The quotations, by permission of the Chapel Hill Press, are from *The Reminiscences of William Preston,* edited by Minnie Clare Yarborough, Chapel Hill, North Carolina, 1933, pp. 7–8.

spurs twinkling in the candlelight, forty-two now, but from a distance still like a fragile boy of sixteen, and at close range with his fever-parched lips and dry sallow skin clinging to the bones of his fleshless fingers, like a very old man.[21] There, too, came John P. Kennedy, author of *Swallow Barn,* tall, robustious William H. Crawford, and the squat, ruddy, square-jawed Minister to England, Mr. John Quincy Adams.

In Dolly Madison's drawing room, Calhoun and his colleagues could exchange ideas with some of the greatest names America had yet produced. Yet they themselves commanded almost equal attention. The older generation was keenly aware of the drive and latent strength in this new crop of statesmen, none yet forty; and John Randolph spoke for public opinion when he said, 'Henry Clay's eye is on the Presidency and my eye is on him.' [22] Clay, Calhoun, and Webster—in that order— few could doubt that in the hands of these three the future history of America was already in the making.

Daniel Webster was the unknown quantity. More than either of his colleagues, his power was in physical presence. With his great head and the magnificent sweep of his shoulders, the dark, brooding eyes that could pierce or burn, he focused attention from the instant he stepped into a room. Many had already succumbed to the musical witchery of his voice; few could say where or for what he stood; but all sensed the untapped depths of his power.

Sheer emotion summed up Henry Clay. It was this impulsive, optimistic, one-time farm boy of 'the Slashes' who personified the new spirit of American democracy, audacious and domineering. No doubts beset him, none of the uncertainties that troubled Webster, nor the introspective questionings that haunted Calhoun. Action he found more congenial than thought; a courtroom quarrel had ended in a fist-fight with the opposition lawyer, for which the Kentuckian had willingly paid his fine of fifteen dollars.[23] Already he had hit upon the conviction that the first responsibility of government was to help its citizens to make money; [24] and the fresh-coined slogan of 'American System' had meanings both for the Western masses, seeking capital and federal aid for the opening of their young empire, and the Eastern capitalists, seeking new sources of raw goods for their factories.

Yet Clay compelled as well by sheer physical magnetism. His charm overweighed his complacent belief that he had never met his superior, and an opponent declined a personal meeting because he would not subject himself to Clay's fascination. Women also were keenly susceptible to the long-legged 'fascinating ugliness' of this blithe 'gamester in politics,' with his gay mouth and eyes that 'could gaze an eagle blind.'

For Calhoun, too, 'the fair' had glances of unabashed interest. His black suits accentuating his height and slenderness, his thick hair falling loose about his temples, and the deep eyes of his Covenanter ancestors now sparkling with eagerness, now dark with emotion, he was a striking figure. Yet the most fervent contemporary tribute to the Southerner's 'personal beauty,' his erect and 'finely made' figure, now neither 'spare nor robust,' his grace and animation, are attributed, not to a woman, but to Josiah Quincy of Boston.[25] For most feminine tastes Calhoun's features would have been too strongly marked, too stern. The impression he gave was far more of drive and strength than of mere good looks. There was a quality of excitement about him, of suppressed fire, of forces held in leash. In him you felt something of the same fierce intellectual vitality that men had known in the young Hamilton.

Even his enemies conceded him to be 'an engaging, attractive man.' He had a disarming modesty with the great, and with his inferiors, whether in age or position, then as later, his manners were not only agreeable, 'but even fascinating.'[26] He was 'an intense and vibrant personality,' [27] interested in books and people and ideas, quick to smile with the exuberance of youth, yet with a mature steadiness of purpose.

All acknowledged his 'genius for leadership.' Already he was coming to be recognized as spokesman for the lower South, interpreter of its aims and ideals. Reserved, almost shy, with no attempts at assertiveness, he could make himself felt in gatherings of men twice his years.

He knew his power. As one South Carolina historian has put it: 'He was a great statesman, a man of pure and high principles, but he believed firmly in himself, nor did his greatness ever exceed the estimate he entertained of it.' [28] In the earlier days he had lain sleepless night after night, wondering if he could succeed in the capital as he had in Abbeville.[29] Now not even the House satisfied his energies.

His fame was becoming nation-wide. In Connecticut, old classmates from Yale and Litchfield had vivid memories of the young man who had shown such 'great abilities and great ambition' from the beginning. A former classmate who was elected to Congress looked forward to a renewal of their acquaintance. He was 'kindly received' and was struck by the impact of Calhoun's personality, but was rapidly convinced that the South Carolinian had 'already given up to ambition what was meant for mankind.' [30]

Calhoun was consciously improving his oratory. During the War-Hawk days, his power had been in logic, physical presence, emotional intensity. His style had been simple, direct, forceful; on the frontier hustings he had long since become master of 'every trick . . . by which a mass of ignorant and turbulent voters' can be held to attention.[31]

But Congress, if turbulent, was not ignorant; and Calhoun well knew how much he had yet to learn of the 'graces and elegances' of public speaking. Even the admiring Ritchie regretfully admitted that Calhoun was 'not eloquent,' and a South Carolina contemporary described the young floor leader as a man of great sensitivity, but 'little imagination' and 'a rapid, though limited eloquence.' He had the advantage, reported the critic, of an excellent education, and 'astonishing powers of memory.' But foremost was his 'charming metaphysical analysis, and . . . an apt sagacity, almost peculiar to him.' [32]

Calhoun was aware of his weaknesses. Wisely, he determined not to aim for the graces which he sensed were alien to him, but to build upon his natural powers. Not style but content would be his aim; not display but simplicity of speech and gesture. His voice was not musical, but it was vibrant and strong; he would cultivate it until it was full and clear and its syllables 'fell pleasantly upon the ear.' He could perfect his diction. The results were effective. Before he left Congress, a journalist would describe him as 'the most elegant speaker who sits in the House,' his gestures graceful and easy, confining himself always to his subject, and having finished what he had to say, being done. Even Lowndes was amazed at his improvement, declaring that he only wanted to see the 'degree of eminence he would reach by practice.' [33]

5

Calhoun threw himself into his Congressional duties with a zest which would have astonished his South Carolina friends who had seen him only a few weeks before. Early in the session which opened December 4, 1815, exhausted by the long strain of war and depressed by the loss of his child, he seems to have had some idea of arranging a plan for the payment of the public debt and then returning permanently to Floride and the farm near his brother Patrick. But ambition was too strong. In the exhilaration of post-war America, his momentary listlessness was swept away. He resumed leadership with the same cool self-confidence of his war days. Only thirty-three, he was still one of the youngest men in the House, but along with Clay, he cracked the whip of authority. Great tasks remained to be done; blueprints for a broadening Union dominated his thinking. Even during the war, in those soaring moments when he had given in to what he frankly admitted was 'the fervour of my feelings,' he had visualized what the Union could become. Peace had given his dreams release, and glowing through even his most routine speeches of the post-war years is his vision for America.

Yet he indulged in none of the highly colored rhapsodies, already glib on the tongues of his companions. Caution restrained him. America could not, must not be subjected to another war. He put no faith in peace treaties. Even in February, 1815, amidst the clamor for peace and return of the service men, he had warned: 'It is easier to keep soldiers than to get them.' Our frontiers and seaports must be kept guarded. Had England foregone the principle of impressment? Not at all; peace in Europe had merely freed her from the necessity of impressment. 'If ever an American citizen should be forcibly impressed,' Calhoun warned, 'I would be ready again to draw the sword.' [34]

6

Hence in his first speech of the peacetime session in December, 1815, Calhoun warned against a repeal of the Act of War, characteristically basing his argument on fine-spun constitutional theorizing. During his remarks he turned briefly to 'that odious traffic,' which would be the burden of so much of his thought in later years. The Constitution had intended that the slave-trade 'be tolerated until 1808. . . . I feel ashamed of such a tolerance, and take a large part of the disgrace, as I represent a part of the Union, by whose influence it might be supposed to have been introduced.' But the restriction was binding on all 'parties to the Constitution.' Control of the slave power did not rest with Congress alone.[35]

He continued his dual theme of militarism and Americanism in subsequent speeches on the Commercial Treaty and the proposed repeal of the Direct (War) Tax. Not 'present ease' was his aim, but 'lasting happiness. . . . We need have no fears of militarism,' he declared. Our people would take up arms, only in defense of their rights, 'not for . . . conquest.' Our danger was apathy. Our people were inactive, 'except in pursuit of wealth.' Would England 'look unmoved upon this prosperity?' We still had 'causes of conflict. . . . If Great Britain has her Wellington, we have our Jackson, Brown, Scott . . . they have plucked the laurel from her brows.'

Our strength was in the Navy. A strong Navy was the safest, cheapest, and most effective means of defense. Our Atlantic coast line was so 'long and weak' that only by a Navy 'can it be effectively defended. . . . We shall have peace then . . . peace with perfect security.'

But we must not forget our military strength. He hinted of compulsory military training in his demand for a longer training period than six months and for troops obtained by 'regular draught' from 'the body of the people.[36] . . . I know that I utter truths unpleasant to those who wish to enjoy liberty without making the efforts necessary to secure it.' An 'indifference to defence was the first symptom of decay.' We must build military roads, 'great roads' for defense and for 'connecting the interests of varied sections of this great country. . . . A certain encouragement should be extended . . . to our woolen and cotton manufacturers.' We must build steam frigates and fortify the Mississippi and the Chesapeake. How these last objectives were to be accomplished 'he would leave to the military men.' [37]

Such aims, he knew, would 'require constant sacrifice on the part of the people, but are they on that account to be rejected?' He would not 'lull the people into false security. . . . Convince the people that measures are necessary . . . and they will support them. . . .' Taxes were not oppressive when laid for prosperity and security, for 'the general welfare. . . . We are charged,' warned Calhoun, 'by Providence, not only with the happiness of this great people, but . . . with that of the human race. We have a government of a new order . . . founded on the rights of man, resting on . . . reason. If it shall succeed . . . it will be the commencement of a new era in human affairs. All civilized governments must in the course of time conform to its principles.' But this nation, the 'youthful Hercules,' must abjure 'love of pleasure' and 'take the rugged path of duty,' or it would end 'in a dreary wilderness.' [38]

7

For the disorder of the currency, too, as the year 1816 opened, Calhoun had a cure, a national bank. The idea was nothing new. It had been tried out continuously between 1791 and 1811, and this latest measure, both in wording and provisions, was startlingly like Alexander Hamilton's plan for a government 'financial agent,' twenty-five years before. As we have seen, the question of a Second Bank had been thrashed out during the war, with Dallas's last 'paper bank,' strongly opposed by Calhoun, missing fire in the excitement of Ghent and New Orleans. Now Secretary Dallas brought the Bank out once more, with enough concessions to Calhoun's ideas for the South Carolinian to introduce the bill and pilot it through the House.

Calhoun's support was based on the very ground upon which he later opposed it, when, in twenty years of operation, the Bank actually aggravated the very evils it was supposed to remove. In theory, Calhoun was no lover of banks, national or otherwise, but the 'trash' or 'rags,' masquerading under the name of currency, which the war had sown broadcast over the country, could not be ignored. Night after night Calhoun was up, pleading, cajoling, persuading one after another member of the opposition. On February 26, 1816, he supported the Bank in a major address, declaring 'The condition of the currency . . . a stain on public and private credit,' and 'opposed to the principle of the federal constitution,' which had permitted only Congress the power to regulate the currency. Now the power was exercised by private banking institutions. Gold and silver had 'disappeared.' There was no money but paper money which was beyond the control of Congress. Banks were issuing inflationary amounts of paper beyond the amount 'of specie in their vaults.' The banks held forty millions in public stock. They were making loans to the government, not as brokers, but as stockholders. And they had been doing so for twelve years.

Naturally, the banks were opposed to the new measure. 'Banks must change their nature,' the South Carolinian cynically observed, 'before they will ever voluntarily aid in doing what it is not their interest to do.' But a national bank, paying specie, would force all banks to do the same. 'The disease is deep; it affects public opinion, and whatever affects public opinion touches the vitals of government.' [39]

The bill was passed and signed April 16, 1816. It was entirely an Administration measure. It provided for a capitalization of only $35,000,000, one-fifth in cash, the remainder in federal stock, of which the government was to subscribe $7,000,000. Dallas got his wish for a close government-bank tieup, with the clause which permitted the government to appoint five out of the twenty-five directors. But Calhoun won out with the provisions that specie payments could not be discontinued, and that the Bank could make no loan to the United States in excess of $500,000, or to the states exceeding $50,000. A final clause compelled the Bank to pay a bonus of $1,500,000 to the government for its franchise. Hamiltonian the measure undoubtedly was, yet as a means to an end it was supported by its old enemy of 1811, Henry Clay, with the very arguments that Hamilton had used.

Auxiliary to his work for the Bank, and at the actual request of the Treasury Department, Calhoun also drew up a plan requiring that all debts to the government be paid entirely in coin, Treasury notes, or notes of the United States Bank. The clamor from the state banks, whose notes were thus excluded, extended into the halls of Congress, and in the House the measure was lost by a single vote.

Once again Calhoun was compelled to appeal to Daniel Webster for aid. The next morning the New Englander introduced his own bill, similar in meaning, similar in wording, and supported it with a speech so logical and persuasive that it was passed by a large majority that very afternoon. Sheer audacity had enabled Webster to win where Calhoun had lost.[40]

8

Then on a warm afternoon in April occurred one of the most disastrous incidents in Calhoun's life.

The South Carolinian was in a committee room, deeply engrossed in work on the Bank problem, when he looked up to find a friend at his side. The man's face was grave. The House was in an uproar. The protective tariff measure, designed not only for the stimulation of the 'infant' American industries which had grown up during the war, but for the actual payment of the war debt, was under attack. Only in January, Calhoun had urged that manufactures be encouraged, but 'still in a military view.'

Would he come into the Chamber now, just for a few minutes and hold back this unexpected tide? [41]

Calhoun hesitated. He had 'determined to be silent' in this debate. He was tired after 'so long and laborious a session' and now only wanted to complete his work and return 'to the bosom of his family.' He had no interest in the question; he was a planter, concerned, like his constituents, only with 'the cultivation of the soil, in selling . . . high and buying cheap.'

The gadfly buzzed on. 'What shall I say?' asked Calhoun wearily. He was not prepared to speak; 'I mean not a verbal preparation, for I have ever despised such; but that meditation and arrangement of thought which the House is entitled to on the part of those who occupy any portion of their time.' [42]

His friend pressed him further. The very 'right' of protection was under challenge. The 'right' of protection. Calhoun's interest snapped to attention, and within five minutes he was on the House floor, saying in haste what he would repent at leisure all his life.

His words were brief—but sufficient. 'Till the debate assumed this *new form*,' he explained, he had not intended to speak at all. But the war had destroyed 'our two . . . leading sources of wealth, commerce and agriculture.' We had no markets. Our cotton goods were unprotected from the competition of goods from the East Indies. 'Neither agriculture, manufactures, nor commerce, separately is the cause of wealth; it flows from the three combined. Without commerce, industry would have no stimulus; without manufactures, it would be without the means of production; and without agriculture, neither of the others can subsist.' Sharply he condemned the theorists who believed in 'the Phantom of eternal Peace.'

'No country ought to be dependent upon another,' he continued. 'When our manufactures are grown to a certain perfection, as they soon will under the fostering care of Government, we will no longer experience these evils. The farmer will find a ready market for . . . all his wants.' The war had compelled America to turn her capital to manufacturing. He was aware of the possible evil in 'dependence on the part of the employed' factory workers, but he could not see that the English soldiers from the manufacturing districts were any worse than the others. The tariff would 'bind together our widely spread Republic . . . the liberty and union of this country are inseparably united. . . . Disunion. This single word comprehends almost the sum of our political dangers, and against it . . . we ought to be perpetually guarded.' [43]

He had left no doubts as to his meaning. Despite his later concessions to a 'small permanent protection,' he was supporting the new tariff primarily as a measure of war reconstruction. It was as a gesture of unity and concession that he offered his support—'not for South Carolina, but for the nation'—convinced, as he was, that the tariff would bring a harmonious balance to the three great interests of the country. He would withdraw his support twelve years later because it had done exactly the reverse. His tactics had changed, not his strategy. Nevertheless, the man who in 1833 would endeavor to restrict Congressional power to tariffs for 'revenue only' had in 1816 taken an unqualified stand for the protective policy so satisfying to the most ardent of high-tariff supporters that his address was framed and tacked upon the walls of taverns and barrooms beside Washington's Farewell Address.

Calhoun himself, despite the inner qualms that were troubling him within a very few years, did not feel compelled to deny the support of Pennsylvania protectionists, who hailed him as their condidate for the Presidency. He did not know that the measure he had offered to the nation as a whole was to be turned against his own people. His error was the error of virtually the whole South; and if 'Mad Jack' Randolph felt the body blow that protection gave, both to agriculture and the 'strict construction' of the Constitution, it was Thomas Jefferson, who from the blue hills of Charlottesville endorsed protectionism and 'joined hands' with Calhoun, Lowndes, and Clay.[44]

9

Despite the routine that absorbed Calhoun in those post-war years, he never lost sight of his goal. The 'broadening Union' was always foremost in his thoughts. He gave expression to his views in an address remarkable for its link between the 'national' and the 'sectional' Calhoun of the historian's creation.

Here are the phrases so often on his lips in the future: 'the selfish instincts of our nature . . . the rival jealousies of the States.' These are the forces which he increasingly saw as threatening the Union—the forces of diversity, the clashing interests of the sections. Now, as always, liberty was foremost with him—in fact, he saw the Union as founded to preserve liberty. When sectional interests should become so diverse as to threaten the liberty of a group of states to follow their own pattern of life, then, the Carolinian foresaw, the Union would fall. In 1816, as in his last years of life, every energy was dedicated to preventing this catastrophe—to seeking methods by which diverse interests might be reconciled—forces which would prevent any states or sections with a numerical majority from thrusting their will upon a minority section.

Calhoun's objectives and fears in 1816 were the objectives of a lifetime; he would change only in his methods. His goal was constant: to preserve the Union, and to hold back all forces which might rend the Union apart. The great size of our country, he told Congress, 'exposes us to the greatest of all calamities, *next to the loss of liberty*—disunion. We are . . . rapidly,—I was about to say fearfully, growing. This is our pride and our danger, our weakness and our strength.—Those who understand the human heart best, know how powerfully distance tends to break the sympathies of our nature. . . . Let us . . . bind the republic together with roads and canals . . . the most distant parts . . . within a few days' travel of th center. . . . A citizen of the west will read the news of Boston still moist from the press. The mail and the press are the nerves of the body politic. By them, the slightest impression made on the remote parts, is communicated to the whole system. . . . If . . . we permit a sordid . . . sectional spirit to take possession of this House, this happy scene will vanish. What is necessary for the common good may apparently be opposed to the interest of particular sections. It must be submitted to as the condition of our greatness. . . . Were we a small republic the selfish instincts of our nature might . . . be relied on in the management of public affairs.' [45]

'What is necessary for the common good may apparently be opposed to the interest of particular sections. It must be submitted to as the condition of our greatness.'

Here, indeed, is the crux of the charge that Calhoun was inconsistent, that the Great Nationalist of 1816 right-about-faced to become the Great Sectionalist of the eighteen-forties. The man who in youth voiced these words would thirty years later become the leader of the minority South's struggle to maintain her own way of life against the majority of the nation.

But Calhoun did not use words loosely. Young as he was, he was a realist. Already he had sensed the dangers to political freedom in the wage-slavery of the workshops. Already he was aware of the danger when 'attachment to party becomes stronger than attachment to country.' His thinking deepened and expanded with the passing years, but it is hard to believe that the whole basis of his political thought overturned. The key to the dilemma is in the phrase, 'What is necessary for the common good.'

For what Calhoun saw as the common good, he had defined clearly, if negatively, in his speech, pointing out 'the greatest of all calamities, next to the loss of liberty—disunion.' Already Calhoun saw what Webster saw, years later, that to the common good liberty *and* union were the ideal. To Calhoun, liberty meant the right of an individual, a state, a section, or 'an interest,' to manage its own affairs—to adopt its own 'peculiar institutions,' unless these institutions threatened the common good. In all sincerity, Calhoun never deemed the peculiar institutions of the South, either slavery or the agrarian way of life, incompatible with the 'common good,' or endangering either the liberty or the union of the country as a whole.

The agitation against slavery, however, and legislative attempts to restrict its extension, he deemed a violation of the South's liberty, and knew from the first that the end would be disunion. Thus, vehemently, he opposed all such agitation and legislation. His 'moral obtuseness' on the slave question may be condemned; but it has nothing to do with his consistency.

What, then, of the Calhoun presented to us by history—the 'Nationalist' of 1817; the 'Sectionalist' of 1850—the man who changed sides? The interpretation simply does not hold up under examination. Calhoun could have made the same speech in 1850 that he had made over thirty years earlier.

The possibility of another war gave further impetus to Calhoun's immediate demand for national unity. 'The common strength is brought to bear with great difficulty on the point that may be menaced by an enemy.' Taxes had been 'drained' from the sections for use in war; only by 'internal trade' could they be restored.

Many essential improvements were on 'too great a scale for States.' States would surely yield their consent for such widespread benefits, but even if they did not, there was always the 'general welfare' clause. 'I am no advocate for refined arguments on the Constitution,' declared the confident Carolinian. 'The instrument was not intended . . . for the logician to exercise his ingenuity on.' The past had provided numerous examples of Congress appropriating money 'without reference to the enumerated powers. . . . Look at Louisiana.' His imagination taking wings, he conjured up a vision of future glories; of enterprises which would one day unite Maine to Louisiana, the Great Lakes to the Hudson; Philadelphia, Baltimore, Washington, Richmond, and Charleston to the west; and finally, the perfection of 'intercourse between the West and New Orleans.' 'Let us conquer space.' [46]

More prosaically in his famous 'Bonus Bill' of the second session of the Fourteenth Congress, Calhoun proposed that the bonus and dividends of the United States Bank be set aside for internal improvements. The measure was passed by the House and sent on to the Senate. A few days later, Calhoun dropped in at the 'President's House' to say good-bye. The session was nearly over, and he was packing for home.

The pale little man in the powdered wig looked at him gravely. He had, he feared, unwelcome news. He would be forced to veto the 'Bonus Bill.'

But why? demanded Calhoun. He had supposed it to be in accord with the Administration's views. Otherwise he would never have subjected the President 'to the unpleasant duty, at the very close of his administration, of vetoing a bill passed by . . . his friends.' Hadn't the President himself urged that Congress exercise all its constitutional powers in the interests of internal improvements?

Ah, yes, said Mr. Madison, in substance, but there was the trouble. The Constitution gave no such latitude as Mr. Calhoun had suggested.

Calhoun protested that his error had been unintentional. He begged the President to reconsider. But Madison refused. On March 3, 1817, the day before he left the Presidential office, Madison returned the bill with his veto and a suggestion that the Constitution be so amended as to provide the necessary power. Hastily the vote was called again, a complete reversal this time, although Calhoun clung to his original position and voted in vain to pass the bill over the Presidential veto. It was an act that he would regret all his life.[47]

10

This was not the first time, however, that Calhoun's zeal had apparently outrun his judgment. Another bill—equally innocent on the surface—had been introduced and passed in 1816, Calhoun supporting it along with nearly everyone else. It provided that Congressional pay be raised from the standard six dollars a day to an annual salary of fifteen hundred dollars.

But the people did not support it. The people were horrified. Was the American taxpayer to reach into his breeches' pockets just to keep a pack of lazy Congressmen chattering up there in Washington? If the job didn't satisfy the present officeholders, there were plenty it would satisfy. A tidal wave of outraged public opinion engulfed the Fourteenth Congress, perhaps the most remarkable assemblage to sit in the national councils until 1850. Few even dared to run for re-election; most of those who did were speedily and permanently retired.

Webster solved the difficulty by shifting his residence from New Hampshire to Massachusetts. Clay was almost lost, and only achieved re-election by going out on the stump and reminding his enraged audiences that if a good rifle flashed once they would try it a second time before throwing it away.[48]

From the South Carolina foothills rolled up a thunderstorm of disapproval. South Carolina now had two quarrels with Calhoun: he had his full share of explaining to do about the tariff, arguing that he had supported it as a 'purely fiscal' measure, but that as a permanent policy, it would never receive his support; and now he must also defend his vote for increased salaries. Suddenly the man who had won his seat almost by unanimous consent in the earlier elections found himself confronted with not one but two opponents, and a grave-faced group of the faithful called on him one evening at Bath in the summer of 1816 and staked out his path of duty.[49]

He had made a terrible mistake, they told him. His whole future career stood in jeopardy. He must not dare venture out on the stump, lest the public wrath be turned against him. He must issue a public statement,

promising to rescind his vote at the next session of Congress—should
he be so bold as to offer himself for re-election—a risk which they by
no means advised. He must admit his error, and promise to mend his
ways.[50]

Calhoun listened, his blood boiling. Unfortunately, we have no report
of what he actually did say; but it is easy to imagine the scene, he looking calmly out of deep-set eyes at the well-wishers, his mouth gone 'tight
and straight as a piece of wire,' but never raising his voice while he talked.
'When I have made up my mind, it is not in the power of man to divert
me,'[51] he once told Duff Green. He had made up his mind. He was
courteous, but firm. He had done nothing of which he was ashamed. Fifteen
hundred dollars? Two thousand would have been no inordinate salary.
He would not back down. He would take the stump and defend his course;
the people would understand.

11

Three months later, at the opening of the 'lame duck' session of 1816, an
almost cockily confident Calhoun walked into the House Chamber. He
had addressed mass meetings at Abbeville and Edgefield;[52] he had come
back vindicated by a triumphant re-election to his seat; and convinced
equally of the people's capacity to understand and his own powers to
persuade.

The offending measure was, of course, immediately brought forth for
the kill. Amidst the hasty scramble of retractions and reversals from
those re-elected under pledge of reform, Calhoun arose and launched
into a defense of his previous vote. Neither trimmer nor weathercock, he
could not resist a sneer at his colleagues' frightened compliance with the
popular will. This was 'a new and dangerous doctrine,' for the first
time broached in the House. 'Are we bound to do what is popular?' He
did not feel bound to obey the instructions of his constituents. 'The constitution is my letter of instruction . . . the solemn voice of the people
to which I bow . . . the powerful creative voice which spake our Government into existence. . . .'

The House, he declared, was the 'only gift of the people.' Yet its 'best
talents,' men 'of the most aspiring character,' strove for positions in the
'departments or foreign missions,' where salaries were higher. 'Gentlemen
say we ought to come here for pure patriotism,' declared the angered
realist. 'It sounds well; but there will be found neither patriotism nor
honor sufficient for continual privations. . . . Our population advances
. . . marriages take place at an early period. Hence'—and here he spoke
from the heart—'the duty to make provision for a growing family. . . .
By inadequate pay, you close the door on some of the most deserving
citizens. Talent, in this country, is particularly from the middling and

lower classes. A young man . . . spends his property . . . in acquiring
sufficient information to pursue a profession.' Should he not receive adequate pay for devoting his 'talents to the service of his country?' Should
'men of inferior capacity be sent here?' Make this House financially comparable with its honors, and 'men of the greatest distinction . . . will
seek it.' [53]

At such a time and under such circumstances, Calhoun's words were
scarcely calculated for popularity. Yet his very defiance commanded admiration. From the opposite side of the House Thomas Grosvenor suddenly arose and said: 'I have heard with peculiar satisfaction the able,
manly . . . speech of the gentleman from South Carolina.' [54]

A bomb could not have struck the House with more effect. Mouths fell
open; pens hovered in midair. Not a man had forgotten the winter morning during the war when the clerk adjourned the House at twelve o'clock,
'the Speaker being absent . . . engaged, it is supposed, in an honorable
. . . endeavor to reconcile a difficulty of a very serious nature between
two members.' [55]

Who were the members? Two empty chairs told the story. They belonged to Thomas Grosvenor of New York and South Carolina's John C.
Calhoun.

A duel was in the offing. The provocation? No one knew. That it was
personal rather than political Calhoun's official biographer indicated years
later,[56] but there had been bad blood between the two for months. Calhoun's nerves had long been tight-drawn. Grosvenor was a bitter Administration critic. The pair had bickered constantly on every conceivable subject from the war program to their tastes in literature.

But the delicate ministrations of Clay arranged 'the affair.' The next
day the would-be combatants were back in their seats. Of the affray,
they had nothing to say then or later. To each other they had nothing to
say for three entire years!

Now, sensing the House's wonder, Grosvenor plunged on: 'I will not
be restrained. No barrier shall exist which I will not leap over, for the
purpose of offering to that gentleman my thanks for the judicious, independent, and national course which he has pursued . . . for the last two
years.' [57]

Coming from his bitterest enemy, this was triumph indeed. It climaxed
Calhoun's career in the House. His words on the allurements of Cabinet
offices were prophetic. When he returned to Washington the next year, it
was as Secretary of War.

IX

Mr. Secretary of War

To ANYONE but a very young and very ambitious man, the position of Secretary of War in the Cabinet of James Monroe would have held small appeal. For the Department was an unquestioned war casualty, buried in a muddled heap of unsettled accounts, amounting to some fifty million dollars.[1] Although it had limped through the late war with a passable degree of efficiency, it was now devoid either of respect or authority. Indeed, the task of its redemption had been turned down by Henry Clay, Andrew Jackson, William Lowndes, and Langdon Cheves, none of whom were inclined to embark upon a ship apparently already sunk. Calhoun had been in Monroe's mind from the start, for he was the avowed favorite of the Army men;[2] but the President preferred a western appointee; and, despite his admiration for Calhoun's talents, feared that his youth and inexperience might mitigate against his success.

Calhoun's friends, even Lowndes, were of the same opinion. There was sincere regret among them that his 'brilliant powers' were to be buried under executive routine.[3] These very doubts only fired Calhoun's desire to put himself to the test. He accepted the post, brought his family to Washington, and moved in with Lowndes for a few months before renting a house on C Street.[4] His loneliness was appeased, but hiring servants, buying furniture, and entertaining notables soon relieved him of any hope that his finances would be improved. In fact, he was soon threatening suit against his Southern debtors in order to meet his living expenses.

The War Department was housed in a narrow brick building on Pennsylvania Avenue, with six chimneys lined across the roof and six pillars adorning the portico. Primitive awnings, sagging wearily in wet weather, shaded the windows; and in sudden heaves would dump gallons of cold water down the neck of Secretary of War Calhoun or anyone else so unfortunate as to be under them. Inside was a refreshing lack of complexity. When Secretary of the Navy Crowinshield was ill, Calhoun merely stepped across the hall and took over his duties.[5]

The young Secretary who strode into his office on the morning of December 6, 1817,[6] was a man with a mission. 'We have much indeed to do,'[7] he wrote General Jacob Brown, shortly after taking office. Valiantly he

resisted all temptation to leap in and reverse the established procedure
of years. He knew his limitations. He had read only one small book of
military science; he had everything to learn and was eager to learn.[8]

'Utility and perfection' were his aims for the Department. These, he
knew, 'must be the work of time . . . with labor and reflection.' And for
over a month he did nothing but study and carry on routine business.[9]
He read. He listened. He humbly questioned the technical experts, slowly
drawing together the information which he later codified into rules that
won the acclaim of Congress and the country.

He took the trouble to make himself agreeable to high ranking officers,
who might have been expected to resent the authority of so inexperienced
a man. And he captivated them. In his official letters it was almost with
apology that he pointed out any errors they might have made. He could
be tactful when reminding General Scott that, despite his honors in the
'late war,' he could not be presented with United States brevets wholesale;
and considerate to Major-General Brown, whom he warned against 'premature exertions after a severe illness,' assuring him that 'much as I desire your services, I still more desire your recovery.'[10] He was sensitive
to the disgrace of the unruly young officer who faced court-martial. 'Believing that his difficulties have arisen from . . . youth, I have determined
to accept his resignation,' was Calhoun's decision.[11] Dismissal would
wreck the young man's future.

Even peppery General Andrew Jackson, smarting from a quarrel with
Calhoun's predecessor, who had transmitted orders directly to subordi-
nates over his head, was soothed by the tact and finesse of the new Secretary. For Calhoun, ignoring Jackson's mutinous command that his men
should obey no orders except those given by him, merely sent the departmental instructions directly to Jackson, as should have been done from
the first. So pleased was the General that 'from that time forth, among
the younger public men, there was no one who stood so high in Jackson's
regard as the Secretary of War.'[12]

By nature Calhoun was endowed with great personal charm, and like
other Southerners, he had no scruples in using it to fulfill his ends. A
friend tried in vain to analyze his power 'to inspire confidence . . . the
highest of qualities in a public man . . . a mystical something which is
felt, but cannot be described.' Another contended that it was 'perhaps
his perfect *abandon,* his sincerity, his confidential manner, his child-like
simplicity, in union with his majestic intelligence,' that so won those 'who
came within his circle.'[13]

The charm was not reserved for high officials. The clerks who saw him
every day, heard his quick footsteps race up the stairs, saw his dark head
bent over his desk, were, with one or two exceptions, his ardent admirers.
One offered to tell him who in the office was betraying secrets to his opponents, but Calhoun merely said: 'My bitterest enemies are welcome to

know all that occurs in my department. I think well of all about me, and do not wish to change my opinion, and as far as . . . information is concerned, I only regret my permission was not asked, as it would have been freely granted.' [14]

2

Calhoun, however, had his full share of faults and weaknesses. The absent-mindedness, which brought him to John Quincy Adams's house early one morning to apologize for having forgotten a dinner invitation of the night before,[15] extended into his work. He carelessly allowed his engineers to award an Army contract to a 'pleasant scoundrel' named Mix, omitting the public advertisement for bids, required by law. Mix's failure was complete, and when denied a chance to continue his misdeeds, he accused Calhoun of having shared the profits with him. A Congressional investigation fully exonerated the Secretary, 'but the story remained to color certain judgments' upon his conduct in office.[16]

Furthermore, Calhoun had the quick, hot temper and touchy pride common to many young Southerners of his era.[17] Not yet had he achieved the self-command of his maturity; and feeling his youth, he must have been especially eager that his personal authority be respected. And occasionally he betrayed an arrogance which embroiled him in three conflicts, two of which were to have far-reaching effects on his life.

First of these was with stalwart Sam Houston. The hard-fighting, hard-drinking Tennessean was no man to be flouted by a Secretary of War. He was recklessly independent, and appeared in Calhoun's office, fresh from the wilderness, with a delegation of Indians, Houston dressed as they were, in a loincloth and blanket.

Something flickered across Calhoun's mobile face as he saw his guests, but even Houston conceded that his Southern charm was at its best; he could not have shown the visitors more warmth and courtesy had they been ambassadors from the courts of Europe.

As the Indians went out, Calhoun signaled to Houston. The door closed, and Calhoun's official courtesy dropped like a mask. His 'passion kindled.' What was the meaning of an officer of the United States Army appearing before the Secretary of War 'dressed like a savage?'[18] Houston took the outburst in sullen silence, but he never forgot it, and never forgave Calhoun.

Next came General Parker, the chief clerk in the War Office. Against the General, Calhoun had nothing more tangible than the fact that he disliked him; in fact, he frankly admitted to General Scott that he was satisfied with the man's work, but he became obsessed with the idea that his chief clerk was talking behind his back. Monroe, indulgent to his War Secretary's vagaries, appointed the clerk Paymaster General, and assured Calhoun that if Parker ever 'treated him ill," he would dismiss him.

But the Administration was not large enough to contain both Parker and Calhoun. Soon the Secretary, taking pains to have a witness present, summoned the General and bitterly demanded to know if he had 'spoken in a spirit of ridicule or censure upon his reports.' Parker, astonished, stammered out that he did not know how to answer, to which Calhoun retorted that he knew very well whether or not he had spoken so, and closed the interview. Shortly afterward, Monroe discharged the Paymaster General, who soon found haven in Crawford's Treasury Department, where he was free to state that 'The management of the War Department had been inefficient and extravagant.' [19]

Calhoun's pettiness in this affair is undeniable, but it is not characteristic. He was not a small man, and seldom again in his long career did he show such petulance and injustice. Usually men's faults did not blind him to their virtues.

The problem of Parker, however, was nothing compared to that of another and far more assertive General. Andrew Jackson was invariably a problem, whether viewed close-up, over the sights of a dueling pistol, or at a distance Indian-hunting in Spanish territory. Now the hour had advanced to meet the man. Down on the Georgia border, Seminoles, unrestrained by the so-called Spanish 'government,' were running amuck in a frontier orgy of burning, scalping, and pillaging. The situation shouted for Jackson, and he knew it. He was aware that merely to clear the Seminoles from Georgia meant nothing, so long as they still camped out in East Florida. Yet for the government to order an invasion would mean war. Jackson sat down, wrote Monroe that the government need not be implicated at all. Let the President hint to Jackson's friend, John Rhea, 'that the possession of the Floridas would be desirable . . . and in sixty days it will be accomplished.' [20]

Monroe was ill when the letter arrived. Later, he claimed he never saw it. Calhoun read it, however, and mentioned that it was a matter for the President's personal attention.[21] And 'Johnny Ray' apparently saw the President, and took some unguarded remark for the desired hint. He passed the word. Meanwhile, Secretary of War Calhoun had written Jackson: 'Adopt the necessary measures to terminate the conflict.' [22]

Jackson proceeded to the border. There he found ample evidence that British and Spanish agents had had their full share in fomenting the Indian uprisings. The Indians he disposed of in short order; then started in on the British and the Spaniards. Within fifty-nine days the job was completed. St. Marks had fallen; Fort Barrancas had fallen; Pensacola had fallen; the Spanish governor was in Jackson's hands; an Englishman named Ambrister, in charge of Indian troops, had been shot; a Scottish trader who had warned of the invasion had been hanged. British prestige, far from protecting the Indians, had proved powerless to save its own citizens; but British and Spanish indignation spoke strongly of war.

The storm broke over the Cabinet, with the blame divided between Secretary of State Adams and Secretary of War Calhoun. The cool Puritan from Massachusetts did not feel any great concern. He was convinced that the Spanish outrages justified Jackson's action, 'but the President and Calhoun were inflexible. . . . Mr. Calhoun,' wrote Adams, 'bore the argument against me.' [23]

Pride, which has been the downfall of uncounted great men, certainly wrought its worst upon Calhoun. He did not actually demand Jackson's court-martial, but an 'inquiry.' [24] As he said later, he did not question either Jackson's 'motives or his patriotism.' But sacrificing the man to the principle cost him dear. 'Calhoun,' remarked the discerning Adams, 'seems to be personally offended . . . that Jackson has set at naught the instructions of the Department.' [25]

Actually the story was more complex. It was a tricky situation, an explosive situation that faced Monroe's Cabinet during those warm June weeks of 1818. It might easily touch off war, and none knew better than Calhoun how miserably unfit for war the country was. Mixed though his motives might be, Calhoun was unaware that Rhea, either by inference or silent consent, had felt himself allowed to set the General in action. He was convinced that Jackson had deliberately transcended his powers and instructions. And even Jackson's ardently friendly biographer, Parton, considered it 'an honor for Mr. Calhoun . . . to call for an inquiry into proceedings which came near involving the country in war.' [26]

The debate continued for weeks, but finally Adams won his point. Jackson was neither disavowed nor 'investigated,' and Calhoun, acquiescing in the majority decision of the Cabinet, dismissed his own opinion from his mind. Official policy had been made; now it must be carried out. In September, he was writing Jackson that 'I concur with you in regard . . . to the importance of Florida to the . . . security of our Southern frontier.' But he warned that, although war with Spain alone would be nothing, there would 'be an English war,' almost certainly. 'A certain degree of caution,' Calhoun reminded the incautious General, would be 'desirable.' [27]

3

Monroe's Cabinet had more problems than General Jackson. Indeed, the personnel of the Cabinet itself furnished enough dynamite potentially to blow up the whole Administration if it were not kept under control. And in control was James Monroe, a 'dull, sleepy, insignificant' looking man, of whom his enemies said, 'He hasn't got brains enough to hold his hat on.' His suit was rusty black, 'his neckcloth small, ropy, and carelessly tied, his frill matted, his countenance wilted with age and care.'[28] He was not one of America's most brilliant Presidents, but he had two qualities which more spectacular leaders often lack—discrimination and diplomacy. He knew good men when he saw them, and he knew how to make them work for the general good.

The Attorney-General was William Wirt, a brilliant Virginia lawyer, socially charming and addicted to study as to a drug. But the outstanding figure of the Cabinet was John Quincy Adams. No man of his times could equal him, both in learning and practical experience. Schools in Holland and Paris, a degree from Harvard, secretary to the Ambassador to Russia at fourteen, and later himself Ambassador to Russia and Germany, United States Senator and Peace Commissioner—these were the highlights of his career. Yet this middle-aged, prim-lipped intellectual was handicapped by a personality which then and later obscured his greatness. He had much of Calhoun's ability, but none of his magnetism. He was cold, tactless, and uncompromising; constitutionally incapable of enjoying himself. 'I went out this evening in search of conversation, an art of which I have never had an adequate idea,' he once confided to his Diary.[29]

Such talents as Adams's were completely overshadowed by the flamboyance of Georgia's blond William H. Crawford, Secretary of the Treasury. His background was not unlike Calhoun's, for he, too, was an Indian fighter's son who had spent his boyhood on the South Carolina and Georgia frontiers. He, too, had attended Dr. Waddel's school and ridden the backcountry law circuit before breaking into politics and the Georgia Legislature. There was no stopping him then—Senator, Minister to France, Cabinet officer, Presidential candidate—all these posts followed in rapid succession, drawing from Adams the bitter comment that Crawford's success had been 'far beyond either his services or his talents.'[30]

Physically he was a giant of a man, strapping, robust, 'roaring with laughter.' At the French court even Bonaparte had been struck by his booming speech and 'grand' manner, and Madame de Staël had responded to his 'enchanting smile' and 'flashing blue eyes.'[31] Though Adams and Calhoun were undeceived by the bland look which half-concealed the hardness of his features, even they underestimated his genius. He could speak with apparent frankness, in language so guarded that it could be interpreted according to the prejudice of any listener, and unlike Calhoun at this period, he knew when to be quiet. Having just missed the Presidential nomination in 1816, he had no intention of permitting the mistake to be repeated. In Calhoun and in the war hero Jackson he discerned potentialities of which they themselves were scarcely aware. Skillfully he played them off against each other, treasuring up Calhoun's impulsive outbursts for future reference, and, according to Adams, instigating 'the whole movement in Congress against . . . Jackson,' the President, and Calhoun's administration of the War Department. And if Monroe himself had entertained any illusions as to Crawford's loyalty, he was relieved of them at the close of his term when the Secretary attacked him as a 'damned, infernal old scoundrel,' at which point the President hit him with a poker.[32]

Calhoun was generally liked by his other colleagues. With Monroe himself the self-confident young Carolinian, whose sparkling eyes and tousled hair made him look younger still, was an especial favorite. The last in choice had become the first in standing, and there is evidence that John Quincy Adams on his White House visits was not overpleased so often to find the President and the Secretary of War walking up and down the lawn together. Regretfully, Adams conceded that Monroe was more inclined to rely upon Calhoun's suggestions than on those of any of his other advisers.

Yet Adams himself liked Calhoun, admiring his philosophical turn of mind, 'sound judgment,' and freedom from 'sectional prejudices.' What the New Englander deplored was that Calhoun's strong convictions were far more determined by constitutional than 'moral considerations.' [33] William Wirt found the Southerner 'a most captivating man . . . ardent, generous, high-minded, brave,' although too intense and impetuous.[34]

But Calhoun's impetuosity was keyed to the times. South America churned with revolution, and Calhoun horrified the cautious Adams by suggesting that the United States sell arms to Colombia to shake off the European yoke and extend her own revolution into Mexico and Peru. Europe, unsated by fifteen years of Napoleonic blood-letting, was looking hungrily toward the straggling republics of the New World. Turkey had sprung upon Greece; France upon Spain. Post-war bitterness, national recklessness, and individual idealism throbbed in the very air. In England, a young nobleman who would give his life in the cause of freedom * had written:

> 'The mountains look on Marathon,
> And Marathon looks on the sea.
> And musing there an hour alone,
> I dreamed that Greece might still be free.'

Calhoun dreamed the same dream. For the United States it was a time of decision. Could a free republic see her sister republics fall victims to tyranny and subjugation? Could peace be preserved in a world at war? Could Spain be stopped by humble consent to her aggressions? Could American freedom and European oppression live side by side? These were the questions Calhoun asked, and it was he alone in the Cabinet who called for American naval forces to aid Greece, and for America to stand up and face the responsibilities of freedom.

In session after session of the Cabinet, with 'powerful eloquence,' Calhoun 'descanted upon his great enthusiasm for the cause of the Greeks; he

* George Gordon Lord Byron.

was for taking no heed of Turkey whatsoever.'[35] Not only was he indifferent to Turkey, but to England and Spain and indeed to all Europe.

He warned of European designs on South America. Vigorously, in the name of American public opinion, he denounced 'any yielding to foreign power,' any appeasement of colony-hungry Spain. 'We should not get any credit for it, if we did.'[36] For those who would disrupt 'all our means of preparation,' in the very face of 'possible attacks of the Armed Alliance,' his scorn was bitter. America must arm and remain armed. 'No political combination that ever existed,' he warned, 'required to be so vigilantly watched as the Holy Alliance. . . . It exceeds all other combinations against human happiness and freedom, which were ever formed. . . . They are on one side and we the other of political systems wholly irreconcilable. The two cannot exist together. One or the other must gain the ascendency.'[37]

Countering his views were Crawford, who held that it is not 'good policy to set . . . other nations at defiance,' and Adams. Between isolationism and 'mingling in every European war,' Adams declared, 'I [see] no other prospect for this nation than . . . washing blood-stained hands in blood.'[38]

Eventually the New Englander and the Carolinian composed their differences. Out of these tense Cabinet sessions came a declaration of foreign policy, a hands-off warning to Europe, a guarantee of protection to South America, a promise that the European political system should never be extended on American soil. It became known as the Monroe Doctrine; but if written by Monroe and Adams, its frank avowal of American responsibilities and American leadership is in no small part due to the influence of Calhoun.

4

Foreign policy dominated Calhoun's individual as well as his Cabinet work. To him the War Office was no mere agency for the transaction of routine business. His was the personal responsibility of eradicating those weaknesses which, but for the grace of God, Napoleon and Andrew Jackson might have handed the country back to England. No man ever learned his lessons more completely than John C. Calhoun, and the lesson of 1812 had been burned into his mind. He knew his own responsibility for leading the country into battle; and her defeats rankled within him. Now, confronting a people sick of war, he grimly warned that 'However removed our situation from the great powers of the world, and however pacific our policy . . . we are liable to be involved in war'; adding that perpetual peace was a dream which 'no nation has had the good fortune to enjoy.'[39]

Peacetime, not war, was the opportunity to build up the Army. Peace was the time to guard against the danger of overwhelming losses. Calhoun neatly punctured the trial balloons of 'experts,' who were shouting the old

European bugaboo of large standing armies. To small countries such armies would undoubtedly be a menace, but the very immensity of the United States precluded such dangers while necessitating adequate protection for the oversized frontier line. The military establishment of 1802, Calhoun reminded his war- and tax-weary countrymen, was larger than the one now proposed for a country doubled in size! [40]

All this sounded very well to the officers and men in the threatened Army and to the generation just too young for the war, and to the realists, like Calhoun himself, who were ashamed of the muddle that had been made. Calhoun's bold words did him no harm, for not yet did America expect her statesmen to say nothing and to please everyone. Calhoun's unabashed independence brought him forward as no mere compliance with public opinion could have done.

Congress was another matter. Committed to reducing taxes and maintaining itself in power, it had not the least interest in Army expansion. Reduction and economy were the watchwords, and reduction and economy were ordered from the Secretary of War.

Calhoun was no spendthrift. He had sharply questioned the undue cost of warships at two thousand dollars apiece. He had been stern in his comments to Lieutenant-Colonel Charles Gratiot that 'the expenses of . . . buildings of a temporary character are much too great. . . . Nothing more than comfort' [41] was required.

The confusion and 'crushing responsibilities' that had confronted him from the moment he took office, Calhoun had faced with a practicality which amazed his friends, who thought his mind too abstract to cope with executive detail. 'Every article of public property . . . ought to be in charge of some person responsible,' he had directed. Thus, 'a very considerable reduction of expenses' could be made. He suggested that even in peacetime each military department have a chief accountable to the government at all times.[42]

To establish this system had necessitated a complete reorganization of the War Department. Far from 'burying' his talents, Calhoun revealed executive abilities which an admiring French army officer compared to Napoleon's, and which placed the Department on so firm a foundation that, ironically enough, it faced the tests of both the Mexican and Civil Wars.[43] In a single year the Department paid out $4,571,961.64, which passed through the hands of 291 disbursing agents, with every penny accounted for. And before leaving office, Calhoun could boast that, although departmental expenses were three times greater than in 1800, the unsettled accounts had been brought down to $4,000,000, and that a sum of $957,356.46 had been saved the government through his system of reorganization.[44]

Efficiency and honesty were not enough for Congress, however. The clamor for tax reduction was making an unholy din; but Calhoun drew a line. Economy was one thing. False economy was another. The 'miser's policy,' he insisted, 'is the worst extravagance,' and 'the best is the cheapest, though the first outlay is larger.' In cutting Army pay checks to a point where men of the greatest talent either resigned or refused to enter the service, he could see no economy whatever. 'Men will not serve for honor alone,' he warned; nor would even the rank and file last with reduced pay and rising prices.

Proposals of economy in the Army's food supply drew his full wrath, but Congress was implacable. Ordered to reduce food costs, Calhoun went into conference with the Surgeon-General and emerged with a plan which not only halved expenses, but actually improved the diet of the soldiers. The standard Army ration was one and a quarter pounds of beef, or three-quarters of a pound of pork, one gill of rum, small amounts of brandy and whiskey, and eighteen ounces of bread a day. With no knowledge of vitamins, balanced diets, or the dangers of alcoholism, except what his own common-sense told him, Calhoun proposed that peas and beans occasionally be substituted for the meat; that to save transportation costs, vegetables and livestock be raised at each Army post, and that in the South men have their bacon and cornbread. Molasses, Calhoun concluded, should replace the 'spirit ration' entirely, and hard liquor be reserved for use before battle 'when great efforts were necessary.' [45]

It was ironic that Calhoun's talents should have been revealed in measures of which he himself disapproved. Army reduction, he reminded Congress, would endanger American safety, both domestic and foreign. It would deprive the Department of essential 'concentration of our depots.' So stringently had he cut his own departmental expenses that his entire budget for the year 1820 was $4,500,000, 'a sum less than the expenditure for the Army alone in the year 1817.' Such a striking proof 'of our efficient organization,' Calhoun believed, would 'go far to save the Army.' [46]

But the Army was not to be saved. Ordered to reduce its numbers, Calhoun drew up a plan 'remarkable' in its recognition of the errors of 1812, but so far in advance of its times that Congress, with characteristic fear of new ideas, shelved it for the duration of Calhoun's term of office.

'At the commencement of hostilities,' he wrote, 'there should be nothing to create.' War should be waged on 'the basis of the peace establishment, instead of creating a new army to be added to the old, as at . . . the late war.' Specifically, he suggested the plan, later adopted, of reducing the number of privates in companies rather than the number of companies, a program successfully used in Germany. Thus, in times of crisis companies in charge of trained officers could be speedily recruited up to combat strength. Although the Army was to be reduced to 6,300 men, in an emergency it could be increased to 11,000 without adding an officer or a company; and, by the addition of only 288 officers, to 19,000 men. He knew his view was unpopular, but he would do his 'duty faithfully without regard to unjust clamour.' He had done his part in reducing expenses. His whole estimated departmental budget for the next year, including West Point, would be only $2,570,000.[47]

5

With West Point, Calhoun had better luck, plus the co-operation of an austere, clear-featured disciplinarian, still in his thirties—Sylvanus Thayer, father of the spindling little school on the Hudson. Since that day in 1802 when ten cadets had sat down to their first classes, French and drawing, philosophy and mathematics had been added to the curriculum; but to both Thayer and Calhoun the school seemed too small. They had no fear of too many graduates for the Army to absorb; for in case of war trained civilians would be far more able to grasp Army details than those without military education.[48]

Yet, eager as Calhoun was for newer and richer blood in the officers' corps, it was quality, not quantity, he wanted. Every prospective cadet was given a thorough 'screening' in the form of a personal interview with the Secretary of War. So high were Calhoun's standards that in a single year, out of thirty-five eager Virginians, he appointed only nine, including Robert Edward Lee, the handsome son of the Revolutionary officer, 'Light-Horse Harry' Lee. Joseph E. Johnston was another Virginia appointee, and a slender youth from Mississippi with square cleft chin and set lips, strangely like Calhoun's own, whose name was Jefferson Davis.

Early in 1819, a student's strike broke out at West Point. Calhoun reviewed the findings of the Court of Inquiry, which upheld Thayer's dismissal of a captain with 'insufficient command of his temper,' and expelled the rebelling student committee as 'mutinous.' But tolerance for the mistakes of youth was strong in Calhoun, and deeming 'youth and inexperience' the cause of the uproar, he ordered Thayer to 'restore' the dismissed cadets.[49]

To Calhoun West Point seemed the future's chance to eradicate the errors of the past. He personally read and suggested books for the classrooms. He urged that talent be drawn to the institution by paying professors according to qualifications, rather than by their military rank. He called for new West Points in the South and West, and again and again demanded that the government establish an artillery school of application and practice, a dream which, before leaving office, he had the satisfaction of seeing realized.

6

The amount of work that Calhoun performed as Secretary of War is prodigious. His correspondence is laden with references to the almost continual 'severe pressure'[50] under which he labored; and even more convincing are the gigantic letter-books of this period, in the National Archives, with their thousands of closely written pages. Fortunately, Calhoun had the gift of quick thinking and quick decisions. But all his energies were challenged by the diversity of his tasks, which ranged from the disposal of stands of 'publick arms,' red with the rust of 1812, to the consideration of proper 'presents to Indians' and 'accomodations for travelers using the road through the Choctaw nation.'

Posts on the Missouri. Posts on the Yellowstone. Commissioners for the Choctaws. Regulations for military storekeepers. Courts of Inquiry. Courts-martial. Supplies for Green Bay, for Sandusky, for Prairie du Chien!

He was unyielding with the fraudulent claims of federal contractors, for to Calhoun, born in the shadow of the Revolutionary horrors, no human specimen was lower than the man who defrauded veterans of the small recompense their country could give them. Upon Pension Agent Stephen Cantrell, who had paid the veterans of Tennessee in depreciated notes from the Bank of Nashville, in which he was the principal stockholder, Calhoun scarcely troubled to waste his contempt.[51]

Indian problems added to Calhoun's cares. He pondered them earnestly, then worked out a program of moderation and firmness, of 'justice' and 'humanity,' which sixty-six years later, Carl Schurz would disinter and 'take the credit' for originating it.[52]

He moved swiftly into action, halting liquor sales, stipulating that fur-trading licenses be granted only to men 'of good moral character' to whom 'a single profitable speculation' would not be of more importance than 'the continuance of peace.' Yet he did not view the 'decaying and degenerating' Indian tribes as objects of terror, but 'of commiseration.' Their wants multiplied by crude contact with civilization, and, their own 'rude arts' lost, he was convinced that they must be absorbed into the 'mighty torrent of our civilization . . . our laws and manners.' Specifically, he called for a division of land among families, with compulsory education in farming skills for the men and in cooking, sewing, and home-making for the girls.[53]

Yet, with increased understanding of the Indians, not as theories but as suffering human beings with their own pride and their own heritage, his program broadened. Ultimately he adopted the plan, first dreamed by Jefferson, of uniting all Indian tribes into one great nation beyond the Mississippi, far from the reach of the white man. To Henry Leavenworth he declared that 'force . . . should it be necessary, must be used to prevent the whites from crossing the boundary line.'[54]

Paradoxically, this white Southern owner of black men, this son of an old-style Indian fighter, actually liked Indians. None of the usual Southern confusion on racial questions appeared to trouble him. Personally he treated Indians as 'gentlemen,' with a courtesy and consideration that came as much from understanding as from knowledge. Yet all Washington must have felt that he was carrying diplomatic protocol a little far on the July day in 1824 when he appeared at a formal party with several chiefs, three squaws, and a six-year-old girl, all gaily adorned in stripes of 'festive' red and yellow paint, or, as John Quincy Adams noted, 'all but naked.' [55]

7

The War Department interlude was symbolic of Calhoun's entire career. His lack of skill in practical politics gained him at once personal glory and the defeat of his greatest endeavors. Night after night bending over maps with William Lowndes,[56] his pioneering blood throbbed to the challenge of a new and broadening Union, in which, to him, the hopes of mankind were centered. In a 'masterly state paper . . . filled with the magnitude' of his subject, he defined America as the 'last and only refuge of freedom.'[57] He called for highways and canals to link the nation together. He sent expeditions to explore the Mississippi and the Missouri Basins. His vision captured the popular imagination, but his plan for exploration of the Yellowstone was wrecked in Congress by a coalition of Crawford, Clinton, and Clay supporters.

To Calhoun the magnitude of his tasks was only a spur to his energies. He drove himself mercilessly, working right through the stagnant heat of a Washington summer, often fourteen or fifteen hours a day.[58] His physique could not meet such demands; he was almost continually overwrought and overtired, and a hasty six weeks' visit to South Carolina in the fall of 1819, where the ruins of two successive crop failures were waiting, did little to restore him.

In Rockingham County, North Carolina, on his return in November, 'burning with fever,' he stumbled into a wayside farmhouse, and for ten days hung between life and death. He had contracted a dangerous case of typhus or typhoid, and run-down as he was, it 'raged with extraordinary violence.'

Floride nursed him, but it was not until the twenty-seventh that the press declared that, although, 'very weak and low,' he would probably recover. Washington breathed more easily. On November 30, the *National Intelligencer* reported that he might be able to travel within ten or fifteen days. Three days later, 'very much reduced,' he arrived in the capital.[59]

He was back at his desk in two weeks, but his health continued 'low,' and it was months before he really regained his strength.[60] Floride took him in hand, saw that he ate properly and on time, and had no hesitation in calling him away from conferences with Mr. John Quincy Adams, if that gentleman's unannounced visits interfered with her meal schedule.[61] He cut his working hours down to six or seven a day, but by midsummer was again ill and exhausted. Monroe, who watched his overenergetic Secretary with almost fatherly concern, offered him the use of his own summer home, but Calhoun refused. Travel, he thought, would be of 'more service' to him than anything else, so the President let him combine business with pleasure in excursions to military posts at Niagara Falls, Sackett's Harbor, Pittsburgh, and even Montreal.

Once returned, Calhoun was, of course, unable to resist doing all the work that had accumulated during his absence, and by the winter of 1820–21 was again working under 'uncommonly severe pressure,' without 'one day's relaxation in months.' [62] The tremendous physical strain upon him was, of course, no secret to his intimates; and that he paid for his undue expenditures of energy is indicated in a solicitous letter from Monroe, addressed to the Mineral Springs in Bedford, Pennsylvania, where Calhoun and his family took several weeks' rest during the fall of 1821. 'I am happy to hear that you have in a great measure recovered your health,' wrote the President. 'The use of the Bladensburg water, with the exercise you take in going there, will soon remove all disease.' [63] But Calhoun's private correspondence shows that his general health remained indifferent throughout his entire period as Secretary of War.

8

If Calhoun's days in the War Department were more strenuous than any he had ever known, Floride was in her element. She was only twenty-five, a tiny 'wren-like' girl, still gay, still pretty. Seven years of exile on a country plantation and the birth of three children had left her French vivacity unchanged. Her dark eyes glowing under embroidered turbans, she was hostess at 'select dinners and balls,' when five rooms might be thrown open for dancing. Sometimes forty people, including the entire Cabinet, Army and Navy officers, and Congressmen, would grace the Calhoun's dinner table.[64]

Or the young couple might attend a ball, their perilous way through the Washington streets lit by two rows of bonfires, their carriage wheels rolling like thunder in the night.[65] Floride might wear a dancing frock, the flounced hem gay with artificial roses. She would lead a cotillion with her tall husband, or, close in his arms, glide away in the new and shocking steps of the waltz.[66] And always the faces were the same: the sprinkling of women on the dance floor, or seated on the horsehair sofas, making up in finery what they lacked in numbers. Floride had sometimes attended dinner parties of ten or twelve where she was the only woman present. Nor were there enough men for society to have its cliques; men who tore each other's politics apart on the floor of Congress in the daytime were card partners at night. At the height of their political squabbles, Crawford,

Adams, and Calhoun were seen at evening parties, talking and joking together.[67]

Although Calhoun 'enjoyed the pleasant social life,' mingling 'more than he ever did afterwards,' he was inherently solitary, and far happier on quiet evenings with his children. 'Our little Irishman Patrick grows finely,' he wrote. 'Anna Maria is a great talker, and a source of much amusement to me.' [68] He liked to read, and not only books of politics or history. Like Jefferson's, his Celtic blood succumbed to the fascination of the strange, wild 'Ossianic' poems, suffused in all the melancholy mists of pagan Ireland, and he read of

> 'Moina with the dark-blue eyes . . .
> Her breasts were like foam on the wave,
> And her eyes were like stars of light . . .
> Thou lookest forward in thy beauty from the clouds,
> And laughest at the storm . . .
> Exult then, O sun, in the strength of thy youth!
> Age is dark and unlovely;
> It is like the glimmering light of the moon,
> When it shines through broken clouds,
> And the mist is on the hills.
> The blast of the North is on the plain;
> The traveler shrinks in the midst of his journey.'

He liked vigorous, intellectual discussions with one or two close friends, and for him to attend small-talk parties was a real concession.

The Calhouns were struggling to adapt themselves to each other. Already months and years of living apart had widened the gulf between their personalities. Hospitable Floride would receive visitors 'with the affection . . . of the nearest relative or friend,' load them with jellies and preserves, and put their children to sleep on her own bed; but she knew that a guest like Mrs. Margaret Bayard Smith came primarily to discuss 'men, measures, and facts' with her brilliant husband, and would gracefully withdraw, leaving the pair undisturbed. 'Mr. Calhoun is a profound statesman and elegant scholar,' Mrs. Smith wrote, 'but his manners in . . . private are endearing as well as captivating. . . . While we conversed, Mrs. Calhoun and Julia played on the piano and at chess.' 'You could not fail to love and appreciate . . . her charming qualities: a devoted mother, tender wife, industrious, cheerful, intelligent, with the most perfectly equable temper' was another first-hand comment.[69]

Proof that the Calhouns were 'truly beloved' came during the illness of their five-months-old baby, Elizabeth. Washington society belles thronged the house, offering assistance; Mrs. Smith sat up two nights with the child; the President's daughter acted as nurse, and Monroe himself called every day. From the first, there was little hope, and the baby's death after ten days of suffering came almost as a relief to the exhausted parents. Calhoun, tight-lipped and silent, sought escape in his work the next day, but it was noted that not he, but the faithful William Lowndes, made the arrangements for the baby's funeral.[70] 'Midst all of the anxiety which must occasionally be felt,' Calhoun later wrote of his children, 'how much more happy you are with them, and how disconsolate you would be without them. . . . I feel it quite a misfortune that we cannot bring them up in Carolina among their relatives.' [71]

For Calhoun these were happy years. He had proved his strength beyond even his own satisfaction. He had given the War Department an importance it had not before possessed, and not since the days of Alexander Hamilton had a Cabinet officer of his youth gained such nation-wide admiration. He had his family, a few close friends, an army of devoted followers, particularly among intellectuals and young men, who responded to his sweeping vision of a 'mighty republic . . . once limited by the Alleghany,' now 'ready to push . . . to the western confines of the continent.' [72] But 'long rambles' with John Quincy Adams, dodging the mudholes along Pennsylvania Avenue, were no substitute for horseback rides across a Carolina plantation. 'My passion for farming is not abated,' he wrote. 'I consider my absence from my farm among my greatest sacrifices.' [73] He was eager to return South, but stronger ties were binding him to Washington. He was restless, eager, unsatisfied. Ambition was stirring within him.

X

The Master of Dumbarton Oaks

To FUTURE GENERATIONS the brick house on Georgetown Heights would be known as Dumbarton Oaks. But to Calhoun, who moved there in 1822, the square Federalist mansion on R Street was 'Oakly,' so named for the grove of trees that threw a cooling shade over the fading pink walls in even the hottest weather.

Oakly bore little resemblance to the Dumbarton Oaks which became world famous in 1944, although in Calhoun's words it was 'a splendid establishment' even then. Charleston-born Floride could have found no fault with this stately mansion, its central hallway 'wide enough for a hay wagon to pass,' its great parlors, and the bright, sunny dining room, overlooking the gardens and greenhouse.[1]

For a large family the place was ideal. For Calhoun it would have been enough merely to see his children's health and spirits improving with 'the fresh air and abundant exercise.' But to him, personally, the place meant more than he could say. He had hungered for the Southern countryside with an almost physical pain; a single day on a farm in Pennsylvania, with its rich soil and fields of oats, wheat, and corn, had inspired him to write page after blotted page of ecstatic comment to his cousin, John Ewing.[2]

Oakly was no farm. But in thirty acres of garden and woodland, a man could stretch his legs. Borne down under as heavy a burden of work as he would ever know, Calhoun felt moments of peace in those shell-pink dawns, with the foliage shining emerald green. Once behind the walls of Oakly, Washington, with its turmoils, was shut away. To the rear was the rise and fall of the hills, to the east the old-fashioned flower gardens, and beyond them fruit trees, crouched low against the sloping earth. A 'Lover's Lane' wound along the stone wall at the orchard's border, and here Calhoun and Floride could walk in the twilights. In the fall the pungent scent of grapes lingered on the air, and Calhoun could write his friend, J. G. Swift: 'My wine has started, finally.'[3]

Calhoun did not own the estate. His mother-in-law had bought it for ten thousand dollars in the fall of 1822, against Calhoun's misgivings. 'The price is low, but as she has no need of it, I fear she will in the long run find it dear,'[4] prophesied Calhoun, who as tenant would pay dearly for every moment of enjoyment that his new home gave him.

It was pleasant to live in Georgetown those days, pleasant and expensive. Old brick mansions, set deep in gardens filled with 'majestic trees and flowering plants,' dotted the hills, superbly indifferent to the newly christened 'streets without houses' that twisted below them. During the winter months the houses were filled with planters from eastern Maryland, who with balls, parties, and dinners 'lived luxuriously in fine old English style.' Two miles beyond lay the race-track, and in November even Congress had been known to adjourn 'at an early hour,' to give the legislators sufficient time for the four-mile walk to the turf, their women, 'decorated as if for a ball,' stumbling along beside them.[5]

Calhoun's expenses were staggering. Floride had been 'dangerously ill' from a miscarriage in 1818,[6] and within the next seven years would bear four more children. In addition, as Calhoun told John Ewing, 'My situation exposes me almost incessantly to company, which greatly increases my expenses.'[7]

The Master of Dumbarton Oaks, the Secretary of War, must live in a style befitting his position. For himself he could dress with 'Spartan simplicity,' but Floride must have her ball gowns of 'elegant white velvet,' or 'muslin trimmed with lace over white satin.' She must have feathers for evening wear at nine dollars the pair. She must have her turbans, ranging from eight dollars for 'the most ordinary head-dress,' to as high as fifteen. And as no 'lady of the *ton*' could be seen in the same ensemble twice, she 'must have a new one almost every time she went into company.' She must and did have a coach and four, and, according to the wife of Secretary Crowninshield, such 'horses could not be fed through a Washington winter for less than seven hundred dollars.'[8]

At frequent intervals Adams's *Diary* notes a dinner party at Calhoun's, a banquet for the members of the British Legation or the departmental heads, an evening party or a ball. And the guest lists were long. As early as 1819, over Calhoun's weary remonstrances, for he had neither time nor energy to call on any but his closest friends,[9] Floride resolved to visit every Congressman's wife in Washington. The Calhouns knew everyone, and everyone came to their parties. Onlookers, huddled in the shadows near the gateway, could watch the great and the near-great—Mr. and Mrs. John Quincy Adams, Mr. and Mrs. William Wirt, President and Mrs. James Monroe—stepping down from their carriages and hurrying up the flight of steps to the columned doorway, where Calhoun, his slender figure dark against the candlelight, stood waiting to greet them. But for the curious bystanders, the most unforgettable moment was the night that a tall, surprisingly fragile figure, with 'stiff and wiry' hair and full uniform, Andrew Jackson, the hero of New Orleans, was the honored guest.

Behind all this flash and frivolity ran a purpose, and as the place was

Washington and the protagonist Calhoun, it is not difficult to guess that the purpose was political.

2

On a night in late December, 1821, carriages rolled to a stop before Calhoun's house. From them descended a group of Congressmen, mostly Pennsylvanians, although there were a few South Carolinians included. They lingered a moment in front, talking in hurried whispers, before proceeding to the door.[10]

A Negro butler took their coats and hats, showed them into a chamber where candles were burning. From a pile of books and papers, Calhoun turned and arose in greeting.

Unfortunately, we have no record of what went on behind those doors that evening. All we know is that the spokesman shot forth a question which Calhoun received 'shaken and irresolute.' All Washington was conjecturing the next day as to why the ambitious Mr. Calhoun should have accepted a proffered nomination for the Presidehcy only with 'hesitation.' Calhoun knew. Lowndes was his best friend; it was Lowndes, not Calhoun, whom the South Carolina Legislature had nominated without a dissenting vote a few months before. Calhoun discussed the matter with Lowndes, protesting that he had not sought the honor, and he only hoped that it would not injure their friendship.[11]

Lowndes was not surprised. Had the Charlestonian put forth one-tenth of the energy expended by Calhoun in his pursuit of the Presidential bubble, his challenge might have been formidable. Papers like the Richmond *Enquirer*, torn between support of Crawford and Calhoun, would have had little hesitation about a man praised as embodying the 'moderation of George Washington.'[12] But Lowndes had no energy or ambition left. He was gravely ill, often lying in bed until one or two in the afternoon, when Calhoun would rouse him for dinner;[13] and press reports described him as 'verging to the grave.' He could smile now at the gibe of Charleston aristocrats, still suspicious of 'Pat' Calhoun's son, that 'Mr. Lowndes had most of the State, but Mr. Calhoun had Pendleton District and Mr. Lowndes.'[14] The Charlestonian knew that his 'nomination' was only a courtesy; that actually only 57 of the 110 members of the Legislature had assembled to vote approval of his name. He could assure Calhoun that if his prospects became 'favorable' undoubtedly South Carolina would turn her support toward him. 'I know him and estimate him too well to be mortified by any preference which they may express for him,'[15] he wrote. And to the surprise of all Washington, the two continued their daily walks together.

Calhoun was not really surprised. It had been good politics in the previous summer of 1820 to thrust all thoughts of rest aside for the tour of military fortifications. Everywhere Calhoun had reviewed troops, inspected coastal fortifications, was dined and wined and showered with attentions of the 'most flattering kind.'[16] In New York Harbor hopeful protectionists had almost forcibly held him for hours in a silk mill on Staten Island, but he emerged uncommitted and unruffled, and went on to visit the Navy Yard, to review the artillery, and, standing at attention, to receive the salute of the marching troops.

In Newburyport, where the bitterness of 1812 still lingered, hospitality for the former War Hawk was at a minimum. The Secretary of War had spent the night in a sedate chamber with a spool bed and a sleigh bureau in the whitewashed pre-Revolutionary Wolfe Tavern. On September 15, he had slipped into Boston unannounced for a night of badly needed sleep before the scheduled three days of festivities. With Daniel Webster at his side and the guns of Forts Warren and Independence booming in salute, Calhoun's carriage rolled through the twisting streets, past the mudflats, the cows on the Common, and the crowds that cheered from the windows of the second-story overhangs. That night a party was held at a square-rigged three-story house on Somerset Street, and over glasses of Webster's best Madeira, the lawyers of Boston listened and lingered as Webster drew out his guest. 'Mr. Calhoun talked much and most agreeably,' recorded one of the group, 'and it was evident to all of us that Mr. Webster desired . . . to show him under the most favorable aspect to his friends.' It was no secret among the young lawyers of Boston after that dinner party that 'Mr. Webster wished Mr. Calhoun to be the next President of the United States.'[17] Calhoun returned to Washington in exuberant spirits. The trip, he said, had been 'useful,' but whether to the country or to himself he failed to specify.[18] If the military fortifications of young America had been on exhibition, so, too, had the Secretary of War.

3

There had never been a Presidential election like that battle of 1824. There would never be one like it again. The jockeying for position started as early as 1820. Almost every top-rank statesman who had not already held the office was running now, and the mere list of candidates sounds like a roll-call of American history. John Quincy Adams, Daniel Webster,* Henry Clay, William H. Crawford, William Lowndes, Andrew Jackson, John C. Calhoun.

Leading aspirant in the nation's opinion, as well as his own, was William H. Crawford of Georgia, who felt that he had been defrauded of the nomination in 1816. A fledgling Congressman, Calhoun of South Carolina, had then supported the claims of Secretary of State Monroe, and

* A Massachusetts 'favorite son,' but, as we have seen, actually in favor of Calhoun.

had lashed out bitterly against caucus nominations which stole the 'rightful' power of choice from the people. Now Crawford had the caucus, undivided. He had the machine. He had the politicians. He had the press. Furthermore, he had, so it was said, the support of Thomas Jefferson himself,[19] a legend which continual repetition has written into history. For Crawford, despite his noisy protestations of Jeffersonianism, was actually the standard-bearer of the slaveholding element, as opposed to Jefferson's 'interior democracy.'[20] The sage of Monticello, realizing as early as 1822 that the final race would be between Adams and Crawford, regarding these gentlemen was 'entirely passive.'[21] 'For all of the gentlemen named as subjects of the future election,' he wrote Thomas Ritchie, 'I have the highest esteem.'[22] Equally noncommittal was President Monroe, despite Crawford's fervent claim of support from the entire 'Virginia Dynasty.' Nevertheless, Crawford had claims, support, and hopes, with more than a scant chance of fulfilling them.

Next came Henry Clay. Clay was campaigning in sheer desperation. Just how much his gambling debts had cost him was not a subject of polite conversation—John Quincy Adams put the sum at twenty-five thousand dollars for the winter of 1823 alone.[23] Without a speedy improvement in his finances, he would be obliged to resign the Speaker's chair and retreat to his Kentucky law practice in order to provide for a family which had increased as rapidly as his means had diminished.

Unknown quantity in the race was 'Old Hickory,' the 'People's Friend,' Andrew Jackson of Tennessee. No one really gave him any serious consideration; that is, no one in Washington. After all, as Henry Clay had asked, did 'killing 2,500 Englishmen at New Orleans automatically endow a man with the qualities of statesmanship?'[24] Calhoun had described the hero of New Orleans as 'a disciple of the school of Jefferson,' but from the heights of Monticello, Jefferson himself hastily disclaimed all responsibility for the fighting General.[25]

Strangely enough, 'the ladies' found both charm and grace in this rough-hewn fighter from the wilds. Webster might argue that at heart Massachusetts preferred Calhoun to Jackson; that Calhoun was 'almost a Northern man.' Yet even Webster conceded that Jackson's manners were 'more Presidential than any of the candidates'; he was 'grave, mild, and reserved. . . . My wife,' he regretfully admitted, 'is decidedly for him.'[26]

Calhoun had no fears. He underestimated the General completely; as late as 1822 he was convinced that the final race would be between himself, Adams, and Crawford. Jackson was his friend, his fervent admirer. Andrew Jackson was for *him*. Calhoun had no objection to the General shooting off a few diversionary fireworks in the Southwest. Old Hickory was popular, and this would be of use in winning votes for Calhoun. Jackson had no desire for office. Had he not himself declared: 'Do they think that I am . . . damned fool enough to think myself fit for President? No, Sir.'[27] Undoubtedly Tennessee's favorite son would settle for a term in the Vice-Presidential chair, and the Southwest could catch seats on the Calhoun bandwagon.

Reports that 'clever propaganda was turning Pennsylvania Jackson mad' did not disturb Calhoun; the manufacturers of that state knew that Calhoun was a sound tariff man. But he did not realize that the people had more votes than the manufacturers, and to expect the people to weigh the merits of a sound tariff against twenty-five hundred dead Englishmen, to say nothing of uncounted dead Cherokees, Creeks, Seminoles, and sundry Spaniards, was asking too much of human nature. Calhoun had not won the Battle of New Orleans.

The Jackson boom was not spontaneous, of course. The more spontaneous Presidential booms appear, the more shrewd have been the manipulations behind them. And the man pulling the strings for Jackson was Major William B. Lewis.

Calhoun had his devoted supporters, but it is doubtful if even the most inflamed of them saw their hero as a combination of Alexander, Julius Caesar, and Napoleon Bonaparte, which was Lewis's idea of the General. Lewis was that rarity, a selfless hero-worshiper. He fought for Jackson because he loved him, and once his seven-year mission was accomplished, he packed his bags for home. Furthermore, he had a talent for moving with· such· stealth that the battle was over almost before his antagonists had felt· the attack.

As Jackson's quartermaster in the old Creek War, Lewis's roots struck deep among the soldiers, the moccasined fighters from the frontier. Through them a 'tremendous and irrepressible demand for the hero of New Orleans' began to spring up in state after state. And while Calhoun read 'sheets of extracts of letters from all parts of the country'—even New England—'shewing his rapid increase of popularity . . .'[28] Lewis was burrowing through a muddy political situation, pulling a string here and a wire there, setting off 'spontaneous' Jackson movements across the country.

And there was John Quincy Adams. By precedent Mr. Adams asserted his rights to the office. He was Secretary of State, and for twenty-three years the Secretary of State had automatically stepped straight into the President's house upon locking up his desk at the State Department. Mr. Adams was expectant, and bitterly resentful of anyone who might challenge his expectations.

4

The America of 1822 accepted the news of Calhoun's candidacy with mixed reactions. Newpapers which had been unstinted in their praise of the youthful Congressman 'who carried the war upon his shoulders,' or 'the most brilliant young cabinet officer since Alexander Hamilton,' dodged the question. 'Impolitic and premature' was the verdict of the Winchester, Virginia, *Republican;* he should wait a couple of terms.[29] Even the Richmond *Enquirer* wondered at the 'superior pretensions' which brought Mr. Calhoun 'unexpectedly . . . forward into a race with so many strong men.' [30]

'His age, or rather his youth,' as Judge Story put it, was the chief factor against him. 'Being but a very young man, he may . . . be of use to his country in a subordinate station,' [31] sneered Crawford's Washington *Gazette,* on which Macon commented: 'I do not call his being too young a solid objection when he will be about eight years older in 1825 than our Constitution requires.' [32] The *Gazette,* however, aware that a lie asserted is still fifty per cent effective when denied, pronounced the Presidential hopeful to be thirty, or five years below the constitutional age requirement. The damage was done, although Calhoun's press retorted that the candidate must have been 'elected to Congress at a very early period . . . as it is now nearly twelve years since he first took his seat in the House.' [33]

Most oldsters regarded Calhoun's ambitions with smiling indulgence. 'A smart fellow,' was Gallatin's dismissal, 'one of the first amongst second-rate men, but of lax political principles and a disordinate ambition, not over delicate in the means of satisfying itself.' He was only forty, restless and striving; what would there be for him in later life? William Winston Seaton put the question; Calhoun's answer came with promptitude: 'I would retire and write my memoirs.' [34]

Yet, to the surprise of the country, the South Carolinian's candidacy took hold. True, Thomas Jefferson was silent, although his fellow Virginian, William Wirt, enthusiastically declared that he would turn Calhoun 'loose' in the Old Dominion 'against any man there but Jefferson.' Certainly, where five candidates were grappling for one prize, any man who commanded as many groups as Calhoun did commanded also the attention, if not the votes of the nation.[35]

Primarily, he was the young men's candidate. 'He has been sneeringly called "the young Mr. Calhoun," ' wrote the Boston *Galaxy.* 'This gives him an advantage.' His alone was 'a mind untainted with the prejudices' of this 'turbulent period.' [36] Though a decade had passed since Calhoun and Harry Clay together had sounded the trumpet-call of the 'Second American Revolution,' there was still about him the vigor, the ardent, pulsating nationalism of the days of 1812. Back in South Carolina, local pride overruled objections on tariffs and internal improvements. It was good campaign talk along the mountain fringes of the Carolinas, and even in Crawford's Georgia, that John Calhoun was a back-countryman still; the son of an Indian fighter and soldier of the Revolution, a man who himself had known the feel of a plow in his hands and a rifle against his cheek.

There were the frontiersmen along the borders and the young, hot-blooded, planting South, aristocratic groups even in Virginia, who in ball-rooms and around banquet tables had found Calhoun's manner far more 'easy' and pleasing than Crawford's booming geniality. There were na-tionalists and business leaders who had thrilled to his plans for internal improvements and protection for 'infant industries'; and, above all, there were the officers and men of the United States Army, whose cause the Secretary of War had championed.

They 'went for him' with a gusto that appalled the conservative elders. His campaign biographers, for the benefit of those neither privileged to see nor hear the Presidential hopeful, described Calhoun closely: the 'lean frame,' the 'brilliant . . . penetrating' eyes, the 'striking' face which so 'lighted up' in moments of feeling, seeming to mirror his very thoughts. 'A stranger in a casual interview,' proclaimed the enthusiast, 'would pro-nounce him no ordinary man.' [37]

An efficient corps of newspaper editors 'sounded his praises throughout the Union.' He was hailed as the 'Father of the Army,' and a 'Star in our political firmament.' He was acclaimed for his 'power of analysis,' his keen understanding of America and Americans, as a whole. Writers stressed the 'stability' of his mind; for genius, which the nation had long conceded to John Calhoun, was something to be admired from a distance; but in the mass mind of popular democracy, mediocrity or 'common-sense,' was far more to be trusted. Charges of 'aristocracy' which his flawless courtesy and lavish style of living had brought down upon him were countered with vehement assurances that his manners were 'plain' and 'unassuming,' and that he gave a 'constant impression of kindliness and good will.' [38]

It was too much. Despite his 'undeniable talent for gaining on stran-gers,' he could not see and impress his personality upon every voter in the United States. Actually his popularity was more with the newspapermen than with the people; the very zeal of his followers wearied the public. 'He has made more noise than all the Presidential candidates put to-gether,' protested an anonymous 'Cassius' in the Columbia, South Caro-lina, *Telescope*. 'If we are to believe one half' of what is said, 'his talents greatly transcend the limits we have heretofore ascribed to the human intellect. Compared with him, even Washington and Jefferson are second-ary characters.' [39]

Calhoun's own self-confidence was supreme. It was no bluff; to his campaign managers he proclaimed: 'I am decidedly the strongest of the candidates.' He was unshaken by a warning that 'We must prepare for new opposition.' [40] Was he not, both in New England and the West, 'clearly' the second choice? Even in South Carolina, was he not now 'universally popular?' [41] Why should he doubt himself; had he ever lost a fight in his life? He would win. He had seen 'not a single line to the contrary.' [42]

5

His personality, not his principles, compelled attention. Where he had stood was clear on the records; where he would stand was a mystery even to himself. The country was in transition, and so was he. The task was great—even for Calhoun's intellect—the task of being a nationalist in the North, a states' rights man in the South—and at peace with his own soul. No doubt the very haziness of his views was an asset to a candidate who must be all things to all men. But Calhoun himself derived no enjoyment from cloudy thinking. While he was fighting a forthcoming tariff bill in Congress and begging Monroe to 'modify expressions favourable to the manufacturers,' in his second inaugural, Calhoun's Washington *Republican* was wooing votes from the pro-tariff forces. 'We must bring our workshops from the other side of the Atlantic,' was the *Republican's* declaration, 'and place our manufacturing establishments alongside of our farms.' [43]

States' rights presented a series of question marks. 'When did Mr. Calhoun announce himself a States' rights man?' asked Daniel Webster, years later. 'Nobody knew of his claiming that character until after the election of 1825.' [44] Yet as early as 1823 Calhoun was writing his friend Swift that 'so far from being the friend of consolidation, I consider . . . the rights of the State . . . essential to liberty. The division of power between the local and federal governments . . . is the most . . . beautiful feature in our whole system.' [45] To Virginia's Congressman, Robert Garnett, he added, 'As much as I value freedom . . . do I value State rights.' [46] Only under this system, in the nation or in the world, could small units survive in safety.

Dimly he perceived what in future years would become the cornerstone of his political philosophy—that the balancing and the protection of the varied 'interests' of the country were essential to liberty. But now, with unwarranted optimism, he was convinced that the Northern states alone comprised 'within themselves all of the great interests . . . commerce and Navigation, agriculture and manufacturing. . . . If they act wisely for themselves,' reasoned Calhoun, 'they . . . must act wisely for the union.' [47]

On constitutional construction his views were conclusive. Any 'doubtful portion of the Constitution must be construed by itself in reference to the . . . intent of the framers of the instrument.' He had taken the stand that he would maintain through life, but it is doubtful that the nation, as yet, even suspected his true opinions.

Internal improvements? How, asked doubting Southerners, could Mr.

Calhoun call for roads and canals on the one hand and strict constitutional construction on the other? Mr. Calhoun's answer was guarded. Had not Jefferson, Madison, Monroe all favored appropriations for internal improvements? Had he, personally, ever done more than urge such appropriations? Did this compel any state to accept them? The government should appropriate funds, 'not as a sovereign . . . but as a mere proprietor. . . . I have never yet,' he said carefully, 'committed myself beyond the mere right of making appropriations.' All of his acts, he contended, were 'covered by the acts of Jefferson.' [48]

6

He played politics when he deemed the occasion necessary. He could write Nicholas Biddle, for instance, of his 'deep solicitude in the prosperity of the Bank,' of his pleasure at Mr. Biddle's presidency of that establishment, and he gave his assurances, later deeply regretted, that if he could 'render aid to the institution, it will afford me much pleasure.' Yet to Garnett he admitted that he had always thought the constitutional power through which the National Bank Bill had been passed, 'the least clear of those exercised by Congress.' The 'late war' had brought about an unconstitutional situation, through which, in practice, Congress had lost its power to fix and regulate the value of the currency. The 'great object' of the Bank Bill had been to restore constitutional law. That Congress actually had power to create a National Bank, he would not say; he contended only that the measure had been 'justifiable in the existing circumstances.' [49]

And it was on political grounds alone that Calhoun, indignant at Congressional attacks, determined to defeat John W. Taylor's aspirations for a second term as Speaker. His choice of a successor did little credit to his sincerity, however, since the puritanical John Quincy Adams was horrified one morning to find Calhoun and a friend joking and laughing about the new Speaker, Philip P. Barbour of Virginia, whom they thought 'as ill-chosen . . . as if drawn by lot.' It is probable that Barbour's subsequent appointment to the Supreme Court by President Jackson did not enhance either Calhoun's or Adams's opinion of his qualities.*

To Adams the situation was no laughing matter. 'You have done yourself ill service,' he sneered. Calhoun sobered instantly.

'Mr. Calhoun,' the Massachusetts prosecutor continued, 'you may thank yourself for it all. You, and you alone, made Mr. Barbour Speaker. . . . You have not forgotten how earnestly I entreated you not to prevent the

---

* Oddly enough, John Quincy Adams, as President, appointed Barbour's brother, James, Secretary of War and then Minister to England.

re-election of Taylor, who had offered friendship . . . to the Administration and would have kept his word.'
Calhoun had the grace to admit that he remembered.
'Well, you succeeded in turning him out, and you have got one ten times
worse in his stead.' [50]

7

On the Missouri question, 'the fire-bell in the night,' Jefferson had called
it, Calhoun was entirely 'available,' having taken no stand at all in 1820
or afterward. Crawford had been less cautious, had definitely asserted
that 'If the Union is of more importance to the South than slavery, the
South should immediately take measures for gradual emancipation. . . .
But if . . . slavery is of more vital importance than . . . the Union
. . . she should at once secede. . . .' [51] Legislature after legislature in the
Northern states was passing resolutions, condemning slavery as a crime.
And at Monticello, Thomas Jefferson, still convinced that emancipation
was inevitable, looked with unfeigned terror on the public demand for
boxing slavery up in the Southern states. Only with the evil dispersed,
only with the ever-increasing numbers of blacks not confined to one area
where they would soon outnumber and terrify the whites, would the South
ever attain the security under which she could voluntarily emancipate, so
he thought, without fear of dominance by the black race.

John Randolph of Roanoke, almost alone in his time, saw what the
abortive Compromise meant and warned unflinchingly, if Congress could
exclude slavery in a territory, over the will of its own people, 'how long
will it be, before two thirds of the States will be free? Then you can
change the Constitution and place slavery under the control of Congress
—and under such circumstances, how long will it be permitted to remain
in any state?' [52]

Calhoun, characteristically, had deplored the 'agitation,' as he was to
do all his life. 'I can scarcely conceive of a cause sufficient to divide the
Union,' he said somberly, 'unless a belief arose in the slaveholding states
that it was the interest of the Northern states to conspire gradually against
their property in the slaves, and that disunion is the only means to avert
the evil.' [53]

Over the Monroe Cabinet, the Missouri question had broken with the
roar of a thunderbolt. To Adams the question was moral, the Compromise
'a law to perpetuate slavery.' To Monroe it was constitutional—a question as to whether a law prohibiting slavery in a territory would not hold
over when that territory became a state. Would not that state then be
prevented from entering the Union on equal terms with the other states?

Calhoun supplied the answers. Personally he thought that Congress could regulate slavery in the territories—a thought that he would deeply regret in later life. He agreed that there was 'no express authority in the Constitution'; perhaps, as President Monroe had pointed out, the 'implied powers' clause was sufficient. But the Missouri Compromise was an expedient necessity. Why worry as to whether the Missouri Bill would prevent slavery 'forever' in the area north of 36°30' or 'merely in the Territorial state'? Why not merely declare the Compromise constitutional? Why, even Mr. Adams could vote for that.[54] The 'practical, aspiring' politician had spoken.

Mr. Adams did vote for it. So did the entire Cabinet. Calhoun's neat evasion had furnished a way out, which was seized upon with gratitude. But it had also left the entire Cabinet with a memory of Calhoun's stand, a memory that he would have done much to obliterate from their minds in the years to come.

8

Washington streets were filled with confident partisans of one or another of the Presidential candidates. Many sported silk waistcoats on which the heads of their heroes were printed from wood blocks: Jackson's hair bristling, Clay smiling confidently, Adams looking out in cool disdain, and Calhoun 'with a touch of defiance.' Henry Clay was swaggering about the capital, arguing 'dogmatically about the tariff' at dinner parties, loudly announcing that he had eight states pledged to his cause. Growled Adams: 'He plays brag, as he has done all his life.'[55]

Equally assured was Calhoun. 'We are doing well,' he exulted to Micah Sterling. 'Our friends were never in better spirits.' Proudly he cited his proofs of strength. North Carolina, New Jersey, Pennsylvania—all were certain; Delaware and Maryland almost so.[56] The very abuse poured upon him seemed proof of his 'rapid and . . . real progress' toward a leading national position. 'I trust,' he declared, 'that I have so acted that my defense will be an easy one to my friends.'[57] Of his 'd——d good-natured friends,' who, so the Philadelphia Gazette reported, had 'nauseated the people' with too frequent mention of his name, he had nothing to say.

Adams, fearful of the Carolinian's threats to his own ambitions, delicately suggested the attractions of the ambassadorship to France. He expected more from Mr. Calhoun—he said—'then from any man living for the benefit of the public service of this nation.'[58] Foreign service would widen his horizons, would make him even more useful. But the shrewd Southerner was not thus to be eased out of his prize, and curtly responded that he lacked the money. Monroe, worn to distraction by the fiercely interlocking rivalries, attempted to ease hostilities by hustling Andrew Jackson out of the country. A Mexican mission was the prize held out to the hero of New Orleans, but here again Andrew Jackson had far more interest in the prospects of Andrew Jackson than in diplomatic bickerings.

The campaign of 1824 was the most bitter, most scurrilous in all American history up to that time. Monroe's legendary 'era of good feeling' was drowned in a torrent of filth and invective, in which newspapers took the lead. The press was 'free' in the eighteen-twenties. Any man could start a paper on a maximum of nerve and a minimum of borrowed credit. Any political promoter could skulk behind the editorial 'we,' or seek protection from duels and lawsuits in the comfortable anonymity of 'Cassius' or 'Vox Populi.' [59] Editors could be as 'easily bought and sold' as bolts of cloth. 'We shall give our whole support,' openly announced the Boston *Galaxy*, later a strong Calhoun organ, 'to him who shall pay the most liberally.' [60]

Personal abuse was 'a mere seasoning of dull editorials. . . . Give a dog a bad name and you hang him!' [61] And with five striving, ambitious men locked in a death-struggle, with eager partisans ready to stoop to anything to elect their favorites, fortunes awaited young men with a distaste for scruples and with venom-dipped pens at auction to the highest bidder.[62]

So 'the gentlemen of the press' went to work. They began with Clay's 'loose morals' and Calhoun's 'loose principles.' They charged that John Quincy Adams had been disinherited for his private and public indiscretions; and added that he walked barefooted to church! They sneered at Calhoun as the 'Army candidate,' the 'Prince of Prodigies,' a dangerous, ambitious man whose election would be 'a calamity.' They snarled at Andrew Jackson. He was a drunkard, a bribe-taker, a swindler, an atheist, an adulterer, and a murderer. He was 'a slave speculator,' and 'a conspirator with the notorious Aaron Burr.' He was a professional duelist, who had tried to assassinate Senator Benton, who '. . . in the town of Nashville . . . deliberately shot down Charles Dickinson . . . and then exultingly wrote: "I left the d——d scoundrel weltering in his blood." ' [63]

Of all the party presses, none was more vitriolic than Crawford's. Calhoun was aware of its aims, and told Adams, 'with great bitterness,' that never in our history had there been a man 'who had risen so high of so corrupt a character, or upon so slender a basis of service,' as Crawford. To this outburst Adams was verbally indifferent, but confided to his *Diary* that Crawford and Calhoun were nothing but 'two famished wolves grappling for the carcass of a sheep'; and that the campaign itself was only 'a system of mining and countermining between Crawford and Calhoun to blow up each other, and a continued underhand working of both, jointly against me . . . at this game Crawford is . . . much superior . . . to Calhoun, whose hurried ambition will probably ruin himself and secure the triumph of Crawford.' [64]

Calhoun was the object of Adams's particular disfavor. The treatment the New Englander had received from Calhoun and his friends was bad enough: 'professions of friendship' on one hand, and secret 'acts of hostility' on the other. For Calhoun, 'dispirited' by the harshness of the Congressional attacks upon him, seeking comfort and advice, Adams could feel sympathy. But for the man, avowedly as ambitious as himself, he could feel only suspicion. 'The relations in which I now stand with Calhoun,' he was soon to write, 'are delicate and difficult.' [65]

Calhoun still made a show of seeking his erstwhile friend's advice. And on a hot day in July, 1822, on his way to a dinner party, he picked up the Secretary of State and unfolded something of what was on his mind. Washington, he said, needed an 'independent newspaper.' [66] The *National Intelligencer* spoke only for Clay and the *Gazette* for Crawford. Adams remained noncommittal. In Calhoun's sudden interest in freedom of the press, he saw the forewarning of a new personal organ—this one to advance the interests of Calhoun alone.

By fall the new Washington *Republican* appeared, and none too soon, for through the summer, with Calhoun the only Cabinet officer in town, the *Gazette* had 'kept up a course of the most violent abuse and ribaldry against him.' Even the fastidious Adams, for all his increasing distrust of the South Carolinian, recoiled from columns of 'the foulest abuse upon Calhoun personally.' [67]

Crawford was exultant. Watching Calhoun day by day, aware of his sensitivity and touchy pride, he was convinced that he knew his man. He knew how the Carolinian writhed under censure, both public and private, and thought him too proud, too much 'the gentleman,' to fight back with the weapons that Crawford himself would use.

He had some surprises coming. For Calhoun was born and bred a fighter. He was perfectly capable of taking care of himself, and in their way his weapons were as deadly as Crawford's.

To surface appearances Calhoun's new Washington *Republican* was a 'literary' sort of paper, remarkably free from the medical and lottery advertisements which filled the columns of rival journals. True, it dwelt far more on the defects of Crawford than on the virtues of Calhoun, but it could state—and with justification—that it would 'make good our premises from which we have drawn our conclusions.' [68]

Crawford's politics, not his personality, drew the South Carolinian's fire. Indignantly he denied Crawford's 'assumption of the Jefferson policy,' and proceeded to condemn his rival out of his own mouth. 'Mr. Crawford,' contended the issue of November 13, 1822, 'has furnished a conclusive proof of his hostility to the Navy;—Vide, his speech—1812—in which he asserts that for this country to maintain a Navy is worse than ridiculous.' Where, indeed, was Mr. Crawford during 'the late war?' The Boston *Galaxy* had the answer: 'He took shelter in a foreign mission.' [69]

Still Crawford's tune blared on. The vulgarity of his attacks appalled Adams; they were 'infamously scurrilous and abusive, not only upon Mr. Calhoun but upon his mother-in-law. This,' declared Adams in sardonic amusement, 'is Mr. Crawford's mode of defensive warfare.' [70]

Calhoun answered with columns of statistics, illustrating the waste and inefficiency of the Treasury Department; Crawford countered with columns of filth. The *Republican* replied with 'firmness and moderation,' answering only the more gross of the political accusations. 'As for the personal charges, it stated with dignity, 'we deem them unworthy of notice.'

Adams watched the by-play admiringly. 'If this press is not soon put down,' he told his *Diary*, 'Mr. Crawford has an ordeal to pass through.' [71]

9

Mr. Crawford did have an ordeal to pass through. It is not a pretty story. In fact, the heat it engendered has scorched the pages of history for a hundred years. Partisans of Crawford and Calhoun have defended their heroes with more ardor than accuracy, casting the two alternately in the hero's or the villain's roles. Bowers,* for instance, gives a vivid picture of Crawford as the injured innocent, and Calhoun, the 'scheming, not overly scrupulous politician,' who stooped low for an underhanded revenge. Calhoun's provocation, however, Bowers does not discuss.

Calhoun's biographer, Styron,† reversed the story. Here Crawford is the scheming villain; Calhoun, the injured innocent. Of the vigorous and wholehearted revenge that Calhoun actually enjoyed, Stryon had nothing to say. Had Calhoun been content to suffer in noble silence, he might indeed have been the marble-pure, unearthly figure that Mr. Stryon and Southern legend would have him be.

But Calhoun was a man. He was a proud, passionate, and intensely ambitious man. His pride had been hurt. His anger had been aroused. Had he scorned to strike back, he would have been far more admirable for the history books—and far less human. Ten years in Washington had left their mark upon the Carolinian. Although he never stooped to political corruption, morally his character was at the lowest ebb of his entire career. It was a very different man from the idealistic young farmer of 1812, with his trust and faith in human nature, who now cynically told John Quincy Adams that 'the passion for aggrandizement is the law paramount of man in society.' Crawford had betrayed him, betrayed his aristocratic lack of suspicion of his fellow men. Now Calhoun took his revenge.

* In *Party Battles of the Jackson Period.*
† In *The Cast Iron Man.*

On the nineteenth of April, 1823, there appeared in the *Republican* the first of a series of documents known to history as the 'A.B. papers.' Ostensibly they were written by a young clerk in the War Office. Actually they were written by Ninian Edwards, an Illinois Congressman and Calhoun supporter, who only belatedly denied responsibility for them.[72]

The papers created a sensation. Here were no mere slurs at political misjudgments, at sloppy bookkeeping, or careless votes on significant questions. Here, in plain, unequivocating language, Crawford was charged with gross irregularities and 'misconduct' in his handling of federal funds as Secretary of the Treasury of the United States.[73]

The public was enraged. There were cries for documents to substantiate the charges. A House committee assembled for an investigation. And Edwards, from his sanctuary as a Minister in Mexico City, produced six more charges of fraud against the hapless Crawford.

How much truth there was in the accusations is beside the point; for actually such 'proof' as there was had been before Congress all the time. What mattered was the impression upon public opinion. Calhoun's revenge was complete, indeed.

He might have spared himself the trouble. Already his confidence had cracked under the first crushing defeat of his career. It happened in Pennsylvania, the high-tariff state where his strength had seemed so assured. In March, 1823, the state convention had met. All had been arranged. With united voice Pennsylvania would endorse the Presidential candidacy of the Secretary of War. Then the bandwagon would begin to roll: New York, New Jersey, New England, all climbing aboard.

The Calhoun men had waited. Secretly the Crawford, the Clay, the Adams men had worked. When the vote was counted, there was no endorsement of John C. Calhoun or anyone else. Pennsylvania would wait —and see.

10

Was President Monroe himself favoring Calhoun? Officially, of course, he could take no stand. Yet his personal fondness for the South Carolinian was no secret to those on 'the inside.' Their understanding was complete. One of the few men in a lifetime to whom Calhoun could sign a letter, 'With sincere affection,' was James Monroe.[74]

Jealousy pricked at Crawford. 'Our Mars has intuitive perceptions,' sneered the bitter Georgian, 'upon fortifications and all other military subjects. These intuitions have involved the President in contests. . . . He [Calhoun] has contrived to make them those of the President, instead of his own.' [75] What Crawford did not say was that Monroe, with his genuine regard for Calhoun's knowledge and intellect, saw no reason why he should withdraw his support from a War Department measure, merely because it was under fire from the Crawford rear guard in the House.

Whomever Monroe may have favored, it was not Mr. Crawford. Crawford had been his 'only serious rival' back in 1816, and now Monroe's failure to endorse his second try 'caused him openly to oppose the President.' As early as 1822, both men had all but reached the breaking point, with 'rumors . . . thick' that the President would demand Crawford's resignation. Extant today in Monroe's papers are several undated drafts, charging Crawford with accusing the President of being 'anti-Jeffersonian,' and openly terming the ambitious Georgian 'the curse of the country.' [76]

Equally clear is the evidence that wherever Monroe could justifiably advance the interests of the Secretary of War, he did so. It was, of course, necessary and proper for the President to make official visits along the Atlantic coast, and it was perfectly proper that the Secretary of War should accompany him. So Calhoun went with the President to Charleston and to a Saint Cecilia ball, and it was Calhoun who sat at the side of 'the last of the cocked hats,' as the velvet-lined Presidential barge, manned by sixteen oarsmen in scarlet waistcoats and white trousers, bumped the dock at Philadelphia. [77]

Even as official escort to General Lafayette in his triumphal tour of America, Calhoun stinted no energies.* From Yorktown to 'Williamsburgh,' from Norfolk on to Richmond, the little group proceeded, to the accompaniment of booming cannon, toasts, cheers, and tears. Calhoun was moved beyond his own understanding at moments when the old officers of the Revolution stumped forward in their faded buff and blue, joining hands and memories with their comrade of forty-odd years before.

The élite of Richmond met the War Hawk of 1812, as well as the old hero of the Revolution, at the dinner and ball which climaxed the General's visit. The dinner itself would have meant little to Calhoun. He was not the kind of man to be overtitillated by the spectacle of girls in a dimly lit room, so 'scantily dressed that they might as well have had nothing on but their petticoats,' and his finicking appetite would have rebelled at the 'great saddles of mutton, roast turkies,' and bacon on which the company supped heavily and uncomfortably. But it was an undeniable pleasure to have as partner Eliza Carrington, one of the prettiest and gayest of the Richmond belles, and to know that the approving eyes of the company were fixed upon the old man in buff, the young man in black, and the girl between them. Eliza, too, felt 'the honor of being attended by Mr. Calhoun and the Marquis. . . . I must not forget to tell you,' she wrote her sister, 'that little Lizzy had the honor of a kiss.' Whether bestowed by the grave Frenchman or the grave Carolinian, Miss Lizzy neglected to say. [78]

* Calhoun's immediate Presidential hopes had at this time been exploded, but his long-range goals were unaltered.

11

Just when during those harassed, overtaxed years Calhoun found time to sit for his portraits is one of the mysteries of his career. But Washington had become art-conscious; and one man, one name, dominated the scene in the early eighteen-twenties—Charles Willson Peale. Not the greatest of American painters, even in his own estimation, but a living legend. He had fought through the Revolution, a youthful Colonel on Washington's staff; had 'scrounged' for food and found his men too starved to eat. He lived through the nightmare of Valley Forge, painting miniatures with skeleton-like fingers almost too stiff to hold the brush. But the picture of Washington's sick, half-naked troops, piling themselves into ice-caked barges on the Delaware—'the most hellish scene I have ever beheld'—he once said, he left for others to romanticize.[79]

Peale invaded Washington in 1819, white-haired and handsome at eighty-four, the man who had pitched horseshoes with Washington and written unsolicited advice on agriculture; now commissioned by Monroe to paint official portraits of his entire Cabinet. So between searches for a fourth wife, he eagerly set to work. 'My late portraits,' he wrote Jefferson, 'are much better than those I formerly painted.'[80]

It was then that he painted Calhoun. As a work of art, this portrait, in the 'hot glowing' colors which the artist had learned from his son, Rembrandt, is undeniably attractive.[81] A century and a quarter later, the colors remain fresh and bright; but as 'a likeness' this thin-faced, smiling young man, with a curling bang splatted in the middle of his forehead, bears little resemblance to the Calhoun the world has come to know.*

It was Rembrandt Peale, Charles Willson's son, who portrayed the real Calhoun, who dominated the Monroe Cabinet sessions, who in a single decade had fought and shouldered his way to the forefront among American statesmen. Peale's style bears little resemblance to his father's. Although Charles Willson may have learned color techniques from him, Rembrandt was utterly incapable of applying them himself. His sensitive and interpretative painting of Calhoun in middle life, which the sitter thought the best likeness ever made of him, is little more than a monotone. What Peale sought was the essence beneath the flesh-tones.

With Calhoun, it was the drive, the fire, the energy, both physical and mental, that counted. Peale captured it all, with bold sweeps of the brush —the massive head which later generations would have called leonine, the resolute mouth and shadowed eyes, restless, searching, and eager, even on canvas.

* Original in possession of John C. Calhoun Symonds of Charleston, South Carolina.

But Calhoun baffled Peale, as he would baffle painters to come. He tried again, and the man who looked out from his new pencil sketch might have been another human being from the Calhoun of the oil portrait. Losing none of the strength of the earlier work, the rugged modeling of head and jaw, the picture was an amazing forecast of the Calhoun of twenty years later. The oil painting was all action; the pencil sketch was all thought.

However, John Wesley Jarvis, not Peale, brought to a focus the moods, conflicts, and diversities of Calhoun. History has dealt harshly with Jarvis. 'Generally considered the foremost painter of his time,' he has come down as a sort of 'licensed buffoon,' void of inspiration, and credited only with his skill in 'catching a likeness.'[82] He was no colorist. At best, his work was uneven, and at worst, suffered perceptibly from his careless habits and hasty production. Thirty-six years old, financially and artistically at his height, he was earning a hundred dollars a day for portraits, of which he turned out five and six in a week. Calhoun had no time for the fifteen- or sixteen-hour sittings which artists of the school of Copley demanded. He could drop in at Jarvis's any time, pick his way through a litter of palettes, decanters, broken tumblers, books, easels, women's petticoats, and musical glasses, tip the suds from a shaving mug, accept a refill in any liquid but water, and wait briefly while the artist dashed a few final strokes on the portrait of his fourth or fifth sitter for the day.

Dark, somber, almost stern, Jarvis's Calhoun is a handsome study. In striking contrasts of light and shadow, the artist stressed the Carolinian's clear-cut features, the steady gaze and glow of the eyes, accented by their deep sockets, and the fine-drawn lines beneath. He was so thin that the hollow temples and gaunt contours of jaw and cheekbones were clear beneath his skin; already there was a hint of how he looked when age and illness had had their way with him.

Jarvis was stirred by the complexities of the man before him. And he caught them in the portrait: the strength that all knew, and the gentleness that only Calhoun's family knew. He sensed the tension beneath the calm, the Puritan austerity, underlying the Southern grace. Here was a man in whose personality the conflicts and diversities of the whole South could resolve themselves. Aristocrat and Highlander had fused their differences.

12

Meanwhile, Destiny had taken a hand in the Presidential race—and eliminated a candidate. Early in September, 1823, the jovial and confident Crawford had left the capital for a vacation. A few days later, his massive figure hidden under a sheet from the eyes of curious onlookers, was carried into Senator James Barbour's house in Virginia. It was a living shell of a man that lay there, a creature that breathed and sighed, but saw and heard and spoke nothing. A stroke and an overdose of calomel, so it was said, had wrought the ruin of the strapping Crawford. He was 'paralyzed in every limb.' [83]

Was his mind gone, too? This was the question that tortured his friends through the days of waiting. But in that motionless form a man still lived and ambition still burned. He was a Presidential candidate still, and the first words that he muttered, days later, were to fight on, for he would never give up. So the Crawford press assembled and reported him recovering from severe illness, and his friends got together and worked out ways of making the news stories seem true. Rumors that he was dying aroused his ire; he had himself carried to his carriage, bolstered with pillows, and driven through the streets of Washington. Eventually he even dragged himself around his house and attended Cabinet meetings, led down the corriders like a child.[84]

It was no use. On the night of February 24, 1824, to the jeers of the anti-Crawford Representatives and their friends, a 'last hope' meeting was held. Slowly, by two and threes, the caucus members straggled in. From the jammed gallery came cries of 'Adjourn, adjourn,' and in alarm someone moved to do so. The red hair of a New York boss named Martin Van Buren glowed in the lamplight; he sprang to his feet and forced down the abortive motion. Eventually sixty-six members arrived and hastily went through the form of nominating Crawford for President and Swissborn Albert Gallatin for Vice-President. Sixty-four cast their ballots for Crawford; but significantly, one hundred and fifty-two party members had remained away.[85] More significant still, this was the death-gasp of the caucus system of nominations.

13

The fall of the Crawford banner did nothing to raise the tattered flag of Calhoun. One week earlier his hopes had been dashed as conclusively as those of his rival. Once again it was Pennsylvania which was to work his downfall. Again the state convention was assembling. Delegates were bombarded with instructions, which almost without exception favored Jackson. Lewis had done his work well. But Calhoun counted on Philadelphia, and there he had a powerful campaign manager in the future Vice-President, George M. Dallas. On February 18, 1824, had come a meeting of the city ward leaders. Dallas had taken the floor. His admiration for Mr. Calhoun was well known, he said, but he could not resist the popular will. The cause of the nation was 'at stake.' The cry was for 'a single illustrious individual,' Andrew Jackson of Tennessee! And with a roar the leaders of Philadelphia went on record for 'Old Hickory.' [86]

The Calhoun Presidential campaign was over. For the first time in his forty-two years the South Carolinian had met defeat. The taste was bitter. 'Taking the United States together,' he was convinced, 'we never had a more favorable prospect than the day we lost the state.'[87]

Probably only Floride knew how much his defeat hurt him, but his despondency was not lost upon even his casual friends. Temporarily he withdrew from society to restore his depleted energies, remaining secluded in 'his house on the hills beyond Georgetown. . . . He does not look well,' Margaret Bayard Smith observed, 'and feels very deeply the disappointment of his ambition.'[88] Little sympathy was wasted upon him. Many saw in him the material for a future President; but he was young yet; he could wait. . . .[89]

14

In May, his old friend, Professor Silliman, arrived from Yale. Calhoun received him with 'great cordiality,' and over the dinner table showed that his defeat had not diminished the energy and contagious enthusiasm that had won him so ardent a following. 'He explained . . . his plans for internal improvement,' Silliman recorded, 'which were extensive and detailed, and included not only a ship-canal between Lakes Superior and Huron . . . but even a cut across the neck of Cape Cod, thus uniting Buzzard's Bay with Massachusetts . . . and saving a dangerous navigation around the Cape.'[90]

Calhoun's retirement was brief. He was too keyed to the political tempo of the times. Spring had scarcely warmed into summer before the astute John Quincy Adams had detected Calhoun's 'game now is to unite Jackson's supporters and mine upon him for Vice-President. Look out for breakers.'[91]

Calhoun's interest in the Vice-Presidency, as such, was listless. He cared 'nothing' about it, he claimed, but the fire of ambition within him would smoulder to the end of his days. Nothing was left for him now but tortuous speculations as to whether the star of his political destiny lay with Adams or Jackson. Necessity compelled a compromise. The Vice-Presidency was a mere stepping stone; the future was what counted. The difficulty lay in convincing New Englanders that he was for Adams and Westerners that he favored Jackson. One New Englander upon whom all his efforts were wasted was the canny Adams, who watched his struggles with sardonic amusement. 'Under-hand' was his one-word summary of them.

But if Calhoun, his ambition fiercely whetted by disappointment, had descended to the wiles of the professional politician in pursuit of his stepping stone, he was not alone. Washington *en masse* had descended into an orgy of dodges and deals and double-talk, the mere summary of which would fill a book. Already it was obvious that the election would be thrown into the House, with the winnings going to him who could gather the votes of the one who would be eliminated.

Clay was out—a poor fourth. Crawford straggled in the rear. The race had narrowed down to Adams and Jackson, with Jackson in the lead. Would Jackson coalesce with Crawford? He would 'support the devil' first. A Clay emissary approached the embattled General and retreated with unmilitary haste. Jackson would 'see the earth swallow him up' before he would fraternize with Henry Clay.[92]

The House would decide. And Henry Clay controlled the House.

Jackson had the votes. But his weak link was Congressman Stephen Van Rensselaer of New York. In a delegation virtually halved between Adams and Jackson supporters, old Mr. Van Rensselaer was uncertain. He had never been certain of anything in his life. Now he was senile and completely under the dominance of his wife. Had he read Humboldt's latest book? someone asked.

'I—I—really am not sure.' Turning to his wife: 'Have I ever read Humboldt's work, my dear?'

She frowned angrily. 'Certainly, you know you have read it.' [93]

However, on that snow-swept election day of 1824, Mrs. Van Rensselaer passed her husband no note of instructions. He sat taut, head bowed, visibly sweating. Upon his vote turned that of New York; upon the vote of New York turned the entire election. Thirteen states were needed for a majority, and New York was the thirteenth state. His was the choice; his the responsibility. God help him, what should he do!

There were plenty with answers. Van Buren hovered about his chair. 'Three times in the course of an hour' Van Rensselaer gave 'his word of honor not to vote for Mr. Adams.' Now there were only five minutes left.

Someone saw Henry Clay arise. Smiling and confident, as always, he strolled down the aisle. He paused before Van Rensselaer, bent and whispered a few words into the old man's ear. A moment later, he resumed his seat as the vote-counting started. Van Rensselaer sat slumped, his eyes closed.

It was God with whom Van Rensselaer credited his decision. He prayed for divine aid. Opening his eyes, he saw a discarded ballot within reach on the floor. He picked it up. On it was the name of John Quincy Adams. God had left His answer.

It was all over. Appalled by the magnitude of what he had done, Van Rensselaer staggered up, stumbled out, crying, 'Forgive me.'

'Ask your own conscience, General, not me,' said a disgusted young follower, turning away.[94]

'The people,' said Humphrey Cobb, 'have been tricked out of their choice.'

'Gentlemen,' John Randolph said, 'the cards were stacked!' [95]

15

John Quincy Adams received the news of his election shaking, the sweat pouring down his face. He could scarcely stand or speak, and for a moment it was actually thought that he would decline.[96] The Congressional galleries had broken into hisses at the news. Only the Negroes hurrahed his elevation, and in the Washington slums only the pelting snow prevented a hostile mass demonstration, with the rotund figure of the President-elect strung up in effigy.

To General Van Rensselaer, God may have seemed responsible for the day's outcome, but the cynical citizenry of Washington attributed events to forces something less than divine. Mrs. Smith could scarcely restrain her wrath that evening at the spectacle of Speaker Clay, 'walking about with . . . a smiling face and a fashionable belle on each arm . . . as proud and happy as if he had done a noble action.' Occasionally someone would toss a glance at the shrinking figure of the New Englander, and remark: 'There goes our "Clay President." ' [97]

16

The people had been defrauded of their choice. This was the sentiment of the American press. 'The Warrior, the Hero, the Statesman, and Republican,' declared Crawford's Washington *Gazette*, 'was discarded for the cold-blooded calculator, the heavy diplomatist, the reviler of Jefferson . . . the haughty, unrelenting aristocrat.' Public opinion had spoken.[98]

History has thoroughly discredited the 'bargain and corruption' yarn. Two months before the count, Clay had revealed that he would throw his support to Adams. Under the Constitution the House was unhampered; it had even been thought that in case of a deadlock 'Mr. Calhoun' might 'come in.' Nevertheless, both in popular and electoral votes, Jackson was the winner. Had Clay thrown the election to him and then accepted the State Department, it is doubtful that there would have been anything approaching such widespread criticism.

No 'bargain' had been made, but Calhoun, along with Jackson and many others, believed it had, a fact which throws a more kindly light on his future conduct if not on his intelligence. To a personal friend he wrote bitterly of 'the wicked conspirecy which brought Mr. Adams . . . into power,' [99] and thus convinced, could find justification for the right-about-face which his political instincts warned him would be essential to his future.

From an Adams popularly elected, Calhoun would have had as much to gain as from the elevation of Jackson. But an Adams elected in defiance of popular will would not only have committed political suicide, but would have dragged his whole following down with him. John Calhoun had no desire to have his prospects tainted. Not the 'bargain,' so much as the appearance of the bargain, was what mattered.

So Calhoun served notice. 'If Mr. Clay should be appointed Secretary of State, a determined opposition to the Administration would be organized from the outset; the opposition would use the name of General Jackson.' Delicately he outlined the choice of public officials that would allay popular suspicion: for Secretary of State, Joel Poinsett; Treasury, Langdon Cheves; War, John MacLean; Navy, Southard.[100]

Adams received the messages in the spirit in which they were sent. His diagnosis was accurate: 'It is to bring in General Jackson as the next President under the auspices of Calhoun. To this end the Administration must be rendered unpopular and odious. . . . I am at least forewarned.'[101]

Meanwhile, Calhoun had safely achieved his 'stepping stone.' On March 4, 1825, in the crowded Senate Chamber, Calhoun arose and spoke a few words. He had been 'called to the Vice Presidency,' he said, 'by the voice of my fellow-citizens.' He promised a 'rigid impartiality' in all the questions that would confront him. 'I am without experience,' he concluded, 'and must often throw myself on your indulgence.'[102]

Mr. Vice-President Calhoun

PERHAPS NO AMERICAN ever filled the office of Vice-President with more dignity, poise, and courtesy than John C. Calhoun, but it is certain that no man ever more successfully tortured two Presidential administrations than he. In a letter to J. G. Swift, dated February, 1826, he warned that if he and his friends did not openly support Adams, they would be denounced as in opposition. 'We must pledge support to Mr. Adams's re-election, and recommend all of those principles for which we have ever contended.' [1] Yet almost simultaneously he stated that the Adams Administration, '*because of the way it came to power* . . . must be defeated at all hazards, regardless of its measures.' [2] In such diversity of opinion his opponents could readily scent political malice; actually Calhoun was not interested in the career of John Quincy Adams one way or another, but he was extremely interested in his own. To fulfill his ambitions he must take a middle course, drawing support from both the warring Adams and Jackson forces.

That he was deep in intrigue many suspected. His very presence as presiding officer was proof.[3] Since the days of Aaron Burr, Vice-Presidents had frequently not even come to Washington during the Congressional sessions, much less made themselves the outstanding personalities of the Capitol. Calhoun might protest that he could not accept his pay without fulfilling the duties of his office; but his driving energies were too well known for that explanation to satisfy. It was obvious that he was keeping himself before the country to increase his popularity. A spectacular quality about him attracted the young men who visited Washington, and his careful cultivation of their admiring friendship was commented upon.[4] Here, indeed, was a man sowing the seeds for a political future. To Josiah Quincy there seemed something defiant in the very way Calhoun threw back his thick, dark hair. Quincy quoted what the 'striking-looking man' of forty-four had said to him: 'You will see, from what I have told you, that the interests of the *gentlemen* of the North and South are identical.' [5]

There was nothing remarkable in this statement. From Washington's day on, the Capital city had acknowledged a government of gentlemen—in fact, one of, by, and for gentlemen. Tacitly government was for the people, but the young men who had spoken for the frontier masses in 1812 were representing the classes by 1825. Langdon Cheves, for example, had come far from his back-country days as an apprentice plowboy. Bald and bespectacled, ruddy and plump from enjoyment of both food and liquor, he was serving as president of that 'capitalistic monster,' the Bank of the United States.[6]

Of the fiery young War Hawks, who had trumpeted America into battle fourteen years before, few remained in Congressional service. Clay was at the State Department. Tuberculosis had finally laid brilliant William Lowndes in his grave. But Calhoun, gazing down from the Vice-Presidential platform, could see familiar faces and faces that would become familiar, faces of men who would dominate the nation's history for the next twenty-five years. By 1827, three future Presidents sat before him in the Senate Chamber. Senator Andrew Jackson had gone growling back to Tennessee to sharpen his claws for bigger game; but the military chieftain's place was stolidly filled by the horse-faced William Henry Harrison, hero of Tippecanoe. Tyler, too, sat nearby, poetic, musical, the aristocrat revealed in every line of his slim body. He would be the last of the old Virginia Dynasty to reach the Presidency. No aristocrat, but the most eligible widower in Washington was the 'yellow-haired laddie,' Martin Van Buren, a chunky young Dutchman from upstate New York, whose frank smile contrasted with shrewd, oversuspicious eyes.[7] He had already shown his talents in the management of Crawford's campaign, and though not yet known as 'The Little Magician of Kinderhook,' his bag of tricks was being rapidly replenished for the next venture.

From Missouri came the burly, black-haired Thomas Hart Benton, gazing pompously over piles of books and papers heaped upon his desk. He and Calhoun were now on good terms, but the utter dissimilarity of their minds and temperaments would have prevented real intimacy, even had politics not thrown them into opposite camps. Calhoun worked from within; Benton, from without. Calhoun reasoned; Benton read. In later days, when the two men were privately terming each other 'humbugs,' Calhoun once remarked, with a personal bitterness rare in him, that Benton would have made a fortune as a writer of quack medicine advertisements.[8] In a later century, he would have been the ideal 'expert' on a quiz program. He made up for his lack of originality by packing his mind with thousands of facts, which he poured forth upon men of far greater mental power.[9] In later years, if Calhoun, always indifferent to minor details, forgot a name or a date, Benton would dispatch a page for some obscure volume in the Congressional Library, open it to the exact chapter and page, copy out the information and send it to the erring Senator with his compliments. From such triumphs he achieved a disproportionate satisfaction. He was overbearing, bombastic, sometimes tedious and dull, yet with magnificent qualities of loyalty and friendship which his ex-dueling opponent, Andrew Jackson, would one day appreciate. Benton's learning had given him a solid grasp of the great financial issues of the day, and in his appreciation of the vast and broadening Union, his vision was not even exceeded by Calhoun's. For all his faults, he had sufficient elements of true greatness to attain a place in history just below Calhoun, Webster, and Clay.

Calhoun himself had helped South Carolina send the boyish-looking Robert Young Hayne to Congress. Only Henry Clay was more dashing than this tall, fair-haired man, with his petulant mouth and laughing gray eyes. There was strength as well as impetuosity in Hayne; but not yet had the lightning passed between him and the swarthy, dreaming New Englander who sat nearby, so lost in his thoughts that someone had to poke him before he could rouse himself to answer to his name on a roll-call.[10]

Daniel Webster, his voice like an organ, his face glowing like a 'bronze statue,' and his eyes deep-set beneath a majestic domed forehead, already deserved the description of 'god-like.' [11] Not yet was he in 'the full maturity of his wonderful powers,' but his vivid imagination was already at work, skillfully identifying the interests of the Northern industrialists with patriotism and liberty. His eloquence was a refreshing tonic to the Vice-President, who spent hours of boredom listening to slow-moving debates which he could easily have turned into action had he been on the floor.[12] For Webster, Calhoun felt keen professional admiration, and once congratulated a friend upon hearing the Massachusetts man 'in one of his grandest moods.' [13]

Yet not even Webster 'attracted the most attention.' A jingle of silver spurs on the floor, the padded footsteps of a slinking hound—and the galleries began to fill.[14] The spectral figure of Calhoun's old adversary of 1812, John Randolph of Roanoke, most fantastic personality in a fantastic era, was striding down the aisle, whip in hand. He had been rapidly 'dying, sir, dying,' for the last fifteen years, but he was still far more alive than his enemies could have wished. Drink, drugs, and disease had had their way with him, however, and a friend described him as 'more like a disembodied spirit than a man adequately clothed in flesh and blood.' [15] His costume was striking: he varied from blue riding coat and buckskin breeches to 'a full suit of heavy, drab-colored English broadcloth, the high rolling collar . . . almost concealing his head,' and the skirts swinging about the white leather tops of his boots. Sometimes he wore a red hunting shirt, or an overcoat which dragged behind him along the carpet, and once he wore six or seven overcoats, which he peeled off, one by one, upon arrival, tossing them in a heap on the floor.[16] This demonstration gave birth to a newspaper story that he was in the habit of dressing and undressing himself on the floor of the Senate.

That he was intoxicated by his own rhetoric is beyond doubt. He might start one of his harangues at four in the afternoon and continue unabated until ten, the Chamber gradually emptying as hunger drew off the Senators. Calhoun alone retained his seat, seldom even changing his position.[17] Meanwhile, Randolph leaped from subject to subject, and in thirty minutes might discuss the superiority of the Church of England to the Episcopal Church of America, the 'revolting racial issue' in *Othello,* the military mistakes of William the Conqueror, the 'adulterous intercourse between the Dowager Princess of Wales and the Earl of Bute,' and a song on the men of Kent, which he said he would have given five thousand pounds to have written.

Viewed from a distance, erect, black-haired, 'a strange fire in his swarthy face,' he still gave his fantastic illusion of youth. His flashing eyes, long, quivering forefinger, and silvery voice, 'fine as the treble of a violin,' had lost none of their witchery, none of their power.[18] Calhoun himself was not immune, characterizing him as 'a man of remarkable genius,' with 'wisdom worthy of a Baker and wit that would not discredit a Sheridan.'[19] But the two men were never intimate. Indeed, in one of his outbursts Randolph addressed Calhoun as 'Mr. Vice-President, and would-be Mr. President of the United States, which God in his infinite mercy prevent.' Calhoun remained utterly impassive and abstracted, 'without once noticing the indecorum to himself or others.'[20] The Vice-President 'actually made love to me,' Randolph once chortled, after a ride home in Calhoun's coach. And despite his long suspicion of the Vice-President's early nationalism, even Randolph finally conceded that he was 'a strong man . . . armed in mail.'[21]

They had sufficient mutual regard to join the same 'mess' for at least one Congressional session, giving Calhoun ample opportunity to study the Virginian's peculiarities. Randolph's tortured, sleepless nights, when he would walk up and down the hallways rapping at doors and submitting any man who happened to be awake to a night-long visit,[22] could not have been unknown to Calhoun, who attributed this nervous excitability to physical causes, and years afterward declared that he had never suspected insanity in Randolph 'by word or act.'[23]

2

This view was particularly annoying to President John Quincy Adams, who sat powerless in the White House, fuming under Randolph's tongue-lashings. Not only had Calhoun declined to call Randolph to order in the Senate; he had exhibited 'the most perfect indifference to whatever was said, good, bad, or indifferent.' His failure to appoint Administration men to committees had been so marked that Randolph himself pushed through a motion, stripping the Vice-President of his appointing power by a vote of 40 to 2; and of his supervision over the Senate journal, 37 to 7![24] (In Calhoun's defense, however, even the President had to admit that the majority of Senate talent was on the opposition side.) But worst of all, with Adam's popularity dropping more rapidly each day, his Vice-President appeared to have found refuge on the bandwagon of Andrew Jackson!

Adams's patience snapped. He took his case to the newspapers, and through the spring and summer of 1826 the public was treated to the spectacle of the President and the Vice-President of the United States, under the pseudonyms of 'Patrick Henry' and 'Onslow,' hurling charges of 'despotism' and 'anarchy' at each other. Though each man took ostensibly high ground, Calhoun saw through the attack immediately, and commented that whether its purpose was to 'arrive at truth . . . or political or personal hostility, the American people must judge.'[25]

The debate lasted for weeks, full of sound and fury and signifying very little. It gave Calhoun an opportunity to deal in logical abstractions, and he did so with a zest that boded little good for the object of his attack. He quickly thrust aside Adams's contention that 'to preside' implied the power to call to order, and turned the debate into a discussion of inherent and delegated powers. House rules specifically granted such power to the presiding officer, but Senate regulations reserved the authority to the members themselves. All the Vice-President could do was to order questionable words 'taken down.' 'I trust that it will never be the ambition of him who occupys this chair to enlarge its powers,'[26] said Calhoun, who gracefully accepted the very powers in question a year later by vote of the Senate.

He strove to put his theories into practice. It is true that at least once he broke his own rule by ordering an overtalkative Senator to take his seat, and when disobeyed wrathfully broke 'a harmless seal frame which stood near him.' It is true that he allowed Randolph to speak in a 'strain of calumny and abuse,' which culminated in nothing less than the notorious Clay-Randolph duel. But as if warned by this incident, Calhoun watched the irascible Virginian thereafter, and once ordered him to take his seat, 'until the Chair decides. . . . The Chair directs the Senator from Alabama to reduce the words to writing.'

'Abruptly,' King of Alabama retorted that he 'would not.' Calhoun, 'pale with agitation,' rose, struck his hand against the desk and shouted: 'The Chair orders the Senator from Alabama to reduce the words to writing.' Both he and Randolph were 'intensely excited,' according to Martin Van Buren,[27] but King was stubborn and unmoved.

Saucily Randolph chortled: 'I shall take the liberty of speaking disrespectfully of Nero . . . and the rest of the host of worthies . . . when I see fit.' All Calhoun could do was to arise and express 'his deep regret that any occurence had taken place . . . calculated to destroy harmony.' He could only follow the rules as written, but 'would ever show firmness in exercising those powers that were vested in the chair.'[28]

3

Even outside the presiding officer's seat, Calhoun had no time for relaxation. At home his rapidly increasing family was harassed with childhood epidemics and accidents. Too bogged down by domestic disasters to take a summer vacation trip south, Calhoun wrote his mother-in-law details of the children's symptoms, concluding: 'Patrick when he got hurt wished for wings that he might fly to you to nurse him.' [29]

On the political front Calhoun was more and more finding himself 'an object of bitter party attacks.' In the winter of 1827 the storm broke. 'A deep laid conspericy to destroy for ever my reputation . . . burst on me,' he wrote. 'An artful charge of participating in the profits of the Mix's contract [while Secretary of War] was got up, and published. . . . I . . . saw the assassin aim and determined to repel it . . . by an appeal to the House, . . . demanding an investigation. It was granted, but the chair, forgetting the first principles of justice, constituted the Committee . . . of hostile materials. They have been about everything except that for which the Committee was created, but . . . they will prove my best friends, for it will be seen, that in whatever condition I found the Department . . . I left it in . . . perfect condition.'[30]

With the confidence of a clear conscience, he bore his 'inquisition' for forty days, emerging with an acquittal so complete that never again, throughout his whole career, was his personal character questioned. The seriousness with which Calhoun took this affair, refusing to preside over the Senate until cleared of the charges, struck the political journals as ridiculous. *Niles' Register* conceded that Calhoun was utterly 'incapable of any such participation,' and chided the Vice-President for submitting to his feelings. If every government official attacked in the press were to exhibit such personal touchiness the House would have nothing more to do but to track down foolish and unbelievable charges.[31]

Calhoun was learning fast in his new position. He was entangled in a maze of politics, of plots and counter-plots, of stolen letters—and always in the background was Crawford; Crawford trying to break both Calhoun's and Monroe's friendship with Andrew Jackson.[32] Only too well did the Carolinian know now that ambition and popularity must be paid for in happiness and peace of mind. Yet even had he been freed from routine political irritations, Calhoun would never really know relaxation and calm again. For during those hours on the Vice-Presidential platform, one of the tremendous mental revolutions, which are the most dramatic experiences life can offer to the man of thought, had been taking place in his brain. In a final flash of realization, clear as the shafts of sunlight from the skylight dome falling across his face, he saw at last that the broadening Union which he loved carried within itself the seeds of another slave system, a system which would chain the agricultural sections of the country in colonial dependency on the industrial North. The battle lines of his future were being drawn.

4

The man, the force that drove Calhoun into his realizations was none other than John Randolph. For with all his vagaries, the Virginian was a realist. As early as 1816, he had seen through the 'tariff humbug,' long before bitter experience had brought a similar comprehension to Calhoun. All the throbbing, storm-tossed issues that were to torment the South and the nation for the next thirty years were passing before Randolph's tortured vision. He knew that the North was coming 'to believe that to prefer industry to agriculture was to be "progressive,"' and that 'the South . . . had accepted the Union on the assumption that the power of government would remain in the hands of the landed classes, who alone have that understanding of tradition, without which no society can be healthy.'[33] Ten years before, his warnings had struck deaf ears, but his powers of prophecy were still unimpaired.

State Rights? Divided Sovereignty? Disunion? 'This government is the breath of the nostrils of the States. . . . To ask a State to surrender part of her sovereignty is like asking a lady to surrender part of her chastity.' We could have disunion in a moment. The voters 'have only to refuse to send members' to Congress, 'and the thing is done.'

Randolph was a humanitarian slaveholder. 'The greatest orator I ever heard was a woman,' he once said. 'She was a slave. She was a mother, and her rostrum was the auction block.'[34] Yet he hurled warnings at those who would tamper with the system. 'We must concern ourselves with what is, and slavery exists . . . it . . . is to us a question of life and death . . . a necessity imposed on the South, not a Utopia of our seeking.'

'We are the eel that is being flayed!' he shouted. 'We of the South are united from the Ohio to Florida, and we can always unite, but you of the North are beginning to divide. We have conquered you once, and we will conquer you again.'

Calhoun listened. Randolph's lurid words were tearing him out of the confidence and certainty of his early public life. His career had perhaps been too much of a triumph for so young a man. Now he was facing defeat, not alone of his personal ambitions, but of all that he held dear. With Randolph, he was among the first American leaders to understand the changing conditions that were swooping down upon the country. 'He was thus, in a critical moment, called on to make . . . a decision which was to shape his destiny, and perhaps the destiny of a whole people.'[35] He had the choice of trimming his sails to catch the popular wind or of resisting the storm. He could become a politician or a statesman. Although political intrigue had played and would continue to play an important role in his life, fundamentally his decision was made on the last day of February, 1827.

His choice was a difficult one, with his record as an avowed high-tariff man. When the wool tariff hung on his deciding vote, his friends begged him to stay away from the chair. By evading the issue, as General Jackson was so adroitly doing, his strength in Pennsylvania would remain unimpaired. But by such evasion the bill would pass, dealing a crushing blow to Southern agriculture. Calhoun did not flinch. He cast his vote against the measure.

In the North, Calhoun's popularity began to collapse. In the South, it rose. But the assertion of his devoted Carolina supporters, that 'neither ancient nor modern annals furnish a nobler example of heroic sacrifice,' and that he had surrendered 'every prospect of the Presidency,'[36] is a masterpiece of exaggeration. Calhoun knew perfectly well that whether or not he supported the tariff, he would not be the next President. However the game was played, the one man in America with the winning hand was Andrew Jackson. And this time Calhoun saw wisdom early, and again postponing his long-range ambitions, accepted 'second place' on the Jacksonian ticket for 1828.

But he could never be President without the support of the South. He was fighting a majority trend, but there was plenty of vitality on the minority side. Since 1824, when Congress had clamped duties on hemp, cotton bagging, and cheap wool for slave clothing, Washington had needed no John Randolph to explain the meaning of the thousands of petitions, memorials, and resolutions in denunciation of high tariffs which came flooding in from the South. For Calhoun the pathway was clear. The tariff of 1816 had taught him his lesson. His consistency in regard to tariffs was open to question, but his fundamental loyalties were unchanged. He was a South Carolinian. Throughout his career he was willing to support measures advantageous to other sections, so long as they did not harm his own state. The tariff of 1816 had not hurt South Carolina. The tariff of 1824 not only hurt South Carolina, but the whole South as well. The times had warranted his stand, and he was consistent according to his own definition. Inconsistency, he once held, was a change of position when there is no change of circumstances to warrant it.[37]

He had gone through a change far greater than his stand on the tariff. His whole concept of government had been torn apart; he saw that in his triumphant self-confidence of 1812, when the shipping interests of New England had been ruthlessly sacrificed to the need for home industries, he had made a grim mistake: that by 'setting up the principle of majority rule, he had armed another section with the power to destroy his own.'[38]

Yet he deplored sectionalism. He would not ask for benefits *exclusively* for his state, or for his section. Laws for the general welfare did not include the enrichment of any part of the country at the expense of another. Yet forced into sectional rivalry by the tightening unification of the industrial North and East, the Southern agriculturalists already knew that their very existence depended upon an alliance with the West. Westerners, on the other hand, had found that their cheap whiskey could steal the New England rum market and had demanded a protective tariff against imports of West Indian molasses. In as simple a move as that had the West become momentarily allied to the East in demanding 'protection.' Conversely, if fifty-one per cent of the country had been supporting the South, and for special economic benefits two per cent had shifted to the North, did that transfer of self-interest endow the majority with divinity? Were the majority and the general welfare synonymous? In the name of good sportsmanship were the entire Southern people to submit to economic conditions which might destroy their livelihood, their capacity to develop to the ends for which Nature had intended them? What dignity existed in this use of government? What moral obligation compelled one great group to submit to another? Was the will of the majority the voice of God?

Calhoun denied it. There was a loftiness in the problems that he now faced, for they dealt with the basic question of loyalty in a government: the source of the obligation to obey. As early as 1820, these questions had tugged at his consciousness, but only now did he have time to study and reflect upon them. His evolution had been slow during years when he was gathering a variety of impressions and experiences. Now he had reached his decision. In defiance of popular sentiment, he denied the validity of a basic and accepted principle of so-called 'free government' in modern times. Triumphant in the twentieth century, it was generally recognized in the nineteenth, 'that the majority ought to be the ruling power.' [39]

As yet Calhoun's opposition was abstract. He had found no solution. But he recognized the great defect of unchecked majority rule in the American system. And he knew that if there was an 'American way,' if there was something inherent in free America, unknown to other nations, it would be a common loyalty, a reciprocal justice, a give-and-take, between its varied economic groups; not the tyranny of the seven million over the six million, but a government of the entire people. The Constitution, so Calhoun believed, had been devised to create such a government of justice, of mutual concession. It was not being so interpreted. But there was more than one possible interpretation.

Calhoun groped for a solution. Though he had advised William Wirt to 'study less' and trust more to original genius,[40] he himself was studying now. He was reading the debates of the Constitutional Convention, learning that the fundamental theory of our government was not based on majority rule, but on checks and balances. He was reading the Virginia and

Kentucky Resolutions. He was spending hours in thought, self-questioning, and reflection. He had learned to divide the powers of his intellect, so that he could lose himself in concentration yet remain aware of matters on the floor. Wrapped in such self-absorption, he could sit ten or twelve hours at a time, without food, without rest, and without leaving the chair, 'motionless as a figure of marble.' Already he looked pale and attenuated, 'as if in bad health,' [41] but as a presiding officer his patience was almost inexhaustible. Only once during a long and arduous session had he betrayed his nervous strain with an outbreak of temper.

5

He had little reason for peace of mind. Day by day he lived under a steadily mounting weight of foreboding, climaxed during the summer of 1827, when a general convention of manufacturers met in Harrisburg, Pennsylvania, to unite all friends of the tariff interest on a program for 1828. Calhoun watched in grim silence. He was still uncertain as to whether Congress had power to encourage 'domestick manufactures,' but he had at this time no uncertainty as to the 'dangerous example of seperate representation, and association of great Geographical interests to promote their prosperity at the expense of other interests, unrepresented, and fixed in another section, which . . . is calculated to . . . make two of one nation. How far the administration is involved in this profligate scheme, time will determine; but if they be, the curse of posterity will be on their head.' [42]

Calhoun could only wait now—wait and look on, as the dickering and horse-trading of the 'boisterous' session of 1828 roared to a close. The protectionists had control of the House. Their bill, as passed, laid duties 'even higher and more indiscriminately than those of the Harrisburg plan.' [43] But the battle was not won without a fight, and the cloying heat of May was closing over Washington before the bill reached the Senate floor.

Here events halted, as the New England Senators revised provisions to suit their commercial and navigation needs. Even so, the outcome looked close—so close that once again Administration leaders prepared a scheme to destroy Calhoun's—and, incidentally, Andrew Jackson's—Presidential hopes. A second tie—so it was rumored—was being arranged for the specific purpose of putting Old Hickory's running mate on record in opposition to the whole tariff program.

Even Calhoun's opponents marveled at his courage. Again he did not shrink from the choice. He would not embarrass General Jackson's prospects for election. He would vote against the bill—so the word was passed through the ranks of the Administration—and instantly withdraw his name 'from the ticket as Vice-President.' The tie was not arranged.[44]

Calhoun was beyond all thought of self now. The actual passage of the so-called 'Tariff of Abominations,' long as he had expected it, shook him to his depths. A friend watched him pacing the floor that night, hour after hour, in a restless frenzy, running his long fingers through his hair until it stood erect all over his head. His first horrified look into the abyss had been too clear; in a glance he had seen impending civil war or the dissolution of the Union, and to a man of his patriotism, these alternatives were equally horrible.

'It was worse than folly,' he said, 'it was madness, itself. With the public debt paid off, the Government could have cut duties in half and still have had ample funds.' Instead, duties were increased, 'on an average nearly fifty per cent,' at the sacrifice of the planters, the farmers, the shipbuilders —all to 'promote the prosperity of a single interest.' [45]

Many historians have contended that slavery was the actual cause of the great cleavage between North and South, climaxed in the bloodshed of the Civil War. Others, such as Christopher Hollis and Woodrow Wilson, have agreed with Calhoun that the tariff issue was basic, 'the great central issue around which all the others revolved'; [46] others still, as the conflict between agrarianism and industrialism, between the cotton capitalism of the South and the finance capitalism of the North.

This is a question of the utmost importance. It could be debated endlessly. Few today would deny that slavery is and was always a great moral wrong. Yet as an institution in the eighteen-twenties, it cannot be judged from the vantage-point of the twentieth century. Many morally upright Southerners—like Calhoun himself—could not see the moral evil of slavery. It is true that at this period there were numerous abolition and emancipation societies in the Southern states; [47] whereas, in the New England of Calhoun's young manhood, slavery had been tolerated, if not condoned.[48] Both North and South, recognition of its evils was now growing; yet as a moral issue it was then, perhaps, in the category of the civil rights problem of today.

It was as an economic question that slavery counted. For, as we shall later see, a cotton-slave economy was depleting the Southern soil and would lead to the outcry for new slave territory and the whole expansionist movement. Farsighted as Calhoun was, it is doubtful that he ever realized this issue in its entirety. Himself a fervid soil-conservationist, he was blind to the drain of the cotton economy on the Southern soil—blaming Southern depression entirely on the encroachments of the Northern rival economy.* Yet if uncertain of the cause, he was aware of the result, and would become foremost among those who demanded new territories

---

* Oddly enough, Western diversified farming, economically and politically, was able to withstand the 'encroachments' of Northern industry, throughout the entire ante-bellum period.

and union of the agrarian South and West as essential to Southern planting prosperity.

From Calhoun's excitement over the tariff question, we can see that
slavery was not now foremost in his mind. What he did see—with his uncanny grasp of fundamentals—was 'the great and vital point' as 'the
industry of the country—which comprehends almost every interest.' [49]
Slavery, the tariff, banking—all were aspects of this one point. The issues
did not make the division; the basic 'geographic dissimilarity' between
North and South created the issues. In almost every aspect of their 'industries,' the expanding North and the retreating South were at odds.

Already Calhoun saw that the South was fated to become a minority in
the nation. And for him the minority question was basic. The Union, as he
interpreted it, was devised for the protection of minorities; majorities
could look after themselves. And the South, an economic minority within
the Union, was being reduced to financial subservience by a hostile voting
majority.

That Calhoun's political theory was designed to cover the peculiar needs
of the slaveholders is undeniable. That slavery was one of the reasons why
his theory was developed is possible. Yet the gist of his doctrine—whatever may have been its conscious or unconscious origins—the protection of
minority rights within the Union transcended the immediate issues of his
own time, however vital they may have been.

Whatever question or combination of questions led Calhoun to focus
his interest on minorities at this period, the tariff was undoubtedly the
immediate cause. Symbolically, at least, its importance can hardly be overestimated. For at this moment the tariff was charged with all the emotions
arising from the beginnings of a fundamental cleavage between North and
South. Economically its importance is less easy to ascertain. Yet it was 'an
oppression to the South' long before the slavery issue became paramount,
and it remained an oppression 'long after slavery was abolished.' [50]

The fight would not be easily determined. Calhoun warned: 'I do not
belong to the school which holds that aggression is to be met by concession. . . . Encroachments must be met at the beginning and . . . those
who act on the opposite principles are prepared to become slaves.' [51]

XII

A Unionist Comes Home

IF ANY AMERICAN had wanted to lay his finger on the pulse of Southern public opinion between 1825 and 1850, he would have found no better place for the purpose than Pendleton, South Carolina. To the casual observer Pendleton might have seemed little more than a sun-baked crossroads village, where raw-boned farmers from the hill-country lounged in front of Tom Cherry's inn and watched the indifferent passage of time.[1] Certain town documents, however, told a different story. The names on the lending library list, the church records, and even the minutes of the Farmers' Society [2] would have been strangely familiar and strangely misplaced. They were Gaillard, Ravenel, Hunt, and Colhoun. They were Prioleau and Pinckney. They were, in short, Charleston.

Pendleton, set deep in the rolling red hills of the up-country, had a summer climate. Not that it was cool, but in the language of the natives, it was 'healthy.' To Charlestonians, some of whom had buried ten children in the periodic ravages of yellow fever and cholera, Pendleton had appeal both for health and agriculture. During the eighteen-twenties, mansion after mansion arose in columned splendor along the banks of the Seneca. Fresh-painted columns gleamed through hedges of bamboo and wild orange; red hills were turning white with cotton.

Here, too, had come the Charleston civilization: the wrought-iron work of William Gaillard, the workshops of cabinet- and carriage-makers, printing presses for the Pendleton *Messenger* and the magazine, *The Farmer and the Planter*. Little girls were subjected to Yankee schoolmarms, French verbs, 'elegant' table manners, and ramrod posture. Little boys from the Military Academy paraded about the Town Square in a glory of gray uniforms and brass buttons. At the inn, Tom Cherry frowned as he urged his Negroes to polish harder and faster until the waxed floor of his ballroom gleamed like new-washed glass in the sun. He had the Eagle Hotel to give him competition now.

Knee-deep in the lush green fields around the village, fat Jersey and Devon cattle placidly chewed their cuds. Blooded horses whinnied and tossed their manes, 'the finest horses in the country,' according to those who owned and bet on them.[3] Beyond the village lay the fairgrounds and,

XII A UNIONIST COMES HOME 173

most important of all, a race-track. Yes, Pendleton had come far in twenty years; from a frontier village it had become the acknowledged center of business, government, and culture for the entire Carolina up-country.

Calhoun knew the locality. He had frequently come up into the hills for hunting and fishing, and to visit his brothers-in-law, John and James Colhoun. By 1826, he had decided that it was time to establish his own home in South Carolina.[4]

As with the Charlestonians, considerations of health influenced his decision. 'The soil is indifferent, but the climate fine,' he told a friend. His baby son, John, had almost died of 'lung fever' during the last winter in Washington and only recovered when brought down into the Carolina foothills.[5] But finances played their part: a lowered income from his farm property, his small salary as Vice-President, and a family of growing children to educate, all added to his burdens. Then, too, his political fences stood badly in need of repair; he had been away from home too long. Favorite though he was in the country as a whole, had he required merely the vote of his native state, it is doubtful whether at this time he could have been elected to office. His long silence during years when the tariff controversy was mounting to fever heat had given local politicians, with whom he was never overpopular, ample opportunity to find him guilty of 'playing politics.'

He was not wholly playing politics in returning to South Carolina, however. 'There were two or three Calhouns, perhaps more,'[6] a friend once wrote. One, driven by ambition, eager to shape his political theories into realities, chose a life of turmoil in the glare of national publicity. The other, home-loving, studious, and retiring, yearned for the slow tempo and richness of daily living to be found in the planter's existence. The two Calhouns had fused their differences in the man who returned to South Carolina in 1826. Personal inclinations had drawn him back, but ambition told him that such a course was a necessity to his political future.

Calhoun had come home. With the one exception of the winter of 1836–37, when his daughter, Anna Maria, was with him, Calhoun never really made a home in Washington again. He returned to the 'messes'; he had no surplus funds with which to maintain two establishments, and was separated 'almost continually' from the wife and children to whom he was so devoted. Yet he was happy; he had 'struck roots' in his native state, where all his true interests were centered. Here he attended church, educated his children, bought his groceries, and got his mail. Here he kept open house for his own and his wife's clans, shared peach cobbler and fried chicken at the homes of his neighbors.

The name of Calhoun gave Pendleton distinction. Yet he was never so much a part of the village—with its glossy city veneer—as of the District outside. The rural aspects of Pendleton most appealed to him. Beyond the village—just as in Abbeville a generation earlier—stretched the last outposts of the Southern frontier. There rose the mountains, reaching back into infinities of space; there lay miles upon miles of forest, wild as when the Indians had roamed their trails. Half an hour's ride from Pendleton and you were in another world, a world of tall pine and clear streams, running with trout; of road trails, glittering with quartz and tangled with briers and passion-flowers. Deep in a clearing stood 'Old Hopewell' Church with its thick walls of native fieldstone, its walnut pulpit and pews and heavily shuttered windows; beyond, the graveyard, where the first generation of up-country pioneers now lay.

Half a century ago this had been untracked wilderness. Here were red-scarred hills, grist mills above the undershot water-wheels, whitewashed farmhouses with high blue ceilings, log barns with corn cribs in the rear.

Here lived the men of Calhoun's own flesh and bone and spirit, the tall men of the hill-country, who held themselves in check for fear of their emotions. Here were the Jeffersonian Puritans, who sought only happiness and the salvation of their souls, asking always of all law: 'Will it leave us alone? Will it leave us free?' [7] On the surface they were a gay people, quick to smile and swift with laughter; but beneath ran streaks of melancholy, of austerity and of mysticism.

These were men 'still close to the pioneers in spirit'; not poor whites, but tough-minded farmers with an instinct for penetrating to fundamentals. They had fought the Revolution knowing well that not England, but the commercial dominance of England, had been their enemy.

They had watched and waited; the fight, they knew, far from being over, had scarcely begun. They had favored the loose alliance of North and South under the Articles of Confederation; but when, as they saw it, 'commercial, financial, and special interests' found the Federation 'too weak to serve their purposes,' their 'suspicions were aroused.' [8]

They remembered Pat Calhoun's denunciation of the new Constitution as 'taxation without representation.' They knew 'the fathers,' not as revolutionists, but as conservatives, men of property, intent on safeguarding the interests of property. For two hundred years the South had been a colonial dependency of Great Britain. Would it exchange its dear-bought freedom to become a colony of the commercial North?

The back-country farmers had fought. They had fought in Virginia, in Maryland, and in the two Carolinas, but they had fought alone. Terrified by their 'Western' radicalism, the planters had scurried to the cover offered by such conservatives as slender, violet-eyed Hamilton, who had understood that prosperity was to be attained only by a stable government controlled by the propertied classes.

But prosperity for big business had not necessarily meant prosperity for agriculture. What the gentlemen of the plantations were slowly realizing was what the Piedmont farmers had known all the time. Between the alternatives of friendship or profits, no hesitation will be made. Federalist leaders—the Whigs of a later day—had formed their alliances, not with their Southern dinner partners, but with the business houses of Great Britain, accepting their leadership in the general advance of an industrial society.

2

The South had not won freedom in '76. It had changed masters. This was why the Piedmont farmers had shied off from the idea of a Federal Union. As a separate country, they could have bargained independently with Old or New England for the cheap manufactured goods they wanted.

Not even the Virginia Dynasty could reverse the Hamiltonian trend. As written, the Constitution might guarantee a federal and not a national government; but would it be interpreted as written? Now, as Jefferson had feared, it seemed that industry and finance were to become the master, not the servants, of agriculture and commerce. That the South was yoked in an unequal Union, by the eighteen-twenties was already becoming apparent.[9] Furthermore, slavery was wiping out any chance for the South to compete with the North industrially. Southern capital was too submerged in the peculiar institution to leave any surplus for untried enterprises. Slavery had doomed the South to remain agricultural.

Basically the Piedmont Southerners were still democrats, still Jeffersonians, but Jefferson's dream of an America of small farms was going up in the smoke of an industrial revolution his eyes had not foreseen; in a gigantic capitalism of big-scale plantations and big-scale industries. Up-countrymen were no longer content to be sturdy yeomen on two-horse farms; they must be planters and gentlemen. North and South, the new cotton economy with its demands for cheap labor was destroying the theory of a free and equal society of all men. Yet there was enough of Jeffersonian opportunity left in the South for the men of strength and drive to walk behind their plows at fifteen and to count their acres by the thousands at fifty.

Earlier, slavery and political prejudice had separated the log-cabin farmers of the frontier from the planters of the coast. Now, through sheer necessity, the planter was slowly reconciling his political differences with the back-country. Day by day, year by year, slavery was drawing the two classes together. A man could raise an extra bale or two of cotton, buy a raw 'hand' cheap, train him, work him, and double his cotton output in a single season. Within ten years he would be pushing on into the big landholding class. He might still spit tobacco and make crude jokes on the steps of the cross-roads store and ride to town in his shirt-sleeves, but he would send his wife to church in a carriage and his boys to the state universities.

It was this class, 'to which the great majority of Southern whites belonged,'[10] that was forging the links of a united South. From this group descended the poor white, the frailer, slower, luckless settler of the pine barrens or the sand hills. And from this class also sprang the big land-holders, the 'great majority,' in fact, of the planters of Virginia, Georgia, and the two Carolinas.[11] Slaves meant money and money meant educa-tion, and education and the tastes of a gentleman were all that the aris-tocrats of Charleston and Virginia had had a few generations earlier. Socially, as well as economically, it was possible, in a very short time, for 'up-country gentlemen' to assume the manners, the habits, and the privileges of the planting class.

No artificial tenant system stiffened relationships. Planters had too many slaveless second cousins in the next county to attempt any false pretenses with their neighbors or 'kin.' Democratic 'to the core,' they would intermarry with the homespun as freely as with the broadcloth.[12]

But economic compulsion aided romance. Pushed to the wall, the older planters were reluctantly compelled to seek allies in the despised 'Western radicals' of a generation before.

Profitable as slavery might seem to the newcomer to the planting class, his shrewd vision was not dulled. Since 1816, he had been buying in a protected market and selling in an open one. The merciless pressures of world capitalism, with its demands on a cotton economy that were stretch-ing his farm into a plantation, had made his choice inevitable. He could be rich or he could be poor. He could be a part of the once-hated 'planting aristocracy'—or its victim. Against the capitalism of the North, his only hope was to join the rival capitalism of the South.

What made the newcomer a potent ally was his inherent level-headed-ness. Shrewdly he had realized that his only chance for self-realization lay in the planting class. He had assumed his new role, full-armed with all his old fears. The enemy was the same. The greater the contrast be-tween his present wealth and his past poverty, the greater the gulf be-tween the profits he made and the profits he should have made. It was easy to become a slaveholder, but easier still to go bankrupt as a slaveholder. And one who had tasted of the sweets of the 'Southern way of life' had no intention of abandoning them.

Thus, on the basis of a common economic interest and a common enemy, Southern unity was being achieved. It was a slow process. It would be two generations before the unification would be complete; and by then, it would be too late.[13]

But what was happening in Pendleton was in a sense happening all over the Southern states. Up-country and low-country met, clashed, and blended. Two civilizations were fusing in South Carolina, and although not typical of the entire variegated pattern of the South, she was as representative as any one state could be. After 1825, she would lead the Southern mind.[14]

Historians would write of the leadership of the slaveholders. The truth was less simple. Neighborhood planters might meet at the courthouse to lay down the laws and nominate one of their number to be Congressman or legislator—in the good old Virginia style—but the newcomer could not be excluded. Often as the sole member of his family to have dressed his log cabin in a coat of white clapboards, he had reached a sort of eminence among his 'kin.'[15] Where he stood today, they might stand tomorrow. He had proved himself, and they would follow him.

What the planters did embody was the fulfillment of the common ideal. The Southern society was a society of gentlemen, not because gentlemen were in the majority, but because the majority aspired to be gentlemen. The leader of the Southern mind must be a gentleman, and the future leader of the Southern mind was John C. Calhoun.

He was fitted to represent the idea. A gentleman by instinct, he made few of the mistakes of most newcomers to the planting class. He was patrician in his very simplicity. If, intellectually, his brilliant mind represented Charleston thought, spiritually and even physically he was one with his own people. He had their gauntness, the loneliness which never left them, no matter how large the crowd around them. Like them, he dreamed of America as the 'perfect State.'[16] Like them, his roots struck far into the earth, and the beauty of the Southern farm life had gone deeper into him than any outsider imagined. If, like Lee and Davis and all the ragged, reckless horde in butternut gray, he would fight to the end for a cause that he logically knew to be lost, it was because, like them, he was fighting not only for a life he lived and believed good, but for a land he loved.

3

It was a beautiful land—this land he loved. It was a vivid, restless, moody land, torn by winds, lashed by rains. In summer, it brooded and dreamed, a blue mist over the mountains, the warm air heavy with the scents of myrtle and magnolia and sweet with the smell of the wild plum. It was a land fitted to its people; it had their energy and their indolence; it had their strength and it held their dreams.

For Calhoun it was once more home. Now his children could live as he had lived, love the life that he loved. They would know another world from Washington, a world of smokehouses and slow, muddy rivers, and the cotton sack dragging from the shoulder of a black man. They would know the taste of tart brown cider and sun-mellowed peaches, of cornbread dripping with country butter and sorghum; the scents of horehound and mint leaves, catnip and rosemary, of fresh-filled hay barns and plowed fields wet with rain. They would know the cry of the screech owl and the liquid ripple of a mocking-bird, the stitch of the cricket on a hot summer night, and the mournful echo of the 'houn' dawg,' baying to an October moon. They would know the richness and color of this Carolina hill-country that even in winter was green as spring, with its box hedges and short-needled cedar and spruce; pines towering black against a hard blue sky, red roads cutting through the hills, and the last pink burning of sunset over a cotton field. They would know the rhythm of wheat in the wind, and the hundred-degree noontime sun, glittering across a sanded yard. They would know the stillness of summer days, the wisdom of silence, and the certainties of stars.[17]

With his people's love of the wind-swept hills, Calhoun hoped to build on the highest hilltop in the region.[18] Unable to purchase it, he moved into a small white dwelling known as 'Clergy Hall,' once the 'old stone church' parsonage, and in more recent years owned by Floride's family.[19]

Clergy Hall was on a high elevation. Mountain winds whipped through the tall cedars that bordered the drive, and rolling fields sloped down toward the Seneca River. Calhoun felt at home instantly. He attended church at Hopewell, but the crudeness of the little meeting-house did not suit Floride's taste, and she herself founded an Episcopal church down in Pendleton. Here the Presbyterian Calhoun came occasionally; and to young Charles Cotesworth Pinckney, who saw him for the first time at the rear of a long line of his children, the slender man with graying hair was a disappointment, for although Vice-President of the United States, he looked no different from other Anderson County farmers. But as he spoke with friends after the service, Pinckney marveled at the change that crossed his features. 'His whole face,' observed the rector's son, 'was alight with genius.' Calhoun revealed a little of the current trend of his thought to Pinckney, when, after some approving comments on the spiritual benefits of public worship, he suddenly remarked: 'Shaking hands with your neighbor at the church door, asking after his family, even remarking that it is a pleasant day—these all have a wonderful power in binding men together.'[20]

Binding the Anderson County men even more closely together, however, was the Pendleton Farmers' Society. Established in 1815 by the planters, for the farmers, no organization in the district was more inclusive. And the minutes show that on an August night in 1826, 'The Honorable John C. Calhoun . . . attended and took a seat.'[21]

Here Calhoun fitted in perfectly. Indeed, from 1839 to 1840 he presided as president in the classic little building with its white-columned portico facing Pendleton Square. It was one of the few organizations to which he ever belonged, for he was that rarity among public men—a non-joiner. But the Farmers' Society especially interested him, for with similar groups throughout the state, it was dedicated to agricultural reform. Its aim was to lead agriculture back to the days of individual plantation self-sufficiency, both in farm and manufactured products, and thus to help allay the effects of the tariff.

Women, as well as men, were included in these aims. Prizes were offered for material spun and woven in the district; from the best bolts of woolen, cotton, or imitation gingham cloth and the best stockings of twilled homespun to the 'best piece linnen Diaper, 6 yds.' As only well-tended or reclaimed land could produce winning crops, prizes were awarded for the greatest output of flint corn per acre, and the best fields of wheat, rye, barley, oats, cotton, peas, and hay. There were awards for the sweetest home-churned butter and the most mellow barrel of cider, for the best yoke of oxen, the finest bull calves and stallions.[22]

'I have turned farmer since my return home,' Calhoun wrote Swift from Pendleton. 'I am wholly absorbed in agriculture to the exclusion of politicks,' was his word to Littleton Tazewell of Virginia a year later.[23] At last he was finding release from the pent-up Washington years. Now he could take time to invent that subsoil plow;[24] to try out the Pennsylvania methods of plowing and planting, watching his 'hands' to see that the ground was so deeply cut and the surface so thoroughly turned that it would be almost impossible for weeds and grass to sprout during an entire summer. He would see that the corn was planted 'about 3 feet apart both ways, as to overshadow and prevent the growth of weeds.'[25] He was even experimenting with plaster-of-Paris as a fertilizer, and with new breeds of cattle and hogs. 'I write to remind you of the cantalope seed, which you promised me,' he informed Tazewell in April, 1827. 'It is a fruit of which I am very fond.'[26] He was in the field from sunrise to sunset, coming home in the evening hot, dirty, tired, and completely happy. Between Congressional sessions, at least, it was almost possible for him to forget that he was Vice-President of the United States.

Had Calhoun ceased to be interested in 'politicks,' however, he would have ceased to be Calhoun. Physical labor alone was not enough to absorb his energies, and the more he threw himself into the farmer's life, the more aware he was of how gravely that life was threatened.

'You are not incorrect in supposing . . . that as much devoted as I am to agriculture, which without affectation is my favorite pursuit,' he admitted to Tazewell, 'I am not so actually absorbed . . . as to have my attention wholly diverted from public affairs. They are in fact intimately blended . . . among the reasons of my attachment to agriculture is, that while it affords sufficient activity for health, it also gives leisure for reflection and improvement.'[27]

Thus he summarized his creed. But he derived neither comfort nor relaxation from his gloomy thinking through that summer of 1827. 'The more I reflect,' he wrote Tazewell, 'the more I dispond.' His mind was beset with the problem that theoretically or practically was confronting every thoughtful Southerner. The question was 'the permanent operation of our system, particularly as affecting the great agricultural interest of the South.'[28]

His own bank account gave him ample cause for concern. He was making good crops; he had never made a bad crop in his life. It was no use. So far as his finances were concerned, he might as well have remained in Washington.

He outlined his plight to his sympathetic brother-in-law, James: 'Our staples scarcely return the expense of cultivation. . . . Land and negroes have fallen to the lowest price, and can scarcely be sold at the present depressed rate. . . . My means have been exhausted. . . .'[29]

What had happened to him he knew was happening to the whole South. His story was the story of his neighborhood, and it was the same whether told in the firelight of a hill-country farmhouse, or on the pillared portico of a Pendleton mansion. 'Never,' he wrote, 'was there such universal and severe pressure on the . . . South.' To what did he attribute the disaster? 'The almost universal excitement among the people of the staple states,' he told Monroe, 'they almost unanimously attribute to the high duties.'[30]

Calhoun shared the popular opinion. His trumpeting of the universal outcry was to give him leadership; it reflects less credit upon his understanding. Undoubtedly the tariff was and continued to be fundamental in the South's distress; and Calhoun's powerful analysis of its ultimate results, not only as an act of economic injustice, but as a symbol of a majority interest trampling down the rights of the minority, is beyond challenge. But the tariff was not the sole cause.

What Calhoun did not see, what he was, in fact, emotionally incapable of seeing, was the role of the cotton-slave economy in the falling prices and general depression. To a few, the acute financial failure of slavery was already apparent; years since, John Randolph had read the story in his own Virginia, in the worn-out tobacco lands, and the great families impoverished by supporting their unemployed and fast-breeding slaves.[31] Now, in South Carolina, prices were falling because land was becoming worthless and Negroes too plentiful to be of value.

The advent of the cotton gin had spelled disaster. With the mills of Manchester and Lowell, of Lancashire and Liverpool, clamoring for cotton, cotton, and more cotton, the South was exporting its topsoil in every bale. The small cotton farmer was doomed; either he became rich quickly and abandoned his exhausted acres for virgin soil to the West or he sank into profitless cropping and poverty.

The South was caught in a relentless treadmill. The demands of the cotton mills meant more Negroes to work more land to raise more cotton; and the ensuing rapid breeding of the slave population as rapidly decreased its value. Hence was created a demand for new slave territories, so that there would be new markets for slaves. Here, indeed, were the germs of ultimate abolition, for a system, never generally condoned in a free country, was becoming more and more intolerable as it overflowed its old boundaries and competed with the cheap labor westward.

That Calhoun understood the danger of one-crop cotton planting, his own efforts at soil conservation prove. But there is no evidence that, either in youth or in age, he perceived the interrelationship of the cotton-slave economy. Yet on the danger of the tariff system, his vision was flawlessly clear. And out of his reflections came the realization of the 'weak point of our system. . . . The part least guarded' under the Constitution required 'the strongest guard.' What was the remedy against the encroachments of 'a combined geographical interest'? [32] Some 'negative' or 'veto' power must be found.

Yet he hesitated. What troubled him were 'the peculiar minor interests' which would remain unprotected; and also the question of 'how far such a negative would be found consistent with the general power . . . an important consideration which I waive for the present.' That such a negative power would exist, were it not for the Judiciary Act of 1789, he was convinced. That Act had wrought 'an entire change in the operation of our system.' Without it, each government would have had 'a negative on the other.' He hammered questions at Tazewell. How had Congress happened to adopt the Act? Did it respect state sovereignty? Would a veto wielded by an important 'interest' be consistent with the Constitution? If not, how *could* 'a great local interest' be defended or controlled? [33]

The Virginian's answers must have been sobering. 'I see and feel, deeply feel, the difficulties which you have so clearly stated,' Calhoun replied to him. 'I . . . am unwilling to consider them insuperable. . . . I have given them much thought during the summer, but confess I do not see my way clear.' Nevertheless, he contended, 'the acknowledged theory of our system' shows the states 'as sovereign and independent as to their reserved rights, as the Union is to the delegated.' He would 'go over the whole ground' with Tazewell when they met in Washington.[34]

4

More interesting even than the labor pains of nullification, which the Tazewell-Calhoun correspondence so vividly illuminates, is the troubled and uncertain state of mind in which Calhoun gave birth to the doctrine. From these letters it is apparent that the reason he defended nullification with such passionate intensity was not because he believed it to be a faultless system, but because of what seemed to him its sheer necessity. As he had admitted, he not only saw but felt, and felt far too deeply. To Monroe, one year *after* his letters to Tazewell, he stated flatly: 'It seems to me that we have no . . . check against abuses, but such as grow out of responsibility, or elections. . . .'[35] This he could write in July, 1828; one month later he had surrendered completely to the most extreme limits of the nullification doctrine.

He was desperate. The safety of the South was at stake. Even Jackson had been compelled to give tacit lip-service to the protectionists, though where Jackson really stood, no one knew; and probably least of all, himself.

Calhoun did much floor-pacing those summer nights, up and down, up and down his great central hallway. Often it was past three before he dropped into his bed for a couple of hours; then he would be up and at his thoughts again.[36] He refused to admit there could be no way out. From his letters we can see the workings of his mind. If the Judiciary Act of 1789 had wrought a change in the American system, weakening the rights of the states, then the change must be reversed. The system must be restored to its 'original purity.'

Calhoun's genius lay in his penetration of cause and effect; his conclusions were not always so much a result of logic as of the basic forces of history. He was far from being blind to the spirit of the age. So far as economic forces went, no man was more aware of it. It may be exaggeration to say that Calhoun 'suffered his very soul to be ground to powder' between the millstones of his emotional desires and his logical realizations, but there is truth in the general principle.[37] In the same vein, an early biographer commented that Calhoun would have been a far happier and healthier man had he been less tortured by his relentless vision.[38]

He faced the tariff question, as he was later to face slavery, aware of the threat it implied, and prepared to rip it out by the roots. It marked the country off into sections, and in sectionalism Calhoun could see only an ever-increasing menace to the permanence of the Union. 'It is dangerous,' he wrote Monroe, 'to see the country divided as it is by sections, and almost unanimously in regard to every great measure, particularly when it may be supposed to originate in the spirit of gain on one side at the expense of the other.'[39] To Tazewell he had been even more explicit. 'On virtually every important question of government,' he pointed out, 'no two distinct nations can be more opposed than this [the staple states] and the other sections.'[40]

The federal character of the American Union, Calhoun believed, would necessitate a veto power wielded by the individual state rather than by the section or interest affected. Only in later years, when the impotency of the individual states endangered the effectiveness of their protest, did Calhoun submit to the inevitable, and organize the region as a conservative check within the Union. For to Calhoun the continued existence of the Union depended on an effective protest, without which he saw that the Southern states would secede. As he would explain more specifically to his friend, James Hammond, in 1831, either nullification by one state or a united protest by the entire South would suffice; but the danger of united action was that, misdirected, its very strength might rend the Union apart.

Despite his fears Calhoun was driven on. Even had he desired to stand by, he would have had no chance. For all through the summer months of 1827 and 1828, he was besieged by up-country leaders and low-country planters, begging his aid in finding a way out.[41]

5

Actually the 'nullification crisis,' as it came to be called, derived very little from Calhoun's abstract doctrine. Mentally and emotionally, South Carolina was already an armed camp; nullification was the result, not the cause. And the man who was whipping the tempers of South Carolina into flame was not Calhoun, but thirty-five-year-old George McDuffie.

His had been a lonely and strange career. It had been Calhoun's older brothers, William and James, who discovered this boy store clerk and blacksmith's apprentice, and sent him to Dr. Waddel's school and to the South Carolina College. Within three years of his admission to the bar, McDuffie was 'the coming man of the South.' Emotionally his powers were 'convulsive.' Like Calhoun he had moments when he came dangerously near to hypnotism, and he shared the older man's quality of 'logic set on fire.'[42] To some this dark, slender man, with his 'cavalier's head,' deep-set blue eyes, and tight fists beating at the air, seemed 'beautiful as an angel,' and a Northern observer commented, 'I never heard such eloquence flow from the lips of mortal man.'[43]

Elected to Congress at thirty-one, like Calhoun he defied John Randolph almost from the day he took his seat. Upon the astounded Virginian he poured a torrent of abuse so 'witheringly pungent' that the enraged Randolph walked out of the Chamber and almost sent him a challenge. 'Lay on, McDuff,' chanted the press admiringly.[44]

Despite rustic manners and sleeves 'out at the elbows,' McDuffie's talents gained him 'admission into exclusive South Carolina society.' He wooed and won a Charleston belle, Mary Rebecca Singleton. One year later, she lay dead beside their newborn child. McDuffie, grim, bitter, fighting off paralysis from an old dueling wound, withdrew into his loneliness. Such of himself as he cared for the world to see, he threw into the 'passionate frenzy' of his speeches.

These speeches were no mere reflections of Calhoun; they were spurs in his sides. It was McDuffie, not Calhoun, who was lashing the people of South Carolina into such fury at their peril that a near-majority was ready to lead the state into secession then and there. It was McDuffie who was charging up and down the state all through the summer of 1828, calling for rebellion, revolution, and forcible resistance. It was McDuffie who fathered the famed '40 bale theory,' contending that under the Tariff of Abominations the South was, in effect, giving the North forty out of every one hundred bales she raised. At Columbia he surpassed himself. Before a tensely expectant group he stood, ripped off his broadcloth coat, tossed it to the ground. 'Doff this golden tissue,' he shrieked. 'It is fit only for slaves!' [45]

6

And thus, during the long summer days of 1828, South Carolina's memorable *Exposition and Protest* was evolved. While South Carolina was criticizing Calhoun for his indifference to her plight, he was hard at work on the doctrine which startled the nation with its declaration that a single state, having entered the Union for the preservation of its liberties, could and would determine when the federal government had violated those liberties.

Just who the leaders were who lounged with Calhoun on the long pillared porch of Clergy Hall * that summer is uncertain. First among them was probably Charleston's little 'Jimmy' Hamilton, forty-two years old, a Major in the War of 1812, now Brigadier-General, commanding twenty-seven thousand well-trained state troops. So wealthy that he owned fourteen cotton plantations, so hot-tempered that he is reputed to have fought fourteen duels, he could control the passions of a mob as skillfully as Calhoun mastered the intellects of its leaders. Yet Hamilton, too, had a mind, cool and clear as his emotions were hot. He would be the campaign manager of nullification, organize the clubs, word the theories in popular language, unflinchingly, as Governor, face the possibilities of civil war, but then and later he considered secession uncalled-for and revolutionary. Of the value of nullification, however, he had no doubts, at all. 'He who dallies is a dastard; he who doubts is damned.'[46]

Equally vehement was the young up-countryman, Francis Pickens, glowering of eye and brow, arrogantly proud of his ancestry, his learning, and his abilities: his boast, 'I have never made myself what the world calls popular.' In his calmer moments he could say, 'As long as we are in the Union, I . . . believe it our duty to discharge all our obligations . . . under it. . . . Our people have been educated to compacts and chartered rights, as a substitute for the sword.' But he was for 'war up to the hilt,' [47] if nullification failed.

Silent and attentive as befitted his twenty-one years was James H. Hammond, cotton planter and slavery champion, who within two years would be editing the nullification paper, the *Southern Times,* and horse-whipping

* Rechristened Fort Hill in 1830. (See A. G. Holmes, 'John C. Calhoun,' *Southern Magazine,* II, No. 10, 1936.)

a Camden editor who chanced to disagree with him. Like his friend, Robert Barnwell Rhett, who had not yet been won over to 'peaceful, Constitutional Nullification,' Hammond already despaired of the Union; for twenty years he was to aim at secession or Southern nation-wide dominance.

From Charleston would have come Robert Young Hayne, for his was to be the responsibility of presenting nullification on the floor of Congress, of which he had this year said: 'The time is at hand when these seats will be filled by the owners of manufacturing establishments.' Legislative interests were no doubt represented by the tall, bushy-haired, up-country Andrew Butler, later Calhoun's Senatorial colleague. And present in spirit, if not in his fat, aging flesh, was Thomas Cooper of Charleston, professor at the South Carolina College, teacher of a generation of Southern hot-heads. His pamphlets of a few years before, denouncing Calhoun for his consolidating tendencies and warning of inherent dangers in the Constitution, had won him a hearing throughout the South; and already he was urging his followers to 'calculate' the value of the Union. Cooper valued the Union 'too little, because he loved liberty too well.' [48]

These, then, were the leaders. Most of them were young; all hot-headed; all aristocrats by choice if not by origin. That they represented South Carolina public opinion is questionable; that they represented the governing opinion is undeniable. Calhoun could lead them; he could not always control them. He drew them together, fused their diversities, through them he held the impetuous state in check. His was the task of allaying the common grievance, of substituting a practical remedy for the hopeless submission of the Unionists and the reckless defiance of the Secessionists, of directing 'the eye of the State to the Constitution . . . for the redress of its wrongs.' [49]

And it was to the Constitution that he and the leaders looked, to the Constitution in what Calhoun called its 'emphatically American' federal character. They looked to the old South Carolina legislative compromise, in which the back-country and the coast, 'two great interests,' were given equal recognition in determining state policy. South Carolina had a government 'of the entire population . . . not of one portion . . . over another portion'; [50] and this, to Calhoun, was an example of the concurrent rather than the numerical majority, of justice for minority groups.

The precedents of nullification were, at least, wholly American. Had not Madison's Virginia Resolutions proclaimed that when a state deemed a law unconstitutional, it was in duty bound to 'interpose' to protect its liberties? Had not the Kentucky Resolutions of Thomas Jefferson asserted that the right of judging was an essential attribute of sovereignty, and that 'In all cases of compact between parties having no common judge *

* To the Nullifiers the Supreme Court was entirely the creature of the national government, no common judge between the government and the states.

each party' could decide for itself? Bold words these, proud words; but whether or not, as Daniel Webster believed, the plan of a Southern Confederacy was already under consideration by more radical Southern leaders,[51] Calhoun was right in preferring a struggle over the question-marks and evasions of the Constitution than one on the fields of battle. On one matter he was determined. If the South were made to suffer the disadvantages of the Constitution, she would also reap its advantages.

7

The result of Calhoun's thinking was a lengthy report to the South Carolina Legislature, which with a few revisions was published in December, 1828, and became known as *The Exposition and Protest*. It attracted little initial attention.[52] It was not remarkable for its readability, yet its importance can hardly be overestimated.

All that the prophet John Randolph had foreseen, all that the backcountry farmers had feared, Calhoun now saw. He saw a 'permanent economic conflict'[53] between North and South, the North determined to become industrial, the South resolved to remain agricultural; the South demanding free trade in an open market, the North demanding exclusion of foreign competition. 'We are the serfs of the system,' the *Exposition* declared, 'out of whose labor is raised not only the money paid into the Treasury, but the funds out of which are drawn the rich rewards of the manufacturers.' To the 'growers of cotton, rice, and tobacco,' it was the same whether the government took one-third of what they raised for the privilege 'of sending the other two-thirds abroad, or one-third of the iron, salt, sugar, coffee, cloth, and other articles,' they required, 'in exchange for the liberty of bringing them home.' The Southern farmer paid for the Northern manufacturer's protection against foreign competition by a loss of his own capacity to compete in the world market. And on the world market his very livelihood depended. Not one-quarter of the Southern agricultural output could be consumed in the United States alone.

Would not Europe answer 'probihition by prohibition,' clamping high duties on Southern rice and cotton? 'Commercial warfare' would mark the end of that system of barter and exchange under which Europe and the South had traded for so long. With three-quarters of her markets destroyed, the South would be forced to sell her surpluses to the North at any price 'the manufacturers might choose to give.' Truly had Calhoun spoken when he warned that the tariff could reduce the 'South to poverty or a complete change of industry.'

With their foreign trade gone, the Southern people would be compelled to abandon the culture of rice, indigo, and cotton, and become 'the rivals, instead of the customers of the manufacturing States.' Yet this would only mean 'ruin in another form.' For if manufacturing should take root in the South, the North 'by superior capital and skill' would 'keep down successful competition. . . . We would be doomed to toil at our unprofitable agriculture, selling on a limited market.' Otherwise, *'those who now make war on our gains would make it on our labor.'*

To a moderate tariff system for revenue, affording incidental protection, the South would agree. 'We have suffered too much to desire to see others afflicted, even for our relief, when it can possibly be avoided. We would rejoice to see our manufacturers flourish on any constitutional principle, consistent with justice,' [54] which to Calhoun was the binding element of the Constitution. But here was the crux of the matter. A uniform law for the whole nation could act with great injustice. Alexander Hamilton had understood. Society, the great Federalist leader had written, must not only 'guard against the oppression of its rulers, but . . . guard one part . . . against the injustice of the other part. . . . If a majority be united by a common interest, the . . . minority will be unsafe." [55]

Now a majority had united in their own common interest. But did not our whole political system rest 'on the great principle involved in the recognized diversity of geographical interests?' Was a free government established for the general welfare, or merely as an 'instrument of aggrandizement . . . to transfer the power and property of one class or section to another'? Calhoun warned: 'No government based on the naked principle that the majority ought to govern, however true the maxim . . . under proper restraint, can preserve its liberty, even for a single generation.'

But theory was nothing without the means of putting it into practice. The Constitution provided the remedy—for the national government, the Supreme Court, to prevent encroachments by the states; for the states, their 'right . . . to interpose to protect their reserved powers.' Critics might object that there was no 'express provision' for such action in the Constitution; what of the Supreme Court's power to declare laws unconstitutional? This was not specifically provided for—likewise, interposition by the states was to be 'inferred from the simple fact that it is not delegated' [56] to the national government.

8

A sheer declaration of anarchy, nullification appeared to its critics: Calhoun himself did not shrink from the fact that he was giving publicity to doctrines which a large majority would consider 'new and dangerous.' [57] Unflinchingly he pointed out how far a sovereign state could go if pressed beyond endurance. Yet he was too realistic to imagine it conceivable that a state could remain in the Union in outright violation of the Union's laws. Nullification did not suspend a law for the nation, but only within the state that protested. It was not an end in itself, but a method of appeal. It gave opportunity for three-quarters of the states in convention to determine whether or not to confer the questioned power upon the Union by constitutional amendment. The nullifying state would then have to obey—or secede.

It may be that the abstract principle of nullification was like starting over a waterfall in a canoe and calling 'halt' halfway down. But Calhoun realized that principles are seldom carried to their ultimate extremes. The calling of a Constitutional Convention, 'the delay—the deliberation,' the national ambitions of state leaders and minority opinions 'within the State,' all would render this 'reserved power' a rare power to be invoked or used. 'Nothing but truth and a deep sense of oppression' would justify such action; otherwise, it would result 'in the expulsion of those in power.' The weakness of his argument, as historians have generally realized, is that with the states the ultimate source of power, should a quarter of them nullify a law that was clearly constitutional, there would be nothing the other states could do.

Calhoun must have known that he would fail. He signed the death-warrant of his own doctrine by his honest admission that under protection 'the capitalist . . . the merchant, and the laborer in the manufacturing States would all . . . receive higher rates of wages and profits'; that with free trade, 'to meet European competition they would be compelled to work at the lowest wages and profits.' Thus was the irreconcilable nature of the conflict revealed.

Yet, in the long run, he was right. He knew that the so-called 'American System' was merely the old European system that would 'ultimately divide society.' He saw the inevitable rise of a politically dominant 'moneyed aristocracy.' 'After we are exhausted,' ran his somber warning, 'the contest will be between the capitalists and the operatives.' The system would eventually destroy 'much more than it would transfer.' A tariff could subsidize industry at the South's expense—a tariff could build producing power, but what about purchasing power? Could the North remain rich by keeping the South poor? 'For the present,' he conceded, 'all was flourishing,'[58] and 'what people would forego practical gains in the present for hypothetical losses in the future?'

9

To James Parton, writing in the aftermath of the Civil War, Calhoun's somber warning seemed little short of lunacy.[59] To later generations it appeared more like prophecy. For all that it feared and forecast, the draining of the wealth of both the West and the South into the coffers of the East, linking political and financial control; the subjugation of agriculture to the demands of the manufacturers; the 'backward' Southern industries, the 'war on the Southern system of labor'—all were to come about as inevitably as the solution to a problem in mathematics. Sociologists, writing of the South a century afterward, all but duplicated Calhoun's words.

Eighty years after Calhoun's last warnings were whispered, it would be admitted that the South had become the nation's 'number one economic problem,' with slaveholding abolished, but not slavery, with eight million poor whites, besides the blacks, huddling in rickety shacks, driven out to shift for themselves when the cotton market fell, living on cornmeal and molasses in a squalor few masters would have permitted to their slaves.*

It is true that throughout Southern history the North has most conveniently served as public whipping-boy for innumerable Southern sins. It is equally true that after the Civil War, many Southern leaders, such as James Orr of South Carolina and Henry W. Grady of Georgia, honestly believed that the agrarian system had been wrong, and that the South should adopt the economy of the victors. Nevertheless, the Old South died, not entirely of its own internal diseases—including the cancer of slavery—but from conquest and destruction. In addition to the tribe who sold out their own section and their own birthright for a few crumbs from the Northern capitalists' table, there were the thousands who by conquest alone were compelled to do so. The embryonic mills, the power sites, the mines, the virgin woodlands and cotton lands had to be sold at fractional value or pledged as collateral to finance capitalists, who for their own profit were trying to develop the South industrially. Appomattox had fixed the pattern of Southern industrial development.

With the last barriers shattered by the guns of the Civil War, a half-century sufficed for ownership of Southern railroad companies, public utilities, natural gas, oil, and metal ore, 'transportation, communication, financial, manufacturing, mining, and finally distributing corporations . . . to be largely held in the great cities of the North East.' [60] By Nature 'blessed with immense wealth,' the Southern people would be found 'the poorest in the country.' Barred, not only by tariff, but by credit and freight-rate barriers from equal industrial development, the region 'would mine its natural riches for goods manufactured elsewhere.' Through absentee ownership many of its natural resources were left undeveloped, artificially held out of competition with resources in other sections. 'Penalized for being rural, handicapped in its efforts to industrialize,' Amer-

* Letter from an Alamance County, North Carolina, farmer, September 14, 1939 (in possession of the author): 'Country folks in this locality have a three-meal ration of side meat (hog-belly) sorgum molasses and cornbread. No variety and plenty pellegra. So it is — the poor must starve.'

ica's 'greatest untapped business market,' wanting to buy, needing to buy, was unable to buy.[61]

Specifically, of course, Calhoun's grim warning that the North would keep down successful Southern industrial competition was prophecy for only ninety years. Since 1920, the tables have been turned. Belated discovery that cheap labor, cheap power, and cheap real estate were all obtainable at the source of the raw materials made manufactures boom in some parts of the South and began draining New England of her livelihood and prosperity.* Yet, in general, the pattern of 1865 was still unaltered. Modern Southern industrial development was still superimposed and colonial; profits and ownership still flowed to New York City. As late as 1945 in the full tide of wartime prosperity, it could be said without denial by Hodding Carter in *The Saturday Evening Post* that 'The South and West . . . still live in economic subordination to a handful of Eastern States.' [62] And Ellis Arnall, writing in the *Atlantic*, could wonder when 'these two great areas' would be 'no longer regarded as colonial appendages to be exploited and drained of all wealth for the support of an Eastern industrial empire.' [63] Behind the very secession movement had been the belief that if industrialism got control of the federal government, it would not only 'exploit agriculture,' but direct the pattern of Southern industrial growth, to the sacrifice of the South's freedom of choice. 'Today,' wrote Frank Owsley, 'we . . . witness the fulfillment of John C. Calhoun.' [64]

Nullification was more than logic-chopping. It was built on a premise, a premise that the North's superior voting power would destroy the economic life of the South, a premise of which 'the Tariff of Abominations was the proof.' [65] It was Calhoun's battle for social values, for a civilization which he sincerely thought to be as perfect as man could devise, and which he saw endangered by forces which, in common with Jefferson, he believed were in contradiction to all right living and a vital threat to the very liberties the Union had been formed to preserve. It was Calhoun's supreme battle in defense of the minority, not only the South of his day, but all the shifting minorities in the complex Union of the future.

Beside the immensity of this question, the Presidential contest of 1828 was 'but an incident . . . the means of a reformation which must take place.' Yet Calhoun must have known that it would not take place; that it was vain to dream of 'a returning sense of justice on the part of the majority,' [66] or of agreement with his thesis on the part of Andrew Jackson. A practical politician, Calhoun understood that, with an election at stake, whatever Jackson's personal feelings, the vote of protectionist Pennsylvania was worth far more than that of little South Carolina. And what would be his own weight with Jackson against the weight of a whole interest, a whole section of the country?

* Vide the Textron row of 1948, as a single example.

Yet, if there was little to hope for from Jackson, from his rival, Adams, there was even less. The election was but a weak chance, but that chance must not be endangered. Hence, the *Exposition* must be held in abeyance, and the fact of Calhoun's authorship with it,* for if he lost the Vice-Presidency, what then would be his influence with Jackson? So South Carolina waited, as the election returns flowed in—a surging tidal wave, 178 to 83—for Old Hickory. And Calhoun himself, although his electoral vote dropped by 11 from his count of 182 in 1824, won easily. 'Nominated unanimously' by the Legislatures of Pennsylvania, New Jersey, Ohio, and Kentucky, he had also received an overwhelming endorsement from the Old Dominion, which he felt to be the greatest triumph of all.[67]

Of the 'rightful power' of his remedy, he had no doubts. It was more than a right—it was 'a sacred duty to the Union, to the cause of liberty over the world,' to establish the principle of nullification. In pledging themselves to uphold the Constitution, men were obliged to prevent its violation. 'They would be unworthy of the name of freemen, of Americans,—of Carolinians . . . if danger could deter them.' [68]

'The ground we have taken,' Calhoun wrote his friend, Duff Green, 'is that the tariff is unconstitutional and must be repealed, that the rights of the South have been destroyed, and must be restored, that the Union is in danger, and must be saved.'[69]

* Calhoun personally was willing that his name be revealed. See *Life*, p. 36.

XIII

Petty Arts

IF GREAT MEN were measured by their success with women rather than with statecraft, the history books would be far less cluttered. There was Washington, for instance; forever proposing to the wrong girls—the ones who would not give him a second glance—and unable to confess his feelings to the one woman he really loved. There was Thomas Jefferson, an affectionate domestic man who lived nearly forty years of single loneliness after the death of his wife, because he had promised her that he would never remarry. There was Abraham Lincoln. And there was John C. Calhoun.

Not that Calhoun lacked the ability to please women. Indeed, he gave them a flattery far more satisfying than the usual toasts to their physical beauty. His appeal was to their minds. Mrs. Jefferson Davis, who knew him well, wrote that, although courteous, he had not a trace of that gallantry characteristic of the period. 'He spoke to a girl on the same subjects as to a statesman,'[1] Mrs. Davis declared. 'He paid the highest compliment which could be paid to a woman,' according to another female contemporary, 'by recognizing in her a soul—a soul capable of understanding and appreciating.'[2] But attracting and understanding are two different matters, as Calhoun never entirely found out—with men as well as with women.

His power over men was undeniable. His courage, both moral and physical, won their unstinted admiration. His lofty principles challenged the imagination, rallied ardent and talented followers to his side.[3] But here indeed was the trouble, according to a friend. 'As a practical statesman, his great defect was that he pursued principles too exclusively. Principles are unerring; but in their practice and application . . . we have to deal with erring man.'[4]

And, incidentally, women!

To Calhoun the world operated along fixed principles, worked out according to mathematical formulae. Now there are such things as fixed principles. And it is true that sometimes men are reasonable and that occasionally the world is reasonable, but very seldom are women reasonable. And here Calhoun made his error. He was himself too charged with emotion to deny the existence of caprice; he granted its power in determining human conduct; but he did believe that in the end reason would prevail. No doubt it did prevail with Calhoun, who had forcibly subjected his emotions to his intellect, but it did not prevail with Andrew Jackson and it did not prevail with Peggy O'Neil Timberlake. Nor did it prevail with Floride Calhoun.

Calhoun was reasonable. To him women's quarrels were unreasonable, and hence unimportant. 'The quarrels of women,' he wearily remarked at this period, 'like those of the Medes and the Persians, admit of neither inquiry nor explanation.' [5] Yet a quarrel between two women was sufficiently important to shake Calhoun's chances of obtaining the Presidency, regardless of the effect it may have had upon history.

One woman was beautiful. We have Daniel Webster's word for that, and Webster was no inexpert connoisseur. The impressions of the young newspaperman, Ben. Perley Poore, were more concrete. The white skin, 'delicately tinged with red,' the dark curls and curving, full-lipped mouth of the Irish barmaid who became the American Pompadour, haunted Poore's imagination for fifty years.[6]

And the other had been beautiful. This explains much. Floride Calhoun was no longer the sprightly girl who had dazzled Washington society a decade before. Women aged early in those days. Floride was only thirty-five, but, by the standards of the times, already a middle-aged woman. She had borne eight children, and now in the winter of 1829 was 'in a delicate condition' once more. Mrs. Margaret Bayard Smith, several years later, could write of Floride's husband that 'his face charmed me,' [7] but the toasts to Floride's beauty had given way to others. There was Mrs. Porter, for instance. And there was Peggy O'Neil.

Peggy had been well if not favorably known in the national capital since her twelfth year, when her rollicking impudence in a dancing contest had won her a smile and a prize from lively Dolly Madison. In earlier years, Andrew Jackson had trotted her upon his knee, and Washington society ladies, between conjectures as to whether Mrs. Jackson would smoke her corncob pipe in the White House or treat the visiting Ambassadors to hers and the General's backwoods dance exhibition of 'Possum up de Gumtree,' pronounced Peggy a 'fit handmaid' for the President's wife. Birds of a feather, you know! [8]

News that Peggy, now the widow of Naval Purser Timberlake, would become the bride of Senator John Henry Eaton of Tennessee set Washington's hair on end. Eaton was practically Andrew Jackson's adopted son, and his first wife had, in fact, been the President's ward. But if shocked, Washington was hardly surprised, for the rumors of the couple's premarital intimacies, climaxed by the rumored suicide of Timberlake, had illumined feminine chit-chat for over five years.[9] No belated wedding ceremony between the dark, explosive Peggy and the lean, auburn-haired

Eaton could right such a series of wrongs. Mrs. Calhoun was no longer
the social queen, but she was the Vice-President's wife, and under her
lead the ladies of Washington preened for battle. 'The ladies . . . will
not go to the wedding,' Mrs. Margaret Bayard Smith wrote, 'and if they
can help it, will not let their husbands go.' [10]

The husbands went. With Jackson to guide them, they were far less
tractable than was expected. Even Calhoun weakened, and called alone
on pretty Peggy,[11] and what those two might have said to each other
would make an interesting addition to history. But it did no good, politically speaking. Henry Clay, inspired alike by Peggy and alcohol, could
not resist a variation on a theme from Shakespeare. 'Time,' said Mr.
Clay, 'cannot wither, nor custom stale her infinite virginity.'[12] This
'pretty wit' shook the men of Washington into hilarious glee, but to Andrew Jackson the affair was no laughing matter. When Vice-President
Calhoun warned the enraged President-elect that 'public opinion' would
not allow Eaton's appointment as Secretary of War, because Peggy would
thus automatically be brought into society, Jackson instantly detected
the feminine hands behind the curtain. 'Do you suppose,' he demanded,
'that I have been sent here by the people to consult the ladies of Washington as to the proper persons to compose my Cabinet?'[13]

Naturally, it was Peggy toward whom the barbs were aimed. Of the
dignified and pleasant John Eaton, there was little criticism. Indeed, it
is doubtful that Peggy's morals, so much as Peggy's origins, were the real
objects of attack. Mrs. Secretary Ingham, for instance, was 'received,'
but she was a lady by birth if not by conduct. Peggy may not have been,
as Jackson so vehemently asserted, 'chaste as a virgin,'[14] but so far as
legal evidence went, his viewpoint could have been as easily proved as
the other. Yet Peggy was unquestionably guilty, guilty of social ambitions
beyond her 'lowly condition,' guilty of beauty unbecoming a matron of
thirty, guilty of wit and conversational charm, to which years of association with Washington leaders had given intellectual polish as well as
picturesque profanity.

'Damn it, I'm off,' exclaimed Peggy on the news of her elevation to
the rank of Cabinet 'lady.'[15] Off, she surely was, on an adventure in
which she shared honors with a proud South Carolina aristocrat in
wrecking a Cabinet, but in, she surely was not. In Washington social
circles there was no seat for Peggy O'Neil. Not even the wishes of the
President-elect could force the ladies to visit one who had 'left her strait
and narrow path.'[16]

Jackson's championship was the puzzle. Outwardly, the ladies laughed
it off, with mischievous hints that Peggy had made another conquest. Had
the history of Rachel Jackson's death been known to them, they would
have indulged in no such suppositions. During her last days the faithful
Rachel, who in error had married Jackson before her divorce from her

first husband had become final, was dragged through the Administration press and held up to public scorn as a strumpet and adulteress. She had died, believing that she was a burden upon his glory. The vicious hatred of the American press had killed her—so Jackson thought. And when, agonized beyond endurance, he had thrown himself upon the new grave in the beating rain, it had been Rachel's friend, Peggy O'Neil, who had comforted him, led him gently into the house, and persuaded him to eat and rest.[17] Would malicious tongues wreck the life of another woman, whom Jackson firmly believed to be as innocent as his own maligned Rachel? Not while there was a drop of red blood left in his body. He was a man who had loved once and loved deeply; he had lived the rough life of the frontier, and yet, to him, womanhood was sacred. Quixotic, ridiculous, if you will, Andrew Jackson, in his championship of Peggy, gave the Southern 'gentlemen' of his day an example of chivalry.

2

Between the two administrations in the winter of 1828 a void of silence descended upon Washington. Like a flickering candle, the Adams Administration made a few spasmodic attempts to lighten its own gloom. Henry Clay, who could not live without the stimuli of success and excitement, donned his 'mask of smiles,' and an artificial animation which carried him through. To his friends he seemed to be going into the customary 'decline'; he was white and thin, unable to sleep without drugs, and alternating between seclusion and a restlessness so intense that he could not even eat at home unless surrounded by friends. Actually he was on the verge of a nervous collapse: the dissipation of a favorite son and the insanity of another, four years of carping criticism from the opposition press, and his own fall from national favor had been too much for even his blithe temperament. He rallied himself finally, and was so spirited, gracious, and gay that friends said he 'was determined we should regret him.'[18] Even President Adams thawed out enough to assume a cordial manner for his last levee, at which, for the first time in his Administration, two drawing rooms were opened for dancing.

Nevertheless, Washington was ominously silent. Most of the Cabinet officers' houses were closed. The winter was very cold. After a driving snowstorm which turned the languid Potomac into a sheet of ice, many of the city's poverty-stricken, starving silently in unheated houses, froze to death. One city newspaper took on the support of a poor family for six weeks, although a society woman protested that to feed the poor was a mere temporary measure and rendered them even more unfit to help themselves when outside help was ended. Congress, mindful of its responsibilities toward the public funds, could of course vote no money for relief, but in answer to an appeal from the *National Intelligencer* took up a collection from the members to purchase fifty cords of wood for distribution where necessary.[19]

It took the ebullient Mrs. Margaret Bayard Smith to shake the city out of its lethargy. She gave a 'small party' at which she saucily mingled the old and the new régime, with as honored guests 'our old friends,' Mr. and Mrs. Calhoun, who alone had accomplished the tightrope feat of walking from one administration into another, 'she as friendly and social, he as charming and interesting as ever.' While some talked in groups and others played chess, Mrs. Smith talked with the two she most admired, 'Mr. Barbour and Mr. Calhoun,' Calhoun discussed the 'late election and the characters of . . . leaders on both sides. I really ought to commit such observations as his to paper, but I cannot find the time,'[20] Mrs. Smith wrote.

The entrance of Mrs. Porter, wife of the Secretary of War, with a smile for one and a nod for another, climaxed the evening. 'No one can see Mrs. Porter but love her,' Mrs. Smith wrote of this sparkling beauty, who in the bleakness of the Adams régime had scored the greatest social success since Dolly Madison.[21] While Mrs. Adams quibbled upon the question of whether to visit or to wait for visits, Mrs. Porter every other week issued hundreds of invitations to her 'Mondays,' with four rooms and a band for dancing. Her open house on 'little Mondays' was equally celebrated; and yet, with all her gaiety and a list of five hundred social calls to make, she would leave a party to visit the Washington slums, and sit for hours in an unheated room by the bedside of a dying woman.

As she entered, she gaily chaffed the Jackson men, and 'carried on a sprightly conversation with Calhoun,' to which, Mrs. Smith declared, 'all around listened with delight.'

'I have not long to stay, so I am determined to . . . enjoy all I can,' she said. 'But no matter'—nodding her head—'if we must go now, we will be back in 4 years, so take it yourselves.'

She wandered away, and Calhoun turned to his hostess. 'What a pity,' he said, 'that all the ladies can not carry it off as charmingly as Mrs. Porter, but some, I hear, take it much to heart.'

'The gentlemen more than the ladies,' Mrs. Smith retorted. 'All the Secretaries are sick . . . with the exception of General Porter.'

Calhoun deplored the mingling of 'personal with political feelings. . . . There is nothing from which I have really suffered in the late conflict,' he said, 'but the division it has created between me and personal friends; as for the abuse of political opponents, that is *nothing*, wounds which leave no scar.'[22]

3

In February, Jackson, evading a celebration, slipped quietly into the city. His army followed him. Day after day the trampled streets became filled with strange faces, bearded, gnarled, weather-beaten. Moccasins padded in the mud; rifles that had seen service with Old Hickory in 1812 flashed in the sun. Daniel Webster studied the faces with fastidious distaste. A 'great multitude,' he commented, 'too many to be fed without a miracle, are already in the city, hungry for office.' Actually, he marveled, they seem to think that Jackson 'has come to save the country from some dreadful danger.' [23]

Later generations, familiar with the free-for-all which concluded Jackson's inauguration, have not shared Francis Scott Key's opinion that the spectacle was 'sublime.' Yet to the women of Washington there was something 'imposing and majestic' in the scene. Twenty thousand people were massed together on the lawn of the Capitol or crowded into carts under the poplar trees along Pennsylvania Avenue, awaiting the appearance of their hero. He came slowly into view, stooped with grief as well as age, his steps hampered by the eager jostling of the crowd.

'There! there! that is he!'

'Which?'

'He with the white head!'

'There is the old man . . . there is the old veteran; there's Jackson!' [24]

He mounted the steps to the portico, standing in silence behind a table covered with red velvet, his loose hair blowing in the wind. Nearby stood the Cabinet officers, the grim and disapproving Chief Justice Marshall, and Vice-President Calhoun, who with a minimum of ceremony had taken his own oath in the Senate Chamber. Slowly Jackson bowed to the people, as brilliant sun rays pierced the mist. Cannon boomed. An answering roar rose from the crowd, then silence as the General read his address. At the close he touched his lips to the Bible and bowed once more, 'to the people in all their majesty.' [25]

There was little majesty and less restraint at the other end of Pennsylvania Avenue, where a mob, a rabble of men, women, and children, blacks and whites, were 'scrambling, fighting, romping' across the White House lawns, leaping from the windows, storming the doors where waiters were ladling out punch. There was no sublimity in the spectacle of fainting women, of bloody noses, and buckets and buckets of broken china and glass. And there was a minimum of majesty inside, where tobacco-chewing frontiersmen, red clay thick on their boots, mounted the damask-covered chairs in the East Room to get a better look at their hero, and where 'a stout black wench' was sitting happily on the floor, eating 'jelly with a gold spoon.'[26] Jackson himself was only saved from suffocation in that swirling mob by friends who formed a human barricade around him. He escaped through a window to Gadsby's Tavern, although he had sufficient energy to climax his day with a dinner party at which he, Calhoun, and other favored political supporters dined on sirloin steak from a prize ox roasted for the occasion.[27] Mrs. Smith summed up the day: 'Ladies and gentlemen, only, had been expected. . . . But it was the People's day and the People's President, and the People would rule.'[28]

The inaugural ball was another matter. There gentlemen did appear, and ladies, too, in wide-skirted, tight-waisted gowns of brocade, piped with coral satin, of blue silk or India muslin, trimmed with white roses and delicate hand-embroidery. Vice-President Calhoun was there, gay and smiling; the Cabinet officers and their ladies were there, and Mrs. Vice-President Calhoun, who did not seem to notice that Mrs. John Henry Eaton, wife of the Secretary of War, was also there.

And right then the trouble began.

4

Peggy was undaunted. She soon called on the Vice-President's lady, and was received with 'civility,' although it cannot be imagined that the visit brought any particular pleasure to either of them. Instantly the question arose: Was Mrs. Calhoun to return the visit?

Here the Vice-President himself enters the story. He was not under the control of his wife. No one ever controlled John C. Calhoun. But neither did anyone, least of all her husband, control Floride Bonneau Calhoun. Already he must have felt the razor edge of her temper, for a tacit understanding that his office was to be a sanctuary seems to have been established between them. Hence, he was startled when Floride flounced into the room the next morning, interrupting his writing to announce: 'Mr. Calhoun, I have determined not to return Mrs. Eaton's visit.'

Calhoun was stunned. He had discussed the subject with his wife, but they had reached no decision, and the very suddenness of her ultimatum shook him. Years afterward, he recalled that the panorama of his future life—the tariff fight, nullification, the break with Jackson—all flashed before his eyes like the vision of a dying man. 'I foresaw the difficulties in which it would probably involve me.' He could not speak. Only his wife's words, sharply repeated, tore him from his reverie. 'I have determined, Mr. Calhoun, not to return Mrs. Eaton's visit.'

Calhoun roused himself. He listened as Floride offered the hardly plausible excuse that she was a 'stranger' in the town, knowing nothing 'of . . . the truth, or falsehood of the imputation' on Mrs. Eaton's character. But if Mrs. Eaton were innocent, she should 'open her intercourse with the ladies who resided in the place . . . and who had the best means of forming a correct opinion of her conduct.' [29]

It was Calhoun's 'vain and silly wife,' who, for her own social gratification, ruthlessly wrecked her husband's career 'at its zenith,' asserted Eckenrode more than a century later; [30] and although he may have exaggerated, Calhoun himself came to believe that 'The road to favor . . . lay directly before me. . . . The intimate relation between General Jackson and Major Eaton was well known, as well as the interest that the former took in Mrs. Eaton's case.'

Yet he adds that he would have felt himself 'degraded' had he sought 'power in that direction.' [31] For by the South Carolina moral code, Floride was right. Floride was the mother of young daughters; what example would it be to them if official rank should prove superior to 'female virtue'; should 'open the door already closed'? In South Carolina, where death alone could sever marriage vows, family rules stipulated that on social questions the woman's decision was law. So with that fatalistic, almost Greek resignation which characterized Calhoun two or three times during his life, in contrast to the defiant, fighting side of his nature, he bowed to the feminine verdict. 'This is a question upon which women should feel, not think,' he said. 'Their instincts are their safest guides.' [32]

Calhoun knew when Floride had made up her mind. Hence, the story handed down by one branch of the Calhoun family may be only legend, but it is completely characteristic of all parties concerned. The story is that a private interview took place between Jackson and the Vice-President.

'You must see . . . that your wife returns Mrs. Eaton's visit,' Jackson is said to have demanded.

'I can't do that, Mr. President,' Calhoun answered.

'You must,' Jackson said firmly.

Calhoun's own stubbornness asserted itself. 'I can't, and I won't,' he retorted.

'If you won't, then I will,' said the undaunted General.

Calhoun suddenly became alarmed. He knew his wife.

'Well, Sir, I'd advise you not to try,' he said.

He could not have chosen better words to arouse the General's defiance. President Jackson is said to have visited the Calhoun dwelling. There he laid down the law. We can see Floride in the miniature painted of her about this time: her heart-shaped face framed by two loops of smooth, dark hair, and a white cap tied under the chin; dark eyes half-hidden under drooping, imperious lids; the chiseled nose and prim little mouth, whose cupid's bow and curves did not conceal its firm determination. She listened in silence, her small head high. Would this backwoodsman dictate the social law to her, to a Bonneau of Charleston? Not likely! His tongue-scourgings could quell armed mutinies; they made not the least impression on one obstinate little woman. She heard him through. She called for the butler. 'Show this gentleman to the door,' she said.[33]

Floride did not stay in Washington to witness the political consequences of her actions. By summer she had retreated to South Carolina, prepared to remain there 'at least for 4 years,' rather than 'endure the contamination of Mrs. Eaton's company.'[34] The damage was complete. Floride could have avoided the whole affair had she wished, for in her 'interesting condition' she could not have been blamed, even by General Jackson, had she chosen gracefully to withdraw from society. She did nothing of the sort. Even had she fully realized the outcome of her stand, it is doubtful that she would have changed.

To Peggy O'Neil it was all politics, and in a large measure she was right. But she was wrong in her belief that Calhoun was playing the general game; he was merely the victim of it. A serious man, he refused to take the Eaton affair seriously. He was looking forward to the next two or three years with deep concern. 'To preserve our Union on the fair basis of equality, on which alone it can stand, and to transmit the blessing of liberty to the remotest posterity is the first great object of all my exertions. . . . These are not the times in which petty arts can succeed. Too many questions are pressing on us. I have ever held them in contempt, and never more than now.'[35]

5

Calhoun was not left in peace to conjecture as to the future, and they were 'petty arts' indeed that diverted him from his course. With his wife gone, he had, as Adams said, taken reluctant leadership of the 'moral party.' To his friends he explained that his position, both as Floride's husband and as Vice-President, obliged him to lead the opposition to Mrs. Eaton. He published a pamphlet upholding his wife's defense of the 'dignity and purity of her sex,'[36] but the chivalry which led him into battle for his own lady prevented him from leveling his guns at the other. Perhaps memories of his youth had left a tender spot in his heart for pretty Irish barmaids. Nevertheless, his defense lacked his usual literary force. He asserted that his wife had never called on Peggy, but Peggy herself countered that Mrs. Calhoun had visited her prior to Eaton's appointment to the Cabinet, and had left her card. We have the word of one woman against another, and can take our choice.[37]

Here mystery enters the scene. Was Peggy, as Jackson said, 'the smartest little woman in America'? or was Perley Poore correct in describing her as a 'mere beautiful, passionate, impulsive puppet,'[38] whose strings were pulled by Martin Van Buren to his own advantage? Probably there was truth in both statements. Peggy could not force her way into Washington society, but neither could society force her to leave until 'her triumph, for so she calls the dissolution of the Cabinet,' [39] was complete. Complete it was. Not a single officer whose wife had insulted her was permitted to keep his seat. And the men of the warring factions, guns in hand, slipped through the Washington streets, silently hunting down their prey. No blood was shed, but several nervous husbands, departing hastily into the obscurity where their wives had already disappeared, averted hostilities. Even Calhoun, true to the best Carolina tradition, is said to have grimly conjectured as to whether or not a duel with Van Buren would relieve the situation. In letters, however, he decided that Van Buren was 'feeble,' though 'artful. . . . I see no cause to fear him.' [40]

But there was cause to fear Van Buren. Van Buren understood that to be or not to be Peggy's friend was the test upon which depended Presidential favor. So he opened his house to Peggy. She was guest of honor at his dinners and balls. At the Russian Ambassador's he escorted her in to dinner before the Dutch Minister's lady, which so enraged that indignant female, she would not go in at all. 'For the whole week, you heard of scarcely anything else,' [41] wrote Mrs. Smith. When Peggy, who took all her griefs and slights to the President, reported this last insult, the Jacksonian reply was characteristic, 'I'd sooner have live vermin on my back, than the tongue of the women of Washington on my reputation.' [42] Meanwhile, the immortal author of 'The Star-Spangled Banner,' once again resorted to verse:

> *'It would grieve me to see our great Master sport*
> *With his dignity for a frail woman in Court.'*

Blithely Van Buren proceeded with his plans. Into Peggy's pretty little ear he whispered that Jackson was 'the greatest man who ever lived,' but warned her not to tell the President, as he would not have him know it for the world. And, of course, Peggy told the General immediately, exactly as Van Buren had planned. Jackson's eyes filled with tears. 'That man loves me,' [43] he declared.

Peggy's power over the President was undeniable. Calhoun admitted it, although his compliment to her abilities hardly soothed Jackson's feelings. 'That base man Calhoun is secretely saying that Mrs. Eaton is the president,' Jackson wrote. And at a public reception in the East Room, Peggy impudently dared the President's wrath, and won even more of his admiration. As Jackson, in his provincial patriotism, was loudly boasting that he had never set foot on foreign territory, Peggy intervened:

'What about Florida, General?'

Hushed, the guests waited for the explosion.

'Oh, that's so, Florida was foreign,' Jackson conceded.

'I guess you forgot that when you *went* there, General,' Peggy said cheerfully. 'Never mind, General, it didn't *stay* foreign long after you got there.' [44]

6

It was the sophisticated and woman-wise Daniel Webster who summed up contemporary opinion: 'The consequences of this dispute in the social . . . world are producing great political effects . . . and may very probably determine who shall be successor to the present Chief Magistrate.' [45]

Subsequent views have been more objective. No doubt Van Buren personally entrenched himself more firmly with Jackson by his attentions to Mrs. Eaton. But to assume thereby that Jackson's choice of a Presidential successor was based on personal grounds would be to dismiss him too lightly.

Actually at this period there was a wider area of political agreement between Jackson and Van Buren than there was between Jackson and Calhoun. And temperamentally, the President and Vice-President were entirely too much alike for comfortable companionship. The break would have come had there never been a Peggy O'Neil. For as we shall see, in Jackson's eyes the enormity of Calhoun's subsequent sins was enough completely to swamp his lack of attention to a pretty barmaid.

If Calhoun had become President, what then? He might have postponed the tariff fight for a few years. He might have strengthened the cause of the states. But he could not have fought the spirit of the age—consolidation—industrialism—standardization—much more successfully in office than outside. Certainly with the South in power, it would have been far more difficult to arouse the Southern States to any consciousness of their long-range dangers.

So Peggy O'Neil may not have greatly changed history, after all. And Calhoun, despite his qualms at Floride's verdict, knew where the primary source of trouble lay—in Martin Van Buren.

XIV

America Grows Up

General Jackson will be here about the 15th of Feb.
Nobody knows what he will do.
Many letters are sent to him;
he answers none of them.
My opinion is
That when he comes he will bring a breeze with him.
Which way it will blow I cannot tell.[1]

THUS WROTE DANIEL WEBSTER on a January morning in 1829, two
months before that fabulous inauguration day when Old Hickory and 'the
People' had taken over the capital.

'When he comes he will bring a breeze with him.' The breeze that he
had brought was the spirit of democracy.

America was growing up. The squalling infant, sired by Washington,
spanked into lusty childhood by Thomas Jefferson, had grown into a gawky
and bumptious adolescence. With the inauguration of Andrew Jackson,
America had rejected its heritage—and found its destiny. For Jackson himself was the symbol of the new America. He was the first truly American
President, the first Chief Executive to spring, not from the Founding
Fathers' classic republican heritage, but from the roaring frontier, from
the very loins of America herself. Jackson owed no responsibility to the
past. To Jackson one word held meaning—democracy.

2

To the self-appointed aristocracy of America, democracy had seemed an
endurable idea when voiced by the undeniably aristocratic Mr. Jefferson of
Monticello. It had seemed a tolerable idea to the parlor-liberals of England, as 'theory in a London drawing room.' But it was something different when presented 'in the shape of a hard greasy paw, and . . . in
accents that breathed less of freedom than of onions and whiskey.' Equality
was ideal, and of course 'we should all be equal in heaven'; but there were

limits when butchers and laborers in dirty shirt-sleeves, calling themselves
gentlemen, were introduced as such to a haughtily bred woman like Mrs.
Frances Trollope.[2]

These were the years when the world came to America. They came in
couples; they came in droves: Alexis de Tocqueville, Captain Marryat,
Captain and Mrs. Basil Hall, Fanny Kemble, Mrs. Trollope, the scientist
Charles Lyell, George Featherstonhaugh the geologist, and many more.
They came; they saw; and they wrote books. Yes, democracy was real; it
lived, breathed, and proclaimed itself America. Even the hypercritical Mrs.
Trollope admitted that 'Any man's son may become the equal of any
other man's son,' a fact conducive to the 'coarse familiarity . . . assumed
by the grossest and lowest . . . with the highest and most refined.'[3] Men
who could not read sent their children to school to become lawyers; children inherited a love of independence and the consciousness that they
were the sons of brave fathers; but in foreign eyes this could not make
them scholars and gentlemen. In foreign eyes Americans were 'deficient in
both taste and learning,'[4] yet few denied their inherent talent and mental
power.

3

But what a country it was, this lusty, roaring young America! New York
on July Fourth—'six miles of roast pig,' lined Broadway in booths, champagne popping within and firecrackers without, the sky showered with
rockets, 'Italian suns, fairy bowers, stars of Columbia, and Temples of
liberty,' all 'America ablaze . . . and all America tipsy.'[5] The toasts to
the heroes of Tippecanoe and New Orleans, to Vice-President Calhoun,
'an able statesman and practical Republican,' to the 'gone coon,' Henry
Clay; 'Like the sun, his splendour hides his spots.'[6]

The gusto, the extravagance of the American taste and the American
language: of 'Leghorn hats large enough to turn the wheel of a windmill';
of 'Brewster's Truly Fortunate Lottery office—Orders thankfully and
promptly executed'; and the small-town drygoods store with its 'Rich
Super Extra Gold List Elegant Blue Cloth.'[7] The backwoodsman who
wanted 'all hell boiled down to a pint,' just to pour down his enemy's
throat. The river boatman who 'rip't up' his Captain with a hunting knife!
Shakers dancing, their wrists raised to their chests, hands hanging down
like the paws of a bear: 'Our souls are saved and we are free from vice
and all iniquity,' which Captain Marryat thought 'a very comfortable delusion at all events.' Waxwork shows of General Jackson and the Battle
of New Orleans, or 'celebrated' criminals 'in the very act of committing the
murder.'[8]

An era was ending. In the New Haven *Herald,* Noah Webster, ears outraged by the new 'American language,' where 'bangup' had become the adjective of esteem, and 'fair dealing and no jockeying' the summary of the moral code, issued an appeal: 'I have devoted a large part of my life to a study of your language. . . . If . . . men choose to write defence and offence with c—or musick with k . . . they have a perfect right to do so; but such irregularity . . . will never deform . . . my writings.' [9]

In the public press Americans could gloat over reports that the tall, war-worn Wellington had so far 'lost his sense of shame, as to forsake his wife to associate with an opera singer.' [10] Democratic America joyfully sneered at British heroes; debunking was a national pastime, although enough hero-worship still survived for the entire citizenry of a Rhode Island village to fight to buy snuff from a jar previously patronized by John Quincy Adams, and to gaze in reverence upon the 'vessel that had contained powder fit to tickle the nose' of an ex-President of the United States.

4

Was there ever a country like it since the world began? Americans thought not. Our 'glorious' future, our 'divine political institutions' were on every lip; and it was 'our weather, our democracy . . . our canvasback ducks,' etc., until the British Mrs. Basil Hall concluded that it was only by the courtesy of Americans that foreigners were permitted to share these enjoyments.[11] But, once more, what a country it was—its contrasts—frontier democracy and Negro slavery, Davy Crockett and John Randolph, North and South—and here, the greatest variances of all!

'A continent of almost distinct nations,' was Mrs. Trollope's observation. 'I never failed to mark the difference on entering a slave state.' [12] The South was different, already the nation's 'other province,' itself as much a patchwork of contrasts as the country at large. Estimates of Southerners ranged all the way from the paeans of those entertained in the manorhouses to Mrs. Basil Hall's peevish dismissal of the 'secondary classes' as 'more disagreeable, gruff, and boorish than anything I ever saw.' [13] South as well as North, there was the same fierce personal individualism, intensified by isolation on a half-won frontier. In the South, even more than in the North, the basic equality of all white men was still real. 'The lower South was a social unit except for the poor slave'; [14] and class brotherhood, bought at the terrible price of black slavery, was strong. Poor Southerners showed little of the grudging ill-will displayed by the man 'of no dollars' in the North, whose services as laborer or servant, for all his theoretical equality, were 'in point of fact' commanded by the man of wealth and power.[15] In the South men of limited ability, who in England would have been swept into factory or mine, still commanded their own persons. If cotton had confiscated the best Southern lands, access to unclaimed pine barrens and foothill farms furnished abundant subsistence for those who would work half-heartedly for a few months in the year. Southerners could fail and still remain free. And for those whose enemy was luck, not indolence, the West lay beckoning always, rich with its promises of cotton lands and great plantations to come.

Diverse goals separated North and South: the North rushing toward its new industrial democracy; the South lagging contentedly behind. Not the development of new enterprises, but the stabilization and extension of the existing plantation economy was the Southern ideal. Politics fitted the facts. Observers of Jackson's democracy, whether foreigners or Southerners, agreed that, although 'the framers of the Constitution . . . intended to establish a Republic, not a Democracy . . . the impulse which General Jackson has given to the democracy of America will . . . always be felt, and impel the government in a more or less popular direction.' The restrictions of republicanism, the checks on the popular will, and the powers of the central government were breaking down in the onrush of democracy. Suspect were men more gifted than their neighbors. In a democracy one man was as good as another; the man who represented, not the ideal but the common strivings, would reach power under popular rule. Once in office, he would not be free to vote according to his own concept of the general good. He was bound by pledges to the pressure groups which had elected him, and was under the threat of future defeat if he acted independently of his makers, the people.[16]

But not in the South. There the Republican ideal still lingered. In Congress, where the growing pains of young America throbbed most sensitively, men strove to interpret the Republican Constitution to fit the demands of the new economy; while the 'gentlemen of the South' sought only to confine the new economy to the limits of the Constitution. In the North men of breeding and education were withdrawing in disgust from popular politics, as 'fit only for blackguards,' or the kind of citizen who read the papers daily at the liquor store to see 'that the men we have been pleased to send up to Congress speak handsome and straight as we choose they should.' [17]

Yet in the South, as we have seen, Jefferson's 'natural aristocracy' still ruled, even if other of his ideals had been less scrupulously maintained.* In the South men trained to rule were still free to rule; and what this

---

* See Clement Eaton's *Freedom of Thought in the Old South* (Duke University Press, Durham, 1940) for account of how Jefferson's bill-of-rights freedoms began to disappear in the ante-bellum South, along with his natural-rights concept that all men were equal.

diversion from the national pattern might mean to the future none dared tell; 'the democratic institutions of the country impelling the people one way, while the aristocratic aspirings of the upper classes' gave them 'an impulse in the opposite direction.' [18]

5

Symbolic of the conversion of America from a republic into a democracy was the struggle for power of its leaders—the progressives against the traditionalists. Behind the scenes in Washington the stage was setting for a mighty drama, a contest of giants that would take shape as a battle for the presidential succession, and would even determine the future course of the Union. And as the nation chuckled over the 'petty arts' of the Peggy O'Neil warfare, back-stage, actors on both sides mouthed their lines, and the long-suppressed hints as to Calhoun's early disapproval of Jackson's seizure of the Florida territory were now dinned into the ears of the receptive General.

'I have always been prepared to discuss it on friendly terms with you,' Calhoun asserted at the height of the quarrel in 1831, and his letters during the days of the campaign four years earlier prove his words. To both Monroe and Major Henry Lee, who was seeking the truth of the 'Florida incident' for a campaign biography of Jackson, Calhoun had written that he would 'cheerfully' give his views in regard to the 'true construction' of Jackson's Florida orders, but only to Jackson himself. 'With you,' he wrote his running mate, 'I cannot have the slightest objection to correspondence on this subject.' [19] But Jackson had indicated no desire for such correspondence. He merely asked Calhoun if the question of his arrest had been considered in the Cabinet, to which Calhoun replied, 'No,' an answer true, as far as it went.[20]

The truth went farther, as we know, and Calhoun had nothing to gain and everything to lose by revealing it. To his credit it can be said that he took the risk and, rebuffed, considered the incident closed. But Crawford thought differently. Crawford had nothing to lose now. A broken man, bitter, he knew that his own Presidential chances were gone. But there was Martin Van Buren to consider. 'Marty' had helped Crawford back in 1824. Had it not been for Calhoun's maneuverings and his own fateful illness, he might well have been in the White House today. If so, it would have been wholly logical to pick Van Buren as his successor. Jackson believed Calhoun to be his friend. What would he say if he knew the truth of those Cabinet sessions of 1819—the truth about his 'honest' and 'noble' friend Calhoun? Revenge was sweet, and revenge in the name of gratitude even sweeter. So in the summer of 1829 Mr. Van Buren visited Mr. Crawford on his Georgia estate, and their hours of conversation were long and confidential.[21] There events were set in motion which were promptly made known to Jackson's old friend, William B. Lewis, who arrived at the White House for a visit in November.

Smoking comfortably after a strenuous day, the President was brought out of a reverie by a carefully casual remark. Lewis was saying that the entire Monroe Cabinet had opposed Jackson's course in the Florida affair.

Jackson shook his head. There was Mr. Calhoun. But Lewis was firm. He had seen a letter 'in which Mr. Crawford is represented as saying that it was not he, but Mr. Calhoun, who was in favor of your being arrested.'

'You saw such a letter as that?'

Lewis nodded. It was now in New York, he added.

'I want to see it, and you must go to New York tomorrow.'[22]

Actually it was a good six months before Jackson saw the letter. But the damage was done. Meanwhile, other events were taking place which contributed to the break. With the same energy with which they had undermined the Adams Administration, Calhoun's supporters, afire with fanatic loyalty, went to work. Typical of their enthusiasm, as well as of their methods, were the activities of Duff Green.

Duff Green was an extraordinary character. A vehement States' Rights Democrat, he consistently opposed secession; a lover of the agricultural South, he was himself the prototype of the twentieth-century business tycoon. His interests embraced railroads, stagecoach lines, land speculation, mining, editing, writing, and iron manufacturing; and in Calhoun's own latter-day liberalism—his recognition of the interdependence of South and West, his calls for railroads and limited but essential Southern industrial development—we can hear echoes of the booming voice of Duff Green.

While this dynamo was devoting his true energies to advancing Calhoun's cause, he was not above accepting the confidence of Jackson during the first years of his Administration. From an actual 'Kitchen Cabinet' member, he became openly and avowedly the leader of the opposition.

Under Jackson's very roof in the winter of 1829, Green had the impudence to tell a Washington newspaper publisher of his plans for the gradual triumph of Mr. Calhoun. Calhoun papers were to be set up in all strategic sections of the country, explained Green, whose own Washington *Telegraph* had long posed as the 'official' Jackson organ; and the instant the formal 'break' came were to join in denunciation of the President.[23] The publisher listened with interest, and immediately reported matters to Jackson, who was unsurprised. He was 'prepared for it.' That his course was already resolved upon is indicated by a private letter on the thirty-first of December, 1829: ' . . . of Mr. Van Buren . . . I have found him everything that I could desire him to be . . . one of the most pleasant men to do business with I ever saw. He . . . is well qualified to fill the highest office in the gift of the people. . . . I wish I could say as much for Mr. Calhoun. You know the confidence I once had in that gentleman. However, of him I desire not now to speak.' * [24]

6

Meanwhile, for the public at large the curtain had risen on the great battle between the agrarian past and the industrial future. And the protagonists were not Jackson and Calhoun, but Daniel Webster and Robert Young Hayne.

Ostensibly listening to a debate on the public lands, which had consumed weeks through the winter of 1829–30, it was only when Hayne dropped the first seeds of the nullification doctrine that Webster, lounging sleepily against a pillar, had stirred with interest. Afterward events moved swiftly. Webster saw the battle in its entirety—above personalities; the meaning of the nullification doctrine he perceived from the first. For Jackson this perception was the luckiest of accidents; for Calhoun a disaster.

A few initial skirmishes preceded the full-scale debate; but news that each combatant would speak—and speak fully—aroused Washington's interest in a dramatic spectacle only less exciting than an appearance of 'mad' Junius Booth or 'Mr. Kean.'

The city was packed. The Indian Queen, Gadsby's, every nameless and forgotten boarding house in Washington was crammed to capacity, argumentative, bickering partisans jostling each other on the staircases, heatedly disputing the relative merits of Jackson and Calhoun, of Webster and Hayne.

By eight o'clock of the morning of January 21, 1830, every seat in the Senate Chamber was filled. All eyes were on Hayne, and how handsome he looked! Boyish and slender in the coarse homespun suit which he had substituted for the hated broadcloth of Northern manufacture, he was a blithe, carefree figure to all appearances, although there was tension under the smile which hovered so lightly across his full lips, and intensity in the flash of his gray eyes. All knew, however, that the taut figure in the Vice-President's chair, listening with an eagerness which he had not shown in years, was the real spokesman of the day. And as Hayne's rhetoric flowed out, plausible, persuasive, not concealing the already familiar arguments of nullification, observers had only to look at the 'white, triumphant face' of the Vice-President to see revealed the secret that was a secret no longer.

* Newly discovered material gives proof of Calhoun's own personal loyalty to Jackson, as late as the summer of 1830. In August, he wrote Virgil Maxcy, an intimate friend, that he was 'much gratified to find that the President has not lost ground in Maryland.' Not until November did he realize the isolation of his position and write: 'I see a great crisis. I pray God that our beloved country may pass it in safety.' See Calhoun's letters to Virgil Maxcy of August 6, 1830, and November 3, 1830, in Galloway-Maxcy-Marcoe papers, Congressional Library.

His deep-set eyes 'shone approvingly,' and now and again a smile broke across his tight lips. Much of the time he was bent over his desk, scrawling hasty, half-legible notes of advice to the speaker, which a few moments later would be carried down the aisle most ostentatiously by one of the page boys.[25] Yet even his vigilance could not save the situation, as Hayne, carried away by his excitement, carelessly misstated a crucial point of the whole nullification doctrine, laying himself open to attack by the weakest of his opponents. Nor was it the weakest who would challenge him. Daniel Webster was waiting.

Few were aware of the error. It was the South's day and the South's victory—or so the Southerners thought. They tumbled out of the Senate Chamber, flushed, ecstatic. That would show 'em! That would show old Jackson and Webster, too! Why, Hayne had demolished him before he even started. Gaily the Southerners proceeded to the taverns and toasted the end of Daniel Webster and his tariff, and the glories of nullification, in glass after steaming glass of punch. It was said that night that you could tell a New England man—and particularly a Massachusetts man—by his downcast face.[26] The battle was won before it was even over.

7

The morning of January 26 dawned, cold and clear. The wind was 'blowing high,' the streets filled with clouds of red dust.[27] Coach after coach rolled up before the Capitol, and the sharp, frozen ruts of winter cut deep into the satin-clad feet of the women as they descended from their carriages into billows of ruffles. Women were everywhere—over one hundred and fifty of them, one observer said—and by the time they had selected their seats, there was scarcely room for a Senator to stand, much less sit down. 'No principle would have had so much attraction. But personalities are irresistable,'[28] Mrs. Smith commented. For although on that day, on that floor, the question of whether the United States were a federal union or a national democracy would be settled, few present troubled to realize it.

The conflict between the personalities, however, was realized completely. And the personalities, people now sensed, were not so much Webster and Hayne as Webster and Calhoun. On the floor stood Webster, dark and imperturbable, and in the chair sat Calhoun, spare, rough-haired, tense as a coiled spring. Although from the beginning Webster held and compelled attention, those who glanced at the Vice-President found in his 'changing countenance' a rich reward. For as the strength of Webster's argument dawned upon the clear-thinking Carolinian, his restlessness became 'very evident'; and as Webster denounced Hayne's call for a union of the agrarian South and West against Northern industrial interests, and proceeded to extol the kind of centralized Union that would protect the manufacturers, Calhoun's 'brow grew dark,' and his face increasingly somber.²⁹

The plea for internal improvements 'nettled him' beyond endurance. 'Too much excited' even to remember his position, his feelings gave way, and time and again he tried to break into Webster's speech. At last he saw his opportunity, and tearing through all rules of parliamentary procedure, curtly demanded if the Senator from Massachusetts was accusing 'the person now occupying the chair' of having changed his position.

Webster was astounded. He turned to the presiding officer, quietly remarked, 'If such change has taken place, I regret it,' and continued where he had left off. The rebuff was complete. He followed up a few moments later with a Shakespearian and pointed warning: 'No son of their's succeeding,' looking steadily at Hayne and then at Calhoun, who 'changed color' and showed some agitation.³⁰

At the eulogy on Massachusetts the excitement rose to its zenith. In the gallery the Massachusetts men wept openly. Even Webster's own emotions, which for all his eloquence were surprisingly sluggish, now stirred. His dark skin warmed; his eyes burned as if 'touched with fire.' And Calhoun, whose mobile face throughout the debate, revealed all the emotions that he strove to conceal, had given way once again. State love —state pride—these were things he could understand, and his own dark eyes were wet with tears.

' . . . Liberty and Union, now and forever, one and inseparable.' It was over. The room hung in a silent spell, petulantly broken by Calhoun himself, with a sharp rap of his gavel, a curt 'Order! Order!' Yes, it was over; and 'no one who was not present can understand the excitement of the scene.' ³¹

8

The second act in the struggle of the Jacksonian democracy was booked for the annual party 'love-feast,' the Jefferson Day dinner, three months later. And here Calhoun and Hayne put their own heads into the trap.

For even Hayne, oddly enough, seemed to have had no doubt that Jackson would lend his support to the doctrine of nullification. That nullification was Calhoun's threat to Jackson seems not to have occurred to him. Of the President's silent support of Webster he had no conception. Jackson was a Southerner. The expanding tariff-industrial program of the North was a threat to Southerners. Thus reasoned Hayne.

Democratic was the choice of a dining place—Jesse Brown's Indian Queen Hotel, known to all Washington by the luridly painted picture of Pocahontas swinging in front, and by the host himself who, enveloped in a huge white apron, personally carved and served the principal dish of the evening.[32] And democratic was the guest-list, for a card had been left at the bar, available to any admirer of the great Jefferson who cared to sign, pay, and get his ticket.[33]

Light blazed from open windows, flashed through the decanters of whiskey, rum, and gin which stood in rows along the weighted table. Within, the air was scented with the usual banquet fare—boned turkey, partridges, canvasback ducks, pickled oysters—and heavy with suspense.[34] At each plate lay evidence of Calhoun's contribution, the interminable list of toasts, ranging all the way from the purest of Jeffersonian doctrine down to 'the doctrine contended for by General Hayne.'[35] Their meaning was clear: to commit the Democratic Party to the principles of nullification. The Pennsylvania delegation entered, took one look, and departed in a body.

Jackson at last, Van Buren at his side. The General was charged with excitement, 'as animated,' Van Buren later said, 'as if he were prepared to defend the Union on a field of battle.'[36] What did it mean? Only three men in Washington knew what was in Andrew Jackson's mind that night. Only Van Buren and Jackson himself knew of the three or four tentative toasts that had gone into the fire, and of the slip of paper bearing one trenchant sentence that lay now next to the President's heart.

Dinner was served. From the head and foot of the central table, Calhoun and Jackson eyed each other, toyed with their food. Course after course was set before them and removed, untouched. Slowly the tension in the room increased. A plot had been uncovered to assassinate Jackson! Calhoun was heading a secret secession movement in South Carolina; already, so it was said, medals had been struck off: 'John C. Calhoun: First President of the Confederate States of America.'[37] And as if by magnetic power, all eyes were drawn to the two central figures, so different and yet so alike, towering head and shoulders above most of the other men in the room, their drawn faces and thin, compressed lips. Each was waiting . . .

Hayne, dapper, buoyant, rapidly recovering from Webster's body blows, arose. His address was an embellished reiteration of the challenge to Webster, adapted for the dinner table. Then came the toasts—twenty-four of them—with Jackson growing more and more stern and Calhoun more and more taut. Finally, Toastmaster Roane:

'The President of the United States.'

Jackson arose, stood waiting for the cheers to die away. He faced Calhoun, and from each side men drew back, leaving the way clear. Van Buren scrambled to the top of a chair to see better what was going on.[38]

Andrew Jackson looked straight into the eyes of John C. Calhoun. 'Our Union—it must be preserved.'[39]

Not a cheer sounded. An order to arrest Calhoun where he sat would not have come with more force.

Jackson raised his glass, and as a man the room arose. All heads turned toward Calhoun. His eyes had gone black; he had the look of a man in a trance. He brushed his hand across his forehead, then reached out, his thin fingers groping. Slowly they closed around the stem of his glass. His hand shook; the amber fluid trickled down the side.[40] 'He's going to pour it out; he's going to pour it out,' someone whispered. The glass steadied; Calhoun drank. Again the burning gaze of the two antagonists met, crossed. Jackson left his seat and walked over to Senator Benton. Hayne hurried to the President's side, and there was a hasty whispering. The room was emptying as if news of an invasion had come from outside.

At last quiet was restored. It was Calhoun's turn now. White-faced, his eyes blazing, he had summoned every resource of his intrepid mind. He would surrender nothing of his creed. He lifted his glass. The words of his own anticlimax came slowly, but his voice was clear:

'The Union. Next to our liberties, most dear.'[41]

He had picked up the challenge. That night, in that room, the lines of Appomattox had been drawn.

9

Looking back in later years, Calhoun could see the relentless succession of events from that inaugural ball, when Floride had not seemed to 'notice the presence of Mrs. Eaton,' to the discomfiting scrawl from President Jackson on a May morning in 1830 which to all practical purposes ended Calhoun's Presidential hopes forever. Even then he scarcely realized what had happened, but the drama had been played to its final curtain. For by now the artfully designed and long-concealed 'letter' of Crawford's was in Jackson's hand.

It was a 'vindictive' document. In it Crawford, skillfully hiding his own undercover campaign against Jackson, laid the entire blame upon Calhoun. Yet Jackson's old friend, John Overton, who read the letter at Jackson's suggestion, was not deceived by it. It was, he said, 'a poor tale . . . scarcely fit to deceive a sensible school boy.'[42] No doubt Calhoun had criticized the General's action. No doubt he had evaded confession, but, unlike Crawford, he had not attempted to throw the blame upon another. To Overton the whole affair was beneath notice. His advice to Jackson was to forget it; but this was the one course which it was impossible for the President to follow.

Jackson was appalled. Convinced that he could read a man's soul in five minutes, he was equally convinced that any man who opposed his actions was his personal, vindictive enemy. Discovery that he had been deceived was a bitter slap at his self-esteem. What made the matter even more painful to this man of 'fanatical friendships' was his long-held impression that Calhoun had been his sole defender in Monroe's Cabinet.[43] Nevertheless, he withheld his fire. He wrote to Crawford, received his version of the affair, and then only, in a 'brief, restrained' note, demanded the truth of Calhoun.

But if Jackson was furious, Calhoun was more so. He was 'determined to keep [his] temper,' as he wrote Virgil Maxcy, 'but not to yield the hundreth of an inch.' Parton, by no means a Calhoun admirer, admits that he could find no evidence whatsoever 'that Mr. Calhoun was guilty of duplicity toward General Jackson.'[44] Publicly or privately, Calhoun had never professed that he approved all of the General's proceedings in Florida, but he was betrayed by his 'desire to stand well.' Disgusted with Crawford's revelation of Cabinet secrets, he lowered himself to his rival's level. Instead of taking the 'correct and dignified' ground of scorning to reveal 'the proceedings of a Cabinet council,' he attempted justification in a tortuous maze of thirty-two closely written pages.[45] Crawford, meanwhile, his memory blurred as to the actual events, after having inoculated Jackson's mind with his initial misstatements, back-tracked, and in a second letter declared that Mr. Calhoun did not actually propose to 'arrest General Jackson.'

Here, indeed, was a loophole through which Calhoun might have squeezed; but he had not apparently sunk so far. Now that the secret was out, he scorned to hold back any of it. If he had used the word *investigation* rather than arrest, his meaning was perfectly clear. How 'could an officer under our law be punished without arrest and trial?'

'The object of a cabinet council,' Calhoun explained, is . . . to form opinions . . . after full . . . deliberations.' Proposals for Jackson's arrest had not been considered. He admitted that his personal belief had been that Jackson had 'transcended his orders,' but that he questioned neither his patriotism nor his motives. Such hair-splitting was, of course, utterly impossible for Jackson to understand.

Calhoun had called for an investigation. The rest of the Cabinet had thought otherwise. At the end the unanimous decision was to uphold the General. 'I gave it my assent and support.'[46] This was more than Crawford did, who, despite his tacit submission to the majority viewpoint, went right on secretly condemning and undermining Jackson through his supporters in Congress. For Calhoun, always a personal admirer of Old Hickory, once the decision had been made, the incident was closed. Thus ran his defense—'truthful, restrained,' plausible enough to those who would labor through it, but still only too clearly the futile struggle of a creature caught in a trap. To Jackson its meaning was clear. Arrest, investigation, or reprimand—it was all the same; in his 'hour of trial' Calhoun was leagued in 'secret council' against him. Bitterly he gripped his pen. 'I had a right to believe that you were my sincere friend, and . . . never expected to . . . say of you . . . *Et tu Brute.* In all your letters as War Secretary you approved *entirely* my conduct in relation to the Seminole campaign. . . . Your letter . . . is the first intimation to me that *you* ever entertained any other opinion. . . . Understanding you now, no further communication with you on this subject is necessary.' * [47]

Calhoun demurred. So far as Jackson was concerned, he was a dead man, but he did not know it. His 'further communications' dragged over months, and before the battle ended, the memories of William Wirt, the dying James Monroe, and the totally indifferent John Quincy Adams had been thrown into the fray.

Yet all was not quite lost. Calhoun put in a tense six months waiting for his chief's anger to cool, but cool it finally did. Not that Jackson felt more kindly inclined toward the South Carolinian; in fact, by October, 1830, he was writing to his daughter-in-law, Emily Donelson, that he had 'long known' of Calhoun's attempts to injure him through the Eaton affair.[48] Yet undeniable steps were being made toward at least an official reconciliation. For the public was confused. Next to that of Jackson himself, Calhoun's popularity was unrivaled, and Jackson might lose much in the South by any open break with his Vice-President.

10

Behind the scenes, mutual friends of the two worked feverishly. Not only John Overton had been disgusted at Crawford's and Lewis's intrigue for the hasty advancement of Van Buren. And loyal as Jackson was to his New York friend, his basic sense of justice came to the foreground. So one autumn day in 1830, as Ralph Earl was painting a portrait of Jackson, the President announced to the omnipresent Van Buren that the estrangement between himself and the Vice-President was ended. The unfriendly correspondence was to be destroyed. 'The whole affair was settled.'

Unruffled in the face of apparent disaster, the Red Fox offered his congratulations. Calhoun was invited to dinner.[49]

Had the South Carolinian been content to let matters rest, history might have been different. But the events of the past two years had gone too deep. Calhoun recognized the whole fight as a struggle for the succession between Van Buren and himself, in which 'Van Buren was ultimately successful as a result of excessive cleverness on his own part, and some shady practices on the part of Lewis and of Eaton.' [50]

* Jackson's letter to Monroe, requesting an unofficial 'go ahead' signal through 'Johnny Ray,' was written nearly two weeks after Calhoun's letter of blanket orders to Jackson to 'take the necessary measures . . . to terminate the conflict' was dispatched. Hence, the Cabinet debate turned on the construction of the orders. (Andrew Jackson to James Monroe, January 6, 1818, quoted in Parton, II, 433; also Calhoun to Jackson, December 26, 1817. *American State Papers, Military Affairs*, I, 690)

Van Buren had tried to destroy him; why, then, should he not destroy Van Buren? Straightway Calhoun proceeded with a humanly spiteful act against his rival, which in the end injured no one so much as himself. The correspondence about his row with the President was his weapon. Why destroy it? Why not publish it and let the world judge as to who had really been the plotters and who the victim? With the aid of Duff Green and Felix Grundy, Calhoun got the formidably bulky documents ready for the press. Eventually Grundy cornered John Eaton in his hotel room and read him the entire manuscript. What changes would please the President? Grundy asked. Eaton suggested several. The men parted with the understanding that the Secretary of War was to explain the matter to Jackson. No disapproval came from the White House, and on February 15, 1831, Calhoun, convinced that he was acting with Jackson's full knowledge, published the entire sorry business in the *Telegraph*. The reaction of the entire Administration press was instantaneous. The *Globe* spoke for all of them: 'Mr. Calhoun will be held responsible for all the mischief which may follow.' [51] Roared Andrew Jackson: 'They have cut their own throats.' [52]

The feminine element had had the last, or rather the silent word. John Henry Eaton, the outraged husband, had deliberately failed to mention Calhoun's plan to Jackson. Peggy O'Neil's revenge was complete.

Calhoun was left to the meager consolation offered by such sympathetic females as Margaret Bayard Smith, who, with 'the light of Mr. Calhoun's splendid eye still lingering' in her imagination, announced that she would 'swear to every word of Mr. Calhoun's letters. They are written with the . . . spirit of a true gentleman, a spirit of rectitude, delicacy and refinement, and I trust he will break the net his enemies have been weaving around him. The impressions of the unprejudiced seem to me to be all in his favor.' [53]

Public opinion did little to help Calhoun. Stripped of power, he still had his term as Vice-President to fill out; and hours in which, 'proud and silent,' he could brood over the misfortunes that had struck him. He was 'burning with resentment.' Of restoring his position with Jackson, he now had no hope at all. Yet during the session of 1831 an event occurred which convinced him that if his own future was blighted, he could do as much for the hopes of the man upon whom he laid the blame—Martin Van Buren.

Van Buren was Minister to England, uttering suave generalities to the men and sweet nothings to the ladies, impressing all with the belief that America could produce diplomats of courtliness—even of culture. His had been an inspired appointment, no doubt, but unfortunately a recess appointment. Final approval must be granted by the Senate, and Calhoun's influence upon the Senate was still strong.

A tie was arranged. In triumph Calhoun cast the deciding vote of rejection, and in triumph descended from the Vice-President's rostrum and his own high standards of conduct:

'It will kill him, sir, kill him dead,' he announced, in glee. 'He will never kick, sir, never kick.'

Instantly Thomas Hart Benton perceived the irony of the situation. 'You have broken a Minister,' he announced confidently, 'and elected a Vice-President.' [54]

How could Calhoun's madness have carried him so far? Even Van Buren himself had not dared hope for such childishness as this. But the damage was done, and the revenge which Calhoun had sought to turn upon his rival was again turned only upon himself.

Administration supporters lost no time in showing their antagonism. The leader among these was John Forsyth of Georgia, who in the midst of debate one day lashed out bitterly at the long-passed attacks of the Calhoun press.

This 'touched the Vice-President on the raw.' He turned to Forsyth. 'Does the Senator allude to me?'

Forsyth looked at him. His voice vibrated through the Chamber. 'By what right does the Chair ask that question?' he demanded; then waited, giving everyone ample time to reflect that actually the Vice-President had no right to speak at all. 'The chair,' runs the old account, 'was awed into silence.' [55]

But Calhoun was beyond all clear thinking now. The clean, bright ambitions of his youth were stained with bitterness. Was it only two years since he had sat here, the friend and acknowledged successor of Andrew Jackson, his 'transcendent abilities' [56] daily praised in the press, his popularity daily increasing, both with the Senate and the country? What had happened? The same room, the same faces—and yet how different! He had waited so long for the fulfillment of his hopes; and he was weary of waiting. Now his prize had slipped from him. He felt that he had been cheated out of it, and he had some right to think so. Men could say that he was still young enough to form an alliance with Clay for future benefits; but what did they know? He did not feel young. Mentally at forty-nine he had yet to reach his full height, but physically, intense thinking was wearing him out.[57] A small boy, taken up to the Vice-President's rostrum, cried out in terror at the 'ghost with burning eyes,' and years later could remember how white Calhoun's face had been, and how dark and blazing his eyes.[58] His face told the story. The dying John Randolph studied him closely. 'Calhoun must be in Hell,' he observed. 'He is self-mutilated, like the fanatic that emasculated himself.' [59]

He was indeed a tortured man. There is tragedy in his bottled-up ambitions, for his desire was not for himself alone. He may have overestimated his responsibilities, but at least he scorned to shirk them. Well did he know the intensity of feeling that gripped South Carolina more firmly with every passing day. Perhaps he knew, too, of John Tyler's letter to Hayne, written on June 20, 1831, with its assertion that if the 'obnoxious' Administration of Adams had been continued, even Virginia would have adopted 'a decided course of resistance,' nullification or secession, if need be.[60]

What could Calhoun now do? Almost alone among statesmen of his time, he was at grips with fundamentals. Nationalist that he was, he would far rather take positive than negative action, work from within rather than from without. It was the dream of his youth, the last hope of his age, that as President he might attempt his own reformation of the government, restoring the Constitution to its 'primitive purity.'

His baffled ambitions had driven him to states' rights, not as the only means of saving the Union, but as the only device by which *he* could save the Union, and the rights of the South within the Union. No choice was left him. As he told James Hammond, so far as his relations with Jackson were concerned, he 'had dissolved all ties, political . . . or otherwise, with him and forever.'[61] Yet if his leadership of the Southern cause and the Southern concept of the Federal Union has any value to modern times, his quarrel with Jackson may even have been providential. Conscious of his powers, so long as any hope of the Presidency loomed before him, he would have been tempted to compromise his principles. Now no political considerations tempered his fervor. He was bitter but free, and he could look to the needs of the South with a single eye.

11

Family affairs added to Calhoun's cares. He had been 'delighted' in 1829 when his oldest boy, Andrew, decided to enter Yale. This had surprised Calhoun, for the boy's distaste for study was so marked that his father had feared to 'force' him, lest he develop a 'permanent disgust' for learning. So backward was he in 'conick sections and Trigonometry' that Calhoun could hope only that he might attain 'respectable . . . standing.'

In letters to his old tutor and friend, James Kingsley, Calhoun had attempted to smooth his son's way. Andrew would rely 'on your kindness for advice and encouragement.' Particularly did Calhoun beg Kingsley's aid in finding a roommate 'of good character.' Andrew, he hastened to add, had always been such a son 'as a parent might desire'; he did not know that he had 'a single bad habit or inclination.' Nevertheless, mindful of the 'secret . . . vice' at Yale in his own student days, Calhoun would deem 'an idle or immoral roommate a great misfortune.' Intellectual improvement was nothing beside 'correct moral deportment.'

For a few months Calhoun relived his own student days. It was 'a source of no inconsiderable pleasure' to him that Andrew was so pleased with Yale. He considered it 'fortunate' that he had placed 'himself . . .

A cartoon drawn during the Presidential campaign of 1832.
Calhoun, Clay, Wirt, and Jackson play at Brag, a form of poker.
Clay has just won the hand with his three aces. *Courtesy of the
American Antiquarian Society, Worcester, Massachusetts*

under the guidance of the same teachers to whose superintendance . . . I owe so much'; that Andrew was 'in the same class with so many of the sons of my old class-mates. . . . I hope that he will cultivate their acquaintance.' Most of all, he was amazed that his boy had become 'fired with an ardent zeal to acquire knowledge.' His 'constant improvement' was shown in every letter which the delighted father read and reread.[62]

Then, late in August, came news as 'painful' as it was 'unexpected.' An 'unfortunate occurence' had 'separated' Andrew and 'many of his classmates' from Yale.[63]

Probably Calhoun never knew the whole story. The 'Conic Sections Rebellion' finds no place in the official histories of Yale College. Yet in the story of the class of 1832 it looms large. For a large proportion of the boys were actively involved in the student mutiny against the teaching of 'conick sections' which resulted in the 'disruption' of the class. Afterward fifty-five students apologized and were reinstated, but Andrew Calhoun was not among them.[64]

For the Calhoun pride had been hurt—on both sides. Once more Andrew's father wrote Kingsley, but his tone was short, almost curt. 'For your kind attention to him . . . my acknowledgement.' One last favor would he ask. Would Kingsley tell Andrew that his father had written him to come home, in case the letter had not yet arrived, and 'knowing how anxious he must be to hear from me.' [65] To the boy himself he gave no rebuke. Between the lines is a tone of indignation. Calhoun was miffed, angry that his son, the son of the Vice-President of the United States, should be 'separated' so summarily. The incident was closed, but Calhoun's relations with his alma mater cooled, and although he took a mild interest in graduate activities throughout his life, it is significant that of his other four boys not one was entered in Yale.

12

It was another one of Calhoun's seven children * that brought relief to his depressed state of mind through these years. Burdened as he was with correspondence, he would still do his fatherly duty by his fourteen-year-old daughter, Anna Maria, in boarding school in the fall of 1831, and away from home for the first time. 'I set you the example of being a very punctual correspondent,' he wrote. 'Yesterday, I received your letter and today I answer it.'

* Andrew Pickens (October, 1811), Floride (January, 1814, died April 7, 1815), Anna Maria (February 13, 1817), Elizabeth (October, 1819, died March 22, 1820), Patrick (February 9, 1821), John B. (May 19, 1823), Cornelia (April 22, 1824), James Edward (April 23?, 1826), William Lowndes (August 13, 1829).

He had not dreamed how much delight Anna Maria's letters would bring him. It was a heart-warming experience to share his thoughts and feelings with his daughter, gently to guide her across the pitfalls that he, too, had known. Yet the correspondence, on Anna's side, at least, had begun under compulsion. He would not scold her for her aversion to writing, for he had good reason to believe it 'in some degree hereditary.' But he was generous enough in his praise to spur her on to a spirited correspondence.

He shared her joys and sorrows with the same understanding that she would give him a few years later. 'I am not surprised that you felt so lonesome at first,' he told her, mindful of his own early days in Litchfield. 'We are never more so, than when in the midst of strangers, but you acted like a philosopher, when, instead of giving yourself up to tears, you set about removing the cause, by forming the acquaintance of those around you.' He added a warning out of his own reserve. 'Form a general acquaintance with all, but be familiar with few . . . worthy of your friendship.'

This was his way of guidance: to praise and encourage her virtues rather than to ferret out her weaknesses. 'With your aversion to early rising, you deserve much praise for not having . . . "missed prayers." I commend your caution in declining to speak of your associates until you have had more time to form your opinion. . . . Much of the misfortune of life comes from hasty and erroneous conceptions of others.'

Nowhere in Calhoun's letters is the Victorian preachiness which so infested parental communications of the period. For Anna's physical well-being he was concerned; he would urge her to guard her health and her posture; but so far as her moral welfare went, she needed no advice; she was his daughter and he trusted and understood her. Almost from the first, between the girl of fourteen and the man of forty-nine, the relationship was far more that of contemporaries than of parent and child. And Anna Maria responded to this gentle guidance. Whatever her hopes, she knew that her father would understand. He wrote her: 'I will . . . send to you the musick which you request. Give a full and fair trial to your voice, but unless it should prove at least pretty good, it would be an useless consumption of time to become a Singer; but do not dispair till you have made a fair trial.'

To his delight he found that this girl, of all his children, had inherited his own clear intellect and his own tastes. 'I am not one of those, who think your sex ought to have nothing to do with politicks,' he told her. 'They have as much interest in the good condition of their country, as the other sex, and tho' it would be unbecoming them to take an active part in political struggles, their opinion . . . cannot fail to have a great . . . effect. . . . I have no disposition to withold political information from you.' Yet in these early letters he still discussed political questions with brevity. He could write her of his health, his eagerness to be home, how painful the long 'seperations' were to him. But the heaviest of his burdens he would not yet lay upon her young shoulders. It was enough for him to have her love and solicitude. He had found a friend in his daughter.[66]

XV

Blue Cockades and Dueling Pistols

To FOREIGN VISITORS in the first third of the nineteenth century, Charleston was the most 'delightful' city in the United States,[1] perhaps because, of all American cities, with the exception of New Orleans, Charleston looked the least American. Heat, damp, and torrential rains had faded the orchids and pinks of the crumbling walls into an 'ancient hue,'[2] fragile and delicately tinted as eggshells. Already war, fires, and hurricanes had given Charleston the time-worn look of an old European city; although some world travelers, looking up the sandy streets where sunlight glanced off bristling yucca and palmettos, and groups of slatternly Negroes lounged at every street-corner, would recall the West Indies or the Orient.[3] If there was a hint of Holland or Flanders in the turn of a gable, those slanting rooftops with their graceful pantiles might have been seen glimmering on some fifteenth-century cathedral in Italy or Southern France.

But most of all, Charleston was an English town. 'We are decidedly more English than any other city of the United States,'[4] boasted Hugh Legaré. Georgian doorways with fluted columns opened onto long, shaded galleries. For Britons, fresh from soot-steeped London and smoke-stained Lancaster, to see Charleston, the mansion houses and the churches of Christopher Wren; to walk into those drawing rooms, with their Doric pilasters and mock-India wallpaper, was like stepping back into an English country town of the eighteenth century or invading the stage-set of a comedy by Farquhar or Congreve.[5] And most British of all were the people themselves, these booted and spurred 'country squires,' with their talk of horses and hunts and races, and the echoes of London tutors sounding in the flatly accented speech of the young men.[6]

And their hospitality! As the scientist Charles Lyell described it, Charleston had 'a warmth and generousness . . . which mere wealth cannot give.'[7] Even little Harriet Martineau, drawing her spinsterish form rigid against the blandishments of these people who traded in human flesh, gave way before such gestures as a carriage at her disposal every day of her visit, tickets to the newest play or lecture on phrenology, and

bouquets of rare hyacinths with her breakfast coffee. Yes, the Charlestonians knew how to make their visitors feel more than at home.[8]

Although society had an unmistakably aristocratic tone, its 'family' demands were flexible. The man himself meant more than his family, and
the aristocratic tradition meant more than the individual man. Old barriers had been broken down by the Revolution, estates subdivided, and
by 1850, merchants and back-countrymen could win their way into the
'charmed circle' of Charleston society.[9] Old names and old families meant
much in theory, but old Charleston warmed to the onrush of new blood;
and in practice there was a place in Charleston for the self-made aristocracy of brains and character. Men like George McDuffie, James Louis
Petigru, and John C. Calhoun, up-countrymen all, and all with Irish blood,
might not lead the dance steps at the Saint Cecilia Ball, but they set the
patterns of Charleston thought. Society was pleasant because it included
all who could make it pleasant and no others. In Charleston money had
its power and family its place, but neither of these alone gave entrée to
breakfast at Joel Poinsett's.[10]

Requirements for an invitation were high: agreeableness in the men,
beauty and charm in the women. And although strangers were welcome,
if they failed to pass the host's tests, they were never invited again.

Here came the Huger cousins, Alfred and Daniel, each slender, tall,
chiseled of feature, Grecian of mind. Here came the Ravenels, the Rut-
ledges, the Porchers. You saw Thomas Grimké—'the walking dictionary,'
writer of ponderous and unreadable articles in the *Southern Review;* and
William Elliott, wildcat hunter and author of the racy *Piscator.* That
dumpy little man with his long head and squinting eyes, his shrill voice
rising now and again into a screech, is the greatest lawyer in America in
the opinion of his Charleston neighbors, and no man in the city is more
beloved. He loves the Union—loves liberty; yet has no faith in the
people's ability to preserve the one or the other. This gentle cynic,
James Louis Petigru, professed no creed; yet when summoned to court
on Good Friday he sternly reminded the judge that only Pontius Pilate
had held a judicial session that day.[11]

One face—one man, although silent and alone—would have compelled
any visitor's attention. Proud, somber, high-bred, it is the face of a
Byron—or of a Greek god. The handsomest man in Charleston is Hugh
Legaré—until he rises to his feet and shambles across the floor, visibly
shrinking from the curious and pitying glances that fall on his dwarfed
body, his shriveled and misshapen legs.[12] Close at his side is a younger
man, an unforgettable face—bitter, sardonic—with square forehead and
arrogantly flaring nostrils, Robert Barnwell Rhett, most brilliant among
them—and most disturbing.

A few faces around Joel Poinsett's breakfast table are already familiar.
Calhoun was there, of course, on the rare occasions when he was in town;

and friends separated from him over the months would be quick to mark the changes that unrelenting labor and strain were working upon him. His slender figure was as lithe, his clear eyes as piercing, as ever; but already he was looking 'haggard and careworn,' far older than his years.[13] Nearby would be young McDuffie, equally tense and overstrung; and debonair Robert Hayne. That huge head and bulging forehead bring back memories, although it is hard to recognize in this rotund figure, Langdon Cheves, the spirited young War Hawk of 1812.[14]

And if ever a man had been born to personify the aristocratic ideal in practice—not in theory—it was the host, Joel Poinsett himself. Grandson of a highly respectable and skillful Huguenot silversmith, who might have found much in common with Boston's Paul Revere, Poinsett's openly admiring allusions to his ancestor were the despair of his low-country wife. 'Manor-born,' she had only accepted the swarthy little man, for whom the poinsettia was named, after she had previously jilted him, married and become a widow, leaving her faithful suitor to years of bachelorhood.

But they were by no means empty years. Poinsett, dark, slender, incredibly delicate in health—he often said that he had been able to live most comfortably for twenty years with only one lung[15]—lived fully and happily as well. He served as Ambassador to Mexico and Secretary of State, alternated between the South Carolina Legislature and the United States Congress. He had been Vice-President Calhoun's messenger to John Quincy Adams, bearing the secret message that if Adams would desist from appointing Clay to the Cabinet, Mr. Calhoun would support the Administration; and later was President Jackson's secret agent in Charleston during the nullification crisis.

At table Calhoun might even have rivaled his host, however; for contemporaries generally agreed with the young Congressman who proclaimed Calhoun 'the most charming man in conversation I ever heard.'[16] At Poinsett's there were no restrictions upon subject matter. At Judge Huger's, too, politics were drunk with the Madeira, and young men in ruffled shirts and flamboyant waistcoats listened with wary intentness as history was discussed by the men who were making it. But it was only in a few Charleston homes that politics prevailed; it was art at the Middletons' and literature at the Prioleaus'.

In a single decade Charleston had reached maturity. Only in 1827 had a scornful townsman denounced the city on the Ashley as 'a scene of inaction' to Calhoun's friend, James MacBride. There was 'no prospect of pleasure in Charleston' for those 'of a highly elevated cast.'[17] But now, how different! The city had its literary groups, its men of letters, such as William J. Greyson of *Defense of Slavery* fame; William Crafts, whose rhymed couplets in *The Raciad* were pronounced to rival Pope's for dexterity of phrase and originality of thought; Grimke, and Elliott. Writing was still deemed a polite accomplishment rather than a means of livelihood; but at the fortnightly gatherings, at Judge Prioleau's, Charleston's most talented voices and intellects shared their thoughts with their admiring contemporaries. Here Charles Fraser, the miniature artist, first voiced his stately reminiscences of Revolutionary days, later published in book form. Hugh Legaré spoke on his absorbing passion, 'The Greek Republics,' and Poinsett on 'The Republics of South America.' Similar evenings flourished at Judge King's, where the host himself was typical of the 'new' Charleston aristocracy. A poor immigrant boy from Scotland, by force of character and self-education he had made himself a leader of the intelligentsia.

But at the name of William Gilmore Simms eyebrows lifted haughtily. Charleston circles had no entrée for this earthy young Elizabethan, with a strong, handsome face and racy speech; a lawyer now, but a slaveless, landless apothecary's apprentice only a few years before. What place did his 'swamp-suckers' and 'Border Beagles,' his 'rapscallions and blackguards,' have in polite society? Britain could call him an American Fielding; an exasperated visitor would cry out, 'If he is not your great man, for God's sake, who is?' Charleston was unimpressed—and unmoved.[18]

Charleston had its art; there was Washington Allston, although he, too, had been snubbed at home until approval had been nodded in European capitals. But his brilliant pupil, Samuel Morse, had arrived in town, to win success in 1818; there was John White with his historical panoramas; and Fraser, the schoolmate and teacher of the great Sully, encompassing so much honesty and power in the limits of the miniature. Portrait artists like John Wesley Jarvis, with gifts for painting gentility into faces where it was important that gentility be seen, were always sure of a welcome in self-conscious Charleston. Portraits, the work of masters like Van Dyck and Reynolds, hung on paneled walls beside those by Lawrence and Sully; it was part of the tradition to patronize both the old and the new. Modern Greek and Italian sculpture loomed white through the hangings of Spanish moss; but there was room, too, for the Greek revivalism of Architect Robert Mills, and for the contemporary American sculptors like Hiram Powers and Clark Mills, whom the Charleston City Council would one day vote a medal of thanks for his marble bust of Calhoun.[19]

Charleston, like Paris, was a woman's town. The ladies set the tone of society; the teatable was the 'center of polished intercourse,' and it was the ladies who sent their compliments and the invitations to tea.[20]

Always the Southern code prevailed. There were beauties, but their charms were displayed only in the drawing room. There were musicians, but they played only for their families and closest friends. Women ruled, but they ruled and warred through their husbands.

Yet Charleston had its salon and its salon queen. She was Mrs. Holland, a beautiful woman, slender and tall, with dark eyes and always a

jeweled fillet around her smooth hair. Men were aware of her white skin
and round arms; women noted the classic drapery of her clothes, the
flowing sleeves and the lace veil over her head. Half Greek in an era
when Robert Mills's temples were foremost in the public mind, her
exoticism and plaintive songs in softly accented Italian and Greek, sung
to the music of a guitar, accounted for much of her charm. But it was
her *savoir-faire* that won the admiration of all. Secure in herself, she rose
above the limitations of poverty, two rooms, and scant furniture. To her
parties came 'eagerly everyone—the very flower of the town.'[21] Undoubtedly Calhoun, too, found his way to her door, took a seat on the
shawl-draped bed or on a soapbox, accepted lemonade and sweet wafers,
and surrendered himself, as all did, to 'the pleasure of spending an evening
with Mrs. Holland.'

2

This was not the Charleston of Calhoun's law-student days. There was
still the same muted, mellow beauty, the same depths of shade under the
old trees on the City Square. There was the same overpowering scent of
crushed figs against crumbling brick sidewalks, and of Pride-of-India
trees, bringing back nostalgic memories of lilac bushes in New England,
twenty-five years before.[22] Again Calhoun could feel his way up the
spiral staircase in the tower of Saint Michael's, look down upon the
slant-roofed city, caught in the embrace of the two shining rivers; hear
the silence and then the jangle of voices as the wind tossed up the sounds
of the street, a hundred and twenty-five feet below.[23]

But Charleston had changed. The protective tariff had done its work.
In the harbor, where but a few years before the ships of the world had
lain scattered like snowflakes, now only an occasional sail whitened and
filled. Rotting and empty were the wharves, once piled with 'London
duffle and Bristol blankets,' 'Spanish segars,' and 'Scotch Snuff in bottles.'[24] Foreign trade was shattered. Poverty had struck the city like a
blight, with grass literally growing in more. than one of the downtown
streets.

Gone was the buoyant, ebullient Charleston of Calhoun's youth. Under
a rippling surface of laughter and gaiety, thought ran deep. Puritanism
had set its mark upon the Charleston of the English tradition; and the old
French ways were overlaid now with a new democratic-aristocracy. It
was the Huguenots and Scotch-Irish who set the new tone of Charleston
society, thoughtful, self-disciplined men, 'conscious that they were living
in the eye of God.'[25]

Hugh Legaré was the living personification of this new 'moral' Charleston. His French blood long since washed out by a passionate infusion of

Scottish Covenanter blood, he was as much the Puritan as Calhoun, 'equally introspective,' and steeped in melancholy. And for every young Carolina buck who proclaimed his belief in the divinity of Christ on the one hand and proudly recounted his amours on the other [26] were two like Calhoun and Legaré, who practiced a 'strict morality,' upholding a Puritanism 'of conduct rather than dogma.' [27]

Legaré knew Charleston's tragedy. He knew that in this small city pulsed the last heartbeats of the eighteenth century, the last American attempt to uphold the aristocratic ideal, to build an ordered and stable society upon the instabilities of a young democracy. Both Legaré and Calhoun understood that the 'new American' industrial democracy was actually neither new nor American. It was the raucous voice of the nineteenth century, with young America as its sounding board. From the first they saw it as a challenge to their civilization.

For with their roots sunk in the soil, up-countrymen and Charlestonians alike were united in their fear of the Northern factory system which 'killed a man's inner glow.' [28] The North could boast of the kind of freedom that saw the mill-hand rise to the mill presidency in a single generation. But what of the hapless thousands who sweated on the workbenches all their lives long for ninety cents a day? Men should control their own time, contended the Southern leaders, develop their own capabilities, rather than speed their bodies and minds to the tempo of machinery. Hence, they clung to agriculture, basing their society on preference rather than reason. Even the Charlestonians had chosen the agrarian life. It was not the merchants and businessmen, the 'year-round' citizenry who gave Charleston its peculiar flavor, but the rice and cotton planters, who lived in the city only three or four months in the year. The representative Charlestonian was an equally representative planter.

In the South the values were set from the top, unlike the North and later the West, where the people made their own way of life, and values were lowered for popular consumption. In the South civilization was a stabilized ideal toward which all white men could aspire, but its ultimate goals they neither could nor wanted to change. For in the South aristocracy was not the possession of the chosen few; it was the ideal of the whole. This was a civilization upon which strong men could make their imprint: aristocratic in its ideal; democratic in the availability of the ideal.

What was America—Northern opportunity or Southern self-realization, Northern democracy or Southern republicanism? Had the South abandoned the American idea, or had the American idea abandoned the South? North and South the gulf was widening. 'Washington left a . . . pure republic . . . it has now settled down into a democracy,' [29] noted Captain Marryat in 1839. Only in the South did that form of government survive in which men chose from the highest those free to think for the lowest. An intellectual aristocracy was not deemed alien to political freedom. The classes were fluid; economically men's interests were one; and socially there was the goal toward which all might aspire.

Charleston had voiced the ideal. And deliberately, knowingly, South Carolina and the whole South had chosen. Not progress toward the unknown, but a reblending of the known. Not industrialism, but agrarianism. Not the future, but the past. The South had chosen and the South was doomed, for when the old and the new clash, the old must in the end give way. Calhoun had yet to learn this, but Legaré understood, and his vision was bitter. He would not be alive on that April day in 1865 when the Charleston ideal would be blown to atoms by the guns of the Civil War. But he knew, nevertheless. 'We are the last of the race of Carolina; I see nothing before us but decay and downfall. . . . I ask of heaven only that the little circle I am intimate with in Charleston be kept together.' [30]

3

This sense of approaching doom which overshadowed the South after 1820 was felt, not only by contemporary visitors, but by many subsequent writers.* Already apparent to the thinking were the two sources of this apprehension, closely if not inextricably interwoven. Fundamental was the fear that a way of life was imperiled; secondly, there was the growing, half-realized, finally acknowledged fear that slavery was threatened. The importance of this question in a study of Calhoun can hardly be overestimated. It is basic in his whole mature career; more important, it is the essence of the often-debated question as to the cause of the Civil War; most important for our own time, it is at the heart of America's present dilemma: the problem of maintaining the essential values of a way of life while shuffling off its evil practices.

No one today would deny the evils of slavery. Few would have denied them in the South before the eighteen-thirties. No doubt modern psychologists would find an undeniable guilt complex in the South's tension and fears, in the very vehemence of its refusals, in the name of economic necessity, to face the evils of the system. It was, in fact, the exact reversal of that unacknowledged sense of guilt among the Northerners; themselves but a generation removed from slave-ownership, slave trading and selling, who could relieve their moral responsibility by joining the outcry of the abolitionists. For this the Southerners could not afford to do. The defense

* See Harriet Martineau's description of the tense and fearful Charlestonians of the eighteen-thirties, their 'want of repose' and restless gaiety in *Retrospect of Western Travel.*

of slavery as a 'positive good' arose as Southern whites became increasingly convinced that without slavery their fundamental society could not survive; and secondly, that by a sudden, unplanned liberation of the slaves, the whole South would be plunged into an era of want, suffering, and social chaos.

The South's fears were realized; the delicate questions, susceptible of solution only by a slow and intricate intellectual process, were instead judged by the violence of war. Since Appomattox, the whole South, both black and white, has been living in the wreckage, working out, not a solution to its problems, but a hand-to-mouth *modus vivendi*. That slavery was smashed, not only by force of arms, but by the righteous fury of a moral crusade, is morally significant, but temporarily, at least, has proved intellectually and practically disastrous. The forced destruction of the existing social system could not alter human relationships.

Whether the South today, in the throes of war-boom prosperity, will sacrifice the remaining values of its way of life by accepting the industrial democracy against which Calhoun fought; or whether it can, at last, work out a new life holding the good of its dream, untainted by either the dark stain of slavery or of industrial tyranny, is perhaps America's foremost problem. Ironically enough, it is at the very moment when the weaknesses of industrial democracy which revolted Calhoun are at last becoming apparent to those who live under the system that it is only too likely to be embraced by the Carolinian's fellow countrymen.

4

But to surrender before the battle began, even with the knowledge that the victory was lost, was not in Calhoun's code. There was a fight worth fighting; there were issues with meaning. There was that fanaticism in Calhoun's Covenanter blood which, with the knowledge that his motives were pure, would drive him on regardless of consequences. He understood what the Southern life meant, and not only was he convinced of its values, but he was confident of the weapons that he would use to defend them. 'I know that I am right,' he said of nullification. 'I have gone over the ground more carefully than I ever did anything before, and I cannot be mistaken.' [31]

For all their Puritanism, Charlestonians had distrusted Calhoun at first. 'A monomaniac consumed by a single idea,' was Legaré's dismissal of the man, who even more than himself would give weight and meaning to the tradition of the city. Legaré could sneer at Calhoun's 'romantic' dreams of a Greek democracy, when his own thoughts dissolved in highly colored visions of a parliament of man and a federation of the world.[32]

Yet he knew, and Charleston would come to know, that what meant the most to them meant the most to Calhoun.

Nullification, however, was still more theory than action. It was 'in abeyance' still. Three years had passed. The tariff was still on the books; Southern profits and Southern power diminishing day by day. And that Calhoun had been no more than a 'quiet onlooker,' during the long years when the crisis was brewing, added to Charleston's distrust of him. His authorship of the *Exposition* was an open secret in South Carolina, if not in the nation, but his failure to acknowledge and legitimize it was a black mark against him. He was playing politics, it was generally conceded, and South Carolina was impatient, and justifiably so. A Columbia editor sounded warning: 'Mr. Calhoun must follow his state. If not, South Carolina does not go with Mr. Calhoun.' [33]

For three years Calhoun had striven to avoid the inevitable. He had tried his personal influence with Jackson and failed. He had forged nullification as a double-edged weapon, as a last hope for the South and as a threat to the North, compelling surrender to Southern terms. It was working in reverse; it was only stiffening Northern determination and Northern resistance. For love of the Union and at grave risk to his popularity among his own people, Calhoun had held the rebellious elements of the state in check. Now the pressures upon him were too strong. If he failed to support South Carolina's war against the tariff, his Southern influence was at an end. Whether or not he endorsed nullification, Jackson had ended his national influence. Only one choice remained. He could seek favor now only at the hands of the South, and the South was pushing him into action.

5

Whether without the safety-valve of nullification, South Carolina would have resorted to outright secession is one of those hypothetical questions impossible to answer. As early as 1829, Poinsett, horrified to discover in Charleston, where actual nullification had gained little ground, a torrent of defiance against the national government, had dedicated himself to the fight to keep South Carolina in the Union. His efforts had been momentarily successful; at the 1830 elections, Unionists had gained control of the Legislature, but their victory was short-lived.

Calhoun's old teacher, Chancellor De Saussure, probably came closest to expressing his state's view when he proclaimed in 1831 that the tariff was against 'the spirit of the Constitution,' and 'weakening the attachment of the South to the Union.' Any outright desire for secession, the Charlestonian dismissed as a fable 'of a distempered imagination,' although he warned that 'ultimately . . . our people would prefer even that . . . to having a government of unlimited powers. . . . We are divided,' he wrote, 'into nearly equal parts, not at all as to the evil . . . but . . . the remedy. . . . If the tariff . . . become the settled policy of the government . . . the separation of the Union will inevitably follow; which I pray God I may not live to see.' [34] And so clearly do the old Chancellor's words reflect Calhoun's fears that it is impossible to doubt that Calhoun visited his home sometime during these months, and unburdened himself to his teacher of years past.

Torn between his nullification theories and his knowledge of the practical concessions that would have to be made, Calhoun's mind was feverishly active. Young James Hammond, dropping in on him at seven o'clock on a March morning in 1831 in Columbia, found him hard at work on a plan for co-ordination of 'the three great interests of the nation.' The North, he told Hammond, was for industry, the South for farming and free trade, the West for internal improvements. He had long favored such improvements. He was for them still, but he doubted their constitutionality. Hence, the Constitution must be amended, and 'the channels of the West' connected with those to the Atlantic. This would unite the South and West, which 'must be reconciled to save the Union.'

As for the tariff, it 'might be so adjusted as to suit the Northern people better than it does now.' The general increase of duties 'had diminished . . . profits . . . by adding to the cost of everything.' But the 'system of plunder . . . the traffic of interests' was 'despicable.' Unless protection were modified, disunion was 'inevitable.'

He spoke bitterly. Hammond listened in bewilderment as Calhoun put on his hat and led him out for a walk, talking rapidly all the while. He wanted, he said, to become 'more Southern.' And at his sudden remark, that Clay's partisans so hated Jackson, they would take Calhoun with 'nullification on his head,' Hammond was startled. He knew what his host meant now.

His opinion was strengthened that evening when the pair met again for tea. Calhoun's unwonted energy of the morning had burned itself out, and Hammond found him 'much less disposed to harangue than usual.' There was 'a listlessness about him which shows that his mind is deeply engrossed,' and to Hammond there was no doubt that it was once more fixed upon the subject of the Presidency. 'He is undoubtedly quite feverish under the present excitement and his hopes.' [35]

6

On a steaming day in late July, 1831, Calhoun, 'goaded into desperation by his opponents,' set pen to paper. He flinched from no premise, no conclusion. His meaning was unmistakably clear. Ours was a union of states, not of individuals. The Constitution was a compact, to which each 'free and independent' State in the Constitutional Convention had separately linked its own citizens. Hence, each state had the right to judge of the power it had delegated, and in the last resort—to use the language of the Virginia Resolutions—'to interpose for arresting . . . evil.' The question was simple. Was our government national or federal? Did it rest on the sovereignty of the states or the unrestrained will of the majority?

Thus, boldly, Calhoun laid his premises. He could still concede that there might be a difference of opinion, still admit that 'The error may possibly be with me.' But now he could see no error. So deeply did he feel the necessity of a way out that the missing link he had once sought hopelessly in agony of spirit, 'be it called what it may—State-right, veto, nullification, or by another name—I conceive to be the fundamental principle of our system, resting on facts historically as certain as our revolution itself.'

It was the past against the present, the ghost of Jefferson against the very much alive John Marshall, who had been piling precedent upon precedent in the years since *Marbury v. Madison* and *Fletcher v. Peck* had established the 'right' of the Supreme Court to declare acts of states or nation unconstitutional. And it was not in the Kentucky and Virginia Resolutions, but in these last years of his life, that Jefferson challenged Marshall, declaring that if the federal and state 'departments' of government were to clash, 'a convention of the states must be called to ascribe the doubtful power to that department which they may think best.'

Here Calhoun rested his case. Ultimate authority, he contended, was not in the national government, 'a government with all the rights and authority which belong to any other government,' but in the power that called that government into being—the states.

He stressed his 'deep and sincere attachment to . . . the Union of these States . . . the great instruments of preserving our liberty and promoting happiness.' Half of his life and all of his public services were 'indissoluably identified' with the Union. 'To be too national' had in the past been considered his 'greatest fault.' No one 'could have more respect for the maxim that the majority ought to govern' than he, but only 'where the interests are the same . . . where laws that benefit one benefitted all.' Where laws helpful to one group, however, were 'ruinous to another,' simple majority rule was 'unjust. . . . Let it never be forgotten that where the majority rules without restraint, the minority is the subject.' Happily we had 'no artificial and separate classes of society.' But we were not exempt from 'contrary of interests,' like this sad 'conflict flowing directly from the tariff.'

Could not the tide be turned? Did the Union itself, 'as ordained by the Constitution,' provide no means of drawing together 'every portion

of our country,' through a common and identical interest? Would this
'contrarity of interests' become subject to the unchecked will of a majority, defeating the whole great end of government—'justice'? To answer
in the affirmative, declared Calhoun, would be to admit that 'our Union
has utterly failed.' Nothing could force him to a conclusion 'so abhorrent
to all my feelings.'

Idealistically Calhoun could hope for 'a state of intelligence so universal and high that all the guards of liberty may be dispensed with except an enlightened public opinion,' acting through the vote. But this
would presuppose 'a state where every class and section . . . are capable
of estimating the effects of every measure, not only as it may effect itself,
but . . . every other class and section; and of fully realizing the sublime
truth that the highest and wisest policy consists in maintaining justice,
and . . . harmony; and that compared to these, schemes of mere gain
are but trash and dross.' Somber experience had taught him that 'we are
far removed from such a state,' and that we must rely on the 'old and
clumsy' mode of checking power to prevent abuse, of 'invoking a constitution to restrain a government, as laws were invoked to restrain individuals.' [36]

Thus, to the South in his so-called 'Fort Hill Letter,' to the North in
five columns in the New York *Courier and Enquirer,* Calhoun gave expression to the 'natural, peaceful, and proper remedy' against grievances
—nullification. But in New York's and the nation's opinion, the remedy
was neither 'natural' nor 'proper.' Its full implications would not be understood until action supplanted words, but already audible were the
sinister overtones that thereafter were to leave upon Calhoun 'a kind of
stain . . . as a public man.'

At best, nullification was a curious and suspect cause, and the unin-
formed among Calhoun's friends were shocked to find that he had not
'repudiated it,' availing himself 'of the occasion to make himself popular.'
To Richard Crallé and Duff Green, who as yet had no concept of how
terribly shattered Calhoun's political fortunes had already become, his
letter was 'like the shock produced by a cold bath.' 'Had it not been
for the cry of Nullification,' asserted Green, with more confidence than
proof, 'Mr. Calhoun would have been nominated by the Anti-Masons,' [37]
a questionable honor indeed.

7

Even in the South, beyond the borders of South Carolina, nullification
was an alien doctrine. Typical was the bewildered Georgia farmer, shut
off in the hills, with no answer to his eager questions, and a ready welcome

for the stranger whose horse's hoofbeats were sounding against the hard-packed clay of the mountain road.

He peered through the dusk at his guest. Was he planter . . . farmer . . . cotton factor, perhaps? It was hard to tell. His horse was a 'strong and servicable' looking animal, the equipment plain, not too ornate for a poor man, or too poor for the well-to-do. As the rider swung down, his host examined him more closely. A tall man, perhaps fifty or fifty-five, and slender, looking 'capable of great physical endurance.' His smile was 'pleasant and winning,' but everything in his speech and manner 'indicated the habit of refined society.'

Yet, almost as if by instinct, he made straight for the end of the porch, where according to country custom a basin of sun-warmed water stood on a shelf and a towel hung on the wall. He doused his face and hands, swept the powdery red dust off his clothes; and then stepped back to his host to 'exchange the courtesies of the day.'

The farmer opened the conversation. Nullification was the question that dominated his thoughts: Calhoun, Hayne, and the rest—he damned them all with complete impartiality. The stranger remained silent, obviously tired. 'He evidently wished to avoid any controversy.' But as his host launched into a dogmatic defense of majority rule, the guest remarked that in nullification minorities claimed no power over a majority; they sought only to rule themselves. 'I do not wish to argue this question,' he added with a smile. 'I suspect that neither one of us would be likely to convince the other. . . . I would prefer to talk with you on more pleasant subjects.'

But the aroused farmer had no intention of losing the battle by default. His persistence gained its object. His guest roused himself at last. He began to talk, slowly at first, then launched into a full-scale defense of nullification complete with illustrations, metaphysical analysis, and the most fervid persuasion. Fascinated, the Georgian watched a transformation grip the man before him. Where only a few minutes before he had been all ease and familiarity, he was now as grave and earnest as a Senator expounding constitutional principles on the floor of Congress. Gentleness was replaced by command. The brilliant eyes were 'fixed with a strange intensity,' and as the speaker's excitement increased, 'bright glances' shot out from under his thick brows. Suddenly the farmer recognized his guest. Only one man in America could look like that.

Swiftly, he turned on him.

'Are you not John C. Calhoun?'

'That is my name.'

'Well, I was sure of it.' [38]

8

Never had Calhoun's popularity among his own people been so high. Even in Pendleton, where he rode two or three times a week to pick up his mail, crowds followed him from the inn and the store to the cramped office of the Pendleton *Messenger*, where he would spend an hour or two chatting with the editor or reading proof of one of his addresses.

The 'Fort Hill Letter' was only one of many that he had to write in these months. Of the abuse hurled at him he took little heed, but misunderstandings or interpretations of his doctrine were of extreme concern to him. These he answered a year later in his 'Letter to Governor Hamilton.' Point by point, he challenged the contentions of his opponents.

The Constitutional Convention had not nationalized our government. It had only raised it from below to the level of the state. Nullification was not secession. With nullification, the state was still within the Union; with secession, it was beyond control. Secession freed the state from its obligations; nullification compelled 'the governing agent to fulfill its obligations.'

States could secede, by nullification, only from the acts of other states, not from their agent. Secession was justifiable only when an entire group of states upheld a measure which defeated the 'general welfare,' for which the Union had been formed.

Consolidation, Calhoun warned, could destroy the Union as effectually as secession. The preservation of the Union depended upon the equilibrium between the states and the general government. Without a check against encroachments beyond the delegated powers, the stronger would absorb the weaker. Such a check was provided by nullification. Had not the granting of power in the Constitutional Convention 'required the consent of all the States,' while to withhold power the dissent of a single state was sufficient? Had not the Founding Fathers specifically rejected measures to prohibit the states from judging the extent of their reserved powers?

The original American system of majority rule, he contended, had meant the concurrent, not the absolute, majority. Even at the Constitutional Convention, not a mere majority of the states, but a majority of the people in each state assured final modification. Nevertheless, he conceded, the practical operation of our government 'has been on the principle of the absolute majority.' A majority of seven million could violate the rights of a minority of six million. 'We see,' declared Calhoun, 'the approach of the fatal hour.'

His cause he believed to be that of 'truth and justice, of union, liberty, and the Constitution.' In the last resort, only a Constitutional Convention of the states could decide whether the national government had abused its delegated power. First nullification, then a convention, these were the legitimate remedies for oppression. But he who 'would prescribe . . . disunion . . . or the coercion of a State,' Calhoun warned, 'will receive the execration of all future generations.' [39]

9

The trouble with 'peaceful, constitutional nullification' was that so few of its adherents were inclined to methods that were either peaceful or constitutional. Calhoun had, in fact, devised nullification, not only as a possible cure-all, but as a safety-valve to divert the pent-up disunionist sentiment in the state. Nevertheless, the very violence of the 'fellow-travelers' under the Calhoun banner was enough to deter 'respectable' numbers of Carolinians from alliance, despite their hatred of the tariff.

Out-and-out Unionists were few; yet they included such men as Thomas Lowndes, Benjamin F. Perry, Theodore Gaillard Hunt, Hugh Legaré, Thomas Grimké, William Drayton, Daniel Huger, James Louis Petigru, and Joel Poinsett. Aside from mere protestations against federal 'outrages,' they had no program. True, Grimké did suggest to the Legislature that if the state believed the tariff unconstitutional, it behooved it to ask other states to join with South Carolina in an appeal for a constitutional amendment. But mere appeals offered no inducement to a people keyed to the thought of secession. Oddly enough, one group of outright secessionists, headed by Langdon Cheves, condemned nullification as too ineffectual and even too illogical. How could you remain in the Union, they argued, and refuse to obey the Union's laws? [40]

From the national—that is to say, the Jacksonian—viewpoint, nullification would have been suspect in any case. It was an idea, a different and an abstract idea, which would have damned it from the start, so far as Jackson was concerned. Calhoun could argue that only secession would destroy the Union; yet both he and Jackson knew perfectly well that secession was the ultimate recourse of the nullification doctrine; and that even the implied possibility of secession furnished opportunity for countless hot-heads to do as well as to dare.

Blue cockades for the Nullifiers! A strip of white cotton on the left shoulder marked the Unionists, who stolidly contested 'every foot of ground.' [41] Candles burned late in Charleston assembly rooms. Tempers were strained. Nullifiers, leaving their hall by way of King Street, sent a request to the Unionists that in order to avoid collision they use Meeting Street, a block below. The Unionists only broke down all intervening fences in their haste to reach King Street, and the two groups met, head-on.

The Unionists always contended that it was a Nullifier who threw the first stone. The stately Drayton pled for self-control, but it was too late. The hot young blood of Charleston was up. Amid charges of 'sneak,' 'renegade,' and 'traitor,' Hugers, Middletons, and Pringles clashed with the followers of Hammond, Hamilton, and Calhoun.

Petigru was struck on the shoulder. Another man's face was split open. 'The Union men,' declared a Nullifier's lady, 'became violent.'[42]

Reverberations echoed through Charleston drawing rooms. No longer did gentlemen linger over the 'delightful perfume' and the 'beautiful wreaths' of vapor which arose from their gilt coffee cups. No longer did they contest the relative merits of Mocha and Java, one reminiscing of Turkey and the coffee beans parching in the tin plates; one remembering the Café des Milles Colonnes and the pretty Parisian *limonadière*, who had passed him his cup. Men now had important matters to think about; and those soft-spoken aristocrats to whom politics had seemed only a polite diversion, never to be brought into the drawing rooms with ladies present,[43] suddenly realized that politics had assumed the same sharp-edged reality known to their Whig and Tory grandfathers.

Nullifiers sneered at men who would 'basely submit to armed invasion and destruction of their rights.' Unionists scornfully wondered if the federal government would submit to defiance from one small state. Once Old Hickory got into action, predicted the Union leaders, he would make 'blue cockades as scarce as blue roses in South Carolina.'

'We can die for our rights,' roared the Nullifiers.

"You will die and not get your rights,' the Unionists countered.[44]

Charleston had become an armed camp. Joel Poinsett's breakfasts were mere partisan rallies now. The dark and dapper little Huguenot with the sharp eyes and bitter mouth had shouldered the task of holding the line for the Union—right or wrong. Actually about all that he could do was to play the part of a high-class spy for the Jackson Administration. Hopelessly outnumbered, devoid of arms, deserted by a near majority of his friends, Poinsett did not lack courage. Slowly he armed his scant ranks; secretly, by night, drilled them. To Jackson he passed on the suggestion that 'grenades and small rockets are excellent weapons in a street fight.'[45] His activities were no secret—but not even the most rabid of Nullifiers dared lay hands on him. Charleston knew that at the first act of outright defiance, a message from Poinsett would be on its way to Washington; the state would be clapped under martial law and Calhoun and the entire South Carolina Congressional delegation arrested for treason and turned over to the courts.

10

November 24, 1832 and the gathering of the clans for the Nullification Convention at Columbia! All were there, 'socially and politically the

élite of the State'—Hayne, Hamilton, Calhoun, Pinckney—and all so
united in purpose that many wondered why the convention should sit
at all.[46]

It was a gaudy assemblage. Outside was the tramp of footsteps, the
rattle of bayonets. Within, spurs jingled and voices soared. Through the
throng moved Calhoun, his face grave with concern. All his pleas for
moderation were forgotten in talk of rockets, bombs, and cannon. If force
were used, South Carolina would 'forthwith . . . organize a separate
Government, and . . . do all other things which sovereign and independent States may of right do.' Sixteen thousand 'back-countrymen,'
roared Robert Preston, 'with arms in their hands and cockades in their
hats [are] ready to march to our city at a moment's warning to defend us.'

At length the convention settled down. The Federal Tariff Act was declared null and void after February 1, unless the government should see
fit to give relief before that time. The 'right' of nullification was clearly
affirmed. Hayne spoke the final word. South Carolina, he asserted, would
'maintain its sovereignty, or be buried beneath its ruins.' [47]

Scarcely had the convention adjourned to reassemble March 11, 1833,
before the Legislature hastily wrote its will into law. The 'revolutionary'
doctrine of nullification was on the books. But not another state dared
go so far; and as a practical policy, the doctrine would never be revived
again until 1842, when Massachusetts would 'nullify' the Fugitive Slave
Law.

Jackson's answer was all but instantaneous. His famed Proclamation
arrived in Charleston on December 10. To the Nullifiers, it came with the
force of a physical blow. Its argument, lucid and fine-spun, struck straight
at the heart of their doctrines. 'The Constitution . . . forms a government, not a league. . . . To say that any State may secede . . . is to
say that the United States is not a nation. . . . Disunion by armed forces
is treason.'

'Fellow-citizens of my native state,' continued the Presidential appeal,
'let me . . . use the influence that a father would over his children.'
Would the proud state of Carolina dissolve 'this happy Union . . . these
fertile fields . . . deluge with blood . . . the very name of Americans
. . . discard?' [48]

'God and Old Hickory are with us,' [49] exulted the Unionists, who would
have settled for Old Hickory alone. Throughout the country the Proclamation sounded like a bugle call. Webster, Story, Marshall, even John Quincy
Adams, aligned themselves on the President's side.

But not South Carolina. For South Carolina it was too late. As Miss
Maria Pinckney put it, 'To count the cost has never been characteristic of
Carolinians!' The threat only 'increased the number and ardor of the
Nullifiers.' If offers of military aid were pouring in on Jackson, volunteers
were also flooding in upon Robert Hayne. Ready and chafing for action

were the 'Mounted Minute Men,' flaunting fresh-polished boots and yellow plumes and 'palmetto buttons of a beautiful pattern.' [50] A generation of young men, their veins throbbing with the blood their sons poured out at Shiloh, Chancellorsville, and Malvern Hill, armed with blue cockades and dueling pistols, were ready to answer the call of their state.

Charleston looked like a military depot. More timid souls clustered before public notices, eagerly reading the advertisements of cheap sugar plantations for sale in Mississippi. Two federal warships haunted the harbor. By December 24, General Winfield Scott and a good-sized body of troops were ordered South, forcibly to guard Fort Sumter and the customs house; and Calhoun bitterly declared that for the first time in history America's guns were pointed inward at her own people.

McDuffie, uninspired by the Christmas spirit, breathed fire. There would be no violence 'unless the driveling old dotard' in the White House were to 'commence indiscriminate attack upon men, women, and children.' [51] Hayne, deep in Hoyt's *Tactics* and problems of pistols, sabers, powder, and ball, that same Hayne who only eight years before had asserted that 'no threat of forcible resistance to the national government should ever be resorted to,' now bared his teeth in a counter-proclamation, insolent, inflammatory. And Poinsett frowned uneasily over Jacksonian promises that were something less than conciliatory. 'In forty days,' the President had written, 'I can have within the limits of South Carolina, fifty thousand men, and in forty days more, another fifty thousand.' [52]

Threats of war and secession were heard on every side. The people were 'ripe for war,' declared one inflated report, 'and the President equally so.' [53]

Were they? Socially an elaborate pretense that all was well still maintained. Officers of the harbor forts had been hastily replaced with men whose military ardors had not been weakened by Southern charm, but these were treated with the same gracious courtesy that had seduced their predecessors. Elderly Commodore Elliott 'became a great favorite with the ladies.' Nullifiers and Unionists might ridicule each other in public; in private, Hamilton and Petigru met to devise means of keeping the peace between the rival factions. 'The leaders of the Nullifiers did *not* desire disunion.' [54] Even Jackson was holding himself in check until nullification had actually taken effect.

Charlestonians had no access to the files of the President's private correspondence, in which he had written Van Buren as early as August that Calhoun's 'best former friends say . . . he ought to be hung.' [55] But it was no secret after the letter to Hamilton that Calhoun would resign from the Vice-Presidency, and no surprise when Robert Hayne stepped down from the Senate to make way for a stronger champion. Such was the excitement that even Calhoun, the stickler for constitutional legalities, wasted no time seeking a way to submit his resignation to the people of

the United States to whom he was, of course, responsible. Instead, he addressed a brief note to Secretary of State Edward Livingston, next in the
line of Presidential succession:

> *Sir,*
> *Having concluded to accept of a seat in the United States Senate,
> I herewith resign the office of Vice-President of the United States.*[56]

To this extraordinary document, neither the Secretary of State nor the
United States government paid the least attention. It was ignored so completely that Calhoun finally wrote Livingston to see if he had received it.
The Senate, too, disdained to recognize the withdrawal of their presiding officer. Instead, they elected a President *pro tempore* and continued
business as usual.

11

Calhoun was literally taking his life into his hands when he said good-
bye to Floride on December 22, 1832, and mounted the stage for Washington. His sheer physical courage, risking death or dishonor, broke down
Charleston's last resistance to his leadership. Even his political opponents
could not now withhold their personal admiration.

At Columbia his friends gathered around him. They clung to his hands,
looked deep into the brooding eyes that 'saw all and revealed nothing.'
What was he thinking? Would he have strength to bear whatever ordeal
Jackson might devise for him? Admirers would have been reassured by
the observation of his friend, Robert Henry, that Calhoun had 'never
appeared in better health,' nor 'calmer and more self-possessed.' At the
report that Jackson would have him arrested the instant he crossed the
Virginia border, Calhoun merely smiled.

'It will not be done,' he said; 'my opponents are too politic to attempt
it'; but in a sudden burst of intense feeling he added: 'As far as myself
and the cause are concerned, I should desire nothing better; it would set
people a-thinking.' [57]

His confidence was assumed. The physical ordeal of his journey was
second only to the fears and questions that tormented his brain during
those weary hours. What lay beyond him? Only rumor answered—scraps
and fragments of rumor, whispers from the waiting clusters of silent figures,
words hastily broken off as his tall figure strode through the doors of the
wayside taverns. He would be arrested. He would never take his seat as
Senator. He would be imprisoned. South Carolina would be invaded. He
would be hanged.

On New Year's Day, 1833, he reached Raleigh, North Carolina. Crowds
gathered beneath his window, and devoted partisans offered him a public

dinner, which he politely declined. There was something of grandeur in his bearing, and men spoke of Luther and the Diet of Worms.

Virginia next, and a message from his old enemy, John Randolph of Roanoke. He was resolved 'personally not to assist in the subjugation of South Carolina, but if she does move, to make common cause against the usurpations of the Federal Government.' No government extending from the Atlantic to the Pacific could exist, Randolph warned. 'There is death in the potion . . . Patrick Henry saw.' [58]

Randolph's words did little to relieve the tension of Calhoun's mind. For his personal welfare he was too proud to admit concern; but the uncertainties confronting both his state and the South at large were torturing him. His conscience was clear; he knew that he had restrained South Carolina and 'restrained himself'; [59] but equally well he knew that in Jackson's mind burned the obsession that Calhoun was the moving spirit of all disorder in the South and should be held accountable for whatever might occur there.

That disorders would occur, Calhoun had no doubt. It was with terrible misgivings that he had adopted his doctrine; for what he did fear was the temper of South Carolina.

His carriage was approaching the Virginia state line. Beyond was Washington—and Andrew Jackson.

XVI

Force and Counter-Force

'GENTLEMEN,' declared the President of the United States, 'there will be no bloodshed.'

His eyes flashing, his seamed face taut, Old Hickory's words crackled with assurance. But his certainty was not shared by the grim, tired group of men clustered before his desk. South Carolina Unionists, themselves ready 'to rush to arms,' they begged the President to desist from force. South Carolina had gone mad! What chance had they, with their scant nine thousand men, against the mass fury of an entire state? The meaning of force was civil war. And civil war meant defeat.

Jackson heard them out in silence. Dramatically he pointed a bony finger at his desk. 'I have in that drawer,' he said, 'the tender of one hundred and fifty thousand volunteers. . . . We shall cross the mountains into . . . South Carolina with a force, which joined by the Union men of that State, will be so overwhelming as to render resistance hopeless. We will seize the ringleaders, turn them over to the civil authorities, and come home. . . . There will be no bloodshed.' [1]

His words were something less than soothing. Even his most ardent admirers were more convinced of the zeal than of the peacefulness of the President's intentions. 'They say,' wrote vivacious Fanny Kemble, 'the old General is longing for a fight.' [2]

Fanny was in Washington. She was spending the tense January days 'charming Henry Clay' and making 'John Marshall weep,' at the 'wretched' little Washington theater, with its 'grotesque mixture of misery, vulgarity, stage finery, and real raggedness.' [3] Americans, accustomed only to the rantings of the dark and sunken-eyed Junius Booth, were not then a theater-broken people. It was scarcely seven years since Kean had been howled down and struck with a dripping 'twist of tobacco,' to which insults a Baltimore audience added 'hisses, yells, and beating the doors and benches with fists, canes, etc.' [4] Now in the 'little box' of a theater,[5] its pit 'completely crammed' with coatless men and nursing women, and the Senatorial boxes adorned with booted legs swinging over the sides,[6] Juliet's balcony scene wove its spell amidst the 'incessant spittings' of the audience.[7]

In Washington in that winter of 1833, two personalities held the public attention. Between them there was no connection. To each the other was unknown. But for sheer relief that January, the tense Washington citizenry took time out from the drama of Calhoun for the light comedy of Fanny Kemble.

At Philadelphia she had played in a too-tight dress which threatened to split from neck to waist at every move, until, in the 'laughing scene,' it 'grinned' open, putting the lacing of her stays, 'like so many teeth,' on display to 'the admiring gaze of the audience.' The house rocked. Slowly turning her hot face, Fanny saw that the eyes and plaudits were not for her, but for the tall and gracefully slender man with tow-colored hair and smiling mouth, who was advancing in a one-man procession down the center aisle—Mr. Henry Clay!

That within a few weeks Fanny's name would be linked with that 'vulgar' man, who had actually passed 'before titled men in England with his hands in his breeches' pockets,' [8] would have never entered Miss Kemble's wildest imaginings. Yet it was under the protection of the flirtatious and fifty-six-year-old father of twelve that Fanny Kemble burst upon Washington.

She had 'never felt anything like the heat of the rooms' or heard 'anything so strange as the questions people ask'; but the grim, erect Jackson, 'a fine old well-battered soldier,' [9] won her unstinted admiration. The talk swirled around her; South Carolina 'in a state of convulsion,' Nullifiers and Unionists battling in the streets, and, it was said, 'lives have been lost.' In horror, Jackson told of a steamer sailing out of Charleston Harbor, her flag upside down! 'For this indignity,' declared the President, 'she ought to have been sunk.' [10]

'So "Old Hickory" means to lick the refractory Southerns,' mused Fanny to her journal. 'Why, they are coming to a Civil War!' [11]

2

The playbills were flapping in the January wind, as Calhoun's coach rolled into Washington. He looked at them with more than usual interest. 'Mr. Kemble and Miss Kemble in The Stranger. . . . Pitt, 50 cents. Gallery 25.' Fanny Kemble. He knew that name. In Charleston it was already the talk that young Pierce Butler of Sea Island was infatuated with her; had given her no respite since her arrival in Philadelphia. Curiosity tugged at Calhoun. Despite his cares, he promised himself one evening's relaxation at a Fanny Kemble performance.

The dreariness of a Washington January was a counterpart to his mood. It was as if he had never been away, as if the sun-gilded palmettos of the South were a dream that would fade from his memory. This was the reality, this frozen and rutted road of which he could scarcely think without aching; the smell and feel of the leather coach curtains that brushed his face at every jolt of the stage; and the dry crackling of the dead leaves still clinging to the black oaks outside. Idly his gaze swept the landscape: the white Capitol looming out of a huddle of rickety shanties; below, the half-finished, scattered red-brick buildings of the town. There was Gadsby's, a crazy-quilt of galleries and staircases, exits and entrances, and finally, the new Jardin des Plantes, full of shrubs now almost a foot and a half high. A fence of wooden palings enclosed last summer's lawn in front of the President's house, now a withered waste of brown grass. At the rear a stretch of unplowed field slanted down to the muddy Potomac. No, nothing had changed; nothing but himself.

Loyal followers had escorted him across the Virginia line into Washington. Now only curious and blank-faced spectators stared as the coach drew up before his boarding house and he stiffly descended. He had scarcely reached his room before he was warned that he would be arrested, and his mail, crammed with drawings of skulls and coffins, did little to quiet his nerves.

More crowds lined the streets the next morning. It was January 4, 1833. The Capitol building was packed. Curious friends and foes thronged the Senate gallery. Calhoun entered the Chamber, deathly pale but calm, with an almost studied deliberation in his walk. Here, too, all was the same—all the familiar little sounds, magnified by his own intensity: the scratching of a quill, the thump of knuckles rapping sand off the wet ink, the click of a key in a desk drawer, and the rustle of a newspaper, tossed down as he passed.

As he sat down, several Southerners gathered around him to shake hands; but it was noticed that many former friends, one of whom had openly urged that he be hanged, held back; and acquaintances turned their heads to avoid his gaze. When he strode forward to be sworn in, lips tight and head high, the curious gazed at each other wonderingly, amazed at the reverential and determined tone in which this 'traitor' swore to 'uphold, defend, and protect the Constitution of the United States.' [12]

Senators, who had been indignant at his 'unbridled audacity' in thrusting himself into a body he planned to overthrow, now softened somewhat. Several who had previously refused to speak came forward and welcomed him to the Senate. He returned their compliments with his usual grace, and the tension in the Chamber relaxed.

3

Washington seethed with rumors. Lights burning late in the White House windows . . . a thudding of hooves down a street . . . of footsteps clattering up the stairs. Into Calhoun's lodgings one midnight burst Congressman Robert Letcher of Tennessee, his friend and the friend of Andrew Jackson. Calhoun sat up. His servant draped a cloak around his shoulders. There he sat, 'drinking in every word' as Letcher's story poured forth. He had been at the White House. He had heard Old Hickory. If one more step was taken, the President promised, 'he would try Calhoun for treason, and if convicted, hang him as high as Haman.' [13]

White, tense, Calhoun was 'evidently disturbed.' But there was nothing that he could do. He was as convinced of the righteousness of his course as his Scottish ancestors had been, and would have gone to the stake for his convictions as readily as they. Furthermore, Andrew Jackson was in exactly the same frame of mind. He had no more intention of backing down than his iron-willed opponent. The two combatants were clashing head-on. Jackson would win: he had the Army; he had the public sympathy, and Calhoun had a neck that would break; but behind him the Carolinian had a state that could throw the whole country into civil war.

4

'Prejudice amounted to a passion against him.' Not since Arnold and Burr had there been 'so sudden and so terrible a fall'; and in all America there was no man whose every act was watched with such 'fearful curiosity.' Nothing, it was believed, could restrain him, neither loyalty nor patriotism; nothing could control his 'mad ambition.' [14]

Calhoun's very look fulfilled the popular idea of a conspirator: the dark face, 'lines . . . deeply gullied by intense thought; a manner at once emphatic and hesitant; determined, yet cautious.' But even Jackson's admirers conceded that he was 'every inch a MAN.' [15] His physical courage was unquestioned. Nothing could shake him—bitter personal hatred, the abusive press, even threats of bodily 'outrage.' Senators marveled at his 'noble bearing,' as, unmoved and unafraid, he walked about the streets of the capital.

For the man himself sympathy ran high. Those who knew him, his loftiness of character, his 'scorn of meanness in man or thing,' could not withhold their personal admiration. 'Mr. Calhoun,' wrote Mrs. Smith, 'will his high soarings end in disappointment and humiliation or be drowned in blood? . . . He is one of the noblest and most generous spirits I have ever met. . . . I am certain he is deceived himself, and believes he is now fulfilling the duty of a true patriot.' [16]

'Those who hated most . . . pardoned those who felt,' noted a contemporary observer. There was something of 'moral sublimity' in this tragedy of fallen greatness; and there were times when the warmth of feeling for Calhoun as a man overrode public indignation. 'Opinion,' declared March, often 'hesitated between hatred and admiration,' adding to the 'interest and anxiety' felt for him. Typical was the confession of a Jackson newspaperman, who entered the Senate 'deeply prejudiced against him. I left it filled with the highest admiration for his talents and patriotism.' [17]

5

But Calhoun asked no sympathy. And what he thought, no one knew. Few of his letters of this period have been preserved. He may have been too busy or too tired to write, or may even have ordered his correspondence destroyed. He did dash off a brief, cheering note to his brother-in-law, James, assuring him that all was 'going well.' [18] The Southern people should be given no pretext for force. Yet his real agitation was plainly revealed on January 16, 1833, the day that Jackson's Message arrived, calling for powder and arms to enforce order in South Carolina.

Calhoun sprang to his feet. His words were bitter. In youth, he told the Senate, he had 'cherished a deep and enthusiastic admiration of this Union.' He had looked 'with rapture' on the beautiful structure of our federal system, but knew always that in the last resort the body that delegated the power could judge of the power. And now, for merely daring to assert the state's constitutional rights, 'we are threatened to have our throats cut, and those of our wives and children.' He stopped, exhausted and shaken. 'No, I go too far. I did not intend to use language so strong.'

The correspondent for the Baltimore *Patriot* looked at him in amazement. 'Mr. Calhoun spoke under a degree of excitement never before witnessed in a parliamentary body. His whole frame was agitated.'

Could this be the cool, the poised, the mild-mannered Vice-President of the United States, whom the press corps had watched for so long? 'It is seldom,' commented the Baltimore reporter, 'that a man of Mr. Calhoun's intellectual power thus permits himself to be unmanned in public . . . the will of such a man usually gets command of his passions.' [19]

A Senator hastily assured Calhoun that the government would appeal to South Carolina's sense of justice and patriotism. 'I am sorry that South Carolina cannot appeal to the sense of justice of the General Government,' retorted Calhoun, and was sharply called to order by several Senators.[20] A moment later, still struggling for composure, he arose again and 'begged pardon for the warmth with which he had expressed himself . . . feeling as he did, he could not have spoken otherwise.' [21] From the White House, Jackson commented: 'Calhoun let off a little of his ire today, but was so agitated and confused that he made quite a failure.' [22]

6

It was sheer agony Calhoun suffered during those weeks. For a man of his make-up—proud, sensitive, high-strung, only a few years back a popular hero, now little more than a pariah, all his dreams and hopes blotted out— his position must have been intolerable. He, the brilliant young Cabinet officer, the confidant of Monroe and Jefferson, now to have old friends shrink back as he passed, to have his name bandied as rebel and traitor, his career ended, his health giving way, all hopes for national glory at an end—this was his sorry lot during those long weeks. And not even his personal fears were uppermost in his thoughts. He had left Floride only slightly improved from 'dangerous illness'; [23] he had delayed his departure for days to watch at her bedside, and concern for her was weighing upon him. But most of all, the terrible responsibility for the outcome of his doctrine hung like a deadweight on his mind.

7

'Thank God for old Jackson,' exulted the Washington *Globe*.[24] Rumors of possible compromise from the headquarters of Henry Clay did nothing to divert the White House intentions. In response to Jackson's demands for action, the Force Bill, described by Calhoun as 'a virtual repeal of the Constitution,' was reported out of the Senate Judiciary Committee, January 21, 1833. Calhoun's friend, Duff Green, the Senate printer, published it in full, impudently bordering his columns in black.

On January 22, Calhoun again took the floor. His answers to Jackson's call for powder and shot was in three resolutions which he presented, declaring: (1) that the states were parties to a constitutional compact; (2) that they had delegated specified powers to the federal agent; and (3) that the states were legal judges of what they had delegated. With logic so finespun that the loss of a single word would destroy the meaning, Calhoun told the Senate that if our system was founded on the 'social compact,' Jackson's arguments were correct; but if we were a 'Union of States,' the Force Bill was not only 'wholly repugnant' to the 'genius' of our system, but 'destructive of its very existence.'

His anger mounted. The Force Bill was an 'outrage.' It was 'the creature warring against the creator.' Nor was it restricted to South Carolina, but if 'there be guilt, South Carolina alone is guilty. Why . . . make the bill applicable to all States? Why make it the law of the land?'.

Not the fate of South Carolina alone was at stake, but the whole American system of government. If the Force Bill be enacted, be it further enacted, was his cry, 'that the Constitution is hereby repealed. . . . It will . . . forever put down our beautiful federal system and rear on its ruins consolidated government.' [25]

Throughout, keenly as he felt, he maintained his self-control. His terse sentences were of 'beautiful structure,' and although he spoke only a few minutes, he proved himself a foe against whom the whole talent of the Administration forces would have to be thrown.[26] Now it was Jackson's turn to humble himself, and to beg Daniel Webster, with whom he had not even been on speaking terms for more than a year, to lead the fight for the government.

Webster held back. He would not speak until the South Carolinian had more fully revealed himself. Days dragged by until Friday, the fifteenth of February, when at last Calhoun arose. History would record that he spoke 'On the Revenue Collection Bill (commonly called the Force Bill).' Actually he was speaking in defense of himself, his state and his cause.

He set the stage dramatically for the great occasion. Pushing some chairs down to both ends of a long desk which stood before the lobby rail, he enclosed himself in a sort of cage where he could pace up and down as he spoke. Close observers saw how rapidly he had aged in the past few months: the chiseled bone structure of his face was clearly visible; the dark lustrous eyes were sunken. His short-clipped hair, brushed back from a broad forehead, was streaked with gray. To some, the gaunt, stooped figure seemed 'the arch traitor . . . like Satan in Paradise'; [27] to others, the 'austere patriot,' with his back against the wall, battling fiercely in defense of violated liberties. To all, despite his tension and defiance, he looked at least the complete orator.

But he did not feel so. Not only had he to defend himself before an audience, hostile and embittered; but to re-evaluate the whole principle of federal government. Intellectually, he knew himself to be fitted for the task, but of his oratory he was less certain; for he was facing, both on the floor and in the galleries, critics spoiled by the eloquence of Webster and Clay, and wholly ready to award their verdict to the most compelling speaker. And as he stood silent a moment in the cold, clear light from the falling snow outside, he wondered if he would be able to speak at all. He was not ill, as Washington rumor had hopefully proclaimed, but days of grueling strain had drained his strength. He was tired, so desperately tired, that, as he frankly told the Senate, he doubted that his physical strength would be sufficient to see him through.[28]

His very admission compelled sympathy. And his first words, disarmingly gentle, were a pleasant surprise. He was speaking in sorrow rather than anger, with a perception of the basic cause of the conflict which eluded him in later years, as he deplored 'the decay of that brotherly feeling which once existed between these States . . . to which we are indebted for our beautiful federal system, and by the continuance of which alone it can be preserved.' But, he asked, had the general government the 'right to impose burdens on . . . one portion of the country, not with a view to revenue, but to benefit another?'

Passionately he denied the 'false statement' that South Carolina's object was 'to exempt herself from her share of the public burdens. . . . If the charge were true—if the state were capable of being actuated by such low and unworthy motives, mother as I consider her, I would not stand up on this floor to vindicate her conduct.' No, 'a deep constitutional question' was at stake. Nothing could be more erroneous than the charge that South Carolina was attempting to nullify the Constitution and laws of the United States. 'Her object is not to resist laws made in pursuance of the Constitution, but those made without its authority.' She did not even claim 'the right of judging of the delegated powers.' [29] but only of the reserved, and only when the Congress encroached upon her own powers and liberties.

Ingeniously he had transposed the entire relationship of accuser and accused. None denied that he had done so 'in innocence.' 'It was evident to all,' declared a Jacksonian supporter, 'that he sought to produce belief from what he himself believed. He could not change facts, but he could interpret them.' [30] He was not an impostor, but a fanatic.

There were moments when he gave way to his feelings, when he startled the Senate with his allusion to 'the mischievous influence over the President,' and to Jackson himself as the man 'false to South Carolina's hopes . . . now the most powerful instrument' to put down both the Southern people and their cause. Men looked at each other in astonishment. His bitterness, his resentment, his overwrought intensity were startling to the most casual observer. Hitherto none in public life had more scorned abuse or indulgence in personalities.[31]

He strongly defended the tariff of 1816 as a revenue measure, despite its few concessions to the protective policy. 'I would be willing to take that act today as the basis of a permanent adjustment.' The American system —and he meant 'nothing offensive to any Senator'—meant only the destruction of a balanced and harmonious Union. Its real meaning was that same 'system of plunder which the strongest interest has ever waged, and will ever wage against the weaker. . . . It is against this dangerous and growing disease' that South Carolina 'has acted.'

Chamber and galleries were hushed. Daniel Webster's head was bent over a paper; he was busily taking notes.

Not alone did the Force Bill declare war against South Carolina, Calhoun continued. 'No. It decrees a massacre of her citizens.' It puts 'at the disposal of the President the army and navy, and . . . entire militia . . . it enables him to subject every man in the United States . . . to martial law . . . and under the penalty of court-martial to compel him to imbrue his hand in his brother's blood.'

'It has been said to be a measure of peace! Yes, such peace as the wolf

gives to the lamb . . . as Russia gives to Poland, or death to its victim. . . . It is to South Carolina a question of self-preservation . . .
should this bill pass . . . it will be resisted at every hazard . . . even
that of death. . . . Death is not the greatest calamity; there are others
. . . more terrible to the free and brave . . . the loss of liberty and
honor . . . thousands of her brave sons . . . are prepared to lay down
their lives in defence of the State, and the great principles of constitutional liberty for which she is contending. God forbid that this should ever
become necessary! It never can be, unless this Government is resolved
to bring the question to extremity, when her gallant sons will stand prepared to perform the last duty—to die nobly.'

'The very warmest oratory ever witnessed,' marveled the correspondent
of the Charleston *Courier,* 'will give . . . but a faint idea of the manner
in which words seemed to come from Mr. Calhoun's inmost soul, and to
agitate him from head to foot in their delivery.' [32] Few could appreciate
the intricacies of his argument. His voice was hoarse, his delivery harsh
and abrupt. But few could remain unmoved by the spectacle of the man
himself, swept by his own intense feelings, with all the emotions that he
strove to conceal mirrored in the dark, shadowed eyes that in moments of
excitement or anger 'flashed with the fire of a soul that burned within
him.' *

A few moments later, brows were wrinkling over one of his subtleties.
Was ours a federal Union, a Union of states, as opposed to individuals?
Our very language afforded the proof. The terms, 'union,' 'federal,' 'united,'
were never applied to an association of individuals. 'Who ever heard of
the United State of New York?' Nor was our federal system built on
divided sovereignty, for sovereignty was of its very nature indivisible. It
was a 'gross error' to confound the exercise of sovereignty with sovereignty
itself, or the delegation of the powers with the surrender of them. To
surrender a portion 'is to annihilate the whole.'

Vehemently he denied that he was 'metaphysical. . . . The power of
analysis . . . is the highest attribute of the human mind . . . the power
which raises men above . . . inferior animals. It is this power which has
raised the astronomer from . . . a mere gazer at the stars to the high
intellectual eminence of a Newton or a Laplace. . . . And shall this high
power . . . be forever prohibited, under a senseless cry of metaphysics,
from being applied to . . . political science and legislation?' They are

---

* Calhoun's emotional power as an orator—his 'logic set on fire'—has been underestimated. 'No one can hear him without feeling,' declared one observer. No one could
see him 'without being moved.' At least two contemporaries insisted that Calhoun
was a 'far more ardent' speaker than Webster, with 'all the feeling and fire . . . which
the New Englander lacked.' (See Grund, *Aristocracy in America,* II, 218, 286, and
281; Perry, *Reminiscences of Public Men,* p. 64; Magoon, *Living Orators,* p. 235;
and Jenkins, *John C. Calhoun,* p. 450.)

'subject to laws as fixed as matter itself . . . the time will come when politics and legislation will be considered as much a science as astronomy and chemistry.'

He swung back to the subject. The Force Bill, they said, must be passed 'because the law must be enforced! The law must be enforced! The imperial edict must be executed!' To preserve this Union by force! 'Does any man in his senses believe . . . this beautiful structure . . . can be preserved by force? . . . Force may indeed hold the parts together, but such union would be the bond between master and slave. . . . It is madness to suppose that the Union can be preserved by force.'

In the midst of 'the tempest and whirlwind of his oratory,' a voice screamed from the gallery: 'Mr. President, I am being squeezed to death!' The almost unbearable tension snapped, and the Chamber rocked with laughter. Only Calhoun, clamped in the vise of his own intensity, stood unmoved and rigid, but his spell was broken. Shortly afterward, 'complaining of a slight indisposition,' he gave way to Daniel Webster's motion to adjourn.[33]

Continuing the next day, Calhoun called for a society organized with reference to its economic diversities, giving 'labor, capital, and production,' each the right of self-protection. His words were prophetic; well did he realize that the political lines of the states did not correspond to the economic groupings of the population. 'Let it never be forgotten,' he added, 'that power can only be opposed by power . . . on this theory stands our . . . federal system.'

The cynicism of this last statement, voiced by the 'first great realist of the nineteenth century,' a disillusioned idealist, who had learned that reason does not prevail, shocked Daniel Webster. It affronted the 'whole latent idealism' of an America, whose thought was based on French theories of the 'innate goodness of man.' It would be a hundred years before America would realize that 'power can only be opposed by power,' and that man, far from being inherently good, was as selfish as Calhoun believed him to be. Paradoxically, if Calhoun's premises were, at the time he uttered them, fifty years in the past, his doctrine was a hundred years to the future. Jackson did not know how to devise measures which would free the states and sections from oppression and yet leave enough authority in Washington for a government. His fear of outlying districts being subordinated to financial centralism was as real as Calhoun's, but he had no plan to avert the evil. Calhoun had ideas on both these questions, but was prevented from experimenting. Both Calhoun and Jackson were struggling to fuse the old ideals of the Constitution with the new realities of an expanding, complex civilization. But only Calhoun was facing the question, not of what the country wanted at the moment, but what it would require in the future.

The basic argument, the South Carolinian concluded, is 'whether ours

is a federal or consolidated government . . . the controversy is one between power and liberty.' He had spoken little more than an hour, but
was worn out from his exertion of the day before; and 'either from the
intensity of his feelings, the want of physical strength, or a deficiency of
vocal power,' was 'unfit for a long . . . sustained effort.' [34]

Comments ranged from a Southerner's enthusiastic declaration that the
speech was not 'surpassed by any recorded in ancient or modern times'
to the scoff of the Charleston *Courier* that he had 'ruined his politics by
his philosophy; and merged the practical statesman in the Utopian
dreamer.' Those who read the text considered the speech reasoned and
calm, although one critic wondered if 'logic can demonstrate any moral
proposition.' An eyewitness declared: 'His gestures and countenance expressed things unutterable, while his language was guarded.' [35]

8

History has dealt more kindly with Calhoun's speech than did his contemporaries. For undoubtedly he marred the strength of his argument by
outbreaks of passion. 'A total failure' was the summary of the Richmond
Enquirer. 'He is too much excited to do even justice to himself.' [36] Accounts generally agreed that he had failed, with the *Telegraph* pointing
out that his mind was 'so much worried.' [37] To Webster even the constitutional argument seemed inconsiderable. 'There is nothing to it,' he
asserted. To a friend he wrote: 'You are quite right about his present
condition. He cannot, I am convinced, make a coherent . . . argumentative speech.' [38]

Which was exactly what Calhoun wanted him to believe. Not even the
strength of his emotions could weaken the Carolinian's 'powers of reasoning . . . almost miraculous,' or the subtlety of his keen mind. Webster
had taken the floor the instant Calhoun had sat down, and with equal
haste had fallen completely into the trap set for him. Ignoring the speech
itself, as Calhoun had hoped that he would do, he took for his text the
three resolutions which Calhoun had presented on January 22. To cheering
galleries the New Englander proceeded to denounce nullification as the
practical end of the Republic and of liberty; to assert that the Constitution was established by the people and not the states; that it acted upon
individuals and not the states. From the White House Jackson exulted:
'Many people believe Calhoun to be demented. . . . Webster handled him
like a child.' [39]

Calhoun refused to be smoked out. On February 24, the Force Bill came
to a vote. Dramatically Calhoun arose. Haughty and defiant, he stalked
out of the Chamber, followed by the entire Southern delegation. Only
John Tyler, who had long since opposed the tariff as 'an appeal to the

numerical majority of the North to grow rich at the expense of the South,' remained to cast his 'Nay.' A few moments earlier Clay had hurried out of the Chamber on the plea of 'bad air.' [40]

9

Two days later, Calhoun, with a gentle reproof to Webster for the 'personal character' of his late speech, opened his reply with the statement, 'I never had any inclination to gladiatorial exhibitions . . . and if I now had, I certainly would not indulge them on so solemn a question.' With a dramatic gesture he lifted a few notes that he had taken on Webster's speech. He apologized for 'the poverty of his language.' He was sorry that his term 'constitutional compact' seemed obscure. But he had high authority, 'no less than the Senator himself.' [41] And he read the phrase from the famous Reply to Hayne.

Word by word, line by line, he tore at Webster's logic. 'Hundreds who could not or would not be convinced by his reasoning' could not withhold their admiration of the 'extreme mobility of his mind.' If the states had 'agreed to participate in each other's sovereignty,' as Webster claimed, how could they agree but by compact? Yet now the New Englander said there was no compact.

If a single state could ordain and establish a Constitution, why not a number of states? The states could not touch the Constitution? What about the power of three-fourths of the states to alter, or even abolish, the Constitution? Power had not been delegated to the people. The people, acting through their states, had delegated their power to the government.

Near Calhoun sat a long, skeleton-like figure, with eyes as dark and brilliant as his own. The dying John Randolph, convinced that his fellow Southerner's arguments were unanswerable, had no fear of Webster. A hat on the table obscured his view. 'Take away that hat,' he said. 'I want to see Webster die, muscle by muscle.' [42]

Calhoun conceded that he was no constitutional lawyer. But he wished to remind the gentleman from Massachusetts that an actual proposal to give the Supreme Court power to determine disputes between the states and federal government had been rejected in the Constitutional Convention! He read from Virginia's ratification of the Constitution, with its unequivocal statement that when delegated powers were perverted against the state, they could be resumed. And suddenly he read from the Massachusetts ratification of 'the compact.'

'Ours has every attribute which belongs to a federative system,' Calhoun concluded. 'It is founded on compact; it is formed by sovereign communities, and is binding between them. . . . The sovereignty is in the parts and not the whole.' [43] Nullification was constitutional. Through suffrage, oppression by rulers was prevented; through nullification, oppression by majorities.

Who had won? Randolph thought he knew. 'Webster is dead,' he crowed. 'I saw him dying an hour ago.' [44] To the galleries the victor was the one whom each individual had happened to hear first; to the country the winner was he with whose doctrines each section or group already agreed. Webster's reasoning was legal, taken from the words of the Constitution; Calhoun's, despite his denials, was metaphysical, arguing from what in the nature of things a government formed for certain defined purposes should be. Between the two concepts was no meeting ground. It was like trying to prove the principles of chemistry through physics. That Calhoun's logic was watertight, few denied. Even Webster conceded the strength of his position, granted that the Constitution was a compact, which Webster still insisted it was not. Trapped by the details of Calhoun's argument, he had been forced to reduce his own contentions to the level of common-sense, demanding whether the American people wanted a government like other governments or a mere league.

If victory belongs, not to him who has proved his case, but to him whose proofs are accepted, the honors went to Webster. Calhoun had shown what the government had been, and what he thought it should be; but Webster had demonstrated what the numerical majority thought and wanted it to be. His was the spirit of the times and of the future.

10

Calhoun might well claim victory on the field of logic. But logic was not the field Andrew Jackson had chosen. The 'Bloody Bill' was law; troops stood ready to march into South Carolina to wrest the federal revenues from their coffers. And if South Carolina resisted, what then of John C. Calhoun?

Clayton of Delaware studied Calhoun's drawn, haggard face. He approached Henry Clay. 'These Carolinians have been acting very badly, but they are good fellows, and it would be a pity to let old Jackson hang them.' he said.[45]

Mr. Clay considered. He did not think the South Carolinians 'good fellows,' and he was not at all sure that it might not mean the salvation of the country if Jackson did hang them. But civil war—Henry Clay did not want a war. Furthermore, pending in the House was a bill which tore his beloved American System to pieces. It might pass. But it would disrupt business. Nor was there much likelihood that it would be accepted by the Calhounites with their present view of the whole tariff question, based not on economics, but on principle. They were in no mood to accept Administration concessions on the one hand and coercion on the other.

But concessions from Henry Clay, from the representative of the manufacturing interests—that would be another matter. Remnants of the American System might even be salvaged. Calhoun could argue the values of
'peaceful, constitutional nullification' until his voice stuck in his throat;
but whether South Carolina seceded or not, war would come at her first
act of civil disobedience. This Henry Clay knew. He knew Andrew Jackson, and he knew the depths of that 'superstitious attachment to the Union,
which marked every act' of Calhoun's career. So Clay put out feelers. Calhoun responded. 'He who loves the Union must desire to see this agitating
question brought to a termination,' he said.[46]

Secretly, at night, the two met. The interviews were 'frosty.' Desperate,
the proud South Carolinian reluctantly accepted terms meted out to him.
Meanwhile, Clay went his way, making public promises to one group,
private pledges to another. On February 13, 1833, he introduced his own
modified tariff bill. 'I have ambition,' he declared, 'the ambition of being
the humble instrument in the hands of Providence to reconcile a divided
people.' As the 'humble instrument' sat down, Calhoun arose and briefly
announced that he would support the compromise. The galleries thundered
with applause.[47]

Northern public opinion was indignant. In Boston the self-termed
'friends of the Union'—that is to say, 'all persons . . . in favor of sus-
taining the labor of the Mechanic, Farmer, Manufacturer, Merchant, and
Shipowner'—met at Faneuil Hall to voice their opposition 'to any legislation' upon the tariff whatsoever by Congress. 'Any honorable conciliation'
they would accept, but 'the protecting system' was 'too closely interwoven
with all the interests of New England' to permit their consent to its
abandonment. The Clay-Calhoun compromise, said the Boston *Courier*,
was 'a palpable attempt to abandon the system of protection.'[48]

From the very way in which Mr. Clay was greeted by Mr. Calhoun, reported the correspondent for the Philadelphia *Sentinel*, 'no man can doubt
that the whole American System . . . is to be abandoned.'[49] The Nantucket *Courier* mourned the 'dissolution and ruin'[50] of the Republic. If
South Carolina would not abandon her course, neither should New England.

The very 'folly and cupidity of the friends of the American System'
furnished the Nullifiers with a 'powerful engine' for 'inflaming the minds
of their followers,' the New York *Evening Post* reminded its readers. South
Carolina had done 'nothing more, except that she is doing it with more
rashness, than some other states have done.'[51] And in Richmond, 'Father
Ritchie,' still bitter at that 'mule remedy' of nullification, which is 'neither
one thing, nor t'other,' defended the South Carolinian against charges 'of
destroying the manufacturers.' Mr. Calhoun would 'never agree to the
passage of any bill which would destroy the capital and skill in the Northern States.'[52]

Although Calhoun agreed to Clay's compromise, he rebelled at a clause on home valuation, and planned to let it pass without his vote, so that his conscience would permit him to attack it later. Unfortunately, John Middleton Clayton of Delaware immediately saw through the scheme, and announced that unless Calhoun voted personally for every clause, offensive or otherwise, he would move to lay the whole measure on the table.

This dose was too much even for Henry Clay. He joined a group of Calhoun's supporters behind the Vice-President's chair and begged that their chief might be spared this humiliation. Clayton was inflexible. 'If they cannot vote for a bill to save their necks from a halter, their necks may stretch,' [53] he said.

'Sweating blood,' Calhoun spent an entire night walking the floor of his room, fighting out the battle between his pride and his duty. The next morning, as Clayton boasted 'I made him do it,' the proud Carolinian stood before the Senate, announced that he was 'acting under protest,' and voted for every section of the compromise bill.

The Administration press chortled with glee. 'A single night,' proclaimed Frank Blair in the *Globe*, 'was sufficient to change Mr. Calhoun's constitutional scruples.' [54]

11

Congress adjourned March 3, 1833. That same day Calhoun started his seven-hundred-mile journey South. His haste was feverish. His one hope was to reach Columbia before the eleventh, when the Nullification Convention was to reassemble—before blood was shed.

For South Carolina had gone beyond him. Force would be met by fire. South Carolina was in no mood to accept the crumbs from Henry Clay's table, certainly not under the very gun-barrels of Andrew Jackson! If the principle of protection was wrong, why recognize it at all? South Carolina was armed. South Carolina was ready. Mr. Clay's tariff could be nullified as easily as the Tariff of Abominations had been.

The weather was raw and cold. Calhoun had hoped to take the packet, despite the qualms natural to one 'who suffers from sea-sickness as much as I do.' But the Potomac was frozen. Chafing at the delay, he abandoned the stage at Alexandria, and climbed into one of the open mail carts which traveled night and day over the half-broken trails.

To the legendary 'ten evils of stage-coaches,' the mail carts could add a dozen more. There were no springs. There were no coverings. There were no seats, and Calhoun, huddled in his waterlogged otter-skin greatcoat, had the choice of sitting on his luggage or on the mail bags, cramping his long legs into the spaces between. Thus he traveled for eight days and nights. Stop-overs were only for fresh drivers and horses; and hasty gulpings of the 'abominably bad . . . brown bread and common doings,' or 'white bread and chicken fixings,' eaten in silence and without complaint, either at the groups of dirty black and bluish-white children who glided in to stare 'as if you were a wild beast,' or at the unsavory fact that the 'lumps of paste' called wheatcakes, resembled nothing so much as 'lumps of clay.' [55]

Such a trip for even a young and robust man would have been almost unbearable. What it must have done to Calhoun is beyond conception. He had taken the precaution, now habitual with him, of placing a sheet of paper beneath his underwear to protect his chest, but it is not surprising that much of his later ill health dates from this period.

Now, aside from possible self-congratulation that the flat Southern terrain precluded the necessity of easing the horses at every high hill by getting out and walking,[56] Calhoun was beyond any concern for his physical well-being. Through swamp water and pine forest, across makeshift bridges of jolting logs, the cart rumbled. The pine torches hissed through the wet nights, the rain and wind beat down upon driver and passenger, with Calhoun too absorbed in his thoughts even to be aware of their effect upon him.

Not even when the cart swayed into Columbia did he rest. He had missed the convention's opening by twenty-four hours, and now made straight for the hall, startling the assembly as he walked in with his mud-splashed clothes and white, drawn face.

He was too tired to speak, but a seat was found for him on the floor. He had not come too soon. The mood of the convention was ugly. On the rostrum stood Robert Barnwell Rhett, voice taunting, nostrils flared in scorn. Openly he shouted for a Southern Confederacy. Openly he defied any delegate there to say that he loved the Union.

Up rose a single, old, one-legged veteran of the Revolution, Daniel Huger. 'It has been the pride of my life,' his voice quavered across the assembly, 'to submit to the laws of my country.' [57]

Through the hall Calhoun's tall figure moved restlessly from delegate to delegate. He pled for patience. He begged South Carolina not to assume the responsibility before history, before the world, for disrupting the dream of a united America. It was no easy task, preaching the gospel of peace to a people booted and spurred for war. He had indeed instructed them in their 'rights.' They had rejected the 'bribe' of a compromise tariff the year before. Many were furious at what they deemed his concessions to Clay; and only a few moments prior to his arrival had put through a resolution of censure against him by a majority of three votes.

Amidst loud cries of 'peacable secession' and pledges of allegiance to the state and obedience only to the national government, Calhoun won his way. By sheer personal persuasion the weary man convinced the delegates that South Carolina's practical objectives had been won. The state had nullified. The tariff had been repealed. To go farther would 'mean a war in the South.' And he 'did not wish it.' [58]

Overnight the mood of the convention changed. On the fourteenth the delegates repealed their nullification of the tariff of 1828. And with war averted, even the Unionists swung over to Calhoun's side. His leadership was restricted, of course, to his own state borders. He was utterly without a party, his career tainted by the very name of nullification. He cared little. Despite the immediate victory, he still had the courage to point out the magnitude of the defeat that had been suffered. It had certainly been no small triumph for a single state to wrest from the federal government the relinquishment of its tariff policy, but the price of nullification had been the triumph of coercion. Nullification of the Force Bill itself, just before the convention's adjournment, was no more than a gesture. The 'Bloody Bill' remained on the books, a precedent for future eventualities; and to all practical purposes, the national government had proved its superiority to the states that created it.

The effects of the struggle were to be felt through the lives of the entire generation then living. It is true that the West and South were already divided on the slavery question. Yet their community of interest on the tariff was one, and as late as 1861 there were many who believed that a Free Trade Act alone would be enough to draw the West into the orbit of the Southern Confederacy. But they were wrong. The tariff fight between Jackson and Calhoun had so divided the agrarian states that the West and South could not stand united before the test of civil war.[59]

Back at Fort Hill, Calhoun could at last relax and seek restoration of his depleted energies. Submerged in the gloom of reaction, he reflected with bitterness on the fruits of his 'victory.' The Democratic Party, he declared, was carrying the principles of consolidation farther than Hamilton had even dreamed. 'The sperit of liberty is dead in the North.' A consolidated, nationalistic government had been legally established under 'the bloody act. . . . It will never be enforced in this State. . . . Carolina is resolved to live only under the Constitution. There shall be at least one free State.' [60]

'The struggle, far from being over,' he wrote, 'has only just commenced.' [61]

XVII

Calhoun at War

'I HAVE HAD BUT LITTLE SPIRIT to write to my friends,' Calhoun confessed to Littleton Tazewell early in 1836. His view of the future was 'hopeless'; he could see only the eventual 'overthrow of our system.' All was coming to a head; and 'the vice, folly, and corruption of this the most vicious, mad . . . administration that ever disgraced the government is about to recoil on the country with fearful disaster.' [1]

Never, before or later, did Calhoun reveal such bitterness. He was so despondent that to him every move of the Chief Executive seemed 'fatal' to the country, and throughout Jackson's second term this mood of depression hung over him. Undoubtedly his personal frustrations tainted his thinking: as John Quincy Adams, studying him across the dinner table, put it: 'Calhoun looks like a man racked with furious passions and stung with disappointed ambition, as undoubtedly he is.' [2] Fifty-four now, at the prime of his intellectual powers, Calhoun was goaded with the conviction that his hopes both for himself and the country were doomed to extinction. Peace, health, and rest had become almost impossible to him. [3]

Yet his despair was not for himself alone, and history would prove how genuine was the basis for his fears. In the tragedy of his baffled ambitions lay baffled also infinite possibilities for the working of American democracy.

The concentration of power in the hands of the Executive he recognized as one of the most disturbing aspects of the Force Bill. Nor was this bill more than one example of Jackson's 'general tendency.' Calhoun clearly saw that Executive authority strong enough to curb the business interest could, in other hands, be united with this same interest, to govern the nation. If Executive authority were recognized as superior to state authority, even for the states' benefit, that same power could be used at another time to work the states' subordination. None knew better than he how powerful were the precedents that the Jackson Administration had already laid down. 'No one,' Calhoun wrote David Hoffman, 'can look with greater alarm than I do, on the attempt of the Chief Magistrate to appoint his successor' (Martin Van Buren). 'Should it succeed . . . resting . . . on the avowed subserviency of the nominee to the will of the President . . . it would afford conclusive proof of the consumation of Executive usurpation over the Government, and the Constitution. . . . Executive . . . power will forever silence the popular voice.'[4] In practice, if not in theory, by popular wish, if not by historical authority, under Andrew Jackson the federated Republic was becoming a unified nation. This was what Calhoun saw, and what he feared.

2

To Andrew Jackson, Calhoun was just one more rival, a hated one, to be sure, but definitely in second place. Jackson had a more potent enemy now, and he could fight the enemy and the issue with equal intensity.

The man was Nicholas Biddle. Democrats of later generations might damn him as un-American, but his philosophy was as old as America herself. Like most of his fellow mortals, Mr. Biddle was no conscious villain. He was merely imbued with the conviction that what was good for Mr. Biddle was, of necessity, good for the country.

Many battles in the coming-of-age of America had already been won. America had surrendered to the principle of majority rule; the only question was, who should control the majority? The battle of the money power still roared on. It was not now a question of freedom against a concentration of power, but of public power against private power, of the masses against the classes. Would the people choose their governors under the guidance of political potentates or of business ones? This was the issue: Jackson and Biddle the contenders.

No two men could have been more unlike. And no one man could have so embodied the united causes of money and aristocracy as the dark, classic-featured, one-time child prodigy, Nicholas Biddle of Philadelphia. When young Andrew Jackson lay half-dead in a South Carolina prison-pesthouse, thirteen-year-old Biddle had just completed the prescribed courses at the University of Pennsylvania. At eighteen he was in France, personally handling the more delicate details of the Louisiana Purchase. A few more years and he was back in America, editing a highly literary magazine and writing a history of the Lewis and Clark expedition, while he built up the biggest banking monopoly America had ever seen. Brilliant in intellect, elegant in dress, fascinating in manner, it was this figure, with the face of a poet and the brain of a financial wizard, who in the 'Age of Jackson' exerted even more personal power than the President. For through its branches and agencies, 'the Bank of the United States ruled the commerce, the industry, and the husbandry of a nation; and Biddle ruled the bank.'[5]

Jackson knew it. There was much Andrew Jackson did not know about the workings of minds like Biddle's, or the intricacies of high finance; yet

of the Bank's tendency to make the rich 'richer by Act of Congress,' he
was fully aware. Furthermore, he was convinced that the Bank had failed
in its 'great end of establishing a uniform and sound currency'—a view
that would have been heartily seconded by Calhoun had he been able to
agree with Jackson on anything at all.

Oddly enough, despite his 'distrust of accumulated capital,' Jackson
had not at first pressed the Bank issue. There were strong Bank men in
his party—even in his own Cabinet. 'I do not dislike your Bank any
more than all Banks,' [6] Jackson told Biddle. It was Daniel Webster and
Henry Clay in their hot haste for an issue who almost 'literally black-
mailed' Biddle into asking Congress for the Bank's recharter four years
in advance of the expiration date in 1836—thus making the Bank the
political football of the campaign of '32.[7]

Jackson took up the challenge. If the Bank was to be an issue, his Veto
Message—a hot blast against the 'rich and powerful' who 'bend the acts
of Government to their selfish purposes' [8]—spoke for the laborer against
the capitalist. The 'Recharter' was lost and the battle was on, with 'the
Monster of Chestnut street'—as Jackson termed the Bank—fighting the
people with their own public funds. Credit barriers were unclamped;
loans to editors and political haranguers were dispensed with prodigal
liberality. Presses were rented and bought. Pro-Bank speeches by Webster,
Clay, Calhoun, and many others were reprinted by the thousands, and
thoroughly enjoyed by the bankers, businessmen, and politicians, who
had acclaimed them in the first place. Factories closed down, and it was
said they would reopen only upon 'the election of Henry Clay.' Unemployment, depression, disaster—all was forecast as the price of the re-
election of Andrew Jackson.

All without avail.

Old Hickory's mind was made up. As the election returns poured in,
he acted to bring matters to a head. His conviction was complete that
if federal funds remained at the disposal of Biddle, he would use them to
'buy up all Congress' and override the Presidential veto in time for the
Bank's recharter in 1836.[9] And Biddle would supply the evidence in his
own handwriting a year later when the state of Louisiana was offered two
million dollars in depression relief as the price for eleven votes in the
House of Representatives! Clay was already on the Bank payroll as an
advisory counsel. Webster was freely supplied with loans; and by the
spring of 1841 would still owe the Bank $111,166.[10] Furthermore, so
many individual Congressmen were already fettered to the Bank's strong-
boxes that the purchase of only a few more votes would have been
necessary.

Jackson's plan was simple: to remove the federal funds from the Bank.
When Secretary of the Treasury Louis McLane declined to comply, he
was transferred to the State Department. When the newly appointed

Secretary, William John Duane, bluntly refused to carry out orders, he found himself removed along with the deposits. That same day—September 23, 1832—Roger Taney had stepped into the office. Seventy-two hours later, federal funds had ceased their flow into the Bank of the United States, with existing deposits already on their way to repositories in the various states. So far as Andrew Jackson was concerned, the incident was closed.

So far as Nicholas Biddle was concerned, it had scarcely opened. Ensuing scenes in the drama were played out on two sets: a tall, stately room in a Greek temple on Philadelphia's Chestnut Street and the tobacco-scented, untidy, upstairs study of the 'President's House,' where Andrew Jackson sat waiting.

Biddle leveled his guns. All that Jackson had feared he might do, he did; and the country was swept by a panic, as it seemed to Jackson 'entirely artificial,' and almost entirely manufactured by that 'hydra of corruption,'[11] the Bank.

The truth was less simple. Biddle was a businessman, and like other businessmen deemed his first duty to be toward his corporation. With the federal funds gone, curtailment of loans was absolutely essential both 'to salvage his own institution' and to safeguard the interests of the depositors.

Yet, if it was Jackson's haste that precipitated the panic of 1833, Nicholas Biddle was no man to by-pass the opportunity to carry the fight through. The contractions were justified; but the reduced discounts and the continually restricted drawings—all within the few months from August, 1833, to September, 1834—were too much. Stocks tumbled; business houses crashed; unemployed laborers walked the streets, cursing the names of both Biddle and Jackson.

Biddle stood firm. With organized capital behind him, with Jackson's wildcat finance as a palpable excuse, Biddle could bring down such wreckage upon the heads of the unsuspecting populace as would make them howl for mercy—or for the recharter of the Bank of the United States, 'which alone had always kept its notes at par with specie and above those of all other banks.' No relief could be offered; for 'Nothing but the evidence of suffering abroad will produce any effect.'[12]

Boston suffered the first bombardments. While merchants pled for a million dollars to pay duties on cargoes that were already at the wharves, the Bank suddenly canceled all discounts and demanded the return of many of its balances in the state banks. In the six months from August, 1833, through January, 1834, the Bank squeezed over eighteen million dollars from a gasping public, one-third of its entire discounts. Small men, small industries, were exterminated, but the pressure also bore heavily upon even the wealthiest establishments. Biddle's own satellites were hit, but they still had money left to buy the support of the wavering, to pay the stage fare to Washington, and in delegation after delegation to climb the stairs to the White House 'den.'

There, white hair bristling high above the heap of letters, petitions, and assassination threats which littered his desk, tobacco-stained teeth clamped upon the stem of his corncob pipe, his thin face gullied with lines of pain, the old man heard his tormentors out.

'Go home, gentlemen, and tell the Bank of the United States to relieve the country by increasing its business.' To others: 'You are a den of vipers and thieves. . . . Should I let you go on, you will ruin forty thousand families. . . . I have determined to rout you out, and, by the Eternal!' —hard fist crashing into a nest of flying papers—'I will rout you out!' To all, one command was the same: 'Go to Nicholas Biddle! The people! The people, sir, are with *me!*' [13]

3

The people were. Congress was another matter. Indignant at the Presidential slurs upon its honor, terrified by a mighty mass of petitions for relief and recharter, Congress rose up that fall, snarling. Hatred of Jackson had become sheer obsession.

The removal of the deposits furnished the ammunition for the Congressional guns. The 'right' of the Secretary of the Treasury to discontinue placing public funds in the Bank was written into the Bank's charter, provided 'satisfactory reasons' were given for doing so. But neither Jackson nor Taney in their united wisdom could produce reasons satisfactory to Congress in its present mood.

The nullification issue postponed the bombardment until the session of 1834. Then Henry Clay opened the festivities. Mr. Clay's efforts were thorough. It took him the better part of three days and twelve pages of small type in *Niles' Register* to express his fears of encroaching Executive power and his hatred of Andrew Jackson. The removal of the deposits was 'an open, palpable, and daring usurpation. . . . We are in the midst of a revolution,' he shouted, 'rapidly tending towards . . . the concentration of all power in the hands of one man.' Soon our government will be 'transformed into an elective monarchy. . . . Thank God, we are yet free.'

His voice sank low. 'People . . . speak . . . in the cautious whispers of trembling slaves.' Soon 'we shall die—ignobly die, base, mean, and abject . . . the scorn and contempt of mankind, unpitied, unwept, unmourned.' Kendall noted that this pathetic climax was greeted 'with repeated cheers and clapping of hands,' the feminine portion of the audience, at least, supplying the tears which Mr. Clay feared would be lacking at his country's demise.[14]

Three days of retaliation were consumed by Benton, who sneered lustily at Clay's call to 'drive the Goths from the temple.' Then came Calhoun.

Unlike his more energetic predecessors, he devoted only an hour and a half to his remarks; yet on the test of statesmanship, he failed as completely as Jackson had done with the tariff measure.

For there is no doubt that John C. Calhoun was as much opposed to the National Bank as ever Jackson could be. His early ties to the Bank could be snapped without fear of retaliation, for they were not financial but political. He knew that the National Bank, which he proudly admitted *he* had fathered, had not grown up as he had hoped that it would. He knew that the Bank was, in part, responsible for the very conditions that it had been devised to prevent. He could oppose it now wholeheartedly. He could and did say, 'We must curb the Banking system, or it will certainly ruin the country.'

But what he could not do was join forces with Andrew Jackson. This would have been the statesmanlike course, but it would have been too much for Calhoun's very human nature to endure. His feelings had blinded him to the fundamentals of a great issue, and the personal hatred between him and Jackson again confused and divided the Southern people, with disastrous results.

Undoubtedly Calhoun was honest in thinking that 'an union of the banking system and the Executive' would be 'fatal' to our country. He was right in his belief that 'an entire divorce between the government and the Banking system' was the only cure, but he had no solutions to offer. His efforts were destructive, not constructive.

He boasted that he was in the 'front rank' of those who, once denounced as 'traitors and disunionists,' were now 'manfully resisting the advances of despotic power.' The officials who had secreted the deposits were 'public plunderers under the silence of midnight.' It had been a 'wanton exercise of power' on the part of the Executive. 'It is not even pretended,' he declared, 'that the public deposits were in danger.'

'If the question merely involved the existance of the banking system,' he would 'hesitate' before he would 'be found under the banner of the system.' But the question was not between the government and the Bank, but between the legislative and the executive branches of the government. Should the President have 'the power to create a bank, and the consequent control over the currency?' This was 'the real question.'

If the Bank was so injurious with Congressional control, what safety would there be for the currency when transferred to local banks, wholly free of control? Calhoun honestly could not see how the government could deposit in state institutions without involving all 'the objections against a bank of the United States.'[15] His reasons for supporting the Bank and attacking the President are plausible and not without much foundation. Yet, knowing the clarity of his vision, his hatred of all forms of money power, it is impossible to avoid the conclusion that his hatred of Andrew Jackson was even stronger.

4

It was Daniel Webster who played the part of a statesman. In March, 1834, he stepped to the foreground. Free from the ambition that nagged at Clay and the bitterness that gnawed at Calhoun, he took a step, bold indeed, considering his own relation to the Bank. His suggestion was a compromise, granting the Bank a six years' lease on life, in which to wind up its business, stipulating, meanwhile, a restoration of the deposits. His speech was the most statesmanlike of the session, but the Senate was in no mood for statesmanship. Calhoun, although eloquent about the distress that 'is daily consigning hundreds to poverty and misery . . . taking employment and bread from the laborer,' wrecking business and whirling financiers 'to the top' of the wheel, condemned Webster's proposal as almost entirely 'objectionable.'

He could boast that 'I do not stand here the partisan of any . . . class . . . the rich or the poor, the property-holder, or the money-holder.' He could warn that whoever had the currency 'under their exclusive control, might control the valuation of all . . . property . . . and possess themselves of it at their pleasure.' He knew that the federal currency had once more degenerated into bank notes, scarcely of more value than the paper they were printed on.

Something had to be done.

But Webster's method was too extreme. He pointed out that even those who thought the tariff unconstitutional had allowed 'upwards of eight years for the termination of the system,' contending that to end it at once would spread destruction and ruin over a large portion of the country. So he offered a counter-proposal, extending the Bank's charter for twelve years, with the value of gold to be established in a ratio of 16 to 1 with silver, and the notes of no bank to be used 'in the [payment of the] dues of the government.' [16]

Six years was long enough for any institution to wind up its affairs, and it is difficult not to believe that Calhoun was actuated by motives little higher than sheer opposition. But it was the Administration that had the votes and the people who had made up their minds, and all attempts at delay only hastened the Bank's end.

The opposition could censure, however, and under Clay's leadership, with whole-hearted support from both Webster and Calhoun, a vote censuring the President's removal of the deposits was put through, 26 to 20. Three weeks later came a reply from Andrew Jackson. He spoke of his old war wounds. He recounted his services to his country. And finally, he denied the Senatorial right to censure him at all.

The pathos of this appeal drew no tears from Calhoun. With a vituperation that he never exceeded, he thrust bitterly at the President. 'Infatuated man! blinded by ambition . . . dark, lawless, and insatiable ambition!' He sneered at the President's appeal to the people 'as their immediate representative,' as allies in his war 'against the usurpations of the Senate.' No 'such aggregate as the American people . . . existed,' Calhoun contended. States were the units of government. 'Why, he never received a vote from the American people!' *

The President had no right to question the Senate. The Senate was the sole judge of its own powers. The President had no right to send a protest! The Senate had no right to receive it.[17]

5

Whatever Calhoun's motives, his fears were real. No man in history ever more clearly warned the nation of the dangers of unchecked Presidential power; and regardless of how much Calhoun may have feared the power of Jackson, he feared Jackson's precedents even more. Fighting from opposite sides and against each other, Calhoun and Jackson had revealed the dual dangers of economic tyranny and federal tyranny to freedom, to the whole federal system itself. Which danger was the more real would long remain a moot point.

The cause of Executive consolidation, Calhoun thought, could largely be traced to 'the fiscal action of the Government. . . . While millions are heaped up in the Treasury . . . constituting an immense fund . . . to unite in one solid and compact band, all, in and out of office, who prefer their own advancement to the publick good, any attempt to arrest the progress of power and corruption must end in disappointment.' And to Calhoun, all—the centralization of Executive power; the encroachments on the rights of the states; Jackson's appointment of his Vice-President and 'successor' in the heat of the new party conventions; the 'extravagant' expenditure of public funds with the resultant increase in votes as thanks for services rendered—all were part of a new pattern to become a perennial problem in American government. Precedents had been set that if not reversed would endow the hitherto federal government with powers undreamed of at the Constitutional Convention.

Jackson, declared Calhoun on February 13, 1835, had invoked, not one-man rule, but a monarchy. 'The nature of a thing is in its substance; and the name soon accomodates itself to the substance.' Sixty thousand employees were on the federal payroll. One hundred thousand, including the pensioners, were dependent upon the federal Treasury for support.

---

* Presidents, of course, are chosen by the Electoral College, the members of which, in that day, were appointed by each state 'in such manner as the Legislature thereof may direct.' (Constitution of the United States, Article II, Section 1.)

Nor did this include the unnumbered thousands, hopeful for future benefits. What better way to build up a dynasty? 'The President wants my vote; and I want his patronage; I will vote as he wishes, and he will give me the office I wish for.'[18] Official patronage alone, Calhoun charged, held Jackson's party together. And no speedier means toward centralization in government could be found.

Calhoun had no praise for Jackson's balancing of the federal budget; indeed, he feared the danger inherent in surplus revenues. Indignantly he countered Benton's suggestion that governmental expenditures be increased. Then would the number be doubled 'of those who live or expect to live by the Government.' He swept aside proposals to turn surplus funds over to the 'pet banks,' to bank-stock speculators in public lands who were 'rapidly divesting the people of the noble patrimony left by our ancestors.' Why not deposit them equally in the treasuries of the states? 'It is objected that such a distribution would be a bribe to the people. A bribe . . . to return it to those to whom it justly belongs, and from whose pockets it should never have been taken . . .?' If left to the government itself, remember the 'thousands of agents, contractors, and jobbers through whose hands it must pass, and in whose pockets so large a part would be deposited.'[19]

6

Calhoun sensed the spirit of the age—but was against it. Furiously he turned upon a statement of James Buchanan's that a national majority could vote down the Constitution and the government of the states; that such was the essence of democracy. This was not Calhoun's America, the America of which he had expressed despair to the Senate, but for which he would fight on. His America was 'not a Democracy,' but a Republic. Ours was a Constitution 'which respects all the great interests of the State, giving each a voice.'[20] He did not deny the rights of rebellion and revolution, but neither could the opposition deny the right of nullification!

America was in transition, and so was he. He had come far, tragically far, from the bright hopeful days when he had trusted the people and trusted the government. A statesman, he had too often played the part of a politician during these crucial years. Politically and personally he had reached the lowest ebb of his entire career.

XVIII

The Age of Jackson

IN ALL AMERICAN HISTORY there is no greater tragedy than the war between Andrew Jackson and John C. Calhoun. Who was to blame is irrelevant. Which was the more guilty, the more prone to let his selfish desire for victory transcend his obligations to the Southern and American people alike, is unimportant. What matters is that, for all their variance on specific issues and means of attaining their ends, those ends were alike.

Most historians have drawn them apart, contrasting Calhoun's theory of the state and Jackson's concept of the nation as the ultimate power in American government. Yet personally, economically, and even politically, these two contenders were alike.

Each bore the marked characteristics of the same race: the thin, wiry bodies, the long heads, bristling with thick, unruly hair; the deep-set eyes, gaunt cheeks, and grim lines of mouth and jaw. They walked alike, with long, swinging strides. They talked alike, for theirs was the vigorous, accented speech of the Southern hill-country, from which all Jackson's roamings, and all Calhoun's years in New England and Washington, could not smooth away the last traces of Scotch-Irish brogue and burr.

They had the characteristic gloominess of their heritage. Each had a remarkable capacity for exaggerating the evil around him. Where Jackson saw the Bank of the United States as 'a hydra of corruption,' and nullification as a sword forged by Calhoun for the express purpose of dividing the Union to make himself President of one-half, Calhoun found nothing but evil in the breezy expansiveness of Clay's 'American System,' nothing but 'deluded' fanaticism in the moral idealism of the abolitionists.

It is true that Jackson's great gift was intuition—delicate, sensitive, uncannily perceptive; and Calhoun's, a mind so powerful, so sharp-edged and clear, despite its narrowness, that in all American history, perhaps, only the intellect of Jonathan Edwards can compare with it. Yet such differences as there were between Jackson and Calhoun were more environmental than temperamental. Jackson was the symbol of the frontier, of the majority mood of America, but Calhoun belonged to a state and a tradition. His very•moral code, unlike Jackson's, was not so much personal as a matter of upholding the standards of his section. Calhoun had studied theories; Jackson knew facts. Jackson was a man of action; Calhoun was a man of thought.

But on economic fundamentals they were in agreement. Although history would record Jackson as the great apostle of democracy and Calhoun as the defender of slavery, Jackson was the greater landowner and slaveholder; and if he ever expressed an opinion against slavery, we have no record of it. What Calhoun and Jackson both knew was that the stronghold of freedom was the landholder, free to vote according to his choice, and not according to the will of an employer, with life and death power over his job. And if Jackson extended his stronghold of freedom to include the landless factory hand; if Calhoun saw the country, not as a battleground between the masses and the classes, but as a unit of discordant minorities, each with a right to freedom and self-realization—both men recognized finance capitalism as the common enemy.

Alike the two men assuredly were. They were alike in their blood and bearing, their reverence for women and affection for children, their love of home and the land; the very intensity with which they felt and thought. And their likenesses made them mortal enemies. They felt exactly the same way about entirely different things. Their patriotism—as each saw patriotism—their adherence to principle, regardless of personal consequences, brought them into headlong conflict. And neither could admit defeat.

Each captured the imagination of the American people. Gallant and reckless warriors both, they had the courage to risk all in order to win all. Hated as they both were, neither was ever despised.

2

Had clear thinking prevailed, had Calhoun and Jackson risen to the statesmanship worthy of them during these troubled times, history might have been very different. Both had muddied the issues: Jackson, by supporting big business on the tariff, while he fought it on the Bank; Calhoun, by doing just the reverse. But these were not the years for clear thinking. It was a time of passions, violent and unleashed, of party battles and personal hatreds. Jackson, sitting knee to knee with Calhoun in the Senate Chamber, attending a funeral, could gloat over the 'peculiar twinkle' in the Southerner's eye, indulging the comforting belief that insanity was breeding in his rival, who would be confined to a lunatic asylum a year or two hence. And Calhoun could brood that Jackson, in his fiendish 'desire to retain power,' was bent 'on a French war,' for had he not said 'that nothing could induce him to take a third term, but a war with France?'[1] Jackson's sturdy pronouncement that American claims against

France would be collected—by force, if necessary—which brought even old John Quincy Adams to his feet cheering, brought no echoes from the bitter Calhoun.

In this year of 1835 there occurred the first outright attempt to assassinate a President of the United States, as a pistol was brandished in the portico of the Senate Chamber, and Harriet Martineau saw the white hands of the would-be killer, 'struggling above the heads of the crowd,' before he was pinioned and dragged down. Such was the madness of the time that within two hours the 'name of almost every eminent politician was mixed up with that of the poor maniac.' ² For Jackson, who had been hastily taken home, looking 'very ill and weak,' had strength enough left to assert that Calhoun and Poindexter were those most guilty. It was their intemperate ravings—so charged the President—that had incited the fanatic into the belief that by murdering Jackson he would rid the country of a cruel tyrant.

The Senatorial response to these accusations was something less than temperate. White with rage, Calhoun stood up in the Chamber and spurned the charge. It was one more attempt of Andrew Jackson to throttle free speech, to muzzle Congress, to stifle even freedom of thought.

The Senate was impressed, but not the American people. It was the 'Age of Jackson' still, and Old Hickory was impervious to all but the ravages of illness and age. For Jackson was one of those Presidents who come twice or thrice in a century, whom the world accepts for what they are,' not for what they do. Declared William Wirt: 'General Jackson can be President for life, if he chooses.' ³

3

Jackson's America had become Jackson's Washington. The city where the national mind was to be formed was becoming the prototype of the national mind. Virile, lusty, raucous, it was only too symbolic of that national democracy which Andrew Jackson had fathered. To the 'aristocracy' of Capitol Hill and Georgetown Heights, it seemed as if America had been overturned. They were wrong. America had not overturned; it had merely overflowed. The people had always been there, but they had never been to Washington before.

They were there now: young mechanics shouting and reeling along Pennsylvania Avenue, unknown Irish laborers, unloved, unmourned, dying where they fell and buried in unmarked graves; weather-beaten frontiersmen who had walked a hundred miles to see Old Hickory; officeseekers by the hundreds, whose expenses home Jackson often paid out of his own pocket.⁴ Lost in the mobs were such potent figures as short, slender, shabbily dressed Frank Blair, the sarcastic and slashing editor of Jackson's Washington *Globe,* or little Amos Kendall, a young man still, but with masses of white hair and white side-whiskers framing his yellowish face, his frail figure slipping through the swirling crowd with 'elfin speed.' Yet those in the know were well aware that these figures were the powers behind Jackson's throne, the shapers of Presidential policy.

Not even they were more feared than a dumpy little woman in calico, a poke-bonnet shading sparkling blue eyes and teeth of glowing white. To see her was to see ladies 'sweep their veils around their faces and men . . . scuttle off, hiding behind their hats.' [5] For this was Anne Royall, the 'widow with the Serpent's tongue,' from whose prying curiosity no bought vote was hidden, no public or private scandal safe.

King Andrew's spies lurked—so it was said—in every drawing room, repeating 'anything said in the least critical of the Administration.' As names were carefully concealed, everyone in society suspected everyone else. Mrs. Smith relieved her feelings at Sunday church services by squeezing back against the Presidential fingers as they gripped the edge of her pew. Henry Clay, 'gracefully reclining on a sofa in the firelight, his face flushed and animated with emotion,' spoke for the opposition: 'There is not in Cairo or Constantinople, a greater moral despotism than is . . . exercised in this city over public opinion. Why, a man dare not avow what he thinks or feels . . . if he happens to differ with the powers that be.' [6]

4

Something less than genteel were the Presidential receptions. The fastidious George Bancroft was of the opinion that 'a respectable woman would have far preferred to walk . . . the streets than subject herself' to the 'revolting scenes' of the White House drawing room. There a bearded and buckskinned frontiersman 'in all his dirt' could force his way to the President, pumping his arm with one hand and flourishing a whip with the other. There the satin-clad toes of the women were muddied and trampled by a veritable army of mechanics and apprentices, 'pouncing upon the wine and refreshments, tearing the cake with . . . ravenous . . . hunger; starvelings, and fellows with dirty faces and dirty manners, all the refuse that Washington could . . . turn forth from the workshops and stables.' [7] And yet in Jackson himself, stooped and frail, proudly indifferent to the loss of his front teeth, there was a dignity, a courtesy if you will, that transcended his surroundings. The people's President he might be; his integrity was his own.

For those of roistering inclinations there was plenty of 'real life' in Jackson's Washington. Around punchbowls, 'large as a Roman bathing tub,' [8] newcomers were saluted with a ladleful of Daniel Webster's 'special mixture' (Medford rum, brandy, champagne, arrack, maraschino, strong green tea, lemon juice, and sugar). [9] For all-night parties were the shadowy

cellars, 'not quite so well furnished as the common resorts of cabmen
. . . in London,' where Negro waiters served oysters, venison, and roast
duck, on dirty tablecloths. Mechanics swaggered in, calling for cheese
and crackers; Kentuckians, 'full of oaths and tobacco juice,' smoked and
spat, only a few inches from young bucks with perfumed hair and imported kid gloves, who discussed women 'in French slang.' [10]

Faro banks lined Pennsylvania Avenue, all the way from the Capitol
to the Indian Queen; and light from dripping sperm candles flickered
faintly against the windows of Senatorial coaches. Out beyond Washington, at Bladensburg, were the race-tracks and the dueling grounds, and
in secret but accessible places were cockpits, where even the President
of the United States might show up to cheer his favorites on.[11]

5

Washington was still a frontier town. For accommodations the public
servant still had his choice of the 'mean insignificant-looking' boarding
houses, or of inns like Gadsby's, whose 'pretensions to aristocracy' rested
on 'four clean walls . . . and rooms agreeable and airy.' [12] Calhoun bore
the common lot without complaint. For his personal comfort he cared
little. He was coming more and more to live in his intellect, 'with no
thought of the body.' [13] But that he was not immune to hardships is indicated by his pleasure the one winter that he was actually comfortable.
He was at 'Mrs Page's on the avenue, nearly opposite to the central
market.' The furniture, rooms, and board were 'very good,' the landlady
'obliging,' and the servants 'excellent.' The mess itself, he told Anna
Maria, was 'dull, but quiet,' which suited him perfectly. After the grind
of the day, he sought only rest or 'agreeable' company, preferably not
'too discordant on political subjects.' One winter he found himself with
a 'temperance mess,' which was congenial enough, except that he was the
only Southerner in the group.[14]

His mess of 1834, however, was neither dull nor harmonious. If Ben:
Perley Poore is to be believed, no more high-powered group of dynamos
ever sat under a Washington rooftree than around the dinner table of the
United States Hotel that winter. Looking about him, Calhoun would have
been stabbed with memories, now twenty years old. For there sat Henry
Clay, his smile as mocking and impudent as in youth; and nearby Daniel
Webster, ponderous now, both in motion and speech. At his side was another Bay Stater, a lanky and long-winded young Congressman named
Edward Everett, overawed by the dual presence of Massachusetts' two
greatest men, Webster and former President John Quincy Adams. Scarcely
less awe-inspiring was the presence of a shaggy graying man of seventy-
nine, Chief Justice John Marshall, now in the twilight of his long career.

Completely unreserved in his opinions, Marshall could confuse intellects as great as Webster's when launched into a display of his fine-spun legalism; but it is doubtful that Calhoun, however, would have permitted himself to be drawn into argument. Nullification was still dangerously near the surface of the minds of each; and each knew the gulf that separated him from the point of view of the other. But Calhoun might have enjoyed the conversation of Justice Story, his eager face mobile as a child's; and ready always to talk for hours to anyone who had the hours to give him.[15]

With Clay and Marshall present, it is easy to believe in the 'flashes of merriment which set the table in a roar,' as Poore described it. But the Washington journalist's further assertion, that 'in their familiar intercourse with each other they had all the tenderness of brethren,'[16] is more pleasant to believe than capable of proof. The story is in the facts; by the end of a single Congressional session the highly charged combination was scattered; and Calhoun was back with the Southerners.

In the stately mansions on Georgetown Heights the gracious manners of old Maryland were still maintained. Even foreign visitors exclaimed at the 'continental ease' of life in the 'Co't end' of Washington, with its roster of 'pleasant, clever people,' who came 'to muse and be amused'; but Calhoun, welcome guest though he would have been in these homes, could not stretch his salary to a point where he could repay hospitality. Society saw little of him now. Maintaining bachelor quarters, and freed from the social responsibilities of the Vice-President or the Secretary of War, he was freed also from the necessity of accepting invitations. Social life in Washington in the eighteen-thirties, as today, was a career in itself; as Amos Kendall observed, 'The "big bugs" here pay no attention to the sun . . . in regulating their meals.' Guests were invited for five, assembled at six, sat down to dinner at eight, nine, or ten, and by eleven were scarcely able to leave the table at all. Now in a state of declared hostilities with the Jackson Administration, Calhoun could hear at second hand of the 'squeeze' at the Postmaster General's, where nearly four hundred people, the women 'too tightly laced and their bosoms and shoulders much exposed,' crammed chairs, closets, and corners of an eight-room house. Undoubtedly with one, at least, of Kendall's opinions, Calhoun would thoroughly have agreed, that 'if there is more extravagance, folly, and corruption any where . . . than in this city, I do not wish to see the place.'[17]

But foreign visitors, steeled to expect the worst of Washington, were all the more appreciative of its occasional beauties. Fanny Kemble, from her bouncing stagecoach, had been struck with the 'mass of white buildings with its terraces and columns,' standing out in sharp relief against a clear sky.[18] Even Mrs. Basil Hall, although finding the city 'as unlike the capital of a great country, as it is possible to imagine,' conceded that the Capitol building itself was 'very commanding and beautiful.'[19] Most surprising was the usually supercritical Mrs. Trollope, who was 'delighted with the whole aspect of Washington: light, cheerful and airy, it reminded me of our fashionable watering places.' She deplored the lagging imaginations of those who mocked because gigantic plans had not yet been put into execution, looking instead at the structural outlines of the 'metropolis rising gradually into life and splendour,' at the 'magnificent width' of Pennsylvania Avenue, with its shade trees, grass, shrubs, and the classic outlines of the public buildings. The foreign legations gave an air of 'tone,' lacking in other American cities. There were no drays or other signs of commerce, and well-dressed men and women sauntered along the avenue, pausing to look into the windows of the shops, or of 'Mr. Piskey Thompson, the English bookseller, with his pretty collection of all sorts of pretty literature, fresh from London.' [20]

6

Nowhere were contrasts more garish than in the House of Representatives. There, against a stately backdrop of fourteen marble columns rising forty feet to the vaulted dome, the actors of Jackson's Washington played their parts, for 'traveling expenses and eight dollars a day.' They lolled in well-stuffed armchairs, tossed their feet to the tops of their desks, whittled, or dug at their nails with four-bladed penknives, 'a large majority with their hats on, and nearly all spitting.' They strode up and down the aisles, dodging the page boys and kicking aside the welter of papers, letters, and envelopes which strewed the carpets; yet were reported to maintain an almost 'perfect decorum.'

From the sidelines only the echoes of voices could be heard, but visitors had early found that the beauty of the House was a reason for 'going again and again'; and that its advantage was that 'you cannot hear in it.' There was indeed much talk of building a glass ceiling to hold the sound, so members could at least 'understand the question before the house'; but then, as now, their remarks were designed primarily for home consumption, and during a single session virtually every member took pains to make three or four 'long-winded speeches about nothing,' littered with screaming eagles, 'star-spangled banners, sovereign people, claptrap, flattery, and humbug.' [21]

Downstairs, in the stuffy depths of the basement, John Marshall, Story, and Gabriel Duvall—old men now, the last ties with the early days of the Republic, struggled valiantly to maintain their judicial decorum, as 'flippant young belles' passed a stream of books up to the desk to be autographed.[22] Above, in the Senate Chamber, a certain dignity prevailed. Senators did not wear hats, nor toss their legs. The Chamber itself was conceded to be 'the finest drawing room in Washington,' and foreign visitors watched in wonder as Senators like Calhoun and Benton struggled through close-packed rows of crinolines, only to find a lady and a box of bonbons already established in their seats.

Henry Clay was the dominant figure of the Jacksonian Congresses. The years had taken their toll of the Cock of Kentucky. He was thinner than ever, his face weather-beaten, and his white hair combed straight back from his temples. 'The face and figure of a farmer, but . . . the air of a divine,' one enthusiast described him. Moderation had become the 'striking characteristic' of the immoderate Kentuckian.[23] Since his nervous collapse he had been compelled to still his storms, and the sticks of peppermint candy which he sucked to sweeten his confessed bad tempers were now as much in evidence as his snuffbox had been only a few years before.[24]

Blond, bland, exasperatingly unruffled, taking snuff or ostentatiously reading a novel when under attack, Martin Van Buren, 'The Red Fox,' lounged in the Vice-Presidential chair. He smiled easily, but his smile did not reach his eyes; he questioned much, but revealed little. Language to him, Perley Poore thought, seemed a means of concealing rather than revealing thought.[25] Behind his silky exterior, he was inflexible, perpetually on guard.

All knew him to be Calhoun's 'evil genius.' Yet the way he smiled and 'fawned' upon the great Carolinian was marked to even the most casual observers. What did he fear? Why should Calhoun be conciliated when it was generally conceded that he had been stripped of all power 'to do mischief'? None who really knew Calhoun, who had plumbed the depths of his cold, proud contempt for Van Buren, had any doubts that if he were 'really dangerous,' he would not be kept quiet by any such appeasement as this.

It was Calhoun, next to Van Buren and Clay, who compelled the most attention from Senate visitors. The modeling of his 'remarkable' head, his taut mouth, his haggard, 'intense, introverted' look, 'struck every beholder.'[26] The 'evidence of power in everything that he said or did,' indeed commanded a sort of 'intellectual reverence'; but with the discerning, this soon turned to 'absolute melancholy,' for only too well did they realize how self-destructive and mischievous all this dammed-up force could be.[27]

Prestige he still had; the prestige of any man who could control a half-dozen votes and the balance of power in the Senate Chamber; but it was of a sinister sort. Well did Calhoun know how long was the road he would have to travel before he would be received again into the trust and affections of the American people.

To Anna Maria he frankly admitted: 'We can do little . . . but to check the *progress* of usurpation.'[28] He would not permit his few followers to merge with the Whigs; he was an outcast from the Democrats;

and in the Senate itself an object of suspicion, far removed from the whole-hearted admiration he had once known. Had it not been for the loyalty of the young men of Carolina, he could scarcely have stood this period at all.

One group, however, gave the lonely Carolinian an ungrudging admiration and even affection. These were the little Senate page boys, the 'rushing, dancing, little Pucks,' Charles Dickens called them; who filled the snuffboxes and kept the sand-dusters full of prepared sand for blotting ink. The victims of supercharged dynamos like Benton, who would send them scurrying down the dark basement corridors of the Capitol in the dead of a midnight session to stagger back with their arms full of dusty folios; they were the willing slaves of those they liked the best. And of all the Senators at this period, the grave and undemanding South Carolinian was the one whom the pages took the most 'delight in serving.'

'Why?' queried James Parton.

'Because he was so democratic,' was the surprising answer.

'How democratic?'

'He was as polite to a page as to the President of the Senate, and as considerate of his feelings.' [29]

Bitter, frustrated, despondent as Calhoun was, he had still his 'natural grace and dignity, inviting approach.' Even his enemies were awed by his intellect, and foreign visitors found him 'secretly acknowledged' as the 'greatest genius in Congress.' [30] Amos Kendall felt the heat of that 'ardent mind,' conceding him to be 'brilliant,' but 'meteoric and eccentric,' seeing nothing in any light but his own. His best friends were baffled by his contradictions; and to Benton it seemed that he had two sets of morals, 'one for private life, which was very good, and another for public life, which was very bad.' [31] 'Abstract propositions' were the only food now for all the 'restless activity and energy of his mind.'

7

At parties, too, guests like Harriet Martineau found Calhoun as restless and disturbing a figure as on the Senate floor. The other luminaries could relax. Clay, who in masculine society would put his feet on the mantelpiece, drinking, chewing, and spitting, 'like a regular Kentucky hog-drover,' was 'all gentleness, politeness, and cordiality in the society of ladies.' [32] Webster, shaking the sofa with laughter, could be the 'life of the company' for four or five hours on end, full of anecdotes, and talking only 'wisdom enough to let us see that he was wise.' [33]

But not Calhoun. Calhoun seldom appeared at these gatherings: those who cared to hear 'a new dissertation upon negative powers' or a further elaboration of the nullification doctrine, with which he was 'full as ever,'

visited him in his rooms. Occasionally he would burst in for a few minutes, haranguing men before the fireside as if they were in the Senate,
putting the minds of his companions upon 'the stretch' with his painful
intensity, leaving them at last to take apart his 'close, rapid, theoretical
talk to see what they could make of it.' [34]

Harriet Martineau marveled at these displays, but the man himself
interested her even more. To her he seemed like an intricate, highly
wrought piece of machinery—'the thinking machine,' his friends called
him. He felt so passionately that he could hear no argument; his mind
had almost lost the power of communicating with other minds. 'I know
no one,' Miss Martineau declared, 'who lives in such utter intellectual
solitude.' Characteristic was his peremptory, arrogant 'Not at all, not at
all,' whenever one of his favorite positions was assailed. [35] His 'moments
of softness,' when reunited with his family, or when reminiscing of his
old college days, the British woman found 'singularly touching,' a relief
as much to himself as to others.

Yet, for 'all his vagaries,' she admired him personally far more than
she did Webster or Clay. The attraction was mutual. One 'of her greatest
admirers,' her abolitionist opinions notwithstanding, Calhoun played host
when his mess gave her a dinner party, which broke up well after eleven
with the singing of Scottish airs. In the plain, deaf little British author
Calhoun found what he needed, a sympathetic listener. To her he poured
out memories of his earliest childhood, of that day, now fifty years past,
when standing between his father's knees 'his first political emotions
stirred within him, awakened by his parent's talk.' When the lioness left
at last, she admitted that Calhoun might have been 'offended if he had
known . . . with what affectionate solicitude' she looked after him. What
destiny could hold for 'that high spirit' and 'a mind so energetic,' she
could not imagine. [36]

8

Benton, 'the fiercest tiger in the Senate,' was of course goading the high-
strung Carolinian all the time. Calhoun, although still 'very impressive'
in debate so long as he kept to his subject, was far too overwrought to
endure attack with any calmness, and would lash back at his tormentor
with painful protestations. 'I have no purpose to serve,' he would shout.
'I have no desire to be here.' He had sacrificed all for his 'brave, gallant
little State of South Carolina. Sir, I would not turn upon my heel to be
entrusted with management of the Government.' As he spoke, his brow
darkened; his eyes burned; his sentences became 'abrupt and intense';
and it seemed to Harriet Martineau that he did not realize how he had
betrayed himself in a few sentences. [37]

His battle with Benton was climaxed when the burly Missourian insulted him with a charge of falsehood. Calhoun spurned it, and from the Senate floor came calls for order. Smilingly Mr. Van Buren declined to pronounce Benton out of order. Webster arose to Calhoun's defense, and appealed to the Senate from the chair's decision. Promptly the Senate voted—24 to 20—to sustain Webster and Calhoun. By nightfall it was all over Washington that Calhoun and Benton would fight a duel; but to Philip Hone, who had watched proceedings from the gallery, it would have seemed just as sensible to challenge a hyena 'for snapping at me as I passed his den.' [38]

Politically, as well as personally, Calhoun's friends were much concerned for him. His bitter displays, they saw, were seriously weakening him. Occasionally he missed a Senate session to visit a sick friend, and with his last strength this man pled with the Carolinian to strengthen his self-control. 'I hear they are giving you rough treatment in the Senate,' he said gently. 'Let a dying friend implore you to guard your looks and your words so . . . no undue warmth may make you appear unworthy of your principles.'

Calhoun was deeply touched. 'This was friendship, strong friendship,' he told Harriet Martineau.

A few days later the friend was dead. Once again Benton struck out at Calhoun, taunting and goading. Calhoun sat silent, breathlessly tense but motionless. For two hours the harangue continued. At last Calhoun regained the floor. He arose, lifted his head, glanced proudly about him, calmly announced that his friends need not fear his being concerned at such remarks; then quietly picked up the threads of his argument at the exact point where he had dropped them. 'It was great!' an observer exclaimed.[39]

9

These were the years when Calhoun's powers as a speaker reached their full flower. And in an age of great orators, Calhoun was the most original. He was not eloquent, as the eighteen-thirties and forties viewed eloquence. Against Webster's bombast Calhoun's taut phrases loom, bare, stripped, as tree branches in winter. In maturity, as in youth, his style was 'tense, crowded, rugged, hard to grasp and to hold.' His words were well chosen, showing the classical discipline of his early studies, 'but he never stopped to pick or cull them in the midst of a speech,' and his diction was frequently attacked as 'careless.' [40]

He cared nothing for effect. There was no grace, no polish, no beauty in those 'fierce and blunt phrases' of his later years, in his 'oblique questionings,' and 'hard reasoning.' Once he had taken time and trouble to win the title of 'the most elegant speaker who sits in the House,'[41] but not now. Now he spoke only to convince, and not a word was wasted. In an age of four- or five-hour harangues, studded with Latin and Greek, Calhoun was refreshingly free from the 'Congressional sin' of 'making everlasting speeches.' He seldom spoke more than an hour, and then in short Anglo-Saxon phrases, flavored with slang and the 'most unsparing irony.'[42]

He was as frugal of gesture as he was of words. Always he sought to conserve his energy. Usually he stood rigid in the central aisle of the Senate, bracing himself against the desks on either side. If aroused, he might pace restlessly up and down. Like Webster and Clay, he was by nature an actor; almost instinctively he knew how to use to 'great effect' his eyes, his body, and the long thin hands of his Scottish heritage. Physically his magnetism was tremendous. His tall figure commanded interest from the moment he arose to speak,[43] and only Webster equaled him in his ability to hold an audience in hushed, expectant silence.

His dress was striking. Ordinarily he preferred boots to shoes, and in winter always wore black, topped off by a high 'beaver,' accentuating his lanky six-feet-two. 'George Washington and I,' he would laugh, when joked about his towering length.[44] In summer, as well as in winter, Senate custom demanded the same costume of heavy black broadcloth; but in summer, Calhoun, alone among his colleagues, was defiantly and comfortably cool in suits of thin nankeen cotton, grown and manufactured in his native South Carolina.[45]

10

Although Calhoun's rapid delivery—averaging about a hundred and eighty words a minute—made him one of the most difficult of all Senate orators to report, he was personally a popular favorite with the press corps. To them he was not only good 'copy,' but a good friend. Newspapermen learned to watch for his shaggy head and tall, stooping figure in the corridors of the Capitol, where he paced back and forth on rainy days, one hand at his back, the other gripping a huge East India handkerchief. Abstracted he might seem to the casual observer, but he treated the reporters with a 'frank, engaging courtesy,' which disarmed all but those who had resolved not to submit to his fascination.[46]

His friends were less appreciative of these interviews. He talked 'too much,' they thought; he laid himself open for attack or hurt. But self-concealment was alien to Calhoun's nature. His code forbade suspicion; as he said, 'I would rather be betrayed, than to suspect on light grounds.'[47]

Yet frank as he was on political matters, his private life and his private thoughts were carefully shielded from view. 'I am willing,' he once said, 'that the whole world should know my heart.' Yet his heart was what he never would reveal, and this innate reticence made him all the more 'an

interesting study,' not only to his friends, but especially to the newspapermen. Personal details of the great held a keen interest for them. A new
note had appeared in Washington journalism, with the publication of such
chatter as 'I know that Mr. Webster dined the other day at the White
House in company with Isaac Hill, and that the dishes were so cooked in
the French style that neither the great man from the Bay State nor the
great man from the Granite State could eat much. . . . The other day I
saw Mr. Calhoun and Mr. Clay shake hands and smile complacently upon
each other; from which I have no doubt that Mr. Calhoun is trying to
conciliate Mr. Clay and bring him over to a coalition of the South and
West against the North and New England. . . . I know that Mr. Calhoun
is a very fast walker and a very fast talker; few can keep up with him,
either in the one or the other.' [48] Jackson's America wanted to know how
its heroes looked, what they read, whom they admired, and what they ate
for breakfast.

Occasionally the press corps would descend to even more intimate matters—Calhoun's sexual life, for instance. That his personal life was as
pure as his public, his worst enemies regretfully conceded. The question
was—why?

It was a far from fastidious age. Men, cooped up seven or eight months
of the year in the dreary and often womanless life of the 'messes,' were
apt to become momentarily forgetful. Pretty diversions in spencers and
ruffled petticoats fluttered their eyelashes on every street-corner, stalking
down their willing prey in the very corridors of the Capitol itself.[49] Calhoun, his intimates knew, 'looked on all selfish and sensual appetites as
united only to brutes, or men who have made themselves so.' [50] Yet he, who
would not even speak to one whose political honor was in question, lived in
the closest personal intimacy with such men as Mississippi's Poindexter,
whose open profligacy was a scandal even in Washington, where sexual
irregularities were the rule rather than the exception. Calhoun was utterly
unshocked and uncritical of his friends' lapses from the moral code. Only
for himself he held no tolerance.

It was all beyond the understanding of the Washington observers, who
cynically ruled out of their conjectures such trivialities as love or loyalty
in marriage. Was it merely, as Parton insisted, that his frail physique exempted him from 'all temptation to physical excesses'? Were his enemies
right in sneering that he was 'too absorbed' in his political schemings to
have energy left for extra-curricular activities? Was there, wondered Ben:
Perley Poore, 'more of the intellectual than the animal in his nature, or
had he subjected his passions through discipline'? And on these interesting
points, not even those who knew Calhoun best dared venture an answer.
Only his latter-day correspondence furnished a clue. 'Life,' in his Cal-
vinist code, 'was a struggle against evil.' Always 'stern repression and
self-discipline' were necessary.[51]

11

Calhoun's only happiness now was centered in his home. His Senatorial duties, he told Anna Maria, were nothing but 'drudgery and confinement'; he was devoid of hope, both for himself and the nation. 'The times are daily becoming worse,' was his despairing cry. 'God knows what is to become of the country.' [52] Never had the little details of family life meant so much to him: Anna Maria's teaching of her younger brothers and sister, her 'little scholars'; Floride's gardening, which he knew would mean so much to 'her health and enjoyment'; young Patrick's 'mechanical genius.'

'Give my love to all and particularly to your Grandmother,' he would write Anna Maria. 'Give me as much . . . news as my old friend Dr. Waddel would in telling one of his long stories. . . . Tell me everything. . . . God bless you all.' If his family saw the number of letters he had to write, they would send him two or three to his one.

To Floride he wrote frequently, but her answers were strangely un-satisfying—'on grave subjects of business, or . . . the welfare of the family.' Often, she did not reply at all. Scattered through his letters to Anna are numerous references, such as 'Tell your mother I have written her several times without hearing from her'; or, 'I have not had a letter from home since I left, tho' it has been a week since my arrival here.' He sent Floride his speech on the 'deposite' question, but there was a wistful note in his words to Anna Maria, that he supposed she would not trouble to read it, as she took 'no interest in such things.'

But Anna Maria never failed him. 'Were it not for your letters,' he wrote her, 'there are a thousand incidents that are daily occurring . . . of which I should remain ignorant. . . . Were it not for you, I would not have heard a word about the Humming birds . . . the vines, their blooms, the freshness of the spring, the green yard, the children's gardens . . . those little . . . details, which it is so agreeable to an absent father to know.' [53]

Physically he was always pent-up in Washington. Wet weather denied him the exercise essential to his well-being, and his thoughts would turn longingly toward the beautiful saddle-horse he had purchased in 1830, 'the best animal I ever mounted.' He feared having him ridden by the boys, or anyone 'who would not appreciate his gait,' but why should the horse, too, be confined because his master was away? 'He will be idle in my absence,' Calhoun once wrote his brother-in-law, James, 'and if you have not one that suits you, you will be welcome to him till my return.' [54]

'I would,' was his wish in the sultry heat of a Washington summer, 'I could be at home and enjoy the fine peaches, which you say are just coming in. You say nothing of the Pears. How do they turn out?' Would

Miller * use the right kind of leather and pegs for the Negro shoes? Would Fredericks * see that the manure was not put on the fields until the earth was 'ready to receive it'? 'You must find your occupation delightful,' he wrote his planter brother-in-law, James. 'I almost envy you. As long as I have been in publick life my attachment to agriculture is not in the least abated. With your fine plantation and various pursuits your time must be fully occupied, and pass away agreeably.' [55]

Nevertheless, the cloud over his days was lifting. For in the fall of 1835, Anna Maria arrived in Washington.

12

Anna Maria was not beautiful. Her portraits show a small girl with dark eyes, a square jaw, and a long and incredibly slender waist; but her few letters which have been preserved radiate wit and warmth and charm. Josiah Quincy, meeting Anna in Washington when she was still in her teens, marveled at the way she could present the Southern cause and the ingenuity with which she parried his questions. 'I have rarely met a lady so skilful in political discussion as Miss Calhoun.' [56] Close companionship with her overintellectualized father had brought her mind into harmony with his; and like many Southern girls of her generation, growing up in the society of thinking men, her education had come, not from French novels and piano tunes, but from learning to think for herself. From her earliest childhood 'the idol' of her father's heart, she could now understand his theories and aims, and he took real pleasure in confiding his problems to her. 'Of course, I do not understand as he does,' she told her governess, Miss Mary Bates, 'yet he likes my unsophisticated opinion.' [57] Actually he relied upon her far more than she realized, and put a far higher estimate upon her mentality than she did herself.

But theirs was no mere intellectual companionship. She entered fully 'into the spirit of his life,' and in these years of crisis and strain he turned to her constantly 'as a never failing source of inspiration and help.' She was more than his daughter. She was his hostess and his confidante—and, above all, his friend. Probably he never loved another human being as he loved Anna Maria; and she herself admits that no one, 'not even he,' knew what he meant to her.[58]

With such intensity of feeling between father and daughter, it is not surprising that Anna Maria's choice of a husband was a moody, highly intellectual farmer-statesman, Thomas Clemson, mentally and temperamentally much like Calhoun himself. What is surprising is Calhoun's attitude toward the affair. Strong as his love for Anna Maria was, it was neither morbid nor possessive. Needing her, as he would never admit the need of any other person, he understood Anna's need, too. Far from re-

* Miller was the Pendleton cobbler; Fredericks, the Fort Hill overseer.

senting the intruder, he merely widened the scope of his own affections and welcomed Clemson into his family.

On a November day in 1838, in the long, sun-dappled parlor of Fort Hill, Calhoun gave his daughter away. The party was of the gayest; the feasting and dancing gave the up-country neighbors something to talk about for weeks. Only the children's governess noticed Calhoun in the background, tugging the ornaments off one of the wedding cakes. These he later wrapped and sent to a child.[59]

13

Anna Maria had returned to South Carolina a year previous to her wedding. But the two winters she had given her father had wrought a change in him, remarkable to even the most disinterested observers. Warmed by her sympathy and companionship, his taut nerves had relaxed; his old-time poise and self-command had begun to return. Gallery observers, terrified by his imperious manner, his flashing eyes and compressed lips, were astounded to find that in private he was 'the mildest of enthusiasts,' and if questioned about nullification could take it 'with perfect good humor,' almost as if he expected to be misunderstood.

The recovery of his self-control in private was having a marked effect upon his influence in public. Now his redirected force could again make itself felt upon the minds and emotions of men. He was no longer the solitary, defiant leader of the 'lost cause' of nullification. On the 'burning questions' of the Bank and slavery, Calhoun had found new issues, and was regaining 'a considerable following . . . throughout the South.' Flocking under his banner were the young Southerners and Westerners of both parties, who saw the ominous meanings these questions held for their sections. 'He is now one of America's greatest leaders,' Lord Selkirk wrote home, and if he were any judge, would soon become 'the most important figure in American politics.' [60]

He was besieged with visitors. Guests might find him, as a young German count did, 'stretched on a couch, from which he arose to give us a warm Southern welcome.' He would immediately introduce 'the subject of politics,' explaining his theories, 'contrary to the usual American practise . . . in the most concise manner, but with an almost painful intensity.' His face, declared one visitor, would assume 'an almost supernatural expression; his dark brows were knit . . . his eyes shot fire, his black hair stood on end, while on his quivering lips' was 'an almost Mephistophelian scorn at the absurdity of the opposite doctrine.' Then, suddenly, he would snap from his mood, become 'again all calmness, gentleness, and good nature, laughing at the blunders of his friends and foes, and commencing a highly comical review of their absurdities.' [61]

Calhoun was himself again.

XIX

Slavery – The Theory and the Fact

CALHOUN was born into the system of slavery. Patrick Calhoun had fixed the destiny of his sons the day that he rode back from a legislative session in Charleston, with Adam, the first Negro ever seen in the Carolina up-country, straddling his horse behind. Black and white faces together had hovered over the baby Calhoun's cradle. All his life his memory would go back to the woman who had nursed him, to Adam's son, Sawney, who had hunted and fished with him. John Calhoun grew up to know the Negroes, not as abstractions, but as only a farmer could know them who had plowed in the 'brilin' sun,' with the black man at his side.

Memories of the system were woven into the fabrics of his day-to-day living. Mornings with Sawney in the spring, when the wind was soft and the fishing rods light in their hands. Frantic, last-minute notes from Floride, reminding him to bring shoes and medicine for the Negroes—a hectic, last-minute search over Washington, swinging himself up into the stage at last, with the bulky package under his arm. A Christmas morning at Fort Hill, when he had called young Cato in to dance, the shaking head, the feet slapping against the floor—and at the end, the bewildered, almost frightened look on the child's face, when Calhoun had handed him a shining, new fifty-cent piece, the first coin he had ever seen.[1]

His bewilderment when the black, sleepy-eyed Hector, the coachman, ran away 'under the seduction . . . of . . . free blacks'; and his anger when 'Alick,' the only male house-servant on the place, gave them 'the slip' when Floride threatened him with a whipping.[2] And never would he forget that swift, stabbing moment of terror when he had broken the wax on a letter in Floride's small, cramped hand, and had read the most dreaded words that any Southern husband and planter far from home could receive: that the Negroes had been 'disorderly,' and that measures must be taken to bring them into subjection.[3]

Details of the system that so horrified outsiders were as natural to Calhoun as his own breathing. Even in the isolated up-country of his youth, he might occasionally have seen the tragic spectacle of Virginia Negroes being herded South for sale: a cart of five or six children, almost 'broiled to sleep'; a cluster of women stumbling forward, their heads and breasts bare, two or three half-naked men 'chained together with an ox-chain'; and behind them always the white man, his pistol cocked. Familiarity with such scenes did not destroy their poignance, however; and in his young manhood Calhoun found consolation only in his belief that slavery was 'like the scaffolding of a building,' which, when it had served its purpose, would be taken down.[4]

In his youth, too, walking along the Charleston waterfront, Calhoun could have caught the reeking whiff that to every Southern man and to every Yankee slave-trader meant only the horror of the slave-ship. He could have gone aboard, have peered into that black hole with its heat and its stench that no white man could describe, have seen the black limbs flailing and coiling like snakes, and the 'torpid' body of a child, crushed lifeless against the ship's side. He may have seen the black flood sweep from the hold, pour out across the decks of the ship, men and women, rabid and fighting with one another for a drop of water; or falling limp beside the rail, 'in a state of filth and misery not to be looked at.'[5]

Whether or not Calhoun ever endured this shattering experience is unknown. It is probable that he did. The changing tide of economics could later make him acclaim slavery as 'a good,' but, illogically, it never qualified his horror at the 'odious traffic,' deliberately stealing and enslaving human flesh. As a Southerner, he was sickened and ashamed at his own accessory guilt; as a slaveholder, and conscious of no crime in being a slaveholder,[6] his sincere effort was to see that the slave-trade was not only outlawed, but actually abolished.

2

Although his strict conscience was untroubled by slaveholding, it did force Calhoun to face his responsibilities as a master with the utmost seriousness. 'Every planter,' he said, 'must answer, not for the institution—for which he is no more accountable than the fall of Adam—but for his individual discharge of duty.' His ideals were high. His severest critics have conceded that he was a 'just and kind master to his slaves,' and an English guest at Fort Hill noted his freedom from any 'vulgar upstart display of authority.'[7] Yet, like all Southern men, he was capable of leaping into swift, decisive action when circumstances of the bitter institution demanded it; and as we have seen, in one or two instances had his slaves whipped and otherwise punished if their misconduct was serious. 'A perfectly humane man,' he yet knew that where slaves were the most indulged, they were the worst servants.[8]

'The proper management and discipline of Negroes,' it was said, 'subjected the man of care and feeling to more dilemmas, perhaps, than any-thing he could find.'[9] For plantation Negroes reflected the character of their owners. Ignorant, brutish, and degraded slaves could usually be traced back to a master of the same qualities. As late as the eighteen-fifties, there were still isolated plantations where Negroes could be found with no more knowledge of civilization than when they had come out of Africa, fifty or sixty years before. But these were the exceptions. Real as the horrors of slavery were, Southern leaders insisted that cruelty was an abuse and not a part of the system; and that the improvement in the condition of the Negro was as marked as in that of any other laboring class. 'I can remember how they were forty years ago—they have im-proved two thousand per cent,' a Virginia planter told the Northerner, Frederick Law Olmsted. 'They are treated much better, they are fed better, and they have greater educational privileges.'[10]

To sensitive men there could be real pleasure in treating their Negroes, not as animals, but as human beings who could be uplifted and developed. Such a master was Calhoun. Aware of how far economic interest went in compelling masters to do their duty by their slaves, to Calhoun there was another equally important side. 'The first law of slavery,' said Debow's *Review*, 'is that of kindness from the master to the slave.'[11] Calhoun sum-marized the dual ideal: 'Give the Planters Free Trade, and let every Planter be the parent as well as the *master* of his Slaves; that is, let the Slaves be made to do their duty as well as to eat, drink, and sleep; let morality and industry be taught them, and the Planter will have reason to be satisfied; he will always obtain seven or eight per cent upon the value of his Slaves; and need never be compelled to the distressing alternative of parting with them unless he allows them by overindulgence to waste his substance.' That Calhoun was personally devoted to many of his Negroes, there is no doubt. To his friend Maxcy, he wrote his sympathy on the death of a servant whose 'character of a slave' was 'in a great measure lost in that of a fine, humble indeed, but still a friend.' Calhoun's main hope for his slaves, expressed again and again in his unpublished correspondence, was that they be 'well and contented.'[12]

Just how many slaves Calhoun owned is uncertain. Estimates run all the way from thirty to ninety, and the truth probably lies between those figures.[13] Constantly he strove to mitigate such evils of the system as he could. His son, Andrew, owned a plantation in the hot black lands of Alabama, and for the sake of the Negroes' health and efficiency, the two men worked out an elaborate system of exchange. Andrew would work the slaves for six months, then send them East for recuperation in the vitalizing air of the South Carolina foothills. His father, meanwhile, would have a second group rested and refreshed, ready for another siege in the tropics. In this way, too, the Negroes were kept 'in the family,' which to Calhoun seemed the most important point of all.[14]

Occasionally Calhoun's solicitude for his servants' family ties would exceed those of the Negroes themselves. Once, when he was sending a family of house-servants to live permanently at Andrew's plantation, a mother rebelled, and declared that she would give up all her children if only she could stay with her master and mistress. Said Calhoun: 'I could not think of her remaining without her children, and as she chose to stay, we retained her youngest son, a boy of twelve.' [15]

3

The 'quarters' at Fort Hill—no cluster of whitewashed log cabins, but a single tenement dwelling of stone—stood just past the great barn, about an eighth of a mile from the 'big house.' To reach them, you took the path from the office down the lawn to a tree-shaded lane which wound by the barn, on the left, to the fields and hills beyond. In a shed before the house steamed a kettle, tended by an aging 'Mammy,' who would take her turn for a week or so minding the children, whose round black heads peered from every window.[16] On some plantations the shouts and giggles might fade into whispers when the master approached, but not at Fort Hill. Calhoun might awe the Senate, but he held no terrors for children, black or white, and they tumbled about his feet, unafraid.[17]

From the pot would come the smell of vegetables and salt meat, for each family had its own garden patch of greens and yams, corn and turnips, supplemented by allotments of meat and corn meal. On some plantations molasses and rice were also distributed; at Fort Hill, the specialties were fresh meat and 'wheaten' bread, which were given out at the Christmas season.[18]

Christmas does not seem to have meant much to Calhoun. Never a 'professing Christian,' his letters seldom mention the day at all. Away from his family, he had no heart for celebration. But at home he could not resist the holiday spirit. There must have been moments, then, when he envied his servants' capacity for sheer physical enjoyment. A fiddler mounted on a dining room chair! One man beating a triangle; another drumming on wood! A plank laid across two barrel tops with a man and woman at opposite ends, laughing at each other. The shuffling feet, the twisting bodies, the cries to the pair on the barrels: 'Keep it up, John! Go it, Nance! Ole Virginny never tire! Heel and toe, ketch a fire!' 'The Negroes had a merry-making in the kitchen, the other evening,' Calhoun wrote Clemson in 1842. '. . . They danced in the kitchen and kept it up until after midnight.' [19]

4

Despite Calhoun's ideals as master, slavery at Fort Hill was more typical than ideal. Fifty years after his death, the old men and women who had been boys and girls in the eighteen-forties could remember their joy when their master came home. Why they were happy, they did not know; all they could say was, 'just 'kase he were Marse John C.'[20]

Fifty years is a long time, long enough for the overseers and the threat of the whip to be forgotten. Out of necessity these evils did exist at Fort Hill. Calhoun had his full share of overseer trouble. Time and again he was compelled to change overseers; often he would complain that they had so neglected things that he had not the least pleasure in looking over the place upon his return from Washington. 'It is so important to me,' he told his cousin, James, 'to have everything satisfactorily arranged before I leave home.'[21]

Running a plantation by remote control bore heavily upon both master and slave. For it was on the plantations where the master was absent, and the overseer had full sway, that many of the worst evils of the system occurred.[22]

Even so high-minded a master as Calhoun was compelled to follow existing practices of the slave system. Punishments were necessarily lighter for a Negro than for a white man.* A killing was manslaughter; rape was merely a trespass. A few idealists, such as Jefferson Davis, introduced trial by jury among their Negroes, but the experiment usually failed. Punishments would be too severe. 'Africans live better under a monarchy,' concluded the *Church Intelligencer*.[23]

Without question Calhoun underestimated the mental potentialities of Negroes. Living completely on an intellectual plane himself, unable even to understand white men on a lower level of thought than his own, he was honestly convinced that physical security was the only 'freedom' that would have meaning to a slave. Steeped as he was in the philosophy of Aristotle, he could not have felt otherwise. Had not Aristotle differentiated between the injustice of slavery based on 'conquest' and 'force of law,' and the slavery of men who could obey reason, but were unable to exercise it?[24] 'Show me a Negro,' Calhoun is reported to have said, 'who can parse a Greek verb, or solve a problem in Euclid,' and he would grant that he was the human equal of the white man. Strange as this statement is, those who judge the ante-bellum slave by the cultivated Negro leaders of the twentieth century, or even the lovable mammies and house-servants of history, can have no concept of the mental and moral condition of the

---

* Except, of course, when the crime was committed against a white man!

semi-savage field hands, often but a generation removed from the Congo.* Even the most ardent of abolitionists quailed before the Negro slaves of the lower type: Olmsted once declared: 'If these women and their children after them were always . . . to remain of the character and capacity stamped on their faces . . . I don't know that they could be much less miserably situated . . . for their own good and that of the world, than they are.' [25]

There was nothing in Calhoun's personal experience to alter his opinion. Once he had freed a slave shoemaker and his family, who, cold and starving in the North, returned and begged to be taken back into bondage. 'When I told him that I would do all I could for him, he seized both my hands in his, and expressed his fervent gratitude,' [26] Calhoun told the story afterward.

It is interesting to speculate on what must have been Calhoun's opinion of a Northern society that could prate of freedom and send starving Negroes back into slavery. Probably, too, the incident did much to confirm Calhoun's belief that to the slave, as to many white men, material security, not political freedom, was the more important.

5

Not the least of the burdens of slavery lay upon the women of the plantation. Men could sit on their porches and argue the virtues of Aristotle and the leisureliness of the Southern way of life by the hour, but women had work to do. Men could sleep like the dead through the black hours of night, when, at a terrified whisper and a damp touch on her shoulder, a woman roused herself, threw a tippet over her nightgown, and hurried down the long hall to the family dining room and the storerooms beyond, searching for medicine bottles in the flickering candlelight—or for a Bible. What did men know of that endless walk to the quarters at two or three in the morning—with that frightened figure at her side, the ruts and rocks that she had never heeded in the daytime cutting into her slippers, and the trees looming up out of the darkness? And then the long hours of watching —the slow smoke of the fire, the tossing, feverish sleep of a sick child, or a dying man. Men had the responsibilities of slavery, or so they said, but what did they know of the work of it? [27]

Floride knew, and for her the day was long. No blessed early morning

---

* There were, of course, as many social and intellectual gradings among the Negroes in their native Africa as among any people, and these differences were reflected in the American slaves and their relative status in the slave-society. As with all peoples, the ignorant lower classes were, of course, in the majority; and many of these were sold to traders by the ruling chiefs and aristocracy. Individuals of higher type, captured as prisoners-of-war, were often included in these consignments.

sleep when her husband's restless stirring roused her at the first pale light
of dawn. While he was off, tramping across the fields for exercise, she
would dress, seizing a few precious moments of leisure to last her through
the hours. A personal maid might attend her, comb out and arrange her
long hair, and lace her stays high under her breasts, perhaps even select
her dress, for there were slave women of impeccable taste, existing only to
wait hand and foot upon their mistresses.[28] But probably no such paragon
existed at Fort Hill. There were too few working 'hands' for the daily tasks
to be easy for anyone.

The instant breakfast was over, work began. Floride might walk down
to the quarters to see that the old woman in charge was not eating the
children's share of food, or might have all the children brought up on the
lawn and fed before her own eyes.[29] She might stroll down to the chicken
yard and listen to tales of 'how twenty-five young turkeys had just tottled
backward and died *so;* or the minks and chicken snakes had sucked half
the eggs'; or it 'looked like there weren't *no* chickens that didn't have just
one toe nicked, somehow.' The question of the chickens was delicate. Originally each Negro family on the place had its own hens, marked by a nicked
toe. The Calhouns' own fowls were supposed to strut through their brief
life span with toes intact; but Floride soon noted that fewer and fewer
chickens were surviving mutilation and more and more eggs were being
brought up for purchase by the family. Her ruling was drastic. Chickens
were banished at Fort Hill, except for the exclusive use of the Calhouns
themselves.[30]

Inspection over, Floride might settle herself in the family dining room,
or on whatever porch was shadiest. There she could consult with Cook to
'make sure . . . if the day were hot, that dinner would be light and cooling'; broth, fowl, beefsteak, perhaps, with salad, asparagus, claret, good
coffee—and ice on the butter-plates. She might be called upon to umpire a
quarrel between little Lafayette and Venus, who had each staked claims to
the same dusting cloth and halted work to roll their eyes and make faces
at each other. Uncle Tom, the coachman, would peer around the corner,
requesting the key to the storehouse that he might get four quarts of corn
for 'him bay horse.' A woman would shuffle in to report that one of the
hands was 'fevered and onrestless'; and Floride herself would again hurry
to the storeroom to measure out the inevitable calomel, and then to hold
the head and slip the spoon into the sick man's mouth, for no slave would
take medicine from the hands of anyone but his master or mistress. Home
again, Floride could ring for a girl to bring her pocket handkerchief, but
five minutes later, she might be running back down the road to the quarters
to attend a field hand who had gashed his foot with a hoe. She knew what
she would have to do. First, she would tie an apron over her dress; then,
with 'no shrinking, no hiding of the eyes,' she would calmly examine the

injured foot, dripping with blood and sweat, superintend a bath, prepare a healing application, and bind it on with her own hands.[31]

Did Northern women spend their entire Christmas season standing in the sewing room, a pair of heavy shears in their hands, cutting out dresses and turbans for their servants, until it seemed that their arms and backs would break in two for weariness? Northern women's joy in having servants to answer their merest whim and call might diminish when they discovered that if they wanted so much as a dress pattern cut, they would first have to tell the slaves how to do it, then show them how, and finally do it themselves.[32]

6

Figures might show that only one-quarter of the Southern whites belonged to the slaveholding class. Undoubtedly the South, like the West, would have produced an agrarian civilization with or without slavery. Yet year by year the tendrils of 'the peculiar institution' were entwining themselves more tightly around the Southern roots.

Certainly slavery helped keep the South agrarian, for it was conceded that to change the Negro over from a farm to an industrial worker would involve a process far slower than the rapid expansion of the industrial system had been elsewhere. Slavery forced the South into its demand for a national political system based on states' rights; for otherwise moralists in a nationalistic, consolidated government would have felt themselves legally responsible for the existence of slavery in South Carolina. Slavery was the Southerner's school for statecraft. It produced men trained to command, a breed that for generations controlled over two-thirds of American elective offices. But the strongest effects of slavery were upon those who bore its burdens, the individual Southerners themselves.

As a Southerner and a leader of Southerners, it would have been impossible for Calhoun to have viewed the Negro problem in the abstract. Even in New England, where he tasted the first theories of abolitionism, he could still have seen the last few Northern slaves walking the streets of New Haven. He knew, if the North forgot, the Northern share in the moral responsibility for the system. Still jingling in Northern pockets were the profits of the slave-ships and the proceeds from selling the Negro South, upon discovery that the Northern climate and labor system were unsuited to him.

Slavery was an economic question. Outsiders looked with horror on the 'forlorn and decaying' villages of the South, on Negro cabins, which a Northern laborer would 'scorn to occupy for an hour.' They saw the worn-out fields, the sagging, empty plantation houses, and the 'poor, degraded white men and women,' with neither farming incentive nor industrial opportunity under the slave system. The mere abolition of slavery, concluded one Northern observer, would 'whiten those . . . abandoned fields.' [33]

There was nothing in history to prove it. Whether slave or free, there would still have remained in the South a huge illiterate population, which might be productive or parasitical, but in either case would have to be provided for. Slavery could be abolished; the problem of Negro labor would still be there. Britain had abolished slavery in Jamaica, but few of the freedmen had chosen to work. They had squatted and starved. What of the great plantations of Santo Domingo, now sinking back into wilderness and jungle—the planters and their families slaughtered in their beds; the former slaves wandering now in poverty and exile—roaming—plundering? Was this dark fate in the Southern stars? [34]

Most important, could the Southern economy stand the financial loss of its 'largest item of capital investment'? Or, as it sometimes seemed to the Southerners, was abolition a deliberate Northern trick to wreck Southern prosperity, to reduce the Southern agricultural system to the status of prostitute for Northern industry; to do, under the semblance of outraged 'morality' what Northern exponents of high tariffs and centralized banking had, so far, been legally unable to do otherwise? That this picture was grossly exaggerated, if not entirely false, was unimportant. Not the fact, but the Southerner's belief, was what counted.

To Calhoun slavery was a practical question. The Negro was the Southern laborer; slavery, the device by which a semi-civilized, alien population had been fitted into the social and economic pattern. Not the relationships of master and slave, but of black and white, was what the system had been primarily designed to regulate. Had slavery not existed in the ante-bellum South, and had the black race been suddenly thrust upon that region, undoubtedly something like slavery would have been created to cope with it.[35]

Not the slave, but the Negro, was uppermost in Southern thinking. Calhoun had thrashed the question over with John Quincy Adams, in Missouri Compromise days, years before. 'What of liberty, justice, the rights of man?' Adams had demanded. Did the Declaration of Independence mean nothing at all?

'The principles you avow are just,' Calhoun had said slowly. 'But in the South, they are always understood as applying only to the white race.'

Adams was silent. Slavery, Calhoun had persisted, 'was . . . the best guarantee of equality among the whites, producing an unvarying level among them.' Under slavery, no white man could dominate another; or, as he pointed out years afterward, 'with us, the two great divisions of society are not the rich and the poor, but the black and the white.'

Adams might have grunted with disgust. Southerners, he charged, gloried in their indolence, were proud of their masterful dominance.

Calhoun had protested. Slaveholders were not lazy. 'I have often held the plough, myself, and so did my father.' Mechanical and manufacturing labor was not 'degrading.' But if he were to hire a white servant in South Carolina, his reputation would be 'irretrivably ruined.' [36]

For slavery was most of all a social question. What the system actually meant in terms of mores, tabus, and fears, no outsider could ever understand. It was the Negro who set the pattern for Southern living and thinking. If, economically, the question was practically unsolvable, socially, it was even more so. For the abolitionists it was enough to blame Southern backwardness on slavery, to attribute the Southerner's overwrought nerves to the fear of insurrection and retribution, perhaps even to the guilty conscience that men who held other men in bondage should have. But a hundred years later, the South was just beginning to emerge from its backward, poverty-stricken condition as 'the nation's number one economic problem.' It was eighty years after the abolition of slavery that David Cohn, one of the most discriminating of Southern thinkers, would describe the sense of 'strain' in the Southern air, 'of a delicately poised equilibrium; of forces held in leash. Here men toss uneasily at night and awake fatigued in the morning. . . . To apply patent remedies is to play . . . with explosives.' [37]

The most ardent Southern admirers could not deny it. The most calloused of casual observers could not escape it. What virtually every Southern woman admitted, every Southern man knew.[38] There was no peace, no safety in the Southern states. And there was no hope for escape.

In the white men of the South a common danger had wrought a common understanding. Taut nerves ran beneath their languid indolence of pose and gesture. They were quiet men, those farmers and planters who lounged through long, hot afternoons on the porches of plantation houses like Fort Hill. Drawling, easy-going, disarmingly gentle, they might appear to visitors like Charles Lyell or Captain Marryat, relaxed under the spell of their hosts' charm. But someone would unwittingly utter a few words, and discover, to his dismay, that on a subject, which once could be discussed freely in the South, not a word could now be said. Men, who but a moment before were urging 'indulgence to their slaves,' flared up in a suddenly 'savage spirit,' speaking of abolitionists in 'precisely the same tone . . . as beasts of prey.' Calhoun's Congressional colleague—short, plump, Northern-born Robert Preston, his red wig askew—would roar that if any abolitionist dared set foot on *his* plantation, he would 'hang him . . . notwithstanding all the interference of all the governments of the earth.' Another soft-spoken cotton planter, calmly and quietly, but unflinchingly, would announce that should any abolitionist visit his plantation, 'I have left the strictest orders with my overseer to hang him on the spot.' [39]

'Fiercely accessory' was the poor white, tobacco-chewing, sweat-stained, standing on the porch of Fort Hill, confident that his white skin alone assured him an invitation to dinner. Fear was the uninvited guest at his own dinner table; he would hide in the pigpen at the rumor of an insurrection, and in a back corner of his cabin lay bags packed for the quickest of getaways if the 'Niggers rose.'[40]

Fear, too, haunted the clear-eyed yeoman hill farmer, who worked in the field beside his one or two black men. 'I reckon the majority would be right glad if we could get rid of the Negroes' was his comment. 'But'—and his words were fraught with meaning—'it wouldn't never do to free 'em and leave 'em here.'[41]

Free them! The very idea was enough to enrage the small planter, the middle-class lawyer, teacher, or doctor, whose ideals, both economic and social, were closest to those of the great planters. And as the landed planter might add, it cost nothing to attack slavery, but he could not listen quietly when outside attacks put in danger 'everything we hold dear in the world.'

Calhoun's sentiments were similar. 'We are surrounded by invisible dangers, against which nothing can protect us, but our foresight and energy.' The difficulty was in 'the diversity of the races. So strongly drawn is the line between the two . . . and so strengthened by the form of habit and education, that . . . no power on earth can overcome the difficulty.'[42] And a hundred years later Cohn would write of 'a society kept going by unwritten and unwritable laws . . . taboos, and conventions. . . . The Southerner's whole society and way of life is conditioned by the . . . Negro. If there has never been a free Negro in the South, it is also true that there has never been a free white . . . the Southerner . . . functions in an environment of which he is a prisoner . . . ' He added: 'If segregation were broken down by fiat . . . I have no doubt that every Southern white man would spring to arms and the country would be swept by war.'[43]

There were sensitive men who writhed under sternness and the rule of fear, who felt themselves degraded by the degradation of the Negroes. When administering punishment, they were tortured by the thought that 'I am violating the natural rights of a being who is as much entitled to the enjoyment of liberty as myself.'[44] Torn by ethical conflict, they were forced to repress their better natures. Continually they mourned the brutalizing effects of the system upon their children. They knew that it was among the more ignorant white classes where 'coarse . . . brutal authority' furnished the 'disgusting' picture of pretty girls laughing as a cowhide whip flicked across the 'nasty mouth' of a suffering slave child, where 'power over the males and females' was 'most demoralizing.'[45] But year by year more of the poorer classes were pulling their way into the slaveholding hierarchy.

The most well-meaning of men were helpless. The more they hated their responsibilities, the more heavily they weighed upon them. 'We are the slaves, not the blacks,' [46] they mourned. Not for them the easy way of the few, who solved their problem by turning their Negroes 'free' to starve or to beg from their neighbors. They would disdain the spirit of the age, the 'judgment of the world,' if necessary, rather than cast the dependent race whom they were 'bound to protect' upon the uncertain mercies of Northern idealism.

Financially the load was staggering. There were the 'cotton snobs' of the Delta, so drowned in acres and slaves that they had no interest in the sliding scale of their bank accounts. But no man could fail to read the tragedy of Virginia in the worn-out tobacco lands, exhausted by two hundred years of crop production for the maintenance of slaves. Slaves had become a crushing burden on the poverty-stricken Virginia masters, who had to feed and maintain them without any work to give them.[47]

All knew that the slave system, as such, gave 'the least possible return for the greatest possible expense.' In hard times the Northern employer could lay off his hands to shift for themselves; the slaves had 'complete insurance against unemployment,' and had to be fed and clothed. A man so unlucky as to own a drunkard or a thief was forbidden by law to sell or to free him. He was, however, guaranteed the duty of feeding and clothing him.

With no possibility of discharge, with little hope of advancement, it was to the Negroes' interest 'to work as little as they can.' Two blacks only do the work of one white, a planter told Charles Lyell. Half the South was employed in watching the other half. Calhoun himself might have seen what the abolitionist Olmsted described—an entire field of women halting work when the overseer had passed, only lowering their hoes when he turned to ride toward them again.[48]

Yet, save for a scattering of yeomen farmers in the hill counties where a black face was never seen, the most difficult of all tasks would have been to convince the average Southerner of the desirability of emancipation. Fear—economic, social, and political—had done its work. Middle- and upper-class planters, and many of the yeomen, were content with the system; and to the arguments of the abolitionists, not even the poor whites gave 'a murmur of response.' Hinton Helper could marshal proofs that the system was enslaving planter and poor white alike, but not even he could insure the farmer from the competition of free, and cheap, black labor.

Southern whites had been well indoctrinated with the less savory side of Northern industrialism. 'A VERY SLIGHT MODIFICATION of the arguments used against the institutions . . . of the South . . . ' Calhoun had said, 'would be . . . equally effectual against the Institutions of the North.' [49] Southern poor whites saw no hope in the grinding wheels of industrialism. Temporarily industry might open new jobs, but as more machines took the

place of men, both in the factory and on the farm, the day would come
when the emancipated Negro and the white workingman would grapple
for the few jobs left to the Southerners. Labor-saving machines seemed
well named; would they not save employers the necessity of hiring labor?
Hence, it was to the interests of the small farmers—and these points were
stressed again and again by their leaders—to co-operate with the planter
in keeping the Negro out of economic competition, and in preventing industrialism from crushing out agriculture. The pernicious competition of
the slave-operated plantations against the small independent farmers was
less obvious.

More, even, than economic arguments, the abolitionists' own zeal ripped
the problem right out of practical politics. As late as 1828, there were
three hundred abolitionist societies *south* of the Mason-Dixon line. As
late as 1831, the whole slave question could be openly debated in the
Virginia Legislature.

It is undoubtedly true that Southerners talked about emancipating far
more than they emancipated. Yet so eminent an historian as Albert J.
Beveridge has argued that, had it not been for the anger and fear aroused
by the abolitionist onslaught, 'it is not altogether impossible that there
would have been no war, and that slavery would in time have given way to
the pressure of economic forces.' Allan Nevins, conceding that abolition,
gradual or otherwise, was impossible in the Deep South, pronounces it
'unquestionably true that the abolitionist madness helped kill all chances
of gradual emancipation in the border states of Maryland and Kentucky.'
In Fredericksburg, Virginia, an active movement for gradual emancipation
was under way when the abolitionists stepped in. The ruin was complete.
Less than a decade afterward, not a single emancipation society remained
south of the Mason-Dixon border.[50]

The abolitionists can, at least, be credited with skill in defeating their
own purposes. Not for them the tedious processes of 'gradual emancipation.' They would not see the nation's honor stained by truckling to slaveholders through federal reimbursement of the planters for the losses abolition would cause them. To them it mattered not that abolition without
compensation would wreck the entire Southern economy and leave the
planters destitute. To them the sin of slavery was all that mattered.

It is essential, of course, to keep a sense of proportion in judging both
abolitionist and slaveholder. The abolitionists' zeal was, in most cases, a
sincere and high-minded moral force. Yet it is easy to understand the attitude of those who were daily told that their financial security, if not their
very lives, depended on the maintenance of a system which the individuals
of that period found already in effect. Human nature being what it is, and
the problem as complex as it was, the Southern attitude toward abolitionists with their inexpensive moral zeal can be readily understood.

'Emancipation, itself, would not satisfy these fanatics,' declared Calhoun.

'That gained, the next step would be to raise the Negroes to a social and political equality with the whites.' [51] The abolitionists dared not deny his words. Early as 1831, incendiary pamphlets were in circulation through the Southern states, demanding the complete political equality of men, many but a generation out of Africa. Openly hot-tongued zealots were calling upon four million slaves to revolt and take over the South for themselves.

Southerners had had more than one grim foretaste of what insurrection might mean. Fresh in memory was 'bloody Monday,' August 22, 1831, when Nat Turner and his followers ran through a Virginia county, leaving a trail of fifty-five shot and murdered, 'but without plunder or outrage,' [52] the *Liberator* commented. And at Natchez the mass-murder of Santo Domingo had been escaped only by the white woman who overheard a Negro telling a nurse-girl to murder the child in her charge. Swiftly the planters organized. Negroes and abolitionists alike were rounded up, strapped to tables, and lashed with blacksnake whips until the blood ran inches deep upon the floor. A gigantic plot for the murder of every white man in the Natchez district and the enslavement of their women was uncovered. Never did the planters breathe easily again.

Abolitionists could attribute Southern tension to a sense of guilt in enslaving the Negro. However true this may be, Southern recalcitrance was at least, in part, the work of the abolitionists themselves. To a world arrayed against the Southern system, no weakness could be admitted, no word of concession said.

7

But there were moments when the whole truth was spoken; and men like those who gathered with Calhoun at Fort Hill strove vainly to find a way through the mesh in which they had entangled themselves. With 'one opinion for Congress, and another for their private table,' they discussed with calm reasoning the evils 'which they could not admit in public.' [53]

Although a man known to abuse his slaves was punished by law and scorned by his neighbors, all knew of the far-distant plantations in the West and Deep South, which the law and public opinion could not reach. There, in a murky, fever-laden heat, where white men's nerves and tempers were drawn to the breaking point, and black men crouched all day in ankle-deep mud, the rawhide coiling over their backs, slavery existed 'in all its horrors.' Dark stories seeped in from those swamps, of masters, intemperate, reckless, indulging their own passions on the helpless creatures over whom they held power of life and death; of slaves fed on cotton seed or hung up by their thumbs; of blood-stained whips as much in use as spurs on a horse. A sadistic master, crazed by heat and the power of his authority, could pull out his Negroes' teeth or cut off their hands.[54]

Generally recognized, except in the North itself, was the fact that Northern newcomers were responsible for many of the cruelties which made slavery notorious in the eyes of the civilized world. For Northerners lacked the understanding of the Negroes' needs and weaknesses as individuals. Northerners looked upon the South as a fabulous empire of landed estates with hundreds of acres and thousands of retainers; Southerners knew that the majority of slaveholders owned but a single Negro family, alongside of whom their owners worked the fields. Calhoun had this heritage. He knew that the Negroes' spirit could be broken by lack of sympathy or overwork; and furthermore, that in the fierce heat of the Southern sun, neither white nor black could expend the energy of a worker in the North. Northern planters, frequently striving for 'a rapid fortune,' made no allowances. They drove the Negroes as they would themselves, blamed their failure on the system of slavery, deserted their responsibilities, and returned North to 'become very loud-mouthed abolitionists.' [55]

Calhoun's own son-in-law, Pennsylvania-born, gave up planting in disgust, with the assertion that 'I can do better for my family and myself . . . than . . . spending my life on a plantation.' Calhoun, however, was shocked by Clemson's proposals to rent out his Negroes at a profit. Sternly Calhoun reminded him that with rented Negroes it would not be to the interest of the planter 'to . . . take good care of them. . . . The object of him who hires,' Calhoun sternly reminded Clemson, 'is generally to make the most he can out of them, without regard to their comfort or health, and usually to the utter neglect of the children and the sick.' Rather than have them thus exploited, if Clemson could not find good masters for them, Calhoun would buy them himself, although to do so would be 'financially disasterous' [56] for him.

And always in the background was the 'disgusting topic' which lay like a deadweight on the conscience of every thoughtful Southerner—the evil of miscegenation. That it existed was freely admitted; even an abolitionist account of these conditions was acknowledged to be 'full of truth.' Yet no abolitionist so scourged the evil as did the Southerners themselves. No abolitionist could understand the feelings of fathers who, whatever their own youthful follies, lived in constant fear of their sons' promiscuous intercourse with Negro women.[57]

Actually the evil was not as widespread as was claimed. For where the sins were confessed in the color of the progeny, British visitors were astounded to find that the 'mixed offspring' in the Southern states of antebellum days was 'not more than two and a half per cent of the whole population,' offering a comparison by no means favorable to their free country.[58]

To an unhardened observer the slave-pen, with its 'likely parcel' of Negroes for sale, on the very spot where horses and cattle had been auctioned off the day before, seemed the most horrible aspect of slavery. Yet the 'calloused indifference' of many slaves themselves, 'very merry, talking and laughing' as they waited to be sold; and the seeming lack of 'offended modesty' was equally repellent.[59] The deepest tragedy of slavery, however, the separation of husband from wife, of mothers from their children, happened less often than Northern visitors believed. Public opinion condemned it. Families were sold in lots 'like books and chairs,' but few would buy a broken-hearted mother without her children. Fathers, however, were sometimes sold from their families, the husbands and wives then being free to take other mates.[60]

8

Granting the desirability of emancipation, argued the Southerner, what was to be done with the Negro after he was free? 'Singular is the contempt . . . in which the free blacks are held in . . . free . . . America,' observed Captain Marryat in 1829. Color alone, the Captain had discovered, made the Negro 'a degraded being' in the land of 'liberty, equality, and the rights of man.' In the slave states, the Britisher had 'frequently seen a lady in a public conveyance with her negress sitting by her,' and no 'objection . . . raised . . . but in the free states a man of colour is not admitted into a stage coach.' Segregation in Northern theaters and churches, Marryat noted, was 'universally observed.'[61]

As early as 1820, in the very capital of 'free' America, Congress had restricted suffrage to white persons. 'The crime of a dark complexion,' declared William Jay, 'has been punished by debarring its possessor from all approach to the ballot box.'[62] In Philadelphia, a wealthy Negro protested and appealed, but was found to be only white enough to pay his taxes.[63]

Harshest of all were the Northern restrictions against education. One-third of the Southern states had laws prohibiting the Negroes from learning to read, but abolitionists were blissfully indifferent to the fact that in the free states most 'academies and colleges' were barred to the Negro, and that colored children were 'very generally' excluded from public schools, in deference to the 'prejudice of leaders and parents.' Only abroad could wealthy young Negroes receive higher education. Connecticut had its Black Act, prohibiting all instruction of colored children *from other states*. In New Hampshire enraged citizens of Canaan passed resolutions of 'abhorrence' at the establishment of a subscription school with twenty-eight white and fourteen Negro students, voting that the building be ripped from its foundations.[64]

Even if the freed Negroes were willing to work for wages, what chance would they have with the 'protection afforded by their present monopoly of labor withdrawn,' and thrown into open competition with the poverty-stricken whites? When a Negro laborer was hired in the North, his fellow workers struck. What would freedom offer the Southern Negro? History would offer the answers.

Actually the Negro of talent sometimes had more opportunity for self-realization in the slave states than in the free. Southerners could point out that exceptional Negroes sometimes made 'large fortunes in trade.' Hired out as cabinet-makers, builders, and mechanics, they paid a part of their wages to their masters and still were able to save for themselves. In Memphis, Thomas Lowe Nichols, a Connecticut physician, was astounded to find a slave entrusted with the sole care of a $75,000 jewelry store. He was free to escape at any time, and in a moment's theft could have been rich for life, but had no desire to break trust. In New Orleans, Dr. Nichols found another slave the head clerk of a leading bookstore, waiting upon 'the ladies' with the courtesy of a Creole courtier. He wore gold studs and a diamond ring; on Sundays he made his 'promenade' on the shady side of Canal Street, with a young slave woman in a gown of costly changeable silk, a blue bonnet and a pink parasol. He had his seat at the Opera, too, in a section especially reserved for 'ladies and gentlemen of colour,' where no common white trash were permitted to intrude.

Most astounding, a slave was the 'head clerk and confidential business man' of one of the largest cotton houses in New Orleans. In New York under freedom, he might have been a whitewasher or a barber, or perhaps have run an oyster-cellar; under slavery, he had his own home, a wife, a family, and all the material comforts he could desire. He could have bought his freedom in an instant, but had no desire to do so.[65] Exceptional as these instances undoubtedly were, they were used by the Southerners to prove that, both economically and socially, even a slave might rise under American democracy.

Northern visitors, however, frequently tempered their moral indignation with telling observations. One was surprised at the 'friendly relations' between the blacks and whites of the South, and the interest and kindliness shown by an entire trainload of white passengers toward a group of Negro railroad workers, en route home to their families for Christmas. 'I constantly see . . . genuine sympathy with the colored race, such as I rarely see at the North,' abolitionist John Abbott was compelled to admit. And he added what Dr. Nichols stood vigorously ready to confirm: 'The slaves are much better off than the laboring classes at the North . . . the poor ones.'[66]

It is true, of course, that 'compulsion to labor' under any system is a violation of human freedom. But what was freedom? asked the defenders of the South. What was slavery? Freedom held a high meaning to Calhoun. To him it meant, not just the absence of tyranny, but the condition which would allow each human being to develop to the highest ends of his nature. And of all varieties of freedom, in the opinion of Calhoun, political freedom was the highest—and the most rare. It was the reward for centuries of striving and growth and unceasing battle against oppression; what would be its fate in the hands of those unused to exercising it? The white man's heritage of liberty stretched back ten hundred years; for untold centuries countless Negroes were slaves in their native Africa.* Two races, almost equal in numbers, physically, culturally, and politically at variance, faced each other. Would the white Southerner dare entrust his freedom to the black? He did not dare, and all history, argued Calhoun, was on his side. The safety of the whole, Aristotle had warned, depends upon 'the predominance of the superior parts.' Calhoun conceded that once the slave had reached a state of moral and intellectual elevation, it would be to the master's interest 'to raise him' to the level of political equality, for he would then 'be destitute of all power' to 'destroy liberty.' Henry Clay, too, spoke for the whole South. 'I prefer the liberty of my own race,' he said. 'The liberty of the descendants of Africa is incompatible with the safety and liberty of the European descendants. Their slavery forms an exception . . . from stern necessity, to the general liberty.' [67]

Calhoun would have scorned to deny that Southern servitude was slavery. But with equal vehemence, and not without reason, he condemned the 'vicious fallacy' of confusing wage labor with free labor. 'I like to attend to things as they are, and not the names by which they are called,' he said. Carlyle had drawn the distinction. 'Free labor means work or starve. Slave labor means work or be flogged.' [68]

Even more bitter was the British Sarah M. Maury, representative of a race of 'freemen,' whose women, stripped to the waist, crawled through the coal mines, butting the wains with their balding heads; whose children, 'harnessed like brutes . . . tugged and strained in the bowels of the earth' for sixteen or seventeen hours at a time, for months 'never even seeing the light of the sun.' Said Mrs. Maury: 'The sole advantage possessed by the white Slaves of Europe . . . is that they have permission . . . to change each naked, hungry and intolerable bondage for a worse . . . this the white man must call liberty.' [69]

Calhoun did not call it so. Liberty held higher meanings for him than

* The Southern insistence on the 'superiority' of the white race was not entirely rationalization to justify the slave system; but was based on an utter ignorance of the Negro in his native Africa. It was not the truth which influenced Southern thinking; but what at that period was thought and reported to be the truth. Twentieth-century research has uncovered African history and culture which was utterly unknown to Calhoun and his time, and which might have made a vast difference in the Southerner's concept of the slave's intellectual potentialities.

freedom for men of superior capacity to exploit the basic inequalities of their fellow men. Was it not more just legally to acknowledge inequalities and to protect men from the selfishness of their fellows? Yes, argued Calhoun, the Northern wage slave was free, free to come South to work in the pestilential swamps at the dangerous tasks at which the life of no valuable slave could be risked; [70] free to hold a job so long as he would vote for the political choice of his employers; free to work fourteen hours a day at seven dollars a week until his health gave way.[71] His earnings were taxed to provide for the paupers and jail-loungers whose 'freedom' permitted them the luxury of not choosing to work; but this burden did not weigh upon the Southern slave. 'Slavery makes all work and it ensures homes, food, and clothing for all. It permits no idleness, and it provides for sickness, infancy, and old age.' [72] Both systems, he insisted, rested on the principle of labor exploitation, but the South had no ugly labor scrap-heap; the master was compelled by law to mortgage his acres, if necessary, to provide adequately for old and sick slaves. The master was responsible to society for the welfare of his slaves; no one was responsible for the freeman but himself.

The paradox was, of course, that slavery for the Negro restricted the freedoms of the whites. Freedom could not live anywhere in a slave society. Free speech, for example, was silent on one subject, slavery, in accordance with one of the strangest gentlemen's agreements in all history. Even of Jefferson's Virginia, with its liberal, humanistic 'free trade' in ideas, Thomas Ritchie could write in 1832 that there had been a 'silence of fifty years.' [73]

Freedom of the press remained—on the books. A few valiant, fiery, individualistic editors like the fighting Quaker, William Swain, of the Greensborough *Patriot,* and a sprinkling in Kentucky, Tennessee, and Western Virginia, dared denounce slavery to the end, and went unscathed. These were the exceptions. Others, less fortunate, suffered boycotts, cancellation of subscriptions, were even shot down in duels! By 1845 the Richmond *Whig* was openly praising the mob destruction of an abolitionist paper in Lexington, Kentucky; although never in the South were there such crimes against the press as the lynching of Lovejoy in Illinois.

'Letters to the editor' urging abolition of slavery were returned as 'too strong for the times.' Yet, despite the pressures of wealth and vested interests and the fears of the poor whites, most of the editors 'sincerely agreed with their readers on the slavery question.' The 'lives of the free Negroes in Southern communities' they saw as a demonstration of their 'unfitness for freedom.'

In Jefferson's time there had been a tolerance toward anti-slavery doctrines. Virtually every great Virginian of the eighteenth century was on record against slavery. At twenty-one, Henry Clay had been openly urging gradual emancipation on the street-corners of Lexington, Kentucky. The Whig planters then, and even later, maintained a tolerance on the question at sharp odds with the newly rich planters of the Democratic persuasion. And in the early years, it was these liberal aristocrats 'whom the common people followed.' [74]

9

Restrictions on suffrage were declining rapidly. By the half-century mark, 47 per cent of the white males voted in the lower South and 66 per cent in the upper; figures comparable to those of 47 per cent in Massachusetts, 67 per cent in Pennsylvania, and 62 per cent in New York. And far from being mere planting aristocrats, the 'great majority' of Southerners were 'hard-working farmers . . . provincial and conservative, but hardly more so than the people of New England or Pennsylvania.' [75]

Not the aristocratic planting society, but the rise of the common man spelled the end of tolerance on the slave question in the South. Jacksonian democracy, with its chants of freedom for the masses, only clamped the Negro the more tightly in his bondage. With the extension of the franchise came contraction of thought. The newcomers had risen too rapidly to assume the patina of a mature culture. They were too closely allied to the lower classes, who, cowering in hatred and in fear, were 'pro-slavery almost to a man.' And as slavery was the economic foundation of the planter life to which they aspired, they countered any threat to the institution which symbolized their goal.[76]

What was the tyranny of slavery? Out in Illinois, a young Whig named Abraham Lincoln defined the tyrannical principle of the institution as 'You work and earn bread, and I'll eat it.' [77] What he did not say was that the principle was the same, whether applied to the agrarian capitalism of the South or the industrial capitalism of the North; and that the fact, not the principle, would conquer the world of the present and the future.

Others were more perceptive. From the New York slums rose the great rabble-rouser, Mike Walsh, with his brassy face and outthrust jaw, youthful, bitter, rebellious. Of birthplace uncertain, of parentage unknown, without money, without education, Walsh was a pioneer of the slums, as was Jackson of the wilderness. For the first time Walsh and his 'Bowery b'hoys,' were to sound the raucous voice of the city streets in American politics.

It was Walsh's brawling news-sheet, *The Subterranean*, which became the first political organ of American labor; and to the horror of the abolitionist idealists, a fervid supporter of the presidential aspirations of

John C. Calhoun. Incongruous the alliance of Southern planters and city slum-dwellers might seem to outside observers, but not to the leaders of the two groups. If Walsh, like Calhoun, could declare that the salvation of labor depended upon the preservation of slavery, it was because he and Calhoun each realized that the slaveholding planters formed the last barrier against the protective tariff with its ominous meanings for agrarian and laboring groups alike.

'Demagogues tell you that you are freemen. They lie; you are slaves,'[78] was the shout of Walsh to his oppressed followers. No man could be free who was dependent only upon his own labor. The only difference between the workman and the Negro slave of the South was 'that . . . one . . . has to beg for the privilege of becoming a slave. . . . The one is the slave of an individual; the other . . . of an inexorable class.' Could the abolitionists produce 'one single solitary degradation' inflicted on the slave that the Northern laborer did not suffer under 'freedom'? Men moralized over the sufferings of the poor Negroes in the South; what of thirteen hundred men in New York City deprived of their liberty, only because they were poor?[79]

Equally disturbing were the caustic truths of the impassioned young preacher-editor, Orestes Brownson of the New York Workingman's Party. Six feet two inches tall and slender, his masses of dark hair thrown back from his face, Brownson was one of the most idealistic of the idealists, one of the most intellectual of the intelligentsia. He had been a Baptist preacher, an admitted agnostic, a dogmatic Unitarian. He had been a supporter of Andrew Jackson, fighting to fit the 'economic equality' of the Jackson program to the political liberties of the Jeffersonians. He was a slashing stump speaker, drawing roars from a crowd at every pause for breath; and his writings were acclaimed by Harriet Martineau as nearer 'the principles of exact justice' than anything she had ever seen. Now in the Boston *Quarterly Review* Brownson lashed out against the hypocrisy of those who would draw distinctions between the two American capitalistic systems of labor. 'Free labor,' he asserted, 'deprived the workingman of the proceeds of labor most efficiently.' Wages were for 'tender consciences . . . who would retain the slave system without the expense, trouble and odium of being slave-holders. . . . If there must always be a laboring population . . . we regard the slave system as decidedly preferable.'[80]

Appeals such as this struck terror to the hearts of Northern business leaders. Actually Calhoun was unable to enlist any serious number of Northern liberals and Northern laborers in his cause; but the psychological effect, just like the psychological effect of the abolitionists in the South, was what counted. Threats of abolitionism, Calhoun's followers could match with threats of labor unionism; 'chattel slavery' was pitted against 'wage slavery.' If the North was a threat to the South, so did the South present a threat to the North.

It was not to be borne. Slavery, a cheap, competitive laboring economy, could be tolerated only so long as it functioned under the kind of tariff and banking legislation that would profit big business. And it was Calhoun, with 'a prescience grown by now almost uncanny,'[81] who saw from the first that slavery alone could furnish the issue which would unite the idealistic anti-slavery forces of the North with the manufacturing interests in a 'moral' crusade against the Southern economy.

He had not long to wait.

10

On New Year's Day in 1831 a 'pale, delicate . . . over-tasked looking man' sat down at a pine desk in a dingy room in Boston where ink had splattered the tiny windows, while from a corner a printing press roared and shook unceasingly, to read his own words, starkly black on the first page of the first issue of *The Liberator*. 'Let Southern oppressors tremble —let all enemies of the persecuted blacks tremble. . . . I will be harsh as truth, and as uncompromising as justice. . . . I am in earnest . . . I will not equivocate . . . I will not excuse . . . I will not retreat a single inch . . . AND I WILL BE HEARD.' On the seventeenth, THE PICTURE appeared, Garrison's concept of a slave auction, incorporating in one searing message all the evils of the years: the sign, 'Slaves, horses, and other cattle to be sold at 12'; the weeping mother, a buyer 'examining her as a butcher would an ox'; the cluster of dapper young men, carefully eyeing their prospective female purchases.[82]

Men had laughed at William Lloyd Garrison. Calhoun did not laugh. He had seen it all as early as 1819, when he had turned, startled, at John Quincy Adams's dogmatic assertion that 'If the Union must be dissolved, slavery is the question upon which it ought to break.' Adams was weary of a Union with slaveholders. Let the North separate from the South, he had suggested; have 'a new Union . . . unpolluted with slavery . . . rallying the other States by . . . universal emancipation.' *

Calhoun had agreed with Adams that emancipation was a 'great objective,' but that it could only come at terrible cost, almost a revolution. And he could not and would not face the thought of disunion 'with all its horrors.'[83] The abolitionist agitation, he saw, would divide the sec-

---

* Oddly enough, twenty-three years later, John Quincy Adams presented to the Senate a petition signed by the citizens of Haverhill, Massachusetts, 'for the adoption of measures peaceably to dissolve the Union.' (See Carl Sandburg's *Abraham Lincoln, The Prairie Years*, Blue Ribbon Books, New York, 1926, p. 183.)

tions with hatred, strike at the heart of the Union both from the North and the South. If the Union were to be saved, he knew, the agitation must be halted—halted by the insistence and the unity of the slaveholders.

So out of his own knowledge and his own forebodings, Calhoun bid the South to 'look to her defenses.' To save the values of the Southern way of life within the Union was the standard he raised; and to save these values, the Southern people must unite within a single party and on a single issue. A unit economically, the South was divided politically and socially, with the majority of its great planters members of the Whig Party, and the masses still followers of Jefferson and Jackson.

Slavery was not the issue Calhoun would have chosen. The tariff would have united both the South and the West, but Jackson and nullification had confused the people on that question. Slavery would be the hardest of all issues to defend, but it was the one the North had chosen.

Only through states' rights, through complete autonomy, could the South hope to preserve its civilization. Once it allowed a single one of its institutions to be subverted by pressure from the outside, the ground had been surrendered. It was not so much abolition to which Calhoun objected as imposed abolition. Slavery was only a symbol, the most inflammatory of symbols, to be sure, but one upon which the whole South could stand united.

Calhoun well knew that the very name of slavery affronted the latent idealism of humanitarians, not only in the North, but in the world at large. In the face of such opposition, even an orthodox religious defense, such as was summarized by the Reverend John C. Coit, Presbyterian clergyman and friend of Calhoun's, was not enough. The Cheraw pastor cited chapter and verse. There was no moral slavery, he contended. Before God, Negroes' souls were equal with whites'. That 'slavery is against the spirit' of Christianity, Thomas R. Dew might insist, but the clergy of South Carolina would not concede even this. How, Coit asked, 'could men dare follow, not the letter but the spirit? Who was to know the spirit but through God's word?' [84]

Calhoun went beyond the Bible for his defenses. Slavery could no longer be termed a necessary evil, because the very admission of evil was a concession of justice in the Northern point of view. But to defend slavery unitedly, without giving hope for its ultimate extinction, of course involved a revolution in Southern thinking. To bring about this revolution was the task of Calhoun's mature years. He was incredibly successful. If slavery was the bulwark of Southern agrarian civilization—as Calhoun contended it was—the North knew now that the South could not be forced into abolition. There would be no surrender. From Yale, Calhoun's one-time friend, Benjamin Silliman, wrote sadly of his old pupil's vindication of 'slavery in the abstract. He . . . changed the state of opinion and the manner of speaking and writing upon this subject in the South,' leaving the region 'without prospect of, or wish for, its extinction.' [85]

To rest the cause of the South upon the crumbling foundation of Negro slavery was the tragic contradiction of Calhoun's career. With him, as with all Southerners, it was an emotional error. Far from being void of emotion, Calhoun was 'a volcano of passion,' and it was this which gave him such a hold over the hearts, as well as the heads, of the Southern people. He felt as his people felt, and his feelings blinded him to the facts.

Slavery he could defend with reason, but could not view with reason. The farsighted prophet who detected the disastrous results of the protective tariff with such accuracy was the same short-sighted Southerner, utterly blind to the financial drain of slave labor. He was the bigot who defended human servitude and the philosopher whose system for the protection of minority rights would appear to many, a hundred years after his time, as the salvation of political democracy. The clear-eyed statesman, who could commend Jefferson's denunciation of the Missouri Compromise for its attempt to define the boundary lines of slavery, was the same broken politician who by 1850 could see no hope for the country he loved, save in an artificial restoration of the 'equilibrium' which time and history and geography had wrecked forever; an incongruous coupling of the agrarian past to the industrial future.

Yet from the first, Calhoun had seen the basic issue: that the triumph of industrialism would bring 'misery to those who lived on the land.' That, logically, he knew his fight to be hopeless had no influence upon him. Sustained by his sense of duty, he battled the very future whose inevitability he foresaw, with the same stubborn, hopeless courage of old Patrick Calhoun in his war with the Constitution. 'As I know life,' he said grimly, 'were my head at stake, I would do my duty, be the consequences what they may.' [86]

11

This was the background to the war that opened on the floor of the Senate in December, 1835, never to end until the last 'gentleman of the South' had left the Chamber in the winter of 1861. What could be, Calhoun had understood from the first. What would be, it was his task to avert. If the abolitionist agitation continued, he was convinced it would rend the Union apart. And it was as the defender of the Union, not of slavery alone, that Calhoun stood in the Senate Chamber during those years of the eighteen-thirties and forties, hurling back the challenge of the Northern states. And looking on that taut, erect figure, white with anger, eyes blaz-

ing, men might doubt his prophecies and conclusions, but never his conviction as to their truth.*

'I ask neither sympathy nor compassion for the slave-holding States,'
was his proud declaration. 'We can take care of ourselves. It is not we,
but the Union which is in danger. . . . We love and cherish the Union;
we remember our common origin . . . and fondly anticipate the common
greatness that seems to await us.' But, 'come what will,' he warned, with
somber prophecy, 'should it cost every drop of blood and every cent of
property, we must defend ourselves.' [87]

Strangely enough, it was not Calhoun but Andrew Jackson who opened
the abolitionist fight upon the Senate floor. Much has been said of Jackson as the great friend of the common man, and of Calhoun as the great
defender of the landed interests. Yet the man who made democracy a
vital and living force in American government never regarded Negro slavery as a violation of that democracy. Not even Calhoun saw the threat
of abolitionist agitation any more clearly than Jackson, nor was he more
capable of favoring thorough and decisive action.

A postoffice fight aroused the President's wrath. In July, 1835, the
citizens of Charleston raided the postoffice, stole and burned a sack of
abolitionist pamphlets; then named a committee to meet with the postmaster to determine what material could not be delivered in the city.
The Charleston postmaster promptly notified the postmaster in New York
to forward no more abolitionist material; and the postmaster in New
York laid the matter before Amos Kendall, Postmaster General of the
United States.

Nullification had been mild, indeed, compared to the Administration's
stand. Jackson, four years earlier, had flatly proposed that abolition
papers be delivered by Southern postmasters only to those who demanded
them, 'and in every instance the Postmaster ought to take the names down,
and have them exposed thro the publick journals as subscribers to this
wicked plan of exciting the slaves to insurrection . . . every moral and
good citizen will unite to put them in coventry.' So, with the full backing of the President, Kendall declared that he would neither direct the
postmaster at New York to forward the incendiary pamphlets nor the
postmaster at Charleston to receive them. Even higher than the laws of
the United States, declared Connecticut-born Kendall, were the individual's
responsibilities to his home community. Meanwhile, Jackson, in his Mes-

* Calhoun's opinions on slavery underwent little change from 1830 to 1850. As the
aim of this chapter is to reveal his state of mind on the entire slave question, his
quotations hereafter are not necessarily arranged chronologically. A question current
in 1837 he might have discussed again more forcibly and effectively in 1848. Through
different years, he might present three or four sides to a question which are here
consolidated under one subject head. The note references clearly indicate the source of
the different quotations; and, of course, in a report of any one specific speech, this
method is not used.

sage to Congress the following December, denounced abolitionists as plotters of a civil war with all its horrors, and recommended passage of a
measure absolutely excluding the circulation of 'incendiary publications
intended to instigate the slaves to insurrection.' [88]

The howls with which Northern liberals greeted this proposal have
long since been forgotten in latter-day liberal veneration of Jackson. Actually this proposition was too much even for Calhoun. He recognized no
'higher law' than the Constitution, with its unmistakable provisions for
freedom of the press, and he knew that if he were a party to its violation for measures that would benefit his own people, he could not invoke
its protection when the South's rights were violated. 'Rights and duties
are reciprocal,' he said. Such was Calhoun's stand, but there were those
who saw in it more than abstract principle. President Jackson's support of
a measure, asserted Senator King, was enough in itself to assure Senator
Calhoun's opposition. Calhoun protested too much. 'I have too little
regard for the opinion of General Jackson and . . . his character, too, to
permit his course to influence me in the slightest degree.' [89]

Nevertheless, it was Calhoun who moved reference of the President's
Message to a special committee, and it was he who was named committee
chairman. On February 4, 1836, he brought in a report declaring freedom
of the mails essential to freedom of the press, and that Congress could
make no law excluding any material whatever from the mails, incendiary
or otherwise. Instead, he offered a counter-proposal. He suggested that
federal postoffice agents be required by law to co-operate with state and
territorial agents in preventing circulation of incendiary material where
such material was forbidden by local law; and that local officials found
guilty of violating their responsibilities by declining to examine suspect
'literature' be denied the protection of the federal government.[90]

It was Henry Clay who detected the fine-spun fallacy in this proposition. If Congress had no power to exclude abolitionist documents from
the mails, he asked, how then could it exclude their delivery through the
mails?

Yet Calhoun's proposition, as well as his objection to the President's,
was based on a fundamental constitutional question. Jackson would give
the national government the power to regulate the mails; Calhoun would
lay on the servants of the national government the obligation to bow to
state laws.

The debate dragged on for months, ending in a 25 to 19 defeat for
Calhoun's bill. The three-way Southern split served only to open the
way for the Northern opposition, who promptly passed a measure, providing fines and imprisonment for any postoffice official who in any way
prevented any material whatever from reaching its destination.

12

Round two involved the abolitionist petitions. The question was not new. Long agitated in the House, the usual practice had been to receive the petitions and to table them instantly. But this was not enough for Calhoun, who stubbornly insisted that such petitions should be refused from the first. Deliberately he was forcing an issue which, it must be admitted, many of the more moderate slaveholding groups preferred not to force at all. If a petition could term slavery 'a national disgrace' in the District of Columbia, why could it not be so termed in South Carolina? If the South had the constitutional right to hold slaves at all, it had a right to hold them in 'peace and quiet,' Calhoun argued. The fight must be waged on the frontier; for, as he put it, 'The most unquestioned right can be rendered doubtful, if it be admitted to be a subject of controversy.' [91]

Nor was it a violation of the right of petition to refuse to receive these 'mischievous' documents. The First Amendment merely deprived Congress of the power to pass any law 'abridging . . . the right of the people . . . to petition the government.' It did not require Congress to accept petitions, Calhoun contended. Had not Jefferson himself ruled that before petitions were presented, their contents must be revealed by the introducer, and a motion made and seconded to receive them? Deprived of its right as a deliberative body to determine what to 'receive or reject,' Calhoun argued, Congress would become the passive receptacle of all that was 'frivolous, absurd, unconstitutional, immoral, and impious. . . . If a petition should be presented, praying the abolition of the Constitution (which we are all bound . . . to protect), according to this abominable doctrine, it must be received.' If the abolitionist societies should be converted into societies of atheists, and petition that a law be passed, 'denying the existence of the Almighty . . . according to this blasphemous doctrine, we would be bound to receive the petition.' [92] If Congress was bound to receive petitions to abolish slavery, why then could it not abolish slavery itself?

Why not indeed? Congress listened. With Calhoun few would even attempt debate. His questions went unanswered. Often he would complain that none would reply to his charges. But not until Abraham Lincoln would America produce a man to answer from first principles arguments based on first principles. To such a man Calhoun would have listened with respect, but to no other.

13

On December 27, 1837, Calhoun took the Senate floor. The resolutions that he introduced flung the issue right in the teeth of the Constitution,

the North, and the Senate itself. They were far from watertight, either in
logic or practicality. As Benton said, they were 'abstract, leading to no
result; made discussion where silence was desirable, frustrated the design of the Senate in refusing to discuss the abolition petitions,' and pro-
moted the very agitation their author deplored.

They were penned in sheer desperation. An attack on slavery anywhere,
declared Calhoun, was an attack on slavery everywhere, an argument true
enough in the abstract, but scarcely possible for a states'-right advocate
validly to support. For if 'intermeddling' by the citizens of one state
with the 'domestic institutions . . . of the others' violated state sovereignty, how then could it be 'the duty' of the federal government 'to
give increased security' to 'domestic institutions'? If slavery could not be
threatened without a violation of state sovereignty, how, then, could it
be protected? [93] Calhoun was caught in the net of his own logic. Many
of his detractors now saw that if the South could only mind its business
by interfering with the business of the North, then slavery was intolerable.[94] Were Northerners free only to criticize the laws of Massachusetts,
but not those of South Carolina? Was it possible for the government to
give increased security to liberty in Connecticut and to slavery in Georgia?

But Calhoun's feelings were too wrought up for any possibility of clear
thinking, even in his lucid brain. 'Is the South to sit still and see the Constitution . . . laid prostrate in the dust?' he demanded furiously.[95] Had
the Alien and Sedition Laws been defeated by 'sitting still and quoting
the authority of the Constitution'? Yet he chided Anna Maria for her
conclusion that it would be 'better to part peacably at once than to live
in the state of indecision we do.' He knew 'how many bleeding pours [sic]
must be taken up in passing the knife of seperation [sic] through a body
politick (in order to make two of one).' Although admitting that 'we
cannot and ought not to live together as we are . . . exposed to the continual . . . assaults' of the North, he was resolved that 'we must act
throughout on the defensive, resort to every possible means of arresting
the evil, and only act, when . . . justified before God and man in taking
the final step.' [96] Yet he had long known that difficult as it was 'to make
two people of one,' if 'the evil be not arrested at the North,' the South
would take the initiative. 'I, for one,' Calhoun declared, 'would rather
meet the danger now, than turn it over to those who are to come after us.' [97]

Day after day, speech after speech, his words poured on. There were
those who saw no danger to the Union in the violation of its most sacred
principles, but only in the words of those who dared foretell the danger.
'If my attachment to the Union were less, I might . . . keep silent. . . .
It is a cheap and . . . certain mode of acquiring the character of devoted attachment to the Union.' [98] But he saw—and he would speak.

'They who imagine the spirit now abroad in the North will die away
of itself . . . have formed a very inadequate concept of its real charac-

ter. . . . Already it has taken possession of the pulpit . . . the schools
. . . the press.' He had no patience with Senators who saw in the aboli-
tion-disunionists nothing but a 'mere handful of females,' interested only
in abolishing slavery in the District of Columbia, while 'they openly
avow they are against all slavery.' [99]

What were the facts? Fifteen hundred abolitionist societies with an average of a hundred members each, increasing at the rate of one a day, 'hundreds of petitions, thousands of publications . . . attacking $900,000,000
worth of slave property and . . . the . . . safety of an entire section of
this Union in violation of . . . pledged faith and the Constitution. . . .'
And yet, we are told, 'if we would keep . . . cool and patient, and hear
ourselves and our constituents attacked as robbers and murderers . . .
without moving hand or tongue, all would be well.' [100]

'We are reposing on a volcano!' Calhoun shouted. The present generation would be succeeded by those taught to hate the people and the institutions 'of nearly one half of this Union, with a hatred more deadly
than one hostile nation ever entertained towards another.' [101] Gone would
be 'every sympathy between the two great sections,' their recollections
of common danger and common glory. The abolitionists were 'imbuing
the rising generation at the North with the belief that . . . the institutions of the Southern states were sinful and immoral, and that it was
doing God service to abolish them, even if it should involve the destruction of half the inhabitants of this Union.' [102]

'It is easy to see the end. . . . We must become two people. . . . Abolition and the Union cannot co-exist. As the friend of the Union I . . .
proclaim it.' [103]

Bitterly he ridiculed the belief of the North that 'slavery is sinful, notwithstanding the authority of the Bible to the contrary.' There was a
period, he reminded the Senators with sarcasm, 'when the Northern States
were slave-holding communities . . . extensively and profitably engaged
in importing slaves to the South. It would . . . be . . . interesting to
trace the causes which have led in so short a time to so great a change.'

What was the Northern concept of liberty? Once it was thought that
men were free who lived in constitutional republics. Now all non-slave governments were free, 'even Russia with her serfs. . . . The term slave . . .
is now restricted almost exclusively to African slavery.' Products of the
Hindus and the serfs were declared free-made, and enjoyed as the products
of freedom. 'To so low a standard has freedom sunk.' [104]

In Northern idealism he saw nothing but sheer fanaticism. The spirit
of abolition was nothing more than that 'blind, fanatical zeal . . . that
made one man believe he was responsible for the sins of his neighbor, that
two centuries ago convulsed the Christian world' and 'tied the victims
that it could not convert to the stake. . . .' [105]

Why, he asked, did the individual Northerner feel himself responsible for slavery? Simply because our government had become nationalized instead of federal, 'the States . . . like counties to the State, each feeling responsibility for the concerns of the other.' Since the Force Bill passage, in practice, the United States had become 'a consolidated government.' His resolutions were 'test' questions, involving the whole theory of the federal system.[106]

14

Calhoun won his battle—on paper. With the specter of actual, practical nullification removed from public view, the Senate, at least, was quite willing to approve the nullification doctrines, and pass five out of six of Calhoun's resolutions, with little material alteration. Whether or not the public would have granted such approval is another matter.

But Calhoun was not content, even with pledging the faith of the federal government toward the maintenance of slavery. His added determination was to secure the safety of the 'domestick institution' under international law.

Since 1830, three American ships, the *Creole, Enterprise,* and *Comet,* traveling to and from Latin American ports, had been held with their cargoes of slaves by British authorities. Since 1830, Presidents Jackson and Van Buren had, in Calhoun's words, 'been knocking—no, that is too strong a term—tapping gently at the door of the British Secretary, to obtain justice.'

Now Calhoun demanded action. Again he resorted to resolutions, in the bitter words of Adams, 'imposing his bastard law of nations' upon the entire Senate, which bowed to his will without a dissenting vote. American property rights had been violated, was his contention. Under the law of nations those vessels 'were as much under the protection of our flag' as if anchored in their home ports. Yet England declared the slave that touched British soil to be thenceforth free. Calhoun, with thoughts of India and Ireland bitter in his mind, could sneer at British distinctions between property in persons and property in things. He could warn that 'it would ill become a nation that was the greatest slaveholder . . . on . . . earth —notwithstanding all the cant about emancipation—to apply such a principle in her intercourse with others.' [107] The British government was obdurate. The greatest maritime power on earth had refused to admit that slavery was recognized by the law of nations, and thus declined the mutual consent upon which all international law rests.

Actually England did release one of the vessels and its human cargo. But the brig, *Enterprise,* which docked after slavery was abolished in the Empire, was never returned. And in 1841 Britain gave freedom to the slaves who had seized the brig, *Creole,* after killing the master in a mu-

tinous uprising. Calhoun was left to the empty victory of having committed the Senate to the stand that a 'domestick institution' was recognized by international law; and to the equally empty satisfaction of
seeing Secretary of State Daniel Webster appeal impotently to Calhoun's
resolutions in his negotiations.

15

That emancipation, gradual or otherwise, would have been extremely difficult—almost impossible—by 1840 is undeniable. Yet had Calhoun
joined with Henry Clay, for instance, in trying to work out a transitional
system; had he devoted the same time and thought to a possible solution that he did to his defense of slavery, his claims upon the gratitude of
his country would be far greater.

For the South the issue would then have been fought in clear-cut terms.
For a South sincerely, if hopelessly, attempting to struggle from the morass
that engulfed her, the world would have had true sympathy. Against her
still would have been ranged the spirit of industrial expansion, the spirit,
perhaps, of the entire modern world, but not the outraged moral idealism
of the nineteenth century. The North would have lost its issue; and slavery would not have obscured fundamentals.

This Calhoun did not see. Not for him the easy way out of Henry Clay,
who could wash his hands of personal responsibility by comforting dona-
tions to a pipe-dream such as the American Colonization Society. Calhoun had too much intellectual honesty to salve his conscience with lip-
service to ideals that denied the facts. Boldly and honestly he faced slavery as a fact and not as a theory. Not his own conscience, but the dilemma
of the South, was what tortured Calhoun. Historians have shown how,
with pitiless clarity, Calhoun saw the doom of his people under the
reaped whirlwind of abolitionist agitation, but did not see that a logical
doom may not necessarily be an inevitable doom.[108] Although history
would prove him tragically right in his somber conviction that abolition
superimposed by the North would wreck the South; he could not see
that slavery, as such, was not basically essential to the South; and that
gradual emancipation by the South itself would have been another matter.

To instinctive Jeffersonians, such as Calhoun was, the dilemma was
more than intolerable. Grimly aware of the inequalities of man, Calhoun and his followers were compelled to reduce Jefferson's philosophy
to the realities of their own time. Why, if Jefferson believed in emancipation, had he waited until his deathbed to free his own slaves? What if
Jefferson had lived until the slave system was so deeply rooted in the
Southern soil that its immediate extrication would mean destruction of
the entire Southern economy; until attempts at enforced abolition from

the North had ruled out all hopes of voluntary abolition from the South? Jefferson had died, haunted with the hopelessness and fear that was creeping like a blight across the Southern people. It is easy to condemn Calhoun for the stain on his otherwise brilliant career; yet, if he had no answer for the most tragic human problem of his time, neither had Thomas Jefferson.

XX

Floride

FLORIDE was lonely.

Standing alone on the north portico of Fort Hill, her eyes moved across the garden and park to the forests and mountains beyond. To Calhoun, she knew, those blue-misted hills meant peace, freedom, all that he longed for in his months in Washington. To her, they were the walls of a prison. She knew this country; she had spent her vacations here as a child. But somehow she had never imagined the emptiness of these winter months when the people of Charleston were gone. . . .

These raw-boned hill-countrymen were not her people; they were proud of Calhoun; he was one of them, but they looked askance at his 'foreign' wife. They stared with cold suspicion at her little Episcopal church in Pendleton. They did not build white columns on their porches nor plant magnolias in the yard. Theirs was the same sturdy stock that had bred Daniel Boone and Davy Crockett; there were cousins of Andrew Jackson's among them; and their anger flared when they heard how Floride had laughed at Rachel Jackson's corncob pipe. As one of them said: 'We . . . wouldn't stand for a Charlestonian making fun of our kin.' [1]

In the course of time, biographers would come to accept the marriage of Floride and Calhoun as ideal. As a matter of fact, it was far more real than ideal. Despite his 'sweet temper,' Calhoun had his full share of faults as a husband. And with the one exception of Mary Todd Lincoln, there is no more baffling or stormy figure among all the historical American wives than Floride Calhoun. There is no doubt that in his own way Calhoun deeply loved her, although, as we shall see, there were trials to overcome.

Did Floride return his affection? There is no actual evidence that she did not, but not a line remains to show that she did. For this omission, Calhoun himself may have been responsible. One historian has asserted that Calhoun deliberately destroyed his personal correspondence 'for the express purpose of keeping it from the prying eyes of biographers.' [2] The fact that he saved Thomas Clemson's impersonal communications, but that nearly all of Anna Maria's charming notes have disappeared, would substantiate this. And the three Floride letters that escaped destruction reveal almost nothing.

Complete certainty of his wife's affections seems to have been something Calhoun never had. From the first months of their marriage, he was complaining that he had received so few letters from Floride, although he had written her so many. He would write two 'within a few days'; he would dream of her at night; his correspondence is threaded with messages like one to Anna Maria: 'Say to your Mother I will write her in a few days; and that I have not received a single line from her in return to the letters, which I have written since I left home.' * ³

Was Floride perhaps pushed into marriage with Calhoun? Her mother was a dominant, if not a domineering woman. She herself had scorned to mate with the inbred aristocracy of Charleston. She had sensed Calhoun's latent genius, almost before he was aware of it himself. He had purpose and drive and fire; she loved him as a son, and sought him as a son-in-law.

But Floride was born into a romantic age and a romantic life, and in her teens was seeking romance. The dark, intense, good looks of Calhoun's youth may have had a potent appeal to more objective femininity, but to Floride there could have been little romance about him. He had been the 'big brother' of the household, hearing her Bible lessons, telling her to be 'a good girl,' sending his love to 'the children.' ⁴ There had been that strange current of affection between him and her mother; she was old enough to have felt it, although she could not have known what it meant. He could talk to her mother as he would to a man; would he ever speak so to her? Would he ever, except in the first flush of courtship, look upon her as more than a child?

She was too young. Calhoun was twenty-nine the year of their marriage, nearly eleven years older than she and, mentally, much more than that. Modern science has revealed how serious, emotionally and physically, such a difference of age can be. Calhoun was a mature man, settled and self-assured. Almost from his wedding day romance seems to have left his mind. Floride was not his sweetheart. She was the keeper of his home, the mother-to-be of his children. For almost from her wedding night she was pregnant.

Life was hard for Floride. During their first year Calhoun was separated from her for three months. During the second year he was nine months away. All during their first six years of marriage, the difficult years when they should have been growing together, they were growing apart. They should have been ironing out their differences; instead, they were developing their individualities. They had their separate roles; hers, the Victorian 'sainted wife and mother'; his, the scholar, the leader, the man-of-affairs. They were thrown back upon themselves, becoming more and more self-sufficient, emotionally and intellectually. Their only tie was in their children. Like Mary Lincoln, Floride might well have said that had

* Calhoun to Anna Maria Clemson, June 28, 1841. Clemson College Papers, written seven weeks after he left for Washington.

her husband been more often at home, she could have loved him better. Of thirty-nine years of married life, Calhoun spent nearly fifteen away from his wife.

There were his years as Secretary of War. Floride had dreamed of Washington, of the gay life there, the parties and balls, and her husband, proud and adoring, at her side. Instead, she had been tumbled pell-mell into the home of Mrs. William Lowndes, who was a Charlestonian and a lady, but almost a stranger. The house was overrun with children. Lowndes was an invalid, far too weak and ill to endure social activities of any kind. And at first Floride had not even had a carriage to ride out in, for as a Congressman, Calhoun had not been able to afford one, and had shared the cost of a horse and buggy with Lowndes.[5] And Calhoun himself overworked and overtired, what time had he for his young wife? He was driving himself to the point of collapse; up at dawn, laboring past midnight, in a one-man attempt to wipe out in his department the accumulated errors of twenty-five years. Afterwards, of course, there had been Dumbarton Oaks . . . the receptions . . . the balls . . . the tributes to her beauty and charm of which she had dreamed; but then it may have been too late.

2

They had returned to South Carolina. And there, Floride was more lonely than ever, lonely in a way Calhoun could never understand. It was not the isolation of Fort Hill which she minded especially, or the perpetual child-bearing, or the continual work, supervision, and responsibility; for these were all part of the Southern life, 'the whole duty of womankind.' But she needed her husband and wanted to be needed by him. She was a Southern belle, spirited, pampered, and spoiled; she was of a generation of women that was worshiped and adored. A gracious hostess, she would entertain her husband's friends, but his way of life she could never share. Hers was the world of balls and teas, of literary afternoons and evenings at the opera, not of political strife and contention. Guests filled the house, but to see her husband, not her; there was conversation, earthy and spirited, but none of the small-talk elegancies of Charleston.

Had she married into her own class—one of those languid, soft-spoken gallants of the low-country, she could have gone into Charleston in the proper season, danced at the Saint Cecilias, entertained and been entertained. But Calhoun was away in the winter and she could not go alone; and if they went to Charleston in the summer, he was always ill. She was the wife of the most popular man in South Carolina; they were besieged with invitations to dinners, dances, barbecues, and balls all over the state, but Calhoun, exhausted from his strenuous sessions in Washington, summarily rejected them.[6]

She longed for her husband's companionship. In youth, even when far advanced in pregnancy, she begged to accompany him in his inspection trips as Secretary of War; but he, more solicitous for her physical than her emotional needs, did not understand. 'Mrs. Calhoun was anxious to accompany me,' he wrote a friend at the start of his 1820 tour. 'I was only deterred from an apprehension that it would be too fatiguing.'[7] She was the kind of woman who, given the chance, would have concerned herself intensely with such matters as her husband's diet and health, with protecting him from undue invasions of visitors, with all the little physical comforts which he needed as much as any man, but heeded scarcely at all.

For her times and upbringing, Floride was perfectly normal. But hers was not a normal marriage, and Calhoun was scarcely a normal man. Like Lincoln, he was 'a genius who made demands,' difficult, complex, highly organized. When problems beset him, he sought only to be let alone, to work them out in 'hours of solitary thought.'[8] Privacy was as essential to him at such times as food and drink; his withdrawals were not deliberate, but instinctive. But this his wife could never understand.

3

Primarily, Floride's trouble was jealousy. As it was obvious that Calhoun had eyes for no other woman, her jealousy was turned upon his work and daily life, and even upon their own children. Calhoun adored his children, and he could not or would not punish them. The extent of his efforts seems to have amounted to once sending a boy away from the dinner table for speaking disrespectfully of a preacher.[9] He believed in training children through example, but unfortunately, he was so seldom at home. Unfortunately, too, he had an overadequate share of theories on child development, which would much later become fashionable, but which played havoc with poor Floride's attempts at discipline. Children, thought Calhoun, in unconscious protest against his own repressed youth, should grow up without control, without restraint. Their bodies should be hardened by sports and exercise, but their minds left untrained until maturity.[10] All this sounded very well, but Floride, with five headstrong boys and two girls to bring up, was obliged to face reality. Although she was by inclination an indulgent mother, upon her shoulders fell the unpleasant part of the disciplinary problems.

The children themselves, who felt only the softer side of their father's nature, of course adored him. Frail little Cornelia openly declared that she loved him better than anyone else. To the boys, he was the 'dearest, best old man in the world.' And as for Anna Maria, we have already seen that in her father's later years, she shared with him a companionship which he gave no other person.[11]

Floride knew it. She was her husband's rival for the affections of their children; and they, in turn, rivaled her for his love and attention. The unpublished Calhoun letters at Fort Hill show Floride continually at war with one or another of the children, and Calhoun futilely trying to make peace. As 'your mother fancies you have evinced coldness towards her,' Calhoun wrote Anna Maria, he urged that she write Floride an especially affectionate letter.[12]

4

For Floride there was but one outlet, the eternal feminine release—her 'nerves.' Her South Carolina contemporaries, it must be admitted, used a stronger word; and even her own descendants have admitted that she was subject to 'fits of temper.'[13] Stories of her rages have seeped through South Carolina legend for a hundred years: of a silver pitcher with a dent in the side where it struck the hard head of its human target; the absence of the family china attributed to similar misusage; hints that Calhoun sought refuge in his office for days on end, not even permitted to re-enter the family dwelling until he had written Floride a note, petitioning her permission to do so.

These are the rumors, and they are doubtless exaggerated. Yet, in later years, even in his unpublished correspondence, there are unmistakable hints that home life was not undiluted serenity. Writing Anna Maria in March, 1844, he told her that a Mrs. Rion had been engaged as housekeeper. 'Thus far, it has been a happy change. Everything has been going on with great harmony about the house. . . . I trust the former unpleasant state of things have passed, not to return, and wish to see harmony all around.'[14]

Certainly he did his own part in keeping the peace. His oldest son once declared that he had never heard Calhoun speak impatiently to a single member of the family. His strongest reproof at one of his wife's outbursts was a gentle, 'Tut, tut, Floride.'[15] which no doubt infuriated her all the more.

Had he fought back, it might have cleared the atmosphere. Instead, he retreated to the office, where Floride was presumably denied admittance, and lost himself in his books and papers and dreams. And, of course, his very capacity for escape annoyed Floride. The more she resented his self-sufficiency, the more self-sufficient he became, spending hours alone in the office or striding in contented solitude over the fields. And she, resentful, jealous of all that took him from her, by her own actions aggravated the very qualities against which she was rebelling.

Most of all, she resented his career. She was proud of him, of course, and had infinite faith in his greatness. But it was only natural that she should

resent the cares and labor which took such toll of her husband's physical
strength and shattered his peace of mind. His career took him from her;
sentenced her to days of isolation and loneliness. And the plantation, too,
justified her feeling that he did not need her, that he had outlets which
she could never share.

Floride raged at his utter masculine superiority. Who ran the plantation while he was away? He could shift the responsibility to her in the
winter months without a by-your-leave; yet, when home, it seemed as if
he thought not a leaf or a blade of grass could grow unless he personally
saw to it. He could praise her 'management,' yet once he was at home,
her activity was relegated to the kitchen and the sewing room. He was
the 'Master of Fort Hill.'

Very well! If she were to be penned up on the plantation, it was she
who would rule. If lines of demarcation were to be drawn, she would
draw them. If his was the plantation, hers was the house.

For the house was hers, she felt. It had been in her family, not Calhoun's. Her frustrated nervous energy demanded outlet; she was 'beset
with the idea of making improvements.' Although her child-bearing days
were over before 1830, she had carpenters at work, hammering, shingling,
adding room after room for the next twenty years. It was neighborhood
legend that every time Calhoun went to Washington, Floride added another room; for, as she said, there wasn't much he could do but pay
for it, once it was there.

Calhoun was distressed by these 'haphazard additions,' but reasoning,
persuasion, outright pleading had no effect upon Floride. In desperation,
the harassed man appealed to his brother-in-law: 'She writes me that she
is desirous to commence an addition to our House . . . on her return
to Pendleton. I think it would not be advisable on many accounts, till
after my return. . . . I have long since learned by sad experience what
it is to build in my absence. It would cost me twice as much and the
work then will not be half as well done. . . . I could build at comparatively small expense, and have it well done under my own eye. I wish you
to add your weight to mine to reconcile her to the course I suggest. I
have written her fully on the subject.'[16]

5

Sometimes a wildness would break across her. She would turn Sunday into
washday, send the Negroes scurrying from house to well-house with heaping baskets, and shock Calhoun's afternoon visitors with lines strung with
billowing petticoats, spencers, and ruffled under-drawers. She would storm
through the house and the grounds, locking every window, every door,
every closet, storeroom, smokehouse, and outhouse on the plantation. She

would call for the carriage and drive off, leaving her husband to break down the doors and do the explaining to the gentlemen of Pendleton when he brought them home for a long-planned dinner party. Was this her answer to the curious fact, noted instantly by a visitor to the plantation, that the key to Calhoun's office was always 'under his immediate control,' with 'no one' permitted to enter it but himself, unless he was there? [17]

Was not the mistress of the plantation *always* the keeper of the keys?

She would stand staring down at the 'fantastic pattern' of her husband's flower garden, which he had laid out with such tender care; for he loved flowers, and always came home with his trunk crammed with exotic cuttings, which he planted with the same zest that he put into his crop experimentations.[18] But Floride did not like it. The garden was hers. He had said so himself. Did he not send her seeds for her flowers and watermelons? What did he, an up-countryman, know about gardens? And the story goes that one night, when he was safely asleep, Floride called out the whole body of slaves, with reinforcements from the neighbors, and by morning had every flower replanted.[19]

6

Calhoun was impervious to Floride's outbreaks. She could not hurt him, because he could not and would not feel himself responsible. He blamed all upon her 'nerves,' which were, indeed, her one power over him. For physically, Floride seems to have been quite a healthy woman. Calhoun, in 1848, weary and 'never free from a cough,' wrote rather enviously of her 'fine health,' and 'excellent' constitution.[20] Nevertheless, the 'attacks of a Nervous Character,' which kept her in bed for periods ranging from two days to four weeks, 'under constant apprehensions of dying,' gave him 'horrible anxiety.' [21]

Consciously or unconsciously, this was exactly what Floride wanted him to feel. He no doubt diagnosed her complaint accurately as 'more from agitation than any other cause'; but a psychiatrist, observing the dramatic ailments of this high-strung ex-belle, her whole family summoned to await the end,* would have had no difficulty in detecting her resentment at the attention and adulation lavished upon her famous husband. For when Floride was the most popular woman in Washington, her temper was 'perfectly equable.' [22]

When she was ill, Calhoun was the kind of husband Floride always wanted him to be. He was tender, solicitous, 'very uneasy about her.' Most important, he was with her, at her bedside. And his sympathy was real.

* It is interesting to note that most of these illnesses took place when Calhoun was at home, not when he was in Washington and Floride was essential to her family and the direction of the plantation

His letters are sifted through with references to the 'severe Nervous condition to which she is subject';[23] written always with great concern and genuine pity. There is not a line that he would have feared to show her.

7

Primarily, Calhoun craved from his wife intellectual companionship, and even his earliest love-letters show that in Floride he was seeking 'beauty of mind' as well as physical fulfillment. But Floride was different, and Calhoun self-absorbed, on the threshold of his career, had not the slightest conception of how to bring her mind into harmony with his.

At first, it did not seem to matter. In the early years of their marriage, with passion alternating with separation, with friends like Littleton Tazewell and William Lowndes, with whom he could exchange ideas, he had sufficient mental stimulation. Then came the Peggy O'Neil episode, and the same tragedy that for years wrecked Calhoun's public hopes tore at the roots of his private life. For he had reached middle age then, and with blood cooled and hopes dimmed, with duty, not glory, the watchword of his future, he turned, too late, to the wife he had unknowingly neglected. Then, if ever, he needed understanding both intellectual and emotional, but it was too late.* As we have seen, the Eaton affair marked a crisis in Floride's own life, and the pride for which she had sacrificed her husband's political prospects dealt no more tenderly with his personal needs.

Never, she had resolved, would she return to Washington until it was freed from the 'contamination' of Mrs. Eaton's presence.[24] And she did not return, not even in that tense January of 1833 when, alone, her husband faced Andrew Jackson and the greatest crisis of his career. And alone he would face every crisis of his life thereafter, down to the stark solitude of his Washington death-chamber, when in far-off Carolina Floride waited hopefully for a summons that came too late.[25]

Calhoun accepted matters philosophically. He was too masculine in temperament to concern himself with feminine whys and wherefores. He needed his family; he missed them keenly, but, if lonely, he could be content, for he had never known anything but loneliness. His solitary childhood had stamped his character for life; he was too self-reliant, too sufficient unto himself.[26]

---

* See Calhoun's letter to Anna Maria quoted on page 281 in which he said that he had sent Floride a copy of his speech on the 'deposite' question, but feared she would not read it as she took 'no interest in such things.'

8

Dark as this side of the story is, one fact is unmistakably clear. Calhoun married Floride because he loved her, and, in his own way, he loved her all the years of his life. She stirred him, baffled him, sometimes amused him, but always knew how to pique and hold his interest. To her, he knew, he was neither the demon that he appeared to one section of the country, nor the demigod that he seemed to the other, but a man and husband, and sometimes a most exasperating one. And being flesh and blood, Calhoun must have occasionally enjoyed being treated as such.

Nor were his longings to be home and 'be quiet' ignored completely. For all her faults, Floride sensed at times that gentleness and affection were necessary. More than once her husband returned to her so broken in health and tormented in mind that no one expected ever to see him in Washington again; yet after a few months of rest and of Floride's nursing, he was back, revived in mind and body.

His letters are crammed with this eagerness to be at home. 'These long seperations . . . from those dear to me . . . are exceedingly painful,' he would write Anna Maria. 'My anxiety to return increases daily . . . a month more and my face will be turned homeward to my great delight. . . . I can scarcely describe my eagerness to see you all.' These are not the longings of a man unhappy at home, although his remark that he found his children 'the great solace of life' may indicate the direction in which his affections primarily lay.[27]

During restless, bitter years when his public life was sheer tragedy, he knew his only happiness with his family. To those who knew him, it was obvious that his 'home had attractions for him superior to which any other place could offer.' There his manners, 'at all times agreeable,' became utterly 'captivating';[28] his shyness, which he concealed under his free-flowing conversation, was completely gone. 'Few men,' declared one observer, indulged their families in 'as free and confidential conversation'[29] as he did. He was most charming when completely himself, and he was completely himself only at home.

If marriage and family ties were only a part of his existence, his feelings were none the less strong. Some even felt that, far from subordinating his family to the demands of office, Calhoun allowed his family affections to become too warm and absorbing. To be at home he neglected social duties almost obligatory to his position. Floride could brood over the times that he had left her alone; yet after thirty-three years of marriage he almost declined a seat in Tyler's Cabinet for fear that he could not persuade Floride to come to Washington with him again.[30]

Henry Clay, indeed, declared that he had never seen a man treat his wife with such 'tenderness, respect, and affection' as Calhoun showed

Floride.[31] He was not the kind of man to have remembered birthdays or anniversaries, but austere as he was in his personal desires, his generosity to his own family was almost more than he could afford. 'You must tell the children,' he would write Anna Maria, 'that I will bring out with me, when I return home, the prettiest books that I can find.'[32] Washington matrons would glance up startled to find the Senator from South Carolina at their side, searching the drygoods counters for the kind of white silk stockings that Floride liked best; or, indeed, any gift that would take her fancy. 'Peace offerings,' the cynical called them.[33]

Tragedy lurks behind his muted words to his son Andrew in the summer of 1847: 'As to the suspicion and unfounded blame of your Mother, you must not only bear them, but forget them. With the many good qualities of her Mother, she inherits her suspicious and fault finding temper, which has been the cause of much vexation in the family. I have borne with her with patience, because it was my duty to do so, & you must do the same, for the same reason. It has been the only cross of my life.'[34]

Yet his fundamental love for his wife lightened the darker side of their marriage. He paid Floride the supreme tribute of obliviousness to her faults. It was upon her virtues that he focused his attention, genuinely admiring her common-sense and energy. 'Whatever your mother does, she does well,' he wrote Anna Maria. 'I have no doubt that her management of the estate will quite discredit mine.'[35] Late in life he told a friend that he had never regretted his marriage; it had been a 'true union of the heart and soul.'[36] Significantly, he did not mention the mind. Even more significant was that he felt called upon to defend his marriage at all.

9

But it was a marriage. Their hours of hardship were flecked with moments of joy. Their memories together spanned nearly a half-century; they had been young; they had known the ecstasy of courtship and of married love; the long, lonely months of separation, the waiting, the hungering, the consolation and release of reunion. Nine children had been born to them, and each had been welcomed with joy. Two had died, and together the father and mother had stood sorrowing beside their bodies. There was the echo of Cornelia's crutches to hold them together, their pride and delight in their boys' brilliance and in Anna Maria's grace and charm. If neither had completely found nor understood the needs of the other, if neither shared the other's innermost thoughts and dreams, if at their moments of deepest loneliness, of greatest tragedy, they were physically and spiritually alone, there was still much that Calhoun and Floride did share. Together, they built a life, a home, a marriage. They were often unhappy. Yet they had their moments of happiness. Their marriage was real, not a Victorian ideal. Probably they were as happy as most couples.

XXI

Years of Decision

IN MAY, 1837, eight weeks after Martin Van Buren took office as President, the financial bubble burst.

For Nicolas Biddle, the collapse was providential. Old Hickory was gone—in retirement at the Hermitage. To Mr. Biddle the panic offered 'an excellent opportunity . . . for securing his former prestige in the financial world.'[1]

So Jackson had killed the National Bank! He had by no means 'killed it dead.' For in March, 1836, one day before the federal charter had expired, America had learned that although 'dead,' the Bank had calmly refused to give up the ghost, 'refused to cease its operations . . . and continued . . . as if in full life.'[2] All that had had to be done was to transfer the notes of the 'defunct' institution to the Pennsylvania Bank of the United States, and to continue 'business as usual.' Mr. Biddle of Philadelphia was ideally situated to reopen his battle for control of the nation's monetary system, but two short months after that March morning when Van Buren had taken the Presidential oath, and the weeping thousands had cheered, not him, but his predecessor, a frail, stooped figure in black, lifting his cane in salute as he stood silent in the wind, his white hair blowing back from his face.

On the morning of May 10, 1837, a card was pinned on the door of a New York bank, reading simply, 'Closed until further notice.' By afternoon Philip Hone, watching the mobs 'swirling outside,' could hear the screams of the trampled women, the curses against Jackson and Van Buren.[3]

For a few days more the Southern banks continued in operation, although *Niles' Register* smelled conspiracy when the banks of Mobile and New Orleans ceased business, even before the arrival of the Northern newspapers![4] Last of all, the vault-like doors of the Greek temple on Chestnut Street closed—'the tomb of many fortunes,' mused Charles Dickens, five years afterward, looking up at the tall columns, ghostly in the moonlight.[5]

The Panic of 1837 was no slump of a year. It was the depression of an era. It was not national; it was world-wide. It was not the work of

Nicholas Biddle, who had suspended merely to protect his funds in the hope of later being invited to restore a sound currency. Nor was it the work of Andrew Jackson, who had heard the rumblings of the approaching storm as early as two years before. Acting by instinct, he had halted all credit sales of the public lands, stipulating in his famed 'Specie Circular' that only gold and silver be accepted in payment for public property. He was right—in principle. But by sucking gold and silver westward, where land sales had tripled from 1834–35, the 'Circular' had proved disastrous in practice.

The combination of wildcat banking and unrestrained wildcat efforts at federal control was too much. The Panic of 1837 climaxed the dizziest, fastest, richest boom era the young Republic had ever known. All over the nation banks had stretched their credit to the limit, passing out millions in paper 'shin-plasters.' To finance the new cotton mills and canals, the railroads and turnpikes, banks had been 'created as if by magic.' Loans were passed out to stockholders before even the capital was paid in. Fictitious deposits were added to the books to increase circulation. Paper dollars to silver were in the ratio of 20 to 1. Small wonder that suspicious British financiers called their loans, tightened credit, and started new specie runs on the hapless banks of America.

Even wilder were conditions in the South, where slaves, plantations, and machinery could all be bought on paper. In Mississippi one man was indebted to the banks for a million dollars! Often not a penny of real capital existed, 'beyond the small sums paid in by the unsuspecting depositors.' [6]

Speculation in government lands had become an orgy. The country was sown with 'plans of new . . . towns, drawings . . . in which every street was laid down and named, churches, theaters, etc.' [7] Men fought for lots in those visionary cities of prairie grass and marsh-muck, paid in notes from a bank, and sold them at a profit a month or two later to men who again paid for them on credit. [8]

First the boom, then the crash! Slowly the great flood moved across America. It was a year before it poured over the Southern back-country, but then through the South, the ruin was 'complete.' It engulfed the Mississippi Delta country, leaving a trail of empty plantation houses, barns, and granaries sagging into ruins, and crudely lettered signs flopping from trees, 'Gone to Texas.' It ravaged the country from New Orleans to Cincinnati, where hungry mobs smashed down doors, tore apart the furniture, looted the strong-boxes of banks and brokerage offices. [9] Eight hundred and fifty banks were closed; three hundred and forty-three never opened again.

The deflation was complete. Securities had become insecurities. Tobacco was worthless, cotton 'below calculation.' [10] Of the fortunes that were lost, of the great business houses that were ruined, the public heard—Nicholas

Biddle saw to that. Of the uncounted, unheeded thousands that suffered and starved and died, of the hopeless young men who wandered the streets seeking work, little was said. No relief came from the government. Free men, free to find or refuse work, did not expect it. It would violate the principles of Thomas Jefferson for the government to repair, by direct grants of money or legislation, losses not incurred in the public service.[11]

But theories filled no stomachs. Not only credit, but actual coin, had almost completely disappeared. Where? No one knew. It was 'systematically suppressed.'[12] Much was sucked into the big cities and sent overseas. Some was bought and sold 'like common merchandise.' Even the federal government bowed to Biddle's 'suspension' orders, unable to use its own gold and silver stored away in those 'closed' banks. It is true that Andrew Jackson had a brilliant idea, pertaining to the gold and silver in the Western land offices. This, the government could pay out to its creditors—and at least maintain prestige. He wrote to Van Buren, but unfortunately that gentleman had already announced that the government's obligations would be paid in paper—paper so far below the value of the debts that Benton foresaw the grim vision of a public debt, 'that horror . . . shame, and mortal test of governments.'[13]

But everyone was making money. Counterfeiting was the sport of the day. Democrats hammered stray bits of copper, brass, and iron into coins ornamented with taunting pictures of the 'whole hog'; Whigs coined tin tokens, engraved with likenesses of Jackson and Van Buren.

Semi-legal bank notes, varying from state to state and section to section, were now the 'sole currency of the country,' 'I O U's from the Treasury,' Captain Marryat called them. The British mariner found New York struggling along on a strange, barter-scrip basis: coins for a glass of brandy brought change in fifteen 'tickets' good for fifteen glasses of brandy. Change from a dinner in an oyster house was good only for more oysters.

'Do you want any oysters for lunch?' Marryat asked his barber.

'Yes.'

'Then here's a ticket and give me two shaves in return.'[14]

Burlesque notes announced themselves as 'the better currency.' A few even reached the Hermitage, taunting Jackson with such slurs as 'this is what you've brought the country to,' and, 'behold the effects of tampering with the currency.' The President's house was infested, polluted, with vulgar cartoons, for the American public, true to earlier and later custom, was convinced that whoever was in power at the time of a catastrophe was responsible. By the time the government pensioned off the old war veterans at a loss of ninety-five cents on the dollar, even loyal Tennessee was turning Whig; and the demand for the return of the United States Bank led Benton to comment dryly that the 'children of Israel were waiting for the fleshpots of Egypt.'[15]

Calhoun understood it. He had seen how far the public credit had been stretched, how the National Bank, by expanding and contracting the currency, by raising and depressing prices, could 'command the whole property and industry of the country.' The 'connection between Banks and Government,' he knew, was 'the source of immense profit to the Banks.' [16] But was it fair, was it just to lend out public funds to profit private individuals?

Now, at last, belatedly, with Jackson out of the picture, Calhoun could regard the question with a single eye. His personal record was clear. No I O U's to the Bank weighted his pockets. True, he had supported the Bank in 1816, but only because, if the government received bank notes as credit, it must have power to regulate their value. And although, a year or two before, he would have supported some kind of temporary bank to 'unbank the banks,' he knew that now the time for halfway measures was past. He was against 'the chartering of a United States Bank, or any connection with Biddles . . . in a word for a complete seperation from the whole concern.' [17]

Henry Clay's appeal for the Bank's revival he viewed with 'withering' scorn. 'The Senator says the country is in agony, crying for "Action, action." I understand where that cry comes from. It comes from . . . men who expect another expansion to relieve themselves at the expense of the government. "Action, action," means nothing but "Plunder! Plunder!" ' and I assure the Senator from Kentucky that he is not any more anxious in urging a system of plunder than I shall be in opposing it.' [18]

2

Visitors to Fort Hill in the summer of 1837 found Calhoun more abstracted than they had seen him in years, his brow furrowed and his face drawn with thought. He was completely uncommunicative. In neither letter nor conversation did he confide in anyone except a few intimates such as Pickens and Hammond. Yet, as Arthur Schlesinger, Jr., has pointed out, with the one possible exception of the Dred Scott case, Calhoun's thinking that summer was perhaps the most important decision reached by an American leader before the Civil War.

Upon it would rest the unity of poor white and planter, which made the Southern stand possible. From it can be traced the origin of the American political system, that strange alliance of city laborers and bosses and Southern agrarians, which was to characterize the Democratic Party for a hundred years. And in it is the test of Calhoun's statesmanship. South Carolina had driven him into nullification a decade before. Now it was he who drove the South where he was convinced it must go.

The scheme was gigantic. Only a dedicated mind could have conceived it. Only a cast-iron will could have carried it through. Single-handed and on his own authority, Calhoun determined to break down the alliance of Northern businessmen and Southern planters, and by union on the States' rights issue to throw the South *en masse* into the Democratic Party, the party of Jefferson—and of Andrew Jackson.

Involved was the defiance of fifty years of Southern history and of nearly three quarters of the Southern planting aristocracy. For the planters had inherited their Whiggery from Federalist ancestors, along with their Hepplewhite chairs and Chippendale tables. They loathed the Democrats. They had mistrusted Jefferson and hated Jackson. They had voted for Henry Clay, and tolerated Calhoun only because of his unflinching devotion to Southern institutions.

The crash had set Calhoun thinking. The interests of gentlemen in all sections, so the Whig leaders preached, were identical. Were they so? Already the South had paused to 'calculate the value of the Union'; now the time had come to 'calculate' the value of the Whig Party. Schlesinger has pointed up the question: Were the interests of the South, of the men who drew their livelihood from the soil, more endangered by the onrush of finance capitalism or by radical laboring democracy? [19]

Had the capitalistic alliance profited the planters of the South? Why, because of the stock-brokers' deflation in London and New York City, were 'rich' landholders in the Southern states without money even for postage stamps? Why had not a Southern bank paid out a dollar in silver or gold since the collapse of Biddle's 'monster'? [20] Why?

Cotton was king, said the Whig planters. Who had crowned that puppet king? London and New York, not Savannah and New Orleans, fixed the price of cotton on the world exchange. The planter sold low on London terms and bought high on the terms of the New York inspired tariff laws. Because of cotton and the tariff and the world bankers, it seemed to Calhoun, the whole South was going into debt.

Again, why?

Southern planters could not borrow on their crop futures from the small and overburdened banks of the South. They had to borrow from New York, which, in turn, borrowed from London, and London and New York both demanded that cotton be pledged as collateral. For the more cotton raised, the lower the price, and the higher the output and profits of the mills in Lowell and Lancashire. Cotton was king. Two million pounds a year in Washington's day; two billion a year by 1860. Cotton was king simply because the banks lent only to those who would grow cotton. Cotton and slavery were fixed upon the South. All else was 'ruthlessly destroyed.' [21]

This vicious cycle in itself would have been enough to convince Calhoun that Southern agriculture was becoming financially prostrated before Northern capitalism. But he saw more. New York dominated 'every phase of the cotton trade . . . from plantation to market.' And year by year new chapters would be added. Southern railroads, Southern mines, even slave-worked plantations, would be taken over by Northern creditors and controlled and managed by Northern capital. To Northern businessmen went forty cents out of every dollar paid for Southern cotton, DeBow asserted; and every profitable branch of the cotton industry—selling, banking, brokering, insurance, freight—all were 'enjoyed' in New York.[22]

Underneath this financial subjection of one great interest by another, Calhoun saw nothing less than the destruction of American political freedom. For he knew that the foundation of political freedom was economic self-sufficiency. A slaveless farmer could be free were he able to raise sufficient food for his own livelihood. But a planter, drowned in cotton, dependent upon the goodwill of his New York banker, could scarcely afford to offend his partner by differing from him politically.

It added up.

Calhoun saw the conflict as Jefferson had seen it, not between the propertied and the propertyless, but between capital built on inflated public paper and bank stock and capital in the agrarian tradition, resting either on individual ownership of the means of production or of the land. Between the two was no common ground. And the 'terrible giant' that would strangle landownership and machine operatives alike was finance capitalism.

As early as 1834, Calhoun had voiced his forebodings. Industry could be productive only as the workers shared in the profits of production. 'Capitalism,' he declared, sought 'to destroy and absorb the property of society. . . . The capitalist owns the instruments of labor, and he seeks to draw out of labor all the profits, leaving the laborer to shift for himself in age and disease.'[23] Was freedom possible where one man was dependent upon another for his livelihood? In the South, all white men, from the swamp squatter to the cotton snob, had at least a mutuality of interest. But in the North, with master and man pitted against each other in a contest for survival, inevitable inequalities, both economic and social, were wrecking the democratic program.[24] And now, what by tradition the capitalist had done to his operative, he was preparing to do to his rival.

The missing pieces were slipping into the puzzle. Certainly the monetary question was as dangerous if not more dangerous than abolition. 'More dangerous than church and state,' Calhoun had termed the union of the banking and the political powers; but only now did he see the picture in its entirety. From this one evil, as he saw it, flowed all the rest. He said, 'the revenue is the State, and those who control the revenue control the State.' Openly, Henry Clay had avowed that the question of the Bank involved 'the disunion of the States themselves.' If so, if the Bank was indispensable to the government, then, indeed, it was stronger than the government. Could 'that favor equality,' wondered Calhoun, 'which gives to one portion of the citizens and the country, such decided advantages over the other?'

Through a national debt and 'loans to Congressmen,' the banking power would have 'a vested interest in the United States of America.' From there on, the program was automatic. Northern business interests—indifferent to minority protests—would control Congress in the name of the Whig Party.

The end, Calhoun concluded, would be the destruction of the American federal system; for States' rights presented irresistible checks to the 'progress' of industrial capitalism. Unwilling to tolerate such frustration of their will, the industrial interests would see to it that there would be a 'government of the absolute majority, which would destroy our system and destroy the South.' [25] The cotton states would have a choice: consolidation or disunion; to the great American experiment, the end would be the same.

This, then, was the question. Would the federal government remain federal? Or would it be taken over by the powers of finance capitalism? The industrial revolution that was transforming America from a rural to an urban society could neither be reversed nor checked. Could it be controlled? Or would the South be an accessory to her own destruction? The sides were lining up—for battle over the body of American democracy.

The Northern program was clear. Primarily, Webster's teachings, discrediting the once generally accepted 'right' of secession, must be drummed into a holy cause. Even as an equal in the Union, the South proved, as Calhoun aptly pointed out, a constant 'conservative check.' Seceded, free to set her own terms, her position would be intolerable to the North. As Myndert Van Schaick, a leading New York merchant and one-time anti-slavery leader, put it: the 'dissolution of the Union would transfer some of our best customers to another market.' Thus, it was absolutely essential to both 'the English money-lender and to his New York jackel that the Union should be preserved.' [26]

It is fantastic to assume, as have some Southern extremists, that the North actually plotted to push the South into secession—thus to insure her conquest and subjugation. War and secession would destroy one of the best markets Northern business had. As Calhoun pointed out with increasing potency during the years, cotton capitalism and finance capitalism, rivals though they were, were at the same time indispensable to each other. And indispensable to both was the preservation of slavery.

Calhoun sensed this last, although he did not fathom its details. For business leaders during most of Calhoun's lifetime were violently opposed to slavery. They had been 'foremost' against its expansion since Missouri Compromise days. They had denounced the representative principle in the Constitution, which counted each slave as three-fifths of a voter. They would term the Texas annexation a 'crowning curse,' with nearly 'every important merchant in New York' joining in a mass meeting calling for 'No annexation of Texas' unless there be 'proper guards against slavery.' [27]

Yet in the four-year period prior to 1850, they indulged in as strange a reversal of political practice and moral principle as is to be found in all American history. The Wilmot Proviso of 1846—with its unequivocating demand that the Missouri Compromise be dropped and slavery forbidden in all territories west of the Rio Grande—worked the right-about-face. Northern business had no intention of losing its Southern market. And the fury over the Proviso measure would show how near secession an aroused and united South might go if pushed to the wall on the slavery question.

But this was only half the story. For the hideous truth is that not Charleston, not Savannah, no Southern port, but New York City itself, became 'the greatest slave-trading mart in the world.' [28]

The illegal slave-trading merchants were the successful merchants. It was they who reaped profits of $175,000 in a single voyage; and the New York business houses that supplied the capital. New York builders launched the ships—one hundred in six months alone. 'The trade' revitalized the New York shipping industry—became 'almost a recognized branch of business.'

Southerners like Calhoun might plead for enforcement of the anti-slave-trade laws. Alexander H. Stephens would wonder if the trade, outlawed by an outraged public opinion since the turn of the century, should not be legalized and restored, as the only possible means of controlling the pitiless horrors of the 'bootleg' slave-trading vessels. And twenty years after this period, Senator William H. Seward of New York, striving hopelessly to tighten the anti-slave laws, admitted that the unconquerable pressure against him came, 'not so much from the Slave States as from the Commercial interests of New York.' [29]

Calhoun was no man to underestimate the humanitarian appeal of the slave question. But he knew equally well that Northern business would support slavery, so long as slavery profited Northern business. The 'great and crucial' point, as he had seen ten years before, was 'the industry of the country.' If the South would sacrifice its patriotism to slavery, so would the North sacrifice its principles to business—this Calhoun understood perfectly. From the Northern moral viewpoint, slavery was 'a great wrong.' But business had 'become adjusted to it . . . millions and millions of dollars . . . would be jeopardised by any rupture between the North and the South.' Abolition, or Southern secession to prevent abolition, would cost the businessman of the North the mighty profits which he gleaned from the slave labor of the South. The North could not 'afford' to let the abolitionists overthrow slavery.[30]

And Northern business had the press, and the power, and the politicians to turn public opinion against abolitionism—thus reasoned Calhoun. Convinced as he was that abolitionism would rend apart the Union he loved, he shrank at no means to avert the disaster. Would the North sit by and watch the South 'destroy a business system which had been built up over so many years'? Aggressions were not to be met by compromises. They could be withstood only by counter-attacks, by an appeal to the cupidity in the heart of man.

If the North could be made to see her own self-interest threatened, then she would back down. Not principles, but profits, Calhoun reasoned, were the keystone to Northern policy. The threat of secession was the South's weapon. If Northern leaders permitted unchecked abolitionist agitation to threaten Southern institutions and Southern prosperity, then the South could equally threaten Northern institutions and Northern prosperity.

Unfortunately, the Southern leaders could not resist flourishing their weapons. 'We join with Northern labor in its resistance to Northern capital,' boasted Francis Pickens. Even more dangerous to the South was Pickens's and Hammond's threat to expose the 'white slaves of the North' by circulating among them, abolitionist style, incendiary pamphlets on the power of the ballot box, and the ways and means by which labor could combine and overthrow its masters. 'When gentlemen preach insurrection to the slaves,' trumpeted Pickens, 'I warn them . . . that I will preach . . . insurrection to the laborers of the North.' Added Hammond, 'Our slaves are hired for life . . . there is no starvation, no begging, no want of employment. . . . Yours are hired by the day and scantily compensated.' [31]

The Northern challenge had been accepted, the Southern challenge thrown down. Calhoun had mapped his program—mapped it on political lines. The union of Whig planters and Whig businessmen must be ended and the South united in a single party—and not just as the junior partner of the North. For only a united South could compel a reckoning.

3

The stand that Calhoun had taken required a degree of moral courage, no less than the physical courage he had displayed five years before. It was not enough to defy the power—political, financial, social—of the entire North; he was now at war with the entire Whig planting hierarchy. Even McDuffie was appealing to the 'wealth and intelligence' of the North for friendship and protection. Thomas Cooper, in constant touch with Biddle, was beating the drums in Charleston, where a speaker was booed down who had declared labor to be 'the only True Source of Wealth.' [32]

Most painful of all to Calhoun personally was the possibility, as a friend warned him, that even his own state might desert him. He faced it characteristically. 'I never know what South Carolina thinks of a measure. I never

CALHOUN IN MIDDLE AGE

From the portrait by G. P. A. Healy in the Museum of Fine
Arts, Richmond, Virginia. *Photograph by the Metropolitan
Museum of Art*

consult her. I act to the best of my judgment and according to my conscience. If she approves, well and good. If she does not, or wishes anyone
else to take my place, I am ready to vacate.' And he said: 'Democracy, as
I understand it and accept it, requires me to sacrifice myself *for* the masses,
not *to* them. Who knows not that if you would save the people, you must
often oppose them?' [33]

Only ghosts walked with Calhoun at Fort Hill in that summer of 1837,
ghosts of Jefferson, of John Taylor, and James Madison, who at eighty-six
had sensed the 'permanent incompatibility of interest between the North
and the South,' which might 'put it in the power of popular leaders, to unite
the South on some critical occasion.' [34]

The occasion had arrived.

Calhoun's stand was not wholly selfless. He was still in his prime, only
fifty-five, and ambition still strong within him. So low had his political
fortunes ebbed during nullification that any open discussion of his Presidential aspirations would have seemed ridiculous. Yet he still had hope, in
a politically united South and a South united to laboring or Western
allies. Consciously, he would not let himself think about the matter; and
when weary, often voiced his hopes that permanent retirement would not
be far off. 'Agriculture,' he wrote wistfully, 'is a delightful pursuit.' [35]

Nevertheless, jealous Whig leaders would confuse his undeniable ambitions with the equally undeniable dangers that confronted Southerners
of all political faiths. Calhoun's coldly realistic, fine-spun thinking was too
subtle for the booted and spurred 'cotton snobs' riding the crest of the
romantic, white-columned, land-poor 'Deep South.' Nor could they have
accepted his doctrines had they understood them, for they knew who held
their purse strings. Not until the eighteen-fifties would they unite, realizing,
too late, that Calhoun had all along known where their power lay.

Unpleasant realities loomed before Calhoun as he arrived in Washington
for the Special Session of the Twenty-Fifth Congress, called by Van Buren
for September 4, 1837, to take action on the financial crisis. The stand he
had chosen meant pocketing his pride, more painful than any other surrender to a man of his proud temperament. It meant doing what he had
not had strength to do with Jackson, allying himself with Martin Van
Buren, whom he hated more than he had ever hated Jackson; for whom,
moreover, he felt a searing contempt. It meant steeling himself against the
taunts of men like David Campbell, who wrote that 'so reckless a game'
as Calhoun's could 'lead to nothing but hopes of reward—probably the
Presidency.' [36] Most of all, it meant being misunderstood; but he was used
to that, and prepared for it. He had made his decision alone. He came back
to Washington to fight it out—alone.

4

During the summer, while Calhoun had been reaching his decisions at home, the panic was running its course. By September, Van Buren was faced with an empty Treasury and a monetary situation shrieking for action. The Whigs and Nicholas Biddle were moving in for the kill. All of Andrew Jackson's war on the Bank, they gloated, all of Biddle's apparent defeat, had borne this fruit of depression; and the people, suffering but unable to understand the complexities of finance, were ready to return to the Bank system.

Van Buren's answer was quite the reverse. Unmoved by abuse, unswayed by demands for either relief or retreat, the realistic little Dutchman stolidly prepared to correct the underlying causes of the *débâcle*.

Jackson's lieutenant could hardly return to the system in the downfall of which he himself had played so large a part. Not a recharter of the Bank, but a complete 'divorce' between the government and banks was what Van Buren requested in his message to the Special Session. Drained by the panic, only six state banks were still paying specie by the fall of 1837. As no government funds could be deposited in non-specie-paying banks, the 'Sub-Treasury' system had been established *de facto*. Now Van Buren requested the legalization and official establishment of the system— the final divorce of government and the 'money power' which Calhoun had decided was essential.

5

So closely had Calhoun guarded his decision that H. L. Hopkins wrote Rives as late as September 11, 1837, that a rumor that Calhoun would support Van Buren's Sub-Treasury Bill 'has caused much anxiety among the Whigs. They cannot believe it, nor can I.' [37] But when the worst was known, and Calhoun on October 3 voiced his support of Van Buren's plan, B. W. Leigh summed up for the chagrined Whigs with the comment that now 'one ought not perhaps to be surprised at anything he may do.' [38]

'He has destroyed himself,' confidently announced one observer, laboring under the belief that his hopes and the facts were synonymous.

'He has thrown himself under a falling party, and will be crushed beneath it.'

'His State will sustain him.'

'Never. He is the victim of blasted ambition, and will never rise again.' [39]

From far-off Charleston, Thomas Cooper sent assurances to the dark man with the classic face in the Greek temple at Philadelphia. 'I am giving you what leading . . . men . . . say. Calhoun is rather borne with than supported. He has talent, but without tact or judgement.' Even McDuffie would 'go with us . . . if it were not for personal regard to Mr. Calhoun.' [40]

Congress was in an uproar. Feverishly Biddle moved 'to instruct the Senate'; to goad Webster and to whip Clay into a filibuster. Actually the whole Sub-Treasury system had been functioning for months 'without causing the slightest disturbance.' [41] None of the evils forecast had occurred—or did occur. But if Calhoun, as charged, had supported the Sub-Treasury as an attempt to weaken Northern business interests, Biddle himself had acknowledged the fact of his grip upon the national economy. 'This insane Sub-treasury scheme,' wrote 'Emperor' Biddle, 'is urged forward to break down all the great interests of the country.' [42]

But Calhoun was not beaten. Actually he had more support than he knew. Even Benton agreed with him that the accumulation of funds in the North 'had enabled that section to . . . make the South tributary . . . for a small part of the fruits of their own labor.' And from the Hermitage bitter Andrew Jackson, railing at the 'combined money power of the aristocracy,' could say, 'I am happy . . . Mr. Calhoun got right. . . . I'll not throw the least shade over him. To err is human, to forgive, divine.' [43]

'My means of control,' Calhoun wrote, near this period, 'is to march directly forward, fearless of consequences . . . to develope our doctrines . . . with the intention of forcing them on those, with whom I act, by controlling publick sentiment.' No ordinary politician's method this, yet, to the astonishment of friend and foe, with virtually the 'whole delegation of South Carolina . . . against the Sub-Treasury Bill,' Calhoun's plan worked.[44]

There was no rest for him in his brief vacation between sessions. He had no time to dream in the lazy, grape-scented air, to watch the blue haze curl around the foothills; or, soft-stepping behind his dogs, hear the whirr of the partridge wings as the birds flashed up from the underbrush. There were too many men to persuade and cajole, crowds pushing in on him, day and night, so that in Columbia on his return trip he sat up past one o'clock to write to Anna Maria.[45]

He had gauged public sentiment accurately. Within twelve months even the most chagrined of Whigs was compelled to admit Calhoun's 'powerful agency in bringing about the present success in some parts of the country.' [46] Watching in silent dismay, not unmixed with wonder, Daniel Webster reported defeat to Biddle. 'Calhoun is moving heaven, earth, etc., to obtain Southern votes for the measure. He labors to convince his Southern neighbors that its success will relieve them from their economic dependence on the North. His plausible and endless persuasion . . . and the power and patronage of the Executive have accomplished more than I thought possible.' Even more remarkable was the public patience, for as to the immediate financial emergency neither Calhoun nor Van Buren had comfort to offer. 'We have had the pleasure of getting drunk,' remarked the South Carolinian, 'and now experience the pain of becoming sober.' [47]

6

He was laboring to his utmost, physically and mentally. He was living in a sort of vacuum of hard work in which the clamor of Washington society sounded in his ears like far-off echoes. What pleasures he had were vicarious. 'I was quite refreshed, my dear Anna,' he wrote, 'with the account you gave me of the . . . wedding parties and gay hours which you have spent. . . . My life for the last month . . . has been one of incessant toil and labour, without relaxation or amusement of any description whatever. I held the fate of the country, by the confession of all, in my hand, and had to determine in what direction I should turn events hereafter. . . . I can say nothing about the gayety of Washington.' [48]

In Congress, however, Calhoun was meeting the sheer fury of Henry Clay. Clay had a right to be angry. Here was Van Buren, his Administration shattered. Here was the Senate, almost equally divided, with Calhoun's following holding the balance of power. And now, at the moment of Clay's greatest triumph, when Biddle seemed about to deliver a staggering blow to the reeling body of Jacksonism, here was Calhoun, the traitor, swinging his forces over to Van Buren's side! The Whigs had saved Calhoun in his own disaster; now he had turned their triumph into defeat. Would Henry Clay sit by? He would not.

Had Clay better understood his erstwhile friend he might have realized that in Calhoun, when personal and political loyalties conflicted, there was no question as to where his duty lay. He would have been forced to admit that Calhoun never pledged himself to the Whig cause. On the contrary, more than once, he had arisen in the Senate to declare: 'I stand utterly disconnected with either one of the great parties now striving for power.' [49] Time and again he had refused to declare himself a Whig, pledged himself only to support any group that accorded with his constitutional views. 'We are determined to preserve our seperate existence,' he had told Pickens in 1834. 'Our position is strong. No measure can be taken but with our assent, where the administration and the opposition parties come into conflict.' [50]

But Clay wasted no time in thinking. In January and February of 1838, his frenzy burst all bounds. He charged into Calhoun with a ruthlessness that appalled even the most hardened of Senatorial observers. 'Turncoat,' was the mildest of the epithets he flung at him. He taunted him with the friends he had lost and the company he kept. He sneered at the 'metaphysical' subtleties of the Calhoun mind; 'too much genius and too little common-sense.' He raked up all Calhoun's somersets and delinquencies: the tariff, the National Bank, internal improvements, not missing one, from 1815 on. And with it all he brought into play his matchless oratorical equipment, the grace of his long, swaying body, the music of his voice, the wit, the ridicule, all the weapons that he employed so skillfully, and that Calhoun possessed not at all.[51]

It was a great show. It was perhaps too good a show. It was merciless. Spectators gasped at Clay's power, but it was Calhoun, silent and unbending, to whom they gave their sympathy. They looked at him with wonder. What was he thinking? Clay's thrusts had hurt him; only *he* knew how deeply. His pride was too touchy, his feelings too intense to bear this attack without pain. And he knew that he was no match for Clay's double-edged repartee, his one, two, and into your vitals, with six wounds bleeding before you could marshal your forces for a single blow. So, when the long-drawn tension of it was over and the Senate stirred, then silenced to hear Calhoun's reply, the Carolinian would not speak . . . not now. He would give Clay as 'good as he sent,' but not for a few days.

On March 10, Calhoun took the floor. It was a high occasion that confronted him and he felt it keenly. Not since 1833 had he so girded himself for an effort. He was fully, perhaps overly, convinced that he was defending himself, not only before the Senate, but before the bar of history.

No one could have been a greater contrast to Clay. He was, as he had always been, 'dignified, restrained, with no effort at display.' Even Benton congratulated him on his high plane of speaking, writing afterward that the address was 'profoundly meditated . . . the style . . . terse, the logic close; the sarcasm cutting. . . . It was . . . masterly.' [52]

Step by step he countered Clay's charges. If he had sired the original National Bank, had he not in 1816 opposed a 'far more dangerous bank,' recommended by Alexander Dallas, founded entirely upon United States stocks, and 'lending our credit to the bank for nothing, and borrowing it back at six per cent'?

He would scorn to denounce a man on account of his intellect, 'the immediate gift of our creator.' He could not accuse Clay of possessing those 'powers of analysis and generalization . . . (called metaphysical by those who do not possess them) which . . . resolve into their elements . . . masses of ideas. . . . The absence of these higher qualities is conspicuous throughout the whole course of the Senator's public life . . . we ever find him mounted on some popular . . . measure which he whips along, cheered by the shouts of the multitude. . . . To the defects of understanding which the Senator attributes to me, I make no reply. . . .

'Instead of leaving not a hair on the head of my arguments, as the Senator threatens . . . he has not even attempted to answer a large portion.' Nor did he 'restrict himself to a reply. . . . He introduced personal remarks. . . . I addressed myself, when I was last up, directly and exclusively to the understanding, carefully avoiding every remark which had the least personal or party bearing. In proof of this, I appeal to you, Senators. . . . But it seemed that no caution on my part could prevent what I was so anxious to avoid. . . . I shall be compelled to speak of myself.' [53]

Suddenly Calhoun's long-constrained passions broke loose. Before a Senate, transfixed with surprise, he stood, every muscle tensed, his forehead wet, his eyes 'flashed lightning.' He had a high stake to plead for, his own reputation; and he pled now in a 'burning flood of indignation,' such as men had not heard from him since the days of nullification.[54] Issue by issue, year by year, he picked up Clay's charges, and hurled them down again. He scorned to recognize as 'his friend' the 'Senator from Kentucky.' He scorned to notice the watered-down version of Clay's remarks, which on a belated second thought the Senator had prepared for the press. He would answer the words as Clay had spoken them.

'The Senator very charitably leaves it to time to disclose my motive for going over! I, who have changed no opinion, abandoned no principle, and deserted no party. The imputation sinks to the earth. . . . I stamp it with scorn in the dust. I hurl it back. What the Senator charges unjustly, he has *actually* done. He went over on a memorable occasion, and did not leave it to time to disclose his motive.' * [55]

The slur was too much for Clay. The battle was on again, day after day, charges and counter-charges, insults and sneers. The Senate was mortified, the galleries delighted, at this spectacle of two of America's greatest Senators, mauling and abusing each other. They rehashed the Compromise of 1833, Calhoun haughtily claiming that it was he who had dictated the terms, he who had 'gloried' in his own strength.

'The Senator from South Carolina was in any condition other than that of dictating terms,' snapped back Clay. 'Those of us who were here . . . recollect well his haggard looks and his anxious and depressed countenance.' He had been forced to yield on point after point. He was helpless. He had even been forced to compromise with 'the Senator from Missouri.'

Calhoun bridled. He shot Clay a look of hatred, so defiant, so wild, that to one observer, writing years afterward, it seemed as vivid as yesterday. 'I feel not the least gratitude towards him,' he declared. The Compromise was 'necessary to save the Senator, politically. Events had placed him flat on his back. . . . The Senator was flat on his back and couldn't move. I wrote more than half a dozen letters home . . . to that effect. *I* was his master. I repeat it, sir, *I* was his master. . . . He went to *my* school. He learned from *me*.'

Clay sprang to his feet. He charged toward Calhoun and men fell back from him as he ran. He brought himself up sharply before the rigid figure

* Reference to the 'bargain-corruption' story.

of the South Carolinian. He drew back. He shook his finger in Calhoun's face. '*He,* my master!' He drew back further, still pointing. '*He,* my master!' He drew back against the wall, arm outflung, voice acid with contempt. '*He,* my master!' and the silence quivered as his voice played across it. 'Sir, I would not own him as a slave!' [56]

7

Particularly infuriating to the Southerner, Henry Clay, were Calhoun's assumptions of Southern leadership. 'What right had the Senator to . . . speak for the whole South?' What right had he even to speak for the 'gallant little State of South Carolina?' Had not even his own colleagues deserted him? He was utterly, completely alone.

Calhoun's head lifted in pride. Yes, he had dared defy South Carolina 'for whom I feel a brother's love.' He had dared to stand alone, 'as the Senator sneeringly says.' But he had had his vindication, and it was from South Carolina herself. 'Resolved,' ran a resolution passed by the Legislature that winter of 1838, 'that this State has seen, with great satisfaction, the steady and consistent adherence of her Senator, John C. Calhoun, to the well-known, avowed, and mature principles of the State, and they accord to him their deliberate and strong approval.' Clay's and Preston's charges against Calhoun of 'going over to the enemy' were indeed 'awkward,' added the Charleston *Mercury,* 'since an immense majority of the people of South Carolina concur with Mr. Calhoun in his opinions as to the currency. . . . Accusations made against Mr. Calhoun apply also to the Legislature and people of the State.' [57]

So now, his voice broken with emotion, Calhoun could proudly say: 'I underestimated the intelligence and patriotism of my . . . noble State. I ask her pardon . . . that, in being prepared to sacrifice her confidence, as dear to me as light and life, rather than disobey the dictates of my judgment and conscience, I proved myself worthy of being her representative.'

Clay remained unmollified. But Calhoun wearied of the give-and-take, if the energetic Kentuckian did not. And it was Calhoun who at last 'pleasantly put an end to it by saying he saw the Senator from Kentucky was determined to have the last word, and he would yield it to him.' [58] Nevertheless, the final honors went to Calhoun. For the Sub-Treasury Bill became law, July 4, 1840, and, although repealed by the Whigs the following year, it was re-enacted in 1846.

8

Burdened though Calhoun was, he did not fail to write long and cheerful letters to Anna Maria. For Anna had been ill since her pregnancy, far more ill than she had dared let her father know, and inadvertently learning the facts, he was 'pained' at this 'mistaken state of feelings. . . . You need never fear, my dear,' he told her gently, 'that I would think you egotistical, should you speak ever so much of yourself. There is nothing that concerns you that is indifferent to me.'

Months dragged into a year, but Anna Maria did not recover. Encouragement, not warning, was the note in her father's letters now. 'Nature was always at work to repair derangements in our system,' and with her youth there was 'much to hope.' He longed to be home 'with you and to aid in keeping up your sperits. . . . These annual absences from those most dear to me are a great drawback which nothing but a deep sense of duty could make tolerable.'

He laid little stress on his political cares. He wrote of what he thought would interest and amuse her, of Lord Morpeth's visit, of his 'Mess,' of the 'sharp . . . clear' weather and the sleighs racing by in the white streets outside. Though 'exceedingly uneasy' about her, he struggled to hide his concern. He sent her his magazines, hoping that she might find something to amuse herself and to pass away the time. He had not read them. 'As highly, my dear . . . as I prize a letter from you,' he told her, 'I do not write this with the view of getting an answer. I know how fatiguing writing must be to you, and you must not think of writing me in reply.'

He wrote her of Charles Dickens, the dandified young Cockney, with his corkscrew curls and glittering rings, whom Washington Irving had dismissed as 'flash as a riverboat gambler.' But Calhoun thought him 'nothing in the slightest degree offensive.' He saw 'a good deal' of both Dickens and 'his lady,' for the Englishman had brought letters of introduction, and although Calhoun knew nothing of Dickens's writings and Dickens nothing of Calhoun's politics, the personal liking between the men was instantaneous.[59]

Of the social festivities of the capital, Calhoun could write little. His health was just adequate for the demands he made upon it; he had no surplus energy for late hours or the slightest irregularity in his living habits. 'I take good care of myself, exercise regularly when I can, and rarely go out in the evening,' he wrote his anxious family.

It was an age of heavy eating, heavy drinking, heavy dosing, and of almost complete disregard for hygienic living. Against this background Calhoun's Spartan régime seems surprisingly modern. He 'detested stimulants.' He scorned doctors or medicines. His addiction—when well past sixty—to three- or four-mile daily walks in the heat of a Washington August, and cold baths in January, astounded his sedentary colleagues, and does more credit to his zeal than to his common-sense; for tuberculosis had already made inroads upon his wiry frame. Early as 1834 he began writing home of the 'distressing' colds, 'accompanied by cough,' which were becoming 'usual' with him. Undoubtedly, his condition was aggravated by his mental agitation; modern psychologists would co-relate the 'dark forebodings' that so haunted his later years with the steady decline of his strength. Yet through his 'judicious dietetics . . . eating and drinking lightly,' [60] and regular hours of rest and sleep, he probably enjoyed better general health than more vigorous men who lived with less restraint.

He, who had been so strait-laced in youth, was now delighted that his boys were going to dancing school. Dancing, he commented, 'was almost indispensable . . . for the happiness . . . of the two sexes. . . . Tell James that he must not dispair of contracting graceful accomplishments. All he wants is to try.' In his brief vacations he grasped eagerly at the pleasures his Washington labors denied him. At an Abbeville party he looked with keen interest at 'a beautiful array of fine-looking fashionable girls, far more than I could have expected.' [61]

Calhoun has never received any undue share of credit for being a ladies' man. Certainly neither then nor later was he a *gallant*. He had a good Southern appreciation of a pretty face and a trim waistline, but there was none of Henry Clay's middle-aged romanticism about him. Yet a contemporary was amazed to find that 'in the company of ladies' this austere figure 'was one of the most interesting and charming men in the world.' [62]

Apparently the ladies thought so. Calhoun had always a strong attraction for women, especially witty, sparkling, intelligent women, like Mrs. Porter and Mrs. Margaret Bayard Smith, or his own mother-in-law. But with girls and young women there was a gentleness in his attitude that was most appealing; it was in such contrast to his iron and fire on the Senate floor. The father who could write with such tender understanding to his sick daughter could show as much interest in a girl's embroidery as in a statesman's politics. Jefferson Davis's young bride, Varina, would find him so fatherly and understanding that in their first five minutes of acquaintance, she was telling him how much she missed her mother! He had a gift for sensing the wishes of those around him and adapting his conversation to them 'with an exquisite tact and grace.' [63]

He took an interest in Angelica Singleton, a gay little belle, steeped in compliments, who being the youngest in the 'Mess' was confessedly 'a wee bit of a pet among them.' Henry Clay was seeking her avidly in marriage for his son, but it was the grave and graying South Carolinian who won her friendship. 'Mr. Calhoun,' she wrote, 'has been very kind to me.' [64]

For Calhoun kindness to Angelica was only an incident in an upheaval that shook Washington at this time, only less than the Sub-Treasury fight. Had John Calhoun sauntered into a Washington drawing room with Peggy O'Neil on his arm, eyebrows could have lifted no higher than at the report that he had called on President Van Buren.

Actually there was nothing else that he could have done. He was keenly aware of 'the awkwardness of defending the political measures . . . of one, with whom I was not on speaking terms.' But he had his full share of explaining to do, even to Anna Maria, who, alarmed at the risk to her father's standing, fully expressed her mind. Calhoun understood. 'So far from being offended, my dear daughter, the sentiments you have ex- pressed but elevate you, if possible, in my estimation.' It was the President with whom he had resumed relations, not 'Mr. Van Buren.' [65]

That he had somerseted at the beginning of a Presidential campaign added to the confusion. He was unswayed by the opinion of Duff Green that the election of William Henry Harrison would open 'the brightest prospects you have ever had.' He paid no heed to the Missourian's gibe that Van Buren would not receive a single vote, 'unless you are mad enough to give him the vote of South Carolina, but I cannot believe that you will commit suicide as this would be.' Mr. Green was soon to learn the truth of Calhoun's warning that, 'having defined my course . . . it is not in the power of man to divert me.' Not only did Calhoun and South Carolina, with their unfailing instinct for a lost cause, vote for Mr. Van Buren; but, although utterly 'retired from the world of fashion and amusement' and at grave risk to his health, Calhoun braved a blinding hailstorm to attend the last Presidential levee, 'a thing I would not have done in such weather, had not the incumbent been defeated.' Few shared Calhoun's quixotic gallantry, however, and at the White House not even the little 'tabby cat' footstools, 'gay with their covering of glazed white chintz and pink roses,' nor the old-fashioned bowls of roses scattered through the drawing room, could dispel the gloom. 'It was thinly attended,' noted Calhoun, 'and, I must say, dull.' Nor were there any refreshments, which he regarded 'as a great want of taste.' [66]

Van Buren's defeat in 1840 was no shock to Calhoun. It was inevitable. For in the first steam-rollered, high-pressure campaign in American history, the country *en masse* had given way to an orgy of trapped red foxes and running raccoons, of log cabins in every town and barrels of hard cider on every street corner. Rallies, twenty thousand strong, gorged on barbecue and cider roared:

> *'With Tip and Tyler,*
> *We'll bust Van's Biler.'*

> *'Ole Tip, he wears a homespun shirt,*
> *He has no ruffled shirt, wirt wirt.*
> *But Matt, he has the golden plate,*
> *And he's a little squirt—wirt, wirt.'*

Calhoun, who had charged Van Buren with no more than being a sneak and 'a weasel,' learned now that his old enemy ate from golden plates, perfumed his whiskers, stuffed his pouter-pigeon form into boned corsets, and wore the carpet bare before mirrors where he surveyed his masculine charms. Under the magic of campaign song and story, even poor old William Henry Harrison, the Virginia aristocrat, was transformed into a cider-guzzling, buckskinned fugitive from the frontier. If the Democrats had their 'hero of New Orleans,' the Whigs had their hero of Tippecanoe, 'and Tyler, too,' the brilliant, horse-faced Virginian, put on the ticket to wean the Jackson-Calhoun forces from the ranks of the Democracy. And for the final onslaught, Daniel Webster 'profaned' the sacred soil of Virginia, weeping loudly that he had not been born in a log cabin! [67]

Even 'the ladies' armed themselves for war, in a display of 'Sub-Treasury brooches,' each cameo adorned with a little strong-box and a tiny blood-hound, chained to the huge locks. 'Mr. Van Buren,' so 'the fair' had explained eagerly, 'wants to set these dogs on your family.' [68]

Having gone through the scurrilities of the Jackson campaign, Calhoun had few illusions as to the ways and means by which popular sovereignty selects its leaders. Yet the horseplay of 'Tippecanoe and Tyler, too,' was enough to shock even him. What lay behind it all?

He might have been enlightened had he glanced at the files of Nicholas Biddle's correspondence. 'Let him' (Harrison), so spake the High Command, 'say not one single word about his principles—let him say nothing. . . . Let no . . . convention—no Town Meeting ever extract from him a single word about what he thinks now, or will do hereafter. Let the use of pen and ink be wholly forbidden.' * [69]

He might have said as much for brain power. America had no time for thinking in those gorgeous and gaudy weeks. The High Command was doing the thinking. The American public was jumping through the hoops.

9

In February, 1841, Harrison, followed by a large and steadily increasing army—this time of office-seekers—arrived in Washington. Calhoun called, and although embarrassed by the President-elect's familiar greeting, 'as if

---

* This directive, actually issued for the 1836 campaign, in which Harrison was defeated, was used to better effect in 1840.

we had been old cronies,' he was struck with how frail and dependent the old man seemed. 'As unconscious as a child of his difficulties and those of his country, he seems to enjoy his election as a mere affair for personal vanity,' Calhoun wrote Anna Maria. 'It is really distressing to see him.'

A day or two later, in his Senate seat, Calhoun felt a tap on his shoulder. He swung around, and 'low and behold it was the President-elect.' Keenly aware of the 'awkwardness of the situation,' Calhoun, with the eyes of the entire Senate fixed upon him, rose and led the way to the lobby, where he was rescued from 'the most familiar kind of conversation . . . by others coming up. I have given . . . this little incident as characteristic. . . . the only hope is that he may be perfectly passive and leave it to the strongest to take control.' [70]

Calhoun was left no time to reflect on who 'the strongest' might be. Within twenty-four hours after Harrison's inaugural, all Washington was laughing over the picture of Daniel Webster, flung on a sofa, exhausted from the labor of killing twelve Roman Pro-Consuls 'dead as smelts' in the inaugural which he had rewritten for Harrison. In the Senate the cock of Kentucky was crowing over his flock as if it were he, and not Harrison, who had been elected President of the United States.

Calhoun watched him warily. Forces of history were swaying them, but it was man against man still: Calhoun, 'in the full glory of his intellectual magnificence,' Clay, in the pride of his political power, but 'restive as a caged lion.' [71]

It was the tariff on which they warred again, still Calhoun knew, 'the most vital of all questions.' Though the problem had been pushed into the background for the past few years, Calhoun was still on guard against the plans of those to whom a high tariff was the very foundation-stone of the 'American system.' Both the argument and the facts were unaltered. Industry still was protected, while cotton, rice, and tobacco were thrown on the market of the world, 'that other branches should have a monopoly at home.' Could not men see that in granting the government power to reward one interest and deny another, they were giving it 'unlimited power over all the . . . business of the country'?

Yet he dismissed suggestions from Benton and Wright that the tax might be reduced on salt, iron, hemp, and lead. To detach items from the whole list would still benefit one industry at the expense of another. If salt were exempted, some other article would bear the additional costs. If the taxes were to be taken off one, they must be taken off all.

He was not for the ruin of the manufacturers. 'There is no one,' he asserted, 'who puts a higher estimate on those arts, mechanical and chemical, by which matter is subjected to the dominion of mind. I regard them as the very basis of civilization, and the principle designed by Providence for the future progress and improvement of the race.' And if he sought justice for the interest he represented, he would be 'ashamed to stand by and see injustice done any other. . . . We cannot, after disregarding the interests of others . . . insist that they shall respect ours.' [72]

But these were mere preliminary skirmishes for the great battle of 1842. For Henry Clay, 'true to his secret, but false to his public, pledges,' had revealed that the compromise tariff of 1833, once thought to be permanent, had only been intended to last seven years! In the new, so-called 'Loan Bill,' Calhoun detected a variation of an old theme. 'They dare not go directly for protection,' he wrote. Instead, they resorted to 'every means to raise the expenditures and to cut off the revenues,' to 'prostrate public credit,' through sheer 'looseness and waste,' artificially to create a need for the tariff 'they could not openly obtain.' The selfishness of the scheme sickened Calhoun, yet he had no illusion of reform. Only too well did he know 'how vain it is to urge arguments against the fixed determination of a party.' [73]

But he would not surrender without argument. Obtaining the floor on March 16, 1842, he smote the crux of Clay's contentions in his first sentences. The betrayal, he declared, was complete. The Loan Bill would 'entirely supersede the Compromise Act.' In theory, he pointed out, the gentleman from Kentucky's resolutions respected every provision of the Compromise of 1833—and in practice violated every one of them! [74]

Even in the heat of her battle, he reminded the Senate, South Carolina had granted six or seven years for gradual reduction, solely to avoid 'ruinous losses' to the manufacturing interests. Now these same interests have 'turned on us.' Overnight, duties were now to be raised thirty per cent, a move justifiable only if government expenditures were raised in the same ratio, and if these expenditures were necessary. 'It must be shown that all possible economy has been done.'

As a high-tariff man, the Senator from Kentucky believed free trade to be among 'the greatest curses' that could befall the country. But had the free-trade experiment failed? Had it drained the country of its resources and energies? Calhoun did not believe it. In the tentative free-trade experiment just completed, what were the facts? Calhoun supplied them. American exports up sixty per cent. Lowell cotton manufactures up twenty-five per cent in a single year. Fifty per cent more in American raw materials were being purchased by American manufacturers; in eight years a double amount of cotton had been shipped into Boston Harbor alone. Yes, 'the great staple interest of the South and the great manufacturing interest of the North may be reconciled.'

Importation of foreign cotton goods, conversely, had dropped fifty per cent in a single year. Yet the cotton manufacturing interests were flooding Congress with petitions for high tariffs. Why? The more duties were lowered, the cheaper the cost of production at home, the larger the market abroad. Tobacco exports? Up forty-three per cent.*

True, all acknowledged the great poverty and 'distress in the Southern regions.' Clay could attribute it to the low tariff, but for Calhoun it was the result of the indebtedness of 'the States, Corporations, and Industry, and the sudden liquidation of . . . currency.' The nation had speculated and lost, but distressed as the South was, cotton was as high as in 1831, and the planters when hard-pressed could furnish themselves with almost all of their physical needs. Nothing was more ridiculous than to blame the national depression on the low tariff.

Free trade, Calhoun concluded, had its foundation in truth itself. Not only did it increase American prosperity. It held the nations together 'in concord.' Severe penalties would follow a departure 'from its laws.'

The debate dragged on through the heat of the summer of 1842, and in spite of Calhoun's vigilance, the Loan Bill was passed. It was a disillusioned and despairing man who spoke the final word. This, he declared, was worse than 1828—worse because it violated the pledge of Henry Clay 'that if we of the South would adhere to the Compromise while it was operating favorably to the manufacturing interests, they would stand by us when it came to operate favorably to us.' During eight years of reduction, 'an extraordinary impulse had been given to every branch of industry—agricultural, commercial, navigating, manufacturing.' Without foreign trade we would have an oversupply of manufactured products for our own country, and our labor would be unemployed. The manufacturers were not alone to blame; the parasitic aspirants for government jobs would support any means to keep the Treasury full—and themselves on the payroll.

The articles for which manufactured goods were exchanged, Calhoun noted, bore light duties; and the articles for which agricultural products were exported bore high duties. For every dollar that went into the Treasury, three went to the manufacturers. The more industry was protected, the more protection was requested.

Rufus Choate retorted that the New England mill-owners were dependent for their very existence on the Loan Bill.

'Is such a state of dependence on . . . Government' consistent with freedom? queried Calhoun. On this issue, he concluded, 'there can be no repose.' [75]

Despite his momentary triumph, Henry Clay was beaten, and he knew it. Destiny had ruled him out on that rain-streaked March day one month after the inaugural of 1841 when the weary Harrison had died, murmuring: 'These applications—will they never cease?' [76] Tyler, the nullifier;

---

* As in the slavery chapter, Calhoun's speeches here are again consolidated without reference to chronology, in order to show his state of mind on certain issues.

Tyler, the states' rights Democrat; the low-tariff man whom Fate had hoisted into the leadership of a Whig Administration—John Tyler was President of the United States.

10

Stripped now of all other power, Clay could still make mischief. He mocked at Calhoun: 'There stood the Senator from South Carolina, tall, careworn, with furrowed brow, haggard cheek, and eye intensely gazing . . .' Calhoun, painfully embarrassed, broke in with a sharp call to order, but the irrepressible Kentuckian went on: 'Looking as if he were dissecting the last and newest abstraction which sprang from some metaphysician's brain, and muttering to himself: "This is indeed a crisis."' The Senate roared as Clay turned his battery on Benton, whom he described as looking 'at the Senator from South Carolina with an indignant curl on his lips and scorn in his eye, and points his finger with contempt, saying: "He calls himself a statesman! Why, he has never produced a decent humbug!"'

Clay wearied of his sport. He could foresee no future for himself in the Senate. So on the last day of March, 1842, he arose to say farewell. He was an old man now, 'a gone coon.' His frail figure drooped. His thin hair was white. The voice, once so vibrant, so bell-like, was low and weary. All mockery, all satire, all bitterness, was gone. To all who had wronged him, he offered his forgiveness. And if in the heat of his youth, in his high passions, he had hurt others, could they not forgive him now?

It was play-acting, of course, but great play-acting. And it was Calhoun, who in six tense years had not even spoken to Henry Clay, who 'gave way,' and stood up, 'the tears running down his face.' As the Senate stared, he crossed the Chamber and held out his hand. The two old friends embraced, only Benton remaining unmoved, showing 'no more emotion,' Parmalee declared, 'than if he had been made of cast-iron.' [77]

'I don't like Henry Clay,' Calhoun said, afterward. 'He's a bad man, an impostor, a creator of wicked schemes. I wouldn't speak to him, but, by God, I love him.' [78] The remark is as revealing of Calhoun as of Clay, of Calhoun's continual conflict between Scotch reason and Irish emotions. Mentally, he disapproved of Henry Clay, but emotionally, he could not withstand him.

11

A few months later, Calhoun himself quietly bowed out of the Senate. Like Clay, he made no secret of his longing for rest and retirement; unlike Clay, he made no attempt to conceal the secret that all America

knew—that both men had retired for the same purpose. Both were awaiting THE CALL. As Calhoun put it: 'It now remains' for the people of
the United States 'to determine how long [I] shall continue in retirement.' [79]

His need for rest was genuine. The strain of the last two summers, six
or seven hours a day in the 'breathless' heat of the Senate Chamber, plus
the hours of study and committee work outside, the mass of visitors and
the weight of correspondence, overwhelmed him under the 'heavy and
exhausting work.' Never had his letters shown such longing to 'be quiet,'
to be 'released,' to be home.

Strategically the moment had come for him to retreat with the honors
of victory. As a Senator, his work was done. With Tyler in the White
House, victory had been raked from defeat. Calhoun saw his one goal, to
restore the old 'State rights Republican doctrines' nearer than he had
dared hope. The tariff still threatened; but the program of Tyler, the retirement of Clay, and his own hopes that in the Executive department he
might bring his full program to fruition, had done much to reinvigorate
his faith in American democracy.

Although he spoke for the America of the past, for the ideal, rather than
the practical, new hope edged his words. 'I am a conservative,' he boasted;
yet there were moments when he was the Calhoun of earlier days. 'I
solemnly believe,' he said, 'that our political system is, in its purity, not
only the best that was ever formed, but the best possible that can be devised for us.' [80]

12

No one but a madman—or Duff Green—would have dreamed of running
Calhoun for the Presidency in 1844. For after the break with Jackson,
Calhoun must have known, even if he later momentarily forgot it, that he
'could never be President.' But his friends were his worst enemies. Unfortunately for his peace, Calhoun inspired in them a loyalty which
could only find expression in striving against all hope and common-sense
to make him the Chief Executive. Calhoun felt keenly that he had no
way of rewarding this devotion. But the majority of them expected no
reward. Like fat, weary Dixon Lewis, they would make Calhoun President,
satisfied that they had done their duty by him and the country, 'and then
. . . retire to a more private and peaceful life.' [81]

In vain did Calhoun protest in letter after letter, public and private,
that he had 'no desire' for the office. His friends knew his deep ambition
and ceaselessly nurtured it. Letters to and from Calhoun reveal that not
since 1822 had so concerted an effort been made, either by his friends or
himself, to win the Presidency.

Foremost among these supporters was Duff Green of Missouri. The Carolinian's defeats, Green regarded only as proof that his own advice had been disregarded. 'Had you been advised by me,' he wrote in 1840, with more assurance than proof, 'you would have been the Candidate in opposition to General Jackson, and elected and the country saved the misery . . . that followed. Had you been advised by me, you would have been the most popular man in the United States.'

Green railed at Calhoun's 'madness' at throwing South Carolina to Van Buren in 1840. He raged at his friend's fastidious aversion to making common ground with the Whigs. A hard-headed realist, who saw elections in terms of personalities rather than issues, it was beyond his understanding why Calhoun, anti-abolitionist, anti-consolidationist, and anti-Bank, could not link his destiny, without regard to 'political principles or views of policy,'[82] to the abolitionist, consolidationist, banking crowd, whose hatred for Van Buren and Jackson was as strong as his. What mattered the party, so long as his own advancement was assured?

Despite their years of friendship, intensified by the marriage of Calhoun's son, Andrew, to Green's daughter, Calhoun's answer was stern. 'I am sure that if your letters would fall into the hands of those who are to come after us, they would infer from . . . the course you recommend that I was a vain, light-headed, ill-judging and ambitious man, ignorant alike of the . . . times and my own strength . . . aiming constantly at the Presidency and destined constantly to be defeated.' Did not Green know that never, 'even in the heat of youthful years,' had he sought honor but through duty? Had he ever 'held out hopes of office to those who follow me?' Had he not for years 'knowingly pursued a course that would sacrifice my popularity . . .? I did not suit the times, nor the times suit me.'[83] Yet now, if his friends still thought that he only could carry to victory the causes for which he had fought so long, 'I will not shirk the responsibility.'

It was 1822 all over again. Once more the promises of support were ripening and falling into his lap—from North Carolina, from Virginia, and even New England—a triumph indeed for the apostle of nullification and slavery. Van Buren had lost the New Hampshire state convention. R. M. T. Hunter was urging New England friends 'to get up an organisation by Congressional districts.' From Lemuel Williams came news of the personnel for the forthcoming state convention of Massachusetts: Boston, sixty delegates for Calhoun, twelve for Van Buren; Essex County, 'the same proportion'; in Salem, '10 to 2,' and 'many other towns favorably heard from.' In New York, where the Irish vote was guaranteed to the son of Patrick Calhoun, excitement reached a fever-pitch. Young Joseph Scoville was swinging Tammany Hall into line. The mere appearance of a letter with the Pendleton postmark at the city post office was known to the partisans of both Van Buren and Calhoun long before it had reached the hands of its recipient.[84] And on a September evening in 1843, burly, black-haired Mike Walsh arose before a huge assembly to proclaim: 'The man of my choice for the next President of the United States is John C. Calhoun.' 'Protracted cheering' followed his words, after which the audience sang out the new campaign song:

> *'Away down Sout' dar, close to de moon,*
> *Dere lives an old chap, dat dey call Calhoun.'* [85]

Even this was not enough to satisfy the ardors of the New York supporters. Elmore wrote Calhoun: 'There is a great desire . . . to know more of you . . . your life and services. Your speeches are inquired after, and most of all yourself. They wish to see and talk with you and hear you speak. These wishes . . . cannot be resisted.' [86]

But Calhoun resisted them. He would sacrifice much to further his ambition, but not even to become President could he conquer his instinctive repugnance to becoming 'a political electioneer. . . . It may be pride, it may be fastidiousness . . . but . . . I cannot help it,' wrote the man, in whom 'Tippecanoe and Tyler, too,' had roused no desire to emulate their example. 'I would be happy to travel quietly, as an individual to see my friends . . . but I am averse to being made a spectacle . . . or to . . . indicate a personal solicitude about the office, which I do not feel.' He would 'abandon no principle. . . . Whether victorious or defeated, it shall be on my own ground . . . I would rather risk defeat than character.' [87]

With a second request he complied. Early in 1843, the first full length 'Life' of Calhoun appeared. The authorship was credited to R. M. T. Hunter, but Rhett contends that the writer was Calhoun himself, and that when he refused to 'father' it, the book was turned over to Hunter. The Virginian was said to have inserted a page or two, presumably the eulogies, and thus became the 'putative author of a work' that brought him more acclaim than any other act of his life.[88]

Any student of Calhoun's literary style can see the difference between his terse, rough-hewn sentences and this smooth-flowing, wordy document. Certainly Calhoun would have had no reason to lie to Anna Maria, and to her he said: 'Mr. Hunter has rewritten . . . so much . . . as to be . . . entitled to the authorship.' And to James E. Colhoun, he wrote of the 'Sketch . . . prepared by some of my friends here.' Undoubtedly he supplied the material and blocked in the outline, and equally, without doubt, the complete structure was edited by hands other than his own.[89] The book is authorized, not autobiographical.

The campaign thundered on. In Pendleton, even the Clay Whigs voiced 'regard for Mr. Calhoun on his principles.' The press of England was looking with admiration on the candidacy 'of one of the most remarkable men in the United States.' In 1843, the Jacksonville, Alabama, *Republican* lifted Calhoun's name to the masthead, stating that his opinion was known on three great issues, the tariff, Texas, and abolition.[90] Had it not been known, his chances would have been far better. The era had ended when the people would choose a President to lead them; now the bosses chose Presidents to be led. Calhoun had every qualification for the office of President except the most essential, which was to have no qualifications at all.

Calhoun himself had read the ending when he wrote Duff Green in 1837: 'the very services, which ought to recommend me . . . constitute insuperable objections to my election.' [91] In the South's view he was the 'acknowledged leader of the Democratic party'; he had ripped it apart, but he had sewn it together again, single-handedly, and stamped it with its old pattern of states' rights and a low tariff. He had won the victory; but none knew better than he that to 'reap the fruits' was 'a task by no means easy.'

As in 1822, it was his own strength that defeated him at last. Valiantly the Calhoun leaders struggled to 'hold in' the young men, lest 'they be indiscreet in their ardor.' Open support, they knew, was paid for by open attack. Wiser than their chief in the ways of politics, they tried to quench the flame they themselves had kindled. They entreated him to 'reflect earnestly and solemnly' on the steps he was to take. An open break now with Van Buren would split the party and focus attention on Calhoun's candidacy. Calhoun was trying to face issues when the essence of politics consisted in avoiding them.[92]

Cracks were running across the smooth surface of his hopes. Would the abolitionist societies unite and throw the balance of power to a man who favored their principles? Clay and Van Buren had promised to 'take care' of their friends; would Calhoun, with his fastidious aversion to spoils, do the same? It was the old, old story, the story to which in his calmer moments, Calhoun had known the ending all along.

A politician was not to be beaten by a statesman. At the almost incredible resurgence of Calhoun strength, the wily 'Red Fox' scuttled from his lair. If he could not defeat Calhoun on Calhoun's ground, it was he, and not the South Carolinian, who had the power to choose the ground.

Van Buren had the party organization. The power of calling conventions lay with the old committees, dating back to the Jackson days. Calhoun's only chance lay in a convention composed, not of party hacks, but of independent delegates from each Congressional district. But should Calhoun be nominated, Rhett predicted, Van Buren would align himself with the Whigs.

As loyal James Hamilton said, 'nothing now remains but to *agitate* and to *agitate deeply*.' Lemuel Williams promised Calhoun's nomination on 'an independent ticket' that would draw 'Whig votes enough to carry Mass., Maine, and New York.' But these ideas were vetoed by Southern party leaders, like Hunter and Elmore, who warned against an open rupture with a party that by some 'act of Providence or the defeat of Van Buren, might yet surrender, if you have not beforehand made that impossible.' [93]

Disgusted by the strife, Calhoun made up his mind. By April, 1844, he resolved not to let his name 'go before a convention . . . which is not calculated to bring out the voice of the party.' Van Buren's convention, he knew, would throw the nomination 'to the large central states,' giving them 'control of the Executive department, the ballot, the vote, and the patronage.' And what was worse, in violation of pledges, New York Democrats were dickering for the support of abolitionist leaders.

He knew what he must do. It was with the advice of friends such as Hunter, who acclaimed his 'mode of delivering truth without offending,' that he sent an Address to the Central Committee in Charleston, and another to the South Carolina Senators, outlining his decision. 'This act of Mr. Calhoun's,' declared the *New Aurora*, 'has done and will do more to elevate him in the estimate of the good . . . and the hardworking than any act of his life.' The Mobile *Tribune* left his name on the masthead as 'one who loves his country.' [94]

It was all over. His friends were warm in their expressions of sympathy. Macey, grieved and mortified at a hint that the South Carolinian might take second place to Van Buren, bitterly declared that he would rather have Calhoun lose a dozen Presidencies than to see 'your great and pure name' so polluted. He had withdrawn so that he might be 'preserved for the future,' his friends assured him; only 'for the present' were the 'cherished hopes' withdrawn. In Virginia his withdrawal had strengthened him in the affections of the people. Even Van Buren supporters would surrender next time. 'The exhibitions of feelings . . . were deep,' wrote Hunter. A 'settled determination' had arisen 'to make you the President next time, should God spare you to us.' [95]

Letters were pouring in upon him from men he had never seen and never would see, men who would fight for him without stint and without reward, solely because 'of our deep and ardent admiration of your talents . . . principles and character.' It was heart-warming to read the words of those who 'were willing to have risked all . . . and be content to fall battling for . . . our choice'; but could not, 'by abuse of your own generous permission to use your name, peril the attainment of the destiny for which you were intended.' [96]

But Calhoun was not interested. Days were dark for him in that young spring of 1844, with his own hopes dying as everything around him throbbed into life. 'They ought not to think of rallying on me at the next election, unless it should be found indispensable in order to preserve our position,' was his word to Hunter. 'I am the last man that can be elected . . . I am now disentangled from the fraudulent game of President making and hope never to have to do anything with it again.' Relentless thoughts were hammering in his brain—1848? He might not even be alive in 1848. He was empty and bitter and very tired. He was ready to retire, so he had written; yet could still tell James Edward: 'The great point is to preserve my character. . . . That may be of service, hereafter; not to run again as a candidate, but in some greater emergency.' Meanwhile— it was time to think about spring planting.[97]

XXII

Calhoun and the Lone Star

MEN TOLD OF A LAND where the green grass swept down to the green sea, with only a line of foam to show where one ended and the other began. Men told of a sea of green grass that swept straight to the horizon and rolled into great waves when the wind blew. Men told of nights, bright as day, when huge stars and glittering fireflies turned the prairie into blue fire, and bathed every wild rose and geranium, every blade of fine wiry grass, in effervescent light. Men told of a lone star hanging over the horizon, leading them on to new dreams and new hopes; men told of a great country, fresh from the hand of God.

Texas.

A man named Stephen Austin had wondered: 'May we not form a little world of our own, where neither religious, political, nor money-making fanaticism . . . shall ever obtain admission?' This was the American dream, and not Stephen Austin's alone. It was the dream of the first Pilgrim who set his foot on the rock at Plymouth, and of the last starving colonist of Roanoke Island. It was the dream of Pat Calhoun and Andrew Jackson, and all the hard-living, hard-fighting, hard-dying men and women who had braved the horrors of the pest-ships and broken their youth against the unbroken wilderness. It was the dream that died as civilizations developed, but was born anew at the opening of each frontier.

Texas had been acknowledged as Spanish territory in the Treaty of 1819, although Henry Clay and his followers were always to contend that the country was included in the Louisiana Purchase. Two years later, Mexico made good her revolt from Spain, and the flag of the Mexican Republic waved over the land of the Lone Star. That same year Americans began pushing along the dusty tracks toward the Rio Grande; twelve thousand of them made the journey in a single decade. They came with Mexico's blessing, and Stephen Austin was free to dream of a yeoman's civilization, a New England in a Southern climate.

But Texas was Southern, after all, and it was inevitable that Southern expansionists should look with covetous eyes upon that land—ripe and waiting for the cotton seed—which could bring them five or six new states, new lands to replace the worn-out earth of the old cotton states, and the political balance of power in Congress. And with the South went slavery, and the fear of approaching slavery drew the desired New England and Swiss and German settlers off to the Ohio country, leaving Texas to those who demanded the enslavement, and not the freedom, of man.

Slavery was even behind the Texan struggle for freedom—the epic of the Alamo. In 1829, indifferent to the outcries of the American settlers, Mexico outlawed slavery, and a year later forbade all further immigration from the United States. It was too late; Stephen Austin's dream was ended. In 1836 came the news that shook the nation, news of the slaughter of four hundred and twelve young men, among them the beloved Davy Crockett, bayoneted to death in a little fort called the Alamo. Texas had declared her independence; but this technicality mattered little. Americans had died in Texas; the little blood-soaked fortress had become a page of American history.

From the Alamo on, it was no longer a question of whether Texas would enter the Union; it was when. 'Reannexation' was 'Manifest Destiny.' By 1836 Calhoun could declare in the Senate that he had decided not only 'to recognize the independence of Texas, but' to favor 'her admission into this Union.' Probably no man did more than Calhoun to bring about annexation; [1] but the actual program did not get under way until the Presidency of John Tyler.

2

Perhaps no American President has been more grossly underestimated than the brilliant Virginian, Tyler. His loyalty to his convictions dragged his name into the mud of party strife and blackened his fame for years to come. Yet, in 1840 at the time of his Vice-Presidential nomination, Tyler's name had 'a charm for the Southern people.' Cultivated, polished, musical, a graduate of William and Mary College at seventeen, he was completely the aristocrat, yet virile in mind and body. With the confidence of birth and position, he gaily flouted social convention, and at his levees introduced guests without regard to precedence, 'most abominably unfashionable.' His Virginia morning custom of an immense julep, 'sparkling with ice,' charmed Southerners and startled New Englanders, as he would take a swallow, then pass the glass to 'a handsome daughter of one of the Cabinet officers,' who sipped and handed it on. In conversational powers, he was said to surpass even Mr. Calhoun.[2]

Nor had Calhoun been more independent and far-seeing. Tyler had remained in the Senate Chamber to vote against the Force Bill, when the less courageous had withdrawn. Tyler had resigned his seat rather than obey the Virginia Legislature's instructions to rescind his vote of censure upon President Jackson. Tyler, not Calhoun, as early as Missouri Compromise days, had seen that slavery would come to turn upon the terri-

torial question. He had fired the opening shots against the tariff and National Bank, as 'an unwarranted extension of the powers of the government and an appeal to the numerical majority of the North to grow
rich' at the South's expense.

Yet it was Calhoun who was credited with these opinions. For it was
the unfortunate truth that what John Tyler said or did mattered very
little. Tyler had every quality that makes for leadership but the quality
of leadership itself. His independence could be dismissed as mere eccen-
tricity or perversity; Calhoun, on the floor of the United States Senate,
defying the threat of arrest in his battle for nullification, captured the
imagination of the Southern people; taking the same stand and voicing
the same opinions, Tyler could lose and Calhoun win an army of supporters.

Cursed as he was with this weakness in personal leadership, Tyler had
done more to weaken than to arouse enthusiasm for the cause of Texas
annexation. But he had the Western vision; to Webster and Ashburton
he had suggested a treaty to annex California and the Far West to the
United States, in exchange for setting the British boundaries at the Columbia River. He had sent Tom Benton's son-in-law, dark, Charleston-
born John Frémont, to explore the Rocky Mountain passes. He had even
given support to Dr. Marcus Whitman, who was leading wagon trains
over the peaks of the mountains to contest the settlements of the Hudson's
Bay Company, far to the North in Oregon.

By 1842, it was a 'public secret' that Tyler was working for the annexation of Texas. By 1843, his haste was feverish. In June, at a 'World
Convention' in London, American abolitionists urged the British Foreign
Secretary, Lord Aberdeen, to encourage abolition in Texas, and a certain
'Mr. Andrews' even suggested that British abolitionists buy the freedom
of Texas slaves, receiving Texas lands in exchange. All this Duff Green
communicated to the Secretary of State, Abel Parker Upshur, in a private
letter that summer, and by August matters were moving swiftly. Tyler,
convinced that England was seeking to wage war against Southern 'institutions,' wrote Minister Waddy Thompson in Mexico that it was being plotted abroad to make 'Texas a dependency of London.'[3] On August 18, Lord Aberdeen told the House of Lords that 'We desire to see
slavery abolished in Texas.'[4]

At Fort Hill, Calhoun kept his finger close on the pulse of events.
Openly he took no part. To the horror of his closest friends, he had a
short while before actually declined the post of Secretary of State, when
Webster's indifference to territorial expansion at last necessitated his
withdrawal from Tyler's official family. The time, Calhoun had said, was
not 'propitious' for Texas annexation; the unpopularity of Tyler was
militating against the drive; but all knew what was really in his mind.[5]
No better issue than Texas could be imagined for a Presidential campaign, and it was as a prospective candidate that Calhoun was kept well

supplied that summer with important information. Ashbel Smith, the Texas Chargé d'Affaires at London and Paris, wrote him details of his conversations with Lord Aberdeen, passing on his lordship's frank admission that Her Majesty's government desired abolition throughout the world; although, of course, without interfering 'improperly' upon the subject. An excerpt from Lord Aberdeen's dispatch to the British Chargé d'Affaires in Mexico offered Great Britain's mediation 'on the abolition of slavery in Texas' as 'a great moral triumph for Mexico.' Britain desired such abolition, 'mainly in reference to its future influence on slavery in the United States.'

Duff Green, too, sent his findings to Calhoun, and both to him and Secretary Upshur, the South Carolinian replied that they could not place 'too much importance upon British designs.' She was using all her 'diplomatic arts,' her whole purpose, Calhoun believed, being for a monopoly of the cotton trade. 'She unites in herself the ambition of Rome and the avarice of Carthage.' [6]

Yet Calhoun still warned against 'premature' attempts at annexation; and when in December, 1843, Thomas Gilmer attempted to draw him out with the words that 'On a question of such magnitude, it is not meet, that a voice, which for more than thirty years has been heard . . . on all public questions, should be silent,' he merely replied that his opinion had often been expressed. Annexation was 'necessary to the peace and security' of both Texas and the United States, and any objections that it would extend slavery 'must be met as a direct attack on the Constitution.' [7] More, he would not say.

Meanwhile, Destiny took a hand in the affair.

3

Among the 'gay, young belles' of the capital in the winter of 1844 was a girl of twenty-four, named Julia Gardiner. She was tall, with a full figure and the bearing of a Greek statue in her flowing gowns. Grecian, too, were the classic lines of her nose and mouth and the poise of her oval-shaped head, crowned with a load of dark braids and a thin gold coronet, set with one pure diamond, which she wore like a star in the middle of her forehead.

But she was no statue. She was radiantly alive, warm color glowing in her cheeks and lips, her round gray eyes under the sweep of dark brow, alert and sparkling. Her gaiety was slightly tempered by the death of President Harrison, but as she wound a bit of black crêpe around her wrist, in token of 'the hero of Tippecanoe,' she certainly never dreamed that she herself would become the First Lady of the United States.

Her preference for older men, however, was marked. Her interest was piqued by that incorrigible bachelor, 'handsome, portly' James Buchanan, who would cast her stealthy glances while adjusting his necktie. She was not even immune to Henry Clay's aging but potent charms. But it was the widower, President John Tyler himself, with his 'high-toned nature and graceful bearing,' who won her warmest 'schoolgirl' admiration.[8]

On February 28, 1844, with spring already greening the hills above Washington, Julia Gardiner was one of a gay group of ladies and officials who boarded the new warship *Princeton* for a trial cruise down the Potomac. Below in the cabin, she sparkled and smiled, a young man on either side. She paid little heed to their chatter; she had eyes only for the tall figure of the President, ears only for his 'sweet, silvery' voice.

Toast after toast was drunk, laughter sounding over the dull roar of the boiler. Secretary Upshur jovially lifted an empty bottle. 'The dead bodies must be removed before I can offer my toast,' he remarked.

Laughing, the captain passed him another bottle. 'There are still plenty of living bodies,' was his answer.[9] A moment later, the Secretary of State swept his cloak about him and started for the deck where Secretary of the Navy Gilmer and Senator Benton were awaiting him. Would the President join them? The President smiled. He preferred to remain below.

It happened—a gigantic roar that split the universe as a large gun exploded. It tossed the ship like a leaf, sent President, men and women tumbling into a struggling heap upon the deck. For a moment the hush held; then rose the sound of screaming.

A man reeled down the ladder. 'The Secretary of State is dead!'

Julia sprang up. 'Let me go to my father.'

Someone held her. The words beat like waves against her numbed brain. Secretary Gilmer was dead. And Representative Maxcy. Senator Benton was hurt, but still living. Mr. Gardiner . . .

Julia struggled to escape. 'My father loved me and would want me near him.' A woman stepped to her side. Her voice broke with pity. 'My dear child, you can do no good. Your father is in Heaven.'

Then Julia Gardiner fainted. A man caught her as she fell, held her against his dark coat, carried her up through the hatch into the air and off the stricken ship. When she came to, she was in President Tyler's arms.

Tyler was fifty-four; Julia thirty years his junior. But he courted her with the ardor of a younger man, and to the hero-worshiping girl, emotionally undeveloped despite her social maturity, he seemed more and more to take the place of the father she had lost. Before the year was out, they were married at a High Nuptial Mass of the Catholic Church in New York, and the wags were singing:

> 'Texas was the captain's bride,
> Till a lovelier one he took;
> With Miss Gardiner by his side,
> He, with scorn, on kings may look.'[10]

4

Secretary Upshur was dead. Upshur had wanted Texas, but he had fumbled. Although proposing a treaty of annexation as early as 1843, he had not dared commit the United States to military protection of the Lone Star Republic should the Mexican and the European Powers find negotiations unpleasant. A dilemma confronted Mr. Upshur the day that Destiny, or an exploding gun, relieved him of all earthly concerns. Who could finish the work? One man took it upon himself . . .

By dawn of February 29, 1844, the self-appointed instrument of Destiny, dour, square-jawed Henry Wise of Virginia, left his rooms. His dull blue eyes were aglow with purpose. To him the tragedy of the day before was providential. Destiny had blazed the trail for the annexation. Without Texas the South was doomed; of this Wise was convinced. Texas could save the South and the Union, and for such an end the audacious Virginian would waste few scruples upon his means.

He hurried to the lodgings of George McDuffie of South Carolina. The Senator was still in bed, but shuffled out in robe and bedroom slippers to receive his guest. Wise whirled upon him. Would Mr. Calhoun take Upshur's post, solely for the annexation of Texas? McDuffie did not think so. Wise persisted. In all probability Mr. Calhoun's name would be sent to the Senate that very day. McDuffie must beg him not to decline. The South Carolinian settled himself at his desk.

A few moments later, Wise arrived at the White House. Leaning against the mantel of the breakfast room was Tyler, shaken and 'humbled at his escape,' a newspaper in his hand. The President greeted his friend in a tremulous voice, then 'turned his face to the wall in a flood of tears.' [11] Wise had no time for sympathy. The moment demanded action. Now all party factions would be stilled and Presidential nominations approved. 'Your most important work is the annexation of Texas, and the man for that . . . is Mr. Calhoun. Send for him at once.'

Tyler stiffened. His pride was still smarting from the rebuff of Calhoun's earlier refusal; he had no desire for a repetition. Nor was he in any mood to have his Cabinet hand-picked for him. His voice was firm. 'No, Texas is important, but Mr. Calhoun is not the man of my choice.'

During breakfast, Wise wrestled with his problem. What if Tyler nominated someone else before Calhoun received McDuffie's letter? What would Calhoun do? What would the President do? His own position would be intolerable. Immediately the tasteless meal was over, he picked up his hat, walked over to the President and bade him 'a lasting farewell. . . . I have done that which will forfeit your confidence,' he announced dramatically. He had done both the President and Mr. Calhoun 'a great wrong, and must go immediately to Mr. McDuffie to apologize.' 'What do you mean?' Wise explained. He had told McDuffie 'to write to Mr. Calhoun and ask him to accept the place of Secretary of State at your hands.' 'Did you say you went at my instance?' 'No . . . but my act as your known friend implied as much, and Mr. McDuffie was too much of a gentleman to ask me. . . . I went . . . without your authority, for I knew I could not obtain it; and I did not tell Mr. McDuffie . . . for I knew he would not have written. . . . I can hardly be your friend any longer, unless you sanction my unauthorized act . . .'

Tyler sprang from his chair, threw both hands over his head. 'Wise, you have not done this thing! You cannot have done this!' He paced the floor, struggling to control his anger. 'You are the most exasperating man . . . the most wilful and wayward. . . . No one else would have done it. . . . You are the only man who could have done it. . . . Take the office and tender it to Mr. Calhoun; I doubtless am wrong in refusing the services of such a man.' [12]

Tyler's surrender was complete. On March 6, he wrote Calhoun that he had 'unhesitatingly' nominated him, in view of his 'great talents and deservedly high standing with the Country at large. . . . I hope,' concluded the vanquished Executive, 'that you will be immediately at my side.' [13]

That same day the nomination was sent to the Senate. Within a few hours all Washington knew that Calhoun was the nominee. On the floor of Congress business was hushed and the clerks droned on unnoticed. Men gathered in groups, whispering and talking. In the House the crowd was thickest around the gigantic four-hundred-and-fifty-pound bulk of Dixon Lewis of Alabama, as man after man pushed through, begging him to write Calhoun to accept. Lewis dipped his quill. 'I have never seen stronger evidence of *complete unanimity* . . . that you are . . . the only man to meet the crisis.' Even the Whigs 'say so.'

He had stirring news before his letter ended. Without Calhoun's knowledge, without even referring his name to a committee, the South Carolinian had been unanimously confirmed as Secretary of State. 'Everyone is delighted,' Lewis concluded. 'The Leaders . . . dislike and dread you . . . but of the Van Buren men . . . I believe that three fourths of them are more friendly to you than to him.' To Crallé he wrote, 'Providence, rather than Tyler, has put Calhoun at the head of this great question.' Of Mr. Wise's assistance to Providence, he had nothing to say. [14]

5

It was spring at Fort Hill, green misting the tree-tops, the gardens a golden blaze of sunlight and forsythia. The winter rains were over now and wind blew through the windows. It stirred the letters on Calhoun's desk, letters from men in all corners of the United States, of all political faiths and all walks of life. They had been pouring in for days, sometimes thirty in a single mail. And all sounded one theme: the Southern hotheads were clinging to the hope of Texas as drowning men to a straw. The Charleston *Mercury* acclaimed Calhoun as 'the moral property of the nation'; even the New York *Herald* and *Niles' Register* stressed the 'entire unanimity' with which the nation sought his services.

Most persuasive were the inducements of personal friends; of Lewis with his hint that 'a ground swell from the people themselves growing out of the Texas question may roll you into the position of a candidate'; the fervor of young Francis Wharton: 'Looking at you once more as the representative of the Union as a whole will open the old fountains of affection. There was a time when Pennsylvania would have voted for you by acclamation—that time may come again. . . . The Secretaryship of War made you the second man in the affections of the nation; the Secretaryship of State will make you first.' [15]

All this clamor dwindled into hollow echoes in the ears of Calhoun. How different this, from 1817! Then he had been a last-minute choice, his best friends distrustful of his abilities; but he himself afire with youth, intensity of purpose, and confidence in his powers. Today his purpose still burned; his self-confidence was heightened, if anything, by his skillful use of his strength. Difficulties were still challenges to him; he never looked at the obstacles, but only at the goal. Of his capacity to carry through what was perhaps the most difficult task of diplomacy since the purchase of Louisiana, he had no doubts at all.

But long-continued defeat had dimmed his enthusiasm for any but the highest office of all—and the most unattainable. He was too old to seek less. He felt that he had only a few years to live; and his months of retirement had not refreshed him, as he had hoped they would. His relentless energies never really let him rest, and he was feeling the physical reaction from years of high-tension labor. To return to the dismal life of the 'Messes' seemed more than he could bear. As he wrote, acceptance would 'break up all my family arrangements, and I have no hope that I can possibly induce Mrs. Calhoun again to return to Washington.' [16]

But what a challenge lay before him! With Texas annexed, the objectives of a lifetime would be near fulfillment; the tightening of bonds between West and South, the restoration of that old equilibrium between the sections, upon which the Union had been built, and without which, he was convinced, it would fall; and, most of all, safety for the South within the Union. Oregon would soon be knocking at the door; and he had long included Oregon in his reckonings. England was the common enemy; he would not sacrifice a foot of American soil to England, not even to save it from Northern domination.

To broaden the bounds of his country, North and South; to win territories, greater, richer, broader than the Louisiana Purchase, this was destiny—the destiny of a virile young country, warring her way in a world of jealous older Powers. Oregon and Texas, 'the peace of the country . . . the salvation of the South,' as McDuffie had said, what man could resist this challenge? Not John Calhoun. He had fought and would fight, since all insisted upon that. He knew what his answer was to be. And who is to blame him, if he dared hope a little for a final triumph to his years of labor; for while life existed, hope lived too. 'I have been compelled most reluctantly to accept the State Department,'[17] he wrote James Edward.

6

Calhoun was blissfully free from any scruples about imperialism in America's attitude toward Texas. Under his federal theories, Texas and all other annexed territories would come in as sovereign and self-governing states. Their freedom was only strengthened by the federal bond. Thus could Calhoun reconcile imperialism with self-determination, although with Texas the theories were shaken by the facts. Majority rule, Calhoun considered tyranny; yet so long as the Union operated upon that principle, the South must keep the majority. Texas supplied the balance—but only as a slave territory, and in utter contradiction to Calhoun's own avowed belief that the people of the state had the right to determine whether they would be slave or free. And he went 'by tortuous ways to get Texas,' not because he wanted Texas to be slave, but because he wanted South Carolina to be free.[18]

Undoubtedly Calhoun believed himself to be speaking the truth when he later said: 'I would have been among the very last individuals in the United States to have made any movement . . . for Texas . . . simply on the ground that it was to be an enlargement of slavery.' He honestly believed that annexation was 'essential to the interest and prosperity of the North.' What effect it might have on slavery, he could not say, but he supposed it would 'wear slavery southwards.'[19] In this he shared the view of both Jefferson and Tyler. Texas would be a 'safety valve' for the Union, by which the threat of black numerical superiority could be removed from the old South, and the blacks diffused among the whites to a point where fear would be removed.

Much of what was to be called diplomacy was nothing but politics, and muddy politics at that. Calhoun was a statesman, and as a statesman would he be adequate to the politics of all this? With his aversion to playing the game for his own profit, would he know how to play it for a cause upon which he believed lay the destiny of the whole South and the whole country?

It turned out that he would. He had not lived in the Washington atmosphere for thirty-odd years without learning the tricks of his trade. To obtain his goal, the friends of Texas annexation must be united. Preferably, they must unite upon a Presidential candidate pledged to annexation—and such a candidate was not to be found among the aspirants of the moment. Slaveholder Henry Clay, who was having trouble enough with his own Northern Whig constituency without throwing in Texas, cut his political throat when he spoke for annexation in the South and against it in the North. This was satisfactory to all concerned until the newspapers of both sections compared notes—and Mr. Clay was defeated before he had even run! Exultant over 'the last of Clay,' Calhoun told a friend: 'Mr. Clay has been a great disturbing power. . . . He has done much to distract the South, and to keep the West out of its true position.' [20] But the Kentuckian's collapse was merely a lucky accident. And in a sudden bold stroke Calhoun sought reinforcements from the man who probably hated him more than any other, Andrew Jackson.

Jackson was dying at the Hermitage. The gallant old warrior was a shattered wreck of seventy-seven now, coughing his lungs away, with a year yet to wait for release from pain and the peace he had never known in life. His flimsy hold on the political leaders of the country was as broken as his body, but he was Andrew Jackson still, and to uncounted ordinary Americans, he was America itself. He was only a symbol, but a symbol who had bled in the Revolution and looked on the face of Jefferson, the symbol of New Orleans and the last invasion of American soil, when redcoats and buckskin had fought it out over the heaped cotton bales. He was the symbol of the dreaming South and the brawling West and their united hope of a new world in the new promised land—Texas.

Like Calhoun, Andrew Jackson had never taken his eyes off Texas. Yet his political heirs were invoking his name while side-stepping the issue in which Jackson himself was most interested. Calhoun understood the situation perfectly. Whatever his personal feelings, he avoided the mistake of underestimating the power of his old enemy. If Jackson would speak, would commit himself openly, the pretensions of his one-time followers would crack wide open, and the highway to the Lone Star state be swept clear.

It would have been asking too much of Calhoun's pride to expect him humbly to seek aid from Andrew Jackson, especially when such aid involved the destruction of Van Buren at the very hands that had made him. Mr. Calhoun's methods were more devious—and more diplomatic. It was he, who two years before had seen to it that Jackson was sent a letter from a Baltimore paper, asserting, first, that the annexation of Texas was essential to the preservation of the American Union; secondly, that England would seize the new Republic if America did not. This dual threat had fanned Old Hickory's embers into flame. He had hunched over his paper. 'I am . . . writing scarcely able to wield my pen, or to see what I write. . . . Had I time and strength I would make it a clear case that . . . we as a nation under the obligations of the Treaty of 1803 are bound to protect Texas as part of Louisiana ceded to us by France. . . . There is no time to lose . . . I am daily growing weaker and shorter of breath.' [21]

This was the letter that eventually found its way into the hands of Secretary of State Calhoun. Van Buren himself was next on the program. Never had Calhoun deceived himself that his renewed 'friendship' with the New Yorker was more than a political necessity. Van Buren's recent flirtations with the abolitionists had openly disgusted him. He must be destroyed. Van Buren had opposed annexation in 1837. Now, with infinite dexterity, Calhoun saw that the question was put to him again. Would Van Buren repudiate his old leader? Or would he recant? Whatever his answer, he would be ruined in one section of the country or the other.

Mr. Van Buren replied in characteristic fashion. He would be glad to see Texas in the Union if such an end could be obtained without war. And as the South had openly declared that it would risk war, both with England and Mexico, for the sake of Texas, Van Buren's answer was as unsatisfactory as Calhoun had hoped that it would be. Back at the Hermitage, Jackson, still speaking 'affectionately' of Van Buren, gave the verdict. The party must choose another man.

7

Both Clay's and Van Buren's statements revealed how deeply the seeds of anti-slavery feeling had penetrated Northern soil. Neither did much to soothe the feelings of the overwrought South. Indeed, throughout the Texas negotiations Calhoun's task was twofold: to get Texas into the Union and to keep the South in.

Never had anti-slavery sentiment been so high. Only two years before, Calhoun himself with 'delicacy' and 'firmness' had staved off one abortive attempt at disunion. He would be the next President, it was understood; the South could wait a little longer. But the tariff was going up; cotton had dropped to four cents a pound; and Calhoun was out of the race by the spring of 1844, giving full rein to the extremists, who had rested their hopes of 'justice' upon his election.

Texas was the last chance. Southern tension was at the breaking point. Letters poured in on Calhoun, roaring threats of secession and disunion, awaiting only his word. South Carolina was ablaze. In May, 1844, at a meeting in Ashley, came the cry to annex Texas 'if the Union will accept it,' or to annex the Southern states to Texas in a Southern confederacy. At Beaufort, a mass meeting threatened that if the South were 'not permitted' to bring Texas into the Union, 'we solemnly announce to the world—that we will dissolve this Union.'

'We hold it to be better,' was the word of a large assembly in Williamsburg, 'to be out of the Union with Texas than in it without her.' Hammond despaired 'of the Union more and more daily. . . . The . . . tariff . . . the sectional hostility to Texas . . . the impertinence of the abolitionists show that North and South cannot exist united.' His Negroes were fully 'aware of the opinions of the Presidential candidates on . . . Slavery and . . . the abolitionists.' There was 'a growing spirit of insubordination . . . they have fired several houses recently. This is fearful—horrible. A *quick* and *potent* remedy must be applied. *Disunion* if *needs be.*' [22]

'Texas or Disunion' was the Fourth of July toast echoing across the South in the summer of 1844, 'and a Southern convention generally called for.' Richmond was suggested, but the hotheads were coolly repelled by the Virginia capital. Next, Nashville was sounded out, but its citizens deplored 'the desecration of the soil of Tennessee . . . by treason against the Union.' The scheme collapsed, but not until the North had been sufficiently alarmed—which may have been the real intention all along. [23]

'It is to us a question of life and death,' wrote Calhoun. Wracked by the agitation, which almost single-handedly he was trying to control, he had no scruples against bringing the North into line through fear, and urged Hammond and other hotheads to voice their sentiments in the press. All America must know the consequences should annexation be defeated.

'I only ask the South to stand by me.' From the North he expected nothing. Bitterly he wrote that the South, with its own interests unchallenged, had supported the North in the Revolution and the War of 1812, but now, when the South asked aid, the North refused. [24]

8

But if Calhoun felt bitterness at the stand of New England, for Old England he felt only contempt. Britain's idealism he saw as nothing but 'a grand scheme of commercial monopoly, disguised under the garb of abolitionism.' He knew of the plight of the women and children, heaving

coal in the British mines, the 'freedom' of the famine-ridden peasants of
India and Ireland. It was under Britain's 'starvation or forced labor' plan
that so-called 'free' Negroes were transported from Africa to the West
Indies, there to 'compete successfully' with American slave labor. Calhoun detected in all this an English attempt 'to restore . . . the slave
trade itself, under the specious name of transporting laborers . . . to
compete . . . with those who have refused to follow her suicidal policy.' [25]

And a generation ahead of history, Calhoun saw right through the
problem that was to torment the future Confederacy. Would England
ally herself with the South? Calhoun could have given the answer. It was
to England's interest that the South remain in the Union, selling her cotton at the prices of the world exchange. It was to England's interest that
slavery cease to compete with the labor of her own colonies. And it was to
England's interest that Texas remain free—a clearing house from which
well-trained agitators could be filtered through the Southern states. England had actual territorial designs on Texas, Calhoun was convinced, as a
site from which she could 'brave at pleasure the American continent and
control its destiny.' [26]

9

To the fastidious eyes of Sir Richard Pakenham, fresh from the London
of Dickens, Disraeli, and plump little Victoria, the crude and lusty American capital must have seemed, as it had to his compatriot, Harriet Martineau, a 'grand mistake.' Certainly, despite the pretensions of the sprawling white Capitol building, topped with its tawdry wooden washbowl of
a dome, Washington, like the nation it symbolized, was still all 'promises.'
Half-hearted attempts had been made at paving a few of the streets, but
most of the avenues were, as yet, 'theoretical,' the passage of which involved an ambitious journey over stiles, ditches, and open fields, until
the weary pedestrian finally attained the few stretches of gravel, ash, or
brick paving, or the loose planks flopping in the mud, which served as
sidewalks.

Surface drains meandered along the roadways. Pigs, geese, and cows,
turned loose to consume the huge piles of garbage heaped up in the streets,
disputed the right of way with delicate femininity in crinolines. Pennsylvania Avenue was still a slatternly jumble of shanties, pigsties, cowsheds,
and hencoops; of boarding houses, hotels, markets, grocery and drug
stores, and a taffy store where the owner 'spat on his hands' to make his
candy crisp—all these jostled sedate brick buildings with fanlit doorways
and bare, half-finished government buildings.

It was April of 1844, the air mild, if not sweet-scented—April after the
long malarial winter, where hot and cold days alternated like beads upon a

string, and the meadows were 'gay with wild flowers,' while the rivers
were still 'sheets of ice.' [27] The languor of a Southern spring was drooping over the city, and if little white boys were energetically chasing stray
chickens, the wiser little black boys drowsed peacefully upon the sunny
curbings, horses' reins slung loosely around their ankles.

Her Majesty's envoy on his way to the State Department pushed his
way among spare, grave-faced New Englanders; clean-shaven Southerners,
immaculate in high stocks and gaily embroidered waistcoats, yet already
betraying the arrogance that was to ruin them; Westerners, one without
a cravat, one with his black hair braided like a woman's, still another in
the coonskin cap and fringed buckskins of the frontier; Indians, blanketed
and gloomy; and a somber chaingang of slave prisoners being moved
slowly forward in an 'enforced march.' And at last, the State Department office on the corner of Fifteenth Street—and Mr. Calhoun.

Seeing him there behind his desk, slender and noticeably stooped, bowing with the 'grace of a younger man,' and a 'courtesy that might have
come from generations of old aristocracy,' the British Minister may well
have wondered what kind of man he was. No breezy 'democratic' fellowship, no hearty joviality here. Although 'charmed' with Calhoun's genial
greeting, he would have felt a barrier between him and the stately Carolinian, which, although 'slight as gossamer, was as impenetrable as granite.' But this quality of reserve would not have been displeasing to an
Englishman. After days in a city raucous with the twang of the frontier
and the nasal whine of New England, the thick-edged Dutch inflections
of New York and Jersey, and the slurred syllables of Georgia and Florida,
he would have highly appreciated Calhoun's 'perfect' enunciation and pro-
nunciation, to which the flavor of the Scots-Irish would have borne a
familiar echo to Pakenham.[28]

But what was he? An 'idea . . . a consecrated purpose' he had long
seemed to the world at large ' . . . in Congress, in Cabinets, on this or the
other side of the throne of American power.' Certainly he looked the
part. He was 'unlike any other man,' with his tight lips and dark eyes
burning into Pakenham's as if to read his very thoughts, yet revealing
nothing of his own; his furrowed brow and thin cheeks, cut deep with
lines of passion and thought—'too intense for compromise.' What could
you make of a mind with all the keen-edged vigor of youth fused to a
finely poised flexibility on every subject but one, and on that one as
'fixed and unchangeable as a law of nature'? [29] To any thoughtful observer
at this period, Calhoun was a fascinating study, but for Pakenham he
was a living challenge to the powers of diplomacy.

Slowly, carefully, with infinite delicacy, the two men felt each other out,
parried, thrust, withdrew. It was America's wish, said Calhoun, to accomplish annexation in a manner 'agreeable' to the interests of both England and Mexico. Sir Richard declined to view any aspect of the situa-

tion as agreeable. Calhoun, calm and undisturbed, closed the interview, firmly declining correspondence.

Next came the Minister from Mexico. Mexico, Calhoun assured her anxious representative, would be well compensated if she renounced her claims. Five million dollars was the sum at which he hinted. But in this 'present' Mexico manifested no interest.

In a second conversation with Pakenham, Calhoun frankly admitted the anxieties of the slaveholding states, outlined details of his offer to Mexico. Why could not England, France, and the United States join in an alliance against all encroachments on the Mexican territory? Pakenham countered with a suggestion that all three bind themselves not to encroach upon the independence of Texas. Calhoun smilingly declined. This did not suit his 'present purpose.' [30]

But it was with the Minister from Texas himself that Calhoun's conversation was most disturbing. The Texas people wanted annexation, but not flamboyant Sam Houston, President of that Republic. Houston could afford to wait. Houston, nursing his grudges against Calhoun, fully conscious of his country's desirability in a colony-hungry world, could play England, France, and the United States off against each other for the best terms and for the best protection and recognition of himself.

And if the United States were to press annexation, 'friendship' and aid from the European Powers would cease. Mexico had never recognized the independence of Texas; she would regard annexation as an unfriendly act, and might take measures. Was the United States prepared to give satisfactory assurance of her intent to defend the soil of her prospective territory?

This was the question that Mr. Upshur had found unanswerable. Death had freed him from the responsibility. Calhoun, who was willing 'to sacrifice everything but his honor to obtain Texas,' [31] would risk even war to obtain his end, but he had no power to commit the United States. Nor did he want Texas to enter the Union as a conquered territory, but as an independent state. However, a United States naval squadron could be placed in the Gulf of Mexico. Extra troops could be sent to the Southwest frontier. 'The President,' Calhoun assured the Texan Minister, 'would deem it his duty to use all the means placed in his power *by the Constitution* to protect Texas from foreign invasion.' The inclusion of three words saved him, for without the support of Congress, the President had no power to declare war. But Calhoun's assurances were enough for the Minister, who at the 'Texas dinner' on May 18, offered a toast to the Secretary of State: 'When he thinks he is right, he will go ahead no matter how great the responsibility; and had he the power, the army would doubtless be ordered right into Texas to repel any attack on her.' [32]

10

Calhoun's activities during the previous few weeks had been intense. On April 22, 1844, he laid before the Senate his Treaty of Annexation, complete with copies of correspondence between Lord Aberdeen and Pakenham, which promised that England would use no 'improper' influence to prevent annexation. Included was his own note to Pakenham, the audacity of which was scarcely paralleled in American diplomatic history. 'I took the broad ground,' he wrote a friend, 'that our policy was to interfere with no other country, and to allow no other country to interfere' with our internal concerns. Actually his ground was far broader. With disconcerting frankness he had thrust the entire responsibility for annexation upon England herself. Even indirect influence upon Texas, he contended, was 'improper.' England's own actions were forcing annexation upon America 'in imperious self-defense.' 'The time is come,' he declared, 'when England must be met on the abolition question.' [33]

Sir Richard Pakenham's response was bitter. It was a misrepresentation to say that the Texas Treaty was the result of British views. British views had been known all along. Furthermore, had not Calhoun himself been an open annexationist as early as 1836?

The charge was true, but Calhoun had the law upon his side. Neither England nor the United States was responsible for Calhoun's private views as a Senator. He was not the Senator from South Carolina now, but the representative of the United States, accountable for no beliefs and no action but those of the government. Furthermore, whatever Britain's views had been in past years, it was only now that they were officially avowed.

Calhoun had saved himself by his ingenious inclusion among the papers laid before the Senate of a Presidential statement that present conditions merely confirmed Mr. Tyler's 'previous impressions.' Naturally, none knew better than Calhoun and Pakenham that negotiations for Texas had been under way for months, wholly on the basis of unofficial 'information.' Even now the secret words of Duff Green bore more weight than the open avowals of Lord Aberdeen, which served as the mere excuse to complete work already begun.

11

But what a storm was stirred up! Reverberations thundered from Downing Street. Great Britain had 'no thought or intention of seeking to act directly or indirectly . . . on the United States through Texas.'

Calhoun's bald assertion that slavery was the issue may have united

the South, but it had as thoroughly united the North, by admitting what
had been suspected from the first. Calhoun's feelings had run away with
him, and the brilliant logician, who had so meticulously shown that slavery was a question pertaining only to the states, now stood before the
nations of the world, openly committing the American government to the
defense of the South's 'domestick institution,' and openly declaring that
an attack on slavery anywhere was an attack on slavery everywhere.[34] He
had wrecked his own best argument.

Fury swept the North. Massachusetts, 'faithful to the compact between the people of the United States,' declared Charles Francis Adams,
saw that 'the annexation of Texas, unless resisted, may drive these states
into a dissolution of the Union.' Whittier frothed with poetic fury at
'slave-accursed Texas.' Calhoun's best friends feared the result of his
boldness. Admirers could contend that his 'open avowal . . . of the real
motives . . . was . . . what the American public expected from the
known candor and high and honorable bearing . . . so . . . admired in
John C. Calhoun.'[35] Yet even they saw that the issue might 'endanger the
Union,' and watched the votes for annexation melt into the mist. Preston
railed that his one-time colleague considered questions only in relation
to the 'elections of 1848'; and 'little Aleck' Stephens saw the whole Texas
scheme as 'got up to divide and distract the Whig Party at the South,'
or to accomplish the 'dissolution of the present Confederacy.' Would
Mr. Calhoun destroy a country of which he could not be chief magistrate?

Not even the South would stand by Calhoun. Who would risk war with
an election in the offing? When the final vote was counted, only sixteen
Senators had dared approve annexation, despite roars from old Andrew
Jackson that 'There was never such treason to the South.' Stephens wondered how Calhoun could dream the Senate was so 'lost to all sense of national honor . . . as to ratify this treaty.'[36] Yet so overwhelming was the
shock of defeat that in a momentary fit of despondency, Calhoun actually
advised Tyler to abandon the whole question, and for weeks the project
lay dormant.[37]

12

Texas alone was enough to tax any one man's powers of diplomacy. But
all through the negotiations, Calhoun had a second personal war on his
hands, with his son Andrew on the one side and Anna Maria's husband,
Thomas Clemson, on the other. Andrew, an Alabama cotton planter, had
unfortunately inherited all of his father's indifference to money, with little
of his scrupulousness in the use of it. Certainly he was no fit business
partner for the dour Thomas Clemson, a stickler for accuracy, strict
ethics, and square bargains. From his embassy post in Belgium, Clemson
constantly harassed his father-in-law with a lengthy list of accusations
against Andrew, and Calhoun, refusing to take sides, attempted solution

by personally shouldering the blame. Apparently he never mentioned matters to Andrew with whom he was on the most affectionate terms and whom he frequently defended against Floride's criticisms. To Clemson he promised payment of 'every cent due you.' Loftily his moralistic son-in-law declined the offer. 'You take upon yourself,' he wrote Calhoun, 'what I think ought to rest elsewhere.' [38]

In common with Calhoun's entire family, Clemson seemed to think that the Secretary of State had plenty of time to manage his family's personal affairs. Calhoun was of the same opinion. He always felt that the strong should bear the burdens of the weak; but he was often very weary, and hinted as much to Clemson, who merely responded: 'I have no doubt your occupations are very laborious. I wish it were in my power to alleviate them.' [39]

The presumptuous Pennsylvanian had no hesitation in asking his father-in-law to ride over his entire plantation, discharge the overseer, see to the Negroes, and arrange for everything that ought to be done. His father-in-law would do so. A letter from Floride: 'Anxiety has been too much for me.' Did he remember that green silk shawl, striped with leaves, which he had brought her from Washington years before? She was afraid that it had been lost at the dyer's. Would he see to it? He would.

A note from James at the University of Virginia. He needed some books. Would his father find them? His father would.

There was Calhoun's brother-in-law, James Colhoun, whose young bride had just died. He must write James. 'My deep condolence to you. . . . I will not attempt . . . consolation. Your bereavement is too great for that. When the wound is so deep, nothing but a change of scene or the gentle hand of time can assuage the pain. You must not think of remaining alone. . . . The scenes around you will but . . . remind you of your loss and convert your grief into bitter gloom. We urge you to make our home your home, at least for some months to come. . . . Your affliction has been great, but you are too young . . . to retire from the drama of life. While health and strength remain we have duties to perform.' [40]

Like many busy men, Calhoun found time and energy to do an enormous number of things. How he managed it was a marvel even to those who knew him best, but Miss Bates, the governess, noted that he wasted no time, and that 'by gathering up the fragments he had enough and to spare.' Small wonder, however, that he was obliged to live by the clock, to rise before dawn to attend to his voluminous correspondence.[41] And small wonder that we find him writing home: 'I feel myself a Trustee for you all.'

But he was never too tired to reach eagerly for the bulky letters with the Belgian postmark, addressed in Anna Maria's angular, illegible script, so like his own; or the tiny, precise lettering of his 'affectionate son,' Thomas Clemson. Clemson was to be presented at Court and had been trying on his 'stiff,' ornate uniform. 'Anna laughs at me a good deal about it,' Clemson wrote, 'and wishes that you were here to see me. She says you would die laughing.'

Gay, teasing notes from Anna Maria, sometimes scrawled across the back of her husband's letters—these were the best of all. 'Seeing so much blank paper going begging,' she would explain, 'I may as well fill it, even with nonsense.' She would dash off bits of chatter about her gowns, her impressions of Paris, and assurances that the children were as 'smart as ever, in spite of all you say to the contrary.' Christmas was coming! What would he like for a present? 'It is not the value of things I know which you will think of. . . . For Mother and Sister there were a thousand things one might send, but you are a man so utterly without fancies that it is hard to know what would suit you.' She had decided upon a black silk cravat, which was 'ridiculous to have sent you.'[42]

Letters of this kind—Anna Maria's assurances that 'I love you all dearly and am crazy to see you'; Clemson's news that 'The little fellow [Calhoun Clemson] often talks of you'—were rare refreshment in Calhoun's overladen days. From home the news was less cheerful. Floride's nervous 'agitated' letters informed him of every article of clothing down to the last pair of pantaloons which she had packed in the boys' trunks, and every symptom of their ailments, which were frequent and severe. The younger boys, especially John and William, were frail, all troubled with ominous chest weakness and 'constant cough.' Like their father, they were brilliant mentally, although, to his regret, none shared his taste for the 'classicks.' John was studying medicine at the University of Virginia, his letters so charming, so filled with enthusiastic descriptions of the University's beauties that Calhoun proudly passed them on to his brother-in-law. John's ill health, however, was a continual worry to his father, and when entering him in the University, he had written at length to the law professor, Henry St. George Tucker, urging that his son 'have the benefit of the best medical advice that can be obtained.' He was 'exceedingly uneasy' about him.[43]

Calhoun was just congratulating himself that he had gotten his two youngest boys confined in a small backwoods college, where 'there will be nothing to divert their attention from study and their morals will be safe,' when he received distressing news. Enforced morality and the charms of learning had been too much for James, who had deserted within two weeks. Calhoun was deeply disappointed. He had planned soon to send the boys to a larger college, but at the moment they were utterly unfit for anything better. In fact, their dislike of Greek and Latin was so intense that their father took time out from the Texas negotiations to write the college president that to make his sons study the hated languages would be a useless waste of time.

Of the restless, headstrong James, Calhoun had great hopes, but he knew his weaknesses. He was reckless and extravagant, easily 'led astray by bad company.' It had been to prevent him from overindulging himself that his father had put him 'in the woods.' 'He has good talents and great ambition,' Calhoun wrote his ever-sympathetic brother-in-law, 'and all that is wanted is to give them the right direction to make him distinguished in life.' With evident foreboding the indulgent father gave way to the boy's pleadings and entered him in the University of Virginia, where surprisingly he became 'much attached to his studies.' By December, 1846, Calhoun was again writing, 'I begin to have much hope of him.' [44] But this most promising of all his boys, although he outlived his father, died young.

13

Despite his years, Calhoun seems to have borne the duties of the State Department with less physical strain than he had undergone during his time as War Secretary. His tasks were no less arduous. As Secretary of State he was virtually 'the master-spirit of the American Government'; and was amazed himself at 'the immense influence' his Department exerted 'on foreign and domestick affairs.' [45] The National Archives give vivid illustration of the tasks that confronted him. There was the diplomatic correspondence, official and unofficial, the parrying and sparring in the interviews; explanations to the Senate that 'no salary attaches to the appointment' of Mr. Duff Green as consul at Galveston. Discovering that the port collectors could not complete their returns in time for the convening of Congress on January first of each year, he set back their date to early in September. He even chose and ordered the books for the Department library: histories of England and of Greece, the *Transactions of the Royal Geographic Society, History of India*, Rardinel's *History of the Slave Trade*, the history of the Oregon territory, and *The Travels of Marco Polo*.[46]

The duties of the Department, he thought, had been 'shamefully neglected.' [47] He tackled them with driving energy. In his scant eleven months of service he endowed the Department with the same clean-cut efficiency that had characterized the War Office when he had closed the door upon it. But he had no surplus strength to fritter on detail—through sheer physical necessity he had at last learned to delegate authority.

Clerks found him 'courteous, affable, and considerate.' He was less irritable than in his younger days, less tense; and although tolerating not 'the slightest carelessness,' toward unintentional mistakes he was unexpectedly 'kind and lenient.' [48]

He took his responsibilities, however, with overwhelming seriousness. He was annoyed by Tyler's happy-go-lucky manner, and made it perfectly plain to the President that he would conduct his own Department in his own way. It was no secret to the departmental underlings that the President and his high-handed Cabinet officer reached a near-rupture over the appointment of an aide to Ambassador William R. King, for Calhoun insisted that the assistant, regardless of his political qualifications, must be able to speak French.

14

Although Calhoun's 'bold,' unhesitating course gave him 'power as a statesman before the civilized world,' he was no ideal Secretary of State as Webster had been. He had neither the means nor the energy to play host at those mighty ten-course dinners which his predecessor had so enjoyed. He was, in fact, excused from arduous social duties. So strongly were his energies concentrated on his main purpose that he had even considered serving without pay if he could have been freed from routine departmental duties and given *carte blanche* on the settlement of the Texas and Oregon questions.[49]

But he was not a recluse. For the last time he went out into that Washington society where, dining on terrapin and canvasback ducks, guests argued the merits of Dante and Virgil, or Byron and Wordsworth, where George Sand was mentioned with 'bated breath,' and *Lady Audley's Secret* was always a secret to the young.[50]

At Presidential receptions it was noted that the Secretary of State was kept busy shaking hands with as many people as Tyler himself. And the President's 'informal receptions' in that most formal East Room, with its row of crystal chandeliers and its enameled paneling, were as popular as Tyler's policies were distasteful. At the President's invitation, fashionable and unfashionable Washington alike attended the Saturday afternoon Marine Band concerts on the White House lawn. There you saw the portly Benton, strolling up and down, looking as if keeping up 'a gentle remonstrance with himself for being so much greater than the rest of the world'; gaunt and crippled George McDuffie of South Carolina, 'formed in the same physical mold as Mr. Calhoun, but bearing aloft a cavalier's head'; Vice-President Dallas, in his black suit and immaculate white cravat, his dark eyes shining beneath heavy black brows, and a mass of curly white hair; and Secretary of State Calhoun, 'tall and gray and thin,' bowing to his friends, his hand upon his heart.[51]

Fully appreciative of the festivities was the President's bride, Julia Gardiner, writing ecstatic notes to her mother of her excitement when the great men of the day were presented to her. 'Her wit, her piquancy . . . bewitching grave and gay, old and young . . . she was one of those born to shine, to carry hearts by storm.'[52] But this was said of her later. Now she was a frightened girl, subjected to the whispered taunts of those who believed she had married the President only because he was the President. And it was Secretary of State Calhoun who played no small part in smoothing her way.

He came to her rescue at her own wedding reception, when Tyler, suddenly engrossed in his responsibilities as President, left Julia alone and uncertain in the middle of the floor. It was Calhoun who stepped to her side, gently took her arm, and led her to the table where he helped her cut and serve her wedding cake. From that time on, the austere Southerner and the 'captain's bride' were 'excellent friends.'

At a crowded dinner table, Julia gaily promised that she would make it a point of honor to see that her friend, Judge John McLean, voted for the Texas annexation. 'There is no honor in politics,' snapped Calhoun. Tyler, whose 'sense of political honor was rigid,' was startled when she repeated the conversation in their bedroom, and asked her, 'almost sternly, "Did Calhoun say that?"' But Julia found nothing in her later knowledge of men or events to change her respect for the Secretary's opinion.

Never had Calhoun's closest friends seen him 'so sociable' as he was these days. At a 'merry' Cabinet dinner, Calhoun at Julia's side made himself 'particularly engaging.' For to her utter amazement, he whispered poetry into her ear 'with infinite sweetness and taste.' Tyler 'could scarcely have been more astonished if an explosion had occurred beneath his feet.' 'Well,' said he, 'upon my word, I must look out for a new Secretary of State, if Calhoun is to stop writing despatches and go to repeating verses.' [53]

15

At the Texas Treaty's rejection in the spring of 1844, the lagging hopes of England and France leaped into new flame. Both nations fairly stumbled over each other in their pledges to 'guarantee' Texas independence. In London, Lord Aberdeen promised the Mexican Minister that if Mexico would recognize Texas, France and England would jointly guarantee the independence of Mexico.

The 'proceedings of other Powers in Texas' was no surprise to Calhoun. Nor were the machinations of bitter Sam Houston any secret to Tyler, who remarked that Houston's 'billing and cooing with England was as serious a love affair as any in the calendar.'

From Bremen, United States Consul Ambrose Dudley Mann revealed a British plot to cut off Texas from all European trade except with herself. 'Would to Heaven,' explained Mann, 'that my country-men could . . . see what I have seen . . . of British diplomacy. With one voice they would exclaim: "Give us Texas, if possible without a War, but give us Texas."' From Paris the American Minister, William R. King, confirmed

Calhoun's belief that 'under the pretext of humanity towards the Slave,' Britain's 'real object' was 'to engross to herself the entire production of Shugar and in a great degree, that of cotton and Rice.' [54] Furthermore, the Empire was 'exerting herself to induce France to make common cause with her.'

'Unofficial'—'Private,' many of these letters were marked, but their information was none the less real. Unofficial, too, had been Captain Marryat's little book, in which he had quoted Dr. Channing Gould's opinion that 'it should be a *sina qua non* with England' that Texas should adhere to the law of abolition which was in force 'at the time that she was an integral part of Mexico. . . . If Texas is admitted into the Union, all thought of . . . abolition . . . must be thrown forward to . . . an indefinite period. . . . If Texas remains independent . . . slavery abolished, she becomes . . . not only the greatest check to slavery, but eventually the means of its abolition.' [55]

Which summarized Calhoun's opinion precisely.

16

Word from Andrew Jackson Donelson, new American Chargé d'Affaires in Texas, helped to spur the Secretary of State's lagging hopes into action. Donelson could give Calhoun at least momentary assurance that Houston's doubts and dodges were being resolved by immediate pressure from Donelson and more remote but equally effective pressure from his old friend at the Hermitage. Carefully circulated through the Texas Congress was assurance that 'the General is still sanguine of the success of . . . re-annexation, and awaits . . . fulfillment of the popular wish in the United States.' The general feeling in the Texas Congress was of 'the best,' Donelson reported. But he sounded a warning: the British and French Ministers at Galveston, 'very active in their exertions against annexation . . . report that no measure consummating annexation can get more than Twenty votes in our Senate. . . . I hope they will be disappointed.' [56] Calhoun's own dismay at the treaty's rejection had been primarily due to shock. He had been amazed at the rebuff from a Senate, which in answer to the 'unanimous voice' of the country (as he believed) had called him to the State office for the express and sole purpose of bringing Texas into the Union. He had been wrecked by his own zeal. It was because he had not answered the unanimous voice of the country, not placed the question on the broad national grounds it deserved, that he had failed in his objective. No Northern Congressman who cared two cents for his re-election would vote for a measure openly committing the entire United States to the endorsement of slavery. Calhoun had not even invoked the diplomatic subterfuges of language by which he could have made the dose tolerable. He had acted avowedly as a slave promoter, and by doing so had played the part, not of a statesman, but of a Southern partisan.

But by autumn of 1844, although positive as ever that Texas was still a slavery question, he had known what he must do. His means must be wholly American. His error had cost time, yet events were moving on his side. In May, dark horse James Knox Polk, Andrew Jackson's 'Young Hickory,' had galloped off with the Democratic nomination on an avowed Texas and Oregon expansionist program. His election by a hairline margin that November was interpreted by Tyler as the demand of 'a controlling majority' of Americans 'in terms the most emphatic,' [57] that annexation be accomplished.

Jackson, Tyler, and Calhoun had all gauged the public will more accurately than a pre-election Congress. Whether slave or free, Texas tantalized the American imagination. In the heat and froth of a Presidential campaign even Northern Democrats could give tacit support to annexation. Northern business leaders saw now the truth of Calhoun's claim that the addition of Texas to the Union would be as profitable, economically, to the North as to the South.[58]

On September 10, 1844, federal forces were ordered to enter Texas for 'protection' against possible Mexican invasion. It was a bold game he was playing, pitting the dying Jackson against the plotting Houston, the Southern slavocracy against the British Empire, uniting the divergent groups and the divergent aims, the cupidity of the American traders, the greed of the Western expansionists, the party ambitions of the Northerners, the life-and-death hopes of the Southerners, all into a single weapon for his purposes.

But of one fact Calhoun was sure. Mexico would not fight. She was penniless, for one thing; for months the American State Department had been dunning her for debts due under the Treaty of 1843, taunting her for her want of honor. By December she would be all but 'prostrated' in 'the midst of a revolution,' [59] as Shannon informed Calhoun.

Mexico would not fight without the aid of Britain, and Britain would not fight to undo a *fait accompli*, Calhoun was convinced. Texas was interesting to England only so long as it remained independent, and her ideals for the Lone Star Republic could not compete with her economic ambitions for Oregon.

In February, 1845, Calhoun's health gave way. He contracted a 'congestive fever,' so severe that for several days his life hung in the balance. Worn out from the months of work, he had little strength to fight infection, and Francis Wharton, who visited him in his bedroom at the United States Hotel, was shocked at his emaciation and weakness. Coughing, his cheeks flushed with fever, his recovery had been visibly thrown back by the necessity of seeing visitors and working at full speed from the moment he had been able to leave his bed. He wrote his family that he was 'completely restored,' but to Wharton he admitted that his health was breaking and that he longed now for nothing but complete retirement.[60]

17

But there was no rest for him in the next four weeks. Time was running short. He knew that he would not return to the Cabinet, even if Polk asked him; and Polk had no intention of asking him, having no desire to shine as the lesser light in his own Administration. He was unmoved by a curt reminder from Duff Green that 'anything necessitating' the departure of Mr. Calhoun would be 'against the principles for which you were elected.' Principles? What had principles to do with elections?

Calhoun knew that he must play to win. He had never admitted failure; he would not do so now. He could not be scrupulous in his methods or instruments. At his shoulder John Tyler sounded the keynote for those last frantic days. It mattered not 'how' annexation was accomplished, 'but whether it shall be accomplished, or not.' [61]

There was a way out, but hitherto Calhoun had hesitated to use it. Several years before, Robert Walker had suggested two means of acquiring territory; either by treaty or by joint resolution of the two houses of Congress. It was upon this second method that Calhoun seized.

Not even McDuffie believed that he would have 'the audacity' to do it. Not even this close friend knew the fanatic determination of Calhoun. No act of his career has been more scourged by history: that Calhoun, the strict constitutionalist, the doctrinaire who had raged in holy horror at Jackson's evasions of constitutional safeguards in the name of the popular will, should interpret the election as a mandate for the admission of Texas, should, in the opinion of many, violate the Constitution, the symbol of 'our peculiar and sublime political system.'

That his move, based as it was on majority opinion and majority rule, was in defiance of his federal theories, cannot be denied. Yet there was nothing more 'unconstitutional' about it than there had been in the purchase of Louisiana forty years before. Neither treaty nor joint resolution was specifically mentioned in the Constitution as the method for acquiring territory; and in signing the treaty for Louisiana, even Jefferson had admitted that, as a 'strict constructionist,' he had 'done an act beyond the Constitution.' [62]

No doubts troubled Calhoun. At his side stood a powerful ally, none other than Daniel Webster, the 'Defender of the Constitution' himself, who insisted that he could see nothing unconstitutional in Calhoun's position. He did feel compelled to add, however, that if the principle were invoked too frequently, America might wake up one morning to find all Canada annexed to the Federal Union.[63]

Calhoun's 'conclusive reason,' however, had little to do with the Constitution. A treaty required the two-thirds vote of the Senate, 'which could hardly be expected, if we are to judge from recent experience.' A joint resolution required but a simple majority of both houses, and thus was 'the only certain mode by which annexation could be effected.' [64] He would not again risk the hazard of defeat under the two-thirds rule. And less partisan history has had admiration for the man who scorned to let a 'small group of wilful men' defeat a great national objective.

18

Calhoun had calculated correctly. By a reasonably safe vote, and with a reasonable amount of approval, Congress did pass the joint resolution. Calhoun sounded the final word, 'act without delay.' On March 19, 1845, the President approved the resolution; the next day the Cabinet met to express its acquiescence. Late on the night of March 3, a few hours before his Presidency ended, John Tyler and Secretary of State Calhoun signed and sent off the dispatch inviting Texas to enter the American Union. Final action would be taken by Polk, but to all practical purposes Calhoun and Tyler had added to the American Union the greatest expanse of territory since the purchase of Louisiana.

Calhoun's work was done. Mindful of his own dismay, when confronted with the immensity of the State Department, he remained in Washington a few days to assist the new Secretary, James Buchanan. On March 10, 1845, as crowds gathered in Texas to cheer the annexation, Calhoun started home. There was nothing in his career of which he was more proud than of this crowning act of his term as Secretary of State.

XXIII

The Master of Fort Hill

WITH THE POSSIBLE EXCEPTION of George Washington, no American statesman has been more thoroughly dehumanized than John C. Calhoun. The 'uncrowned king' of South Carolina has suffered the fate of the 'father of his country' in having his virtues magnified into pomposities, his faults gilded by hero-worship. It took a hundred years to excavate George Washington from the layers of priggish perfection under which the idolizing Weems had buried him. And John Calhoun's Parson Weems was Miss Mary Bates.

This little New England schoolmarm, who came to Fort Hill as governess to the Calhoun children, worshiped her great employer. She confided her interpretations of him to a little pamphlet entitled 'The Private Life of John C. Calhoun,' which contains the undoubted proof that a man can be a hero to his children's governess if not to his valet. Yet in her attempts at deification, Miss Bates is responsible for a statement that has darkened Calhoun's name for seventy years. 'I never heard him utter a jest,'[1] she declared. Perhaps she never did. Probably her own atmosphere was sufficiently chilling to cool her idol's moments of warmth. But John Quincy Adams in his *Diary* more than once deplored Calhoun's tendency to joke on serious political matters and his outbursts of mirth at inopportune moments of Cabinet debate;[2] and Anna Maria Clemson and James Edward Colhoun were also aware of Calhoun's unmistakable flashes of humor.

Miss Bates was apparently distressed that so abstemious a man as her famed employer did not share her enthusiasm for the principles of the Christian Temperance Union. Perhaps she was blissfully unaware of his youthful days when he was happily raising his own grapes and making his own wine, but there was no mistaking his meaning when he 'kindly' told Miss Bates that he believed she was carrying things 'a little too far.' He had small 'relish' for whiskey, brandy, or rum, which he regarded more as medicine than beverages,[3] but he was fond of claret and served it at his dinner table. It must have been difficult for her to reconcile this with her belief that he was superior 'to those things which the natural heart

most craves . . . he was so purely intellectual, so free from self-indul-
gence . . . he did not even indulge himself in a cigar.' [4]

Calhoun did not indulge himself in cigars. He happened to prefer his
tobacco in other forms. He took snuff, perhaps without the dash and flair of
Henry Clay, but often enough to give rise to a slogan, 'When Calhoun took
snuff, South Carolina sneezed.' [5] And at Fort Hill his morning smoke was
something of a ritual. Every day after breakfast young Cato was sent to
the kitchen with a pair of tiny wire tongs to pick up a live coal for his
master's pipe. While Calhoun was 'lighting up,' the boy would lug a
bucket of cold water to the office and make it ready for the day's work. [6]

An outside office was a fixture on the Southern plantation, where unwritten law declared that the overseer must never enter the dwelling
house. At Fort Hill it was a tiny white clapboarded structure behind the
living-room ell, with a miniature porch and four white columns across the
front. Only one story high, it was kept endurably and damply cool by
the icehouse in the cellar, and the shade from Admiral Decatur's varnish
tree, Henry Clay's arbor-vitae, and Webster's hemlock, all standing near,
and all gifts to Calhoun through the years. Inside was a somber, untidy
man's room, the gloom of oak-painted walls, bookcase, and pine table
accented by the tall black mantel over the fireplace. There was a comfortable lounging chair, a cabinet with a secret compartment, where Calhoun kept his private correspondence, and a massive, scarred, mahogany
desk, on which he wrote his nullification papers and his book, and at which
he devoted one or two whole days a week merely to answering his mail.
On the one handsome piece of furniture in the room—a carved rosewood
table, with a top of black-veined, Italian marble—were heaped letters
from celebrities all over the world: politicians, scholars, poets, philosophers,
and preachers. But near the table was a wastebasket, and this, too, was
usually filled with letters, these from unknown or anonymous writers, some
frankly hero-worshiping, others of censure or abuse. Whatever their nature,
Calhoun threw them away, scarcely read, from which fate the fan mail,
at least, was secretly rescued by Anna Maria or Cornelia. [7]

The bookcase extended out into the room, its contents available from
either the front or the back. Here were practically all the books in the
family, for Floride, who was no great reader, got her *Tales of the Good
Woman, Bluestocking Hall,* and *Sailors and Saints* from the Pendleton
Library Society; [8] but all Calhoun's marked and worn favorites were there:
Plutarch and Aristotle; the farmer's poet, Virgil, the histories of Rome and
of Poland, his Plato, in which he once declared could be found the whole
Constitution of the United States, the old volume on the diseases of cattle
which Floride had brought him at the time of their marriage, a modernized
version of the Bible, and the 'Ossianic' poems. [9] On the wall hung a large
chart which he had bought for the amusement and instruction of his
children. A fascinating curiosity it was, made up of revolving disks, which

asked various questions on American history and geography, with different answers for each of the states. Deer antlers and bearskins alternated with great maps of South Carolina, Texas, and the Louisiana Purchase; a picture of Calhoun's 'best friend and worst enemy,' Henry Clay, hung near an autographed pose of Davy Crockett, hero of the Alamo.

A ship model of the *Constitution* adorned the mantel; in a corner Cornelia's little crutches often leaned against her father's jointed fishing rod, for she spent hours with him, frequently writing to his dictation. The relation between Calhoun and this little girl was especially tender. A fall from a swing had injured her spine, and her years had been spent in agonizing waits and examinations in doctors' offices, her parents' hopes rising as their finances dwindled. But not even the great Philadelphia surgeon, Dr. Philip Syng Physick, could 'restore' Cornelia. Although crippled, she was content; she was 'bright,' although not intellectual. 'I am especially relieved to know Cornelia has become fond of her books,' Calhoun once wrote home, 'as I had almost despaired that she ever would.'[10] When at home it was he who nursed her, petted her, spoiled her, granted her the freedom of his 'sacred' office and his newspapers. And if she opened and read his favorite magazines, even when he was longing to see them, he refused to have her disturbed until she had finished.

2

No one really knew Calhoun who did not know him at Fort Hill. Fort Hill was the symbol of all in life that he prized. Understanding his love for his plantation, we can understand all the surface vagaries and inconsistencies of his career. 'After all,' he said, 'there is no life like a farmer's life, and no pursuit like that of agriculture.'[11]

Unlike Webster at Marshfield, Calhoun was no 'squire' or 'laird' to his Pendleton neighbors. He had no artificial rules such as Webster enforced at home, forbidding all discussion of law or politics. Political discussion was as essential to these Southern farmers as eating or sleeping. To Webster, Marshfield was the escape; to Calhoun, Fort Hill was the reality. Webster's biographer was puzzled by 'the representative of bankers and manufacturers' finding his 'chief delight in agriculture.'[12] In Calhoun were no such tensions. He moved among his neighbors, 'the great Mr. Calhoun,' a 'lion even in the neighborhood of his own house,'[13] yet one of them. Intellectually few of his contemporaries knew or understood him, but emotionally he was a man whom they could all know and understand.

For so complex a man Calhoun's wants were very simple. Good health, good crops, and his family, were all that he asked of life. At Fort Hill he was content, at peace with himself and in harmony with his entire existence. He loved it all, the quiet hours with his books, his visitors, the flower garden where bloomed the cuttings that he himself had planted and chosen, the long twilights on the porch, when brush-fires glowed against the darkness. 'He knew the zest of life,' declared his cousin James, 'only and fully at his home.' [14]

In the work of the farm he found outlet for all his energies, and at the height of the planting season was often in the saddle from seven-thirty in the morning until the dark of night. The days were not long enough for all that he wanted to do. Whether he kept the usual planter's day-book is unknown, but some idea of his problems can be obtained from a study of the plantation-book of his friend, William Lowndes. There would be the distribution of the blankets, of the 'pease' and potato allowances, the allotments of rice and corn, the problems of ditching and the new 'head Dam'; the problem of how many bushels of seed to the acre. [15]

With his analytical mind Calhoun might have figured out, as Lowndes did, the number of 'hands' used to make shingles and of coopers to make barrels, estimating that 'two fellows should fell 20 trees per day,' and that 'in threshing a whole day 2 Men or 3 Women should thresh 1200 sheaves.' [16] Where Lowndes had drawn a plan for his new cotton gin, Calhoun might have drawn a rough outline of his new grist mill. Nor could the distribution of the specialized work of the plantation be entirely left to the overseer's decision. It required time and thought to weigh the abilities and inclinations of each young 'hand' so that plowman, weaver, carpenter, cooper, herdsman, driver, wagoner, shoemaker, and wheelwright might be most usefully and efficiently fitted into the economic unit of the plantation-state.

What most amazed those who thought of Calhoun as a dreamer and theorist was the hard-headed practicality with which he farmed. [17] Twenty years in Washington had cost him nothing of his almost instinctive skills and understandings of the land. He dared to be different, to experiment. Everything that the land would grow he planted: figs, melons, pear trees, mulberries. A hollow in one of the bottoms, where the stagnant water lingered, troubled him. He finally planted it in rice, and to the amazement of the neighborhood, drew an annual yield enough to supply his entire family.

Occasionally his interests spurted in strange directions. He tried cattle-breeding, crossing a dark, red, humpbacked 'sacred cow' to the swamp cattle of the marsh lands. Another year it was grapes; and by sheer persistence, he made the 'first successful attempts at grape culture in that part of the country.' One year it was silkworms, and for months the family was subjected to an invasion of cocoons, dropping unheralded from the shelves of every closet, barn, storehouse, and outbuilding on the plantation. Net result: three silk suits for Calhoun.

He even pitted himself against soil erosion, the most terrible problem the Southern farmer had to face. That the plantation system was wasteful, even its devotees knew; year by year you could watch the spread of the 'old fields,' washed and worn away by thundering rains and careless cotton planting. But Calhoun had a solution. His neighbors might shake their heads with amusement when he planted peavines with the corn, sowed the fields with Siberian wheat and the lawns with Bermuda grass. They wondered at his carefully terraced hillsides and 'peculiar' methods of 'ditching, drainage, and planting.' But they read their answer in the earth itself. In years when rain splashed their fields with gullies and the streams ran red with topsoil, Calhoun's land lay unbroken and his yield was as rich as before.[18]

It was not all easy. There was the year of the big drought, with the cotton 'small and backward' and the corn 'low.' There was the year of the big yield when the bolls swelled on the vines and the corn shot up as if reaching for the sun that gave it growth. But that, too, was the year when cotton tumbled below five cents a pound; and market news brought from a late steamer cost Calhoun two thousand dollars, just after he had made five hundred dollars' worth of improvements. But on the whole the land gave him rich return for his care. That even in a drought he could make an average crop if the work were under his own supervision, he wrote Clemson, 'speaks pretty well for my farming.'[19]

At Fort Hill were the best quarters, the best breeds of stock, and the finest crops in the entire county. A 'model farm' was the verdict of the members of a learned agricultural committee, who inspected the place in 1844. They watched as the lanky owner staked off his graded ditches, gauged the width of the fireplaces and the cross-sweep of ventilation in the long stone quarters, and looked with unconcealed admiration on the fat red Devon cows, imported from England a few years before. Yet for Calhoun, the incurable perfectionist, their praise was not enough. The chafing knowledge that he could give only a fraction of his time to the work he loved most dulled the edge of his enjoyment; and to James Colhoun he once burst out, 'If I had not been in public life, my crop would easily be a thousand bales.'[20]

3

His retirement from the State Department in 1845 gave him six consecutive months at Fort Hill. For one half-year, he could give himself up to the sheer enjoyment of the life he loved. Now time was not marked off by days on a calendar, but by the pulse and rhythm of the life about him. It was March when he came home, and the red clay hills looked deceptively barren and bare. Finished were the tasks of winter: the slaughtering of the hogs, the hauling of ice and wood, and the turning of the low ground stubble. It was cotton-planting time now; a yoke of oxen were slowly plowing around the rugged slopes; the 'hands' were hard at work, drilling oats, rolling and cutting logs, clearing ground, and burning brush. Now and then the fires went out of control, and Calhoun would be out fighting the flames with his Negroes and the help of such few neighbors as might see the blur of smoke against the sky.[21]

By April, the 'hands' were walking up and down the fresh-cut rows, 'drapping corn.' The last of the spring labors were completed: the rails hauled up, the briars cut, more rows plowed, more drilling for cotton and for corn. June and July were the months of hoeing and hilling, of plowing the corn and cutting the oats, of scraping down the cotton and thrashing the grain. The old fields were green; across from the house on Fort Hill the harvested wheat was standing in shocks. August—and the fierce, slow heat of deep summer, even the air from the mountains languid and warm— it was resting time now, the time of family reunions and all-day 'sings'; and Calhoun, looking on the curving rows of cotton flowers in their pink bloom, might have thought of his own boyhood when he had known the meaning of heat and thirst and the weariness and deep exhausted sleep that comes after an August day in a cotton field.[22] And there was still work to be done, oats to be hauled and stacked, fodder to be pulled, extra buckets of water to be drawn from the well, buckets of milk to be lowered into the cool darkness.

September was still planting time and picking time, time to sow the turnips and dig the yams, time to pick the cotton. By October, the last white sack, dragging along the row behind the field hand, lay flat and empty; the great wagons were loaded; mules moved forward, heads bent, neck and back muscles straining; huge wheels creaked and groaned their way down the red, rutted road to the gin.

In the evening, time flowed more slowly; Calhoun walked, instead of rode, sometimes a rifle in his hands, or a stick, as long as his vigorous strides. Work was stilled; he could take the road down by the quarters, look across the cornfields to the hills beyond, white with their load of cotton. Or he could walk down the path to the river, where the garnet clay shifted off into red, into rose, into yellow sand and mud; and the pine trees in stern blackness crowned the ridge of the hill. Where steep little hills rushed down to narrow ravines at the bottom, he could look down on the floating softness of dogwood petals. A few steps more—and the Seneca glinted through the tangled branches; and the warm pink undertone of the river-bed glowed through the silvery rush of water.

Calhoun had 'gazed in rapture' on some of the most beautiful scenery in the land. He knew the sea-green mist on the Litchfield hills in the spring, the great fields of Pennsylvania with their stout cattle and their ripe warm earth exposed to sun and plow. He had looked on the green valleys and softly rolling hillsides in southern Virginia, where the first generation of American Calhouns had broken soil and built their cabins and dreamed their dreams. But nothing could mean so much to him as Fort Hill itself, the river, the hills, the flame-streaked sunsets, the giant red oaks veiled in mist, the fruit orchards, the fields of swaying grain, the green pastures in their dark borders of pine, the forests and the mountains beyond. Nothing on earth had such power to stir him and to bring him peace.

4

The house seemed a part of its surroundings. Long, narrow, and white, it rambled across the top of a hill. From the left a double-row of cedars swung in a half-circle to the north portico; at the lower right, above a high stone cellar, stood the spring-house, where milk, butter, and cream were kept cool even on the hottest days.

A flower garden, bordered with wild-orange trees, lay in front of the house, and spreading from it were smaller beds, hemmed in ten-inch box. A vast park of virgin oaks and towering poplars surrounded the garden, and beyond, in all directions, lay panoramic sweeps of beauty. Far to the left, like white birches against the green, rose the spires of Pendleton. From the rear descended a wooded valley. Ahead, sixty miles distant into North Carolina, surged the mighty range of the Blue Ridge, now dark and clear, now fading back into layers of mist.

It would be all changed a hundred years later. The brick dormitories of Clemson College would close in from three directions, with gray uniformed cadets hurrying through the park where the deer and the bear had run two centuries before. Amidst the hurly-burly of a college campus, only the house in its tiny plot of box-patterned lawn was the same. Coming upon it suddenly at night, it would gleam out of the darkness, its white walls and tall white columns keeping the same remote look of withdrawal that Calhoun must have known. There was still the gentle slope to the roof, the massive chimney crumbling against the side, the forsythia bushes spraying into fountains of yellow bloom. Behind the cedars and the veiling of the locust trees, the house stood unchanged. Nothing could shatter its aloof beauty, its look of infinite peace.

It was later, more pretentious generations that would call Fort Hill a mansion. Actually it was only an overgrown farmhouse with little architectural distinction unless it were the beautifully carved mantels from Charleston. Except for the broad central hallway, it hardly differed from the gaunt sturdy farmhouses of New England.

Coils of trumpet vines and rambler roses around the windows and a green latticework of vines stretching from column to column on the porches softened the dwelling's austerity. The dominant impression the house gave was strangely like that of Calhoun himself. It combined

FORT HILL

The earliest view now known, taken in the latter part of
the 19th Century. The house had at this time changed very
little since Calhoun's day. *Courtesy of Mr. J. C. Littlejohn,
Clemson, South Carolina*

the strength of the pioneering log cabins with the simplicity of a Greek temple. Here the most haughty of coastal planters or the plainest of back-country farmers could feel perfectly at home.[23]

Floride's 'improvements' had resulted in a startling informality of design. What looked like the front door under the stately north portico was actually the back; the front was at the side! But once within, not even the most discriminating of Charlestonian visitors could have found fault with the long drawing room between the two columned porches. Here hung the family portraits, Anna Maria with a secret smile on her lips and old Mrs. Floride Colhoun, bushy-haired and wild-eyed as she had been in life. Below were grouped striped silk-velvet chairs, and at the fireside an elaborately carved chair presented to Calhoun by the King of the Belgians. A glittering candelabrum cast a soft glow on the hand-knit lace curtains. It was a gracious room, a beautiful room, but designed for company—and for Floride. It is difficult to imagine Calhoun cramping his long legs into the confines of the mohair and mahogany sofa with the twisted dolphin feet, while Floride tinkled waltzes on the spinet. He would have preferred the porches, following the shade from side to side of the house; or, if the company was too assertively masculine for family taste, there was always the privacy of his own sanctum, the office.

The state dining room across the hall was a long room, low-studded and stately as its name, with a high black mantel brooding at one end and a high narrow sideboard at the other. This buffet—beyond all else the most beautiful piece of furniture in the house—was Calhoun's pride. It had been given to him by Henry Clay, who owned its twin, and was made —so legend said—of mahogany from the cabin of the frigate *Constitution,* a fitting gift from one War Hawk to another.[24]

Here were the green decanters, the red wine bottles, the plain silver re-flected in the sheen of the two Duncan Phyfe tables. Each one was five by twelve feet, and they could be pushed together for those fabulous twenty-nine-course banquets on which county legend lingers—and which may actually have taken place once or twice in twenty-five years.

A lone guest might join Floride and her husband at the round mahogany table in the family dining room. This was the old kitchen of simpler days, and to Calhoun probably seemed the pleasantest room in the house. Here, from the north windows, was the best view of the mountains he loved; and even on damp days there was cheer in the leaping flames of a great six-foot fireplace with its wide, brick hearth and swinging crane. Here, too, banished from the more formal rooms, were the rough-hewn heir-looms from Calhoun's up-country boyhood, the pine paneled cupboard, the ladder-backed chairs, the spinning wheels. For Calhoun, this was a room redolent with memories.

Upstairs guest room after guest room straggled across the house. Furnish-ings were a hodge-podge of canopy beds, spool beds, with post spools gigantically swollen in accordance with Floride's attempts at furniture design, the sleigh bed of their early married days, French mahogany bureaus and 'modern' black walnut ones with marble tops. But to strangers the novelty would have been found in the small rooms next the bedrooms, for here were dour, tin, bathing tubs, approximately the size and shape of the latter-day Western sombreros—awesome objects, for of course it was well known that bathing in a tub gave you 'lung-fever.'

Calhoun and Floride slept downstairs. Their chamber, long and over-looking the rear flower garden, opened from a little nursery for the youngest child; and where now Anna Maria's doll-bed and dresser were kept for old memory's sake. The furniture was depressing; a huge black walnut bed, headboard towering to the ceiling, matched to a wardrobe, equally grim, and both of Floride's design.

The hallways Calhoun had stamped with the mark of his own person-ality. Along the walls hung the antlers of the deer he had shot; below, spread on tables, were newspapers sent to him from all corners of the country and displayed for the benefit of his guests. Here in these halls he walked at night when grappling with thought, or on days when rain made outdoor exercise impossible—the doors flung open to the porches beyond and the air soaked with the scents of grass and roses and the pungency of boxwood.[25]

Everything about Fort Hill was designed to make a guest feel completely at home. Whatever the fluctuations of the cotton market or Calhoun's bank account, 'open house' was the rule. Any guest, whether in 'broadcloth or jeans,' was welcome to stay the night, and was received with an open-handed generosity that left Charlestonians—themselves no mean hosts—reminiscing about the 'hearty hospitality' at Fort Hill, years after Cal-houn's death. The dining tables staggered with food; 'everything of Southern production,' one observer thought; and although Calhoun never took undue interest in what he ate, he was not immune to the allurements of 'excellent coffee,' 'delicious cream,' and hot, snow-white hominy grits, swimming in country butter. The choicest dishes were selected for the visitor, but for a guest who had the ill judgment to decline an invitation to family prayers, Calhoun's command was peremptory: 'Saddle the man's horse and let him go.'[26]

5

The state dining room was a favorite gathering place for the young people of the neighborhood, and night after night kin and 'kissing kin' jostled each other around the tables. At one party a wild duck was placed before a gangling youth, who was requested to carve and serve it. Gamely the boy plunged a knife and a fork into the back with such zeal that it took off on its last flight, landing right in the silken lap of a cousin, Martha Calhoun.

Conversation ceased. Every eye was fixed on the stern face of the host. He neither moved nor spoke. In a second burst of courage the boy addressed him: 'It wouldn't have happened, sir,' he said, 'except the duck had have been wild.' [27]

Calhoun relaxed into a broad grin. The crisis was over, and the friends and cousins of the Calhoun boys continued to have the freedom of Fort Hill. For Calhoun's sons there was no such loneliness as their father had known. Boys were everywhere, dashing under the carpenter's ladders, sprawled on the porches, or astride their horses on the cedar-needled driveway. Calhoun on his rounds would frequently stop to tease them for reading so many 'trashy' novels or to argue the comparative merits of rifles and double-barreled shotguns, which latter, he asserted, he would never waste upon a squirrel.

Calhoun liked to talk to boys. He had a gift for drawing them out, for meeting them on their own ground. One of his son's friends he threw completely off his guard, listening to his youthful political theories, then modestly submitting his own. Suddenly the boy realized that he was 'listening to the greatest mind of the day,' and halted, overcome with embarrassment, despite Calhoun's understanding attempts to relieve it. Calhoun's nephew, Ted, must also have been overwhelmed when his uncle, discovering him badly in need of a haircut, told him to wait, dashed in the house, grabbed Floride's shears, and leading the youngster into the back yard speedily hacked off all surplus locks.[28]

6

But only when Anna Maria was at home was her father's happiness complete. With her, who had shared his burdens, he now shared his joys, giving way to moments of 'frankest gaiety' never seen by his closest friends, and least of all by his biographers. Not the 'Roman Senator,' but the father with the 'sweet smile,' the 'affectionate voice,' the 'unbending firmness of principle' united to 'the yielding softness of a woman,' where only his feelings were in question—this was the Calhoun Anna Maria knew. Interests that he shared with her are strange, indeed, in a man supposedly concerned only with cotton and slavery.

'He loved and found pleasure in simple things,' Anna Maria wrote. 'No one loved or appreciated more music, poetry, or the beauties of nature.' She was not with her father when he had stood silent and awe-struck, moment after moment, before the majesty of the mountain ranges of North Georgia. But she watched him thrill with 'all the delight of the most imaginative poet' at the fury of a mountain storm or the panoramic sweep of river, forest, and hill. His tastes were instinctive, not cultivated, but none the less real.[29] No one would have suspected him of hidden artistic yearnings, yet under Clemson's tutelage 'his latent artistic abilities' were manifested in a discriminating choice of minor pieces of European art which began to appear on the walls of Fort Hill. Clemson dabbled in art himself, not entirely unsuccessfully, as his somber landscapes and still lifes at Clemson College reveal; but the neighborhood legends that tell of Calhoun, equipped with umbrella and palette, trying his own paint brushes, are probably nothing more than legend.[30]

7

At dusk neighbors and relatives would begin dropping in: Francis Pickens, Colonel Drayton, John Ewing Colhoun, and his brother, James Edward, one by one would mount the steps, find chairs, perhaps draw them down to the south end of the portico where they could breathe the fresh, poignant scent of Calhoun's favorite mimosa. A Washington politician staying over-night at Fort Hill might join them; and in his hard-muscled and sun-bronzed host, around whose eyes were the pleasant curving lines of an outdoor man he would hardly have recognized the 'pale, slender, ghostly-looking man' who black-robed strode along the streets of the capital. In Washington, Daniel Webster had marveled at his South Carolina col-league's indifference to recreation.[31] He would have marveled all the more could he have been at Fort Hill with the young British scientist, Feather-stonhaugh, leisurely eating a supper of cottage cheese and cream with his distinguished host; and seen the 'cast-iron man' lounging back in his chair, eyes half-closed, indulging in pleasant conjectures as to whether that lov-ing young couple across the river were really engaged, after all.[32]

Here on this shadowy porch, littered with saddles and children's toys, newspapers and a forgotten rifle or two, a Negro's fingers plucking away at a guitar, and a dog's tail thumping against the floor, Calhoun could at last be content. Here in the soft, throbbing darkness, he smiled and talked and laughed sometimes, savoring the rich beauty of plantation life.

What did they talk about? An old 'day-book,' belonging to one of the up-country planters, its jumble of ragged news clippings, scrawled nota-tions, and quaint recipes splashed with the brown stains of age, gives a cross-section of what a Southern planter of the eighteen-forties was talk-ing about and thinking about. Contrary to Northern conjecture, it was not slavery alone. The lull before the storm was heavy over the South; even Calhoun, judging by his correspondence, had turned his thoughts to party politics, and many Southerners could still explain away abolitionist at-tacks as mere jealousy of a competing labor system.

But the Southerner still had capacity for self-criticism. He would discuss the French philosopher, Alexis de Tocqueville, and his accusation that no country in the world had 'so little true independence of mind . . . as America,' the nation that had 'refined the arts of despotism' and drawn a circle around freedom of thought. He would discuss the New York *Independent's* accusation that Charleston was the most illiterate city in the United States, with the lowest school attendance, the highest percentage of infant mortality, the highest death rate, the lowest wage scale. These were the figures. They did not tell of the yellow fever that periodically ravaged Charleston. They did not contrast the New York public school with the Southern tutor, or give the huge predominance of Southern over Northern men in the American universities and colleges. The South was not aiming to teach the masses, but to train leaders—for the South and for the nation.[33]

For a man so burdened, Calhoun gave generously of his time. He had the gift of leisureliness, of making you feel that his hours were no more important than yours. What made Fort Hill hospitality so pleasant was the ease with which guests were fitted into the family circle. The work of a plantation could not be halted, so visitors joined the Calhouns in their routine, accompanying their host on long horseback rides over the quartz-strewn roads or 'the ladies' to church services in Pendleton. They would listen to the talk, so different from that in the North, a foreign visitor thought, 'liberal and instructive,' with no thought of gain. 'I would not be rich in America,' Calhoun declared with vehemence, 'for the care of my money would distract my mind from more important concerns.' His newly discovered gold mine at Dahlonega, Georgia, which so excited his friends, only mildly interested him. 'I know,' he said, 'that there is nothing so uncertain as gold.'[34]

Guests came to see—and remained to admire. 'The most perfect gentleman I ever knew,' was Featherstonhaugh's estimate of his host. So gracious were Calhoun's manners that, almost angrily, William Smith, a violent political opponent, complained that Calhoun had treated him with such kindness, consideration, and courtesy that 'I could not hate him as much as I wanted to do.'[35]

And yet there was a lack, a paradox in his nature. It was young Featherstonhaugh, who, meeting him only once, saw what those closest to him could not see. He had, declared the Englishman, 'an imperfect acquaintance with human nature.' He was 'baffled by those inferior to himself.'[36]

The tragedy of Calhoun is in these two sentences. Had he seen less clearly, he would have understood far more. How could a man who could 'grasp the most intricate questions without difficulty,' be expected to understand the halting and often baffled mental processes of the average man in the street? Penetrating to essentials with an almost intuitive rapidity, it was impossible for him to understand that what was so clear to him was blurred to others. Add to this a Calvinistic conscience and a schooling in the dirt and bitterness of partisan politics, and small wonder that the tragic defect of his personality was that he suspected the moral motives of men who differed from him. That they could be honestly mistaken never occurred to him. Tortured with forebodings over the logical outcome of the abolitionist agitation, for example, he could not understand why others did not see. Had he been less brilliant as a man, he might have been more useful as a statesman.

Politically he controlled more through an intellectual mastery of the leaders than by conquering the understanding of the masses. He could win men, fascinate them, draw them to him, but in the final analysis he did not understand them. It was only his natural sympathy and consideration that gave the illusion of his doing so. He held his tremendous personal following among the Southern people through an emotional rather than an intellectual comprehension.[37]

8

Few of his friends could meet him on his own ground. Given a visitor who fired his intellect, like keen-witted Benjamin Perry, Calhoun would sweep his work aside, and from ten in the morning until dinner at night would never leave his chair and never stop talking. 'He was in high spirits,' Perry wrote of one of their interviews, 'and his conversation was truly fascinating. . . . It was natural . . . and cheerful, amusing and instructive, giving and taking, calling in the whole of his life's experience, thought, and learning. He . . . described his contemporaries, told anecdotes of Randolph, Lowndes, Jackson, Polk, Benton, and others.' He praised the officers of the Army. He described his course in Congress. 'He liked very much to talk of himself, and he always had the good fortune to make the subject captivating to his listeners.' [38]

Perhaps no single facet of Calhoun's nature so accounted for his personal charm as his conversational power. Conversation was a cultivated art in South Carolina, yet Calhoun, with none of the advantages of foreign travel or the urban polish of Charleston, was in this the acknowledged leader of them all. 'There has been no man among us,' asserted one, 'who had more winning manners in conversation . . . than Mr. Calhoun.' The 'indescribable fascination' in his way of talking was one reason why South Carolina so loved him. 'Could he have . . . conversed with every individual in the United States,' declared the enthusiastic Hammond, 'none could have stood against him.' And not only South Carolinians paid tribute. 'There was a charm in his conversation not often found,' said Henry Clay. 'It was felt . . . by all . . . who . . . conversed with him.' [39]

In the close encounters of 'informal debate . . . none could withstand him.' He could anticipate arguments before they were uttered, shatter them, and run them through. Nor did he antagonize his listeners. He won by conceding every point that he could, and by giving so serious an argument that listeners were flattered by the implied compliment to their understanding. If not too swept away, Calhoun might even halt in the midst of some fine-spun analysis to ask 'kindly, "Do you see?" ' But few attempted to reply. They 'listened and admired.' [40]

All topics seemed within his range: politics, history, art, philosophy, science, literature, athletics. His sweep of interests is reminiscent of Jefferson's. He could turn from the discussion of a popular novel (which he had not read) to the subject of racial origins or the exploitation of India. 'I have never been more convinced of Mr. Calhoun's genius,' remarked one visitor, 'than while he talked to us of a flower.' [41] He could captivate a blacksmith with his understanding of ironworking or horseshoeing; he could hold a whole dinner table in amazement as he traced the entire history of fig culture. He would discuss any subject at all, whether he knew anything about it or not, with results that were sometimes disturbing to an expert.

There was the sea captain, for instance, who was explaining the direction of trade winds across the equator. Calhoun doubted; Calhoun did not agree. He broke in with his own theories on the direction of trade winds across the equator, speaking with such logic and eloquence that he won the entire table over to his side. The equatorial winds, however, unimpressed by Calhoun's argument, continued their journey across the equator in exactly the direction that the less eloquent sea captain had said that they did. Had Calhoun's political enemies been present, they might have seen in his little triumph proof of one of his greatest weaknesses: the failure to examine his premises with the care and effort he put into his logical deductions, thus arriving at the 'most startling conclusions.' [42]

There were times, too, when Calhoun's 'somber outlook' led him into 'remote regions of the mind,' untraversed and incomprehensible to any but the most intellectual of listeners. Occasionally he would overwhelm with his 'too detailed knowledge.' He would give way to his 'zeal as a propagandist,' become angular of phrase and stark of thought, his ideas outrunning his language. Some found his argumentativeness wearying, agreeing with Parton that his mind was as arrogant as his manners were courteous. There were listeners who had no desire to listen, no wish to sit at Calhoun's feet and hear wisdom 'flow from his lips in a continual stream.' Calhoun had his faults, both as man and conversationalist. He was often overstrenuous, but he was never dull. And such was the impact of his charm that an abolitionist could write, 'He was by all odds the most fascinating man in private intercourse that I ever met.' [43]

Lacking time to be a scholar, Calhoun was still 'infinitely better read' than was generally suspected. He read a great deal, and what he read he absorbed so completely that to many it seemed as though he did not read at all. He seldom gave quotations; his mind appeared to work wholly from within, untouched by outside influences. 'It was more like a spring than a reservoir,' [44] one observer declared.

Without having read Goethe, he amazed a listener by duplicating the German master's interpretation of the character of Hamlet! Of novels he knew nothing. A woman lent him one, and as he flipped over the pages, he remarked that it was the first book 'of the kind' he had ever seen! (Whatever he and Charles Dickens discussed, it was not Mr. Pickwick.) [45]

Often in his reading he sought too much for stray facts which suited his own preconceived notions, while 'the weightiest fact of contradiction' might be impatiently brushed aside. His favorite books were, of course, history, but he liked any kind of works on government, empires, travel, international conflicts, and 'the improvement and decline of the races.' But he was far more of a thinker than a reader, and according to Jefferson Davis 'spent hours at a time in solitary thought.' [46]

9

He had a deep interest in religion. More than one historian has agreed with the contemporary journalist who asserted that, born a century earlier, Calhoun might well have become the 'Jonathan Edwards of the South.' He had just the kind of 'acute metaphysical Scotch intellect' to have 'revelled in theological subtleties,' and revel in them he did; although, with his limited knowledge of science and utter reliance on the powers of reason, it is not surprising that his early faith had become seriously shaken. But whatever his doubts and broodings, he kept them to himself.[47]

He would never join a church. Blameless as his life appeared to be, 'conscientious scruples' troubled him, and he held back from a conviction of his 'personal unfitness.' His pastors, however, had no doubts as to his piety, and one who discussed religion with him 'was astonished to find him better informed than himself on those very points where he had expected to give him information.' [48]

His manner was reverent in church, and friends thought him 'much disturbed by any inattention in others.' But he had his lapses. Charles Cotesworth Pinckney was startled one Sunday to look up from his sermon and find Calhoun with his eyes closed, apparently asleep or absorbed in his own thoughts. The rector smiled. 'You are counting electoral votes,' he thought; 'you have not heard a word.' After the service the pastoral coach stopped to pick up the long-legged statesman who was already well into his four-mile walk home. Scarcely had Calhoun sat down before he leaped full-armed into the rector's sermon, discussed it, disputed it, and took it apart, point by point.

He was an intensive Bible student. The Hebrew people fascinated him: their origin, their history, and their race. He even longed to study their language that he might read the Old Testament 'in the original,' and his 'abrupt energy' led him to making a 'theoretical grammar' of Hebrew nouns and verbs. He is said to have believed the Biblical prophecies and to have paused wonderingly at the grim words: 'With a great army . . . the king of the North shall come . . . and take the most fenced cities; and the arms of the south shall not withstand.' [49]

XXIV

America in Mid-Century

IT WAS IN THE FALL OF 1845 that John C. Calhoun set out to take a look at America. The trip was long overdue. His inspection tours of the nation he had helped build were over. Not for twenty years, since his days as Secretary of War, had he been north of the Mason-Dixon line nor west of Alabama. And in those twenty years America had reached maturity. In 1825 it had been the potentialities of the young Republic that had challenged the imagination. Now it was the realization.

Scattered over the South and New West by the half-century mark were 2,400,000 farmers, planters, and dairymen. But their number was topped by the 2,500,000 bankers, businessmen, and industrial workers, including financiers, ironmongers, whalebone-makers, flax-dressers, and 'makers of philosophical instruments.'[1] Already the industrialists outvoted the farm, and the destiny of America was fixed for the next hundred years.

Even the statistics were charged with excitement. In 1820 there were 9,500,000 Americans; by 1840 the number had almost doubled, and ten more years would add another 5,000,000.[2] In 1820 212,000 residents of the Eastern states were factory workers; by 1840 the number increased by 278,000. Of these over 200,000 were women, working ten or twelve hours a day at wages approximating $6.50 a week—the standard rate in the mills of Massachusetts. Employers' profits averaged forty-three per cent.

Agricultural output still outstripped the industrial. Farm crop values for 1850 amounted to $1,600,000,000, but the industrial figures edged near at $1,013,336,436.[3] The decade was roaring on to a thundering climax. The swollen veins of Boston were thumping with the warfare of diverse blood types, as Brahmin blue and Irish red met, clashed, and curdled. The result was not destruction but invigoration; and a jump in population from 66,000 to 114,000 within fifteen years. In New York, too, thanks to foreign blood transfusions and the absence of birth control, the story was the same: a gain of 100,000 in fifteen years.[4]

The city loomed on the skyline of the American consciousness. In the South there was Galveston, 'bright and new,' with its tropical gardens and orange trees, its sandy streets, glittering with pebbles and shells;

Montgomery, 'a city of palaces and gardens . . . built upon more hills than Rome'; and Memphis, where 'sable belles and sooty exquisites' flashed a 'thousand rainbows of color' on Sunday afternoon promenade. Southern women were expressing horror at 'living too long a time at the plantations,' because, like Calhoun's own Floride, they pined for the city where they could enjoy 'luxury and amusement.'[5] Farming involved setting your life in a pattern and planning ahead; farming demanded stability, but America had swung into speed tempo.

New York was Mecca to the new Pilgrims of Progress. 'In every place,' wrote Captain Marryat, 'you will meet with some one whom you have met walking on Broadway. Americans are such locomotives.' Railroads cobwebbed the East; they spun their way from Boston to New York, from Philadelphia to Pittsburgh, from Washington to Baltimore. For them iron production had leaped from an annual tonnage of 165,000 to 347,000 within ten years.[6]

America was on the move. Lights from the campfires of Carolina 'movers' flickered in the waters of the Ohio River; caravans of wagons were moving into Illinois, Indiana, Missouri—the women, the children, the teams of oxen and horses, the brood mare and her foal, and the men with the long rifles on their shoulders. New states were thundering at the doors of the Union; they were shouldering their way into the national councils; their power could completely push aside the pretensions of the old Thirteen. Michigan, Wisconsin, Arkansas, Florida, Iowa, Texas. And beckoning always onward—the dream, the promise, the untapped magnitude of Oregon.

It was the era of oyster cellars and chin whiskers and prim rows of blue-stocking girls in the classrooms at Oberlin College. It was the age of contrasts; of sod huts on the prairie and Greek temples on the bayou; of twelve-year-old New England girls working from dawn to dark in the cotton mills and of twenty-year-old New England boys filling the classrooms at Columbia College for the new course in 'Superintendents of manufacture.' It was the time of expansion and the time of invention; it was a time for greatness and an age of pettiness. 'Gentlemen,' proclaimed the keeper of the Mississippi River hotel, before starting the roll-call of the menu, 'We are a great people.'[7]

Foreign visitors still came to look and wonder at democracy in action. As an ideal, they found it even more vehemently asserted than in Jackson's time, but far less of a living reality. Those who had won its profits had been the first to betray its principles. 'Love of liberty and country I found infinitely stronger among the laboring classes,' declared a German visitor, amazed at the 'contempt and hatred of American institutions' he found among the self-appointed 'upper classes.'[8] Another German, Professor Frederick Von Raumer, thought America's 'universal love for the republican form of government a strong bond of union . . . so that neither what is peculiar nor what is general can exclusively prevail.' But he was disturbed by the lack of 'taste for humanity . . . in the best society in America.' [9]

Even more perceptive was the great French student of democracy, de Tocqueville. America he saw as a country not of freedom but of fear— fear of unleashed democracy, fear of slavery, fear of finance capitalism. In the Southern states, he found, little was said. 'But there is something more alarming in the taut forebodings of the South than in the clamorous fears of the North.' [10]

Not even Calhoun looked with more concern on democracy's 'inadequate securities' against 'the tyranny of the majority' than did de Tocqueville on the inevitable subjection of 'the provinces to the metropolis,' and the consequent rise of 'a class who without the economic security of land ownership' [11] would deem money the ultimate power in government.

The vicious circle was complete. Men, who but for industrial democracy would still have bent their backs to the plow or over the workbench, fought now to hold back the very forces that had swung them into power. They knew how precarious was their foothold on security; if democracy could make them, it could as easily elevate their own mill hands. Democracy was openly hated now, and none feared and hated it more than those who without its help would have been nothing at all. Money alone could breast the tide. Money could pay the boat fares of famine-starved Irishmen, who were only too delighted with American slums and fifty cents a day; men and women who should be content to remain as servants and who could more easily be denounced for their 'ridiculous notions of liberty and equality . . . and for pretending to enjoy the same privileges as our born citizens.' Money could distinguish the 'herd' from the 'aristocracy.' So the men of the cotton mills and the corporations grappled for more money, money for a family dynasty, money for social position and economic power, money to guarantee their exception to the rule of shirt-sleeves to shirt-sleeves in three generations.[12]

Money was the credo of American existence. Money was the measuring rod of a man's worth, the 'only . . . secure distinction.' With two thousand dollars in the bank, the wife of a grocer, turned India merchant, could set up as a lady 'of the *ton*,' give parties to people she had never met and exclude her own relatives. But her position was precarious. The rise or fall of a single stock on the Exchange, and a dozen families would be excluded from the pale of fashion, and a dozen more would emerge as candidates for 'imaginary honors.' Tired husbands could not retire. Money-making was an end in itself. Men who would scorn to cheat at cards would swindle on the Exchange. In no country, reported the widely traveled Thomas L. Nichols, had he seen faces 'furrowed with harder lines of care,' or 'so little enjoyment of life,' as in America. Never, declared an Englishman, had he heard Americans talk without the word *dollar* invading the conversation.[13] Why, asked a Bostonian, waste the time of an intelligent boy in four years of 'moonshine' and 'abstractions' at college when he could learn as much in six months in a counting house? Our merchants, he contended, are 'the most respectable part of the community. . . . The art of making dollars . . . has given them a higher standing in society than they could have acquired by all the philosophy in the world.'[14]

A New Yorker added his testimony: 'In this city there is no higher rank than that of a rich man.' Out of the class-consciousness and class-strife of the eighteen-thirties, out of the smoke and the steam, had risen a new American society of which the whole basis was financial, and in which each 'gentleman ranked according to the numerical index of his property.'

Aristocracy its shareholders called themselves, and frantically, feverishly, they worked to prove themselves aristocracy, 'sneering at the liberal institutions of their country,' dedicating themselves to convincing Europe that in America an unrecognized nobility did exist and that they were it.[15]

Upon these posturings and posings, with little girls in school cutting their own playmates as soon as their fathers could dress them for better company, foreign visitors looked with unconcealed amusement. For the 'white-gloved democrat of the South' with his aristocratic bearing, they could have respect; they could even admire the unpretending mechanics of Boston; but for the 'ungloved aristocrat' of the North, to whom not the aristocratic tradition but dollars and cents were of primary importance, they had only contempt. An aristocracy to be tolerable, foreign visitors reminded Americans, must either 'protect the lower classes' or set them an example of courtesy and learning.[16]

New York, in general, and the women of New York, in particular, assumed the leadership of the new society. Only a few blocks from the new mansions ran alleys knee-deep in mud and rows of 'hideous tenements' where 'free' Negroes huddled over smouldering charcoal fires and a smell of 'singeing clothes or flesh' hung always in the murky hallways. But milady of society lolled on 'silk or satin furniture' in carpeted drawing rooms, cluttered with 'portfolios, knick-nacs, bronzes, busts, cameos, alabaster vases' and illustrated copies of 'ladylike rhymes bound in silk.' She rose at nine, breakfasted at ten, 'pottered' for three or four hours, walked and shopped along the four-mile, brick-paved stretch of Broadway, dined, pottered again until six, when she could start on her toilette for dinner. And what a fragile, feminine, mincing little creature she was, her feet crammed into 'miniature' slippers, her neck, face, and arms whitened with 'pulverized starch,' heaps of false hair piled on top of her head, and a 'pale rose-colored bonnet' teetering on top of it all. Yet the 'exquisite beauty' of the American women of the eighteen-forties excited the admiration of the most discriminating of foreign visitors.[17]

But beauty was restricted to their person. Certainly it was not in their homes where beauty and vulgarity had become synonymous terms. Nor was it in their conversation, which foreign visitors thought wanted charm, grace, and polish. Not that the 'young woman of amiable deportment' lacked priming for the social world. 'A little of everything' was the educational rule: French, bookkeeping, economic history, constitutional law, natural theology, mental philosophy, geometry, technology, 'arches and angles and compliments . . . magnetism and electricity'; music and drawing, penmanship, and Virgil, too, all gave milady assurance that she need 'never be embarrassed in society.' She could play 'The Storm' on the spinet, read such 'literary trash' as 'Stanzas by Mrs. Hemans,' or a 'garbled extract' from Moore's *Life of Byron,* but Chaucer and Spenser were dismissed as unintelligible; and Byron was not fit to read. *The Rape of the Lock?* The very title! Shakespeare? 'Shakespeare, madam, is obscene,' lacking in 'the refinement of the age in which we live.' [18]

Occasionally the rococo façade gave way. A young coxcomb in 'exquisite' London-made dress would invite the ladies to smell his hair, which he could assure them was scented with 'real Parisian perfume.' A society girl would taunt a pretty rival, sneering at her dress as 'not worth seventy-five cents a yard,' and at the 'unlicked cub' with her. Good manners in other countries, observed a European, consist in putting everyone at ease, 'which could be done without undue familiarity,' but here those who were rich 'seem determined upon making everyone that is poorer than themselves feel his inferiority.' [19]

2

Tremendous was the impact of this new-rich middle class upon the national economy. America was paying heavily for her substitution of wealth and 'progress' for freedom and self-realization. 'Eminently selfish,' declared Charles Lyell, was the policy of states like Massachusetts, where manufacturers persistently demanded a protective tariff, indifferent to its effect upon world trade, or 'other parts of the Union.' * Three or four heavily populated states, Lyell observed, could enforce their protective program at the expense 'of a dozen less populated agricultural states, whose interests are in favor of free trade.' [20]

Yet in this same Massachusetts and all over New England, small farms were crude, unkempt, 'crippled with debt and mortgages.' New England farmers, lured by the abolitionist outcry, went on blindly voting for the Whigs and high tariffs. They paid no heed to Jackson's and Calhoun's

---

* This observation was made more than a hundred years before Massachusetts' Governor Paul A. Dever visited President Harry S. Truman in 1949 to request a higher protective tariff for the Massachusetts woolen industry!

warnings that 'the small farmers, mechanics, and laborers, were the real possessors of the national wealth,' nor to their call to unite with the city laborers and the Southern farmers against the capitalists and corporations who 'could make their own class interests prevail against division.' [21]

It was not majority rule in America now. It was money rule. Few wealthy men actively embroiled themselves in the maelstrom of political strife; for knowingly the 'mudsills' could never have been prevailed upon to vote for them. But there were men of popular appeal like Daniel Webster, honestly convinced that the industrial way was the American way. There were men eager for office who would pay in services for a nomination, and there were others poor enough to sell their vote for a day's food. And if a popular leader of generous aims should slip into power, would not money persuade him where his political sympathies should lie? A gentleman could cut no figure in Washington merely upon his Congressional salary.

Meanwhile, the new potential of America, the teeming workers of the East, surrendered to a new type in American politics. The 'boss' had the food, the basic human necessities that industrial 'progress' had failed to supply. Men of coarse wit and rowdy eloquence, like hard-bitten Mike Walsh, found followers willing to vote as they directed and as often as they required. Embittered by the betrayal of men who but a few years before were 'their own kind,' the working masses looked with understandable suspicion on that sprinkling of men, brilliant, learned, and generous, who might still have been willing to serve them. Thus was one more obstacle thrust in the way of Calhoun's fight to carry on what Jackson had begun, to fit Jefferson's ideals to the economic realities, to unite divergent groups against the common enemy.

Not first in 1865, but as early as 1845, bribery, vote-purchase, and corruption were rules of American politics. 'The best character that can be given any candidate is that he is so rich that he does not need to steal,' asserted the New York *Tribune*. 'Theft has become the peculiar vice of our public men.' Hundreds of thousands were pilfered by state officials in Ohio. In Maine a pastor was appointed State Treasurer, and coolly helped himself to a hundred thousand dollars plus his salary. The New York *Herald*, in disgust, issued warning that the 'foul disgrace to our free institutions' would be 'a cause against democracy throughout the civilized world.' [22]

Washington was a 'sink of corruption.' Dearily Dr. Nichols looked back to the day when 'the Senate of the United States was considered as high above . . . suspicion' as the British Parliament. Men of conscience like Calhoun were sickened by the dishonesty about them. Yet continuously he pled with his followers to continue their public service. 'No one of your talents . . . ought to think of retiring,' he wrote Hammond. 'If the . . . worthy retire, the . . . worthless will take their place. Our destiny, and that of our posterity is involved in our political institutions and the conduct of the Government.' The duty of the 'enlightened and patriotick' was to 'devote their time and talents to the country.' [23]

Few had stomach to follow his lead. Day by day Jefferson's 'natural aristocracy,' the professional, literary, and scientific men, were withdrawing themselves from contamination. Others of talent, who a generation earlier would have found self-realization in politics, now, recognizing that money was the badge of esteem, set themselves to the business of amassing it.

Darkly true had been Calhoun's prophecy of a decade before when he had told the Senate that the law of supply and demand governs the moral as well as the economic world. 'If a community demands high mental attainments, and allots honors and rewards that require their development, creating a demand for . . . justice, knowledge, patriotism, they will be produced.' Instead, America was allotting her public honors to those unfavorable to the development 'of the higher . . . qualities, intellectual and moral.' How could the 'rising generation' fail to feel this 'deadening influence. . . . The youths who crowd our colleges and behold the road to . . . distinction terminating in a banking house, will feel the spirit . . . decay within them.' Who would have ambition 'to mount the rugged steep of science as the road to honor and distinction' when the highest point they could attain would be 'attorney to a bank'? [24]

Not even the South had escaped infection. Big business compelled big agriculture; year by year the demands of cotton mills in Old and New England were fixing slavery more and more irrevocably upon the Southern states; and the dark tide was creeping on, over the rich bottom lands of Alabama and Mississippi, across Louisiana and Arkansas, to the borderlands of Texas. Slavery was becoming more cruel, more ruthless. Just as the corporation had brought a mechanical impersonality into the old relation of employer and workman, so were the absentee landlords freed from personal responsibility for their Negroes' welfare. Levee plantations were too hot and too unhealthful for a white man's residence for more than a few months in the year. Laws for the Negroes' welfare still remained on the books, but who would hear the slave's cry for help or uncover the secret horrors hidden in the murky swamps? [25] Profit was of primary importance in this new-rich segment of Southern society. What chance for personal knowledge of the Negro had these hard men of the Mississippi frontier or the Northern businessman turned cotton planter? It was these 'cotton snobs,' as the older and more conservative Southerners called them, who confused money with character, power with responsibility. It was they who built the rococo temples with the forty-foot façades; who sported velvet-lined coaches, driven by coachmen with rich livery and bare feet; who whipped their Negroes and damned the abolitionists; who prated of the purity of white Southern womanhood and debauched black Southern womanhood. These were the men whose fifteen-year-old sons drank, smoked, gambled, and whored with a perfection that made Europeans compare them to men of twenty-five in their own countries.[26] These were the men who would gamble away their plantations in a single night, whose security was so hair-trigger they would duel at the quirk of an eyebrow or the flicker of a smile; the men who made Southern pride and Southern arrogance interchangeable terms.

To foreign visitors the true spirit of aristocracy was in the integrity of the small planters and the farmers of the yeoman class from which Calhoun himself had sprung. But if the 'cotton snobs' mistook the outer trappings for the essence of the aristocratic tradition, if their talk at table was more of horses and hounds than of Shakespeare and Milton, their avowed aims were in keeping with the planter tradition. 'In a few years,' was their optimistic prediction, 'we shall be the richest people beneath the bend of the rainbow, and then the arts and sciences will flourish to an extent unknown on this side of the Atlantic.'[27]

Only an American could have trumpeted this extravaganza, but its aim was uncompromisingly Southern. If the new Southerner had succumbed to the money-mania as much as his Yankee cousins, at least he had some idea for his money's disposal. And in this sentiment alone is proof of the wedge that was slowly but relentlessly driving North and South apart. Southern ends were more excessively Southern than ever before. Sensitive, self-conscious, watchfully on the defensive, the South was withdrawing into herself. If, on the one hand, she was racing to build her railroads and even an occasional cotton mill; on the other, she was accentuating her local culture, her agrarian tradition, all that cut her off, not only from the North, but from the whole main stream of world 'progress.' If Southern values were to survive at all, Southern leaders argued, they could not be compromised. And year by year the gulf between the two sections was widening, dividing the South from the North so radically 'as to render it culturally and economically a separate nation.'[28]

In the flood of this tide stood Calhoun. What he sought was not Southern cultural predominance over the rest of the nation, but Southern survival in a Republic loosely enough united for the 'peculiar institutions' of each section to survive without the feeling of personal responsibility on the part of the inhabitants of the other sections. But to intensify Southern culture, on the one hand, and to weave it into the fabric of a national pattern that became more divergent every passing day, was beyond the powers of any man. Said a Southerner: 'The Southern people . . . rather than let this Union be dissolved . . . will drive into Canada every . . . abolitionist, every disunionist.' Said a Northerner: 'South Carolina approves of allowing a man to flog his servant . . . Massachusetts does not. South Carolina approves of selling pretty girls at auction . . . Massachusetts does not. . . .'[29] Between such gulfs of opinion was any common ground possible?

The tragedy was that North and South did not know each other, and, heated as each side was by prejudice, had less and less desire to know each other. Few Northerners could travel in the Southern states. Their opinions were formed by the press and the church which condemned slavery in particular and Southerners in general, without stopping to realize that two-thirds of the white Southerners actually owned no slaves at all.

The contempt was even more eloquent South than North. No better barometer of public opinion can be found than in the Fourth of July toasts of a single year and a single state, South Carolina in 1845. 'South Carolina. Star of the first magnitude . . . revolving on her own axis, shining with no borrowed light, her creed, let us alone.' 'Northern abolitionists . . . unfit to be citizens of our great Republic.' 'Grain crops and manufactories . . . the present policy of South Carolina.' 'The abolitionists. Negro sons and daughters-in-law to the whole of them.'

And this: 'May the Southern States soon have a President of their own and that President be John C. Calhoun.'[30]

Calhoun was keenly sensitive to the pressure of the new times. Although outwardly he had himself changed his course, he was the first to recognize the changes in the course of the country. As early as 1837 he had been aware that 'the lower classes had made great progress to equality and independence. Such change . . . indicates great approaching change in the political and social condition of the country . . . the termination of which is difficult to be seen. Modern society seems to me to be rushing to some new and untried condition. . . .'[31]

He knew that an era was ending. He had lived to see the evolution of his country from Jefferson's dream of a classless pastoral republic to the reality of a class-ridden industrial democracy. He had seen the birth of modern American society.

Traditional history would mark the Civil War as the dividing line between the old and the new America. But the facts and figures speak otherwise. The war was not the battle between the Southern and the Northern concepts of America. The war did not decide whether the industrial or the agrarian ideal would prevail for the nation. Time and the world had decided. The America of the North had won. The South would fight, not for dominance but for survival. And all the characteristics of so-called 'modern' America: the standardization of society, the increasing corruption of politics, the rising ascendancy of the laborer over the farmer as the common denominator American, the triumph of unrestrained majority rule—all that would be written down as the result of the Civil War was not so much the result as the cause. Not Abraham Lincoln but

Andrew Jackson was the father of modern America. The Civil War was merely the legitimization of the birth.

3

Upon this new, industrialized, fast-moving America, Calhoun looked with mixed feelings of horror and admiration. He was no dreaming traditionalist, bent on mewing up his country in a pastoral oasis of farms and plantations, linked by half-blazed forest trails. He had approved the new cotton mills. He could not see a map but that his eyes and brain visualized canals, highways, railroads, drawing the diverse sections into one. Industrial progress meant as much to him as to any man; what troubled him were the fortunes being amassed by the few and the change in American purposes and thinking that the fortunes had brought. Would industrial progress—this was the question that nagged at his brain—would industrial progress mean better living for the many or enrichment of the few? He foresaw the worst. Unchecked, unrestrained industrialism would destroy the Union and wreck the South.

But in the West there was hope. Its vast breadths, its unmeasured potentialities for an agrarian economy, linked in values to the older South, linked even closer by rail line and steamboat, was a prospect to stir the imagination. The North might dream of making agriculture subservient to the demands of an Eastern industrial empire; Calhoun's counter-check was to use the new industrialism as a means of enriching and improving the united agrarian economy of the South and West. Realist to the bone, he knew that the South's only chance of survival was to invoke the means of its rivals. He must defeat majority rule by majority rule. If, practically speaking, the Union was to be operated for the promotion of group interests, then his group interests must receive their share.

Indeed, the Civil War itself has frequently been described as a struggle between the North and South for the dominance of the new West. No Southern leader would, of course, acknowledge that the Old South was finished; that the tobacco-cotton economy had so depleted the soil of Virginia, Georgia, and the Carolinas that the only hope of continued prosperity was in surrender of the West to slavery. Boxed up, the South was ended economically as well as outvoted politically. Yet subconsciously this realization was a driving impetus behind the expansionist movement, plus the realization that as the public opinion of the North united against the South, the Southern states must maintain—state by state—a numerical equality with the North, a necessity which Calhoun realized perfectly.

Yet, blind as the Carolinian was on the economics of the slave question, on the facts of human nature he was far wiser than his fellows. Texas had taught him a lesson. Regardless of Southern needs, Northern opinion, he knew, would limit the spread of avowedly slave territory. Hence, his effort to restate the expansionist question in agrarian rather than slavery terms; and to find a common economic ground by which the agricultural states of the South and West could stand politically united. But as fast as the South demanded new allies for her system, so would the North demand allies for hers—and the irrepressible conflict loomed nearer.

4

Calhoun's interest in the West went back to 1835 when he had written a Georgia Congressman that 'a judicious system of railroads would make Georgia and Carolina the Commercial centre of the Union.' By 'proper exertions,' he had pointed out in a subsequent letter, 'the two States could turn half of the commerce of the Union through their limits.' With 'one great road of uniform construction,' an 'immense intercourse' would take place between the West 'and Southern Atlantick ports.' And at the outlet would stand not New York, but Charleston. 'The advantages of New York are not to be compared with it.' [32]

Thus, in a few enthusiastic sentences had Calhoun given birth to the program to which he would devote the energies of his middle years. Fundamentally his aim was unchanged—to preserve the integrity of the South within the Union. But his means were changing. Already he saw that if the Southern life was to be preserved, some surrender to the spirit of the age must be made. If money was the means of power, then the South must share in the 'mighty flood of prosperity' that the age of railroads would bring. Linked together in distance and commerce, the West and the South could withstand the encroachments of industrial power.

How could this great aim be accomplished? Already a route was clear in Calhoun's mind: the little railroad at Athens, Georgia, extended to the Tennessee River, where the paddleboats lashed the tawny water into foam; then on to Nashville and the steamboats down the Cumberland; across the Ohio and to St. Louis where the Mississippi and the Missouri met. From this main line must run several branches: one south to the Chattahoochee near Columbus, Georgia, 'to meet the projected railroads from Montgomery and Pensacola'; another down the Tennessee to join the Decatur Railroad, around the Muscle Shoals and thence by the 'projected' railroad to Memphis; 'another between the Tennessee and Nashville to Cincinnati,' and finally one 'from . . . the Ohio to Lake Michigan.' 'Projected,' imaginary, but still 'the most important and magnificent work in the world.' [33]

Georgia thought otherwise. Georgia financiers had evinced no interest in extending their railroads for the benefit of Charleston. Hence, the question

was, Where should the route start—along the valley of the French Broad
River, through North Carolina, as suggested by Robert Young Hayne, or
by the little-known 'Carolina Gap,' along the old Cherokee Path in a bee-
line from Charleston to Nashville and on to St. Louis, as urged by Calhoun?

That Hayne's route—serving, as it did, the entire Carolina up-country
—was more advantageous to his own state, a single glance at the map will
reveal. But Calhoun, bent on his grand design of 'uniting . . . two sections,' was thinking beyond the borders of Carolina. It was to the Far
West that the South must look, not to Cincinnati or Lexington, whose
natural trade outlets were not South Carolina, but Maryland and Virginia.
Basically both Hayne and Calhoun sought the same end—intersectional
unity through trade; but where Hayne indulged in roseate dreams that
rail lines between Kentucky and Ohio would make for social ties and
affection between the sections that might even allay the Northern repugnance to slavery, Calhoun's plan dealt far more with practical economics.
Actually his railroad scheme was only a part of his long-range program
for a balanced and broadening Union, voiced first in his days as a Congressman and as Secretary of War, and to be climaxed with his Memphis
Memorial of 1846.

Politically, of course, Calhoun's plan was inadvisable, because from a
superficial standpoint it slighted his own state. But he was no man to be
deterred by such considerations. Back in 1836 he had determined that the
Carolina Gap was the direct highway to the West, far superior to Hayne's
alternative French Broad route. Well, he had decided, he would see for
himself. Only if he proved to himself that he was right, could he demonstrate the truth to others. Maps were not enough. He would walk the first
stage of his route, across the mountains from Fort Hill to the mouth of the
North Carolina river, Tuskaseegee.

To another man the scheme might have seemed fantastic. To the 'active,
energetic' Calhoun nothing was impossible that he had set his mind upon.
And in mid-September, 1836, accompanied by his friends Colonel James
Gadsden and William Sloan, he had started for the mountains.

To Calhoun the experience had been exhilarating. Now he could give
full play to his long unfulfilled desire to be an engineer. His mathematical
eye and brain gauged the elevation of the bluffs and ridges, and by the
time his survey was over, the whole great 'rout' was spread out like a map
in his mind: the 'decents' and crossings, the unbuilt rail lines, and the
navigation on the 'Western Waters.'

Up there, in that vast world of towering peaks and smoky ranges,
Washington seemed very far away. Here was the pure, ice-needled water,
the keen air, the pungent scent of pine needles warm in the noontime sun.
All his senses were alert, for even as his eye marked the slope and elevation

of the prospective gradings, he would be aware of the footprints of a wolf on the banks of a stream and of the rustling in the brush.

Down below, temperatures still hung at the ninety mark. Here already the maple leaves were dipped with the sunset, and the leaves of beeches were deepening from pale yellow to warm gold.[34] Carpets of color were strewn across the distant ranges; the translucent air steeped every leaf and every blade of grass in a richer hue. At dusk the haze darkened from smoke-blue to purple; at dawn clouds clung to the downward slopes, swirling away like smoke, revealing range after range as if through a veil.

Here in the hills, time had dropped back fifty years. Here still was the half-won frontier, the clay-chinked cabins of the old Abbeville district of Calhoun's boyhood. Here was a world long known and forgotten—of leaf tobacco drying on the mantel and strings of red peppers swinging from smoke-stained rafters. Here were the quilting frame and the spinning wheel, the cedar water-bucket and the split-bottomed mountain chairs, cut from fine-grained white oak. From the table would come the familiar sound of sucking swallows and clattering knives; from the fireplace the scent of broiling venison and of cornpone, wrapped in shucking and baked black under a layer of hot ashes.

Calhoun surrendered easily to the informal mountain hospitality. He could count himself lucky when he shared a room merely with his traveling companions, for in some cabins sixteen might be bedded down in a single chamber.[35] Even in the taverns a traveler was regarded as unreasonably fastidious who objected to bedclothes which had 'only been used a few nights,' or a sudden awakening as the landlord ushered a stranger into his bed.[36] So Calhoun took it with equanimity when aroused one midnight by a peremptory 'Move furder thar, old horse,' and found the rural mail carrier climbing into bed with him.

In the morning, he lay abed longer than was his wont, savoring the long-lost memories, the September air, spiced with pine. From the room beyond came the sounds and smells of breakfast, the clatter of the bucket, and a faint breath of wood smoke, stealing through the loose-laid logs of the partition. He was roused, at last, by his hostess. Without ceremony she thumped over to the bed, told him to get up, climb the ladder into the loft, and fetch her down a ham for his breakfast. And without a demur the Senator obeyed.

She didn't know he was the great John Calhoun. He hadn't bothered to tell her. But at the close of the mountain visits, Colonel Gadsden gratified their hostess's curiosity. She bustled up to Calhoun and looked him searchingly up and down.

'Well,' was her disappointed verdict, 'you look just like other folks.' Then, hopefully, 'I guess you have a pretty wife to home, h'ain't you?'

Smilingly Calhoun replied that the next time he came to the mountains, he would bring Mrs. Calhoun with him, and she could see for herself.

'Well, I guess she has plenty of pretty bed coverlets to home now, h'ain't she?'

At this, the author of a thousand speeches was speechless.[37]

At the mouth of the 'Tuskyseege,' the long trek ended. Now even Calhoun realized how laborious the nine days of incessant walking and searching had been. But his enthusiasm was aglow. Results had been 'eminently favorable, far more' than even he had anticipated. He threw himself into the work of preparing a 'statement of facts' for the Pendleton *Messenger*. Meetings must be held immediately in Abbeville, Edgefield, and 'Orangeburgh.' The route, he was convinced, had 'a decided preference over all other routes,' and nothing but suitable efforts were required to 'ensure its success.'

He was not unaware of the obstacles that confronted his dream. He listed them as two: 'the want of concert, and the want of funds,' the second a disturbing factor, indeed, when one considered how the men with funds might easily divert his plans into their own channels. Of the 'want of concert,' he had no fear; against it he would pit his energy and his persuasiveness.

For a brief while it seemed as if in his long-range aims he might succeed. His Carolina Gap route could obtain no general support, but agreement with Georgia seemed in the offing, and in Columbia leading railroad financiers expressed enthusiasm over the very route through Georgia to the Tennessee that he had recommended three years before, at which time he had not been able to get a single man in the state to agree.[38] Calhoun was, of course, nominally a director of the embryonic Louisville, Cincinnati, and Charleston Railroad, but a man more temperamentally unfit to enjoy such letterhead honors can hardly be imagined. As he told Duff Green, when turning down the proffered chairmanship of a mining corporation: 'Of all things . . . I have the least taste for money-making . . . in particular the branch connected with stock, exchange, or banking. . . . You must see how illy qualified I am for the task . . . and how exceedingly irksome its duties would be to me. . . . I would infinitely prefer . . . to take the place of Chief Engineer at the head of the Mining Department . . . to develop . . . so fine a deposite would at least require so much reflection and energy as to absorb the attention.' [39]

To the 'great object of uniting the West and the South Atlantick ports,' he had willingly lent his name—until he discovered that it was only his name that was wanted. South Carolina and Georgia would not be 'one,' not even for their mutual benefit. Sensing this, Calhoun had striven, as we have seen, to find some other route 'as far West as possible, without touching Georgia,' but could not convince the financiers of his own state. He had tried to see the advantages of other routes; nor had he relied upon his own judgment alone. But the 'great object' he could not and would not relinquish, and neither South Carolina nor Georgia saw what lay behind his pleas. While South Carolina struck out for herself along the route of the French Broad, Georgia adopted almost the entire route Calhoun had suggested, 'but . . . looking wholly to her own interests.' While South Carolina was still debating ways and means, Georgia's route to the West would be completed at low cost, with consequent lower rates for transportation; and with its connection to the Tennessee, its branches would draw the trade from Knoxville and the entire West, 'in preference to ours, even if it was completed.' [40]

Calhoun had been bitterly disappointed. The 'mighty flood of prosperity' that he had predicted, would now break over Georgia alone. And on October 28, 1838, he had submitted his resignation to Robert Young Hayne. A note of genuine regret sounded through his words. South Carolina's French Broad route, he was convinced, would collapse in 'complete and disasterous failure.' He would not share in the responsibility. 'No one would rejoice more than myself to find that you were right,' he told Hayne. 'We are all in the same ship, and must share alike in the good or bad fortune of the State.' Charleston, he was still convinced, 'had more advantages for Western trade than any other city on the Atlantic.' South Carolina must look to the Far West, to the Tennessee, not the Ohio. She must—but she would not.

'You cannot possibly feel more pain in differing from me, than I do in differing from you,' he assured Hayne. 'Our differences shall never effect our personal relations.' [41]

Thus formally ended Calhoun's connections with Southern railroading, but not his interest. In 1839 he was writing an Illinois Circuit Judge that Charleston had far greater advantages for trade than New York, and that the 'line of communication' must be 'through the Tennessee River.' Could not Illinois take the lead? 'I have long had the completion of this great line of communication much at heart,' he confessed; 'and have been surprised, when I reflect on the vast . . . portion of the Union interested, that it has attracted so little attention.' [42]

5

Disappointed though he had been, his interest in routes and rail lines and all modes of communication continued unabated in subsequent years. Maps fascinated him; the pioneering blood stirred in his veins; and visitors to Fort Hill in the forties would often find him on the north portico with maps spread out before him and he questing their secrets with all the eagerness of youth. 'You evince good judgement,' he wrote Anna in Belgium, 'in preferring a new and growing country to an old . . . one . . . there is something heartsome . . . in . . . a new country. Indeed, so strongly do I feel the charms of a growing and improving country, that I would be much disposed to place myself on the very verge of the advancing population and growth . . . were I to follow my inclination.'[43]

If only he were young!

If he were young, he told a group in the summer of 1845, he would settle over there—in the North Georgia country. He swept a long finger down the map from Greenville and Seneca to the tiny speck marking the southern end of the rail line running northwestward from the old Cherokee country on into Tennessee. This was the place, he announced—Terminus, or Marthasville, or whatever they were calling it now. Give it a few years and you'd see a railroad running from that spot to the Ohio country and on to the Pacific coast beyond. Just wait, he said in substance, and you'd see Terminus the great railroad center of the Southeastern United States. Yes, that's where he would go, if he were young again!

His friends listened, with deference but skepticism. That was like old Calhoun for you! What gentleman could *ever* imagine living in that brawling mudhole, with its one railroad office, one sawmill, and two stores? They were changing its name again now—Marthasville it had been for the last year or two, and now it was rechristened again—what *was* the name, anyway? Oh, yes, Atlanta—Atlanta, Georgia, that was it.

Calhoun's means permitted him little surplus travel. But in the fall of 1845 came the chance he had dreamed of. He was chosen a delegate to a 'South-Western convention' at Memphis, called to promote the unity and development of the economic resources of both the South and the West. Here, at last, was a concrete step toward his great goal. And it was with high enthusiasm that he arrived at his son's Alabama plantation that fall for a tour that became little less than a march of triumph.

Celebrations were climaxed in New Orleans. There in the old Creole city where Andrew Jackson had reigned as hero, his deadliest enemy was mobbed by cheering crowds whenever he ventured into the streets. Anyone who wanted a personal interview received it, and visitors crowded his rooms merely to see and hear him.

The excitement was exhilarating. Friends, aware of his serious illness only a few months before, found him looking remarkably well. He reveled in the beauty of the exotic old city; its narrow streets and high-walled houses, the wrought-iron lacework, the old market in the shadows of the high archways. At the harbor even his fears for the decay of Charleston would have dimmed, for there, row on row, hiding the brown water of the Mississippi, lay an 'array of steamboats, gorgeous river palaces, from inland ports a thousand miles distant,' flatboats, rafts, loaded with hemp, wheat, corn, pigs, furs—all the treasures of the West pouring into the world market at New Orleans.[44] Small wonder that Calhoun's pulses leaped; his vision grew; he saw New Orleans as the great American port of call for all Latin America, the Mississippi as the life-artery of the

Union; and could not and would not believe that the day of the South's prosperity and greatness was at an end.

In Mobile he had declined all public celebrations, but in New Orleans, at the behest of the city dignitaries, he accepted a public dinner, and could not resist writing Clemson that he was received 'everywhere in a manner sufficient to gratify the feelings of . . . the most illustrious. . . . All parties everywhere united, without distinction, in a demonstration . . . not exceed[ed] by that shown to General Jackson in . . . the same places. . . . I everywhere was received as the guest of the place, and passed without expense . . . through every town to and from Memphis.' [45]

6

Most popular of all the modes of 'locomotion' in that year of 1845 was river travel. In theory this was a means of transportation that appealed to Calhoun. Since 1815, when he had written Floride of the ease and safety of the steamboat in which you were 'moved on rapidly without being sensible of it,' [46] he had longed for a line straight from Charleston to Washington.

River boats varied all the way from the crude 'hell afloat' steamers of the West, where the sun poured through the overhead and the furnace burned through the deck, to the river palaces of the lower Mississippi, broad-beamed and flat-bottomed, complete with a hurricane deck for lovers, a library of 'histories, voyages, biographies, sermons, reviews, and the latest novels,' a barber shop, and a two-hundred-foot drinking saloon. There the traveler could find comfortable sofas, marble-topped tables, and swinging chandeliers; the art connoisseur might note the paneled walls with their 'hand-painted' scenic murals. Less inviting were the ladies' cabins, where the gentler sex, if alone, sat in fixed, silent rows with their reticules and little baskets in their laps, their faces 'the images of philosophic indifference.' The rocking chairs were invariably occupied by the mothers, who rocked, suckled their young, and wearily voiced unrealized threats of 'I'll switch you,' to children 'so wild and undisciplined, as to be the torment of all who approached them.' [47]

Had Calhoun sought America over, he could not have found a better cross-section of his country than on the deck of a river steamboat. All were there: dissolute young planters; stock actors grumbling at the smallness of their wages and parts; firm-lipped governesses from New England traveling alone to some far-distant plantation; card-players who would rather collect their winnings than get off at their stops; politicians, statesmen, riff-raff, gentlemen. And for all—all but the unfortunate 'deck passengers,' who slept like dogs on the bare planking below—equality was the rule. Men of rank, of the most gentle manners and superior education, found themselves treated with no more 'deference and respect' than the rudest backwoodsman, whose coin and whose rights were as good as any man's. Only to 'the lady' was homage paid, and she, whether 'rich or poor, mistress or maid,' had 'a right to the best, to the head of the table.' Calhoun and a hundred other hungry men might lean on their chairs and wistfully watch their fricasseed chicken and hot rolls cool while a beruffled Miss lingered in the cabin to twist her last curl about her finger— but this was her privilege as a woman.[48]

As travel went in 1845, the river boat was enjoyable. There were, of course, certain objections. Calhoun might have noted that the deck of the gentlemen's cabin, like that of the Senate Chamber, was not only deep in carpet but steeped in tobacco juice. As a newcomer to river travel, he might have voiced fear that the boiler had burst at the first 'frightful' discharge of steam, but would have laughed with the others when the birds in the branches overhead, hardened to 'progress,' were shown completely unfrightened by the snortings of a steamboat. And he would have soon accustomed himself to the sounds and smells of travel, the grate of the bottom against a sandbar, the ripping of planks by a snag, and the smell of the sperm lamps in the evening.

At dusk most of the passengers would 'go below.' Some read; others played cards, and there were stewards who 'knew the secret of juleps.'[49] At ten the curtains were drawn. Not enough room in the ladies' cabin? Then we'll cut off a slice from the men's. The gentlemen could draw lots for the berths that were left.

Calhoun would have cared little whether or not his number came up. There was a surplus of him for the bed; the 'neat little cot' of the steamboat was built only for a five-foot-ten limit. There would have been little chance for sleep in any case, what with the 'suffocating' air and the heat from the boiler; the smells of sweat and starch, brandy and tobacco, and the constant talk of those who 'could neither sleep themselves, nor allow others' to do so. There was little rest even, in that din of crying babies, the 'tremor from the machinery, the puffing of the waste pipe,' and the 'endless thumping of the billets of wood on their way to the furnace.'[50]

Calhoun might have preferred to spend the night on deck with a group of his fellow travelers, talking the 'eternal politics' of shipboard, hearing the varied but eternal reiteration: 'The Northern democracy must join with the South and elect a Southern President, or the Union is gone forever.'[51] Or he could seek solitude at the ship's rail. Overhead was air of such purity that the moss-draped trees at the water's edge, the white gleam of the prow, even a sagging river landing, stood out in 'tenfold beauty,' and the very stars no longer seemed the same. Below lay the 'muddy Mississippi,' quivering in the pale candlelight beauty of the moon. He would draw back finally, seek a seat on a trunk, and join the passengers at talk until breakfast.

Ponderously the steamer moved upstream. At a landing a Negro might signal, tell the boat to wait 'till Master was ready.' Later would come a stop for sugar and then for thundering bale after bale of cotton. At either side of the broad, brown highway of water were the 'wretched-looking' waterfront villages of the Mississippi, where woodcutters' huts teetered on rotting green piles and gaunt-ribbed cows and pigs stumbled knee-deep in water. In a cabin doorway would lean a woman, 'the very image of dirt and disease,' her face bluish white, 'her squalling baby on her hip-bone.' And as the mighty steamer passed, the mud-streaked children would pause from their play and stand staring, lifting faces of the same 'ghastly hue.' [52]

Swamp and forest and jungle closing in, and then a tunnel of oaks, golden streamers of sun lacing the dark earth below; and at the end the towering columns of a Doric temple, now pink, now yellow, now white in the falling light. Bon Sejour, Ormond, Uncle Sam, Ashland—the glorious pageant thundered by.

7

In November, Calhoun arrived at his destination—the Memphis Convention. There, as president, he sounded the keynote with a plea for harmony, for unity above party feelings. A single purpose dominated his mind: the union of South and West as a counterbalance to Northern majority rule.

Southern values could survive only if linked economically to the agricultural West, he told the convention. West and South, the common treasure-trove from which Northern capital was drawn, must unite on a national policy. In such a cause, what did the labels of Whig and Democrat matter? He spoke with an eloquence rare in his later days, his stooped body drawn erect, his deep eyes glowing as if they gave off 'light in the dark.' [53] Once again he voiced the dream of 'balanced industry,' of a balanced union; but now his views were startling. Congress must protect commerce on the Mississippi, he told the delegates. The great river was really an 'inland sea.' Congress had power to regulate commerce 'among the several states'; thus, with federal aid, and the consent of the states involved, could the Mississippi become the fountainhead of a mighty flood of prosperity for the Southern and Western states. It was the youthful, nationalistic Calhoun of an earlier era who made these ringing demands, but it was an aging man in declining health who finally broke off, 'becoming very hoarse,' against prolonged and repeated calls to go on.

Only in the cool of the aftermath, with the speaker's personal spell shattered, did the states' rights men exchange glances of wonder and dismay. This was not states' rights, this interdependence of one state upon another, and of the combination upon the whims or generosity of the federal government. This was nothing more than Clay's old internal improvements program, dusted off and refitted—and for what? Undoubtedly for the Presidential campaign of 1848 and the aspirations of Mr. John C. Calhoun.

Calhoun himself was insistent that his program rested upon the 'strictest state rights doctrines.[54] He wasted no thoughts on the similarity between federal aid for manufacturers and federal aid for Southerners. His program was practical, not doctrinaire. What bewildered his following was the division between his immediate and his long-range aims, his means and his ends.

For it was the regional and the economic interests of the country that Calhoun recognized as dominant now. In theory the Union was built on states; in practice it was now operating in terms of sections. No state could stand alone. Every right the individual state might possess, plus the united strength of the South itself, was not enough under the system of majority rule. To survive within the Union, the South must find allies with whom she could rule the Union.

Calhoun was too farsighted to deceive himself as to how long an alliance between the agrarian West and South against the industrial North would endure. No man more acutely realized the power and onrush of the industrial movement. What he sought was time, a temporary alliance by which the industrial democracy might be held in check long enough to achieve such constitutional reforms as would insure the South's and the West's safety—within the Union.

He was fighting to win. But the mental intricacies of the man who has been called the most 'subtle' of all American statesmen were beyond his own times and his own admirers. The nationalism of this new program horrified them. The prophet had gone astray. As Jefferson Davis viewed it, his reversal had something of the effect which would have been produced by Moses altering the Ten Commandments.[55]

Assuredly Calhoun was right in thinking that the man who was the candidate of a single section alone could never be President. But what he gained in the West, he probably lost in the South. Soon Thomas Ritchie was openly denouncing him, and from South Carolina, from the Southern Review, and even from his own cousin, Francis Pickens, came 'rude' attacks against him.

The American Review, commenting on Calhoun's 'Memphis Memorial,' prepared for submission to Congress, conceded that 'there is a power about Mr. Calhoun's name and position, which would make it worse than bad taste to regard any State paper slightingly that comes from his pen'; but was amazed at the 'jumble and confusion' of his ideas. He was one of the 'master-minds of this country and age,' asserted the Review; he had voiced a principle of 'transcendent moment,' but encumbered it with technicalities. How could Mr. Calhoun find his authority for the development of state rivers and harbors in the Congressional power to regulate commerce 'among the several states'? Was not this a clause, not of privilege, but of restriction? Where was the great 'strict constructionist now'? [56]

Calhoun paid little heed. The questioned portion of the Constitution, he contended, was not clearly understood. He had defined the line between 'internal and external improvements,' had endeavored 'rigidly' to restrict the government to the powers belonging to the 'external relations of the states.' [57] But even more important, as he revealed to his brother-in-law, this constitutional doubt was the 'only barrier . . . that remains between the Union of the South and West,' and in the consummation of this ideal, not even the Constitution would stand in his way.[58]

8

By December, 1845, Calhoun was back at Fort Hill, but only for a few days. A re-election to the Senate awaited him, a prospect which pleased him not in the least. His trip had tired him more than he would admit; he had developed a cough at Memphis which he was unable to shake; and a physician who looked him over shook his head, warning him that he required complete rest.[59]

Concern for his health, however, was the least of Calhoun's worries. For years he had had too little money in his pocket, and had lived too close to the border-line of comfort. Now with falling farm prices and doctors' bills and a family of boys to educate, Calhoun was facing genuine financial disaster. His account-books were beginning the sorry story of ever-mounting costs and ever-mounting debt that was to dog his last years; a story, incidentally, that was being told and retold on every farm and plantation all over the South. It is surprising that Calhoun did not seek personal excuse in the common tragedy; but his Puritan code forbade him to blame anyone but himself.

Plantations, he knew now, could not be run by remote control; and within two years he would be writing frantically to Andrew to find some way to raise money 'to meet our engagements.' Soon he would be forced to the tragic alternative of mortgaging Fort Hill. But embarrassed as he was, he had withstood an offer of a loan from Abbott Lawrence, which he felt was offered more on the security of his character than on the value of his cotton futures.[60] In Washington, Daniel Webster gallantly offered him a loan. Calhoun declined. 'Ah,' said Webster with a smile, 'Nature made me a Cavalier of Massachusetts and you a Puritan of South Carolina.'

Calhoun had no wish to be 'forced into the Senate again.' [61] Once back in harness, he sensed that he would never be free. 'Private life has many charms for me,' he told Duff Green, 'and it will be difficult for me to retire at any time hereafter.' [62] But the pressure upon him was almost irresistible, and his stand at Memphis had only heightened the clamor from all sections of the country. He had been so long in public life that entire generations had grown up with no memory of the country without him. 'We regard the absence of Mr. Calhoun as a national calamity,' declared the New Orleans *Jeffersonian Republican.* 'No man now living is so familiar with the great science of finance.' [63] The call was national, not for the slaveholder and the Southerner, but for the nation-builder, the progressive statesman with his 'lively interest in all industrial improvements.' At Memphis he had indeed forever wrecked his chances of peace and retirement. The program demanded the leader.

Undoubtedly Calhoun meant what he said, however, when he wrote James Edward that 'strong as the pressure was,' he would never have considered returning to public life had he not had 'a deep conviction that there was great danger of a war . . . [with England] and that I might do something to avert so great a calamity.' No one, he believed, could realize the disasters which war would bring. 'I fear neither our liberty nor constitution would survive.' [64]

It was this fear, the conviction that his statecraft was essential to ward off conflict, that accounted for much of the public outcry for his services. 'It is the South that demands it. It is Virginia that calls for it; it is the Constitution that needs it,' trumpeted the Fredericksburg *Recorder.* 'He must pluck the weed of ambition from his breast.' [65]

This last shaft struck home. Age, illness, defeat—nothing could kill or cure Calhoun's ambition. That fall, James Hamilton would be in New York lining up a 'Calhoun committee' to support the South Carolinian's candidacy should the election of '48 be thrown into the House. That the Presidential question was tantalizing his mind is undeniable; as he admitted to Armistead Burt: 'I may lose much for the Presidency.' He could not get through without 'giving and receiving blows, and losing much of the good feelings now felt by all.' Not even President Polk, he believed, really wanted war, but there were many in the Administration who did; and the President was not of the fiber to resist their importunities. The people, he knew, wanted peace; but he knew that it was the leaders and not the people who made Presidential candidates. He could not let himself think about that. 'I would have been unworthy of the high place in which my friends desire to place me, had I yielded to such considerations.' [66]

He was aware, too, of his responsibilities to the program he had set in motion at Memphis. He had conceived it; he alone could bring it to realization on the floor of Congress. To the Charleston *Mercury* it seemed to embody the very 'hope of the future'; to Calhoun himself it seemed the strongest of all possible guarantees against disunion. And to prevent disunion he would 'make any personal sacrifice.' It was with these hopes of staving off a war and uniting the South and the West that he pulled himself once more into the swaying confines of the stagecoach and set his face toward Washington. He did not despair. 'I have with me,' he wrote Andrew, 'the wise and patriotick of all parties; and I shall be supported by the almost united voice of Virginia and S.C. with the most talented portion of the South, and the convictions of my own mind.' [67] Nor did the prospect of the dreary, comfortless months ahead appall him as in recent years. For with him in the coach were Floride and Cornelia.

XXV

A Nation-Sized American

CALHOUN WAS GROWING OLD. Not yet sixty-four when he returned to
Washington for that stormy winter session of 1846, he looked ten years
more. He had become the Calhoun of the schoolhouse textbooks, stooped
and hollow-chested, his gray hair thrown back from his forehead and hanging in masses about his neck and temples. Over him hung 'an air of utter
weariness,' although there were moments still when he showed an energy
that his 'wasted frame scarcely indicated as possible.'

So long as he remained at Fort Hill, breathing pure air, taking the rest
and exercise that he knew to be essential to him, Calhoun's tuberculosis
remained dormant; but back in the maelstrom of the capital he broke
rapidly. He could not conserve his energy. Accumulated years seemed only
to have tightened his nerves and intensified his mental processes. His every
action was quick, and when he spoke it was still as though 'no words
could convey his speed of thought.'[1] It was his intensity which troubled
his friends most; for they knew how fiercely his emotions, even when
bottled up, drained his vitality.

It was at this period that he burst out: 'If you should ask me the
question' what 'I would wish engraved on my tombstone, it is *Nullification*.' The crisis, now thirteen years past, had left scars upon him that he
was only beginning to reveal. Only now could he speak of how much his
state's loyalty had meant to him in those dark hours. 'South Carolina alone
stood by me. She is my dear and honored State . . . South Carolina has
never mistrusted nor forsaken me. . . . Mine she has ever been.' He 'hung
upon her devotion,' recorded the startled woman to whom he made these
confidences, 'with all . . . the tenderness . . . with which a lover dwells
upon the constancy of his mistress . . . his breath . . . quick and short;
his proud head flung back, and his voice subdued by emotion.'

Worn out though he was, it was only too plain that his ambition was not
dead. His protestations were too vehement. 'I cannot describe to you, I
cannot express the indifference with which I regard the Presidential Chair.'
He added, 'with a scornful smile,' 'I will not sacrifice the shadow of a
principle for its possession.'

Not the South, but the country, was now foremost in his thoughts. To his friends it seemed extraordinary that this austere man, unskilled in the arts of party politics, could have become 'the representative of interests which . . . are in contra position to each other,' uniting and guarding each, and 'preserving entire the integrity of all.' [2] For the South his platform was peace, free trade, and a lowered tariff. For the North he offered the raw materials of the West and new land for the young men now grubbing away at the rocky New England soil. And for the West his program had been outlined at Memphis—railroads, harbor ports, commercial union with the South, 'Manifest Destiny.'

2

Washington in 1846, a 'rambling, scrambling village,' with hovels elbowing mansions from Georgetown to the Capitol, still had 'that uncomfortable air of having been made yesterday.' But it was depressing no longer. Green blinds were fastened 'outside all the houses, with a red curtain and a white one in every window.' Calhoun noticed that more and more public buildings were going up 'in a handsome style of Greek architecture,' but not yet were the vacant fields and sand-lots filled in, and the 'would-be metropolis' still looked like 'some projector's scheme' which had failed.

In the spring the Capitol grounds were aflame with roses, tulips, and a single peony bush bending under the weight of nearly a hundred flowers, many of them six inches across. Here in the early afternoons passers-by could see Thomas Hart Benton's invalid wife, sitting on a bench with Old Bullion whispering into her ear or picking bouquets of wild flowers to place in her hands. There were the night parties at Boulanger's, where you could still get Maryland oysters and Virginia terrapin, the 'best brandy in America,' and Madeira that dated back to pre-Revolutionary days; and there were the Marine Band concerts on Wednesday afternoons on the White House lawn. On Saturdays they were held under 'a clump of trees on the enclosed green between the President's house and the war office'; [3] and here, descending from carriage after carriage, came the Washington great. You saw Pennsylvania's James Buchanan, tall and fair, 'his good looks marred only by the nervous jerking of his head . . . his unwilling footsteps . . . just upon the boundary of middle age.' Arm in arm would be the strapping six-footer, 'Bob' Toombs of Georgia, with his 'beautiful hands' and mane of black hair tossed back like Danton's, and frail little Alexander Stephens, beardless, wrinkled, with his piping voice and his 'virile mind.'

Among the crowds moved dapper Nathaniel Willis of the *Society Letters,* looking, with his monocle, more like a duke than a reporter for the New York *Daily Mirror;* Webster, talking 'agreeable nonsense' to the girls; red-faced old John Quincy Adams, with 'a young lady'; Calhoun, 'smiling and happy' with a gentleman. 'Of course, Mr. Calhoun and Mr. Webster were the most distinguished looking men,' commented Mrs. Robert Tyler, the ex-President's daughter-in-law.[4]

Society was as informal as it was gay: the scent of Rhine wine, the gentlemen pledging the ladies, a Senator stuffing himself into a fur coat to play Santa Claus, or tall, swaybacked Jefferson Davis rising to sing a Christmas song. All Washington chuckled for weeks over the frightened look in the pale blue eyes of the dumpy little Swedish author, Fredericka Bremer, as at an evening party Webster, somewhat the worse for wine and wearing a white linen waistcoat which made him 'appear unusually large,' arranged himself before her in his most 'stately' oratorical pose, his hand upon his heart, and in his Senatorial voice boomed: 'Madam, you have toiling millions, we have boundless area . . .'

'Y—e—s, very moch,' the startled Miss Bremer interrupted, the purple ribbons on her lace cap bobbing; but at that moment Jefferson Davis hustled out the would-be orator of the evening.[5]

There was plenty to talk about in the crowded drawing rooms: the *bon mot* of a Washington wit, who, upon receiving a note from a society woman whose ideas of spelling were purely theoretical, had commented, 'Do you not think that, with such difficulty about spelling, it was kind in her to try it?'—the crowds of tourists staring at the new private bathtubs in the National Hotel—and Mr. Morse's 'machine' that made the 'wires talk.' But pre-eminent in public attention was the first American World's Fair —the National Exhibition of 1845. Each state had sent exhibits to the ramshackle, roughly clapboarded room which stretched two full blocks on C Street. Calhoun, with his zest for scientific improvements, probably paused longest before the 'sewing jenny . . . that stitches like the hand-work,' and, watching closely, he could see a needle ply through a strip of cloth, sewing 'a pretty good seam.'[6]

He might have stopped, too, to chat with Mr. and Mrs. Jefferson Davis and ex-President Tyler, who were taking turns drinking from a tin cup into which Tyler had milked the prize cow. Calhoun, it seems, took Davis's 'little wife' more seriously than did her own husband. At any rate, he favored her with long letters in which he discussed political questions with as much depth and care as if she were a contemporary. Varina was much flattered, but to her distress found that Calhoun's handwriting, 'though neat,' was so illegible that she could scarcely make out a word. She finally bundled up a sheaf and took them over to Calhoun's lodgings for his interpretation. He gazed at them sadly. 'I know what I think on these subjects,' he said, 'but I cannot decipher what I wrote.'[7]

3

In 1848, after House sessions were adjourned, a young Whig Congressman, long and lank, with lined cheeks, rough black hair, and a cravat twisted beneath his ear, would slip into a Senate gallery seat and listen to Calhoun with profound attention. It was style more than content that interested him. In the era of Webster's and Clay's ornate bombast, Calhoun's austere style was regarded as highly unorthodox if not inferior to the booming eloquence around him. But Abraham Lincoln of Illinois thought otherwise. With instinctive taste, he was pruning his own flamboyant style, stripping off the surplus wordage, and frankly reshaping his sentences into the clean-cut phrases he admired in Calhoun.[8]

4

Although society flooded in upon Calhoun at his lodgings, he could take no part in the Washington gaieties at all. His seclusion was of necessity, not choice. He had mellowed with the years, and now looked with wistful eyes on the pleasures which his limited strength would not permit him to enjoy. 'I like balls, they are beautiful things,' he told a friend in the winter of 1846, 'but now I have a cough . . . and I fear the evening air.' [9]

Deliberately Calhoun was rationing the time left to him. 'I have made an allotment of these years,' he said, 'a portion for America, a portion for my own private affairs, (for I am a planter and cannot afford to be idle) and a portion I have reserved for peculiar purposes, connected only with myself.' [10] He knew now that he would die in harness, for Washington still whispered of his indignation when young Representative Isaac Holmes carried to him Polk's praise for his 'high talents,' and the offer of the 'Mission to the Court of St. James's, with its ostensible transfer of the Oregon question . . . entirely to his charge.' Instantly Calhoun's perceptions had penetrated the ruse. Every muscle in his face went tense. 'No, sir—no,' he said. 'If the embassies of all Europe were clustered into one, I would not take it at this time . . . here ought to be the negotiations, and here will I stand.' [11]

5

'War is almost upon us,' was the cry of Lewis Cass in December, 1845. After twenty-five years' joint and peaceful occupation of the great 'Oregon country,' stretching from Wyoming to Alaska, America was risking all, for all, or for nothing. 'Fifty-Four-Forty or Fight' had been Polk's campaign cry; this fact lay behind Calhoun's refusal of the British mission. * The

* Despite the campaign oratory, President Polk had made an offer to Britain of compromise on the forty-ninth parallel, in the summer of 1845. This was summarily rejected, and to save face, Polk felt compelled to resume his original position. Hence, his hands were tied, and any future moves toward compromise would have to come from outside his Administration backed by a groundswell of public opinion.

'joint occupancy' was ended; by arms, or by pen, the question would be settled, and it would be settled 'here.'

The nerves of the nation were taut with fear. In Charleston, where Calhoun stopped for a few days on his way North, the excitement was 'great,' and the despondency even more so. What wish had the South Carolina slaveholder to shed his blood in a fight against his best customers, a fight for new 'free soil' for the North? And while Calhoun sat in a Charleston drawing room, trying to compose his thoughts and balance a teacup, as the feminine chatter swirled and eddied about him, a woman burst out with the one question that was on everybody's mind: 'Do you think there'll be a war?'

Conversation ceased, every eye fixed on the guest of honor. Calhoun evaded the question. He had been away from Washington a long time, he said. He had not received any official documents. Gradually the excitement died down and he arose to take his leave. An eager group followed him to the door, among them his own former family governess, Miss Mary Bates.

Turning swiftly to her, Calhoun whispered: 'I anticipate a severe seven months' campaign. I have never known our country in such a state.'

'Oh, Mr. Calhoun,' Miss Bates exclaimed, 'do all you can to prevent it!'

He nodded. 'I will do all, in honour, I can do.' He was silent for a long moment. His face was dark with thought, his eyes shadowed, and 'bending a little forward, as if bowed with a sense of his responsibility and insufficiency, he added, speaking slowly and with emphasis . . . as if questioning with himself: "But what can one man do?"' [12]

What one man could do it was his task to do. A driving purpose was holding him up in his work, was almost keeping him alive. He had, indeed, come to live 'almost bodilessly on something in his mind, the nourishment of crowding ideas, or a driving task.' [13] His time was short.

The selflessness of his goal was known to all. Calhoun, when confronted with personal tributes from Buchanan, Polk, and even Benton,* was touched to tears. Momentarily even party feelings were stilled in his presence. Not even in his brilliant young days as Secretary of War had he stood so high.

All eyes were on him, this abstracted man, 'carelessly dressed,' hair 'indifferently combed,' walking the streets absent-mindedly.[14] 'Now the advocate of war and now of peace . . . now branded as a Traitor; now worshipped as a Patriot . . . now withstanding Power, and now the People; now proudly accepting office; now as proudly spurning it; now goading the Administration; now advising it,' now the defender of states' rights, and now of the indestructibility of the Union—his unsolved contradictions all served to focus public attention on him.

* Benton hated Calhoun, yet conceded him to be 'a great and pure man.'

His fame had become world-wide. 'If this distinguished Statesman could be prevailed upon to visit England either in a public or a private capacity,' recorded Sarah Maury, 'he would command more admiration and interest than any other of Europe or America.' [15]

Peace or war—the responsibility, he felt, rested upon him. He knew how dangerous to his own future his task would be. Temptation was beckoning from every side. He had only to ride the popular wave, to throw himself with Polk and the Democratic battle-cry, to regain his old power in the party, to rally the land-hungry Northern democracy to himself and his cause. In following, not defying, public opinion, 'manifest destiny' might sweep him into the 'President's House,' at last.[16]

Conversely, he could rally his Southern following, confused now by his course at Memphis. He could denounce all expansion of free territory as a menace to slave security, split open the Democratic Party, turn the slave-holders against Polk, and gain for himself a sweet revenge. And had ambition been as strong within him as his enemies said, one of these alternatives would have been his course.

Instead, he faced the jeers from the West that he would accept their help for Texas, but would not repay the compliment with 'all' of Oregon. He defied the anger of imperialists, who sneered that he would have risked war had Oregon been another Texas. And he gambled his popularity in the South, which saw danger in every foot of new territory.

He was for 'all of Oregon' that could be won without war. He knew that it was destiny that Oregon should become a part of the American Union. He had fought for Oregon in the State Department; he would fight for Oregon now. To his very bones, he knew, just as he had known with Texas, what Oregon meant and would mean to the United States of America.

6

It had been Jefferson who had foreseen 'a great, free, and independent empire,' spreading out across the western half of the American continent. Not the Westerner, Jackson, who had cried, 'concentrate our population; confine our frontier.' Not Clay, or Webster, or virtually any of the Northern statesmen, most of whom never saw a future for the West. Calhoun had none of Webster's ability to color his visions in a tropic glory of language that could fire the emotions and warm the heart. Yet it was he, and not the New Englander, whose vision spanned a continent.[17] And it was in no small part due to him, who won more by demanding less, that we gained our great Northwest realm.

Oregon had become a part of the American legend. Oregon was the Western Star, burning in the dreams of two generations of restless, land-hungry Americans. But all that country, all that virgin richness, was under the grip of the Hudson's Bay Company of Her Majesty's Empire, a monopoly that could sell fifty per cent cheaper than any independent American trader could afford.

From 1812 to 1832, scarcely a single American had ventured into the Oregon country. But not all the propaganda of the Hudson's Bay Company as to the worthlessness of the land, nor all the sedate articles in the *Edinburgh Review,* which dismissed the whole vast territory as not 'capable of cultivation . . . not worth 20,000 pounds to either power' [18]—nothing could kill the legend.

Oregon was the country of purple twilights, of sunsets two hours before midnight and dawns two hours later. Oregon was the country of meadows, purple with camas, and of plains, blue with flax. It was the country of the thundering buffalo herds, of the cone-shaped peak of Mount Saint Helena, of cliff walls towering six thousand feet above the valley of the Columbia, of giant ferns and dogwood, heavy and sweet as magnolia blossoms. 'The trees bend with fruit in Oregon,' whispered the legend. 'Camas bread grows in the ground. . . . Money grows out there . . . and featherbeds grow on the bushes. . . .' [19]

7

In 1832, the 'Bostons' in their leather pantaloons and white wool caps built Fort Hall on the Snake River, and blond Nathaniel J. Wyeth, laughing into the deep-set eyes of Dr. John McLoughlin of the Hudson's Bay Company, announced the American purpose of settling Oregon. Great Britain, he said, would only keep it 'as a great English hunting park.'

Swiftly the wily doctor denied this. Englishmen would settle Oregon from overseas. As for America, 'when you have levelled the mountains, cultivated the desert, annihilated distance, not before.' [20]

By 1840, the St. Louis trappers were winding over the pack trails and seeping down into the country. One year later, an exploring squadron sailed down the Columbia, the Stars and Stripes waving bright against the gray walls of rock. American geologists poured out, stood squinting at rocks, soil, hills, and even the stars. Impudent seamen sold a surplus load of liquor to Dr. McLoughlin, then invited him to join them at a celebration of the Fourth of July!

Back in Washington, South Carolina's George McDuffie expressed his cynicism. Seven hundred miles this side of the Rocky Mountains was completely uninhabited. Rain never fell. Such wastes could never be conquered by American men.[21] Yet as early as 1836 the intrepid Bonneville had taken a covered wagon to the junction of the Snake and Columbia Rivers. By summer of the same year, two wagons were rumbling across the desert. Dr. Marcus Whitman, with his young bride and one other couple,

armed with a plow and two rifles, were crossing the mountains, fording
the rivers, gambling their lives and plighting their futures to reveal an
empire to America.

They had smelled the scent of the same shaggy pines under which Meriwether Lewis had lain. Their swaybacked wagons had rolled through Great
South Pass into the Rockies, where a few bronzed mountaineers, who had
seen no white woman since they had last looked into the faces of their
mothers, stood wondering at the yellow hair and soft pregnant body of Nar-
cissa Whitman. Their oxen's hooves scarred the earth beside the prints of
the antelope and the buffalo; they crossed the seared plains of the Snake;
they saw the rolling white caps of the Cascade Range, and in midstream
a naked Indian crouched, spearing salmon from a rock. They had conquered the impossible; two women and a pair of covered wagons had
crossed the Rocky Mountains.

By the fall of 1842, 'all along the borders,' the talk was of Oregon.
Fifty men and twelve women on pack-horses, their wagons abandoned at
Green River, crossed the mountains that year. More were on the way. And
at Puget Sound, forearmed with ten pounds sterling, plus housing materials,
cows, sheep, oxen, farm tools, and seed, the citizens of Her Majesty's
Government were pouring in, twenty-three families the first year. The race
was on—for an empire one-third as large as all Europe.

8

Even the legend could not equal the reality. It was like a caravan of
ancient times, that straggling line of dingy, white-topped wagons, those
herds of cattle and oxen and horses, those men and women and children.
It was a new world into which they were moving, with only the sky and
the stars, the coming of day and of night, of winter and of spring, to
remind them of what they had known before.

For those that came first there were the 'naked praries,' stretching from
sunrise to sunset, the shouts of the last white man at the last outpost at
Fort Lage, the plow banging against the wagon outside, and the churn
thumping within. By day was the crackle of sagebrush; by night, of the
new flames, as the long train curved into a circle, 'each wagon following
in its track, the rear closing on the front until its tongue and ox-chains' [22]
would reach from one to the other, and in the circle's center rose the camp-
fire, red-painted against a black sky.

Men and women and children—all were there—with youth and vigor
in them, with flexible muscles that, braced to the jog of the wagon seat
all day, could still dance to the fiddle strains of 'Pretty Betty Martin' by
night; or young mothers enduring the pain-lashed rhythms of child-birth.
Aged women, their gaunt-knuckled hands loose in their laps, swayed back

and forth in cane-seated rocking chairs; and old men whose bleached eyes had sighted rifles over the cotton bales at New Orleans; whose fathers had fought with Putnam and Greene, and whose older brothers had broken the frontiers of Ohio and Missouri and Boone's Kentucky, now painfully unwound blood-stained strips of their ragged trousers from feet cut to ribbons, as they stumbled barefoot through the snow across the Blue Mountains.

Faces were etched in the firelight: the smile and swagger of the South, the long hard bones of New England; faces of men who would sit in the Senate and build and unbuild governments, men who would found cities with names like Tacoma and Sacramento; not Northerners now, nor Southerners, nor Kentuckians, nor Rhode Islanders, but Americans united in one hope and one purpose, grumbling a little, questioning:

'Why don't the government protect us?'

'Oregon don't count in politics, so long's the nigger question's on the boards. . . . Webster was talking of trading it off for a cod-fishery when we left.'

'Uncle Sam is dozing while England takes the country.'

9

At dawn the great 'horse-canoes' stirred; the ox-whip snapped; the cry sounded: 'Close up! Close up! The Indians could kill all in the forward wagons before you'd know it, and then come back and scalp the last one of you fellows here behind.' The wagons groaned and swayed. The long snake inched on. Fort Laramie, Fort Bridges, Fort Hall, and Cayuses with food-packs hanging from the plump sides of their ponies. Forty dollars for the last barrel of flour! And the warnings:

'Look out for the Crows.'

'Beware of the Blackfeet.'

'The Sioux will oppose you.'

'You can't get the wagons through. There you see the ones abandoned last year.'

Winter was coming. There would be no water in the Rocky Mountain desert. The wolves were so thin you could count the ribs in their sides. You could never get through the Snake country. The Blue Mountains were worse than the Rockies. . . .

'That's all bosh,' Marcus Whitman said.

Onward the caravan moved. Hooves and feet stumbling against the skeleton of an abandoned plow, a Windsor chair, or the sun-bleached circle of a wagon wheel. Through the shallow center of the River Red. 'Up the Platte and towards the Yellowstone.' New names, fresh-flavored on the American tongue: Clackamas, Motallas, Klickitats, Flatheads,

Bannocks, Nez Perces, Walla Walla. 'If those Injuns ever combine against us, we're lost.' [23]

Fever. Cholera. Dysentery. Graves unmarked beneath the long grass of the prairie. Folk legend became fact and then history. 'The cowards never started, and the weak died on the way.' [24]

The day came—the day came when they saw it all: the great valley of the Columbia, seamed with a streamer of gold, the river ablaze in the setting sun. Below rose the lodge fires of the Cayuse; above, in the pink light towered the peaks of Mount Hood and Mount Helen and the long sprawl of Adams, glistening in the first fall of winter snow.

Journey's end for Marcus Whitman's first wagon train was at Fort Vancouver on the north bank of the Columbia. There, one day after their arrival at the Cascades, down the river came the rafts and canoes of the immigrants. Winter rain poured upon them. Above, eagles circled and screamed. But all eyes were fixed on the mighty bulk of the fortress itself, its green terraces sloping upward, its posts rising twenty feet into sharp points to gut any Redskin bold enough to scale them. They could see the log tower in the northwest corner, raindrops glistening on the bristling cannon, the huge brass padlocks of the stockade gateway, and the bonfires steaming along the river bank where a man was standing.

All knew his name. There, in a two-storied white frame house, safe behind the walls of the fort, with a shipload of Boston liquor untouched in his cellar, there, with his Scott and his Shakespeare and his Burns, Dr. John McLoughlin had reigned for nineteen years as governor of the Hudson's Bay Company. He was sixty-five now; he had lived on in the wilderness outpost until his long hair hung in white masses about his stern, strong face, and his eyes peered dimly from behind gold-rimmed spectacles. Hard-bitten, wily, a benevolent despot, McLoughlin ruled his little empire with a tolerance grown from long familiarity with men's needs. Indians came and went freely into the stockade; and for five to fifteen blankets, depending upon her comeliness, a trader of the Company could purchase a copper-skinned slave whose duties were by no means confined to the daytime. Of Dr. McLoughlin himself it was said: 'He is a good man, but one-man power is not American.'

Dr. McLoughlin had thrown Fort Vancouver open to his uninvited guests. He had been expecting them since the day before when a canoe shot over the Cascades and a breathless 'Engine' gulped out the story of a thousand 'Bostons camp by Mount Hood.'

Stunned, the old man had raised his hand. He had made the sign of the cross. When he spoke, his voice was hushed: 'What manner of men are these that scale the mountains and slide down the Rivers as the Goths of old slid down the Alps?'

Gods though they may have seemed to Dr. McLoughlin, in that glittering moment they were but men and women after all, sick, and ragged, and hungry. And in his moment of defeat, the Scotsman had not forgotten his gallantry. That night, twenty-five pounds of flour for each family had been brought into the American camp. With it came luxuries so long sacrificed they were almost forgotten—syrup and sugar and even tea. Pay?—that was something to talk about later. And among the women, one sentiment was breathed: 'God bless Dr. McLoughlin.'

Spring brought McLoughlin's own farm implements and wheat-seed. Fall brought the clink of his coins as sunburned and smiling Americans carried the young harvest into the walls of the stockade. Out in the harbor a lank Missourian pulled his way up the side of a British man-o'-war. 'We've come from Missouri across the Rocky Mountains. We've come to settle in Oregon and rule this country.'

The Captain glanced at the unkempt hair, the sallow, leathery face. 'I've sailed into every corner of the globe and have seen most of the people on it, but a more uncouth . . . bolder set . . . than you Americans I never met before.' [25]

A year rolled away. And in the center of the rich Oregon farm country, near Fort Vancouver, stood a village, complete with library, lyceum, and the first Protestant church west of the Rockies. A village had been born, boastfully and promisefully named Oregon City. A new America had grown up in the wilderness, and it had been plows and not guns that had won an empire.

10

They swarmed into Calhoun's office, the young scouts, the trail-blazers with the new beards on their faces, the huntsmen with the spring-trap muscles and moccasined feet, soft-padding as the paws of wilderness animals. And held by his own eager questioning, they talked until on the maps that lay open before him the few thin lines glistened with flowing river water and the unmarked spaces peaked themselves into mountain ranges or smoothed into sun-seared plains; and he, too, could hear the winds of the West thundering in the rocky crags and the wagon wheels echoing across six thousand miles of stillness.

So it was no dream, after all, that great country; it was all there, just as Meriwether Lewis had seen it, and as Calhoun had dreamed it, while poring over maps with William Lowndes in the old war office, twenty-five years before. Not since 1812 had such enthusiasm, such fervor, gripped him. 'Look at the mighty Mississippi,' he had exclaimed to a British visitor. 'Twenty hundred miles you may travel on his waters; go on for days and nights and see no change; it is a valley that would contain all Europe.' For he was not afraid of bigness. And he was not afraid of progress, though men who saw in him nothing but the personification of the slavery question would say that he was. Yet, if on that one issue his views were as unyielding and provincial as the little state from which he came, on the surging destiny of America his vision was broad as the nation it spanned.

'Mr. Calhoun,' declared a foreign visitor, 'you are a great experiment.' 'We are more,' he flashed back boyishly. 'We're a great hit.'

11

Yet his exultancy was not unmixed with fear. What could the future hold for such restlessness, such drive as had this sprawling young country of his. 'The past is gone; the present is no more; the future alone is ours.' What lurked in that future? Would this untapped greatness, this unspent strength, turn upon itself and rend apart its own greatness? This was his fear. 'We Americans are the most excitable people on earth; we have plenty to eat and drink so we seek war for sport that we may exhaust ourselves and our exuberance.' [26] And now in the winter of 1846, with expansionists still beating the battle drum of '54:40 or Fight'; with warm-blooded Southerners casting covetous eyes on the tropic empire of Mexico and looking hopefully toward the rich farmlands of the Far West; with the covered wagons rolling across the prairies like floodwaters over a broken dam, Calhoun's great fear was of complete disaster, of an unwarranted, unsuccessful, useless war with England and the loss of the entire territory. Nor was his opposition to Polk's cry of 'All of Oregon or none' mere personal opposition to the President, for all that he said and feared he had said and feared two years before.

Aside from the moral or humanitarian aspects of an imperialistic war which troubled Calhoun far more than in the hot days of his youth, he was convinced that the result was far more apt to be 'none' of Oregon than 'all.' As early as 1842, he had spoken on the question, in words touched with the fervor of his vision, yet weighted with warnings against acts that might lose America the entire territory.

Denouncing a bill for immediate seizure of the entire territory, he based his argument on the immensely practical and compelling fact that England could move an army to the western frontier far more easily than could the United States. There were the Empire troops in China; six weeks could see them at the Oregon frontier. There were the British troops in Persia and in India. As for us, it would take us six months alone to send a fleet around the Horn. 'As certain as we regard our right to be,' was Calhoun's warning, 'she regards hers as not less so . . . if we assert our right, she will oppose us by asserting hers . . . the result would be inevitable . . . the territory would be lost.'

Nevertheless, he was utterly opposed to America's giving up her rightful claims. He rebuked Webster for his indifference to the potentialities of the country. 'My object is to preserve and not lose the territory. I do not agree with my eloquent colleague that it is worthless. . . . He has under-rated it . . . its commercial advantages . . . will, in time, prove great.'

Soon, asserted the enthusiastic Carolinian, all the ports of Japan, China, Persia, would be thrown open to American trade. And our routes would no longer be around the storm-whipped Horn, but through that new and 'worthless' territory of Oregon. 'Time is acting for us,' he proclaimed. 'It will maintain our right . . . without costing a cent of money or a drop of blood.'

'Our population is rolling towards the shores of the Pacific,' continued Calhoun. 'It is one of those forward movements which leave anticipation behind. In thirty-two years the Indian frontier has receded a thousand miles to the West . . . the impetus . . . forcing its way restlessly, westward . . . soon—far sooner than we anticipate . . . will reach the Rocky Mountains, and be ready to pour into the Oregon Territory;—when it will come into our possession without a struggle.' Then, he concluded, 'it would be as useless for England to protest our claims, as it was now for us to contest hers.'

If we could not seize all of the territory by renewing the existing treaty for joint occupation, neither could England. But he would give unqualified support to that portion of the bill which would extend American civil jurisdiction over our own citizens. 'I am opposed to holding out temptation to our citizens to emigrate to a region where we cannot protect them.'

Westerners could charge that he was opposed to the extension of American territory. The accusation was unjust. Had not the South declared that he was unduly favoring the West when he had introduced the public domain bill? His desire was to promote the interest of the whole country. 'In opposing the measure,' he had concluded, 'I not only promote the interest of the Union generally, but that of the West, especially.'

It was a ringing speech, and it captured the emotions of those who read it and heard it. Momentarily Calhoun had been able to restrain the madness, but now the whole job had to be done over again. And 'the odds,' Calhoun confessed, 'are greatly against me.' [27]

'All of Oregon or none'—was it rallying cry or battle cry? Immediate notice to England was the demand of the extremists—the formal and final severing of that joint occupancy by which England and America together had uneasily shared the giant territory for twenty-eight years.

To Calhoun the joint occupancy was the 'trump card' of the entire question.[28] Legally, under the terms of the Treaty of 1818, either party could abrogate the agreement on twelve months' notice; actually Cal-

houn was convinced that 'unqualified notice' would 'almost certainly lead
to war.'²⁹ To avoid such a conflict with the most powerful nation on
earth was now his consuming purpose.

His hopes were low. The extremists were 'bold and decided.' The South,
torn between the Whigs, Calhoun, and Polk, was hopelessly divided; and
even Calhoun's own supporters had 'but little resolution.' What interest
had the South in those vast wastes of land which any thinking man knew
that Nature had ordained as 'free' soil? But Calhoun could not withdraw.
'Fatal' to the South, as well as to the nation, he thought, would be a war
of aggression, in which Southern men would shed their blood for free
states. It was 'manifest destiny' that these states belong to the Union,
but not the territory north of the forty-ninth parallel, and not at the cost
of a war.

Calhoun's reliance was on the silent majority, not of the Senate, or of
the House, but of the people themselves. The people, he believed, did not
want war. Peace would not lose Oregon; peace would win it. He dusted
off an old phrase from John Randolph of Roanoke. 'A wise and masterly
inactivity,' he believed, was still the surest claim to title.³⁰

12

Calhoun had scarcely checked in at the United States Hotel that December in 1845 when he was summoned to the White House. From the
Presidential version of what followed we learn that Calhoun was 'in a
good humor,' and 'talked in a pleasant tone.' Actually, however, very little
was said. Each understood the insignificance of the interview. For Polk
to have failed to invite Calhoun to a conference would only have stressed
the party rift that threatened from the moment of Calhoun's entry into
Washington.

Polk may still have borne a grudge against Calhoun for having robbed
his Administration of the glory of the Texas annexation. His conscience,
too, may have troubled him at his own hasty repudiation of the talents
of this man, who he uncomfortably sensed was superior to himself. Calhoun had been flouted; Calhoun owed him nothing. Calhoun had votes
enough to wreck the President's program and ambition to match his own.
And the men had not talked three minutes before Mr. Polk felt the iron
beneath the velvet glove, and learned that once Calhoun's mind was settled
upon a subject, 'it was useless to press it.'³¹

And Calhoun, what of him? He had reason, perhaps, to bear a grudge
against the President, but he would have scorned to indulge it. 'It was not
in the power of Mr. Polk to treat me badly,'³² he had proudly written
Anna Maria on the eve of his dismissal from the State Department.

That Polk was actually seeking to involve the country in war, Calhoun did not believe for a moment. What he did see was the President as the victim of his own campaign promises. To save the country from war, without the loss of the Oregon territory; and to take upon himself the post of public whipping boy, who could be safely blamed for the loss of 'Fifty-Four-Forty' was the position Calhoun decided to assume. It was a difficult position, but to accept it imposed an equally difficult task upon the President.

In the Senate, debate sputtered and simmered. From the gallery a frightened Englishwoman watched. It was a Westerner, this time, who was openly urging war. 'Calhoun sat quietly, but was visibly chafed.' He rose at last, with 'words of peace and praise for England,' the first time in a month that the name of England had been uttered without anger.[33] She leaned back in silent gratitude, tears pouring down her face.

Calhoun was unswayed by the hysteria around him. The tide for 'immediate notice,' he knew, was too strong to be withstood. What he hoped was that the notice might be qualified by 'making it a condition . . . that it shall be accompanied with the offer of the 49th parallel.' That 'the British government would agree' had been his opinion since January, 1846.

Yet a British offer on the same basis, he doubted could be or would be accepted by the President, 'unless Congress should express an opinion, which would make it his duty; in so awkward a condition is Mr. Polk placed.' Polk could scarcely repudiate his pledges. Thus, to bring pressure upon Congress, which would in turn bring pressure on Mr. Polk, was Calhoun's aim. A way must be opened through which the President could support compromise.[34]

13

The date was the sixteenth of March, 1846. By eight in the morning, the crowd began to gather around the doors of the Capitol. Before noon the galleries and passages were clogged with a panting, close-packed mass of eager and perspiring humanity. 'Thousands' were unable to get into the building at all. As Calhoun sat down for roll-call, a wave of anxiety swept over him. Not since the 'Force Bill' days had it been like this. Now he was old. What if he should fail? [35]

At last the stiflingly hot room was silent. Calhoun arose. He stood still a moment, erect and poised, showing no sign of his tension. Then he began, quietly as always, promising at the outset that he would 'abstain from all personalities and everything calculated to wound the feelings of others, but shall express myself candidly on all subjects.' His words were soothing, strangely calm. Peace or war, he declared, was not the issue. It was not a question of war, but of time. Opinion was too divided for war, and were not these divisions of opinion, even in regard to our actual title to the territory, 'strong reasons why the conflict should not be settled by an appeal to force?'

Oregon was far from Great Britain. Free trade, extended throughout the Pacific area, he believed, would in the end 'prove the strongest inducement to emigration,' and the plows of emigrants were a far surer claim to title than guns. Oregon's settlers, he believed, would contend as fiercely for their trade rights as the New Englanders had done before the Revolution. 'Should we restrict, by our high Tariff . . . their infant trade, they might,' he hinted, 'readily find a power prepared to extend to them all the advantages of free trade, to be followed by consequences not difficult to be perceived.'

'I know,' admitted Calhoun, 'that in the existing state of the world, wars are necessary . . . that the most sacred regard for justice, and the most cautious policy cannot always prevent them. When war must come, I . . . appeal to my past history to prove that I shall not be found among those who . . . falter; but . . . I regard peace as a positive good and war as a positive evil. . . . I shall ever cling to peace, so long as it can be preserved consistently with . . . safety and honour.' The war would be a struggle for mastery between 'the greatest power in the world . . . against the most growing power,' but it would not protect the citizens of Oregon. 'It would sacrifice' American 'brethren and kindred. We have encouraged them to emigrate, and I will not give a vote which would . . . ruin them. . . . War . . . would be disastrous. If we did conquer Canada, New Brunswick, and Nova Scotia,' observed Calhoun, mindful of the grim lesson of 1812, 'it would require ten years.' Of the human suffering he would not speak. It would have 'but little effect in deterring a brave people.' But a two-ocean Navy, six or seven armies, one on the Mexican border to meet an enemy bought and trained by the British Empire— was America prepared for the cost of these? Yes, and an inflationary paper currency, and a public debt of six or seven hundred millions, the whole falling on the back of labor, 'while a large amount would go into the pockets of those who struck not a blow!' This was the cost of war. The War Hawk of 1812 had indeed learned a lesson.

Talk of States' Rights would be ended, he warned his Southern listeners, and of a Federal Republic. Modern war required a consolidation of powers. We would become 'a great national, consolidated Government . . . a military despotism.'

But there need be no war. The question could still be compromised, and on the basis of the forty-ninth parallel. North of there, none of our citizens were settled. Morally we had no right to more. Establish that line, and we 'give our citizens in Oregon peace and security.'

A new note sounded in his voice. He was not speaking of Oregon now, but of 'one world,' a world as yet unborn. 'Chemical and mechanical discoveries and inventions have multiplied beyond all former example—adding to the comforts of life in a degree far greater and more universal than was ever known before.' Steam has 'reduced the Atlantic to half its former width.' Electricity 'has been made the instrument for the transmission of thought by lightning itself. Magic wires are stretching themselves in all directions over the earth, and when their mystic meshes shall have been united . . . our globe itself will become endowed with sensitiveness—so that whatever touches on any point, will be instantly felt on any other.' On the horizon of the world was 'the dawn of a new civilization.' Would the two powers, farthest in advance in this great world movement, 'sacrifice their mission to fulfill God's destiny,' in a senseless struggle to determine their military superiority? No, Calhoun declared. 'Powerful causes' were already in operation 'to secure a lasting . . . peace between the two countries by breaking down the barriers which impede their commerce. . . . Free trade between England and America would force all other civilized countries to follow in the end.' With a blinding flash of insight into the economic selfishness that would foster wars upon wars years after his own hopes and forebodings had ended forever, Calhoun presented the practical program that could make 'One World' more than an ideal. Free trade 'would . . . diffuse a prosperity greater and more universal than can well be conceived and . . . unite by bonds of mutual interest the people of all countries. I regard . . . free trade . . . in the dispensation of Providence as one of the great means of ushering in the happy period foretold by inspired prophets when war would be no more.' [36]

He sat down. It was all over. Had he failed? The faces, swarming about him, hands grasping, seizing, pulling his own, congratulations from even 'the most violent of the 54:40 men' gave him his answer. For the practical result of his efforts, he would have to wait weeks, months perhaps, but the human triumph was sweet. In this triumph of sheer patriotism, freed from the sectional bias which had necessarily dominated so much of his thinking, he had reached the pinnacle of his career.

One man did not approach his side. Such a concession for his touchy South Carolina pride would have been too much to endure. Instead, William Preston, who had succeeded McDuffie in the Senate, but had not been on speaking terms with his colleague since Sub-Treasury days, rushed into the House Chamber and up to Representative Holmes of Massachusetts, declaring: 'I must give vent to my feelings. Mr. Calhoun has made a speech which has settled the question of the North Western boundary. All his friends—nay, all the Senators have collected around to congratulate him . . . he has covered himself with a mantle of glory.' [37]

It would have been asking too much of Mr. Polk to have expected him to admit the need of any door being open for him. For the man who had openly and unfortunately declared that 'no compromise which the United States ought to accept can be effected,' [38] surrender now would have been a surrender of face. 'He has embarrassed the Administration on

the Oregon question,' wrote Polk of Calhoun. He wanted to be President.
He wanted to be in the Cabinet. Thwarted, he sought now only to unite
'the Calhoun faction' with the Whigs, to divert and control the Administration from the outside, if he could not do so from within, reasoned
Polk.

Once again Calhoun was summoned to the White House. This was an
interview even more delicate than the one before. 'In a fine humour,' Calhoun met the occasion head-on. No more ticklish problem had ever teased
his diplomacy: this need to offer the President aid without admitting the
need for aid, to show his superior voting strength and yet retain the
semblances of Administration friendship. He sparred carefully, assuring
Polk of his 'desire to assert our rights' in the Oregon territory, not lingering to dispute over just what his and Polk's diverse conceptions of 'rights'
might be. He spoke of restraint and peace, but between him and Polk,
at least, peace was tenuous, and when the guest left, Polk was convinced of his opposition to him. It did not matter. Calhoun had won, and
Polk knew that he had.[39]

14

In Calhoun's opinion, Polk accepted defeat with no particular grace. 'The
Oregon question,' Calhoun wrote Clemson, by April 25, 1846, 'will ere
long be settled, and war avoided. . . . This great change has been effected by the Senate against the entire influence of the Executive.' [40]

Thereafter all happened according to Calhoun's plans and forecast. On
April 27, Congress passed a resolution empowering the President to 'give
notice' at his discretion. Notice was given on May 21, accompanied, as
Calhoun had hoped, by Polk's own offer of the forty-ninth parallel as a
basis for settlement.

Lord Pakenham's prompt refusal did nothing to weaken the confidence
of Calhoun. British pride must be salvaged—but British public opinion
would demand a settlement. Lord Aberdeen's instructions from London
climaxed the issue. Six months after Calhoun's preliminary resolutions of
December 30, 1845, the Senate belatedly agreed with him and with Great
Britain that the forty-ninth parallel did not 'abandon the honor, the
character, or the best interests of the American people.' Senate approval
of a British treaty was voted 41 to 14. And nationally Calhoun had never
performed a greater service for his country.[41]

He gave way to his pleasure and pride in a letter to Clemson. 'It is to
me a great triumph. When I arrived here, it was dangerous to wisper 49,
and I thought to have taken a hazardous step in asserting that Mr. Polk
had not disgraced the country in offering it. Now a treaty is made on it
with nearly the unanimous voice of the Country.' [42] But he received with

due modesty the tribute of a British visitor that 'You are very dear to England for the sake of this peace and free trade.' Calhoun was surprised. 'I did not think my name was even known in England, where I myself have never been.' He added: 'The British government has exhibited the greatest wisdom. . . . Matters could not have been arranged, had there been exasperation.' [43]

Observers noted that there was no personal exaltation in his look, no triumph in his words. He seemed abstracted, absorbed with the problems that confronted him. He had indeed much upon his mind. Momentarily he had been triumphant that spring; he had been happy; he had even dared hope for a few brief days that his life's work, his life's ambitions, were nearing realization. Goal after goal that he had striven for—tariff, Sub-Treasury, 'publick lands,' and, most important of all, the growing unification of South and West—'All the great measures I have advocated,' he wrote James Edward, 'are in a fair way of being consummated.' [44] For the first time in years, he had looked forward to the future; he had even dared hope that for now and for all time the Union might be preserved . . .

15

But by the summer of 1846 it was all over.

Six months earlier, in January, with war or peace trembling in the scales of the Oregon negotiations, John M. Clayton of Delaware approached the South Carolinian. Had Mr. Calhoun heard? Polk had ordered General Zachary Taylor to the Rio Grande. That meant war with Mexico!

Calhoun stood, transfixed with horror. 'It can't be; it's impossible,' he had exclaimed. The Rio Grande? As Secretary of State, Calhoun, fighting for every foot of territory America could rightfully claim, had never dreamed of demanding the Rio Grande boundary. The river was nearly a hundred miles from any territory which America could justly claim.

Calhoun understood this plot. During the discussions for the annexation of Texas he had promised Mexico an honest negotiation—on the 'most liberal and satisfactory terms . . .' on 'all questions which may grow out of this treaty.' According to Mr. Polk, 'liberal' terms granted every foot of the disputed territory to Texas; and further, for the prevention of any future conflict, Mexico must sell New Mexico and California to the United States. Refused, Polk was trying to force the sale, and had chosen the advance to the Rio Grande to overawe Mexico by show, or to conquer her by force. The audacity of the scheme swept over Calhoun.

'The Senate should move a restraining resolution against the President,' he said.

'Do something,' urged Clayton.[45]

Calhoun shook his head. His position on the Oregon question prevented him. War with England would be worse than war with Mexico, and if war with England were to be prevented and Oregon added to the Union, he must maintain relations with the Administration. He could not antagonize Polk further. Calhoun's 'error' of judgment has been condemned here; for it has been claimed that Polk must have known that England would compromise on Oregon before he would have dared provoke Mexico.[46] Yet Calhoun contended that had 'the British proposition been delayed 5 days, until the news of our declaration of war against Mexico had arrived, the Settlement would not have been made.'[47]

It was for 'others' to lead the battle against Polk, Calhoun contended; although 'others' had no intention of doing so. Behind the scenes that spring, amidst rumors of a naval seizure of California, Calhoun worked feverishly, but to no avail. On Saturday, the ninth of May, came the news that the President had been waiting for. American and Mexican troops had skirmished on the eastern bank of the Rio Grande, and, according to Mr. Polk, 'war exists . . . notwithstanding all our efforts to avoid it . . . by the act of Mexico herself.'[48]

16

All day Sunday, May 10, 1846, Calhoun was hard at work, going to the lodgings of friend after friend, begging them to get ready, to stand by. There must not be war. There could not be war. War would mean the intervention of England and of Europe, perhaps the loss of the entire Oregon country. War should not be waged for territory, but for honor, persisted Calhoun, forgetful of his own highly colored dreams of Canada, thirty-odd years before. The ground to be taken, he told his friends, was a complete separation of the necessary defense supplies from any actual declaration of war. A border incident was not a war. Supplies could be voted to the Army without a declaration of war. Time was short, but negotiations were still possible.

All too quickly the night passed. Monday morning, before packed Houses of Congress, the President's words were read. Calhoun sat in a mounting sickness of despair as the clerk's voice rang out the Presidential call to repel invasion, 'to avenge the honor of the United States Army.' The President had done his work; over in the House, amidst a storm of confusion, Southerners and Northerners alike, unable to disentangle defense from war, brushed aside Calhoun's pleading, reasoned words of the night before, and voted for a declaration of war.

In the Senate for a few moments, Calhoun and his supporters held the upper hand. They divided the Administration bill, sending the sections on military preparation to the Military Affairs Committee, and the declaration of war to the Committee on Foreign Affairs. Then there was nothing to do but wait. At last Thomas Hart Benton arose, walked out of the Chamber in the direction of the Military Affairs Committee room. A few minutes later he returned, a slip of paper in his hand. It was the bill of the House of Representatives, and it called 'for a declaration of war.'

Hopelessly Calhoun rose to his feet. His eyes swept the Chamber. He received not a look of encouragement. The story on almost every face was the same—impatience, eagerness, excitement, anger. It was too late. But he knew what he had to say.

If Congress would wait only a few hours—a single day . . . if it would move 'dispassionately, quietly, and with calm dignity.' He might as well have tried to hold back a hurricane. He was shouted down; he only wanted delay, they accused. 'I seek no delay,' Calhoun retorted. He would vote instantly for the necessary military supplies if they were only separated from a declaration of war. But he could not vote for war. Only Congress could make war. Not the President of the United States! It would set a precedent, he prophesied, which would 'enable all future Presidents to bring about a state of things in which Congress shall be forced . . . to declare war,' [49] however opposed to its own conviction. It would divert the warmaking power from Congress to the President. 'The doctrine is monstrous.'

A vote for war against Mexico would be a vote for war upon the American Constitution. A mere border brawl, unauthorized by either government, was no cause for war. 'I cannot do it,' shouted Calhoun. 'I know not whether there is a friend to stand by me.' His whole body trembling, his eyes burning, he crashed his white, skeleton-like hand against the top of his desk with such violence that from all corners of the room men looked to see if it had been shattered by the blow. 'Sooner than vote for that lying preamble,' he shouted, 'I would plunge a dagger through my heart.' [50]

17

Calhoun's passionate outburst stopped nothing and no one but himself. The country was at war within ten minutes after he had dropped into his chair. But his words had broken like thunderclaps over the heads of the Southern leaders. Virtually all of them—Lewis, McDuffie, young Jefferson Davis—all were for war. Before Calhoun had risen, he had been his section's 'idol,' and nationally his position was strong. The winning of Oregon for the North and Texas for the South, his wooing of the West with his stand at Memphis, the preservation of peace with England—all had lifted him once more to his old eminence. Probably he could never have been President, as he must have known, but certainly he stood nearer the goal than he had in the past twenty years. This was the man whom even the New York *Journal* could hail as the 'Saviour of his country,' declaring that he needed only to stand still, and 'as sure as the day comes . . . will '49 see him where his deserts long since should have placed him.' [51]

And now—his worst enemies saw that this was no ruse; his terrible sincerity was evident to the most casual observer. Deliberately he was throwing away the Presidency, it was generally believed, and for what? The cause was lost before it was voiced; why lose himself with it? And it was the South, that same South which he had offended at Memphis and with his drive for Oregon, the South which had loyally stood by him, that he had now grievously wounded. Could he not see what he had done? Could he not see the rich fruit that was hanging over the Southern states, an empire for slavery? Could he not see that all Mexico was below the Missouri Compromise line, that the old balance of power would be settled forever—and in the South's favor? It was the South that he had offended; the South would not support him now.

All over the South the clamor broke out. Even the Edgefield *Advertiser,* in that tense-strung June of 1846, warned that 'beloved as Mr. Calhoun was' he could not 'hold his people's affections, unless he supported the war.' He, of course, had no intention of doing anything else. 'Now that we are in . . . we shall do our duty,' he wrote Conner. 'I give it a quiet but decided support.' The problem was how to bring it to 'an honorable termination.' The Presidential question? 'It ought to be wholly dropt.'

Conditioned though he was to years of public abuse, the attacks from his own 'kingdom' hurt him. Keenly painful was the betrayal of his own cousin, Francis Pickens, who delivered a searing attack on Calhoun's war course as 'wanting in fidelity to the country.' But Pickens was not South Carolina, and in Edgefield resolutions implying condemnation of Calhoun's stand were 'laid on the table by a unanimous vote' almost as soon as introduced. 'South Carolina never speaks until Mr. Calhoun is heard' was the rebuke of the Charleston *Courier.* The loyal *Mercury,* not only gave whole-hearted support to Calhoun's stand for a defensive war, but printed in full a Pennsylvanian's justification of the Southern leader against the attacks of the Northern press. 'Mr. Calhoun has followed more closely in the footsteps of the immortal Jefferson than any of the living Statesmen.' [52]

And on that war-heated Fourth of July, with blood high and bluster loud, all over South Carolina, between the customary tributes to 'woman,' 'the flag,' 'the memories' of Washington, Jefferson, and even Jackson, Calhoun was still the favorite toast of state-wide celebrations. He was the 'favorite son of South Carolina,' 'the Statesman that weathered the storm.' He was 'the pride of his State,' his 'Country's Pilot,' 'surpassed by none,' and 'too profound to be appreciated.' There was praise even for his stand on the war, and for the Oregon settlement, 'another link of the chain which should bind him to his country.' His slanderers? They were 'asses and owls.'

But all this was small comfort to Calhoun. South Carolina's tributes were to him as a man, beloved in spite of his stand, and not because of it. He knew the truth. He knew the temper of the Southern people. South Carolina was burning with the fever of war. If on one page of the *Mercury* he could find praise for the courage of his stand, on another was the story of the ladies of Charleston spurring their young men on to 'punish the outrage,' with a banner for the 'Avengers,' on which 'Blood for Blood' had been stitched by their own dainty hands.[53]

'The military feeling of the country is . . . very high,' Calhoun wrote Clemson. 'The people are like a young man . . . full of health and vigor, and disposed for adventure . . . but wanting wisdom. . . . While I admire the spirit, I regret to see it misdirected.' To his son, Andrew, he wrote more openly, hinting at his fear of European intervention, his nervous handwriting clearly betraying agitation and strain. 'Never was so momentous a measure adopted with so little thought.' If not quickly ended, the war would be a disaster.[54]

18

His dismay was twofold. The war in itself was enough; a ruthless, heartless grab for territory, under the flimsiest pretext of defense against invasion; but that was not all. Too well did Calhoun know the young hot South. Already in his possession was a secret oath, sworn by volunteers all over the South and Southwest, who for years had been pledging themselves to enlist as soldiers in a plot for the annexation and 'conquest of Mexico.' Calhoun's private belief was that, if conquered, Mexico might even be held by the United States 'as an independent country.' 'Keep this to yourself,' he wrote Andrew. 'I have never whispered it to anyone.'[55] This, perhaps, would be the nucleus of a Southern Confederacy, but such a misbegotten monstrosity would have no support from John C. Calhoun.

Of one outcome he was certain. Mexico annexed would mean the destruction of the Union. Mexico was the 'forbidden fruit.' Shortsighted on the slavery question in general Calhoun undoubtedly was, but in this one aspect he penetrated the future with terrible accuracy. If he knew the temper of the South, that young South which had surged beyond him, so, too, did he know the determination of the North. Since the annexation of Texas, he had well known, the last piece of admittedly slave territory had been added to American soil. Northern public opinion would never permit it otherwise. Nor was more necessary. It was understood that Texas would be divided into four to six slave states. Even with

Oregon open to the North, the South's interests were protected by the line of the Missouri Compromise.

The balance of power was close, but safe. Calhoun was frank enough in admitting his belief that, although the institutions of the South could be preserved, they could never be extended. The South's genius, he contended, was not in further expansion but in the development and strengthening of her own landed society.[56]

And now! Now that hard-won margin of safety that he had gained over the cries of 'slave-accursed Texas,' with the give-and-take of the diplomatic tables, was to be offered up as a sacrifice to a gigantic theft. Not content with security, the South wanted all—and would lose all. Calhoun could not read the future, nor did he care to do so. He shrank from it. Yet he has been called 'the one man in the country' during those wild hours 'who understood what was going on.' Here was the end of constitutional rights and protected minorities. A territory would be won which the North would never see slave and the South would never see free. Disunion or submission would be the South's alternatives. The outcome no man could see. 'The curtain is dropt,' Calhoun said, 'and the future closed to our view.'[57]

XXVI

The Rising Storm

NEVER had Calhoun been more despondent than when he returned to the capital in the winter of 1846. For the first time in his long career he, who for a generation had battled against all odds and against all hopes, now seemed 'stricken with terror, almost with despair.' So long as any door was open to him, so long as any action of his could stave off disaster, he would seize at the weakest straw held out to him. Now it was over. It was the end of the truce, the gentlemen's agreement, by which North and South for a quarter of a century, through a geographic line, had held in check a principle. The curtain had lifted, and even he shrank from what he saw behind it.

For in the hot summer of 1846 a Pennsylvania Democrat, blond, boyish of face, precise of diction, had arisen in the House of Representatives. His name was David Wilmot, and the Proviso that he introduced demanded without equivocation that slavery should never be permitted in any territory to be won in the Mexican War.

The oil was on the flames. The warfare was in the open; step by step, battle by battle, a contest North and South for every inch and every foot of new American soil.

The Proviso passed the House, but was defeated in the Senate. It was not defeated, however, in the country. It was fought and rehashed and wrangled over in every store and polling booth and newspaper in America, at every fireside and every political gathering. It bred a 'rancorous bitterness.' To the North the Wilmot Proviso became the sole objective of the Mexican War. To the South it was the 'reddest flag that could have been waved in the face of the Southern bull.'[1]

To Calhoun it was the end.

It was the death-knell of the Union; it was 'abolition in a new and dangerous form.' That the Proviso had been technically 'killed' meant nothing. The challenge to the South had been thrown down. As 'all the North,' Calhoun perceived, 'is opposed to our having any part of Mexico,' some other way would be found.

'The present Scheme of the North,' wrote the bitter Carolinian, 'is that the South shall do all the fighting and pay all the expenses, and they to have all the conquered territory.' Both Northern parties were determined 'that no part of the Territory . . . shall be for the benefit of the South,' but were perfectly willing 'that our blood and treasure shall be expended. . . . We are to be made to dig our own grave.'[2]

The damage was done now, and Calhoun would throw his last strength into a battle for his own. Would Southern men stand by and see the mighty empire they had won revert to the North, a weapon for their own destruction? They would not, and neither would he. The invasion of Mexico had been a great wrong, a wrong precipitated, he knew, by Southern arrogance and Southern ambition, but by all laws of justice in national dealings, the South had at least equal rights in the conquered territory.

It was, he insisted, a question of right and wrong. Could a majority of partners exclude the minority? 'Can that be right in Government, which every right-minded man would cry out to be base and dishonest in private life? . . . Would it deserve the name of free soil, if one half of the Union should be excluded when it was won by joint efforts?' These, he admitted, 'are questions which address themselves more to the heart than to the head.'[3]

Calhoun had longed not to return to Washington that winter. He was desperately tired. His cough was wearing at him night and day, and although, as yet, he had no 'bad symptoms,' such as fever, night sweats, or pain in the chest, he knew perfectly well what was wrong with him.[4] Only rest and freedom from strain could check the progress of his disease, but he knew that there would never be rest for him again in this world. Almost his only respite came in moments when he could read a few straggling sentences in seven-year-old Calhoun Clemson's childish scrawl, and write in answer: 'My dear Grandson, Your letter made your Grandfather very happy. He was happy to hear from you; happy to learn that you are well, and to see that you could write so pretty a letter.' He sent it to 'Grandmother in South Carolina, that she might be made happy too by reading it.'[5]

'Everyone on this side of the Atlantic,' wrote Anna Maria from Belgium, 'seems to look to you to elevate the country out of the mire. . . . Do try to keep Polk and Co. in order for the rest of the 4 years.'[6]

Yet he had nothing to offer. What had to be done was plain; he told Anna Maria that the territorial scheme of the North must be defeated, 'even should the Union be rent asunder.' As for himself, 'I desire above all things to save the whole; but if that cannot be, to save the portion where Providence has cast my lot.'[7]

But how? 'I confess,' he would admit, 'I do not see the end.'[8]

2

Like Lee, Calhoun might well have said that duty was the most beautiful word in the English language; what he did say was that he would do his 'duty, without regard to consequences personal to myself. If our institutions are to be overthrown, I am resolved, that no share of the responsibility shall rest on me.' He was glad that he would not live to see the outcome, glad that he was 'an old and broken man.' But only to Anna Maria would he reveal the depths of his despair. 'You must not suppose that . . . I am impelled by the hope of success. Had that been the case, I would long since have retired from the conflict. Far higher motives impel me; a sense of duty;—to do our best for our country, and leave the rest to Providence.' For posterity's opinion he cared little. He saw no reason why it should be wiser than the past. 'In resisting wrong, especially where our country is concerned,' he told his daughter, 'no appreciation of my efforts is necessary to sustain me.'

To Calhoun the fear of enforced abolition or emancipation was now becoming overwhelmingly real. It would come, as he pointed out, 'in the worst possible form; far worse than if done by our own act voluntarily.'[9] Fifteen or twenty years earlier, gradual emancipation might conceivably have been possible as an act of the South itself, involving no loss of position; but this neither Calhoun nor any of the foremost Southern leaders of that day had had the wisdom to see. The younger and more resilient Davis saw it; as late as 1846 he declared in the Senate that the problem was 'one which must bring its own solution. Leave natural causes to their full effect, and when the time shall arrive at which emancipation is proper, those most interested will be most anxious to effect it. . . . Leave the country to the South and West open'; the slaves pressed by a cheaper labor would spread to the tropic regions (to be gained by the Mexican War), 'where less exertion . . . will enable . . . them to live in independent communities.' However, Davis warned, 'They must first be separated from the white man, be . . . elevated by instruction; or, instead of a blessing, liberty would be their greatest curse.'[10]

3

Undoubtedly Calhoun was right in his conviction that it was too late to back-track now. Forcibly to destroy slavery was to destroy the political power and the economic and social foundations of a whole people. Whether or not slavery was essential to the South, it was essential to the South to have the power to maintain slavery. If the North could control the one, she could control all. This was the issue, the tragedy, that slavery had become the proving ground of the South's fight to maintain her rights as a minority within the Union.

It was the Mexican War, of course, that in 1846 commanded Calhoun's immediate attention. The implications of the Wilmot Proviso had turned the taste of the conflict bitter upon Southern lips. Now, too late, Southern politicians realized how terribly right their leader had been when he had stood out against the conflict. President Polk's hasty attempts to end the struggle by an abortive offer of three million dollars in payment to Mexico, for lands that the American forces would otherwise overrun, further stamped the struggle as a Southern imperialistic venture. No one in the North desired that blood be shed for a Southern slave empire; nor did the more temperate public opinion of either section wish the brawling slave question to be thrust forward again.

To North and South alike, the war had become, in Calhoun's words, 'embarrassing'; the difficulty now was how to get out of it with American honor unimpaired and American territorial ambitions secured. Calhoun, on the twentieth of January, 1847, observed: 'All now acknowledge the war's folly. . . . I never stood higher or stronger than I now do.' [11]

His analysis was overoptimistic. A few farsighted individuals had perceived the tragedy from the first; Webster, who was to lose a son in the holocaust, would have cast a negative vote had he been in Washington at the time of the declaration of war. From Lexington, Kentucky, Henry Clay challenged Polk's declaration, that war exists by the act of Mexico, as 'palpable falsehood.' [12] Nevertheless, a young Whig Representative who dared two weeks after his entry to Congress to offer a series of so-called 'Spot Resolutions' in 'opposition to his own government,' was hailed as the 'Benedict Arnold' of his district! His charges were that Polk's claims to the disputed territory were 'the sheerest deception'; that the American boundary was not at the Rio Grande, and that the only citizens whose blood was shed were soldiers advancing into disputed territory. Condemned as 'base, dastardly, and treasonable,' [13] Abraham Lincoln heard his law partner's warning that his career was at an end.

4

Amidst the cries for conquest and vengeance of these years, Calhoun's was the voice of justice and restraint. In a series of moderate and 'statesmanlike' speeches during the winters of 1847 and 1848,* futilely he voiced the plea that America never take 'one foot of territory' by an aggressive war. Not alone did he oppose the war because of its disastrous consequences for Southern slave interests. Not the sufferings to Mexico alone but the damage to the American spirit was the theme he stressed. A terrible sincerity underlined his words. There is 'a curse,' he warned, 'which must ever befall a free government' which holds other men in subjection. 'With me the liberty of the country is all.' To preserve its 'free popular institutions . . . to adopt a course of moderation and justice towards all

* Here, as in previous chapters, several speeches have been grouped and consolidated to cover certain issues, rather than always being presented in exact chronology. See notes for this chapter.

other countries . . . to avoid war whenever it can be avoided' would 'do more to extend liberty by our example over this continent and the world generally, than would be done by a thousand victories.' [14]

His were no empty fears. So hungry was the ambition of imperialists, North and South; so fierce the urge to plant the Stars and Stripes far to the South, even to Central America, that Webster had called upon Congress to withhold war supplies until the conflict could be proved clearly justifiable. At his side stood Calhoun. 'If fight we must,' he pled, 'let us fight a defensive war' with the least sacrifice of men and money. What were our acknowledged aims? To repel invasion, to establish the Rio Grande as the boundary of Texas; and to obtain indemnities for the claims of our citizens. Already our first two objectives had been accomplished. A defensive policy would make the Mexicans feel this conflict less a war of race and religions, Calhoun contended. Why should we invade Vera Cruz to 'compel the Mexicans to acknowledge as ours what we already hold?' We could conquer these 'proud, unconquerable people'; but would our conquest bring a cessation of guerrilla warfare? Would conquest bring true peace? And what of the men to be expended—the heat—the yellow fever —the broken bodies? 'Can you as a Christian,' Calhoun appealed to each and every Senator, 'justify' giving a vote to its continuance?

He closed with a characteristic warning: he was aware of the determination of the non-slave states that no slavery would be permitted in the new territories. 'Be assured,' he concluded, 'if there be stern determination on one side to exclude us, there will be determination sterner still on ours, not to be excluded.' [15]

Despite the shift in public opinion, Congressional opinion, then as now was not to be diverted by speechmaking. Calhoun's plan was more theoretical than possible. Feelings had gone too high. Passive resistance would have been a practical impossibility in the face of the enraged Mexicans, embittered from the crushing American victories during the early months; nor was 'masterly inactivity' calculated to keep the American armies content amidst heat, disease, and enemy sniping. But that Calhoun's challenges had made a strong impression was proved to him by the 'fierce war' they drew upon him from the Administration supporters.[16]

Presidential ambitions, taunted Turney of Tennessee, were responsible for the Senator's opposition to the Mexican War. Hotly Calhoun refuted the charge. 'The Senator is entirely mistaken. I am no aspirant—never have been. I would not turn on my heel for the Presidency, and he has uttered a libel upon me.' [17] Benton, too, shot arrows into his old enemy, charging that it was none other than the Senator from South Carolina who was 'the author of the present war.' War was the inevitable outcome of the annexation of Texas.

Calhoun arose to the challenge. 'I trust there will be no dispute hereafter as to who is the real author of annexation,' he proudly declared. He had had competition for the honor, but now, 'since the war has become unpopular, they all seem to agree that I . . . am the author of annexation. I will not put the honor aside.' [18]

He, of course, denied that the Texas annexation was the cause of the war. He had been negotiating with the Mexican Commissioners. Had he remained as Secretary of State, he contended, he would have settled the boundary question in a manner definite and satisfactory both to Mexico and the United States. Yet there is justice in Benton's charge. For the Texas annexation was but one more example of Calhoun's faculty for involving his state, his section, and his country in situations which only his own intellect could unravel and which he had no guarantee whatever that he would be permitted to unravel.

5

The war on the battlefield, however, Calhoun and all Congress knew was minor compared to the seething controversy over the division of the spoils. To 'force the issue upon the North' was now Calhoun's driving aim. And the North had decided, he proclaimed. There would be no more admission of slave states. No slavery would be permitted in the territories. In all but the Senate—in the House, in the Electoral College—the South was in the minority. Soon a state would be entered north of Iowa and another north of that, and even in the Senate the strength of the South would be broken. 'We shall be at the entire mercy of the non-slaveholding States.'

The time for compromise, Calhoun believed, was over. He had sought to have the line of the Missouri Compromise extended to the Pacific. This was the course he had suggested to his friends. 'Let us not be the disturbers of this Union.' His efforts had been futile; twice the extension of the Missouri Compromise line had been voted down.

Now he saw his error. Madison had been right when he proclaimed the Compromise 'without a shade of constitutional authority.' It had never been binding upon the South. The South had agreed to it for the mutual harmony and peace of the Union. For surrendering her 'rights' in the territories, she had been promised the return of her fugitive slaves; yet no state but Illinois had 'freely' given them up.[19]

What now? 'God only knows.' The Constitution upheld the Southern side. The debates of the Constitutional Convention offered proof that we were a federal, not a national, government, 'the best Government, instead of the most despotic.' It was this 'constellation of nations' which the Constitution had been written to protect.

The Constitution itself, for example, empowered Congress to legislate for the District of Columbia. Here was added proof of the federal theory. For the District of Columbia was specifically exempted from the sovereignty and control ascribed to the states. All else, all territory, with the single exception of the public lands, was the property of 'the people of the several States. . . . They are as much the territory of one State as another, of Virginia as of New York. They are the territories of all, because they are the territories of each; and not of each, because they are the territories of all.' And as the Constitution could 'give no preference or advantage to one State over another,' so it could give no advantage to 'one portion of the Union over another.' The rights of the states were the rights of the territories—no more, no less.[20]

Was there hope in the Constitution? There was none in compromises, subject as they were to the shifting whims of the Congress and the people. Congressional compromise, he warned, would only 'lull us to sleep again, without removing the danger.' That the Constitution itself was a thing of compromises, resting ultimately upon that same shifting will of the people, he never stopped to consider. 'Let us adhere to the Constitution' was his plea. 'The Constitution is a rock. . . . I see my way in the Constitution. . . . Let us have done with compromises. Let us go back and stand upon the Constitution.'

If Congress denied the South its 'constitutional rights,' Calhoun would leave the matter to his constituents. 'I give no advice. But I may speak as an individual member of that section of the Union. . . . There is my family . . . there I drew my first breath; there are all my hopes. I am a Southern man and a slaveholder, a kind and merciful one, I trust, and none the worse for being a slaveholder.' He would not 'give up . . . one inch of what belongs to us as members of this great Republic. The surrender of life is nothing to sinking down into acknowledged inferiority.' Somberly he warned: 'The day the balance between the two sections . . . is destroyed, is a day . . . not far removed from revolution, anarchy, and Civil War.'[21]

On February 19, 1847, Calhoun laid before the Senate four resolutions which stripped the argument to the essentials: the declaration that the territories were the joint property of the states: that Congress, the states' agent, could make no discrimination which would deprive any state of its rights; that any such law would violate the Constitution, states' rights, and the equality of the Union; and finally, that men have a right to form their state governments as they see fit, the only power of Congress being to see that those governments were republican.[22]

'We foresee what is coming,' Calhoun said. The 'greatest of calamities' was not insurrection, but something worse. '. . . We love and revere the Union; it is the interest of all—I might add the world—that our Union should be preserved.' But the conservative power was in the slaveholding states. In contrast to the labor wars of the North, Southern labor and capital were identified. In conflicts between the two, the South would be on the conservative side. Cunningly he appealed to the cupidity of the

Northern industrialists and their Congressional representatives. 'Gentlemen
. . . warring on us . . . are warring on themselves!' They, not the
Southerners, were creating the excitement. 'All we ask,' concluded Calhoun, asking the impossible, 'is to be let alone.' [23]

There is tragedy in his baffled appeal. Where was the great liberal of
only a few years before who had so clearly perceived industrial capitalism
as the avowed enemy of Northern labor and Southern farmer alike, and
who was forging a political realignment on that realization? In his appeal
to 'Gentlemen, North and South,' he was abandoning his own hard-won
allies. Upon the preservation of Southern rights, he was convinced, turned
all minority rights; and to save these he would not scruple even to use
Northern capital as an instrument against itself.

But not even the giant intellect of Calhoun could play the game two
ways. Northern capital, stiffened against his onslaughts of the past, was
scarcely receptive to his belated wooing now. He was, indeed, right in
his realization that slavery profited the capitalist of the North; but if so,
he could hardly present the South at the same time as the ally of the
laborer and the enemy of the North. Realist that he was, he had temporarily shifted his means to attain his ends; but he could not do so without
confusing the stand of the South and his own status as a defender of the
liberties and not of the enslavement of men. He was trapped by the
dilemma of his time.

                                      6

His very resolutions flung the issue in the teeth of the North. 'Abstractions,' Benton called them, 'firebrands to set the world on fire.' [24] Actually
they showed masterful political strategy. They were adopted by numerous
Southern Legislatures. The Senate, it is true, received them with 'disfavor,'
but Calhoun never pressed for their passage. Apparently he had not even
intended to do so.

They accomplished their objective, however. They had been written, not
for the Senate but for the country; their deliberate purpose, to frighten the
Northern and Southern imperialists out of their dreams for the annexation
of Mexico! If the North saw that the Southern determination that all
Mexico would be slave was as firmly rooted as the Northern decision that
she would be free, would she then be so eager to annex all Mexico? Thus
Calhoun reasoned, and thus he won. Although the threat of the Wilmot
Proviso had certainly been effective in dimming the fervor of the Southern
imperialists, Calhoun was convinced that it was his resolutions that saved
Mexico, 'turned the tide and brought the Union to a disavowal.' [25]

So far as the South was concerned, however, Calhoun knew that the
Mexican territory was only half the picture. To him it was no surprise in

the session of 1848 when the bills for territorial governments for Oregon came in under the banner of free soil. And the stand that he took was the logical consequence of Mr. Wilmot's theory. If the North would permit no slavery in New Mexico, then the South could permit no freedom in Oregon. Had not the principle of the Missouri Compromise been abandoned, he would never have pressed the question. As he told Polk: 'He did not desire to extend slavery . . . but he would vote against a bill with slavery restricted, on principle.' [26]

Logically no choice was left him. He knew perfectly well that Oregon, under the law of nature, as Webster pointed out, would never be slave territory. Why, then, could not the South be permitted the enjoyment of its 'rights'? In theory the few Southerners who might migrate to Oregon could take their slaves with them. And this was a right that must be insisted upon. For if Congress could prohibit slavery anywhere—this was Calhoun's warning—then, logically, Congress could prohibit it everywhere.

7

Nor could Calhoun support Henry Clay's resolutions of 1848, specifically allowing slavery in the territories. Congress had no more power to permit than to abolish the institution, he contended, and to acknowledge the one right would be to recognize the other.

Clay bridled. Did anyone deny the *right* of Congress to prohibit slavery? 'Yes,' Calhoun answered steadily, 'I deny it.'

The abolitionists, he charged, were striving for a 'general principle' that hereafter no territory should be created in which slavery should not be prohibited. In the face of such determination, how could men submit to the Senator from Kentucky's stand that the abolition of slavery would be 'inexpedient'? Inexpedient! He whirled upon the New England Senators. Did they not believe slavery a sin? How could you justify a sin in terms of expediency?

'Far higher ground must be taken . . . as high as that assumed by those determined madmen.' Only thus could they be shown that 'while they are acting in the name of morals and religion, they are . . . violating the most solemn obligations, political, moral, and religious.'

He had acknowledged surrender. The North had had the choice of weapons and had chosen to fight on moral grounds. To defend slavery in terms of expediency now would be like 'extinguishing a conflagration that mounted to the clouds by throwing a bucket of water on it.' Fire could only be fought with fire, power with power. To apologize for slavery was to admit its evil. Once slavery had been thought an evil; not now. Now it 'was the most . . . stable basis for free institutions in the world.' [28]

8

This was 'the platform of the South,' the heresy that Calhoun flung in the face of the North and its leaders during the debate over the territories of New Mexico and Oregon. He began with restraint enough. It was safe to cite Jefferson's belief that 'Congress had no power to regulate the condition of . . . men comprising a State. This is the exclusive right of every State.' Jefferson's words meant little; it was only his name that mattered.

But it would have been impossible for Northerners to have understood the sudden chill arrogance that gripped the man before them, the taunts at his Southern colleagues for losing their dignity as equals among equals. 'You are woefully degenerated from your sires.' Strange, too, were the sneers at menial tasks; not 'the poorest or the lowest' Southern man would perform them. 'He has too much pride . . . and I rejoice that he has. They are unsuited to the spirit of a free man.' Yet no man felt degraded by working in the field with his slave.

And there was sheer heresy in his flagrant repudiation of the very words of the Declaration of Independence. There were men who listened, patriotic and sincere, who in the stark honesty of Calhoun's words saw how wide, how impassably wide, the gulf between North and South had become. So long as a common belief held men together, the Union might survive; but now, under the ruthless realism of Calhoun's hammer-strokes, the very spiritual foundations of the Union were shattering. 'Men were not born free and equal,' he was saying. 'Men are not born. Infants are born. . . . While infants they are incapable of freedom.'

Relentlessly he tore at the beliefs born of Revolution, the bases of the Declaration of Independence, Rousseau's free and natural man. Man was not born in a state of nature, Calhoun contended. He was born subject to the limitations of the society in which destiny had placed him. The safety of society was paramount to the liberty of the individual. Yet government, necessary to protect men from the threat of anarchy, had 'no right to control individual liberty beyond' what was necessary for the safety of society.[29]

Thus did Calhoun justify the enslavement of the Negro. For in the South of his day he believed neither economically, socially, nor politically would there have been safety with the Negro free. Furthermore, if the citizenry were 'ignorant, stupid, debased,' by so much must governmental power be greater and individual freedom less. As a people rose in intelligence and in their understanding of liberty, governmental power would become less 'and individual liberty greater.'

Jefferson had been wrong in his 'false view' that men utterly unqualified to possess liberty were 'fully entitled' to it. It was 'a great mistake' to sup-

pose 'all people . . . capable of self-government.' Vehemently Calhoun
condemned the idealists who deemed it 'the mission of this country . . .
to force free governments on all the people of this continent and over the
world.' Free governments, he declared, with the recent histories of France
and Germany fresh in his mind, 'must be the spontaneous wish of the
people . . . must emanate from the hearts of the people.' Liberty was
'harder to preserve . . . than to maintain.' To bestow liberty upon all
men, 'without regard to their fitness either to acquire or maintain it,' would
deny it to those entitled to it; and would do more 'to retard the cause of
liberty than all other causes combined.' [30]

Thus, in words of harsh realism, did Calhoun lay bare the platform of
the South. Talk of this kind was scarcely calculated to lull the abolitionists
into a peaceful surrender of the contested territories into the hands of the
slaveholders. Calhoun's feelings had gone beyond his control. None more
than he deplored the 'agitation' of the slavery question; yet none more
than he threw so much fuel upon the fire.

9

Week after week, month after month, session after session, the fight
dragged on. It rose to a feverish pitch in the steamy midsummer of 1848 as
nerves and tempers and sweat-soaked bodies battled to hold the Union
together. Calhoun, buoyed up by his determination, labored through the
summer. Surprisingly enough, his precarious health stood by him; he felt
better than he had in several years, and his friends thought he looked unusually well. He was tired, however, and admitted to Andrew that his
engagements left him no leisure for relaxation, 'which I greatly need and
desire.' [31]

He voiced the stand of the South on June 16, 1848, speaking in opposition to a bill excluding slavery 'forever' from the entire Oregon territory.
With increased vehemence he denied that Congress had the requisite power.
That the Constitution established slavery in the territories, he never had
the temerity to assert; but the right of slaveholders to bring their property
to any territory of the United States, organized or unorganized, he claimed
as guaranteed under the Constitution. And even more important than the
rights of slavery, he contended, was the self-defense of the South. All that
the North was seeking was the balance of power. From then on, it would
be easy to enforce abolition; with abolition enforced, all states' rights, all
Southern self-determination, would be at an end. His contentions were
effective; the bill was lost.

The battle, however, had just begun. By mid-July, with the tacit consent of Calhoun, a compromise was evolved. In Oregon the slavery question would be decided by the territorial legislature. In New Mexico and

California it would be left to courts, composed almost entirely of Southern men. At an all-night session on the twenty-seventh, the Senate passed the bill, but in the House it was defeated, not by the abolitionists, but by little Alexander Stephens of Georgia, who, for reasons best known to himself, moved that it be laid on the table. The battle was on again.

A second bill, prohibiting slavery in Oregon, was ready by August. All through the night of the thirteenth the sleepy Senators growled and wrangled in the stifling Chamber, voting its passage by dawn in sheer exhaustion. Calhoun had seen it coming; he had been at the White House all the evening before, pleading with Polk for a veto. Polk refused. He was President of the United States, not of the South, and it was unjust to keep the people of Oregon stranded without a government, merely because of the slavery question. Furthermore, the President warned the impetuous Carolinian, the nation was now too 'inflamed' for a veto.[32] Nothing could be done.

All Calhoun's efforts had gained him nothing but a deeper place in the affections of the Southern people. His very name could not be mentioned in a routine speech from Mississippi to Virginia without throwing an entire audience into wild applause. If he stepped onto a public stage, the whole hall would rise in tribute. He inspired a fanatic loyalty in his followers. He stopped in Cheraw, South Carolina, wearing the chin-whiskers which he had grown to protect his throat early in the eighteen-forties. Within a month all the male citizenry of Cheraw had sprouted goatees! At Saratoga Springs, a South Carolina Whig pleased William H. Seward by upbraiding 'the renegade Democrat,' Martin Van Buren, 'the great man of New York.' Seward then thought, 'as a brother Whig,' he would please his companion by attacking Mr. Calhoun, 'the great man of South Carolina.' But scarcely ten words were out before the Southerner had flown into 'a great passion,' swearing that 'no man should abuse Mr. Calhoun in his presence.'[33]

He was 'the great Southerner,' the South's popular hero. In Columbia, in the fall of 1848, he caused a sensation; and out at the University the little brick chapel was crammed with eager students. They were struck with his appearance, for he stood before them erect and sparkling-eyed, with all the untapped energy of youth in every word and in every movement of his 'sinewy frame.' Buoyed up by his driving purpose, his 'contagious enthusiasm' struck fire from his young listeners.[34] But he had no cheer to offer them. 'The bitter,' he knew, was 'yet to come.'[35]

XXVII

The Statesman and the Man

FROM HIS SEAT in the press gallery, reporter Oliver Dyer looked across the Senate Chamber with unfeigned distaste. Young Mr. Dyer was bitter. The previous summer he had attended the Whig Convention of 1848 where he had seen his idol, Henry Clay, the gallant 'Harry of the West,' now seventy-one years old, thrown once more upon the scrap-heap of rejected Presidential candidates, his last hope of obtaining a lifetime goal forever obliterated. And who was responsible? Not the party hacks, but the men of Dyer's own age, who had wisely calculated that in the awarding of party spoils they would have nothing to win from Clay.[1] He had been in public life too long; the old friends would reap the rewards. So Clay had been discarded for a novice in politics, with no debts to the past, a new version of the old military hero theme, pipe-chewing, hard-bitten 'Old Rough and Ready,' Zachary Taylor of Buena Vista fame.

This was the end, thought Dyer. New faces were moving among the old, new voices echoing in Senate and House. In the Senate, there was Jefferson Davis, on crutches from a crippling wound at Buena Vista. From Illinois came little Stephen A. Douglas with his giant head and giant mind; and in the new seat for the 'Senator from Texas' loomed the 'noble figure and handsome face' of the ex-President of the Texas Republic, Sam Houston.[2] The third and fourth generation of American statesmen these, with unspent greatness in them; but for the younger spectators, the newcomers to the gallery, it was the old-timers, Benton, Clay, Calhoun, and Webster, who sent excitement quivering through their nerve ends.

These were the men born when the guns of the Revolution were booming out their last salutes at Saratoga and Yorktown, when the Constitution was but an unmapped jumble of ideas in the minds of Madison and Hamilton. These men had grown up during the Presidencies of Washington and Adams; they could remember Jefferson and Monroe and Randolph—all the vanished giants of the golden age. Theirs was the second generation of Americans, the link between the colonial past and the national industrial future. To look at them was to look at living history. They were old now, Clay and Calhoun perceptibly breaking, but among the new faces and the new names they towered like giants as they had overshadowed eight of the Presidents who had served with them.

2

Of all, there was none whom time had touched more lightly than Daniel Webster. His body had thickened, his hair grown thin and gray, but the wonderful bronze sheen of his skin still glowed, and the great eyes seemed darker and more brooding than in youth.[3]

He saved his strength by wasting none of it on routine. Unlike Calhoun, who was never known to leave his seat except for illness, Webster scorned to risk his health by sitting in the deadly air and cramped space of the Senate Chamber, and appeared only to speak or answer roll-call. Between-times you saw him walking majestically to and fro in the lobby, his hands clasped behind his back. He seldom spoke, but was seemingly aware that those who saw him were overawed by him. His dignity had become little short of portentous, and his conversation was as stately as his body. For political small-talk and the men who talked it, he had only scorn. It was the clergymen and the constitutional lawyers who found a welcome from Daniel Webster; and he spoke to the highest, not the lowest, levels of his listeners.

There were some, however, who had the ill grace to quibble that Webster's taste for admiration was something less fastidious than his oratory, and who recoiled in disgust from the droves of bankers, stock-jobbers, and industrialists who would tip gallery officers to give them the best seats in which to sit nodding their heads sagely at the Websterian profundities and the Websterian Latin, which few of them could understand. The defender of the Union he might well be; but all knew that he was also the great 'conservator of wealth against unfavorable legislation.'[4]

Liberals mourned Daniel Webster, just as they mourned Calhoun's 'political decadence.' They mourned his lost opportunities, the sluggishness, both intellectual and moral, which left him halted just at the gateway of true greatness. 'The victory won, he would lapse into indifference.' Had he seen the opportunities seized upon by lesser men, would he have been the great American of his age? Many thought so; others feared that had his will-power matched his intellect, he might have set himself up as a dictator. But it was Daniel Webster who had shown the nation the philosophy of government that was the partner of its new philosophy in economics. By harnessing its claims in the sacred name of the Union, he had made industrial progress a holy and a national cause.

Furthermore, it was generally agreed that without Webster in the Senate, 'Calhoun would have carried everything before him.'[5] No one but Webster had the intellect to cope with the assaults of the great Carolinian. And he could do so without offense, either to Calhoun or to Calhoun's followers. Aloof, ponderous though he was, no other Senator was on such good terms with all his colleagues.

3

Age had little effect upon 'Old Bullion' Benton, survivor of a duel with Andrew Jackson. With his burly frame and his booming voice, in which you could almost hear the whirr of the tomahawk, about him still was the aura of frontier days when men gouged and knifed each other. Every morning he scrubbed his body down to the hips with a rough horsehair brush, and every evening completed the operation from hips to feet, afterwards being vigorously 'curried down' by his body-servant. His skin was like leather, his muscles like iron. 'Why, sir,' he would roar, 'if I were to *touch* you with that brush, sir, you would cry murder, sir.' Why did he do it? 'The Roman gladiators did it, sir.' [6]

There was a kind of flamboyant magnificence about him. By sheer bulldog persistence he had shoved and elbowed his way into the front rank of American statesmen. Intellectually his abilities were acquired rather than innate; and it was said of him that he 'carried the Congressional Library in his head.' His respect for facts and figures was profound; and he had only scorn for subtleties that he could not understand. 'What are the facts?' was his perpetual demand. 'Give us the facts.' [7]

There was something laughable in the childishness of Benton's ego, in his boast: 'Yes, sir, General Jackson was a great man, sir. . . . He was of great use *to me*, sir.' Even the reporters smiled at his claim that his rhetorical exuberances were a favorite study and inspiration for young men.[8] But few could help but admire the bulldog courage of the man, who, as his state became 'more Southern,' himself became more unionistic, setting himself in defiance of his section, his time, and his constituency.

He was a terrible man in anger. The ruthlessness of the Indian fighter, the 'gleam of the scalping knife,' was in his bitter mockery and his 'rasping squeal' of sarcasm. Since the day when he had stood up before Henry Foote, shouting, 'Fire, assasin, fire,' he had wasted neither conciliation nor courtesy upon his enemies. 'Mr. President, sir . . . I never quarrel, sir; but I sometimes fight, sir; and whenever I fight, sir, a funeral follows, sir.' [9]

Yet all marked the tenderness he lavished upon his insane wife. No one who saw could forget his gentleness on the evening when, entertaining a French Prince and other distinguished guests, Mrs. Benton in a négligée, rambled into the room and stood staring lovingly at her husband. Talk halted. All looked on as Benton arose, took her by the hand, and, with the 'majesty of a demi-god,' presented her to the Prince and the visitors.[10] Then he drew a hassock to his chair, seated her, gave her his hand to play with, and went on talking as before.

Politically Henry Clay was his abomination. Even to the most casual observer it was a marvel how deeply he could hurt the high-strung Kentuckian. Clay, his long body trembling, his eyes blazing, would jump to his feet, 'to puncture the Senator's balloon,' lashing out with scornful invective, raking up bitter memories, till his friends would intervene, only to be turned aside with a curt 'Sit down, sir, sit down; I can take care of myself.' [11] And Benton, sitting nearby, would turn and win the debate with a pitying smile. Only one man was—apparently—unmoved by the Benton blusterings, and this was John C. Calhoun.

4

Of all the Senate 'giants' in the dying years of the eighteen-forties, none attracted more spectators to the gallery than Calhoun. And of all the spectators at the turbulent sessions of 1848, none was so eager to see Calhoun as reporter Oliver Dyer.

Dyer hated Calhoun. Calhoun, he knew, was a bad man, the defender of human servitude, the fomenter of all the outcry for disunion and secession. What would such a man look like? Face after face, Dyer searched in his eagerness to get a look at the 'Great Nullifier.'

His appearance satisfied Dyer completely. With his masses of hair and gaunt figure, the piercing eyes and strong, stern features, he looked, asserted the young abolitionist, like 'a perfect image and embodiment of the devil.' Had Dyer found a copy of his likeness in *Paradise Lost*, he would have accepted it as the masterpiece of an artist with 'a peculiar genius for Satanic portraiture.'

Benton, meanwhile, had been discussing a petition that the Wilmot Proviso be applied to the citizens of New Mexico territory, a petition which, it was generally suspected, he himself had fathered. Suddenly the 'scattered and indifferent attention of the Senate focussed.' The murmuring undertone of conversation ceased. Calhoun had risen to his feet. Every eye was turned upon him. The petition, he declared, was 'impudent and insolent,' an 'insult to the Senate and the country.'

Yet all was said with 'an exquisite courtesy.' The 'bell-like sweetness and resonance of his voice,' his ideas, presented so clearly that no one could help but understand them, were a 'revelation' to Dyer. 'Spontaneously,' he wished that Calhoun were an abolitionist, 'so that we could have him talking on our side.'

Guilt-stricken, he glanced at Benton. But time had done no more to appease Benton's 'rancorous' hatred of his old enemy from South Carolina than to moderate his feelings toward Clay. With salty relish he rolled out epithets at his opponent: 'the Great Secessionist,' 'the Great Nullifier,' the 'Great Disunionist.' His words were bitter, deliberately insulting. Dyer waited to see the flare-up of Calhoun's anger. But 'he treated it with absolute indifference.' Not by motion or look did he reveal that he had heard a single word. Thus did Calhoun's hard-won self-control now stand by him.[12]

Finally Calhoun resumed the floor. Occasionally he 'warmed into vehemence,' but his courtesy never waned. And in the gallery sat Dyer, confused, indignant at himself. Against his every principle, against his will, all his 'personal feelings' were drawn to Calhoun's side. Even the Carolinian's face seemed to have undergone a change. No longer did he look like a devil, but a sincere patriot, conscientiously devoted to what 'he believed to be right.' Horrified, Dyer struggled for his bearings. It was no use. 'The change went on in spite of all that I could do.' [13]

Calhoun sensed the young man's response. And on New Year's Day, 1849, Dyer received an invitation to visit the Southern Senator at his lodgings. Calhoun was ill that day, too ill even to leave his rooms. But his active mind craved employment, and having been struck with the ease with which Dyer transcribed the rapid flow of Senate debate, he had requested the young reporter to give him a lesson in shorthand.

The visit lasted from noon until sundown. Gently Calhoun chaffed his visitor for a 'mistake' common to most newsmen who reported his speeches, which 'annoyed' him.

'What is that mistake?' Dyer asked.

'They make me say "this Nation," instead of "this Union,"' Calhoun replied. 'I never use the word Nation.* We are not a nation, but a Union, a confederacy of equal and sovereign States. England is a nation, but the United States are not a nation.'

The gates were opened for political discussion. Question after question Dyer fired at his host, and Calhoun answered them, gradually unfolding to the fascinated young man his entire political philosophy. 'Charmed with his manner,' Dyer relaxed, and impulsively blurted out the one question that was actually on his mind. 'What kind of a man,' he asked, 'was General Jackson?'

A change flashed over Calhoun's face. Dyer could have bitten out his tongue. 'Had I not been so young and inexperienced . . . I could not have asked such a question.' Calhoun was silent. Dyer looked into that white, quiet face. There was no bitterness there and no hatred, only the lost, withdrawn look of a man steeped in memories. Minutes passed. At last he roused himself, and the look in his 'luminous' eyes and the gentleness of his voice, Dyer could remember forty years afterward. 'General Jackson was a great man,' he said.[14]

Dyer was won completely. He studied into his hero's early years. 'No man in America,' he concluded, 'ever started his career with brighter, nobler promise than did that gifted, pure-souled young South Carolinian.' How could such a man believe in human slavery? What had happened to

* Calhoun did frequently use the word *nation* in his early speeches.

him? Harriet Martineau had called him 'a cast-iron man'; yes, he could see how a stranger might have received that impression.[15] His ideas on different subjects, Dyer noted, were so 'rigidly separated from one another, that the man himself seemed to be a different personage at different times, according to the question . . . before him. His faculties . . . were a confederation, and everyone of them was a sovereign faculty which could think and act for itself.'[16]

The more Dyer knew Calhoun, the better he liked him. Calhoun's cousin, James Edward, had noted that he was 'never exacting, despite his force of character.' If 'a man was attacked in his presence, he would seek for something to justify praise.'[17] To Dyer his 'kindness of heart' seemed 'inexhaustible.' He seemed 'so morally clean and spiritually pure . . . that it was a pleasure to have one's soul get close to his soul—a feeling,' Dyer hastened to add, 'that I never had for any other man.' To the hero-worshiping Westerner there was a kind of elemental wholesomeness about the great Carolinian, 'as fresh and bracing as a breeze from the prairie, the ocean, or the mountain. . . . He was inexpressibly refined, gentle, winning; yet he was strong and thoroughly manly . . . invincibleness pervading his gentleness. . . . I admired Benton; I admired Clay still more; I admired Webster, on the intellectual side, most of all; but I loved Calhoun.'[18]

5

Reading over Dyer's effusions today, it is easy to pigeonhole him as a mere psychological case-study in hero-worship. But this starry-eyed enthusiast cannot be dismissed so easily. For on an inflated and overeulogistic scale, he had succumbed to a force in Calhoun which can neither be understood nor denied, but, above all, cannot be ignored. For in it is the key to his power. Von Holst, Calhoun's most critical biographer, in reducing his subject's personal traits to three, lists as the most dominant his 'especial fascination over young men.'[19]

It was uncanny. With political opponents, it was even deadly. For, although it was Calhoun's purpose to win men's intellects, too often he could only succeed in confusing their emotions as he had done with poor Oliver Dyer.

Nor was Dyer the only abolitionist to succumb to what Pinckney had described as Calhoun's 'ethereal, indescribable charm.'[20] There was young John Wentworth, the 'infant of the House of Representatives,' who had stood horror-stricken before the huge stockade near the lower gate of the Capitol, where human merchandise was herded behind a fence, like cattle in a stockyard. His nerves had quivered to the harsh voice of the auctioneer, the naked black flesh cowering before the gaze of the crowd, even the very chewing of the 'jaw-breaker' crackers which the auctioneer would cram into the slaves' mouths to show how strong their teeth were. And it was as the avowed defender of this human serfdom that he saw and heard Calhoun for the first time. 'Mr. Calhoun spoke like a college professor,' he noted. 'His position was stationary and he used no gestures. His pale countenance indicated the cloister. His voice was silvery and attractive, but very earnest.' And as the young man listened to those plausible premises and the even more plausible deductions, his resolves broke down. Confronted with Calhoun's logic, it was impossible to avoid his conclusion. 'If a stranger should select the Senator, irrespective of doctrine,' he asserted, 'who came nearest to being a saint,' he would select Mr. Calhoun.

As he had done with Dyer, so, too, with John Wentworth, Calhoun sensed the young man's response. So Wentworth, too, received an invitation to Calhoun's rooms. Calhoun gave him no harangue, none of the lectures with which he often indulged his admiring listeners. Instead, he spoke of Wentworth's own Chicago, of Fort Dearborn and his work with the officers there during his days in the War Department. His language was 'seductive'; his eyes shone as he spoke of the Mississippi and the Great Lakes, the 'inland seas of America'; of the vast, untapped West, 'the natural ally of the South.' Wentworth sat enthralled. 'He was,' he said afterward, 'the most charming man in conversation I ever heard.'

Hours later, Wentworth stepped into the night. In one hand he held a present Calhoun had given him, an autographed copy of the Senator's life and speeches. Like so many before and after him, for that night, at least, John Wentworth was a lost man. Abstractedly he started down the street and ran straight into Senator Thomas Hart Benton. One look at the young man's face and Benton guessed where he had been. His 'rage was unbounded.' He declared that he could repeat every word Calhoun had said. 'It was Mr. Calhoun's custom,' he explained, 'to early procure interviews with young men and to instill into their minds the seeds of nullification.' [21]

The charge was true. As one South Carolina historian summed it up: 'Calhoun possessed pre-eminently that power of personality which enforces ideas, independent of their wisdom. It is this personality which still holds the imagination.' It was the same power which would be felt almost a hundred years later in the personal appeal of Franklin Delano Roosevelt.

And with it all was 'that burning intellectual energy,' that resilience, that high-powered tension of a mind that never grew old. Webster himself was awed by the power of Calhoun's intellect, declaring that he could have 'demolished Newton, Calvin,' or even John Locke as a logician. Dr. Abraham Venable of North Carolina, called in as Calhoun's physician, instantly declared that he had 'ceased to wonder' at the effect his exalted intellect had upon his followers. 'How could you put that man in competition with anybody else?' exclaimed enthusiastic young Albert Rhett of Charleston, on meeting Calhoun for the first time. 'Such an intellect . . . is a more wonderful creation than any mountain on earth.' Looking into the depths of those steady eyes with their strange power to draw and hold your own, feeling the heat of that ardent mind, men were trapped by a power they could not analyze, a force they could not understand.[22]

Calhoun was aware of his power. Did he have any ulterior motive in exerting it? Undoubtedly. But it was not to win votes for himself; it was to impress men with the righteousness of his cause, so to fire their imaginations that, dazzled by Calhoun, they would take up the cause that he held 'dearer than light or life.' He had pledged himself to nothing less than a single-handed battle to reverse the will of the American people.

The scheme was fanatic, of course. Yet the measure of Calhoun's greatness is how nearly he approached his goal. 'No man in America,' declared the wondering Wentworth, 'ever exerted the influence over this country that Mr. Calhoun did.'[23]

Not force, but persuasion, was Calhoun's weapon now; not anger, but gentleness. The bitterness, the storm and the fury that had swept over him in the thirties, was harnessed to his one overwhelming purpose. Through grim experience he was learning what lesser men knew by instinct: that the most flawless logic ever devised could not convince a man against his will. To attempt robbery of a man's beliefs only aroused his determination to cling the more closely to them.

Calhoun at late last had come to the knowledge that few men were creatures of reason like himself. They were creatures of prejudice, and their reasoning consisted in finding defenses for their prejudices. Logically Calhoun could prove that disunion and Southern destruction would be the result of the abolitionist frenzy. But how could he turn men's wills against abolition? Only by winning the individual leaders. How could he arouse young Southerners to the danger that confronted them? If he won their hearts, then only could he conquer their intellects. He had realized all except the most important thing of all. He did not realize that, for every individual he convinced against the will of the majority, the stiffer would become the will of the majority not to be convinced.

With men equipped to appreciate it, Calhoun's intellectual power was as deadly as his emotional. Converts like Orestes Brownson, who preferred Calhoun's unabashed adherence to the cause of slavery to the hypocritical mouthings of men who saw slavery only in labor systems other than their own, were frightening to the whole liberal school of American thought. Calhoun's ideas had long been popular among Southern college professors, who were systematically drilling them into the minds of their students. But by the eighteen-forties they were gaining 'strong' footholds among 'scholars of the North,' such as Dartmouth's President Nathan Lord, who 'seemed incapable of resisting the seductive reasoning of his perceptive, comprehensive mind.'[24]

'If he could but talk with every man, he would . . . have the whole United States on his side,' it was declared. He was fighting with the energy of a hundred men; he was winning every battle; and with every battle won, the certainty increased that he would lose the war.

But he fought on, nevertheless. By day and by night he was accessible to all who sought him; and men found in his simplicity a blessed relief from the lordly Congressmen with their pompous ways. But these same Congressmen, Wentworth asserts, would not permit their constituents to leave Washington without asking: 'Have you seen Mr. Calhoun? Do you think of leaving without seeing Mr. Calhoun?' [25]

Bitterly his friends resented the time and energy he lavished upon men who meant nothing to him. What did it mean? They knew how self-contained he was, how he shrank both from 'the praise and gaze of the multitude.' They knew the limitations of his physical strength; and that once at home, he would scarcely stir from his plantation all summer long. 'I am an object of as great curiosity to people outside of a circle of five miles in this State, as anywhere else,' he once said. 'Not one man in a hundred in this State ever saw me.' [26] Where Henry Clay would cross the street to meet a crowd, Calhoun would cross to avoid one. In later years this passion for privacy became a complex with him. If he stopped at an inn and was told that it was full, he would leave immediately, although the mere whisper of his name would have given him the freedom of the house. Nor did he tell his name to the wayside farmer who denied him a glass of water 'to quench his feverish thirst,' although, when the man discovered that he had refused 'the great Mr. Calhoun,' he declared that he would have run miles to 'gratify his wish.' [27]

6

He was one of the most difficult 'of all American leaders to understand.' To Amos Kendall he seemed the most inconsistent of statesmen, although always insisting that 'he was entirely consistent.' What could you make of such a man: a nationalist, who made a holy cause out of states' rights; 'a legalist who understood the law only as a defense against majorities'; a reactionary who insisted that slavery was the soundest foundation of liberty—and a liberal who as early as 1848 called for 'dispensing altogether with electors,' and for the voters 'to vote by electoral districts direct for the President and the Vice-President, the plurality of votes in each district to count one,' and the state to be recorded in favor of the candidate winning a majority of the districts? [28]

Calhoun's smaller-minded friends found comfort in checking off the great man's undeniable faults: his moments of 'morbid melancholy,' his intellectual arrogance, his willingness to be contradicted only when confident that he could refute the contradiction, the 'hasty desultory reading' with which he supported his ideas. They charged that he 'thought for the State,' vengefully crushing out 'all independence of thought below him.' [29]

This is a charge difficult to prove. Scarcely a prominent South Carolinian of the day—Legaré, Poinsett, Huger, McDuffie, Perry, Petigru, Preston, Thompson, Pickens—avoided political differences with Calhoun and they all survived, politically as well as personally. With Senator William Preston, who had so admired Calhoun in youth, the break was particularly sharp. It was during the Sub-Treasury fight, in which Preston 'acted with Clay throughout' and attacked Calhoun with bitterness. Calhoun declined to answer him. 'Nothing,' he had declared, would force him to forget 'what is due the State' and 'to exhibit the Spectacle of her two Representatives in the Senate quarreling with each other.' [30]

Calhoun was not spiteful. He was a good hater, as his feuds with Benton and Jackson show, but his animosities were political, not personal, and in all the reams of his private correspondence there are few lines of vengefulness. He was more hurt than angered by unjust attack, but he wasted little energy in battling his opponents. Nor did he need to do so in South Carolina; the state took care of them for him. South Carolina would tolerate no animosity toward John C. Calhoun. More than one opponent actually left the state, so vehement was the opposition to all who declined to pay tribute in 'The Kingdom of Calhoun.' Preston's brilliance achieved his re-election to his Senate seat, but many of his 'warmest' friends refused to speak to him again after his attack on Calhoun.[31]

Yet even the loyal Rhett felt that Calhoun parted too easily from friends whose principles differed from his own. He was loyal personally, yet when the choice came between friendship and principle, he did not hesitate. Conversely, intense as his hatreds might be, as with Van Buren in 1840, he could put them aside in the pursuit of his goal. Issues, not personalities, dominated him.

XXVIII

No Compromise With Destiny

No COMPROMISE! This was the message that Calhoun had brought back to South Carolina in the spring of 1847. No compromise with destiny! Unity alone could save the South now. 'Let us show at least as much spirit in defending our rights,' he pleaded, 'as the Abolitionists have evinced in denouncing them.'[1]

He had arrived in Charleston on March 7. A 'warm, and enthusiastic' reception awaited him. On the night of the ninth he spoke from the stage of the Harmony Hall Theater; he was hoarse from a severe cold, but already the meeting had been postponed two days and could not be delayed longer. The theater was packed, and the street outside; hundreds had been turned away.[2] Those within listened with strained attention.

'Let us profit by the example of the abolitionist party,' and like them 'make the destruction of our institutions the . . . issue,' was Calhoun's plea. If slavery was evil, it was an evil in the abstract, just as government was an evil, but preventing more evil than it inflicted. For slavery, good or bad as it might be, was the only means, so Calhoun contended, 'by which two races so dissimilar . . . can live together, nearly in equal numbers, in peace.'

'Party madness,' Calhoun charged, was behind the abolitionist movement. So evenly divided were the parties in the North that the small abolitionist group held the balance of power and could even force the nomination of Presidential candidates favorable to its interests. Thus, to be elected, a Northern candidate must espouse abolitionism.

Power could be countered by power. In the North both parties were united against the South. Hence, in the South, both parties must unite against the North, forming 'a new constitutional party.' Thus, if the Northern parties found themselves unable to win a victory in the Electoral College, one or the other, composed of those who consider slavery evil but 'love the Constitution,' would swing over to the Southern side.

Economically, Calhoun reminded the audience, it was the North that profited from the Union. The South could take care of itself. But the South had no 'desire to be forced on our resources. . . . Our object is perfect equality with other members of the Union.' Delay would prove 'fatal.' Now 'the political ties' were still strong. But further bitterness, further alienation, North and South, would narrow the choice to two: subjection or submission.

'We have the Constitution on our side,' Calhoun concluded. 'I have never known truth . . . fail . . . in the end.'[3]

Applause thundered against his ears. Glowing, exhilarated, he left the stage. Floride was waiting for him. They returned to their rooms, where he wrote a long letter to Duff Green, pouring out his triumph. 'I have just returned from addressing a very large and enthusiastick meeting . . . the largest ever held here. . . . I never have been received even here with greater unanimity and enthusiasm.'[4]

But the party leaders were not convinced. In Washington, a few weeks later, President Polk confided to his diary that 'Mr. Calhoun has become perfectly desperate in his aspiration to the Presidency, and has seized upon this sectional question as the only means.' He was not only 'unpatriotick and mischievous, but wicked. I now entertain a worse opinion of Mr. Calhoun than . . . ever. . . . He is wholly selfish. A few years ago he . . . threatened to . . . dissolve the Union on account of the tariff.' Now 'he selects slavery to agitate the country.'[5]

Scarcely less scathing were the comments of Calhoun's own friend, James H. Hammond, who wrote William Gilmore Simms: 'His object is to gain Southern votes for himself for President. . . . It will be said that he agitates the slavery question for selfish purposes. . . .' And when in August, 1848, Calhoun braved heat and fever to return to Charleston and repeat his warnings that secession would be the logical result of abolitionist agitation, the clamor against him grew louder. His attempts to restrain the public demand for a Southern convention, or at least to have some state other than South Carolina initiate the call, drew a bitter taunt from the fiery Robert Toombs: 'Calhoun stands off . . . in order to make a party all his own, on slavery. . . . Poor old dotard, to suppose he could get a party now on any terms.'[6]

There was certainly a shade of truth, if not of justice, in these accusations. A Southern convention or a Southern party would focus the united opinion of the section against the North, but the party could only profit the ambitions of Calhoun. It is preposterous to assume that he whipped up the slavery question for the purpose of riding into the White House on it; but undoubtedly he was willing to take advantage of an existing situation to further his Presidential chances.

2

Calhoun's love was for the South and the way of life in the South. He made no secret of this. 'Strong as is my attachment to the Union, my attachment to liberty and the section where Providence has cast my lot is still stronger.' [7] Yet, as Jefferson Davis said, his 'affections clung tenaciously to the Union.' Nearly 'forty years of my life have been devoted to the service of the Union,' he could pridefully declare. 'If I shall have any place in the memory of posterity, it will be in consequence of my deep attachment to it and our federal system of government.' [8] To him the Union meant far more than the mere linking together of the states; it meant the Constitution, embodying the liberties in the government. Furthermore, it was within the Union that his beloved South had flowered. For the Union to be destroyed, either through consolidation by the North or by secession of the South, would mean that a great experiment in freedom had failed.

The federal theory, Calhoun felt, was America's unique contribution to government. And the very essence of the federal system was its protection of minority rights. Calhoun knew that the world was watching the American experiment. Could a country of peoples, diverse in their economic, social, and even moral patterns, dwell together in a political Union for the general welfare of all; with each group free to live as it would, so long as it violated none of the privileges and rights of another group? This was what American freedom meant to Calhoun and to the South, and this was what he thought it meant to the Founding Fathers.

And if the South seceded to preserve those constitutional rights which she had once thought would be protected within the limits of the Union, it would still mean that the great experiment had failed. Only as a last resort would the thought of secession be tolerable. For he explained: 'As I believe a good government to be the greatest of earthly blessings, I should be averse to the overthrow of ours, even if I thought it greatly inferior to what I do.' [9]

Once more, too, the other side of the picture appeared. Slavery had endured under the protection of the American flag; but how would it fare isolated in a Southern Confederacy? Would a world, outraged by the anachronism of slavery in any place or form, welcome into the family of nations a country avowedly built upon that foundation? Politically and economically might not an independent South meet world-wide ostracism? And in a severed Union Southern 'rights' in the territories could scarcely be more than academic. Calhoun was too honest and farsighted to dupe himself into the belief that slavery could be preserved by destruction of the Union. At best it could only exist under the protection of the Union. Yet he did not shrink from the final alternative. Disunion he saw as a threat rather than a program; but he was aware that for the threat to be effective in the eyes of the North, the South must be united.

3

Slavery was only a part of his program. He defended slavery, not only because he deemed it essential to the Southern way of life, but because the

ability of the South to maintain it against the will of the Northern numerical majority was a test case. Calhoun pitted states' rights against consolidation, because states' rights were the cornerstone of the federal system, and
only under a federal system could the true Union, and the South within it,
be preserved. Although he was aware of the need of a central government,
consolidation, with its unrestrained popular democracy and unrestrained
majority rule, held for him the same terror that it had held for the Founding
Fathers. And now: 'God knows we are tending too rapidly towards consolidation.' [10]

He staked his lines on the offensive. Not the South, which defended
only its constitutional rights, but the Northern abolitionists, were the
fomenters of disunion. To destroy the rights of the South was to destroy
the living spirit of the Union. Passionately Calhoun, all through the winters
of 1847, '48, and '49, pled with the Senate to face 'the magnitude of the
existing danger.' As early as ten years before, he had seen, 'clear as the
noonday sun, the fatal consequences which must follow if the present
disease be not . . . arrested. . . . This'—and he stressed his words—'is
the only question of sufficient magnitude . . . to divide this Union, and
divide it, it will, or drench the country in blood.' [11]

So intense was Calhoun's indignation at the abolitionist 'fanaticks' that
it even carried over into his social relations. He who, according to Wentworth, never 'did or said an uncivil thing,' now worked out an elaborate
code for dealing with men whose opinions would endanger the Union. If
one of them were to ask him a civil question, he would give him a civil
answer, but 'nothing more.' He would not himself start a conversation with
one. If an abolitionist offered him his hand, 'he should take it.' But he
would never offer his own hand. Wentworth himself, who during his ad-
vocacy of the Texas annexation had 'received a great many hearty shakes
from the hand of Mr. Calhoun,' now found that he 'received only those
shakes which I went after, knowing the terms.'

To the horror of Washington society, Calhoun's followers *en masse*
adopted the new code. Thus was added one more difficulty to the 'mixed'
parties of Northerners and Southerners, which had already developed
something of the atmosphere of a smouldering powder barrel. Calhoun himself indulged his whim with little offense, but not all his supporters had
'the culture and the refinement that the great South Carolinian had.' [12]

Nor had Calhoun patience with followers who became hardened to the
abolitionist assaults. When no rebuke was offered a bill seeking protection
for an abolitionist paper, Calhoun arose and wearily gave the 'word of
command.' This, he declared, was nothing more than 'a masked attack
upon the great institutions of the South, upon which not only its prosperity,
but its very existence depends.' He had hoped that the younger men might
'rise to the South's defense.'

There was pathos in his voice. It seemed 'as though the veteran sentinel had grown weary of his lonely watchtower.' Hastily Jefferson Davis assured the Senator from South Carolina that it was only 'from deference to him, who has so long . . . stood foremost in defense of the South,' that he had remained silent. He had only wished to follow 'the indignation which he has expressed so well.' [13]

4

Calhoun was not always left to fight his battles alone. Not even the law was safeguard for the Southerners now. Virtual 'nullification' by Massachusetts and other Northern states of the constitutional provisions for the return of fugitive slaves put the bitterness of the entire slaveholding South beyond measure. Even Calhoun's colleague, Andrew Butler, the seldom-speaking 'other Senator from South Carolina,' burst into a heated attack of retribution.

In his seat Daniel Webster stirred. A murmur rippled across the surface of the Chamber. The great domed forehead began to rise above the heads of the crowd.

'Webster's up, and he's mad,' was the message flashed by rumor telegraph all over the Capitol. The gallery began to fill. Webster stood awaiting his audience, head bowed and hands clasped behind his back. At last he spoke. He looked straight at Butler. 'If the honorable member shall . . . inform the Senate . . . on what occasion' Massachusetts 'has broken the compromises of the Constitution, he will find in me a COMBATANT on that question.'

It was the word 'combatant' that counted. He spoke it, Dyer declared, as if it weighed ten tons. And as he spoke, he lunged forward, his dark face aglow, his arms raised. And in that moment of outrage and passion, to one observer, he seemed only to show what 'a magnificent human being God's creative hand can fashion.'

Butler was getting up. He was muttering: 'I'll answer the gentleman; I'll answer the gentleman.'

Alarmed, Calhoun sprang to his friend's side. But it took all his strength and that of several other Senators to hold the enraged Butler in his seat. Slowly the Senate quieted. Only one man could handle Daniel Webster, and he turned to him now, uttering a few, soft-spoken sentences, with an air of almost childlike innocence, and yet with the most 'consummate skill.' [14] As if by sleight-of-hand, he turned the whole angry controversy into the closely reasoned, constitutional argument, in which he and Webster had engaged so many times before. So the Senator from Massachusetts believed that the Constitution had been respected? Did Webster deny that the Constitution extended to the territories? Was this an admission that if the Constitution *did* extend to the territories, the South would be protected?

Webster's attention shifted from Butler with a jerk. He had never made any such admission, he growled. The Constitution was 'the supreme law of the land.'

'Supreme law of the land?' repeated Calhoun. 'The territories of the United States are a part of the land.' Where our flag went, there went also the Constitution. How could we have any authority beyond the Constitution? 'Is not Congress the creature of the Constitution?' The territories were the property of the thirty-three states. 'The South asks no higher ground to stand upon.'

Cornered, Webster admitted that the 'fundamental principles' of the Constitution did apply to the territories. Nevertheless, he added, the Supreme Court had declared that the Constitution itself did not extend to the territories.

Calhoun feigned incredulity. If the Constitution did not extend to the territories, how, then, could Congress exercise any power over them, to prohibit slavery or to allow it?

'It is granted in the Constitution . . .,' gasped Webster, 'the power to make . . . laws for the territories.'

Calhoun was exultant. 'That proves the proposition false, that the Constitution does not extend to the Territories.' Where else could Congress have obtained the power to legislate for them, save from the Constitution itself? Would 'the Senator . . . with his profound talent' deny that the Constitution was the 'supreme law' of the territories? Would the Senator admit, for instance, that titles of nobility (specifically forbidden by the Constitution) could be granted in California?

Webster, irritated, declined to answer. The territories were not a part of the United States. 'Never.'

Calhoun's guard fell. 'I had supposed that all the territories were a part of the United States. . . . At all events,' he added hastily, 'they belong to the United States.'

Webster ended the duel in triumph. 'The colonies of England belong to England, but they are not a part of England,' he said.

Calhoun persisted. 'Whatever belongs to the United States they have authority over.' The extension of the Constitution to the territories, he insisted, would be a shield to the South.[15]

5

Calhoun had more ammunition in reserve than mere appeals for help in silencing abolitionist agitation. Convinced as he was that selfishness was the mainspring of human nature, his determination was reached. He would not rely on words alone. He would pit the North against itself, use the Northern businessman to checkmate the Northern abolitionist, thus compelling concessions that would never be made voluntarily.

Now would be the North's turn to 'calculate the value of the Union.' Who reaped the profits of the Union? The business leaders of the North. Who would lose if the Union were divided? The business leaders of the North. 'Strike out the products of slave labor—the great staples of cotton, rice, tobacco, and sugar—and what would become of the commerce, the shipping, the navigation . . . the manufactures of the North, and the revenue of the Government? What would become of the North's great commercial and manufacturing towns, and her vast tonnage and shipping, crowding every harbor and afloat on every sea?'

The North could deny the constitutional rights of the South. What if the South denied the constitutional rights of the North? Supposing, until justice were 'rendered the South,' all Southern ports and railway lines were closed to the North? Supposing the Northwestern states could be detached from the Northeastern by leaving open only those river and rail lines which connected West and South? Then the South could enjoy free trade, set her own price for cotton, corn, and tobacco, build ships to rival New England's in every port in the globe—and all at the North's expense! [16]

It was a bold scheme, an unworkable, impractical scheme. Most of all, it was an inflammatory scheme, and there were those who agreed with Benton that this was indeed the break-up of the Union. But it had no such meaning to Calhoun.

He knew that he had the power of mind—yes, and of emotion—to sway those men who sat before him. But what were they but representatives, after all? Of what use to convince their reasons and to leave unswayed their constituents' passions? Defeat would be only postponed. Laws passed would be only paper. Not Congress, but the people would decide the final issue.

What of the tariff, for instance? The tariff was not the issue of the day; it was not even foremost in Calhoun's own thoughts. On paper its battle had been won long ago, and yet how empty that victory was! Relief from tariff pressure had only intensified abolitionist agitation. Men, hungry for money and power, were not to be deterred by the mere lowering of a tariff. There were other ways—new states could be admitted, states safe for Northern interests, and the guarantee of such safety would be the exclusion of slavery.

They were all tangled together, the tariff, the territorial question, and outright abolition; and all were means to one end. Deliberately, Calhoun was convinced, the North had violated the constitutional compact for its own economic advantages—but would it be prepared to lose the South entirely? Nothing, he believed, would restrain it but the fear of lost profits —and he proposed to make that fear real. The North's 'unbounded avarice,' he contended, 'would . . . control them.'

Actually it was the threat which served his purpose. His strategy had been masterly. His appeals had been to the deepest instincts of every American group: to the patriots who hated slavery, but rallied to the defense of the Union; to the ambition of party leaders who by courting the abolitionists would lose the South; to the cupidity of business groups whose profits would be wrecked by a divided Union. With it all, he had backed up his threats by an increasingly united 'determination of the South to maintain her rights.'[16] The agitation, he knew, would not cease of itself.

Yet, masterly as his reasoning had been, it was flawed in its basic premise. Two could play at the same game. A united North could counter a united South. The more Calhoun stiffened the South's resistance, the more impressive his gains in legal concessions by force of threat and in defiance of public opinion, the more that opinion united against him. What he did not see was that even the Constitution had been a thing of compromises; and not even the Constitution could transcend the will of the people to uphold it.

6

He was working far in excess of his strength. By 1848, he was showing unmistakable signs of heart disease, but he refused to let down; as Nathaniel Willis commented: 'Mr. Calhoun lives in his mind; with no thought of the body.'[17] Early in the winter he contracted bronchitis and was in bed for weeks. His friends helped nurse him, and found him at once the most docile and the most exasperating of patients. Actually he was as little trouble as a sick man could be, for he feared only to make trouble, and would lie quietly all day, 'asking for nothing.' But he could not and would not shut off the working of his intellectual machine; and the doctor, Representative Abraham Venable of North Carolina, witnessed with grave concern 'the influence of his mighty mind over his weak physical structure.' Like 'a powerful steam engine on a frail bark, every revolution of the wheel tried its capacity for endurance to the utmost.' To those who watched at the Carolinian's bedside it seemed that he was literally 'thinking himself into the grave.'[18]

His burdens were indeed heavy. But boldly he faced the alternatives that confronted him. To him the preservation of the Union meant the preservation of the Constitution. 'I go to preserve the Union, but when I see that the . . . rights . . . of the South are to be sacrificed, I will . . . when I deem the case hopeless, move that the South rise and separate for their own safety.'[19]

Hopeless he would not yet deem the case. He had worked out a plan during those long weeks in bed; and at his call sixty-nine Southern Senators and Congressmen met in the Senate Chamber on the twenty-third of December, 1848. There a committee of fifteen was appointed, and from these a sub-committee with Calhoun at its head. To them Calhoun presented the first draft of his 'Address of the Southern Delegates in Congress to their Constituents.' Its object, he contended, was 'not to cause excitement, but to put you in full possession of all the facts necessary to a full . . . conception of a deep-seated disease, which threatens great danger to you. . . .'

Briefly, in terse, bitter, but restrained language, he repeated the old story of the rights and wrongs of the South. Once more he warned that if the North had the power to 'monopolize . . . the Territories,' she would soon have the majority power to 'emancipate our slaves under color of an amendment to the Constitution.' Then would the slaves be enfranchised to vote, and with these political allies, the dominance and subjection of the South would be completed.

Never had Calhoun's vision so pierced the mists of the future. In a flash of insight he had looked beyond the field of Appomattox, had seen 'consequences unparalleled in history,' the overthrow of the Southern whites, the slaves raised to power on the shoulders of Northern politicians. He saw the South in ruins, prostrate, poverty-stricken; for her subjugation, he knew, could come only at the climax of a 'bitter' conflict between the people of the two sections. He knew that the South would resist 'without looking to consequences.' [20]

History was to divide sharply as to the purpose of this tragic appeal. As usual with Calhoun's warnings, it was 'understood and appreciated by the masses,' but not by the politicians.[21] It was published throughout the South, but leaders stood off aghast; their aim being to avoid issues rather than to create them. Horace Mann spoke for the North: 'Many of the most intelligent men,' he wrote, 'believe Mr. Calhoun is resolved on a dissolution of the Union.' [22]

No act of Calhoun's career was to be more misunderstood, either by his own contemporaries, or by posterity, than his stand in this hour of decision. And only by realizing what was in his mind in the winter of 1848–49, is it possible to throw any light upon this 'obscure chapter in politics.' For Calhoun, 'in his very last stage . . . saw two things, neither of which are yet upon the broad page of history—that Southern nationalism was a real force, and that the only way to keep it from destroying the Union, was to organize it within the Union.' [23] Far from being the 'moving cause of excitement,' as many believed him to be, intimates like Beverly Tucker and Hammond well knew that for over twenty years his had been the power that had restrained the hotheads.[24] He had checked the 'Bluffton movement' in 1844. He had restrained the 'premature' demand for a Southern Convention that same year, hoping that the election of a Democratic President would provide a solution to Southern problems. Always his aim had been 'to turn the flank of the secessionists . . . to circumvent rather than to express' their aims.[25]

Concessions, he knew, must be made. But all his acts during these final months—his calls for unity through the Southern Address and a Southern Convention at Nashville; his dream of a 'dominion status' for the South, hinted at in his last speech, and indicated in the book he left behind him; his choice of a conservative and patriot as his successor, rather than a man who would make good his threats; the 'deepening agony' of his last days, when he seized frantically on any straw of hope—all give somber testimony to the one hope that had gripped him through a lifetime. Through 'love of the Union, he had tried every expedient, possible or impossible, rather than advise the South to resort to the plain remedy of secession.' To the last he would hope for the 'preservation of the Union upon the terms he had suggested.'[26]

Those who now taunted him as disunionist and party politician are scarcely above suspicion themselves. For not ten months later, these same men would be openly howling the inevitability of disunion. Southerners must 'stand by their arms'; must 'fight or submit'; these were the watchwords of the winter of 1850. That same Robert Toombs, the Georgian who condemned Calhoun as a traitor, would stand up in Congress not one year later openly declaring: 'I am a disunionist.' Even Alexander Stephens would add that he saw 'no hope to the South from the Union.'[27]

Circumstantial evidence, at least, would indicate that in both parties were die-hard radicals whose actual fear of Calhoun's plan was that *it might work*. The North *might* be brought to a halt; Southern secession *might* be averted. And knowingly or unknowingly, the Whig moderates would play right into the extremists' hands. By thwarting Calhoun's plans for Southern unity, they robbed the extremists of any justifiable hope that Southern rights might be preserved without secession.

Calhoun's Southern sub-committee met January 13, 1849. From the first, the Whig members balked; as they admitted later, they had taken part only that they might undermine the movement. It took all Calhoun's efforts, after hours of heated debate, to secure ratification of the Address by a single vote. Two days later, eighty Southerners gathered in the Senate Chamber behind closed doors, and all Washington seethed with excitement.

Calhoun's aims were not understood. A 'regular flareup' broke out, with Calhoun challenging the bull-necked, bushy-haired Whig leader Toombs, who flashed back that the union of the South meant only the break-up of the national Union. Another Whig taunted Calhoun with the desire to be President—a charge so ridiculous now that it could not even make him angry. 'The Presidency,' he said softly, 'is nothing.' But the evening closed in an uproar, with Whigs and even Democrats refusing to sign Calhoun's desperate appeal.[28]

Up to the White House the next day went Calhoun. He was overwrought, speaking in 'excited tones' of the Texas Representatives, declaring that they had 'betrayed the South.' But he received no sympathy from Mr. Polk, who let him understand 'distinctly' that he would give 'no countenance to any movement which tended to violence or disunion.' Congress was the place to settle disputes, not agitated mass meetings, with addresses to 'inflame the country.' To Polk it seemed wholly unjustifiable that with any reasonable prospect of peace by Congressional action, the Southerners should withhold their co-operation. Calhoun, he felt, was bent on forcing the issue and did not even 'desire that Congress should settle the question.' [29]

Polk was right; but what he could not see, and what the Whig group could not see, was that 'no Congressional settlement was possible.' Any kind of makeshift legislation would only be undone at the next session by the wrath and dictates of an aroused public opinion. Only the reversal of Northern public opinion could save the South now, and only an aroused and united South could frighten the North into such a reversal. Thus reasoned Calhoun. The Northern people must themselves will a settlement before any settlement could endure.

7

He alone could not force the reckoning. The strain of those tense weeks had exhausted his strength. On the morning of January 19, 1849, he arose, whipped up his waning energies with a cold bath, then walked to the Capitol. The morning was windy and raw. The hot, stagnant air of the Senate Chamber struck him like a blast furnace and his head spun. Dimly he saw Stephen A. Douglas approaching, with someone on his arm. Calhoun stood up, acknowledged the introduction, and collapsed at the Little Giant's feet.

He recovered in a moment. Fearful only of the concern his family would feel for him, he hurriedly wrote them, begging them not to believe the 'exaggerated' reports in the papers. A doctor had been summoned, had mumbled something about a 'want of tone in his system,' advised him to 'live more generously,' and to remain quiet. He now felt 'fully as well as usual.' [30]

Doggedly he determined to resume his seat the next day. Again he walked to the Capitol, but, faint and weak, he could not stay out the morning. For the next few days he was confined to his room.

The collapse of their leader struck terror into the hearts of the Southerners. Without his guiding hand their whole program was in danger. They reminded the public sternly that his illness was caused by his own friends, visiting him 'injudiciously,' keeping him up night after night far past twelve o'clock. In the columns of the Washington newspapers his agitated followers pled that the great Carolinian be given a chance to rest and recover; above all, that he be left alone.

For all his determination, Calhoun was too ill to attend the meeting on January 22, when his banner was trodden underfoot by the Southern Whigs. Courting friendship and unity with their fellow Whigs in the North, they were able to triumph: 'We have completely foiled Calhoun in his miserable attempt to form a Southern party.' The defeat did not come without a fight; there was 'not only warm but . . . red-hot debating.' But only two Whigs offered their signatures, and several prominent Democrats disclaimed any obligation to vote for the 'whittled-down . . . weak milk and water address,'[31] which was all the Whigs had left of Calhoun's appeal. Not yet would the South unite.

But Calhoun refused to surrender. Any device that would postpone the day of retribution, that would restrain the onward march of the North even momentarily, leaving hope for future action, he could support with his whole heart. 'We have done all we could to unite the South on some common ground,' he wrote. Against the 'whole weight' of the Southern Whigs, the entire Administration group, and the 'hacks' of the Democratic Party, 'it was doing much to get 49 signers.'[32]

On January 24, Calhoun was back in the Senate, looking 'ill and anxious.' He could neither rest nor sleep; he was 'worn out with anxiety.' A few days later he fainted again, and was carried into the Vice-President's office, where Rhett found him sitting on the sofa, his coat and waistcoat off. It was a raw cold day.

As Rhett entered, Calhoun held out his hand and said: 'Ah, Mr. Rhett, my career is nearly done. . . . The great battle must be fought by you younger men.'

'I hope not, sir,' Rhett answered quickly, 'for never was your life more precious, or your counsels more needed for the guidance and salvation of the South.'

Tears filled Calhoun's eyes and ran unheeded down his haggard cheeks. 'There indeed, is my only regret at going,' he said. 'The South—the poor South! God knows what will become of her!'

Rhett begged Calhoun to put on his clothes. He shook his head. 'I can't,' he said. 'I'm burning up. Wait until I'm cool.'[33]

He was burning himself out in the fire of his own intensity. His friends begged him to stay out of the Senate Chamber, and after a few days his health seemed to improve, but no one believed that he would ever be able to return to Washington for another session.

8

Then came word from Anna Maria. She was in New York, only able to remain in the country for a few weeks. She longed to see her father. And Calhoun braved the strenuous journey to New York City, where he had not been for years. His visit was all but secret; he had no energy for entertaining or for being entertained. But in answer to Anna Maria's plea for a picture of him to put in her locket, he accompanied her one cloudy March afternoon to the Fulton Street Gallery of Matthew Brady, who had already won national fame for his work in the new 'art' of photography.

Brady had photographed them all—the dying Jackson; the buoyant and freckled Clay; Webster, who had walked in upon him announcing pompously: 'I am here, Mr. Brady; I am here. Do with me as you will.' But none of his subjects had interested him more than Calhoun. He studied him as Anna Maria 'delicately' arranged his hair and cloak for the sitting; the square forehead, the deep, 'cavernous' eyes—'startling,' Brady found them; they 'almost hypnotized me.' He was struck by the Southerner's appearance of 'great age.' Calhoun was sixty-seven, but strain and illness had aged him years beyond that.

Calhoun talked while the equipment was being brought up, showing a knowledge of the scientific process of photography which amazed not only the onlookers but Brady himself. At last the intricate system of locks and clamps, in the cage where the poser had to place his head, was ready. Three shots were taken. The first was almost instantaneous; but in the second, the clouds had thickened above the skylight overhead, and Calhoun, obliged to stand motionless for several minutes, 'wearily remarked upon it.' The picture was a failure, and with some hesitation Brady asked the Senator if he would mind posing again. Calhoun glanced at Anna Maria, then very 'readily consented.' [34]

The results were startling. Only a trace of the Carolinian's youthful good looks now lingered. He was so thin that his high cheekbones almost pierced the skin, and his long hands were transparent. Here was the Calhoun the world has come to know: proud, defiant, unbroken, his cloak swept dramatically around him, the shaggy hair, which had resisted all Anna Maria's attempts to comb, hanging loose about his bent shoulders. Out of the portrait he gazes, his dark eyes burning across a century, on his face the look of a prophet, a tortured prophet who sees nothing in the future but the defeat of all that he fights for and holds dear.

9

Never had spring been more beautiful in South Carolina. And never, even in youth, had Calhoun's senses responded more eagerly. The young bloom of the jessamine and dogwood, the forest, 'just clo[th]ing itself with green,' the contrast between 'being pent up in a boarding house in Washington and breathing the pure fresh air of the country . . . made fragrant by the blossoms of Spring,' [35] was almost more than he could bear.

The cycle of the seasons circled around him. With his farmer's eye he gauged the progress of his crops. The weather generally had been too cold and wet for cotton, but his looked well; in fact, with his hillside drains and curving rows, was 'really handsome.' Even the 'old field' past the barn was green as a meadow. Beyond, far as the eye could see, stretched a hundred and twenty-five acres of oats, one single 'unbroken mass of green.' The 'big bottom' opposite was covered with 'a superb crop of corn'; and farther still rose Fort Hill, the harvested wheat, 'standing in shocks. . . . Everything,' he wrote Anna Maria, 'looks beautiful.' [36]

A visiting reporter was left breathless by the rigors of Calhoun's schedule: rising at four or five o'clock, a long ride over the plantation, letter-writing until breakfast, and then work in the office until one or two in the afternoon. He was driving himself as hard as in his youth, and the expenditure of physical energy alone would have put a young and robust man to shame. He took all necessary care of himself, he assured Anna Maria, 'except being rather more overtasked than I could wish.' To Clemson, he confessed: 'I walk three or four miles every day; and write 6 or 7 hours on an average.' [37] He was drawing recklessly on his last reserves in order to finish the tasks before him. Too keyed up for sleep, night after night, as in the nullification days, he walked the hallways of Fort Hill, relentless thoughts hammering at his overactive brain.

He paid for this feverish energy with days of complete reaction when he was too weak to leave his room or for Floride to permit anyone to see him but his closest friends. Grimly he would not even admit that he was ill. 'There is no foundation in the report to which you alude,' he coldly wrote a friend, his shaky handwriting so hair-fine and delicate that the strokes scarcely marked the paper. 'My health is as good as usual.' [38]

10

The time had come for the last mighty drive to unite the South. Hour after hour the leader sat in his office, mapping strategy. Never again would his enemies dare charge that all his efforts were mere devices to hoist himself into the Presidency. Not even those at the ends of his strings dreamed that his was the master hand that was pulling them. Even the ostensible leader of the cause, Henry J. Foote of Mississippi, believed that the whole idea of a Southern Convention had originated in his own brain. It was the sovereign state of Mississippi that had answered to the South's cry for joint action, not 'South Carolina, or her statesmen,' so Foote happily believed. Not until two years later did he discover that far from Calhoun having written only to him on the subject, the old South Carolinian's correspondence had been 'pretty extensive'; and indeed that the whole

CALHOUN IN HIS LAST YEARS
From a daguerreotype by Matthew Brady, in the National Archives

framework of the Convention had been 'more or less' worked out 'by his great intellect.' As Sam Houston dryly observed, if 'South Carolina had never existed, Mississippi would never have thought of it.' [39]

It was in answer to newly aroused Southern sentiment that Calhoun had set the wheels of a convention in motion. As early as 1837 he had thought a Southern Convention indispensable as a means of impressing the North; [40] by 1848 he was advocating it again. The collapse of the Southern Address movement had only strengthened his conviction. The time had come. The leaders had failed to speak. No matter. The North would be far more stirred by a movement straight from the angered masses of the South than by any political address.

Only an 'unbroken front could repel Northern aggressions.' The Convention would 'discharge a great duty we owe our partners in the Union . . . to warn them . . . that if they do not . . . cease to disregard our rights . . . the duty we owe to ourselves and to our posterity would compel us to dissolve the partnership.' [41]

Calhoun had gauged public sentiment far more closely than his Senatorial opponents had done. Legislature after Legislature—Virginia, Florida, Missouri, North Carolina—passed resolutions in defiance of the Wilmot Proviso. Virginia laid the groundwork for a special session should the Proviso be passed. Democrats swept the elections in Georgia and Alabama. In accordance with a plan, privately suggested by Calhoun, delegates from the districts and parishes of South Carolina met in Columbia on May 14, 1849, and appointed a central committee of 'Vigilance and Safety' to co-operate with similar committees in other Southern states should the need arise.

Though ostensibly Mississippi took the lead, it was almost in Calhoun's words that in the fall of 1849 the call for the Convention was issued. The place chosen was Nashville, Tennessee; the date, June, 1850. Calhoun was jubilant. The Convention would be 'the most important movement that has yet been made . . . it may still be hoped,' he wrote Mathews, 'that the Union will be saved.' [42] The South was stirring from its long sleep; it would never relax again.

But not even this great task absorbed Calhoun's energies. 'All the time left me,' he wrote Anna Maria, was devoted to the completion of his book on the 'Science of Government,' which he had started in 1842, but had been compelled to lay aside. He 'ought not to delay . . . any longer.' [43]

Like all authors, Calhoun longed for some appreciation of his efforts, perhaps for the audience that he sensed he would not live to see. Chafing against the intellectual solitude which had enclosed him for years, his thoughts turned to one of whom he had truly said: 'It is a satisfaction to come into contact with a man of intellect who understands you.' Daniel Webster would see the point of his arguments; he would be 'sure to admit their force. . . . Better send him a manuscript copy,' he told his secretary, Joseph Scoville. Webster would not dispute his findings. 'Webster has sense. He has never attempted to answer any argument of mine.' [44]

Family affairs pressed in for his attention. Clemson, as usual, was relieving his own burdens by laying them upon Calhoun; and the older man, as usual, accepted them without complaint. He made his customary summer survey of Clemson's deserted plantation, listened to the younger man's continual whine that he longed to be 'done with Southern property,' and resisted pressure for a quick sale or rental of the hapless Negroes.[45] This was routine, but by midsummer Calhoun's peace was shattered once more, as in the past, by a bitter money quarrel between his son Andrew and Clemson. What made matters worse, the year before Floride had turned on her own son.

'I regret it,' Calhoun had written, 'I regret it profoundly.' [46] He loved Andrew; whatever he had done, he was his own flesh and blood. And he also loved Clemson for Anna Maria's sake. Silently he bowed his head to his son-in-law's charge that he was trying to 'protect' his son, expressed gratitude for gifts of 'excellent' imported wine and brandy, and no rebuke for Clemson's slurs against his 'way of doing business.' Without reproof, even to Andrew, Calhoun shouldered the burden, mortgaged Fort Hill more heavily, and pledged his crop against his son-in-law's losses. 'You cannot be more anxious to have what is due you,' he wrote, 'than we are to pay it.' [47]

11

Slowly the seasons turned. Autumn burned across the hills; leaves fell one by one from the oak trees like drops of sunlight. It had been a damp summer; 'dust never rose on the place from . . . April to August,' [48] Calhoun had written. Yet all the South had flowered into life. Not in ten years had there been a richer harvest.

Once more Calhoun stood by to superintend the gathering of his crop. His loving care of the land, 'manuring and good cultivation,' as he explained to Clemson, had reaped a rich reward. He could take pride in a corn field tilled and plowed for fifty years and now yielding up its three thousand bushels. The wet lowlands he had planted in rice, and gathered one hundred and thirty bushels. Sixty bales of cotton had been picked from one hundred and thirteen acres.

Despite his financial burdens, he could leave home with an easy heart. He had a 'first-rate' overseer, 'who takes as much interest as I do in everything about the place.' [49] His work was over. So now he stood in the light-glow of late October, for the last time watching the cotton wagons roll out of sight around the curve.

There was the smell of dead leaves and of brush fires and of pine needles

warmed in the sun. The flaming sunset dimmed. Wild ducks massed in
formation, beating their way across a colorless sky.

The long summer was over.

12

He was 'very comfortably quartered,' Calhoun wrote his family from
Washington in November, 1849, 'at Hill's boarding house,' where he had
stayed several times before. His large and airy room was on the ground
floor, with Armistead Burt within calling distance next door. Hill's itself
was a grim and comfortless-looking structure, three stories high with a
front chimney on either side and a long ell at the back. But it awakened
memories in Calhoun. Already its brick walls were steeped in history,
for it was here that Congress had crowded in during those grim days of
1814, after the burning of Washington. Here, too, within a few years
Southern men would lie in chains, for the 'Old Capitol' was to become
'Old Capitòl Prison' of Civil War days. And there at last would rise a
temple to freedom, for it was upon this site that the white marble building
of the Supreme Court was one day to stand.

Its location, 'the most protected and best in Washington,' was what
pleased Calhoun. Only a block distant rose the steps of the Capitol. This
meant much to a man who knew so well 'the bleakness of the walk' up
the hill in windy weather, the danger of getting overheated in the heavy
clothing of the Washington winter, and of 'cooling off too suddenly,' upon
entering the Senate Chamber.[50]

Much of the time he was unable to leave his room. He toiled feverishly
in an effort to see his book—his life-work—finished at last. To Anna
Maria he expressed regret for not writing her 'as frequently as formerly.
. . . Be assured that it has not been caused by any abatement of affection
towards you. It is . . . simply . . . that I have been overburthened with
writing . . . labor, which you know, I have ever been especially averse
to.' His personal correspondence, she knew, included nine people in his
own family. In addition, he had written during the summer 'between 400
and 500 pages of foolscap,' and now was devoting most of his 'spare time'
to preparing the book for the press. The 'discourse, or disquisition'—he
had not yet named it—was already being copied. The discourse on the
Constitution was 'much more voluminous,' but the 'rough draft' was
finished. If only he could get it done before Congress adjourned . . .[51]

Occasionally he fell into reminiscence. Burt, who admired him greatly,
both as man and leader, was a sympathetic listener. And once, when the
two were alone, in a rare moment of self-revelation, Calhoun unburdened
himself of a memory that had haunted him for forty-odd years. He spoke
of his youth, of his law-circuit days, and of a girl in an old tavern at a
cross-roads.[52]

13

The Senate Chamber, too, was showing signs of the years. There were the same two stoves, rusty and steaming with their load of hickory wood, the same foul air, too stagnant even to heat, the streams of tobacco juice trickling across the floor. Men sat shivering, with their hats on and blankets pinned at their throats. Others reeled in, warm and half-drunk, from the notorious 'Hole-in-the-Wall,' which was in the Capitol, itself.

On the few days he was able to drag himself to the Senate at all, Calhoun's eyes searched the faces around him. There was a fever, an exhilaration in the air, that he had known before. But never, even in 1812, had it been like this. New faces and new names now: Mississippi's violent young Foote, the 'Free Soil' Senators, Chase of Ohio and the caustic Seward of New York, Douglas of Illinois and Bell of Tennessee—and yet the tense look on their young faces was one Calhoun would have recognized instantly. These, too, like the War Hawks of 1812, were men who had grown up on the edge of danger. War talk had been free then; it was pent-up now, but all the more terrible for that. Once that same excitement had quivered through his own nerves; now he knew only despair. For now the enemy was not an instrument of unity but of destruction; not from without but from within the Union's own borders.

Around him, too, were the men with whom he had shared his life, his despairs and his exaltations, men whom he had alternately fought and loved. There sat Benton, dropping his eyes before Calhoun's gaze, Houston, in his Indian blanket and moccasins, he who had reigned as King in Texas, now whittling time away with slow sharp strokes of his knife. Nothing could rouse him from his lethargy but the appearance of a woman, preferably Varina Davis, to whom he would rise, bow, and greet with his fervid 'Lady, I salute you.' Later he would draw from his pouch one of the little wooden hearts he carved, and hand it over with a flourish: 'Lady, let me give you my heart.' [53]

Webster sat nearby, chin sunk in his collar, his thin hair hanging limp over his great head, the deep eyes seldom flashing now, but burning with a 'steady, awful glow.' And there, in all his old pride of command, aquiver with eagerness, sat that 'same old coon,' Henry Clay. [54]

For Henry Clay was back, and not even the drama of his departure could match the drama of his return. He was seventy-three, only recently recovered from injuries suffered in a stagecoach accident, but his slender body was still erect, and 'about the corners of his capacious mouth . . . the bewitching smile' of his youth still played. [55] He was white-haired now; thirty-eight years had passed since the blithe, buoyant 'cock of Kentucky' had sounded the trumpet call for the Second American Revolution, but he was Henry Clay still, born to lead and to command. He had come back to save his country, and aflame with this purpose, old age had dropped from him like a cloak.

In the rough-and-tumble of Senate debate, men marveled to see how little Clay had lost of his old power. He was still at his best when flashing taunts, such as his gibe at Calhoun, who in a misguided moment had proclaimed that 'a mysterious Providence had brought the blacks and whites together for their mutual betterment.' Clay wasted no words on his response. 'To call a generation of slave-trading pirates a mysterious Providence,' he declared, 'was an insult to the Supreme Being.' [56]

Old as he was, Clay's eye had not ceased to rove. It paused upon Amelia Burt, the pretty twenty-year-old niece of Calhoun, who accompanied her uncle to Congress mornings and sat beside him on a hassock. One evening Clay dropped in at Mrs. Hill's. The corridor was dark, but he found Amelia and reacted instantly, according to instinct and habit. Breaking free, she burst into the sitting room. 'Oh,' she exclaimed, 'I have been kissed by the great Mr. Clay!'

The great Mr. Calhoun failed to share her enthusiasm. He laid down his paper. He shook his finger at her. 'Amelia,' he warned, 'don't you put your trust in that old man.'

Party bickerings had lost all interest for the old Kentuckian. Bitterly he snapped at a group of Boston business leaders: 'Don't talk to me about the tariff . . . when it is doubtful if we have any country . . . lay aside your sectional jealousies . . . cease exasperating the South . . . cultivate a spirit of peace. Save your country, and then talk about your tariff.'

At dinner one night he sank into a silence so heavy that a friend said: 'Mr. Clay . . . are you angry at everybody?'

'That is just it,' Clay replied. 'Here is our country upon the very verge of a Civil War which everyone pretends to be anxious to avoid, yet everyone wants his own way, irrespective of the . . . wishes of others.' At that very dinner table, he declared, were enough variations of opinion to settle the whole question. 'Come, gentlemen . . . let me lock you all in, and I remaining outside, will . . . present any plan of concert that you may agree upon to the Senate and advocate it. . . .' [57]

14

Next to the advent of Clay himself, Calhoun's return to the capital that winter had stirred the most sympathy and interest on the part of the citizenry. And they were shocked at his appearance; 'he was so pale and thin,' one observer wrote, that 'he looked like a fugitive from the grave.' [58]

Weak though he was, he sat 'bolt upright,' as always, resting his arms on the arms of his chair.[59] He was literally taut with concern. He had been ill almost from the day of his arrival in Washington; his condition was aggravated by the fever of his mind, for all—the worst that he had prophesied and feared—was thundering down upon the country with 'fearful disaster.'

The cords of the Union were frayed and breaking. It took seventeen days for the House to elect a Speaker. Thundering at the door of Congress were petitions for the freedom of the territories, for the abolition of slavery, for 'the dissolution of the Union' itself. Petitions from the North, not the South. And if the Southern Bob Toombs, black hair bristling, words rapping like machine-gun fire, could shout in the frenzy of debate, 'I am for disunion,' it was the Northern abolitionist, Wendell Phillips, who could coolly write: 'We are disunionists.' [60]

Out of the whirlwind and the frothings the true issues loomed. President Taylor's annual message was read; openly it advocated a return to 'that old odious system of monopoly which has been so effectively put down by the people.' By December 23, the Washington *Daily Union* was quoting the 'merchant princes' of Boston in denunciation of low tariff rates as 'monstrous to manufacturers.' The farmer, bitterly declared the *Union*, would be satisfied, but 'notwithstanding . . . exorbitant profits,' the Whig businessmen were 'clamoring for more protection.' [61]

Now, at last, the South understood what Calhoun had been telling them all these years. His 'fondest hope' that party lines would be erased in common action against a common danger seemed 'about to be realized.'

'The South is aroused to dissolve the Union immediately,' declared the Columbia *Telegraph*. 'The two great political parties have ceased to exist in the South . . . so far as slavery is concerned,' proclaimed the Richmond *Enquirer*. 'With united voices they proclaim . . . the preservation of the Union if we can, the preservation of our own rights if we cannot.' 'We are afraid,' added the Richmond *Republican*, a Whig organ, that 'these men will find the South in earnest when it is too late.' [62]

It was the former conservatives who now seemed most aroused. Even little Alexander Stephens now admitted: 'I see . . . no hope to the South from the Union.' [63] The time for words and resolutions was over. The time for uniforms and gunpowder had arrived.

15

'The Southern members are more determined and bold than I ever saw them. Many avow themselves to be disunionists,' [64] sadly wrote Calhoun on the twelfth of January, 1850. That he had united the South in defiance of submission was somber comfort to him in the face of the dying Union. Who would reap the whirlwind he had sown? Had he trained his followers too well? Would men, trained to think of secession only as a threat, by the same relentless process of reasoning that he had outlined seize upon it as an end in itself? Had he, in his desperate struggle to save the Union, wrought the weapon, not for its preservation, but for its destruction?

And the North—the unification of the South had not persuaded it to moderation, as Calhoun had thought that it would do. Force had bred force; fire was answered with fire. 'The North shows no disposition to desist from aggressions' was Calhoun's weary admission. 'They now . . . claim the right to abolish slavery in all the old States, that is those who were originally members when the Constitution was adopted.' [65] Disunion or submission—he had named the alternatives, but he could not face them. If only he could hold out until June, when the Southern Convention would assemble!

Friends who visited Calhoun in his room saw plainly that he was 'a broken down man.' Sick and despondent, tortured with forebodings, his 'mind was as luminous as ever,' and his spirit that 'of a patriot.' [66] Intimates heard him 'breathe out' the love for the Union that his pride forbade him to display before those who called him traitor and secessionist. He could write, 'disunion is the only alternative'; [67] yet bowed under the weight of what he thought was his personal responsibility, he could not give the word of command.

The problem was to be solved for him. From his sick-room, he heard of the winter-night meeting of Clay and Webster. Clay would offer 'what he calls a compromise.' [68] Calhoun had no hope of it; a compromise now would be nothing. And even had he been so mistaken as to think otherwise, Stephen A. Douglas's ill-fated amendment of the session of 1849, seeking to extend the Missouri Compromise line to the Pacific, would provide evidence enough. Supported by both Davis and Calhoun, the resolution had passed the Senate. But the storm of outraged letters, telegrams, and petitions flooding in from the North frightened the House into beating the measure down. Could not men understand that it was not Congress, but public opinion, that ruled America?

16

Wrapped in flannels and looking weak and ill,[69] Calhoun was in his seat on the raw January day on which the old Kentuckian dragged himself up the steps of the Capitol, murmuring: 'our country is in danger, and if I can be the means of saving her, my health or my life is of little consequence.' [70] And no one who saw or heard could have been unmoved, as drawing his frail figure erect, summoning every last resource of his strength and eloquence, Clay proudly proclaimed: 'This Union is my country; the thirty states are my country; Kentucky is my country . . . if my own State should raise the standard of disunion, I would go against her . . . much as I love her.' [71]

Probably Clay's specific proposals were as distasteful to himself as they were to Calhoun; yet he pressed them with the desperation of the patriot who saw no other way open. He threw sops to both sides; for the North, a free California, an established western boundary line for Texas, squatter sovereignty in New Mexico and Utah, and the abolition of the slave-trade in the District of Columbia; for the South, an ironclad fugitive slave law, unrestricted slave-trade between the Southern states, and a guarantee that slavery would never be abolished in the District of Columbia without the consent of Maryland. Upon a foundation of existing realities and mutual concessions, the compromise was wrought; but could not Clay see that each burning question was a mere symptom of the disease which ravaged the country? And without detecting and removing the cause, would not a more virulent attack break out again within five or ten years?

Nevertheless, Clay won. Probably Calhoun did not realize it at first; he was taken severely ill a day or two after the address, and when he rallied, weeks later, the damage was done. To the Democrats, who shrank from Calhoun's forcing of the issue, Clay's moderation offered an honorable alternative. Furthermore, his way out was nothing short of ideal to the Whig extremists like Toombs; for in Calhoun's plans for a constitutional settlement, the fire-eaters feared that there might actually be a settlement, and their dreams of Southern empire would be shattered. Under the cover of compromise, they would have time to work on the waverers, to unite the whole South for secession and a Southern Confederacy.

They were wrong. Statistical matters about which no gentleman concerned himself were against them. Ten years later would be ten years too late. Only Calhoun had understood 'If the South is to be saved, now is the time.' [72] Meanwhile, in the name of patriotism, Clay had divided the South and ended the last possibility of a successful united stand against Northern domination.

17

The time had come for Calhoun to choose his successor. And his choice was not the fiery Rhett, but Jefferson Davis of Mississippi. This is not surprising, for the 'man who looked like Calhoun' was like him, enough so to be of his own flesh and blood. Gaunt, bushy-browed, clear-eyed, Calhoun and Davis resembled each other, not only in appearance, but in character, nerves, temperament, and intensity of purpose. Both were planter-scholars, men to whom the life of the intellect was more rich and meaningful than the exterior world could ever be. Both agreed on basic values in living, the agrarian values, without which, Jefferson had said, no civilization could be healthy. They knew one kind of life and from it drew their strength and philosophy; knew it to be worth living for and fighting for.

They had been friends since Calhoun's War Secretary days; intimates, since Davis's entry into the Senate. No man so won Davis's admiration as Calhoun. Like William Rutherford, Jr., Davis saw his 'beau ideal' of a statesman in the man who, 'with a disease that was rapidly carrying him to the grave,' had rejected all appeals to 'remain quietly at home' and returned to the Capitol to 'renew his labors in defense of the Constitution and the preservation of the Union.' [73] It was Davis who shared Calhoun's questioning and struggles during those dark days; and never had Calhoun found a more willing listener.

Calhoun's own affections warmed to the younger man. All over America the Mississippian had been cheered as a popular hero since that day at Buena Vista, when, with his foot shattered and his boot filling with blood, he had clung to his saddle and rallied his men to victory. But even more than his physical courage, Calhoun admired Davis's integrity and independence, and the fortitude that drove him on through days and nights of grueling legislative work, although in continual ill-health and almost never free from pain.

But the qualities that were virtues in Calhoun were intensified into vices in Jefferson Davis. Calhoun's sensitivity was Davis's nervous irritability; the 'iron will' of the South Carolinian, in Davis was sheer stubbornness. With all his master's overwhelming confidence in the powers of his intellect, Davis lacked the intellect which would have warranted the confidence. The time that Calhoun had put into thought, Davis put into books. Hence, his accumulation of facts was great, but once that was exhausted, he had small powers of abstract reasoning to fall back upon; and as his biographer points out, his study seemed only to give him a knowledge of results, without comprehension of how the results had been achieved.[74] Thus, he could deny nullification and yet accept states' rights, which had sprung from the same premises; where Calhoun's political philosophy was rooted in a grimly realistic understanding of cause and effect, Davis's was only doctrinaire.

Of human nature, too, Davis had less understanding than Calhoun. Proud and touchy, he seemed cold where Calhoun was merely grave. Davis had none of Calhoun's ingenuous ability to cloak abstractions in the guise of simple truths; nor had he Calhoun's uncanny power for winning men's intellects through their emotions. He could not control men who differed from him; he sought to bend them to his will. He could not delegate authority, nor conciliate and rally men of diverse opinion, as Calhoun had done, drawing from each the strength that would suit his own central purpose. Davis was no creator of causes; he could only lead the cause ready-made. He was a man temperamentally and idealistically akin to Calhoun, but the difference between them was the difference between talent and genius.

In selecting Davis, instead of Rhett, as his successor, Calhoun's emotions had betrayed him into a tragic mistake. With the South united at last in recognition of its danger, the need was for a leader who realized, as Calhoun did, that now was the time 'to force the issue upon the North.' Rhett understood this perfectly. But Davis was not only chained by Calhoun's own emotional affection for the Union, but lacked the relentless foresight of the older man. Davis, though disclaiming all patchwork compromise measures, would fail to join Rhett in rallying the South to a stand at Nashville the following summer. He would waste the next ten years in holding off disunionist sentiment in the South and in futile attempts to find constitutional means of hampering the strength of the North.

18

The report was current in Washington through February, 1850, that Calhoun himself would answer Clay, would rally his strength in a last plea for the Constitution above compromise, for the South's safety within the Union. But few believed it. He appeared in the Senate occasionally, 'looking pale and ghastly,' the newsmen observed, 'and ought not soon to venture upon a speech.' Most of the time he was in bed, 'too weak even to hold a pen.'[75] Yet the report persisted. He had dictated his speech; he would deliver it on March fourth.

News that the great Carolinian would rise, almost from his deathbed, to voice his last warnings against the self-destruction of the American Union, 'early crowded the galleries and even the floor of the Senate' with 'a brilliant and expectant audience.' Long before convening time at noon, all exits were blocked. Nearly every Senate seat was occupied by 'a representative of the fairer . . . portion of humanity,' as the New York *Tribune* correspondent noted, and it was necessary to take a vote to legalize their presence. The crowd was 'smaller than when Clay spoke,' but it was 'nevertheless very dense.'[76]

A hush rested over the throng. Voices sunk into whispers; faces were tense with anxiety. Again and again eyes turned to the empty seat between James Whitcomb of Indiana and Jefferson Davis—Calhoun's chair.[77] At last there was a stir at the door. The crowd parted. Leaning upon the arm of his friend, James Hamilton, Calhoun entered the Chamber with slow, dragging steps and sank into his seat, his head bent, white hands clenching the arms of his chair. In the gallery sat men and women who could remember him when he had first walked into the House in October, 1811, dark-haired and erect, and tears now filled their eyes.

Now he was almost too weak to stand alone. It was some minutes before he was able to drag himself to his feet.[78] For a moment he stood, glancing proudly about the Chamber where he had ruled for so long. Once more the familiar faces rose before him. At last he spoke. He thanked the Senate for the 'very courteous way in which they have permitted me to be heard today,'[79] then passed a manuscript over to Senator James Mason of Virginia.

The speaker arose. Wind was blowing through an open window. Against the silence, Mason's voice rang out the somber words of Calhoun's dying message, while at his side its author sat 'like a disembodied spirit,' a long, black cloak wrapped about his emaciated form, his head unwaveringly erect, his rugged features as white and motionless as if sculptured in marble.[80]

It was like a great funeral ceremony with the corpse sitting by. For death was written on Calhoun's face and there were those who feared that its shadow was hanging too over the Senate of the United States, the South, and the whole country.[81]

In those last words, in the tragic summary of Calhoun's lifelong hopes and fears, there was neither passion nor abuse; no threats, no anger. His words were muted, 'curiously gentle,' and yet somehow all the more terrible for that. They held the hopelessness of despair. He had nothing to say except what he had said so many times before, but now for the first time the Senate could listen and understand. Was it only fourteen months since Toombs had dismissed Calhoun's warnings and calls for a united South as a mere 'miserable attempt' to form a Southern party, eventuating in a wrecked Union and a Southern Confederacy, with John C. Calhoun at its head? Was it only last June that the Whig, Humphrey Cobb, indignant at Calhoun's attempts to unite the South in the Democratic Party, had dismissed the South Carolinian as 'our evil genius,' warning that 'unless he is stopt . . . we shall be overwhelmed in the fall elections'? Elections! Party labels! What did they matter?[82] Now at last, and too late, the South could take Calhoun's words at their face value, and understand the somber truth of what he had been trying to tell them all along.

Now, at last, no one doubted his sincerity. No human yearnings could longer torment that spectral figure, that 'ghost with burning eyes.' With nothing but the grave before him, he had surrendered none of his convictions, 'yielded not an inch of his creed.'

Now, for the first time, Northerners and Southerners knew that Calhoun had spoken the truth when he had bitterly declared that he who warned of danger was not the creator of that danger. If it were true that his insistence that the South assert her 'rights' had aroused an equal determination on the part of the North, it was also true that he had neither created slavery nor the South's adherence to slavery; that in the hands of a more passionate man, slavery might well have bred a civil war years before. He had failed because no one man can accomplish the impossible. The most ironclad constitutional theorizing cannot hold in check the onrush of economic progress and ambition, especially when such ambition is drenched in moral idealism. Had his patriotism been more narrow, had he ruthlessly endeavored to preserve the South against the Union, or the Union against the South, he might have won. But in looking to all, he had lost all. The Union was lost and the South would rally, neither to save it nor to save herself. It was no consolation to him that now even his enemies could agree that he had 'clearly vindicated himself from the charge that he desired disunion.' [83] This was no traitor, tearing his country apart to feed his vanity, but a broken-hearted patriot.

His first words struck the keynote of despair. 'I have . . . believed from the first that the agitation of slavery would, if not prevented . . . end in disunion.' What had endangered the Union? 'The immediate cause is the almost universal discontent' of the South, 'the belief of the people that they cannot remain . . . in the Union.' What was the 'great and primary cause? . . . The equilibrium between the two sections, as it stood when the Constitution was ratified,' had been destroyed. Once each section had had the means to protect itself against 'the aggressions of the other . . . now . . . one section has the exclusive power of controlling the Government,' and the other no means of protection.

Had this destruction been the operation of time, the South would not have complained. But it was the work of government, 'of the common agent of all . . . charged with the protection . . . of all.' From the Ordinance of 1787 to the Missouri Compromise, and now in the Oregon and Mexican territories, the South had been deliberately excluded from the lands belonging to all. Tariff revenues, drawn from Southern funds, had put 'hundreds of millions of dollars' into the pockets of Northern industrialists. New industries were daily springing into birth; had Southern funds been spent in the section from which they were drawn, the South, too, could have won immigrants, have increased her population, and maintained her numerical superiority.

Finally, the government's own actions had concentrated 'all the powers of the system into itself.' The process had commenced 'at an early period of the Government; and proceeded until it absorbed virtually its entire powers. . . . The Government claims . . . the right to decide . . . as to the extent of its power . . . it also claims the right to resort to force to maintain . . . power. . . . What limitation can possibly be placed upon the powers of a government claiming and exercising such rights?' How could the states maintain the powers which the Constitution had reserved to them? From a Federal Republic in actual practice the government had been changed 'into a great national consolidated democracy . . . as despotic in its tendency as any absolute Government that ever existed.'

The Northern states were in ascendancy over every department of the government. The Southern states had no means by which they could resist. Yet this might be tolerated were it not for the great diversity of economic interests which separated the two peoples.

The whole North, declared Calhoun, was against slavery. The most extreme condemned it as mortal sin. The least regarded it as a 'stain' on the national character. But to the South the institution was basic. The relationship between the two races was entangled with the entire social organization. If destroyed, it would subject the two peoples to the greatest calamity, and the entire section 'to poverty and wretchedness.'

Slowly, step by step, he outlined the rise of slavery agitation: the growth of the abolitionist societies; the wooing of the two great political parties, making concession after concession to abolitionist demands in their eagerness for power; the state laws which openly nullified the fugitive slave provisions; and finally, the movement to exclude slavery and the South from every new territory to be added to the Union.

Only one more step remained. That was the emancipation of the black race in the Southern states. Already the South was confronted with the single question: abolition or secession. But secession was not necessary to tear the Union apart. Already the work of destruction was under way. The cords of faith and fellowship and plighted troth, which the people of the States had woven together for their 'general welfare,' for the creation of one Union, were snapping one after another. Soon the 'whole fabric' would fall asunder. Already the spiritual ties were broken: the great church fellowships—the Methodists, the Baptists, the Presbyterians—met in fellowship no more. North and South, the great faiths had divided; only the Episcopalians remained united.

Now the political parties were splitting off into sectionalism, Calhoun pointed out, ignoring his own efforts to bring about that particular situation. Soon every cord of the Union would be snapped—but the bond of force itself. But what true union was the union of force? Only a union of free, independent and sovereign states was worthy of the sacred name.

How could the Union be saved? Not by eulogies. Southern assailants could cry out the name of the Union, but if they 'loved the Union, they would be devoted to the Constitution. It made the Union—and to destroy the Constitution would be to destroy the Union.' A true lover of the Constitution would neither violate it nor permit others to do so.

Nor could it be saved by eulogies on 'that illustrious Southerner whose mortal remains repose on the western bank of the Potomac.' He was one of us, 'a slaveholder and a planter.' He was devoted to the union with England, not as an end, but 'as a means to an end. When it was converted into the means of oppression, he headed the movement of resistance. . . . I trust . . . we have profited by his example.'

The South had no compromise to offer, no platform but the Constitution.

Could the Union be saved? 'Yes, easily. The North has only to will it to achieve it.' She must concede the South equal rights in the new territories. She must give up the fugitive slaves—and cease the 'agitation of the slave question.' Furthermore, she must concur in a constitutional amendment, restoring 'the original equilibrium between the two sections.' He knew that the North would not 'will it,' and that to the necessary amendments she would never concur.* But he had no more to offer. The South had no more to offer. 'The South asks for justice, simple justice, and less she ought not to take.' If the North would not agree to a settlement, let her say so, and the states could 'part in peace.' If she would not permit secession, 'tell us so, and we shall know what to do,' when faced with the alternatives of 'submission or resistance.' As for himself, he had, at least, the comfort of knowing that come what might, he was free from all personal responsibility.[84]

* Even Daniel Webster recognized the strength of Calhoun's position. Speaking in Washington on July 4, 1851, Webster warned that if the Northern states refused, 'wilfully and deliberately,' to obey the fugitive slave provisions of the Constitution, 'the South would no longer be bound to observe the compact.' (In 1833, Webster had vehemently denied that the Constitution was a compact.) 'A bargain cannot be broken on one side, and still bind the other side.' Curtis, *Webster*, II, p. 519.

XXIX

When Rome Survived

CALHOUN HAD SPOKEN for posterity. It was for later generations to acclaim his speech as the most powerful warning delivered by a Southern leader before the Civil War. Only that war itself, history's proof of his prophecies, would lift the curtain on meanings that baffled even his Southern listeners at the time. His words would not be forgotten. The time would come when they would be remembered with terror and shrinking, but their meaning was not then understood.

None doubted the terrible sincerity of this dying message; none but felt a cold chill of fear at that spectral figure before them. 'Impressive as were his words,' Nathan Sargent commented, 'his own appearance was infinitely more so.' [1] None doubted the sincerity of the South, united at last. But it was not yet united in realizing the depths of its danger.

Slowly Senate and spectators roused themselves. A stir rippled across the long-held quiet. Only then did Calhoun move, his dark eyes 'glowing with meteor-like brilliance,' as anxiously he searched face after face, as if to read the effect of his words. With his friends there was no question; his intellect they regarded as 'superior to any other of past or present times,' [2] but this was not the answer he was looking for.

Webster stepped to his side, then Henry Clay. Once more the *Triumvirate* stood together behind the Vice-President's desk. Then a group of Calhoun's fervent young admirers closed in on him. He 'received them with cordiality, his eyes shining with a new brightness,' a reporter noted, and a few minutes later could clearly be heard exhorting them to 'at any rate . . . be men.' [3]

His energy quickly waned. Two friends hurried to his side and gently supported him out of the Chamber. A hush fell over the room—and suddenly, spontaneously, the entire Senate and gallery arose and stood in tribute. [4]

For all their unfaltering logic, the tragic appearance of the author had weighted Calhoun's words with an emotional, rather than a logical, appeal. To many it seemed impossible that his thinking was not darkened by his physical condition. It was a sick, a dying man who had looked so darkly into the future. The future was not dark. Never had it been so bright. No one, asserted the Bay State's Governor Davis, looked to see the country break in two except Calhoun, 'who . . . has brooded so long on the subject.' The people 'cannot believe in the probability of danger,' declared the *National Intelligencer*. 'There are so many signs of an unprecedented national prosperity.' New York's Philip Hone, also aware of the wave of Northern prosperity rolling in from the white-capped cotton fields, read the Calhoun appeal and tossed it aside in impatience. 'This is probably his last kick and the sooner he is done kicking the better.' [5]

To the Philadelphia *Public Ledger* the speech was a 'firebrand . . . far inferior to his former efforts.' It was repetitious, containing nothing which he had not said before; a criticism true enough, although it failed to appreciate that Calhoun had spoken in summary. The stark realism of his words offended the *Ledger's* sensibilities. Was this 'glaring materialism, this arbitrary exclusion of progress,' the true essence of our political system? [6]

Only the New York *Herald* grasped the significance of the words. The speech was 'a masterly survey,' the most important, so far 'as its effects are to be considered, that has ever been delivered in the Senate.' The 'wrongs of the South' were set forth without appeal 'to the sympathies of one section, or to the passions of the other.' His exposé of the fraying religious and social ties between the two sections was 'startling.' [7]

The North Carolina *Standard* wished only that the South had believed Calhoun fifteen years earlier. 'He goes deeper into the cause of things than any other man.' No one had been so 'green,' was the comment of the Fayetteville, North Carolina, paper, as to believe that the call for the Southern Convention was sounded at the behest of Mississippi. It was from South Carolina, 'and . . . in Mr. Calhoun's speech, we have a revelation of the purpose. . . . It is to demand . . . impossible concessions . . . that if not granted . . . the South will secede.'

'Reckless' was the verdict of the Wheeling *Gazette*. Calhoun's address was 'characteristic of one whose daring spirit, though it may have aroused and excited a multitude, could never lead or control them.' The Marysville *Eagle* condemned the South Carolinian for pointing out dangers without remedies. He was now, declared the paper, 'about to encounter the eternal world.' Let him not go down as a disunionist, 'in the blackness of eternal night.' [8]

2

Aglow with excitement, Calhoun finally returned to Hill's boarding house. He could neither rest nor relax. Instead, he wrote his friend, H. W. Conner: 'My speech . . . was read today. . . . My friends think it among my most successful. . . . I have made up the issue between North and South.

If we flinch, we are gone; but if we stand fast . . . we shall triumph, either by compelling the North to yield to our terms, or declaring our Independence of them.' [9]

Exhausted, he lay abed the next day. By afternoon came disquieting news. Fiery young Foote, the Mississippi Whig, had taken advantage of Calhoun's absence to engage in a personal misinterpretation of his opinions. Calhoun's address, Foote claimed, had been 'hurtful' to the South and to the Union in whose cause it was delivered. It was not representative. The South did not despair of the Union. What right had Mr. Calhoun to speak for the South and the Southern leadership?

Calhoun was indignant. When well, he 'rose superior' to censure or · abuse, but in his weak and depressed condition the attack assumed gigantic proportions. So they thought him too feeble to 'repel . . . his antagonists!' Grimly, he dragged himself from his bed and out into the watersoaked air of a Washington March.

Mrs. Jefferson Davis, sitting on a stool on the floor of the Senate, saw him come in, 'supported on each side by a Senator,' breathing 'in short gasps,' his eyes 'lustrous with fever,' but his 'eagle glance swept the Senate in the old lordly way.' As he passed Varina, he gave her 'one burning hand,' whispered, 'My child, I am too weak to stop,' and dropped into his chair.

Benton had risen. Now he hesitated, took one look at his old enemy and said gently, 'I have nothing to say.'

But Foote indulged in no such delicacy. For over an hour he 'baited' the dying leader, while Benton kept up an indignant whisper: 'No brave man could do this infamy. Shame! Shame!' Davis and several other Senators tried to spare Calhoun the strain of replying, but without avail. Bending his tall body over the desk, as 'he found his strength failing,' Calhoun 'spoke to the point,' his voice weak, but his meaning unmistakably clear.[10] 'I have never pretended to be the leader of any man,' was his reply to Foote's accusations. 'When I speak, I speak for myself upon my individual responsibility.'

He was plainly 'much agitated.' [11] 'It is in vain,' he protested, 'for any man to say he loves the Union if he does not protect the Constitution; for that is the bond that made the Union.' But the Constitution had been misinterpreted. The South could no longer live in the Union on terms of equality without a 'specific guaranty that she shall enjoy her rights unmolested.'

Foote retorted that he believed the question could be settled in ten days.

'I agree with our ancestors,' was Calhoun's reply. 'They thought liberty required guaranties.'

Foote countered Calhoun's charges of the day preceding. He could not believe that all the North was hostile or opposed to the South.

'More or less hostile,' snapped Calhoun. If it came to a stand, all

Northern factions would unite against the South. 'Unless there be a provision in the Constitution to protect us . . . the two sections of this
Union will never live in harmony.'

'I talk very little about whether I am a Union man or not,' said Calhoun softly. 'I put no confidence in professions. . . . I challenge comparison with any man here. . . . I appeal . . . if there be any man who
has abstained more carefully from . . . a violation of the Constitution.
. . . If I am judged by my acts, I trust I shall be found as firm a friend
of the Union as any man within it.'

'There are two ways of treating the subject:—one is by speaking, and
the other by acting. Of the two, the latter is most effective. . . . If any
Senator . . . chooses to comment upon what I have said, I trust I shall
have health to defend my . . . position.' [12]

The effort had been 'too much for his exhausted frame.' [13] He sank back
into his chair, and to Varina Davis it seemed that he 'would die on our
hands with a little more.' [14] Quickly, his friends gathered around, half-led
and half-carried him off the floor, drove him home, and put him to bed;
and for the next forty-eight hours he was perfectly content to remain there.

3

On March 6, 1850, a stately, slow-moving figure, his great head sunk upon
his chest, mounted the steps of Hill's boarding house. In the background
bystanders whispered. Daniel Webster was calling upon Mr. Calhoun.

Webster had 'an exalted opinion' of Calhoun's genius. He considered the
South Carolinian 'much the ablest man in the Senate,' the greatest man,
in fact, that he had met in his entire public life. Most of all, however, he
cherished him as a personal friend. Despite years of political differences,
there still existed between them 'a great deal of personal kindness.' [15] Webster could not conceive how such a man could have enemies so bitter.
Aware of the Southerner's steadily ebbing strength for several years past,
he had endeavored to reconcile Benton to him, but the gruff old Missourian
was obdurate.

'Webster,' he had said, 'don't you mention that to me. . . . I won't be
reconciled to Calhoun—I won't, sir. . . . I won't have anything to do
with him. . . . My mind is made up, sir. . . . Anybody else, but not Calhoun. He is a humbug, and I won't do it sir.' [16]

Now the two men faced each other, Webster in his familiar blue coat
and buff breeches, to a casual observer still the commanding figure of his
prime; though an old friend like Calhoun would have noted the thinning
hair and thickening body; Calhoun, his strength now completely gone,
lay flat on his back, 'ghastly pale,' his face 'cut deep with lines of suffering
endured in silence.'

Solicitously Webster inquired after his health—perhaps with his old greeting—'How do the men of '82 stand on their pins?' Calhoun shook his head silently.[17]

Webster broached the subject of his own forthcoming speech. Calhoun's eyes burned with eagerness. He wished he could hear it. Webster hoped that he would be able to return to the Senate. He was particularly anxious that his South Carolina friends be present. Calhoun shook his head. He felt that he would never leave his bed again.[18]

It was the seventh of March, 1850. Webster had been speaking only a few moments. Save for the deep, booming cadences of his voice, the Senate Chamber was still. Even the plumed fans had ceased to move. All eyes were fixed on his majestic form, his dark, somber face. Only Peter Harvey, a reporter, saw the 'tall gaunt figure' in the black cloak, with the 'deep cavernous black eyes and . . . thick mass of snow-white hair' enter the Chamber from the Vice-President's office and slowly drag himself toward the nearest seat. He swayed as he approached it; and a Senator sprang to his side and helped him into an easy-chair, where he sank, trembling, scarcely able to move.

Webster had not seen him. But suddenly he referred to 'the distinguished and venerable Senator from South Carolina, who is unfortunately prevented by serious illness from being in his seat today.'

Calhoun stirred. Bending his head and shoulders forward, he struggled to rise and interrupt, but sank back, while Webster's flow of rhetoric continued undisturbed. A few moments later, Webster referred again to 'the eminent Senator from South Carolina, whom we all regret so much to miss from such a cause from his seat today.'

This was too much for Calhoun. Eyes gleaming, nervous hands grasping at the arms of his chair, abruptly he summoned the last of his fleeting energies, pulled his frail body erect, threw back his head, and in a voice hollow, ghostlike, yet clear in every corner of the Chamber, proudly announced: 'The Senator from South Carolina is in his seat.' [19]

Webster started. He turned, and his eyes filled with tears. Not in his wildest moments had he dreamed that his friend would rise from what he actually believed to be his deathbed, to hear his words. Touched beyond expression, he impulsively extended his hands and bowed low.[20] Later in the address, Calhoun interrupted for a short defense of his stand on Texas, and at the conclusion again briefly took the floor. He spoke now with 'surprising resonance' of voice, and the correspondent of the New York *Tribune,* who had visited him in his room a few days before when he could scarcely whisper, recorded with amazement that 'You would have sworn, had you heard him, that his lungs would last for years.' [21]

His words were conciliatory. A year or two before, he would have insisted that the South's abstract rights to slavery in all sections be fully maintained; but now, in the face of the ominous reality that confronted him, he would sacrifice his abstractions, even adhere to the line of the Missouri Compromise, if only the lands possible to slavery could be opened to slavery. As for the rest, he agreed with Webster: 'Leave that portion of the country more natural to a non-slaveholding population to be filled by that description of population.'

'No man,' Calhoun concluded, 'would feel more happy than myself to believe that this Union should live forever. . . . I . . . believe that I have never done one act which would weaken it, that I have done full justice to all sections.' But if the Union could not be broken, that in itself would be enough to prove its tyranny. And broken, it could be. 'Great moral causes will break it, if they go on.' [22]

Great moral causes! Not consolidation. Not secession alone. Slavery had become a moral cause to the people of the North. As such, the Union was already broken, not in paper contracts and compacts, but in the plighted spiritual troth upon which even the Constitution itself rested.

What he did know was that Daniel Webster, in supporting the Clay Compromises, had won. It mattered not that his repudiation might result, that already Northern editorials were speaking of 'traitorism' and 'betrayal,' the Boston *Post* admitting that opinion on his stand was 'conflicting, even among his friends,' the New York *Tribune* warning that Webster's address 'has . . . received no solid mark of approval from the North.' [23] To the South Daniel Webster was the North. He was the North offering conciliation, and it was difficult, indeed, for Southerners to remember Calhoun's merciless logic when Webster spoke of unity and patriotism. Few Northern papers were circulated in the South now, and for the South, as a whole, Webster's olive branch was guarantee enough.

Virtually the entire Southern press applauded Webster's words. Conversely, many condemned Calhoun's insistence on a constitutional amendment as 'impracticable,' if not actually mischievous. The necessity was now at an end, the Virginia *Free Press* declared. Even Calhoun's own Charleston *Mercury* praised Webster's address as 'noble in language, generous and conciliatory in tone.' Significantly it added: 'Mr. Calhoun's clear and powerful exposition would have had something of a decisive effect, if it had not been so soon followed by Mr. Webster's masterly playing.' [24] Not even to save herself would the South secede now. Webster's assurances had blinded her to her danger.

But they did not blind Calhoun. He knew the futility of Congressional concessions unbacked by the voluntary desire of the people. As he said: 'It is impossible to execute any law of Congress until the people of the States shall co-operate.' [25]

On March 18, in a wavering hand Calhoun signed a letter to Conner, predicting that the effect of Webster's words would be only temporary. 'He could not sustain himself at the North with either party,' Calhoun stated.

'Can anything more clearly evince the utter hopelessness of looking to the North for support, when their strongest man finds himself incapable of maintaining himself on the smallest amount possible of concession to the South; . . . and on points too clear to admit of constitutional doubt?' [26] Yet the speech had been sufficient for its immediate purpose. 'If Mr. Calhoun's speech made a deep impression here,' stated the New York *Herald*, 'Mr. Webster's has made a deeper.' [27]

4

Under the spur of his purpose, Calhoun's waning energies were accelerated. He answered to roll-call on the eighth, and on the tenth wrote Clemson that his health had so much improved that he was able to take his seat in the Senate 'and a part in the discussions.' Only warm weather and exercise were essential to a 'full restoration' of his strength.[28] He was in his seat on the eleventh, leaning back with scorn on his face as William H. Seward arose to proclaim a 'higher power' than the Constitution, which would give Congress the right to determine whether the individual states be slave or free. Calhoun heard him out in silence, remarking afterward, 'With his ideas, he is not fit to associate with gentlemen.' [29]

On the thirteenth of March, Calhoun walked into the Senate Chamber for the last time. His eyes were calm, though vigilant, his body erect, his voice 'by no means indicating the degree of physical weakness which did, in fact, possess him.' [30] The 'fine old Celt was a warrior every inch of him,' declared the correspondent of the New York *Tribune*. Quietly, and without ostentation, he took his seat, but he 'stirred a deep feeling among the onlookers.' His condition was known to all, and there was something about him now which spoke only too plainly of the nearness of death. To his ardent young Southern admirers he had 'the heroism of a martyr'; to Daniel Webster he was 'a Senator of Rome when Rome survived.' [31]

During the afternoon he had a long talk 'on the exciting topics of the day' with a young Representative, who in early youth had drawn inspiration from Calhoun's words of 'kindness and encouragement,' and who now found 'the same kind feelings . . . still manifested towards me by the veteran statesman.' [32] Perhaps it was during this momentary diversion that Henry Foote took opportunity to open his attack again. The weary Carolinian re-entered the Chamber just in time to hear the word 'disunionist' flung at him.

'Disunionist? Did he call me that?' he demanded bitterly.

Ashamed, Foote attempted explanation. But Calhoun's blood was up, and although in evident physical pain, he threw himself into the debate, taking on antagonist after antagonist. His voice was no longer 'clear as a trumpet'; it was 'quivering from weakness and husky with emotion,' but

his unconquerable will-power remained unbroken.[33] He was summoning all
his strength for replies. The reporters looked on in amazement. 'Even in
his strongest days,' they knew, 'such antagonism would have taxed his
energies.'[34] Now he was at the point of collapse. Foote, whom even his
friends thought was 'too severe on Mr. Calhoun,' begged him to wait until
tomorrow. Calhoun gave him a single glance. 'I do not know,' he said
quietly, 'that an opportunity will then be afforded me of saying what I
desire to say.'[35] Instantly the Senate hushed into silence.

Calhoun hesitated, then apologetically announced: 'I regret very much
that the state of my health does not permit me to enter fully into the
argument. . . . I shall be under the necessity of economizing my words
as well as my strength.'

He turned to Foote. 'Can the Senate believe,' he demanded, 'that the
South is safe while one portion of the community holds entire possession
of the power of the Government to wield it for their own benefit?' Why,
the disease would be 'fatal, if not arrested.'

Foote repeated his charge that Calhoun was making up a new issue without consulting the other Senators.

'I never consulted with any Senator in my life when about to make a
speech,' retorted Calhoun indignantly. He would consult when there was
a 'new issue.' The Senator from Mississippi was 'too impatient.'

'I am but imitating the example of the Senator,' was Foote's reply.

Calhoun's answer was tart. 'I am considerably older than the Senator,
and am therefore rather more entitled to give advice.' Sharply he rebuked
Foote for his association with men whose doctrines meant disunion.

Foote reminded Calhoun of the courteous necessity of being on good
terms with the other Senators.

'Well, I am not on good terms with those who are for cutting our throats,'
flashed back Calhoun. He would not even speak to a man who dared
say there was a 'power higher than the Constitution. . . . I will say good
morning . . . or shake hands . . . if he thinks . . . to offer his hand,'
but that was all he would have to do 'with those who entertain opinions and
doctrines such as he has avowed.' Calhoun paused, glanced down at his
thin black cloak, and retreated toward the door. He flung a final word.
This was the extent of his intercourse with 'those who I think are endangering the Union.'[36]

The turmoil had utterly exhausted his strength. He remained in bed,
'gradually sinking,' one newspaper reported, and unable to see anyone.
'He is not only sick, but dispirited,' declared the New York *Herald*, but he
could not rest. Day by day opinion was crystallizing on the Compromise
measures, and the rising tide of excitement penetrated his sick-chamber.
Flooding in on the dying man was abuse such as that in Garrison's *Liberator*, which dubbed him the master-tyrant, 'uppermost among the damned.'
If he were sane, which Mr. Garrison doubted, then he was 'an adulterer,

a thief, a barbarian . . . and a man-stealer,' privately, 'publicly, and at wholesale.' Calhoun would have wasted little self-pity on such ravings, but what did hurt was commentary like that of the New Orleans *Bee*, which announced 'the public sentiment of 9/10ths of the . . . South will rebuke the opinion of Mr. Calhoun and stamp it as calumny.' Even the Charleston *Mercury*, still praising Webster's speech, thought 'it no longer . . . impossible to bring this sectional contest to a close.' [37] With every passing day opinion crystallized more rapidly. Out of sixty Southern newspapers only fifteen would even agree to support the forthcoming Convention.

'Mr. Calhoun is deserted on all sides,' reported the *Public Ledger*.[38] The 'sad, ungrateful experience' of these last days wounded Calhoun deeply. He 'loved his country; he loved the Union'; and now to be misunderstood was almost more than he could bear. He had labored to forestall the 'irrepressible conflict.' But he knew that to temporize would only increase the evil which he sought to remove. Most of all, he was convinced that the future was dependent upon existing causes. His consolation was that in the end, he might be appreciated.

'You are a very unpopular man,' declared a visitor.

Calhoun eyed him calmly.

'I am, among politicians, but not among the people, and you will know this when I am dead.' [39]

5

He had spoken truly. North and South alike, an entire nation, was following the reports of Calhoun's illness. Not even their hatred of his policies could diminish their admiration of the man. 'That which will interest' our readers most 'is the sad news concerning Mr. Calhoun's health,' wrote the New York *Herald* correspondent on the twenty-third.[40] He spoke for virtually the entire Washington press corps. Scarcely a telegraphic communiqué went out of the Capitol that March without word as to Calhoun's condition. For an entire generation of reporters and young Representatives, there was no memory of Washington without John C. Calhoun. They could not face the thought of his death. Frantically they seized on the faintest pretext for hope. 'The republic must make up its mind to lose the great South Carolinian,' reported the *Herald* on March 21. 'He will live,' triumphed the same paper four days later. 'His mighty mind has actually gained the mastery over . . . the body.' He would 'live long enough to use up those political donkeys who have been kicking what they supposed to be a dead man.' A few days afterward, the columnist was compelled to admit that the Carolinian had suffered a relapse, but added, 'I cannot make up my mind yet that he is going to die.' [41]

6

Calhoun himself cared little. 'I put a high value on renown,' he had told
Anna Maria; but he would not have wished to live, or that his memory
and words should outlive the thing he loved. What tormented him now
every hour was the conviction that he had failed, not only to save the
Union, but the South. All would be lost. 'The reward,' he had said, 'is in
the struggle more than in victory . . . I hold the duties of life tó be
greater than life itself, and that in performing them manfully, even against
hope, our labor is not lost. . . .' But was it not? He had spent a lifetime
trying to effect by example what he could not do through principle; he
had told the world what the South was and the North, and how the North
was trying to destroy the South, 'blindly, perhaps, but still actually.' [42]
He had united the South in momentary realization of its danger, but had
lacked the strength, physical and political, to rally the dissident forces for
a stand.

He had stressed the futility of compromise because his hopes still lay
in the June Convention and his own domination of it. Now he knew that
even the Convention would be useless. Webster's overtures had divided the
South, and the great question must be settled now, while he still lived,
if at all. But he knew it would not be settled. The Compromise would be
accepted, and the question 'patched up for the present, to brake out again
in a few years.' [43] Calhoun knew his South even when it had gone beyond
him. When the Compromise was overruled, when the Congress of the
future refused to be bound by the acts of the past, then at last would this
young 'new' South snap its bonds—and then it would be too late! Secession was practicable only while the South had had strength to make good
the threat and to stand alone—and now was the last chance. Only now
had the South strength to compel the constitutional guarantees that could
insure her safety in the Union. These young men, dreaming of a rich slave
empire stretching on into Cuba and Mexico, could they not see that time
and destiny were not their friends? Drunk on cotton, they looked at their
acres, not at the trade statistics; lost in their dreams of future grandeur,
they failed to gauge the present growth of the North. They did not hear
the humming roar of machines, the whisper on the wind that an outraged
public opinion would never see another foot of slave territory annexed to
free soil; or a great slave republic share the continent. They would hear
and see only when the temple of the Union crashed, and like Samson, they
were buried in the ruins.

7

'What do you see in the future?' Judge Beverly Tucker asked the dying prophet.

'Dark forebodings, and I should die happy if I could see the Union preserved,' was Calhoun's reply. But he did not see it. 'The Union is doomed to dissolution . . . within twelve years,' he told Mason. 'The probability is, that it will explode in a presidential election.' [44] It was a terrible thing. 'The dissolution of the Union,' he told W. H. Parmalee, 'is the heaviest blow that can be struck at civilization and representative government.' [45]

He utilized his last energy in adding the final touches to his book, that strange summary of his entire life's experience and thought. This, heralded as 'the greatest effort of his mind,' he would leave behind him, as if even from his grave to refute the charges of those who libeled him as traitor and disunionist; as if to prove that even in his last hours his weary mind was still searching for a way to reconcile irreconcilables, to achieve an impossibility. [46]

8

He could not stand the exertion. On March 17, the New York *Herald* reported his hours 'numbered.' He could sit up in bed and argue fiercely, but ten minutes of such exertion would prostrate him for hours. Anxiously his son John hovered over him. A doctor, he knew that his father could not live long in the 'contaminated atmosphere' of Washington. Son and friends agreed on Lynchburg, Virginia, with its rural quiet and clean mountain air. It was decided to move him the next Wednesday if he survived 'till that time.' [47]

All but his closest friends were now barred from the sick-room. He was forbidden to discuss political questions, but insisted on talking about slavery, and even when so weak that the power of speech had almost left him, his brain worked on.

Exhausted from such strain, his nerves finally gave way, and to a friend who seized a brief interview he seemed 'almost demented.' His mind was racked with the problems of disunion. If Virginia seceded, where would the District of Columbia go? Could it be transferred to Maryland and Maryland turned over to the North? Fragments of this interview seeped into the Washington rumor-pool, and a scoffer declared that Calhoun was dying in giving birth to the Southern Confederacy. [48]

9

Early in the week he was better. His fever left him; his appetite improved. He was keenly interested in the approaching trip to Lynchburg, and was already making plans for his recovery and return to the Senate. On Wednesday he sat up, and in handwriting surprisingly firm addressed a note to his colleague, Butler, possibly the last letter he ever wrote. 'I suppose the debate etc. on Mr. Clay's resolutions will go on for at least this week before a vote is taken on them. But should it not, as I am desirous of being heard in the debate, I must request the favour of you to have them postpone to some early day next week, say Tuesday, by which time my strength, I think, will be sufficiently restored to enable me to speak.' [49]

To speak once more, to lead one more fight, was the single purpose that kept him alive. He had no real illusions as to his recovery. But he did hope that by force of will he could hold off the end until he had made one last plea. 'He will spare no efforts to preserve the South if he cannot preserve the Union,' declared the North Carolina *Standard*. On the twenty-third, the Philadelphia *Ledger* reported 'his mind . . . as active as ever . . . he is at this moment engaged in dictating another speech.' Already Washington rumor had decided what he was going to say. 'Firmly and . . . honestly persuaded that the Union ought to be dissolved,' declared Morehead to Crittenden, Calhoun was preparing 'every strong argument,' showing that 'the only salvation of the South is by disunion.' [50] But he was writing no speech, although he did dictate a few resolutions to his secretary. Loose in structure, repetitious both of themselves and of what had gone before, they contained no new insights and no solution of the terrible problem.

10

On March 27, the snow was falling in Washington. It was spring at Fort Hill, and lying back against his pillows, eyes resting on the white monotony outside, Calhoun could see it all: the fountains of yellow forsythia on either side of the driveway, the cedar boughs swaying in the wind, the gentle slope of the roof and the cool white columns. Almost he could hear the jingle of bridle reins and the thud of hooves on the drive, Floride's shears as she knelt over her rosebushes, or Anna Maria's voice, hushed against the sounds of a spring evening. A statesman was dying, Washington said, but a man was dying, too.

Characteristically, on what he felt the most, he would have said the least. He knew that his life would be written down as tragedy. Yet he had not been 'an unhappy man.' He had loved life; he had 'battled with its small joys and cares'; he had known much sorrow; but there were moments when he had felt shafts of pleasure, keen as pain. Lying prostrate now, feeling his strength flowing from him, he had time to look inward and remember. Faces, long vanished, haunted his memory: Tapping Reeve with his hand on his back, dreaming down a country road in Litchfield; Jefferson in the hall of Monticello; shriveled 'Jemmy' Madison and fatherly James Monroe; Randolph of Roanoke, with his whirling forefinger and glittering eye. Faces of friends welled up in his memory, friends loved with an intensity a man could not give in later life: Jimmy MacBride under the elms of Yale and pale William Lowndes and all those ardent and eager young Carolinians of the twenties who had rallied to his standard with selfless, unswerving devotion.

He had found happiness in his children and his children's children. He had lived a quiet life and a very simple one; yet from that very simplicity he had drawn a contentment and a strength that stood by him always. Whatever he had done, he had done with his whole heart. He had lived as intensely as he had felt and thought, and in his way of life had found the fountain-spring of all his thinking and believing. And there was much to think about and remember in those quiet hours with the wet snow clotting against the window-panes; the worn red hills of the South and the mountains hazed in 'a powder that was blue,' the black walls of pine, the scent of mimosa and of pennyroyal, the white-starred shimmer of dogwood in a Southern April and the smile of a girl of sixteen with black hair and dancing eyes, a girl that he had called Floride—all that he had loved and would never see again.

He knew that he was going to die. He was not afraid. He had long known how tenuous was his hold upon existence, and it was this very knowledge which had driven him on. As early as ten years before, despite his later digressions, he had told his brother-in-law James that he felt himself too old to do justice to the Presidency; and from that day through his private letters like a theme ran the words, 'My time must soon be through.'[51]

He had known when he kissed Floride at Fort Hill in November, when he had looked back on all that he loved, that he would never come home again. To a friend he had confided that he knew 'death was near, much nearer than he was willing to have his family know,' and added that he wished to give all the time he could spare from public duty to 'preparation for death.' *[52]

'Sternly and positively' he had forbidden that his family should know

---

* Preparation for death, with Calhoun, apparently meant to 'make his peace with God.' So far as practical affairs went, he died, leaving no will. The mortgage on Fort Hill was paid off with the ten-thousand dollars raised by Charleston admirers to buy Calhoun a yacht for a sea-voyage 'to restore his health.'

of his condition. He would not want Floride, he said sharply, 'put to any inconvenience.' [53] He loved his family devotedly, but there was no question where his duty lay. To have them at his side, with all their sympathy, their fears for his safety, would 'unnerve him' entirely, perhaps to a point where he could not go on. He could not let himself be torn with emotion. As he said, 'he could not bear to see their grief.' [54]

Until the last week, although burning with fever and worn out with a cough that tore at him night and day, he continued to write calm, hopeful letters to Anna Maria and Clemson, assuring them that his health was improving. As they could not come to him, why should they worry about him? Almost to the end his resolution held; then the human ties were too strong. On March 23, the press reported that he had at last 'consented to send for his family.' [55]

11

News that the great Carolinian was on his deathbed had sent the young Senate chaplain, C. M. Butler, aflame with evangelical zeal, hurrying to Hill's boarding house to bring this restless soul before God. Through a half-open doorway he caught a glimpse of the sick man, pale, emaciated, his head propped by pillows and his eyes piercing and restless as ever. Calhoun would not see him. He was obdurate, almost angry. 'I won't be told what to think!' he exclaimed. Religion was a 'subject I've thought about all my life.'

Proud, solitary, independent of any intellect but his own, Calhoun refused even spiritual assistance in these last days. His religious pilgrimage had been a strange one. Always devout, yet never 'professing' Christianity, his life had been a search for the faith which would fill the needs of his soul and yet satisfy the demands of his reason.[56] Reacting against the stern Presbyterianism of his youth, caught midway between the Calvinism of the up-country and the deism of the intellectual Jeffersonian groups, he had drifted into attendance at his wife's Episcopal church, of which it was said in Carolina that this was 'the only way to Heaven for a gentleman.'

His conflicts and questionings had made him an interesting study to pastors who watched his thoughtful face during services. Even his friends had no idea where he stood. Some believed him a deist, others a Swedenborgian. Furthermore, he gave money to build the Unitarian church in Washington and 'on the first roll of this Washington parish' can be found his name. 'Unitarianism,' he announced with characteristic dogmatism, 'is the only true faith and will ultimately prevail over the world.' [57] Yet when Rhett, concerned over his spiritual welfare, urged him to 'seek God in Christ,' Calhoun was silent 'to an appeal which would have meant much to him in earlier years.' [58]

Now, with his days drawing to a close, the stern old Calvinistic doctrines of his youth once more reasserted their power. He was stirred by the revival of Presbyterianism through the Southern states, and to those who knew him best it seemed that his doubts had at last been resolved. Dr. Venable questioned him about the time and manner in which best to meet death. And he answered, with the old-time faith of his boyhood: 'I have little concern about either; I desire to die in the discharge of my duty; I have an unshaken reliance upon the providence of God.' [59]

12

By Saturday, March 30, he was much weaker and very restless. He sat up for a couple of hours, and toward evening stimulants so revived him that he discussed slavery with fervent interest. But late at night, when apparently at rest, he said to Scoville: 'Read very low some of the papers which I said I wished in the morning, as I am very feeble.' Obediently the clerk gathered some of the last pages of manuscript upon which Calhoun had been working and began to read aloud, but soon made a pretext to stop. 'Very well, you can read me the rest tomorrow,' Calhoun said.

He lay quietly for a time, but at twelve-thirty his heavy breathing alarmed his son. He could not sleep; his pulse was faint, but he refused any stimulants. 'You had better get some sleep,' he told his son. The young man lay down, but an hour later was roused by his father's faintly spoken: 'John, come to me.' He was much weaker now and holding out his arm said, 'I have no pulse.' No, he had not rested, but he was in no pain. He wanted his son to lock up his watch and the manuscript. This done he relaxed, and suddenly remarked: 'I have never had such facility in arranging my thoughts.'

John looked at him with concern. 'You're overtasking your mind with thinking,' he warned.

'I cannot help from thinking about the country,' Calhoun replied.[60]

13

What was he thinking? Not about himself and the terrible problem that his own death would solve for him. Not even his beloved South was foremost in his thoughts now. Broken-hearted by his own forebodings, he was hoping still that some way, somehow, the Union might be saved and the South within it. At last he spoke. 'If I had my health and my strength to give one hour in the Senate, I could do more for my country than at any previous time in my life.' [61]

'For my country.' What new thought had come to him? Had he devised some plan that he believed might yet hold back the forces of history, destiny, and the inevitable? Few historians have thought so. With the sole exception of the hint in his letter to Butler, there is nothing in his last writings more than the desire and the will for some unfound solution. Whatever his secret, it died with him. One word yet he might have spoken, but this even dying despair 'could not wring from his lips.'[62] 'Disunion' was the word he did not speak.

Minute by minute time ticked away. Venable left to seize a few hours' rest. Richard Crallé arrived to take up the watch.

The pitiful bareness of the sick-room, the lack of all feminine care and attention struck the young clerk to the heart. From the mantelpiece the 'sickly glow' of a single tallow candle outlined wardrobe and bed, flickered dully against a lump of cold boiled rice, a glass of water, and another of dried prunes, 'the sole death-bed conveniences of John C. Calhoun.' There was a party at Hill's that night, and disturbed by the 'loud sounds of revelry,' Calhoun tossed restlessly about, although he 'uttered no murmur.' Occasionally the door would creak open and a merrymaker would look in to ask if he still lived.

Throwing himself on a couch, Crallé fixed his eyes on Calhoun's 'still and pallid face.' The majesty of the long, solitary figure on the bed, 'prostrate, almost unable to move,' and 'struggling for every breath,' was not lost upon Crallé. He had loved Calhoun as a father. And now, if only there were 'a thousand little comforts, a thousand kind and soothing attentions,' with which he could ease his last hours!

There was nothing that he could do. And where were all the others, Crallé wondered. What feminine hand had 'smoothed his pillow'? What 'kind sympathies' had offered him 'delicacies of food'? Where was 'the friendship . . . the gratitude for a long life of privations, charities, and public service'? 'They entered not the portals of that desolate chamber.'[63]

Not even the aged Negro body-servant was there, who had waited upon Calhoun since his young War-Department days. For thirty years they had shared each other's lives and moods; they had been young and grown old together; separated only by room and by color, they were dying together; and the slave would go before the master.

A glimmer of light edged its way around the drawn curtains. It was five o'clock. Calhoun roused himself. John stepped to the bed and asked him how he felt. 'I am perfectly comfortable,' he said.

An hour passed. Once more Calhoun beckoned his son to his side. Grasping the boy's hand, Calhoun looked deep into his eyes, moved his lips, but could not speak.

The door opened. A few friends filed past the bed and each one Calhoun took by the hand. As Abraham Venable approached, Calhoun held out his wrist, his intent gaze searching the younger man's face.

'You are pulseless, sir, and must take some wine,' Venable said.

Calhoun motioned to the wardrobe, then raised his head, took the glass in his hand and drained it. Again he held out his arm. A moment later, Venable gently laid it down. 'The wine,' he said, 'has produced no effect.'

Calhoun gave Venable one long searching look, his eyes incredibly clear and keen. He understood. Quietly he leaned back, adjusted his head on the pillow, placed his hand on his chest, and lay waiting. Bending over him, Venable watched the face of the dying man. It was 'calm . . . composed,' unafraid. Already the deep lines of suffering were smoothing themselves away, but the dark eyes, their luster undimmed, unflinchingly met his own. 'He was conscious to the last moment.' [64]

The room was very still. A pale blur of dawn lay on the floor. Outside wet boughs creaked in the March wind. The early morning ring of hooves sounded against the pavement. Inside was only the sound of that slow breathing—slower—slower—one long breath—and then silence. It was a quarter past seven on Sunday morning, and in Charleston the bells of Saint Philip's and Saint Michael's rang out, calling the people to worship. A few moments later, the 'magic wires' in the telegraph office began to click, and in state after state of the American Union the letters were spelled out: 'Mr. Calhoun expired at fifteen minutes past seven this morning . . . to the last, his eyes retained their brightness.' [65]

14

'Universal regret' was the statement of the New York *Herald*. 'Affliction and sorrow hang like clouds over the federal city,' wrote the correspondent of the Philadelphia *Ledger*. Bitterly opposed to Calhoun personally, he was compelled to admit that the old Carolinian was 'one of the ablest men this country has produced.' [66]

At Yale College, ruddy-faced, grizzled Benjamin Silliman, 'the great Silliman' now, opened his diary. Nearly half a century had passed since the young teacher and the young student had together explored the mysteries of the 'new' science in a classroom on Chapel Street. 'John C. Calhoun died this morning . . .' wrote Silliman, 'calm and in perfect possession of his reason. Nothing is quoted regarding his soul or his prospects for another life.' [67]

In Albany Dr. Alexander Stephens, he who as a gangling boy in his teens had thrilled to Calhoun's 'young eloquence,' watched the flag over the Capitol of the state of New York fall to half-mast. For years, Dr. Stephens had followed the career of his old fellow student, his admiration mingled with concern. For he had a physician's understanding of Calhoun's make-up, physical as well as mental; and to him his friend's death was plainly 'an intellectual death . . . an overworked mind dwelling too long on one . . . object,' a terrible lesson 'to intense thinkers.' [68]

And far off in Belgium, Anna Maria, sensing the desolation of that lonely bedchamber, mourned bitterly that she could not have had the melancholy satisfaction of soothing her father's last hours. 'Did you know,' she wondered, 'what an aching void your death would cause in your daughter's heart?' [69]

In the Senate, on Monday, the task of announcing what all knew fell to tall, white-haired Alexander Butler. Each Senator had his own concept of Calhoun. To Butler it was his colleague of the past few years, ill, and aware that he could live for only a short while, yet 'the least despondent man I ever knew.' He had met death with complete 'realization of what was passing,' but 'with his usual aversion to professions . . . said nothing for mere effect upon the world.' [70] His last hours had been in keeping with his entire life.

Henry Clay took the floor. Memories were flooding in on him—of a youthful friendship, unstained by the bitter quarrels of later years; of the young floor leader in that first War Congress, 'a star bright and brilliant'; of Madison's Secretary of War, so deeply and unashamedly in love with his young wife; of the fellow orator, with his flashing eyes and 'torrent of mighty rhetoric, which always won our admiration even if it did not bring conviction to our understandings.' His principles, however they might have differed from ours, Clay declared, 'will descend to posterity under the sanction of a great name. . . . Mr. Speaker, he is gone. . . . He is now an historical character.' [71]

Then the third member of the broken triumvirate arose. Jefferson Davis sat nearby, and never had he seen 'Mr. Webster so agitated'; never had he heard his voice so falter, 'as when he delivered the eulogy on John C. Calhoun.' [72] For Webster, too, those early days of the War Congress had meaning. 'We were both young men,' he said reminiscently. He touched on Calhoun's 'originality and vigor of thought,' his 'superior dignity,' his courtesy to others. 'Whatever his aspirations,' Webster declared, 'they were high, honorable, and noble. . . . There was nothing groveling or low, or meanly selfish that came near the head or the heart of Mr. Calhoun.' [73]

15

The funeral services were on Tuesday, the day that he had hoped to return to his seat once more. Instead, he lay in state in the middle aisle of the Chamber, his coffin covered with a black velvet pall, light slanting across his pale features. Outside, spring had come; it was a warm clear day. The Senate Chamber was crowded. In the gallery sat 'several ladies of Mr. Calhoun's family . . . in deep mourning.' Floride had arrived, but too late.

The chaplain pronounced the short, formal, funeral service. Near the coffin sat the bearers, Webster, Mangum, Cass, King, Berrien, and Henry Clay, his face working with 'visible emotion.' Slowly Daniel Webster arose to speak the few words that his feelings allowed him. Involuntarily he glanced at Benton. Benton had refused to speak, and sat now, his back turned, twirling his spectacles in boredom. At the close of the service, the bitter old Missourian spoke: 'He is not dead, sir; he is not dead. There may be no vitality in his body. But there's plenty in his doctrines.' [74]

16

At the Washington docks, the crowd was waiting. It was April 22, a still warm day. Before them loomed the steamer *Baltimore*, cabins, masts, and smokestack all draped in black. From behind moved the hearse, its twelve black horses led by Negro mutes. There were the dim notes of martial music; there was the tolling of the church bells. Silently the pageant moved forward; the waiting hundreds saw Daniel Webster, his dark face shadowed with grief, and Jefferson Davis, his head averted. Silently the crowd watched, as the body of a young West Point cadet, a Congressman's son from Alabama, was hoisted to the deck. Beside it was laid a second coffin, 'partially shaped' to the long body of Calhoun.[75]

The church bells were tolling as the *Baltimore* moved slowly out onto the waters of the Potomac. They were tolling across the river at Alexandria, where the flags hung at half-mast, and at Washington's Mount Vernon, and at Fredericksburg, where the minute guns boomed.

They were tolling through the late afternoon twilight in Richmond, as an 'immense throng stood in utter silence' before a row of carriages and footmen in black livery with bands of white cambric about their hats and sleeves. A hearse, drawn by four black horses, and followed by the long parade of family carriages, moved through the empty streets to Jefferson's Capitol. There the next morning the Governor released the 'Guard of Honor,' and delivered the body of Calhoun to 'the committee of 25.' 'Virginia will mingle her tears with those of Carolina,' he said. The 'spontaneous outpouring of our population yesterday' was only 'a slight manifestation of the exalted admiration' which the state felt for the 'genius' who had departed. 'I knew him well, and esteemed him for those virtues which won the heart of the nation.' [76]

The bells were tolling in Petersburg, where business was stilled, and from black-draped houses men and women filed into Saint Paul's Church for a short memorial service. They were tolling that afternoon in Wilmington, as the flags drooped at half-mast and the minute guns boomed, and a double line of citizens stood uncovered in the hot sun, watching a white horse draw through the narrow streets all that remained of Monroe's Secretary of War, who had last visited them, ardent and young, a quarter of a century before.

South of Wilmington the *Baltimore* moved along a tangled back-drop of pine and swamp, but as the smoke lifted gray banners of approach against the sky, bells sounded from the tiny hamlets along the water's edge, and cannon boomed. At one isolated farm a single old man stood waiting. His head was bare. His hands rested on a small pine tree which he had draped in black. Behind him stood two Negroes, their heads uncovered and bent.[77]

From the deck of the *Baltimore,* Thursday morning, Abraham Venable gazed over the harbor of Charleston to the misted towers and walls beyond. It was like a city of the dead. There was not the stroke of a hammer nor the sound of a voice; only the slow booming of the guns and the slow solemnity of the church bells broke the stillness. To Venable, looking in wonder, this proudest city in America, now humbled in grief, spoke a language that went to his heart. Only the five little ships in the harbor, moving up and down, their colors lowered to half-mast, and the hearse and 'vast multitude of mourners . . . bore witness' that in the city the pulse of life still beat.[78] South Carolina's king had come home.

The *Baltimore* docked at noon. A Guard of Honor in full mourning, with white scarfs across their shoulders, stepped forward. The iron casket was lifted and placed within a funeral carriage, 'spread over with a pall of black velvet, enflounced in silver with the escutcheon of the State of South Carolina in the centre and four corners.'[79]

The muffled drums rolled. The bells tolled. Six black horses drew the catafalque through the empty streets. Behind moved the funeral procession—twelve ex-Governors and Lieutenant-Governors, the military escort, Calhoun's wife and children, the neighbors from Pendleton, the last few old soldiers of the Revolution.

At Citadel Square, Venable saw such a spectacle as he had never seen before and would never see again. Mourning thousands stood in silence, their heads uncovered, bowed before the funeral carriage of 'their pride and their hope, laid low.'[80] Over them hung the 'hush of death'; behind them brooded the front and battlements of the Citadel, all draped in black. Not a sound could be heard but the tramping of the horses, the tolling of the bells, the relentless rumble of the drums.

From the Square the procession moved through the city gates down Boundary Street (now Calhoun Street), overhead the draped 'escutcheon of the State,' and beneath it the words, 'Carolina Mourns.'[81] Even the palmetto trees were swathed in black; every store and building and church was hung with mourning; every door and every window closed. From the Citadel to the City Hall not a voice, not a sound, broke the stillness. Not a curtain was raised; not a face looked out. All were in the procession outside, or mourning silently within.

The procession ended at City Hall. Within, the building was darkened and draped, with palmettos arched over the entrance. The coffin was placed beneath a canopy, supported by Corinthian columns and surmounted by three pale eagles, holding the crêpe in their beaks. Calhoun's friends, who knew his 'simple tastes,' [82] had been pained by the grandeur, had feared that solemnity would be lost in display. But the genuine outpouring of the people's grief overshadowed the pomp and ritual of Victorian convention. For a day and a night he lay in state, and for a day and a night thousands passed by. Railroad and steamship companies had given free passage to all mourners, and they came in droves, men and women and children, the young and the old, the Charleston great and the hill-country farmers, shoulders bowed with work and boots red with clay; the white and the black, all moving in a single unbroken line. Only the women lingered, and upon the coffin they tossed their cloth-of-gold roses until the entire bier and all the space around it was covered with a carpet of flowers.[83]

17

And it was the man as much as the statesman that his state and the whole South loved. It was the intimate human details of his personality that Carolinians a hundred years after his death were talking about and remembering. They would whisper about his youthful romances, shake their heads over his wife's tantrums, sadly admit that he and she were 'not congenial.' They would argue about his health and his bushy hair, wondering still if he could change the color of his eyes in moments of excitement or anger. In the drawing rooms of Charleston, beside the paintings of Sully and of Lawrence, it was the portraits of Calhoun, no matter how damaged or crude, which hung in the place of honor, and to which men and women pointed with pride. He had become a sort of great-grandfather to the entire state, known as well and affectionately to those who had never seen him as if he had died only yesterday—or had never died at all. In no other state, not even in Jefferson's Virginia, is there that strange bond between the dead and the living.

They 'felt things' about Calhoun in South Carolina. They feel them still. Those in his own time were grateful that 'we have lived in his age, that we have seen him and heard him and known him. We shall delight to speak of him to those who are rising to fill our places.' But why did they love him so? Most of them had never known Calhoun. Few had seen him. Yet they mourned his passing 'with a sense of loss almost personal.'

If strangers paid tribute to his intellectual powers, Carolinians extolled his moral worth. They looked up to him because he was 'a good man, modest and unassuming,' his 'greatness and goodness allied.' [84] He was not a typical Southerner; there were few in any age like him. Yet in his way of living and philosophy of life he had summed up 'a whole people and a whole civilization.'

They loved him because he was one of them. His people and theirs had traveled in the same covered wagons, rolling down from Virginia. Like them he had drawn his strength from the red earth and the rock-bound hills; like them, behind all his talk of tariffs and slavery and states' rights, his every act and his deepest love went back to the land and the life on the land. Few Southerners had understood nullification; all Southerners could understand the reasons behind nullification. He was a man who had known and loved one way of life, and had given all his strength in a fight for the kind of America in which that way of life could endure.

South Carolina had loved Calhoun even when he had flouted and defied her. He had been a statesman, not a politician; his task had been to lead, not to follow, public opinion; to sacrifice himself 'for the people, not to them.' Of humble origin, he had held aloft the aristocratic ideal; not the aristocracy of accident of birth, or of wealth; but the aristocracy of brains and strength and character, which few could reach, but toward which all could aspire.

Like Jefferson, he believed that man's ends lay in his political destiny; that the goal of democracy was not equality, but equity; not to press men down into a common mold, but to give them release to develop to the fullest limits of their natures.

For the deference he exacted, the people, in their turn, exacted a statesman's conduct from him. He was above their bickerings and battles. When he descended to the politician's level and took the stump to defeat a Congressman who had opposed him, it was he, in the person of his candidate, who was soundly defeated. He was not expected to interfere in the state's internal concerns; and so the public firmly and sternly reminded him.

18

The last rites of all were simple. No ornate funeral carriage, but bare-headed young men carried the body of their great king to the grave in the west cemetery of Saint Philip's churchyard. There in the shadow of the brick walls, crumbling under their streamers of ivy, the mighty dead of South Carolina slept; proud names, Charleston names, with no up-country outlander among them. It was not the resting place Calhoun would have chosen. He would have preferred the wind-swept hills. But the citizens of Charleston had appealed to his family that 'the remains of him we loved so well be permitted to repose among us,' there in the Westminster Abbey of the South. 'Nowhere on earth,' wrote Jonathan

Daniels, seventy-seven years later, 'is there a sweeter or nobler place for sleep.' [85]

He was the South incarnate. He never thrilled to the notes of 'Dixie,' or watched the Stars and Bars unfurl against the Southern sky. The flag of the American Union hung above his grave. Yet it was his spirit that fired the Southern cause. For it was the Southern way of life, not states' rights, or slavery, or the tariff, for which the South fought—and Calhoun had been its greatest defender. The South would have fought without him; but the 'lost cause' for which it battled was his. And if the shade of old John Brown tramped with the armies of Grant and Sheridan, marching with the ragged followers of Lee and Stonewall Jackson was the gaunt, fiery-eyed ghost of John Calhoun.

On the square of white marble in Saint Philip's churchyard was cut the one word, CALHOUN. It was enough; he would not have asked for more. But there was no tribute 'of which he would have been more proud' than the gibe of a bitter Yankee soldier, standing in triumph in Saint Philip's churchyard in April, 1865, with the bomb-shattered ruins of Charleston around him: 'The whole South is the grave of Calhoun.' [86]

XXX

Minority Champion

NEVER WAS SLEEP more troubled than Calhoun's in the quiet churchyard. For months after his burial, the men and women of Charleston hovered about the tomb, heaping it daily with fresh wreaths and flowers. It became a sort of shrine, and in the sixties as Sherman marched from the mountains to the sea, a company of soldiers was stationed to guard it night and day. Finally, when the mutter of guns sounded around Charleston and shells smashed into the besieged city, the sexton of Saint Philip's, with a single assistant, dug up the body and reburied it by night beneath the church, lest the victorious troops of the North commit desecration. And there, unknowing, in the triumph of victory, came the bitter Yankee soldier with his epitaph; and in April, 1865, William Lloyd Garrison himself, to strike his hand against the white marble and proclaim: 'Down into a deeper grave than this, slavery is gone, and for it there is no resurrection.'[1]

As late as 1910, Southern die-hards could be found lingering about the tomb of Calhoun, declaring that the South would have won if only he could have been its leader, and even the old Negroes would 'tell stories of his unparalleled greatness.' He was still the South's uncrowned king; yet scarcely twenty years afterward 'thousands' of Northern visitors yearly made pilgrimages to his tomb.[2] Dead nearly three-quarters of a century, the Southern leader was coming into his own.

'He will speak,' had declared an unknown eulogist, 'most potently from the grave.' Not even the prophet himself had uttered prophecy truer than that. Behind him when he died, unfinished but blocked out, were his two books—*A Disquisition on Government* and *A Discourse on the Constitution of the United States*—to which he had literally given his last days and almost his last hours. Upon them his claim to fame is assured. For here, stripped of the day-to-day issues of his own time, is the essence of his entire political philosophy, the sum of all his living and thinking. Here is what latter-day critics would hail as perhaps the most powerful defense of minority rights in a democracy ever written.

It was a somber prophecy for later times, a haunted warning for his own. Yet in his own day it was neither heeded nor understood. The South

Carolina Legislature issued the work, together with his speeches, in a de luxe edition which was placed in reverence on Southern shelves, but how wide a reading audience those six abstract, closely written volumes obtained during the years of war and strife, it is not difficult to surmise. As for the victorious North, it had no desire to read or heed the warnings of the vanquished. Yet, as has been observed, when a man like Calhoun puts his last breath into a warning for his people, the people themselves are the losers if they do not hear what he has to say.[3]

2

The first book is superior to the second, which is diffuse, repetitive, clearly showing the illness of its author. Yet even the second is extraordinary. It is too much to claim, as do the most fervid Southern enthusiasts, that these books rank with Aristotle's, but with the single exception of the *Federalist Papers,* they represent America's most remarkable contribution to political thought.

In the *Disquisition* Calhoun outlined what he conceived to be the principles of government in general, and of democratic government in particular. In the *Discourse* he illustrated these principles by means of the Constitution and the American federal theory—and here is where the difficulties begin. For none knew better than Calhoun how vastly America had outgrown the federal pattern; and that the interests, once represented by states and later by sections, would soon be scattered across the entire country. By 1850, Calhoun had realized that although politically states' rights were a safeguard, economically they were not enough. Von Holst points out how in the end Calhoun repudiated what had been supposed to be his entire political philosophy;[4] fifteen years after his passing, a generation of Southern young men would die in the name of states' rights, mistakenly supposing that they were dying in the name of Calhoun.[5]

For passionate as was Calhoun's love for South Carolina; convinced as he was that the state was the unit upon which America was built, this organization still, to Calhoun, was a means and not an end. He was fighting, not for the original American pattern, but for the general federal theory; but this not even his most devoted admirers could understand. And not the federal theory alone, but the justice which the federal theory was devised to maintain, was to Calhoun the essence of America. America had outgrown states' rights—the usurpations of majority rule proved this—thus the theory must be reworked upon a new pattern.

This explains the confusion that distorts the second volume of Calhoun's mighty work. How could a country, which had embodied its theory in a pattern, maintain the theory without the pattern? Yet Calhoun's very recognition of this dilemma is the measure of his greatness as a statesman. It was not the Union that mattered so much as the purpose behind it. Calhoun was not doctrinaire; his aim was to make democracy work.

The purpose of his book was threefold: to save the South, to save the Union, to save the federal principles of the Union. All, he knew, were indispensable, one to the other. He knew that 1850 was the last chance for the South and West to rally behind a constitutional amendment which he thought would 'protect the South forever against economic exploitation.' He knew that ten years later would be too late. Within the Union, unconquered, the South could form a barrier against the final triumph of industrial centralization and unchecked majority rule; without, all would be lost.

Thus, in his last days, with haunted vision and in agony of spirit Calhoun had thrust against the forces which challenged the Union. The right to secede, as a last resort, hopeless as secession might be, he did not deny: 'That a State, as a party to the constitutional compact, has the right to secede . . . cannot be denied by anyone who regards the Constitution as a compact—if a power should be inserted by the amending power, which would radically change the character of the system; *or if the former should fail to fulfill the ends for which it was established.'* [6] Yet, practically, he knew that the South's only hope was in the Union.

3

Calhoun saw the country politically as 'a democratic Federal republic, democratic not aristocratic, federal not national . . . of states, not of individuals.' [7] He saw it as a government, not of the numerical majority, but of the concurrent majority—with each major group in society having a voice in the legislation affecting it, as in the legislation affecting the whole.

Economically, his ideal was not an agrarian, but a balanced, economy. The numerical supremacy of factory workers over farmers, of industrialists over planters, he considered had nothing to do with the rights and powers belonging to each group. The one was not the slave of the other; all were essential to the maintenance of a sound and healthy economic system.

For Calhoun, America was a protest against the European spirit, against an aristocracy of birth, against the artificial aristocracy of accumulated wealth 'and the decadence of men.' The South, although conservative, static, at odds with the dynamic and expanding North, he saw as the symbol of this protest. Already the South was an anachronism, a minority voice against the majority will, but still the last barrier against the rising, middle-class, standardized civilization which was sweeping the world in the wake of the Industrial Revolution.

Future events would prove to many how terribly right he had been. A century later Harold Laski would find an America committed to the evaluation of men by what they had rather than what they were—to the pursuit of wealth rather than of happiness as the chief end of man.

To Calhoun the American system was an experiment in diversity. It was based upon the right of peoples to choose their own way of life, economic and social, and to live it, regardless of the majority pattern. America's freedom was in her differences. Under the federal political system, as written, different civilizations, granting that they could agree on principles involving the common interest and common safety of all, could live together.

In the South a special civilization had developed. It was a Southern civilization, common only to that region and representative of it. Yet it was under the American system that it had grown to fruition; and it was authentically American.

With the secession of the South, the great American experiment would be at an end. As a political philosopher and as a patriot, Calhoun could not bear to see it end. Furthermore, in the American system Calhoun saw principles applicable to the entire world, to all mankind. One of the earliest advocates of 'One World,' he was, however, wise enough to know that there could never be one pattern of culture for the world. In a world where 'progress in matter,' as he had long foreseen, had outstripped moral development,[8] you may say that you must have one standard of values to exist, but it does not follow either that you will have the values or continue to exist. As a practical statesman, Calhoun was not so much interested in what you have to have, or should have, as in what you could have.

Any government, national or world-wide, that crushes men into a single pattern, he deemed a despotic government. This was the principle invoked by every conqueror through time; and for the United States, for example, to impose on the world one system of industrial capitalism, whether good or evil, would be adoption of the tyrannical belief that the world could only exist under one system. Half a century before Adolf Hitler was born, Calhoun had the wisdom to know that although men may agree on general principles of safety, a world system based upon one country's concept of freedom, denies others the very right of choice which is essential to freedom.

4

A world federal government, Calhoun might see as desirable and possible. But he would have laughed at what the world, or the post-Civil War United States, considered to be a federal government. Federal, as a working word in the American vocabulary, has indeed been dead since the

Civil War. For federal involved the rights of peoples to control their own affairs in their own localities; and the same federal principle which protected the South as a minority voice in the United States could be readily invoked in a world federal government today.

Governments, Calhoun had always contended, were formed to protect minorities; majorities could look after themselves. As written, the Constitution had been an attempt to protect minority rights. In a federal Union the South was a constant conservative check against the national advances of 'liberalism' and 'progress.' Thus, for the majority, it was necessary to strip her of the power to say how the Constitution was written. It was necessary to abolish the federal theory, and what could not be done by law was finally done by war.

The demolition work was complete. 'Conquered and subjugated,' the Southern people, as a latter-day statesman pointed out, were relegated to be 'drawers of water and hewers of wood.' [9] The war that was to 'free' the Negro had left a back-wash of eleven million Southern men and women, both black and white, who eighty years after the guns of Sumter and Shiloh were still, were living on cash incomes of less than two hundred and fifty dollars a year.[10] The South, which knew that democracy flourished only under an economy in which 'private property was widely distributed, individually owned, and personally managed,' had become the country of which it could be said that '85 per cent of Georgia is owned by people outside.' [11]

By the twentieth century, the 'Colonial status of the South,' sensed by the suspicious 'Pat' Calhoun and his backwoodsmen, prophesied and outlined by John Calhoun, had become a recognized, and, it was to be feared, a permanent status. By near the half-century mark, John Gunther could report that more Southern industries and more Southern resources were 'being transferred to Northern control month by month.' * [12]

War had left a whole people despoiled, a whole land laid waste. Yet hand in hand with the Northern victory came the grimmest, most ironic joke of all. For by bleeding and defrauding the South, it finally became evident that the industrialists were bleeding and defrauding themselves. High tariffs had walled out their world markets, and their greatest home market could not afford to buy what they made. The seed of future depressions was sown in the Southern states, as was foreseen by Franklin D. Roosevelt when he warned that the 'economic unbalance in the Nation as a whole' was 'due to this very condition of the South.' [13] Here, indeed, was proof of Calhoun's doctrine that only by aiding, not by subjecting his fellows to his will, can man assure prosperity for himself.

'The South . . . the poor South . . .' Not even in his wildest imaginings had Calhoun foreseen the desolation that became the truth. But he

---

* Nor was this 'Colonial status' reversed by the trend of Northern-owned industries southward, through the nineteen-forties.

sensed it, nevertheless. He had seen the beginning of the end, and his life's struggle had been to avoid that end. He had warned; and his warnings were heeded too late. And viewing the grim lesson of the 'Colonial' South today,* bleeding still from wounds unhealed after eighty years, would have filled Calhoun with fear as to the fate of 'backward' minority peoples under the rule of a world government unless it were firmly based on the federal principle. It is fortunate, perhaps, for the peoples of the world that America developed a philosopher who believed that superior to progress was the right of individuals to choose whether they would be progressive or not; and that federalism was a system—and not a word.

5

Calhoun's love was for liberty. (He, of course, shared with Henry Clay and virtually the entire Southern leadership of his day, the conviction that the Negro slave formed 'an exception . . . from stern necessity, to the general liberty.') Yet 'the more enlarged and secure the liberty of individuals,' he declared, 'the more perfectly' government fulfilled 'the end for which it was ordained.' [14] Like Jefferson, he knew that the manufacturer must be placed 'by the side of the agriculturist,' but industrial progress he would have measured, not by its profits to the few, but by its benefits to the many. He had no illusions that the capitalistic system of labor exploitation, North or South, had arisen with any social benefits in mind. He knew that 'in point of fact' every 'wealthy and civilized' portion of society lived upon the labor of another class. Capitalism, either as Northern industrialism or Southern slavery, he viewed realistically as a force too great to be eliminated. Yet as a statesman it was his task to find means to control it. Such was the purpose of a free government, Jefferson had declared, to 'restrain men from injuring each other . . . and . . . not take from the mouth of labor, the bread it has earned.' Or, as Calhoun put it: 'He who earns the money has a just title to it against the universe.' [15]

6

Calhoun had early realized that political freedom and economic security, far from being opposed, actually were counterparts of one another. 'Liberty and security,' he said, 'are indispensable.' If liberty left 'each free to

* Despite the much-heralded talk of 'equalization' of freight rates in recent years, Southern industry was still paying tribute as late as 1948. For example, to send 100 pounds of textiles 808 miles from Holyoke, Massachusetts, to Cincinnati, Ohio, cost $2.54; to send the same amount 808 miles from Shreveport, Louisiana, to Cincinnati cost $3.13.

pursue the course he may deem best to promote his interest and happiness . . . security gives assurance to each, that he shall not be deprived of his exertion to better his condition.' [16]

If not all secure men were free (as in the case of the slaves), Calhoun reasoned, it was equally true that no free man was insecure. Without economic security political freedom was a mockery. Was the penniless, landless, hopeless 'poor white' free? * Was the laborer free whose livelihood depended upon his subservience to the political will of his employer? Was any man free with no security that his work would reap rewards, that his children would have the same right as 'privileged' children to health, to education, to normal adult development—regardless of depressions and cotton markets?

Realist that he was, Calhoun well knew that men would readily sacrifice their liberty to make sure of 'protection' or security. Had he not told Benjamin Perry that men would choose protection in preference to liberty? He knew human nature. He knew that 'you could not eat the Constitution.' He knew that men, although called voters and citizens, thought 'material things more important than freedom.' [17] There might be men (a minority of them) to whom abstract political freedom was the highest of all earthly blessings; but even for these few there would be no lasting liberty without the security of the many. Hence Calhoun favored the kind of political system which would at least guarantee to the worker the economic security possessed by a Negro slave. The test of a free government, he would have declared, was the measure of protection it granted its weakest individuals.

Calhoun's life, his talents, all that was in him, he consecrated to the task of 'handing down the Constitution as pure as when he found it.' No man was a more sleepless guardian against its violation, no man more untiring in his efforts to restore its supremacy over 'the Congress, the Executive, and the People.' [18] To him the Union had been devised for certain ends, enumerated in the Constitutional Convention. Through the 'peculiar Federal structure' of our government, America's freedoms were protected. If ours was a government, not of men, but of law, the Constitution was the ultimate law. If our Union were to endure, then the Constitution could not be used to defeat the ends it had been written to maintain.

So reasoned Calhoun. And so runs the explanation of his lifelong struggle to 'restore our government to its original purity and to keep it within the limits of the Constitution.' The Constitution, as written, had devised new principles which, evolved, might mean new freedoms for all men. This was the kind of America he fought to preserve. 'I don't want to destroy the Union,' was his continual cry, 'I only wish to make it honest.' [19]

* Calhoun failed, of course, to take into account the fact that much of the poverty and landlessness of the 'poor white' was due to the large-scale plantation system and the draining of the land from the cotton economy.

If he be a disunionist who insists upon constitutional guarantees above
the will of the people, upon the ultimate authority of law above men,
then Calhoun was a disunionist. Logically, he was right. There is no freedom where a simple majority can dispense with constitutional safeguards.
If a popular majority were to become the ultimate law, then, as Jefferson
had realized, the Constitution would be so much waste paper. Men could
talk of freedom while they violated the constitutional provisions that
authorized slavery, but Calhoun knew, only too well, that if constitutional
law could be set aside at will to free the blacks, it could as easily be disregarded to enslave the whites.

7

Despite all the guarantees of its written Constitution, however, none
knew better than Calhoun that the United States was far from immune to
the dangers that had destroyed all free republics of the past. Totalitarianism was not a word in his vocabulary—oligarchy would have been his
nearest approach to it—but he was aware of its meanings nevertheless. In
every past age, democracies had drifted steadily toward consolidation,
and consolidation meant the destruction of the local rights and freedoms
that the republic was created to preserve. Only a federal as opposed to
a national system of government could prevent this; and the future colonial subjugation of both the South and West would prove an interesting
object lesson to idealists who pinned their faith in mere political democracy without restraints.

It is true that for both the South and West the exploitations of big
business during New Deal days were considerably eased by a government with power to oppose them. Yet even here the South profited primarily because a party favorable to its interests wielded the power. Had
the reverse been true, the states had no reserved powers by which the
processes of consolidation could have been checked.

8

To a truly federal Union, Calhoun asserted, 'consolidation and disunion'
would be equally destructive.[20] And the one would be the result of the
other. Southern aspirations to nationalism, although the outgrowth of
real encroachments and real dangers, were in themselves as great a danger
to the Union as the forces they opposed. Calhoun had long tried to siphon
this Southern nationalism off through the individual states, but without
success. Only in later years, as we have seen, had he realized that the
only way to keep it from destroying the Union was to consolidate the

Southern element. And to this end a constitutional amendment was essential, for the old spirit of mutual interest and mutual affection was gone.

America's very individuality was its worst danger. As Calhoun put it, 'the more extensive and populous the country, the more diverse the . . . pursuits of its population, and the richer . . . and more dissimilar the people, the more difficult it is to equalize' the action of government, especially 'in reference to the varied and diversified interests of the community.' Nothing was more easy than oppression under the cloak of laws 'which on their face appear fair and equal.' [21] Here, in a line, was the history of the tariff struggle; of the whole country, in fact, between the Revolution and the Civil War.

With haunted vision the prophet had read the future. He had not flinched, not withdrawn from the darkness that he saw. Grimly he set himself to solve the problem that had wrecked every constitutional republic of the past—to find ways to prevent men from oppressing each other and from wrecking that justice which the Union had been devised to preserve.

How, he asked, in substance, 'can we construct a working machine for the democratic state, without bestowing upon the majority an absolute dictatorship?' Like Jefferson, he could say that 'the right of suffrage is the . . . primary principle in . . . a constitutional government,' [22] but unlike the Virginian, Calhoun's faith in suffrage and the numerical majority alone was not uncritical. Suffrage could do no more than guarantee the responsibility of the elected to the group that elected them. If the common interest were the same, suffrage would be enough. But instead, there was a continual 'struggle . . . between the various interests to control the government.' [23] If one was not strong enough, a combine would be 'formed between those whose interests are most alike.' The dominant class would serve 'its class interests . . . would be the rulers . . . the minority . . . as much the . . . subject portion, as are the people in a monarchy.' [24]

No justice, Calhoun contended, written constitution or none, could be preserved without restraints. 'It is idle, worse than idle, to attempt to distinguish . . . between a government of unlimited powers, and one professedly limited, but with an unlimited right to determine the extent of its powers.' [25] Yet such, men were beginning to claim, was the structure of the United States.

He had seen as early as nullification days the error in our Constitution, that the 'Federal government contains . . . no provisions by which the powers delegated could be prevented from encroaching on the powers reserved to the several States.'

Why has this fundamental omission been made? Calhoun would have said that it was due to a faulty concept of human nature, and of this the Jeffersonians were the most guilty. It was they who had written equality alone, not equity, into the Declaration of Independence. Equality of citizens 'in the eyes of the law,' Calhoun of course deemed 'essential to liberty in a popular government.' [26] The non-voting citizenry—the Negroes, the women and children—he saw as comparable to the passengers on a ship; not directing the passage, but sharing in the privileges and the protections of the voyage.[27]

To Calhoun equality too often meant only an equal chance for the unequally endowed to compete for a goal. Not equity, but *laissez-faire*. Not protection, but exploitation. And this tragedy had occurred through the Jeffersonians' second faulty concept of human nature. Steeped as they were in the idealism of the French Revolutionary philosophers, they had assumed that an ideal government made ideal men; that the evil in the world was not from men, but from the institutions that held them down. Men were inherently good; and by this fallacy the Jeffersonians had blinded themselves to the danger of unchecked democracy becoming the very source of its own destruction.

For all men were not inherently good, and the institutions that crushed them were themselves man-made. Had the doctrine of inherent goodness been true, then an assumption of equality might have been possible. Recognizing the divine equality of human souls, men of talent would voluntarily have protected, not exploited, those with whom Nature had been less generous.

But the Hamiltonians had understood. Throughout the ages realists of their ilk had perceived the true nature of man. They had understood it and they had exploited it. At seventeen Hamilton had perceived what Calhoun only realized at thirty-seven: that 'a vast majority of mankind is entirely biassed by motives of self-interest,' [28] and that by this interest must be governed.

Bitter experience had opened Calhoun's eyes. Freedom, he knew, was not to be saved by denying the dangers to freedom. An ideal government did not make ideal men. Thomas Jefferson and the French theorists could not do in a generation what Christianity had been unable to do in eighteen hundred years.

Yet where the Hamiltonians, to gratify the aims of the few, would use the facts of human nature to exploit the many, Calhoun would use the same facts to protect all men from one another. If men were selfish, selfishness should be recognized, and when acknowledged, it could be controlled.

Defiant of the French Revolutionary theory of man 'in a state of nature,' Calhoun turned to the facts. Man, he contended, existed only in the social state, and the social state necessitated government. Yet man had 'a greater regard for his own safety and happiness than for the safety or happiness of others'; and 'hence, the tendency to a universal state of conflict,' if not prevented by some controlling power.[29] Government would be completely unnecessary if men truly loved their neighbors as themselves.

Self-interest, Calhoun knew, could be as ruthless in a democracy as in a monarchy. Bitterly he ridiculed 'the folly of supposing that the party in possession of the ballot box and the physical force of the country could be successfully resisted by an appeal to reason, truth, justice, or the obligations of the Constitution.' [30]

Had not all history taught him otherwise?

What could be done? Calhoun, at least, had an answer. Any political ideal, he contended, was useless, unless built upon a foundation of the facts. And he tore at the facts with a realism that left the last of Jefferson's idealistic concept of men in 'shreds and tatters.' [31] He re-examined the teachings of the fathers, substituted economic realism for abstract humanitarianism; and based his democratic faith upon a new foundation.

What he proposed was a blending of the two dominant trends of American thought, the Jeffersonian ideal upon the Hamiltonian foundations. Not rejecting majority rule, but expounding it and providing for its control, he worked out a corollary to Jefferson's thought and suggested constitutional reforms that 'might prove the salvation of political democracy in America.' [32]

His basic solution, the substitution of the 'concurrent' for the numerical majority, was revolutionary—perhaps his most revolutionary contribution to political thought.[33] His aim was a government, not 'of a part over a part,' but of 'a part made identical with the whole.' [34] How could this be done? By consulting the voice 'of each interest or portion of the community, which may be unequally or injuriously affected by the action of the government,' before putting laws into operation. 'Each division or interest' should have 'either a concurrent voice in making and executing the laws, or a veto on their execution.' Thus would the different interests be 'protected, and all conflict and struggle between them prevented.' [35]

Calhoun was, of course, sufficiently realistic to know that although in theory he sought 'the sense of the entire community,' necessarily only 'a few great and prominent interests' could be thus represented.[36] Nevertheless, legislation would be more just if enacted by a nation-wide majority of farm, laboring, and financial groups than by a majority of the one over the other.

In a modern application of his plan, the 'concurrent veto' seems, of course, the stumbling-block. Yet this objection is lessened if we reject the twentieth-century concept of the term 'veto,' for which Calhoun would have had only scorn, and remember that under his nullification theories a state could suspend a law only in relation to itself, not for the rest of the country. And in time of war, Calhoun realized that, Constitution or no Constitution, freedom was at an end, although undoubtedly he would have preferred that the Constitution admit this truth explicitly. His own words were clear: 'Government . . . must in the present condition of the world, be clothed with powers sufficient to call forth the resources of the community, and be prepared at all times, to command promptly in all emergencies . . . large establishments . . . both civil and military . . . with well-trained forces in sufficient numbers. . . .'[37] 'Liberty must always be subject to power which prevents from internal or external dangers. . . . Liberty must yield to protection; as the existance of the race is of greater moment than its improvement.'[38]

However, in time of peace, Calhoun knew that there was no justice without self-determination. It was not democracy when '51% of the people have a moral right to coerce 49%.'[39] To put the matter into terms of our day, would there be any moral sanction for the re-establishment of slavery, provided that a majority could be induced to vote for it?

Calhoun, 'bolder and more logical than Jefferson,'[40] feared centralized government no less than unrestrained industrialism, but he knew it was a *fait accompli*, and hence must be recognized and controlled. Again, a realist, he saw that 'We must take men as they are, and do the best we can with them. . . . If all were disinterested patriots, there would be no difficulty in running or managing the political machine, and very little credit in doing either.'[41]

If a free government could rest only upon the realization of the Christian ideal of brotherhood and unselfishness, then, Calhoun feared, we should never have a free government. Men could be free, however — even with selfish human nature unchanged—if they had but wisdom enough to understand themselves. Self-interest could be the best promoter of compromises. When men realized that their own interests would be lost unless they allowed their fellows to protect themselves, then only would agreements be reached. A democracy based on the principle of the concurrent majority, Calhoun believed, would unite the most conflicting elements, 'and blend the whole in one common attachment to the country. . . . Each sees and feels that it can best promote its own prosperity by . . . promoting the prosperity of the others.' For antipathy and rivalry would be substituted the ideal of 'the common good.'[42]

Complicated? Yes. The unrestrained government of a numerical majority, Calhoun readily admitted, had the 'major advantage of simplicity.'[43] Constitutional governments were complex, and the higher and freer they were, the more complex they became. He did not deny that a 'mutual negative' might lead to collision and conflict, might even momentarily render government 'incompetent.' Liberty from the oppression of a majority, however, seemed to him well worth the dangers. Furthermore, each minority would, in turn, be restrained in the use of its 'veto' by its own internal minorities. Another restraint would be the inevitable reluctance to break the lines of the great political parties.

Because of his appreciation of the complexities of a government at once democratic and free, Calhoun insisted it be run by those intelligent and informed enough to deal with its difficulties.

Here, indeed, is the very foundation of his defense of slavery. For where Jefferson loved freedom too much to deny it to the least of men, Calhoun loved it too much to surrender it to those who he thought might endanger it. He had lived to see the new birth of tyrannies in 'free' Jamaica and Santo Domingo; the abortive and short-lived birth of freedom in Germany; the return of imperial despotism to France. Freedom, he knew, was not a grant, but an accomplishment; lasting, not when superimposed from without, but only as it grew from within.

He believed completely that the encroachments of the rich were 'more destructive to the state than those of the poor'; but he felt sure also that a forced political equality among those of unequal capacity would only deny liberty to those most fitted to uphold and maintain it. It would mean a government of the lowest rather than of the highest elements in the citizenry. The natural 'inequality of condition,' he claimed, gave an 'impetus to those on top' to maintain themselves, and to the others 'to press forward' into their places. 'This gives progress its greatest impulse.' But to 'force the front rank back to the rear, or attempt to push forward the rear . . . would effectually arrest . . . progress.' [44]

Jefferson himself had called for a government of the 'natural aristocracy,' and had declared that a government of landowning farmers was the best; of 'mechanics' the worst. It was also Jefferson who advocated majority rule. The changed complexion of our population in half a century, however, had made these demands incompatible. In a nation where 'mechanics' and industrialists were in the majority, it was assured that in an unrestrained democracy they would govern.

The question that was the 'major problem' of Calhoun's day is the major problem of our own. The realism, as well as the inevitability, of Calhoun's basic premise has been shown by the rise of a sort of minority control, 'not unlike his concurrent veto.' Our modern pressure groups—farm bloc, silver bloc, labor bloc, and all the many others—are an 'extralegal and unsatisfactory' attempt to protect minority interests. [45] The objections to the activities of these groups, which we so frequently voice, are due to their extralegal quality and the consequent difficulty of controlling them. Calhoun, by regularizing and embodying in law these inevitable minority aspirations, would have made them at once more effective and more controlled.

Calhoun visualized a Congress of strictly defined group representation, in which each group would have final say on questions primarily affecting itself. Instead of viewing one another as competitors, each group, he felt, would come to realize that its prosperity was directly dependent upon the rights and prosperity of the other. As Herbert Agar has said, 'Perhaps no democracy can avoid tyrannizing over its minority groups, unless it is willing to adopt some system similar to Calhoun's concurrent veto.' [46]

Similarities will be observed between Calhoun's plan and the legislative representation of varied 'interests' which we have seen in the twentieth-century 'corporate states,' such as Mussolini's Italy. The evil which corrupted these states does not, of course, argue that all their institutions were evil. It does go to show that neither Calhoun's nor any other system can provide adequate safeguards against man's persecution of his fellows.

Calhoun was right in thinking that his plan would strengthen democratic processes. He was wrong in thinking it a cure-all. His concurrent veto for major economic groups might prevent the oppression of the farmer by the industrial laborer, or of the laborer by the manufacturer. It might guarantee the poor white a livelihood; it could not save the Negro from lynch law. It might ease class lines on the basis of poverty or injustice; it could not erase color lines or religious prejudices.

We have seen the efforts of minority groups to protect their 'interests' by 'pressure groups.' The philosophy underlying Calhoun's proposals has also become a dominant, if extralegal, force in our great political parties and within the government itself. Perhaps the basic rule of American political parties is to utilize, reconcile, and absorb the diverse interest groups which compose them. The obscurities and contradictions which so often compose their platforms are but practical attempts to compromise these divergent demands. For their mutual benefit each group tacitly binds itself to tolerate the interests of the others, both in writing a 'flexible' platform and in choosing an 'available' candidate.

Within the government the Cabinet posts and 'special interest agencies' are in their essence representatives of group interests. And in the halls of Congress we daily observe that mutual 'courtesy' and compromising coalition which tend to prevent the enactment of laws damaging to the 'interests' of a regional or economic group.*

All this Calhoun would have codified and enacted into law, and as Herbert Agar has pointed out, 'A modern adaptation of Calhoun's plan, giving to the major economic interests . . . the concurring power . . . might go far towards removing both class and economic distinctions.' Meanwhile, we put up with the unrestricted, extralegal 'rule' of group interests 'until we are prepared to give interest groups a positive voice in lawmaking.' [47]

A statesman's value is relative, after all; and judged by later times, and his meaning for them, Calhoun stands in the first rank of men America has produced. For as thinker and prophet, he was more important for later times than for his own.

---

* For a further elaboration on the operation of the concurrent majority system today, see John Fischer's interesting article, 'Unwritten Rules of American Politics,' in *Harper's Magazine*, November, 1948.

He knew that in his day he would fail.

He knew that he was setting himself against, not only the growing strength of the industrial North, but the forces of history, the spirit of the age. He saw that spirit as a whole 'and challenged it as a whole.' He knew that his own name and his own fame would go down to ruin. He did not care. He would not have wanted even his name 'to outlive the thing he loved.' His concern was for fundamentals, for the principles of free government which he believed to be as basic and unyielding as the principles of scientific truth. Politics he saw as a science for the development and freedom of man; and in writing his books, just as he thought, 'without fear or favor,' his hope was to lay 'a solid foundation for political science.' [48]

For him there was only the duty to point out the truth as he saw it. Truth, he knew, was more important than success, and he was content to do his duty 'without looking further.' He knew, as his successor, Jefferson Davis, knew, that the principle for which he contended was 'bound to reassert itself, although it may be at another time and in another form.' [49] Sustained by the tenets of that Calvinistic faith which had enveloped him from boyhood, he faced the gathering darkness, unafraid.

THE END

☆

Notes
Bibliography
Index

☆

NOTES

I. THE HERITAGE

1. W. H. Sparks, *Old Times in Georgia: The Memories of Fifty Years*, 108–109.
2. Ben Robertson, *Red Hills and Cotton: An Upcountry Memory*, 121–122.
3. Sparks, 69.
4. John C. Calhoun to Anna Maria Clemson, March 7, 1848, in the *Correspondence of John C. Calhoun*, J. Franklin Jameson, ed., in the *Annual Report of the American Historical Association* for 1899, II, 744–745. (Cited hereafter as *Correspondence.*)
5. Sparks, 14, 16.
6. D. H. Fleming, *The Story of the Scotch Covenanters*, 72, 76.
7. Sparks, 16–17.
8. David Ramsay, *History of South Carolina*, I, 452.
9. See J. B. O'Neall, *Annals of Newberry*, 244–245; John S. Jenkins, *Life of John Caldwell Calhoun*, 21.
10. James Parton, *Famous Americans of Recent Times*, 117–118.
11. Calhoun to Miss Nancy Calhoun, May 30, 1847. Copy in possession of Miss Lilian Gold, Flint, Michigan.
12. John H. Logan, *History of the Upper Country of South Carolina*, I, 150.
13. William P. Starke, 'Account of Calhoun's Early Life,' in the *Annual Report of the American Historical Association* for 1899, II, 67–68. (Cited hereafter as Starke.)
14. Anonymous, *Life of John C. Calhoun*, 5. (Cited hereafter as Calhoun, *Life.*)
15. Jenkins, 22.
16. Parton, 118.
17. *Ibid.*

18. Christopher Hollis, *The American Heresy*, 83.
19. Calhoun, *Life*, 5.
20. Starke, 69.
21. *Ibid.*, 70–71.
22. Calhoun, *Life*, 5.
23. Jenkins, 24; Starke, 72.
24. Parton, 186.
25. Calhoun, *Life*, 5.
26. Charleston *City Gazette and Daily Advertiser*, March 7, 1796.
27. Wills of South Carolina, I, 37, in South Caroliniana Library, University of South Carolina, Columbia.
28. Hamilton Basso, *Mainstream*, 47–48.
29. Sparks, 24–25.
30. Elbridge S. Brooks, *Historic Americans*, 292.
31. Starke, 73.
32. *Ibid.*, 32.
33. Robertson, 64.
34. Basil Hall, *Travels in America*, II, 230; Ulrich B. Phillips, *Life and Labor in the Old South*, 124.
35. Robertson, 57–58, 223.
36. James Edward Colhoun, quoted in Starke, 75.
37. Starke, 68.
38. Jenkins, 25.
39. Starke, 75.
40. *Ibid.*, 73.
41. South Carolina *Gazette*, May 10, 1798, in Clemson College Papers.
42. Fort Hill neighborhood tradition. See also Walter L. Miller, 'Calhoun as a Lawyer and Statesman,' *The Green Bag*, XI, no. 5, 197, 424.
43. Starke, 77.
44. Miller, *The Green Bag*, XI, no. 5, 147, 424.
45. Starke, 77–78.

II. FOR GOD AND TIMOTHY DWIGHT

1. Christopher Hollis, *The American Heresy*, 83.
2. Hamilton Basso, *Mainstream*, 47–48; William E. Dodd, *The Cotton Kingdom*, 100.
3. Twelve Southerners, *I'll Take My Stand*, 111.
4. William P. Starke, 'Account of Calhoun's Early Life,' *Correspondence*, 77.

5. J. E. D. Shipp, *Giant Days; or The Life and Times of William H. Crawford*, 167.
6. J. G. Swift, *Measures, Not Men*, 5.
7. Starke, 80.
8. Calhoun to Alexander Noble, September, 1801, printed copy in the office of the South Carolina Department of Education, Columbia, South Carolina.

9. William E. Dodd, *Statesmen of the Old South*, 83–84.
10. J. W. Barber, *Views of New Haven*, 4.
11. Students' Treasury bills, 1799–1808, manuscript in MSS. Division, Yale Library.
12. J. B. Reynold, Samuel H. Fisher, Henry B. Wright, *Two Centuries of Christian Activity at Yale;* quotation from James Kingsley, *Yale College*, I, 118.
13. *The Laws of Yale College*, chap. 2, p. 8, in Yale Rare Book Room. (Hereafter referred to as *Laws*.)
14. Samuel G. Goodrich, *Recollections of a Lifetime*, I, 348–349.
15. Treasurer's Records, Dec. 8, 1802, in MSS. Division, Yale Library.
16. *Laws*, chap. 2, p. 9.
17. *Ibid.*, chap. 8, pp. 24–27.
18. Calhoun to William P. Starke, quoted in Starke, 80.
19. Alexander Fisher to Caleb Fisher, Jan. 16, 1813, and Dec. 30, 1809, Fisher Papers, Yale Library.
20. *Laws*, chap. 3, p. 16.
21. Reminiscences of Dr. Alexander Stephens, quoted in manuscript records of the Linonian Society, Yale Library.
22. Swift, 5–6.
23. *Laws*, chap. 9, pp. 11–12.
24. *Ibid.*, chap. 8, p. 11.
25. Ezekiel P. Belden, *Sketches of Yale College*, 145.
26. *Laws*, chap. 3, p. 13.
27. Belden, 147–148.
28. *Ibid.*, 149.
29. Alexander Fisher to Caleb Fisher, June 18, 1813, and Aug. 12, 1814.
30. Calhoun to Alexander Noble, Oct. 15, 1804, *Correspondence*, 94.
31. T. S. Green, *Catalogue of Yale College Library*.
32. George P. Fisher, *The Life of Benjamin Silliman*, I, 34–35.
33. *Connecticut Journal and Herald*, Oct. 27, Dec. 10, 1803.
34. Timothy Dwight, Jr., *Memories of Yale Life and Men*, 321.
35. *Ibid.*, 40.
36. Manuscript diary of Daniel Mulford, April, 1801, to Dec., 1807, entry for July 4, 1805, in Yale Library.
37. Reynold, *Two Centuries of Christian Activity at Yale;* quotation from Bagg, *Four Years at Yale*, 17; see also Fisher, *The Life of Ben-*

38. *Brief Memories of the Class of 1802;* see also Fisher, I, 53; and E. C. Tracy, *Memoirs of the Life of Jeremiah Evarts*, 21.
39. Records of the Yale College 'Moral Society' for April 11, 1816, quoted in *Two Centuries of Christian Activity at Yale*.
40. Frederick Marryat, *Diary in America*, 68 (one-volume American edition).
41. Goodrich, I, 354.
42. Marryat, 226.
43. Belden, 48.
44. Franklin B. Dexter, *Biographical Sketches of the Graduates of Yale College*, V, 647, 676.
45. R. Gibson to James MacBride, April 18, 1817, MacBride Papers, MSS. Division, Library of Congress.
46. Calhoun to James MacBride, Feb. 16, 1812, and Dec. 15, 1812, MacBride Papers, MSS. Division, Library of Congress.
47. Calhoun to Micah Sterling, April 1, 1818, Calhoun Papers, MSS. Division, Library of Congress.
48. R. D. French, *Memorial Quadrangle*, 157.
49. Hermann von Holst, *John C. Calhoun*, 6.
50. Fisher, II, 50.
51. *Ibid.*, II, 97.
52. Reminiscences of Dr. Alexander Stephens in manuscript records of Linonian Society.
53. Manuscript records of the Alpha Chapter, Phi Beta Kappa, Yale College, July 11, 1803, in Yale Memorabilia Room.
54. *Ibid.*, July 25, 1803.
55. *Ibid.*, Dec. 19, 1803.
56. Calhoun to Isaac Townsend, Feb. 30, 1827, in records of Alpha Chapter, Phi Beta Kappa.
57. Manuscript records of Alpha Chapter, Phi Beta Kappa, Dec. 5, 1803, and Dec. 20, 1803.
58. Manuscript records of the Linonian Society and the Brothers in Unity in MSS. Division, Yale Library.
59. Calhoun to William H. Storrs, June 15, 1840, copy in manuscript records of Brothers in Unity at Yale.
60. Wilbur L. Cross, *Connecticut Yankee*, 148.
61. Manuscript records of the Linonian

Society at Yale, entries for Nov. 31, 1803; June 13, 1803; Aug. 1, 1803; and March 2, 1804.
62. Manuscript records of the Brothers in Unity at Yale, June 13, 1803.
63. Manuscript records of Alpha Chapter, Phi Beta Kappa, in Yale Memorabilia Room; entries for Sept. 5, 1803; July 13, 1802; Nov. 15, 1802; and Feb. 7, 1803.
64. Roger S. Boardman, *Life of Roger Sherman*, 332.
65. George F. Hoar, *Autobiography of Seventy Years*, 8.
66. Goodrich, I, 348–349.
67. J. G. Swift, 6.
68. Fisher, II, 97.
69. Timothy Dwight, Jr., *Decision of Questions*, 99, 42.
70. John S. Jenkins, *The Life of John Caldwell Calhoun*, 31.
71. See the 'Scheme of the Exercises for the Public Commencement, Yale College, Sept. 21, 1804.' In MS. Division, Yale Library.
72. Walter Miller, 'Calhoun as a Lawyer and Statesman,' *The Green Bag*, XI, 201–202.
73. Anson Phelps Stokes, *Memorials of Eminent Yale Men*, II, 199.
74. New Haven *Herald* and New Haven *Register*, July 17, 1804, and Aug. 21, 1804.
75. Calhoun to Jeremiah Day, Dec. 2, 1822. Calhoun Papers, Yale University.
76. Calhoun to Benjamin Silliman, March 20, 1818. Calhoun Papers, Yale University.
77. Calhoun to Benjamin Silliman, Aug. 14, 1825. Calhoun Papers, Yale University.
78. Calhoun to D. Daggett, Dec. 14, 1826. Calhoun Papers, Yale University.

III. YEARS OF GROWTH

1. Calhoun to Alexander Noble, Oct. 15, 1804, *Correspondence*, 93–94.
2. James Parton, *Famous Americans of Recent Times*, 56.
3. Calhoun to Mrs. Floride Colhoun: Sept. 26, Aug. 12, and Dec. 23, 1805, *Correspondence*, 95–96, 98, 101.
4. Parton, 56.
5. William P. Starke, 'Accounts of Calhoun's Early Life,' *Correspondence*, 83.
6. South Carolina tradition.
7. Calhoun to Mrs. Floride Colhoun, June 12, 1810, and Oct. 1, 1809, *Correspondence*, 115, 113.
8. Original in Calhoun Papers at Calhoun College, Yale University.
9. Anecdote quoted in Starke, 84
10. John Quincy Adams, *Diary*, IV, 70; also Calhoun to James Monroe, June 24, 1820. Calhoun Papers, Library of Congress.
11. Calhoun to Mrs. Floride Colhoun, July 22, 1805, *Correspondence*, 94–95.
12. Descriptions drawn from *Memories of Horace Bushnell, passim; Personal Memories of E. D. Mansfield*, 122; S. G. Goodrich, *Recollections of a Lifetime*, I, 126–127; Thomas L. Nichols, *Forty Years of American Life*, I, 23.
13. Calhoun to Mrs. Floride Colhoun, July 22, 1805, *Correspondence*, 95.
14. Frederick Marryat, *Diary in America*, 68.
15. Goodrich, I, 74, 78–79, 81, 83; Nichols, I, 27.
16. This description is drawn from Samuel H. Fisher's *The Litchfield Law School, passim*.
17. Calhoun to Mrs. Floride Colhoun, July 22, 1805, *Correspondence*, 94–95.
18. Lyman Beecher, *Autobiography*, I, 224.
19. *Ibid.*, 124, ff.
20. Goodrich, I, 117.
21. Calhoun to Mrs. Floride Colhoun, Dec. 23, 1805, *Correspondence*, 101.
22. Calhoun to Mrs. Floride Colhoun, Sept. 9, 1805, and March 3, 1806, *Correspondence*, 97 and 103.
23. Marryat, 72.
24. The story of this friendship, handed down in the annals of the Calhoun family of Connecticut, was received from Miss Lilian Gold, Flint, Michigan, great-granddaughter of Dr. John Calhoun of Cornwall.
25. Nichols, I, 60; II, 125. See also Marryat's description of white slave auctions in 1789, 88.
26. Calhoun to Mrs. Floride Colhoun, Aug. 12, 1805, and July 3, 1806, *Correspondence*, 95–96, 106.
27. Calhoun to Mrs. Floride Colhoun, Sept. 9, 1805, and to Andrew Pick-

ens, Nov. 24, 1805, *Correspondence,* 97 and 100.

28. J. G. Swift, *Measures, Not Men,* 6.
29. Calhoun to Mrs. Floride Colhoun, June 2, 1806, *Correspondence,* 105.
30. Calhoun to Mrs. Floride Colhoun, Sept. 11, 1806, *Correspondence,* 107.
31. Amos Kendall, *Autobiography,* 22, Goodrich, I, 86, 133; and Nichols, I, 23, 18.
32. Calhoun to Mrs. Floride Colhoun, Jan. 19, 1806, *Correspondence,* 102; and Calhoun to H. Seymour, June 2, 1822, Calhoun Papers, Library of Congress.
33. Calhoun to Mrs. Floride Colhoun, Aug. 12, 1805, *Correspondence,* 96.
34. Harriet Martineau, *A Retrospect of Western Travel,* I, 227–228.

35. Peter Neilson, *Recollections,* 253.
36. Mrs. St. Julien Ravenel, *Charleston: The Place and the People,* 379.
37. Basil Hall, *Travels in North America,* II, 191.
38. Calhoun to Mrs. Floride Colhoun, Dec. 22, 1806, *Correspondence,* 108.
39. These quotations are taken at random from issues of the South Carolina *Gazette* through the years 1806, 1807.
40. Gerald Johnson, *Andrew Jackson: A Portrait in Homespun,* 48. (College Caravan edition.)
41. Calhoun to Mrs. Floride Colhoun, undated, 1807, in Calhoun Papers, Clemson College, South Carolina.
42. Calhoun to Mrs. Floride Colhoun, Dec. 22, 1806, *Correspondence,* 108.

IV. THE BIRTH OF A PATRIOT

1. William P. Starke, 'Account of Calhoun's Early Life,' *Correspondence,* 85.
2. Ben Robertson, *Red Hills and Cotton,* 1.
3. Starke, 85.
4. James Parton, *Famous Americans of Recent Times,* 124.
5. Anecdote quoted in William Meigs, *The Life of John Caldwell Calhoun,* I, 47.
6. J. Belton O'Neall, *The Bench and Bar of South Carolina,* I; Bowie quoted, 283–284.
7. Joseph Rogers, *The True Henry Clay,* 36.
8. Calhoun to Mrs. Floride Colhoun, April 6, 1809, *Correspondence,* 110.
9. See J. Belton O'Neall, *The Annals of Newberry,* 19–20; *The Bench and Bar,* 96; Lucius Little, *Ben Hardin,* 32–34; Frederick Marryat, *Diary in America,* 232; Mrs. Basil Hall, quoted in *Three Englishwomen in America,* ed. by Una Pope-Hennessey, 236; W. H. Sparks, *Old Times in Georgia,* 482.
10. Anecdote quoted in Charles M. Wiltse's *John C. Calhoun, Nationalist,* 43.
11. See William E. Barton, *The Lineage of Lincoln,* 297–298.
12. Samuel G. Goodrich, *Recollections of a Lifetime,* I, 182.
13. *Ibid.,* I, 86–87.
14. The figure is usually given as twelve, but Luke Hanks died in 1787, and in the first census at

'Ninety-Six,' in 1790, Mrs. Ann Hanks was named as head of a family of five males and six females. It has been said that in any group of half a dozen Hanks girls, at least one would be named Nancy. Although Nancy Hanks of Kentucky and Nancy Hanks of Anderson County, South Carolina, were probably connected, the exact relationship would be too involved to trace. See Barton, *The Lineage of Lincoln,* 297–298.
15. Calhoun to Mrs. Floride Colhoun, Oct. 1, 1807, *Correspondence,* 109.
16. Columbia (S.C.) *State,* July 12, 1896.
17. G. W. Symonds, 'When Calhoun Went A–Wooing,' *The Ladies' Home Journal,* May, 1901.
18. Starke, 86; see also Fletcher Pratt, *The Heroic Years,* 183.
19. Calhoun to Miss Floride Colhoun, Sept. 28, 1810, *Correspondence,* 122.
20. William E. Barton, *The Paternity of Abraham Lincoln,* 266.
21. Mary Bates, *The Private Life of John C. Calhoun,* 30–31.
22. Barton, *The Paternity of Abraham Lincoln,* 137.
23. Gamaliel Bradford, *As God Made Them,* 110.
24. Manuscript reminiscences of James Edward Colhoun, Calhoun Papers, Clemson College.
25. Judgment Roll, No. 286 in the Judge of Probate's office for Anderson County, South Carolina.

'State of South Carolina. County of Anderson . . . application for partition. . . . The land of Luke Hanks, decd.' See also, Barton, *The Paternity of Abraham Lincoln*, 222–224.

26. LeConte quoted in Claude G. Bowers, *The Tragic Era*, 348.
27. Charleston *City Gazette and Daily Advertiser*, Jan. 4, 1809.
28. Benjamin F. Perry, *Reminiscences of Public Men*, 90–91.
29. *Ibid.*, 92.
30. Don C. Seitz, *The Also-Rans*, 55.
31. *Ibid.*
32. Manuscript records of the South Carolina State Legislature in State Archives Building, South Carolina

Historical Commission, entries for Dec. 5, 1809, and Dec. 12, 1809.
33. Huger quoted in Benjamin F. Perry, *Reminiscences of Public Men*, 92.
34. House Roll, Legislative Records, Nov. 8, 1809.
35. 'Rules' printed in Legislative Records, Nov. 28, 1808.
36. Legislative Records, Dec. 5, 1804.
37. Parton, 125; Starke, 87.
38. David D. Wallace, *History of South Carolina*, II, 375.
39. Calhoun, 'Discourse on the Constitution,' *Works of John C. Calhoun*, Richard K. Crallé, ed., I, 400–406.
40. Herbert Agar, *The Pursuit of Happiness*, 193.

V. OF COURTS AND COURTING

1. Frederick Marryat, *Diary in America*, 232; W. H. Sparks, *Old Times in Georgia*, 482.
2. Calhoun to Mrs. Floride Colhoun, April 6, 1809, *Correspondence*, 110.
3. *Idem*, June 25, 1809, *Correspondence*, 111.
4. So the tradition is handed down in the Calhoun family. A written account can be found in G. W. Symonds's article, 'When Calhoun Went A–Wooing' in *The Ladies' Home Journal*, May, 1901.
5. Calhoun to Mrs. Floride Colhoun, June 25, 1809, *Correspondence*, 111.
6. R. D. French, *Memorial Quadrangle*, 158–159.
7. *Ibid.*, 159.
8. Calhoun to Mrs. Floride Colhoun, July 18, 1809, *Correspondence*, 112.
9. Calhoun to Mrs. Floride Colhoun, Jan. 20, 1810, *Correspondence*, 114.
10. William P. Starke, 'Account of Calhoun's Early Life,' *Correspondence*, 86.
11. Calhoun to Mrs. Floride Colhoun, Jan. 20, 1810, *Correspondence*, 114.
12. Mrs. St. Julien Ravenel, *Charleston, the Place and the People*, 427–429.
13. Caroline Howard Gilman, *Recollections of a Southern Matron*, 297.
14. *Ibid.*
15. Mrs. St. Julien Ravenel, 427–429.
16. Basil Hall, *Travels in North America*, II, 190–191.
17. Mrs. St. Julien Ravenel, 396.
18. Calhoun to Mrs. Floride Colhoun, June 12, 1810, *Correspondence*, 114–115.

19. *Idem*, 115.
20. *Idem*, July 27, 1812, *Correspondence*, 118.
21. E. P. Poe, sketch of Calhoun in clipping from Anderson (S.C.) *Observer;* in Clemson College Library.
22. Calhoun to Mrs. Floride Colhoun, Nov. 23, 1812, *Correspondence*, 125.
23. *Idem*, June 12, 1810, *Correspondence*, 115.
24. *Idem*, July 27, 1810, *Correspondence*, 117.
25. *Idem*, Sept. 7, 1810, *Correspondence*, 119.
26. *Idem*, July 18, 1810, *Correspondence*, 117.
27. Starke, 88.
28. Calhoun to Mrs. Floride Colhoun, July 27, 1810, *Correspondence*, 117–118.
29. Calhoun to Miss Floride Colhoun, Sept. 28, 1810, *Correspondence*, 121–122.
30. Calhoun, *Life*, 8.
31. Calhoun to Miss Floride Colhoun, Sept. 28, 1812, *Correspondence*, 121–122.
32. This ending is quoted from the Symonds article in *The Ladies' Home Journal* for May, 1901. He gives no authority, and it is not included in the copy in the Starke sketch from which E. P. Jameson took his copy. However, the original has disappeared.
33. Clothes for a 'Pic-Nic' are described in the Charleston *Courier*, Jan. 1, 1807.

34. A typical outing on the Cooper is described by Caroline Howard Gilman, 257–258.
35. Calhoun to Miss Floride Colhoun, Sept. 28, 1810, *Correspondence*, 122.
36. Starke, 89.
37. Calhoun to Mrs. Floride Colhoun, Sept. 13, 1810, *Correspondence*, 120.
38. Starke, 89.
39. Mrs. St. Julien Ravenel, 390.
40. Caroline Howard Gilman, 164.
41. *Ibid.*, 165–168.

42. Charleston *Courier*, Jan. 3, and Jan. 14, 1807.
43. Calhoun to Mrs. Floride Colhoun, Sept. 7, 1810, *Correspondence*, 119.
44. Charleston *Courier*, Jan. 7, 1807.
45. Calhoun to Mrs. Floride Colhoun, May 8, 1811, *Correspondence*, 122–123.
46. Calhoun to Miss Floride Colhoun, Sept. 28, 1811, *Correspondence*, 121–122.

VI. THE SECOND AMERICAN REVOLUTION

1. Bernard Mayo, *Henry Clay: Spokesman for the New West*, 402.
2. Survivor of Fort Madison quoted in Lexington (Ky.) *Reporter*, April 4, 1812.
3. Gaillard Hunt, *John C. Calhoun*, 35.
4. Joseph Rogers, *The True Henry Clay*, 157.
5. Calhoun to James MacBride, Sept. 13, 1811, MacBride Papers, Library of Congress.
6. *Diary of William Dunlap*, Feb. 19, 1805, II, 386.
7. *Ibid.*, Feb. 28.
8. Amos Kendall, *Autobiography*, 300.
9. Benjamin F. Perry, *Reminiscences of Public Men*, 51–53.
10. *Annals of Congress*, 12th Congress, 1st Session, 332–333.
11. Newburyport (Mass.) *Herald*, Nov. 6, 1811.
12. Calhoun, *Life*, 8.
13. Calhoun to James MacBride, Feb. 16, 1812, MacBride Papers, Library of Congress.
14. Henry Adams, *History of the United States*, VI, 125–126.
15. Calhoun, Report of Nov. 29, 1811, *Works*, V, 1–6, *passim*.
16. *National Intelligencer*, Nov. 28, Dec. 5, *et seq.*, 1811.
17. Philadelphia *Aurora*, December 14, 1811.
18. *National Intelligencer*, Nov. 28, Dec. 5, 1811.
19. Newburyport (Mass.) *Herald*, May 29, 1812.
20. William Bruce, *John Randolph of Roanoke*, I, 381, 417.
21. Cited in Richmond *Enquirer*, December 21, 1811; quoted in Hartford *Courant*.
22. *Annals of Congress*, 12th Congress, 1st Session, 422, 441, 525.
23. Calhoun, *Works*, II, 19.

24. William C. Preston, *Reminiscences*, 7–9.
25. Newburyport (Mass.) *Herald*, Nov. 11, 1811.
26. Calhoun to James MacBride, April 18, 1812, MacBride Papers, Library of Congress.
27. Excerpts quoted in Hugh Garland, *Life of John Randolph*, I, 288–297, *passim* (13th edition).
28. *Ibid.*, I, 296.
29. *Ibid.*, I, 306.
30. John S. Jenkins, *Life of John Caldwell Calhoun*, 47; Calhoun, *Works*, II, 1–13.
31. Richmond *Enquirer*, Dec. 24, 1811.
32. Newburyport (Mass.) *Herald*, Nov. 8, 1811.
33. James Parton, *Famous Americans of Recent Times*, 127.
34. Augustus J. Foster Papers, Library of Congress; MS. Diary, I, Feb. 12, 1812, and April 15, 1812; also MS. Notes, I, 30–31.
35. Calhoun to Mrs. Floride Colhoun, Dec. 21, 1811, *Correspondence*, 124.
36. Foster, MS. Diary, I, Dec. 14, 1811.
37. *Ibid.*, April 5, 1812.
38. *Ibid.*, April 15, 1812.
39. *Annals*, 12th Congress, 1st Session, 848–850; see also J. A. Bayard to A. Bayard, Jan. 25, 1812, in *Annual Report of the American Historical Association* (1913), 189.
40. Mayo, 431–432.
41. E. P. Thomas, ed., *The Carolina Tribute to Calhoun*, 389.
42. Foster, MS. Diary, I, May 8, 1812.
43. James Madison to Thomas Jefferson, April 3, 1812, in *Writings of James Madison*, II, 531.
44. Calhoun to James MacBride, April 18, 1812, MacBride Papers, Library of Congress.
45. Sidney H. Gay, *James Madison*, 307.

46. Foster, MS. Diary, I, May 19, May 22, May 23, 1812; also MS. Notes, I, 156.
47. Newburyport (Mass.) *Herald*, May 29, 1812.
48. Foster, MS. Diary, I, June 1, 1812.

49. Henry Adams, *History*, VI, 125–126.
50. Foster, MS. Diary, I, June 7, 1812.
51. *Ibid.*, June 17, 1812.
52. Henry Adams, *History*, VI, 125 ff.
53. Foster, MS. Notes, I, 168.

VII. YOUNG HERCULES

1. Marquis James, *The Raven, Sam Houston*, 27, 28.
2. James Parton, *Life of Andrew Jackson*, I, 414–418.
3. Gerald Johnson, *Andrew Jackson: A Portrait in Homespun* (College Caravan Edition), 86.
4. Quoted in *Correspondence of Andrew Jackson*, John S. Bassett, ed., I, 220–223.
5. Benjamin F. Perry, *Reminiscences of Public Men*, 53.
6. Calhoun to James MacBride, Dec. 15, 1812. MacBride Papers, Library of Congress.
7. *Annals of Congress*, 12th Congress, 1st Session, 139.
8. Claude M. Fuess, *Daniel Webster*, I, 138, 123.
9. *Ibid.*, I, 155.
10. Samuel Lyman, *Daniel Webster*, I, 51.
11. Fuess, I, 160.
12. Calhoun, 'Speech on the Army Bill,' Jan. 14, 1813, *Works*, II, 43.
13. The descriptions of life in Washington are drawn from the *Letters of Mary Boardman Crowninshield*, 21, 41; the correspondence of William Lowndes in the Lowndes Papers, Library of Congress; and in Mrs. St. Julien Ravenel's *Life of William Lowndes, passim;* Foster, MS. Diary, I, 12; and the *National Intelligencer*, Dec. 13, 1813.
14. *National Intelligencer*, Aug. 26, 1813; Foster, MS. Notes, I, 11.
15. Fletcher Pratt, *The Heroic Years*, 181–182.
16. Amos Kendall, *Autobiography*, 95.
17. Mrs. St. Julien Ravenel, 108.
18. Quoted in Mrs. St. Julien Ravenel, 86.
19. Commonplace Book of William Lowndes, Lowndes Papers, Library of Congress.
20. Quoted in Mrs. St. Julien Ravenel, 184.
21. 'Extract of speech by Mr. Tod of Massachusetts,' in Lowndes Papers.

22. Undated news clipping from *Southern Patriot and Commercial Advertiser* in Lowndes Papers.
23. *Ibid.*
24. Mrs. St. Julien Ravenel, 87.
25. Calhoun to James MacBride, Feb. 2, 1813. MacBride Papers, Library of Congress.
26. Calhoun to Mrs. John C. Calhoun, March 1, 1812, *Correspondence*, 125.
27. *Idem*, Feb. 7, 1814, *Correspondence*, 126.
28. *Idem*, Nov. 23, 1812, and Feb. 7, 1814, *Correspondence*, 125, 126.
29. Calhoun, 'Speech on Merchants' Bonds,' Dec. 4, 1812, *Works*, II, 37.
30. *National Intelligencer*, Aug. 23, 1814; Winder's Narrative, American State Papers, Military Affairs Manuscript Division, I, 552–553.
31. Dolly Madison Papers, Library of Congress, notations for Aug. 23 and Aug. 24, 1814.
32. Margaret Bayard Smith, *First Forty Years of Washington Society*, 100, 114.
33. Dolly Madison Papers, Aug. 23, and Aug. 24, 1814.
34. Sarah A. Emery, *Three Generations*, 212.
35. Eye-witness accounts of the invasion of Washington are in the *National Intelligencer*, Aug. 30, Sept. 1, 2, 8, and 15, 1814. See quotation on 'the Cossacks' in a London newspaper, cited in Arthur Stryon's *The Cast-iron Man: John C. Calhoun and American Democracy*, 76–77; also Stilson Hutchins Moore and Joseph West Smith, *The National Capital*, 96, 99–100.
36. Sarah Emery, 213–214.
37. *National Intelligencer*, Sept. 2, 1814.
38. *Ibid.;* see also Margaret Bayard Smith, 112.
39. *National Intelligencer*, Oct. 19; also Petersburg (Va.) *Courier*, Oct. 25, 1814.
40. J. G. Swift, *Measures, Not Men*, 15.

41. George T. Curtis, *Life of Daniel Webster*, I, 43. The anecdote is attributed to George Ticknor, who heard it from Webster, himself.
42. Calhoun, 'Speech on Loan Bill,' Feb. 25, 1814, *Works*, II, 90–91, 55.
43. Fuess, I, 168; *The Writings and Speeches of Daniel Webster* (National Edition), XIV, 69.
44. Fuess, I, 168.
45. James Madison, quoted in J. P. Kennedy, *Memoir of William Wirt*, I, 339; Henry Adams, *History*, VIII, 231.
46. Calhoun, 'Speech on the Loan Bill,'

Feb. 25, 1814, *Works*, II, 94, 95, 98, 79.
47. *Idem*, 116.
48. *Idem*, 91, 102, 89.
49. *Idem*, 91.
50. Calhoun to James MacBride, Feb. 12, 1815. MacBride Papers, Library of Congress.
51. *Idem*, Feb. 12, 1815.
52. Samuel G. Goodrich, *Recollections of a Lifetime*, I, 22–23.
53. Foster, MS. Notes, II, 148–149; 160–162; see also MS. Diary, I, April 20, 1812; Dec. 22, 1811; April 8, 1812; and April 17, 1812.

VIII. A BROADENING UNION

1. Thomas L. Nichols, *Forty Years of American Life*, I, 363; Albert Gallatin to Matthew Lyon, May 7, 1816, in Henry Adams, *Life of Albert Gallatin*, 560.
2. Calhoun, *Works*, II, 134.
3. Calhoun to Mrs. Floride Colhoun, April 9, 1815, *Correspondence*, 128–129.
4. *Idem*.
5. Calhoun to Mrs. John C. Calhoun, *Correspondence*, 129.
6. Vernon Parrington, *The Romantic Revolution in America*, v.
7. Charles A. Beard, *Economic Origins of Jeffersonian Democracy*, 12, 18.
8. James Parton, *Famous Americans of Recent Times*, 128.
9. Calhoun, Speech on 'The Loan Bill,' Feb. 25, 1814, *Works*, II, 101.
10. Calhoun, speech on 'Merchants' Bonds,' Dec. 4, 1812, *Works*, II, 37.
11. Christopher Hollis, *The American Heresy*, 87.
12. William E. Dodd, *Statesmen of the Old South*, 142.
13. Hollis, 87, 88.
14. Margaret Bayard Smith, *First Forty Years of Washington Society*, 96.
15. *Letters of Mary Boardman Crowninshield*, 57.
16. *Ibid.*, 15, 16, 23, 35, 51.
17. William C. Preston, *Reminiscences*, 5–6.
18. Anne H. Wharton, *Social Life in the Early Republic*, 38.
19. Amos Kendall, *Autobiography*, 300.
20. Preston, 7–8.
21. Josiah Quincy, *Figures of the Past*, 210.
22. Ben: Perley Poore, *Reminiscences*, I, 68–69.

23. *Ibid.*, 54.
24. Parrington, 141.
25. E. F. Ellet, *Court Circles of the Republic*, 100.
26. Parton, 126.
27. Theodore D. Jervey, *Robert Young Hayne and His Times*, 51.
28. Gerald Johnson, *John Randolph of Roanoke*, 186.
29. Walter Miller, in *The Green Bag*, XI, 276.
30. Samuel G. Goodrich, *Recollections of a Lifetime*, II, 407.
31. Parton, 130.
32. Correspondent for Charleston *Courier*, quoted in New York *Evening Post*, March 12, 1814.
33. Mrs. St. Julien Ravenel, *The Life and Times of William Lowndes*, 230.
34. Calhoun, speech on 'The Military Peace Establishment,' Feb. 27, 1815, *Works*, II, 117–123.
35. Calhoun, speech on 'The Treaty-Making Power,' Jan. 4, 1816, quoted in John S. Jenkins, *Life of John Caldwell Calhoun*, 63, 75.
36. Calhoun, speech on 'The Direct Tax,' Jan. 31, 1816, quoted in Jenkins, 104–117.
37. Calhoun, address on 'Commercial Treaty,' quoted in Jenkins, 65–73.
38. Calhoun, address on 'The Direct Tax,' April 4, 1816, *Works*, II, 152.
39. Calhoun, speech on 'The Bank Bill,' Feb. 26, 1816, *Works*, II, 153–162.
40. Claude M. Fuess, *Daniel Webster*, I, 184–185.
41. Calhoun, *Life*, 19.
42. Jenkins, 118.
43. Calhoun, speech on 'The New Tariff Act,' April 6, 1816, *Works*, II, 163–173.

44. Thomas Jefferson to Benjamin Austin, Jan. 9, 1816, Jefferson *Correspondence*, X, 10.
45. Calhoun, *Works*, II, 160.
46. Calhoun, speech on 'The Bonus Bill,' Feb. 4, 1817, *Works*, II, 186–196.
47. Jenkins, 138.
48. Benjamin F. Perry, *Reminiscences of Public Men*, 55.
49. Calhoun, *Life*, 23.
50. Jenkins, 134–135.

51. Calhoun to Duff Green, May, 1839, *Correspondence*, 429.
52. Calhoun, *Life*, 23.
53. Calhoun, speech on 'The Compensation Bill,' Jan. 17, 1817, *Works*, II, 174–185.
54. Jenkins, 136.
55. New York *Evening Post*, Dec. 28, Dec. 31, 1813.
56. Calhoun, *Life*, 23.
57. Jenkins, 136.

IX. MR. SECRETARY OF WAR

1. *Niles' Weekly Register*, March 27, 1824.
2. Calhoun to James Monroe, Dec. 9, 1827, *Correspondence*, 252.
3. Calhoun, *Life*, 24, 72; Mrs. St. Julien Ravenel, *The Life of William Lowndes*, 230; John S. Jenkins, *The Life of John Caldwell Calhoun*, 141–142.
4. John Quincy Adams, *Diary*, IV, 136.
5. *Ibid.*, IV, 144.
6. Calhoun to William F. Buyers (first official letter), Dec. 8, 1817, War Office, Military Book, IX, 423, National Archives.
7. Calhoun to Jacob Brown, July 29, 1818, Brown Papers, Library of Congress.
8. Calhoun, *Life*, 25.
9. *Ibid.*, 25; Jenkins, 142.
10. Calhoun to Jacob Brown, Nov. 3, 1821, Brown Papers, Library of Congress.
11. Calhoun to Sylvanus Thayer, March 7, 1818, War Office, Military Book, IX.
12. James Parton, *Famous Americans of Recent Times*, 139.
13. Mary Bates, *The Private Life of John C. Calhoun*, 30–31.
14. Calhoun, *Life*, 27.
15. J. Q. Adams, *Diary*, V, 236.
16. *Niles' Weekly Register*, XXII, 251–263, 279–282; *ibid.*, XXXI, 292, 293–302, 305, 394–407; *ibid.*, XXXII, 18.
17. Theodore D. Jervey, *Robert Young Hayne and His Times*, 51–52.
18. Marquis James, *The Raven*, 44.
19. J. Q. Adams, *Diary*, V, 527.
20. Andrew Jackson to James Monroe, Jan. 6, 1818, quoted in James Parton, *Life of Andrew Jackson*, II, 433.
21. James Monroe to Calhoun, May, 19, 1830, quoted in Parton, *Andrew Jackson*, II, 435. See also letter of Calhoun to Monroe, May 26, 1830, *Correspondence*, 273.
22. Calhoun to Andrew Jackson, Dec. 26, 1817, Orders in Seminole War, American State Papers, Military Affairs, I, 690.
23. J. Q. Adams, *Diary*, IV, 108, 113.
24. Calhoun to Andrew Jackson, May 28, 1830, *Niles' Weekly Register*, XL, 21.
25. J. Q. Adams, *Diary*, IV, 107, 108, 113.
26. Narrative of William B. Lewis written to James Parton, Oct. 25, 1859, and quoted in Parton, *Andrew Jackson*, III, 312. See also J. Q. Adams, *Diary*, IV, 366–371.
27. Calhoun to Andrew Jackson, Sept. 8, 1818, in War Office, Military Book, IX.
28. Samuel G. Goodrich, *Recollections of a Lifetime*, I, 401–402.
29. J. Q. Adams, *Diary*, IV, 281.
30. *Ibid.*, IV, 315.
31. Parton, *Andrew Jackson*, II, 345.
32. Bennett Champ Clark, *John Quincy Adams: Old Man Eloquent*, anecdote cited, 178.
33. J. Q. Adams, *Diary*, IV, 144–145, 162, 221; V, 374.
34. John P. Kennedy, *Memoir of William Wirt*, II, 185.
35. J. Q. Adams, *Diary*, IV, 276.
36. *Ibid.*, V, 172, 70–71, 275.
37. Calhoun to Henry S. Dearborn, June 8, 1824, *Correspondence*, 218–219.
38. J. Q. Adams, *Diary*, V, 279.
39. Calhoun, report on 'The Reduction of the Army,' Dec. 12, 1820, *Works*, V, 93.
40. *Idem*, Dec. 14, 1818, *Works*, V, 25–40, *passim*.
41. Calhoun, *Life*, 24–25.
42. Calhoun, *Works*, V, 34, 84–85, 88.
43. Gaillard Hunt, *John C. Calhoun*, 45.

44. See report on 'The Expenses of the Army and Military Academy,' March 5, 1822, Calhoun, *Works*, V, 115–122; and report on 'The Reduction of the Army,' Dec. 12, 1820, *ibid.*, V, 86–87.

45. Calhoun, report on 'The Reduction of the Army,' Dec. 14, 1818, *Works*, V, 35–37.

46. Calhoun to Jacob Brown, Nov. 12, 1820, Brown Papers, Library of Congress.

47. *Idem.*

48. Calhoun, report on 'The Military Academy at West Point,' Feb. 25, 1820, *Works*, V, 72–80, *passim*. See also the report on 'An Additional Military Academy,' Jan. 29, 1819, *ibid.*, V, 54–57.

49. Calhoun to Sylvanus Thayer, Jan. 15, 1819, War Office, Military Book, IX.

50. Calhoun to Jacob Thompson, Nov. 10, 1824, in Brown Papers, Library of Congress.

51. Calhoun to Stephen Cantrell, July 30, 1823, War Office, Military Book, XI. See also Calhoun to Elbert Anderson, Aug. 12, 1824, in American State Papers, Indian Affairs, II, No. 12, National Archives; also *Correspondence*, 155, 159.

52. Christopher Hollis, *The American Heresy*, 89.

53. Calhoun, report on 'Indian Trade,' Dec. 8, 1818, *Works*, V, 18, 19; see also *ibid.*, V, 139; and report on 'Civilizing the Indians,' *ibid.*, V, 69–70.

54. Calhoun to Henry Leavenworth, December 29, 1819, *Correspondence*, 167.

55. J. Q. Adams, *Diary*, VI, 402–403.

56. Mrs. St. Julien Ravenel, *The Life of William Lowndes*, 31.

57. Calhoun, report on 'Roads and Canals,' Jan. 14, 1819, *Works*, V, 40–54.

58. Calhoun, *Life*, 30.

59. *National Intelligencer*, Nov. 20, 23, 26, 30, and Dec. 4, 1819.

60. Calhoun to John E. Colhoun, Dec. 12, 1819, Calhoun Papers, Clemson College.

61. J. Q. Adams, *Diary*, IV, 495.

62. Calhoun to John E. Colhoun, Oct. 23, 1820, *Correspondence*, 178–179; see also to Micah Sterling, July 24, 1820, John Gribbel Collection, Philadelphia; *Correspondence*, 183, 185, 187, 201–202, 205, 207, 209, and 212.

63. James Monroe to Calhoun, Sept. 24, 1821, *Writings of James Monroe*, VI, 198.

64. J. Q. Adams, *Diary*, IV, 197, 512, 524; Margaret Bayard Smith, *The First Forty Years of Washington Society*, 171.

65. Margaret Bayard Smith, 254.

66. Ben: Perley Poore, *Reminiscences*, I, 73–74.

67. Margaret Bayard Smith, 268–269.

68. Calhoun to John E. Colhoun, July 23, 1821, Calhoun Papers, Clemson College.

69. Margaret Bayard Smith, 144–145, 147, 152; Josephine Seaton, *William Winston Seaton of the National Intelligencer*, 135–136; William M. Meigs, *The Life of John Caldwell Calhoun*, I, 280.

70. Margaret Bayard Smith, 149.

71. Calhoun to John E. Colhoun, May 27, 1823, *Correspondence*, 207.

72. Calhoun to John E. Colhoun, Dec. 27, 1821, *Correspondence*, 197.

X. THE MASTER OF DUMBARTON OAKS

1. Grace D. Ecker, *A Portrait of Old Georgetown*, 249–250.

2. Calhoun to John E. Colhoun, Sept. 27, 1821, *Correspondence*, 197.

3. Calhoun to J. G. Swift, May 10, 1823, *Swift Correspondence*, T. R. Hay, ed., in 'John C. Calhoun and the Presidential Campaign of 1824,' *American Historical Review*, XL, Oct. 1934, and Jan. 1935, 82–96, 287.

4. Calhoun to John E. Colhoun, Oct. 22, 1822, Calhoun Papers, Clemson College.

5. Stilson Hutchins and Joseph Moore, *The National Capital*, 317–318.

6. Calhoun to John E. Colhoun, Nov. 8, 1818, Calhoun Papers, Clemson College.

7. *Idem*, Sept. 28, 1823, *Correspondence*, 213–214.

8. *Letters of Mary Boardman Crowninshield*, 25, 35, 21.

9. J. Q. Adams, *Diary*, IV, 480–481.

10. *Ibid.*, V, 466–468, 478.

11. Mrs. St. Julien Ravenel, *The Life of William Lowndes*, 227, 230.

12. *Southern Patriot and Commercial Advertiser*, Feb. 4, 1823.
13. William Lowndes to Mrs. Lowndes, Jan. 14, 1821, Lowndes Papers, Library of Congress.
14. Thomas Hart Benton, *Abridged Debates*, VII, 12.
15. Mrs. St. Julien Ravenel, 227–230.
16. Calhoun to John E. Colhoun, Oct. 23, 1820, *Correspondence*, 178–179.
17. George T. Curtis, *The Life of Daniel Webster*, I, 176–177.
18. Calhoun to John E. Colhoun, Oct. 23, 1820, *Correspondence*, 178.
19. Margaret Bayard Smith, *First Forty Years of Washington Society*, 163.
20. W. P. Cresson, *James Monroe*, 453.
21. Jefferson to Thomas Leiper, April 3, 1824, *The Writings of Thomas Jefferson*, Paul Leicester Ford, ed., X, 299.
22. Jefferson to Thomas Ritchie, Jan. 7, 1822, *Writings*, X, 203.
23. J. Q. Adams, *Diary*, V, 58–59.
24. Ben: Perley Poore, *Reminiscences*, I, 23.
25. Gerald Johnson, *Andrew Jackson* (College Caravan Edition), 192.
26. Daniel Webster, *Correspondence*, I, 216.
27. Augustus C. Buell, *A History of Andrew Jackson*, II, 157.
28. Virgil Maxcy to R. S. Garnett, Nov. 16, 1823, in *American Historical Review*, XII, 599–601.
29. Winchester (Va.) *Republican*, July 20, 1822.
30. Richmond *Enquirer*, quoted in *Southern Patriot and Commercial Advertiser*, Feb. 4, 1822.
31. Washington *Gazette*, July 24, 1822.
32. Macon to Fisher, April 23, 1823, Fisher Papers, University of North Carolina Library.
33. Washington *Republican*, Sept. 25, 1822.
34. Josephine Seaton, *William Winston Seaton*, 162.
35. James Parton, *Famous Americans of Recent Times*, 141.
36. Boston *Galaxy*, Sept. 26, 1823.
37. J. G. Swift, *Measures, Not Men*, 45.
38. *Ibid.*
39. 'Cassius' in Columbia (S. C.) *Telescope*, quoted in pamphlet, *An Examination of Mr. Calhoun's Economy*, Dec. 1823.
40. Macon to Fisher, April 23, 1823, Fisher Papers, University of North Carolina Library.

41. Calhoun to Macon, March, 1823, Fisher Papers, University of North Carolina Library.
42. *Idem.* See also *American Historical Review*, XI, Oct. 1934. Calhoun to Virgil Maxcy, April 1, Aug. 6, and Nov. 2, 1823, in Virgil Maxcy Papers, MSS. Division, Library of Congress.
43. Washington *Republican*, Nov. 16, 1822; J. Q. Adams, *Diary*, V, 238.
44. Arthur Stryon, *The Cast-Iron Man*, Webster quoted, 119.
45. Calhoun to J. G. Swift, April 29, 1823; Aug. 24, 1823, *Swift Correspondence*.
46. Calhoun to Robert Garnett, July 3, 1824, *Correspondence*, 219–223.
47. *Idem.*
48. See Calhoun's letter to Robert S. Garnett, July 3, 1824, *Correspondence*, 219–223, *passim;* also Calhoun to J. G. Swift, Aug. 24, 1823, *Swift Correspondence*.
49. *Correspondence*, 221–222.
50. J. Q. Adams, *Diary*, VI, 301; V, 523–524, 452.
51. J. E. D. Shipp, *The Life and Times of William H. Crawford*, 168.
52. Randolph, quoted in *Annals*, 18th Congress, 1st Session, 1308; see also Stryon, 91.
53. J. Q. Adams, *Diary*, IV, 524.
54. *Ibid.*, V, 36, 9, 10, 12.
55. *Ibid.*, VI, 315.
56. Calhoun to Micah Sterling, Jan. 5, 1824, Calhoun Papers, Library of Congress.
57. Calhoun to Thomas Rogers, June 9, 1822, Fisher Papers, University of North Carolina Library.
58. J. Q. Adams, *Diary*, VI, 477.
59. Amos Kendall, *Autobiography*, 201.
60. Boston *Galaxy*, Jan. 18, 1822.
61. Francis Grund, *Aristocracy in America*, II, 178–179.
62. J. Q. Adams, *Diary*, V, 238; Frederick Marryat, *Diary in America*, I, 164–167 (British edition).
63. *We, The People*, Oct. 25, 1828.
64. J. Q. Adams, *Diary*, VI, 57; V, 315, 515, and 525; also Henry Adams, *Albert Gallatin*, 599.
65. J. Q. Adams, *Diary*, VI, 42.
66. *Ibid.*, VI, 46–48.
67. *Ibid.*, VI, 43, 47, 63.
68. Washington *Republican*, Nov. 13, 1822.
69. *Ibid.*, Nov. 20, Nov. 23, 1822.

70. J. Q. Adams, *Diary*, VI, 62.
71. Washington *Republican*, Sept. 18, 1822; J. Q. Adams, *Diary*, VI, 64.
72. Claude G. Bowers, *Party Battles of the Jackson Period*, 107–108, 89–90; J. Q. Adams, *Diary*, V, 315–326, *passim*.
73. J. Q. Adams, *Diary*, V, 315–326, *passim*.
74. Calhoun to James Monroe, July 26, 1820, Calhoun Papers, Library of Congress.
75. William H. Crawford to Albert Gallatin, May 13, 1822, in Henry Adams' *Life of Albert Gallatin*, 580.
76. Cresson, *James Monroe*, 457; J. Q. Adams, *Diary*, V, 525; also *Writings of Monroe*, VI, 287.
77. E. F. Ellet, *Court Circles of the Republic*, 98.
78. Eliza C. Carrington to Mrs. James McDowell, Nov. 16, 1824, Carrington-McDowell Papers, Library of Congress.
79. J. T. Flexner, *America's Old Masters*, 190, 197.
80. H. T. Tuckerman, *The Book of the Artist*, 299.
81. *Ibid.*, 62.
82. Samuel Isham, *The History of American Painting*, 108.
83. Shipp, 174.

84. J. Q. Adams, *Diary*, V, 272; VI, 394–400, 408.
85. *Niles' Weekly Register*, XXV, 405.
86. *Franklin Gazette* (Philadelphia), Feb. 19, 1824.
87. Calhoun to Virgil Maxcy, Feb. 27, 1842, Virgil Maxcy Papers, MSS. Division, Library of Congress.
88. Margaret Bayard Smith, 164.
89. Parton, 140.
90. George P. Fisher, *The Life of Benjamin Silliman*, II, 107.
91. J. Q. Adams, *Diary*, VI, 279, 273.
92. Andrew Jackson, *Correspondence*, III, 355; Marquis James, *Andrew Jackson*, II, 27.
93. Margaret Bayard Smith, 185.
94. Martin Van Buren, *Autobiography*, 150, J. C. Fitzpatrick, ed.; Margaret Bayard Smith, 192.
95. Margaret Bayard Smith, 181; Shipp, 185.
96. Margaret Bayard Smith, 186.
97. *Ibid.*, 190–193.
98. Washington *Gazette*, Nov. 29, 1825.
99. Calhoun to Littleton Tazewell, July 1, 1827, Calhoun Papers, Library of Congress.
100. J. Q. Adams, *Diary*, VI, 506–507.
101. *Ibid.*, VI, 506–507.
102. *National Intelligencer*, March 5, 1825.

XI. MR. VICE-PRESIDENT CALHOUN

1. Calhoun to J. G. Swift, Feb. 29, 1826, *American Historical Review*, XL, 300.
2. Nathan Sargent, *Public Men and Events*, I, 108.
3. Ben: Perley Poore, *Reminiscences*, I, 136–137.
4. Josiah Quincy, *Figures of the Past*, 263.
5. *Ibid.*, 241.
6. Benjamin F. Perry, *Reminiscences of Public Men*, 241.
7. Poore, I, 203–204.
8. Varina Howell Davis, *Jefferson Davis: A Memoir*, I, 270; Perry, 45; Charles Cotesworth Pinckney, 'Calhoun From a Southern Standpoint,' *Lippincott's Magazine*, LXII, July, 1898.
9. Oliver Dyer, *Great Senators of the United States*, 203–207, *passim*.
10. Harriet Martineau, *Retrospect of Western Travel*, I, 165.
11. Dyer, 253–254.
12. Poore, I, 63.

13. Perry, 64.
14. Poore, I, 68–69.
15. Quincy, 210–212.
16. Poore, I, 69; Quincy, 213.
17. Norwich (Conn.) *Courier*, April 19, 1826.
18. Henry Adams, *John Randolph of Roanoke* (Standard Library Edition), 298; Quincy, 210.
19. 'Onslow to Patrick Henry,' Calhoun's *Works*, VI, 347.
20. Norwich (Conn.) *Courier*, April 19, 1826.
21. Henry Adams, *John Randolph*, 286; Hugh Garland, *Life of John Randolph*, II, 267–268.
22. Thomas Hart Benton, *Thirty Years' View*, I, 473; also Coalter's Executor vs. Randolph's Executor, Clerk's office, Circuit Court, Petersburg, Va.
23. *Idem.* Calhoun quoted in Coalter's Executor vs. Randolph's Executor, Clerk's office, Circuit Court, Petersburg, Va.

24. Norwich (Conn.) *Courier*, April 19, 1826.
25. Onslow, *In Reply to Patrick Henry* (pamphlet), Washington, 1826.
26. *Ibid.*
27. Martin Van Buren, *Autobiography*, 209–210.
28. Poore, I, 70.
29. Calhoun to Mrs. Floride Colhoun, Feb. 14, 1827, *Correspondence*, 233–235.
30. Calhoun to James Edward Colhoun, Feb. 14, 1827, *Correspondence*, 239–240.
31. *Niles' Weekly Register*, XXII, 251, 279; XXXI, 292; American State Papers, Military Affairs, II, 431–449.
32. Calhoun to James Monroe, Dec. 9, 1827, Dec. 22, 1827, Jan. 3, 1828, March 7, 1828, May 1, 1828, July 10, 1828; *Correspondence*, 251–253, 254, 255, 260, 263, and 266.
33. Christopher Hollis, *The American Heresy*, 98.
34. Quincy, 213.
35. J. H. Hammond, in *The Carolina Tribute to Calhoun*, J. P. Thomas, ed., 297.
36. *Ibid.*, 297.
37. Calhoun, *Works*, II, 109.
38. 'Calhoun and the Divine Right of the Majority,' Nathaniel W. Stephenson, Scripps College Papers, 30, 31.

39. *Idem.*
40. Hollis, 84.
41. Poore, I, 136.
42. Calhoun to James Edward Colhoun, Aug. 26, 1827, *Correspondence*, 247–251.
43. Calhoun, *Life*, 33–34.
44. *Ibid.*, 44.
45. *Ibid.*, 33.
46. *Ibid.*, 32.
47. Allan Nevins, *Ordeal of the Union*, 148–149; see also Henry Clay's speech on 'The Abolition Petitions,' Feb. 7, 1839, in *The Life and Speeches of Henry Clay*, I, 411–412; and Joseph Lumpkin to Howell Cobb, Jan. 21, 1848, in *Annual Report of the American Historical Association*, 1911, 294–295. Dr. James A. Padgett of Washington, D. C., formerly of the History Department, University of North Carolina, declares that in 1830 there were 100 'manumission societies' in North Carolina alone. 'By 1850 it was against the law to belong to one.'
48. Theodore D. Jervey, *Robert Young Hayne and His Times*, 167.
49. Calhoun, *Works*, VI, 31.
50. Hollis, 108; John P. Pritchett, *Calhoun and His Defense of the South*, 31–32.
51. Calhoun, *Works*, II, 626.

XII. A UNIONIST COMES HOME

1. 'Old Pendleton' in Charleston *Sunday News*, April 30, 1905.
2. Manuscript records of the Pendleton Farmers' Society, Clemson College.
3. Walter Miller, 'Calhoun as a Lawyer and a Statesman,' *The Green Bag*, XI, 327–328.
4. Calhoun to Christopher Van Deventer, July 23, 1827, *Correspondence*, 246.
5. Calhoun to James Edward Colhoun, Dec. 24, 1826, *Correspondence*, 237–238.
6. Oliver Dyer, *Great Senators*, 186.
7. Ben Robertson, *Red Hills and Cotton*, 9, 128–129.
8. Benjamin B. Kendrick, 'The Colonial Status of the South,' reprinted from *The Journal of Southern History*, VIII, No. 1, Feb. 1942, p. 6.
9. *Ibid.*, 11–12.
10. William E. Dodd, *Life and Labor in the Old South*, 32.
11. Benjamin B. Kendrick and Alex Mathews Arnett, *The South Looks at Its Past*, 41.
12. Dodd, 32.
13. *Ibid.*, 16.
14. *Ibid.*
15. *Ibid.*, 32. See also W. J. Cash, *The Mind of the South*, 20–21, 41, 61.
16. Robertson, 75.
17. *Ibid.*, 60, 64–65, 71, 59, 90, 135–137, 178, 223.
18. Calhoun to Mrs. Floride Colhoun, June 14, 1826, *Correspondence*, 235–236.
19. Calhoun to John E. Colhoun, June 14, 1826, *Correspondence*, 236–237; and to James Edward Colhoun, Dec. 24, 1826, *Correspondence*, 237–240.
20. Charles C. Pinckney, 'Calhoun from a Southern Standpoint,' *Lippincott's Magazine*, LXII, July, 1898.
21. Manuscript records of the Farmers' Society, August, 1826, *passim*, Clemson College.
22. *Ibid.*, *passim*.

23. Calhoun to Littleton Tazewell, April 1, 1827, Calhoun Papers, Library of Congress.
24. W. H. V. Miller, contemporary sketch, 'Calhoun as a Farmer,' undated clipping in Clemson College Papers.
25. Calhoun to John E. Colhoun, Sept. 27, 1821, *Correspondence*, 196–197.
26. Calhoun to Littleton Tazewell, April 1, 1827, Calhoun Papers, Library of Congress.
27. *Idem.*
28. *Idem*, July 1, 1827.
29. Calhoun to James E. Colhoun, May 4, 1828, *Correspondence*, 264–265.
30. Calhoun to James Monroe, July 10, 1828, *Correspondence*, 266–267.
31. James Parton, *Famous Americans of Recent Times*, sketch on John Randolph, *passim*.
32. Calhoun to Tazewell, July 1, 1827.
33. *Idem*, Aug. 25, 1827.
34. *Idem*, Aug 9, 1827.
35. Calhoun to James Monroe, July 10, 1828, *Correspondence*, 266.
36. Frank A. Dickson, Jr., on Calhoun, in Anderson *Independent*, Dec. 15, 1929. See MS. clipping in Clemson College Papers.
37. See Gerald Johnson, *The Secession of the Southern States*, 57–67, *passim*.
38. Hermann von Holst, *Life of John C. Calhoun*, 164–165.
39. Calhoun to James Monroe, July 10, 1828, *Correspondence*, 62.
40. Calhoun to Littleton Tazewell, Nov. 9, 1827, Calhoun Papers, Library of Congress.
41. Calhoun, *Life*, 35.
42. W. H. Sparks, *Old Times in Georgia*, 83.
43. Benjamin F. Perry, *Reminiscences of Public Men*, 77.
44. Sparks, 84–90, *passim*.
45. Perry, 77, 79.

46. *Ibid.*, 131, 143–147.
47. *Ibid.*, 177.
48. Theodore D. Jervey, *Robert Young Hayne and His Times*, 167.
49. Calhoun to Virgil Maxcy, Sept. 11, 1830, Virgil Maxcy Papers, Library of Congress.
50. Calhoun, *Works*, I, 400–406.
51. Webster to B. F. Perry, April 10, 1833, quoted in George T. Curtis, *Life of Daniel Webster*, I, 458.
52. Parton, 148.
53. Christopher Hollis, *The American Heresy*, 95.
54. Calhoun, 'The South Carolina Exposition,' *Works*, VI, 1–32, *passim*.
55. *The Federalist*, no. LX.
56. Calhoun, 'The South Carolina Exposition,' *Works*, VI, 32–46, *passim*.
57. Hollis, 103–104.
58. Calhoun, 'The South Carolina Exposition,' *Works*, VI, 17, 19, 25.
59. Parton, 150.
60. Kendrick, 'The Colonial Status of the South,' 17.
61. The National Emergency Council, *Report on Economic Conditions in the South*, 8, 49, 54, 60, and 61.
62. Hodding Carter, 'Chip on Our Shoulder Down South,' in *The Saturday Evening Post*, 219: 18–19 (Nov. 2, 1946).
63. Ellis Arnall, 'The Southern Frontier,' *Atlantic Monthly*, Sept., 1946, 29–35, *passim*.
64. Frank L. Owsley, 'Pillars of Agrarianism,' *American Review*, March, 1935.
65. Hollis, 97.
66. Calhoun, 'The South Carolina Exposition,' *Works*, VI, 55.
67. Calhoun to James E. Colhoun, Jan. 28, 1828, *Correspondence*, 256–260.
68. Calhoun, 'The South Carolina Exposition,' *Works*, VI, 56.
69. Calhoun quoted in *Niles' Weekly Register*, XXXV, 61, Sept. 20, 1828.

XIII. PETTY ARTS

1. Varina Howell Davis, *Jefferson Davis: A Memoir*, I, 213, 221.
2. Mary Bates, *The Private Life of John C. Calhoun*, 23.
3. Ben: Perley Poore, *Reminiscences*, I, 46.
4. Hammond quoted in *The Carolina Tribute to Calhoun*, 373.
5. Poore, I, 124.
6. *Ibid.*, 123.

7. Margaret Bayard Smith, *The First Forty Years of Washington Society*, 234.
8. Queena Pollack, *Peggy Eaton: Democracy's Mistress*, 77; Margaret Bayard Smith, 253.
9. Queena Pollack, 77.
10. Margaret Bayard Smith, 253.
11. See Calhoun, 'Mr. Calhoun's Reply to Mr. Eaton,' *Works*, VI, 437.

NOTES: CHAPTERS XIII AND XIV

12. Gerald Johnson, *America's Silver Age*, 11.
13. James Parton, *Life of Andrew Jackson*, II, 329.
14. Queena Pollack, 100.
15. *Ibid.*, 116.
16. Margaret Bayard Smith, 240; also 256–257, 277, 303.
17. Margaret Eaton, *Autobiography*, 72–73.
18. Margaret Bayard Smith, 277.
19. *Ibid.*, 283.
20. *Ibid.*, 268.
21. E. F. Ellet, *Court Circles of the Republic*, 140.
22. Margaret Bayard Smith, 268–270, *passim*.
23. Webster to Mrs. Ezekiel Webster, Feb. 19, 1829, quoted in George T. Curtis, *Life of Daniel Webster*, I, 328, 340.
24. Margaret Bayard Smith, 289, 293.
25. *Ibid.*, 291.
26. James Hamilton, Jr. to Martin Van Buren, March 5, 1829, Van Buren Papers, Library of Congress.
27. Poore, I, 95.
28. Margaret Bayard Smith, 295.
29. Calhoun, 'Reply to Mr. Eaton,' *Works*, VI, 437–439.
30. J. H. Eckenrode, *The Randolphs*, 251.
31. Calhoun, *Works*, VI, 437.
32. From clipping in Calhoun Papers South Caroliniana Library.
33. Calhoun family tradition.
34. See J. Q. Adams, *Diary*, VIII, 159.

Actually, Mrs. Eaton furnished a convenient excuse for Floride's withdrawal, because of family responsibilities. Floride was, in fact, planning to return to Washington for the winter of 1830–31, but was kept at home by the illness of her mother. See Calhoun's letters to James Edward Colhoun, Dec. 3, 12, and 14, 1830, Calhoun Papers, Clemson College. See also Margaret Bayard Smith, 290–292.

35. Calhoun to Patrick Noble, Jan. 10, 1829, *Correspondence*, 269; Calhoun to Christopher Van Deventer, March 20, 1829, *ibid.*, 271.
36. Calhoun, 'Reply to Mr. Eaton,' *Works*, VI, 437–439.
37. Queena Pollack, 54–55.
38. Poore, I, 122, 130.
39. Margaret Bayard Smith, 320.
40. Calhoun to Samuel L. Gouverneur, March 30, 1830, *Correspondence*, 271.
41. Margaret Bayard Smith, 305–306.
42. Queena Pollack, 144.
43. Poore, I, 130–131.
44. See Jackson's letters to Andrew Donelson, July 10, 11, 1831, in *Jackson Correspondence*, IV, 310–311, 311–312; also letter to Colonel Howard, Aug. 4, 1831, Jackson Papers, second series, Library of Congress.
45. Martin Van Buren, *Autobiography*, 377–379; also *Jackson Correspondence*, IV, 245, and Poore, I, 125.

XIV. AMERICA GROWS UP

1. George T. Curtis, *Life of Daniel Webster*, I, 337; William O. Lynch, *Fifty Years of Party Warfare*, 357.
2. Frances Trollope, *Domestic Manners of the Americans*, 109.
3. *Ibid.*, 109.
4. Frederick Marryat, *Diary in America*, 258–260 (American edition).
5. Norwich (Conn.) *Courier*, May 9, 1826; Marryat, 32–33.
6. Norwich (Conn.) *Courier*, April 26, 1826.
7. *Ibid.*, Sept. 6, 1826.
8. Marryat, 35–36, 81, 151.
9. New Haven (Conn.) *Herald*, quoted in Norwich (Conn.) *Courier*, April 12, 1826.
10. *National Banner*, quoted in Norwich (Conn.) *Courier*, April 26, 1826.

11. Mrs. Basil Hall, quoted in *Three Englishwomen in America*, 94; Frances Trollope, 138.
12. Frances Trollope, 30, 153.
13. Mrs. Basil Hall, 283.
14. William E. Dodd, *The Cotton Kingdom*, 33; W. J. Cash, *The Mind of the South*, 345, 67.
15. Frances Trollope, 190.
16. *A Voice from America to England, by an American Gentleman*, 10, quoted in Marryat, 10–11, and Basil Hall, *Travels in North America*, II, 8, 40.
17. Frances Trollope, 96.
18. Marryat, 9.
19. Calhoun to Major Henry Lee, April 30, 1828, in *Jackson Correspondence*, IV, 368–369; Calhoun to Jackson, *ibid.*, 368–369; Calhoun to Monroe,

Dec. 9, Dec. 22, 1827, Jan. 3, March 7, April, and July 10, 1828, *Calhoun Correspondence,* 250–256, 260–264, and 266.

20. James Parton, *Life of Andrew Jackson,* II, 368–369.
21. W. H. Sparks, *Old Times in Georgia,* 57–58.
22. Parton, III, 322–325.
23. Thomas Hart Benton, *Thirty Years' View,* I, 128.
24. Jackson to Overton, Dec. 31, 1829, *Jackson Correspondence,* IV, 108.
25. Charles W. March, *Daniel Webster and His Contemporaries,* 118–119.
26. Frances Kemble, *Journal,* I, 88.
27. Margaret Bayard Smith, *First Forty Years of Washington Society,* 309.
28. *Ibid.,* 310.
29. March, 138–139; also 115–127, *passim.*
30. *Ibid.,* 148; see also Ben: Perley Poore, *Reminiscences,* I, 115–116.
31. March, 148.
32. Nathan Sargent, *Public Men and Events,* I, 52–53.
33. Poore, I, 43–44.
34. Frances Trollope, 240; Amos Kendall, *Autobiography,* 282.
35. *United States Telegraph,* Jan. 28, 1830.
36. Martin Van Buren, *Autobiography,* 413.
37. See Sargent, I, 175. This libel, given voice by Kendall, printed by Blair, repeated and circularized through the entire Nullification crisis and thereafter, was utterly without foundation; although it undoubtedly reflected wishful thinking on the part both of the Southern extremists and of the Jacksonians, who used it as 'proof' of Calhoun's 'disloyalty.'
38. Van Buren, 414.
39. Parton, *Andrew Jackson,* III, 284.
40. Van Buren, 415.
41. *United States Telegraph,* April 17, 1830.
42. John Overton to Jackson, June 16, 1830, *Jackson Correspondence,* IV, 151.
43. Sparks, 152.
44. Parton, *Andrew Jackson,* II, 57–58. Calhoun to Virgil Maxcy, Aug. 1, 1831, in Virgil Maxcy Papers, Library of Congress.

45. Calhoun to Andrew Jackson, May 29, 1830, in *Works,* VI, 362–385.
46. *Idem,* 370–372.
47. Jackson to Calhoun, July 19, 1830, *Jackson Correspondence,* IV, 399.
48. *Idem,* Oct. 24, 1830, *Jackson Correspondence,* IV, 387.
49. Van Buren, 377–379.
50. Marquis James, *Andrew Jackson: Portrait of a President,* chap. 10, 535, note 6.
51. Washington *Globe,* Feb. 11, 1831.
52. Jackson to C. J. Love, March 7, 1831, *Jackson Correspondence,* IV, 245.
53. Margaret Bayard Smith, 334.
54. Benton, I, 215, 219.
55. Sparks, 56.
56. *Ibid.,* 55.
57. James Parton, *Famous Americans of Recent Times,* 153.
58. Andrew Pickens Calhoun to William Meigs, quoted in Meigs, *Life of John Caldwell Calhoun,* II, 78.
59. John Randolph to Jackson, March 28, 1832, *Jackson Correspondence,* IV.
60. John Tyler to Robert Young Hayne, June 20, 1831, Tyler Papers, Library of Congress.
61. Calhoun to James H. Hammond, March 18, 1831, quoted in Memorandum by Hammond, *American Historical Review,* VI (July, 1901), 741–745.
62. John C. Calhoun to James Kingsley, Oct. 12, 1829, and Jan. 22, 1830, Calhoun Papers, Yale University. (The first letter is at Calhoun College.)
63. *Idem,* Aug. 30, 1830.
64. See 'A Circular Explanatory of the recent proceedings of the Sophomore Class in Yale College, New Haven, August 1830,' in folder, 'Papers of Class of 1832,' MSS. Division, Yale University Library; also *1832 Class Book,* Edited by Edward E. Salisbury, introduction; also 47–50.
65. Calhoun to James Kingsley, Aug. 30, 1830, Calhoun Papers, Yale University.
66. Calhoun to Anna Maria Calhoun, Jan 11, 1831, Dec. 30, 1831, and March 10, 1832; *Correspondence,* 278–279, 308, 315–316.

XV. BLUE COCKADES AND DUELING PISTOLS

1. The Duc de Liancourt quoted in Charles Fraser's *Reminiscences*, 54–55.
2. *Ibid.*, 34.
3. Harriet Martineau, *Retrospect of Western Travel*, I, 227–228.
4. Vernon Parrington, *The Romantic Revolution in America*, 109.
5. Basil Hall, *Travels in North America*, II, 190.
6. Charles Lyell, *Travels in North America*, I, 157–184, *passim*.
7. *Ibid.*, II, 246.
8. Harriet Martineau, I, 225, 228.
9. Fraser, 55.
10. Francis Grund, *Aristocracy in America*, I, 19. See also Fraser, 55, and Jonathan Daniels, *A Southerner Discovers the South*, 332.
11. Benjamin F. Perry, *Reminiscences of Public Men*, 246–250; 362.
12. *Ibid.*, 253–255.
13. Caleb Atwater, *Remarks on a Tour to Prairie du Chien*, 289.
14. Perry, 245.
15. Mrs. St. Julien Ravenel, *Charleston, The Place and the People*, 31.
16. John Wentworth, *Congressional Reminiscences*, 20.
17. R. Gibson to James MacBride, April 18, 1817, MacBride Papers, Library of Congress.
18. Parrington, 125.
19. W. J. Cash, *The Mind of the South*, 93.
20. Fraser, 51–52.
21. Mrs. St. Julien Ravenel, 481–482.
22. Fraser, 116; Peter Neilson, *Recollections*, 249.
23. Caroline Howard Gilman, *Recollections of a Southern Matron*, 156.
24. Charleston *Courier*, Jan. 1, 14, 1807.
25. Vernon Parrington, *The Romantic Revolution in America*, 109–110.
26. Caroline Howard Gilman, 94.
27. Parrington, 109–110.
28. Ben Robertson, *Red Hills and Cotton*, 96.
29. Frederick Marryat, *Diary in America*, 10.
30. Parrington, 123.
31. Calhoun to Samuel Gouverneur, Aug. 18, 1831, *Correspondence*, 299–300.
32. Parrington, 120.
33. Columbia *Telescope*, June 10, 1831. William Meigs, *The Life of John Caldwell Calhoun*, I, 424, 430, 435.

34. De Saussure to Silliman, Nov. 1, 1830, Fisher, *Life of Benjamin Silliman*, I, 334.
35. Manuscript journal of James Hammond, March 18, 1831, in Library of Congress.
36. Calhoun, 'Fort Hill Letter,' quoted in John S. Jenkins, *The Life of John Caldwell Calhoun*, 161–187, *passim*.
37. Duff Green to Richard Crallé, Oct. 10, 1831, Green Papers, Library of Congress.
38. *American Whig Review*, autumn, 1832.
39. Calhoun, 'Letter to Governor Hamilton,' quoted in Jenkins, 195–232, *passim*.
40. Perry, 244.
41. Mrs. St. Julien Ravenel, 451.
42. Mrs. St. Julien Ravenel, 451–452.
43. Caroline Howard Gilman, 143.
44. Mrs. St. Julien Ravenel, 451.
45. Joel Poinsett to Andrew Jackson, Nov., 1832, *Jackson Correspondence*, IV, 488.
46. Mrs. St. Julien Ravenel, 451–452.
47. Manuscript proceedings of the Nullification Convention, *passim*, in State Archives, South Carolina Historical Commission.
48. James D. Richardson, *Messages and Papers of the Presidents*, II, 640–656, *passim*.
49. James O'Hanlon to Jackson, Dec. 20, 1832, *Jackson Correspondence*, IV, 504.
50. Hayne to Francis Pickens, Dec. 26, 1832, *American Historical Review*, VI, 756.
51. George McDuffie to Richard Crallé, Dec. 26, 1832, Crallé Papers, Library of Congress.
52. Andrew Jackson to Poinsett, Dec. 9, 1832, *Jackson Correspondence*, IV, 498.
53. Mrs. St. Julien Ravenel, 455.
54. *Ibid.*
55. Jackson to Van Buren, Aug. 30, 1832, *Jackson Correspondence*, IV, 470. Calhoun's letter of resignation is quoted in Gaillard Hunt's *John C. Calhoun*, 159–160.
56. Mrs. St. Julien Ravenel, 454; also Robert Henry in *The Carolina Tribute to Calhoun*, 230.
57. Quoted in Arthur Stryon, *The Cast-Iron Man*, 185.

58. See 'John C. Calhoun and the Secession Movement of 1850' in Herman
V. Ames, *Proceedings of the American Antiquarian Society*, April 1919,

19–50, *passim;* also, Beverly Tucker
to James Hammond, March 25, 1850,
quoted in *The William and Mary
Quarterly*, XVIII, 44–46.

XVI. FORCE AND COUNTER-FORCE

1. Amos Kendall, *Autobiography*, 631.
2. Fanny Kemble, *Journal*, I, 87.
3. *Ibid.*, 99.
4. Providence *Record*, quoted in Norwich (Conn.) *Courier*, May 31, 1826.
5. Fanny Kemble, I, 86.
6. Frances Trollope, *Domestic Manners of the Americans*, 271.
7. Fanny Kemble, I, 99.
8. *Ibid.*, I, 33–34; 29.
9. *Ibid.*, I, 33–34.
10. Silas Wright to Martin Van Buren,
Jan. 13, 1833, *Jackson Correspondence*, IV.
11. Fanny Kemble, II, 25.
12. Charles March, *Daniel Webster and
His Contemporaries*, 191.
13. Thomas Hart Benton, *Thirty Years'
View*, I, 342–344; Nathan Sargent,
Public Men and Events, I, 241;
and Ben: Perley Poore, I, *Reminiscences*. Although the truth of this
incident has been denied, Jackson's
correspondence gives ample testimony that the thought of hanging John C. Calhoun, either as a
threat or a pleasing daydream, was
continually in his mind. That some
kind of midnight visit did take place
is probable, on the testimony of
several, not unbiased, political reporters of Calhoun's day. It had,
however, no political effect; and is
quoted here merely as local color.
Undoubtedly, it added to Calhoun's
nerve-strain; it had no influence
whatever on his course of action, for
he knew Andrew Jackson well
enough to be aware of what was in
his mind all along.
14. W. H. Sparks, *Old Times in Georgia*,
59.
15. March, 225.
16. Margaret Bayard Smith, *The First
Forty Years of Washington Society*,
341–342.
17. March, 227.
18. Calhoun to James Edward Colhoun,
Jan. 10, 1833, *Correspondence*, 323.
19. Baltimore *Patriot*, quoted in Richmond *Enquirer*, Jan. 22, 1833.
20. March, 201.

21. *Congressional Debates*, 22d Congress,
2d Session, Jan. 15, 1833.
22. Charles J. Stillé, 'Joel R. Poinsett,'
in *Pennsylvania Magazine of History and Biography* (1885), XII,
284–285.
23. *United States Telegraph*, Jan. 5,
1833.
24. Washington *Globe*, Jan. 3, 1833.
25. Boston *Courier*, Jan. 29, 1833.
26. March, 195.
27. Ben: Perley Poore, *Reminiscences*, I,
140.
28. See *United States Telegraph*, Feb. 15
and Feb. 16; Feb. 18 and Feb. 19,
1833.
29. Calhoun, speech on 'The Revenue
Collection Bill,' *Works*, II, 197–261,
passim.
30. March, 227.
31. *Ibid.*, 338.
32. Charleston *Courier*.
33. Washington *Globe*, Feb. 16, 1833.
34. *Ibid.*, Feb. 17, 1833; also Charleston
Courier.
35. Charleston *Courier*, Feb. 23, Feb. 25,
1833.
36. Richmond *Enquirer*, Feb. 21, 1833.
37. *United States Telegraph*, Feb. 26,
1833.
38. Daniel Webster to Judge Hopkinson,
Feb. 19 and Feb. 15, 1833, in Edward Hopkinson Collection, Philadelphia.
39. Jackson to Joel Poinsett, Feb. 17,
1833, *Jackson Correspondence*, V,
18.
40. March, 248.
41. Arthur Stryon, *The Cast-Iron Man*,
196–198, *passim*.
42. Charleston *Mercury*, March 27,
1833; *United States Telegraph*, Feb.
26, 1833; John S. Jenkins, *John
Caldwell Calhoun*, 313.
43. Calhoun, *Works*, II, 276–278, 285–
286, 291.
44. Walter Miller, 'Calhoun as a Lawyer and Statesman,' *The Green Bag*,
XI, 276.
45. Benton, I, 342.
46. Richmond *Enquirer*, Feb. 16, 1833.
47. *Ibid.*

48. Boston *Courier*, Jan. 18, 1833.
49. Philadelphia *Sentinel*, Feb. 18, 1833.
50. Nantucket *Courier*, quoted in Boston *Courier*, Jan. 31, 1833.
51. New York *Evening Post*, quoted in Boston *Courier*, Feb. 19, 1833.
52. Richmond *Enquirer*, Jan. 3, 1833.
53. Sargent, I, 234.
54. 'The Ten Evils of Stage-coaches,' in *The Ladies' Repository* (Dec. 1856), 753.
55. Frances Trollope, 217; Calhoun to Franklin Elmore, November 24, 1840, Calhoun Papers, Library of Congress; Frederick Marryat, *Diary in America*, 149.
56. Thurlow Weed, *Autobiography*, 139.
57. Perry, 135; see also *Reminiscences of Public Men*, Second Series, 223.
58. New York *Herald*, April 5, 1850.
59. Philip S. Foner, *Business and Slavery*, 284.
60. Calhoun to Christopher Van Deventer, March 24, 1833, *Correspondence*, 324.
61. Christopher Hollis, *The American Heresy*, 107.

XVII. CALHOUN AT WAR

1. Calhoun to Littleton Tazewell, Jan. 24, Jan. 16, and Feb. 9, 1836, Calhoun Papers, Library of Congress.
2. Hermann von Holst, *John C. Calhoun*, 164.
3. James Parton, *Famous Americans of Recent Times*, 57.
4. Calhoun to David Hoffman, Nov. 4, 1835, *Correspondence*, 347–348.
5. Marquis James, *Andrew Jackson, Portrait of a President*, 250.
6. Nicholas Biddle, *The Correspondence of Nicholas Biddle*, Reginald C. McGrane, ed., 93–94.
7. Claude G. Bowers, *Party Battles of the Jackson Period*, 213.
8. *Ibid.*, Jackson quoted, 219–220.
9. Gerald Johnson, *Andrew Jackson* (College Caravan Edition), 144.
10. Nicholas Biddle to Alexander Porter, June 14, 1834, *Correspondence*, 235–236; see also Webster's letters in New Hampshire Historical Society Collection.
11. John Spencer Bassett, *Life of Andrew Jackson*, II, 635.
12. Nicholas Biddle to William Appleton, Jan. 27, 1834, *Correspondence*, 219; Bowers, 311.
13. Hugh R. Fraser, *Nicholas Biddle and the Bank*, 19.
14. Amos Kendall, *Autobiography*, 395–397.
15. Calhoun, speech on 'The Removal of the Public Deposits,' Jan. 13, 1834, *Works*, II, 313, 325, 338–339, 333–334; Calhoun to Tazewell, Feb. 9, 1834, Calhoun Papers, Library of Congress.
16. Calhoun, speech on 'The Proposition of Mr. Webster to Recharter the Bank of the United States,' March 21, 1834, *Works*, II, 349, 345, 348, 363, 365. In this speech, acclaimed by Benton as restoring debate 'to the elevation that belonged to the Senate,' Calhoun actually agreed to vote for Webster's motion, 'objectionable' as he found it; but his objections apparently convinced Webster, who personally withdrew the motion. No action was taken on Calhoun's counter-suggestion.
17. Calhoun, speech on 'The President's Protest,' May 6, 1834, *Works*, II, 415, 417, 418–425.
18. Calhoun, speech on 'Executive Patronage,' Feb. 13, 1835, *Works*, II, 446–465.
19. Calhoun, speech on bill 'To Regulate the Public Deposits,' May 28, 1836, *Works*, II, 534–568.
20. Calhoun, speech on 'The Admission of Michigan,' Jan. 5, 1837, *Works*, II, 613.

XVIII. THE AGE OF JACKSON

1. See William Meigs, *The Life of John Caldwell Calhoun*, II, 118.
2. Harriet Martineau, *Retrospect of Western Travel*, I, 161–162.
3. See *The Diary of Philip Hone*, Bayard Tuckerman, ed., I, 76–77. A vivid description of the House of Representatives can be found in Marryat's *Diary in America*, 89–90.
4. Frances Trollope, *Domestic Manners of the Americans*, 176, 228–229.
5. Harriet Martineau, I, 155–156.
6. Margaret Bayard Smith, *First Forty Years of Washington Society*, 301.

7. M. A. DeWolfe Howe, *The Life and Letters of George Bancroft*, 196; Bancroft to Mrs. S. D. Bancroft, Dec. 27, 1831; Marryat, 90–91.
8. Francis J. Grund, *Aristocracy in America*, II, 265.
9. Ben: Perley Poore, *Reminiscences*, I, 87.
10. Grund, II, 186–187.
11. Poore, I, 61, 191.
12. See Grund, II, 184–185. Detailed descriptions of the discomforts of Washington boarding houses of the period may also be found in Fanny Kemble's *Journal*, Harriet Martineau's *Retrospect of Western Travel*, and Frances Trollope's *Domestic Manners*.
13. Nathaniel P. Willis, *Hurry-Graphs*, 180–181.
14. Calhoun to Anna Maria Calhoun, Jan. 25, 1838, *Correspondence*, 390–391; also Calhoun to Anna Maria, Dec. 18. 1839, *ibid.*, 436–437.
15. Harriet Martineau, I, 149.
16. Poore, I, 343–344.
17. Amos Kendall, *Autobiography*, 280–282; see also Poore, I, 50–52; and Marryat, 89.
18. Fanny Kemble, *Journal*, II, 87.
19. Mrs. Basil Hall, *The Aristocratic Journey*, quoted in *Three Englishwomen in America*, 165.
20. Frances Trollope, 176–177.
21. Fanny Kemble, II, 89; see also Marryat, 89–90, and Frances Trollope, 177, 183.
22. Harriet Martineau, I, 144–145.
23. *Ibid.*, I, 179.
24. Poore, I, 143–144.
25. *Ibid.*, I, 189; 202–204.
26. James Parton, *Famous Americans of Recent Times*, 124.
27. Harriet Martineau, I, 147–148.
28. Calhoun to Anna Maria Calhoun, May 14, 1834, *Correspondence*, 336.
29. Parton, 124.
30. Grund, II, 321.
31. Kendall, 629–630.
32. Grund, II, 212.
33. Hone, *Diary*, Dec. 8, 1835, I, 177.
34. Harriet Martineau, I, 147.
35. Parton, 142.
36. Harriet Martineau, I, 147–149, 241.
37. *Ibid.*, I, 181–182.
38. Just who would have issued the challenge is a mystery. For Calhoun, stung to fury, repaid Benton with compound interest, in perhaps the most bitter outbreak of his career.

See Hone, *Diary*, Feb. 17, 1835, I, 133; also Charleston *Courier*, Feb. 23, 1835.
39. Harriet Martineau, I, 149–150.
40. John S. Jenkins, *John Caldwell Calhoun*, 450.
41. James C. Jewett to Gen. Dearborn, Feb. 5, 1817, in *William and Mary Quarterly Historical Magazine*, XVII, no. 2, Oct. 1908, 139–144.
42. Grund, II, 321.
43. New York *Evening Post*, Feb. 19, 1838; Boston *Post*, Dec. 16, 1833.
44. South Carolina tradition.
45. Poore, I, 136–137.
46. Arthur M. Schlesinger, Jr., *The Age of Jackson*, 53; W. H. Milburn, *Ten Years of Preacher Life*, 152–153.
47. Calhoun to Duff Green, March 28, 1844, *Correspondence*, 722–723; to James H. Hammond, April 24, 1841, *ibid.*, 490.
48. Mrs. E. F. Ellet, *Court Circles of the Republic*, 162–163.
49. Nathan Sargent, *Public Men and Events*, II, 239; I, 173.
50. Richard Crallé, undated reminiscences of Calhoun in Crallé Papers, Library of Congress.
51. Parton, 106; Poore, II, 64, 136; Calhoun to Anna Maria Clemson, March 7, 1848, *Correspondence*, 745.
52. Calhoun to Christopher Van Deventer, Feb. 7, 1836, *Correspondence*, 357–358.
53. Calhoun to Anna Maria Calhoun, April 3, 1834, May 14, 1834; also to Thomas Clemson, Dec. 13, 1840; to Anna Maria Clemson, June 28, 1841; to Thomas Clemson, July 23, 1841; to Anna Maria Clemson, March 20, 1842; *Correspondence*, 333, 335, 336–337, 468, 480, 482, 506; also to Mrs. Clemson, June 23, 1837, Calhoun Papers, Clemson College.
54. Calhoun to James E. Colhoun, Nov. 30, 1830, Calhoun Papers, Clemson College.
55. Calhoun to Thomas Clemson, Aug 8, 1841, *Correspondence*, 486; Calhoun to James Edward Colhoun, Feb. 8, 1834, *ibid.*, 331–332.
56. Josiah Quincy, *Figures of the Past*, 263.
57. Mary Bates, *The Private Life of John C. Calhoun*, 10.
58. Anna Maria Clemson's reminiscences of her father in Clemson College Papers.

59. Bates, 9.
60. A. C. Cole, *The Whig Party in the South*, 48; the Earl of Selkirk to Jean, Countess of Selkirk, Jan. 8, 1836, in Charter Room, St. Mary's

Isle, Kirkudbright, Scotland, quoted in preface to John P. Pritchett's *Calhoun and His Defense of the South.*
61. Grund, II, 321.

XIX. SLAVERY—THE THEORY AND THE FACT

1. Reminiscences of Cato as told to Mrs. Francis Calhoun, in Mrs. Francis Calhoun Papers (privately owned), Clemson College.
2. Calhoun to Charles J. Ingersoll, Aug. 4, 1818, *Correspondence*, 136–137; and Calhoun to James Edward Colhoun, Aug. 27, 1831, *ibid.*, 301.
3. Calhoun to John Ewing Colhoun, Jan. 15, 1827, *Correspondence*, 240–241.
4. J. K. Paulding, *Letters from the South*, I, 117; see also James Parton, *Famous Americans of Recent Times*, 119.
5. Robert Walsh, *Notices of Brazil*, II, 477–490, *passim.*
6. Calhoun, *Works*, IV, 339–349; II, 133.
7. *Ibid.*, III, 631; Hermann von Holst, *John C. Calhoun*, 5.
8. Basil Hall, *Travels in North America*, II, 200.
9. B. MacBride in *The Southern Agriculturist*, III, 175.
10. Frederick Law Olmsted, *Journey Through the Slave States*, 106.
11. *Debow's Review*, XV, 257–277.
12. Sarah M. Maury, *The Statesmen of America*, 378; also Calhoun to Virgil Maxcy, March 18, 1822, Virgil Maxcy Papers, Library of Congress.
13. Parton, 120.
14. *John C. Calhoun*, pamphlet of the State Department of Education, Columbia S. C.
15. Mary Bates, *The Private Life of John C. Calhoun*, 20–21.
16. Mrs. Basil Hall, quoted in *Three Englishwomen in America*, 220.
17. Cato's reminiscences, Mrs. Francis Calhoun Papers.
18. *Ibid.*
19. See Frederick Law Olmsted, *The Cotton Kingdom*, II, 73; Charles Lyell, *A Second Visit to the United States*, I, 263; also Calhoun to Thomas Clemson, Dec. 30, 1842, Calhoun Papers, Clemson College.
20. Cato's reminiscences.
21. Calhoun to James Edward Colhoun,

Oct. 7, 1835, Calhoun Papers, Clemson College.
22. Frances Kemble, *Journal*, II, 338.
23. 'A Southern Churchwoman's View of Slavery,' in *Church Intelligencer*, Nov. 22, 1860.
24. See *The Carolina Tribute to Calhoun*, 234.
25. Olmsted, *Journey Through the Slave States*, 385.
26. Bates, 21.
27. Frances Trollope, *Domestic Manners of the Americans*, 199; Caroline Howard Gilman, *Recollections of a Southern Matron*, 54.
28. *Church Intelligencer*, Nov. 22, 1860.
29. Lyell, *Travels in North America*, I, 157–184, *passim.*
30. Slave reminiscences in Mrs. Francis Calhoun Papers.
31. Caroline Howard Gilman, 181, 50–51, 54, 293; Mrs. Francis Calhoun Papers, and Lyell, *A Second Visit to the United States*, I, 265.
32. *Church Intelligencer*, Nov. 22, 1860; see also Frances Butler Leigh, *Ten Years on a Georgia Plantation*, *passim.*
33. John S. C. Abbott, *Slavery, South and North*, 142, 154, and 161.
34. Lyell, *Travels*, I, 22.
35. Allan Nevins and Henry Steele Commager, *History of the United States*, 214–215.
36. See John Quincy Adams, *Diary*, IV, 530–531; V, 5–11, 13.
37. David Cohn, 'How the South Feels,' *The Atlantic Monthly*, Jan. 1944, 47–51.
38. Fanny Kemble, *Journal*, II, 393.
39. Frederick Marryat, *Diary in America*, 193; Lyell, *Travels*, I, 157–184; A. C. Cole, 'The Whig Party in the South,' in *The Annual Report of the American Historical Association*, Washington, 1913; and Grund, *Aristocracy in America*, I, 30.
40. Olmsted, *The Cotton Kingdom*, II, 111.
41. *Ibid.*, 110.
42. Calhoun, quoted in Von Holst, *John C. Calhoun*, 141.

43. Cohn, 'How the South Feels,' *Atlantic Monthly*, Jan. 1944, 47–51.
44. William Garnett, July 12, 1805, in papers of Thomas Ruffin, *North Carolina Historical Commission Publications*, I, 80.
46. Hall, II, 260.
47. Marryat, 190; Hall, II, 218.
48. Amos Kendall, *Autobiography*, 502; W. H. Sparks, *Old Times in Georgia*, 34; Marryat, 194; Lyell, *A Second Visit to the United States*, I, 72; Olmsted, *The Seaboard Slave States*, 385.
49. *Freedom's Defense* (pamphlet), Worcester Antiquarian Society.
50. Albert J. Beveridge, *Abraham Lincoln* (Standard Library Edition), II, 19; Allan Nevins, *Ordeal of the Union*, I, 148–149.
51. Calhoun, *Works*, II, 623; VI, 'The Southern Address,' 285–313.
52. See issues of *The Liberator*, Aug. 1831.
53. Marryat, 194.
54. Abbott, 74; Olmsted, *Seaboard Slave States*, 385; Harriet Martineau, *Slavery in America*, 29; Marryat, 190, 193, 195; and Lyell, *A Second Visit*, I, 181–182.
55. *Church Intelligencer*, Nov. 22, 1860.
56. Calhoun to Thomas Clemson, Sept. 1846, Calhoun Papers, Clemson College.
57. Marryat, 190–191; Thomas Dew, *Pro-Slavery Argument*, 228–229.
58. Lyell, *A Second Visit*, I, 271–272.
59. James Sparks, *Old Times in Georgia*, 111.
60. Lyell, *A Second Visit*, I, 209–210; Mrs. Basil Hall, *The Aristocratic Journey*, quoted in *Three Englishwomen in America*, 210.
61. Marryat, 82.
62. *Ibid.*, 83; also William Jay, *Miscellaneous Writings on Slavery*, 371–394, *passim*.
63. Marryat, 83.
64. William Jay, *Miscellaneous Writings on Slavery*, 371–394, *passim*.
65. Thomas L. Nichols, *Forty Years of American Life*, II, 278–280; see also Lyell, *A Second Visit*, II, 71.
66. Abbott, 75, 78, 85–86.
67. Robert Henry, quoted in *The Carolina Tribute to Calhoun*, 234–235; also Henry Clay, Speech on 'The Abolition Petitions,' Feb. 7, 1839, in *Life and Speeches of Henry Clay*, II, 418.

68. Calhoun, *Works*, IV, 517; Dodd, *The Cotton Kingdom*, 63; Parrington, *The Romantic Revolution*, 100.
69. Sarah M. Maury, *The Statesmen of America*, 365.
70. Lyell, *A Second Visit*, I, 82.
71. *Ibid.*, 241.
72. William J. Grayson, *The Hireling and the Slave*, preface, vii, viii.
73. Richmond *Enquirer*, Jan. 19, 1832.
74. Clement Eaton, *Freedom of Thought in the Old South*, 174–175; 162, 21, 111.
75. *Ibid.*, 63.
76. J. D. B. DeBow, *The Interest in Slavery of the Southern Non-Slaveholder*, 10.
77. Quoted in Carl Sandburg's *Abraham Lincoln: The Prairie Years* (Blue Ribbon Edition), 403.
78. *The Subterranean*, Sept. 13, 1845.
79. *Congressional Globe*, 33d Congress, 1st Session, 1224.
80. Orestes Brownson in Boston *Quarterly Review*, July, 1840.
81. Christopher Hollis, *The American Heresy*, 110.
82. *The Liberator*, Jan. 1 and Jan. 17, 1831.
83. John Quincy Adams, *Diary*, IV, 530–531.
84. John C. Coit, quoted in *The Carolina Tribute to Calhoun*, 149ff.
85. George Fisher, *The Life of Benjamin Silliman*, II, 98.
86. Gerald Johnson, *The Secession of the Southern States*, 61; also George F. Cushman, 'John C. Calhoun,' *Magazine of American History*, VIII, 612–619.
87. Calhoun, speech on 'Abolition Petitions,' March 9, 1836, *Works*, II, 488–489.
88. Jackson to Amos Kendall, Aug. 9, 1835, *Jackson Correspondence*, V, 360–361.
89. Calhoun, *Works*, II, 515.
90. See Calhoun's speech on 'Deputy-Postmasters,' April 12, 1836, *Works*, II, 509–533.
91. Calhoun, speech on 'Reception of Abolition Petitions,' Feb. 6, 1837, *Works*, II, 627.
92. Calhoun, speech on 'The Abolition Petitions,' March 9, 1836, *Works*, II, 481–482; see also Thomas Hart Benton, *Thirty Years' View*, II, 135, 138.
93. See text of Resolutions of Dec. 27, 1837, Calhoun's *Works*, III, 140–142.

94. Hollis, 119.
95. Calhoun, *Works*, III, 145.
96. Calhoun to Anna Maria Calhoun, Jan. 25, 1838, *Correspondence*, 391.
97. Calhoun, *Works*, III, 154; also, *ibid.*, II, 486.
98. *Ibid.*, III, 154.
99. *Ibid.*, speech on 'The Reception of Abolition Petitions,' Feb. 6, 1837, *Works*, II, 629; *ibid.*, III, 170–171.
100. Calhoun, 'Remarks on Resolutions,' Dec. 27, 1837 ff.; *Works*, III, 159–161.
101. *Ibid.*, III, 155; II, 629.
102. *Ibid.*, III, 163–164.
103. *Ibid.*, II, 629; also *The Carolina Tribute to Calhoun*, 361.
104. Calhoun, *Works*, IV, 516–517.

105. *Ibid.*, III, 148–152, 177.
106. *Ibid.*, 142.
107. Calhoun, remarks on the 'Case of the brigs, Comet, Emporium, and Enterprise,' Feb. 14, 1837, *Works*, III, 10–12.
108. Gerald Johnson, *Secession of the Southern States*, 61. Marryat, 194–195, points out that slavery was working its way westward; and forecast that within 'twenty or thirty years [1860–1870] . . . provided . . . these states are not injudiciously interfered with,' the upper South and possibly even Tennessee and South Carolina would 'of their own accord, enroll themselves among the free states.'

XX. FLORIDE

1. Ben Robertson, *Red Hills and Cotton*, 98, 102.
2. Gerald Johnson to author.
3. Calhoun to Mrs. John C. Calhoun, March 1, 1812, *Correspondence*, 124–125. See also letters to Anna Maria Calhoun, Sept. 8, 1837, and June 28, 1841, *Correspondence*, 379 and 480; and June 23, 1837, Calhoun Papers, Clemson College.
4. Calhoun to Mrs. Floride Colhoun, Dec. 23, 1805, Jan. 19 and April 13, 1806, *Correspondence*, 101, 102, and 105.
5. Mrs. St. Julien Ravenel, *The Life of William Lowndes*, 83–84.
6. See Calhoun to Mrs. Floride Colhoun, Dec. 22, 1806, *Correspondence*, 108; to Thomas Holland, July 2, 1833, *ibid.*, 324; to David Hoffman, Nov. 4, 1835, *ibid.*, 347–348; to Frederick H. Sanford, Feb. 23, 1841, *ibid.*, 476.
7. Calhoun to Jacob Brown, Brown Letter Book, BR2, Aug. 1, 1820, Brown Papers, Library of Congress.
8. John S. Jenkins, *Life of John Caldwell Calhoun*, 448.
9. Walter Miller, 'Calhoun as a Lawyer and Statesman,' *The Green Bag*, XI, 330.
10. Oliver Dyer, *Great Senators of the United States*, 168–170.
11. Varina Howell Davis, *Jefferson Davis*, I, 213; Mary Bates, *The Private Life of John C. Calhoun*, 9.
12. Calhoun to Anna Maria Clemson, July, 1848, and March and August,

1844, Calhoun Papers, Clemson College.
13. Patrick Calhoun to author, May 6, 1943. (Patrick Calhoun of Pasadena, California, was the son of Andrew P. Calhoun, and thus the grandson of both John C. Calhoun and Duff Green. Born in 1856, he spent his early childhood at Fort Hill, and after the death of his father, lived with Duff Green in Georgia, accumulating a fund of reminiscences and lore on the Calhoun family. He died in 1943.)
14. Calhoun to Anna Maria Clemson, March, 1844, Calhoun Papers, Clemson College.
15. Patrick Calhoun to author, May 6, 1943.
16. Calhoun to James Edward Colhoun, April 21, 1838, *Correspondence*, 395–396.
17. Clipping from the Washington *Daily Union*, Aug. 18, 1849, on the personal habits of John C. Calhoun.
18. Clipping, by Frank Dickson, Jr., from Anderson *Independent*, in Clemson College Papers.
19. Fort Hill tradition.
20. Calhoun to Anna Maria Clemson, Feb. 1848, Calhoun Papers, Clemson College.
21. Calhoun to Thomas Clemson, July, 1842, Calhoun Papers.
22. See letter of Calhoun to Clemson Dec. 3, 1842 in Calhoun Papers, Clemson College; and to T. R. Matthews, Aug. 18, 1845, Calhoun

Papers, Library of Congress, in which he referred to 'a severe illness of Mrs. Calhoun with an attack of a nervous character which confined her to bed for more than a month.'

23. Calhoun to James Edward Colhoun, undated, Calhoun Papers, Clemson College.
24. See John Quincy Adams, *Diary*, VIII, 159; also Margaret Bayard Smith, 290–292. It is true, however, that family responsibilities tended to keep Floride at home in later years, and that on several occasions she spent a winter with her husband in the 'messes.' However, she was not with him in his times of greatest crisis and strain, and in the last years did not come to Washington at all.
25. See Crallé Papers on death of Calhoun, in Library of Congress.
26. See Elbridge Brooks, *Eminent Americans*, 292; Christopher Hollis, *The*

American Heresy, 83; and Jenkins, 25.
27. See Calhoun's letters to Anna Maria Calhoun, Feb. 13 and March 10, 1832; May 14, 1834; to Mrs. Clemson, Jan. 3, 1841, *Correspondence*, 312, 316, 336, and 472.
28. Sarah M. Maury, *The Statesmen of America*, 376–377.
29. Bates, 8.
30. Letter of Calhoun, March 9, 1844, *Correspondence*, 574.
31. Henry Clay in *The Carolina Tribute to Calhoun*, 9–10.
32. Calhoun to Anna Maria Calhoun, April 3, 1834, *Correspondence*, 333–335.
33. South Carolina tradition.
34. Calhoun to Andrew Pickens Calhoun, April 12, 1847, Calhoun Papers, Duke University Library.
35. Calhoun to Anna Maria Calhoun, April 3, 1834, *Correspondence*, 334.
36. E. E. Poe, clipping on Calhoun in Clemson College Papers.

XXI. YEARS OF DECISION

1. See Reginald C. McGrane, *The Panic of 1837*, 40–70, *passim*.
2. Hugh R. Fraser, *Nicholas Biddle and the Bank*, 62–75, *passim;* McGrane, 177.
3. Philip Hone, *Diary*, I, 256–257.
4. See issues of *National Intelligencer*, May 1–10, 1837, p*assim*.
5. Charles Dickens, *American Notes* (Library Edition), 282.
6. McGrane, 25.
7. Frederick Marryat, *Diary in America*, 18–19.
8. Hermann von Holst, *History of the United States*, II, 216; William M. Gouge, *Fiscal History of Texas*, 75.
9. Cincinnati *Inquirer*, Jan. 12, 1842.
10. *Niles' Weekly Register*, LII, 166.
11. Calhoun, *Works*, III, 227.
12. Fraser, 34; Thomas Hart Benton, *Thirty Years' View*, II, 26.
13. Benton, II, 20, 26, 27.
14. Marryat, 18.
15. Benton, II, 250.
16. Calhoun, *Works*, III, 75. See also Calhoun's speech on the 'Bill to Separate the Government from the Banks,' *Works*, III, 102–122, *passim*.
17. Calhoun to James Edward Colhoun, Sept. 7, 1837, *Correspondence*, 377.

18. Calhoun quoted in Benton, II, 250.
19. Arthur M. Schlesinger, Jr., *The Age of Jackson*, 246–247.
20. *North American Review*, Jan. 1844, and *National Intelligencer*, Feb. 24, 1842.
21. Christopher Hollis, *The Two Nations*, 205, 204.
22. J. D. B. DeBow, *Industrial Resources of the Southern States*, III, 93; London *Times*, Oct. 2, 1859; Thomas P. Kellett, *Southern Wealth and Northern Profits*, 98.
23. See Calhoun's speech on 'The Removal of the Deposits,' *Works*, II, 309–343; also Albert Brisbane, *A Mental Biography*, 222.
24. Vernon Parrington, *The Romantic Revolution in America*, vi.
25. Calhoun, *Works*, III, 96; speech on the 'Issue of Treasury Notes,' Oct. 3, 1837, 115ff.; also Calhoun to R. H. Goodwyne, *Niles' Weekly Register*, Sept. 29, 1838.
26. New York *Journal of Commerce*, June 13, 1850.
27. Philip S. Foner, *Business and Slavery*, 16; Hone, II, 54; New York *Evening Post*, April 25, 1844.
28. London *Times*, quoted in New York *Tribune*, Sept. 29, 1860.

29. New York *Post*, April 16, 1861; *Journal of Commerce*, May 5, 1860; New York *Times*, Nov. 24, 1854; and *Annual Report of the American Anti-Slavery Society*, 1858, 56.
30. Samuel J. May, *Recollections of the Anti-Slavery Conflict*, 127–128.
31. Schlesinger, 246–248; Francis Pickens, quoted in House, Oct. 10, 1837, *Register of Debates*, 25th Congress, 1st Session, 1393–1395.
32. Schlesinger, 231.
33. New York *Herald*, April 1, 1850; Calhoun to Orestes Brownson, Oct. 31, 1841, quoted in Orestes Brownson, Jr., *Brownson's Early Life*, 302.
34. Benton, II, 132–133.
35. Calhoun to Andrew Pickens Calhoun, April 5, 1838, *Correspondence*, 394.
36. David Campbell to William C. Rives, Oct. 3, 1838, Rives Papers, Library of Congress.
37. H. L. Hopkins to William Rives, Oct. 3, 1838, Rives Papers.
38. B. W. Leigh to John J. Crittenden, June 5, 1838, Crittenden Papers, Library of Congress.
39. Mrs. E. F. Ellet, *Court Circles of the Republic*, 244.
40. Thomas Cooper to Nicholas Biddle, May 14, 1837, in *Biddle Correspondence*, 279.
41. Reginald C. McGrane, ed., *The Correspondence of Nicholas Biddle*, 266; see also Claude M. Fuess, *Daniel Webster*, II, 67.
42. McGrane, 226.
43. Andrew Jackson to Frank Blair, Aug. 12, 1841, *Jackson Correspondence*, VI.
44. Calhoun to James Hammond, Feb. 23, 1840, *Correspondence*, 448–450.
45. Calhoun to Anna Maria Calhoun, Dec. 10, 1837, Calhoun Papers, Clemson College.
46. David Campbell to William C. Rives, Oct. 31, 1838, Rives Papers, Library of Congress.
47. Daniel Webster to Nicholas Biddle, in McGrane, *Biddle Correspondence*, 301; Calhoun, *Works*, III, 228, 243.
48. Calhoun to Anna Maria Calhoun, Sept. 30, 1837, *Correspondence*, 380.
49. Calhoun, *Works*, II, 310. See also letters to Francis Pickens, Jan. 4, 1834, *Correspondence*, 328.
50. Calhoun to Pickens, Dec. 12, 1833, and Jan. 4, 1834, *Correspondence*, 326–329.

51. Ben: Perley Poore, *Reminiscences*, I, 205.
52. Benton, II, 97ff.
53. Calhoun, speech on the 'Independent Treasury Bill,' March 10, 1838, *Works*, III, 249–250, 273–275, 277.
54. John S. Jenkins, *Life of John Caldwell Calhoun*, 378.
55. Calhoun, *Works*, III, 269; see also *Congressional Globe*, 25th Congress, 2d Session, March 10, 1838, 176–181.
56. Benton, II, 122–123.
57. See Gaillard Hunt, *John C. Calhoun*, 244; Charleston *Mercury*, June 7, 1838; *Niles' Weekly Register*, LIV, 339.
58. Calhoun, *Works*, III, 270–271.
59. Calhoun to Anna Maria Clemson, May 30, 1840, *Correspondence*, 458; Jan. 3, 1841, *ibid.*, 470–472; June 28, 1841, *ibid.*, 478–480; March 20, 1842, *ibid.*, 506.
60. Calhoun to Anna Maria Clemson, March 20, 1842, *Correspondence*, 505; to Francis W. Pickens, Jan. 4, 1834, *ibid.*, 328; to Anna Maria, May 14, 1834, *ibid.*, 337; *idem*, Sept. 8, 1837, *ibid.*, 379; *idem*, Dec. 18, 1839, *ibid.*, 437; to Thomas G. Clemson, July 11, 1841, *ibid.*, 481; see also New York *Herald*, April 1, 1850; Jenkins, 448.
61. Calhoun to Anna Maria Clemson, April, 1839, and Dec. 1841, Calhoun Papers, Clemson College.
62. W. H. Parmalee, 'Recollections of an Old Stager,' *Harpers' New Monthly Magazine* (Oct. 1873), 757.
63. Mary Bates, *The Private Life of John C. Calhoun*, 9–10; Varina Howell Davis, *Jefferson Davis*, I, 213; and Parmalee, 757.
64. Angelica Singleton, March 13, 1838, and March 4, 1839, Angelica Van Buren Papers, Library of Congress.
65. Calhoun to James Edward Colhoun, Feb. 1, 1840, *Correspondence*, 445; to Anna Maria Clemson, Feb. 13, 1840, *ibid.*, 445–448.
66. Duff Green to Calhoun, Aug. 21, 1840, *Correspondence*, 828–829; Calhoun to Duff Green, May, 1839, *ibid.*, 427–429; and Calhoun to Anna Maria Clemson, Jan. 3, 1841, *ibid.*, 470–471.
67. See Arthur Stryon, *The Cast-Iron Man*, 241–242.
68. Varina Howell Davis, I, 190.
69. Quoted in W. E. Woodward's *A New American History*, 428.

70. Calhoun to Anna Maria Clemson, Feb. 17, 1841, *Correspondence*, 475.
71. Poore, I, 254, 291.
72. Calhoun, speech to 'Reduce Certain Duties,' Feb. 23, 1837, *Works*, III, 45–46; see also *ibid.*, III, 377, 451; *ibid.*, IV, 103, 46.
73. Calhoun, *Works*, IV, 150.
74. *Ibid.*, IV; speech on 'Mr. Clay's Resolutions,' *ibid.*, 100–101, 103; see also *ibid.*, 2, 109, 115, 120, 126, 127, 134–135, 174.
75. Calhoun, *Works*, IV, 171–172, 173, 207.
76. Poore, I, 266, 273.
77. Parmalee, 758–760.
78. Anecdote in Joseph Rogers, *The True Henry Clay*, 250.
79. Calhoun to James H. Hammond, Nov. 27, 1842, *Correspondence*, 522.
80. Calhoun, *Works*, II, 614.
81. Dixon Lewis to Richard Crallé, March 14, 1842, Crallé Papers, Library of Congress.
82. Duff Green to Calhoun, Aug. 21, 1840, *Correspondence*, 828.
83. Calhoun to Green, July 27, 1837, *Correspondence*, 375.
84. Lemuel Williams to Calhoun, Sept. 6, 1843, *Correspondence*, 874–876; and Joseph Scoville to Calhoun, Oct. 25, 1842, *ibid.*, 855–856.
85. Quoted in Charleston *Mercury*, Sept. 10, 1843.
86. Franklin H. Elmore to Calhoun, Nov. 2, 1842, *Correspondence*, 857–861.

87. Calhoun to R. M. T. Hunter, July 10, 1843, *Correspondence*, 540–541; and to Duff Green, Sept. 8, 1843, *ibid.*, 545–547.
88. See Hunt, 251.
89. Calhoun to Anna Maria Clemson, Feb. 6, 1843, *Correspondence*, 540–541; and to Duff Green, Sept. 8, 1843, *ibid.*, 545–547.
90. Jackson (Ala.) *Republican*.
91. Calhoun to Duff Green, July 27, 1838, *Correspondence*, 376.
92. Edward Block to Calhoun, Sept. 1, 1843, *Correspondence*, 868–871.
93. James Hamilton to Calhoun, Nov. 21, 1843, *Correspondence*, 891–894; Lemuel Williams to Calhoun, Sept. 6, 1843, *ibid.*, 874–878; Franklin H. Elmore to Calhoun, Jan. 13, 1844, *ibid.*, 911–912.
94. Calhoun to George McDuffie, Dec. 4, 1843, *Correspondence*, 552–555; see also *New Aurora* and Mobile *Tribune*, Jan. 27, 1844.
95. Robert B. Rhett to Calhoun, Dec. 8, 1843, *Correspondence*, 898–900; Virgil Maxcy to Calhoun, Dec. 10, 1843, *ibid.*, 898–900; R. M. T. Hunter to Calhoun, Feb. 6, 1844, *ibid.*, 927–931.
96. James A. Seddon to Calhoun, Feb. 5, 1844, *Correspondence*, 923–924.
97. Calhoun to R. M. T. Hunter, Feb. 1, 1844, *Correspondence*, 564; to Duff Green, Feb. 10, 1844, *ibid.*, 564; to James Edward Colhoun, Feb. 7, 1844, *ibid.*, 566–567.

XXII. CALHOUN AND THE LONE STAR

1. Hermann Von Holst, *Calhoun*, 222, 234.
2. Ben: Perley Poore, I, *Reminiscences*, 303; Thomas L. Nichols, *Forty Years of American Life*, II, 168.
3. *American Historical Review*, XIII, 311–312.
4. London *Morning Chronicle*, Aug. 19, 1843.
5. Leon Tyler, *Letters and Times of the Tylers*, II, 330.
6. Calhoun to Upshur, Aug. 27, 1843, text in National Archives.
7. Thomas W. Gilmer to Calhoun, Dec. 13, 1843, *Correspondence*, 905; Calhoun to Gilmer, Dec. 25, 1843, *ibid.*, 559.
8. Tyler, II, 226e; *ibid.*, III, 194.
9. E. F. Ellet, *Court Circles of the Republic*, 356.

10. Tyler, II, 226e; *ibid.*, III, 197.
11. Poore, I, 278.
12. There are numerous contemporary accounts of this meeting of which the most authentic are Henry Wise, *Seven Decades of the Union*, 221 ff.; Frank G. Carpenter, 'A Talk With a President's Son,' in *Lippincott's Magazine*, IV, 420; Tyler, II, 244; and Poore, II, 315.
13. Tyler to Calhoun, March 6, 1844, *Correspondence*, 438–439.
14. Dixon Lewis to Calhoun, March 6, 1844, *Correspondence*, 935–938; and Dixon Lewis to Crallé, March 19, 1844, Crallé Papers, Library of Congress.
15. *Niles' Weekly Register*, March 23, 1841; Dixon Lewis quoted in *Correspondence*, 938; and Francis

Wharton to Calhoun, March 8, 1844, *ibid.*, 939–940.

16. Letter of Calhoun, March 9, 1844, *Correspondence*, 573–576.
17. George McDuffie to Calhoun, March 5, 1844, *Correspondence*, 934–935; also Calhoun to James Edward Colhoun, March 19, 1844, Clemson College Papers.
18. Allen Tate, *Stonewall Jackson: The Good Soldier*, 381.
19. Calhoun addressing Daniel Webster in Senate, March 7, 1850; Calhoun to Wharton, *Correspondence*, 644.
20. Calhoun to Francis Wharton, Sept. 17, 1844, *Correspondence*, 615–617.
21. Jackson to A. V. Brown, Feb. 12, 1843; reprinted in Richmond *Enquirer*, March 22, 1844.
22. Thomas Hart Benton, *Thirty Years' View*, II, 617; see Marquis James, *Andrew Jackson: Portrait of a President*, 484.
23. James Hammond to Calhoun, May 10, 1844, *Correspondence*, 953–955.
24. Calhoun to Francis Wharton, May 28, 1844, *Correspondence*, 592–594; also Calhoun to George W. Houk, Oct. 14, 1844, *ibid.*, 624–625.
25. Calhoun to Francis Wharton, May 28, 1844, *Correspondence*, 592–594.
26. *Idem.*
27. Harriet Martineau, *Retrospect of Western Travel*, I, 144, 160.
28. Oliver Dyer, *Great Senators of the United States*, 185.
29. *Ibid.*, 185; Sarah M. Maury, *The Statesmen of America*, 345–346; Martineau, I, 244–245.
30. See Samuel F. Bemis, ed., *The American Secretaries of State*, V, 'John C. Calhoun,' by St. George L. Sioussat, sketch, *passim*.
31. Tate, 237.
32. See Von Holst, 231; also Texas Instructions, Department of State, I, 1837–1845, Calhoun to W. S. Murphy, April 13, 1844, National Archives; also *Niles' Weekly Register*, LXVI, 232; and W. S. Murphy to Calhoun, April 29, 1844, *Correspondence*, 947–948.
33. Calhoun to J. R. Mathews, May 9, 1844, Calhoun Papers, Library of Congress.
34. Senate Document 341, 28th Congress, 1st Session, 48. See also Von Holst, 236 and 242.
35. John Greenleaf Whittier, *Poetical Works*, 'To a Southern Statesman,' I,

208; 'Letter on Texas' (pamphlet), Hamden, in Worcester Antiquarian Society; also William Preston to John J. Crittenden, Jan. 28, 1844, Crittenden, Papers, Library of Congress.
36. Letter of Alexander H. Stephens, May 17, 1844, Stephens Papers, Library of Congress: also William Preston to Crittenden, Jan. 28, 1844, Crittenden, Papers, Library of Congress.
37. Tyler, II, 330; Calhoun, *Works*, IV, 333–335, 358–359; Calhoun to J. R. Mathews, July 2, 1844, Calhoun Papers, Library of Congress.
38. Calhoun to Thomas Clemson, Jan. 1843, Calhoun Papers, Clemson College.
39. Thomas Clemson to Calhoun (undated), Calhoun Papers, Clemson College.
40. Calhoun to James E. Colhoun, June 29, 1844, Calhoun Papers, Clemson College.
41. Mary Bates, *The Private Life of John C. Calhoun*, 9, 30–31; Varina Howell Davis, *Jefferson Davis: A Memoir*, I, 275.
42. Anna Maria Clemson to Calhoun (undated), Calhoun Papers, Clemson College.
43. Calhoun to Henry St. George Tucker, March 31, 1843, *Correspondence*, 526–528.
44. Calhoun to John E. Colhoun, Dec. 16, 1844; to James Edward Colhoun, Oct. 2, 1845, Calhoun Papers, Clemson College.
45. Calhoun to Anna Maria Clemson, May 22, 1845, *Correspondence*, 656–657.
46. Legislative Archives, State Department Messages, Feb. 6, 1845; Legislative Archives, *ibid.*, Dec. 9, 1844; and Texas Instructions, National Archives, Aug. 13, 1844, XV.
47. Calhoun to Anna Maria Clemson, May 22, 1845, *Correspondence*, 657.
48. W. H. Parmalee, 'Recollection of an Old Stager,' *Harpers New Monthly Magazine* (Oct. 1873), 756.
49. Letter of Calhoun, March 9, 1844, *Correspondence*, 575–576.
50. Varina Howell Davis, I, 221–224.
51. E. F. Ellet, 310–311; Varina Howell Davis, I, 271, 220.
52. E. F. Ellet, 357.
53. Tyler, III, 197–199.
54. *Ibid.*, II, 433, 336, and 436. See also

Ambrose Mann to Calhoun, Oct. 31, 1834, *Correspondence*, 982–986; William R. King to Calhoun, Oct. or Nov., 1844, *ibid.*, 986–990.

55. Frederick Marryat, *Diary in America*, 197.
56. Letters of Andrew Jackson Donelson to Calhoun, Jan. 27 and 30, 1845, *Correspondence*, 1019–1022, 1023–1024.
57. Von Holst, 251, 234.
58. Calhoun to Thomas W. Gilmer, Dec. 25, 1843, *Correspondence*, 559–560.
59. Calhoun to William Shannon, Sept. 11, 1844, Legislative Archives, XV, Department of State; William Shan-

non to Calhoun, Feb. 7, 1845, National Archives.
60. Calhoun to James Edward Colhoun, Feb. 16, 1845, Calhoun Papers, Clemson College; Francis Wharton's notes for Feb. 18 and Feb. 20, 1845, *Correspondence*, 644.
61. Von Holst, 247, 254; also Duff Green to James Knox Polk, Jan. 20, 1845, Polk Papers, Library of Congress; and Eugene I. McCormac, *James Knox Polk*, 287–288.
62. David S. Muzzey, *A History of Our Country*, 218.
63. Tyler, II, 153.
64. Von Holst, 255.

XXIII. THE MASTER OF FORT HILL

1. Mary Bates, *The Private Life of John C. Calhoun*, 8.
2. Mrs. Margaret Bayard Smith, *The First Forty Years of Washington Society*, 268–269; John Quincy Adams, *Diary*, V, 452.
3. Calhoun to J. G. Swift, May 10, 1823 and Oct. 30, 1823; see also Calhoun to Anna Maria Clemson, Dec. 18, 1839, *Correspondence*, 436; and April 10, 1849, *ibid.*, 763.
4. Bates, 12.
5. Walter L. Miller, 'Calhoun as a Lawyer and Statesman,' *The Green Bag*, XI, 271; also Charleston *Mercury*, June 20, 1846.
6. Cato's reminiscences, quoted in Mrs. Francis Calhoun Papers, Clemson College, South Carolina.
7. See description of Fort Hill by Mrs. Patrick H. Mell, Charleston *Sunday News*, April 30, 1905; also Bates, 14.
8. Records of the Pendleton Library Society, Clemson College, South Carolina, including membership and book lists.
9. See list of books in Calhoun's library in Clemson College Papers; also Walter L. Miller in *The Green Bag*, XI, 330.
10. Calhoun to Anna Maria Calhoun, April 3, 1834, *Correspondence*, 334.
11. Calhoun to Anna Maria Clemson, March 24, 1840, Calhoun Papers, Clemson College. A part of this letter is printed in *Correspondence*, 451.
12. Claude M. Fuess, *Daniel Webster*, II, 333, 335, 343.
13. Interview with Calhoun in Washington *Daily Union*, Aug. 18, 1849.

14. Reminiscences of Calhoun by James E. Colhoun, April, 1850, manuscript in Calhoun Papers, Clemson College.
15. Plantation Day-Book of William Lowndes, 1802–1822, 18, 19, manuscript in Lowndes Papers, Library of Congress.
16. *Ibid.*
17. Sarah M. Maury, *The Statesmen of America*, 363.
18. W. H. V. Miller, 'Calhoun as a Farmer,' printed, clipped article, dated 1843, in Clemson College Papers. See also the Report of the Committee on Farms for the Pendleton Farmers' Society, *Southern Cultivator*, III (July, 1845), and Calhoun's letter to James Edward Colhoun, Feb. 26, 1832, *Correspondence*, 313, in which he estimated that soil erosion was costing South Carolina, alone, about $20,000,000 yearly. Calhoun's own skill as a soil cultivator blinded him to the destructive effect of the cotton-slave economy on the Southern soil generally; for, as an individual, he had proved that with proper care such erosion could be controlled. He did not see that to the average cotton speculator the availability of cheap land and cheap labor made soil-conservation measures appear unnecessary.
19. Calhoun to J. R. Mathews, Aug. 18, 1845, Calhoun Papers, Library of Congress; also Calhoun to Clemson, 1845, Calhoun Papers, Clemson College.
20. Reminiscences of James E. Colhoun, April, 1850, Calhoun Papers, Clemson College.

21. Clipping by Frank A. Dickson, Jr., from Anderson (S. C.) *Independent,* Dec. 15, 1929, in Clemson College Papers.
22. Ben Robertson, *Red Hills and Cotton,* 222–223.
23. Walter L. Miller, *The Green Bag,* XI, 328.
24. Fort Hill tradition.
25. Bates, 9; Miller, 328; Washington *Daily Union,* Aug. 18, 1849.
26. Mary Baker Chesnut, *A Diary from Dixie,* March 11, 1861.
27. George Washington Featherstonhaugh, *Canoe Voyage up the Minnay Sotor,* II, 267–269.
29. Told the author by Mark Bradley of the Clemson College Faculty, who heard it from 'Ted' himself.
29. Reminiscences of Calhoun by Anna Maria Clemson, April, 1850, printed copy in Clemson College Anderson.
30. Article by Dickson in Anderson (S. C.) *Independent,* Dec. 15, 1929; see also 'John C. Calhoun's Home Life,' Anderson (S. C.) *Daily Mail,* Oct. 23, 1926.
31. Maury, 373; William Mathews, *Oratory and Orators,* 312–313; Daniel Webster in *The Carolina Tribute to Calhoun,* 11–12.
32. Featherstonhaugh, II, 247–272, *passim.*
33. Planter's Day-Book (anonymous), in Clemson College Library.
34. Featherstonhaugh, II, 270–272; Bates, 10; Maury, 377; in Gamaliel Bradford's *As God Made Them,* 103; also Dixon Lewis to Crallé, June 10, 1840, Crallé Papers, MSS. Division, Library of Congress.
35. Featherstonhaugh, II, 270; Benja-

min F. Perry, *Reminiscences of Public Men,* 80–81.
36. Featherstonhaugh gives an excellent appraisal of Calhoun's character in his sketch, II, 247–272, *passim.* See also Maury, 382–384.
37. Robert Barnwell Rhett, in *The Carolina Tribute to Calhoun,* 371.
38. Perry, 45–46.
39. See Holmes, quoted in *The Carolina Tribute to Calhoun,* 27, 31; Hammond, *ibid.,* 321; Clay, *ibid.,* 9–10.
40. Bates, 14.
41. Maury, 238.
42. Perry, 44.
43. John S. Jennings, *John Caldwell Calhoun,* 453; James Parton, *Famous Americans of Recent Times,* 142; Henry, quoted in *The Carolina Tribute to Calhoun,* 237; and John Wentworth, *Congressional Reminiscences,* 21, 31.
44. James E. Colhoun, 'Reminiscences of Calhoun' (manuscript), April, 1850; Charles C. Pinckney, 'Calhoun From a Southern Standpoint,' *Lippincott's Monthly,* LXII (July, 1898).
45. Henry S. Foote, *Casket of Reminiscences,* 78; see also R. M. T. Hunter Papers, Virginia State Historical Library.
46. Parton, 142; Jenkins, 448; Jefferson Davis in *North American Review,* CXLV (1887), 246 ff.
47. Parton, 122.
48. Miller, *The Green Bag,* XI, 330; Hammond in *The Carolina Tribute to Calhoun,* 323; Bates, 27.
49. Bates, 26; Miller, *The Green Bag,* XI, 329; and Charles C. Pinckney in *Lippincott's Monthly,* LXII (July, 1898).

XXIV. AMERICA IN MID-CENTURY

1. J. D. B. DeBow, *Statistical View of the United States,* 126–128.
2. *World Almanac* (Official Census, 1945), 129.
3. DeBow, 165.
4. DeBow, 192. See the following breakdown of figures in the official *Seventh Census* (J. D. B. DeBow, editor), Washington, 1853: agricultural workers, exclusive of slaves, 2,400,583; workers in manufacturing and commerce, exclusive of women and children, 1,596,265; nonagricultural workers (male), 993,620, totalling 2,589,885 for non-agricul-

tural workers; also 381,408 employed in miscellaneous occupations.
5. Thomas L. Nichols, *Forty Years of American Life,* I, 208–209, 224, 235, 248; Frederick Marryat, *Diary in America,* 141.
6. Marryat, 41; Carl Sandburg, *Abraham Lincoln: The Prairie Years* (Blue Ribbon Edition), 64.
7. Charles Lyell, *A Second Visit to the United States,* II, 160–161.
8. Francis Grund, *Aristocracy in America,* II, 70.
9. Frederick von Raumer, *America and the American People,* 491–496.

10. Alexis de Tocqueville, *Democracy in America*, I, 483.
11. *Ibid.*, 333.
12. Grund, I, 114, 117.
13. *Ibid.*, 45, 102–103; Nichols, II, 194; and Frances Trollope, *Domestic Manners of the Americans*, 242.
14. Grund, I, 33–34, 45.
15. *Ibid.*, 195; von Raumer, 491–496.
16. Grund, II, 167.
17. *Ibid.*, I, 72–73; Frances Trollope, 177, 240.
18. Von Raumer, 491–496; Frances Trollope, 67–68.
19. Grund, I, 197; II, 18.
20. Lyell, *Travels in North America*, I, 57.
21. Nichols, II, 135–151, *passim*.
22. *Ibid.*, II, 141, 143, 145, 147.
23. Calhoun to James H. Hammond, April 18, 1838, *Correspondence*, 394–395.
24. Gustavus Pinckney, *John C. Calhoun*, 94–95.
25. Frances Trollope, 195.
26. W. J. Cash, *The Mind of the South*, 20, 5, 9, 42, 44, 46, 69.
27. *Ibid.*, 21, 67, 382, 20, 29; see also von Raumer, 491–496; and Grund, II, 70–71.
28. Benjamin B. Kendrick and Alex M. Arnett, *The South Looks at Its Past*, 69.
29. John S. C. Abbott, *Slavery, North and South*, 178–179.
30. Charleston *Mercury* and Charleston *Courier*, July 5, 6, and 7, 1845.
31. Calhoun to James H. Hammond, Feb. 18, 1837, *Correspondence*, 367.
32. Calhoun to William C. Dawson, Nov. 24, 1835, *Correspondence*, 349–351; and to A. S. Clayton, Nov. 24, 1835, *ibid.*, 352.
33. Calhoun to Duff Green, Aug. 30, 1835, *Correspondence*, 344–346.
34. Frances Trollope, 97.
35. *Ibid.*, 161.
36. Thurlow Weed, *Autobiography*, I, 143.
37. Dave G. Sloan, *Fogy Days, Then and Now*, 73–74.
38. Calhoun to James E. Colhoun, Nov. 11, 1836, *Correspondence*, 364; Sept. 2, 1836, *ibid.*, 363; Sept. 19, 1836, *ibid.*, 363; to William C. Dawson, Nov. 22, 1835, *ibid.*, 349; to James Edward Colhoun, Oct. 27, 1837, *ibid.*, 381.
39. Calhoun to Duff Green, July 27, 1837, *Correspondence*, 374–375.

40. Calhoun to J. S. Williams, Oct. 17, 1835, *Correspondence*, 347; to F. Carter, Nov. 26, 1835, *ibid.*, 353; to Robert Young Hayne, Nov. 17, 1838, *ibid.*, 451.
41. Calhoun to Hayne, *Correspondence*, 451.
42. Calhoun to Sidney Breese, July 27, 1839, *Correspondence*, 430.
43. Calhoun to Anna Maria Clemson, Nov. 21, 1846, *Correspondence*, 711–712.
44. Fort Hill tradition; Basil Hall, *Travels in North America*, II, 280; and Nichols, I, 181–182; Lyell, II, 104–105.
45. Calhoun to Thomas Clemson, Dec. 13, 1845, *Correspondence*, 674.
46. Calhoun to Mrs. John C. Calhoun, Nov. 29, 1815, *Correspondence*, 129.
47. Marryat, 130; Hall, II, 94; Lyell, II, 163–164; and Calhoun to F. H. Elmore, Nov. 24, 1840, Calhoun Papers, Clemson College.
48. Nichols, II, 72, 15; I, 120; Marryat, 130.
49. Hall, 94.
50. Frances Trollope, 34; Marryat, 125.
51. Nichols, II, 147, 15; I, 120, 221–223.
52. Lyell, II, 122–123; Frances Trollope, 38; and Nichols, II, 109.
53. Sarah M. Maury, *The Statesmen of America*, 345–346.
54. Calhoun to James Edward Colhoun, July 2, 1846, *Correspondence*, 698.
55. J. Hamilton Eckenrode, *The Randolphs*, 249, 251; Varina Howell Davis, *Jefferson Davis*, I, 207.
56. *American Review*, Jan. 1848.
57. Calhoun to J. L. M. Curry, Sept. 14, 1846, *Correspondence*, 725–726.
58. Calhoun to James Edward Colhoun, July 2, 1846, *Correspondence*, 698–699.
59. Calhoun to Thomas Clemson, Oct. 1845, Calhoun Papers, Clemson College; Sarah M. Maury, 378; Varina Howell Davis, II, 274.
60. Calhoun to Abbott Lawrence, May 13, 1845, *Correspondence*, 654–655.
61. Calhoun to Thomas Clemson, October, 1845, Calhoun Papers, Clemson College.
62. Calhoun to Duff Green, Oct. 18, 1845, Duff Green Papers, Library of Congress.
63. New Orleans *Jeffersonian Republican*.
64. Calhoun to James Edward Colhoun,

Jan. 16, 1846, *Correspondence*, 675–677.
65. Fredericksburg (Va.) *Recorder*, quoted in Lynchburg (Va.) *Republican*, Oct. 14, 19, 1845.
66. James Hamilton to Calhoun, Oct.

12, 1846, *Correspondence*, 1090–1092; and Calhoun to James Edward Colhoun, Jan. 16, 1846, *ibid.*, 676.
67. Charleston *Mercury;* also Calhoun to Andrew P. Calhoun, Jan. 16, 1846, *Correspondence*, 677.

XXV. A NATION-SIZED AMERICAN

1. Sarah M. Maury, *The Statesmen of America*, 375.
2. *Ibid.*, 350, 382–384.
3. E. F. Ellet, *Court Circles of the Republic*, 309.
4. *Ibid.*, 310–311, 321–323.
5. Varina Howell Davis, *Jefferson Davis*, I, 416–418.
6. *Ibid.*, I, 253–255.
7. *Ibid.*, I, 214.
8. A. J. Beveridge, *Abraham Lincoln* (Standard Library Edition), II, 5.
9. Sarah M. Maury, 384–385.
10. *Ibid.*, 376.
11. W. D. Porter, quoted in *The Carolina Tribute to Calhoun*, 401; Holmes, 30.
12. Mary Bates, *The Private Life of John C. Calhoun*, 25.
13. John Temple Graves, *The Fighting South*, 41.
14. Sarah M. Maury, 381; Nathaniel Willis, *Hurry-Graphs*, 180–181.
15. Sarah M. Maury, 380.
16. Porter, in *The Carolina Tribute to Calhoun*, 400–401.
17. Claude M. Fuess, *Daniel Webster*, II, 151, 155.
18. *Edinburgh Review*, LXXXII, 240.
19. Eva E. Dye, *McLaughlin and Old Oregon*, 275.
20. *Ibid.*, 13.
21. William Barrows, *Oregon: The Struggle for Possession*, 195.
22. *Ibid.*, 246.
23. Eva E. Dye, 239, 253–254.
24. Carl Sandburg, *Abraham Lincoln: The Prairie Years* (Blue Ribbon Edition), 22.
25. Eva E. Dye, 261, 284.
26. Sarah M. Maury, 379, 376.
27. Calhoun, speech on 'The Treaty of Washington,' Aug. 28, 1842, *Works*, IV, 212–238, *passim;* on 'The Oregon Bill,' Jan. 24, 1843, *ibid.*, IV, 238–258, *passim.*
28. Calhoun to John W. Mason, May 30, 1845, *Correspondence*, 659–663.
29. Eva E. Dye, 234; Calhoun to James H. Hammond, Jan. 23, 1846, *Correspondence*, 678.

30. Calhoun, speech on the 'Treaty of Washington,' Aug. 28, 1842, *Works*, IV, 212–238.
31. James Knox Polk, *Diary*, II, 283.
32. Calhoun to Anna Maria Clemson, May 22, 1845, *Correspondence*, 656–657.
33. Sarah M. Maury, 374.
34. Calhoun to Thomas G. Clemson, Jan. 29, 1846, *Correspondence*, 680; idem, March 23, 1846, *ibid.*, 685–687.
35. Calhoun to Anna Maria Clemson, March 26, 1846, *Correspondence*, 684–685.
36. Calhoun on 'Giving Notice to Great Britain,' March 16, 1846, *Works*, IV, 258–290, *passim.*
37. Holmes in *The Carolina Tribute to Calhoun*, 230.
38. Calhoun to James Hammond, Jan. 23, 1846, *Correspondence*, 678.
39. Polk, I, 344.
40. Calhoun to Thomas G. Clemson, April 25, 1846, *Correspondence*, 688–689.
41. Porter, in *The Carolina Tribute to Calhoun*, 401.
42. Calhoun to Thomas G. Clemson, June 11, 1846, *Correspondence*, 697.
43. Sarah M. Maury, 370–380, *passim.*
44. Calhoun to Thomas G. Clemson, July 11, 1846, *Correspondence*, 700–701; to James Edward Colhoun, July 29, 1846, *ibid.*, 701–702.
45. Calhoun to Andrew Pickens Calhoun, July 14, 1846, Calhoun Papers, South Caroliniana Library.
46. Hermann von Holst, *John C. Calhoun*, 276–277.
47. Calhoun to James Edward Colhoun, July 2, 1846, *Correspondence*, 698–699.
48. *Idem*, May 29, 1846, *Correspondence*, 692–694.
49. Calhoun to H. W. Conner, May 15, 1846, Calhoun Papers, Library of Congress.
50. Christopher Hollis, *The American Heresy*, 135.

51. The New York *Journal of Commerce,* quoted in the Charleston *Mercury* for March 23, 1846, called Calhoun 'among the greatest statesmen of the age.'
52. Calhoun to Thomas G. Clemson, June 11, 1846, *Correspondence,* 697. Charleston *Mercury,* May 19, June 17 and 20, 1846.
53. Charleston *Mercury* and Charleston *Courier,* issues for July 5, 6, and 7, 1846. See also James Gregorie to Calhoun, May 23, 1846, *Correspondence,* 1083–1085; James Hamilton to Calhoun, Oct. 12, 1846, *ibid.,* 1090–1096.
54. Calhoun to Thomas G. Clemson, undated, Calhoun Papers, Clemson College; and to Andrew Pickens Calhoun, July 14, 1846, Calhoun Papers, South Caroliniana Library.
55. James Gregorie to Calhoun, May 23, 1846, *Correspondence,* 1084; also Calhoun to Andrew Pickens Calhoun, Dec. 1, 1847, *ibid.,* 741.
56. Allen Tate, *Stonewall Jackson,* 37–38.
57. Calhoun to Andrew Pickens Calhoun, May 14, 1846, *Correspondence,* 690–691; and Calhoun to H. W. Conner, May 15, 1846, Calhoun Papers, Library of Congress.

XXVI. THE RISING STORM

1. Oliver Dyer, *Great Senators of the United States,* 35.
2. Calhoun to H. W. Conner, Jan. 14, 1847, Calhoun Papers, Library of Congress.
3. Calhoun, *Works,* IV, 502–503.
4. Calhoun to Andrew Pickens Calhoun, Jan. 16, 1846, Calhoun Papers, South Caroliniana Library.
5. Calhoun to John Calhoun Clemson, December 27, 1846, *Correspondence,* 740.
6. Anna Maria Clemson to Calhoun, undated, in Calhoun Papers, Clemson College.
7. Calhoun to Anna Maria Clemson, Dec. 27, 1846, *Correspondence,* 715–716.
8. Calhoun to Duff Green, Nov. 9, 1847, *Correspondence,* 740.
9. Calhoun, speech on 'The Amendment to the Oregon Bill,' Aug. 12, 1848, *Works,* IV, 530; also to Anna Maria Clemson, March 7, 1848, *Correspondence,* 744–745.
10. Varina Howell Davis, *Jefferson Davis,* I, 407.
11. Calhoun to Thomas G. Clemson, January 30, 1847, *Correspondence,* 717.
12. Henry Clay, public address in Lexington, Kentucky, Nov. 13, 1847.
13. A. J. Beveridge, *Abraham Lincoln* (Standard Library Edition), II, 125–127; 135–136.
14. Calhoun, *Works,* IV, 413, 420.
15. Calhoun, speech on 'Three Million Bill,' Feb. 9, 1847, *Works,* IV, 304–305, 317, 319–320, 323.
16. Calhoun to Thomas G. Clemson,
    Feb. 17, 1847, Calhoun Papers, Clemson College.
17. Calhoun, 'Reply to Mr. Turney,' Feb. 12, 1847, *Works,* IV, 328.
18. Calhoun, 'Reply to Mr. Benton,' Feb. 24, 1847, *Works,* IV, 362–364.
19. Calhoun, speech on 'The Oregon Bill,' June 27, 1848, *Works,* IV, 479–511.
20. *Ibid.,* 483–496.
21. Calhoun, 'Resolutions on the Slave Question,' Feb. 19, 1847, *Works,* IV, 348–349.
22. Calhoun, *Works,* IV, 347–348.
23. *Ibid.,* IV, 361.
24. Thomas Hart Benton, *Thirty Years' View,* II, 697.
25. Calhoun, speech on 'The Oregon Bill,' June 27, 1848, *Works,* IV, 479–511.
26. James Knox Polk, *Diary,* IV, 17–22, 297–300.
27. Calhoun, *Works,* III, 184, 180; II, 630, 631; IV, 361.
28. *Ibid.,* III, 190.
29. Calhoun, *Works,* IV, 505; also Benton, II, 697.
30. Calhoun, speech on 'The Oregon Bill,' June 27, 1848, *Works,* IV, 494–495, 507 ff.
31. Calhoun to Andrew Pickens Calhoun, undated, summer of 1848, Calhoun Papers, South Caroliniana Library.
32. Polk, IV, 72–74.
33. Benjamin F. Perry, *Reminiscences of Public Men,* 319.
34. Charleston *Mercury,* Dec. 8, 1848.
35. Calhoun to Anna Maria Clemson, Aug. 13, 1847, *Correspondence,* 736.

XXVII. THE STATESMAN AND THE MAN

1. Oliver Dyer, *Great Senators of the United States*, 70–76, *passim*.
2. Varina Howell Davis, *Jefferson Davis*, I, 282.
3. Benjamin F. Perry, *Reminiscences of Public Men*, 65–67.
4. John Wentworth, *Congressional Reminiscences*, 33–35.
5. Harriet Martineau, *A Retrospect of Western Travel*, I, 165; Dyer, 286, 291–292.
6. Dyer, 198–202.
7. Francis Grund, *Aristocracy in America*, II, 215.
8. Varina Howell Davis, I, 270.
9. Wentworth, 48.
10. Dyer, 216.
11. Varina Howell Davis, I, 272–273.
12. Dyer, 291–292.
13. *Ibid.*, 150–152.
14. *Ibid.*, 170–172.
15. Harriet Martineau, I, 243–246.
16. Dyer, 186.
17. Manuscript reminiscences of Calhoun by James Edward Colhoun, April, 1850, Calhoun Papers, Clemson College.
18. Dyer, 187.
19. Hermann von Holst, *John C. Calhoun*, 5.
20. Charles C. Pinckney, 'Calhoun From a Southern Standpoint,' in *Lippincott's Monthly* (July, 1898).
21. Wentworth, 7, 21–22, 20.
22. Webster quoted in Lyon Tyler's *The Letters and Times of the Tylers*, II, 153; Venable in *The Carolina Tribute to Calhoun*, 76; and Robert B. Rhett, quoted in Charles C. Pinckney's sketch.
23. Wentworth, 22.
24. *Ibid.*
25. *Ibid.*, 20.
26. New York *Herald*, April 1, 1850.
27. Wentworth, 25; Henry, in *The Carolina Tribute to Calhoun*, 238.
28. Calhoun to Franklin H. Elmore, Oct. 16, 1848, Calhoun Papers, Clemson College.
29. Perry, 49.
30. Calhoun to Armistead Burt, Jan. 24, 1838, *Correspondence*, 389.
31. J. J. Crittenden to Alexander H. Stephens, Sept. 4, 1848, Stephens Papers, Library of Congress; Beverly Tucker to James Hammond, March 13, 1847, Hammond Papers, Library of Congress; see also entries in Hammond's journal for August, 1845, Library of Congress.

XXVIII. NO COMPROMISE WITH DESTINY

1. Calhoun, 'Charleston Address,' March 9, 1847, *Works*, IV, 3.
2. Calhoun to Thomas G. Clemson, March 12, 1847, *Correspondence*, 720.
3. Calhoun, 'Charleston Address,' March 9, 1847, *Works*, IV, 3ff.
4. Calhoun to Duff Green, March 9, 1847, *Correspondence*, 718–719.
5. James Knox Polk, *Diary*, II, 458–459.
6. Hammond to Simms, March 21, 1847, quoted in Herman V. Ames, 'John C. Calhoun and the Secession Movement of 1850,' in the *Proceedings of the American Antiquarian Society*, April 1919, 19–50; also Ulrich B. Phillips, 'The Correspondence of Robert Toombs, Alexander H. Stephens, and Howell Cobb,' *Annual Report of the American Historical Association* (1911), 139–196.
7. Calhoun, speech on 'Amendment to the Oregon Bill,' Aug. 12, 1848, *Works*, IV, 531.
8. Perry, 61; Jefferson Davis in *North American Review*, CXLV, 259 ff.
9. Calhoun, *Works*, IV, 532.
10. J. L. M. Curry, 'Principles, Utterances and Acts of John C. Calhoun, Promotive of the True Union of the States,' in *University of Chicago Record*, III, 101–105.
11. Calhoun, 'Speech on Abolition Petitions,' Feb. 6, 1837, *Works*, II, p. 630.
12. John Wentworth, *Congressional Reminiscences*, 24.
13. Varina Howell Davis, *Jefferson Davis*, I, 365.
14. Oliver Dyer, *Great Senators of the United States*, 289–292.
15. *Ibid.;* also Calhoun, 'Speech on Territorial Governments,' Feb. 24, 1849, *Works*, IV, 535–542.
16. See letter of Calhoun to Percy

Walker, Oct. 23, 1847, in *National Intelligencer*, June 27, 1855; also *Works*, IV, 534.

17. Nathaniel Willis, *Hurry-graphs*, 180–181.
18. Abraham Venable, in *The Carolina Tribute to Calhoun*, 36.
19. Quoted in New York *Herald*, April 1, 1850.
20. Address, quoted in Charleston *Courier*, Feb. 1, 1849.
21. John S. Jenkins, *John Caldwell Calhoun*, 453.
22. Mann, quoted in Christopher Hollis, *The American Heresy*, 139.
23. Nathaniel Wright Stephenson, 'Calhoun and the Divine Right of the Majority,' Scripps College Papers, Claremont (California, 1930), 51.
24. Letter of Beverly Tucker to James Hammond, March 25, 1850, in *William and Mary Quarterly*, XVIII, 44–46.
25. Stephenson, in Scripps College Papers, 32, 34.
26. *Ibid.*, 51; Calhoun to Mrs. St. George Campbell, in manuscript memoirs of R. M. T. Hunter; and *William and Mary Quarterly*, XVIII, 46; see also *Mentor*, V, 1 (March 15, 1917), and Hollis, 140.
27. See Henry Foote's *War of the Rebellion*, 79–82; Robert Toombs, quoted in *Congressional Globe*, 31st Congress, 1st Session; Louis Pendleton, *Alexander H. Stephens*, 96–116, *passim*; Richmond *Enquirer*, Feb. 12, 1850.
28. Robert Toombs to John J. Crittenden, Jan. 22, 1849, in *Annual Report of the American Historical Association* (1911), 139–196, *passim;* also Hollis, 137.
29. Polk, Jan. 16, 1849, IV, 285–292, *passim*.
30. Calhoun to Thomas G. Clemson, Jan. 20, 1849, Calhoun Papers, Clemson College.
31. Thomas Metcalfe to J. J. Crittenden, Jan. 23, 1849, and Robert Toombs to Crittenden, Jan. 22, 1849, Crittenden Papers, Library of Congress.
32. Calhoun to Henry W. Conner, Feb. 2, 1849, Calhoun Papers, Library of Congress.
33. Robert B. Rhett quoted in *The Carolina Tribute to Calhoun*, 369.
34. Roy Meredith, *Mr. Lincoln's Camera Man*, 24–25.

35. Calhoun to Anna Maria Clemson, April 10, 1849, *Correspondence*, 763.
36. *Idem*, June 15, 1849, *Correspondence*, 767.
37. *Idem;* also Calhoun to Thomas G. Clemson, June, 1849, Calhoun Papers, Clemson College.
38. Calhoun to J. R. Mathews, June 20, 1849, Calhoun Papers, Library of Congress.
39. Henry J. Foote, quoted in *Congressional Globe*, 32d Congress, 1st Session, 134–135.
40. Calhoun to J. R. Mathews, Jan. 7, 1837, Calhoun Papers, Library of Congress.
41. Calhoun to John R. Means, April 13, 1849, *Correspondence*, 765.
42. Calhoun to J. R. Mathews, June 20, 1849, Calhoun Papers, Library of Congress.
43. Calhoun to Anna Maria Clemson, June 15, 1849, *Correspondence*, 767–768.
44. See Columbia (S. C.) *Transcript*, Aug. 6, 1851; also New York *Herald*, April 1, 1850.
45. Calhoun to Thomas G. Clemson, June, 1849, Calhoun Papers, Clemson College.
46. Calhoun to Anna Maria Clemson, July, 1848, Calhoun Papers, Clemson College.
47. Calhoun to Thomas G. Clemson, Dec. 8, 1849, Calhoun Papers, Clemson College, partly quoted in *Correspondence*, 776.
48. Calhoun to Thomas G. Clemson, Oct. 14, 1849, Calhoun Papers, Clemson College.
49. Calhoun to Anna Maria Clemson, June 15, 1849, *Correspondence*, 767.
50. Calhoun to Armistead Burt, Nov. 5, 1849, *Correspondence*, 773–774.
51. Calhoun to Anna Maria Clemson, Dec. 31, 1849, *Correspondence*, 776–777.
52. D. J. Knotts to W. E. Barton, Sept. 1, 1919, quoted in W. E. Barton, *The Paternity of Abraham Lincoln*, 135.
53. Varina Howell Davis, I, 282; Oliver Dyer, 289.
54. Washington *Daily Union*, Aug. 23, 1849.
55. Thomas L. Nichols, *Forty Years of American Life*, II, 184; E. F. Ellet, *Court Circles of the Republic*, 408.
56. *Congressional Debates*, XIII, Part 1 (1836–1837), 5.

57. Wentworth, 25–26.
58. New York *Herald,* March 6, 1850; Nathan Sargent, *Public Men and Events,* II, 363.
59. Sargent, II, 363.
60. *The Liberator,* March 22, 1850.
61. Washington *Daily Union,* Dec. 25, 1849; Dec. 23, 1849.
62. Columbia (S. C.) *Telegraph;* Richmond *Enquirer;* see issues for 1849–1850.
63. See Pendleton, 94–116, *passim,* for statement of Alexander H. Stephens's general sentiments.
64. Calhoun to Andrew Pickens Calhoun, Jan. 12, 1850, *Correspondence,* 780.
65. *Idem.*
66. W. H. Parmalee, 'Recollections of an Old Stager,' in *Harpers New Monthly Magazine* (Oct. 1873), 758.
67. Calhoun to James H. Hammond, Feb. 16, 1850, *Correspondence,* 781.
68. Calhoun to Thomas G. Clemson, Feb. 6, 1850, *Correspondence,* 781.
69. Philadelphia *Public Ledger,* Feb. 18, 1850.
70. Ben: Perley Poore, *Reminiscences,* I, 363–364; Carl Schurz, *Henry Clay,* II, 364.
71. Henry Clay, *Works,* IX, 397–398.
72. Calhoun to James Hammond, Jan. 4, 1850, *Correspondence,* 779.
73. William Rutherford, Jr., to Howell

Cobb, April 16, 1850, *Annual Report of the American Historical Association* (1911); also Jefferson Davis in *North American Review,* CXLV, 246.
74. Elizabeth Cutting, *Jefferson Davis: Political Soldier,* 81.
75. Philadelphia *Public Ledger,* Feb. 18, 1850.
76. Charles A. Dana in New York *Tribune,* March 6, 1850.
77. *Congressional Directory,* H. V. Hills, ed., 1850.
78. Sargent, II, 363.
79. *Congressional Globe,* March 4, 1850, v. 21, 31st Congress, 1st Session, 455 ff.
80. G. W. Julian, *Political Recollections,* 87; Wentworth, 23; New York *Tribune,* March 6, 1850.
81. Hollis, 141.
82. Ulrich B. Phillips, ed., 'The Correspondence of Robert Toombs, Alexander H. Stephens, and Howell Cobb,' in *Annual Report of the American Historical Association* (1911), 139–196; also Cobb to James Buchanan, June 17, 1849, Buchanan Papers, Library of Congress.
83. William Rutherford, Jr., to Howell Cobb, April 16, 1850; also Philadelphia *Public Ledger,* April 2, 1850.
84. Calhoun, speech on 'The Slavery Question,' March 4, 1850, *Works,* IV, 542–573, *passim.*

XXIX. WHEN ROME SURVIVED

1. Nathan Sargent, *Public Men and Events,* II, 363.
2. Ben: Perley Poore, *Reminiscences,* I, 366; Philadelphia *Public Ledger,* March 5, 1850.
3. New York *Herald,* March 5, 1850.
4. Varina Howell Davis, *Jefferson Davis,* I, 458.
5. Philip Hone, *Diary,* March 5, 1850, 375.
6. Philadelphia *Public Ledger,* March 7, 1850.
7. New York *Herald,* March 5, March 6, 1850.
8. North Carolina *Standard,* Wheeling (Va.) *Gazette,* Maysville (Ky.) *Eagle,* March 7, 1850.
9. Calhoun to H. W. Conner, March 4, 1850, Calhoun Papers, Library of Congress.
10. Varina Howell Davis, I, 457.
11. New York *Herald,* March 6, 1850.

12. Calhoun, 'Reply to Foote,' March 5, 1850, *Works,* IV, 574–578.
13. Richard Crallé, reminiscences of Calhoun, in Crallé Papers (undated), Library of Congress.
14. Varina Howell Davis, I, 458.
15. Webster, in *The Carolina Tribute to Calhoun,* 11–12.
16. Peter Harvey, *Reminiscences and Anecdotes of Daniel Webster,* 231.
17. Jefferson Davis, in *North American Review* (1887), 259.
18. Harvey, 219.
19. *Ibid.,* 220–222.
20. Varina Howell Davis, I, 461.
21. New York *Tribune,* April 3, 1850.
22. *Congressional Globe,* March 7, 1850, v. 21, 31st Congress, 1st Session, 483.
23. Boston *Post,* quoted in Washington *Daily Union,* March 15, 1850.
24. Charleston *Mercury,* March 16, 1850.

25. *Congressional Globe,* March 7, 1850, v. 21, 31st Congress, 1st Session, 483.
26. Calhoun to H. W. Conner, March 18, 1850, Calhoun Papers, Library of Congress.
27. New York *Herald,* March 8, 1850.
28. Calhoun to Thomas G. Clemson, March 10, 1850, *Correspondence,* 783.
29. New York *Herald,* March 16, 1850.
30. Webster, in *The Carolina Tribute to Calhoun,* 11.
31. New York *Tribune,* April 3, 1850; George P. Fisher, 'Webster and Calhoun in the Compromise Debate of 1850,' *Scribner's Magazine* (May, 1905); Webster, in *The Carolina Tribute to Calhoun,* 11.
32. Rusk, in *The Carolina Tribute to Calhoun,* 13.
33. John S. Jenkins, *John Caldwell Calhoun,* 441.
34. New York *Herald,* April 1, 1850.
35. *Ibid.,* March 16, 1850.
36. *Congressional Globe,* v. 21, 31st Congress, 1st Session, 464ff.; New York *Herald,* March 16, 1850.
37. New York *Herald,* March 16, 1850; also *The Liberator,* March 15, 1850.
38. Philadelphia *Public Ledger,* March 8, 1850.
39. Mary Bates, *The Private Life of John C. Calhoun,* 14.
40. New York *Herald,* March 23, 1850.
41. *Ibid.,* March 21, March 26, March 28, 1850.
42. Calhoun to Anna Maria Clemson, March 7, 1847, *Correspondence,* 744–745; John Perry Pritchett, *Calhoun and His Defense of the South,* 20.
43. Calhoun to Thomas G. Clemson, March 10, 1850, *Correspondence,* 784.
44. See Arthur Stryon, *The Cast-Iron Man,* 355; also J. B. Curry, 'Principles, Utterances and Acts of John C. Calhoun, Promotive of the True Union of the States,' in *University of Chicago Record,* III, 101–105.
45. W. H. Parmalee, 'Recollections of an Old Stager,' *Harper's New Monthly Magazine* (Oct. 1873), 758.
46. Christopher Hollis, *The American Heresy,* 140.
47. New York *Herald,* March 16, March 17, 1850.
48. *Ibid.,* March 25, 1850.
49. Calhoun to Andrew Butler, March

27, 1850, Calhoun Papers, Library of Congress.
50. Philadelphia *Public Ledger,* March 23, 1850; G. S. Morehead to J. J. Crittenden, March 31, 1850, Crittenden Papers, Library of Congress.
51. Manuscript reminiscences of James E. Colhoun, April, 1850, in Calhoun Papers, Clemson College.
52. Bates, 20.
53. Richard Crallé's reminiscences of Calhoun, Crallé Papers, Library of Congress.
54. Bates, 22.
55. Philadelphia *Public Ledger,* March 23, 1850.
56. Walter Miller, 'Calhoun as a Lawyer and Statesman,' *The Green Bag,* XI, 330.
57. Josephine Seaton, *William Winston Seaton,* 158; also, John C. Proctor, ed., *Washington, Past and Present,* II, 826–827.
58. Robert Barnwell Rhett to Calhoun, Dec. 8, 1843, *Correspondence,* 899–900.
59. Abraham Venable, in *The Carolina Tribute to Calhoun,* 319.
60. Washington *Daily Union,* April 3, 1850.
61. James Hammond, in *The Carolina Tribute to Calhoun,* 319.
62. Robert Barnwell Rhett, in *The Carolina Tribute to Calhoun,* 370.
63. Crallé's reminiscences of Calhoun, Crallé Papers, Library of Congress.
64. Abraham Venable, in *The Carolina Tribute to Calhoun,* 37.
65. Charleston *Mercury,* March 31, 1850.
66. New York *Herald,* March 31, 1850; Philadelphia *Public Ledger,* April 2, 1850.
67. George Fisher, *Life of Benjamin Silliman,* II, 97.
68. Alexander H. Stephens, quoted in *The Carolina Tribute to Calhoun,* 88–91.
69. Reminiscences of Calhoun by Anna Maria Clemson, copy in Clemson College Papers.
70. *Ibid.,* also Alexander Butler, in *The Carolina Tribute to Calhoun,* 1–8.
71. *Ibid.,* Henry Clay quoted, 9–10.
72. Varina Howell Davis, I, 461–462.
73. Webster, quoted in *The Carolina Tribute to Calhoun,* 11–12.
74. New York *Tribune,* April 3, 1850; Washington *Daily Union,* April 3, 1850; W. H. Parmalee, 758; Phila-

delphia *Public Ledger,* April 3, 1850; Oliver Dyer, *Great Senators of the United States,* 213.

75. Varina Howell Davis, I, 462; Mary Bates, 28.
76. 'Report of the Committee of Twenty-Five,' in *The Carolina Tribute to Calhoun,* 39–51.
77. *Ibid.,* 51.
78. *Ibid.,* Venable quoted, 76.
79. Jenkins, 444.
80. *The Carolina Tribute to Calhoun,*

Venable quoted, 80–81; Porter quoted, 383.
81. *Ibid.,* 'Narrative of the Funeral Honors,' 65–88, *passim.*
82. Mary Bates, 28.
83. Varina Howell Davis, I, 463.
84. Fred A. Porcher, quoted in *The Carolina Tribute to Calhoun,* 271, 281; also Pritchett, 20.
85. Jonathan Daniels, *A Southerner Discovers the South,* 330.
86. Hollis, 145.

XXX. MINORITY CHAMPION

1. Claude M. Fuess, *Daniel Webster,* II, 228.
2. *Ibid.,* 228.
3. Hamilton Basso, *Mainstream,* 56; John P. Pritchett, in *Calhoun and His Defense of the South,* and Christopher Hollis, in *The American Heresy,* also give full discussions of Calhoun's political theory.
4. Hermann von Holst, *John C. Calhoun,* 346.
5. James Parton, *Famous Americans of Recent Times,* 175.
6. Calhoun, 'Discourse on the Constitution,' *Works,* I, 301.
7. *Ibid.,* 112–113.
8. Calhoun to Anna Maria Clemson, Nov. 21, 1846, *Correspondence,* 712.
9. John Gunther, *Inside U.S.A.,* Ellis Arnall quoted, 775.
10. Virginius Dabney, *Below the Potomac,* 291.
11. Benjamin B. Kendrick, *The Colonial Status of the South,* 16.
12. Gunther, 673.
13. *Report on Economic Conditions in the South* (pamphlet), Franklin D. Roosevelt quoted, 1.
14. Calhoun, 'Disquisition on Government,' *Works,* I, 59.
15. Calhoun, speech on 'The Revenue Collection Bill,' Feb. 15, 16, 1833, *Works,* II, 234; also Frank L. Owsley, 'Pillars of Agrarianism,' *American Review,* March, 1935.
16. Calhoun, 'Disquisition on Government,' *Works,* I, 52–55.
17. Benjamin F. Perry, *Reminiscences of Public Men,* 46; Hollis, 144.
18. J. L. M. Curry, 'Principles, Utterances, and Acts of John C. Calhoun, Promotive of the True Union of the States,' *University of Chicago Record,* VI, 104ff.
19. Calhoun to James Edward Colhoun,

quoted in letter of Alfred Huger to Isaac S. Nichols, Feb. 18, 1869, Calhoun Papers, Library of Congress.
20. Calhoun, 'Discourse on the Constitution of the United States,' *Works,* I, 142.
21. Calhoun, 'Disquisition on Government,' *Works,* I, 14–15.
22. *Ibid., Works,* I, 12.
23. *Ibid., Works,* I, 15, 16.
24. *Ibid., Works,* I, 23.
25. Calhoun, 'To the People of South Carolina,' *Works,* VI, 133.
26. Calhoun, 'Disquisition on Government,' *Works,* I, 55.
27. John C. Coit, quoted in *The Carolina Tribute to Calhoun,* 181.
28. Vernon Parrington, *The Colonial Mind,* 298.
29. Calhoun, 'Disquisition on Government,' *Works,* I, 4.
30. *Ibid., Works,* I, 33–34.
31. Vernon Parrington, *The Romantic Revolution in America,* 70; see also Basso, 69.
32. Herbert Agar, *The Pursuit of Happiness,* 193.
33. Basso, 58.
34. Calhoun, 'Disquisition on Government,' *Works,* I, 30.
35. *Ibid., Works,* I, 25.
36. *Ibid., Works,* I, 26, 27.
37. *Ibid., Works,* I, 17.
38. *Ibid., Works,* I, 55.
39. Agar, 199; also Nathaniel Wright Stephenson, 'Calhoun and the Divine Right of the Majority,' Scripps College Papers, 35.
40. Charles M. Wiltse, 'Calhoun and the Modern State,' *Virginia Quarterly Review* (Summer, 1937), 396–408, *passim;* Agar, 191.
41. Calhoun to James Edward Colhoun, May 29, 1846, *Correspondence,* 693.

42. Calhoun, 'Disquisition on Government,' *Works*, I, 48–49.
43. Calhoun, 'Discourse on the Constitution,' *Works*, I, 268–270.
44. *Idem, Works*, I, 77, 55, 57.
45. Agar, 197.
46. *Ibid.*, 219.
47. *Ibid.*, 198.
48. Hollis, 82; also Calhoun to Anna Maria Clemson, June 15, 1849, *Correspondence*, 768.
49. Edward Pollard, *The Lost Cause*, 749.

BIBLIOGRAPHY

NEWSPAPERS

Anderson (S. C.) *Independent.*
Anderson (S. C.) *Observer.*
Boston *Courier.*
Charleston *City Gazette and Daily Advertiser.*
Charleston *Courier.*
Charleston *Mercury.*
Charleston *Sunday News.*
Columbia (S. C.) *Telegraph.*
Columbia (S. C.) *Telescope.*
Connecticut *Journal and Herald.*
Franklin Gazette (Philadelphia).
Jackson (Ala.) *Republican.*
Lexington (Ky.) *Reporter.*
The Liberator (Boston).
London *Morning Chronicle.*
Lynchburg (Va.) *Republican.*
Maysville (Ky.) *Eagle.*
Mobile *Tribune.*
National Intelligencer (Washington)
Newburyport (Mass.) *Herald.*

New Haven *Herald.*
New Haven *Register.*
New York *Evening Post.*
New York *Herald.*
New York *Journal of Commerce.*
New York *Tribune.*
Niles' Weekly Register (Baltimore).
Norwich (Conn.) *Courier.*
Philadelphia *Aurora.*
Philadelphia *Public Ledger.*
Richmond *Enquirer.*
South Carolina *Gazette.*
Southern Patriot and Commercial Advertiser.
The Subterranean (New York).
United States Telegraph (Washington).
Washington *Daily Union.*
Washington *Gazette.*
Washington *Globe.*
Washington *Republican.*
We, The People (Washington).

PERIODICAL MATERIAL

Ames, Herman V., 'John C. Calhoun and the Secession Movement of 1850,' *Proceedings of the American Antiquarian Society* (April, 1919), 19–50.

Anonymous, 'Freedom's Defense' (pamphlet), in Worcester Antiquarian Society Library.

Anonymous, 'Mr. Calhoun's Parliamentary Eloquence,' *United States Democratic Review*, XIV (1844), 120–122.

Anonymous, 'Political Portraits with Pen and Pencil—John C. Calhoun,' *United States Democratic Review*, II (1838), 65–84.

Anonymous, 'Peggy O'Neal; or the Doom of the Republic,' *Southern Review*, XII (January–April, 1873), 213–231; 281–297.

Annual Report of the American Anti-Slavery Society (1858), 56.

American Review, commentary on the Memphis Memorial, Jan. 1848.

American Whig Review, anecdotes of Calhoun and nullification, autumn, 1832.

Arnall, Ellis G., 'The Southern Frontier,' in *Atlantic Monthly* (Sept., 1946), 29–35.

J. A. Bayard to Andrew Bayard, in *Annual Report of the American Historical Association* (1913).

'Calhoun as Seen by His Political Friends,' *Southern Historical Association Publications*, VII, 425.

'John C. Calhoun,' pamphlet of the State Department of Education, Columbia, South Carolina.

Calhoun to Judge Charles Tait, *Gulf States Historical Magazine*, I (Sept. 1902), 98–100.

Cohn, David, 'How the South Feels,' *Atlantic Monthly* (Jan. 1944), 47–51.

'Committee on Farms for the Pendleton Farmers' Society,' in *Southern Cultivator*, III (July, 1845).

Curry, J. L. M., 'The Calhoun Letters: A Review,' *Southern Historical Association Publications*, V, 159–163.

Curry, J. M., 'Principles, Utterances, and Acts of John C. Calhoun, Promotive of the True Union of the States,' *University of Chicago Record*, VI, 104–105.

Davis, Jefferson, 'Life and Character of the Honorable John Caldwell Calhoun,' *North American Review*, CXLV, 246–260.

Dunlap, William, 'Diary of William Dunlap,' in *Publications of the New York Historical Association*, II (1930), 376ff.

Fisher, George P., 'Webster and Calhoun in the Compromise Debate of 1850,' *Scribner's Magazine* (May, 1905).

Hamden, 'Letter on Texas,' pamphlet in Worcester Antiquarian Society Library.

Hammond, James, 'Memorandum,' *American Historical Review*, VI (July, 1901), 741–745.

Hay, T. R., ed., 'John C. Calhoun and the Presidential Campaign of 1824,' *American Historical Review*, XL (Oct. 1934 and Jan. 1935), 82–96; 287ff.

Holmes, A. G., 'John C. Calhoun,' in *Southern Magazine*, II, no. 10 (1936).

Hunter, T. M. T., 'Memoirs of R. M. T. Hunter,' in *William and Mary College Quarterly*, XVIII, 44–46.

James C. Jewett to General Dearborn, Feb. 5, 1817, in *William and Mary College Quarterly*, XVII, 139–144.

Kendrick, Benjamin B., 'The Colonial Status of the South,' in *The Journal of Southern History*, VIII, no. 1 (Feb. 1942). Also printed separately as pamphlet.

MacBride, B., in *The Southern Agriculturist*, III, 175.

Miller, Walter, 'Calhoun as a Lawyer and Statesman,' *The Green Bag*, XI, no. 5 (May, 1899); no. 6 (June, 1899); no. 7 (July, 1899); no. 7 (Aug., 1899); and no. 8 (Sept., 1899), 197–202; 269–272; 326–337; 376; and 424.

'The Memphis Convention,' report in *Debow's Review*, XV, 257–277.

National Emergency Council, 'Report on Economic Conditions in the South,' pamphlet.

Owsley, Frank L., 'Pillars of Agrarianism,' *American Review* (March, 1935).

Parmalee, W. H., 'Reminiscences of an Old Stager,' *Harpers' New Monthly Magazine* (Oct. 1873).

Perry, B. F., 'John C. Calhoun,' in *The Land We Love*, VI, 397–403.

Phillips, Ulrich B., ed., 'The Correspondence of Robert Toombs, Alexander H. Stephens, and Howell Cobb,' in the *Annual Report of the American Historical Association* (1911), 139–196.

Pinckney, Charles C., 'Calhoun From a Southern Standpoint,' *Lippincott's Monthly*, LXII (July, 1898).

Ruffin, Thomas, Papers quoted in *North Carolina Historical Commission Publications*, I, 80.

'A Southern Churchwoman's View of Slavery,' *Church Intelligencer*, Nov. 22, 1860.

Stephenson, Nathaniel, 'Calhoun and the Divine Right of the Majority,' in Scripps College Papers (1930), Claremont, Cal.

Stillé, Charles J., 'Joel R. Poinsett,' *Pennsylvania Magazine of History and Biography*, XII (1885), 284–285.

Symonds, G. W., 'When Calhoun Went A-Wooing,' *The Ladies' Home Journal*, May, 1901.

Tucker, Nathaniel Beverly, to St. George Tucker, March 25, 1850, *William and Mary Quarterly*, XVIII, 44–46.

Wiltse, Charles M., 'Calhoun and the Modern State,' *Virginia Quarterly Review* (Summer, 1937), 396–408.

MANUSCRIPTS

Alpha Chapter, Phi Beta Kappa, manuscript records, Yale University.

American State Papers, Indian Affairs, I and II, National Archives.

American State Papers, Military Affairs, I, II, III, and IV, National Archives.

Anonymous, Planter's Day-Book, Clemson College Papers.

Jacob Brown Papers, Library of Congress.

James Buchanan Papers, Library of Congress.

Mrs. Francis Calhoun Papers, Clemson College, South Carolina.

John C. Calhoun Papers, Clemson College Library.

Calhoun Papers, Duke University.

Calhoun Papers, Library of Congress.

Calhoun-Noble Papers, Library of Congress.

Calhoun Papers, South Caroliniana Library.

Calhoun Papers, Yale University.

Carrington-McDowell Papers, Library of Congress.

Confidential Letters, War Office, I, National Archives.

H. W. Conner Papers, Library of Congress.

Richard K. Crallé Papers, Library of Congress.

John J. Crittenden Papers, Library of Congress.

Timothy Dwight. Notes by Professor J. Day on 53 sermons in the College Chapel, October 1798–1805.

John H. Eaton Papers, Library of Congress.

Franklin H. Elmore Papers, Library of Congress.

Jeremiah Evarts, Manuscript Diary, Yale University.
Alexander M. Fisher Papers, Yale University.
Charles H. Fisher Papers, University of North Carolina Library.
Augustus J. Foster Papers, Library of Congress.
Duff Green Papers, Library of Congress.
Gideon and Francis Granger Papers, Library of Congress.
James H. Hammond Papers, Library of Congress.
Edward Hopkinson Collection, Philadelphia.
Andrew Jackson Papers, Library of Congress.
Jackson Papers, Second Series, Library of Congress.
Linonian Society Papers, 1790–1881, two boxes; also records, 1797–1811, vols. 3 and 4, Yale University.
William Lowndes Papers, Library of Congress.
James MacBride Papers, Library of Congress.
John McLean Papers, Library of Congress.
Dolly Madison Papers, Library of Congress.
Virgil Maxcy Papers, Library of Congress.
James Monroe Papers, Library of Congress.
Daniel Mulford Diary, April, 1801, to Dec., 1807, Yale University.

Nullification Convention Proceedings, in manuscript, State Archives, South Carolina Historical Commission.
Pendleton Farmers' Society, manuscript records, Clemson College Library.
James Knox Polk Papers, Library of Congress.
Papers of Class of 1832, Yale University.
William Rives Papers, Library of Congress.
Scheme of the Exercises for the Public Commencement at Yale College, Sept. 12, 1804, Yale University Library.
Senate and House Documents, 40th Congress.
South Carolina Legislature, manuscript records (1800–1812), in State Archives Building, South Carolina Historical Commission.
Alexander H. Stephens Papers, Library of Congress.
Students' Treasury Bills (1799–1808), Yale University.
Texas Instructions, Department of State, I (1837–1845), and Legislative Archives, Department of State, XV, National Archives.
Robert Toombs Papers, Library of Congress.
Angelica Singleton Van Buren Papers, Library of Congress.
Martin Van Buren Papers, Library of Congress.
Wills of South Carolina, I, South Caroliniana Library.

BOOKS

Abbott, John S. C., *Slavery, South and North*. New York, 1860.
Abdy, Edward S., *Journal of a Tour Through the United States*. 2 vols. London, 1835.
Adams, Henry, *History of the United States*. 9 vols. New York, 1890.
Adams, Henry, *John Randolph of Roanoke* (Standard Library Edition), Philadelphia, 1898.
Adams, Henry, *Life of Albert Gallatin*. Philadelphia, 1879.
Adams, John Quincy, *Memoirs of John Quincy Adams*, Charles Francis Adams, ed. 12 vols. Philadelphia, 1874–1877.
Agar, Herbert, *The Pursuit of Happiness*. Boston, 1938.
Annals of Congress, Gales and Seaton, eds. 42 vols. Washington, 1834–1856.
Annual Report of the American Historical Association (1893), 'Missouri Compromise.'

Anonymous, *Life and Speeches of Henry Clay*. 2 vols. New York, 1943.
Ambler, Charles H., *Thomas Ritchie: A Study in Virginia Politics*. Richmond, 1913.
Armstrong, James L., *General Jackson's Youthful Indiscretions*.
Ashley, J. M., *Reminiscences of the Great Rebellion*. Toledo, 1890.
Atwater, Caleb, *Remarks on a Tour to Prairie Du Chien*. Columbus, 1831.

Baldwin, J. G., *Party Leaders*. New York, 1885.
Bancroft, Frederic, *Calhoun and the South Carolina Nullification Movement*. Baltimore, 1928.
Barber, J. W., *Views of New Haven*. New Haven, 1825.
Barrows, William, *Oregon, The Struggle for Possession*. Boston, 1884.

Barton, William E., *The Lineage of Lincoln*. Indianapolis, 1929.

Barton, William E., *The Paternity of Abraham Lincoln*. New York, 1920.

Bassett, John Spencer, *The Life of Andrew Jackson*. 2 vols. in 1. New York, 1931.

Basso, Hamilton, *Mainstream*. New York, 1944.

Bates, Ernest S., *The Story of Congress*. New York, 1936.

Bates, Mary, *The Private Life of John C. Calhoun*. Charleston, 1852.

Beard, Charles A., *Economic Origins of Jeffersonian Democracy*. New York, 1915.

Beecher, Lyman, *Autobiography of Lyman Beecher*. 2 vols. New York, 1871.

Bemis, Samuel F., ed., *The American Secretaries of State and Their Diplomacy*. 10 vols. New York, 1927–1929.

Benson, Allan L., *Daniel Webster*. New York, 1929.

Belden, Ezekiel P., *Sketches of Yale College*. New York, 1843.

Benton, Thomas Hart, *Abridgment of the Debates of Congress*. 16 vols. New York, 1861.

Benton, Thomas Hart, *Thirty Years' View*. 2 vols. New York, 1854–1856.

Beveridge, A. J., *Abraham Lincoln* (Standard Library Edition). 4 vols. Boston, 1928.

Biddle, Nicholas, *The Correspondence of Nicholas Biddle*, Reginald C. McGrane, ed. Boston and New York, 1919.

Binns, John, *Recollections*. Philadelphia, 1843.

Biographical Dictionary of the American Congress.

Boardman, Roger S., *Life of Roger Sherman*. Philadelphia and London, 1938.

Bowers, Claude G., *Party Battles of the Jackson Period*. Boston, 1922.

Bowers, Claude G., *The Tragic Era*. Boston, 1929.

Bradford, Gamaliel, *As God Made Them*. Boston, 1929.

Brief Memories of the Class of 1802. New Haven, 1863.

Brownson, Henry F., Jr., *Brownson's Early Life*. Detroit, 1898.

Bruce, William C., *John Randolph of Roanoke*. 2 vols. New York and London, 1922.

Bryan, Wilhelmus B., *A History of the National Capital*. 2 vols. New York, 1914–1916.

Buell, Augustus C., *A History of Andrew Jackson*. 2 vols. New York, 1904.

Bushnell, Horace, *Life and Letters of Horace Bushnell*, Mary S. Cheyney, ed. New York, 1880.

Butler, William A., *A Retrospect of Forty Years*. New York, 1911.

Caldwell, Erskine, *You Have Seen Their Faces*. New York, 1937.

Calhoun, John C., *Correspondence of John C. Calhoun*, J. Franklin Jameson, ed., *Annual Report of the American Historical Association* (1899), II. Washington, 1900.

Calhoun, John C., *Works of John C. Calhoun*, Richard K. Crallé, ed. 6 vols. New York, 1854–1857.

Cash, W. J., *The Mind of the South*. New York, 1941.

Chesnut, Mary B., *A Diary From Dixie*. New York, 1905.

Clark, Allen C., *Life and Letters of Dolly Madison*. New York, 1914.

Clark, Bennett Champ, *John Quincy Adams, 'Old Man Eloquent.'* Boston, 1932.

Clay, Henry, *The Works of Henry Clay*, Calvin Colton, ed. 10 vols. New York and London, 1904.

Cobb, Joseph B., *Leisure Labors*. New York, 1858.

Cole, Arthur C., *The Whig Party in the South*. Washington, 1913.

Comegys, J. P., *Memoir of John M. Clayton*. Wilmington, 1882; in Papers of the Historical Society of Delaware.

Congressional Globe (Blair and Reeves, eds.). 111 vols. Washington, 1834–1873.

Cresson, W. P., *James Monroe*. Chapel Hill, N. C., 1946.

Craighead, J. C., *Scotch and Irish Seeds in American Soil*. Philadelphia, 1878.

Cross, Wilbur L., *Connecticut Yankee*. New Haven, 1943.

Crowninshield, Mary B., *Letters of Mary Boardman Crowninshield*. Cambridge, 1905.

Cunningham, Clarence, *A History of the Calhoun Monument*. Charleston, 1888.

Curtis, George T., *Life of Daniel Webster*. 2 vols. New York, 1870.

Cutting, Elizabeth, *Jefferson Davis, Political Soldier*. New York, 1930.

Dabney, Virginus, *Below the Potomac*. New York, 1942.

Daniels, Jonathan, *A Southerner Discovers the South*. New York, 1938.

Davis, Varina Howell, *Jefferson Davis: A Memoir*. 2 vols. New York, 1890.

DeBow, J. D. B., *Industrial Resources of the Southern States.* New Orleans, 1852–1853.

DeBow, J. D. B., *The Interest in Slavery of the Southern Non-Slaveholder.* Charleston, 1860.

DeBow, J. D. B., *Statistical View of the United States.* Washington, 1854.

de Tocqueville, Alexis, *Democracy in America.* New York, 1904.

Dew, Thomas R., *Review of the Debate in the Virginia Legislature, 1831–1832.* Richmond, 1832. Reprinted in *The Pro-Slavery Argument.* Charleston, 1852 (pp. 287–490).

Dexter, Franklin B., *Biographical Sketches of the Graduates of Yale College.* 6 vols. New York.

Dexter, Franklin B., *Student Life at Yale Under the First President Dwight.* Worcester, 1918.

Dickens, Charles, *American Notes.* (Library Edition.) Boston, 1871.

Dodd, William E., *The Cotton Kingdom.* New Haven, 1919.

Dodd, William E., *Statesmen of the Old South.* New York, 1911.

Dwight, Timothy, Jr., *Decision of Questions.* New York, 1833.

Dwight, Timothy, Jr., *Memories of Yale Life and Men.* New York, 1903.

Dye, Eva E., *McLoughlin and Old Oregon.* Chicago, 1900.

Dyer, Oliver, *Great Senators of the United States Forty Years Ago.* New York, 1889.

Eaton, Clement, *Freedom of Thought in the Old South.* Durham, 1940.

Eaton, Mrs. Margaret O'Neil, *The Autobiography of Peggy Eaton.* New York, 1932.

Eckenrode, J. H., *The Randolphs.* New York, 1946.

Ecker, Grace D., *A Portrait of Old Georgetown.* Richmond, 1933.

Ellet, E. F., *Court Circles of the Republic.* Philadelphia, 1869.

Emery, Sarah A., *Three Generations.* Boston and New York, 1872.

Featherstonhaugh, George W., *A Canoe Voyage up the Minnay Sotor.* 2 vols. London, 1847.

The Federalist. New York, 1864.

Fisher, George P., *The Life of Benjamin Silliman.* 2 vols. New York, 1866.

Fisher, S. G., *The True Daniel Webster.* Philadelphia, 1911.

Fisher, Samuel H., *The Litchfield Law School.* New Haven, 1933.

Fleming, D. H., *The Story of the Scotch Covenanters.* Edinburgh, 1904.

Flexner, T. J., *America's Old Masters.* New York, 1939.

Foner, Philip S., *Business and Slavery.* Chapel Hill, N. C., 1941.

Foote, Henry S., *Casket of Reminiscences.* Washington, 1874.

Foote, Henry S., *War of the Rebellion.* New York, 1866.

Forney, John W., *Anecdotes of Public Men.* New York, 1873.

Fraser, Hugh R., *Nicholas Biddle and the Bank.* New York, 1936.

Fraser, Charles, *Reminiscences.* Charleston, 1854.

French, R. D., *Memorial Quadrangle.* New Haven, 1929.

Fuess, Claude M., *Daniel Webster.* 2 vols. Boston, 1930.

Garrison, Wendell Phillips, and Francis Jackson, *William Lloyd Garrison.* New York, 1885.

Garland, Hugh, *The Life of John Randolph.* 2 vols. New York, 1851. (Edition referred to is the thirteenth, complete in one volume, with two parts. New York, 1874.)

Gay, Sidney H., *James Madison.* Boston, 1884.

Gilman, Caroline Howard, *Recollections of a Southern Matron.* New York, 1852.

Goodrich, Samuel, *Recollections of a Lifetime.* 2 vols. New York, 1886.

Gouverneur, Marian, *As I Remember.* New York, 1911.

Gouge, William M., *The Fiscal History of Texas.* Philadelphia, 1852.

Graham, Henry, *The Social Life of Scotland in the Eighteenth Century.* 2 vols. London, 1900.

Graves, John Temple, *The Fighting South.* New York, 1943.

Grayson, William J., *The Hireling and the Slave.* New York, 1856.

Green, Edwin L., *George McDuffie.* Columbia, 1936.

Green, Samuel Swett, *The Scotch-Irish in America.* Worcester, 1895.

Green, T. S., *Catalogue of Yale College Library.* New Haven, 1791.

Griswold, Rufus W., *Prose Writers of America.* Philadelphia, 1849.

Grund, Francis J., *Aristocracy in America.* 2 vols. London, 1839.

Gunther, John, *Inside USA.* New York, 1947.

Hall, Basil, *Travels in North America*. 2 vols. Philadelphia, 1829.

Hamilton, Ernest W., *The Soul of Ulster*. New York, 1917.

Harvey, Peter, *Reminiscences and Anecdotes of Daniel Webster*. Boston, 1877.

Hazelton, George C., *The National Capital*. New York, 1902.

Healy, George P. A., *Reminiscences of a Portrait Painter*. Chicago, 1894.

Hills, H. V., ed., *Congressional Directory*. Washington, 1850.

Hoar, George F., *Autobiography of Seventy Years*. 2 vols. New York, 1903.

Hollis, Christopher, *The American Heresy*. New York, 1930.

Hollis, Christopher, *The Two Nations*. London, 1935.

Holmes, Alester G., and Sherrill, George R., *Thomas G. Clemson: His Life and Work*. Richmond, 1937.

Holst, Hermann von, *Constitutional and Political History of the United States*. 8 vols. Chicago, 1876–1892.

Holst, Hermann von, *John C. Calhoun*. Boston, 1882.

Hone, Philip, *The Diary of Philip Hone, 1828–1851*, Bayard Tuckerman, ed. 2 vols. New York, 1889.

Hough, Emerson, *Fifty-Four Forty or Fight*. Indianapolis, 1909.

Houston, David F., *A Critical Study of Nullification in South Carolina*. Cambridge, 1896.

Howard, O. O., *Zachary Taylor*. New York, 1892.

Hunt, Gaillard, *John C. Calhoun*. Philadelphia, 1908.

Hunter, R. M. T., *Life of John C. Calhoun*. New York, 1843.

Hutchins, Stilson, and Moore, Joseph, *The National Capital*. Washington, 1885.

Howe, Mark A. DeWolfe, *Life and Letters of George Bancroft*. New York, 1908.

Isham, Samuel, *The History of American Painting*. New York, 1905.

Jackson, Andrew, *Correspondence of Andrew Jackson*, John S. Bassett, ed., 7 vols. Washington, 1926–1935.

James, Marquis, *Andrew Jackson: Portrait of a President*. Indianapolis and New York, 1937.

James, Marquis, *The Raven, Sam Houston*. Indianapolis, 1929.

Jay, William, *Miscellaneous Writings on Slavery*. Boston, 1853.

Jay, William, *View of the Federal Government in Behalf of Slavery*. New York, 1839.

Jefferson, Thomas, *The Writings of Thomas Jefferson*, Paul Leicester Ford, ed. New York, 1899.

Jenkins, John S., *Life of John Caldwell Calhoun*. Auburn and Buffalo, 1850.

Jervey, Theodore D., *Robert Young Hayne and His Times*. New York, 1909.

Johnson, Gerald, *Andrew Jackson: A Portrait in Homespun*. (College Caravan Edition.) New York, 1936.

Johnson, Gerald, *America's Silver Age*. New York, 1939.

Johnson, Gerald, *Secession of the Southern States*. New York, 1933.

Julian, George E., *Political Recollections*. Chicago, 1884.

Kettell, Thomas P., *Southern Wealth and Northern Profits*. New York, 1860.

Kemble, Frances A., *Journal of Frances Kemble*. 2 vols. Philadelphia, 1835.

Kendall, Amos, *Autobiography of Amos Kendall*. William Stickney, ed. Boston, 1872.

Kendall, Edward A., *Travels Through the Northern Part of the United States*. 2 vols. New York, 1809.

Kendrick, Benjamin B., and Arnett, Alex Mathews, *The South Looks at Its Past*. Chapel Hill, N. C., 1935.

Kennedy, John P., *Memoir of the Life of William Wirt*. 2 vols. Philadelphia, 1852.

Laws of Yale College. New Haven, 1800.

Leigh, Frances Butler, *Ten Years on a Georgia Plantation*. London, 1883.

Little, Lucius, *Ben Hardin*. Louisville, 1887.

Logan, John H., *History of the Upper Country of South Carolina*. Charleston and Columbia, 1859.

Longacre, James B., and Herring, James, eds., *The National Portrait Gallery of Distinguished Americans*. 4 vols. New York and Philadelphia, 1835.

Lyell, Charles, *A Second Visit to the United States*. New York, 1849.

Lyell, Charles, *Travels in North America*. 2 vols. London, 1845.

Lyman, Samuel F., *Daniel Webster*. Philadelphia, 1859.

Lynch, Denis Tilden, *An Epoch and a Man: Martin Van Buren and His Times*. New York, 1929.

Lynch, William O., *Fifty Years of Party Warfare*. Indianapolis, 1931.

Mabee, Carleton, *The American Leonardo: A Life of S. F. B. Morse*. New York, 1943.
Madison, James, *Letters and Other Writings of James Madison*. 4 vols. Philadelphia, 1867.
Magoon, E. L., *Living Orators in America*. New York, 1849.
Mansfield, E. D., *Personal Memories of E. D. Mansfield*. Cincinnati, 1879.
March, Charles W., *Daniel Webster and His Contemporaries*. New York, 1852.
Martineau, Harriet, *Autobiography*. Boston, 1877.
Martineau, Harriet, *Retrospect of Western Travel*. 2 vols. London and New York, 1838.
Mathews, William, *Oratory and Orators*. Chicago, 1879.
Marryat, Frederick, *Diary in America*. 2 vols.
Maury, Sarah M., *The Statesmen of America*. Philadelphia, 1847.
May, Samuel J., *Recollections of Our Anti-Slavery Conflict*. Boston, 1869.
Mayo, Bernard, *Henry Clay: Spokesman of the New West*. Boston, 1937.
Mayo, Robert, *Political Sketches of Eight Years in Washington*. Baltimore, 1839.
Meigs, William, *Life of Charles J. Ingersoll*. Philadelphia, 1897.
Meigs, William, *The Life of John Caldwell Calhoun*. 2 vols. New York, 1917.
Meredith, Roy, *Mr. Lincoln's Camera Man*. New York, 1946.
Milburn, W. H., *Ten Years of Preacher Life*. New York, 1859.
Monroe, James, *Writings of James Monroe*. 7 vols. New York, 1902.
Muzzey, David S., *A History of Our Country*. Boston, 1939.

Neilson, Peter, *Recollections*. Glasgow, 1830.
Nevins, Allan, and Henry Steele Commager, *History of the United States*. New York, 1943.
Nichols, Thomas L., *Forty Years of American Life*. 2 vols. London, 1864.

Ogg, Frederick, *The Reign of Andrew Jackson*. New Haven, 1919.
Olmsted, Frederick Law, *The Cotton Kingdom*. 2 vols. New York, 1861.

Olmsted, Frederick Law, *A Journey in the Back Country*. New York, 1869.
Olmsted, Frederick Law, *A Journey Through the Slave States*. New York, 1853.
Olmsted, Frederick Law, *A Journey in the Seaboard Slave States*. New York, 1904.
O'Neall, J. B., *Annals of Newberry*. Charleston, 1859.
O'Neall, J. B., *Biographical Sketches of the Bench and Bar of South Carolina*. 2 vols. Charleston, 1859.

Parrington, Vernon, *The Colonial Mind*. New York, 1927.
Parrington, Vernon, *The Romantic Revolution in America*. New York, 1927–1930.
Parton, James, *Andrew Jackson*. 3 vols. Boston, 1866.
Parton, James, *Famous Americans of Recent Times*. Boston, 1874.
Paulding, J. K., *Letters from the South*. New York, 1817.
Peck, Charles H., *The Jacksonian Epoch*. New York, 1899.
Pendleton, Louis, *Alexander Stephens*. Philadelphia, 1908.
Perry, Benjamin F., *Reminiscences of Public Men*. Philadelphia, 1883.
Perry, Benjamin F., *Reminiscences of Public Men*. Second Series. Philadelphia, 1889.
Phillips, Ulrich B., *Life and Labor in the Old South*. Boston, 1929.
Phillips, Ulrich B., *Robert Toombs*.
Pinckney, Gustavus M., *Life of John C. Calhoun*. Charleston, 1903.
Polk, James K., *Diary of James K. Polk*. 4 vols. Chicago, 1910.
Pollard, Edward, *The Lost Cause*. New York, 1868.
Poore, Ben: Perley, *Reminiscences of Sixty Years in the National Metropolis*. 2 vols. Philadelphia, 1886.
Pollack, Queena, *Peggy Eaton, Democracy's Mistress*. New York, 1931.
Pope-Hennessy, Una, *Three Englishwomen in America*. New York, 1931.
Pratt, Fletcher, *The Heroic Years*. New York, 1939.
Preston, William C., *Reminiscences of William Preston*, Minnie C. Yarborough, ed. Chapel Hill, N. C., 1933.
Pritchett, John Perry, *Calhoun and His Defense of the South*. Poughkeepsie, N. Y., 1937.
Prime, Samuel, *The Life of S. F. B. Morse*. New York, 1875.

Quincy, Edmund, *Life of Josiah Quincy.* Boston, 1874.

Quincy, Josiah, *Figures of the Past From the Leaves of Old Journals.* Boston, 1883.

Ramsay, David, *History of South Carolina.* Charleston, 1809.

Ravenel, Mrs. St. Julien, *Charleston, The Place and the People.* New York, 1906.

Ravenel, Mrs. St. Julien, *The Life and Times of William Lowndes.* Boston, 1902.

Register of Debates in Congress, Gales and Seaton, eds. 14 vols. Washington, 1825–1837.

Reynold, J. B., Fisher, S. H., and Wright, H. B., *Two Centuries of Christian Activity at Yale.*

Richardson, James D., *Messages and Papers of the Presidents.* 20 vols.

Robertson, Ben, *Red Hills and Cotton: An Upcountry Memory.* New York, 1942.

Rogers, Joseph, *The True Henry Clay.* Philadelphia, 1904.

Rush, Richard, *Occasional Productions.* Philadelphia, 1860.

Salisbury, Edward F., ed., *1832 Class Book.* New Haven, 1880.

Sandburg, Carl, *Abraham Lincoln: The Prairie Years.* (Blue Ribbon Edition.) New York, 1926.

Sargent, Nathan, *Public Men and Events.* 2 vols. Philadelphia, 1875.

Schlesinger, Arthur M., Jr., *The Age of Jackson.* Boston and New York, 1945.

Schurz, Carl, *Life of Henry Clay.* 2 vols. Boston, 1887.

Seaton, Josephine, *William Winston Seaton.* Boston, 1871.

Seitz, Don, *The Also-Rans.* New York. 1928.

Shipp, J. E. D., *Giant Days: The Life and Times of William H. Crawford.* Americus, Ga., 1909.

Singleton, Esther, *The Story of the White House.* 2 vols. New York, 1907.

Sloan, Dave M., *Fogy Days, and Now.* Atlanta, 1891.

Smith, Ashbel, *Reminiscences of the Texas Republic.* Galveston, 1876.

Smith, Justin H., *The Annexation of Texas.* New York, 1911.

Smith, Margaret Bayard, *The First Forty Years of Washington Society.* Gaillard Hunt, ed. New York, 1906.

Smith, W. H., *A Political History of Slavery.* New York, 1903.

Sparks, W. H., *Old Times in Georgia: The Memories of Fifty Years.* Philadelphia, 1870.

Stewart, David, *The Highlanders of Scotland.* London, 1885.

Stokes, A. P., *Memorials of Eminent Yale Men.* New Haven, 1914.

Stillé, Charles J., *The Life and Services of Joel R. Poinsett.* Philadelphia, 1886.

Stryon, Arthur, *The Cast-Iron Man: John C. Calhoun and American Democracy.* New York and Toronto, 1935.

Swan, Mabel M., *The Athenaeum Gallery.* Boston, 1940.

Swift, J. G., *Measures, Not Men.* New York, 1823.

Schouler, James, *History of the United States.* 6 vols. Washington, 1880–1891.

Tate, Allen, *Jefferson Davis, His Rise and Fall.* New York, 1929.

Tate, Allen, *Stonewall Jackson: The Good Soldier.* New York, 1928.

Taussig, Frank W., *The Tariff History.* New York, 1896–1898.

Thomas, E. P., ed., *The Carolina Tribute to Calhoun.* Columbia, 1857.

Tradesman's Travels in the United States. London, 1842.

Trollope, Frances, *Domestic Manners of the Americans.* New York, 1832.

Tucker, H. T., *The Book of the Artist.* New York, 1867.

Tyler, Lyon G., *The Letters and Times of the Tylers.* 3 vols. Richmond, 1884–1896.

Tracy, E. C., *Memoir of the Life of Jeremiah Evarts.* Boston, 1845.

Twelve Southerners, *I'll Take My Stand.* New York, 1930.

Van Buren, Martin, *The Autobiography of Martin Van Buren,* John C. Fitzpatrick, ed., *Annual Report of the American Historical Association* (1918), II. Washington, 1920.

Von Raumer, Frederick, *America and the American People.* New York, 1846.

Wallace, D. D., *History of South Carolina.* 4 vols. New York, 1934.

Walsh, Robert, *Notices of Brazil.* 2 vols. London, 1830.

Weed, Thurlow, *Autobiography of Thurlow Weed.* Harriet A. Weed, ed. 2 vols. Boston, 1884.

Webster, Daniel, *The Writings and Speeches of Daniel Webster.* 18 vols. Boston, 1903.

Wentworth, John W., *Congressional Reminiscences*. Chicago, 1882.

Willis, Nathaniel P., *Hurry-Graphs*. New York, 1851.

Wiltse, Charles M., *John C. Calhoun: Nationalist*. Indianapolis, 1944.

Wiltse, Charles M., *John C. Calhoun: Nullifier*. Indianapolis, 1949.

Wise, John S., *Recollections of Thirteen Presidents*. New York, 1906.

Wise, Henry, *Seven Decades of the Union*. Philadelphia, 1827.

Woodward, W. C., *A New American History*. New York, 1936.

World Almanac, Official Census, 1945.

Wycoff, Henry, *Reminiscences of an Idler*. Chicago, 1882.

Wharton, Anne Hollingsworth, *Social Life in the Early Republic*. Philadelphia, 1902.

INDEX

In case you want to see the world.

At American Express, we're here to make your journey a smooth one. So we have over 1,700 travel service locations in over 120 countries ready to help. What else would you expect from the world's largest travel agency?

do more

http://www.americanexpress.com/travel

AMERICAN
EXPRESS

Travel

And just in case.

We're here with American Express® Travelers Cheques and Cheques *for Two*.® They're the safest way to carry money on your vacation and the surest way to get a refund, practically anywhere, anytime.
Another way we help you...

do more ®

AMERICAN EXPRESS

Travelers Cheques

Through a land bank and other conservation organizations, more than a third of the 12×3-mi island's acreage is protected from development, and more parcels are continually acquired for preservation as open lands. Most of these areas, marked with signs on the roadside, are open to the public for nature walks, hiking, bird-watching, or swimming; some are accessible by bike via paved paths.

In town (there is, by the way, only one) you'll find many first-class art galleries, crafts shops, and boutiques, along with a number of historical museums and fine restaurants. Beyond are the moors—swept with fresh salt breezes and just a hint of bayberry, wild rose, and cranberry—and miles of clean, white-sand beaches. The breezy openness of Nantucket, along with its location 30 mi out to sea, gives the island a feeling of isolation and allows a respite from the rush and regimentation of life elsewhere. The style of the place—though long a bastion of the very wealthy—is decidedly casual and low-key.

Summer, of course, is the main season: Everything is open, and the beaches beckon. Yet much remains open in spring and fall, when crowds are thinner and prices lower. Spring (which can be wet and foggy) brings so many daffodils that its arrival is welcomed with the Daffodil Weekend festival, which features, among other events, an antique-car parade down a route lined with millions of the blooms. In fall the weather is still lovely, and the moors are covered with a mantle of purple, brown, and rust. Shops stay open through Nantucket Noël—a month of holiday events such as house tours, historical walks, carolers in period costume, concerts, and plays. After that, winter appeals mainly to those hearty souls who love solitude, stark landscapes, romantic inns with fireplaces, and freshly harvested scallops.

Places to Go, Sights to See

Coatue-Coskata-Great Point. An unpopulated spit of sand comprising three wildlife refuges, Coatue is open for picnicking, surf casting, or just enjoying the

surroundings. Coskata's beaches, dunes, salt marshes, and stands of oak and cedar provide a habitat for birds. Because of dangerous currents, swimming is strongly discouraged, especially within 200 yards of Great Point Light. The refuge is reached via the gatehouse at the end of Wauwinet Road by foot or by four-wheel-drive vehicle, for which you need a permit (tel. 508/228–2884). *Ara's Tours* (tel. 508/228–1951) runs daily Great Point excursions, as well as history and ecology tours of the island.

Cranberry Bogs. Between Siasconset and town are two working bogs surrounded by conservation land—especially pleasing in October, when the bright red berries are harvested by flooding the bogs. The Milestone Bog is off Milestone Road (with a parallel bike path); off the Polpis Road is the Windswept Cranberry Bog, which has a parking area.

Eel Point (tel. 508/228–2884 for the Nantucket Conservation Foundation). Accessible only by foot (take a right off the Madaket bike path onto Eel Point Rd.), this unspoiled conservation area 6 mi from town has a beautiful beach. This small stretch of land has the harbor on one side, shoal-protected ocean on the other, and low grasses with wild grapes, roses, and bayberries in between. The area attracts vast numbers of birds, and the extensive sandbar makes the water clear, calm, and shallow; the surf fishing is good.

First Congregational Church (62 Centre St.; closed mid-Oct.–mid-June). Climb the 92 steps of the 120-ft tower for a view of moors, ponds, beaches, islands, and the winding streets and rooftops of town.

Hadwen House (96 Main St., tel. 508/228–1894; closed Labor Day–mid-June, except for limited hrs). A guided tour of this all-white, porticoed Greek Revival mansion—one of a side-by-side, nearly matching pair known as the Two Greeks—points out the grand circular staircase, fine plasterwork, marble fireplace mantels, and other architectural details. Regency, Empire, and Victorian furnishings are accented with 19th-century portraits and decorative objects. Across the street are the famous *Three Bricks*—identical, elegant brick mansions set off by white-columned Greek Revival porches, built between 1836 and 1838 by whaling merchant Joseph Starbuck for his three sons; his daughter married William Hadwen, builder of the Two Greeks.

Nantucket Whalewatch (Hy-Line dock, Straight Wharf, tel. 508/283–0313 or 800/942–5464, or 800/322–0013 in MA) runs naturalist-led whale-watching excursions in season.

Oldest House (Sunset Hill, tel. 508/228–1894; closed Labor Day–mid-June, except for limited hrs). The most striking feature of this 1686 saltbox, the island's oldest structure, is the massive central brick chimney with its brick horseshoe adornment. Other highlights are the diamond-pane leaded-glass windows, enormous hearths, and cutaway panels that show 17th-century construction techniques.

Old Mill (tel. 508/228–1894; closed Columbus Day–Memorial Day). At the top of South Mill Street is this 1745 Dutch-style octagonal windmill, built with lumber

from shipwrecks. When the wind is right, the mill's wooden gears still grind cornmeal, which is for sale. The white sails flying on this hilltop site are a joy to behold.

Siasconset. You can reach this village of pretty lanes with tiny rose-covered cottages and driveways of crushed white shells by a road or a level, 7-mi, bike path. An actors' colony around the turn of the century, today 'Sconset (as it's known) offers a sandy, uncrowded beach, three fine restaurants, a box-lunch place, and a few services such as a liquor store and a market (everything shuts down come autumn).

Whaling Museum (Broad St., tel. 508/228–1736). Set in an 1846 spermaceti-oil refinery, this museum gives you the real feel of Nantucket's whaling past. Exhibits include a fully rigged whaleboat, harpoons, scrimshaw, a whale skeleton, replicas of cooper and blacksmith shops, and a 16-ft-high lighthouse prism.

Beaches

Children's Beach is a calm harborside beach, an easy walk from town, with a park and playground. A short, easy bike ride from town (or you can take a shuttle bus), lively **Jetties Beach** is popular with families for its calm surf, snack bar, Windsurfer rentals, and tennis courts. **'Sconset Beach** (or **Codfish Park**), reached via the 'Sconset bike path or a shuttle, is a golden-sand beach with moderate to heavy surf. Three miles from town by bike path or shuttle bus, **Surfside** is the premier surf beach, with a wide strand of sand.

Restaurants

Chanticleer (9 New St., 'Sconset, tel. 508/257–6231; closed Mon. and Columbus Day–Mother's Day), serving classic French fare, is generally considered the island's top restaurant. Lunch in the rose garden, with a flower-bedecked carousel horse in the center, is a delight. The in-town top spot is the **Club Car** (1 Main St., tel. 508/228–1101; closed Dec.–mid-May), with flawless Continental cuisine, and a piano bar in an attached railway car. The **Brotherhood of Thieves** (23 Broad St., no phone), a very Old English pub restaurant, attracts long queues for its convivial atmosphere—thanks partly to the live folk music at night and to the hundreds of beers, ales, and exotic alcoholic concoctions available from the bar.

Reservations Services

DestINNations (tel. 800/333–4667), **House Guests Cape Cod and the Islands** (Box 1881, Orleans 02653, tel. 508/896–7053 or 800/666–4678), **Martha's Vineyard and Nantucket Reservations** (Box 1322, 73 Lagoon Pond Rd., Vineyard Haven 02568, tel. 508/693–7200 or 800/649–5671 in MA), **Nantucket Accommodations** (Box 217, Nantucket 02554, tel. 508/228–9559).

Visitor Information

Nantucket Chamber of Commerce (Pacific Club Bldg., 48 Main St., Nantucket 02554, tel. 508/228–1700), **Nantucket Information Bureau** (25 Federal St. 02554, tel. 508/228–0925).

Centerboard Guest House

8 Chester St. (Box 456), Nantucket 02554, tel. 508/228–9696

The look of this inn, a few blocks from the center of town, is unique on the island. In the high-ceilinged guest rooms, white walls (some with murals of moors and sky in soft pastels), blond-wood floors, white or natural wood furniture, white slatted shutters, and natural woodwork with a light wash of mauve tint create a cool, spare, dreamy atmosphere. There's more white, still, in the lacy linens and fluffy comforters on the feather beds, each mounded with four pillows. Restrained touches of color are added by small stained-glass lamps, antique quilts, dishes of pink crystals, and fresh flowers.

The large Room 4 has a queen-size bed, a sofa, and an oversize shower; Room 2 has two antique brass and white-painted iron double beds. The small but pleasant studio apartment is suggestive of a cabin on a ship, with a galley kitchen, two double beds in a berthlike alcove, a separate twin bed in its own cubbyhole (fun for a child), a dining area, and a private entrance.

The first-floor suite is a stunner. Its large living room evokes the house's Victorian origins, with an 11-ft ceiling, the original parquet floor, a working fireplace topped by an elaborately carved oak mantel, and antique accents (a carved duck, a tapestry fire screen, lighting fixtures, and books). A nice modern touch is the wet bar. A lush hunter-green and rose Asian carpet, a sofa bed, and upholstered chairs nicely complement the eggplant-color walls and the richness of the wood. Off the small separate bedroom, with a custom-built, cherry, four-poster bed topped by a high fishnet canopy, is a well-appointed bath with a whirlpool tub and highly polished dark-wood cabinetry set off by a rich green marble floor.

Manager Kim Gloth, an Ohio native, is enthusiastic about living on Nantucket, and her enthusiasm is evident in the way she tends to the needs of her guests. Unobtrusive yet available to remedy any problem, her cheerful disposition sets the mood here. Each morning she sets out cold cereals, fruit, muffins, Portuguese bread, teas, and coffees in the sunny dining room amid such artistic touches as a sand-and-shell assemblage under glass and an 18th-century corner cupboard spilling antique blue and purple dried hydrangeas.

🏠 *4 doubles with bath, 1 studio apartment, 1 suite. Air-conditioning, TVs, phones, minirefrigerators in rooms; beach towels. $165, suite $285; Continental breakfast. AE, MC, V. No smoking, no pets. 2-night minimum weekends.*

Century House

10 Cliff Rd. (Box 603), Nantucket 02554, tel. 508/228–0530

When you arrive at the Century House, innkeeper Jean Heron greets you with considerable warmth and energy in the cozy sitting room, which is stuffed with comfortable furniture and artwork depicting Nantucket scenes. She and her husband and fellow innkeeper, Gerry Connick, bought the inn in 1984 to get away from corporate life.

The sprawling, late Federal–style building, built in 1833 by a sea captain (it is the oldest continuously operated guest house on the island), is in the residential part of the town's historic district. A wide veranda with rocking chairs wraps the front and sides of the house.

Guest rooms are very casual, homey, and bright, with wallpapers and fabrics in the Laura Ashley light-floral style, such country furnishings as wicker and painted wood, and wide-board floors or wall-to-wall carpeting. Down comforters and canopy or spindle beds add touches of luxury. Bathrooms have marble tile floors; some have tubs.

A breakfast buffet—highlighted by homemade granola, coffee cakes, fruits,

juice, bagels, muffins, fresh-baked breads, and cinnamon-flavor coffee—is served in a pine-paneled country kitchen or on the veranda.

🏨 *14 doubles with bath. TV in sitting room. $125–$195; Continental breakfast, afternoon happy hr. MC, V. No smoking, no pets.*

Cliff Lodge

9 Cliff Rd., Nantucket 02554, tel. 508/ 228–9480

In 1995 Debby Bennett bought the lodge because it was "already beautiful" and then used her flair and warmth to create an enchanting getaway. The big, bright, airy guest rooms are done in sky blue and crisp white and have pastel hooked rugs on spatter-painted floors, country curtains and furnishings, light floral wallpapers, and white-eyelet linens. Built in 1771, the lodge preserves lots of old-house flavor, in moldings, wainscoting, and wide-board floors. Modern touches are room phones and small TVs tucked in cupboards. Some baths are very small. The very pleasant apartment has a fireplace in the living room, a private deck and entrance, and a large eat-in kitchen.

In addition to the attractive common rooms, both with wood-burning fireplaces, guests may take afternoon tea or cocktails on the sunporch, the garden terrace, or the roof walk, with a great view of the harbor. And there's parking available—a rarity in town.

🏨 *10 doubles and 1 single with bath, 1 apartment. Guest refrigerator and coffeemaker, beach towels, croquet, barbecue grill. $125–$165, apartment $225 ($1,450 weekly); Continental breakfast. MC, V. No smoking, no pets. Closed Jan., weekdays in Feb.*

Corner House

49 Centre St. (Box 1828), Nantucket 02554, tel. 508/228–1530

Fluffy down comforters and plenty of down pillows, pretty linens, and firm mattresses on interesting beds (antique, reproduction, canopy, brass, tall-post) practically guarantee a sweet night's sleep at this B&B a block or so from town center. The 1790 main inn has wide-board floors that carry the patina and the cracks and tilts of age. The living room and original keeping room each have walls of detailed Colonial woodwork; the living room has a fireplace. Sandy Knox-Johnston and her British husband and fellow innkeeper, John, join guests for a convivial afternoon tea in the keeping room, on the wicker-filled screened-in porch, or in the garden terrace.

Inn accommodations vary widely. In the main house some tiny third-floor rooms have rough plaster walls and exposed beams; others have separate sitting areas or daybeds in alcoves, perfect for reading. In a nearby post-and-beam house designed by Sandy, a still-practicing architectural restorer, skylighted pine-beam cathedral ceilings rise over upstairs rooms with sleeping lofts.

🏨 *14 doubles with bath, 2 suites. Fans, air-conditioning in all rooms; TVs, minirefrigerators in some rooms; beach towels. $115–$185; Continental breakfast, afternoon tea. MC, V. No smoking in rooms, no pets. Closed Jan.–Mar.*

Jared Coffin House

29 Broad St., Nantucket 02554, tel. 508/ 228–2400 or 800/248–2405, fax 508/228– 8549

Amid the shops, restaurants, and activity of downtown stands this perennial favorite—loved because of its location, dependability, conveniences, and class. It consists of six structures dating from

the 18th century to the 20th, and all are well maintained and landscaped.

The landmark main inn is the most impressive. In 1845 Jared Coffin, a wealthy shipowner, built this glorious three-story redbrick Greek Revival with a portico, a parapet, a hip roof, and a cupola (ask for a key to go up in it and check out the panoramic view). In 1847 it became a stopover for travelers, in 1961 the Nantucket Historical Trust restored it, and today it is watched over by Phil and Margaret Read—owners since 1976.

The first-floor public rooms are elegant, yet welcoming—with Asian rugs and antique Sheraton and Chippendale furniture, portraits, clocks, and lace curtains. In cool weather you can sit by the fire sipping drinks brought to you from the basement bar and restaurant, the Tap Room. Breakfast and dinner are served in the formal restaurant, Jared's, a lovely, high-ceilinged room with salmon walls, pale-green swag draperies, Federal antiques, and chandeliers with frosted-glass globes.

The main house's 11 guest rooms have Asian carpets and a blend of 19th-century antiques and reproductions, including gilt-wood mirrors, upholstered chairs, and carved four-poster pineapple beds. The second-floor corner rooms are the largest (they have sitting areas), and the front corner rooms have more windows. The inexpensive single rooms—a rare commodity on the island—are small but tastefully done. The small, clean, and comfortable rooms of the Eban Allen Wing, all with private baths and TVs, also cost less than other rooms.

The Harrison Gray House, an 1842 Greek Revival across Centre Street, is the most popular part of the inn, offering bigger rooms—many with sitting areas and large baths—as well as a common living room and a sunporch with a TV. Both this and the 1821 Henry Coffin House have queen-size canopy beds. The Daniel Webster House, built in 1964, with uninspired decor by Ethan Allen, is adjacent to the outdoor café and has a second-floor lobby and a small deck at the back, where you can relax and have a drink or read the paper.

🏨 *52 doubles with bath, 8 singles with bath. 2 restaurants; TV, phones in all rooms; minirefrigerators in some rooms. $150–$200, singles $85; full breakfast. AE, D, DC, MC, V.*

Martin House Inn

61 Centre St. (Box 743), Nantucket 02554, tel. 508/228–0678

New Yorkers Ceci and Channing Moore bought this refurbished B&B in 1991, after Channing left a career in banking. Built in 1803 as a mariner's home with dormers and a widow's walk, Martin House is just off the main thoroughfare and offers mostly spacious rooms with white lacy curtains, four-poster or canopy beds, and Asian and dhurrie rugs. A large first-floor room, just off the entrance hall, has an exceptional tobacco-leaf pattern, a four-poster bed with cloth canopy and backing, and a tiny bathroom. The coveted Room 21 on the second floor offers a queen-size canopy bed, a sofa, a minirefrigerator, a wood-burning fireplace, and a porch that overlooks the backyard. The country-look third-floor rooms are under the eaves and could be bumpy business for tall folks.

You can eat your breakfast of home-baked breads and muffins (including raspberries from the backyard patch), granola, and fruits in the formal dining room, on the veranda, or in the living room (which has a fireplace, piano, sofa, and cozy window seats).

🏨 *9 doubles with bath, 2 doubles and 2 singles share 1 bath. TV in living room. $95–$160, single $50–$55; Continental breakfast. AE, MC, V. No smoking, no pets. 2-night minimum in peak season.*

Seven Sea Street

7 Sea St., Nantucket 02554, tel. 508/228-3577, fax 508/228-3578

This inn on a quiet side street in the center of town was built in 1987 in the Colonial style and has a widow's walk (take a seat up there for a great harbor view, or relax in the Jacuzzi). Though the all-new furnishings are also in period styles and antique colors (Federal blue, Colonial red), the place has a bit of a Scandinavian look. A post-and-beam construction in light pine and red oak, it features exposed-beam ceilings, pine-trimmed white walls, and highly polished wide-board floors. Each room has a desk area, a braided rug, a queen-size pencil-post field bed with a fishnet canopy and quilt, a rocking chair, and a bathroom with a two-seat fiberglass stall shower and brass fittings. One of the rooms can be made into a suite, with a sofa bed in an adjoining sitting room.

One of the two small common rooms has a Franklin stove; the breakfast room has a fireplace, as well as a microwave and a coffeemaker that you can use. There is also a small library in one of the common rooms, with comfy chairs in which to curl up and read. Innkeepers Matthew and Mary Parker used to produce *Nantucket Journal*, a magazine on island living.

🏠 *11 doubles with bath. Cable TV, phones, minirefrigerators in rooms; whirlpool bath. $155–$185; Continental breakfast. AE, D, MC, V. No smoking, no pets. 2-night minimum weekends, 3-night minimum holidays.*

76 Main Street

76 Main St., Nantucket 02554, tel. 508/228-2533

Built by a sea captain in 1883 as a residence, this gracious B&B sits just above the bustle of shops on mansion-lined upper Main Street. The original mansard roof has been obscured in front (though not at the sides) by an unfortunate Federal-style facade with a fretted parapet and platinum gray shutters on the white wooden siding. But don't let this quirky exterior fool you.

The serpentine granite staircase leads to a beautiful Victorian entry hall that's all shiny rich wood—from the elegant patterned floor to the elaborately carved cherry staircase. Massive, dark-stained redwood pocket doors with bull's-eye moldings close the hall off from the sitting room and the former dining room/parlor, now the two best guest rooms. These two rooms share the hall's emphasis on fine wood as well as its high ceilings. Room 3 has a two-tone wood floor, a carved armoire, and twin four-poster beds set off by Asian-style blue-and-white wallpaper. Spacious Room 1 has three large windows, upholstered chairs, brass lamps, and a bed with an eyelet spread and canopy.

The second- and third-floor hallways, with maple and oak flooring topped with Asian rugs and runners, lead to rooms that are not as grand as those on the first floor but well furnished nonetheless: Ethan Allen reproductions, braided rugs, handmade quilts over all-cotton sheets, country curtains, and light patterned wallpapers. Everything sparkles. Some rooms on the dormer-punctuated third floor have skylighted baths, casement windows, or window seats.

In a one-story, motel-like annex out back (built in 1955, when the facade was added), you'll find six rooms with private entrances. Although they have low ceilings, they're large enough for families of as many as five and have been brightened with new plastering and white bedding. Furnished in a more Colonial style, with industrial carpeting, pretty wallpapers, and velour-upholstered armchairs, they're available in season only.

Owner Shirley Peters usually officiates over the inn's breakfast buffet, which is set out on a long wooden table in the breakfast room or out back on the flagstone patio.

🏨 18 doubles with bath. Cable TV, minirefrigerators in annex rooms. $140–$150; Continental breakfast. AE, MC, V. No smoking, no pets.

Summer House

17 Ocean Ave. (Box 880), Siasconset 02564, tel. 508/257–4577, fax 508/257–4590

Those hoping to get away from it all might look to this bastion of easy classiness in the village of Siasconset, 7 mi from town. Here, across from 'Sconset Beach, stand some rose-covered, gray-shingle, 1- and 2-bedroom cottages of the Summer House complex. Each is furnished in a casual yet elegant style with romantic English-country motifs—white walls, Laura Ashley floral print curtains and upholstered armchairs, and English stripped-pine antiques. Some cottages have fireplaces or kitchenettes, and most have marble baths with whirlpools.

The inn's restaurant—with its wicker furniture, abundance of flowers and windows, and paintings of Nantucket scenes—serves creative American cuisine that emphasizes seafood and attracts a stylish clientele. In season you'll hear someone tickling the ivories each night in the bar-lounge. You can break the fast on a shaded porch overlooking the gardens and the sea. On the oceanside you'll find a pool, with a café that serves light lunches and frozen drinks.

🏨 8 cottages with bath. Restaurant, bar, café, pool, private beach. 1 bedroom $360–$425, 2-bedroom $500–$525; Continental breakfast. AE, MC, V. No pets. Closed Nov.–late Apr.

Ten Lyon Street Inn

10 Lyon St., Nantucket 02554, tel. 508/228–5040

In 1986 Ann Marie and Barry Foster opened this B&B on a quiet street about a five-minute walk from the town center.

Barry completely rebuilt the three-story Colonial-style house from its foundations; Ann Marie used her decorating skills—from upholstering to antiques restoration—to make this an eye-pleasing place. Inside the gate, exotic bulbs, lilacs, and other perennials curve around the lawn and pink and peach roses climb the trellises against the house's weathered gray shingles.

Barry, an electrical contractor, wanted the house to have a historical feel, so to the smooth white-plaster walls and ceilings and light-wood moldings he added golden-pine floors in planks of varying widths, salvaged Colonial-era mantels, and hefty antiqued-red oak ceiling beams.

Guest rooms have a spare, uncluttered look yet are warmed by details. The white walls create pristine surroundings for exquisite antique Asian rugs in deep colors and such choice antiques as an English-pine sleigh bed or a tobacco-leaf four-poster. Chairs are upholstered in English florals, and there are bits of lace as well. The beds have hand-stitched quilts, down comforters, and all-cotton sheets (which Ann Marie actually *irons*). Bathrooms are large, white, and well appointed, with maize-and-white-striped floor runners and delicate wall hangings from Ann Marie's native Austria. Several baths have deep claw-foot tubs with separate showers; all have antique porcelain pedestal sinks and brass fixtures.

Large, lush Room 1 has a 19th-century French-country tester bed romantically draped in gauzy white mosquito netting, stunning red Turkish carpets, potted palms, gilt mirrors, and little antique gilt-wood cupids on either side of the bed.

Ann Marie provides a healthful Continental breakfast, served in the garden during summer and at a long table in the breakfast nook in winter; the muffins are low in sugar and fat, the jellies low in sugar, yet all is delicious. Common areas include a small upstairs sitting room and

a living room with a book-filled cabinet and an Asian carpet.

🏠 *7 doubles with bath. $135–$195; Continental breakfast. MC, V. No smoking, no pets. Closed mid-Dec.–mid-Apr.*

The Wauwinet

Wauwinet Rd. (Box 2580), Nantucket 02584, tel. 508/228–0145 or 800/426–8718, fax 508/228–7135

An exquisite setting, impeccable furnishings, and extensive amenities characterize this luxurious 19th-century inn. A minute's walk through the dunes leads to miles of Atlantic beach; you'll find little else here at the gateway to the Coatue–Coskata–Great Point Wildlife Preserve (an innkeeper-run Land Rover tour of the preserve is included in the room rate). Transportation to town, 8 mi away, is provided by jitney or the new 26-passenger launch *Wauwinet Lady.*

Each guest room is decorated in country/beach style, with glazed wall treatments or light wallpapers, wall-to-wall carpeting, custom hand-painted furniture, stripped pine or other antiques, and comfy upholstered chairs. The restaurant, Topper's, is one of the island's best, serving new American cuisine in a summerhouse setting. The patio is especially nice at sunset. An elegant breakfast is brought to your room or served in the restaurant.

🏠 *25 doubles with bath, 5 cottages. Restaurant, bar; air-conditioning, TV/ VCRs in rooms; turndown service, room service, business services, concierge, video library, 2 tennis courts, sailboard and Sunfish rentals/lessons, croquet, mountain bikes, picnic cruises, Jeep tours, ferry pickup. $250–$500; full breakfast. AE, DC, MC, V. No smoking, no pets. 3-night minimum summer and holiday weekends. Closed Dec.–Mar.*

Westmoor Inn

Cliff Rd., Nantucket 02554, tel. 508/228–0877, fax 508/228–5763

At this yellow Federal mansion, you'll find a tradition of gracious entertaining that was established when the Vanderbilts built it as their summerhouse in 1917. The entry, with its sweeping staircase, conveys the imposing air of a manor house. Off the entry is the living room, in which you'll find a grand piano and a games table, and a sunporch with white-wicker chairs and a TV (for those inevitable rainy days).

Outside, the wide lawn has Adirondack chairs and a garden patio behind 11-ft hedges—the perfect place to lounge on a summer day. A mile from the shops and restaurants and just a short walk from an uncrowded ocean beach and the Madaket bike path, the inn is a good choice for those who want space and seclusion.

Guest rooms are bright and white and have eyelet comforters and pillows, framed botanicals, old prints, and some very nice antiques. Third-floor rooms have lots of dormers and angles, with stenciling on the white eaves. The second floor features highly polished wideboard pine floors. Most baths are modern, though a few need updating (old, metal shower units and tile floors)—specify if it matters to you. One first-floor suite has a giant bath with an extralarge Jacuzzi and French doors that open onto the lawn. The third-floor master bedroom, with its king-size bed and queen-size sofa bed, has a broad view of moors and the ocean beyond to the north; to the east it looks onto a neighbor's private baseball diamond.

Mornings you gather with other guests in a room that has a glass ceiling and walls for a buffet of yogurt, fruit salad, granola, croissants, home-baked scones or nut breads, juices, and more. Tables are set with white damask, flowers, and white china. There are also such thought-

ful touches as ramekins of jams and butter, a bowl of ice around the milk pitcher on the buffet, daily newspapers, and soft classical music. After a day of exploring the island, you can gather with others yet again for a predinner wine-and-cheese reception.

▥ *14 doubles, 3 apartments with kitchens. Bicycles, beach towels. $155–$255; Continental breakfast, wine and cheese. AE, MC, V. No smoking, no pets. 3-night minimum mid-June–mid-Sept. Closed early Dec.–Mar.*

White Elephant

Easton St. (Box 359), Nantucket 02554, tel. 508/228–2500 or 800/475–2637, fax 508/325–1195

For years a hallmark of service and style, the Elephant offers above all a choice location on Nantucket Harbor. All that separates it from the bobbing boats is a wide lawn that has a large pool, a whirlpool spa, and a waterside café.

Rooms in the deck-wrapped main hotel have stenciled-pine armoires, sponge-painted walls, and floral fabrics. The Breakers offers more luxurious accommodations, with harbor-view walls of windows, minibars, and minirefrigerators. Some rooms have French doors that open onto the lawn or a deck—*very* romantic.

Groups of cottages done in the English country style, some with full kitchens, are next to the hotel or in a nearby pine grove. The entire property has been renovated, and everything is fresh and new.

▥ *48 doubles with bath, 32 1- to 3-bedroom cottages. Restaurant; lounge; cable TVs, phones in all rooms; air-conditioning, VCRs, minibars, minirefrigerators in some rooms; room service; concierge; heated pool; croquet court; putting green, boat slips. $245–$495, cottages $325–$650; breakfast extra. AE, D, DC, MC, V. No pets. Closed Nov.–Apr.*

Boston

Newbury Guest House

New England's largest city and the cradle of American independence, Boston was established in 1630, decades before the republic it helped to create. Its most famous buildings are not merely civic landmarks but national icons; its great citizens are not the political and financial leaders of today but the Adamses, Reveres, and Hancocks who live at the crossroads of history and myth.

At the same time, Boston is a contemporary center of high finance and higher technology; a place of granite and glass towers rising along what once were rutted village lanes. Its enormous population of students, artists, academics, and young professionals has made the town a haven for foreign movies, late-night bookstores, racquetball, sushi restaurants, and unconventional politics.

Best of all, Boston is meant for walking. Most of its historical and architectural attractions are in compact areas, and its varied and distinctive neighborhoods reveal their character and design to visitors who take the time to stroll through them.

Places to Go, Sights to See

Boston Common is the oldest park in the United States and was once used for grazing cows. Across Charles Street from the Common is the *Public Garden,* where the famous swan boat rides are given on the 4-acre pond.

The **Charlestown Navy Yard** (tel. 617/426–1812) is the home of the USS *Constitution,* nicknamed Old Ironsides, a designated national historic site. In addition to the *Constitution,* visitors may tour the USS *Cassin Young,* a World War II destroyer; the museum; the commandant's house; and the collections of the Boston Marine Society.

The Esplanade, a strip of park that runs along the Charles River for the entire length of the Back Bay, is home to the *Hatch Memorial Shell,* where the Boston Pops plays each summer. More than a pleasant place for a stroll, a run, or a picnic, the Esplanade is home port for the fleet of small sailboats that dot the Charles River Basin and for the *Union Club Boathouse,* private headquarters for the country's oldest rowing club.

Faneuil Hall and **Quincy Market** face each other across a small square thronged with people at all but the wee hours. In this indoor-outdoor mall you'll find a plethora of shops, souvenir vendors, restaurants, bars, and dance clubs.

The 70-acre **Franklin Park Zoo** (Dorchester, tel. 617/442–2002) features an excellent walk-through aviary, and the Tropical Forest Pavilion, home to gorillas and 32 other species of mammals, reptiles, birds, and fish.

The 2½-mi **Freedom Trail** (tel. 617/242–5695) is marked on the sidewalk by a red line that winds its way past 16 of Boston's most important historic sites. The walk begins at the Freedom Trail Information Center on the Tremont Street side of Boston Common. Sites include the State House, Old Granary Burial Ground, King's Chapel, Old State House, Boston Massacre site, Faneuil Hall, Paul Revere House, Old North Church, Copp's Hill Burying Ground, and the USS *Constitution.*

Two blocks west of the Museum of Fine Arts (*see below*) is the **Isabella Stewart Gardner Museum** (280 The Fenway, tel. 617/566–1401), a trove of spectacular paintings, sculpture, furniture, and textiles. At the center of the building is a magnificent courtyard, fully enclosed beneath a glass roof in which there are always fresh flowers.

The **Museum of Fine Arts** (465 Huntington Ave., tel. 617/267–9300) features an extensive American art collection, including important works by John Singer Sargent, Winslow Homer, Edward Hopper, and John Singleton Copley. It has an extensive collection of Asiatic art, and its assemblage of antique musical instruments is world renowned. This museum also hosts major traveling exhibitions.

The **Museum of Science** (Science Park, on the McGrath/O'Brien Hwy. near Leverett Circle, tel. 617/723–2500) features more than 400 exhibits on astronomy,

astrophysics, anthropology, medicine, computers, earth science, and more. Also on the premises is the **Mugar Omni Theater** (tel. 617/523–6664), a state-of-the-art film projection and sound system with a 76-ft, four-story, domed screen.

Central Wharf is the home of the **New England Aquarium** (tel. 617/973–5200) where you'll find seals, penguins, a variety of sharks, and other sea creatures—more than 2,000 species—some of which make their homes in the aquarium's four-story, 187,000-gallon observation tank, the largest of its kind in the world.

Beaches

Although Boston is on the water, the nicest beaches are outside the city. However, there are local public beaches such as **Malibu Beach**, in Dorchester, and **Pleasure Bay**, in South Boston. Call for information on these Metropolitan District Commission–run beaches (tel. 617/727–5114). Several excellent beaches a short distance from the city make lovely day trips: **Nantasket Beach**, in Hull; **Crane's Beach**, in Ipswich; **Plum Island**, in Newburyport; and **Wingaersheek Beach**, in Gloucester.

Restaurants

Boston offers something for every taste and wallet size. **Julien** (250 Franklin St., in the Hotel Meridien, tel. 617/451–1900) offers some of the finest classic French cuisine in town. **Durgin-Park** (5 Faneuil Hall Marketplace, tel. 617/227–2038) serves homey New England fare in a casual, if noisy, atmosphere. **Biba** (272 Boylston St., tel. 617/426–7878) is an inventive and enormously popular restaurant that has new American fare. **Ristorante Lucia** (415 Hanover St., tel. 617/367–2353) is considered by some aficionados to be the best Italian restaurant in the North End. **Legal Sea Foods** (Park Plaza, 35 Columbus Ave., tel. 617/426–4444; Prudential Center, 800 Boylston St., tel. 617/266–6800; and several other locations) serves the seafood for which Boston is famous. The lively **East Coast Grill** (1271 Cambridge St., Inman Sq., Cambridge, tel. 617/491–6568) offers creatively spiced seafood, salads, and barbecue, while the upscale and innovative Provençal-inspired **Hamersley's Bistro** (553 Tremont and Clarendon Sts., tel. 617/423–2700) helps make the South End Boston's latest popular restaurant district. **Figs** (42 Charles St., Boston, tel. 617/742–3447; 67 Main St., Charlestown, tel. 617/242–2229) specializes in gourmet pizza.

Nightlife and the Arts

The **House of Blues** (96 Winthrop St., Harvard Sq., Cambridge, tel. 617/491–2583), owned by Dan Akroyd, among others, is the spot for live blues music. In Boston, **Axis** (15 Lansdowne St., tel. 617/262–2437) features urban, underground dance music; **Avalon** (tel. 617/262–2424), right next door, offers Top 40 dance tunes and gay nights on Sunday. For jazz try the **Regattabar** (1 Bennett St., in the Charles Hotel, Harvard Sq., Cambridge, tel. 617/661–5000) or **Scullers** (400 Soldiers Field Rd., in the Doubletree Guest Suites Hotel, Brighton, tel. 617/783–

0811). **John Harvard's Brew House** (33 Dunster St., Harvard Sq., Cambridge, tel. 617/868– 3585) is a well-stocked alehouse. The **Comedy Connection** (Faneuil Hall Marketplace, Boston, tel. 617/248–9700) books national and local talent.

The **Bostix** ticket agency in Copley Square and Faneuil Hall (tel. 617/482–2849 or 617/723–5181) sells half-price, day-of-show tickets to theater, dance, and music events.

Reservations Services

Bed & Breakfast Agency of Boston (47 Commercial Wharf, Boston 02110, tel. 617/720–3540 or 800/248–9262, fax 617/523–5761), **Bed & Breakfast Associates Bay Colony Ltd.** (Box 57166, Babson Park Branch, Boston 02157, tel. 617/449–5302 or 800/347–5088, fax 617/449–5958), **Bed and Breakfast Cambridge and Greater Boston** (Box 1344, Cambridge 02238, tel. 617/262–1155 or 800/888–0178, fax 617/227–0021), **Bed and Breakfast Reservations: North Shore, Greater Boston, Cape Cod** (Box 35, Newtonville 02160, tel. 617/964–1606 or 800/832–2632, fax 617/332–8572), **Greater Boston Hospitality–A Bed and Breakfast Reservations Service** (Box 1142, Brookline 02146, tel. 617/277–5430), **New England Bed and Breakfast, Inc.** (1753 Massachusetts Ave., Cambridge 02138, tel. 617/498–9819).

Visitor Information

Greater Boston Convention and Visitors Bureau (2 Copley Pl., Suite 105, Boston 02116, tel. 617/536–4100 or 888/SEE–BOSTON, fax 617/424–7664), **Massachusetts Office of Travel and Tourism** (100 Cambridge St., 13th floor, Boston 02202, tel. 617/727–3201 or 800/447–MASS, fax 617/727–6525).

Beacon Hill Bed and Breakfast

27 Brimmer St., Boston 02108, tel. 617/ 523-7376

Susan Butterworth had owned this six-story, brick Victorian row house with huge bay windows in Beacon Hill for more than 20 years, when her sons left for college, and she decided to turn it into a B&B. The historic neighborhood is characterized by narrow, twisting streets lit by gas lamps and lined with trees.

Guest rooms are enormous, with great oriel windows, built-in bookshelves, and fireplaces (alas, nonworking). Rooms contain some Victorian antiques—one has a metal four-poster bed—but upstairs there's a more contemporary theme, with loud navy and white check wallpaper in the hallways and undistinguished modern furniture and beige couches in the bedrooms. Breakfast is served downstairs in a large room with red decor, Victorian antiques, and a bay window that overlooks the river.

The B&B has no parking available, and since you can walk to everything from this central location, don't bring the car. If you do, a nearby parking lot charges $15 for 24-hour parking.

🏠 *3 doubles with bath. Air-conditioning, TVs in rooms; elevator for luggage. $150–$200; full breakfast. No credit cards. No smoking, no pets.*

The Bertram Inn

92 Sewall Ave., Brookline 02146, tel. 617/ 566-2234 or 800/295-3822

Built in 1903 as a private home, the Bertram Inn is an elegant Victorian mansion on a quiet Brookline street, a few minutes' walk from the subway and a 10-minute ride to the center of Boston. The impressive entrance hall features a grand staircase and heavy, carved rock-ing chairs; to the left, a sitting and breakfast room is warmed by an elaborate fireplace. A stunning guest room on this floor has a big, marble working fireplace; lead-pane windows; heavy curtains; and cherry paneling. Other bedrooms have Victorian antiques, bookshelves, Asian rugs, working brick fireplaces, and pedestal sinks.

In 1993 owner Bryan Austin renovated the second floor, adding more private baths, and also redecorated the porch, where breakfast is served in summer. This is a quiet, calm place to stay within easy reach of the city—and you can park your car for free!

🏠 *11 doubles with bath, 3 doubles share bath. Air-conditioning in some rooms; phones; cable TV in all rooms; free parking. $69–$174; Continental breakfast. AE, MC, V. Smoking on porch only.*

A Cambridge House Bed-and-Breakfast

2218 Massachusetts Ave., Cambridge 02140, tel. 617/491-6300 or 800/232-9989, fax 617/868-2848

Massachusetts Avenue is a busy, four-lane thoroughfare, but this 1892 yellow-clapboard house, listed on the National Register of Historic Places, is set well back from the street. As you cross the wide front porch and enter the hallway, the outside noise and bustle vanish into a calm, well-ordered, Victorian glow.

In fact, the ground floor public rooms are the house's best features: They're dominated by gloriously carved cherry paneling and massive fireplaces. The living room and parlor, where a buffet breakfast and afternoon snacks are served, show off elegant Victorian couches, a corner china cabinet with silver coffee service, and hardwood floors with Asian rugs. Across the hall, the former dining room has been converted to a guest room, with the distinctive carved paneling and a canopy bed. Overall, the

inn's peaceful, sophisticated ambience is not well suited to families with young children.

A paneled stairway featuring portraits and a grandfather clock on the landing leads to the second floor. The first room at the top of the stairs has thick carpets, a canopy bed, a working fireplace, and padded walls covered in fabric that complement the beige-and-cream bed skirts and drapes. Other guest rooms are furnished with canopy or sleigh beds, fireplaces, and Victorian antiques. Most rooms in the carriage house, while tastefully furnished, are extremely small; despite wall-size mirrors installed in some to create a sense of space, you can only just walk around the bed.

Ellen Riley bought the house in 1985 and intended to use it as a private residence. She converted a couple of rooms into guest accommodations "just for fun," and got carried away by the B&B spirit. When she's not around, the inn is managed by polite, helpful innkeepers.

The house is just four blocks from the nearest subway station, and Harvard Square is two stops away. There are plenty of shops and restaurants in the immediate vicinity, and 15 minutes on the subway will take you into the heart of Boston. And there's free parking.

🏠 *12 doubles with bath, 1 single with bath, 3 doubles share 2 baths. Air-conditioning, cable TV, phones in rooms; free parking. $109–$250; buffet breakfast, hors d'oeuvres, soft drinks. AE, D, DC, MC, V. No smoking, no pets. 2-night minimum weekends May–Oct.*

82 Chandler Street

82 Chandler St., Boston 02116, tel. 617/482–0408 or 888/482–0408

Located in Boston's recently revitalized South End—on a quiet, tree-lined street of tall, redbrick row houses—this B&B is just a five-minute walk from the city center, a 10-minute taxi ride from the airport, and around the corner from Amtrak's Back Bay station. Constructed in 1863, the building sits on former tidal marshlands that were filled in to provide housing space for the city's growing middle class. Its mansard roof and brown stone are trademarks of 19th-century Boston homes.

Owners Denis Coté and Dominic Beraldi bought the house in 1978 and, after major renovation, turned it into apartments. In 1983, however, when one tenant moved out, they decided to try their hand at innkeeping. According to Denis, a social worker for 25 years, innkeeping is a positive kind of social work, "but more enjoyable, since you're helping people to have a good time, rather than to survive!"

A full breakfast, including pancakes, French toast, or crepes, is served family style in the big, sunny penthouse kitchen, which has exposed-brick walls, plants, skylights, and windows that overlook the city's rooftops. The bedroom across the stairwell is the Room with a View: Its wide bay window looks out on downtown Boston and several landmark skyscrapers. The walls are exposed brick, the floors are polished pine with Asian rugs, there's a working marble fireplace, and a skylight in the bathroom. Ask for this room first when making reservations (especially since all rooms cost the same).

The 82 Chandler Street inn is very much an "up and down" house: all other guest rooms open off the staircase and are color coded with green, red, blue, or yellow schemes. Front rooms have large bay windows, and two have working fireplaces; all are spacious and sunny, with white enamel and brass headboards, pedestal sinks, Asian rugs, and a kitchen area with refrigerator.

Ever devoted to his guests' well-being, Denis provides a wealth of tourist information, directions, and advice on the best sights to see. Although you can use two nearby parking lots (costing $16–$18 per day), parking is problematic

throughout Boston, and you're better off without a car.

🏠 *3 doubles with bath, 2 studios for short-term rental. Air-conditioning, phones, kitchen areas in rooms. $95–$160; full breakfast. No credit cards. No smoking, no pets. 2-night minimum Apr.–Nov.*

The John Jeffries House

14 Embankment Rd. at Charles Circle, Boston 02114, tel. 617/367–1866, fax 617/742–0313

Named for the father of modern ophthalmology, the John Jeffries House was built about 100 years ago as part of the neighboring Massachusetts Eye and Ear Infirmary; in 1987 the square, four-story, brick building was converted into a large inn. The managers have created a friendly, stylish ambience—one that's typified by the downstairs parlor (where breakfast is served), with its wing back chairs, fireplace, polished pine floors, thick Oriental rugs, and 24-hour coffee service. The common areas and some guest rooms were redecorated, recarpeted, and refurnished in 1996, while the third-floor bedrooms were updated in 1997; they contain Victorian-style furnishings and brass fixtures, and most rooms have kitchen facilities. Many of the bedrooms are rather cramped; for more space, ask for one of the reasonably priced two-room suites that combine a small bedroom with a tiny parlor area.

The inn sits at a major intersection, but triple-glazed windows keep out the noise. One side of the John Jeffries faces characterful Charles Street, at the bottom of Beacon Hill.

🏠 *23 doubles with bath, 12 singles with bath, 11 2-room suites. Air-conditioning, TVs, phones in rooms; kitchen facilities; reduced rates at local parking garage. $80–$135; Continental breakfast. AE, D, DC, MC, V. No smoking in public areas and some rooms, no pets.*

The Mary Prentiss Inn

6 Prentiss St., Cambridge 02140, tel. 617/661–2929, fax 617/661–5989

Originally built in 1843 as a country estate for Cambridge resident William Augustus and his new wife, Mary Prentiss, this yellow Greek Revival house sits on what is now a narrow residential street just off busy Massachusetts Avenue. Innkeeper Charlotte Forsythe and her architect husband, Gerald, opened the inn in 1992 after extensive renovations that included adding a new wing and a spacious oasis of a deck. Some rooms have wide-board pumpkin-pine floors, antique armoires, original wooden shutters, Asian rugs, and either four-poster or cannonball beds. Charlotte collects old photographs of young children, which are displayed throughout the inn.

A full breakfast—which may include fresh fruits, blintzes with strawberry sauce, quiche, or fresh-baked muffins—and afternoon tea are served in front of the fireplace in the breakfast room, or in mild weather, on the deck. Located ½ mi north of Harvard Square and a four-block walk from the Porter Square subway station (15 minutes to downtown Boston), the inn is just steps from the neighborhood's many eclectic restaurants, clothing stores, and one-of-a-kind gift shops.

🏠 *13 doubles with bath, 5 suites. Air-conditioning, cable TV, phones in all rooms; wet bars in some rooms; limited free parking. $89–$179; full breakfast. AE, MC, V. No smoking, no pets. 2-night minimum some weekends, 3-night minimum holidays and college commencement weekends.*

Newbury Guest House

261 Newbury St., Boston 02116, tel. 617/437–7666, fax 617/262–4243

This trio of elegant redbrick and brownstone row houses was built in 1882 as private homes in Boston's fashionable Back

Bay, still *the* place to live in Boston. A father-and-son team, Nubar and Mark Hagopian, bought the first four-story house in 1990, and after extensive restoration and renovation, opened it as a B&B in January 1991. Not surprisingly (considering the location, the price, and the quality of the inn), business went well, and in 1994 the Hagopians expanded into the two neighboring buildings.

The location of this inn is perfect: Newbury Street—famous for its gas streetlamps, broad sidewalks, leaded windows, and neat front gardens—is the city's smartest shopping street, home to a wide selection of clothing stores, antiques shops, art galleries, hair salons, sidewalk cafés, restaurants, and trendy bars. It's also a short walk to the Public Garden, Boston Common, Copley Square, and many other attractions.

The first-floor lobby features an arched stained-glass window, hand-painted in the 1880s by an artist from Tiffany's. Stained-glass panels also adorn the entryway doors. Guest rooms open off the beautifully carved oak staircases of these tall, narrow houses. Several rooms have cherry four-poster or sleigh beds, non-working fireplaces, and intricately cut plaster moldings; all feature reproduction Victorian furnishings, dark-stained pine or oak floors and rugs, queen-size beds, and prints from the Boston Museum of Fine Arts.

Throughout the house, "bay" guest rooms have couches and oriel windows that overlook Newbury Street; less expensive traditional rooms have wing chairs and are smaller.

A Continental breakfast of breads and pastries is served in the dining room with its Victorian furnishings; in summer guests can eat outside on the brick patio.

There's metered street parking just outside, and the inn offers a limited number of spaces to guests for $10 per night. You don't need a car here, but if you will have one, reserve a space in advance.

▦ *32 doubles with bath. Air-conditioning, cable TV, phones in rooms; limited parking (fee). $85–$155; Continental breakfast. AE, MC, V. No pets. 2-night minimum weekends.*

North Shore

Harbor Light Inn

The sliver of Atlantic seacoast known as the North Shore stretches from the grimy docklands of Boston's northern suburbs, past Rockport's precariously perched rows of wooden fishing shacks, to the fine Federal mansions of proud Newburyport, which is just south of the New Hampshire border. These North Shore towns present a world of contrasts: Salem claims a history of witches, millionaires, and maritime trade; Rockport is home to many artists' studios; and its neighbor, Gloucester, serves as a workaday port with a substantial fishing fleet. In Newburyport redbrick storefronts give way to clapboard fishing cottages along a sandy road leading to dunes, beaches, extensive salt marshes, and numerous nature reserves.

During the short summer season, and in early fall, you'll experience the region at its brightest—and busiest. Most past visitors will probably remember the towns as bustling, sunglasses-and-sandwich-shop meccas, where finding a room is almost—but not quite—as difficult as finding a parking space. In the long, peaceful off-season months, you'll find it nearly as hard to locate a room—not because the inns are full, but because some businesses in the region close down after

October. Winter and early spring have much to offer nature lovers, hikers, and those in search of scenic seaside tranquility. Locals enjoy the summer on the North Shore as much as visitors. The offerings at this time of year are what vacations are about: beaches, ice cream, crafts shops, seafood, boats, museums, nature trails, and top-quality country inns.

Places to Go, Sights to See

Crane's Beach. Near Ipswich, this white stretch of sand, over 5 mi long, is part of a 735-acre nature reserve that incorporates a salt marsh. Here, as at other North Shore beaches, biting flies invade on intermittent "bug days" throughout the summer.

Gloucester. The town's most famous landmark is the statue of a man at a ship's wheel, facing the ocean, dedicated to those WHO GO DOWN TO THE SEA IN SHIPS. The monument is fitting, for Gloucester, the oldest seaport in the nation, is still a major fishing port. The town is also home to Rocky Neck, the oldest working artists' colony in America, and close to a number of excellent white sandy beaches.

Marblehead. The small seaside town was founded by fishermen from Cornwall, England, in 1629, and the twisting, narrow streets of the historic district resemble those in typical Cornish fishing villages. Today the town is one of the major east coast yachting centers. The redbrick *town hall* (Washington St., tel. 781/631–0528) contains the well-known patriotic painting *The Spirit of '76*.

Newburyport. Some of the finest Federal mansions in New England line the streets of this small town. They were built by prosperous 19th-century sea captains when Newburyport was a thriving port, famous for its clipper ships. The town's redbrick center has been completely revitalized and is now a shopping area. In the restored Customs House on the waterfront, the *Maritime Museum* (25 Water St., tel. 978/462–8681) has shipbuilding exhibits. A causeway connects Newburyport with *Plum Island* (tel. 978/465–5753 for U.S. Fish and Wildlife Service), which has a long sandy beach and a wildlife refuge.

Rockport. At the tip of Cape Ann, Rockport was originally a fishing village, but it developed as an artists' colony in the 1920s. Today it's an arty, touristy New England town, with an incredible concentration of galleries and fine crafts stores, attracting large crowds in the summer.

Salem. Salem may not be the prettiest town on the North Shore, but it's rich in history. The infamous witchcraft trials took place here in 1692, and the *Salem Witch Museum* (Washington Sq. N, tel. 978/744–1692) accurately portrays the hysteria that engulfed this Puritan community. Later on Salem became a prime U.S. port with trade links to China and India. Salem's merchants were America's first millionaires, and their mansions still flank the streets. The *Salem Maritime National Historic Site* (174 Derby Rd., tel. 978/740–1660), operated by the National

Trust, is beside Derby Wharf. Tours take in the Customs House, the Government Warehouse, and historic shipowners' homes. The *Peabody and Essex Museum* (East India Sq., tel. 978/745–1876), the country's oldest continuously operating museum, houses a fine collection of exotic items brought back by merchant ships. Visitors should also stop off at the *House of Seven Gables* (54 Turner St., tel. 978/744–0991), immortalized by Salem-born author Nathaniel Hawthorne in his novel.

Whale-Watching. The whales are so numerous between May and October that you're practically guaranteed to see at least half a dozen, and on "good" days you may well see 40 or more. Several companies run trips from Gloucester. Excursions also depart from Salem and Newburyport.

Restaurants

Seafood is the North Shore specialty, from deep-fried clams "in the rough" to haute-cuisine lobster dinners. Rockport is a dry town, with no liquor stores and no alcohol available at restaurants, but you can usually bring your own. Recommended seafood restaurants include **White Rainbow** (65 Main St., tel. 978/281–0017), in Gloucester; the **Landing** (81 Front St., tel. 781/631–6268), beside Marblehead Harbor (outdoor dining in summer); and **Scandia** (25 State St., tel. 978/462–6271) and **David's,** at the Garrison Inn (*see below*, tel. 978/462–8077), both in Newburyport.

Nightlife

Live blues and rock bands play at the **Grog** (13 Middle St., Newburyport, tel. 978/465–8008), Thursday through Sunday nights. **David's,** at the Garrison Inn (*see below*, tel. 978/462–8077), has live entertainment on weekend evenings.

Reservations Services

Bed and Breakfast Associates Bay Colony Ltd. (Box 57166, Babson Park Branch, Boston 02157, tel. 617/449–5302 or 800/347–5088, fax 617/449–5958), **Bed and Breakfast Reservations: North Shore, Greater Boston, Cape Cod** (Box 35, Newtonville 02160, tel. 617/964–1606 or 800/832–2632, fax 617/332–8572).

Visitor Information

The umbrella organization for the whole region is the **North of Boston Visitors and Convention Bureau** (17 Peabody Sq., Peabody 01960, tel. 978/977–7760, fax 978/977–7758). The following cover more specific areas: **Cape Ann Chamber of Commerce** (33 Commercial St., Gloucester 01930, tel. 978/283–1601), **Greater Newburyport Chamber of Commerce and Industry** (29 State St., Newburyport 09150, tel. 978/462–6680), **Marblehead Chamber of Commerce** (62 Pleasant St., Box 76, Marblehead 01945, tel. 781/631–2868), **Rockport Chamber of Commerce** (3 Main St., Box 67, Rockport 09166, tel. 978/546–6575), **Salem Visitors' Center** (2 New Liberty St., Salem 01970, tel. 978/740–1650).

Addison Choate Inn

49 Broadway, Rockport 01966, tel. 978/546-7543 or 800/245-7543, fax 978/546-7638

Rockport offers an excellent selection of inns, and the Addison Choate is one of the best. Shirley Johnson, an interior designer, bought the inn in 1992 with her husband, Knox, a landscape architect, and together they set about enhancing the historical character of an already attractive property.

Made of white clapboard, the long, narrow, two-story house, built in 1851, was the famed site of Rockport's first bathtub. The living room has a Greek Revival mantel, cozy reading nooks, and Classical antique and modern furnishings. A Continental breakfast with home-baked goods is served in the dining room; in summer you can sit on the porch and gaze at the inn's perennial garden.

Spacious rooms in the main inn have big, tiled bathrooms. The navy and white Captain's Room has a dark-wood, four-poster, canopy bed; polished pine floors; handmade quilts; Asian rugs; and paintings of ships. The Chimney Room has a white brick chimney, wide-board floors, a Victorian oak bureau with a mirror, and a rocking chair with a hand-woven seat. Other rooms contain Hitchcock rockers and headboards, spool beds, filigree brass beds, quilts, local paintings, and wooden antiques. The third-floor Celebration Suite was converted from a loft, and its two huge windows have sea views over the rooftops. The bedroom has wide-plank pine floors, patterned fabrics, white wicker furniture, a TV, and a refrigerator.

Beyond the main building, the former stable house contains two one-bedroom apartments, and still farther back is a fenced-in swimming pool. The large apartments offer first-floor living space and kitchens; one contains an iron spiral staircase leading to a bedroom with cathedral ceilings, wooden beams, and a skylight; the other has a loft bedroom, stained-glass windows, and a patio.

Knox's hobby since childhood has been bird-watching, and he offers guided birding tours in the greater Rockport area. The inn, which is not suitable for young children, is a minute's walk from the town center and two blocks from the Rockport–Boston railway station.

🏠 *5 doubles with bath, 1 suite, 2 1-bedroom apartments. Air-conditioning in some rooms, pool, free parking. $85–$130; Continental breakfast. D, MC, V. No smoking, no pets. 2-night minimum weekends mid-June–mid-Sept. and some holidays, 3-night minimum July 4 weekend.*

Amelia Payson Guest House

16 Winter St., Salem 01970, tel. 978/744-8304

The Amelia Payson Guest House is within walking distance of Salem's main attractions—only a block or so from the many museums in the historic district and a brief stroll across the common from the town center and the sea. Built in 1845 for Amelia and Edward Payson, the Greek Revival house has bright, airy rooms with floral-print wallpaper, brass and four-poster canopy beds, nonworking marble fireplaces, and white wicker furnishings. The parlor downstairs contains a grand piano, while upstairs a reading room is full of visitor information. A Continental breakfast of fresh fruit and home-baked breads is served in the elegant dining room (too elegant for families with little ones!). Ada and Don Roberts bought the building in 1984, restored it, and have been operating it successfully as an inn since 1985.

🏠 *3 doubles with bath, 1 studio with kitchenette. Air-conditioning, TVs in rooms, free parking. $75–$125; Continental breakfast. AE, MC, V. No smoking, no pets. 2-night minimum weekends May–Oct. Closed Jan.–Feb.*

Clark Currier Inn

45 Green St., Newburyport 01950, tel. 978/465-8363

Built by shipping merchant Thomas March Clark in 1803, this three-story clapboard mansion is a typical example of the Federal architecture for which Newburyport is famous. The interior has been completely renovated to reveal many period splendors, such as polished wide-plank floors, window seats, original Colonial-style shutters, woodstoves, and a Federal "good morning" staircase—so-called because two small staircases join at the head of a large one, permitting family members to greet one another on their way down to breakfast.

Guest rooms, named after former owners or residents of the house, are all spacious and carefully decorated in period style and with Federal antiques. Some feature pencil-post beds, and one contains a sleigh bed dating from the late 19th century. Many of the rooms have fireplaces with carved-wood surrounds, but these are not in use. Typical of the Federal home, ceilings become lower as you reach the upper stories, so in first-floor rooms the ceilings are 11 ft high but only 7 ft on the third floor, where guest bedrooms are converted from former servants' quarters; upstairs, the ambience is less formal but still authentic.

Bob Nolan, an international banker and currency trader in New York City, and his wife, Mary, a political science teacher at Rutgers University in New Jersey, stepped out of their high-stress jobs back in 1990 to take on the Clark Currier. They wanted a more family-oriented lifestyle for themselves and their daughter, Melissa. Since taking over, they've opened up the ground floor to create a large living room with a working fireplace, antique desks couches, and bookcases. A second-floor library has books and writing desks and a display of antique toys on the landing outside. The inn offers a buffet-style breakfast of breads and muffins, afternoon tea, complimentary sherry in the evening, and such in-room extras as candy dishes—restocked daily by Melissa. In summer you can eat in the garden with its rocking chairs and gazebo.

🏨 *8 doubles with bath. Air-conditioning, TV in garden room, free parking. $85–$155; Continental breakfast. AE, D, MC, V. No smoking, no pets.*

Eden Pines Inn

48 Eden Rd., Rockport 01966, tel. 978/546-2505, fax 978/546-1157

Built in 1900 as a private summer cottage, Eden Pines stands so close to the ocean that the whole place seems about ready to sail off to sea—in fact, two of the wood decks already did, which prompted owner-managers Inge and John Sullivan to build a stormproof brick deck that has survived for years. The house looks out to the twin lights of Thatcher's Island; below the deck lie rocks and the raging (or lapping) waves. The Sullivans bought the inn nearly 30 years ago, and they use its location to the utmost. The large bedrooms have great ocean views, and six out of seven have secluded balconies. Rooms are eclectically furnished with a mixture of modern rattan or wicker, some canopy beds, and a few older pieces picked up at antiques shops. A fresh look predominates, however, with pastel blue, green, or yellow walls; modern floral fabrics; bright white moldings; and pastel-tone carpets. One room has a nonworking white brick fireplace. Most of the large bathrooms offer marble baths or vanities and brass fixtures.

Downstairs, the living room has a stone fireplace with a stone surround and dark-stained, pine-paneled, and white papered walls. The breakfast room, with its white trellises and wood-plank walls, opens onto the oceanside deck; the room's huge windows provide excellent sea views.

For even better ocean vistas, take a look at the Sullivans' other property just

down the street, the four-bedroom Eden Point House, which they rent by the week. It stands on a rock, surrounded by the sea on three sides, and is done in a contemporary, open-plan design, with a semicircular living room; a stone, floor-to-ceiling fireplace surround; a high cathedral ceiling; and a large, modern kitchen.

Eden Pines Inn and Eden Point House are a five-minute drive from Rockport center, and two minutes by car from the nearest beach.

🏠 *7 doubles with bath. Air-conditioning, cable TV in rooms; croquet. $100–$165; Continental breakfast. MC, V. No smoking, no pets. 3-night minimum holiday weekends. Closed mid-Nov.–mid-May.*

Garrison Inn

11 Brown Sq., Newburyport 01950, tel. 978/465-0910, fax 978/465-4017

This square, four-story, Georgian red-brick was first constructed as a private home in 1809 and became an inn around the turn of the century. Set conveniently on a small square, a few blocks from Newburyport's downtown and the waterfront, the Garrison is a high-quality inn with excellent dining. This somewhat formal inn will appeal to travelers who enjoy business-style conveniences, including cable TV, telephones, in-room coffee-makers, and complimentary newspapers. Spacious rooms contain Colonial reproductions, and exposed walls show off Newburyport's famous redbrick. The best guest rooms are the unusual top-floor suites; furnished with 19th-century reproduction couches and wing chairs, they have fireplaces and are on two levels, with either a contemporary spiral staircase or a Colonial staircase leading from the sitting room to the sleeping area.

The two restaurants, David's and Downstairs at David's (under separate management), are top of the line both for food and service, and they offer a child-

care facility where kids can play and eat while parents enjoy a meal in peace!

🏠 *17 doubles with bath, 7 suites. 2 restaurants, air-conditioning, cable TV in rooms and lounge. $97.50–$175. AE, D, DC, MC, V. No-smoking rooms available, no pets.*

Harbor Light Inn

58 Washington St., Marblehead 01945, tel. 781/631-2186, fax 781/631-2186

On a bustling narrow street at the heart of Marblehead's historic district, this Federal-style inn competes with the Clark Currier Inn in Newburyport as one of the classiest, most relaxing, and most authentic inns on the whole of the North Shore. If you take the Harbor Light Room and stand on tiptoe, you can see the lighthouse in the harbor; otherwise you'll only have an occasional glimpse of the sea. Nevertheless, you're bound to be impressed with the building's interior—wide-board floors, chintz chairs, silver ice buckets and candy bowls, original shutters that fold into the wall, and Chinese rugs. As for the beds, you can choose between a pencil-post bed and a hand-carved mahogany four-poster bed with a floral canopy. Bathrooms have huge mirrors and skylights, and some contain whirlpool baths as well.

The old building dates from the early 1700s, with one wing constructed in the 19th century. When innkeepers Peter and Suzanne Conway bought the place in a state of disrepair in 1986, they opened up the third floor and added a completely new section to the back of the house. They're veteran, energetic innkeepers, whose hard work and attention to detail have resulted in a luxurious inn with excellent amenities but undisturbed original features. The character of the rooms varies tremendously—those in the earlier structure have more original features, such as arched doorways, working fireplaces, and wide-board floors. On the third floor, however, rooms have skylights, exposed brick, cathedral ceilings,

and wooden beams. In the new addition, rooms are modern in concept and in decor, and some have decks.

In 1992 the innkeepers bought the building next door and over the next year expanded the inn, adding seven more big, beautiful bedrooms with working fireplaces, four-poster beds, and painted wood paneling. One room has an old-fashioned bathroom with a claw-foot tub; the top-floor rooms have exposed beams and large, modern bathrooms. The inn has two parlors with Chippendale furniture, wing chairs, and open fireplaces; Continental breakfast is served in the dining room. Sophisticated, older children may enjoy the elegant atmosphere, but it's best to leave the littlest ones at home.

🛏 *20 doubles with bath, 1 suite. Air-conditioning, cable TV in rooms; meeting room; pool. $95–$245; Continental breakfast. AE, MC, V. No smoking in public rooms, no pets. 2-night minimum weekends July–Oct., 3-night minimum holiday weekends.*

Harborside House

23 Gregory St., Marblehead 01945, tel. 781/631–1032

In Marblehead's historic district and overlooking the water, Harborside House was built in 1850 by a ship's carpenter. Susan Livingston has lived here more than 30 years and has operated the house as a successful B&B since 1985. This is what the British mean by *B&B*: a family home, with two upstairs bedrooms turned over to guests. Visitors share a downstairs living room, which has a working brick fireplace and wood paneling, and eat a breakfast of home-baked goods and homemade cereal in a pleasant dining room or on the deck. Bedrooms have polished wide-board floors and Asian rugs. One twin-bedded room has perfect views over Marblehead Harbor with its hundreds of sailboats; the other, with a double bed and antique dressing table, overlooks a lovely garden. Susan, who works as a dressmaker

from home, is a considerate and interesting host, providing information folders about the area as well as in-room journals where you can write about the highlights of your stay. This cozy house (too cozy to accommodate families with young children) is a short walk from all of Marblehead's attractions and offers parking space, a much-sought-after commodity in the historic district.

🛏 *2 doubles share bath. TVs in rooms, free parking. $65–$85; Continental breakfast, afternoon tea. No credit cards. No smoking, no pets.*

Inn on Cove Hill

37 Mt. Pleasant St., Rockport 01966, tel. 978/546–2701 or 888/546–2701

This immaculate, well-maintained inn is on a pretty hillside street, just two minutes' walk from the center of Rockport. The square, Federal-style house was built in 1791, reportedly with money from a cache of pirate gold discovered at nearby Gully Point. Although some guest rooms are small (a few are really tiny), they're so carefully decorated in the Federal style—white draperies and spreads, bright flowery print papers, and white painted brass headboards—that they can be called "cozy" with a clear conscience. Other rooms have such details as Laura Ashley floral-print wallpapers, patchwork quilts, unfinished wooden antiques, canopy and half-canopy beds, spool beds, iron door latches, wooden bathroom fixtures, wide-board floors, and pastel-tone Asian rugs. Two rooms in an 1850s addition have been furnished in the Victorian style, with brass and wicker, and one bathroom contains an original claw-foot bathtub and bathroom set. The overall country style is executed with taste: You won't be ambushed by duck pillows or rag dolls at every turn.

The second and third floors are reached via two narrow spiral staircases; the front staircase has 13 steps, representing the original 13 colonies. (Owing to

the stairs, this place isn't suitable for young children; even if you plan to stay in one of the first-floor bedrooms, you should still leave the kids at home.) Both upper stories have decks, and the third floor affords a good view over the rooftops to Rockport Harbor and Bearskin Neck.

The guest lounge retains its original wide-board pine floors and dentil cornice moldings; furnishings include a mixture of Federal-style antiques, velvet wing chairs, and rockers as well as more modern matching couches. There's no public breakfast room, so a rather scanty Continental breakfast (fresh muffin, juice, and coffee) is served on Wedgwood or Royal Doulton English bone china in your bedroom or in the garden at tables around an old pump.

Innkeepers John and Marjorie Pratt spent their honeymoon here and returned years later to buy the place. They've been running the inn since 1978, and in that time have done a good deal of restoration, removing 1950 cover-up features to expose original wood paneling and floors. The Pratts are excellent hosts with a great sense of humor.

▦ *9 doubles with bath, 2 doubles share bath. Air-conditioning, fans, TVs in rooms. $50–$105; Continental breakfast. MC, V. No smoking, no pets. 2-night minimum July–Aug. and weekends May–June and Sept.–Oct. Closed mid-Oct.–mid-Apr.*

Miles River Country Inn

823 Bay Rd. (Box 149), Hamilton 01936, tel. 978/468-7206

Staying in Gretel and Peter Clark's sprawling 24-room Colonial home amid acres of lawns and gardens is like being a guest at a private country estate. The double living room that opens to a glass-enclosed porch adorned with New Orleans iron filigree, the open kitchen with a multiwindowed corner where breakfasts are served, and the simple country-style bedrooms (several with fireplaces) all look out to the ponds, fields, and gardens where Gretel has planted 60 types of perennials. She also collects fresh eggs from her chickens for breakfast and often serves muffins or scones with fresh honey from the bees she keeps.

The Clarks opened their home to guests in 1991 after their children had all left, and they welcome families. Four of the rooms, furnished primarily with antiques from Peter's family, are named for the children who formerly occupied them. The quiet town of Hamilton, a horse-lovers' mecca, hosts world-class polo matches. Crane's Beach and the Essex area antiques shops are only a few miles away, and the Cape Ann beaches are an easy drive.

▦ *5 doubles (1 can be rented with an adjacent area that has a single bed) with bath, 2 doubles share bath. Air-conditioning, TV in sitting room. $84–$195; full breakfast. AE, MC, V. No smoking, pets by prior arrangement only. 2-night minimum weekends June–Sept. Closed Christmas wk.*

Sally Webster Inn

34 Mt. Pleasant St., Rockport 01966, tel. 978/546-9251

Sally Webster was a member of Hannah Jumper's so-called Hatchet Gang, which smashed its way through the town's liquor joints one evening in 1856 and turned Rockport into the dry town it remains today. Sally lived in this house for much of her life, and guest rooms are named after members of her family. The inn, run by David and Tiffany Muhlenberg, is classy, small, and relaxing—so plan to visit without the kids. Bedrooms contain pineapple four-poster, canopy, or spool beds; some have pine wide-board floors with Indian and Belgian rugs and nonworking brick fireplaces that shelter old curiosities such as a cranberry rake or a bread bin. Other furnishings include Chippendale, Sheridan, and Queen Anne antiques.

A Continental buffet breakfast is served in the long, narrow dining room in winter and on the patio in summer. The guest lounge is known as "Sally's share," because she inherited it after her father's death. It has a grandfather clock, a brick fireplace with custom tile work, and paintings by Rockport artists. The inn is a couple of minutes' walk from the center of town.

🏠 *8 doubles with bath. $55–$97; Continental breakfast. D, MC, V. No smoking, no pets. 2-night minimum weekends June–Oct. Closed mid-Dec.–Jan.*

Seacrest Manor

99 Marmion Way, Rockport 01966, tel. 978/546-2211

The motto here is "decidedly small, intentionally quiet," and Seacrest Manor certainly lives up it (best to leave the wee ones at home). The 1911 clapboard mansion sits on a hill overlooking the sea, surrounded by carefully tended gardens. Inside you'll find two long sitting rooms with leather chairs, bookshelves, dark green silks, and a huge wall mirror from the old Philadelphia Opera House. The hall and stairway are festooned with paintings by local artists—some of which depict the inn. The simply furnished guest rooms feature white bedspreads, brick (nonworking) fireplaces, floral wallpapers, and wood paneling. Some rooms have sea views, while others have large decks.

By the working fireplace in the dining room, a kingly breakfast is served on Wedgwood crockery. Innkeepers Dwight MacCormack and Leighton Saville are justly proud of their culinary delights (especially the spiced Irish oatmeal with chopped dates). Many special touches enhance your stay: complimentary newspapers, a shoe-shine service, custom toiletries, and nightly turndown service.

🏠 *6 doubles with bath, 2 doubles share bath. Cable TV in rooms. $88–$138; full breakfast, afternoon tea. No credit cards.*

No smoking, no pets. 2-night minimum weekends, 3-night minimum holidays. Closed Dec.–Mar.

Seaward Inn

44 Marmion Way, Rockport 01966, tel. 978/546-3471 or 800/648-7733

At the end of a quiet promontory a mile south of Rockport, this cedar-shingled inn built at the turn of the century lies just across a narrow lane from the sea. In the main building the medium-size rooms have Colonial furnishings; the best of these at the front provide an ocean view. Third-floor bedrooms offer sloping ceilings and old-fashioned, beige-tone, floral-print wallpapers. Common rooms include a large winterized porch with a flagstone floor (where an espresso bar was added in 1997), a lounge with a piano and an open fireplace, and three dining rooms—one with a brick floor and bay windows. The New England–style breakfasts include home-baked breads, and dinners emphasize local seafood.

Breakers, across the street, is a shingled house on the ocean. Its nine rooms are particularly spacious. One suite features a working fireplace, another has a private deck, and a third opens onto the lawn facing the sea. Another nine-room building and eight cottages are also for rent, some with pine paneling and working fireplaces.

🏠 *38 doubles with bath. Restaurant. $115–$175; full breakfast in peak season, Continental breakfast off-season. AE, D, MC, V. No smoking in main inn, no pets. Closed Nov.–May.*

The Tuck Inn

17 High St., Rockport 01966, tel. 978/546-7260 or 800/789-7260

Named not for the pun, but for the Tuck family who first ran it in 1948, this friendly establishment reopened in 1992. Despite stiff competition among established Rockport inns, this one quickly

became a favorite. The Wood family, who make excellent hosts, knew they'd have to do some work on the near-derelict 1790s Colonial house when they bought it in 1991—they had to deal with dry rot and ended up restoring the place from the cellar to the rafters. In 1994 the Woods also purchased the adjoining building, a 1767 Colonial house, which they restored and now rent as two efficiency units—one with a microwave, and one with a full kitchen.

In the main inn immaculate bedrooms have wide-board pine or carpeted floors, quilted bedspreads, and nonworking fireplaces made from the local granite that once made Rockport famous. They're furnished mostly in mahogany, with a mixture of Colonial and Victorian antiques that include some pineapple four-posters and a couple of Empire pieces. Scott, an accountant and antiques dealer and Liz, a registered dietician, have three teenagers and welcome guests with little ones. They bake a spectacular breakfast buffet that often includes Scott's favorite rhubarb bread.

🏨 *10 doubles with bath, 2 suites, 1 apartment. Air-conditioning, cable TV in rooms; pool, free parking. $55–$115; Continental breakfast. MC, V. No smoking, no pets. 2-night minimum weekends May–Oct.*

Yankee Clipper Inn

96 Granite St., Box 2399, Rockport 01966, tel. 978/546–3407 or 800/545–3699, fax 978/546–9730

The white Georgian mansion that forms the main part of this imposing, perfectly located Cape Ann establishment stands surrounded by gardens, challenging the waves from a rocky headland. Constructed as a private home in the 1930s, this three-story oblong building with big square windows has been managed as an inn by one family for more than 50 years. Guest rooms in the mansion vary in size, but they're generally large; because the sea is on three sides, most

rooms have fabulous views. Many also offer weatherized porches, such as the one that wraps around the enormous suite where John and Jacqueline Kennedy stayed when the late president was still a Massachusetts senator. Furnished with Queen Anne– and Victorian-style reproductions, the rooms contain four-poster or canopy beds, chaise longues, and wicker porch furniture.

Across the lawns in a newer structure called the Quarterdeck, picture windows in all the rooms provide impressive ocean views. Modern and stylish, the spacious (some are huge), well-designed rooms have floral wallpaper, seascape paintings, large bathrooms, and sitting areas with wing chairs and modern couches.

On the other side of the street from the main inn is the Bullfinch House, an 1840 Greek Revival home, appointed with dark wood antiques, floral wallpapers, lacy curtains, and pineapple four-poster beds.

Guests dine at the main inn on a sunny porch with wrought-iron chairs, again overlooking the sea. Just behind the porch, the lounge has a huge fireplace with a mahogany surround and large floral stencils at either side. Dusky pink tones, pink velvet couches, and heavy-framed painted portraits re-create a Victorian atmosphere. Below the lounge a conference center caters to business clientele. The well-managed inn has a friendly staff, and careful touches abound—the outdoor swimming pool, for example, is attractively landscaped and virtually invisible from the road. The Yankee Clipper is more than 1 mi north of Rockport, so guests will need transport in and out of town.

🏨 *21 doubles with bath, 5 suites. Restaurant, air-conditioning, phones in all rooms; TVs in some rooms; whirlpool baths, pool. $99–$249; full breakfast in peak season, Continental breakfast off- season. AE, D, MC, V. No smoking, no pets. Closed mid–Dec.–Feb.*

The Pioneer Valley

Deerfield Inn

The Pioneer Valley, a string of historic settlements along the Connecticut River from Springfield in the south up to the Vermont border, formed the western frontier of New England from the early 1600s until the late 18th century. The fertile banks of the Connecticut River first attracted farmers and traders. Today the northern regions around Amherst, Deerfield, and Greenfield remain rural and tranquil, supporting fruit farms and other agricultural businesses as well as small towns and villages with typical New England architecture. Farther south, power mills, factories, and the earliest industrial cities in North America developed along the river; here the landscape is less scenic, though it is still of great historic interest. Pioneers in education came to this region, too, to found America's first college for women. Today five major colleges, as well as numerous smaller institutions and well-known preparatory schools, are in the region, which has a thriving cultural and artistic community life.

Places to Go, Sights to See

Amherst. Three of the valley's five major colleges—the University of Massachusetts, Amherst College, and Hampshire College—are here, and not

surprisingly, Amherst caters to youthful tastes, reflected in its numerous bookstores, bars, and cafés. The town was also the home of poet Emily Dickinson; the poet's *Homestead* (280 Main St., tel. 413/542–8161) can be visited by appointment.

Historic Deerfield. A peaceful village with a violent past, Deerfield lies near the north end of the Pioneer Valley, a short drive east on Route 5 from I–91. In 1675 Pocumtuck Indians attacked the community of newly settled farmers in the Bloody Brook Massacre, killing or driving out every white inhabitant. Returning pioneers were set upon again in 1704, by the Indians and the French together, and only one house—the Indian House—survived that raid intact. Ironically, it was torn down in 1848 because there were no funds for its restoration; a replica was constructed in 1929 and can now be visited, as can 12 other 17th- and early 18th-century house museums (The Street, tel. 413/774–5581) along the main thoroughfare. Some contain antique furnishings and decorative arts; others exhibit collections of textiles, silver, pewter, and ceramics.

Mt. Tom State Reservation. One of several reservations in the Pioneer Valley, *Mt. Tom* (tel. 413/527–4805), off Route 5, has 20 mi of hiking trails and facilities for orienteering, fishing, cross-country skiing, and ice-skating. Nearby, the *Mt. Tom Ski Area* (tel. 413/536–0516) offers downhill skiing in winter and a summer resort with a wave pool and alpine slide.

Northampton. This small town is the site of Smith College, which opened in 1875 with 14 students; today it accommodates almost 3,000 women undergraduates. Northampton was also the longtime home of the 30th U.S. president, Calvin Coolidge. He practiced law here, served as mayor from 1910 to 1911, and returned to the town after his presidential term. A leaflet detailing walking tours around the historic city is available from the Northampton Chamber of Commerce and Visitors' Center (99 Pleasant St., tel. 413/584–1900).

Old Sturbridge Village. About 20 mi east of Springfield, Sturbridge Village is the star attraction of central Massachusetts. A model New England village of the early 1800s with 40 buildings, Old Sturbridge (tel. 508/347–3362) covers a 200-acre site and is one of the best period restorations in the country—it shouldn't be missed. Working exhibits include a 200-year-old newspaper printing press, a blacksmith and forge, a water-powered wool-carding mill, and a sawmill. In the elaborately furnished individual houses, "interpreters" in period costume demonstrate skills such as spinning and cooking and talk about 18th-century life. You can ride the streets in a horse-drawn carriage and visit a farm and a village store.

South Hadley. Mount Holyoke College, the first women's college in the United States, was founded here in 1837. Surrounded by spacious grounds and mellow brick buildings, the *College Art Museum* (tel. 413/538–2245) contains exhibits of Asian, Egyptian, and classical art. Poet Emily Dickinson, born in nearby Amherst, studied here.

Springfield. The largest city in the Pioneer Valley, Springfield is a sprawling industrial town where modern skyscrapers rise between grand historic buildings.

Its main claim to fame, however, is that Dr. James Naismith invented basketball here in 1891. The *Naismith Memorial Basketball Hall of Fame* (W. Columbus Ave., tel. 413/781–6500) honors the game's greatest celebrities and has a cinema, a basketball fountain (instead of water, there are basketballs), and a moving walkway from which visitors can shoot baskets. At the museum quadrangle near downtown are four other museums (tel. 413/263–6800 for information about any of them): the *Connecticut Valley Historical Museum*, which has a genealogy library and rotating exhibits that highlight local history; the *George Walter Smith Art Museum*, with a private collection of Japanese armor, ceramics, and textiles; the *Museum of Fine Arts*, with French impressionist paintings; and the *Springfield Science Museum*, which has aviation exhibits, a planetarium, an ecocenter with fish and other wildlife in their natural habitats, and a dinosaur hall.

Restaurants

A number of inns in the Pioneer Valley offer traditional dining, featuring such New England specialties as seafood, pot roast, rack of lamb, and Indian pudding. Recommended inns are the **Deerfield Inn** (*see below*, Deerfield, tel. 413/774–5587), the **Whately Inn** (193 Chestnut Plain Rd., Whately, tel. 413/665–3044), **Wiggins Tavern** (36 King St., Northampton, tel. 413/584–3100), and the **Publick House** (*see below*, Sturbridge, tel. 508/347–3313).

Nightlife

The collegiate population ensures a lively club and nightlife scene in the Pioneer Valley. Popular spots include **Iron Horse** (20 Center St., Northampton, tel. 413/584–0610), with music of one style or another (folk, blues, jazz, Celtic, rock) seven nights a week; and **Pearl Street** (10 Pearl St., Northampton, tel. 413/584–7771), which presents live music several nights a week and is the area's largest dance club.

Reservations Service

Berkshire Bed and Breakfast Homes (Main St., Box 211, Williamsburg 01096, tel. 413/268–7244, fax 413/268–7243).

Visitor Information

Franklin County Chamber of Commerce (395 Main St., Box 898, Greenfield 01302, tel. 413/773–5463, fax 413/773–7008), **Greater Springfield Convention and Visitors Bureau** (1500 Main St., Box 15589, Springfield 01115, tel. 413/787–1548 or 800/723–1548, fax 413/781–4607), **Worcester County Convention and Visitors Bureau** (33 Waldo St., Worcester 01608, tel. 508/753–2920, fax 508/754–8560).

Pick up the phone.
Pick up the miles.

1-800-FLY-FREE

Now when you sign up with MCI you can receive up to 8,000 bonus frequent flyer miles on one of seven major airlines.

Then earn another 5 miles for every dollar you spend on a variety of MCI services, including MCI Card® calls from virtually anywhere in the world.*

Is this a great time, or what? :-)

Urban planning.

The Allen House

599 Main St., Amherst 01002, tel. 413/253-5000

Dozens of bed-and-breakfast inns fall under the general term of "country-style"—and a few do have good antiques and interesting decor. But inns that are restored with historic precision and attention to every last detail are rare indeed: The Allen House, honored with a Historic Preservation Award from the Amherst Historical Commission in 1991, is one of them.

Alan Zieminski, a biochemist at the University of Massachusetts, has lived in the 1886 Queen Anne stick-style house since the late '60s. He bought it in 1988, and once he and his wife, Ann, began to put their vague ideas of restoration into practice, the project took on a life of its own. Along with Alan's brother, Jonas, the family soon became experts in the Aesthetic period—a Victorian movement heavily influenced by trade with Japan.

Guest rooms are museumlike representations of the Aesthetic era. They have impressive period wallpapers, and sunflowers, the Aesthetics' emblem, are everywhere. Furnishings include some original Charles Eastlake pieces, such as the matching burled-walnut headboard and dresser in the upstairs Eastlake room; other rooms have Eastlake reproductions, wicker "steamship" chairs (replicas of those used aboard steamships of this era), pedestal sinks, screens, carved golden oak or brass beds, goose-down comforters, painted wood floors, and claw-foot tubs. Public areas are just as impressive: The breakfast room has Anglo-Japanese reproduction wallpapers and an intricately carved fireplace; its floor is covered with grass reed matting imported from Japan. The sitting room floor also has reed matting, which is topped by an 1880s Oriental hand-stitched rug.

When the Zieminskis bought the house, it was a kind of time capsule of original,
if faded, relics. The upstairs hallway is lined with pictures found stashed away in a locked room. Modern advantages are tourist information, poetry books, afternoon tea, a hearty cooked breakfast, and free pickup service from the nearby train and bus stations. The inn is a short walk from the center of Amherst, rates are reasonable, and the hosts—who seem a little overwhelmed by what they've achieved—are extremely pleasant company.

🏨 *7 doubles with bath. Air-conditioning, phones in rooms; free parking. $45–$135; full breakfast, afternoon tea. AE, MC, V. Smoking on veranda only, no pets. 2-night minimum in summer, 3-night minimum foliage and special college events weekends.*

Brandt House

29 Highland Ave., Greenfield 01301, tel. 413/774-3329 or 800/235-3329, fax 413/772-2908

Perched on a hill in a residential neighborhood near downtown Greenfield, this white-clapboard, 1890s Victorian is designed for porch lovers. The large living room, which has a fireplace and a white overstuffed couch, opens onto a huge porch where you can relax in wicker chairs or a swing. At the front of the house, the porch offers sunset views toward the Berkshires. A second-floor sunroom, with its microwave, refrigerator, TV/VCR, and big comfy chairs, is a cozy indoor alternative.

The simply decorated guest rooms have feather beds with white-eyelet covers; walls that are painted pastel pinks, greens, or blues; and polished wood floors with Asian or dhurrie rugs. Two of the large second-floor rooms have working fireplaces, and one has a whirlpool bath and a lead-glass window. Downstairs, a wooden pool table dominates a guest lounge, where owner Phoebe Compton, who opened Brandt House in 1988 after raising her children and leaving her computer sales position in Boston, provides

notebooks stuffed with restaurant menus and information about area attractions. Breakfast at a huge oak table in the sunny dining room may include fresh-baked scones or coffee cake, homemade granola, and fresh fruits; on weekends eggs Benedict, frittatas, French toast, or other hot dishes are also served.

🏠 *6 doubles with bath, 2 doubles share bath. Air-conditioning, cable TV, phones in all rooms; VCRs in some rooms; tennis court. $90–165; Continental breakfast (weekdays), full breakfast (weekends). AE, D, MC, V. No smoking.*

Clark Tavern Inn

98 Bay Rd., Hadley 01035, tel. 413/585–1900

The 1740s Clark Tavern was a ferry way station that provided overnight lodging at its original location on the Connecticut River in Northampton. In 1961, when the inn was slated for demolition, two Hadley residents bought the wood-framed building, disassembled it, and meticulously reconstructed it at its current site. Pioneer Valley natives Ruth and Mike Callahan—she's an intensive-care nurse and he's a physician's assistant—purchased the rebuilt tavern and in 1995 opened their authentically restored, romantically appointed Colonial B&B.

Canopy beds piled with pillows in the larger bedrooms face working fireplaces, where two wine glasses and a corkscrew wait on the mantle (romantic touches that are also clues to leave the children at home). The third room is smaller, but it overlooks the gardens and goldfish pond instead of the sometimes-noisy Bay Road. TV/VCRs hidden in wooden armoires and modern bathrooms with hand-painted stenciling blend with the wide-board floors, wing chairs, pewter light fixtures, and other Colonial-style furnishings. Ruth's breakfast specialties include lemon–poppy seed muffins and spiced apples, which she serves—by candlelight—in the dining room, on the screened terrace by the pool, or in your

guest room. In the evening you can relax by the fire in the sitting room, where there is also a refrigerator stocked with complimentary snacks and beverages.

🏠 *3 doubles with bath. Air-conditioning, cable TV/VCR in rooms; outdoor pool. $95–$135; full breakfast. D, MC, V. No smoking, no pets.*

Deerfield Inn

81 Old Main St., Deerfield 01342, tel. 413/774–5587 or 800/926–3865, fax 413/773–8712

Perfectly situated on a street that's lined with museums, the peaceful Deerfield Inn, with its columned facade and white-clapboard exterior, harks back to a gentler era. Built in 1884, it was substantially modernized after a fire in 1981, which explains the square, spacious guest rooms—reminiscent of more modern hotels. The style and grace of the light, airy interior owe much to the flair and imagination of the young, enthusiastic innkeepers, Karl Sabo and his English wife, Jane, who bought the place in 1987, leaving their fast-track lives in New York's Greenwich Village for "something different."

The couple has worked hard on redecoration; for example, they've had reproduction period wallpapers custom designed for the reception room, tavern, and many of the bedrooms. Guest rooms have light floral themes and are furnished with sofas, bureaus, eclectic Federal-style antiques, and replicas of Queen Anne beds and Chippendale chairs. Some rooms have four-poster or canopy beds. Green, quilted "TV cozies" hide the televisions when you don't want the modern world to intrude.

The large, sunny, first-floor dining room is elegantly decorated with Federal-style chairs and antique side tables and is graced with candlelight in the evening. The contemporary American cuisine is first-rate, giving the inn a well-deserved reputation for dining. Specialties change

with the seasons, but they may include Atlantic salmon served over spinach-studded angel hair pasta or maple-glazed boneless pork loin. A cheerful café that opens onto the terrace serves inexpensive sandwiches and salads during the day.

The inn is formal enough to make your stay a special event, but friendly enough to create a relaxed and welcoming atmosphere. Just down the road are the dozen 17th- and early 18th-century house museums of Historic Deerfield (*see* Places to Go, Sights to See, *above*), which provide year-round lectures and tours. The Barnard Tavern has a ballroom with a fiddlers' gallery and several hands-on displays: You can climb into the rope bed and write on the slates. The Memorial Hall Museum has displays about the Native American Pocumtuck as well as relics from the village's history.

🏨 *23 doubles with bath (2 rooms wheelchair accessible). Restaurant; café; lounge; air-conditioning, TVs, phones in rooms. $169–$241; full breakfast. AE, DC, MC, V. No smoking, no pets. Closed Dec. 24–26.*

Lord Jeffery Inn

30 Boltwood Ave., Amherst 01002, tel. 413/253–2576 or 800/742–0358, fax 413/256–6152

This Victorian-style brick inn—all gables and green shutters—is on the common between the town center and the Amherst College campus. Despite its central location, the lodging remains quiet and calm. Public rooms have Colonial furnishings, and the lounge has an open fireplace. The inn's large restaurant—with its white beams, its chandeliers, and its open fireplace—serves first-rate new American cuisine. Most guest rooms have simple cream- or pastel-painted plaster walls and Colonial reproductions; some have bright patchwork quilts and nonworking fireplaces.

Be sure to call ahead for reservations; the Lord Jeffery is usually fully booked during key college weekend events. Ask for a room with a balcony that overlooks the garden courtyard or a first-floor room that opens onto the garden.

🏨 *40 doubles with bath, 8 suites. Restaurant; tavern; air-conditioning, cable TV, phones in rooms. $79–$153; breakfast extra. AE, DC, MC, V. No smoking in public areas and some guest rooms.*

Northfield Country House

181 School St., Northfield 01360, tel. 413/498–2692 or 800/498–2692

Andrea Dale gave up her position as an executive at Saks Fifth Avenue in favor of the quiet life. She found tranquility in Northfield Country House, and so will you. This big English manor house sits atop a small rise on 16 acres and overlooks the countryside and Northfield village. Thick woods border the long curving driveway, and landscaped gardens surround the house. Andrea, a welcoming but discreet host, has renovated extensively, rebuilt porches, and added an outdoor pool. Northfield was constructed about 100 years ago by a shipbuilder, which accounts for the abundance of such handcrafted woodwork as the heavy paneling and thick chestnut beams in the open-plan living room. Guest rooms vary in size—avoid the smallest ones, which are former servants' quarters. Rooms contain Victorian antiques, brass beds, chairs, and mirrors, and the best have working fireplaces with stone surrounds. The "family suite," two small bedrooms that share a foyer and bath, is a good choice for parents traveling with older children.

🏨 *3 doubles with bath, 2 doubles share bath, 1 suite. Outdoor pool. $60–$120; full breakfast. MC, V. No smoking in rooms, no pets. 2-night minimum graduation weekends.*

The Publick House and Colonel Ebenezer Crafts Inn

Rte. 131, On-the-Common, Sturbridge 01566, tel. 508/347-3313 or 800/782-5425, fax 508/347-5073

Although both these establishments are operated by the same management and have a wide variety of amenities, they also have very distinct styles. The Publick House, founded (confusingly enough) by Ebenezer Crafts in 1771, is a sprawling old place. Its extensive dining rooms are lighted by pewter chandeliers and offer traditional Yankee fare—from individual lobster pies to double-thick loin lamb chops. Three meals are served daily year-round. Accommodations at the Publick House consist of fairly small, olde-worlde guest rooms with wide-board floors (uneven, of course), some canopy beds, and simple wooden antiques. Next door, the Chamberlain House has suites done in the same style; you'll find more contemporary, motel-style rooms at the nearby Country Lodge.

Just over 1 mi away, the Crafts Inn is a quiet alternative to the hustle and bustle of the Publick House. A restored Colonial farmhouse built in 1786, it features eight spacious guest rooms with canopy or four-poster beds, antique desks, painted wood panels, and polished hardwood floors. Third-floor rooms have sloping gable ceilings. Downstairs, you can mingle with other guests in the library, on the sunporch, or in the large lounge, which has Colonial furniture and an enormous brick fireplace; there's also an outdoor pool. Breakfast consists of baked goods, and afternoon tea is also served.

🏨 *17 doubles with bath (Publick House); 1 double with bath, 3 suites (Chamberlain House); 100 doubles with bath (Country Lodge); 8 doubles with bath (Crafts Inn). 3 restaurants, bar, air-conditioning, meeting rooms, tennis court, outdoor pool, shuffleboard, playground (Publick House); air-condition-* ing, outdoor pool (Crafts Inn). $59–$155; Continental breakfast (Crafts Inn only; breakfast extra at Publick House, Chamberlain House, Country Lodge). AE, DC, MC, V. Smoking in bar and some rooms (Country Lodge only), pets allowed in Country Lodge.

Sturbridge Country Inn

530 Main St. (Box 60), Sturbridge 01566, tel. 508/347-5503, fax 508/347-5319

This white 1840s building has a Greek Revival facade more evocative of a grand municipal edifice than the farmhouse that this once was. Guest rooms, all of which have working fireplaces, are furnished with Colonial reproductions that blend with the modern design. And every room has a whirlpool bath.

Upstairs, Rooms 7 and 8 are good choices. One has wicker furnishings, the other brass; both have a sunporch, exposed hand-hewn beams, and steps that lead down from the whirlpool bath to a large bedroom. The suite occupies the entire third floor and has cathedral ceilings, a large whirlpool bath in the living room, a wet bar, and big windows. (Check the skylights on rainy days, however; there have been problems with leaks.) Try to avoid the small first-floor rooms; the plumbing gurgles, and whirlpool tubs upstairs tend to reverberate downstairs.

Innkeeper Patricia MacConnell, whose brother owns the establishment, has a light Continental breakfast set up for you in the first-floor lounge. Here you'll also find an open fireplace and Colonial-style furnishings and decor that blend remarkably well with the open, 20th-century floor plan and cathedral ceilings. The innkeepers try to maintain a romantic atmosphere that is not suitable for young children. In summer you can relax—despite the street noise—in the garden gazebo, and Old Sturbridge Village is just a short walk away. Next door, the Stageloft Repertory Theatre performs from June through October.

🏨 *8 doubles with bath, 1 suite. Air-conditioning, cable TV, fireplaces, whirlpool baths in rooms; VCRs in some rooms. $69–$159; Continental breakfast. AE, D, MC, V. No smoking in rooms, no pets.*

Sunnyside Farm Bed and Breakfast

21 River Rd., Whately 01093, tel. 413/665-3113

Although you and the other guests have the whole second floor of this 1864 farmhouse to yourselves, hosts Dick and Marylou Green make you feel very much a part of the family. The yellow house with black shutters and an attached red barn has been in Marylou's family for generations and was once operated as a tobacco farm. Now the fields are leased to the Nourse Strawberry Farms, where you can pick your own in season.

Country-style guest rooms range from tiny to large—the biggest is at the front and is furnished with twin beds and country maple antiques that were either handed down by the family or bought at auctions. Framed fine-art prints hang on the walls, and all rooms have views across the fields. On the first floor, you're welcome to watch TV with the Greens in the living room or curl up with a book in the small library. Breakfast, which is served family style in the dining room, often includes homemade jams and muffins, berries, eggs and bacon, or pancakes.

🏨 *5 doubles share 2 baths. Pool. $45–$95; full breakfast. No credit cards. No smoking, no pets.*

Yankee Pedlar Inn

1866 Northampton St. (Box 6206), Holyoke 01040-6206, tel. 413/532-9494, fax 413/536-8877

The Yankee Pedlar has grown outward from a central mustard-color clapboard building. It now consists of several annexes of superbly decorated guest rooms

as well as an "opera house" for dances and banquets. Rooms have four-poster beds, Currier and Ives prints, nightstands, desks, and other antiques. The spaciousness of the suites, some of which have nonworking fireplaces, makes them worth the minimal extra cost. The all-pink Victorian-style bridal suite is an extravaganza of deep carpets, lace, draperies, and mirrors; it even has Victorian valentines on the mantelpiece and bird cages. For simpler quarters, ask for a room in the neighboring carriage house, where you'll find classic canopy beds, rustic antiques, cathedral ceilings, and exposed beams.

Antiques in the public rooms include a pre–Prohibition Era bar, decorative wood panels from the local (now demolished) Kenilworth Castle, a collection of copper pots, and dozens of old photographs of the region. Thursday through Saturday evenings there's live entertainment in the bar, which is equipped with a popcorn machine configured like a street vendor's cart. The place feels like a classy Victorian-era London pub. In addition to renovating all the rooms when he bought the inn in 1994, Martin Clayton also refurbished the Oyster Bar and Grill Room restaurant, which has a wall mural depicting the dining area and many of its long-time employees. Martin was also responsible for expanding the inn's banquet facilities and function rooms.

Although the inn stands at a major intersection, rooms near the road have triple-glazed windows that keep out the noise. The location isn't ideal for those seeking a quiet getaway, but it is convenient. The inn is close to I–91 and only a short drive from several colleges, including Mount Holyoke, Smith, Amherst, and the University of Massachusetts.

🏨 *18 doubles with bath, 10 suites. Restaurant, bar; air-conditioning, cable TV in rooms; 8 banquet rooms. $65–$125; Continental breakfast. AE, D, DC, MC, V. No pets. Closed Dec. 25.*

The Berkshires

Blantyre

The Berkshires—about 2½ hours by car from both Boston and New York—embrace some of the most attractive countryside in Massachusetts: rolling hills, extensive woodlands, and characteristic New England villages. The county has been a popular vacation destination since the mid-1800s, when wealthy New Yorkers and Bostonians built their summer "cottages" here, and it continues to attract its fair share of wealthy weekenders from the big cities. Though many of the older mansions have now been converted into schools or hotels, much of their elegance and interesting architecture has been preserved.

One of the best (if busiest) times to visit the area is in fall, when the gentle, tree-covered slopes are ablaze with colorful foliage. Summer is another peak period, with the Berkshires' vibrant and varied cultural life in full swing. The annual series of concerts at Tanglewood has become New England's best-known music festival, but this event is accompanied by a host of other regional musical and theatrical performances in a variety of settings. In winter the region is popular for its family-oriented downhill ski areas and for its cross-country skiing.

With all these advantages, the region is hardly undeveloped. You'll find dozens of country inns, ranging from deluxe palazzi and baronial castles requiring evening dress at dinner to relaxed country farmhouses with homemade jam for breakfast. Despite the abundance of accommodations, during the Tanglewood Festival rooms are scarce, rates are high, and the narrow roads are frequently jammed. The influx of affluent travelers keeps prices up, whether you're shopping for antiques or reserving a motel room.

Places to Go, Sights to See

Great Barrington. The biggest town in the southern Berkshires is a mecca for antiques hunters, as are the villages of South Egremont, just south on Route 23, and Sheffield, south on Route 7.

Hancock Shaker Village (Rte. 20, 5 mi west of Pittsfield, tel. 413/443–0188). Founded in the 1790s, the village of Hancock thrived in the 1840s, when 300 Shakers made their living farming, selling seeds, making medicines, and producing household objects. The best buildings to visit here are the Round Stone Barn, with its labor-saving devices, and the Laundry and Machine Shop, with its water-powered instruments.

Lenox. At the heart of the "summer cottage" region, Lenox and its environs fairly burst with old inns and majestic buildings: Particularly worth visiting are *The Mount* (2 Plunkett St., tel. 413/637–1899), former summer home of novelist Edith Wharton, the first woman to win the Pulitzer Prize; *Chesterwood* (4 Williamsville Rd., Stockbridge, tel. 413/298–3579), where sculptor Daniel Chester French spent his summers for 33 years; and *Arrowhead* (780 Holmes Rd., Pittsfield, tel. 413/442–1793), the house where Herman Melville wrote *Moby Dick*. *Tanglewood* (tel. 413/637–5165 mid-June–Sept. or 617/266–1492), on a hillside clearing among 200 acres (much of it forested), is the summer home of the Boston Symphony Orchestra and site of the world-class festival that draws thousands of music fans each July and August.

Mt. Greylock. The highest peak in Massachusetts (3,491 ft) is surrounded by the Mt. Greylock State Reservation (50 Rockwell Rd., Lanesborough, tel. 413/499–4262 or 413/499–4263), which encompasses 10,327 acres and has facilities for bicycling, fishing, hiking, horseback riding, and snowmobiling.

Stockbridge is an archetypal New England small town, with a history of literary and artistic inhabitants—one of the most famous was painter Norman Rockwell. The *Norman Rockwell Museum* (tel. 413/298–4100), with the largest collection of Rockwell originals in the world, opened in 1993, 2 mi outside Stockbridge on

Route 183. Several miles east on Route 20, *Jacob's Pillow* (George Carter Rd., Becket, tel. 413/243–0745), billed as "America's oldest dance festival," hosts celebrated contemporary dance performers during the summer months.

Williamstown. This north Berkshire town is dominated by the grand, weathered stone buildings of Williams College. The *College Art Museum* (Main St., tel. 413/597–2429), emphasizing American and contemporary art, and the *Sterling and Francine Clark Institute* (225 South St., tel. 413/458–9545), with paintings by Renoir, Monet, Pisarro, and Degas, are worth visiting. Williamstown is at the westernmost point of the *Mohawk Trail*, a 67-mi scenic stretch of Route 2 that takes in several interesting sights, including the Western Gateway Heritage State Park and Hail to the Sunrise, a monument to Native Americans. The route follows a section of a former Native American path that ran from the villages of western Massachusetts to New York's Finger Lakes.

Restaurants

Many of the best Berkshire restaurants are at country inns that focus primarily on traditional and New England cuisine. Lobster, regional game, and such favorites as rack of lamb are the most common fare. Some inns require formal dress at dinner. You'll find good restaurants (*see below* for addresses) at **Gateways Inn** (tel. 413/637–2532), the **Candlelight Inn** (tel. 413/637–1555), and **Wheatleigh** (tel. 413/637–0610), in Lenox; the **Williamsville Inn** (tel. 413/274–6118), in West Stockbridge; and **The Orchards** (tel. 413/458–9611), in Williamstown.

Nightlife

The emphasis in the Berkshires is definitely on classical entertainment; however, the **Lion's Den** (tel. 413/298–5545), downstairs at the Red Lion Inn in Stockbridge (*see below*), has folk music and contemporary combos every evening, and the **Williams Inn** (on the Green, junction of Rtes. 2 and 7, tel. 413/458–9371), in Williamstown, has live entertainment on weekends, with jazz on Saturday night.

Reservations Services

American Country Collection of B&B (1353 Union St., Schenectady, NY 12308, tel. 518/370–4948 or 800/810–4948, fax 518/393–1634), **Berkshire Bed and Breakfast Homes** (Main St., Box 211, Williamsburg 01096, tel. 413/268–7244, fax 413/268–7243), **New England Hospitality Network** (Box 3291, Newport, RI 02840, tel. 401/849–1298 or 800/828–0000, fax 401/849–1306), **Nutmeg B&B Agency** (Box 1117, West Hartford, CT 06127, tel. 860/236–6698 or 800/727–7592, fax 860/232–7680).

Visitor Information

Berkshire Visitors Bureau (Berkshire Common, Pittsfield 01201, tel. 413/443–9186 or 800/237–5747, fax 413/443–1970), **Lenox Chamber of Commerce** (Lenox Academy Building, 65 Main St., Lenox 01240, tel. 413/637–3646), **Mohawk Trail Association** (Box 2031, Charlemont 01339, tel. 413/664–6256).

Apple Tree Inn

10 Richmond Mountain Rd., Lenox 01240, tel. 413/637–1477, fax 413/637–2528

This country inn has a fantastic setting on a gently sloping hillside with marvelous views over the Stockbridge Bowl and Laurel Lake. It's also across the street from Tanglewood's main gates. In fact, you're so close to the music festival that you don't even need a ticket—you can listen to concerts from the inn's own gardens amid 450 varieties of roses and surrounded by 22 acres of apple orchards.

The main building, constructed in 1885, has public areas that are furnished with Victorian antiques, including a massive wooden bench. You enter through the parlor, with its arches, Persian rugs, open fireplace, velvet couches, and grand piano. In the tavern oak-paneled walls support a collection of old tools and a water buffalo head that stares out over the fireplace. The main restaurant, a circular 1960s addition, has a marqueelike ceiling with spokes of lightbulbs. Picture windows afford excellent views of the lawns and orchards.

Upstairs, guest rooms are furnished with antiques, including four-poster and brass beds, Victorian washstands, and wicker pieces. Four rooms have working fireplaces, and several have window seats with fabulous views. The generally spacious rooms have unusual shapes that add to their character; this is particularly true of rooms on the top floor, which have eaves, gables, and skylights. It's best to avoid some of the smaller rooms, especially Room 5 (Woodside), which is over the kitchen and can be hot and noisy. The nearby lodge has 21 motel-like rooms.

The Apple Tree Inn has an interesting past, and once belonged to Alice of the Arlo Guthrie song "Alice's Restaurant"—though she catered primarily to diners, not guests. Owners Joel Catalano and Sharon Walker relocated from New York City when they bought the inn in 1996.

🏨 *10 doubles with bath, 2 doubles share bath, 2 suites (inn); 21 doubles with bath (lodge). Restaurant, tavern, air-conditioning in rooms, cable TV in suites and lodge rooms, pool, tennis court. Inn: $60–$300; lodge: $55–$165; Continental breakfast. AE, D, DC, MC, V. No pets. 2-night minimum weekends, 3-night minimum weekends July–Aug. and Oct.*

Blantyre

16 Blantyre Rd. (off Rte. 20), Lenox 01240, tel. 413/637–3556, fax 413/637–4282

Surrounded by 100 magnificent acres, the palatial Blantyre was built in 1901 and has a Tudor style that is unique to the region (its design is based on an ancestral Scottish home). Senator John Fitzpatrick and his family, who also own the Red Lion Inn in Stockbridge, acquired the estate in 1980 and with it the mammoth task of restoration. Some of the furnishings in the great hall are original, as are the plaster relief ceilings, the intricately carved oak paneling, and the leather-backed wallpaper.

Although the hall, with its heavy wooden furnishings (including a rocking horse in full heraldic gear), appears imposingly solemn, the long, cream-tone music room next door evokes a lighter mood, with inlaid chess tables, an antique Steinway grand piano, a harp, antique Dutch and Italian cabinets, and exquisite chairs and couches. Doors open onto a terrace set with tables overlooking two large, perfectly manicured croquet lawns.

Staying at Blantyre is an expensive proposition, so make the most of it by reserving one of the five largest rooms in the main house (and by leaving the children at home). Although the entire property is stylishly finished, rooms in the carriage house and cottages don't quite

compare with these spacious accommodations, which have hand-carved four-poster beds, bay windows, high ceilings, working fireplaces, chintz chairs, over-stuffed chaise longues, boudoirs, walk-in closets, and Victorian bathrooms. The huge Paterson Suite has two bathrooms; a sitting room with a fireplace; a pineapple four-poster bed; and pale green wallpaper, linens, and draperies. If the larger main-house rooms are booked, the smaller Ashley Suite or the carriage house's split-level suites beside the pool are next best.

The first-rate service rests in the hands of Scottish manager Roderick Anderson. The many extras include bathrobes, toiletries, newspapers, turndown service, and mineral water, cheese, and fruit.

🖼 *13 doubles with bath, 10 suites. Restaurant; air-conditioning, cable TV; phones in rooms; room service; pool; whirlpool bath; sauna; 4 tennis courts; 2 croquet lawns; walking trails. $240–$650; Continental breakfast. AE, DC, MC, V. No pets. 2-night minimum Oct. and on weekends. Closed early Nov.–mid-May.*

Brook Farm Inn

15 Hawthorne St., Lenox 01240, tel. 413/637–3013 or 800/285–7638, fax 437/637–4751

This big beige-clapboard Victorian is named after a literary community that emerged near Boston in 1841, and, like its namesake, it has become a gathering place for poets, who hold readings and classes here. The library, with its dark wood antiques, Asian rugs, and open fireplace, contains 750 volumes of poetry and about 75 poets on tape. Joseph Miller, who bought the inn in 1992 with his wife, Anne, inherited the literary tradition with reservations. "I was afraid of it," he admits. "My background is in construction—what did I know about poetry? But it really has a life of its own, and now I thoroughly enjoy it."

Guest rooms contain four-poster and canopy beds, wing chairs, and old bureaus; six rooms have working fireplaces, and all rooms have an excellent collection of reading materials. The most distinctive room is in the garret; it was converted from an old loft and has skylights, exposed beams, floral-print fabrics, and wall stenciling. (Note that this inn is not suitable for children, particularly during the busy summer and fall seasons.)

🖼 *12 doubles with bath. Air-conditioning in all rooms, ceiling fans in most rooms, pool. $80–$195; full breakfast, afternoon tea. D, MC, V. No smoking, no pets. 3-night minimum weekends July–Aug. and some holidays, 2-night minimum weekends Sept.–June.*

The Candlelight Inn

35 Walker St., Lenox 01240, tel. 413/637–1555

Two doors down from Gateways Inn (*see below*) on "inn row" in Lenox, this 1885 B&B exudes style without stuffiness. Eating is particularly important here—there are four dining rooms, and they range in style from an airy space with arched windows and a sun terrace to a darker, old-world room with a large fireplace, paneled walls, and exposed beams. In summer tables are set up in a pleasant courtyard. The menu features such specialties as house-cured gravlax, grilled veal chop, and confit of duck. Older children with sophisticated palates may enjoy this inn, but leave the little ones at home.

The large bedrooms have floral-print wallpapers and Colonial and Victorian antiques, including wing chairs and writing desks. Rooms on the top floor have sloping ceilings and skylights. An original polished-wood linen cabinet adorns the second floor sitting room, which also has blue couches and a TV. The inn, which Rebecca Hedgecock has owned since 1987, is a short stroll from the middle of Lenox.

🏨 *8 doubles with bath. Restaurant, bar, air-conditioning, TV in sitting room. $60–$168; Continental breakfast. AE, MC, V. No pets. 3-night minimum weekends July–Aug. Inn and restaurant closed Tues. in winter.*

Cliffwood Inn

25 Cliffwood St., Lenox 01240, tel. 413/637–3330 or 800/789–3331, fax 413/637–0221

This exquisite Colonial-style building on a residential side street was built in the 1890s for an ambassador to France. Inside you'll find many European touches, such as the oval dining room with its similarly shaped windows and Belgian, French, and Italian 15th- and 16th-century antiques brought back from the Continent by owners Joy and Scottie Farrelly. The Farrellys are also dealers in fine antique reproduction furniture and have 30 or so of these pieces at the inn. The living room features inlaid wood floors, huge wall mirrors, a white marble fireplace, Asian rugs, and a 15th-century Italian desk. In summer breakfast is served on the outside veranda overlooking the pool.

On the second-floor landing, the custom-made bookcase matches arched windows and dentil moldings. Six of the seven guest rooms have working fireplaces (one is in the bathroom), and most contain canopy beds. One room offers a simple, Amish-made, net-canopy bed made of golden oak. Persian and Chinese rugs cover the oak and pine floors, and top-floor rooms are graced with sloping roofs and windows in the eaves. Because of all the antique furnishings, this inn is not suitable for young children.

🏨 *7 doubles with bath. Air-conditioning, indoor and outdoor pools. $78–$213; Continental breakfast (no breakfast winter weekdays), wine and cheese. No credit cards. Smoking on veranda only, no pets. 3–4-night minimum July and Aug. weekends, 3-night minimum some holidays.*

Dalton House

955 Main St., Dalton 01226, tel. 413/684–3854, fax 413/684–3560

Although the original house is 170 years old, this reasonably priced establishment has been modernized, and offers a simple alternative to the more traditional area inns. Inside the pink-clapboard house with mint green shutters, you can mingle with other guests in a split-level sitting room that has a cathedral ceiling and skylight, exposed beams, pine floors, and a freestanding fireplace. You'll dine outside on the deck or in a sunny new breakfast room with pine chairs and tables.

Most bedrooms are in the 1967 wing of the main house. They're cheerful, if small, with orange-and-brown floral-print drapes and wallpapers. Suites and rooms in the recently converted carriage house are larger and have period furnishings, wicker chairs, and floral bedspreads; some have exposed beams. Gary and Bernice Turetsky opened this B&B in 1975 and eventually sold their florist business to go into innkeeping full-time. Families with older children may find this inn, in a bustling village dominated by Crane's paper mills, comfortable.

🏨 *9 doubles with bath, 2 suites. Air-conditioning, TV, phones in rooms; pool; picnic area. $58–$115; Continental breakfast. AE, MC, V. No smoking, no pets. 2-night minimum summer and fall weekends.*

Field Farm

554 Sloan Rd. (off Rte. 43), Williamstown 01267, tel. and fax 413/458–3135

Neither your average B&B nor your typical Berkshire cottage estate, this former home of art collector Lawrence H. Bloedel has been owned by the Trustees of Reservations since 1984 and is now managed by innkeepers Sean and

Jean Cowhig. The stark geometric exterior of this modern (1948) structure, with its cedar shingles painted beige, contrasts unromantically with the region's profusion of period homes. But consider its advantages: 296 acres of private, wooded grounds containing a pond, a pool, a tennis court, and trails for hiking or cross-country skiing. The place is not yet well known, and because it has only five guest rooms, staying here is like living on your own country estate.

The interior is unashamedly square in shape, and the house, designed as a sort of display case for Bloedel's art collection (which went to the Williams College museum after his death), feels a bit like a modern museum. In 1994 the college returned eight pieces on long-term loan, and they are now displayed in the public areas. Most of the 1950s oak, cherry, and walnut furniture was handmade by Bloedel, while other pieces were designed especially for the house—even the plastic doorknobs were custom made, quite a coup in the 1940s. Modern sculptures decorate the gardens. The first-floor guest room and upstairs master bedroom are huge, and all bedrooms have modern furnishings and big picture windows with views over the grounds toward distant hills. Three bedrooms have private decks, and two have working fireplaces surrounded by custom-made tiles depicting animals, birds, and butterflies.

Downstairs in the large public sitting room, you'll discover another working fireplace and more modern art. You can use the pantry, which has a refrigerator, toaster, and wineglasses, to make your own lunch, snacks, or cocktails; the veranda is a good place to enjoy a breakfast of fresh breads with homemade jams, granola, eggs, or French toast or to sip an afternoon drink.

▥ *5 doubles with bath. Pool, pond (fishing poles available), tennis, cross-country skiing. $100; full breakfast. D, MC, V. Smoking on decks and verandas only, no pets.*

Gateways Inn

51 Walker St., Lenox 01240, tel. 413/637–2532 or 888/GWAYINN (492–9466), fax 413/637–1423

A formal, elegant inn with a superb restaurant, Gateways was built in 1912 by Harley Procter (of Procter and Gamble) as a summer home that he called Orleton. The oblong white-clapboard mansion resembles—fittingly enough—a bar of Ivory soap. Today the place is only steps from the center of Lenox, though in Procter's day it was surrounded by 7 acres of lawns with formal gardens, a carriage house, and a tennis court.

You sense the elegance as soon as you step into the impressive entrance hall with its oval windows; from here a grand mahogany staircase with a skylight leads to the second-floor guest rooms. The best of these, in the east corner, is the Fiedler Suite, named after Tanglewood and Boston Pops conductor Arthur Fiedler, who stayed here regularly. It has two working fireplaces (one in the bedroom, one in the sitting room) and a large dressing room off the bathroom. Several other quarters have fireplaces, and one—the Romeo and Juliet Room—has a king-size sleigh bed under a skylight. All rooms have light period-reproduction wallpapers, Colonial and Victorian antiques, and four-poster or canopy beds. The west-corner room has an eight-piece maple and black-walnut Victorian bedroom set.

Public rooms downstairs include a small parlor with Colonial furnishings and two dining areas: the main dining room and the smaller Rockwell Room, named after painter Norman Rockwell, who dined in a sunny corner here every week. Owners Fabrizio and Rosemary Chiariello, self-described "corporate refugees" from New York City who took over the inn in 1996, have redone the dining room with simple russet-tone walls. In warmer months less formal dishes—pasta with seasonal vegetables, lobster ravioli, and

grilled Portobello mushrooms—complement the inn's more traditional fare. The Gateways has an elegant ambience; it's best to leave children at home.

🏨 *11 doubles with bath, 1 suite. Restaurant; air-conditioning, cable TV, phones in rooms. $105–$325; Continental breakfast. AE, D, DC, MC, V. Smoking on porch only, no pets.*

The Gables Inn

81 Walker St., Lenox 01240, tel. 413/637–3416 or 800/382–9401

Another venerable Walker Street inn, this accommodation is famous because it was home to novelist Edith Wharton for two years before she moved into the Mount, her new "cottage" down the road. Built in 1885, the Queen Anne-style mansion has been renovated extensively. Experienced innkeepers Frank and Mary Newton refurbished the eight-sided library—where Wharton wrote short stories—and refurnished the bedrooms with authentic, 19th-century antiques. (Because of all the antiques, this inn is not suitable for children.)

The room where Wharton once slept has a big four-poster bed with a pink-and-white canopy, a mauve sofa, and a rich Asian rug. Several rooms have a theme: The Show Biz Room has old posters of Hollywood movies and signed photos of film stars; the Edith Wharton Suite has a four-poster, a carved-wood fireplace, a sitting area, and two pedestal sinks in the large bathroom. Fresh-baked breads and pastries are served under the chandelier in the elegant dining room. More modern touches are the indoor pool with a whirlpool and the tennis court.

🏨 *14 doubles with bath, 4 suites. Air-conditioning, cable TV in rooms; VCR in suites. $80–$210; full breakfast. D, MC, V. No smoking in guest rooms or breakfast room, no pets. 3-night minimum during Tanglewood, 2-night minimum fall and holiday weekends.*

Ivanhoe Country House

254 S. Undermountain Rd. (Rte. 41), Sheffield 01257, tel. 413/229–2143

The Appalachian Trail runs right by this B&B, and, according to host Carole Maghery, who has been taking in guests here since 1969, deer graze on the lawn in winter. The house was built in 1780, and various wings were added at later dates, creating various levels with curious staircases and passageways throughout. The ample guest sitting room contains antique desks, a piano, and comfortable couches; it's also well stocked with reading material.

Most guest rooms are large and have pleasant country views; some have balconies or porches. All rooms are furnished with antiques, and some with brass beds and fireplaces. There is no dining room, so plan to take breakfast in bed. Dick Maghery used to raise golden retrievers on the house's 20 acres of grounds. The canine-friendly family has two retrievers now and also accepts guests' pets.

🏨 *9 doubles with bath, 2 suites with kitchens. Air-conditioning in some rooms, pool. $55–$110 (dogs $10 extra); Continental breakfast. No credit cards. 2-night minimum weekends July–Labor Day, 3-night minimum holiday weekends.*

Merrell Tavern Inn

1565 Pleasant St. (Rte. 102), South Lee/Stockbridge 01260, tel. 413/243–1794 or 800/243–1794, fax 413/243–2669

Believe it or not, this Federal-style red-clapboard building with a columned facade remained uninhabited for almost 100 years. When the present owners bought it in 1981, they restored the building and installed heat, running water, and electricity. In the process they created one of the most authentic inns in the Berkshires—one that's on the National Register of Historic Places.

Owners Charles and Faith Reynolds are retired schoolteachers who were honored with a Preservation Award from the Massachusetts Historical Commission in 1982. They have recently delegated their innkeeping duties to resident manager Pamela Hurst.

Built about 1794 and turned into a stagecoach inn in 1817, the lodging is blessed with some good-size guest rooms. They have polished wide-board floors, area rugs, painted-plaster walls, iron door latches, and mellow wood antiques. Most beds are pencil four-posters, and some have simple white canopies. Three rooms contain working, Count Rumford–style, wood-burning fireplaces. The necessity of abiding by a 500-year covenant that protects the building's historic status means small (but beautifully decorated) bathrooms—on the third floor, where rooms were built in the shell of the old ballroom, some bathrooms are housed in the former drovers' sleeping quarters.

The original keeping room, now the guest parlor, has a beehive oven as well as a large cooking fireplace with a Franklin stove. A breakfast of pancakes, French toast, or omelets is served in the original tavern room, which contains an open fireplace and the only complete "birdcage" Colonial bar in America. Look for the 19th-century detail: The wood grain on the bar and the doors is hand-painted, not natural; the pulley wheels on the ceiling were used to raise and lower the original candle chandelier (now in a Boston museum). The inn is about a mile east of Stockbridge, beside busy Route 102, but it's well back from the road. Behind the building, 2 acres of landscaped gardens with a gazebo descend gently to the Housatonic River.

🏠 *9 doubles with bath. Air-conditioning, TV room, phones in rooms. $75–$165; full breakfast. MC, V. No smoking, no pets. 3-night minimum summer and holiday weekends, 2-night minimum other weekends. Closed Dec. 24–25.*

New Boston Inn

Jct. of Rtes. 8 and 57, 101 N. Main St., Sandisfield 01255, tel. 413/258–4477, fax 413/258–4234

This distinctive gray-clapboard building with bright red trim is the oldest inn in the Berkshires. It was built as an inn in 1737 (a large extension was added in 1796) and has remained one ever since. The present owners bought the place in 1984 and have carried out extensive restoration and renovation work. Original interior features include the 24-inch king's boards that make up the floor of the tavern room and bar and the unfinished pine and maple panels and corner cupboard on the wall. The sloping door frames, floors, and ceilings are a constant reminder of the age of the building, as is the large, blue-and-white second-floor ballroom, part of the 1796 extension. This room now serves as a gathering room for guests and has two fireplaces, a TV, and an antique billiard table.

Guest rooms feature Colonial-style furniture, wide-board floors, painted-wood beams, and cedar-lined closets; most have beautifully executed stenciling on the walls (a favorite design is the Shaker tree of life). Country-style breakfasts include eggs, bacon or sausage, and pancakes or French toast. The inn is in the tiny village of Sandisfield, in a quiet corner of the southern Berkshires.

🏠 *8 doubles with bath. Tavern, TV room. $95; full breakfast. AE, D, MC, V. Smoking in tavern only. 2-night minimum weekends mid-May–Oct.*

The Orchards

222 Adams Rd. (Rte. 2), Williamstown 01267, tel. 413/458–9611 or 800/225–1517, fax 413/458–3273

The first impression is not too auspicious—a pale-orange stucco exterior; no orchards; and a location amid motels, gas stations, and supermarkets on a commercial strip of Route 2, a mile from the

center of Williamstown. But try to reserve judgment until you're inside this small, fancy hotel, built in 1985. Church pews and a heavy wooden pulpit adorn the corridors, and the lounge offers thick carpets, fresh flowers, and an open fireplace surrounded by an 18th-century carved-oak mantel.

Some guest rooms have four-poster beds, and some have fireplaces; all have English antiques and uniform beige wallpapers with floral patterns. Business travelers will appreciate the in-room desks, bathroom phones, and discreetly hidden TVs. Vacationers should note that there's little difference between the least expensive rooms and those in the middle price range. But try to avoid a room with a parking-lot view.

🏨 *49 doubles with bath. Restaurant, tavern; air-conditioning, cable TV/VCRs in rooms; room service, pool, exercise room with sauna and whirlpool. $160–$225; breakfast extra, afternoon tea. AE, DC, MC, V. No pets. 2-night minimum weekends July–Oct., 3-night minimum college commencement weekends.*

The Red Lion Inn

30 Main St., Stockbridge 01262, tel. 413/298–5545, fax 413/298–5130

Nobody can write about the Berkshires without including this grande dame of New England inns, built in 1773 and situated in the heart of Stockbridge. Numerous famous people have stayed here—including five U.S. presidents, writers Nathaniel Hawthorne and Henry Wadsworth Longfellow, and more-modern legends from John Wayne to Bob Dylan—and the place was frequented by artist Norman Rockwell, who lived just around the corner. The wood-beamed restaurant, its tables set with pewter, is a stylish place to dine on traditional New England fare and Continental specialties. That said, you should note that many guest rooms are small, and those in the main building open off a long, dark corridor. Accommodations in

the numerous annexes are more appealing. Rooms are traditionally decorated, with floral wallpapers and curtains from the mail-order store that's owned by the innkeepers and operates out of the inn. Other furnishings include Early American and Victorian antiques, rocking chairs, Asian rugs, and Rockwell prints. A polite and pleasant staff operates the Red Lion, which has been owned by the Fitzpatricks since 1968.

🏨 *65 doubles with bath, 18 doubles share bath, 28 suites. 2 restaurants, 2 bars; air-conditioning, TVs, phones in rooms; exercise room; meeting rooms; pool. $87–$165, suites $167–$355; breakfast extra. AE, D, DC, MC, V. Smoking allowed only in Lion's Den pub and some guest rooms, no pets. 2-night minimum weekends July–Oct.*

River Bend Farm

643 Simonds Rd., Williamstown 01267, tel. 413/458–5504 or 413/458–3121

One of the oldest buildings in the Berkshires, this property was constructed in 1770 by Colonel Benjamin Simonds, a founder of Williamstown and a commissioned officer of the Berkshire militia during the American Revolution. The restoration of River Bend Farm is totally authentic, and it is listed on the National Register of Historic Places. A stay here transports you to another era.

You enter through the kitchen (called the keeping room) and are greeted by an open-range stove and an oven hung with dried herbs. Chairs hang on pegs on the walls Shaker style, and the room is filled with 18th- and 19th-century country antiques, from wooden washtubs and spoon racks to flatirons and cooking implements. Also downstairs is a small formal sitting room with a fireplace, but "formal" only means the walls are plastered—upstairs it's another story. Bedroom walls consist of wide wood panels, some of them painted in their original colors (owners Dave and Judy Loomis, who restored the building,

scraped their way through layers of paper and paint to discover them). Others are whitewashed or made of simple, scrubbed, wide planks, as are the floors and doors. Window treatments are tab curtains (no hooks, just cloth loops) of unbleached muslin. Accurate Colonial-style reproductions of candle chandeliers hang from the ceilings, and sconces with candles are fixed to the walls. Some rooms have brick (nonworking) fireplaces and antique four-poster or canopy beds. Other antique pieces include a spinning wheel here, a wing chair or a chamber pot there.

Speaking of chamber pots . . . the farm's only disadvantage is that four guest rooms share two bathrooms, one of which is on the ground floor. The first-floor bathroom is an absolute Aladdin's cave of utilitarian antiques, including washbowls, jugs, lamps, butter tubs, and hanging herbs.

Outdoors you have access to the river for canoeing, and you can visit a warm spring pool, ¼ mi upriver. Williamstown is about an eight-minute drive away.

🏠 *4 doubles share 2 baths. $80–$100; Continental breakfast. No credit cards. No smoking, no pets. 2-night minimum during college events weekends. Closed late Oct.–Mar.*

Rookwood Inn

11 Old Stockbridge Rd. (Box 1717), Lenox 01240, tel. 413/637-9750 or 800/223-9750, fax 413/637-1352

This painted lady on a quiet street near the center of Lenox was built in 1885 as a summer "cottage" for a wealthy New York family. The Rookwood perfectly recreates the Victorian era, with striking period wallpapers, matching linens, chaise longues, and heavy carved couches. In 1992 the former owners added three rooms, cleverly incorporating a second turret into the addition, which makes it difficult to spot where the old building ends and the new one begins. Eight spacious bedrooms contain working fireplaces, all chambers are furnished with Victorian antiques, and some have brass or four-poster beds. The old turret rooms have the most interesting configurations, particularly the room on the top floor; steps lead into the turret, which contains a daybed and has windows on all sides. The elegant first-floor lounge offers reading material, an open fire, and a screened porch with wicker furniture.

Owners Amy Lindner-Lesser and Steve Lesser relocated from the Philadelphia area with their two daughters after purchasing the inn in 1996. Steve, a former social worker who recently graduated from the Restaurant School in Philadelphia, is the chef. His specialties include Mexican eggs with salsa, creamy breakfast lasagna, and stuffed French toast.

🏠 *19 doubles with bath, 2 suites. Air-conditioning, TV in common area. $75–$275; full breakfast and afternoon tea. AE, D, MC,V. No smoking, no pets. 3-night minimum weekends July–Aug. and holidays, 2-night minimum weekends during fall foliage season.*

The Turning Point Inn

3 Lake Buel Rd. (R.D. 2, Box 140), Great Barrington 01230, tel. 413/528-4777

This 200-year-old inn—once a stagecoach stop between New York City and Boston—has been in the Yost family for 20 years. They have renovated the house completely, turning the upstairs ballroom into guest rooms and converting the barn into a two-bedroom cottage, which contains modern furnishings, a full kitchen, and a screened porch. Despite remodeling, the old building retains its fair share of narrow passageways, twisting staircases, sloping floors, and peeling paint.

You can get to know fellow guests in the large living room, which has two fireplaces and a piano, or the kitchen, which has a bread oven; chestnut planks from

the old walls were used to make the breakfast tables. Healthful morning meals feature such items as multigrain hot cereals and home-baked muffins or cakes.

Bedrooms, with uneven wide-board floors, tend to be small, and several have sloping roofs; they contain eclectic antiques, and some have Colonial-style beds. The inn is close to swimming, boating, horseback riding, hiking trails, and skiing.

🏠 *4 doubles with bath, 2 doubles share bath, 1 cottage. Fans in rooms, TV in lounge, cross-country ski trail. $80–$100 (full breakfast), cottage $200 (breakfast extra). AE, MC, V. No smoking, no pets. 2-night minimum weekdays, 3-night minimum weekends July–Aug.*

The Weathervane Inn

Rte. 23, South Egremont 01258, tel. 413/ 528–9580 or 800/528–9580, fax 413/528– 1713

The open fireplace and beehive oven in the lounge of this friendly, family-run inn date from the 1760s, when the original building was constructed. Most of the additions were made in 1830, although the current innkeepers added new bedrooms downstairs and recently converted the carriage house into three more rooms. The formal parlor next to the lounge features striking reproduction wallpaper, and guest rooms are decorated in a Colonial style, with stencils, country curtains, wreaths, Norman Rockwell prints, and rocking chairs. The inn has a varied past and at one period served as a dog kennel—one of the guest bathrooms incorporates an original dog-size bathtub! Country-style breakfasts are served in the sunny dining room overlooking the lawn.

🏠 *10 doubles with bath, 1 suite. Dining rooms, air-conditioning, TV/VCR in lounge, pool. $95–$195; full breakfast and afternoon tea. AE, D, MC, V. No smoking indoors, no pets. 3-night min-imum during Tanglewood and holiday weekends. Closed Dec. 20–26.*

Wheatleigh

Hawthorne Rd., Lenox 01240, tel. 413/ 637–0610, fax 413/637–4507

Wheatleigh was built in 1893, a wedding present for an American heiress who brought nobility into her family by marrying a Spanish count. Set among 22 wooded acres, this mellow brick building, based on a 16th-century Florentine palazzo, is nothing short of baronial. Step into the great hall: The sheer style of the open staircase, the balustraded gallery, and the large Tiffany windows are breathtaking. Everything here is vast, including the beds. Guest rooms have high ceilings, intricate plaster moldings (more than 150 artisans were brought from Italy to complete the detailed decoration), and English antiques; nine have working fireplaces with big, elegant marble surrounds.

Though it has much to recommend it, Wheatleigh has suffered from a mixed reputation over the years, with rumblings about the service and the unconventional—some say tasteless—mixture of antique and modern styles. The furnishings have been toned down to mostly classical pieces, the place has been repainted, and the rooms were refurbished in 1993 to give the inn an elegant new front. The service too seems up to scratch, with general manager François Thomas in charge, and virtually anything is available to guests, from in-room massage to breakfast in bed. The rarefied environment is not well suited to young children.

The main restaurant, another huge room with elegant marble fireplaces and cutglass chandeliers, has an excellent reputation for its "contemporary classical" cuisine; the $55 or $68 prix-fixe menus (with 18% service charge) include roast antelope, pheasant, rabbit, and lobster; the Grill Room also serves full meals in a more casual setting.

🏨 *17 doubles with bath. 2 restaurants; air-conditioning; TV/VCRs, phones in rooms; room service; tennis; pool; fitness room; massage room. $175–$565; breakfast extra. AE, DC, MC, V. No pets. 3-night minimum during Tanglewood and holiday weekends.*

Whistler's Inn

5 Greenwood St., Lenox 01240, tel. 413/ 637–0975, fax 413/637–2190

Elegant, ornate, and somehow exotic, Whistler's Inn stands apart from its nearby competitors, with lavish Louis XVI antiques in the parlor; heavy, dark wood furniture in the baronial dining hall; and African artifacts in the office. Innkeepers Joan and Richard Mears, with their easy style, maintain an extraordinary ambience at this English Tudor mansion, built in 1820 by railroad tycoon Ross Wynans Whistler.

The Mearses, who have owned Whistler's since 1978, are widely traveled hosts and great conversationalists. Richard, a published novelist, and Joan, formerly a teacher of art and English, continue to work on new writing projects.

Public rooms are impressive, with Chippendale furniture, ornate antiques (including Louis XVI palace mirrors, candelabra, clocks, and love seats), chandeliers, original artwork, Persian rugs, and marble fireplaces. A Steinway grand piano graces the music room/parlor, and next door is a well-stocked library, where you can partake of complimentary sherry, port, or afternoon tea. The dining room or the sunporch provides a restful setting for breakfast. Be sure to peek at the Mearses' first-floor office—it features many souvenirs brought back from their travels, including African pieces and a large wooden elephant puppet from a maharaja's palace.

Guest rooms are attractively decorated with designer draperies and bedspreads. They vary in size from the large master bedroom to two small chambers beneath the eaves. All are furnished with antiques (one has a Chippendale armoire), and some have working fireplaces. Most rooms have superb views across the small valley that includes 7 acres of private gardens, a croquet lawn, and a badminton court. This peaceful place is only a short walk from the center of Lenox.

🏨 *14 doubles with bath. Dining room, air-conditioning in most rooms, phones in all rooms, croquet, badminton. $90– $225; full breakfast, afternoon tea. AE, D, MC, V. No smoking, no pets. 3-night minimum weekends July–Aug. and Oct.*

The Williamsville Inn

Rte. 41, West Stockbridge 01266, tel. 413/ 274–6118, fax 413/274–3539

Situated a couple miles south of West Stockbridge, this inn was purchased in 1990 by Kathleen Ryan and her daughter, Gail, from New York. With backgrounds in acting and real estate, they've combined their talents to re-create the atmosphere of an 1790s farmhouse, complete with extensive vegetable and flower gardens. In warm weather they create a sculpture garden with works by local artists placed at various spots on their broad lawn.

Guest rooms have wide-board floors, embroidered chairs, and four-poster and canopy beds—all in the 18th-century American style; several chambers also contain working fireplaces, and those beneath the eaves have sloping roofs. The former barn has been turned into spacious guest rooms that have a country look and four-poster or brass beds and woodstoves.

Four dining rooms with fireplaces overlook the surrounding woodland. The chef, Susan Donaghey, serves gourmet country cuisine with produce from the garden. Seasonal specialties include sorrel and red onion tart or wild leek, asparagus, and potato soup, followed by swordfish in Moroccan tomato sauce or roast duck with duck-leg confit seasoned

with green olives and rosemary. On the grounds you can play horseshoes, croquet, badminton, and volleyball.

▥ *15 doubles with bath, 1 suite. Restaurant, bar, air-conditioning, pool, tennis. $105–$185; full breakfast. AE, MC, V. No smoking, no pets. 3-night minimum July–Aug., 2-night minimum Oct. and holiday weekends.*

Windflower Inn

684 S. Egremont Rd., Great Barrington 01230, tel. 413/528–2720 or 800/992–1993, fax 413/528–5147

Barbara and Gerald Liebert of Vermont bought this inn in 1980 as a 25th wedding-anniversary present to themselves; they still enjoy running the place with the help of their daughter and son-in-law, Claudia and John Ryan.

A comfortable, casual atmosphere prevails, yet the inn is professionally managed. Barbara and Claudia—both former chefs—do all the cooking, and everything is homemade, often with produce and herbs from the inn's organic garden. Breakfasts are served either in the sunny dining room or on the screened porch. The living room has a big fireplace, a cloverleaf marble coffee table, and couches, while a second sitting area with a piano opens onto the porch. Bedrooms vary in size, but most are spacious; they're furnished with four-poster beds and filled with antiques, including Victorian washing jugs and bowls. Several rooms contain working fireplaces; the most impressive one has a stone surround that takes up an entire wall. Outside, the nearly 10 acres of land include a large lawn, a picturesque pond, and a swimming pool.

▥ *13 doubles with bath. Air-conditioning, TVs in rooms; pool. $100–$170; full breakfast, afternoon tea. AE. Smoking in living room only, no pets. 3-night minimum summer weekends and holidays, 2-night minimum other weekends in foliage season.*

Vermont

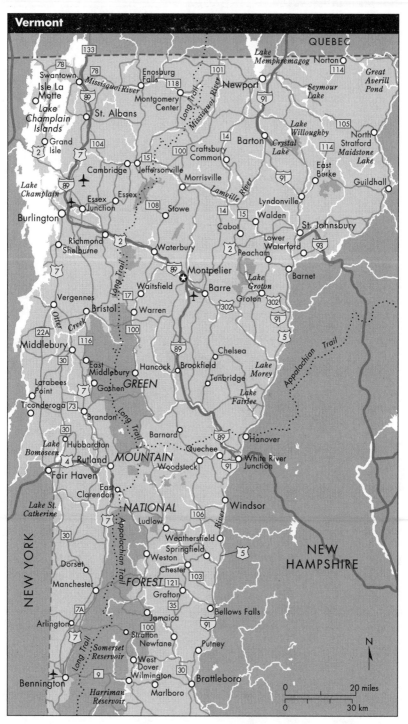

Vermont

QUEBEC

Lake Memphremagog
Norton
Great Averill Pond

133
78
78
89
Swantown
Isle La Motte
Lake Champlain Islands

Missisquoi River

Enosburg Falls
Montgomery Center

St. Albans

Long Trail
101
118
Newport
91

Seymour Lake

114

104
2
7
Grand Isle

Missisquoi River

14
Barton
Lake Willoughby
Crystal Lake
105
North Stratford
Maidstone Lake

100
Craftsbury Common

114
East Burke
Guildhall

15
Jeffersonville
Cambridge
Morrisville

Lamoille River

Lyndonville

Lake Champlain

89
Essex Junction
Essex
108
Stowe

14
15
Walden
Cabot

St. Johnsbury

Burlington

Richmond
Shelburne

2
Waterbury

2
Peacham
Lower Waterford
93
Barnet

7

Long Trail

Montpelier
89
Waitsfield
Barre

Lake Groton
Groton
302
302
91

Vergennes
Bristol
17
Warren

Otter Creek

100
5

22A
116
Middlebury

89
Chelsea

30
East Middlebury
Hancock
Brookfield
Lake Morey
Appalachian Trail

Larabees Point
7
Goshen
GREEN
Tunbridge
Lake Fairlee

Ticonderoga
73
Brandon

Long Trail

30
Hubbardton
Lake Bomoseen
Barnard
89
Quechee
Hanover

4
Rutland
MOUNTAIN
Woodstock
White River Junction
91

Fair Haven

Lake St. Catherine
East Clarendon

NATIONAL
River
Windsor

NEW YORK

7
Ludlow
106

30
Weathersfield
Springfield
5

Dorset
Weston
Chester
103

FOREST
121
Grafton

NEW HAMPSHIRE

Manchester
Appalachian Trail

7A
35
Bellows Falls

Arlington
100
Jamacia
91

7
Stratton
Newfane
Putney

Somerset Reservoir
West Dover
Wilmington
30

9
Brattleboro

Bennington
Marlboro

Harriman Reservoir

N

0   20 miles
0   30 km

Southeastern Vermont

Kedron Valley Inn

There are no big cities in southeastern Vermont. On the contrary, this is a region where, even more than the rest of the state, charm is on a small scale. Once you leave I–91, which parallels the Connecticut River along the state's eastern edge, the countryside is a marvelous patchwork of small towns and surrounding farms.

What brings visitors back year after year are the varied pleasures of the different seasons. Summer means driving, biking, or hiking along tree-shaded back roads or trails; stopping at a small country store for a cool drink; shopping for handmade crafts both traditional and contemporary; or just sitting on the front porch doing nothin' much. Autumn, with every hill a palette of color, is peak season—the time of year when the region is practically overrun with leaf peepers checking the daily foliage reports and creeping along the highways gasping at every new vista. Winter brings skiers as well as those whose idea of a winter sport is drinking cocoa by a roaring fire. Spring's shoots of greenery may exhilarate those who have been cooped up all winter and are eager for a drive in the country, but most locals think of it simply as

"mud season," when thawing snow turns roads to muck and many businesses close to make necessary repairs.

But it doesn't really matter during which season you visit: At any time of year southeastern Vermont is an ideal place to escape to a quieter way of life, if only for a day or two.

Places to Go, Sights to See

Billings Farm and Museum (Rte. 12, ½ mi north of Woodstock, tel. 802/457–2355). The exhibits in the reconstructed farmhouse, school, general store, and workshop demonstrate the daily activities of early Vermont settlers. It is financed by the same Rockefeller money that has helped preserve the town of *Woodstock*, 4 mi west of Quechee, with its tree-lined village green, its exquisitely preserved Federal houses, and its covered bridge.

Catamount Brewing Company (58 S. Main St., White River Junction, tel. 802/296–2248; Windsor Industrial Park, Windsor, tel. 800/540–2248). Vermont isn't lagging behind in contributing to the country's newfound passion for quality beer: Catamount is the state's largest craftbrewery, especially after the opening of their second establishment in Windsor. The company makes a blonde ale, an American amber, and a dark porter, as well as a wide range of seasonal and specialty brews. Tours and tastings are available.

Grafton. This almost-too-picturesque village at the intersection of Routes 35 and 121 got a second lease on life when the Windham Foundation provided funds for the restoration of most of the town's crisp white 18th- and 19th-century houses; you might also note the absence of power lines and telephone poles. It now ranks among the most charming hamlets in the state. About 12 mi south on Route 30 is Newfane, whose town green also is a perennial favorite; the *Newfane Country Store* (tel. 802/365–7916) has a wonderful selection of quilts and homemade fudge.

Green Mountain Flyer (tel. 802/463–3069). This train takes visitors on a 26-mi round-trip from Bellows Falls (on the Connecticut River about 12 mi east of Grafton) to Chester and Ludlow in cars that date from the golden age of railroads. The journey goes through scenic countryside that includes the Broadway Mills Gorge. It is also possible to begin your excursion from Chester; call for departure times and fares.

Kelley Stand Road. This backcountry forest road runs from Arlington to just north of Mt. Snow on Route 100 and accesses the *Long and Appalachian trails,* as well as *Grout Pond Recreation Area* and *Somerset Reservoir*—both ideal picnicking and boating spots.

Molly Stark Trail (Route 9). Running from Brattleboro to Bennington, this is the principal east–west highway through southern Vermont. Along the eastern half of the road lies Marlboro, home of the annual summer *Marlboro Music*

Festival of classical music, which draws musicians and audiences from around the world. The *Southern Vermont Natural History Museum* (tel. 802/464–0048) atop Hogback Mountain, has sweeping views of the countryside and houses the Luman Nelson New England Wildlife Collection, a fascinating and comprehensive taxidermy display of New England game.

Quechee Gorge. The 165-ft drop to the bottom of the 1-mi-long Quechee Gorge (6 mi west of White River Junction) is an impressive sight, and many visitors picnic nearby or scramble down one of several descents to get a closer look. Nearby, in the village of Quechee, the *Simon Pearce* glassblowing factory (Main St., tel. 802/295–2711) houses a pottery workshop, a retail shop, and a restaurant with a wonderful view of the Ottauquechee River.

Vermont Country Store (Rte. 100, tel. 802/824–3184). More a way of life than a retail store, this old-fashioned emporium in Weston still sells such nearly forgotten items from the past as Lilac Vegetal aftershave, Monkey Brand black tooth-powder, Flexible Flyer sleds, Vermont Common Crackers, pickles in a barrel, and tiny wax bottles of colored sugar water.

Restaurants

At **Simon Pierce** (Main St., tel. 802/295–1470), in Quechee, the sparkling glassware from the studio downstairs accents Irish specialties inspired by the owner's background. The **Four Columns Inn** (West St., tel. 802/365–7713), in Newfane, is well known for its exquisite, regionally inspired cuisine. The **Common Ground** (25 Elliot St., tel. 802/257–0855), in Brattleboro, is the place to go for a funkier, down-to-earth vegetarian meal. In the Mt. Snow area, **Doveberry's** (Rte. 100, West Dover, tel. 802/464–5652) serves authentic northern Italian dishes in a dark, inviting red-carpeted room; **Two Tannery Road** (Off Rte. 100, Tannery Rd., West Dover, tel. 802/464–2707) is another local favorite, serving variations on Continental cuisine in an 18th-century restored farmhouse; **Le Petit Chef** (Rte. 100, Wilmington, tel. 802/464–8437) has French fare and a warm, casual atmosphere.

Nightlife and the Arts

The **Weston Playhouse** (Rte. 100, on the village green, tel. 802/824–5288) is a local favorite for a summer night's drama, as is the **Saxtons River Playhouse** (Saxtons River, tel. 802/869–2030). Try the **Mole's Eye Cafe** (High St., tel. 802/257–0771), in Brattleboro, for live music: Folk on Wednesday and danceable R&B, blues, or reggae on weekends.

Reservations Service

Vermont Centerpoint Reservation Service (Box 8513, Essex 05451, tel. 802/872–2745 or 800/449–2745).

Visitor Information

Great Falls Regional Chamber of Commerce (Box 554, Bellows Falls 05101, tel. 802/463–4280), **Mt. Snow–Haystack Region Chamber of Commerce** (Main St., Box 3, Wilmington 05363, tel. 802/464–8092), **Quechee Chamber of Commerce** (Box 106, Quechee 05059, tel. 802/295–7900 or 800/295–5451), **Vermont Chamber of Commerce** (Dept. of Travel and Tourism, Box 37, Montpelier 05602, tel. 802/223–3443), **Vermont Travel Division** (134 State St., Montpelier 05602, tel. 802/828–3326 or 800/VERMONT), **White River Area Chamber of Commerce** (Box 697, White River Junction 05001, tel. 802/295–6200), **Woodstock Area Chamber of Commerce** (4 Central St., Woodstock 05091, tel. 802/457–3555).

The Chester Inn at Long Last

Main St. (Box 589), Chester 05143, tel. 802/875-2444 or 888/243-7466, fax 802/875-6414

In 1997 Mary Ann and Bill Kearns left careers as a caterer and an attorney to move from California with their five daughters to this Victorian country inn. Although not overly luxurious, this grand old lodging invites respect as the focal point of Chester's small town center. Guest rooms are decorated simply (many have memorabilia and quilts on the walls), and bathrooms are small. The Dickens Room, whose bed has a high, carved headboard, is the most spacious, and the Audubon and Tiffany rooms offer access to the second-story porch. Bookshelves in the large wood-paneled library invite inspection. Guests often gather for after-dinner drinks near the enormous fieldstone fireplace in the pine-floor lobby. The spectacular mahogany bar with its marble top gives the dining room a turn-of-the-century opulence; dinner here might feature broiled swordfish steak—marinated in an Asian sauce—with jalapeño-peach chutney. Breakfast, which is also served in this room, always includes Mary Ann's homemade baked goods and such entrées as salmon scrambled eggs.

The town of Chester is fairly sleepy. If you have an interest in history, you'll enjoy strolling through the nearby "stone village," a cluster of privately owned Civil War–era stone houses that town legend says may have been part of the Underground Railroad.

⊞ *26 doubles with bath. Restaurant, TV in public area, 2 tennis courts. $110; full breakfast. MC, V. No smoking, no pets. 2-day minimum some holidays and foliage season weekends. Closed 1st 3 wks of Apr., 2 wks in Nov.*

The Deerhill Inn

Off Rte. 100, Valley View Rd. (Box 136), West Dover 05356, tel. 802/464-3100 or 800/993-3379, fax 802/464-5474

Up on a ridge, this English country-style inn has public areas with west-facing windows and views of the valley below and the ski slopes across the way. Longtime Deerhill Valley residents, Linda and Michael Anelli can provide a wealth of information on activities in the area. After successfully owning and operating a restaurant for six years, the Anelli's bought the Deerhill Inn in 1994 and have embraced their roles as innkeepers. The decor is bright and cheery; incredible attention to detail is evident in every corner of the inn. A huge fireplace dominates the living room, while English hand-painted yellow wallpaper, a garden-scene mural, emerald green carpet, and collections of antique plates accent the dining rooms. Each guest room has an endearing quality: One has an Asian bedroom set, and another has a high ceiling and a Laura Ashley decor; many have fireplaces or hand-painted murals. The four balcony rooms are the most spacious and great views. Michael is the chef and serves upscale comfort food that might include fresh fish, veal medallion with wild mushrooms in a lemon cream sauce, or a black pepper sirloin steak. Breakfast is equally inviting; early risers might get a show from the birds that gather at the feeders outside the large dining room windows.

⊞ *13 doubles with bath, 2 suites. Restaurant, TV/VCR in common area, pool, tennis court. $90–$260; full breakfast. AE, MC, V. No smoking, no pets. 2-night minimum most weekends.*

Eaglebrook of Grafton

Main St., Grafton 05146, tel. 802/843–2564

Tired of conventionally charming country decor? Marge and Eli Prouty have combined a historic house and well-preserved antiques with touches of city sophistication. With the collection of abstract art and the contemporary cathedral-ceiling sunroom overlooking the Saxtons River, the elegant retreat feels like a home that might have been featured in a glossy interior-design magazine.

Of special interest are the pastel watercolor stencils in the hallways, done by an itinerant stenciler in 1840 and restored during the 1950s. Fireplaces with soapstone mantels are everywhere; there are seven in all. Blue-checked fabric gives one of the rooms a French-provincial air; another leans toward American country; a third has a Victorian flavor. Bathrooms are new and comfortable, and the second-story balcony has a view of Bear Mountain. In summer the lushly landscaped stone terrace is a perfect place to sip sherry in the evening or partake of the buffet breakfast served from a long Mennonite table and warmed by the large cooking fireplace complete with a beehive oven.

▥ *1 double with bath, 2 doubles share bath. $80–$85; full breakfast. MC, V. No smoking, no pets. Closed Christmas wk.*

Four Columns

West St. (Box 278), Newfane 05345, tel. 802/365–7713 or 800/787–6633, fax 802/365–0022

With its village green surrounded by pristine white buildings, Newfane has often been called the quintessential New England town, and the Four Columns is part of the reason. Erected in 1832 for a homesick Southern bride, the majestic white columns of this Greek Revival mansion are more intimidating than the Colonial-style rooms inside. Room 1, in the older section, is the most private, with a large seating area and an enclosed porch that overlooks the town common. Room 3 has a double whirlpool bath, and seven of the rooms have gas fireplaces. The Honeymoon Room has a large, marble-tiled bathroom complete with a woodstove and a daybed. New innkeepers Pam and Gorty Baldwin left jobs in Manhattan, as a paper merchant and book publisher, so they could own and operate a business together and raise their daughter in Vermont. They have furnished the guest rooms with antiques, brass beds, and quilts. The inn's restaurant, decorated with antique tools and copper pots, became famous under the direction of a former White House chef, René Chardain; his successor, Greg Parks, has maintained the restaurant's high standards and added his own seafood specialties to the menu.

▥ *15 doubles with bath. Restaurant; tavern; air-conditioning; TV in public area; phones, cassette players in all rooms; outdoor pool; hiking trails; 2 trout ponds. $110–$195, full breakfast; $210–$295, MAP (mandatory during foliage season). AE, D, DC, MC, V. No smoking, pets by prior arrangement. Closed Dec. 24–25.*

Governor's Inn

86 Main St., Ludlow 05149, tel. 802/228–8830 or 800/468–3766

The atmosphere at this formal little retreat just 10 minutes from the Okemo Mountain ski area is high Victorian. Everything from the vest-pocket lobby, where afternoon tea is served, to the innkeepers' collection of antique teacups and chocolate pots evokes a turn-of-the-century elegance. As visitors learn during Deedy Marble's orientation tour, the governor in question is Vermont governor William Wallace Stickney, who in 1890 had the house built as a wedding present for his wife; the bride and groom's portraits still hang near the faux-marble fireplace in the living room. These romantic beginnings haven't been

forgotten by innkeepers Deedy and her husband, Charlie, who have created an appealing hideaway for honeymooners and couples celebrating anniversaries. The new third-floor suite is very private and has fantastic views of the mountains, a whirlpool tub, and an enormous floral daybed. Room 7 comes with a telescope for stargazing or watching skiers descend the slopes. The Marbles' thoughtful attention to detail is evident everywhere: the inn's wide-plank pine floors gleam; lace-trimmed floral-chintz duvets on the beds match the sheets, and terry-cloth robes hang in the closets; arriving guests find glasses and miniature cordials in their rooms; and the inn's special chocolates appear every evening when the beds are turned down.

The hosts take as much pleasure in entertaining their guests as in providing a restful atmosphere. It was partly because they had become so proficient at orchestrating elaborate dinner parties for friends that they finally left management jobs in 1981 to open an inn. Before welcoming their first guests, however, they decided to hone their skills at Roger Verge's famed cooking school in the south of France. As a result of the Marbles' training (and their flair for presentation), the six-course dinners at the Governor's Inn border on the theatrical. Fresh-faced waitresses in floral skirts, white high-neck blouses, and mobcaps announce each course. Guests dine by candlelight with table settings of antique bone china and sterling silver and often linger over meals that might include hot wine broth, Cornish hens with cinnamon glaze and apple and pâté stuffing, and Edwardian cream with raspberry sauce. The award-winning apple pie is especially recommended. Charlie is in charge of breakfast, which often includes his signature rum-raisin French toast.

🏨 *8 doubles with bath, 1 suite. Restaurant, air-conditioning, game room. $190–$240 MAP, afternoon tea; B&B rates available. MC, V. No smoking, no pets. 2-night minimum weekends, 3–4 night minimum holidays and at Christmastime. Restaurant closed Mon.–Tues. and Apr.*

Hickory Ridge House

Hickory Ridge Rd. (R.D. 3, Box 1410), Putney 05346, tel. 802/387–5709 or 800/ 380–9218, fax 802/387–5387

Innkeepers often have interesting backgrounds, but Steve Anderson's may be one of the most unusual; in his pre-Vermont life, he was both a professor and chimney sweep. He and wife Jacquie Walker have since turned a stately 1808 Federal mansion into a homey B&B in which the unusually spacious rooms reflect the original owner's fortune. Putney was one of the centers of the 1960s back-to-the-land movement, and traces of that ethos are still evident in the vegetarian breakfasts served at Hickory Ridge. Home-baked breads, stuffed pumpkin pancakes, and various soufflés are some of the inn's specialties.

The rooms feature country farmhouse decor that is simple yet comfortable; four of them have fireplaces. Rag rugs cover pine floors, lace curtains hang in the windows, and walls are painted in cheerful pastels. Rooms in the newer section, merely 100 years old, have low ceilings, but they're as comfortable as the rest of the B&B. Bathrooms have large tubs, a rare and welcome amenity. Perennial gardens ring the property, and ski trails wind through 12 acres of surrounding woodland.

🏨 *3 doubles with bath, 4 doubles share 3 baths. TV in public area. $50–$95; full breakfast. MC, V. No smoking, no pets. 2-night minimum holiday weekends.*

The Inn at Sawmill Farm

Rte. 100 (Box 367), West Dover 05356, tel. 802/464-8131 or 800/493-1133, fax 802/464-1130

Staying at this aristocratic inn in the Haystack Mountain–Mt. Snow ski region is like being a guest at the country home of a British lord whose family fortune is still intact. In 1968 architect Rodney Williams and his wife, Ione, an interior designer, bought a dairy farm that dated from 1897, but don't expect a rugged rural retreat. The decor here may be country, but it's the kind of country featured in glossy home-and-garden magazines: There's a polished copper milk tank used as a table base, a plaid carpet, a brick foyer decorated with a horse collar and farm tools, and chamber music piped into the low-ceilinged reception area. The atmosphere is on the formal side—the owners prefer that men wear jackets in the public areas after 6 PM—and caters to a select clientele. Guests like to congregate around the huge fireplace in the living room in winter with their afternoon tea or stroll by one of the two ponds when it's warm.

Wallpaper in the guest rooms matches the bedspreads and upholstery; one room might be all soft pastels, another bright with vibrant hues. The carpet is thick enough to swallow high heels. The beds all have down comforters and might be decorated with a tiny lace pillow, or a wall might display a framed quilt sample. Some bathrooms have whirlpool tubs. The 10 rooms in the main building are somewhat smaller than the remaining rooms (some are suites), which have working fireplaces and are in buildings scattered throughout the 28-acre property.

The Williamses' son, Brill, presides as chef in the two restaurants, one of which is a formal dining room with six tables, an antique sideboard, Early American portraits, Queen Anne furniture, and a baby grand piano. In the second, a green-houselike area, simple whitewashed timber pillars contrast nicely with silver napkin rings. The wine list has won numerous awards and has more than 160 labels. The menu features such entrées as roasted semiboneless *poussin* with apple and sausage stuffing or rack of lamb for two with mint sauce. A breakfast specialty is shirred eggs with Vermont smoked ham and cheddar cheese.

🏠 *20 doubles with bath. Restaurant, air-conditioning, TV in public area, pool, tennis court, 2 trout ponds. $340–$425; MAP. AE, MC, V. No smoking, no pets. 2-night minimum weekends. Closed Apr.–mid-May.*

Inn at Weathersfield

Rte. 106, Weathersfield 05151, tel. 802/263-9217 or 800/477-4828, fax 802/263-9219

In this rambling Colonial farmhouse, built in 1795, visitors are greeted in the entry by Terry and Mary Carter and by the smell of hot apple cider simmering in an iron kettle over an open hearth. The wide-plank floors, brick beehive oven, and candlelight lend authenticity to this keeping room. The Carters enhance the Early American feel by illuminating the common areas with candles—seven dozen tapers daily.

The 10 rooms and two suites are distinctly decorated with period antiques, and each is inspired by and named after a famous love story; one room even contains a glass case displaying gifts Terry's grandmother received at her wedding. In the Twelve Oaks Room, swaths of lace over the iron bedstead form a canopy anchored by a bouquet of dried flowers. Wuthering Heights has yellow rag-roll-painted walls; a faux-marble fireplace; three skylights; and a private deck. A camelback trunk sits at the foot of a four-poster bed in one room; a stenciled Windsor chair and hardwood floors lend simple grace to another. Eight rooms have working fireplaces, and Colonial spareness doesn't preclude such modern

comforts as electric blankets. Some bathrooms are small and have 1940s-style fixtures, though one of the suites does have a two-person whirlpool. The inn has several gathering areas, including a tavern, a library, a formal parlor, and a lounge called the Prentis Room.

In the afternoon there's a lavish English tea, complete with homemade pastries and hors d'oeuvres served from silver chafing dishes. This is only a warm-up for dinner, which might include rack of lamb—with mustard, herbs, and raspberry sauce—or salmon Wellington. On the weekends there's often dinner music on the dining room's grand piano. At Sunday breakfast you are often treated to a poetry reading by Harold Groat, an eighth-generation Vermonter.

🏨 *10 doubles with bath, 2 suites. Restaurant, TV/VCR in game room, exercise equipment, sauna, pool table. $185–$225; MAP, afternoon tea. AE, D, DC, MC, V. No smoking, no pets. 2-night minimum most weekends, 3-night minimum holiday weekends.*

Juniper Hill Inn

Juniper Hill Rd. (R.R. 1, Box 79), Windsor 05089-9703, tel. 802/674–5273 or 800/359–2541, fax 802/674–2041

An expanse of green lawn with Adirondack chairs and a small pond sweeps up to the white-columned portico of this Greek Revival mansion. Built at the turn of the century by William Maxwell Evarts, the grandfather of the distinguished book publisher Maxwell Evarts Perkins, the structure is now a national landmark. The central living room, once the ballroom, has hardwood floors, oak paneling, Asian carpets, wing chairs and sofas, and a massive 15-ft-long oak table—one of the home's original furnishings. There are also two more-intimate common areas—the sitting parlor and the library—to suit your mood. An impressive staircase sweeps up past a large Palladian window to the

spacious guest rooms, some of which have fireplaces, marble sinks in the bathrooms, and brass or four-poster beds. Many rooms have views of the distant hills; one even has a small porch. The rooms are all decorated with Edwardian and Queen Anne furnishings.

Breakfast and dinner (a four-course candlelighted affair) are served in the stately mauve-color dining room. There is also a smaller private dining room for special occasions. Both rooms have fireplaces. You can tour Windsor's Old Constitution House, where the document that made Vermont an independent republic was signed, or explore the Windsor-Cornish covered bridge, the longest in New England. Innkeepers Rob and Susanne Pearl also can recommend hiking and cross-country ski trails in the area.

🏨 *16 doubles with bath. Restaurant, TV in public area, ceiling fans, pool, hiking and cross-country ski trails nearby. $90–$150; full breakfast, afternoon refreshments. D, MC, V. No smoking, no pets. Closed Apr., 2 wks in Nov.*

Kedron Valley Inn

Rte. 106, South Woodstock 05071, tel. 802/457–1473 or 800/836–1193, fax 802/457–4469

A strong sense of family strikes visitors as soon as they step into Max and Merrily Comins's inn; in 1985 they moved from New York and began the renovation of what in the 1840s had been the National Hotel, one of the state's oldest. Mannequins in the entry hall wear the antique wedding dresses of Merrily and her grandmother, the couple's collection of family quilts is scattered throughout the inn, and framed antique linens deck the walls. But the dresses and quilts are not the only reason for the inn's familial flavor. This is one of the rare antiques-filled inns that welcomes children, who are encouraged to build sand castles on the pond's small beach.

Refugees from the big city will find the country charm they're looking for in the hand-stenciled walls and four-poster canopy beds with white-chenille bedspreads and peony-patterned pastel sheets. Many rooms have either a fireplace or a Franklin stove, some have whirlpool tubs, and each is decorated with a quilt. One room has a walk-in safe built when the inn was a stagecoach stop. Two rooms have private decks, another has its own veranda, and a fourth has a terrace overlooking a stream that runs through the inn's 15 acres. Families often are housed in one of six units in a one-story log building at the back of the property. Here the rooms are lined up ski-lodge style and are more rustic than those in the main house. They're decorated with a mix of antiques and reproductions.

The lounge is rather small, but the porch is ample and perfect for lazing away an afternoon in a rocking chair. The dining room, where Max serves as host in the evenings, specializes in French dishes with a nouvelle twist: fillet of salmon stuffed with herb seafood mousse in a puff pastry or a boneless breast of chicken studded with roasted pistachio nuts, sautéed and served with a light beurre-blanc sauce.

The bustling town of Woodstock is nearby for strolling or shopping, as is Kedron Valley Stables—an operation not affiliated with the inn—which offers trail rides and lessons. Depending on the season, mountain biking, hiking, and cross-country skiing are just out the door.

🏠 *26 doubles with bath. Restaurant, lounge, TV in rooms, swimming pond. $120–$215; full breakfast. AE, D, MC, V. 2-night minimum weekends, mid-Sept.– late Oct. and Dec. 24–Jan. 1; 3-night minimum holiday weekends. Closed Apr.*

The Old Tavern at Grafton

Rte. 121, Grafton 05146, tel. 802/843–2231 or 800/843–1801, fax 802/843–2245

White-columned porches wrap around both stories of the Old Tavern's main building, creating an impressive facade. The history here is even more impressive. It has been an inn almost continuously since it was built in 1801, and the old guest register bears signatures of such prominent visitors as Daniel Webster and Nathaniel Hawthorne. Yet the Old Tavern hardly shows its age. In 1963 the Windham Foundation began to buy and restore historic homes like this one in and around Grafton. Thanks to the foundation, you can now indulge in creative idleness amid perfectly preserved white-clapboard buildings. Why not stroll to the stream that flows through the center of town; linger on the Old Tavern's porch; take a horse-drawn carriage tour; or read the notices on the bulletin board at the general store?

The inn's main building has 14 rooms, the oldest just above the lobby. There are also 22 rooms in the restored Windham and Homestead houses across the street and 7 guest houses, all with full kitchens. Main building guest rooms evoke New England's 18th-century frontier days. Each is decorated with country antiques; some have crocheted canopies or four-poster beds that could easily be as old as the inn itself. The newer rooms are generally sunnier and are decorated with bright pastels.

There's a well-stocked library off the main building's lobby, and the Phelps Barn in the back houses a comfortable tavern with authentic English pub furniture; you may want to stop by for afternoon tea. Both spots have brick fireplaces that invite you to linger long after dinner. Although breakfast is served in the solarium, there are also two dining rooms—one with Georgian furniture and oil portraits, the other with rustic paneling and low beams. Both

serve inspired New England cuisine: grilled choice sirloin steeped in McNeill's stout and a blend of spices or fresh spinach and egg fettuccine tossed with bay scallops, shrimp, and littleneck clams in a lightly brandied Parmesan cream sauce. Some offerings use cheddar cheese made just down the road at the Grafton Village Cheese Factory.

The trail system at Grafton Ponds, the Tavern's Nordic ski and mountain bike center, covers close to 2,000 acres. In winter skiing is guaranteed because of a state-of-the-art snow-making system.

🏠 *36 doubles with bath, 7 guest houses. Restaurant, lounge, TV in public area, game room, swimming pond, tennis courts, hiking, ice-skating, snowshoeing, tubing, cross-country skiing, mountain bikes. $125–$165 rooms, $500–$710 guest houses; Continental breakfast. MC, V. Smoking only in Phelps Barn, no pets. Closed Apr.*

Parker House

16 Main St., Box 0780, Quechee 05059, tel. 802/295–6077

Beside the Ottauquechee River and only minutes from the famous Quechee Gorge, the 1857 Parker House has a very picturesque setting. Although the two common sitting rooms are small and unexciting, the guest rooms are furnished in Victorian splendor, with soft peach and blue pastels predominating. Emily's Room has a marble fireplace, and Rebecca's Room has a matching armoire and dressing table with dyed-rosewood inlaid in a delicate floral pattern. From Joseph's and Walter's rooms you can see the river.

Innkeepers Barbara and Walt Forrester both have backgrounds in food. She's a pastry chef, and he's a graduate of the Culinary Institute of America, so the food is as delectable as the surroundings are posh. American comfort food, featuring New England products, is served in the intimate formal dining rooms that

are furnished with mauve and cream linens and are illuminated by candles. The terrace, which is used in summer and fall and is more casual, offers a spectacular river view. You are welcome to use the facilities of the Quechee Country Club, including a first-rate golf course, tennis courts, indoor and outdoor pools, and cross-country and downhill ski trails. You can also stroll next door to the Simon Pearce factory to watch glassblowers and potters at work and to buy their wares.

🏠 *7 doubles with bath. Restaurant, air-conditioning in some rooms, TV in public area, golf, swimming, skiing nearby. $100–$125; full breakfast. AE, MC, V. No pets. 2-night minimum during foliage season, commencement weekends, Christmas, and other holidays.*

Whetstone Inn

South Rd., Marlboro 05344, tel. 802/254–2500

A favorite of visitors to (and sometimes performers at) the Marlboro Music Festival, the 200-year-old Whetstone looks like a Colonial farmhouse might if it were decorated by Marimekko. This inn's beginnings as a stagecoach tavern are reflected in the pewter mugs that hang over the dining room mantel, the powder-horn rifle, and hand-hewn roof timbers. But the stenciled curtains, wide-plank floors, and Revolutionary War–era antiques are cheek to cheek with Scandinavian-style wall hangings and furnishings reminiscent of the '50s.

Innkeepers Harry and Jean Boardman are avid music lovers; the library has an extensive (and eclectic) record collection, as well as volumes of Thoreau, Tolstoy, Zola, Hugo, and Proust. Rooms added over the centuries have created a rabbit warren upstairs. All the rooms are light and furnished with a combination of antiques and family hand-me-downs. Jean is the breakfast cook; she also serves dinner on weekends and concert nights.

🏨 *8 doubles with bath, 4 doubles share bath. Restaurant, kitchenettes in 3 rooms, swimming and skating pond. $65–$95; breakfast extra. No credit cards. No smoking in public areas, pets allowed. 3-night minimum holiday and festival weekends.*

Windham Hill Inn

Windham Hill Rd. (10 mi north of Newfane), West Townshend 05359, tel. 802/874–4080 or 800/944–4080, fax 802/874–4080

If you happen to drive up a winding dirt road in the middle of nowhere on a summer's evening and hear strains of Bach or Vivaldi emanating from a rambling brick 1825 farmhouse, you'll have stumbled upon the Windham Hill Inn. The music room, the largest of the many public areas, has an 1888 Steinway grand piano and an 800-title CD collection; it also has its own deck.

Since 1993, innkeepers Pat and Grigs Markham have made extensive renovations, creating an exquisite country retreat. There's rarely a reason to leave the 160-acre property: Swimming, tennis, hiking, cross-country skiing, snowshoeing, and ice-skating are all here. If you'd rather, you can just curl up with a book on a window seat and take in the view of the West River valley.

The Markhams have retained the integrity of the old and incorporated the convenience and comfort of the new. Decadent, elegant touches abound. Guest rooms have antiques, cherry pencil-post canopy beds made by a local craftsman, fluffy comforters, and handmade quilts. Most rooms have fireplaces or Vermont Castings stoves, and several have large soaking tubs with gleaming oak handrails and brass fixtures. Don't let the weathered boards and uneven floors of the barn deceive you: The barn loft rooms are the newest and most luxurious. The Center Room has a cupola with a 360-degree bird's-eye view. The floor-to-ceiling bay window is the signature of the South Room.

The scene from the Frog Pond Dining Room is classic Vermont—a sloping meadow, still waters, and a stone wall that trails off in the distance. Enjoy the view while you feast on such dishes as ravioli with asparagus-artichoke filling in fumé blanc sauce or grilled mustard-seed-encrusted lamb loin with rosemary-Merlot sauce.

🏨 *21 doubles with bath. Restaurant; air-conditioning, phones in rooms; TVs in common rooms; pool; skating pond; tennis court; hiking; snowshoeing; cross-country ski trails. $230–$385; MAP, service charge included. AE, D, MC, V. No smoking, no pets. Closed Apr. and wk before Christmas.*

Southwestern Vermont

West Mountain Inn

This is where Vermont's tradition of rebellion and independence began. Many towns founded in the early 18th century as frontier outposts or fortifications became important trading centers. The state's second- and third-largest cities are here: Rutland is historically tied to the marble industry, and Bennington is where the Green Mountain Boys fought off both the British and the claims of New Yorkers—a battle some say their descendants are still fighting.

Because the southwest corner is a major gateway to Vermont, parts of the area also have a city sophistication: Many of the people who sought to escape New York's hustle and bustle have resettled here and brought with them radicchio, vintage wines, and marketing studies. Most residents, however, are determined to preserve the quality of life that lured them here, even as they go about giving a certain polished perfection to the image of an unspoiled paradise.

Arlington (about 15 mi north of Bennington) is proud of its association with Norman Rockwell, who lived here for 14 years; many of the models for his portraits of small-town life

were his neighbors here. A drive up Route 7A skirts along the eastern edge of the beautiful Green Mountain National Forest.

Places to Go, Sights to See

Bennington. Here, at the Catamount Tavern, Ethan Allen organized the Green Mountain Boys, who helped capture Ft. Ticonderoga in 1775. In 1777 American general John Stark urged his militia to attack the Hessians across the New York border: "There are the Redcoats; they will be ours or tonight Molly Stark sleeps a widow!" Now Vermont's third-largest city, Bennington has retained much of the industrial character it developed in the 19th century, when paper mills, gristmills, and potteries formed its economic base.

A Chamber of Commerce brochure has a self-guided walking tour through *Old Bennington,* a National Register Historic District just west of downtown, where impressive Greek Revival and sturdy brick Federal houses stand around a village green. In the graveyard of the Old First Church, the tombstone of poet Robert Frost proclaims: I HAD A LOVER'S QUARREL WITH THE WORLD. The *Bennington Museum* (W. Main St., tel. 802/447-1571) has a rich collection of Americana. Devotees of folk art will want to see the exhibit of the work of Grandma Moses, who lived and painted in the area. The museum is also known for its collections of glass (including some fine Tiffany specimens) and early Bennington pottery. Those in search of more recent examples of clay creations can visit the *Bennington Potters Yard* (324 County St., tel. 802/447-7531), which has a large store of seconds for sale.

Green Mountain National Forest. The 275,000 acres of Vermont's largest single wilderness area extend into the center of the state, providing scenic drives, picnic areas, campsites, lakes, and hiking and cross-country ski trails. The territory includes the 255-mi Massachusetts-to-Canada *Long Trail* (popular with serious hikers). The *Green Mountain Club* (tel. 802/244-7037) is a source of information about good places for day hikes and picnics.

Manchester. This has been a popular summer retreat since the mid-19th century, when Mary Todd Lincoln visited. *Manchester Village*'s tree-shaded marble sidewalks and stately old homes converted to B&Bs reflect the luxurious resort lifestyle of a century ago, while *Manchester Center*'s upscale factory-outlet stores appeal to the 20th-century's affluent ski crowd drawn by nearby Bromley and Stratton mountains.

Hildene (Rte. 7A, tel. 802/362-1788), the summer home of Abraham Lincoln's son Robert, is on the 412-acre estate of the former chairman of the board of the Pullman Company. His descendants lived here as recently as 1975. Tours include a walk through the 24-room Georgian Revival mansion and the elaborate formal gardens. The *Southern Vermont Art Center* (West Rd., tel. 802/362-1405), with its ever-changing exhibits and musical events, is also worth a visit.

Vermont Marble Exhibit (4 mi north of Rutland, tel. 802/459–2300). Here you can see masons transform rough stone into slabs, blocks, and decorative objects. This fascinating process is a *very* popular attraction.

Restaurants

Those who seek classic French cuisine in Old Bennington go to **Four Chimneys** (West Rd., tel. 802/447–3500), while those in search of down-home eats or all-day breakfasts head to the **Blue Benn Diner** (Rte. 7N, tel. 802/442–5140). The **Arlington Inn** (Rte. 7A, tel. 802/375–6532) has one of the most respected restaurants in the state, and **Wildflowers** (West Rd., tel. 802/362–2568), in the Reluctant Panther Inn in Manchester, has long been known for its elegant cuisine. **Laney's** (Rte. 11/30, tel. 802/362–4456), in Manchester, is a lively, contemporary place that has an open kitchen with a wood-fired brick oven, and **Bistro Henry's** (Rte. 11/30, tel. 802/362–4982), just up the road, has classic and innovative bistro fare such as braised lamb shank with balsamic glazed onions and garlic mashed potatoes. **Chantecleer** (Rte. 7A, East Dorset, tel. 802/362–1616) is refined and elegant, with entrées such as chateaubriand and veal chops.

Nightlife and the Arts

The **Dorset Playhouse** (tel. 802/867–2223 or 802/867–5777) hosts a resident professional troupe in summer and has performances by a community group in winter. In winter the Vermont Symphony Orchestra performs at Manchester's **Southern Vermont Art Center** (West Rd., tel. 802/362–1405), which is also the site of summer concerts. Try the numerous bars and clubs around the Killington and Mt. Snow ski areas for dancing and live music.

Reservations Services

Bennington Area Chamber of Commerce (Veterans Memorial Dr., Bennington 05201, tel. 802/447–3311), **Chamber of Commerce–Manchester and the Mountains** (R.R. 2, Box 3451, Manchester Center 05255, tel. 802/362–2100 or 800/752–9199), **Vermont Centerpoint Reservation Service** (Box 8513, Essex 05451, tel. 802/872–2745 or 800/449–2745).

Visitor Information

Bennington Area Chamber of Commerce (*see* Reservations Services, *above*), **Chamber of Commerce–Manchester and the Mountains** (*see* Reservations Services, *above*), **Rutland Region Chamber of Commerce** (256 N. Main St., Rutland 05701, tel. 802/773–2747), **Vermont Chamber of Commerce** (*see* Southeastern Vermont, *above*), **Vermont Travel Division** (*see* Southeastern Vermont, *above*).

Arlington Inn

Rte. 7A, Arlington 05250, tel. 802/375–6532 or 800/443–9442, fax 802/375–6534

The Greek Revival columns at the entrance of this carefully restored railroad magnate's home give the building an imposing presence. The rooms, however, are anything but intimidating. Their cozy charm is created by claw-foot tubs in some bathrooms, linens that coordinate with the Victorian-style wallpaper, maple ceilings, and the original moldings and wainscoting. The main section of the inn was built in 1848 by Martin Chester Deming, and rooms here are named after members of his family. The decor features Victorian antiques, massive headboards that tower over sleepers, and etched-glass shades on bronze Victorian oil lamps. The carriage house, built at the turn of the century and renovated in 1985, blends country French and Queen Anne period furnishings with folk art. The parsonage next door was added to the inn in 1996. It features hand-carved cherry furniture, TVs hidden in armoires, and phones in all the rooms. The main inn is separated from the road by a spacious lawn, so all guest rooms are quiet.

Innkeepers Deborah and Mark Gagnon traded their life in the financial world (he was in banking, she is a CPA) for this quiet New England town in 1994. While emphasizing the mansion's gracious social and historical significance, they have upgraded the rooms with such modern conveniences as queen- and king-size beds; rooms in the carriage house have become more inviting, with overstuffed chairs. Their efforts in the dining room are also commendable. In addition to using products from Vermont farms, such as buffalo raised in Manchester and pheasant from Dorset, the chef also prepares raised game, including antelope from Texas. Polished hardwood floors, green napkins and walls, candlelight, and soft music complement the elegant food. The Gagnons put on a full country breakfast, which is served in a marble-tiled solarium at the back of the inn.

Arlington is Norman Rockwell country, and the inn is within walking distance of a small exhibit devoted to his work.

🏠 *16 doubles with bath, 3 suites. Restaurant, lounge, air-conditioning, TV/VCR in public area, tennis court. $70–$195, full breakfast. AE, D, DC, MC, V. No pets. 2-night minimum most weekends. Restaurant closed Mon., Dec. 24, Jan. 1.*

The Battenkill Inn

Rte. 100 (Box 948), Manchester Village 05254, tel. 802/362–4213 or 800/441–1628, fax 802/362–0975

The hearts carved into the outside trim were final touches on this architectural gem that was built in 1840 as a wedding present; the rosebushes surrounding the grounds are a modern-day toast to that romance. Recently taken over by Laine and Yoshi Akiyama, who left careers with Disney Imagineering to begin an innkeeping adventure, this refurbished inn exudes all the elements you'd expect from a New England B&B.

Deep red wallpaper and dark green prints lure you into the dining and sitting rooms. Original wooden door and window frames, polished oak floors, and a grand curving walnut staircase all allow you to forgive the rather small bathrooms. Rooms in the rear have decks that look out toward a meadow and the Battenkill. The attentive hospitality and the breakfasts are fast becoming this inn's hallmarks. Raspberry-and-cream cheese-filled French toast is a favorite, and everything is made with low- or nonfat ingredients when possible.

🏠 *11 doubles with bath. Air-conditioning. $85–$155; full breakfast. AE, MC, V. No smoking, no pets.*

Blueberry Hill Inn

*Rte. 32, Goshen 05733, tel. 802/247–6735
or 800/448–0707, fax 802/247–3983*

If you're looking for a true escape affording total peace and quiet, you have found the perfect repose. Located in the Green Mountain National Forest and only accessible by dirt road, Blueberry Hill is an idyllic spot. The Colonial building is bordered by lush gardens, a stream, an apple orchard, and a pond with a wood-fired sauna on its bank. Many of the rooms have views of the surrounding mountains; all are furnished with antiques, quilts, and hot water bottles to warm winter beds. Rooms in the back of the inn are entered by a brick walkway through a greenhouse of blooming plants. Three rooms have lofts that can accommodate additional guests; the Moosalamoo Room is in a private cottage and also has a loft and a small sitting room. The open kitchen is a gathering spot and always has a jar full of the inn's famous chocolate-chip cookies. Tony Clark, innkeeper for more than 20 years, often joins guests for cocktails by the living room fireplace.

Blueberry Hill is probably best known for its ski touring center, which turns into a mountain biking mecca in the summer. There are also 45 mi of marked hiking trails. Robert Frost lived in this area, and the inn is not far from a nature trail that has Frost quotations posted along the way.

▦ *7 doubles with bath, 5 quadruples with bath. Restaurant, cross-country skiing, hiking, mountain biking, sauna. $95–$164 per person, MAP; B&B rates available. MC, V. No smoking, no pets. Closed Apr.*

Cornucopia

Rte. 30 (Box 307), Dorset 05251, tel. 802/867–5751 or 800/566–5751

The Cornucopia has only a few guest rooms, and this enables innkeepers Linda and Bill Ley to truly pamper their guests. You are welcomed into this 1880 Colonial house with champagne; a wake-up tray with flowers and coffee or tea served in English bone china is available in the morning; and at night you'll find a chocolate-covered butter crunch on your pillow. All rooms have Crabtree & Evelyn toiletries, terry robes, and either down comforters or quilts; three rooms have fireplaces, and most have canopy or four-poster beds. The entire first floor is a comfortable public area decorated with antiques and several grandfather clocks; the solarium overlooks English country gardens. The private cottage in the backyard has a loft bedroom with skylights, a living room with a cathedral ceiling and a fireplace, a full kitchen, and a patio.

The gourmet candlelighted breakfast always includes fresh fruit and might be followed by maple-swirl French toast soufflé or pecan, sausage, and apple crepes. The inn is an easy stroll from the center of historic Dorset village, with its crisp white buildings and town green.

▦ *4 doubles with bath, 1 cottage. Air-conditioning, phones. $115–$225, includes gratuities; full breakfast, afternoon refreshments. AE, MC, V. No smoking, no pets.*

1811 House

Rte. 7A (Box 39), Manchester 05254, tel. 802/362–1811 or 800/432–1811, fax 802/362–2443

Classic Colonial good looks and friendliness make the 1811 House the most enviable place to stay in town. The inn's handsome brown clapboard main building anchors the north end of Manchester Village, the charming alter ego of the outlet scene that is a mile north in Manchester Center. The contrast makes this inn that much more of a haven, where you could easily pass the day sinking into one of the common room's armchairs or strolling through the back lawns and gardens—if you ever leave your room at all, that is. Antiques, old portraits and

horse paintings, and wide-plank floorboards give the place an irresistible English country house atmosphere.

Parts of the inn date from 1770, and it has been in operation as a hostelry since 1811—the only break in service was when Abraham Lincoln's granddaughter used it for a summer house. She was among the New York elite who spent their summers in Manchester at the turn of the last century. The inn and other buildings in the village still have that aristocratic air.

Most of the guest rooms are spacious and have writing tables; six rooms have working fireplaces. The three rooms that face the town green have wonderful old fixtures in their bathrooms. Among them, the Robinson Room has its own porch with mountain views and a marble-walled shower room, and the front-corner Mary Lincoln Isham Room has a bed with a canopy of white chenille and is decorated with floral wallpaper and matching drapes. The view of the lawns and distant hills from its porch is splendid. Bathrooms in the separate cottage's three rooms (which are good for families) are the most modern.

Owners Bruce and Marnie Duff have done much to refine the 1811 house; their antiques and decorative touches are particularly appealing. Marnie and her staff present full, rich, and very tasty breakfasts—with scones, eggs and bacon, and potatoes and mushrooms—and Marnie makes delicious monster cookies that you'll find on the bar every afternoon. Bruce is an expert on single-malt scotches, and his cozy, English pub–style bar has the largest selection of them in the state—53 varieties strong. The bar area has a dartboard and is open to nonguests evenings 5:30–8. In the kitchen you can help yourself to tea or coffee all day. For Thanksgiving and on occasional gourmet weekends, Marnie prepares elaborate dinners.

▦ *11 doubles with bath, 3 cottage rooms. Bar, air-conditioning. $110–$200; full breakfast. AE, D, MC, V. No smoking, no pets. 2-night minimum weekends, holidays, and during foliage season. Closed Dec. 25.*

Hill Farm Inn

Just off Rte. 7A (R.R. 2, Box 2015), Arlington 05250, tel. 802/375-2269 or 800/882-2545

Just off Route 7A, this homey inn still has the feel of the farmhouse it once was. The mix of sturdy antiques and hand-me-downs, the spinning wheel in the upstairs hall, the paintings by a Hill family member, the jars of homemade jam that you can take away—all convey the relaxed, friendly personalities of innkeepers George and Joanne Hardy. Room 7, the newest, has a cathedral ceiling with beams and a porch with a view of Mt. Equinox; the rooms in the 1790 guest house provide guests with added privacy. The cabins are popular with families in summer.

An inn since 1905 and one of the first in the area, the Hill Farm's proximity to the Battenkill River has lured trout enthusiasts for decades. In fact, the surrounding farmland was deeded to the Hill family by King George III in 1775, and the farm is said to be one of the oldest in the state. It is now protected from development by the Vermont Land Trust. Hill Farm is also part of a wetlands restoration project that will add a pond and raised walkway from the inn to the surrounding marshland, enabling you to watch different forms of wildlife without disturbing the habitat.

▦ *6 doubles with bath, 5 doubles share 3 baths, 2 suites, 4 cabins (in summer only). Restaurant, TV in public area. $75–$125; full breakfast. AE, D, MC, V. No smoking, pets allowed only in cabins and 1 suite. 2-night minimum most weekends, 3-night minimum holiday weekends.*

The Inn at Ormsby Hill

Rte. 7A (R.R. 2, Box 3264), Manchester Center 05255, tel. 802/362–1163 or 800/ 670–2841, fax 802/362–5176

Built in 1764, this large Federal-style inn served as a hideout for Ethan Allen when he was pursued by British soldiers and later for slaves on the Underground Railroad. Innkeepers Chris and Ted Sprague are gracious hosts; their extensive renovations to the historic building have created interesting, romantic spaces. Guest rooms are done in bold colors and are furnished with antiques as well as a canopy or a four-poster bed. Many rooms have fireplaces that can be seen from the bed as well as the whirlpool tub; some rooms have a view of either the Green or Taconic mountains. The Taft Room has a vaulted ceiling, a sitting area, a fireplace, a double whirlpool, and a two-person shower. The Library Room has an original hand-hewn beam ceiling.

Sumptuous breakfasts are served in the sunlighted conservatory. Chris, a renowned chef, creates entrées such as risotto with pancetta and grilled Portobello mushrooms or baked orange French toast. The meal always ends with a dessert. If you're here on a Friday night, you can partake of a buffet supper that includes hearty soups and stews; on Saturday a four-course gourmet dinner is served.

🏠 *10 doubles with bath. Air-conditioning, phones in rooms; TV in common area. $115–225; full breakfast, afternoon tea. AE, MC, V. No smoking, no pets.*

Molly Stark Inn

1067 E. Main St., Bennington 05201, tel. 802/442–9631 or 800/356–3076, fax 802/ 442–5224

A stay at this Queen Anne–style B&B is like a stay with old friends. Innkeepers Reed and Cammi Fendler have created a truly relaxed atmosphere. Gleaming hardwood floors beckon you to a kitchen where you can prepare tea or coffee and grab a home-baked brownie or two before settling into a wing-back chair in front of the wood-burning stove.

Guest rooms are small (the attic suite is the largest of the lot) but charming: Antique quilts, claw-foot tubs, and thoughtfully placed country furnishings recall New England of a few generations ago. The secluded cottage—with its 16-ft ceiling, king-size brass bed, gas-powered stove, two-person Jacuzzi, and huge window facing the woods—is as romantic as it gets. Reed's genuine hospitality and quirky charisma delight guests as do his tasty full country breakfasts (known to feature cinnamon-apple, cheddar-cheese quiche), served in a new sunroom.

🏠 *4 doubles with bath, 2 triples with bath, 1 cottage. Air-conditioning in some rooms, ceiling fans in all rooms, TV in public area. $70–$95, cottage $145; full breakfast. AE, D, MC, V. No smoking, no pets. 2-night minimum weekends and holidays.*

Reluctant Panther

West Rd. (Box 678), Manchester 05254, tel. 802/362–2568 or 800/822–2331, fax 802/362–2586

Such luxurious touches as goose-down duvets and Pierre Deux linens are the norm here. The Colonial-style building dates from the 1850s, but rest assured that innkeepers Maye and Robert Bachofen have renovated with an eye toward modern convenience. Though soft grays and peach are the colors used throughout, be sure to check out the leaf-pattern wallpaper in the office (it's made from real leaves!). Furnishings are an eclectic mix of antique and contemporary. Ten rooms have fireplaces—the Mary Porter, Mark Skinner, and Ethan Allen suites even have two, one in each of the bathrooms. Suites have whirlpools; two have a double Jacuzzi. The best views are from Rooms B and D,

though Room J has windows on three sides. All rooms include a welcoming half-bottle of red wine.

The inn's restaurant, Wildflowers, has long been known for its elegant cuisine. Robert, former director of food and beverages at New York's Plaza Hotel, upholds that tradition magnificently. A huge fieldstone fireplace dominates the larger of the two dining rooms; the other is in a small greenhouse with five tables and night-blooming flowers. Wildflowers has the best selection of port in the state.

🆘 *12 doubles with bath, 5 suites. Restaurant; lounge; air-conditioning, phones, cable TV in rooms. $178–$375, MAP; B&B rates available. AE, MC, V. No smoking, no pets.*

South Shire Inn

124 Elm St., Bennington 05201, tel. 802/ 447-3839, fax 802/442-3547

Don't be discouraged when you drive through a rather mundane residential area to get here. This magnificent Victorian estate in a quiet neighborhood exhibits the same kind of craftsmanship evident in the grandiose summer homes of Newport. Canopy beds in thickly carpeted rooms, ornate plaster moldings, lead-glass bookcases, 10-ft ceilings, and a carved-wood fireplace in the library create turn-of-the-century grandeur.

Furnishings are antique except for reproduction beds, which provide for a little contemporary comfort. The four carriage house rooms are more modern and have high ceilings, fireplaces, and whirlpool tubs. The hayloft suite has exposed wooden beams and skylights. Innkeepers Kristina and Timothy Mast have placed a small journal by each bed so visitors can record memories of their stay. The full breakfast, which might include fresh fruit, homemade muffins, and the innkeepers' choice of stuffed French toast or pancakes, is served in the white wedding cake of a dining room. It's only

a short drive from the inn to Old Bennington, and you're within walking distance of the bus depot and downtown stores.

🆘 *9 doubles with bath. Air-conditioning, phones in all rooms; whirlpool baths in some rooms; TV in public area. $80– $165; full breakfast. AE, MC, V. No smoking, no pets. 2-night minimum most weekends.*

West Mountain Inn

River Rd. off Rte. 313, Arlington 05250, tel. 802/375-6516, fax 802/375-6553

This 1840s farmhouse, restored over the past 13 years, sits on 150 secluded acres. And everywhere you turn there are reminders of owners Wes and Mary Ann Carlson's idiosyncratic enthusiasms. Take the llama ranch on the property, which started as a hobby, or the small African violets in the guest rooms, which you can take home with you. A small pond is stocked with exotic goldfish, and squirrels feed outside the inn's windows. The Adirondack chairs on the front lawn are perfect for contemplating a spectacular view of the surrounding countryside, and in winter the sloping lawn practically cries for a sled.

Plush carpets, quilted bedspreads, fresh fruit in pottery bowls, trail maps, and copies of the books of local author Dorothy Canfield Fisher are among the luxurious guest-room touches. Rooms 2, 3, 4, and 5, in the front of the house, afford the same panorama as the front lawn (though there are almost no bad views in the place); the three small nooks of Room 11 resemble railroad sleeper berths and are perfect for children. A new children's room is brightly painted with life-size Disney characters and is fully stocked with games, stuffed animals, and a TV with a VCR. A spacious conference room has also been added with a cathedral ceiling, a fireplace, and a full kitchen.

You can gather in the library for happy hour, nibble on complimentary hors d'oeuvres, such as chicken fingers and fruit, and get acquainted with other guests before moving into the low-beamed, candlelighted paneled dining room for a six-course meal. The menu offers creative country cuisine with interesting little twists. Aunt Min's Swedish rye and other flavorful breads, as well as desserts, are made on the premises. Tables by the windows offer a splendid view of the mountains—a view that goes a long way toward promoting inner peace.

🏨 *15 doubles with bath, 3 suites. Restaurant, bar, air-conditioning, TV and phones in public area, children's room, hiking and cross-country ski trails. $145–$244; MAP. AE, D, MC, V. No smoking, no pets. 2-night minimum weekends.*

Wilburton Inn

River Rd., Manchester 05254, tel. 802/ 362–2500 or 800/648–4944, fax 802/362– 1107

This stone Tudor mansion could be the setting for one of those murder mysteries in which the detective names the killer as lightning flashes and thunder pounds. The estate sits on 20 acres of rolling manicured lawn, and the dining room and outdoor terrace overlook Battenkill Valley. Rooms are spacious and elegant, and many have outstanding mountain views; some have chenille-covered canopy beds, hand-painted murals, fireplaces, and whirlpool tubs. There are also separate cottages. The public areas are as elaborate as a railroad magnate's fortune would permit: Witness the ornately carved mantel, the mahogany paneling, the stained-glass dining-room door, the sweeping stone staircase to the lawn, and the Asian rugs on hardwood floors. Owners Albert and Georgette Levis, who are also the proprietors of the Wilburton Art Gallery, have placed contemporary sculpture on the grounds.

The menu has such offerings as cornmeal-encrusted rainbow trout with a hazelnut brown butter and broiled scallops of lamb with a garlic-rosemary sauce. You'll eat in the formal dining room amid the cherry paneling and beams while seated royally on dark green leather chairs. Breakfast, which is served in a more casual dining area, includes fresh fruit, baked goods, and views of the valley.

🏨 *34 doubles with bath. Restaurant, air-conditioning, TV in lobby and some rooms, pool, 3 tennis courts. $120–$205; full breakfast, afternoon tea. AE, MC, V. No smoking, no pets. 2-night minimum holidays.*

Northern Vermont

Inn at Round Barn Farm

Northern Vermont, where much of the state's logging and dairy farms can be found, is a land of contrasts: It has both the state's largest city and the state capital as well as some of New England's most rural areas and many rare species of wildlife. Its recorded history dates from 1609, when Samuel de Champlain explored the lake now named after him. A strong Canadian influence can be felt here: Montréal is only an hour from the border, and Canadian currency and accents are encountered often.

In the Northeast Kingdom, as former U.S. senator George Aiken dubbed the northeastern section of the state, you'll find many areas that have more cows than people and a Yankee accent so thick it's almost unintelligible to a flatlander (which may be part of the point). Those who wander through the forested hills and farmland often feel as if they've stepped into the Vermont of 100 years ago; harsh winters and geographic isolation have kept major development away—so far.

Vermont's largest population center, Burlington, was named one of the country's "dream towns" by Outside *magazine. This is where you can find it all: a real job, a real life, and the real*

big outdoors. Burlington also has the cultural sophistication you would expect to find only in a major city, an appealing quality due in part to the 20,000 students from the area's five colleges (including the University of Vermont) but also because of the many culture-addicted "city people" who have moved up here in droves and want the best of both worlds. For years it had the nation's only Socialist mayor (who is now the nation's only Independent congressman).

Places to Go, Sights to See

Ben and Jerry's Ice Cream Factory (Rte. 100, Waterbury, tel. 802/244–5641). Ben and Jerry began selling homemade ice cream from a bus in the 1970s. Today their Waterbury headquarters, which gives tours of the factory and explains ice cream making, has become one of the state's most popular attractions.

Burlington. Its pedestrian mall, waterfront parks, restaurants with eclectic cuisines, and high level of artistic activity make the state's largest city appealing to nearly everyone. The *Flynn Theatre* (153 Main St., tel. 802/864–8778) is the cultural heart and schedules various music, dance, and theater productions. Stroll down *Church Street* to soak up the local color and stop by one of the several cafés with outdoor tables.

Lake Champlain. Formerly the focus of the shipping industry, this area has become a major center for outdoor recreation. The Lake Champlain islands are replete with beaches and water sports facilities. North of Burlington, the scenic drive through the islands on Route 2 begins at I–89 and travels north through South Hero, Grand Isle, and Isle La Mote to Alburg Center.

Montpelier. The impressive gold dome and massive granite columns of the *Vermont State House* (State St., tel. 802/828–2228) belie the intimate scale of the legislative chambers within. You can tour the House Chamber and the even smaller Senate Chamber, which looks like a rather grand committee room. Next door is the *Vermont Museum* (109 State St., tel. 802/828–2291), which contains exhibits about early Vermont life.

Mt. Mansfield. The highest elevation (4,393 ft) in the state can be reached by car, hiking trail, or gondola; the mountain resembles the profile of a man lying on his back. *Smugglers' Notch*, a spectacular but somewhat harrowing narrow pass over the mountain, is said to have sheltered 18th-century outlaws and their booty in caves, a few of which can be seen from the road.

Shelburne Farms (Rte. 7, tel. 802/985–8686). Founded in the 1880s as a private estate, the 1,000-acre property just south of Burlington is now an educational center devoted to the responsible stewardship of agricultural and natural

resources. You can tour a working dairy farm, listen to nature lectures, or stroll on the grounds, which were landscaped by Frederick Law Olmsted, the creator of New York's Central Park and Boston's Emerald Necklace.

Shelburne Museum (Rte. 7, tel. 802/985–3346). The 35-building complex has one of the country's finest collections of Americana, including early houses and furniture, fine and folk art, farm tools, Audubon prints, and even a private railroad car from the days of steam.

Restaurants

Storm Café (Frog Mill Hollow, tel. 802/388–1063), in Frog Hollow in Middlebury, features an eclectic regional cuisine and outdoor tables that overlook the Otter Creek falls. The **Daily Planet** (15 Center St., tel. 802/862–9647) and **Isabel's** (112 Lake St., tel. 802/865–2522), both near the bustling pedestrian mall in Burlington, feature globally influenced fare. Situated in an 1860s barn with soaring hand-hewn rafters, the **Common Man** (tel. 802/583–2800), at Sugarbush ski area near Waitsfield, offers fine European-style dining and seasonal game specialties. **Miguel's Stow-Away** (Sugarbush Access Rd., Sugarbush, tel. 802/583–3858; Mountain Rd., Stowe, tel. 802/253–7574) makes its own chips and salsa and has innovative Mexican food that's especially satisfying après-ski. In Stowe the **Stowe Inn at Little River** (123 Mountain Rd., tel. 802/253–4836) serves burgers, pastas, and salads in a contemporary setting, while **Whiskers** (1652 Mountain Rd., tel. 802/253–8996) has a tremendous salad bar and in summer, seating amid perennial gardens.

Nightlife and the Arts

Catamount Center for the Arts (60 Eastern Ave., tel. 802/748–2600), in St. Johnsbury, offers a vast array of theater, dance, and musical performances. The **Flynn Theater** (153 Main St., tel. 802/864–8778), a grandiose old structure, is the cultural heart of Burlington and includes in its scheduling the Vermont Symphony Orchestra. The **Valley Players** (tel. 802/496–9612), in Waitsfield, and **Stowe Theater Guild** (tel. 802/656–0090), in Stowe, stage both dramas and musicals. In Burlington try the **Vermont Pub and Brewery** (College and St. Paul Sts., tel. 802/865–0500) for jazz, blues, and folk music or **Club Toast** (165 Church St., tel. 802/660–2088) and the **Metronome** (188 Main St., tel. 802/865–4563) for dancing. **Nectar's** (188 Main St., tel. 802/658–4771) is always jumping to the sounds of local bands and never charges a cover.

Reservations Services

Stowe Area Association (Box 1230, Stowe 05672, tel. 800/247–8693), **Sugarbush Reservations** (tel. 800/537–8427), **Vermont Centerpoint Reservation Service** (Box 8513, Essex 05451, tel. 802/872–2745 or 800/449–2745).

Visitor Information

Addison County Chamber of Commerce (2 Court St., Middlebury 05753, tel. 802/388–7951), **Central Vermont Chamber of Commerce** (Box 336, Beaulieu Pl., Barre 05641, tel. 802/229–5711), **Greater Newport Area Chamber of Commerce** (The Causeway, Newport 05855, tel. 802/334–7782), **Lake Champlain Regional Chamber of Commerce** (60 Main St., Suite 100, Burlington 05402, tel. 802/863–3489), **Smugglers' Notch Area Chamber of Commerce** (Box 364, Jeffersonville 05464, tel. 802/644–2239), **Stowe Area Association** (Box 1230, Stowe 05672, tel. 802/253–7321 or 800/247–8693), **Vermont Chamber of Commerce** (*see* Southeastern Vermont, *above*), **Vermont Travel Division** (*see* Southeastern Vermont, *above*).

Beaver Pond Farm Inn

Golf Course Rd. (R.D. Box 306), Warren 05674, tel. 802/583-2861

A peaceful drive down a country lane lined with sugar maples brings you to this small, restored, 1840 farmhouse. Overlooking rolling meadows, a golf course, and, in winter, cross-country ski trails, the setting is very nearly perfect. Innkeepers Betty and Bob Hansen bought the house as a second home almost 20 years ago, and, realizing they had an idyllic, beautiful spot, they decided to turn it into an inn.

A full breakfast that may include orange-yogurt pancakes is served at an oblong walnut table; a low wooden buffet lines the wall and holds four generations of china. Dinner is also offered three nights a week; favorites are the goat cheese soufflé and chicken stuffed with roasted red peppers served with a scallion, plum, and wine sauce. Guest rooms are decorated simply, and all have down comforters and ample bathrooms. The focal point of the inn is the huge deck, where you can lounge about gazing at the mountains and meadows after, of course, having spent the day hiking or golfing or skiing—it's all just steps from the front door.

▦ *4 doubles with bath, 2 doubles share bath. Golf, hiking, ski trails nearby. $72– $104; full breakfast. MC, V. No smoking, no pets. Closed mid-Apr.–late May and early Nov.*

Black Lantern Inn

Rte. 118, Montgomery Village 05470, tel. 802/326-4507 or 800/255-8661, fax 802/ 326-4077

When you drive to within 6 mi of the Canadian border to a town so small you can pass through it in one minute, you don't expect to find yourself sitting down to a candlelight dinner of pan-seared salmon with red pepper sauce or grilled lamb Margarite. But that's just what you find at the Black Lantern. Though the feeling is country, little touches of sophistication abound: a bowl of potpourri on an antique nightstand, weathered wood used in renovation, a marble-top table in a sitting room. The bar and other common areas are made cozy and intimate by the low ceilings, Asian rugs, and wood or gas stoves. Built in 1803 as a hotel for mill workers, the Black Lantern has been providing bed and board ever since. Rita and Allen Kalsmith, the innkeepers for more than 20 years, are proud of the continuity and of the building's spot on the National Register of Historic Places.

Many guest rooms have pine headboards, lace curtains, and ceiling fans. The suites in the newly renovated building next door are painted with a subtle rag-rolled finish and have large sitting rooms. Some also have the original wide-plank wooden floors. Although not far from the Jay Peak ski area, this is a true getaway. The rugged countryside of the Northeast Kingdom is waiting to be explored, including the seven historic covered bridges of Montgomery.

▦ *10 doubles with bath, 6 suites. Restaurant, bar, TV/VCRs in some rooms, whirlpool baths in suites, cross-country skiing and hiking nearby. $85– $145, full breakfast. AE, D, MC, V. No smoking, no pets.*

Edson Hill Manor

1500 Edson Hill Rd., Stowe 05672, tel. 802/253-7371 or 800/621-0284, fax 802/ 253-4036

This 1939 mansion, built in the style of a grand French Canadian country estate (the original plan was an architectural blend of Colonial Georgian and French provincial) on 200 acres, has the feel of a family compound owned by a rather horsey uncle. The spacious pine-paneled living room has an exquisitely tiled fireplace and a view of the sweeping lawn. Most rooms in the main building have fireplaces; all are done in an American

Colonial style, with antique and reproduction furnishings, pine paneling, and oil landscape paintings. The newer rooms in the carriage houses in the back are decorated similarly but have newer plumbing and a bit more privacy.

Most guests spend a lot of time outdoors on the 40 mi of bridle paths; the on-site riding center becomes a cross-country skiing center in winter. You select from a breakfast menu that includes such old standbys as pancakes, French toast, and bacon and eggs. You can also feast on innovative American dishes at the manor's outstanding restaurant, with its walls of windows and its painting of a wildflower meadow and an ivy-covered stone arch.

🏨 *25 doubles with bath. Restaurant, pool, stables, pond. $75–$170; full breakfast. AE, D, MC, V. No pets. 5-night minimum at Christmastime, 3-night minimum Presidents' Day weekend.*

Fox Hall Inn

Rte. 16, Barton 05822, tel. 802/525–6930, fax 802/525–1185

In Vermont moose are the subjects of passionate debate these days, and innkeepers Sherry and Ken Pyden are in tune with this interest. Throughout this 1890 cottage-style inn, which is listed on the National Register of Historic Places, you'll find a lot of moose miscellany, including a child's moose rocker and, of course, a moose head above the fireplace mantel.

Guest rooms are bright and furnished simply with wicker and quilts. The two turret rooms are spacious and have expansive views of fjordlike Lake Willoughby. The generous wraparound veranda also overlooks the lake and is well appointed with swinging seats and comfortable chairs—the perfect place to listen to the loons on a summer evening. Nearby Mt. Pisgah and Mt. Hor provide opportunities for hiking, and the lake offers canoeing, swimming, and fishing in summer and cross-country skiing and skating in winter.

🏨 *4 doubles with bath, 4 doubles share 3 baths. Hiking and cross-country ski trails, canoes, paddleboat. $60–$90; full breakfast, afternoon snacks. MC, V. No smoking, no pets. 2-night minimum during foliage season.*

The Gables Inn

1457 Mountain Rd., Stowe 05672, tel. 802/253–7730 or 800/422–5371, fax 802/253–8989

This Federal farmhouse, built in the mid-1800s, grew over time (a new wing here, a stairway there) to become a warren of charming rooms filled with American country antiques. Guest rooms have four-poster beds with white lace canopies, rag rugs on wide-plank floors, and little touches added by owners Sol and Lynn Baumrind. The tiny sunroom filled with plants and wicker is just the spot for sipping your morning coffee; a wood-burning stove gives a warm glow on winter evenings.

Rooms in the carriage house are modern and spacious, with cathedral ceilings, fireplaces, and whirlpools. The Riverview Suites have fireplaces, double whirlpool tubs, TV/VCRs, and minikitchens. Lynn's generous breakfasts, served until noon, are legendary; summer guests enjoy it outdoors. Dishes might include Portobello-mushroom Benedict with roasted red-pepper Hollandaise or French toast stuffed with cream cheese, walnuts, and molasses.

🏨 *17 doubles with bath, 2 suites. Restaurant, air-conditioning in all rooms, TV in some rooms and public area, hot tub, pool. $65–$200; full breakfast. AE, MC, V. No smoking, no pets.*

Green Trails Inn

Main St., Brookfield 05036, tel. 802/276–3412 or 800/243–3412

The two 1790 and 1830 farmhouses that form this inn are the focal point of a sleepy yet stubborn town that has voted several times to keep the village's dirt roads. On a 17-acre estate, the inn overlooks Sunset Lake and the longest floating bridge east of the Mississippi. Green Trails was started in the 1930s by Jessie Fisk, one of the first female professors at Rutgers University. Current innkeepers Mark and Sue Erwin maintain a relaxing atmosphere of quiet, comfortable country elegance.

A massive fieldstone fireplace dominates the living and dining area; the common rooms are filled with antique clocks, soothing music, and flowers. Guests rooms are simply furnished with quilts and a smattering of Early American antiques; one corner room in the 18th-century house is decorated with original wall stenciling and has a whirlpool. Meals represent home cooking at its best; rates always include a gourmet breakfast, and in the winter you can also request dinner. The Erwins maintain 30 km (19 mi) of cross-country ski trails, and snowshoeing, fishing, swimming, canoeing, hiking, and biking are all available nearby. You can also opt for a tranquil walk down a tree-shaded country road.

🏠 *8 doubles with bath, 6 doubles share bath. Whirlpool baths in some rooms. $79–$130; full breakfast. MC, V. No smoking, no pets.*

Inn at Montpelier

47 Main St., Montpelier 05602, tel. 802/223–2727, fax 802/223–0722

Until 1988 if you had wanted to stay in the state capital, you had your choice of large chain hotels or small motels. But then came Maureen and Bill Russell, who renovated a spacious, yellow, Federal brick house only a short walk from the center of town. Built in 1828, the inn was designed with the business traveler in mind, but the architectural details, the antique four-poster beds and Windsor chairs, and the piped-in classical music also attract visitors whose most pressing business is deciding how late to sleep (never a problem in the tranquil historic district).

The formal sitting room—with its large marble fireplace, cream-color woodwork, and tapestry-upholstered wing chairs—has a stately Federal feel to it, as if the original owners were about to glide down the polished staircase in rustling taffeta and black knee breeches. The wide, wraparound Colonial Revival porch, with its octagonal section, is especially conducive to relaxing and is one of the inn's most notable features.

Guest rooms in the frame building across the driveway are as elegant as (even slightly larger than) those in the main building. Each building has a small pantry where you can prepare coffee, store food, and/or grab a midnight snack. All rooms (some have fireplaces) are done in a mix of antique and reproduction furniture and rich floral decorator fabrics; the walls are often hung with original artwork, some of it by local artists. Maureen's Room has a sundeck; others have sitting rooms. The soft rose-color decor and the marble fireplace make the dining room a luxurious place to breakfast on fresh-baked goods.

🏠 *19 doubles with bath. Air-conditioning, TVs, phones in rooms; meeting rooms. $99–$169; Continental breakfast. AE, D, DC, MC, V. No smoking, no pets.*

The Inn at the Round Barn Farm

E. Warren Rd. (R.R. 1, Box 247), Waitsfield 05673, tel. 802/496–2276, fax 802/496–8832

Wedding parties have replaced cows in the big round barn here, but the Shaker-

style building still dominates the farm's 85 acres of countryside. As the picture albums attest, the process of restoring the 1910 12-sided barn involved jacking up the entire structure and putting in a new foundation. The result is one of the 12 remaining round (at least, dodecahedral) barns in the state; it's used for summer concerts, weddings, and parties and is on the National Register of Historic Places.

It was the barn that first caught the Simkos' eye; they had owned a ski house in the Mad River valley for 15 years and had driven past it frequently. Looking for a place to retire from the family floral business, they bought the property in 1986. Although the Simkos have since semiretired from innkeeping as well, their daughter, AnneMarie, remains on hand as the wedding coordinator. Resident innkeepers Chris and ShariLynn Williams hail from Canada and bring an entrepreneurial energy and flair to the place.

Guest rooms are in the 1806 farmhouse that overlooks several landscaped ponds and rolling acreage. Guest rooms are plush, with eyelet-trimmed sheets, new quilts on canopy or sleigh beds, Neutrogena toiletries, brass reading lamps, and floral drapes that match the wallpaper. The Richardson Room has low windows with mountain views, skylights, a canopy and headboard done with matching fabric, a gas fireplace, a large whirlpool tub, and a hand-painted mural. The equally luxurious Joslin Room also has a steam shower. Breakfast, served in a spacious room with exposed hand-hewn beams, might be French toast or cottage-cheese pancakes with a maple-raspberry sauce. Guests often gather by the fireplace in the cream-color library to discuss the day's activities—biking, hiking, canoeing, skiing, and the like—and to relax with a glass of sherry.

🏨 *11 doubles with bath. TV in public area; whirlpool baths, steam showers in some rooms; indoor lap pool. $115–$220; full breakfast. AE, MC, V. No smoking, no pets. 2-night minimum weekends.*

Inn on the Common

On the common, Rte. 14, Craftsbury Common 05827, tel. 802/586–9619 or 800/ 521–2233, fax 802/586–2249

In 1973 when Penny and Michael Schmitt left New York's Fifth Avenue and investment banking behind to renovate this early 19th-century Federal building, they spared no expense. Beyond the white picket fence and inside the inn are Scalamandré reproductions of historic wallpapers, Crabtree & Evelyn toiletries, thick plush carpets, and a 250-label collection of vintage wines. Adirondack chairs are placed throughout the long backyard to take advantage of mountain views.

One of the inn's three white-clapboard buildings is directly on the common; the other two, the main building and the South Annex, are just off it. Each has no more than six rooms, so the feeling is intimate. Families are often housed in the South Annex, which has a VCR with a large selection of films and a kitchenette with a microwave and a refrigerator. Though a few rooms are on the small side, all are beautifully detailed, with quilts on the beds, swag draperies with trim that complements the wallpaper, and bathrobes in the closets; some rooms have fireplaces or gas stoves. Room 3, in the main building, has the best views and a large bathroom.

Breakfast, which might include bacon, muffins, pancakes, and French toast, is served overlooking the rose garden in summer. Afterward you can visit the nearby 140-acre sports center, where, in addition to facilities for cross-country skiing in winter and water sports in summer, you'll find naturalists eager to offer information on local wildlife. Dinner is served only to inn guests at communal tables; help yourself at the bar before and after the meal.

Be sure to reserve well ahead of time for a stay here. This is one of the most highly regarded inns in the state and

may be booked as much as a year in advance for peak seasons.

🏨 *16 doubles with bath, 1 suite. TV/VCR in living room, pool, tennis. $220–$280, MAP; $15 charge per pet. AE, MC, V. No smoking. 2-day minimum during foliage season.*

Lareau Farm Country Inn

Rte. 100 (Box 563), Waitsfield 05673, tel. 802/496–4949 or 800/833–0766, fax 802/496–7979

Surrounded by 67 acres of pasture and woodland and just an amble away from the Mad River, this collection of old farm buildings appeals both to outdoor enthusiasts and those simply seeking a rejuvenating country retreat. There's lots of history here—the original settler is buried on the property—that innkeepers Susan and Dan Easley love to share. They also provide information on exploring the area: you can take a 1-mi stroll with the help of a detailed walking guide they've created.

Although the inn has been around since the late-18th century (the oldest part dates from 1790), the furnishings are an eclectic mix—Victorian sofas, Asian rugs, handmade quilts. The effect is always country and always casual. The many-windowed dining room is the most inviting space. Here, you'll be served a family-style breakfast at one of four massive oak and cherry tables. Sitting on the covered porch in an Adirondack chair, staring at horses in pastures out back, is the epitome of peace. You can also explore the big jazz-recordings collection, swim in the river, take a horse or sleigh ride, and stroll through beautiful gardens. American Flatbread, the warm and lively restaurant in the barn next door, serves great pizza made using organic ingredients (open Friday and Saturday only).

🏨 *11 doubles with bath, 2 doubles share bath. TV in sitting room, whirlpool bath in 1 room, swimming, sleigh rides. $75–$125; full breakfast. MC, V. No smoking, no pets.*

Rabbit Hill Inn

Rte. 18 (Box 55), Lower Waterford 05848, tel. 802/748–5168 or 800/76–BUNNY, fax 802/748–8342

Upon arriving here, you'll find that the door will swing open, and you'll be welcomed (often by name) into enough warmth to melt away the stress of even the most difficult journeys. The Rabbit Hill Inn, on 15 wooded acres, has been receiving guests since its days as a stagecoach stop on the Montréal–Portland route. Innkeepers Brian and Leslie Mulcahy are dedicated to upholding a long-standing tradition of gracious hospitality.

The Mulcahy's fondness for the gentility of days past is expressed in the formal, Federal-period parlor, where mulled cider from the fireplace crane is served on chilly afternoons. The low wooden beams and cozy warmth of the Irish pub next door create a comfortable contrast that's carried throughout the inn: Guest rooms are as stylistically different as they are consistently indulgent. The seven suites (the Mulcahy's call them "fantasy chambers") have double whirlpool tubs and fireplaces; most contain a whimsical secret (a hidden door, perhaps) in their design. The Loft, with its 8-ft Palladian window and its king-size canopy bed, is one of the most requested. The abundant windows, Victrola, and working pump organ with period sheet music make the Music Chamber another favorite. Rooms toward the front of the inn have views of the Connecticut River and the White Mountains in New Hampshire; those in the Carriage House are smaller but more private.

In the elegant dining room, chef Russell Stannard prepares eclectic, regional cuisine that might include grilled sausage of Vermont pheasant with pistachios or smoked chicken and red-lentil dumplings

nestled in red pepper linguine. Heart-healthful meals, reviewed by a dietician, are also offered. The bountiful country breakfast includes a buffet of home-baked coffee cakes and muffins, quiches, and fresh fruits.

🏠 *15 doubles with bath, 6 suites. Restaurant, pub, air-conditioning in most rooms, whirlpool baths in some rooms, TV in public area, walking and cross-country ski trails, canoes. $189–$289, MAP; B&B rates available. AE, MC, V. No smoking, no pets. 2-night minimum weekends, 3-night minimum holiday weekends. Closed 1st 2 wks in Apr. and 1st 2 wks in Nov.*

Swift House Inn

25 Stewart La., Middlebury 05753, tel. 802/388–9925, fax 802/388–9927

Andrea and John Nelson didn't exactly intend to open an inn when they did; they were looking at inns with the idea of buying something in 10 years, after John retired from IBM's finance department. But on the way to the airport to return to New Jersey one day in 1985, they stopped by the big white Federal home set atop a sweeping expanse of lawn, and their decision was made. They've made the Swift House Inn one of the most elegant in the state. The Nelsons have since retired, but their daughter, Karla Nelson-Loura, is now the innkeeper.

The patrician air here is no coincidence; the inn was the private home of two of Middlebury's most prominent families: the Swifts, who built the oldest section of the house in 1814, and the Stewarts, one of whom married the grandson of the original owner and lived in the home until 1943. As a result of the long private ownership, elegant detailing has been well preserved. The richly ornamented cherry paneling and trim glow in the dining room, where the bright purple and green grape–clustered wallpaper is an exact reproduction of the pattern installed in 1905. Guest rooms are also luxurious. The Swift Room not only has a private porch but also retains the built-in, brass, wall phone Mrs. Swift installed so she could—believe it or not—listen to church services. White-eyelet-trimmed sheets, gathered lace curtains, floral chintz draperies that match a wing chair, a fresh carnation in a bedside vase—the attention to detail gives the impression that this is still an affluent family's private home.

The carriage house was converted in 1990 and is recommended for families; the rooms are very spacious and have enormous bathrooms with whirlpool baths. One rooms has French doors that open onto a patio. Rooms in the gatehouse are closer to the road and therefore a bit noisier.

In the dining room an attentive staff serves an adventurous menu that might include grilled citrus-marinated duck breast with roasted beet coulis or angel hair pasta with fresh mushrooms and marinara sauce.

🏠 *21 doubles with bath. Restaurant; air-conditioning, TVs in most rooms; phones in all rooms; sauna, steam room, meeting room. $90–$185; Continental breakfast. AE, D, DC, MC, V. No smoking, no pets. Restaurant closed Tues.–Wed.*

Wildflower Inn

Darling Hill Rd., Lyndonville 05851, tel. 802/626–8310 or 800/627–8310, fax 802/626–3039

Nearly every room in one of the inn's four buildings gets a piece of the 500 acres of incredible views. Sitting atop a long ridge that affords panoramic vistas in every direction, this rambling complex of old buildings—which date from 1796—was a working dairy farm until innkeepers Mary and Jim O'Reilly bought it in 1985. Guest rooms in the restored Federal-style main house, as well as in the carriage houses, are decorated simply with both reproductions and contemporary furnishings; some have their own porch.

The most spacious rooms are suites called The Meadows, situated in what used to be the blacksmith shop. The inn is family oriented in every respect, with a petting barn, planned children's activities, a children's room that even has dress-up clothes, and a kids' swimming pool. In winter the place quiets down and caters more to cross-country skiers. Meals feature hearty, country-style food, with homemade breads and vegetables from the garden.

🏨 *12 doubles with bath, 10 suites. Restaurant, game room, children's playroom, pool, hot tub, sauna, hiking and cross-country ski trails, pony and sleigh rides, skating and fishing pond, tennis court, batting cage, petting barn. $79–$220; full breakfast. MC, V. 2-night minimum weekends. Closed Apr. and Nov.*

The Willard Street Inn

349 S. Willard St., Burlington 05401, tel. 802/651–8710 or 800/577–8712, fax 802/651–8714

In 1996 innkeepers Beverly and Gordon Watson purchased this home built for a state senator circa 1880. High in Burlington's historic hill section, this grand house incorporates elements of Queen Anne and Colonial Georgian styles. The stately foyer is paneled in cherry and leads to a formal sitting room with velvet drapes. The solarium has marble floors, myriad plants, and big velvet couches to relax on while you contemplate the views of Lake Champlain. Both rooms have pianos. Some guest rooms have views of the lake and canopy beds; all have antiques and down comforters.

After breakfast—perhaps of baked orange French toast in a triple sec glaze—in the dining room, you can stroll down the exterior marble staircase for a walk in the English gardens. The inn's off-site restaurant, Isabel's, is a short distance away on the waterfront.

🏨 *7 doubles with bath, 8 doubles share baths. Cable TV and phones in rooms. $75–$200; full breakfast, afternoon tea. AE, D, MC, V. No smoking, no pets.*

Ye Olde England Inn

433 Mountain Rd., Stowe 05672, tel. 802/253–7558 or 800/477–3771, fax 802/253–8944

From the outside it would be easy to think that someone had merely slapped an English veneer on this inn. Not so. Owners Chris and Lyn Francis *are* British and have fitted the inn out in a style worthy of royalty. Regal golden lions guard the entrance, and a red London call box stands outside the door. Royal portraits in the lobby, signs that say TO THE LOO, and hunting prints throughout make you want to stand up and sing *God Save the Queen*. The rooms in the main inn are small but well appointed with delicate pastel Laura Ashley furnishings, deep-pile carpeting, brass headboards, and wicker baskets. Ten new suites in the Bluff House have lounges with fireplaces and oversize whirlpool tubs. Some also have decks or patios with mountain views.

Chris is a polo fanatic—his local team has been known to play matches in the snow—and Pickwick's Polo Pub doubles as the inn's trophy room. It's fun to view the team photos and polo regalia on the walls while sampling the outstanding selection of single-malt scotches or one of the 150 rare ales. The dining room can provide Welsh rarebit for breakfast as well as standard American fare.

🏨 *17 doubles with bath, 10 suites, 3 cottages. Restaurant; pub; air-conditioning, TVs, phones in all rooms; whirlpools in some rooms; hot tub; pool. $98–$158, cottages $150–$205; full breakfast, afternoon tea. AE, D, MC, V. Pets by arrangement. 2-night minimum weekends.*

New Hampshire

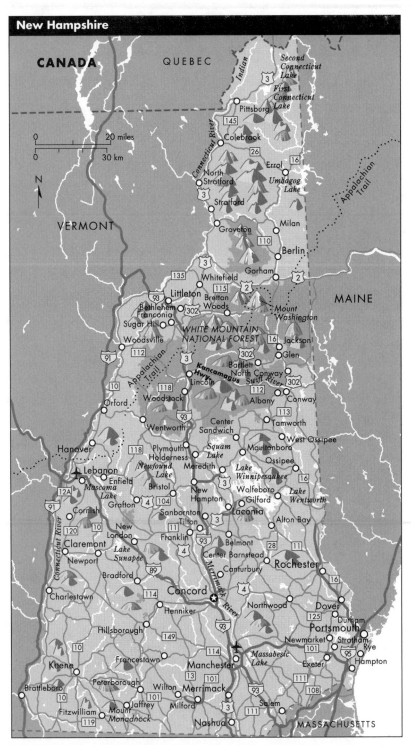

New Hampshire

The Seacoast

Rock Ledge Manor

Tucked between the long Atlantic frontiers of Maine and Massachusetts, New Hampshire's 18-mi shore is a microcosm of pleasure. This brief span contains beaches for swimming and exploring; a quintessential boardwalk; and ideal spots for surf and deep-sea fishing, whale-watching, and boating. Go inland a few miles, and you find Colonial villages and farms. The region's very compactness makes it an ideal vacation spot—you can stay wherever you like and always be within a half hour of any attraction. Though many of the best restaurants are in Portsmouth near the waterfront, a B&B downtown, on the ocean in Rye or Hampton, or farther inland is still convenient for dining out.

The history of the nation is linked with this craggy shore. Scottish fishermen created a settlement at Odiorne Point in 1623. Captain Kidd, Miles Standish, and Captain John Smith were early visitors to the Isles of Shoals. When Portsmouth—a Colonial city with a royal governor in residence—stood Tory at the time of the Revolution, Exeter wholeheartedly supported the patriot cause and became, for 30-odd years, the capital of New Hampshire. Both Portsmouth and Exeter have well-preserved historic houses. In Portsmouth you can visit the

*John Paul Jones House, among others, on the Portsmouth
Trail walking tour. In Exeter, at the American Independence
Museum, you will see the place where residents came for
safety from Indian attack as well as to plot the overthrow of
British rule.*

*Portsmouth has a warren of curious streets near the harbor—
perfect for shopping or just exploring. At Prescott Park a
nearly continuous round of concerts, fairs, and special events
attracts the summer visitor. Head inland, and you will find
pick-your-own apple orchards and berry patches. Durham,
just 10 mi up the river from Portsmouth, is the home of the
state university, where musical and theatrical performances
take place regularly. Route 4, west of Durham, is a worthy
antiques strip, with shops and barns that overflow with dusty
treasures.*

Places to Go, Sights to See

American Independence Museum (1 Govenor's La., Exeter, tel. 603/772–2622).
Housed in the Ladd-Gilman house, next to Phillips Exeter Academy, the museum
celebrates the birth of our nation. The house served as the governor's mansion for
John Taylor Gilman when Exeter was the state capital. The story of the Revolution
unfolds during each guided tour.

Great Bay Estuary. This tidal bay is just out of sight of the tourist coast. Bird
lovers may find snowy egrets, herons, and in the winter, eagles. The *Great Bay
Wildlife Refuge* (336 Nimble Hill Rd., Newington, tel. 603/431–7511) is a place
to go early in the morning with your camera and plenty of insect repellent. In
addition to the main entrance in Newmarket, you can enter the refuge in
Stratham and Durham.

Hampton Beach Casino (169 Ocean Blvd., Hampton Beach, tel. 603/926–4541;
open mid-Apr.–Oct.). Seven acres of entertainment—from shooting galleries and
video games to concerts by name artists—and four water slides make up this
beachside complex. The food spots here are good for snacks or lunch; head
elsewhere for dinner.

Harbor, Island, and Whale-Watching Cruises. From May to October *Seacoast
Cruises* (Rye, tel. 603/964–5545 or 800/734–6488), *Isles of Shoals Steamship
Company* (Portsmouth, tel. 603/431–5500 or 800/441–4620), and *Portsmouth
Harbor Cruises* (Portsmouth, tel. 603/436–8084 or 800/776–0915) offer narrated
trips to the Isles of Shoals and whale-watching and other specialty cruises.

Seacoast Science Center at Odiorne Point State Park (Rte. 1A, Rye, tel. 603/ 436–8043). Tide pools and nature walks at the mouth of Portsmouth Harbor are even better after a stop at the science center, which traces the area's natural history back to the Ice Age. The park encompasses 350 acres of nature trails and rocky shore. Picnic areas invite you to bring your own lunch.

Strawbery Banke (Marcy St., Portsmouth, tel. 603/433–1100). At this waterfront museum complex, costumed interpreters staff 11 of the more than 40 historic houses; some of the docents even give demonstrations on crafts such as broom tying and spinning. Also on the grounds are gardens, a gift shop, and an eatery.

Beaches

The town of Hampton, on Route 1A, encompasses several sandy beaches: One is opposite and one south of the resort's high life. Seashell Stage is an amphitheater where you can catch music of all kinds. There's a public dock and fishing, too. **North Beach** and **North Hampton Beach** are good for swimming.

Jenness Beach, in Rye, is less frantic than the beaches in Hampton. The seacoast's three state parks are also in Rye. **Rye Harbor State Park** has picnic areas and saltwater fishing. **Odiorne Point** was the site of the first European settlement in New Hampshire (1623) and has a science center with wonderful tide pools. **Wallis Sands State Beach** is one of the best beaches in the area.

Restaurants

Locals love the light seafood and homemade desserts at **Karen's** (tel. 603/431– 1948), on Daniel Street in Portsmouth. Watch the sunset as you try the bouillabaisse at the **Oar House** (tel. 603/436–4025), also in Portsmouth, on Ceres Street. You can enjoy harbor views and the tastes of Naples, Italy, at **Porto Bello** (Bow St., tel. 603/431–2989). **Ron's Landing at Rocky Point** (tel. 603/929–2122), on Route 1A in Hampton Beach, offers beachgoers an elegant choice for dinner. The menu includes fresh seafood, beef, veal, and pasta dishes. For the classically informal, **Newick's Lobster House** (tel. 603/742–3205) is an always-crowded fresh-seafood place on Dover Point Road, Dover.

Visitor Information

Exeter Area Chamber of Commerce (120 Water St., Exeter 03833, tel. 603/ 772–2411), **Greater Dover Chamber of Commerce** (299 Central Ave., Dover 03820, tel. 603/742–2218), **Greater Portsmouth Chamber of Commerce** (500 Market St. Extension, Portsmouth 03801, tel. 603/436–1118), **Hampton Beach Area Chamber of Commerce** (836 Lafayette Rd., Hampton 03842, tel. 603/926– 8717), **New Hampshire Division of Parks and Recreation** (Box 856, Concord 03301-0856, tel. 603/271–3254 or 603/224–4666), **New Hampshire Office of Travel and Tourism Development** (Box 1856, Concord 03302, tel. 603/271–2343 or 800/944–1117).

Exeter Inn

90 Front St., Exeter 03833, tel. 603/772–5901 or 800/782–8444, fax 603/778–8757

The Exeter Inn is enough to make you wish you were a preppy—or had a preppy to visit. The redbrick Georgian-style inn is owned by and only slightly removed from the prestigious Phillips Exeter Academy. A stay here puts you in the historic district of this Colonial town (Exeter was the capital of New Hampshire during the American Revolution) and just about midway between Newburyport, Massachusetts, and Portsmouth, New Hampshire.

This could be a fusty place, but it is not, thanks largely to innkeeper Carl Jensen, a hotel professional with an eye for detail. It is a very well-managed, dignified, small hotel with large rooms furnished with antiques appropriate to the building's Georgian design, such as pineapple-carved pencil-post beds. The award-winning, solarium-style restaurant has a fig tree growing in its center and a notable Sunday brunch.

▦ *48 doubles with bath, 1 suite. Restaurant; air-conditioning, cable TV, phones in rooms; fitness room; sauna; meeting rooms. $79–$169. AE, D, DC, MC, V. 2-night minimum Parents' Weekend (late Oct.).*

The Governor's Inn

78 Wakefield St., Rochester 03867, tel. 603/332–0107, fax 603/335–1984

Once the residence of former governor Huntley Spaulding, this beautifully restored 1920 mansion is now operated as an inn by the Ejarque family. The ambience is impressive but not imposing: You may descend an elliptical staircase to eat your breakfast crepes next to French windows on the sunporch, but the guest room you left behind will probably have been casually furnished in white wicker and adorned with light, bright floral wallpaper. Two rooms in the original section have working fireplaces. Rooms in the newer west wing have white walls and modern hotel-room decor that is comfortable but not unique.

The inn restaurant—an end in itself—is open to the public. The fixed menu may start with curried butternut soup with apples, continue with New Zealand rack of lamb glazed with apricots and pistachios or baked rainbow trout filled with savory seafood stuffing, and end with coconut cake with Grand Marnier and oranges.

The inn is roughly halfway between Portsmouth and Lake Winnipesaukee. The White Mountains are only a 45-minute drive north; the beaches are a 30-minute drive south.

▦ *8 doubles with bath, 1 3-bedroom apartment. Restaurant; tavern; air-conditioning, cable TV, phones in rooms; meeting room; ballroom. $78–$128; full breakfast. AE, D, MC, V. No smoking, no pets.*

Highland Farm Bed and Breakfast

148 County Farm Rd., Dover 03820, tel. 603/743–3399

You may find yourself humming the score from *Brigadoon* during your stay at Highland Farm. The three-story B&B, housed in a pre-1850 farmhouse, has a thistle for a logo, and Bobby Burns is quoted on the flyer. Scones for breakfast? You bet. You can have them in the dining room or, in warm weather, on the porch overlooking the rose garden and plum trees.

Noreen Bowers opened her four-chimney, redbrick Victorian to guests because she so enjoyed staying in B&Bs during her own travels. The Highland is a formal sort of house, with a parlor, a wood-paneled library, and, in back, a sunroom that faces south toward the river. The bedrooms are large (two of them can accommodate an extra person), with

hooked rugs and antique beds. In winter you can cross-country ski and in summer hike on trails along the river. Rural though the location may be, it's only 2 mi to historic Dover and a tad farther to the food and entertainments of Portsmouth.

🏠 *2 doubles with bath, 2 doubles share bath. Cable TV/VCR in library. $90–120; full breakfast. MC, V. No smoking, no pets.*

Inn at Christian Shore

335 Maplewood Ave., Portsmouth 03801, tel. 603/431-6770

Mariaelena Koopman, a former art dealer, had her eye on the Inn at Christian Shore for several years before she bought it in 1996. The off-white Federal house (circa 1800) a few blocks outside Portsmouth's historic district needed some work, but she has made steady progress raising it to her standards. Although there are six guest rooms, one is small and is only offered as a second room for families. The other rooms are large and furnished with antiques in keeping with the building's Federal style.

Breakfast is served in the dining room, which has a beamed ceiling, a trestle table with Windsor chairs, and small tables for two with wing chairs. Although originally from Argentina, Mariaelena loves New Hampshire and is a gold mine of information on local restaurants and historic Portsmouth.

🏠 *4 doubles with bath; 1 double, 1 single share bath. Air-conditioning, cable TV in rooms; free parking. $40–95; full breakfast. MC, V. No smoking, no pets.*

Martin Hill Inn

404 Islington St., Portsmouth 03801, tel. 603/436-2287

The yellow Martin Hill Inn was built in downtown Portsmouth in 1820 and its

Guest House in 1850, so it is no wonder that guests feel at home visiting the Colonial houses and historic waterfront of this charming old city.

It was on their second visit to the inn that Paul and Jane Harden found it was for sale. Within the week they resigned their managerial jobs and became innkeepers. "Gardening has become the only hobby we have time for," Paul says.

The two houses are now connected by a flower-lined brick walk, patio, and water garden. Both have bedrooms large enough to contain a sofa and are rather formal in feeling, with Asian rugs and fine Colonial antiques, including canopy and four-poster beds with pineapple carvings. In the Guest House three suites are decorated in Victorian country style, with flowered-chintz drapes and spindle or brass-and-iron beds. The Greenhouse Suite has a solarium and a private entrance. The inn is on a major street that quiets down at night.

🏠 *4 doubles with bath, 3 suites. Air-conditioning, free parking. $80–$115; full breakfast. MC, V. No smoking, no pets.*

Moody Parsonage Bed and Breakfast

15 Ash Swamp Rd., Newmarket 03857, tel. 603/659-6675

Moody Parsonage, built in 1730 for John Moody, the first minister of Newmarket, is a most welcoming B&B. Today's world and worries seem far away in this red-clapboard house where a spinning wheel sits on the landing, and you can still see the original paneling, staircases, and wide-plank pine floors. Five fireplaces— the one in the dining room is always ablaze on chilly mornings—are cozy reminders of days when the seacoast was on the edge of the wilderness.

Owner Deborah Reed grew up in the Parsonage, returning to it after 35 years of marriage and residences that spanned

the globe from Germany to Washington State. A retired registered nurse, she eased into innkeeping by first opening her house to University of New Hampshire students. Now she says she has "discovered that a B&B is definitely in the caregiving category."

All rooms are accented with such family antiques as rush-seat and wing chairs, electrified oil lamps, iron-bound wooden trunks, and copper kettles. One bedroom and bath are on the first floor. The other three rooms are upstairs and share a bath. Two of these are connected and make a good arrangement for a family, but the number of irreplaceable antiques makes this B&B a less-than-ideal choice for families with young children. The first-floor bedroom and two upstairs have working fireplaces.

Fresh flowers are everywhere. "With 2 acres to care for, I guess you could say my hobby is gardening, and I enjoy every minute of it," Deborah says. She also refinishes furniture when time permits.

You are only a 15-minute drive from the museums and restaurants of Durham, Exeter, and Portsmouth and the beaches and boardwalk of Rye and Hampton; Newmarket itself is only 2 mi south. Other options include a shopping mall or two, the facilities of the Great Bay Athletic Club, and the Rockingham Ballroom with its performances of big band music. Or you can sit on the Parsonage lawn and watch the golfers tee off at the course across the street.

🏠 *1 double with bath, 3 doubles share bath. Air-conditioning. $60–$70; Continental breakfast. No credit cards. No smoking, no pets.*

Oceanside Inn

365 Ocean Blvd., Hampton Beach 03842, tel. 603/926–3542, fax 603/926–3549

The small Oceanside Inn is just on the edge of action-oriented Hampton Beach. Weekly fireworks and concerts and the total boardwalk ambience of cotton candy and street performers make for a lively July and August. If you want to people-watch without having to dodge the crowds or just want to stare at the waves, head for the inn's second-floor veranda.

Owners Debbie and Skip Windemiller also recommend off-season (June and September–early October) stays, when the beach is quiet and the Oceanside is about the only thing still open. Then there might even be a fire burning in the breakfast café or the living-room library, and Skip will have time to talk about his past adventures as a freestyle ski instructor. Despite the Oceanside's quintessentially commercial location, Debbie has deftly decorated the rooms with her own eclectic collectibles to create a turn-of-the-century private-home atmosphere. Some rooms have views of the ocean, and soundproofing makes the Oceanside Inn a quiet oasis even during the high season.

🏠 *10 doubles with bath. Air-conditioning, TV/VCRs, refrigerators, phones, hair dryers, safes in rooms; free parking; beach chairs and towels. $90–$135; full breakfast. AE, D, MC, V. No smoking, no pets. Closed mid-Oct.–mid-May.*

Rock Ledge Manor

1413 Ocean Blvd. (Rte. 1A), Rye 03870, tel. 603/431–1413

Built between 1840 and 1880 as part of a major seaside resort colony, Rock Ledge Manor is pure Victorian gingerbread. The white, gambrel-roof house with black shutters overlooks the Atlantic just south of Wallis Sands State Beach. In the distance you can see the Isles of Shoals.

The previous owners turned their oceanfront home into a B&B in 1982 and then sold the established business to Stan and Sandi Smith in 1997. "I've always loved B&Bs and the ocean," says Sandi, "so this is a dream come true."

In the breakfast room, with a view of the sea, the table is set formally with china and linens—the way the morning meal was served a century ago. Off the breakfast room, a delightfully old-fashioned sunroom full of plants is just the place to retire to with the morning papers. Or you might prefer to let the breeze ruffle your pages on the wide wraparound porch.

Two bedrooms are on the ground floor and two on the second, all with ocean views. Marble-top sinks and dressers are part of the authentic Victoriana, as are the brass-and-iron beds and the languidly turning paddles of the ceiling fans.

You may have to reserve well in advance in summer, when many returning guests come for a week or more, but Rock Ledge Manor is open year-round, and the seacoast is gloriously uncrowded in the spring and fall. You are only 5 mi from historic Portsmouth, with its museums, galleries, restaurants, and year-round schedule of special events.

🏨 *2 doubles with bath, 2 doubles with ½ baths, shared shower. $80–$90; full breakfast. No credit cards. No smoking, no pets. 2-night minimum holidays and weekends.*

Sise Inn

40 Court St., Portsmouth 03801, tel. 603/ 433–1200 or 800/267–0525 (reservations only), fax 603/433–1200

This elegant Queen Anne inn has the amenities of a complete hotel, and it's in the heart of town just blocks from the waterfront, Strawbery Banke, and many shops and restaurants.

Antiques and fine period reproductions throughout recapture the 1880s (when the house was built by a prosperous merchant), and the handsome bedrooms and suites have been featured in countless home and design magazines. Rooms in the older part of the inn have high ceilings and interesting architectural features

such as bow windows. Every room is different, though all have tables, desks, antique wardrobes, and such luxury touches as professionally done flower arrangements. A few rooms have whirlpool baths. Room 310, a suite, is typical of the rooms in the older section; it has French doors separating the bedroom from the sitting area and comfortable chairs upholstered in soft blues and creams.

The inn is one of a handful geared for visitors with disabilities. All three floors are serviced by an elevator, and some of the bathrooms are equipped with railings.

🏨 *26 doubles with bath, 8 suites. Air-conditioning, cable TV/VCR, phones in rooms; whirlpool baths, fireplaces, stereos in some rooms; meeting rooms; free parking. $105–$175; Continental breakfast. AE, DC, MC, V. No smoking in some rooms, no pets.*

The Victoria Inn

430 High St., Hampton 03842, tel. 603/ 929–1437

When innkeepers Nick and Tara Di-Tillio gave up working for large hotel chains to focus on the people side of the business, they found the Victoria Inn exactly to their liking. With only three double rooms, it is small enough to allow them to get to know their guests, but its popularity as a wedding spot keeps things lively even during the so-called slow season.

Calling this romantic Victorian is an understatement for this 1875 carriage house. A gazebo beckons from the garden, and the sunroom just over the front door belongs to a honeymoon suite done in blue and white (lots of lace and a brass king-size bed complete the picture). The Lilac Room and Peach Suite are done in the colors Victorians loved best. The formal mauve and cream of the Victoria Room sets off its dark woods. Franklin Pierce, the 14th U.S. president, had a summer home next door and is remembered in the Pierce Room.

A full breakfast of French toast with cream cheese and walnuts or mushroom scrambled eggs with brie is served on the enclosed porch that feels a part of the garden.

3 doubles with bath, 3 doubles share bath. Air-conditioning, cable TV, phones in rooms; free parking; public beach nearby. $75–$95; full breakfast. MC, V. No smoking, no pets (kennel nearby).

The Lakes Region

The Tamworth Inn

When glaciers retreated from New Hampshire, they left
behind a gift of fresh water: more than 1,300 lakes and
ponds and 1,000 mi of streams. Although lakes are scattered
throughout the state, the concentration of 273 parcels of water
in the center—including 72-square-mi Lake Winnipesaukee—
has been singled out as the Lakes Region.

Winnipesaukee means "smile of the Great Spirit," a name as
appropriate today as when it was an abundant fishing ground
for Native Americans. Its shores and those of its satellite
lakes hold such varying vacation delights as bustling
boardwalks and utter isolation, the nation's first summer
resort at Wolfeboro, and one of its oldest summer theaters.
Nearly all the region's 42 towns touch water, and boating can
mean a canoe, a cruise ship, and all manner of craft in
between.

The Lakes Region covers a big area, and each section has its
advocates. Wolfeboro is a been-coming-here-forever place with
an all-ages crowd whose members meet old friends for Sunday
brunch at the inn or make the rounds at the antiques shows.
The west side of Lake Winnipesaukee has honky-tonk Weirs

Beach, where teenagers hang out while their elders browse in
art galleries and crafts shops in Meredith and Moultonboro.
Laconia is a former manufacturing and trading center
that still functions as the region's business hub. North of
Winnipesaukee, Squam Lake perhaps is best remembered for
the movie starring Katherine Hepburn and Henry Fonda, On
Golden Pond, which was filmed on its shores.

In September when the explosive colors of autumn start south
from the Canadian border and move through New Hampshire,
the lakes are blue mirrors that reflect the reds and golds of the
season. Winter is the time for ice fishing and iceboating on
Lake Winnipesaukee and for skiing at Gunstock.

Places to Go, Sights to See

Castle-in-the-Clouds (Rte. 171, Moultonboro, tel. 603/476–2352 or 800/729–
2468). The estate of eccentric millionaire Thomas Gustave Plant in the Ossipee
Mountains is a special place. Tours of the 16-room stone mansion show how Plant
managed to spend $7 million to build it in 1911. You can ride horseback, hike in
the woods, take a paddleboat on the pond, and tour the bottling plant for Castle
Springs water, too.

Canterbury Shaker Village (Southwest of Lake Winnipesaukee, off Rte. 106 at
288 Shaker Rd., Canterbury, tel. 603/783–9511). The Canterbury community,
established in 1792, is now a living museum of Shaker life. You can lunch on
Shaker food in the *Creamery* restaurant and take escorted tours through many of
the 24 buildings. There are candlelight dinner tours of the village as well, by
reservation.

Gilford/Gunstock. The largest public beach on Lake Winnipesaukee is the
waterfront of Gilford town, and if you take Route 11A to *Gunstock Recreation
Area* (tel. 603/293–4341 or 800/486–7862), you will have a choice of outdoor
playgrounds, an Olympic-size swimming pool, fishing, paddleboats, horseback
riding, and special events. Gunstock also has a family campground with 300 tent
and trailer sites, where pets can be unleashed.

Museum of Childhood (Off Rte. 16 in the historic district, Wakefield, tel. 603/
522–8073). This charming museum displays a one-room schoolhouse from 1890,
model trains, antique children's sleds, teddy bears, and 3,000 dolls.

Science Center of New Hampshire (Junction of Rtes. 113 and 25, Holderness,
tel. 603/968–7194). Live indigenous beasts—from bears and bobcats to reptiles
and bald eagles—are sometimes seen on the center's trails and enrich the static
natural-science displays. The ¾-mi nature trail is a favorite of all ages.

Weirs Beach. Fun and games by the hundreds, bowling lanes by the dozens, water slides, and all the cotton candy and pizza you can eat make this a natural target for teens. On summer evenings music blares and skyrockets zoom. Lake cruises are offered by *Mt. Washington Cruises* (tel. 603/366–5531).

Restaurants

Hickory Stick Farm (tel. 603/524–3333), in the woods near Laconia, specializes in roast duckling with sherry-orange sauce. The **Woodshed,** tel. 603/476–2311), in Moultonboro, features prime rib in a converted barn. **Le Chalet Rouge** (tel. 603/286–4035), on the west side of Tilton not far from the toe of Silver Lake, is a modest dining room that serves simple but authentic country French food. Look to the **Tamworth Inn** (*see below*), in Tamworth, for new American cuisine and to the **Crystal Quail** (202 Pitman Rd., tel. 603/269–4151), in Center Barnstead, for very intimate country French dining.

Nightlife and the Arts

Barnstormers (tel. 603/323–8500), the Equity summer theater in Tamworth, has an eight-week season mid-July–Labor Day. The **Tamworth Inn** (tel. 603/323–7721) across the street offers dinner-theater packages. Moonlight dinner-dance cruises are offered by the **M/S *Mount Washington*** (tel. 603/366–5531). **Meredith Station** (tel. 603/279–7777) is an 1849 railroad-station-cum-pub with a DJ and dancing overlooking the lake.

Visitor Information

Lakes Region Association (Box 589, Center Harbor 03226, tel. 603/253–8555), **New Hampshire Division of Parks and Recreation** (*see* Visitor Information *in* The Seacoast, *above*), **New Hampshire Office of Travel and Tourism Development** (*see* Visitor Information *in* The Seacoast, *above*), **Wolfeboro Chamber of Commerce** (Railroad Ave., Wolfeboro 03894, tel. 603/569–2200).

The Blanchard House

55 Main St. (Box 389), Center Sandwich 03227, tel. 603/284-6540

The pristine white 18th- and 19th-century houses that line the streets of tiny Center Sandwich give the town a timeless, unruffled air even during the hustle and bustle of foliage season. It may be this tranquillity that has attracted so many resident craftspeople.

The 1822 Colonial-style Blanchard House has only two guest rooms (they share a bath), but each is large and has its own dressing room. The spare elegance of the rooms reflects the time period of the house, as do the Indian shutters in the parlor, the wide-board floors throughout, and the stone walls in the gardens.

Catherine Hope, who owns this B&B with her husband, Roric Broderick, is a descendent of the original owner, Augustus Blanchard. The canopy on the bed in the stenciled room was made by her grandmother, and many of the quilts and linens are also heirlooms. Since her family has lived in Sandwich for generations, Catherine loves to help her guests discover its many pleasures.

🛏 *2 doubles share bath. Fireplaces in common areas, access to lake beach. $87.50; full breakfast. MC, V. No smoking.*

Ferry Point House

100 Lower Bay Rd., Sanborntorn 03269, tel. 603/524-0087

This red Victorian farmhouse, hidden on a quiet road off Route 3 south of Laconia, was built in the 1800s as a summer retreat for the Pillsbury family. The white wicker chairs and hanging baskets of flowers make the 60-ft veranda facing Lake Winnisquam perfect for relaxing and listening to the loons; you can do the same in the gazebo at the water's edge.

Nearly all of the rooms have views of the lake, along with Oriental-style rugs, painted-wood floors, ceiling fans, and antique Victorian furniture. Innkeeper Diane Damato is proud of her gourmet breakfasts, and rightly so. Baked apples with cheese, fresh muffins, and breakfast crepes with fresh fruit and New Hampshire maple syrup are among her specialties.

Guests are offered homemade baked goods and a cool drink on arrival, and complimentary sherry is available in the living room. A paddleboat, a rowboat, and inner tubes await those who are anxious to get in the water.

🛏 *6 doubles with bath. Cable TV/VCR in living room; guest phone; 2 fireplaces in common areas; swimming, fishing, and boating in lake. $85-95; full breakfast. No credit cards. No smoking, no pets. Closed Nov.-Apr.*

The Inn on Golden Pond

Rte. 3 (Box 680), Holderness 03245, tel. 603/968-7269, fax 603/968-9226

Ever since *On Golden Pond* was filmed at Squam Lake in the early 1980s, the lake's reputation as the "best-kept secret in New Hampshire" has been in jeopardy. Bill and Bonnie Webb, who have owned the Inn on Golden Pond since 1984, know the area well. In fact, Bill is a former president of the nearby science center and a town selectman. He can tell you where to take an early morning nature walk, and if you want the ultimate in quiet—except for the occasional call of a loon—he suggests a third-floor room in the back. Because the emphasis here is on peace and quiet, preteens might find the atmosphere too calm for their liking.

Whether you're in the old wing (circa 1879) or the new (circa 1988), white clapboards cover the outside, and you'll find braided rugs and country curtains throughout. The comfortable rooms are named after birds and animals found in the region, and each has a print, pillow, or other touch in keeping with its name.

🏨 *7 doubles with bath, 1 suite. Cable TV in common room, game room in summer. $90–$140; full breakfast. AE, MC, V. No smoking, no pets.*

The Inn on Newfound Lake

Rte. 3A (1030 Mayhew Turnpike), Bridgewater 03222, tel. 603/744–9111, fax 603/744–3894

This cream-color 150-year-old guest house faces the east shore of Newfound Lake. The rooms are small but bright, with Victorian antiques, four-poster or canopy beds, and claw-foot tubs in the old-fashioned baths. Larry Delangis and Phelps Boyce purchased the inn in 1994 and continue to embellish it.

All the inn folks share an enthusiasm for spring-fed Newfound Lake, acclaimed as the third-cleanest lake in the world. Front rooms have lake views, but you can also watch the reflected sunset from the dining rooms and the front porch. Boats are for rent at the north shore marina. The inn has its own beach.

In addition to the pleasures of Newfound Lake, the White Mountains and Lake Winnipesaukee are easy to reach on day trips, and antiques and handicrafts abound in nearby Plymouth. On rainy afternoons the indoor shuffleboard and basketball hoop in the barn get a workout, and the old piano is kept in tune.

🏨 *22 doubles with bath, 6 doubles share 3 baths, 2 suites. Restaurant, cable TV/VCR in living room, game room, whirlpool bath, exercise room, swimming. $55–$105, suites priced on request; Continental breakfast. AE, D, MC, V. No smoking except in restaurant, no pets. 2-night minimum weekends June–Oct.*

Manor on Golden Pond

Rte. 3 and Shepard Hill Rd. (Box T), Holderness 03245, tel. 603/968–3348 or 800/545–2161, fax 603/968–2116

Built between 1903 and 1907 by Isaac Van Horn, a developer from Florida, this yellow manor house is nestled among the trees on Shepard Hill overlooking Squam Lake. It has welcomed guests since the 1930s when it was owned by Harold Fowler, a renowned *Life* magazine photographer, who made it into a vacation colony for others of his ilk. Many guest rooms in the main house have lake views, as do the cottages (best for families) and the carriage house rooms.

The wealth of polished dark wood and large fireplaces in the common areas, antiques from Great Britain, and rooms named for the likes of Wellington, Churchill, and Victoria all contribute to the English-manor ambience. Thirteen acres, three on the water, provide plenty of space to enjoy the serenity of Squam Lake—the very serenity that led this lake to be used as the setting for the 1981 film *On Golden Pond.*

Owners David and Bambi Arnold like to pamper their guests, so all the rooms have special touches like hair dryers, magnifying mirrors, padded hangers, Godiva chocolates, and Crabtree & Evelyn toiletries. Some rooms, like Savoy Court, have private decks and fireplaces. Four rooms have oversize whirlpool tubs, too.

Guests can enjoy a before-dinner drink in the Three Cocks Pub, a cozy bar with copper-top tables and a rooster motif. Five-course dinners are served either in the manor's dining room or the former billiards room, and the menu changes nightly. A typical meal might feature grilled herb-crusted rabbit in phyllo with a merlot demiglace sauce or roasted Statler chicken breast stuffed with mushroom duxelles and served with purple passion rice pilaf. The desserts are equally decadent: caramel-and-apple napoleon with vanilla-bean ice cream or a chocolate sampler with chocolate-raspberry truffle cake, chocolate turnover, and chocolate crème brûlée.

🏨 *17 doubles with bath in main house, 4 2-bedroom cottages. Restaurant; pub;*

air-conditioning, cable TV in rooms; swimming pool; tennis courts; canoes; paddleboats; fishing; cross-country skiing. $190–$325; MAP. AE, MC, V. No smoking, no pets. Cottages and carriage house closed mid-Oct.–July.

Mary Chase Inn

Rte. 3 (Box 94), Holderness 03245, tel. 603/968–9454

Perched on a ledge is this 1895 Victorian, complete with a turret and a wraparound porch. The lovely cream, light green, and white house, once a convalescent home, had fallen into disrepair when John and Phyllis Chase bought it from his elderly aunt. After two years of restoration the inn opened in 1995.

There's a fireplace in the dining room and in one of the two parlors, which are separated by pocket doors. Antique furniture appropriate to the building's time period fills the guest rooms, each named after one of John's aunts. Flowered wallpapers, lace curtains, and hardwood floors add to the Victorian feel. The suite has a fireplace, a private balcony, and a claw-foot tub. A full breakfast is served either in the dining room or on the porch, both of which have a view of Little Squam Lake.

In summer guests can enjoy the tranquillity of Squam and Little Squam lakes or visit the region's antiques and crafts shops. Winter brings cross-country skiing and skating, and the downhill ski areas of the White Mountains are less than an hour away.

▥ *4 doubles share 2 baths, 1 suite. TV, phone, minirefrigerator in common areas. $85–$125; full breakfast. MC, V. No smoking.*

The Nutmeg Inn

80 Pease Rd., Meredith 03253, tel. 603/279–8811, fax 603/279–7703

All the rooms are named after spices and are decorated accordingly. The walls of Sage, for example, are just *that* shade of green; and should you wonder how the innkeepers, Kathleen and Horst Sieben, managed to find a shower curtain to match the squares of the quilt, the answer is that the quilt was handmade to match the curtain.

The Nutmeg has been a stagecoach tavern, a working farm, part of the Underground Railroad, and a private school. Kathleen loves old houses and has made a full-time job out of renovating this one, doing much of the work herself.

The Cape-style house was built in 1763 by a sea captain who dismantled his ship and used the timber for the beams. He also paneled what is now a dining room with illegal "king's boards," those extra-wide cuts reserved for royal needs. An 18th-century ox yoke, said to have been used during the original construction, is bolted to the wall over a huge fireplace, and the wide-board floors are also original.

▥ *7 doubles with bath, 2 doubles share bath, 1 suite. Air-conditioning, TV/VCR in sitting room, working fireplaces in some rooms, pool. $65–$95; full breakfast. MC, V. No smoking, no pets. 2-night minimum weekends and holidays. Closed Nov.–mid-May.*

Red Hill Inn

Rte. 25B (RFD 1, Box 99M), Center Harbor 03226, tel. 603/279–7001 or 800/573–3445, fax 603/279–7003

An amiable clutter of memorabilia from the first half of the 20th century makes this redbrick mansion on Overlook Hill an unusual country inn. A high school yearbook from the '40s, puzzles and board games from the '30s, and mysterious gewgaws and whatnots from the '20s are what a fortunate houseguest, as if in an old movie, might discover.

When Rick Miller and Don Leavitt found Red Hill, it was a complex of vandalized buildings on the 60-acre campus of a de-

funct college. Happily they did not heed the advice to tear it down but began the salvation and restoration of the main house, the farmhouse, and the stone cottage—all part of a grand summer estate and working farm built in the early 20th century. Outdoor porches were converted into bathrooms and matchstick-paneled sitting rooms, the latter with sweeping views of meadows, mountains, and Squam Lake. Period furniture and even books popular when the inn was a private house were acquired and set in place. Fourteen of the rooms have either woodstoves or fireplaces.

In the inn's four dining rooms, guests quickly discover that chef Elmer Davis loves dessert. On any given night the waitstaff must recite close to a dozen choices, including his famous vinegar pie (which is sweeter than it sounds), windswept chocolate torte, and Kentucky High Pie. But before you get that far, whet your appetite with the cranberry-glazed brie, perhaps, and feast on one of two dozen seafood, lamb, or duck entrées. Many of the herbs used in these dishes are grown in the large on-site garden, which has everything from the ordinary (parsley, thyme, chives) to the extraordinary (hyssop, Egyptian onion, winter savory, and sweet woodruff). In your room you'll find a map of the garden and histories of the herbs grown in it.

After dinner you can head for the popular Runabout Lounge in which a 1940 Chris-Craft speedboat—the same model as the boat in *On Golden Pond*—has been halved to form the bar. But the best way to end a day at the Red Hill Inn is to grab a book and a cup of tea and watch the sun set over Squam Lake from the great bay window in the common room.

🏠 *16 doubles with bath, 5 suites. Restaurant; lounge; TV/VCRs, phones in rooms; whirlpool baths; cross-country skiing, snowshoeing. $90–$170; full breakfast. AE, D, DC, MC, V. No pets. 2-night minimum weekends.*

The Tamworth Inn

Main St. (mailing address: 15 Cleveland Hill Rd.), Tamworth 03886, tel. 603/323–7721 or 800/642–7352, fax 603/323–2026

Tamworth village is synonymous with the Barnstormers Playhouse, summer-night entertainment no one—visitor or resident—would think of missing. Just down the street, the tower of the venerable Tamworth Inn is nearly as well known.

Phil and Kathy Bender, who bought the rambling 1830s Victorian in 1988, have achieved a rare balance. This haven for rest and refreshment since stagecoach days is now where townspeople come for a wedding in the gazebo, new American cuisine in the dining room, or a casual evening in the pub.

Behind the inn, gardens and lawn taper to Swift River. Here Kathy has put her former profession of landscape architect to work, making the most of the romantic gazebo setting with plants and flowers indigenous to New England. Phil, a former banker, manages and cohosts the inn.

The Benders have reduced the total number of rooms in favor of all private baths and more suites. All are furnished with a mixture of 19th-century country antiques and early 20th-century pieces.

In winter fires crackle on the hearths of the dining room, library, and living room, and pots of potpourri in water sit over warming candles. In the pub regulars swap ice-fishing stories around the Franklin stove. In summer you can hang out with the theater cast and crew at the 20-by-40-ft outdoor swimming pool. You can also carry a good book down to the hammock by the river and forget the world completely.

Morning coffee will be brought to your bedroom, if you like. When you amble at leisure to the cheery corner breakfast room you can help yourself to juice, cereal, home-baked breads and muffins, Kathy's special eggs, or French toast.

🏠 *9 doubles with bath, 7 suites. Restaurant, pub, TV/VCR in library and pub, pool, fly-fishing. $95–$130, full breakfast; $120–$160; MAP. MC, V. No smoking. 2-night minimum holidays.*

The Wakefield Inn

2723 Wakefield Rd., Wakefield 03872, tel. 603/522–8272 or 800/245–0841

When you turn off Route 16 and drive east to the historic district of Wakefield, time and traffic vanish. A New England miracle? Well, no, but the Wakefield Inn is listed on the National Register of Historic Places for good reason. This Federal-style building is as square and substantial as a fully rigged ship—precisely what its seagoing builder demanded. He also insisted it be an unconventional three stories high, so he could have the tallest house in the village, and he originally built two houses side by side. Soon the two were joined, and later, a wraparound porch was added.

All this and more you learn from Harry Sisson, who shares innkeeping and ownership with his wife, Lou. The Sissons came to New Hampshire from Connecticut. "We moved in, and the first thing I had to do was cater a wedding reception," Lou recalls. Wedding receptions are numerous here (the village church is across the street). Two doors away is the Museum of Childhood (*see* Places to Go, Sights to See, *above*). Inn guests receive free passes.

Inside the inn there are surprises: a three-sided fireplace in the dining room; a freestanding spiral staircase (no supporting center pole) that is one of the few in the United States. The Indian shutters and wide-plank pine floors are also typical of the late-Colonial era. Upstairs, the guest rooms are named after important 19th-century visitors, such as poet John Greenleaf Whittier or local notables. Throughout the inn are framed tintypes of unsmiling New Englanders. Some pictures the Sissons found in the attic; some are the gifts of inn guests. Many of the subjects are unknown, the "instant ancestors" of the flea market.

All the bedrooms are large—several have an extra bed and are ideal for families—with views of the mountains and countryside or of the historic village. Forget your toothbrush? No matter. Baskets of "most likely to be forgotten" items sit on hall stands, inviting you to help yourself.

Lou's handmade quilts provide the decorative center for the bedrooms. She also holds special quilting weekends at the inn, assuring guests they will return home with completed (or nearly so) quilts of their own.

🏠 *5 doubles with bath, 2 suites. TV/VCR in living room. $55–$75; full breakfast. MC, V. No smoking in rooms, no pets. 2-night minimum holidays.*

The Wolfeboro Inn

90 N. Main St. (Box 1270), Wolfeboro 03894, tel. 603/569–3016 or 800/451–2389, fax 603/569–5375

A landmark lakeside inn with the amenities of a complete resort, the Wolfeboro is a short stroll from the galleries, shops, and sights of the historic village. The original white-clapboard house with green shutters faces Main Street, but extensions overlook Wolfeboro Bay.

Structural additions have been made since the inn's beginnings in 1812: Rooms in the newest wing are a tad brighter, and many have balconies or decks. The oldest part of the inn includes some original bedrooms with fireplaces (decorative), as well as the venerable Wolfe's Tavern. The main dining room has Windsor chairs, a working fireplace, and paneling from the 1760s. In the old tavern there is an oven fireplace, and the serving staff can offer 40 brands of beer from all over the world.

Many guests are lake regulars (and remember coming here as children). Everything is available for a prolonged lake holiday, from the inn's excursion boat (no charge to guests for boat trips or any other amenity) to many other sports facilities. In winter you can try cross-country skiing, skating, ice fishing, and iceboating.

41 doubles with bath, 3 suites, 1 1-bedroom apartment. Restaurant; tavern; air-conditioning, cable TV, phones in rooms; elevator; room service 11 AM–11:30 PM; private lake beach; excursion boat; fishing; conference facilities in inn or on boat. $79–$229; Continental breakfast. AE, MC, V. No pets.

The White Mountains

Notchland Inn

The White Mountains, the highest peaks in the northeast United States, are a rugged range where rock climbers and alpine skiers feel at home. Although 80% of this region is taken up by the White Mountain National Forest, vigorous outdoor pursuits are not all the area has to offer.

Villages founded in the 1700s came to full bloom in the late 19th century, when the elite of Boston, New York, and Philadelphia headed north in private trains to Bethlehem and Bretton Woods. Today visitors from all over the world come to the Mt. Washington valley for shopping sprees at the designer-outlet boutiques of North Conway and to enjoy the serenity of country inns. The variety of regional architecture is astounding: English Tudor–style mansions, Colonial farm-houses, gingerbread-trimmed public buildings, and dairy barns and carriage houses converted into shops and lodgings.

Story Land theme park and the history museum of Heritage New Hampshire are pleasant diversions for families. The subtle sophistication of Jackson Village begins at the red covered bridge that is its gateway; the town offers infinite possibilities for romantic retreats.

*From Sugar Hill's Lupine Festival in mid-June to Lincoln's
New Hampshire Highland Games in mid-September, festivals
and events crowd the summer weekends. The Eastern Slope
Playhouse, also in North Conway, is an archetypical
summer theater, with a professional company performing
Broadway musicals. Galleries and antiques cooperatives are
concentrated here, too.*

*The spectacular scenery of the Presidential Range and its
gorges makes simple sightseeing an end in itself. The area is
vast enough to absorb the hordes of summer visitors and still
leave isolation for those who seek it, particularly in the
mountain, valley, and lakeside villages between Route 16
and the Maine border.*

*Though summer is the busiest season for the region, the first
and second weekends of October are dense with foliage
viewers. Do not be so cavalier as to try for these dates
without reservations, and a year ahead is not too early to
book a special inn. Foliage season is followed by a lull before
the first snows bring skiers. Then, among seasonal special
events, there is a 60-km (36-mi) inn-to-inn Hot Chocolate Run
for the cross-country set in Jackson as well as sleigh rides,
slaloms, and snowmobiling. For alpine skiers the lifts and
runs of Waterville Valley, Loon Mountain, Attitash/Bear
Peak, Cannon Mountain, Wildcat, Black Mountain, and Mt.
Cranmore are household words.*

Places to Go, Sights to See

Kancamagus Highway. Route 112 stretches 34 mi from Lincoln to Conway with
only one exit: Bear Notch Road to Bartlett. It is considered the prime foliage-
viewing road in New England, but at any time of year it is a beauty. You can take
self-guided trails to overlooks.

Mt. Washington. The weather station on top of the highest mountain in the
northeast (6,288 ft) has recorded a world's record in wind velocity (231 mph)
and temperatures that rival the Antarctic. You can reach the summit via the *Mt.
Washington Auto Road* (call 603/466–3988 for road conditions) from Route 16,
Pinkham Notch, or via *Mt. Washington Cog Railway* (tel. 603/846–5404 or 800/

922–8825, ext. 7) from Bretton Woods, mid-April–October, weather permitting. You can also walk.

Old Man of the Mountains. The symbol of New Hampshire is a 40-ft-high outcrop of rock (actually five separate ledges) that bears an acute resemblance to a human profile and is 1,200 ft above Profile Lake in Franconia Notch. This is the Great Stone Face of Nathaniel Hawthorne's famous short story, and there are several designated viewpoints from which to gaze at it. Other sights of the glacier-carved notch are the *Basin*, a 20-ft pothole at the base of a waterfall; the *Flume*, a granite chasm nearly 800 ft long with a stunning series of waterfalls and pools; and *Echo Lake*, where you can try the acoustics over a picnic lunch. *Cannon Mountain Aerial Tramway* (tel. 603/823–5563) operates from Memorial Day to late October. You ascend 2,022 ft in five minutes to the Summit Observation Platform, then follow trails to other outlooks. The *New England Ski Museum* (tel. 603/823–7177) is at the foot of the tramway.

White Mountain National Forest. More than 1,300 mi of trails make this spectacular combination of rugged mountains and wooded valleys heaven for hikers and mountain climbers. More than 300 species of animals and birds live here, while an additional 120 species pass through regularly. In winter you can ski, snowshoe, or try ice climbing; in summer swim, canoe, fish, and camp; any time of year enjoy the quality of life in a protected wilderness covering nearly 758,000 acres. The *Appalachian Mountain Club* (tel. 603/466–2725) has its home base at Pinkham Notch.

Restaurants

Many country inns, such as those listed below, serve dinner to the public as well as to their lodgers, but remember that the lodger always comes first, so reservations are imperative. New England contemporary cuisine is served at the **Inn at Thorn Hill** (*see below*), in Jackson, the **1785 Inn** (*see below*), in North Conway, and **Darby Field Inn** (Bald Hill, tel. 603/447–2181), in Conway. The **Scottish Lion** (Rte. 16, Main St., tel. 603/356–6381); in North Conway, serves oatcakes with every meal.

Reservations Services

Jackson Resort Association (tel. 800/866–3334), **Mt. Washington Valley Central Reservation Service** (tel. 800/367–3364), **Mt. Washington Valley Chamber of Commerce Travel & Lodging Bureau** (tel. 603/356–5701 or 800/ 223-7669), **Reservation Service of the Country Inns in the White Mountains** (tel. 603/356–9460 or 800/562–1300). For referrals (not direct reservations) in communities around Berlin, contact the **Northern White Mountains Chamber of Commerce** (tel. 800/992–7480).

Visitor Information

Mt. Washington Valley Visitors Bureau (Box 2300, North Conway 03860, tel. 603/356–3171 or 800/367–3364), **New Hampshire Division of Parks and Recreation** (*see* Visitor Information *in* The Seacoast, *above*), **New Hampshire Office of Travel and Tourism Development** (*see* Visitor Information *in* The Seacoast, *above*), **White Mountains Attractions** (Box 10, North Woodstock 03262, tel. 603/745–8720 or 800/346–3687), **White Mountain National Forest** (719 N. Main St., Laconia 03246, tel. 603/528–8721 or 800/283–2267).

Adair

80 Guider La., Bethlehem 03574, tel. 603/444-2600 or 888/444-2600, fax 603/444-4823

Frank Hogan, a Washington, DC, trial lawyer, built this gambrel-roof, Georgian Revival mansion in 1927 as a wedding gift for his only daughter, Dorothy Adair Hogan. In 1992 Patricia and Hardy Banfield converted the house to an inn and now run it with their daughter, Nancy. Adair delights guests who come to stroll in its gardens and enjoy the many pleasures of the White Mountains.

A gathering room just off the entry hall has a large fireplace, Asian rugs, and plenty of easy chairs and sofas. An honor bar for guests is in the Granite Tap Room, along with another fireplace and a pool table that dates from the era when Adair was built. A collection of vintage hats that the Banfields found in one of the attics decorates the stairway and hall leading to the guest rooms.

Each room has a garden or a mountain view, Lindt chocolates, and a mixture of elegant antiques and antique reproductions. Seven guest rooms have fireplaces or fireplace stoves, and the Kinsman Suite has a king-size sleigh bed, a fireplace stove, a private deck, and a two-person Jacuzzi tub. As the emphasis here is on elegance and romance, families with children would be happier elsewhere.

Each morning a full breakfast with the likes of fresh fruit, eggs Benedict, raspberry pancakes, and fresh popovers is served in the breakfast room or on the patio. The separately owned Tim-Bir Alley Restaurant serves dinner except during the off-season months of November and April through early May. On a typical night, you could try corn and smoked-salmon pancakes with tomato salsa followed by quail with a maple Balsamic glaze and apple cranberry relish. Save room for desserts such as pecan-crusted apple fig tart with whipped maple cream or chocolate cheese strudel topped with white chocolate sauce.

▦ *7 doubles with bath, 2 suites. Restaurant (dinner only); cable TV/VCR, phone in common area; tennis court, snowshoeing. $135–$220; full breakfast. AE, MC, V. No smoking, no pets.*

The Covered Bridge House

Rte. 302 (Box 989), Glen 03838, tel. 603/383-9109 or 800/232-9109

This simple tan Colonial sits on the banks of the Saco River just a few minutes' drive from bustling North Conway. The inn gets its name from the covered bridge over the river that is part of the property and houses innkeeper Nancy Wanek's crafts and gift shop. Nancy and her husband, Dan, moved here from New York in 1994, seeking a business they could run together that would allow them to spend time with their son, Brian. They've never regretted the move.

The inn is decorated with braided rugs, half-wall paneling, hardwood floors, and Nancy's stenciling. Rooms have quilts, rocking chairs, and a variety of country touches that create a cheerful, but not fussy, atmosphere.

There's a small beach on the river for swimming or tubing in the summer. In winter the cross-country ski trails of Jackson are nearby, as are the downhill areas of Black Mountain, Attitash/Bear Peak, and Mt. Cranmore.

▦ *4 doubles with bath, 2 rooms share bath. Cable TV, phone in common area; fishing; river swimming. $49–$79; full breakfast. AE, D, MC, V.*

Foxglove, A Country Inn

Rte. 117, Sugar Hill 03585, tel. 603/823-8840, fax 603/823-5755

It seems appropriate that this rambling turn-of-the-century home is next to Lover's Lane in the village of Sugar Hill. Beautiful sunsets, cozy rooms, and lush

gardens with hammocks for relaxing all make Foxglove an ideal romantic getaway The atmosphere, the special attention provided by the Boyds, and the wealth of antiques make this the perfect inn for couples or for singles looking for a little pampering.

Innkeepers Janet and Walter Boyd work hard to delight their guests. The gourmet breakfast is different every day, as is the china on which it is served. The common areas are decorated in a country-French style with Louis XV and XVI pieces, and the lilacs on the hall wallpaper are so lush that you may catch yourself taking deep breaths looking for the distinctive scent.

Guest rooms range from the sophisticated Serengeti Room, which has animal print linens, an antique chandelier with carnival-glass shades, and black and brass fixtures in the bath, to the cozy Blue Room, where a king-size bed swathed in blue and white complements the blue fleur-de-lis wallpaper.

🏠 *6 doubles with bath. Dinner by request, cable TV in common area. $85–$145; full breakfast. MC, V. No smoking, no pets.*

The Franconia Inn

1300 Easton Rd., Franconia 03580, tel. 603/823–5542 or 800/473–5299, fax 603/823–8078

The Franconia is a white-clapboard rambler built as an inn in 1934 when the original 18th-century farm homestead was destroyed by fire. Just across the road are its glider field and tennis courts; stables for nine horses are next door.

Alec and Richard Morris, brothers and third-generation innkeepers, bought the property in 1981 and began to turn it into the complete resort it is today. Do you want to swim? Ride? Fly? Hike? Ski? Or just relax on the screened porch? Want a king-size Jacuzzi tub in your suite? Everything is right here on 107 scenic acres in Easton Valley.

Guests can enjoy the fireplace in the beam-ceiling living room, a cozy game room, and a lounge with a big-screen TV. Rooms are decorated in designer chintzes, and many have canopy beds. The Inn Suite comes with a fireplace stove and a wet bar; family suites have two bedrooms with a bath in between.

🏠 *31 doubles with bath, 3 suites. Restaurant, cable TV/VCR in lounge, movie room, game room, hot tub, pool, 4 tennis courts, sleigh rides, cross-country skiing (instruction and equipment rentals), bicycles, croquet, horseback riding (fee), snowshoeing (equipment rentals), ice-skating rink, soaring center, privileges at nearby 9-hole golf course. $98–$158, full breakfast; $145–$205, MAP. AE, MC, V. No pets. Closed Apr.–mid-May.*

The Horse & Hound Inn

205 Wells Rd., Franconia 03580, tel. 603/823–5501 or 800/450–5501

This 1838 farmhouse, on a back road near Franconia Notch and Cannon Mountain, was expanded in 1946 by an Englishman who envisioned living the sporting life and operating a traditional country-house hotel on the side.

Today's owners, Jim Cantlon and Bill Steele, both formerly professional hoteliers from Virginia, are comfortable with that image. "It also seemed a good place to spread out all the things we had collected over the years," Jim says. "We both enjoy cooking and gardening generally, and Bill makes great desserts."

Dogwood-pattern china graces the tables of the paneled dining room, with its working fireplace and windows that look out on the terrace and lawn. The cuisine is Continental with a French emphasis, though there are English grills on the menu too. Upstairs the bedrooms are named for the artwork hung on their walls: the Audubon Room, the Currier & Ives Room, and the Garden Room. An eclectic mix of antiques, flowered wallpapers, and hardwood floors all combine

to create a comfortable ambience in the rooms, some of which have a view of the mountains.

▦ *6 doubles with bath, 4 rooms share 2 baths. Restaurant, cable TV in lounge, phones in rooms, cross-country ski trails. $70–$80; full breakfast. AE, D, DC, MC, V. Closed Apr.–mid-May and Nov.*

Inn at Crystal Lake

Rte. 153 (Box 12), Eaton Center 03832, tel. 603/447-2120 or 800/343-7336, fax 603/447-3599

This charming Victorian, built in 1884, has 11 guest rooms named and color coded for gemstones, including the emerald, the garnet, and the aquamarine. The Ruby Room is a real beauty, with its 1850 Honduras mahogany canopy bed and matching dressing table.

The yellow inn with its green shutters, hanging baskets, and white wicker porch furniture is set in a quiet village; it looks like a page from a calendar. Once a private home owned by Nathaniel Palmer—who designed dresses that were then sewn by the ladies of Eaton and sold to the summer tourists—the inn is now in the capable hands of Richard and Janice Octeau.

The beach on Crystal Lake is within walking distance, and Richard and Janice keep a canoe and paddleboat for you to use. In winter opportunities for skating and cross-country skiing are nearby. A game area, a fireplace, and a 60-inch television in the common room are nice for cool evenings.

▦ *10 doubles with bath, 1 suite. Cable TV/VCR in common area, canoe, paddleboat, lake swimming. $80–$110; full breakfast. AE, D, MC, V. Smoking only in lounge, no pets. 2-night minimum holidays.*

Inn at Thorn Hill

Thorn Hill Rd. (Box A), Jackson 03846, tel. 603/383-4242 or 800/289-8990, fax 603/383-8062

Romantic is a word you hear a lot at Thorn Hill, the mansion designed by Stanford White, the Gilded Age's most famous architect. Although the inn may feel like your own isolated and special place (the view of Mt. Washington is superb), staying here puts you within walking distance of shops, galleries, and many outdoor activities.

Jim and Ibby Cooper, owners and proprietors, came to Thorn Hill from hospitality and education careers in California, Texas, and Florida. Their older children—excited to be involved—fit right in with a lifestyle that seems less a business than a constant round of entertaining good friends. Yet the elegant past is never far away. A suite in the main house features a mannequin wearing an 1870s wedding dress. In one bedroom a blue velvet fainting couch is an invitation to swoon; spectacular Asian rugs and electrified Victorian oil lamps are everywhere.

The rooms in the carriage house have a Victorian country-style decor. The open fireplace and overstuffed sofas of the Great Room encourage you to sprawl, and rather than the formality of the Steinway baby grand piano in the main-house drawing room, the carriage house offers an outdoor hot tub. Three cottages—beloved by honeymooners—have fireplaces, whirlpool baths, and other romantic touches.

Thorn Hill is a year-round retreat. In spring, summer, and autumn there are wildflowers and pine forests as well as swimming, hiking, and fishing. In winter you can step directly from the inn's waxing room onto the 150-km (93-mi) Jackson Ski-Touring cross-country trail network or ski downhill at five major areas nearby. You can toboggan on the property, or, if you prefer, have a horse-drawn sleigh pick you up at the door.

Thorn Hill's dining room is known throughout the valley for its contemporary New England cuisine and its wine list—as well as the candlelight.

🏠 *14 doubles with bath, 2 suites, 3 cottages. Restaurant, pub, air-conditioning, terry-cloth robes, turndown service, cable TV/VCR in the parlor, meeting room, badminton, shuffleboard, pool, croquet, horseshoes, cross-country ski trails, sleigh rides, tobogganing. $120– $220, full breakfast; $150–$250, MAP. AE, D, DC, MC, V. No smoking, no pets. 2-night minimum foliage, Christmas, and winter weekends, B&B only midwk in Apr.*

The Lavender Flower Inn

1657 Main St. (Box 328), Center Conway 03813, tel. 603/447–3794 or 800/729–0106

The outside of this 1850s farmhouse-turned-B&B is done in five shades of lavender, and if you time your visit for mid-June, you will see beds of blue and white iris at their full glory. The iris motif is repeated inside, from wallpaper and prints to shower curtains. Gardening is one of the shared hobbies Ray and Noreen Berthiaume enjoy to the fullest now that they have left the corporate world for innkeeping and small-town life. They are always expanding the herb garden and have also added heirloom rosebushes. In addition, Ray restores antique furniture. Notice, in particular, the old Turkish fainting couch and the Victorian tables and beds made of mahogany or cherry. From Center Conway you can go shopping or skiing in the Mt. Washington valley one day, down to the lakes the next. Portland, Maine, is only an hour away. In winter you can snowmobile or cross-country ski from the inn.

🏠 *3 doubles with bath, 4 doubles share 2 baths. Cable TV in living room. $50– $98; full breakfast, snacks. AE, D, MC, V. No smoking, no pets. 2-night minimum holiday weekends.*

The Mulburn Inn

2370 Main St., Bethlehem 03574, tel. 603/ 869–3389 or 800/457–9440, fax 603/869– 5633

The 1913 Tudor-style mansion—with its circular driveway, stone porticoes, and 3 acres of grounds—stands at the east end of Bethlehem. It was once a summer cottage known as Ivie Estate and has such notable architectural details as imported tile around the fireplaces, stained-glass windows, and ornate mantels.

The Milburn is large enough to provide third-floor living space for owners Tim and Lisa Skeels, their two young boys, and Tim's mother, Twila Skeels, and still have seven large, airy bedrooms for guests on the second floor. The rooms are named after peaks in the Presidential Mountain range. Each is distinctive: The Monroe has its closet in a disused elevator; the Madison has its pineapple-post bed set in the round of a turret; the Adams has a 7-ft-long tub in the bathroom; the Pierce sleeps up to five. Year-round sports and all the sights of Franconia and the White Mountains are close at hand.

🏠 *7 doubles with bath. Cable TV/VCR in common room, 2 18-hole golf courses nearby. $55–$80; full breakfast, afternoon tea. AE, D, MC, V. No smoking, no pets.*

Notchland Inn

Rte. 302, Hart's Location, Bartlett 03812, tel. 603/374–6131 or 800/866–6131, fax 603/374–6168

There are llamas in the barn at Notchland Inn, and these unique animals are just one of the surprises that await you here. This mountain lodge estate overlooks the Saco River valley at the entrance to Crawford Notch. It was built in 1852 by Samuel Beamis, a Boston dentist, and is constructed of locally quarried granite and native timbers. Beamis, a lifelong bachelor, bequeathed it to his

loyal caretaker, whose children began to take in summer guests. Notchland became a year-round inn in 1983.

Subsequent renovations have added a new wing with a gourmet restaurant and a gazebo by the duck pond. An old schoolhouse has become a two-suite guest house with working fireplaces; early photographs of the surrounding mountains hang on the walls. The main house retains high ceilings, wood floors, fireplaces, and other 19th-century touches. The bedrooms have armoires, wing chairs, antiques, and fireplaces.

Les Schoof and Ed Butler, the current owners, bought the inn in 1993 when they moved here from Manhattan. They have brought their own touches, such as the award-winning perennial gardens and Cocoa, a lovable Bernese mountain dog.

Watching the seasons unfold from this mountainside vantage point is irresistible despite the fact that the house has a sad history—Samuel Beamis built it to soothe a broken heart; a marker in the living room tells of Nancy Barton, who in 1788 DIED IN A SNOWSTORM IN PURSUIT OF HER FAITHLESS LOVER on the edge of the property. You can try whitewater canoeing in springtime, hiking and trout fishing in summer. There are ice-skating on the inn pond in winter and miles of trails for cross-country skiing.

▦ *7 doubles with bath, 5 suites. Meeting rooms, outdoor hot tub, river swimming, hiking and cross-country ski trails. $100–$130, full breakfast; $146–$210, MAP (mandatory on weekends). AE, D, MC, V. No smoking, no pets. 2-night minimum weekends except Apr.–June.*

The 1785 Inn

Rte. 16 (Box 1785), North Conway 03860, tel. 603/356–9025 or 800/421–1785, fax 603/356–6081

This white Colonial with blue trim is one of the oldest structures in Mt. Washington valley. It was a "publick house" right from the start and so popular the roof had to be raised—literally—to accommodate more guests. Becky and Charlie Mallar restored the inn completely when they exchanged their careers in education for innkeeping. Their restaurant and its wine cellar continue to win prizes. In fact, the only thing debatable about the inn is which window has the best view of the mountains. Each room is different, not only in its coordinated colors, but in the varied Colonial-to-Victorian antiques and country-style furnishings. Rooms on the back are quietest, and Room 5, with a king-size bed, has a wonderful view.

▦ *11 doubles with bath, 5 doubles share 2 baths, 1 suite. Restaurant and bar, air-conditioning, cable TV in bar and suite, cable TV/VCR in living room, fireplaces in public rooms, room service, pool, cross-country skiing and hiking trails, volleyball, shuffleboard, tennis court. $70–$180; full breakfast. AE, D, DC, MC, V. No smoking in main dining room or in bedrooms, no pets. 2-night minimum during foliage season.*

Snowvillage Inn

Stuart Rd. (off Rt. 153, south of Conway), Snowville 03849, tel. 603/447–2818 or 800/447–4345

From 1,000 ft up Mt. Foss, the span of the Presidential Range at sunset appears hand-colored. No wonder Barbara and Kevin Flynn find this spot ideal for their inn. For hikers, skiers, readers, and environmentalists as well as lovers of good food, Snowvillage is alluring.

The guest rooms (including one with 12 windows) are in the main house, in an old carriage barn–library, and in a new lodge, where every room has a working fireplace. Each has been named for a writer or literary genre and contains appropriate bedside reading. Although many of the fascinating pictures and accessories are Tyrolean, the architecture is New England farmhouse, and the buildings are a cheerful cranberry red with white trim.

Asian rugs, wing chairs, good reading lights, knotty pine paneling, and welcoming homemade chocolate-chip cookies will make you feel cared for. Breakfast includes a high-energy fitness minimenu as well as such items as pumpkin pancakes and omelets. Special guided hikes with gourmet food can be arranged, right down to a five-course champagne lunch.

In winter there are snowshoeing and professional instruction in cross-country skiing, and at any time of year Kevin is ready to point out a trail through the blueberry barrens or map out the way to the area's numerous antiques and discount-shopping meccas. Guests have resident beach privileges at Crystal Lake, minutes away.

The four-course candlelight dinner might begin with Mediterranean fish soup or mussels Provençale. The bulk of the menu relies on such country-French mainstays as duck à l'orange and roasted rack of lamb. Save room for the silk pie, which regulars rave about, or even some pumpkin cheesecake.

18 doubles with bath. Restaurant, meeting rooms, resident privileges at lake, tennis court, volleyball, horseshoes, hiking trails, sauna, cross-country skiing (equipment rental/lessons), snowshoeing (equipment rental). $129–$229; MAP. AE, D, DC, MC, V. No smoking, no pets.

Sugar Hill Inn

Sugar Hill Rd. (Box 954), Franconia 03580, tel. 603/823–5621 or 800/548–4748

The late film star Bette Davis used to visit old friends in this house before she bought her own place, Butternut Farm, nearby, so it is logical that the largest bedroom with the best view is called the Bette Davis Room. Each of the rooms in this 18th-century white-clapboard inn has charm (note the oak-and-maple dresser in Grandma's Room and the original sugar-maple floors), and the setting on the side of Sugar Hill is bucolic. Rag or hooked rugs, rocking chairs, quilts,

and well-chosen antique accent pieces of varying periods add to the inn's welcoming atmosphere.

Jim and Barbara Quinn, former Rhode Islanders, own the inn now. Daughter Kelly and son-in-law Stephen share the responsibilities of running it. Jim cooks the bountiful country breakfasts, while Stephen bakes all the breads and makes dinner for inn and restaurant guests. Barbara and Kelly handle the details of day-to-day operations and decorating. The Quinns are also involved in the Franconia community, especially the Sugar Hill Museum, where there is Bette Davis memorabilia on display, along with the work of local artists.

10 doubles with bath in main house, 6 doubles with bath in 3 cottages. Restaurant, air-conditioning in dining room, guest phone in common area, fireplace stoves and TVs in cottages. $90–$145, full breakfast and afternoon tea; $215–$255, MAP during foliage season. MC, V. No smoking, no pets. 2-night minimum during foliage season and Christmas wk.

Sunset Hill House

Sunset Hill Rd., Sugar Hill 03585, tel. 603/823–5522 or 800/786–4455, fax 603/823–5738

Perched on a 1,700-ft ridge that gives guests a stunning view of both the Presidential Range to the east and Vermont's Green Mountains to the west, Sunset Hill House is known for the fiery glow that plays out over the White Mountains at the end of each day—the hill and the inn were both named for these beautiful sunsets.

After innkeeper Michael Coyle bought this Second Empire house in 1993, he spent six months on renovations. The interior is done in bright floral patterns without seeming frilly or precious. Each of the three large common areas has its own feel: a formal sitting parlor, a lively music parlor, and a very informal game room with a TV and VCR. Outside, the

30-by-30-ft deck looks out to the Presidential Range. Although every room has a view of mountains, some have bay windows that make perfect reading nooks. Two rooms are suites with Jacuzzis. The innkeeper's favorite is Room 201, which has two bay windows.

Expect homey, friendly service from Michael and his wife, Tricia. Guests who stay for the Thanksgiving weekend usually take part in the holiday work bee to ready the inn for the Christmas season. Other inn events include a Valentine theme weekend, a Maple Sugaring weekend in March for tapping trees and boiling sap, and a lupine festival held each June when the hillside is awash in lavender blooms.

The multicourse breakfast, served in the inn's dining room where all tables have a view of the mountains, includes items such as banana-stuffed French toast, and melt-in-your-mouth blueberry muffins. The dinner menu favors such complex dishes as roast rack of lamb with a granola-mustard crust, split and finished with port wine–peppercorn sauce or sesame sugar-crusted chicken breast. The lighter tavern menu features sandwiches, nachos, and pizza.

🏠 *27 doubles with bath, 3 suites. Restaurant, tavern, cable TV/VCR in common area, phones and ceiling fans in rooms, heated pool, 9-hole golf course, cross-country ski trails, snowshoeing. $80–$160, full breakfast; $137–$232 MAP. AE, D, MC, V. No smoking, no pets. 2-night minimum during foliage season and holiday weekends.*

Whitneys' Inn

Rte. 16B (Box 822), Jackson 03846, tel. 603/383–8916 or 800/677–5737, fax 603/383–6886

In 1992 Robert and Barbara Bowman bought this casual country retreat at the foot of Black Mountain and set about making it better than ever. In winter you can walk to the ski lifts; the rest of the year you can enjoy other regional attractions such as Story Land and the Heritage New Hampshire theme museum.

The 1842 farmhouse has two additions—a deluxe wing and a chalet—and two cottages; all have plain country furnishings and lots of pine. The rooms are comfortable, but not elegant, so you can set your ski boots in a corner or lean your poles against the wall without worrying about the decor. The 200-year-old brown barn is used for large functions and as a game room in summer. It houses an original shovel handle used on the mountain's first overhead tow lift as well as a collection of historic ski photos. Upstairs is an après-ski bar.

🏠 *20 doubles with bath, 8 suites, 3 2-bedroom cottages. Restaurant; pub; cable TV in lounge; pub; game room; fireplaces in cottages; TV, minirefrigerators in some rooms; meeting rooms; pond; tennis. $50–$110, full breakfast; MAP available. AE, D, MC, V. No smoking in dining room. 2-night minimum holidays and weekends Jan.–Mar., July–Aug., mid-Sept.–mid-Oct.*

Western and Central New Hampshire

*The hills in the southwest corner of the state are gentler than
the fierce granite ledges of the White Mountains. Perhaps
that's why 3,165-ft Mt. Monadnock remains the second-most-
climbed mountain in the world, after Japan's Mt. Fuji.*

*Everything seems softer and slower paced here. Although
other parts of the state have become home to outlet malls,
theme parks, and fast-food restaurants, this section has
resisted the trend. Roads meander along rivers, each town
has a common that seems even greener and more pristine
than the last, and townsfolk take time to chat with visitors.*

*If you follow the Connecticut River north through countryside
made familiar by Maxfield Parrish, you'll come to Hanover,
home of Dartmouth College. Near pristine Lake Sunapee the
League of New Hampshire Craftsmen holds the oldest (and
possibly the best) crafts show in the nation for a week every
August. And tiny Fitzwilliam remains a well-preserved haven
for lovers of Colonial and Federal architecture.*

*Most of the attractions here are natural or historic. Hiking,
cross-country skiing, canoeing, and fishing are all popular
pursuits. Downhill skiers will enjoy the Pat's Peak and
Sunapee ski areas.*

Places to Go, Sights to See

Christa McAuliffe Planetarium (3 Institute Dr., New Hampshire Technical
Institute, Concord, tel. 603/225–3381). This planetarium was named for the
teacher who was killed in the *Challenger* space shuttle explosion in 1986. Shows
on the solar system and space exploration use computer graphics, sound
equipment, and views through the 40-ft dome telescope.

Fort at No. 4 (Rte. 11W, Cornish, tel. 603/826–5700). In 1747 when this fort
withstood a massive attack by 400 French soldiers, it was a lonely outpost on the

periphery of Colonial civilization. Today it's the only living history museum of the French and Indian War.

Monadnock State Park (Off Rte. 124, Jaffrey, tel. 532–8862). This popular park is home to Mt. Monadnock, from which—on a clear day—you can see the Boston skyline. The only way to the top is on foot, but there are a variety of trails that vary in level of difficulty.

Museum at Lower Shaker Village (Rte. 4A, Enfield, tel. 603/632–4346). The legacy of the Enfield Shakers, including their implements and their crafts, is preserved here. A self-guided walking tour leads through the 13 buildings in the complex.

Museum of New Hampshire History (6 Eagle Sq., Concord, tel. 603/225–3381). This recently expanded museum houses an original Concord Coach built during the 19th century when more than 3,000 of them were built in Concord. At the time this was about as technologically perfect a vehicle as you could find—in fact, many say it's the coach that won the West. Other exhibits provide an overview of New Hampshire's history, from the Abenaki Indians to the early settlers of Portsmouth and up to the current times.

Saint-Gaudens National Historic Site (Off Rte. 12A, Cornish, tel. 603/675–2175). Once the home, studio, and gallery of sculptor Augustus Saint-Gaudens (1848–1907), this site now also has full-size replicas of the artist's bronzes scattered throughout 150 acres of gardens.

Restaurants

Try the **New London Inn** (tel. 603/526–2791), on Main Street in New London, for a nouvelle-inspired menu. **Home Hill Country Inn** (tel. 603/675–6165), on River Road in Plainfield, off Rt. 12A about 10 mi south of Hanover, serves both classic and nouvelle French cuisine in a country setting. **Henry David's** (tel. 603/352–0608), on Main Street in Keene, is a good place for soup and a sandwich. Peterborough's **Latacarta** (tel. 603/924–6878), on School Street, draws those looking for an interesting low-fat, low-cholesterol meal.

Reservations Service

Lake Sunapee Business Association (Box 400, Sunapee 03782, tel. 603/763–2495 or 800/258–3530).

Visitor Information

Monadnock Travel Council (48 Central Sq., Keene 03431, tel. 603/352–1303), **New Hampshire Division of Parks and Recreation** (*see* Visitor Information *in* The Seacoast, *above*), **New Hampshire Office of Travel and Tourism Development** (*see* Visitor Information *in* The Seacoast, *above*), **Peterborough Chamber of Commerce** (Box 401, Peterborough 03458, tel. 603/924–7234).

Amos A. Parker House

Rte. 119 (Box 202), Fitzwilliam 03447, tel. 603/585-6540

"Oh, what's this?" are words Freda Houpt hears a lot from her guests. Great bunches of her own dried flowers hang from the beams in the Great Room of the Amos A. Parker House. The eye-stopping garden, which slopes to the river behind the house, attests to the favorite hobby of its energetic owner, who also volunteers at the Smith College Botanic Garden. On the roadside a genuine liberty pole shows the house's history as a meeting place for revolutionaries. Today's kitchen and Great Room were the original cabin (circa 1700), but by 1780 the shelter had grown to a family home requiring six (still working) fireplaces and a beehive oven in the dining room.

Rooms have good reading lights, comfortable chairs, and a mix of antiques. Elaborate flower murals by local artists Debra Luoma and Brenda Duval decorate the hallway and some of the rooms. From the inn you can stroll downhill to the Fitzwilliam Green, with its ring of 18th-century houses and overflowing antiques stores. Minutes away are Rhododendron State Park and the all-faith outdoor Cathedral of the Pines.

🏠 *2 doubles with bath, 2 suites. TV/VCR and phone in common area, tennis courts and cross-country ski trails nearby. $80–$90; full breakfast. No credit cards. No smoking, no pets. 2-night minimum holidays.*

The Benjamin Prescott Inn

Rte. 124, 433 Turnpike Rd., Jaffrey 03452, tel. and fax 603/532-6637

A working dairy farm surrounds this 1853 Colonial farmhouse, making guests feel like they are miles out in the country rather than just minutes from the center of historic Jaffrey Village. The landscape here is so appealing that novelist Willa Cather, who spent many summers in Jaffrey, chose the Old Burying Ground as her final resting place.

Innkeeper Jan Miller is an award-winning quilt maker, and you'll find samples of her work throughout the inn, along with husband Barry's ship models. Jan is also an accomplished candy maker, and guests will find her homemade chocolates waiting for them each evening. The third floor suite has a king-size four-poster canopy bed, double beds built into alcoves under the eaves, a bathroom with pocket doors, and a balcony that overlooks the farm. Despite the farmlike setting and the large rooms, this B&B is not appropriate for families with preteens.

You can prepare for a day of antiquing or climbing Mt. Monadnock with a full breakfast featuring Welsh miner's cakes, baked French toast with apples or peaches, or an egg-and-sausage casserole.

🏠 *6 doubles with bath, 3 suites. Air-conditioning in 2 rooms, cross-country skiing, hiking, snowshoeing. $65–$130; full breakfast. AE, MC, V. No smoking in rooms.*

The Birchwood Inn

Rte. 45 (Box 197), Temple 03084, tel. 603/878-3285, fax 603/878-2159

Rufus Porter, the early 19th-century itinerant painter, did the mural that decorates the dining room of the Birchwood Inn. Although the inn began operating around 1775 at the crossroads that forms the small town of Temple, it is believed that the current brick building with its attached white-clapboard barn was built about 1800.

You'll revel in the inn's eclectic antiques—from the Steinway square grand piano to the wind-up Edison phonograph. Each guest room has a different theme: The Train Room has vintage model trains on the shelves and photos of trains on the walls; the Editorial Room

has antique typecases and framed copies of newspapers with famous headlines.

Owners Judy and Bill Wolfe share the work of running the inn. "Bill likes to cook, and I like to bake," says Judy. Breakfast is served in the restaurant, as is dinner, which consists of a choice of three entrées and two appetizers. A typical evening's fare might include she-crab soup, lobster bisque, filet mignon, and roast duckling with Grand Marnier sauce.

🏠 *5 doubles with bath, 2 doubles share bath. Restaurant (dinner only), TV in common area. $60–$70; full breakfast. No credit cards. No smoking. Closed 1 wk in Apr. and 1 wk in Nov.*

Candlelite Inn

5 Greenhouse La., just off Rte. 114, Bradford 03221, tel. 603/938–5571

The country-Victorian Candlelite Inn was built (circa 1897) to welcome summer visitors who came to enjoy the tranquility of the towns surrounding Lake Sunapee at the turn of the century. Guests come for the same reason today.

The sunroom has a view of the pond and the vegetable and herb gardens and is the setting for puzzles and games in the evening. Innkeepers Marilyn and Les Gordon provide snacks and on cool nights, keep a fire going in the woodstove. Rooms are named by the colors used to decorate them: blue, rose, lavender, yellow, green. The Peach Room, one of the largest, has an antique brass bed, frothy lace curtains, a double etched-mirror armoire, and an antique sewing machine. In the Yellow Room, a small suite, a hunter green comforter on a cherry Colonial bed provides a nice counterpoint to the sunny walls.

Breakfast, served in the sunroom or in the dining room, is a multicourse affair that even includes dessert. Some of Marilyn's favorite dishes are gingerbread pancakes, French toast made from cin-namon-swirl bread and served with an orange-and-banana sauce, and raspberry-topped lemon pie.

🏠 *6 doubles with bath. Swimming, boating, fishing, cross-country and downhill skiing nearby. $70–$100; full breakfast. AE, D, MC, V. No smoking, no pets.*

The Chase House

Rte. 12A (R.R. 2, Box 909), Cornish 03745, tel. 603/675–5391 or 800/401–9450, fax 603/675–5010

Salmon P. Chase, Lincoln's secretary of the treasury and then chief justice of the Supreme Court, was born in this 1775 Federal-style house on the banks of the Connecticut River. A National Historic Landmark, the house has been meticulously restored, and a 30×40 ft gathering room with a fieldstone fireplace and a minstrel loft has been added by salvaging the attic of an 1810 garrison house. Perennial gardens and a fruit orchard complete the bucolic setting.

Innkeeper Barbara Lewis bought the Chase House in 1991 and finished the addition in 1992. With her partner, Ted Doyle, Barbara enjoys introducing guests to the Connecticut River valley and sharing the history of the house and its celebrated early occupant.

The common areas provide plenty of homey touches: Nooks hold minirefrigerators stocked with soft drinks, a countertop has the makings for coffee or tea (if it's not already made for you), and a cookie jar invites you to indulge a sweet tooth. The gathering room, with exposed beams, a hardwood floor, and a huge fireplace, has a TV and VCR as well as a variety of games. A small office for guests provides a private place to work or make phone calls. You can even keep up your fitness regime using the aerobic equipment in the exercise room.

Guest rooms have Asian rugs, antique armoires, quilts on the beds, and high ceilings. All except the Kate Chase Room are named after Lincoln's cabinet members—including the bridal suite, which is named for Edwin Stanton, Lincoln's secretary of war. The Gideon Welles Suite offers a queen-size pineapple-post bed, a walk-in closet, and a settee under windows that provide a view of the fruit trees.

Breakfast is served in one of two dining rooms—both with fireplaces—or on the patio, depending on the weather and the number of guests. The Amish friendship bread pancakes and the popovers are especially popular.

🛏 *4 doubles with bath, 2 doubles share bath, 2 suites. Air-conditioning in some rooms, cable TV/VCR in common rooms, exercise room, river swimming, canoeing, snowshoeing (equipment available). $95–$135; full breakfast. MC, V. No smoking, no pets. Closed Nov.*

Colby Hill Inn

3 The Oaks (Box 779), Henniker 03242, tel. 603/428-3281, fax 603/428-9218

The friendly greeting by inn dogs Bertha and Delilah, both Great Dane–Labrador mixes, sets the tone for the Colby Hill Inn. The cookie jar is always full, and the welcome mat is always out at this rambling 1795 farmhouse that was once a stagecoach stop in the town of Henniker.

Four of the rooms have fireplaces, including Room 6, which also has a queen-size canopy bed and delicate rosebud wallpaper. All have a mix of antiques and Colonial reproductions. The carriage house rooms are less formal—with exposed beams, white walls, and country furnishings. Outside, the garden gazebo and the shaded flagstone patio around the swimming pool are two favorite places to relax on summer afternoons. In winter guests enjoy downhill skiing at nearby Pat's Peak or cross-country skiing from the door of the inn.

The menu in the dining room changes frequently, but it always includes chicken Colby Hill: boneless breast of chicken stuffed with lobster, leeks, and Boursin cheese. Other options might included Australian lamb encrusted with mustard and fresh herbs or New England seafood pie.

🛏 *16 doubles with bath. Restaurant (dinner only), cable TV/VCR in common areas, phones in rooms, pool, fishing, tennis courts (across street), snowshoeing, cross-country skiing (not groomed). $85–$165; full breakfast. AE, D, DC, MC, V. No smoking, no pets.*

The Hancock Inn

33 Main St. (Box 96), Hancock 03449, tel. 603/525-3318, fax 603/525-9301

Hancock, north of Peterborough on Route 202, has been called one of New England's prettiest villages—and for good reason. Every house on Main Street is listed on the National Register of Historic Places, including the gray-clapboard, mansard-roof Hancock Inn. Although it has had several names over the years, the Hancock Inn began as a tavern in 1789, making it New Hampshire's oldest continuously operating inn.

The former tavern room is now a common room with a fireplace, an antique checkerboard, braided rugs, and period murals. Named for a stencil artist who lived in Hancock in the 1820s and whose work once graced the inn, the Moses Eaton Room was stenciled by innkeeper Linda Johnston using one of Eaton's original designs. In the Rufus Porter Room, an 1825 Porter mural depicts rural New England. Some guests have remarked that the village of red and white houses depicted in the mural is not unlike Hancock itself. In addition, the room has a cheery, gas fireplace stove; an antique trunk; and a four-poster bed. All the rooms have handmade quilts, antiques, and other period appointments. TVs are hidden under cozies with small signs that say, CAUTION:

DO NOT REMOVE UNLESS YOU WISH TO RE-
TURN TO THE 20TH CENTURY.

After retiring from nearly 20 years of
innkeeping in North Conway, Linda and
her husband, Joe, gave up retirement in
1991 to take over the Hancock. They
truly appreciate the inn's history and are
happy to share it with guests. Because
that history permeates even the walls,
the Johnstons believe that children
under 12 would find the atmosphere re-
stricting.

The chef also keeps history in mind via
a menu that includes such updated New
England fare as Shaker cranberry pot
roast with garlic mashed potatoes, Down
East Maine crab cakes served on juli-
enne vegetables, and corn-crusted rainbow trout with herbed Parmesan
couscous.

Guests come to the Hancock Inn to enjoy
an area that might well be more rural
than it was 200 years ago. Opportunities
for hiking, cross-country skiing, and
swimming are all close. Or you might
prefer to just sit on the wide porch and
listen as the Paul Revere bell in the
nearby meetinghouse chimes the hour.

⊞ *11 doubles with bath. Restaurant
(dinner only); air-conditioning, cable
TV, phones in rooms; swimming, boating, fishing, and tennis within walking
distance. $106–$172; full breakfast. AE,
D, DC, MC, V. No smoking, no pets.*

Hannah Davis House

*186 Depot Rd., Fitzwilliam 03447, tel.
603/585-3344*

The fragrance of baking bread sets the
mood for this 1820 gray Federal house
with black shutters only steps from
Fitzwilliam center. In Kaye Terpstra's
kitchen-hearth room, the old beehive
oven no longer functions, but elsewhere
in the house four fireplaces all work, and
the oversize bathrooms have tubs with
cat's-paw feet and brass fittings. The
enormous hanging scale in the kitchen is

a reminder of the country store the Terp-
stras owned elsewhere before opening
their B&B. Kaye, a former social worker,
and Mike, who was an engineer, now pursue cooking and carpentry.

In returning the house to its original
form, Mike has saved much of the old
glass as well as the T-over-T doors and
chair-rail wainscoting. A screened porch
off the kitchen is a place for guests to
relax with a cool drink and enjoy the picturesque spires and rooftops that, just
beyond the trees, surround Fitzwilliam's
classic village green.

Four of the generally large, light, airy
rooms have fireplaces. The first floor
suite has a king-size bed, a sitting room
with a camel-back sofa—complete with
an afghan and fireplaces in both rooms.
A private entrance and private porch
make this a true retreat. The Popovers
Room also has its own deck, high ceilings, a queen-size antique cannonball
bed, and a fireplace that can be seen from
both the bed and the sitting area. Even
the smaller rooms have antique beds and
plenty of cozy touches.

Kaye's mouthwatering breakfasts may
include omelets stuffed with bacon,
cream cheese, tomato, and herbs or
crepes with parsley sauce; homemade
granola, applesauce, and breads round
things out. When you return from a day
of hiking, antiquing, or sightseeing, a
snack of fruit, cheese, and crackers
awaits you. Bedtime turndown service
brings Kaye's homemade cookies.

⊞ *3 doubles with bath, 3 suites. Cable
TV/VCR in common area. $60–$115; full
breakfast. MC, V. No smoking, no pets.*

Home Hill Country Inn & French Restaurant

*River Rd., Plainfield 03781, tel. 603/675-
6165*

If a slice of the French countryside could
be magically set down on 22 acres of
woods in rural New Hampshire, you

might call it Home Hill. French native Stephan du Roure and his wife, Victoria, a native of Plainfield (on River Rd. off Rte. 12A, about 10 mi south of Hanover), own the white-brick Federal mansion on a bucolic spot beside the Connecticut River.

Victoria, who trained at the Ritz in France, has charge of the kitchen, while Stephan handles the three dining rooms and the guest rooms. One of the dining rooms, the Kemper Room, is decorated with Stephan and Victoria's collection of Kemper Blue plates from Brittany. A fleur-de-lis stencil carries the French influence into the lounge. Guest rooms in the main house have stenciling, wide-plank pine floors, and brass or antique beds. A newly renovated carriage house contains two rooms and a luxurious suite, and another guest house overlooks the swimming pool. An arrangement of nine tee boxes and three greens creates a small golf course. Just across the river in Vermont, Mt. Ascutney offers convenient downhill skiing.

🏠 *6 doubles with bath, 3 suites. Restaurant (dinner only, closed Sun.–Mon.), lap pool, tennis court, skating rink, cross-country ski trails, 9-hole golf course. $105–$150; Continental breakfast. MC, V. No pets. 2-night minimum holiday weekends and during foliage season.*

The Inn at Maplewood Farm

447 Center Rd. (Box 1478), Hillsborough 03244, tel. 603/464–4242 or 800/644–6695, fax 603/464–5401

This white-clapboard 1794 farmhouse looks nearly as perfect on the side of Peaked Hill today as it did 200 years ago. From the moment you set foot on the Inn at Maplewood farm's 14 acres—tucked away on a quiet country road—you feel transported back in time. White wicker chairs on the columned front porch invite you to sit, enjoy the after-noon, and watch the cows graze in a nearby pasture.

Inside, you'll think you've returned to glory days of radio broadcasting—rather than the Colonial era—when you see the Simoes' collection of antique radios. All the radios in the parlor work, as do the ones in the bedrooms. Every evening and any time by request, innkeepers Laura and Jayme Simoes start up their own 100-watt transmitter and treat guests to favorite old-time radio shows, from *Fibber McGee and Molly* to *The Shadow* with Orson Welles.

Rooms combine a mix of antiques and quilts with modern bathrooms and blissful peace and quiet. Three rooms have fireplaces. In the Garden Suite, a queen-size canopy bed, a fireplace, a skylight over the bathtub, and a sitting area with flowered cushions on wicker furniture make the room almost too inviting to leave.

The Inn at Maplewood Farm has won several awards for its innovative three-course breakfasts. Laura and Jayme pride themselves on using local produce, eggs, and dairy products—and on making everything from scratch. On a typical morning you might be served chilled cantaloupe and strawberry soup with candied violets, lemon-blueberry scones, and cream-basil shirred eggs with maple-glazed ham.

The pastimes are mostly rural in nature: hiking, swimming in the local pond, fishing, cross-country skiing, searching out the covered bridges, and picking apples, blueberries, or strawberries in season. But the Franklin Pierce Homestead, Canterbury Shaker Village, and the Mt. Kearsarge Indian Museum are all within easy driving distance as well.

🏠 *2 doubles with bath, 2 suites. TV/VCR in common area, guest kitchen with refrigerator and coffeemaker. $75–$125; full breakfast. AE, D, DC, MC, V. No smoking. Closed Apr.*

Rosewood Country Inn

*67 Pleasant View Rd., Bradford 03221,
tel. and fax 603/938–5253*

In 1991 when Leslie and Richard Marquis found the former summer resort that is now the Rosewood Country Inn, the long-abandoned building had been gutted and was filled with debris. In pursuing their dream of owning an inn, they hadn't intended to take on such a drastic renovation project, but they were quick to see the 12-acre property's potential. Today the Victorian country house glistens with fresh beige paint, and rose-color shutters adorn each of the 126 new windows.

Inside, a formal living room in dove gray, rose, and white sets an elegant tone, as do the three-course breakfasts served in the dining room with china, crystal, and candlelight. In the slightly more casual Tavern Room you can indulge in tea and homemade treats in the afternoon, and there are complimentary sherry and chocolates in each guest room as well. You'll find Leslie's stenciling—in a variety of patterns—throughout. In the Bridal Suite, a wicker settee beckons from a bay window nook, and silk flowers woven into the canopy make the bed into a true bridal bower. Antiques, such as the bed warmer in the Williamsburg Room, make interesting accent pieces.

▦ *11 doubles with bath, 1 suite. Cable TV/VCR in common area, lake, cross-country skiing, snowshoeing, downhill skiing nearby. $69–$140; full breakfast. AE, MC, V. No smoking.*

Zahn's Alpine Guest House

Rte. 13, Mont Vernon (mailing address: Box 75, Milford 03055), tel. 603/673–2334, fax 603/673–8415

Tucked into a wooded area on Route 13 between the towns of Milford and Mont Vernon is a little bit of Austria in the form of Zahn's Alpine Guest House. Flowers trail from boxes that line the second floor balcony, which circles the chalet and is protected by the overhanging roof. Inside, a blue-tiled *Kachelofen* (tile oven), built by a local Bavarian master builder, warms not only the breakfast room but also the rest of the inn.

Bud and Anne Zahn often led bike and ski groups through Bavaria during Bud's years as an importer of Bavarian goods. After retirement they missed meeting new people, so they built the inn on a secluded section of their dairy farm. They've used their knowledge of southern Germany and Austria to find antique farm furniture such as the carved wood and green glass armoire in Room 2 as well as the Alpine carpets and other accessories used to decorate other rooms. Even the dishes in the breakfast room are made by an Austrian potter and decorated with Alpine flowers. Rooms have double beds or European-style oversize twin beds that can be combined to make a king-size bed.

▦ *8 doubles with bath. TVs, phones in rooms; minirefrigerator, coffeemaker in common area. $65; Continental breakfast. AE, MC, V. No smoking in rooms.*

Maine

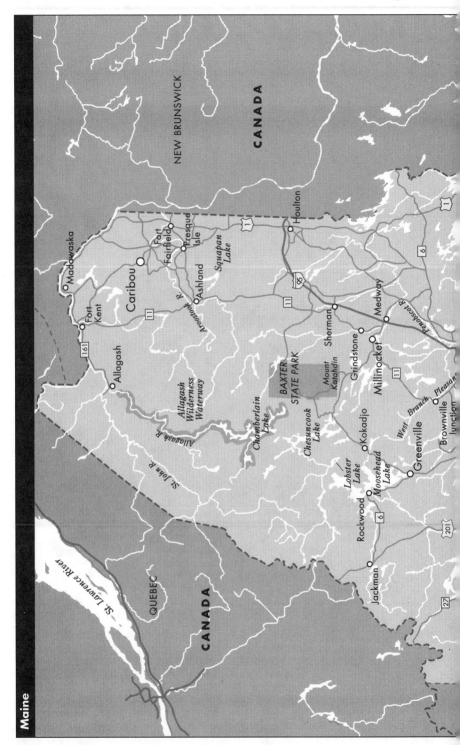

Maine

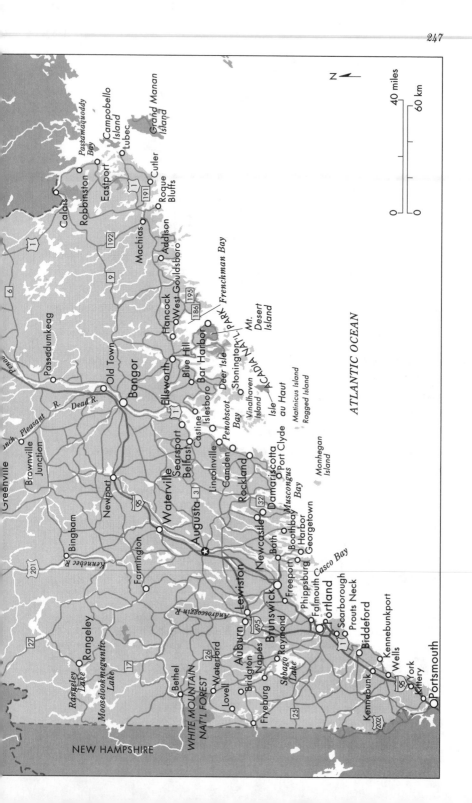

The Southern Coast

The Captain Lord Mansion

Maine's southern coast is no secret to visitors. Within easy striking distance of the big cities, with the biggest sand beaches in Maine and the warmest water (hardly tropical, but less frigid than points north and east), the southern coast towns fairly swarm with tourists in summer. York Beach, Ogunquit, and Wells Beach are summer colonies whose raison d'être is sand.

Farther inland, along Route 1, the highway that runs the length of the Maine coast from Kittery to Fort Kent, are older and more dignified villages: York, which has a historic district on the national register, and serene, dignified Kennebunkport, the retreat of former president George Bush and site of the area's most gracious old homes and a number of varied shops.

If you've come for bargains, head to Kittery, where you'll find a host of factory outlets. Wells also has a smattering of outlets along Route 1 as well as flea markets, antiques stores, and barns crammed with old books.

Crowning the region is Portland, an extremely manageable small city with a good art museum, an impressive selection of

restaurants and shops, and a restored downtown waterside district known as the Old Port Exchange. You can take a cruise of the harbor or a ferry to one of the Calendar Islands (so called because British mariners thought there were 365 of them).

The southern coast may lack the lonely, wind-bitten starkness of points Down East, but it compensates with a fine overlay of civilized amenities—museums, galleries, restaurants, restored old homes—and, of course, those long sand beaches.

Places to Go, Sights to See

Kennebunkport Historic District. Kennebunkport has the prettiest sea captains' homes in the region—nobly proportioned Federal and Greek Revival houses on Spring, Maine, Pearl, and Green streets, with fanlights, hip roofs, columns, and high windows. *Walking tours* (tel. 207/967-2751) depart from Nott House on Maine Street on Tuesday and Friday mornings in July and August.

Marginal Way. On this mile-long public path, there are views of Ogunquit behind you and the rolling surf in front of you.

Old Port Exchange is Portland's restored waterfront district of old brick warehouses converted to trendy shops and restaurants. Leave yourself a couple hours to wander down Market, Exchange, Middle, and Fore streets. On *Custom House Wharf* you can soak up some of the older, rougher waterfront atmosphere.

Perkins Cove. This neck of land connected to the Ogunquit mainland by a pedestrian drawbridge contains a jumble of sea-beaten fish houses that the tide of tourism has transformed into shops and galleries.

Portland Museum of Art (7 Congress Sq., tel. 207/775-6148). This is one of the finest art museums in New England, with a strong collection of Maine landscapes and seascapes by such masters as Winslow Homer, John Marin, Andrew Wyeth, and Marsden Hartley. Homer's *Pulling the Dory* and *Weatherbeaten,* two quintessential Maine coast images, are both here. The modern Charles Shipman Payson Wing was designed by I. M. Pei & Partners in 1983. Also part of the museum complex is the *McLellan Sweat House,* at 111 High Street, a fine example of the Federal style.

Seashore Trolley Museum (Log Cabin Rd., Kennebunkport, tel. 207/967-2800). The display of streetcars (1872–1972) includes trolleys from major metropolitan areas, all beautifully restored. Best of all, you can take a trolley for nearly 4 mi.

York Historic District includes a number of 18th- and 19th-century buildings clustered along York Street and Lindsay Road. You can purchase tickets to enter

all the buildings at *Jefferds Tavern* (Junction of Rte. 1A and Lindsay Rd., tel. 207/363–4974), a late-18th-century inn that has been restored.

Beaches

York's **Long Sands** is the most commercial beach. The sand is a bit lighter and finer at Ogunquit (a jump north) and Wells Beach (another jump north). **Drake's Island Beach,** in Wells, adjoins a stretch of salt marsh protected by the Rachel Carson National Wildlife Refuge. In the Kennebunk area, **Goose Rocks Beach** is the biggest—and a favorite of families with young children. **Gooch's** and **Middle Beach** attract a lot of teens. **Kennebunk Beach** has a small playground and thus a crowd of tots and moms. **Old Orchard Beach** has an amusement park and pier. **Scarborough Beach** and **Crescent Beach state parks** are popular with greater Portland residents; the latter is a good choice for families with toddlers.

Restaurants

Ogunquit's **Hurricane** (Perkins Cove, tel. 207/646–6348) offers first-rate cooking and views of crashing surf. The **White Barn Inn** (Beach St., tel. 207/967–2321), in Kennebunkport offers Continental fare with a Down East accent. For fresh seafood you can't beat Portland's **Street & Co.** (33 Wharf St., tel. 207/775–0887). For a funkier atmosphere try **Katahdin** (106 High St., tel. 207/774–1740), also in Portland, where the eclectic menu includes fresh fish as well as home-style favorites.

Reservations Service

B&B of Maine (377 Gray Rd., Falmouth 04105, tel. 207/797–5540).

Visitor Information

Convention and Visitors Bureau of Greater Portland (305 Commercial St., Portland 04101, tel. 207/772–4994), **Kennebunk-Kennebunkport Chamber of Commerce** (173 Port Rd., Kennebunk 04043, tel. 207/967–0857), **Kittery-Eliot Chamber of Commerce** (191 State Rd., Kittery 03904, tel. 207/439–7545), **Kittery Tourist Information Center** (Rte. 1 and I–95, Box 396, Kittery 03904, tel. 207/439–1319), **Ogunquit Chamber of Commerce** (Box 2289, Ogunquit 03907, tel. 207/646–2939), **Wells Chamber of Commerce** (Box 356, Wells 04090, tel. 207/646–2451), **The Yorks Chamber of Commerce** (Box 417, York 03909, tel. 207/363–4422).

Black Point Inn

510 Black Point Rd., Prouts Neck 04074, tel. 207/883-4126 or 800/258-0003, fax 207/883-9976

The shingle-style Black Point Inn was built in the late 1800s and has been owned by the Dugas family since 1972. It sits at the tip of exclusive Prouts Neck, with views over Scarborough Beach to open ocean on one side and over Ferry Beach to Pine Point and Old Orchard Beach on the other. Rambling public rooms, furnished with Early American antiques include a well-respected dining room, where you take breakfast and dinner (jacket and tie required for dinner) daily, and a lounge with entertainment. Guest rooms, most with spectacular views and about a dozen with fireplaces, are upstairs and in four cottages on the property.

You can laze on the beach or beachcomb; stroll the cliff walk, which passes by artist Winslow Homer's studio and through a bird sanctuary; swim in the ocean or the heated outdoor saltwater pool; or just find a quiet spot to take it all in. A new addition in 1998 will house a spa with an indoor lap pool, mud baths, and a steam room. You also have privileges at the Prouts Neck Country Club, which has an 18-hole PGA golf course and 14 tennis courts.

🏠 *74 doubles with bath, 20 suites. Restaurant; bar; air-conditioning, TVs, phones in rooms; indoor and outdoor pools; spa; golf and tennis nearby; bicycles; boating; croquet; volleyball. $250–$400; full breakfast and dinner. AE, D, MC, V. No pets. 3-night minimum. Closed Dec.–Apr.*

Bufflehead Cove

Gornitz La. (Box 499), Kennebunkport 04046, tel. 207/967-3879

Bufflehead Cove offers the serenity and space of a country location (fields, apple trees, waterfowl) just five minutes from Kennebunkport's Dock Square. The turn-of-the-century gambrel-roof house, built on the banks of the Kennebunk River, has the warm feel of a home that has always been loved, cared for, and comfortably lived in. Indeed, Kennebunkport natives Harriet and Jim Gott raised their family here before transforming the place into a B&B. Harriet runs the inn with daughter Shannon Gott Pearce; Jim is a fisherman.

It would be easy to laze the day away in the Adirondack-style furniture on the porch or in the hammock strung between trees at the river's edge. Just below the porch is a dock with rowboats for your use. Inside the house, bay windows in the beamed living room and dining room maximize the view. Curl up on the Victorian sofa in front of the fieldstone fireplace or in one of the deep cushioned window seats. An elegant, gourmet breakfast is served either in the dining room, which has a "rug" hand-painted on the floor, or in fine weather on the porch.

The Balcony Room—which has a gas fireplace, a two-person whirlpool tub, and a large partially screened balcony that overlooks the river—is the most popular in the house. Honeymooners prefer the private location of the Hideaway Suite, with its own deck beside the river. Romantic touches include a two-sided stone fireplace that separates the living room from the bedroom and a two-person whirlpool tub with a skylight above. The Cove Suite, also with a balcony and a fireplace, has a mural that depicts the view up and down the river. All rooms have hand-painted artwork on the walls by Maine artist Dyan Berk and tile work in the bathrooms and around fireplaces by local artisan Lou Lipkin. Similar touches are planned for three deluxe rooms, all to have fireplaces and water views, which will be added for 1999.

🏠 *2 doubles with bath, 3 deluxe doubles with bath planned, 3 suites. Robes in rooms, private dock, rowboats, beach permits. $135–$250; full breakfast,*

evening wine and cheese. D, MC, V. No smoking, no pets. 2-night minimum. Open by reservation only Jan.–Mar.

The Captain Lord Mansion

Corner of Pleasant and Green Sts. (Box 800), Kennebunkport 04046, tel. 207/967–3141, fax 207/967–3172

Of the mansions in Kennebunkport's historic district that have been tastefully converted to inns, the 1812 vintage Captain Lord Mansion is hands down the most stately and sumptuously appointed. The three-story, pale-yellow house sits in the middle of a manicured lawn in the historic district. The inn has an air of formal—but never stiff—propriety, seen to best advantage in the refined Gathering Room, which looks like a period room (Chippendale) in a museum, except for the guests lounging before the hearth.

Innkeepers Bev Davis and Rick Litchfield, former advertising executives, are far more laid-back than the house they meticulously restored. They chat and joke with you over family-style breakfasts served informally at the two harvest tables in their cheerful country kitchen.

Bev and Rick rescued the Captain Lord Mansion from its Victorian gloom and refurbished it with crisp, authentic Federal decor. Guest rooms, which are named after old clipper ships, are large and stately. Ship Lincoln, to many minds the finest room in the house, with a step-up four-poster bed and damask-covered walls, is also the room in which the inn's benign resident ghost appears (only women have ever seen her). Bark Hesper, on the third floor, is a whimsical country-style room, quainter and smaller than the downstairs rooms, with green dot-and-flower wallpaper and leafy views out the windows.

Bev and Rick seem always a step ahead of other area inns, and in 1997 they added the Captain's Suite, which is a monument to hedonism. From the king-size lace canopy bed you can watch flames dance in the gas fireplace. You step from the hydro-massage shower onto heated marble floors. In the spa room you and your loved one can unwind in the two-person whirlpool tub in front of another fireplace or ride the exercise bicycle and watch TV. It's all decorated in deep reds with gold accents, including a chandelier in the spa.

The Captain Lord is a pleasing base from which to venture forth on forays to Kennebunkport's architectural treasures, the shops of Dock Square, or the sand beaches lining the chill Atlantic.

🏨 *16 doubles with bath. 11 rooms with fireplaces and phones, gift shop, TV room. $149–$349; full breakfast, afternoon tea. D, MC, V. No smoking, no pets. 2-night minimum weekends, 3-night minimum holiday weekends.*

The Captain's Hideaway

12 Pleasant St. (Box 2746), Kennebunkport 04046, tel. 207/967–5711, fax 207/967–3843

Tucked away on a quiet street in Kennebunkport yet just a five-minute walk from busy Dock Square is this intimate, romantic B&B with just two rooms. Innkeepers Judith Boulet and Susan Jackson, both nurses, came to Maine to buy a house at Goose Rocks and ended up owning the Captain's Hideaway, a Federal cottage in Kennebunkport's historic district.

The downstairs Garden Room has a fireplace, a small whirlpool tub, and a private patio entrance—the lilacs outside set the room's theme. Furnishings include a canopy bed, hand-painted furniture, and a delicately carved swan table with glass top. Upstairs, the Captain's Room has gas fireplaces (one in the bedroom, one in the bathroom), an antique king-size canopy bed, and a large whirlpool. Equally inviting is the living room, with Margaret Furlong angels on dis-

play. A collection of Teddy bears adds a whimsical touch. Judith and Susan pamper you with homemade chocolates and a formal breakfast served on china and crystal, with candles, music, and perhaps a fire in the fireplace.

🏠 *1 double with bath, 1 suite. Cable TV, phones, refrigerators with beverages in rooms; beach chairs, towels, picnic lunches available. $199–$249; full breakfast. MC, V. 2-night minimum weekends.*

Edward's Harborside Inn

Stage Neck Rd. (Box 866), York Harbor 03911, tel. 207/363-3037

Sunlight reflecting off the water dances over the white wicker in the sunporch lobby of Edward's Harborside Inn. This turn-of-the-century B&B is at the harbor's edge and just a two-minute walk from the beach. Rooms range from those with shared baths to elaborate suites—one with a fireplace, one with a large whirlpool tub, and another that's ideal for families. Most rooms have sweeping views of the Atlantic Ocean out the front, boat-filled York Harbor to the side, or both. White Adirondack chairs beckon you to the manicured lawn surrounded by a picket fence with a trellis through which you pass to reach the inn's deepwater dock.

Third-generation innkeeper Jay Edwards purchased the inn in 1982. "I grew up in the business and learned what to do and what not to do," he says. One thing he doesn't do is elaborate breakfasts; guests help themselves to a simple Continental buffet served on the porch. Though Jay employs a resident manager, he stays involved in daily operations and enjoys being the "schmoozing host," he says.

🏠 *3 doubles with bath, 4 doubles share 2 baths, 3 suites. Air-conditioning, cable TV, phones in rooms. $90–$220; Continental breakfast, afternoon tea. MC, V. No smoking, no pets.*

The Maine Stay Inn and Cottages

34 Maine St. (Box 500A), Kennebunkport 04046, tel. 207/967-2117 or 800/ 950-2117, fax 207/967-8757

On a quiet residential street a short walk from Dock Square is the Maine Stay Inn, its Italianate main house (circa 1860) listed on the National Register of Historic Places. Additions over the years have included the cupola, the wraparound porch, the pair of sunburst crystal-glass windows, the detailed interior moldings, and the magnificent flying staircase. Innkeepers Lindsay and Carol Copeland bought the inn in 1989, leaving banking careers in Seattle to bring their young family to New England.

Although somewhat small, Room 14, in the rear of the house and overlooking the garden, offers quiet and a private entrance and patio. Suite 12 has plenty of windows to let in the early morning sun (there's even a stained-glass window in the bathroom). This suite and another, as well as one room, have fireplaces. Families often prefer the cottages, which have kitchens (five have fireplaces, too) and offer a bit more privacy. Cottage guests can choose to have their breakfast delivered to them.

🏠 *4 doubles with bath, 2 suites, 11 cottages. Air-conditioning, cable TV in rooms; whirlpool tub in 1 room; croquet; jungle gym. $135–$215; full breakfast, afternoon tea. AE, D, MC, V. No smoking, no pets. 2-night minimum weekends.*

Riverbank on the Harbor

11 Harmon Park Rd. (Box 1102), York Harbor 03911, tel. 207/363-8333, fax 207/ 363-3684

Riverbank on the Harbor delivers what its name promises. The white-clapboard, shingle-style cottage, built in 1890, sits on the edge of York Harbor in a neighborhood of expansive homes, shade

trees, and flowering gardens. Innkeeper Marie Feuer offers five rooms with king-size beds. The house is so tastefully furnished that it was the site of the Old York Historical Society's 1994 Decorator Showcase. The Balcony Room makes up for its lack of a private bath with a small balcony—furnished with a petite wicker settee—that overlooks the harbor. Marie serves a full breakfast in the spacious living-dining room, which extends from one end of the house nearly to the other and is decorated with turn-of-the-century furnishings. On inclement days a fire may be lighted in the fireplace.

Riverbank offers a much appreciated and quiet respite after a day of prowling through Kittery's outlets; sunning on nearby York Beach, a 10-minute walk away; or touring York's historic district.

🏨 *2 doubles with bath, 3 doubles share 2½ baths. $120–$150; full breakfast. MC, V. No smoking.*

Rockmere Lodge

40 Stearns Rd. (Box 278), Ogunquit 03907, tel. 207/646-2985

With a location midway along Ogunquit's famed Marginal Way and views that seem to go as far as England, the Rockmere Lodge is an ideal retreat from the hustle and bustle of Perkins Cove or the shops and restaurants of downtown Ogunquit, both just a ½ mi away. Partners Andy Antoniuk and Bob Brown rescued the 1899 Victorian shingle-style cottage, which had been turned into apartments, and completely renovated it. The skills Andy had amassed from owning a gift basket business and store in Connecticut and also designing sets for theater productions came in handy when the two retired here in 1992. Andy has redone some rooms no less than four times in six years: "I like guests to be surprised," he says, adding that Bob tries to keep him out of wallpaper stores.

The house faces the sea, and it's difficult to drag yourself away from the wrap-around porch with its white wicker furniture and hanging baskets of flowers. Inside the front door the mood changes abruptly to high Victorian. Forest green, navy blue, and rich burgundy mix in the striped wallpaper, Asian rugs, and upholstery. Bob and Andy have furnished the living room with family antiques, such as the Victorian sofa, and pieces they've purchased over the years, including a desk from New York's Plaza Hotel, three carved straight-back chairs that once graced a church altar, and a grandfather clock with a Waterford crystal pendulum. The nutcrackers that guard the Italian tile fireplace are holdovers from Andy's shop. At Christmas they're joined by others, and the house is decorated with a special tree in every room. (Note that given all the antiques and delicate pieces, this inn is not suitable for children.)

Guest rooms all have prized corner locations and are large and airy; all but one have excellent water views. Room 7 has hand-painted decoration on the door and the window frames that matches the mirror frames and dressers. Room 6 has the best views and brings the outdoors in with an arbor motif in green, white, and purple and a green iron bedstead with ivy strewn through the frame. The Lookout sitting area on the third floor is a wonderful retreat, with views to Kennebunkport.

🏨 *8 doubles with bath. Ceiling fans and cable TV in rooms; beach within walking distance. $100–$150; Continental breakfast. AE, D, MC, V. No smoking, no pets. 2-night minimum weekends and holidays.*

York Harbor Inn

Rte. 1A (Box 573), York Harbor 03911, tel. 800/343-3869, fax 207/363-7151

On Route 1A directly across from the ocean, the rambling white-clapboard York Harbor Inn has sprouted various ells and wings and a carriage house over the course of three centuries, but some-

how they all come together. At the inn's heart is a mid-17th-century fishing cabin, with venerable dark timbers and a fieldstone fireplace. The cabin was brought over from the Isles of Shoals on a barge in 1637 and now serves as the inn's parlor. It's suitably furnished with antiques and reproduction pieces from a variety of periods. White holiday lights strewn across the dark cathedral ceiling add a festive air. Breakfast is served in the dining room, which overlooks the Atlantic.

Most rooms are done in a Colonial style, and a handful have fireplaces and whirlpool tubs. Room 14, in the carriage house, is decorated in navy and green and has a four-poster pineapple bed and an Empire dresser. Innkeeper Gary

Dominguez calls Room 13 the "L. L. Bean room"; its decor is reminiscent of a Maine hunting lodge, done in forest green with accents such as pine cones and a stuffed pheasant. Like other rooms in the front of the inn, it has a deck with ocean views (the views improved in 1997 when a row of rental houses was replaced with an ocean-front park). From across the street you can access a ¾-mi trail that runs along cliffs overlooking the ocean.

▦ *24 doubles with bath in inn; 11 doubles with bath, 1 suite in carriage house. Restaurant; pub; air-conditioning, cable TV, phones in rooms; gift shop. $89–$225; Continental breakfast buffet. AE, MC, V. No smoking, no pets.*

Mid-Coast

East Wind Inn & Meeting House

North of Portland the long, smooth arcs of sandy beaches all
but vanish, and the shoreline takes on the jagged, rocky aspect
that seems quintessentially Maine. Long bony fingers of land
point south into the ocean; alongside them flow great rivers—
the Kennebec, the Sheepscot, the Damariscotta—their upper
reaches draining and filling with the tides. To the fingertips
cling the scenic lobstering villages and resorts of South
Harpswell, Newagen, Pemaquid Point, and Port Clyde.

The larger towns of the mid-coast are looped together by Route
1. Freeport, less than a half hour north of Portland, is an
entity unto itself, a town made famous by a store: L. L. Bean,
which began with a pair of waterproof boots and has become a
shopping mecca for the entire world. In the wake of L. L.
Bean's success, scores of upscale factory outlets have opened.

Brunswick, a good-size city with some 27,000 people, is best
known for Bowdoin, its fine liberal arts college. Bath, 12 mi
up the 150-mi Kennebec River, has been a shipbuilding center
since 1607. The Bath Iron Works continues the tradition, and
the Maine Maritime Museum preserves its history.

Wiscasset bills itself as the prettiest town in Maine and lives up to its advertising. Well situated on the Sheepscot River, it brims with antiques shops, old white-clapboard houses, and historic churches.

The Boothbays—consisting of coastal Boothbay Harbor, East Boothbay, Linekin Neck, and Southport Island, and the inland town of Boothbay—are the most visited mid-coast towns, attracting hordes of vacationing families and flotillas of pleasure craft. Boothbay Harbor was an old fishing and boatbuilding town that now calls itself the Boating Capital of New England. Tourism peaks during the Windjammer Days in late June, when vessels of all sorts glide into the harbor in full sail.

When you need a blast of pure ocean air, head down the Pemaquid Peninsula to its terminus—an immense, striated shelf of granite angled into the sea. Here rises the Pemaquid Point Light (1824), one of the most photographed and painted (and visited) structures in Maine. A jump east will take you to the St. George Peninsula, where the small towns of Tenants Harbor and Port Clyde preserve the spirit of old Maine: harbors filled with lobster boats and green-black spruces framing views of the outer islands. Port Clyde is the major port of departure for trips to Monhegan Island, where lobstermen coexist peacefully with artists.

Places to Go, Sights to See

The **Bath Maine Maritime Museum** (243 Washington St., tel. 207/443–1316) will fascinate all who have a taste for things nautical. The museum's collection includes ship models, journals, photographs, and other artifacts relating to Maine's three centuries of shipbuilding.

Boothbay Harbor is the region's boating and yachting center, with numerous boat tours and deep-sea fishing trips departing from the town's piers off Commercial Street.

Bowdoin College Museum of Art (Walker Art Building, Brunswick, tel. 207/725–8731) has a fine collection of Dutch and Italian old masters, Gilbert Stuart portraits, and Winslow Homer engravings, etchings, and memorabilia.

Colonial Pemaquid Restoration (Rte. 1, tel. 207/677–2423). On the way to Pemaquid Point, stop at this important archaeological site. Excavations at Pemaquid Beach began in the mid-1960s and have turned up thousands of artifacts from Native American and early Colonial settlements, including the foundations and remains of an old customhouse, a tavern, a jail, a forge, and some houses.

L. L. Bean (Rte. 1, Freeport, tel. 800/341–4341). The store that Leon Leonwood Bean started in 1912 has grown into a retail empire that attracts millions of shoppers a year. Across the street from the main store, Bean has opened a factory outlet for second-quality and discontinued merchandise. L. L. Kids, a new offshoot, opened in 1997.

Montsweag Flea Market (tel. 207/443–2809). Between Bath and Wiscasset on Route 1 there's a wonderful flea market that sells antiques, collectibles, and odds and ends—up to and including kitchen sinks. It's open weekends from mid-May to the end of October, and also on Wednesday and Friday from mid-July to mid-September.

The **Pemaquid Point Light** (1824) stands atop a dramatic chunk of striated granite and commands a stunning view of the sea and islands. Although the coastal rock formations are less dramatic at the *Marshall Point Lighthouse*, near Port Clyde, the views are just as fine as at Pemaquid Point and the crowds far thinner.

Beaches

Popham Beach State Park (Phippsburg, tel. 207/389–1335), at the end of Route 209 south of Bath, is one of the larger beaches in the mid-coast region: 1½ mi of sand divided into three stretches. In addition, the park has salt marshes, where wading birds congregate, extensive dunes, and a picnic area.

Reid State Park (Georgetown, tel. 207/371–2303), on Georgetown Island off Route 127, has a stretch of sandy beach as well as tidal pools, rocky outcrops, a nature area, and picnic tables.

Restaurants

The **Robinhood Free Meetinghouse** (Robinhood Rd., tel. 207/371–2530), in Georgetown, offers well-prepared classic and new American fare in a beautifully renovated meetinghouse. In South Freeport the **Harraseeket Lunch** (Main St., tel. 207/865–4888), a bare-bones lobster pound next to the town landing, serves fried seafood as well as lobsters. **Kristina's Restaurant & Bakery** (160 Centre St., tel. 207/442–8577), in Bath, offers new American cuisine and is popular for Sunday brunch. The **Anchor Inn** (on the harbor, tel. 207/529–5584), in Round Pond, serves mostly seafood in a casual dining room and screened-in porch overlooking a boat-filled harbor.

Reservations Service

B&B of Maine (377 Gray Rd., Falmouth 04105, tel. 207/797–5540).

Visitor Information

Bath–Brunswick Area Chamber of Commerce (45 Front St., Bath 04530, tel. 207/443–9752; 59 Pleasant St., Brunswick 04011, tel. 207/725–8797), **Boothbay Harbor Region Chamber of Commerce** (Box 356, Boothbay Harbor 04538, tel. 207/633–2353), **Damariscotta Region Chamber of Commerce** (Box 13, Damariscotta 04543, tel. 207/563–8340), **Freeport Merchants Association** (Box 452, Freeport 04032, tel. 207/865–1212).

The Briar Rose

Box 27, Rte. 32, Round Pond 04564, tel. 207/529-5478

Fred and Anita Palsgrove ran an antiques business outside Washington, DC, before moving to Maine in 1986. The Briar Rose was an impulse buy they've never regretted. "We were meant to live here," Anita declares. It's easy to see why they fell in love with the place: The three-story, mansard-roof structure overlooks the harbor and village of Round Pond, a sleepy enclave of artists, craftspeople, fishermen, and shipbuilders, a short drive or bike ride from Pemaquid Point.

Two large guest rooms and one suite, each with a view of the harbor, are light and airy, decorated with period antiques and country collectibles, braided and rag rugs, and floral wallpaper. Added touches include Anita's display boxes of women's sewing notions, Dutch whimsies, Easter things, and a framed lace collection. An old-fashioned country breakfast (multigrain pancakes or baked eggs with herbs and vegetables from the garden) is served in the cheerful blue and white dining room, which is furnished with American country antiques and has harbor views.

It's a short walk to Round Pond Lobster, a waterfront lobster shack with picnic tables on the dock, or the waterfront Anchor Inn for lunch or dinner.

🏠 *2 doubles with bath, 1 suite. $65–$85; full breakfast. No credit cards. No smoking, no pets. Open by reservation only in winter.*

The East Wind Inn & Meeting House

Mechanic St. (Box 149), Tenants Harbor 04860, tel. 207/372-6366, fax 207/372-6320

If you've read *The Country of the Pointed Firs*, Sarah Orne Jewett's charming sketches of coastal Maine, you may have an eerie sense of déjà vu as you drive the 10 mi down Route 131 into Tenants Harbor. Not much has changed since Jewett wrote here at the turn of the century: the neat little white-clapboard houses set in tangles of tall grass and beach roses, the narrow harbor from which the nearly black evergreens rise like sawteeth, the distant glimpse of islands and open water.

Set on a little knob of land overlooking the harbor and islands, the three-story, white-clapboard East Wind Inn has, in the course of its 130 years, served as a sail loft and mason's hall. Today it's hard to imagine it as anything other than the perfect rustic inn, complete with wraparound porch. Innkeeper Tim Watts gave up his work as an accountant to buy the East Wind in 1974, and in his yearlong renovation, he was careful to leave its innocence and simplicity very much intact.

You stay either in the inn or the meetinghouse, a converted ship captain's house just up the hill. The inn's front rooms command a view of sunrise over the islands. The bedrooms are furnished with a hodgepodge of simple Early American-style brass bedsteads and pine chests; oak and mahogany furnishings give the meetinghouse rooms more of a Victorian air. All the rooms are appealingly plain, as is the inn's living room, with its baby grand piano, nautical charts, and comfortable sofas and easy chairs. The three apartments in the Ginny Wheeler Cottage, added in 1996, are fancier and have private decks and fabulous views. Two have fireplaces, and all have kitchens.

The East Wind's restaurant overlooks the harbor, and the menu fittingly emphasizes fresh fish. From the inn you can drive (or bike) to Port Clyde for a picnic at the Marshall Point Lighthouse. Other options include a day trip to Monhegan or an afternoon with the Wyeths at the Farnsworth Art Museum, in Rockland.

🏠 *1 double with bath, 14 doubles share 4 baths, 1 suite in inn; 8 doubles with bath, 2 suites, 1 apartment in meeting-house; 3 apartments in Wheeler Cottage. Restaurant; TVs in suites, apartment, and living room; phones in all rooms; conference room. $90–$275; full breakfast. AE, D, MC, V. No smoking in restaurant. Closed Dec.–Apr.*

Five Gables Inn

Muray Hill Rd. (Box 335), tel. 207/633–4551 or 800/451–5048

Boothbay Harbor bills itself as the Boating Capital of Maine. Its narrow streets are lined with T-shirt and trinket shops as well as upscale boutiques and respected galleries. Whale-watching, puffin-watching, deep-sea-fishing, and tour boats crowd the harbor. Indeed, there's plenty to keep you busy here for days, but at night the Five Gables Inn, in East Boothbay, just 3½ mi away, provides a quiet respite (best to leave the kids at home).

Continuously operated as an inn since it was built in the late 1800s, the Five Gables offers pleasant (though small) rooms decorated with period reproductions; all have ocean views, and some have fireplaces. Owners Mike and De Kennedy, a graduate of the Culinary Institute of America and an artist, respectively, purchased the inn in 1995, coming to Maine from Atlanta and bringing a touch of southern hospitality with them. They are updating the inn and redecorating to maximize room size and views.

Although the multicourse breakfast is served in the spacious common room, guests often take it to tables on the large wraparound porch, which has views over the colorful gardens to Linekin Bay. Paths lead to the waterfront.

🏠 *16 doubles with bath. Cable TV in common room, 2 moorings. $90–$135; full breakfast, afternoon refreshments. MC, V. No smoking, no pets.*

The Flying Cloud

River Rd. (Box 549), Newcastle 04553, tel. 207/563–2484, fax 207/563–8640

Alan and Jeanne Davis looked at 60 potential B&Bs before finding the Flying Cloud. But as soon as they walked through the door, Jeanne explains, they looked at each other and said, "This is it." They retired from careers with Washington, DC, nonprofits to become innkeepers. And Alan, a history buff, plans to write a book about the Civil War.

The house, a 1790 Cape with an 1840 Greek Revival–style addition, is named after the clipper ship *Flying Cloud*, which set a speed record in 1851 on its maiden voyage from New York to San Francisco. (There's an authentic model of this vessel in the formal dining room.) The five bedrooms are named after the *Flying Cloud*'s ports of call—London, New York, San Francisco, Melbourne, and Hong Kong—and each is decorated with memorabilia from the Davises' travels to those cities. Four of the rooms have views of the tidal Damariscotta River.

Furnishings include family antiques and reproduction and current pieces, as well as Jeanne's finds at local auctions, antiques shops, and Elmer's Barn—a legendary shop where she found the living room's brass chandelier stuffed in a coffin. You can relax either in front of the living room fireplace or by the cozy parlor woodstove.

Breakfast is served in the formal dining room or on the front deck, which has river views. Your morning meal may include Maine blueberry, raspberry, or blackberry pancakes; scrapple; grits; fresh fruits; juices; cereal; and yogurt.

🏠 *4 doubles with bath, 1 suite. TV/VCR in sitting room. $65–$95; full breakfast, afternoon refreshments. AE, D, MC, V. No smoking, no pets. 2-night minimum holiday weekends.*

The Isaac Randall House

Independence Dr., Freeport 04032, tel. 207/865-9295

Freeport, dominated by the L. L. Bean empire and scores of upscale outlets, is a surprising place to find country inns. The Isaac Randall was the first, and it remains the most inviting.

Situated on a pleasant 5-acre lot just outside town, the circa-1829 inn has a classic hip roof and twin chimneys. Inside you'll find a country kitchen, where breakfast is served family style (blueberry pancakes and banana-lemon bread stand out), and bedrooms with quilts, pumpkin-pine floors, and a mix of Victorian antiques and country-style pieces. The Rose Room, with a brass bed, working fireplace, fan quilt, and ornate mirror, has a superior corner location. The Pine Room has a rustic country feel and a huge copper tub. The Loft Room, with its king-size bed and cable TV, offers the most privacy. The fire-engine-red caboose in the backyard is popular with families. Rustic compared with the rest of the inn, it has a bedroom, two built-in bunks, a bathroom, and original fixtures. If your room doesn't have a fireplace or a woodstove (only four do), you can warm yourself by the family room stove.

🏠 *8 doubles with bath, 1 suite. Airconditioning, cable TV/VCR in family room, cable TV in 6 rooms, phones in all rooms, small kitchen and refrigerator for guest use, outdoor hot tub, playground. $100-$125; full breakfast. D, MC, V. No smoking. 2-night minimum holiday, children's camp, and graduation weekends.*

The Marston House

Main St. (Box 517), Wiscasset 04578, tel. 207/882-6010 or 800/852-4137

The Marston House is in the heart of Wiscasset, Maine's self-proclaimed "prettiest village," which is considered by many to be the antiques capital of the midcoast region. Owners Sharon and Paul Mrozinsky moved from California in 1987 to open the Marston House antiques shop. In 1988 they opened the B&B in the detached 19th-century carriage house, which Paul, an architect, had renovated.

Guests cherish the quiet and the privacy here. Although small, the two carriage-house rooms offer a quiet retreat from the hustle and bustle of Wiscasset's Main Street. Both have private entrances, fireplaces, and private baths and are simply furnished with Shaker and Colonial-style pieces. There are no common public rooms. Room 2 overlooks the garden. Room 1 gets the morning sun and overlooks a side street and eclectic antiques shop. The rooms can be joined by opening a door between them, a popular option for families.

Breakfast is delivered to the room each morning in a wicker basket and includes fresh fruit, freshly baked muffins, and freshly squeezed juice; hot cereals and granola are served in cooler weather. In fine weather guests often take breakfast to the garden.

🏠 *2 doubles with bath. Terry-cloth robes. $85; Continental breakfast. AE, MC, V. No smoking, no pets. Closed Dec.-Apr.*

Mill Pond Inn

50 Main St., Nobleboro 04555, tel. 207/563-8014

On a residential street in Damariscotta Mills, just inland from Damariscotta, innkeepers Sherry and Bobby Whear greet you enthusiastically at the Mill Pond Inn. Sherry, the romantic, points out the sunset view over Damariscotta Lake and the hammock in the willows by the pond. Bobby, the boating and birding enthusiast, presses a pair of binoculars on you to see the loons, and dashes off for photos of the bald eagles that nest nearby. Clearly, this couple is mad for Maine, for their rambling gray-shingle

house, and for the millpond and birds at their back door.

Sherry's penchant for the romantic shows up in the softly feminine decor, with quilts, lots of fluffy pillows, floral and striped wallpapers, and fresh flowers in all the rooms. The Eagle's Nest, on the third floor, has the best water view, dark wood furniture, original beams, and a rather low ceiling. If you're game, Bobby will take you fishing at dawn in his restored 1957 Lyman Lapstrake. (Note that given the waterfront location, this B&B is not suitable for young children.)

🏠 *5 doubles with bath, 1 suite. Cable TV/VCR in game room, deck, bicycles, boats, canoes, horseshoes, skating, swimming. $80; full breakfast. No credit cards. Smoking on ground floor only, no pets.*

The Newcastle Inn

60 River Rd., Newcastle 04553, tel. 207/563-5685 or 800/832-8669, fax 207/563-6877

Like so many innkeepers, Howard and Rebecca Levitan decided to break with their previous careers—his as a lawyer, hers in sales—to find a better lifestyle. Both had ties to Maine, and in 1995 they purchased the Newcastle Inn. They've redecorated in a French country style, enlarging and adding whirlpool baths and gas fireplaces to some rooms and beautifying the grounds, which slope down to the Damariscotta River. For two weeks in June, lupines bloom here, and they have become the inn's theme.

Rooms are named after lighthouses along the Maine coast. Both Matinicus Rock, which has a two-person whirlpool tub, and Tenants Harbor have quiet, back-of-the-house locations, gas fireplaces, and river views. Floral wallpapers offset the Asian rugs for a comforting yet elegant atmosphere. Pemaquid Point offers the best view in the house from its queen-size canopy bed; it also has a gas fireplace

and two-person whirlpool tub. Monhegan is the grandest in the house: It has a four-poster, king-size, rice bed (its posts are carved to look like sheaves of rice); a large gas fireplace; and burgundy-and-navy paisley wallpaper that complements the room's Asian rug. (Owing to all the carefully selected and meticulously arranged furnishings, you should leave your wee ones at home.)

The front living room is an inviting place to rest or plan a day's adventure, but the rear sitting room is even more delightful: It's cozy and has a fireplace and a river view. The small adjacent pub, with its vibrant red walls, teal accents, and Southwestern artwork, should seem out of place here, but somehow it blends well.

In fine weather breakfast—perhaps eggs Benedict or cinnamon-raisin French toast stuffed with ricotta cheese—is served on the deck overlooking the river. The inn also offers three- or five-course prix-fixe dinners in its dining rooms; you will need to make reservations.

Newcastle is a town with more charm than action; but the inn makes a convenient base for forays to Boothbay Harbor or Pemaquid Point or for a quiet afternoon of canoeing on the river. In summer the inn's sunporch, with white wicker furniture and ice-cream-parlor chairs, makes a particularly appealing spot to contemplate the Damariscotta River and congratulate yourself for having found such a special place.

🏠 *13 doubles with bath, 2 suites. Restaurant, pub, TV in den, whirlpool tubs in 1 room and 1 suite, turndown service. $95–$200; full breakfast. AE, MC, V. No smoking, no pets. 2-night minimum peak holiday weekends.*

Popham Beach Bed & Breakfast

Beach Rd. (HC 31, Box 430), Phippsburg 04562, tel. 207/389-2409

Peggy Johanessen calls the B&B she's created in a former Coast Guard station a work in progress. If you're willing to overlook peeling paint and a few unfinished rooms, it's a gem. How can it miss with a waterfront location on Popham, one of Maine's prettiest beaches?

The red-roofed building topped with a watchtower was constructed in 1883 as a U.S. Lifesaving Station; it was taken over by the Coast Guard in 1935 and decommissioned in 1971. Guest rooms in the front of the house have marvelous views: the Library Room, with hardwood floors and natural wicker furniture, is where boats were once stored; the Bunk Room, with marine-blue carpeting and plenty of white wicker, is the largest in the house. You can relax in the airy living room, furnished with a hodgepodge of pieces and a woodstove that provides warmth when needed.

The quiet location allows you to hear the waves breaking on the shore and a bell buoy clanging at sea. It's a short walk to Civil War-era Ft. Popham or to Spinney's, a casual beach restaurant that serves lobster.

▥ *3 doubles with bath, 1 double shares bath, 1 suite. $80-$145; full breakfast. MC, V. No pets. 2-night minimum weekends July-Aug. Closed Nov.-Apr.*

The 1774 Inn

Parker Head Rd., Phippsburg Center 04562, tel. 207/389-1774

The 1774 Inn, also known as the McCobb-Hill-Minott House, predates the Declaration of Independence. The four-square Colonial, built in 1774 and on the National Register of Historic Places, is considered an outstanding example of a pre-Revolutionary mansion. Architecture buffs will savor the interior detailing: Indian shutters, wainscoting, ceiling rosettes, and crown moldings. Antique fiends will covet the family pieces, such as the silk and damask chair, the Empire sofa, and the Chinese music cabinet (but children may not be as appreciative of such items; best to leave preteens at home).

Debbie and Joe Braun opened the inn in 1996, after retiring from careers in the Maryland House of Representatives. They're not the first residents with political connections: Maine's first U.S. congressman, Mark L. Hill, lived in the house from 1782 to 1842. The house is on a bend in the Kennebec River and has four large corner guest rooms—two with fireplaces, two with river views—all furnished with antiques or reproduction pieces. The Brauns plan to finish the attic and provide access to the cupola and to add three guest rooms in the ell that connects the house to the barn.

Breakfast is served before the fireplace in the formal dining room. Fresh fruit and home-baked muffins or breads will whet your appetite for such entrées as Maine blueberry pancakes with bacon or sausage.

▥ *4 doubles with bath. TV/VCR in den. $85-$125; full breakfast. No credit cards. No smoking.*

The Squire Tarbox Inn

Rte. 144 (RR 2, Box 620), Wiscasset 04578, tel. 207/882-7693, fax 207/882-7107

As you drive the 8½ mi from Route 1 down Route 144 and onto Westport Island, you may wonder if you made a wrong turn as the signs of civilization peter out into lush rolling hills, woods, and a sprinkling of farmhouses. Then the reassuring champagne-yellow clapboard front of the Squire Tarbox looms into view, and you know just where you are: deep in the country at one of Maine's most serene inns.

"This is a really nourishing place," says innkeeper Karen Mitman with a soft smile while in a rocking chair next to the fireplace, beside the grandfather clock. "People come here to reflect, to walk in the woods, to look at the birds." They also come to watch Karen and her husband, Bill, milk their goats and to sample their delicious goat cheese, served each night. For the Squire Tarbox is not only an inn, and on the National Register of Historic Places, but it's also a working farm, with a small herd of goats, a horse, laying hens, and a few donkeys. "We are goat missionaries who rent rooms," Karen says.

Karen and Bill had hotel experience in Boston, but none as goat farmers, when they bought the inn in 1981. Yet somehow they seem to have been in the rambling Federal house forever. Some of it dates from 1763 and some from 1820, and among the downstairs public rooms are a rustic dining room—where dinner is served fireside beneath old ships' beams—and a music room with a player piano.

Of the bedrooms, Room 1, in the main part of the house, is choice—a huge room with king-size bed, braided rugs on pumpkin-pine floors, and an antique footlocker. The attached barn has four rooms that are more rustic in feel and smaller than the inn rooms, but also more private. Room 11 is the best for privacy, with gray-green woodwork, more space than the other barn rooms, and a view of the pasture.

When you tire of strolling around the property and bird-watching from the deck, ask the Mitmans to direct you to the shops of Wiscasset, the Maritime Museum at Bath, the lobster pier and scenic back roads of Five Islands (good for biking), and the beach at Reid State Park. Of course, if you're really weary, you could just rest in front of a fireplace in one of the common rooms.

▦ *11 doubles with bath. Restaurant, TV in den, rowboat, farm animals. $154–$230; MAP, goat cheese in evening. AE, D, MC, V. No smoking, no pets. Closed late Oct.–mid-May.*

Around Penobscot Bay

Eggemoggin Reach Bed and Breakfast

*To purists the Maine coast begins at Penobscot Bay—
everything to the south and west is part of "vacationland,"
where fish houses have been converted to T-shirt shops and
sand beaches invite un-Maine-like lounging and easy entry
into water that is warm enough in which to swim. But at
Penobscot Bay, Maine's largest and, to many minds, most
beautiful bay, things change. The vistas over the water are
wider and bluer. The shore is a chaos of granite boulders,
cobblestones, and gravel, punctuated by so-called pocket sand
beaches, which look small enough to scoop up in a child's
shovel. The water is numbingly cold. Presiding over the bay
are the Camden Hills, looming green over Camden's
fashionable waterfront and turning gradually bluer and
fainter as you move farther away.*

*Chic, sleek Camden is the most popular destination on
Penobscot Bay, and it also offers the most amenities: inns
ranging from bucolic to sumptuous; musical and theatrical
entertainment; scores of gift shops; skiing in winter; and in
summer, of course, the world-famous fleet of windjammers.
Less frivolous, but perhaps more representative of the
hardworking spirit of the bay, is Belfast, a jump up the coast,*

which has a couple of blocks of handsome brick buildings and some very fine Greek Revival houses.

Searsport, another jump northeast, bills itself as the antiques capital of Maine. Bargains may be hard to come by in the shops that line Route 1 here, but in summer, vast flea markets spring up, with merchandise ranging from old china to new hardware.

Route 1, which follows the west side of the bay, can get a little frenzied during the summer. Far more serene are the back roads that wind through the juts and jags of land on the bay's east side. Routes 175 and 166 take you through woods with increasingly stunning water views until the roads terminate at historic Castine. Here you should give yourself a few hours (or days) to wander amid the tidy white-clapboard houses and churches; to soak up the atmosphere at the picturesque harbor; or to walk down to Dyce's Head Lighthouse for vistas out to islands, water, and back to the Camden Hills. Blue Hill, about 15 mi east of Castine, is another coastal town that's perfect for leisurely strolls, and it also has the region's greatest concentration of pottery workshops and art and crafts galleries. The back roads between Brooklin, at the southern tip of the peninsula, and Blue Hill offer some fantastic biking.

Deer Isle is connected to the peninsula by a high, narrow bridge. Take a deep breath and cross it: The island yields many treasures, including the craftspeople who congregate here when the Haystack School of Crafts is in session. At the far end is Stonington, a rough seafaring town with a handful of galleries and shops. From here you can take the mail boat to Isle au Haut, where there's a remote, but beautiful, section of Acadia National Park.

Though Penobscot Bay itself may be too painfully cold for a plunge, it is wonderfully soothing to gaze at it from the villages, woods, and rock peninsulas nearby.

Places to Go, Sights to See

Camden Harbor. The Camden Hills rise right over this town, which also has a terrific view of Penobscot Bay, the islands, and the windjammers that put it on the nautical map. If you wish to hike in the hills, drive north on Route 1 to *Camden Hills State Park* (tel. 207/236–3109).

Castine and Blue Hill. These are quintessential, small New England towns of white-clapboard houses, white steepled churches, ancient elms and maples, and dreamy water views. Blue Hill has more crafts shops (pottery is a local specialty); Castine has a greater range of architectural styles (Main and Perkins streets have the finest houses), a prettier harbor, and an astoundingly long, bloody, and varied history, with painted signs posted around town recounting most of it.

Maine State Ferry Terminal. Hop a ferry at the Rockland Terminal on Route 1 for a day trip or longer sojourn to the islands of Vinalhaven or North Haven, both ideal for bicycling, or to the tiny outer island of Matinicus.

The **Owl's Head Transportation Museum** (Rte. 3, Owl's Head, just south of Rockland, tel. 207/594–4418) has an extensive collection of antique aircraft, cars, and engines. On weekends some of the planes are flown by volunteers, and beginning in May biweekly events are held: car auctions, rallies, and fly-ins.

Penobscot Marine Museum (Church St., Searsport, tel. 207/548–2529). Allow plenty of time to explore the 10 buildings, which display sea captains' portraits, lots of scrimshaw, navigational instruments, and treasures from the China trade.

William A. Farnsworth Library and Art Museum (19 Elm St., tel. 207/596–6457). Rockland has one of the finest art museums in Maine, with a strong collection of landscapes and portraits by Andrew, Jamie, and N. C. Wyeth; Winslow Homer; Rockwell Kent; and Louise Nevelson (who was born in Rockland). A new Wyeth Center was expected to open in 1998. Other offspring of the museum include a number of galleries on Main Street and nearby side streets.

Haystack Mountain School of Crafts (Deer Isle, tel. 207/348–2306). A short drive from Deer Isle Village brings you to this renowned crafts school on the shore in a striking modern building designed by Edward Larrabee Barnes. The school's extensive grounds include a long stretch of pink-granite coastline, where you can pick your way among the boulders for a hike or birding expedition.

Isle au Haut. From Stonington you can take a passenger ferry for Isle au Haut (tel. 207/367–5193 for information), more than half of which is part of Acadia National Park. Far more remote than the main section of the park on Mount Desert, Isle au Haut offers a true escape into the wilds of cobble beaches, hushed birch and spruce woods, and 17½ mi of trails that clamber over the island's high central spine. Camping, by reservation (write to Acadia National Park, Box 177, Bar Harbor 04609), is available in lean-tos at Duck Harbor. The island's sole inn is about halfway between the park and the small village of Isle au Haut.

Stonington. Stonington, at the southern tip of Deer Isle, is a fishing village of weathered houses. Main Street has a smattering of gift shops and galleries, which look a bit incongruous in this rough port town. The real draw here is the waterfront—a jumble of piers, lobster co-ops, warehouses, and views of the archipelago of tiny, spruce-clad islands known as Merchants Row.

Beaches

Lincolnville Beach, north of Camden, has a small strip of sand that's on Penobscot Bay and, unfortunately, right on Route 1 as well. **Laite Memorial Park and Beach** offers bay swimming off Camden's upper Bayview Street. Castine has a small sandy beach on Penobscot Bay, about ¼ mi west of the junction of Routes 166 and 166A.

Restaurants

Blue Hill boasts two excellent choices: **Jonathan's** (Main St., tel. 207/374–5226), serving imaginative American cuisine with an emphasis on fresh Maine foods, and **Firepond** (Main St., tel. 207/374–9970), with a romantic setting—ask for a table on the porch overlooking the stream—as well as excellent Continental fare. The **Landing** (Buck's Harbor, 207/326–8483), in South Brooksville (between Castine and Blue Hill), offers classic cuisine with elevated views over the harbor. For Continental cuisine head to **Jessica's** (2 S. Main St., Rte. 73, tel. 207/596–0770), in Rockland, a European bistro in a cozy Victorian setting. In Rockport, the **Sail Loft** (tel. 207/236–2330), with unsurpassed views of the town's quaint harbor, offers a varied menu emphasizing seafood; it's also a popular Sunday brunch spot.

Reservations Services

B&B of Maine (377 Gray Rd., Falmouth 04105, tel. 207/797–5540), **Camden Accommodations** (77 Elm St., Camden 04843, tel. 207/236–6090).

Visitor Information

Blue Hill Chamber of Commerce (Box 520, Blue Hill 04614, no phone), **Castine Town Office** (Court St., tel. 207/326–4502), **Deer Isle–Stonington Chamber of Commerce** (Box 268, Stonington 04681, tel. 207/348–6124), **Rockland Area Chamber of Commerce** (Public Landing, Box 508, Rockland 04841, tel. 207/596–0376), **Rockport-Camden-Lincolnville Chamber of Commerce** (Box 919, Camden 04843, tel. 207/236–4404).

Blue Hill Inn

Union St. (Box 403), Blue Hill 04614, tel. 207/374-2844 or 800/826-7415, fax 207/374-2829

On Union Street amid other old white-clapboard buildings, this dignified, time-burnished Federal inn is perfectly in keeping with the spirit of its location: subdued, refined, but not overly fussy.

Owners Mary and Don Hartley are a soft-spoken couple who decided to give innkeeping a try after working as psychologists in Ohio. They have carefully kept intact the inn's pumpkin-pine and painted floors and its fireplaces and have furnished the guest rooms with a hodgepodge of Empire and early Victorian pieces, including marble-top walnut dressers, Asian rugs, and wing chairs.

The full breakfast served here will fuel you for the day, and you'll want to return for dinner—this place is known for its meals. At the nightly reception, you'll be fed hors d'oeuvres in the garden or by the living room fireplace. Then, in the rather plain dining room, you'll be served a candlelighted, five-course meal that features local produce, meat, fowl, and seafood. When you return to your room, you'll be pleased by the turned-down bed coverings; in the four guest rooms with fireplaces, fires will be ready for you to light if the evening is cool.

▦ *11 doubles with bath, 1 apartment with fireplace and kitchen. Air-conditioning on 3rd floor. $140–$175; MAP. MC, V. No smoking, no pets. 2-night minimum weekends July–Oct. Closed early Dec. and Jan.–Mar.*

Buck's Harbor Inn

Rte. 176 (Box 268), South Brooksville 04617, tel. 207/326-8660, fax 207/326-0730

Peter Eberling left a career in industrial advertising, and his wife, Ann, left a career in aerodynamics—she designed wings—to escape Los Angeles. They purchased the Buck's Harbor Inn, built in 1901 as an annex for a resort hotel, "on a lark" in 1976 and opened it for business in 1982. Although furnished mostly with traditional country pieces and braided rugs, there are a few surprises collected from the Eberlings' travels, such as the Eskimo print and a Guatemalan Mayan grave rubbing.

This is a nonfussy, traditional B&B, with large corner guest rooms. Peter and Ann give a warm welcome that extends to children, as long as they don't "jump on the bed," Peter says with a grin. You can relax in front of the woodstove in the living room or in the sitting room and library on the third floor, where Peter says he often hides. A full cooked-to-order breakfast is served on the airy porch, which offers glimpses of the harbor over the gardens and croquet court.

▦ *6 doubles share 2½ baths. $65–$75; full breakfast, dinner available Sat. in winter. MC, V. No smoking, no pets in summer.*

The Camden Maine Stay

22 High St. (Rte. 1), Camden 04843, tel. 207/236-9636

The Greek Revival Camden Maine Stay (no relation to the Maine Stay in Kennebunkport) sits among other homes listed on the National Register of Historic Places, just a few minutes' walk from the center of Camden.

Native Mainer Captain Peter Smith, a former U.S. Navy pilot, his wife, Donny, and her twin sister, Diana Robson, have furnished the house with antiques, collectibles, and Asian rugs, many acquired during Peter's 15 years overseas. The quietest rooms are at the back of the house, away from Route 1. Spacious Room 8 has a private patio, a woodstove, and a large window seat; the Clarke Suite has a sitting room with gas fireplace in the front of the house and a rear bedroom with brass cannonball bed.

Peter often provides information on what to do in Camden, throughout the state, and in the rest of New England. Always attentive to detail, his advice can include itineraries, mapped-out routes, and dining recommendations.

🏨 *7 doubles with bath, 1 suite. Cable TV/VCR in common room. $90–$115; full breakfast, afternoon goodies. AE, MC, V. No smoking, no pets.*

The Castine Inn

Main St. (Box 41), Castine 04421, tel. 207/326–4365, fax 207/326–4570

The well-respected Castine Inn acquired new owners in 1997, and the young energetic couple haven't missed a beat. Amy and Tom Gutrow wanted to escape New York City, where she was a lawyer and he a chef. Both grew up in rural areas, Amy in Vermont and Tom in Michigan, and both wanted to return to a simpler lifestyle. Amy wanted New England, Tom wanted water, and both wanted an existing inn. The Castine Inn fit the bill.

The stately yellow-clapboard inn celebrates its 100th anniversary in 1998. The living room is warm and welcoming, with a curio cabinet filled with beachcombing finds as well as comfortable chairs and a fire burning in the Count Rumford fireplace on cool evenings. It's the kind of place in which you can let out a huge sigh and relax. Off the lobby there's a snug little pub, the perfect spot for an evening rendezvous.

Rooms are simply furnished, some with Colonial reproductions. Those on the third floor are the biggest and command the finest views. From one side you see the harbor over the inn's formal garden, from the other you overlook the town and more gardens.

If you wonder what the view looks like in entirety, head to the spacious dining room, where there's a wraparound mural of the town and harbor. Tom, who trained with top chefs in New York and Paris, has added his own touches to the inn's most popular dishes (such as the crabmeat cake with mustard sauce appetizer). For his entrées he uses *fresh* local foods, so the menu changes regularly. At breakfast you have a choice of such dishes as apple-bread French toast and a herbed goat cheese omelet.

Castine is a perfect New England small town that invites you to linger, stroll along Main Street down to the harbor, or out along Perkins Street, past Federal, Greek Revival, and shingle-style houses to the lighthouse. The sea air and exercise will make the return to the Castine Inn and its hearty dinners all the more enjoyable.

🏨 *15 doubles with bath, 2 doubles with detached bath, 3 suites. Restaurant, pub, sauna. $85–$135; full breakfast. MC, V. No smoking in dining room, no pets. 2-night minimum July–Aug. Closed Nov.–Apr.*

Edgecombe-Coles House

64 High St. (HCR 60, Box 3010), Camden 04843, tel. 207/236–2336, fax 207/236–6227

The Edgecombe-Coles is a plush, beautifully decorated B&B on the residential northern edge of Camden. This rambling white-clapboard house (whose sections date from the late-18th to the late-19th centuries) is set well back from Route 1 at the top of an open grassy rise with views of Penobscot Bay.

Terry and Louise Price, who hail from San Francisco, bought the house in 1984 after vacationing in Maine one bright, crisp autumn. Their passion for antiques is evident in the Empire sofa and oil paintings in the living room. You'll get an idea of the Prices' excellent sense of design in the superb Sea Star Room, which has a king-size canopy bed with blue patterned bedding, a cream rug, a picture window looking out on the bay, and a fireplace. A full breakfast is served in

the formal dining room or on the front porch when weather permits.

▦ *6 doubles with bath. Portable air-conditioners available, TV/VCRs in rooms, cable TV in den, cross-country ski trails. $130–$190; full breakfast, afternoon tea. AE, D, MC, V. No smoking, no pets. 2-night minimum weekends July–Aug.*

Eggemoggin Reach Bed and Breakfast

Herrick Rd. (R.R. 1, Box 33A), Brooksville 04617, tel. 207/359–5073, fax 207/359–5074

Approached by a long, wooded drive, Eggemoggin Reach Bed and Breakfast stands on a point behind which shimmer the waters of Eggemoggin Reach. After summering in the area for years, Michael and Susie Canon built the post-and-beam Maine farmhouse in 1988 as a family retreat. They furnished it with an assortment of antiques, Asian rugs, and such simple decorative pieces as duck decoys and ginger jars. In 1993 they opened their home to guests. The house has an open plan, and every room overlooks the water. The living room's large brick fireplace keeps the chill off on cool evenings; the smaller den, with its woodstove, is the perfect place to escape the gloom of a rainy afternoon.

Breakfast is served buffet style in the living-dining room. It includes juices, muffins, and a hot entrée such as oven-baked apple pancakes, Charleston House French toast, or sour-cream breakfast cake. On warm days most guests choose to breakfast outside on the large covered deck, part of which is screened in. The lovely view here and from the upstairs suite is over the Reach to Little Deer Isle and Pumpkin Island Lighthouse.

The third-floor Wheelhouse Suite is spacious and elegant, with white walls and off-white carpeting. There's a king-size bed in the bedroom, and the large, comfortable living room has a sofa bed and an extra single bed.

The inn's two one-room cottages, Port Watch and Starboard Watch, face Deadman's Cove. Both have efficiency kitchens, woodstoves, bathrooms with cedar showers, and private screened porches. Each also has a king-size bed and a small sitting area with a love seat, a table, and chairs.

Similar in design, but larger and with a better view, are the six rooms, two per floor, in the gambrel-roof annex. Two have woodstoves, and on the upper floors the rooms can be connected through common sitting areas, a popular option for couples traveling together.

The Canons love to entertain, and if six or more guests desire, they will arrange for a shorefront picnic, with lobster delivered right to the dock. There's plenty to explore nearby, including Deer Isle, Blue Hill, and Castine.

▦ *6 doubles with bath, 1 suite, 2 cottages, 1 apartment. TV/VCR in living room, rowboat, canoe, dock, mooring. $140–$165; full breakfast. MC, V. No smoking, no pets. 2-night minimum weekends June 15–Labor Day. Closed mid-Oct.–mid-May.*

Goose Cove Lodge

Goose Cove Rd. (Box 40), Sunset 04683, tel. 207/348–2508 or 800/728–1963, fax 207/348–2624

When life seems too complicated, you can always head to the Goose Cove Lodge in the quiet community of Sunset, just outside Deer Isle. With its private location at the end of a dirt road overlooking Penobscot Bay and abutting nature conservancy lands, it's the kind of place where you can forget that the rest of the world exists.

Owners Dom and Joanne Parisi preside over a talented, service-oriented staff. Dom was president of an energy con-

servation management company in western Massachusetts, where Joanne operated a restaurant and worked as a caterer. They decided to improve the quality of their lives and began a search for a simple, rustic natural resort with '90s-era amenities—including fine dining. They found it here.

The main lodge, built as a nature camp in the 1940s, is rustic and homey, with a big fieldstone fireplace, a library, and a small bar on one level and the dining area a few steps down. What takes center stage here is the sweeping view of Penobscot Bay and the islands: no signs of development, just towering pines, rocky shores, a narrow beach, and boats. Guests rooms in the lodge and at the front of the attached wing all have this view as do most of the cottages, which are nestled in the pines throughout the inn's 21 acres. Cottages are simply furnished with country pieces, collectibles, and reproductions—perhaps a braided rug, a rocking chair, or a lobster-trap table—and have woodstoves or fireplaces that are prepared each day by the staff. Some have kitchenettes, and all have decks or granite ledge patios.

Guests truly appreciate the quiet and the natural environment. Dom leads weekly nature walks, and the lodge provides maps for trails on its property and the nature conservancy's adjacent 50-acres, where at low tide you can walk out to an island via a sandbar.

The inn is renowned for its dining room (rates include breakfast and dinner from May through October), which serves creative renditions of classic fare using Maine ingredients. With the exception of the weekly lobster bake on the beach, young children, infants to age 12, eat dinner separately from their parents, entertained by the lodge's staff from 5:30 to 8. Teenagers eat together in the adult dining room.

▦ *2 doubles, 2 singles with bath; 8 suites; 13 cottages. Restaurant, children's program, beach, bicycles, canoes, hiking trails, sea kayaks, 24' sloop (available for rent). $170–$260; full breakfast, hors d'oeuvres, 3-course dinner. AE, D, MC, V. 2-night minimum off-season, 3-person minimum for cottages July–Aug. Closed mid-Oct.–mid-May.*

Homeport Inn

Rte. 1, E. Main St., Searsport 04974, tel. 207/548-2259

Searsport is one of the antiques centers of Maine, and the Homeport Inn's opulent Victorian environment puts you in the mood to rummage through beautiful old things. Route 1 traffic roars by just beyond the front garden (complete with pseudoclassical statuary), but the inn is so solid and stately that this won't bother you. This 1861 ship captain's house—home of Dr. and Mrs. George Johnson (and their intriguing cat Casper and dog Tina)—is filled with heirlooms and has an air of privacy and formality.

Ceilings are immensely high, and the public rooms sparkle with polished hardwood, crystal candelabra, and gold. Guest rooms are large, and some have canopy beds and fleur-de-lis wallpaper. Those downstairs and at the back of the house have private decks, good light, and views of the bay. Families prefer the two-bedroom housekeeping cottage. A substantial breakfast, served on the inviting glassed-in porch or deck, will give you a good start for a morning at local shops, flea markets, or the Penobscot Maine Museum, just ½ mi away.

▦ *7 doubles with bath, 3 doubles share bath, 1 2-bedroom cottage. Fans in rooms, croquet, badminton. $55–$75, cottages $500 per wk; full breakfast. AE, D, MC, V. Smoking limited, no pets.*

Inn on the Harbor

Main St. (Box 69), Stonington 04681, tel. 207/367-2420 or 800/942-2420, fax 207/367-5165

Retired jewelry designer Christina Shipps purchased the Inn at the Harbor

in 1995, tastefully renovating it and updating the electrical, heating, and plumbing systems. Innkeeper Janet Blanchette, a Stonington native, runs the inn and is quick to help you find the best the area offers. Galleries, shops, and restaurants are just out the front door, and the boat to Isle au Haut is a 15-minute walk away.

The inn's expansive deck hangs over the harbor and is a popular guest hangout. In nice weather you might enjoy your Continental breakfast or afternoon cappuccino here.

Each room is named for a schooner that often visits the harbor. The nicest is the *Heritage*, which has a granite fireplace, a king-size bed, and a chaise lounge in front of a large picture window and its harbor view. Ask for a room on the harbor side; street-side rooms have no view and aren't very quiet at night.

🎏 *13 doubles with bath, 1 suite. TVs and phones in rooms. $100–$125; Continental breakfast. AE, D, MC, V. No smoking, no pets. Closed Jan.–Mar.*

The John Peters Inn

Peters Point (Box 916), Blue Hill 04614, tel. 207/374–2116

When you turn down the narrow lane and catch your first glimpse of this country inn, you may wonder whether your car has slipped into some bizarre wrinkle in the time–space continuum. The John Peters, with its four colossal Doric pillars and its views over green fields to the head of Blue Hill Bay, looks like something out of Tidewater, Virginia.

On closer inspection you will see that it is actually a classic brick Federal mansion, built in 1810, to which the columned porch was added in the 1930s. No matter. The John Peters is unsurpassed for its privacy, its tastefully decorated guest rooms, and the whimsical informality of its innkeepers, Barbara and Rick Seeger. Rick gladly left an engineering job in Massachusetts for what the Seegers describe as their "fantasy utopia" just outside the town of Blue Hill.

More often than not, you will be greeted excitedly by the resident Welsh terrier, DOC (for disobedient canine), before Barbara or Rick escorts you into the living room with its two fireplaces, books and games, baby grand piano, and traditional furniture. Asian rugs, which the Seegers collect, are everywhere. (Given the furnishings, this inn is not suitable for children.) Huge breakfasts in the light, airy dining rooms include the famous lobster omelet, served with lobster-claw shells as decoration. After breakfast you can lope down the hill to your boat or stroll into Blue Hill for a morning of browsing in the pottery and crafts shops.

The Surry Room, a standout guest room (though all are lovely), has a king-size bed, a fireplace, a maple chest, a gilt mirror, and six windows with delicate lace curtains. The Blue Hill Room is immense and has a wet bar and mini-refrigerator, an Empire sofa, a four-poster bed, a deck, and a view of Blue Hill Bay. In this room you can have breakfast served to you in bed. The large rooms in the carriage house, a stone's throw down the hill from the inn, have dining areas, cherry-wood floors and woodwork, wicker and brass accents, and a contemporary feel. Four have decks, kitchens, and fireplaces—real pluses. But at the John Peters, nothing is a minus, except having to say good-bye.

🎏 *6 doubles with bath, 1 suite in inn; 6 doubles with bath in carriage house. Phones in 4 carriage-house rooms, swimming pool, canoe, sailboat, pond, 2 moorings. $105–$165; full breakfast. MC, V. No smoking, no pets. Closed Nov.–Apr.*

The Keeper's House

Box 26, Isle au Haut 04645, tel. 207/367–2261

Perched on a rocky outcropping, with the Isle au Haut Lighthouse out the

front door and a cool evergreen forest out the rear, is the Keeper's House. This whitewashed island lighthouse inn is a restorative place. It's best to come if you want to heal body and mind and if you have a penchant for reading by the warm glow of an oil lamp, discussing world affairs by the woodstove, and sharing experiences around the dining room table. (Those who adore Laura Ashley or who can't survive without a hair dryer, phone, or TV, take note.)

When Jeff and Judy Burke purchased the house in 1984, it had been abandoned for 50 years. Experienced innkeepers, they knew the work involved would be arduous, but they also knew people would come. Guest rooms are spacious and simply furnished with a mishmash of antiques and country pieces, many of which came with the house. There are four rooms (each with a water view) in the main house; one in the woodshed; and a rustic, romantic retreat called the Oil House, about 100 yards down the shore from the main house. Once used to store oil for the lighthouse light, it's now a simple, whitewashed room—just large enough to hold a bed—with a private deck hanging over the rocks. It comes complete with a cold-water spigot, an outdoor shower, and a private "outhouse" up the hill.

Judy's full-course meals consist of fresh and whole-grain foods. She serves evening hors d'oeuvres by the living room woodstove, and she can pack you a lunch to eat while you explore—either on foot or on the inn's bicycles—the island and its section of Acadia National Park. Jeff will offer tips on where to go: Choose from rugged hiking trails or a mountain climb that rewards you with panoramic views over cliffs and crashing surf—Jeff says this is where you expect to hear Mary Martin belting out a song. Or head to an unmapped part of the park that offers a more Zen-like experience— a place where, Jeff says, "All your questions will be answered."

🏠 *4 doubles share 2 baths in main house, 1 double shares bath in woodshed,*

1 double with cold-water spigot, outdoor shower, outhouse. Bicycles. $250–$285; full breakfast, lunch, dinner. No credit cards. 2-night minimum July–Aug.

Pilgrim's Inn

Main St., Deer Isle 04627, tel. 207/348–6615, fax 207/348–6615

The pleasures of Deer Isle—back roads and tidal coves, pink granite and dark green spruce, sleepy villages and unspoiled fishing harbors—sink in slowly, and so does the charm of the Pilgrim's Inn. This barn-red, four-story structure (circa 1793) with a gambrel roof is set just a few feet from the road; there's a millpond out back, and the harbor is across the way. A stay at this inn is more than pleasant. Its specialness has to do with the sweet aroma of breads and cakes baking that greets you at the door, with the way the light reflects off the water, with the simplicity and appropriateness of the furnishings, with the bright splashes of flower beds set in green lawns, and, of course, with its hospitable owners.

Innkeepers Jean and Dud Hendrick have lots of experience working with people. Dud was the lacrosse coach at Dartmouth for 13 years, and Jean has a background both in counseling and in working with food. When they got married, they wanted a job they could do together, and they found it here. They have brought a spirit of ease, warmth, and unerring good taste to the Pilgrim's Inn.

The water is visible from nearly all the guest rooms, which have English fabrics and generous proportions. One favorite, Room 8 on the second floor, has country pine furniture, a tall headboard, and three bright windows. Room 5, with its cherry four-poster bed and chest of drawers and its burgundy-and-white color scheme, is also popular.

The inn's formal parlor, with its beige Asian rugs and pale sofas, is cool and stylish. But guests tend to congregate

downstairs in the rustic taproom, which has huge fireplaces, pine furniture, braided rugs, parson's benches, and a bay window with pond views. The attached barn has been converted to a dining room—a big, rustic, romantic space with original barn-wood walls and farm implements on display. Repeat guests to the inn are rewarded with a complimentary package of goodies, but you hardly need that incentive to return.

🏨 *10 doubles with bath, 2 doubles and 1 single share bath, 2 cottages. Restaurant, TVs in cottages, gift shop. $140–$190; full breakfast, dinner. MC, V. No smoking in rooms, no pets. Closed mid-Oct.–mid-May.*

Victorian Inn

Sea View Dr. (Box 258), Lincolnville 04849, tel. 207/236–3785 or 800/382–9817

Although it's less than 10 minutes from downtown Camden, the Victorian Inn feels a world away with its quiet setting well off Route 1 (but on the water side). Former New Yorkers Ray and Marie Donner purchased the inn in 1992 and run it with the help of their teenage son and daughter.

The inn was built as a summer cottage in 1881 for the Sawyer family, which moved in year-round when it fell into financial hardship. It was the first house in town to have indoor plumbing. The original well is still in operation for outside watering. Ray's former career as a heavy construction manager and Marie's as a gift basket designer have served them well here in updating and decorating of the inn. They've created a private retreat with such romantic touches as canopy and brass beds, lace curtains, braided rugs, white wicker furniture, and floral wallpapers.

You can relax on the wraparound porch with views over island-studded Penobscot Bay. You'll get the same view from the cozy living room, which has one of the inn's nine functional fireplaces. You'll

find another in the entry foyer and still another in the formal dining room with crystal chandelier. Roy has also added a fireplace to the glassed-in breakfast room in the turret, which overlooks the water. Five guest rooms also have fireplaces.

The Victorian Suite, with a canopy bed and a turret sitting room, is the favorite, but the small Bay Room, with an antique sleigh bed, has the best views. For privacy and space, ask for the Sawyer Suite; it wraps around the third floor and has a balcony and a loft.

Most days find guests out strolling through the gardens, sitting in the gazebo, and enjoying the fine sea air and heady views. At night you can retreat to the second floor sitting room's window seat, let out a deep sigh, and watch the stars dance over Penobscot Bay.

🏨 *4 doubles with bath, 2 suites. Air-conditioning on 3rd floor; phones, hair dryers, toiletries, robes in rooms; turndown service on request; safe available. $135–$245; full breakfast. AE, MC, V. No smoking, no pets. 2-night minimum mid-June–mid-Oct. weekends.*

Whitehall Inn

Rte. 1 (Box 558), Camden 04843, tel. 207/236–3391 or 800/789–6565, fax 207/236–4427 in season

Camden's best-known inn was built in 1834 as a ship captain's home. At the turn of the century it began its life as an inn, and another wing was then added. You'll sense the long history of civilized comfort as you cross the wide, cheery porch and walk through the decorous lobby on the soft, time-faded Asian rugs. The location is ideal: midway between the shops, restaurants, and windjammers of Camden and the trails of Camden Hills State Park. Penobscot Bay opens up across the road.

Siblings J.C., Chip, and Heidi Dewing grew up at the inn, and now—along with J.C.'s wife and their uncle, Don Chambers—manage it. "What we try to do here is preserve what the inn has always been," J.C. says, adding that there have only been four innkeepers since Ruth Barrett Ordway opened it in 1901.

The Whitehall is dear to the hearts of literary folk: Edna St. Vincent Millay, a Rockland girl, came here in the summer of 1912 to recite her poem "Renascence" and launch her literary career. The Millay Room, just off the lobby, contains Millay memorabilia.

The inn's loyal adherents cherish its high-toned, literary aura and that everything looks the same year after year—right down to the old-fashioned phones connected to an ancient switchboard with plugs. Still, newcomers may be disappointed by the small, sparsely furnished rooms, with their old dark-wood bedsteads, Currier and Ives prints, clawfoot bathtubs, and not much else in the way of style.

Though the Whitehall has a countrified stateliness, you'll hear the traffic on Route 1 unless you get a garden-facing room in the rear wing. The rooms in the Victorian annexes, the Maine and the Wicker house across Route 1, offer more seclusion; their quiet back rooms face the water. The dining room is open for breakfast and dinner, and the menu is heavy on home-baked goods and local fish and produce.

🏠 *35 doubles and 5 singles with bath, 4 doubles share 2 baths. Restaurant, cable TV in public room, phones in rooms, meeting rooms, tennis court, shuffleboard, golf privileges. $135–$175; full breakfast, dinner. AE, MC, V. No pets. Closed mid-Oct.–mid-May.*

The Youngtown Inn

Rte. 52 and Youngtown Rd., Lincolnville 04849, tel. and fax 207/763-4290

Manuel and MaryAnn Mercier have turned the Youngtown Inn, a white Colonial farmhouse built in 1910, into a French-inspired country retreat that's off the beaten track yet just 10 minutes from Camden. Manuel, a chef, was born in Paris and has trained in Cannes, in New York, and on cruise ships. He met MaryAnn, a stockbroker, in Copenhagen.

Upstairs the guest rooms are simple and airy and are furnished with pieces such as a painted armoire, a sleigh bed, and a green-metal canopy bed. The suites have fireplaces and all rooms open onto decks with views of the rolling countryside.

The well-respected restaurant, which takes up the first floor, serves classic cuisine. Breakfast is a treat—perhaps crepes with farmer cheese and blueberries, French toast stuffed with apples, or potato pancakes with smoked salmon and scrambled eggs, and of course croissants. Dinner entrées may include rack of lamb with fresh thyme or pan-seared pheasant breast with foie gras mousse. Also downstairs is a cozy pub. After dinner you can retreat to the upstairs sitting room, with its fireplace and TV.

Lake Megunticook, Fernald's Neck Nature Preserve, and Camden Hills State Park are all nearby.

🏠 *3 doubles with bath, 2 suites. Restaurant, air-conditioning in 2 rooms, fireplaces in 2 suites, TV in sitting area. $99–$140; full breakfast. AE, MC, V. Closed Jan.*

Down East

Claremont Hotel

Mount Desert Island, home to most of Acadia National Park, is one of Maine's crown jewels. In the mid-19th century, wealthy summer visitors were drawn here by the spectacular landforms, dramatic coastline (including the only fjord on the east coast), and deep-water harbors. Early in the 20th century, much of the finest land on the island was enshrined as the 33,000-acre national park, which today lures more than 4 million visitors annually. In the Great Fire of 1947, more than 17,000 acres burned on the island, including 10,000 within the park; 67 summer "cottages" were destroyed, including many along what was known as Millionaires Row. The fire—which followed on the heels of the Great Depression, the introduction of income taxes, and World War II—marked the end of an era on the island. Of the summer homes left untouched by the flames, many are now inns; although the island is still a favorite among the superwealthy, it has opened its arms to everyone.

Not surprisingly, the hordes of tourists have left their mark on the landscape. Bar Harbor, the upper-class 19th-century resort turned 20th-century tourist town, fairly swarms with motels, gift shops, restaurants, and places to buy upscale sportswear.

With a little effort, however, you can still enjoy the granite headlands, freshwater lakes, hiking trails, and wildflower-choked meadows of Acadia in relative peace. On the quieter west side of the island—in the villages of Somesville, Southwest Harbor, and Bass Harbor—lobstermen's boats bob alongside yachts. On the offshore islands, including Swans Island and the Cranberry Islands, traffic jams are unknown and the silence of a summer day is interrupted only by the putt-putt of a lobster boat. And even the island's east side, where Park Loop Road hugs the shore, empties considerably in the off-season. Natives claim that October is the best month to visit.

Northeast of Ellsworth, Maine's coastal geography changes: powerful tides carve away the rugged coastline, blueberry barrens roll over the countryside. The T-shirt and curio shops, fancy galleries, and man-made attractions so prevalent along Route 1 south of here all but disappear. It's rural coastline, mostly undeveloped, with plenty of access points and mesmerizing views.

GrindstoneNeck, a summer "cottage" colony in Winter Harbor, gives a taste of what Bar Harbor must have been like before the great fire. At Schoodic Point, a remote section of Acadia National Park, waves break on enormous slabs of granite and basalt jumbled on the shoreline. Both Prospect Harbor, on Route 186, and Corea, on Route 195, are quiet fishing villages that appear locked in an earlier time.

Machias is the largest town in the region and is home to a campus of the University of Maine. From here you can detour on Route 191 to Cutler, where the wire towers of the Naval Communications Station seem an otherworldly presence. At the other end of Route 191 is Lubec, home of Quoddy Head State Park, the easternmost point of land in the United States, marked by candy-striped West Quoddy Head Light. The 2-mi path along the cliffs here is both mystical and magical and offers magnificent views of Grand Manan island. From Lubec

*you can cross the International Bridge to Campobello and
tour President Franklin D. Roosevelt's summer home and, at
low tide, walk out to East Quoddy Head Lighthouse,
distinguished by its red cross.*

*The area from Lubec to Eastport has the biggest tides in the
country. Boats that ride the water even with docks at high tide
drop as much as 30 ft at low tide and must be accessed by steep
gangways. At the Pleasant Point Indian Reservation you can
purchase authentic sweet-grass baskets for a fraction of what
they cost elsewhere. Eastport is home to a thriving aquaculture
business that specializes in salmon. For a taste to bring home,
visit Jim's Smoked Salmon on Washington Street. It will be a
pleasant reminder of your visit to Maine's bold coast. You can
cross the border to Canada in Calais and make a pleasant day
trip to the resort community of St. Andrews-by-the-Sea.*

Places to Go, Sights to See

Acadia National Park. For a quick introduction to the park, stop off at the Hulls
Cove visitor center for brochures and maps, and then take the Park Loop Road.
You'll pass immense piles of granite rubble on the east shore; dramatic Otter
Cliffs, with ocean views to the horizon; Jordan Pond, ringed by mountains; and
the entrance to the road up to 1,530-ft Cadillac Mountain. Consuming popovers on
the lawn of the Jordan Pond House restaurant is an island tradition.

Great Wass Island Preserve. You can have the Maine coast to yourself at this
1,540-acre nature conservancy—home to rare plants, stunted pines, and coastal
raised peat bogs—at the tip of Beals Island. Trails lead through the woods and
emerge onto the undeveloped, raw coast, where you pick your way along the
rocks and boulders before retreating into the forest. Maine's Bureau of Parks and
Recreation operates 9 mi of trails about 4 mi east of Cutler on Route 191. Like
those at Great Wass, the *Bold Coast* trails are uncrowded and cross undeveloped
terrain. In Eastport the short trail to *Shakford Head* provides a fine view over
Cobscook Bay and out to Lubec, the aquaculture salmon pens, and construction
on the new port facility. The *Moosehorn National Wildlife Refuge* has sections
near Calais and Dennysville—excellent places for viewing migratory birds.

Roosevelt Campobello International Park. To reach this Canadian park by
land, you cross the International Bridge from Lubec. Stop at the information
booth for details on the tides—specifically, when you will be able to walk out to
East Quoddy Head Lighthouse—as well as on walking and hiking trails. You can

also tour the Roosevelt Cottage, which was presented to Eleanor and Franklin as a wedding gift.

Ruggles House (1 mi off Rte. 1 in Columbia Falls, no phone). Built by wealthy Thomas Ruggles in 1818, the house's distinctive Federal architecture, flying staircase, Palladian window, and woodwork—supposedly done over a period of three years by one man with a penknife—are worth a look.

Somes Sound. The only fjord on the east coast takes a long, deep bite out of Mount Desert Island, with mountains rising on either side. Somesville, at the head of the sound, is a perfect white-clapboard village. Northeast Harbor, on the east side of the sound's entrance, is a posh yachting center. You can hop a ferry here for the Cranberry Isles, which command superb views of the mountains and harbor small villages of fishermen and summer communities of artists and academics. Southwest Harbor, on the west side of Somes Sound, is a good base for exploring nearby mountains and lakes.

Beaches

Sand Beach, off the Park Loop Road on Mount Desert Island, has mountains rising behind it and hiking trails departing from its east end. The crowds on hot summer days can be forbidding. **Echo Lake,** near Southwest Harbor, offers freshwater swimming. **Roque Bluffs State Park,** in Roque Bluffs, has both cold-water ocean swimming from a pebble beach and warmer freshwater swimming in a pond with a sand beach.

Restaurants

In Bar Harbor, **Porcupine Grill** (123 Cottage St., tel. 207/288–3884) offers new American cuisine in an antiques-filled setting, while the menu at **George's** (7 Stephen's La., tel. 207/288–4505) is Mediterranean inspired. Tea at the **Jordan Pond House** (Park Look Rd., tel. 207/276–3316) in the park is a century-old tradition featuring oversize popovers with homemade strawberry jam. East of Acadia, in Hancock, **Le Domain** (Rte. 1, 207/422–3395) has authentic French cuisine and perhaps the best wine list in Maine.

Reservations Service

Bed & Breakfast of Maine (377 Gray Rd., Falmouth 04105, tel. 207/797–5540).

Visitor Information

Acadia National Park (Box 177, Bar Harbor 04609, tel. 207/288–3338 or 207/288–4932), **Bar Harbor Chamber of Commerce** (Box BC, Cottage St., Bar Harbor 04609, tel. 207/288–5103 or 207/288–3393 mid-May–mid-Oct.), **Eastport Chamber**

of Commerce (78 Water St., Eastport 04631, tel. 207/853–4644 late May–mid-Sept.), **Lubec Chamber of Commerce** (Box 123, Lubec 04652, tel. 207/733-4522), **Machias Bay Area Chamber of Commerce** (Box 606, Machias 04654, tel. 207/255–4401), **Mount Desert Chamber of Commerce** (Box 675, Northeast Harbor 04662, tel. 207/276–5040), **Schoodic Peninsula Chamber of Commerce** (Box 381, Winter Harbor 04693, tel. 207/963–7658 or 800/231–3008).

Brewer House

Rte. 1 (Box 94), Robbinston 04671, tel. 207/454-2385 or 800/821-2028

In 1827 Captain John Nehemiah Marks Brewer built an ornate, columned, Greek Revival house across from one of his shipyards. In 1990 Estelle and David Holloway left the Chicago area and purchased the house, which had been empty for 10 years. "We were attracted by the wonderful nothingness of it," she exclaims. Estelle, who had a business specializing in architectural antiques, was also attracted by its carved Grecian moldings and Ionic pilasters, its four marble fireplaces, its silver doorknobs, and its elliptical staircase. No wonder the building is on the National Register of Historic Places.

The house is furnished with family treasures and unusual antiques. She describes the cluttered look as "European style, made up of inherited family pieces that don't necessarily match." No matter, what takes precedence here is the view out the floor-to-ceiling windows that look across Passamaquoddy Bay to St. Andrews-by-the-Sea in Canada. Sue Lynn (the rooms are named after the Holloways' children) is the best in the house, with a section of hand-carved paneling from the Palmer House hotel in Chicago serving as the headboard for the king-size bed.

▦ *2 doubles with bath, 2 doubles share bath, 1 apartment. $60–$85; full breakfast. MC, V. No smoking, no pets.*

Claremont Hotel

Claremont Rd. (Box 137), Southwest Harbor 04679, tel. 207/244-5036 or 800/244-5036, fax 207/244-3512

A stay at the four-story, yellow-clapboard Claremont evokes the long slow vacations of bygone days. It was built as an inn in 1884, and today John Madeira, Jr., who manages it for the McCue family, welcomes guests as they've always been welcomed; in summer he is joined by a large, youthful staff. This complex of a main house, 2 guest houses, and 12 cottages is at the end of a quiet road yet just a short stroll from bustling Southwest Harbor. In warmer months you can play croquet on the lawn (the August tournament is a highlight) or partake of cocktails at the boathouse. Year-round, you'll enjoy spectacular views of Somes Sound.

The main hotel was completely renovated several years ago, but traditionalists will be hard pressed to notice any changes (it was pieced back together under the direction of a historic preservationist). Although some public rooms seem underfurnished, the stone fireplaces and the wicker and straight-back chairs in the library and sitting room are in keeping with Southwest Harbor's rugged, fishing village character. Light streams through the picture windows in the large, rather formal dining room (open to the public for dinner), making it a fine place to plan a day of hiking in the national park, biking on the network of carriage paths, or sailing on Somes Sound.

Guest rooms are painted in mottled pastels but retain their simplicity. The views through gauzy white curtains are unforgettable—there's nothing like the sight of the silvery sound at dawn. Some of the rustic guest houses and cottages have the same view.

▦ *24 doubles with bath in main house, 5 doubles with bath in Phillips House, 1 suite in Clark House, 12 cottages. Restaurant, air-conditioning in dining room, cable TV in parlor, phones in rooms, tennis court, croquet, bikes, dock, rowboats, moorings. $120–$155; full breakfast (MAP rates only mid June–mid-Sept.). No credit cards. No smoking in rooms, no pets. Hotel and dining room closed mid-Oct.–mid-June, cottages closed late Oct.–mid-May.*

The Crocker House Inn

Hancock Point Rd., Hancock 04640, tel. 207/422–6806, fax 208/422–3105

Once one of 70 inns in the thriving summer community of Hancock Point, this century-old, shingle-style cottage set amid tall fir trees was abandoned for 20 years. Richard Malaby rescued it in 1980, and he has been restoring it ever since. The pine-paneled living room is furnished with comfortable floral-pattern couches and chairs and an old upright piano. Guest rooms in the main inn have a mix of country-style furniture; oak, brass, and iron beds; oak washstands; quilts; floral- or Colonial-pattern wallpapers; and stenciling. The carriage house has two rooms: spacious Room 14 has a king-size bed and is done in shades of teal, rose, and blue; Room 15, ideal for families, is decorated in soft pastels and has two brass double beds, a brass daybed, a TV room, a small library, and a large Jacuzzi. The inn's dining room serves up a full breakfast (buttermilk pancakes are a specialty here) and is also open for dinner.

Although none of the rooms has a water view, the Crocker House is only 200 yards from the water on either side and 800 yards from the end of the point. It's a good jumping-off point for excursions to Acadia's Schoodic Point and spots farther up the coast.

🖼 *11 doubles with bath in main house; 1 double, 1 quintuple with bath in carriage house. Restaurant, TV room, phones in rooms, Jacuzzi, bicycles, kayaks. $100–$130; full breakfast. AE, D, MC, V.*

Inn at Bay Ledge

1385 Sand Point Rd., Bar Harbor 04609, tel. 207/288–4204, fax 207/288–5573

Jeani and Jack Ochtera, corporate refugees from Massachusetts, operated another inn in Bar Harbor before purchasing the Bay Ledge in 1993. Origi-nally built as a minister's house in the early 1900s, it became an inn in the 1940s and was famous for it's cliff-top location. "It's five minutes from town but feels 100 miles away," Jeani says. You'll see what she means as you descend the 76 steps to the rocky beach and its Cathedral Rock and cavelike Ovens formations (given the cliff-side site, this inn isn't appropriate for young children). With such a peaceful location, no wonder it was once a spa (be sure to take a dip in the oceanfront pool and whirlpool or spend time in the sauna or the steam room).

The Ochteras have filled the house with antiques, paintings and prints by local artists, Asian rugs, and Jeanni's collection of baskets. Guest rooms in the main house have four-poster or canopy beds, featherbeds, and down comforters; three have whirlpool baths, and most have dreamy ocean views. The pine-paneled living room has a brick fireplace and a rustic lodge feel. It opens into the sunroom, which has wicker furniture and yet another fireplace and is where a multi-course breakfast (homemade granola, muffins, fruit, and such entrées as French toast stuffed with peaches and cream) is served. Hidden in the evergreens across the street from the main inn are three cottages; two have fireplaces.

🖼 *7 doubles with bath, 3 cottages. TV/VCR in upstairs common room, steam room, sauna, outdoor pool and whirlpool, private beach. $85–$150 rooms, $150–$250 cottages; full breakfast, afternoon refreshments. MC, V. No smoking, no pets. 2-night minimum mid-June–Oct. Closed mid-Oct.–mid-May.*

Inn at Canoe Point

Hulls Cove (Rte. 3, Box 216), Bar Harbor 04609, tel. 207/288–9511

Those in search of seclusion, intimacy, and privacy will find it at this 1889 Tudor-style house that's pinned between rocky shore and woods at Hulls Cove, only 2 mi from Bar Harbor. Innkeepers Tom and Nancy Cervalli moved here in

1996 from nearby Southwest Harbor, where they operated another B&B. It's obvious from their manner that they've been at this for awhile: they're relaxed and friendly innkeepers with keen eyes for detail.

The large Master Suite is the favorite of most guests because of its size, its fireplace, and its French doors that open onto a waterside deck. The smaller Garden Room has a private entrance and windows on three sides with both water and woods views. The inn's large living room has huge windows, a granite fireplace, and, just outside, a deck that hangs out over the water. (Note that the rocky oceanfront location and the intimate atmosphere make this inn inappropriate for children.)

▦ *3 doubles with bath, 2 suites. Cable TV in common room, private beach. $135–$250; full breakfast, afternoon refreshments. D, MC, V. No smoking, no pets.*

The Island House

Clark Point Rd. (Box 1006), Southwest Harbor 04679, tel. 207/244-5180

Ann Bradford, certainly one of the sweetest and most tactful people in the B&B business, makes the Island House in Southwest Harbor a truly special place to stay. Sitting by the fireplace in her snug living room with its wide-plank pumpkin-pine floor and Asian rugs, Ann loves to recount the history of how her white-clapboard house near the harbor was once a grand inn—the first on the island—and how it shrank over the years. She moved in back in 1969 and began taking in guests 15 years later.

Guest rooms are full of air and light and have such plain, old-fashioned Maine touches as white-painted furniture and sheer white curtains. Honeymooners will appreciate the carriage house suite, with its loft bed, skylight, kitchenette, and serene treetop view. Anne serves a hearty breakfast (dishes include baked eggs accompanied by cheese and sausage balls) and happily shares her knowledge of where to go and what to do.

▦ *4 doubles share 3 baths, 1 suite. Cable TV in parlor and carriage house. $70–$95; full breakfast. MC, V. No smoking, no pets.*

Island View Inn

Rte. 1 (HCR 32, Box 24), Sullivan Harbor 04664, tel. 207/422-3031

Midway between the main section of Acadia National Park on Mount Desert Isle and the Schoodic Point section is the aptly named Island View Inn. The waterfront, shingle-style cottage with a wraparound porch was built in 1888 and is rumored to have been designed by John Calvin Stevens. Upon entering, your eyes go directly to the rear windows, which frame Cadillac Mountain rising above Frenchman's Bay. Then you'll notice the stone fireplace that rises more than two stories. On either side of it are built-in seats that invite you to curl up with a good book from the small library. A leather couch faces the fireplace, and there's an assortment of other antiques and country pieces, most original to the house.

Upstairs in the main inn are four spacious rooms and one slightly smaller room. All open onto a deck, though only two—the Bird and Ships rooms—have water views. A small room above the kitchen in the ell also has a water vew. If your room doesn't have such a vista, rest assured that you can see the bay from the large dining table, where you'll find a hearty breakfast of eggs or French toast accompanied by muffins and meat waiting for you each morning.

▦ *6 doubles with bath. Fans in rooms, beach access, canoe, dinghy, 18' sloop (rental). $60–$90; full breakfast. D, MC, V. Smoking restricted. Closed mid-Oct.– late May.*

Le Domaine

Rte. 1 (Box 496), Hancock 04640, tel. 207/ 422-3395 or 800/554-8495

Nine miles east of Ellsworth, on a rural stretch of Route 1, you'll find a little slice of French dining and lodging sophistication that's as welcome as it is improbable. Owner-chef Nicole L. Purslow trained at the Cordon Bleu and apprenticed in Switzerland. Here, in the Maine countryside, she whips up classic haute cuisine dishes, the perfect accompaniments to which are bound to be hiding amid the more than 40,000 bottles of French vintage in the wine cellar. Meals are served in an elegant dining room whose white walls and dark wood accents are evocative of a French château. A massive brick fireplace dominates one end of the room, and family coats-of-arms, posters of France, and shiny copper pots are displayed throughout.

Although Le Domaine is known primarily for its restaurant, the small, French country–style guest rooms are just as inviting. All have chintz fabrics, wicker furnishings, and simple desks and sofas near the windows; four have balconies or porches over the gardens. The inn owns 100 acres situated halfway between Mount Desert Isle and Schoodic Point. With so much space, the great outdoors will surely beckon you for a walk along the inn's paths or for a game of badminton on the lawn.

🏠 *7 doubles with bath. Restaurant, air-conditioning in 4 rooms, radios and fruit in rooms. $200; MAP. AE, D, MC, V. No pets. Closed late-Oct.–mid-May.*

Mira Monte

69 Mt. Desert St., Bar Harbor 04609, tel. 207/288-4263 or 800/553-5109, fax 207/ 288-3115

Built as a private summer home in 1864, the Mira Monte has all the trappings of Victorian leisure, including columned verandas and spacious grounds. Marian Burns, one of the very few native innkeepers in Bar Harbor, knows Acadia intimately, having spent a lifetime hiking in the park and helping to establish the Wild Gardens of Acadia. Her own knack for gardening shows in the lush flower beds, formal and informal, that surround the inn.

Guest rooms have four-poster beds, gilt mirrors, and velvet fainting couches. The hodgepodge decor is offset by such thoughtful touches as double-glazed windows to reduce road noise and fresh flowers to add a bit of cheer. Ten rooms have private balconies or decks; nine rooms and two suites have fireplaces. A separate guest house has not only the two suites—complete with kitchenettes and two-person Jacuzzis—but also a housekeeping apartment. Marian serves a full buffet breakfast in the dining room, though in warm weather you may prefer to eat on the garden terrace.

🏠 *12 doubles with bath, 2 suites, 1 apartment. Air-conditioning, cable TV, phones in rooms; VCR in library and suites. $125–$180, apartment $950 per wk; full buffet breakfast, afternoon refreshments. AE, D, MC, V. Smoking restricted. 2-night minimum. Closed late Oct.–early May. (In winter suites available as weekly rental housekeeping units.)*

Oceanside Meadows

Rte. 195 (Box 90), Prospect Harbor 04669, tel. 207/963-5557

Along the sleepy road to Corea, nearby where author Elizabeth Dickinson Rich made her home, is a magnificent sand beach set off by dunes. If it catches your attention, you'll likely miss the rambling white-clapboard farmhouses that compose Oceanside Meadows on the other side of the road. Owner Sonja Sundaram, a geologist-geographer with a teaching background, met her husband, Ben, a marine biologist who hails from Scotland, at an environmental studies program in Bermuda. Together they have

extensively renovated the original house, built by Captain George Allen in 1860, and taken over the Sands, the 1820 inn next door. They are well on their way to their goal of building an environmental education center on the property. "We have dunes, beach, forest, ponds, a salt marsh, and tidal pools," Ben says, adding there are six bald-eagle nesting sites on the nearly 200-acre property.

Rooms are comfortably furnished with country furniture as well as ornately carved mahogany pieces that Sonja brought back from her travels to India. Both houses have comfortable living rooms; the Sands has a full kitchen for guests' use as well as a music room with a piano. You can see the water from rooms in the front of both houses. Room 5 in the main house, built into the eaves and decorated in pink and blue, has an excellent view of the beach. In the Sands, Room 1 has a private deck overlooking the water, a cathedral ceiling, and a magnificent chest from India that was hand-carved and inlaid with ivory; Room 5 has the best view of the bay; and Room 7, built under the eaves on the third floor, is popular with honeymooners.

The elegant multicourse breakfast includes such dishes as chilled mango-lime soup and waffles with gorged pears; all use fresh herbs and edible flowers from the inn's organic gardens. After eating, you can go moose spotting on the nature trails to the marsh, walk along the shoreline to a lighthouse, or just sit on the beach and listen to the waves.

🏠 *13 doubles with bath, 1 suite. $95–$105; full breakfast. AE, MC, V. No smoking. Closed Nov.–May.*

Peacock House

27 Summer St., Lubec 04652, tel. 207/733-2403

The Victorian Peacock House, built in 1860 and on a quiet residential street in Lubec, was home to four generations of the Peacock family before Chet and Veda Childs purchased it in 1989. They run it with their daughter, Debra. Chet, raised in nearby Eastport, was returning home after a career that included 30 years in the military and 10 in the corporate world. During those years he and Veda, a Texan, traveled to Europe and often stayed in B&Bs; they decided they wanted one of their own.

The Margaret Chase Smith Suite, named after the former Maine senator, is done in shades of blue and rose and has a brass queen-size bed and Asian rugs. The bright, cheery Summer Room has a white iron-and-brass bed and a wicker armchair. Both offer partial water views through lace-curtained windows.

The comfortably furnished common rooms include a family room with TV/VCR and a bar stocked with mixers, a library with Civil War prints and a gun cabinet (this inn is not suitable for young children), and a parlor with a fireplace. Veda serves a full breakfast—perhaps, eggs Benedict or apple-cinnamon pancakes—in the dining room on table settings that change daily.

🏠 *5 doubles with bath. Air-conditioning on 1st floor. $72.50–$85; full breakfast, afternoon tea. No pets, smoking in family room only. Closed mid-Oct.–mid-May.*

Pleasant Bay Inn and Llama Keep

West Side Rd. (Box 222), Addison 04606, tel. 207/483-4490

Some people, says innkeeper Lee Yeaton, turn around as soon as they hit the dirt road that leads to the Pleasant Bay Inn and Llama Keep. Despite this, Lee and his wife, Joan, strive to retain the rural nature of their property, which slopes down to Pleasant River and is home to a herd of llamas. The Yeatons bought the land in the mid '80s, trading careers in insurance and real estate for llama keeping. They built the Cape-style

house to take advantage of the river views and gave it an open plan so rooms flow from one to another.

In the evening you can relax in the family room in front of the fire, perhaps watching TV or a movie. The library is a quiet place to read. Upstairs, the three comfortable guest rooms are decorated with antiques and such country touches as duck decoys and bird sculptures; all rooms have water views.

You're welcome to stroll the nature paths on the property, which winds around a peninsula and out to Pleasant Bay. And you can even take a llama with you for company.

🏨 *1 double with bath, 1 double and 1 quadruple share bath. $45–$75; full breakfast. MC, V. No smoking, no pets.*

The Tides

119 West St., Bar Harbor 04609, tel. 207/ 288-4968, fax 207/288-2997

The trouble with staying here is that you're tempted never to leave the grounds despite all the attractions of Bar Harbor and Acadia National Park. The oceanfront, 16-room, Greek Revival–style "cottage," built in 1887, is in Bar Harbor's historic district and is listed on the National Register of Historic Places. Joe and Judy Losquadro purchased The Tides in 1996, after running another inn in town. Prior to that they were in Washington, DC, where Joe entered the corporate world after a 20-year naval career.

The back veranda, more an outdoor living room than a porch, hints at the house's grandeur. Henry Link wicker furniture is grouped in front of an outdoor fireplace that has a painting hanging over its mantel. Beyond the semicircular porch's vine-covered columns and rails, a landscaped lawn slopes down to the water. Breakfast, perhaps Acadian buckwheat blueberry pancakes, is served here in fine weather. On chilly days you may prefer to eat in the formal dining room, with its fireplace and its long, cushioned seat built into a curved wall of windows that overlook the bay. The formal living room, decorated in blue and white, opens onto the veranda and shares the same views.

The suites are grand both in size and amenities: All have cable TV; CD players; and such details as patterned, lead-glass, interior shutters in the windows. The Master Suite and the Ocean Suite have ocean views, sitting areas, and gas fireplaces. The third-floor Captain's Suite lacks a fireplace but has the best views over Frenchman's Bay. In the informal upstairs living room, you can curl up by the fire with a book, set up a jigsaw puzzle, or examine Judy's collection of nutcrackers.

🏨 *1 double with bath, 3 suites. Air-conditioning on 3rd floor, guest refrigerator in dining room. $125–$265; full breakfast. D, MC, V. No smoking, no pets.*

Ullikana

16 The Field, Bar Harbor 04609, tel. 207/ 288-9552, fax 207/288-3682

The Ullikana is an oasis of calm and quiet in busy downtown Bar Harbor. In the garden of this traditional timber, stone, and stucco cottage is a piece of modern sculpture. This unusual blend of traditional and modern continues inside, where the decor juxtaposes traditional antiques with more contemporary country pieces, abstract art with folk art, and vibrant color with French country wallpapers. The result, says co-owner Roy Kasindorf, "is like a marriage. It's a reflection of Hélène and I." The contrasts are shocking, but they work.

Roy and Hélène are a vibrant couple who have breathed new life into this 1885 estate. She ran the French program at the United Nations School in New York, and he worked in commercial photography. On a visit to the Maine coast, they stumbled upon the Ullikana. "I thought it was a disaster," he recalls, but "Hélène fell in love with it."

Room 3 mixes dark woodwork and a teal floor with pink floral-and-striped wallpaper and a pink sofa. It's a spacious room with a fireplace, a water view, and a large bath with claw-foot tub. Audrey's Room is a private retreat decorated in lilac-blue florals, and it has an exposed-beam cathedral ceiling, a tin king-size bed with a cameo of cherub angels, and a fainting sofa. From the claw-foot tub in the oversize bathroom, you look out to the islands. Room 5 is done in a French country motif, with rose toile de Jouy wallpaper and drapes and a fireplace. French doors open to a covered deck that overlooks the water. (Owing to all the antiques and artwork, this inn is not suitable for children.)

Breakfast—perhaps poached pears in red wine sauce followed by puffed pancakes with raspberries and blueberries—is served in the dining room, where deep red walls are set off by a teal-green floor and bright pastel dishes. On cool mornings a fire in the hearth takes away the chill. In the afternoon refreshments are served in front of the living room fireplace (you'll also find fireplaces in the foyer and two other guest rooms).

▦ *10 doubles with bath. $115–$195; full breakfast, afternoon refreshments. MC, V. No smoking, no pets. Closed Nov.– May.*

The Weston House

26 Boynton St., Eastport 04631, tel. 207/ 853–2907 or 800/853–2907

Jett and John Peterson offer comfortable, elegant lodgings in Eastport, one of the first towns in the country to see the sun rise. The couple came here from California in 1985 and purchased this 1810 Federal-style home, filling it with antiques and turning it into a gracious B&B. The Petersons' two dogs, a West Highland terrier and a Scottish terrier, will greet you enthusiastically, adding to the feeling of welcome.

Throughout the house are antique clocks, including a grandfather in the hall and a half-dozen or so others that John winds daily. Jett is a marvelous cook who makes excellent use of herbs from her garden and other local produce. Breakfast is served in the formal dining room, and it's accompanied by classical music. The meal begins with fresh fruit or juice and may include blueberry bread and an entrée such as eggs with locally smoked salmon or pancakes with apricot syrup. With advance notice, Jett will prepare box lunches or serve an elegant four-course dinner. Port and sherry are always available in the parlor as are games and magazines. The family room, with a fireplace and a TV, is a casual place to plan the day's activities.

Upstairs, five guest rooms share 2½ baths. The nicest are the Audubon Room and the Weston Room, both of which are in the front of the house and overlook the gardens, the town of Eastport, and the Passamaquoddy Bay. The Weston Room, done in soft pastels, has a working fireplace, a king-size four-poster bed, an antique rocker, a love seat, and cable TV. The Audubon Room is named for its most famous guest, John J. Audubon, who stayed here in 1833.

The Weston House is centrally located for day trips to Campobello or St. Andrews-by-the-Sea. There are a number of walking trails, and the Moosehorn National Wildlife Refuge is nearby. Eastport offers the easternmost Mexican restaurant in the country and salmon—it's worth coming for the annual Salmon Festival in early September. You can purchase authentic sweet-grass baskets at the Indian reservation on Pleasant Point.

▦ *4 doubles and 1 single share 2½ baths. TV/VCR in family room, terry-cloth robes in rooms. $60–$75; full breakfast. No credit cards. No smoking, no pets.*

The Western Lakes and Mountains

The Waterford Inne

The first sign of Maine's lake country appears less than a half hour from Portland: peacock blue mountains ascending at the end of a long, gleaming runway of water; the soft, graceful boughs of white pines interlaced along the shore; a lone canoe leaving its wake across the reflections of cumulus clouds. Because Maine tapers to a point at its south end, the Sebago–Long Lake region is just 40 mi northwest of Portland, the Oxford Hills area an additional 12 mi to the north, and the Rangeley Lakes region is just 1½ hours from Bethel. Though the lakes and hills seem a world away from the coast, you can, in fact, dip into them on a day trip.

Summer, of course, is the prime season for the lakes, when the morning cries of the loons are quickly drowned out by the buzz of motorboats and water-skiers, and boats line up to pass through Songo Lock, connecting Long Lake with Sebago Lake, creating a 42-mi inland waterway. Fisherfolk crowd the shores in pursuit of trout and salmon, and highways thicken with traffic, particularly on July and August weekends when parents visit their children at the many local camps.

Winter is a more contemplative time of year here. Downhill skiers have their choice of Shawnee Peak, just 6 mi west of Bridgton; the expansive Sunday River Ski Resort, near Bethel, and its sister area, Sugarloaf/USA, in the Carrabassett Valley; and remote Saddleback, in Rangeley. Cross-country skiers can head off just about anywhere—across frozen lakes or onto the fields fringing the perfect small town of Waterford, a National Historic District where white clapboard and green shutters are mandatory. Though Waterford and its sister towns of North, South, and East Waterford don't offer much to do aside from basking on small lake beaches in summer, gazing at hillsides ablaze with foliage in fall, cross-country skiing in winter, and swatting blackflies in spring, it really doesn't matter. You come here to relax in the serenity of picturesque surroundings.

As you meander west and north, the Oxford Hills give way to the mightier and loftier White Mountains, which reach their apex across the border in New Hampshire's Presidential Range. The Maine side, however, may well command the finest view, especially just around sunset. When the sun descends into the jagged mountaintops, it doesn't matter what season it is. You can congratulate yourself year-round on having found a very special corner of Maine.

Places to Go, Sights to See

Bridgton. Though not a very appealing town in its own right, Bridgton is the antiques center of the region, with a number of shops on Main Street and on the fringes of town.

Center Lovell. Less than 10 mi due west of Waterford is the town of Center Lovell, which is perched above the dark water of Kezar Lake. Though you won't see much of the lake from Route 5, the main road through town, you will be rewarded with a magnificent view of the White Mountains.

Fryeburg. Although less than 15 minutes from the bustling factory outlets of North Conway, New Hampshire, sleepy Fryeburg, home to a private academy of the same name, is a world away. The lazy Saco River, perfect for canoeing, cuts through town, with the Presidential Range of the White Mountains as a backdrop.

Kezar Lake, tucked away in a fold of the White Mountains, has long been an exclusive hideaway for the rich; recently a couple of inns have opened this unspoiled scenery to more visitors.

Rangeley has lured fisherfolk and winter-sports enthusiasts for a century to its more than 40 lakes and ponds and 450 square mi of woodlands.

Sabbathday Lake Shaker Museum (Rte. 26, New Gloucester, tel. 207/926–4597). Though a bit off the beaten track, the museum is worth a detour for its displays of Shaker architecture and design, including the 1794 meetinghouse; tools; farm implements; furniture; and crafts in tin, textile, and wood. The Shaker community at Sabbathday Lake is one of the oldest and most active remaining in the United States and the last one in Maine. Members continue to raise vegetables and culinary and medicinal herbs.

Songo Lock. Near Naples, the Songo Lock (tel. 207/693–6231), 2½ mi south of Route 302 on Songo Locks Road, permits passage from Sebago Lake to Long Lake by way of Songo River and Brandy Pond. It is the only surviving lock of the Cumberland–Oxford Canal.

Waterford is a National Historic District and the most picturesque of the collection of villages known as the Waterfords. It's so small you can stroll all around town in no time—from the Congregational church, past the general store, to the small sand beach on Keoka Lake.

Beaches

Sebago Lake State Park (tel. 207/693–6613 June 20–Labor Day; tel. 207/693–6231 Labor Day–June 19), on the north shore of Sebago Lake, attracts anglers. It has a large sand beach, boat ramps, and a separate camping area. **Rangeley Lake State Park** (tel. 207/864–3858), on the south shore of Rangeley Lake, has superb lakeside scenery, swimming, picnic tables, a boat ramp, showers, and camping.

Restaurants

Lake House (*see below*), in Waterford, features creative American cuisine. For a musical treat, try **Quisiana** (*see below*), in Center Lovell, where the staff, recruited from the top music schools in the country, serves new American cuisine and stages an after-dinner performance in the lakeside music hall. In Raymond the **Olde House** (Rte. 85, tel. 207/655–7841) has an extensive Continental menu and a romantic atmosphere. At the **Oxford House** (*see below*), in Fryeburg, ask for a table with a sunset view over the White Mountains to enjoy Continental fare. The **Sudbury Inn** (Lower Main St., tel. 207/824–2174), in Bethel, offers classic Continental fare and formal dining upstairs and pizza and a casual pub-type atmosphere downstairs. The **Country Club Inn** (tel. 207/864-3831), built in the 1920s on the Mingo Spring Golf Course in Rangeley, lures diners to its remote hilltop location with excellent dining and sweeping lake and mountain views.

Reservations Services

B&B of Maine (377 Gray Rd., Falmouth 04105, tel. 207/797–5540), **Bethel Area Chamber of Commerce** (*see* Visitor Information, *below*).

Visitor Information

Bethel Area Chamber of Commerce (Box 121, Bethel 04217, tel. 207/824–2282), **Bridgton–Lakes Region Chamber of Commerce** (Box 236, Bridgton 04009, tel. 207/647–3472), **Naples Business Association** (Box 412, Naples 04055, tel. 207/693–3285), **Rangeley Lakes Chamber of Commerce** (Box 317, Rangeley 04970, tel. 800/MT–LAKES).

The Admiral Peary House

9 Elm St., Fryeburg 04037, tel. 800/237–8080 or tel. and fax 207/935–3365

The clay tennis court is one of the first things you notice when you pull into the Admiral Peary House driveway. It's what lured owners Ed and Nancy Greenburg, avid tennis players and experienced innkeepers, away from the motor lodge they operated in nearby Intervale, New Hampshire. Prior to that, both taught school in Canada. Ed is originally from Montréal; Nancy, from Indiana.

The gambrel-roof house, built in 1865 and once home to arctic explorer Admiral Robert Edwin Peary, is a perfect showcase for Nancy's antiques, many of which have been in her family for generations. Mac, the resident border terrier, welcome's you warmly as you enter the bright, airy kitchen. Breakfast is served here family style and may consist of sour-cream blueberry pancakes, stuffed French toast with apples, or the quichelike penguin pie. You can relax by the kitchen woodstove or explore the antiques-filled rooms in the front of the house. Most guests, however, retreat to the living room in the converted barn to lounge in front of the fire, watch TV, or play pool. In nice weather guests also gather on the adjacent screen porch to watch tennis matches or use the outdoor hot tub.

Many of the bedrooms have quilts handmade either by Nancy or her grandmother. The spacious North Pole Room offers the most privacy. Decorated in sage and rose hues, it's built into the barn's eves and has a soaring window that overlooks the backyard. It would be easy to spend the day lazing in the king-size brass bed.

Canoeing the lazy Saco River or hiking in the White Mountains are both popular ways to spend a day; tennis buffs can play a game, get a lesson, or just practice with the ball machine. Shoppers will enjoy the outlets in nearby North Conway, New Hampshire.

🛏 *6 doubles with bath. Air-conditioning, TV and pool table in living room, guest refrigerator, hot tub, bicycles, tennis court. $98–$118; full breakfast. AE, MC, V.*

Augustus Bove House

Corner of Rtes. 302 and 114, Naples 04055

Dave and Arlene Stetson fell in love with the lakeside village of Naples on their honeymoon in 1977. "We came every summer after that," Arlene says, and in 1984 they purchased the Augustus Bove House. As parents of 8, grandparents of 12, and foster parents of 23, they've found that innkeeping comes naturally.

The rambling brick house, built in the 1820s and originally known as the Hotel Naples, sits just across from the Naples Causeway on Long Lake. During its heyday, Arlene says, Joseph P. Kennedy, Enrico Caruso, and Howard Hughes stayed here. The spacious King Room, which has an excellent lake view and a king-size bed, is most popular, followed by the third-floor Blue Room, with a queen-size bed, a lake view, and an antique armoire.

Arlene's artwork, including velvet theorem paintings and reverse paintings on glass, covers much of the inn. She also runs an antiques, crafts, and fabrics shop during the summer months. Her full breakfasts (eggs, pancakes, or French toast; fruit; muffins; and bread) are served in two small dining rooms, one with a table for eight, the other with a table for six. In fine weather don't hesitate to eat out on the deck.

🛏 *2 doubles with bath, 4 doubles share 2 baths. Air-conditioning, TVs in rooms; hot tub; gas fireplace in living room; beach access; shop. $79–$89; full breakfast. D, MC, V. No smoking.*

Bear Mountain Inn

Rte. 35, South Waterford 04081, tel. 207/583-4404

"I want people to feel comfortable, to throw off their shoes and lounge as if they're in their own home," declares Lorraine Blais, who left a career as an interior decorator and shop owner in Boca Raton, Florida, to relocate to Maine's lakes region. A vivacious woman with a sharp eye for detail, her decorating skill is evident throughout the farmhouse-style Bear Mountain Inn, which she discovered "by accident" and purchased in 1996. "I'm the Martha Stewart of Maine," she proclaims, and she fits the bill.

The pine-paneled living room, with its stone fireplace and lodgepole-pine furniture, invites relaxing. The inn's bear theme begins here: The coffee table is a piece of glass balancing atop the paws of an upside-down bear; in a corner is a stuffed black bear. Each bedroom is named after a bear, and each bears Lorraine's creative touch, perhaps swirled plaster ceilings, beds made from barn siding, a hand-painted dresser, a hand-made silk tree, or a hand-carved headboard. The furniture is a mixture of antiques and country pieces. Most spacious and private is the Fuzzy Bear Room, with a Jacuzzi in the bathroom and a nice view of the lake.

Lorraine brings coffee and juice to the second-floor entertainment center, for early risers; the center is also well stocked with complimentary munchies, beer, wine, soda, and mixers. There's a microwave here as well as a portable phone that you can take to your room. Breakfast is served in a country-style dining room that's divided by a massive stone fireplace. Lorraine prefers whole-grain, organic foods, and much comes from her own garden. Breakfast might include whole-wheat waffles with bananas and apples or a soufflé with goat cheese and natural herbs. She makes her own cereals and serves turkey bacon.

The inn's splendors continue outdoors on its 43 acres, which include a private beach on Bear Lake, barbecue facilities where guests toast marshmallows at night, and hiking trails on Bear Mountain across the street. There are also a horseshoe pit and volleyball, badminton, and croquet setups. Despite all these activities, this inn is not a place for young children.

🏠 *2 doubles with bath, 4 doubles share 2 baths, 1 suite. Air-conditioning in 3 rooms, TV in living room, beach, canoes, sailboat, hiking, horseshoes, croquet, badminton, volleyball, cross-country skiing, snowmobiling. $85–$160; full breakfast. MC, V. No smoking.*

The Bridgton House

2 Main St., Bridgton 04009, tel. 207/647-0979

The Bridgton House has been through a lot since 1815, including remodeling in 1860 and fires in 1896 and 1914. It was a private home when Joan Opper and Lois Patterson purchased it in 1994 and re-opened it as an inn. "We each had five kids," Joan says. "We figured it couldn't be any worse." Indeed, they've found it nearly "effortless." They've redecorated with floral wallpapers and a nonfussy collection of antiques and country pieces.

The green-trimmed, white clapboard-and-shingle cottage is on Main Street, an easy walk to stores, restaurants, and Highland Lake. Room 5 is the nicest, with a bench that stretches under four consecutive windows, a small sitting area, a walk-through closet to a private bath, and a quiet, back-of-the-house location.

A full breakfast of baked French toast with apples, homemade breads, fresh fruits and the like is served on the wraparound front porch with a screened-in gazebo in fine weather or in front of the dining room woodstove on inclement days.

🏨 *3 doubles with bath, 3 doubles share 2 baths. Cable TV, ceiling fans in rooms; fireplace in living room; beach access. $85–$90; full breakfast. No credit cards. Closed Nov.–Apr.*

Grant's Kennebago Camps

Kennebago Rd. (Box 786), Rangeley 04970, tel. 207/864–3608 in summer, 207/ 282–5264 in winter, 800/644–4815 out-of-state

It would be hard to find a more peaceful or more restful setting than that offered by Grant's Kennebago Camps. Accessed by a gated private gravel road or by floatplane, this traditional Maine "sporting camp" has been continuously operating since 1905, when city "sports" came to Maine's lakes and mountains for fresh air and fishing. Kennebago provides both, with a lakeside setting on pristine Kennebago Lake, prized by fly-fishermen. Knotty pine cabins are spread out along the lake and in the woods. Each has a private boat and dock, a woodstove, and a screened porch.

You take three meals in the cheery central dining room overlooking the lake, where you can choose entrées from a rotating menu. The staff, like the guests, returns year after year.

Hiking, mountain biking, canoeing, fly-fishing, and sailing are the primary pursuits. On inclement days you can retreat to the TV lounge, curl up with a book, or head to Rangeley.

🏨 *18 cabins with bath. Restaurant; TV/VCR in lounge; no charge for mountain bikes, sailboats, Windsurfers, hiking packs, canoes; charge for motor and boat, portage, floatplane rides, fly-fishing instruction, and guide service; fly shop; children's playground; day care available. MC, V for deposit only. Closed Oct.–late May.*

Lake House

Rtes. 35 and 37 (Box 82), Waterford 04088, tel. 207/583–4182 or 800/223–4182, fax 207/583–6978

Though not actually on a lake, the Lake House is near several (Keoka Lake is a stone's throw away, and Long Lake is 5 mi south), and it's right in the middle of the tiny, picturesque town of Waterford. The most Victorian in style of the area inns, the Lake House has a carpenter Gothic front with a pleasant screened porch and guest rooms that some may find a touch cluttered.

The inn's long history includes stints as a private home; periods as an inn (Mickey Rooney, Claudette Colbert, and Judy Garland have stayed here); and, in the mid 19th-century, service as the Maine Hygienic Institute for Ladies. Today, Michael Uhl-Myers operates the inn and restaurant, which is open to the public for dinner and serves entrées such as roast duckling in a romantic setting (best to leave your children at home).

The spacious, bright Grand Ballroom Suite has a four-poster bed, a stained pine floor, and a bathtub that's in the center of the room. Those who seek privacy might ask for the one-room cottage behind the inn.

🏨 *4 doubles with bath, 1 cottage. Restaurant, fireplace in sitting room, coffeemakers in rooms. $84–$130, full breakfast. MC, V. No smoking, no pets. Closed Apr. and Nov.*

The Noble House

Highland Rd. (Box 180), Bridgton 04009, tel. 207/647–3733

Set on a hill crest amid massive white pines, this grand but utterly unpretentious house was built on a quiet residential street near town by a Maine state senator in 1903. Jane Starets runs the

inn with her husband, Dick (when he isn't at work as a commercial pilot), and the summertime help of their four children.

You cross the wide porch to enter a simply appointed parlor with a comfortable sofa, wing chairs, and a grand piano. Behind the parlor is the formal dining room, where an abundant breakfast buffet (fruit, eggs, pancakes, baked goods) is usually served.

The guest rooms don't quite measure up to the elegance of the public rooms: Most are small and a bit spartan in their furnishings. The Honeymoon Room, however, has a good lake view, a whirlpool bath (as do three other rooms), white wicker furniture, and fresh flowers.

A real asset is the dock across the street on Highland Lake, with chairs and a hammock and the view of Mt. Washington and the Presidential Range rising in the distance.

🏠 *6 doubles with bath, 3 doubles share bath. TV/VCR in lounge, floating dock for swimming, croquet, canoe, paddleboat. $78–$125; full breakfast. AE, MC, V. No pets. 2-night minimum weekends. Open only with reservations mid-Oct.–mid-June.*

The Oxford House

105 Main St.,, Fryeburg 04037, tel. 800/261-7206 or 207/935-3442

The Edwardian-style Oxford House was built as a private home in 1913 on part of the foundation of the Oxford Hotel, a summer resort that burned in 1906. John and Phyllis Morris purchased the house in the 1985 and turned it into an inn. The two previously ran an inn in nearby North Conway, New Hampshire, but sought a quieter location to raise their two children, Bennett and Garvin.

Magnificent cypress woodwork and floral wallpapers decorate both the public rooms and the bedrooms. From both Room 3 and the Sewing Room you can watch the sun set behind the Saco River valley and the Presidential Range of the White Mountains; Room 1 is spacious but lacks this view. All are decorated with country pieces. Breakfast is served in the glassed-in dining room, which has the same view. The well-respected restaurant is open to the public for dinner year-round and for lunch in the summer. There's also a pub in the basement with a full bar and a pool table.

🏠 *4 doubles with bath, 1 double with bath across hall. Restaurant, pub, TV in rooms. $78–$98; full breakfast. AE, D, DC, MC, V.*

Quisiana

Pleasant Point Rd., Center Lovell 04016, tel. 207/925–3500, fax 207/925–1004

Music lovers will think they've found heaven on earth at this delightful but rustic lakeside resort, which is staffed by students and graduates of some of the finest music schools in the country. Every evening a performance is staged in the lakeside music hall; shows run the gamut from Broadway revues to piano recitals to operas. And on Tuesday evening the chamber ensemble plays during the weekly cocktail party on the point. But the music isn't the only reason to come. You'll also enjoy the clean air and the crystal clear waters of 10-mi-long Kezar Lake. The lake is mostly undeveloped, and across it you can see the Presidential Range of New Hampshire's White Mountains.

This old-fashioned family retreat has been in existence since around 1915 and has been operated by Jane Orans and her son, Sam, since 1984. It's the kind of place families come to year after year, always staying in the same lodgings. Legend has it that one couple waited years for their turn until another couple passed away, enabling them to move up to a shorefront cottage.

You choose from 2 lodges and 32 cottages, some nestled in the pines and

others perched on the lake's edge. Each cottage is simply decorated with wicker and maple pieces accented with Waverly fabrics, and some have fireplaces. Of the guests who return, "90 percent request the same cottage," Jane says. "They think theirs is the perfect one." There are two large sand beaches to enjoy as well as a variety of watercraft and three clay tennis courts. Use of most facilities as well as three meals daily are included in the rates.

▦ *11 doubles with bath in 2 lodges, 32 cottages. Nightly musical performances; 3 clay tennis courts; 2 beaches; no charge for canoes, sailboats, rowboats, lake kayaks, Windsurfers; charge for fishing guides, waterskiing, lake tours, boat motors. $110–$155 per person; breakfast, lunch, dinner. No credit cards. 1-wk minimum in high season. Closed Sept.– mid-June.*

The Waterford Inne

Chadbourne Rd. (Box 149), Waterford 04088, tel. and fax 207/583-4037

The tiny white-clapboard and green-shuttered villages known as the Waterfords have fine country inns, but the Waterford Inne stands out for its breezy hilltop location and for its warmly convivial owners, Rosalie and Barbara Vanderzanden, a mother-and-daughter innkeeping team.

Back in the mid-1970s Barbara and Rosalie were schoolteachers in New Jersey and avid world travelers, when they decided they wanted a change of lifestyle and geography. As Barbara tells it, they had been looking all over Maine when a real estate agent showed them what was to become the Waterford Inne. They made an offer on the spot. "It was the feeling of the house that settled it," Barbara reminisces. She has preserved the

secluded feeling of the house by purchasing adjacent property as it becomes available. "When people ask me what I'm going to do with it," she says, "I tell them 'nothing.' "

The property was a dairy farm in the 1820s, and 40 years later a prominent lumber family bought it. With open fields all around, huge pine trees fringing the fields, an orchard out back, and a big red barn off to the side, the place retains vestiges of its farming heritage and its decades serving as a wealthy family's hideaway.

Barbara and Rosalie have done a superb job renovating the gold-painted, curry-yellow-trimmed house. The sitting room is cozy, with dried flowers hanging from exposed beams, a sofa facing the woodstove, and barn-board walls.

The bedrooms have lots of nooks and crannies. Nicest are the Nantucket Room, which has whale motif wallpaper and a harpoon, and the Chesapeake Room, with a private porch; a woodstove; pumpkin-pine floors; a king-size bed; and ducks, ducks, ducks. A converted woodshed has five additional rooms, and though they have slightly less character than the inn rooms, four of them have sunny decks.

The Vanderzandens enjoy trading travel tips with their guests and directing them to area lakes, ski trails, and antiques shops. They will prepare elaborate dinners by prior arrangement. Pets are welcome, but there is an extra charge.

▦ *6 doubles with bath, 3 doubles share bath, 1 suite. TV in common room, apple picking, antiques shop, cross-country ski trails, ice-skating pond, badminton. $74–$99; full breakfast. AE. No smoking in dining room. Closed Apr.*

The Great North Woods

Great rewards await those who take the time to venture to Maine's Great North Woods, where undeveloped lakes, pristine rivers, towering forests, and blue mountains attracted naturalists such as Thoreau a century ago and continue to attract environmentalists and outdoor enthusiasts today.

In the early 1800s Maine's seemingly endless forests were seen as a source of potential wealth by timber barons, who felled the trees and sold them to lumber-starved Europe. Rivers became Maine's earliest highways—a way of reaching otherwise impenetrable forests. Then the rivers were dammed to power lumber mills.

When motorized vehicles came into vogue, roads were built and "sports," as the wealthy summer visitors from the city were labeled, came to hunt, fish, and relax. Sporting camps sprung up on lakes and rivers to cater to the sports' needs, and resort hotels were built for those who came to escape the heat, lured by the promise of clean, cool air, and clear water.

They come for the same reasons today. The rivers dammed for power mills now provide reliable white water for rafting, canoeing, and kayaking. Remote lakes, streams, and ponds still offer unparalleled fishing. Hiking trails lace the region: Mt. Katahdin, in Baxter State Park, the crown jewel in Maine's state park system, is the terminus for the famed Appalachian Trail.

Most of Maine's Great North Woods is owned by paper companies. The roads are private and gated, although visitors are welcome, and an access fee is charged. Keep in mind that most private roads are gravel at best. You leave all connection to services behind when you enter. Logging trucks have the right-of-way, so if you see one bearing down on you, pull over and let it pass. The rewards of travel here, however, are many,

and sightings of moose, deer, bear, and other creatures are frequent, especially at dusk.

Towns are small, few, and far between. Greenville, on Moosehead Lake's southwestern shore, is the region's hub. It has the area's best selection of lodging and restaurants as well as shops, boat rentals and excursions, a medium-size ski area, miles of hiking trails, and unsurpassed views: Try the Lily Bay Road, which heads to Millinocket, for views over Moosehead and the chance to see moose, deer, and other wildlife. The road passes through paper-company lands and by remote lakes, the Penobscot River—prized by rafters and kayakers as well as fishermen—and Baxter State Park.

Places to Go, Sights to See

Baxter State Park. Few places in Maine are as remote, or as beautiful, as Baxter State Park and the Allagash Wilderness Waterway. The 201,018-acre park, a gift from Governor Percival Baxter, surrounds 5,267-ft Katahdin, Maine's tallest peak and the terminus of the Appalachian Trail.

The Forks. At the confluence of the Kennebec and the Dead rivers, this is Maine's white-water rafting capital, although it is increasingly popular with snowmobilers. *Raft Maine* (tel. 800/723–8633) has information on outfitters and lodging and rafting packages. For a short hike head to Moxie Falls.

Kineo. Kineo is easy to pick out from many vantage points on Moosehead Lake. This site of a once-thriving resort community is marked by a sheer cliff that rises 789 ft above the lake. The formation looms just across the narrows from Rockwood, where you can rent a boat for the short ride there—a pleasant day trip. You can hike on moderate or difficult trails to the top of the cliff, or you can play a round a golf.

Kokadjo. This tiny town about a half hour east of Greenville on the Lily Bay Road is famous for its sign: THIS IS GOD'S COUNTRY. WHY SET IT ON FIRE AND MAKE IT LOOK LIKE HELL?

Moosehead Marine Museum (tel. 207/695–2716) has exhibits about the local logging industry and the steamship era on Moosehead Lake. Through the museum you can book tours aboard the *Katahdin*, a 1914 steamship (now diesel). The 115-ft vessel fondly called *The Kate* carried passengers to Kineo until 1942 and was used by loggers until 1975.

Squaw Mountain Resort (tel. 207/695–1000) This respectable alpine ski area offers a step back in time: It's a family-oriented hill with downright cheap rates.

New owners have upgraded the lifts and invested in snow-making equipment. Hike or ride the chairlift to the summit in the summer to take in the views of Moosehead Lake and on a clear day, Mt. Katahdin.

Beaches

Lily Bay State Park (tel. 207/693–6613 late June–Labor Day, 207/693–6231 Labor Day–late June), on the north shore of Sebago Lake, attracts anglers. It has a large sand beach, boat ramps, and a separate camping area.

Restaurants

Thompson's (Rte. 201, tel. 207/672–3245), in Bingham, offers a step back in time in both decor and prices. Slip into one of the booths and order the special, perhaps meat loaf, and save room for the homemade desserts. At the **Road Kill Cafe** (Rte. 15, tel. 207/695–2230), in Greenville Junction, the motto is WHERE THE FOOD USED TO SPEAK FOR ITSELF. Choose from Brake and Scrape sandwiches, Bye-Bye Bambi Burgers, and the like in this casual eatery overlooking Moosehead Lake. The **Greenville Inn** (*see below*) offers formal dining in a Victorian mansion on the lake.

Reservations Service

B&B of Maine (377 Gray Rd., Falmouth 04105, tel. 207/797–5540).

Visitor Information

Baxter State Park Authority (64 Balsam Dr., Millinocket 04462, tel. 207/723–5140), **Jackman Moose River Chamber of Commerce** (Box 368, Jackman 04945, tel. 207/668–4171), **Moosehead Lake Region Chamber of Commerce** (Rtes. 6 and 15, Box 581, Greenville 04441, tel. 207/695–2702), **North Maine Woods** (Box 421 Ashland 04732, tel. 207/435–6213), **Upper Kennebec Valley Chamber of Commerce** (Box 491, Bingham 04920, tel. 207/672–4100).

Chesuncook Lake House

Rte. 76 (Box 656), Chesuncook Village, Greenville 04441, tel. 207/745-5330 or 207/695-2821 for Folsom's Air Service

Chesuncook Lake House gives meaning to the Maine adage "You can't get there from here." This remote, rustic inn has been an outpost of civilization in the otherwise rugged wilderness since 1864. You can travel here by boat, an 18-mi journey; by floatplane from Greenville or Bangor; or on foot—it's a 5-mi hike over a rough woods road.

Chesuncook Village was formed around 1820 and hit its heyday in the 1860s, when it boasted a population of around 200, most of whom worked in the woods. Chesuncook Lake House was built as part of a farm where food and hay were grown to feed timber workers and their animals. When roads began to replace river drives, the village began to die. Today Chesuncook Village is on the national register as a historic site.

Paris-born Maggie McBurnie came here in the early 1950s after marrying Bert, who grew up here. She took to it immediately and decided to remain even after Bert passed away in 1997. A small but strong woman, she provides three full meals daily—solid New England fare with a French accent, and many of the ingredients come from her gardens.

The living room is furnished with a jumble of comfortable but worn chairs and sofas, an upright piano, and a large woodstove that keeps everything cozy on cooler nights. The walls and ceiling here, as in the dining room, are tin. Upstairs are four small, simply furnished guest rooms that share two baths. Although all have lake views, from the two front rooms you can gaze down the lake at Mt. Katahdin.

The remote location means no electricity and no phones. You must entertain yourself, but given the wilderness playground out back and the lake out front,

that's easy to do. It may take you a few days just to adjust to the quiet and learn to relax. "Relaxing is an art," Maggie says. "You have to work at it." For such work, Chesuncook Lake House is the place to be.

▦ *4 doubles share 2 baths. Boats, motors (rental). $85; breakfast, lunch, dinner. No credit cards. Smoking on porch only. Closed mid-Oct.–May.*

Greenville Inn

Norris St. (Box 1194), Greenville 04441, tel. 207/695-2206

The Greenville Inn, a gray-clapboard Victorian with white and maroon trim, sits atop a hill on the outskirts of Greenville. Its exterior grandeur hints at its interior magnificence. Ornate cherry and mahogany woodwork, Asian rugs, and stained glass set the tone at the inn, which was built as a private home around 1890 for a lumber baron and reportedly took 10 years to build.

Today Elfi Schnetzer runs the inn with the help of her daughter, Susie, and son, Michael. They have updated the house yet preserved its architectural details: the intricately carved woodwork; the huge leaded, stained-glass window depicting a spruce tree; the relief walls; wrought-iron doorknobs; and original relief tile-work in the baths.

The downstairs common rooms are punctuated with Victorian-era touches: an intricate leaf-and-vine pattern carved into the oak mantle and mirror in the front sitting room, inlaid floors in the parlor, original stained-glass light fixtures, and tile-inset fireplaces throughout. It all sounds dark and somber, and, in parts, it is, but the view out the windows to Moosehead Lake lightens the mood.

Guest rooms are lighter and, although not gay, certainly brighter than the public rooms. Grandest is the second floor Suite 21, where it would be easy to spend

a day curled up on the window bench gazing at the lake or an evening stretched out on the wicker sofa before the tiled fireplace. The bath is original to the house and has an unusual, marble, needle-nose spray shower as well as a deep tub. Room 23, done in blue, beige, and red, also has a lake view and a tile-and-wood fireplace as well as a king-size bed. The inn also has six simple pine cottages as well as a carriage house suite that's ideal for families, but given the antiques within the main house, the inn isn't suitable for young children.

Breakfast is a lavish Continental buffet that includes fruit, yogurt, cereal, baked goods, and ham and cheese.

🏠 *4 doubles with bath, 2 suites, 6 cottages. Restaurant (dinner only, closed in winter), cable TV in suites and cottages. $125–$195; Continental breakfast. D, MC, V. No pets.*

Inn at the River

Rte. 201 (HCR 63, Box 24), The Forks 04985, tel. and fax 207/663-2181

Although most of the white-water rafting companies that operate in The Forks offer lodging, there was no nonaffiliated B&B until the Cost family—Bill, a river guide, his wife, Cori, and their eight children—opened the Riverside Inn in 1997.

Built in the New England farmhouse style so prevalent in this area, the inn offers simply decorated, comfortable—although small—rooms. Some have private screened porches, some have Kennebec River views, and some have whirlpool tubs. Room 10, decorated in blues and greens, has a king-size bed with a star-pattern quilt and a wrought iron headboard in a grape-leaf pattern. Room 2 is wheelchair accessible and opens onto the front porch, which runs the length of the house.

Guests relive the day's adventures in the small pub, which has a bar and a few tables, or in the great room, with its parquet floor and massive stone fireplace. A full country breakfast is served in the adjacent dining room, where dinner is also available in the summer and on select evenings in spring and fall. A small kitchenette on the second floor is always stocked with complimentary juice, sodas, coffee, and cookies.

🏠 *10 doubles with bath. Pub, TV/VCR in library. $90–$110; full breakfast. MC, V. No pets. Closed mid-Oct.–Apr.*

The Lodge at Moosehead Lake

Lily Bay Rd. (Box 1167), Greenville 04441, tel. 207/695-4400, fax 207/695-2281

Just outside Greenville on a hill overlooking Moosehead Lake, this inn is a final vestige of civilization before the wilderness. After a day of hiking, boating, skiing, or white-water rafting, it's a welcome retreat. Jennifer and Roger Cauchi had careers in hotel and event management in Pennsylvania but wanted a change. "We couldn't explain what we wanted," Jennifer says, "but we knew it when we saw it, and this was it."

The inn, a former summer estate built in 1917, brings the outside in, with decorations that include antlers, small evergreens, pinecones, and branches. Nearly every room has a patterned twig border or other accent that Jennifer painstakingly created by hand. This is not, however, a rustic retreat: off-white carpeting, Asian rugs, and soothing earth tones make it luxurious and welcoming.

All rooms have air-conditioning; whirlpool spas; fireplaces; TV/VCRs; and hand-carved, four-poster, queen-size beds that depict the animal or theme for which the room is named (Totem, Loon, Bear, Moose, and Trout). Although Moose and Totem are the largest rooms, Bear has a private deck. Four rooms have water views—the sunsets over Moosehead Lake are spectacular. Three

new suites, added in the carriage house in 1997, offer such touches as a swinging bed and glass doors that open to a patio and gardens. Guest rooms also have such thoughtful amenities as coffeemakers, wineglasses, ice-filled coolers, makeup mirrors, hair dryers, scales—even pillows for the hot tub.

The Cauchis serve a full gourmet breakfast in the expansive, light-filled dining room overlooking Moosehead Lake. In the evening you can sit on the deck (which also has a lake view) in front of the great room's massive stone fireplace or in adjacent Toby Room, with its English Toby mug collection. Downstairs is a game room with a pool table.

🏨 _5 doubles with bath, 3 suites. Airconditioning coffeemakers, hair dryers, whirlpool baths in rooms. $250–$350; full breakfast, afternoon hors d'oeuvres, dinner (in off-season). D, MC, V. No smoking, no pets._

Sky Lodge

Route 201, Moose River 04945, tel. 207/668-2171, fax 207/668-9471

In the 1940s planes landed on the Sky Lodge's 1,750-ft runway while guests watched from a rooftop gallery. The massive log cabin, built in 1929 as a private home for a New York multimillionaire, was reputed to have secret closets and tunnels to hide bootleg liquor. And some say that Al Capone stayed here. You can sense the excitement and intrigue of those bygone days in the great room, which has soaring fieldstone fireplaces at either end; two, mirror-image, curving staircases leading to a balcony that rims the second floor; and a beamed cathedral ceiling. The soft glow of polished wood is everywhere; bear skins, a moosehead, a wooden canoe, and snowshoe furniture complete the decor.

Guest rooms in the lodge aren't as splendid as the great room (indeed, they need a little sprucing up). Nevertheless, some, such as spacious Room 1, have fireplaces and are welcoming in their simplicity. The Sutro Suite has two fireplaces: one in its sitting room and one in its bathroom—right next to a big old-fashioned tub.

A Continental breakfast buffet is served by the fireplace in the restaurant, which is also open to the public for dinner. Breaking your fast on the dining room porch, with its views of the rolling countryside, is a great way to start the day.

🏨 _5 doubles, 2 triples with bath; 2 suites. Restaurant. $99–$125; Continental breakfast. AE, D, MC, V. Closed Oct.–June._

Directory 1: *Alphabetical*

Directory 2: *Geographical*

Connecticut

Bristol
Chimney Crest Manor
34
Deep River
Riverwind *36*
East Haddam
Bishopsgate Inn *34*
Essex
Griswold Inn *35*
Farmington
The Barney House *34*
Greenwich
The Homestead Inn *6*
The Stanton House Inn
9
Ivoryton
Copper Beech Inn *35*
Kent
The Country Goose *42*
Ledyard
Stonecroft *28*
Litchfield
Tollgate Hill Inn &
Restaurant *44*
Madison
Tidewater Inn *28*
Middlebury
Tucker Hill Inn *18*
Mystic
Harbour Inne &
Cottage *25*
Steamboat Inn *27*
New Canaan
The Maples Inn *8*
Roger Sherman Inn *8*
New Haven
Three Chimneys Inn
10
New Milford
The Homestead Inn
15
New Preston
The Boulders *14*
Hopkins Inn *16*
Noank
The Palmer Inn *26*
Norfolk
Greenwoods Gate *42*
Manor House *43*
North Stonington
Randall's Ordinary *27*

Norwalk
Silvermine Tavern *9*
Old Greenwich
Harbor House Inn *6*
Old Lyme
Bee & Thistle Inn *24*
Old Lyme Inn *26*
Ridgefield
The Elms Inn *15*
Stonehenge *18*
West Lane Inn *18*
Riverton
Old Riverton Inn *43*
Salisbury
Under Mountain Inn *44*
The White Hart *45*
Simsbury
Simsbury 1820 House *37*
Stonington
Antiques &
Accommodations *24*
Lasbury's Guest House
26
Washington
The Mayflower Inn *17*
Westbrook
Captain Stannard House
25
Talcott House *28*
Westport
The Cotswold Inn *6*
The Inn at National Hall
7
Woodbury
The Curtis House *14*
House on the Hill *16*

Maine

Addison
Pleasant Bay Inn and
Llama Keep *287*
Bar Harbor
Inn at Bay Ledge *284*
Inn at Canoe Point *284*
Mira Monte *286*
The Tides *288*
Ullikana *288*
Blue Hill
Blue Hill Inn *270*
The John Peters Inn *274*
Bridgton
The Bridgton House *295*
The Noble House *296*

Brooksville
Eggemoggin Reach Bed
and Breakfast *272*
Camden
The Camden Maine Stay
270
Edgecombe-Coles
House *271*
Whitehall Inn *276*
Castine
The Castine Inn *271*
Center Lovell
Quisiana *297*
Chesuncook Village
Chesuncook Lake House
302
Deer Isle
Pilgrim's Inn *275*
East Boothbay
Five Gables Inn *261*
Eastport
The Weston House *289*
The Forks
Inn at the River *303*
Freeport
The Isaac Randall
House *262*
Fryeburg
The Admiral Peary
House *294*
The Oxford House *297*
Greenville
Greenville Inn *302*
The Lodge at
Moosehead Lake *303*
Hancock
The Crocker House Inn
284
Le Domaine *286*
Isle au Haut
The Keeper's House
274
Kennebunkport
Bufflehead Cove *251*
The Captain Lord
Mansion *252*
The Captain's Hideaway
252
The Maine Stay Inn and
Cottages *253*
Lincolnville
Victorian Inn *276*
The Youngtown Inn *277*

Jaffrey
The Benjamin Prescott
Inn *239*
Meredith
The Nutmeg Inn *222*
Mont Vernon
Zahn's Alpine Guest
House *244*
Newmarket
Moody Parsonage Bed
and Breakfast *213*
North Conway
The 1785 Inn *234*
Plainfield
Home Hill Country Inn
& French Restaurant
242
Portsmouth
Inn at Christian Shore
213
Martin Hill Inn *213*
Sise Inn *215*
Rochester
The Governor's Inn *212*
Rye
Rock Ledge Manor *214*
Sanborntorn
Ferry Point House *220*
Snowville
Snowvillage Inn *234*
Sugar Hill
Foxglove, A Country
Inn *230*
Sunset Hill House *235*
Tamworth
The Tamworth Inn *223*
Temple
The Birchwood Inn *239*
Wakefield
The Wakefield Inn *224*
Wolfeboro
The Wolfeboro Inn *224*

Rhode Island

Block Island
Atlantic Inn *68*
Barrington Inn *68*
Blue Dory Inn *69*
Hotel Manisses *69*
Rose Farm Inn *70*
The 1661 Inn & Guest
House *70*
Surf Hotel *71*

Narragansett
The Richards *61*
Stone Lea *63*
Newport
Admiral Fitzroy Inn *53*
Cliffside Inn *53*
Elm Tree Cottage *54*
Francis Malbone House
54
The Inn at Castle Hill *55*
The Inntowne *55*
Ivy Lodge *56*
Sanford-Covell Villa
Marina *56*
Victorian Ladies *57*
South Kingstown
Admiral Dewey Inn *61*
Watch Hill
Ocean House *61*
Weekapaug
Weekapaug Inn *63*
Westerly
Shelter Harbor Inn *62*

Vermont

Arlington
Arlington Inn *190*
Hill Farm Inn *192*
West Mountain Inn *194*
Barton
Fox Hall Inn *201*
Bennington
Molly Stark Inn *193*
South Shire Inn *194*
Brookfield
Green Trails Inn *202*
Burlington
The Willard Street Inn
206
Chester
The Chester Inn at
Long Last *179*
Craftsbury Common
Inn on the Common *203*
Dorset
Cornucopia *191*
Goshen
Blueberry Hill Inn *191*
Grafton
Eaglebrook of Grafton
180
The Old Tavern at
Grafton *184*

Lower Waterford
Rabbit Hill Inn *204*
Ludlow
Governor's Inn *180*
Lydonville
Wildflower Inn *205*
Manchester
1811 House *191*
Reluctant Panther *193*
Wilburton Inn *195*
Manchester Center
The Inn at Ormsby Hill
193
Manchester Village
The Battenkill Inn *190*
Marlboro
Whetstone Inn *185*
Middlebury
Swift House Inn *205*
Montgomery Village
Black Lantern Inn *200*
Montpelier
Inn at Montpelier *202*
Newfane
Four Columns *180*
Putney
Hickory Ridge House
181
Quechee
Parker House *185*
Stowe
Ye Olde England Inn *206*
Waitsfield
The Inn at Round Barn
Farm *202*
Lareau Farm Country
Inn *204*
Warren
Beaver Pond Farm Inn
200
Weathersfield
Inn at Weathersfield
182
West Dover
The Deerhill Inn *179*
The Inn at Sawmill
Farm *182*
West Townshend
Windham Hill Inn *186*
Windsor
Juniper Hill Inn *183*
Woodstock
Kedron Valley Inn *183*

W YOU TRAVEL, *H*ELP IS NEVER FAR AWAY.

From planning your trip to

providing travel assistance along

the way, American Express®

Travel Service Offices are

always there to help

you do more.

American Express Travel Service
Offices are found in central locations
throughout the United States.
For the office nearest you, please call
1-800-AXP-3429.

do more **AMERICAN EXPRESS**

Travel

http://www.americanexpress.com/travel

© 1997 American Express Travel Related Services Company, Inc.